## EDITORIAL BOARD

UNIVERSITY CASEBOOK SERIES®

# CRIMINAL LAW

**FOURTH EDITION**

*by*

RICHARD J. BONNIE
Harrison Foundation Professor of Medicine and Law
Professor of Psychiatry and Neurobehavioral Sciences
Director, Institute of Law, Psychiatry & Public Policy
University of Virginia

ANNE M. COUGHLIN
Lewis F. Powell, Jr., Professor of Law
University of Virginia

JOHN C. JEFFRIES, JR.
David and Mary Harrison Distinguished Professor of Law
University of Virginia

PETER W. LOW
Hardy Cross Dillard Professor of Law Emeritus
University of Virginia

FOUNDATION PRESS

444 Cedar Street, Suite 700
St. Paul, MN 55101
1-877-888-1330

Printed in the United States of America

**ISBN:** 978-1-60930-391-4

# PREFACE

The fourth edition of this casebook is significantly new. The most dramatic change concerns the treatment of conspiracy and complicity. In most American jurisdictions, conspiracy triggers two quite different kinds of criminal liability. It is an anticipatory crime, analogous to attempt, that punishes agreeing to commit a crime in advance of actually engaging in the proscribed conduct. It also functions as an alternative to complicity in imposing liability for the conduct of another. This overlap between conspiracy and complicity presents a major teaching challenge. Both doctrines must be covered for a coherent account of liability for the conduct of another, but teaching them separately results in time-consuming redundancy and confusion.

Our solution is presented in the all-new Chapter VI, "Liability for the Conduct of Another," which integrates these two doctrines. The basic materials on complicity build on the Supreme Court's 2014 decision in *Rosemond v. United States*. The chapter then deals with two key issues common to both conspiracy and complicity. The first is the old question of possible liability for knowing aid to (as distinct from purposeful participation in) the criminal venture of another. The second is the rule of natural and probable consequences, which in many jurisdictions extends an accomplice's or co-conspirator's liability to additional offenses that foreseeably grew out of the original commitment.

After dealing with several other issues related to conspiracy and complicity, Chapter VI ends with an obviously optional but very interesting section on RICO. The inevitable complexity of those materials is offset by their great importance. Those who can find time to cover them will be well rewarded.

That leaves the inchoate function of conspiracy, which has been moved to Chapter V. After a thorough exploration of the crime of attempt, Chapter V considers its relation to solicitation, complicity, and conspiracy. These materials cover conspiracy as an anticipatory offense, both in its doctrinal requirements and in its analytic relation to attempt.

We have also made significant changes to the coverage of sex offenses in Chapter IX. The chapter begins with a new main case, which explores the historical and evolving meaning of "force" and "nonconsent" in the law of rape. The materials also cover some of the common and vexing sexual assault allegations on the contemporary scene, including those that arise when a complainant claims to have been too intoxicated to consent to sex. Finally, the chapter reproduces and describes, at relevant points, the proposed revisions to the Model Penal Code's sexual assault provisions, the tentative draft of which was published in 2014.

We have also added new materials on "stand-your-ground" laws, including a surprising and interesting main case.

The rest of the book has been revised and tightened in many small ways. Numerous cases have been replaced by cases that are more recent or, we think, more teachable. Many notes have been carefully revised and edited for clarity and accessibility. The chapter sequence has been changed to a more logical order. And overall length has been shortened by nearly 100 pages.

In short, we have questioned every aspect of the prior edition and have sought replacement and improvement when we saw a better way. We hope we have succeeded in this ambition, and invite users of the casebook to let us know if they see places where additional improvements can be made.

RJB

AMC

JCJR

PWL

April 2015
Charlottesville

# SUMMARY OF CONTENTS

# TABLE OF CONTENTS

# TABLE OF CASES

The principal cases are in bold type.

# TABLE OF MODEL PENAL CODE REFERENCES

UNIVERSITY CASEBOOK SERIES®

# CRIMINAL LAW

FOURTH EDITION

# CHAPTER I

# THE PURPOSES OF PUNISHMENT

This book is about the substantive criminal law. It is about that body of law, mostly statutory, that defines the components of criminal liability. Broadly speaking, there are three main elements in the definition of crimes: the criminal act (or actus reus), the criminal state of mind (or mens rea), and the absence of a legal justification or excuse (such as self-defense or insanity). The cases and materials that follow examine each of these elements in detail. The aim is to explore not only the content of the criminal law but also—and more important—the rigorous analytic relationships among its component parts and the ways in which lawyers and judges reason about crime definition and coverage.

When first-year students encounter the phrase "criminal law," they are likely to expect something entirely different. They are likely to expect the body of law, mostly constitutional in origin, that governs police investigation and interrogation. Restrictions on search and the seizure of evidence and the famous *Miranda* warnings are familiar to everyone who watches TV. In most law schools, the rules governing these matters are covered in a separate course called Criminal Procedure. Although criminal procedure and the substantive criminal law are deeply connected, their sources and modes of reasoning are surprisingly different—so much so that there is little to be gained in treating them together. This book is therefore not concerned with pre-trial police investigation but focuses squarely on what must be proved at trial in order to condemn someone as a criminal.

This book is also not much concerned with the social problem of crime. Rates of criminal behavior fluctuate over time, for reasons that are often hard to identify, and so do societal responses to crime. In the United States, the number of persons incarcerated for crime is quite high. In 1980, when the first edition of this book was being prepared for publication, the number of persons in prison in the United States was 319,598.[a] By the end of 2013, this number had grown to 1,574,741, an increase of almost 500% (although a decrease from the peak prison population in 2009).[b] The United States now has the highest rate of incarceration in the world, with 716 of every 100,000 residents in prison.[c] Of the world's major powers, Russia has the second highest incarceration rate—475 of every 100,000 residents in

---

[a] In 1980, the total number of people under the supervision of the criminal justice system, which includes persons in prison, in jail, on probation, and on parole, was 1,840,400. Bureau of Justice Statistics, U.S. Dep't of Justice, Sourcebook of Criminal Justice Statistics 2003, at 478 tbl. 6.1, available at www.albany.edu/sourcebook/pdf/section6.pdf.

[b] Bureau of Justice Statistics, U.S. Dep't of Justice, Prisoners in 2013, at 2 tbl.1 (Sept. 2014, available at www.bjs.gov/content/pub/pdf/p13.pdf. At the end of 2012, the total number of people under the supervision of the criminal justice system was 6,937,600. Bureau of Justice Statistics, U.S. Dep't of Justice, Correctional Populations in the United States, 2012, at 1 (Dec. 2013), available at www.bjs.gov/content/pub/pdf/cpus12.pdf.

[c] Roy Walmsley, Int'l Centre for Prison Stud., World Prison Population List 1 (10th ed. 2013), available at www.prisonstudies.org/sites/prisonstudies.org/files/resources/downloads/wppl_10.pdf.

prison.[d] By contrast, in England and Wales, the rate is 148; in Canada, 118; and in France, 98.[e] These comparisons raise urgent questions of public policy. They relate primarily to the *severity* with which crime is punished and secondarily to the *range of conduct* proscribed as criminal. Despite the obvious importance of these issues, they are not closely connected to the analytic structure of the criminal law and so receive only incidental treatment in this book. The focus here is on the first step in understanding the criminal justice system—the manner in which the law defines criminal behavior and the defenses it recognizes to what otherwise would be a crime.

## INTRODUCTORY NOTE ON THE PURPOSES OF PUNISHMENT

For many years, criminal law scholars have identified four main goals of punishment: retribution, deterrence, incapacitation, and rehabilitation. However, there are at bottom only two competing philosophical theories regarding the purpose of punishment. Each theory represents a complex series of moral assertions and aspirations for the criminal justice system. Each rests on a distinct understanding of human nature and of the causes of criminal activity.

The first theory, which is associated with the retributive function of punishment, is deontological in nature. According to this view, "the institution[ ] of punishment [is] justified by the rightness or fairness of the institution . . . not by the good consequences such institution may generate."[a] For the deontologist, the justification for punishment is the moral culpability (or desert) of persons who violate the criminal law. The second theory of punishment is utilitarian in nature, and is associated with the goals of deterrence, incapacitation, and rehabilitation. According to this view, punishment is threatened and imposed in order to achieve beneficial social consequences, namely, to prevent or minimize criminal behavior.

For purposes of clarity, these materials will focus separately on each of these theories and their practical implications for the criminal process. But it bears emphasizing that the criminal justice system rests on a mixture of these philosophies. That is, while it is possible to envision a system wholly governed by deontological premises or one that relies solely on utilitarian policies, neither of these positions dominates the existing system to the exclusion of the other. Rather, the system makes a series of significant, if uneasy, compromises between them. Moreover, the purposes of punishment are historically contingent in the sense that different justifications are emphasized at different times.[b] While retributive impulses may wane and instrumental goals wax, or vice-versa, the system nonetheless remains committed to a mixture of justificatory principles.

Of course, the criminal process itself does not negotiate these compromises by means of an abstract philosophical dispute. To the contrary, the process does its work by punishing real people in specific cases. Some people serve terms of probation, perhaps accompanied by a short term of incarceration; others go to jail or prison, perhaps followed by a period on parole;

---

[d] Id.

[e] Id. at 3, 5.

[a] Michael S. Moore, The Moral Worth of Retribution, in Ferdinand Schoeman, Responsibility, Character, and the Emotions 182 (1987).

[b] See Albert W. Alschuler, The Changing Purposes of Criminal Punishment: A Retrospective on the Past Century and Some Thoughts about the Next, 70 U. Chi. L. Rev. 1 (2003).

others are forced to pay fines; and still others are put to death for their crimes. For that reason, it is useful to have factual contexts in mind when exploring why our culture commits its resources to punishing criminals. The cases to be studied in subsequent chapters of this book will provide numerous situations that test the appropriate limits of the criminal law. The following situations serve as an introduction. They are variations on a theme. In each case, a child dies. The questions for the criminal justice system are whether someone should be punished for the death and, if so, the relative harshness of the penalty that should be imposed.

## TESTING CASES

### 1. DONTE PHILLIPS

Sarah Davis picked up 2-year-old Donte Phillips and drove him to his day-care center. Davis was the director of the center, which was run by a local church and provided services to low-income families. Donte was the only passenger in the center's van that day. Davis and Donte arrived at the center at 8:30 a.m. Donte remained in the van until 4:00 p.m., when his aunt came to take him home. After a frantic and fruitless search for the boy on the center's grounds, Davis realized that she must have left him in the van. She screamed and rushed to the van, where she discovered Donte's lifeless body. The doctor who performed the autopsy attributed the death to heat stroke. In a statement made to investigators, Davis said that when she arrived at the center, she observed other children running around the grounds. Concerned for their safety, she parked the van and went to check on them, forgetting about Donte for the rest of the day. Davis's colleagues characterized her as sensitive, conscientious, and extremely upset about Donte's death. They attributed her mistake to the fact that both the church and day-care center were struggling financially, and Davis was performing a variety of different jobs in an effort to keep the facility from closing.[a]

### 2. MIKEY WARSCHAUER

At 8:30 on a sunny August morning, Mark Warschauer parked his car in a lot outside his office at the University of California, Irvine. He locked the car and went about his routine as vice-chair of UCI's Department of Education. He returned to the car shortly before noon, where he found police and paramedics tending to a baby's body lying on a stretcher. When Warschauer realized that the dead child was his ten-month-old son, Mikey, he collapsed. Campus police had been summoned at 11:30 a.m. by students who spotted the baby strapped into his safety seat in the back seat of the car. The police reached the baby quickly by smashing the rear windows of the car, but, by then, Mikey had been dead for at least an hour. A pediatrician analogized what Warschauer had done to "putting a child in a greenhouse." Warschauer explained that, on the morning of Mikey's death, he was tired. He and his wife, Keiko Hirata, who was a part-time political science professor, had worked late on a research paper, and Mikey woke them up crying in the early morning hours, cranky over the process of being weaned from his mother's milk. When Warschauer left home that morning, he had intended to drop Mikey at day care before heading to his campus

[a] See Brad Schmitt & Dorren Klausnitzer, Toddler Likely Didn't Suffer, Examiner Says, The Tennesean, June 18, 1994.

office, but he forgot to do so. The couple had no set schedule for taking Mikey to day care. Some days, Hirata did the job. On other days, such as the day of Mikey's death, the chore fell to Warschauer. It had not been easy for Warschauer and Hirata to conceive a child, and they underwent fertility treatments for several years before Mikey was born. They called their son their "miracle baby," and their family and friends agreed that no parents were more attentive or devoted to their child's safety and welfare. Reflecting later on the moment when he first saw Mikey's body, Warschauer sobbed, "It was like death. A knife in my heart. . . . My life as I knew it was over. I knew right then, our happy lives had ended."[b]

### 3. MICHAEL AND ALEX SMITH

Susan Smith drove her car to a boat ramp on a lake near her home in Union, South Carolina, and sent the car into the lake. Smith's two young sons were inside the car, strapped into their car seats. Then, Smith ran to a nearby home and reported that her sons had been kidnapped. For nine days, Smith stuck to that story in interviews with the police, and she appeared on national television to plead for the boys' safe return. Ultimately, Smith confessed that she had drowned her sons, and police divers found her car with their corpses inside it. In her confession, Smith mentioned that she had been distraught because her boyfriend had broken up with her, saying that he was not ready to be a parent. Smith also told the police that she had gone to the lake intending to take her own life, but when the car started rolling into the water, she found that she could not go through with her suicide plan. When Smith was six years old, her father committed suicide. Smith attempted suicide when she was 13. After this incident, a psychologist recommended that Smith be hospitalized for depression, but her mother and stepfather refused. When she was 16, her stepfather began sexually molesting her. Smith's stepfather admitted to police that he had fondled her, but no criminal charges were brought because Smith and her mother did not want him to be prosecuted.[c]

### 4. IMANI AND JASMINE LAWREY

Khalimba Berry found her daughters, three-year-old twins, dead inside her car, which was parked outside her apartment building in Atlanta, Georgia. The cause of death was hyperthermia. That morning, Berry had returned home from her night-shift job, fed her children breakfast, and watched television with them. At noon, Berry went to sleep, leaving the twins in the care of their 11-year-old brother. When she woke up two hours later, Berry could not find the girls. Berry and her neighbors searched the apartment complex for two hours, with no success. Berry then telephoned 911, and the dispatcher suggested that she check her car. She went to the car, and found her children's bodies. She screamed and held them in her arms. Investigators believe that the girls were playing in the car and that they accidentally locked themselves in.[d]

---

[b] See Rachanee Srisavasdi, No Charges, But a Life Sentence of Grief, Orange County Register, Oct. 9, 2003; Joel Zlotnik, Jeff Rowe, & Laylan Connelly, Professors' Baby Found Dead in Car in UCI Lot, Orange County Register, Aug. 9, 2003.

[c] See, e.g., Twila Decker, The Many Faces of Susan Smith, The Dallas Morning News, May 10, 1995, at 5c.

[d] See Bill Montgomery, Autopsy: Twins Died of Heat Exhaustion, Atlanta Constitution, June 10, 1995, at B6.

## 5. DEVON AND DUSTIN DUCKER

One summer morning, at around 3:30 a.m., Jenny Bain Ducker drove to a Holiday Inn in McMinnville, Tennessee, to visit several co-workers who were staying there. Ducker's two young sons accompanied her to the motel, and she left the boys, who were sleeping in their car seats, alone in the car for about ten hours. In the motel, Ducker drank beer and played video games with her friends. According to Ducker's companions, she left the motel room periodically, presumably to check on the boys. However, at some point she fell asleep, due to the combined effects of the beer and prescription medicine she was taking for bronchitis. When she woke up, it was 1:00 p.m. She immediately went to her car and found that one of her sons appeared to be dead. She rushed the boys to the hospital, where both were pronounced dead from heat exhaustion. Ducker and the boys' father were married briefly; both were high school dropouts. According to her ex-husband, Ducker was a neglectful mother. He thought that she drank too much, and he said that he had been planning to seek custody of the boys because he suspected that she was abusing them physically. Ducker's parents pointed out that until recently she had worked the night shift at a local factory; night-shift workers frequently make early morning social visits. Moreover, the children of other factory workers regularly stayed up late and slept during the day, when their parents did.[e]

## 6. FRANCES KELLY

One morning after breakfast, Kevin Kelly took six of his thirteen children out in the family van to do errands. Kelly's wife was visiting family in Ireland, and he was staying at home from his job as an engineer to take care of the children. Kelly and the children returned to their home on Zimbro Avenue in Manassas, Virginia, at about noon, and Kelly asked three of the older children, including his 17-year-old son, Anthony, to take care of the little ones. Kelly spent the rest of the day doing chores and errands around the house, including fixing the backyard fence, ferrying children to and from school, washing clothes, and preparing meals. At about 7:30 p.m., neighbors discovered the body of Kelly's youngest child, 21-month-old Frances, strapped into her car seat in the van. During the day, the temperature inside the van probably reached 140 degrees. Friends and neighbors said that Kelly was a devoted father and a deeply religious man. As one neighbor put it, Kelly's children were his whole life. But other neighbors remarked that this was not the first time that Kelly had lost track of one of his children. Several months earlier, Kelly had left his four-year-old son behind in a video store. The child was restored to the family only after the police used rental records to locate all customers who had come to the store that day; when the police called Kelly, he rushed over to pick up his son. On another occasion, Frances was found wandering by herself down Zimbro Avenue. A police officer brought her home and warned the Kellys to be more careful.[f]

---

[e] See State v. Ducker, 27 S.W.3d 889 (Tenn. 2000).

[f] See, e.g., Josh White, Jury Says Father Should Get Jail, The Washington Post, Dec. 5, 2002, at B1.

## 7. JONATHAN PERRY COURTNEY

Donna Mutyambizi parked her car outside a home in North Laurel, Maryland, for her first day on the job as house cleaner. Although she had been warned not to do so, Mutyambizi left her 17-month-old son, Jonathan Courtney, alone in the car. She cracked the car windows to provide ventilation, and she placed a bottle of water and cereal near the child's car seat. She checked on him twice and each time found him sleeping. When she returned to the car about three hours later, the boy was lifeless. She asked a neighbor to help resuscitate the child, but he already had died from hyperthermia. Initially, Mutyambizi told the police that she had brought her son into the house with her. Later, she admitted that she had left him alone in the car, and she explained that she did so because she had no money for a babysitter. She had asked her estranged husband for money, but he refused to give her any. Mutyambizi's husband claimed that she could afford to pay a babysitter, but he said that she had lost confidence in the person who had been caring for the child. When Mutyambizi was 6 years old, her father shot and killed her mother; thereafter, she was raised by several different foster parents. Mutyambizi's own marriage was unhappy. She and her husband argued frequently, and they separated about six months before their child's death. Friends characterized Mutyambizi as a doting parent, and they said she was very worried about making ends meet following her separation from her husband. At the time of Jonathan's death, Mutyambizi was pregnant with her second child.[g]

## 8. QUESTIONS AND COMMENTS

The following series of notes outlines the major goals of punishment. Consideration of their scope and relative importance is critical in determining the proper disposition of a criminal charge against the protagonists described above. Consider how they should be applied not only to the situations described above but as well to other cases as they are encountered in the rest of this book.

## NOTES ON RETRIBUTION

### 1. INTRODUCTION

The retributive function of punishment presupposes that human actors are responsible moral agents who are capable of making choices for good or evil. People who make evil choices deserve to be punished. This premise is normative; it does not admit to empirical verification or refutation, nor does it depend on pragmatic justification. According to retributivism, it is right to punish one who offends against societal norms because it is wrong to violate these norms. The same point is sometimes put in terms of expiation. It is essential for the offender to right the wrong or, in the vernacular, to "pay" for the crime. The offender "owes a debt to society" for retributive reasons; having violated societal norms, the offender must now atone by suffering punishment for the transgression.[a]

---

[g] See Michael Rezendes, Maryland Woman Caught in a Cycle of Sorrow, The Washington Post, July 13, 1989.

[a] Cf. H.L.A. Hart, Punishment and Responsibility 158–59 (1968):

A famous proponent of retributivism is Sir James Fitzjames Stephen, a 19th-century English judge and historian of the criminal law. His view was:

> [N]o one in this country regards murder, rape, arson, robbery, theft, or the like, with any feeling but detestation. I do not think it admits of any doubt that law and morals powerfully support and greatly intensify each other in this matter. Everything which is regarded as enhancing the moral guilt of a particular offence is recognized as a reason for increasing the severity of the punishment awarded to it. On the other hand, the sentence of the law is to the moral sentiment of the public in relation to any offence what a seal is to hot wax. It converts into a permanent final judgment what might otherwise be a transient sentiment. The mere general suspicion or knowledge that a man has done something dishonest may never be brought to a point, and the disapprobation excited by it may in time pass away, but the fact that he has been convicted and punished as a thief stamps a mark upon him for life. In short, the infliction of punishment by law gives definite expression and a solemn ratification and justification to the hatred which is excited by the commission of the offense. . . . The criminal law thus proceeds upon the principle that it is morally right to hate criminals, and it confirms and justifies that sentiment by inflicting upon criminals punishments which express it. . . .
>
> These views are regarded by many people as being wicked, because it is supposed that we never ought to hate, or wish to be revenged upon, any one. The doctrine that hatred and vengeance are wicked in themselves appears to me to contradict plain facts, and to be unsupported by any argument deserving of attention. Love and hatred, gratitude for benefits, and the desire of vengeance for injuries, imply each other as much as convex and concave. . . . The unqualified manner in which [these views] have been denounced is in itself a proof that they are deeply rooted in human nature. No doubt they are peculiarly liable to abuse, and in some states of society are commonly in excess of what is desirable, and so require restraint rather than excitement, but unqualified denunciations of them are as ill-judged as unqualified denunciations of sexual passion. The forms in which deliberate anger and righteous disapprobation are expressed, and the execution of criminal justice is the most emphatic of such forms, stand to the one set of passions in the same relation in which marriage stands to the other. . . .[b]

The perspective expressed by Stephen is deeply embedded in the vocabulary of the criminal law. We speak in terms of "guilt" or "innocence." We talk about "punishment," "blame," and "responsibility." Words like

---

This . . . conception of punishment . . . makes primary the meting out to a responsible wrongdoer of his just deserts. Dostoevsky passionately believed that society was morally justified in punishing people simply because they had done wrong; he also believed that psychologically the criminal needed his punishment to heal the laceration of the bonds that joined him to his society. So, in the end, Raskolnikov the murderer thirsts for his punishment.

[b] James Fitzjames Stephen, 2 A History of the Criminal Law of England 81–82 (1883).

"murderer," "rapist," "pedophile," "burglar," "thief," "convicted felon," carry deeply stigmatic overtones, attesting perhaps to the most significant moral disapprobation that society can express. Stigmatic labels of this intensity and with these consequences are not applied to one who commits a tort, who breaks a lease, or who breaches a contract. Civil remedies and sanctions do not carry the same meaning as a criminal conviction.[c]

Critics of retributivism insist that the angry and vengeful emotions identified by Stephen do not provide a moral justification for punishment. For example, David Dolinko argues that by valorizing "anger and hatred as . . . proper bases for punishment," retributive theory "invites the public and the legal system to indulge the passion for revenge untroubled by moral qualms."[d] Some modern proponents of retributive theory have responded by distinguishing retribution from a simple thirst for revenge. Michael Moore insists that the retributive urge springs from a virtuous (rather than "wicked") emotion, and thus provides a moral foundation for the attribution of criminal blame.[e] He explains:

> When we make a retributive judgment . . . we need not be motivated by [revenge]. Our concern for retributive justice might be motivated by very deep emotions that are nonetheless of a wholly virtuous nature. These are the feelings of guilt we would have if we did the kinds of acts that fill the criminal appellate reports of any state.

Moore invites readers to imagine how they would feel if they committed a vicious crime, say, a brutal homicide, and he suggests that, in such a case, the only virtuous response would be to "feel guilty unto death. . . . One ought to feel so guilty one wants to die." Moore also argues that it is appropriate, indeed, respectful, to hold actual wrongdoers, no matter what their socio-economic hardships or psychological shortcomings, to the same high standards to which we hold ourselves. "If we experience any reluctance to transfer the guilt and desert *we* would possess," had we committed a brutal crime, to the criminal offender, "we should examine that reluctance carefully." By blaming the offender as harshly as we would blame ourselves, Moore insists, we are giving the offender "the benefit each of us gives himself or herself: the benefit of being the subjective seat of a will that, although caused, is nonetheless capable of both choice and responsibility."

## 2. RETRIBUTION AND THE BLAMEWORTHY ACTOR

The central ethical predicate of retributivism raises questions about who should not be punished as well as questions about who should be. Does it follow from retributivism that people who are not responsible moral agents should not be punished? How is one to determine whether a person is a responsible moral agent? Does it also follow that punishment is unjust

---

[c] In an admirable essay prepared for first-year students on the threshold of studying criminal law, Henry Hart explained that "[w]hat distinguishes a criminal from a civil sanction and all that distinguishes it, it is ventured, is the judgment of community condemnation which accompanies and justifies its imposition." Henry Hart, The Aims of the Criminal Law, 23 Law & Contemp. Probs. 401, 404 (1958).

[d] David Dolinko, Three Mistakes of Retributivism, 39 U.C.L.A. L. Rev. 1623, 1652 (1992).

[e] See Michael S. Moore, The Moral Worth of Retribution, in Responsibility, Character, and the Emotions, 179, 212–15 (Ferdinand Schoeman ed., 1987).

if the underlying misconduct was not the product of free and voluntary choice? How is that determination to be made? How should the law deal with situational circumstances that undermine or override an individual's capacity to make a free and voluntary choice?

These questions are covered in detail in chapters to follow. But for now it should be understood that traditionally the criminal law has answered them through narrowly framed inquiries about the actor and the circumstances surrounding the misconduct. As for the important threshold question of who "qualif[ies] as a blameworthy moral agent," the law's general response is: "Everyone except for the very young, the very crazy, and the severely mentally retarded."[f] As for whether situational circumstances may negate free choice, the law withholds blame only if the actor's capacity to choose a lawful option was constrained by overwhelming external pressures. Here, the classic example is the actor who is threatened with serious bodily harm or death if the crime is not committed. As these references illustrate, the criminal law treats the vast majority of accused persons as fit candidates for punishment, notwithstanding their internal failings or situational difficulties. As Michael Moore's essay suggests, retributivists insist that such treatment is morally justified, indeed required.

Some have argued that retribution endorses a theory of responsibility that is empirically false and morally deficient. According to this view, crime is produced not by offenders' vicious choices, but by vicious circumstances in which offenders are born and forced to reside by an uncaring society. By attributing misconduct to offenders' choices—rather than to their impoverished circumstances—retributive theory allows the community to avoid its responsibility for poverty and related cultural ills. For example, in a provocative lecture delivered in 1975, Judge David Bazelon warned that the criminal process would lose its moral credibility unless it became sensitive to the productive relationship between social injustice and crime.[g] To force the system to confront "society's own conduct in relation to the actor," Bazelon suggested that jurors be allowed to acquit in cases where the crime was caused by "physiological, psychological, environmental, cultural, educational, economic, and hereditary factors," rather than by the accused's free choice. Although Bazelon's primary claim was that the victims of poverty and racial discrimination often may not justly be blamed for committing crimes, he conceded that his determinist view of human conduct would be implicated in a wide variety of cases. Thus, he wondered, "whether a free choice to do wrong can be found in the acts of a poverty-stricken and otherwise deprived black youth from the central city who kills a marine who taunted him with a racial epithet," or "in the act of a 'modern Jean Valjean' who steals to feed his family."

Bazelon's proposal has attracted some favorable commentary,[h] but most scholars disagree. In Stephen Morse's view, for example, the empirical and normative assumptions underlying Bazelon's determinist model are flawed. First, Morse argues that Bazelon's assertions concerning the causes of crime "are wrong. . . . [W]e do not understand *any* of the causes of crime. There are various factors which have a strong positive correlation

---

[f] Peter Arenella, Convicting the Morally Blameless: Reassessing the Relationship Between Legal and Moral Accountability, 39 U.C.L.A. L. Rev. 1511, 1521 (1992).

[g] David L. Bazelon, The Morality of the Criminal Law, 49 S. Cal. L. Rev. 385 (1976).

[h] See Richard Delgado, "Rotten Social Background": Should the Criminal Law Recognize a Defense of Severe Environmental Deprivation?, 3 Law & Ineq. J. 9 (1985).

with violent crime, such as youth and poverty. But social science is not yet ready to make firm causal statements."[i] Second, and more important, the definition of responsibility applied by retributive theory rests on an ethical, rather than factual, basis:

> . . . There is no bright line between free and unfree choices. Harder and easier choices are arranged along a continuum of choice: there is no scientifically dictated cutting point where legal and moral responsibility begins or ends. Nor is there a higher moral authority which can tell society where to draw the line. All society can do is to determine the cutting point that comports with our collective sense of morality. The real issue is where society ought to draw the line of responsibility—and by whom it should be drawn.

Additionally, for Morse and for some others, Bazelon's determinist judgments are unethical because they erode the state's respect for individual autonomy. Even where an offender is faced with a very hard choice to obey the law, Morse continues, it is "respectful to the actor to hold the actor responsible. . . . [S]uch a view treats all persons as autonomous and capable of that most human capacity, the power to choose. To treat persons otherwise is to treat them as less than human."

To illustrate another ethical dilemma created by Bazelon's proposal, his critics ask a practical question, namely, what would the community do with the large numbers of dangerous persons acquitted on grounds of non-responsibility? Since the community could not tolerate the release of such persons—they would remain a significant threat to public safety—the system inevitably would replace criminal punishment with other more "repressive measures," including coercive therapy and preventive detention of potentially dangerous actors. This, they conclude, is a less acceptable result than that provided by the traditional criminal law.

Critical race and feminist scholars and practitioners have refocused Morse's question about the political constituents who should inform the criminal law's definition of responsibility. When Morse asked the question "by whom" the line of responsibility should be drawn, he was referring to the appropriate allocation of authority between legislatures and courts; his claim is that legislators, not jurors, should identify the moral standards that govern the allocation of criminal blame. By contrast, when critical race and feminist commentators ask this question, they are concerned to demonstrate that legislatures, as well as courts, traditionally have been dominated by affluent white men. Since that is the case, these critics claim that the definition of responsibility serves the political interests of such men, not of African-Americans, women, or the members of other marginalized groups. In particular, they argue, the proposition that criminal blame is respectful of individual autonomy protects only those who already possess the social and economic resources to exercise meaningful choices. While it is too early to identify the ultimate impact of such arguments, they have inspired a number of law reform movements, including efforts to make self-defense doctrine more sensitive to the experiences of women and minorities, and to revise charging and sentencing policies that have a disproportionate impact on African-American offenders.

---

[i] Stephen J. Morse, The Twilight of Welfare Criminology: A Reply to Judge Bazelon, 49 S. Cal. L. Rev. 1247, 1261 (1976).

## 3. RETRIBUTION AND GRADING: PROPORTIONALITY

Retribution places an important limitation on the application of criminal blame, namely, the principle of proportionality. Blame is a question of degree. To say that it was bad for someone to do something suggests the further question: How bad? A simple illustration makes the point. Most would agree that a petty thief should not be punished as severely as the person who kills for money. But why not? Our impulse that life imprisonment for the petty thief is grossly disproportionate to the offense is derived from a retributive evaluation of the behavior. The degree of wrong-doing involved in such a case does not justify such extreme punishment. In the language of retribution, this offender did not "deserve" to be punished so severely.

The substantive criminal law implements the principle of proportionality in at least two ways. First, the system "grades" offenses, i.e., legislatures establish the relative severity of different crimes in the abstract. For centuries, the law has incorporated the idea of proportionality by classifying crimes as felonies or misdemeanors. Today, legislatures also grade offenses by establishing a maximum penalty that can be imposed upon conviction, and the relative seriousness of a given offense can be determined by comparing that sanction with those authorized for other offenses. Current legislative grading schemes are considerably more complicated than the traditional distinction between felonies and misdemeanors. For example, the Federal Sentencing Guidelines distribute crimes according to their relative seriousness among 43 different offense levels.

Second, the principle of proportionality requires some assessment of whether a sentence actually imposed fairly reflects the blameworthiness of the individual wrongdoer and the gravity of his or her particular crime. The question here is whether an authorized penalty is or is not disproportionate for a particular crime, in the light of all of the surrounding circumstances. Most sentencing schemes give judges some discretion to consider case-specific factors when determining an offender's penalty.

Critics of retributive theory argue that the principle of proportionality provides no method for calibrating sentences with the type of precision that the criminal justice system requires:

> [I]t has long been a stock objection to retributivism that there is simply no workable way to determine just *what* punishment a criminal deserves. Retributivists very commonly direct us to make punishments 'proportional' to crimes by punishing a more serious crime more severely than a less serious one. Unfortunately, this prescription by itself cannot tell us what punishment any particular crime actually deserves, even if we could rank every crime in a single scale from least to most serious.[j]

Likewise, sentencing officials have commented on the practical difficulties they confront when trying to rationalize their sentencing decisions according to the principle of proportionality. As the United States Sentencing Commissioners put it in the United States Sentencing Guidelines Manual 3 (2014):

---

[j] David Dolinko, Three Mistakes of Retributivism, 39 U.C.L.A. L. Rev. 1623, 1626 (1992).

> [A] sentencing system tailored to fit every conceivable wrinkle of each case can become unworkable. . . . A bank robber with (or without) a gun, which the robber kept hidden (or brandished), might have frightened (or merely warned), injured seriously (or less seriously), tied up (or simply pushed) a guard, a teller or a customer, at night (or at noon), . . . in an effort to obtain money for other crimes (or for other purposes), in the company of a few (or many) other robbers, for the first (or fourth) time that day.

Of course, as proponents of retributivism remark, the principle of proportionality does not claim to provide "an invariant, objective deserved punishment for each offensive act." In the view of these commentators, one of the strengths of retributive theory is its sensitivity to contemporary community morality. "It is possible in any society to rank the seriousness of criminal offenses and to assign to each a punishment that the society at that time considers proportional to the seriousness of the offense. This is then the deserved punishment at that time and place."[k]

## 4. RETRIBUTION AS A LIMITING PRINCIPLE

As the previous Notes explain, retributivist philosophy treats punishment of blameworthy wrongdoers as an ethical imperative. Retribution *requires* punishment whether or not the punishment produces beneficial social consequences. Subsequent Notes explore the consequentialist position that punishment is justified when it achieves social benefits. It is important to understand at the outset, however, that many consequentialist philosophers accept the ethical postulates of retribution as *limiting* the occasions for, and severity of, punishment that otherwise would be justifiable on purely utilitarian grounds.

For these philosophers, retribution alone is not a sufficient justification for punishment, but they believe that the criminal process achieves good consequences by incorporating retributive premises. For example, H.L.A. Hart explains that the retributivists' definition of human beings as responsible moral agents serves "values quite distinct from those of retributive punishment." Thus, even if the criminal law were to be designed strictly along utilitarian lines, Hart believes that it would continue to endorse retributive thinking. He offers two examples of the social benefits of this position. First, by insisting that people have the power to choose how they behave, the criminal law enhances their ability to control their lives:

> [It allows us] to predict and plan the future course of our lives within the coercive framework of the law. For the system which makes liability to the law's sanctions dependent upon a voluntary act not only maximizes the power of the individual to determine by his choice his future fate; it also maximizes his power to identify in advance the space which will be left open to him free from the law's interference. Whereas a system from which responsibility was eliminated so that he was liable for that which he did by mistake or accident would leave each individual not only less able to exclude the future interference by the law with his

k Stephen J. Morse, Justice, Mercy and Craziness, 36 Stan. L. Rev. 1485, 1492–93 (1984).

life, but also less able to foresee the times of the law's interference.[1]

Second, by adhering to retributive premises about individual responsibility for misconduct, the criminal law commands widespread public acceptance because those premises describe the way people treat each other in our culture. "[P]ersons interpret each other's movements as manifestations of intention and choices, and these subjective factors are often more important to their social relations than the movements by which they are manifested or their effects." When one person strikes another, Hart argues, "[i]f the blow was light but deliberate, it has a significance for the person struck quite different from an accidental but much heavier blow." He concludes that:

> This is how human nature in society actually is and as yet we have no power to alter it. The bearing of this fundamental fact on law is this. If as our legal moralists maintain it is important for the law to reflect common judgments of morality, it is surely even more important that it should in general reflect in its judgments on human conduct distinctions which not only underlie morality, but pervade the whole of our social life. This it would fail to do if it treated men as merely alterable, predictable, curable or manipulable things.

## NOTES ON GENERAL DETERRENCE

### 1. INTRODUCTION

Deterrence encompasses two distinct concepts, namely, *special* deterrence and *general* deterrence. *Special* deterrence, sometimes called deterrence by intimidation, refers to steps taken to dissuade particular offenders from repeating their crimes. By bringing the costs of lawless behavior to the offenders' attention, the criminal sanction is intended to induce them to refrain from such conduct in the future. *General* deterrence, often called general prevention or deterrence by example, refers to the impact of criminal punishment on other persons. The idea is that members of the public will be deterred from criminal behavior once they see the consequences suffered by those who commit crimes.

Both special and general deterrence rest on the notion that human actors calculate pain and pleasure when choosing among alternative courses of conduct. If the costs of crime are set high enough to assure that the gains to be derived from it are not profitable, the rational person will not commit crimes. Deterrence theory explicitly concedes that human conduct is caused by a variety of factors, and places punishment for crime heavily on the scale.

### 2. THE CONCEPT

In The Rationale of Punishment 19–41 (1830), Jeremy Bentham outlined the classical concept of deterrence:

> Pain and pleasure are the great springs of human action. When a man perceives or supposes pain to be the consequence of an act, he is acted upon in such a manner as tends, with a certain

---

1 H.L.A. Hart, Punishment and Responsibility 180–83 (1968).

force, to withdraw him, as it were, from the commission of that act. If the apparent magnitude, or rather value* of that pain be greater than the apparent magnitude or value of the pleasure or good he expects to be the consequence of the act, he will be absolutely prevented from performing it. The mischief which would have ensued from the act, if performed, will also by that means be prevented. . . .[a]

General prevention is effected by the denunciation of punishment, and by its application, which, according to the common expression, *serves for an example*. The punishment suffered by the offender presents to every one an example of what he himself will have to suffer if he is guilty of the same offence.

General prevention ought to be the chief end of punishment, as it is its real justification. If we could consider an offence which has been committed as an isolated fact, the like of which would never recur, punishment would be useless. It would only be adding one evil to another. But when we consider that an unpunished crime leaves the path of crime open, not only to the same delinquent, but also to all those who may have the same motives and opportunities for entering upon it, we perceive that the punishment inflicted on the individual becomes a source of security to all. That punishment, which, considered in itself, appeared base and repugnant to all generous sentiments, is elevated to the first rank of benefits, when it is regarded not as an act of wrath or of vengeance against a guilty or unfortunate individual who has given way to mischievous inclinations, but as an indispensable sacrifice to the common safety. . . .

All punishment being in itself evil, upon the principle of utility, if it ought at all to be admitted, it ought only to be admitted in as far as it promises to exclude some greater evil.

Bentham's famous argument captures the utilitarian focus of general deterrence. Unlike retribution, deterrence is not backward-looking in the sense of exacting vengeance for a crime. Rather, it is forward-looking in the sense of preventing or reducing the incidence of future offensive behavior.[b] The central utilitarian premise is that society has the right (and the obligation) to take measures that protect its members from harmful behavior.

### 3. THE CRIMINAL AS RATIONAL CALCULATOR

Bentham himself remarked that critics of his theory doubt that criminal offenders perform the rational calculations that the theory presupposes. The critics concede that the rational calculator model may have some explanatory power for crimes committed for financial gain, but they believe it

* I say *value*, in order to include the circumstances of *intensity, proximity, certainty*, and *duration*; which magnitude, properly speaking, does not. . . .

[a] As Bentham says later, "[t]he profit of the crime is the force which urges a man to delinquency—the pain of the punishment is the force employed to restrain him from it. If the first of these forces be the greater, the crime will be committed ["that is to say, committed by those who are only restrained by the laws, and not by any other tutelary motives, such as benevolence, religion, or honour"]; if the second, the crime will not be committed."—[Footnote by eds.]

[b] See Kyron Huigens, The Dead End of Deterrence, and Beyond, 41 Wm. & Mary L. Rev. 943, 945 (2000).

is wholly unrealistic when applied to crimes motivated by a passion other than greed. By contrast, modern economists support Bentham's assumption that criminals, including those motivated by passions other than cupidity, respond to incentives. As Isaac Ehrlich puts it, "willful engagement in even the most reprehensible violations of legal and moral codes does not preclude an ability to make self-serving choices."[c] Ehrlich offers the following formula to measure the likelihood that a particular actor will decide to participate in criminal activity:

> [The decision] can be viewed as motivated by the costs and gains from such activity. These include the expected illegitimate payoff (loot) per offense . . . ; the direct costs incurred by offenders in acquiring the loot (including the costs of self-protection to escape punishment) . . . ; the wage rate in an alternative legitimate activity . . . ; the probability of apprehension and conviction . . . ; the prospective penalty if convicted . . . ; and finally one's taste (or distaste) for crime—a combination of moral values, proclivity for violence, and preference for risk. . . .

Ehrlich combines these components in an "overall expected net return per offense," which is the expected payoff of the crime, minus the direct costs of committing it, minus the foregone wages of legitimate activity, and minus—most important—the prospective penalty. The last element, the prospective penalty, is the product of multiplying the probability of conviction (which is always less than one) times the threatened penalty. "For crimes that do not involve any material gain," Ehrlich concludes, "the net return is negative; it can be viewed as the price of crime to the offender."

As this analysis illustrates, contemporary economic theory is far more sensitive to the diverse determinants of criminal activity than Bentham's blunt assertion that "every one calculates." However, some critics insist that economists will not provide useful suggestions about how to deter crime until they develop a model that is faithful to the psychological characteristics of the persons whom the law most wants to deter. According to John DiIulio, for example, what is needed is a model that takes account of the fact that many young criminals

> are almost completely incapable of deferring gratifications for the sake of future rewards. In their lives, there has never been a stable relationship between doing "what's right" and being rewarded and doing "what's wrong" and being punished. . . . Their lived experience, the most powerful teacher of all, counsels that kids who look ahead, stay in school and "do the right thing" often end up just as jobless, hopeless and miserable as kids who do crime.[d]

DeIulio argues that economists have never fully taken into account the "extraordinary degree to which today's young street criminals are present oriented, and the extent to which they do crime for fun as well as for profit. " 'You never think about doing thirty,' " one young prisoner told me, " 'when you don't expect to live to thirty.' "

DeIulio believes that some offenders are impervious to rational calculation. Imagine, he says, "a radically present-oriented young man who is

---

[c] Isaac Ehrlich, Crime, Punishment, and the Market for Offenses, 10 J. Econ. Persp. 43 (1996).

[d] John J. DiIulio, Jr., Help Wanted: Economists, Crime and Public Policy, 10 J. Econ. Persp. 3, 16–17 (1996).

also unable to feel joy or pain at the joy or pain of others." Such an offender does not fear the future prospect of arrest and punishment. Moreover, if he is part of a gang, "going to prison is very nearly a good 'career move.'" And while the negative consequences of crime seem remote, "the things he gets for behaving criminally . . . —money, drugs, status, sex—are their own immediate rewards."

DeIulio therefore rejects the rational calculator model of deterrence. "Models that assume that young urban street predators are but a highly impulsive breed of middle-aged economics professors are not only intellectually idle, but (should anyone actually be foolish enough to act on them) downright dangerous. The reality simply does not fit the theory. . . ."

## 4. HOW MUCH PUNISHMENT WILL DETER?

Critics of deterrence often complain that the theory does not offer a precise standard by which to measure the kind or amount of punishment that the law should inflict. What types of assessments should legislators and judges make when designating sentence levels or selecting the punishment for a particular crime? If deterrence is the goal, why not simply impose uniform, severe penalties for all crimes? Is proportionality a relic of retributive thinking that deterrence theorists rebuff?

Richard Posner has considered these questions.[e] He begins by thinking about the appropriate penalty for murder. Since the cost to the victim is so high, even life imprisonment might not seem sufficient. One might think, however, "that the important thing is not that the punishment for murder equal the cost to the victim but that it be high enough to make the murder not pay," and surely life imprisonment meets that test. The flaw in this analysis is that it "implicitly treats the probability of apprehension and conviction as one. If it is less than one, as of course it is, then the murderer will not be comparing the gain from the crime with the loss if he is caught and sentenced; he will be comparing it with the disutility of the sentence discounted by the probability that it will actually be imposed."

The key insight here is that the severity of a threatened penalty must be discounted by the probability of its actually being imposed. Where that probability is low, there is a case for heavy penalties for those actually caught and convicted. But, Posner asks, is this result "fair"? Some go "scot-free," while others serve lengthy terms for the same misconduct. Posner responds to this concern by remarking that

> to object to this result is like saying that all lotteries are unfair because, ex post, they create wealth differences among the players. In an equally significant sense both the criminal justice system that creates low probabilities of apprehension and conviction and the lottery are fair so long as the ex ante costs and benefits are equalized among the participants. Nor is it correct that while real lotteries are voluntary the criminal justice "lottery" is not. The criminal justice lottery is voluntary: you keep out of it by not committing crimes.

As Posner notes, the proximity and certainty of punishment—the probability of conviction and imposition of a criminal sanction—affect

[e] Richard Posner, An Economic Theory of the Criminal Law, 85 Colum. L. Rev. 1193, 1209–13 (1985).

deterrence as much as the magnitude of the penalty. Johannes Andenaes has spoken to the relationship between these factors: "Even the simplest kind of common sense indicates that the degree of risk of detection and conviction [are] of paramount importance to the preventive effects of the penal law. Very few people would violate law if there were a policeman on every doorstep."[f] Of course, exceptions would occur. Some crimes are the result of passion or frenzy that disregards all consequences. Some criminals—political assassins, for example—may be willing to accept even certain penalties. "But there is good reason," Andenaes concludes, "to believe that certainty of rapid apprehension and punishment would prevent *most* violations."

## 5. MEASURING DETERRENCE

As explained above, retribution is a theory of punishment whose validity does not depend on empirical verification. By contrast, the central premise of deterrence theory—that punishment discourages crime—invites empirical validation. Starting in the 1960s, social scientists and legal scholars began undertaking studies designed to verify empirically the deterrent effects of criminal sanctions. All share the intuition that punishment has a deterrent effect. As John DiIulio has observed, "On drives to academic conferences I have noted that even criminologists who have critiqued deterrence theories pump their brakes when a highway patrol car appears."[g] However, the scientists also agree that policymakers should design sentencing systems on the basis of evidence, not hunches. To date, there remain large gaps in empirical knowledge of the links between punishment and the criminal behaviors the punishment is designed to deter.

In 1978, Daniel Nagin reviewed the empirical literature on general deterrence in a report prepared for the National Research Council. In the body of its report, the Panel on Research on Deterrent and Incapacitative Effects stated that it could not "yet assert that the evidence warrants an affirmative conclusion regarding deterrence." The Panel emphasized that its conclusion did "not imply support for a position that deterrence does not exist, since the evidence certainly favors a proposition supporting deterrence more than it favors one asserting that deterrence is absent."[h] In his report for the Panel, Nagin explained that the jury was still out with respect to the magnitude and even the existence of a deterrent effect, and he suggested that policymakers should proceed cautiously because the data were not accurate enough to support any particular set of recommendations for penal sanctions:

> [D]espite the intensity of the research effort, the empirical evidence is still not sufficient for providing a rigorous confirmation of the existence of a deterrent effect. Perhaps more important, the evidence is woefully inadequate for providing a good estimate of the magnitude of whatever effect may exist. . . . Certainly, most people will agree that increasing sanctions will deter

---

[f] Johannes Andenaes, The General-Preventive Effects of Punishment, 114 U.Pa.L.Rev. 949, 960–70 (1966).

[g] John J. DiIulio, Jr., Help Wanted: Economists, Crime and Public Policy, 10 J. Econ. Persp. 3, 16 (1996).

[h] Report of the Panel on Research on Deterrent and Incapacitative Effects, in Deterrence and Incapacitation: Estimating the Effects of Criminal Sanctions on Crime Rates 7 (Alfred Blumstein et al. eds. 1978).

> crime somewhat, but the critical question is, By how much? There is still considerable uncertainty over whether that effect is trivial (even if statistically detectable) or profound. Any unequivocal policy conclusion is simply not supported by valid evidence.

The Panel called for caution in arguing for heavier penalties in order to achieve greater deterrence: "Policy makers in the criminal justice system are done a disservice if they are left with the impression that the empirical evidence, which they themselves are frequently unable to evaluate, strongly supports the deterrence hypothesis." . . .

At the turn of the century, Daniel Nagin updated his review of the empirical research and again concluded that the data were too fragmentary to support specific policies such as more severe terms of imprisonment for particular crimes.[i] In his more recent essay, Nagin did revise his earlier findings in one important respect. This time, he found that the research supported the "more emphatic conclusion that the collective actions of the criminal justice system exert a very substantial deterrent effect." However, Nagin explained that even this more robust conclusion has very limited implications for formulating policy because official interventions to prevent crime "involve targeted and incremental changes. So for policy makers the issue is not whether the criminal justice system in its totality prevents crime but whether a specific policy, grafted onto the existing structure, will materially add to the preventive effect." In the end, one can say, the marginal deterrent effect of specific changes in punishment for specific crimes is likely beyond empirical verification.

### 6. DETERRENCE AND BLAMEWORTHINESS

Bentham argued that punishment ought not to be inflicted in cases where it would be "inefficacious." For example, he remarked that punishment "cannot act so as to prevent the mischief" in cases "of extreme infancy, insanity, and intoxication." H.L.A. Hart has responded that deterrence theory alone does not support Bentham's position that "restriction of the use of punishment to those who have voluntarily broken the law is explicable on purely utilitarian lines":

> Bentham's argument is in fact a spectacular non sequitur. He sets out to prove that to *punish* the mad, the infant child or those who break the law unintentionally or under duress or even under "necessity" must be inefficacious; but all that he proves (at the most) is the quite different proposition that the *threat* of punishment will be ineffective so far as the class of persons who suffer from these conditions is concerned."[j]

It is possible, Hart continued, that although the *threat* of punishment would not affect some offenders, the actual *infliction* of punishment on them might help motivate others. "If this is so and if utilitarian principles only were at stake, we should, without any sense that we were sacrificing any principle of value or were choosing the lesser of two evils, drop from the law the restriction on punishment entailed by the admission of excuses."

---

[i] Daniel S. Nagin, Criminal Deterrence Research at the Outset of the Twenty-First Century, 23 Crime & Just. 1, 3 (1998).

[j] H.L.A. Hart, Punishment and Responsibility 18–20 (1968).

This objection to Bentham's reasoning, Hart argues, is not merely fanciful:

> Any increase in the number of conditions required to establish criminal liability increases the opportunity for deceiving courts or juries by the pretence that some condition is not satisfied. When the condition is a psychological factor the chances of such pretence succeeding are considerable. . . . The belief that such deception is feasible may embolden persons who would not otherwise risk punishment to take their chance of deceiving a jury in this way [and] a criminal who actually succeeds in this deception will be left at large, though belonging to the class which the law is concerned to incapacitate.

Although Hart's argument could be taken to suggest that utilitarians should abandon blameworthiness as a necessary condition for punishment, he does not carry it that far, and others agree. Reinforcing the perception that crime is a blameworthy enterprise adds significantly to its deterrent effect. Louis Michael Seidman adds that the criminal sanction functions best as a deterrent when it reflects community intuitions about culpability.[k] He observed:

> Richard Posner [draws an analogy between the criminal process and a lottery.] Posner may or may not be correct about optimal enforcement levels, but he surely misunderstands the point of his own analogy. Many people have no moral qualms about playing the lotteries, and those who have a taste for risk will play them even when the odds are substantially unfavorable. . . . The evidence is all around us that large numbers of people are willing to play the crime game when the threatened punishment no longer communicates moral disapproval. From the disastrous effort sixty years ago to enforce Prohibition to the current and growing difficulty in deterring tax evasion, it is clear that people do not respond solely to the risk of loss unassociated with moral blame.

## NOTES ON INDIVIDUAL PREVENTION

### 1. INTRODUCTION

It is convenient to collect the remaining purposes of punishment under the rubric of individual prevention. The ultimate objective—prevention of future crimes—remains the same. But the focus shifts from the effect of criminal sanctions on the general public to what can be done, usually at sentencing, to keep particular offenders from engaging in crime again.

### 2. SPECIAL DETERRENCE

Special deterrence refers to steps taken to discourage individual offenders from repeating their misconduct. It is conceptually distinct from rehabilitation, although a criminal sanction may be intended to serve both objectives simultaneously. The justification for a sentence to probation, for example, might be both to discourage future crimes by exposing the

[k] Louis Michael Seidman, Soldiers, Martyrs, and Criminals: Utilitarian Theory and the Problem of Crime Control, 94 Yale L. J. 315, 332–33 (1984).

offender to potential sanctions and to accomplish rehabilitative objectives by the conditions of probation and their enforcement through supervision.

The literature on special deterrence is scant. Most studies of prison effectiveness focus on rehabilitative programs or incapacitative goals rather than on the isolated effect of special deterrence. To the extent that special deterrence is considered on its own terms, some commentators argue that high recidivism rates demonstrate that punishment is not an effective special deterrent. There may be types of offenders, to be sure, whose future behavior is unaffected by imprisonment, and these offenders may comprise the bulk of the prison population. But a premise of some sentences is that some offenders may learn from the fact of conviction or from realistic exposure to the possibility of punishment. The so-called "split sentence" has become more widely used in recent years on just this theory.[a]

### 3. INCAPACITATION

At first glance, incapacitation appears to be a foolproof method of crime prevention in that it avoids some of the more vexing empirical questions posed by deterrence theory. In a word, incapacitation "works": no further offenses outside the prison itself can be committed by an offender who is incarcerated. But incapacitation as an independent goal of punishment provides no justification for incarcerating offenders who would not commit another crime anyway. The challenge is distinguish those offenders who are potentially recidivist from those who are not.

There can be little doubt that current sentencing policy in the United States relies more on incapacitation than can be justified in this manner. A cursory examination of the statistics reproduced at the beginning of the Chapter reveals as much. Legislators in recent decades have passed numerous tough sentencing initiatives, including so-called "three strikes" laws.[b] The use of mandatory minimum sentences has also been very much on the rise.

These initiatives can be criticized on the ground that the system is not equipped to make the predictions of future dangerousness on which this use of incapacitation must least partly be based. There is a "widespread and growing consensus" among behavioral scientists that "clinical

---

[a] A "split sentence" is a sentence that uses a short jail term to give the offender a taste of confinement followed by a period of probation. See Federal Sentencing Guidelines Manual 8 (2014), available on line at http://www.ussc.gov (The United States Sentencing Commission approved the split sentence on the ground that in some cases "the definite prospect of prison, even though the term may be short, will serve as a significant deterrent, particularly when compared with pre-guidelines practice where probation, not prison, was the norm.").

[b] Under the "three strikes" approach to sentencing, offenders who commit the requisite number of crimes of a specified kind (usually felonies) are sentenced to life terms. John DiIulio described and responded to one criticism of this approach, namely, that it is both inefficient and unfair because persons convicted of several trivial violations may be incarcerated for life:

> [F]indings on the amount of serious crime committed by probationers and parolees and the failure of intensive supervision programs have led some to conclude that three-strikes laws are the "only answer." . . . Opponents [of three strikes measures argue that such laws will] lead to the lifetime incarceration of mere "nonviolent" offenders. . . . The much-publicized 1994 case of the California felon whose "third strike" was stealing a slice of pizza in a mall sounds positively damning until you get all the facts. The facts are that this man had four prior felony convictions in nine years, five suspended sentences, and numerous bouts on probation.

John J. DiIulio, Jr., Help Wanted: Economists, Crime and Public Policy, 10 J. Econ. Persp. 3, 14 (1996).

predictions of violence have more than chance validity."[c] But the question posed by relying on recidivist potential as the basis for imprisonment is the extent to which false positives should be tolerated.[d]

Since the system is incapable of identifying recidivist offenders with perfect accuracy, reliance on incapacitation raises difficult ethical questions. What margin of error is acceptable in making predictions of future criminality? If there is only a 30 percent chance that a violent offender with certain characteristics will commit another violent offense, is incapacitation appropriate? For how long? Until the chances are reduced to 10 per cent? Until there is *no* chance? These problems are exacerbated where the predicted future offense does not involve violence. For how long should a petty thief be incapacitated if there is a 90 percent chance of future petty thefts? By itself, incapacitation as a method of preventing future crimes by the incapacitated person may justify sentencing the thief to a term of life imprisonment. On the other hand, empirical studies suggest that certain kinds of killers are virtually certain not to repeat their crimes. For them, punishment based on a need for incapacitation to prevent future crime would not be justified at all.

The system resolves some of these problems by basing sentences on multiple objectives. Both retribution and general deterrence, for example, may demand substantial punishment notwithstanding a prediction that the particular offender is not likely to commit crimes in the future.

Norval Morris offered a theory of criminal punishment that explicitly combines retributive and incapacitative goals. Punishment should rest primarily on retributive grounds, with incapacitation serving as a useful subsidiary objective. In Morris's view, when crimes of serious violence are involved, the criminal process should take account of predictions of future dangerousness even if "the best we can do at present is to predict one in three, in the sense that to be sure of preventing one crime we would have to lock up three people."[e] Thus, once an offender has been convicted and a range of *deserved* punishments identified, it is proper for judges to rely on predictions concerning the offender's dangerousness when selecting a sentence from within the specified range. The idea is that the judge will sentence offenders predicted to be recidivists to the maximum deserved term, while imposing the minimum deserved term on offenders who are unlikely to repeat their crimes.

Morris discussed some of the ethical questions raised by his approach in the context of hypothetical criminals *X* and *Y*, who have identical records and have committed the same crime: Suppose, he said, that *Y* had a job, a supportive family, and some education, while *X* lacked all of the above. Even without direct empirical evidence, it is clear that criminals such as *Y* have a "much lower base expectancy rate of future violent criminality."

---

[c] John Monahan, Clinical and Actuarial Predictions of Violence, in West's Companion to Scientific Evidence (D. Faigman et al. eds., 1996).

[d] Recidivism assessments rely on a range of offender characteristics identified by social scientists as predictive of future dangerousness. Such factors include "age of initiation of criminal careers, drug use, [length of time spent unemployed], and prior criminal record." Panel on Research on Criminal Careers, National Research Council, Criminal Careers and "Career Criminals" 5 (Alfred Blumstein et al. eds., 1986). Consultants for the National Research Council evaluated several of these assessment instruments and found that they produced a rate of false positives that ranged from less than 30 percent to 60 percent.

[e] Norval Morris, Incapacitation Within Limits, in Principled Sentencing 140 (Andrew von Hirsch & Andrew Ashworth eds., 1992).

From that Morris concludes that *X* should be held longer than *Y*, but he immediately recognized the problem with that result:

> [T]he reality in this country at this time will be that my apparently aseptic principles will grossly favor the wealthy to the detriment of the poor, and will be used to justify even more imprisonment of blacks and other underclass minorities than at present obtains .... The sad fact is that in our society predictors of violence are not racially neutral.... [W]hen black youths move into the middle class their crime rates are just the same as those of white youths. It is the black underclass, left behind, which has these enormously high rates of imprisonment and jailing and very much higher rates of violence.... And what else is characteristic of the inner-city ghetto? Much else that distinguishes our criminal *X* from our criminal *Y*—school absenteeism, unemployment, functional illiteracy, generations on welfare, no supportive families. Blackness and a higher base expectancy rate of violence overlap.

What conclusion should one draw from that overlap? Many would say that decisions should not be based on predictions of dangerousness at all if, as is true in America today, they are racially skewed. Morris "sympathizes" with that objection but does not accept it. "The criminal justice system cannot rectify racial inequalities and social injustices," he argues, and "[w]e cannot properly close our eyes to the different threats that criminal *X* and criminal *Y* pose to our community." What is needed, he says, is vigilance to ensure that predictions about violence are based on "validated knowledge" and not on stereotypes or prejudice.

Theories of punishment that combine retributive and incapacitative premises create yet another puzzle. Retributive theory dictates that criminal *X* and criminal *Y*, in the Morris construct, both "deserve" to be punished because each voluntarily chose to commit a crime. None of the facts about criminal *X*'s impoverished background diminishes legal responsibility for the offense, even though *X* should perhaps be regarded as less culpable because environmental factors made it so much more difficult to live in a law-abiding manner. According to incapacitation theory, on the other hand, criminal *X* is an appropriate candidate for enhanced punishment because the circumstances suggest a greater chance of reoffending. Herbert Packer concisely summarized the dilemma:

> The case for incapacitation is strongest in precisely those areas where the offender is least capable of controlling himself, where his conduct bears the least resemblance to the kind of purposeful, voluntary conduct to which we are likely to attach moral condemnation. Baldly put, the incapacitative theory is at its strongest for those who, in retributive terms, are the least deserving of punishment.[f]

## 4. REHABILITATION

The literature concerning rehabilitation[g] as a goal of punishment has tended to fluctuate between extremes of optimism and pessimism.

---

[f] Herbert Packer, The Limits of the Criminal Sanction 50–51 (1968).

[g] In 1980, a panel of the National Research Council offered the following helpful definition of rehabilitation:

According to the rehabilitative model that was in place in the middle of the last century, criminal conduct is caused by the pathology of individual offenders. During the 1960s, some psychiatrists offered exuberant praise for rehabilitation as a humanitarian intervention that would cure offenders and return them to law-abiding ways. As Karl Menninger remarked, the psychiatric community had developed numerous successful therapeutic techniques, designed to enhance an individual's "impulse control and life satisfaction." He anticipated and responded to critics of his approach:

> "But you were talking about the mentally ill," readers may interject. . . . Do you mean to imply that willfully perverse individuals, our criminals, can be similarly reached and rehabilitated?" . . . Do I believe there is effective treatment for offenders, and they *can* be changed? *Most certainly and definitely I do.* Not all cases, to be sure, [but] I believe the majority of them would prove to be curable. The willfulness and the viciousness of offenders are part of the thing for which they have to be treated. These must not thwart the therapeutic attitude. . . .[h]

This model of rehabilitation prompted sharp criticisms, and, by the 1970s, the optimistic attitude had begun to fade. Some philosophers even raised ethical objections to the proposition that offenders should be rehabilitated rather than punished. For example, Herbert Morris argued that the notion that crime is an event caused by the offender's sickness is "basically at odds" with norms that structure not only the criminal process, but also our entire way of life.[i]

At least as important as these ethical questions were practical concerns. Starting in the 1970s, social scientists began studying the empirical basis for the claim that offenders can be cured of their vicious propensities, and the early reports were disappointing. In an influential survey, sociologist Robert Martinson reviewed the scientific research on rehabilitation that was published between 1945 and 1967. His assessment of the efficacy of rehabilitative programs was decidedly negative, as was his opinion of the design of treatment studies. Martinson stopped short of concluding that "nothing works" to rehabilitate offenders, but just barely: "*With few exceptions, the rehabilitative efforts that have been reported so far have had no*

---

> The definition . . . involves three aspects[:] the desired outcome, the intervening variable(s) to be the assumed target of the rehabilitative treatment, and the intervention itself. [R]ehabilitation [is] the result of any planned intervention that reduces an offender's further criminal activity, whether that reduction is mediated by personality, behavior, abilities, attitudes, values or other factors. The effects of maturation and the effects associated with "fear" or "intimidation" are excluded, the result of the latter having traditionally been labeled as "specific deterrence."

Panel on Research on Rehabilitative Techniques, National Research Council, New Directions in the Rehabilitation of Criminal Offenders 8 (Susan E. Martin et al. eds., 1981).

[h] Karl Menninger, The Crime of Punishment 259–62 (1968). Potential treatments for offenders included "[p]sychoanalysis; electroshock therapy; psychotherapy; occupational and industrial therapy; family group therapy; milieu therapy; the use of music, art, and horticultural activities; and various drug therapies." Menninger also recommended that offenders receive other kinds of assistance to enhance the treatment effect, including advice concerning leisure activities, physical exercise, social companions, and job opportunities.

[i] Herbert Morris, Rehabilitation and Dignity, in Principled Sentencing 17 (Andrew von Hirsch & Andrew Ashworth eds., 1992).

*appreciable effect on recidivism*."[j] Martinson did concede that some programs might be working and that researchers may have failed to identify rehabilitative effects because of flaws in their experimental methodology. He also agreed that some of the underlying therapies might be imperfectly designed and poorly administered. Nonetheless, he doubted that rehabilitation was a legitimate goal of punishment:

> It may be . . . that there is a more radical flaw in our present strategies—that education at its best, or that psychotherapy at its best, cannot overcome, or even appreciably reduce the powerful tendency for offenders to continue in criminal behavior. Our present treatment programs are based on a theory of crime as a "disease"—that is to say, as something foreign and abnormal in the individual which can presumably be cured. This theory may well be flawed, in that it overlooks—indeed, denies—both the normality of crime in society and the personal normality of a very large proportion of offenders, criminals who are merely responding to the facts and conditions of our society.

Martinson's way of framing the debate and his skeptical conclusions cast a long shadow over rehabilitation studies and programs. For many years, the nuances of his position were lost on criminal law policymakers, who took away only the message that "nothing works." Martinson himself performed a subsequent study, which led him to "withdraw [his] conclusion" that rehabilitation has " 'no appreciable effect on recidivism.' "[k] This time, Martinson found, some kinds of interventions, including especially supervised parole, are effective in reducing rearrest rates. Likewise, other commentators continued to urge that there are "good reason[s] for not completely abandoning a faith in rehabilitation." First, "a number of studies have shown that improvements *can* be effected in failure rates." Second, the primary "reason why treatment has so often been shown to have no effect . . . is simply that none has been given."[l] "Why would one expect that one hour per week of group therapy with a poorly trained leader and unwilling participants would produce a major behavior change in incarcerated felons, especially considering the powerful effect of the prison background."[m] According to this view, rehabilitation can be effective, at least for some categories of offenders, but only if the community is willing to devote substantial resources to the development and implementation of new treatment programs. Moreover, to be effective, these new programs had to include some interventions designed to ameliorate the social and economic conditions, as well as the psychological ones, that contributed to offenders' propensity to relapse.

In recent years, the literature on rehabilitation has adopted a much more moderate outlook, with scholars and policymakers beginning to express a renewed sense of optimism about the potential efficacy of treatment programs. By the turn of this century, social scientists began "consistently

---

[j] Robert Martinson, What Works?—Questions and Answers About Prison Reform, 35 Pub. Int. 22, 25 (1974). [Emphasis in original.]

[k] Robert Martinson, New Findings, New Views: A Note of Caution Regarding Sentencing Reform, 7 Hofstra L. Rev. 243, 252–54 (1979).

[l] Stephen Brody, How Effective Are Penal Treatments?, in Principled Sentencing 12 (Andrew von Hirsch & Andrew Ashworth eds., 1992).

[m] Panel on Research on Rehabilitative Techniques, National Research Council, New Directions in the Rehabilitation of Criminal Offenders 9 (Susan E. Martin et al. eds., 1981).

reject[ing] the 'nothing works' proposition. Instead, they have argued that there are empirically established conditions under which treatment can work for some kinds of offenders,"[n] including juveniles, drug-addicted offenders, and sex offenders. For some criminologists working in the twenty-first century, the research on rehabilitation is both sophisticated and encouraging, and the problem is "not a nothing-works research literature with nothing to offer, but, rather, a correctional system that does not use the research available and has no history of doing so."[o] Mark Lipsey and Francis Cullen argue that there is one powerful reason for policymakers and legislators to be more attentive to the new treatment data when designing correctional systems:

> The preponderance of research evidence . . . supports the general conclusion that rehabilitation treatment is capable of reducing the reoffense rates of convicted offenders and that it has greater capability for doing so than correctional sanctions. The volume of research and the consistency of the findings of the systematic reviews make this a sufficiently sound general conclusion, bordering on beyond a reasonable doubt, to provide a basis for correctional practice and policy. The gap between this body of research and current practice and policy, however, is large and not easily bridged.[p]

It appears that lawmakers in some states have begun to heed these calls, in part because they agree that some forms of treatment work and in part because their courts are overwhelmed with criminal cases involving recidivist offenders. To choose just one salient example, a number of jurisdictions have begun to experiment with so-called "drug courts," which integrate substance abuse treatment directly into criminal case processing. One author explains why officials in Delaware moved to create drug courts:

> A study conducted in 1987 revealed that a large proportion of arrestees in several major urban areas tested positive for illegal substances. When the Delaware drug court was in the design stage, a study of the State's prisoners revealed that 80% needed substance abuse treatment. Researchers were also finding that when addicted offenders used drugs, they were among the most active perpetrators of other crimes. At the same time, it was becoming established that if treatment reduced drug use by criminally involved addicts, it would also reduce their tendency to commit crime. Research was also proving that compelled treatment was as effective as voluntary treatment. Delaware would find, and other research would confirm, that in-prison treatment based on the therapeutic community model dramatically affects drug use and recidivism.[q]

As for whether drug courts will have a "major effect on public safety" or prove to be "just another failed criminal justice fad," only time,

[n] Gerald G. Gaes, Correctional Treatment, in The Handbook of Crime & Punishment 712, 714–15 (Michael Tonry ed., 1998).

[o] Mark W. Lipsey & Francis T. Cullen, The Effectiveness of Correctional Rehabilitation: A Review of Systematic Reviews, 3 Ann. Rev. L. Soc. Sci. 297, 315 (2007).

[p] Id. at 314.

[q] Richard S. Gebelein, The Rebirth of Rehabilitation: Promise and Perils of Drug Courts, in 6 Sentencing & Corrections: Issues for the 21st Century 3 (U.S. Dep't of Justice, Office of Justice Programs, Nat'l Institute of Justice, 2000).

additional research concerning treatment design and implementation, and the devotion of significant resources will tell.

# CHAPTER II

# THE CRIMINAL ACT

## SECTION 1: THE CONDUCT REQUIREMENT

### INTRODUCTORY NOTES ON THE REQUIREMENT OF CONDUCT

1. THE REQUIREMENT OF CONDUCT

Traditionally, crimes are said to consist of a guilty act done with a guilty mind—in language often used in the criminal law, an actus reus accompanied by a mens rea. The former requirement is so foundational that it is rarely put in issue. Though there are certainly cases where the required conduct is minimal, there are virtually no examples in Anglo-American law of punishment without conduct.[a]

The requirement of conduct is a matter of great significance to the conceptual structure of the penal law. The traditional understanding is succinctly stated in Glanville Williams, Criminal Law: The General Part 1 (2d ed. 1961):

> That crime requires an act is invariably true if the proposition be read as meaning that a private thought is not sufficient to found responsibility. . . . "So long as an act rests in bare intention," said Mansfield, "it is not punishable by our laws"; and this is so even though the intention be abundantly proved by the confession of the accused.

As the quotation suggests, it has long been established that criminal liability may not be premised on a mere intention or bare desire to do wrong. Increasingly, the requirement of conduct is also taken to bar the infliction of punishment for a mere personal characteristic or status.[b] Instead, criminal liability is reserved for behavior. At least within the confines of the Anglo-American tradition, the starting point for any definition of any crime is a statement of proscribed conduct.

Adherence to a conduct requirement does not limit the penal law to the redress of positive acts. As is illustrated later in this Chapter, a failure to act may be punished in situations where the law prescribes an affirmative duty to act. Examples include crimes punishing the failure of parents to

---

[a] Glanville Williams, Criminal Law: The General Part 11 (2d ed. 1961), reports but one example in English law. In Larsonneur, 97 J.P. 206 (C.C.A. 1933), a French woman was prosecuted for being "found" in England without permission. She was "found" there because she was arrested in Ireland, handed over to English police, and "found" in an English jail cell after the English police put her there. She was sentenced to three days imprisonment with a recommendation of deportation.

[b] The Supreme Court held as much in Robinson v. California, 370 U.S. 660 (1962). Robinson was convicted for being "addicted to the use of narcotics." The Supreme Court held, in effect, that it was unconstitutional to convict him based on his status as an addict, though he could, of course, be prosecuted for the acts of using narcotics. This meaning of the case was effectively confirmed in Powell v. Texas, 392 U.S. 514 (1968). See generally Eric Luna, The Story of *Robinson*: From Revolutionary Constitutional Doctrine to Modest Ban on Status Crimes, in Criminal Law Stories 47 (2013). The vagueness doctrine, considered later in this Chapter, is also aimed, at least in part, at forbidding punishment for mere status.

care for infant children, the failure of a lifeguard to attempt a rescue, or the failure to file a tax return when required by law. Possession—a condition begun by an act of acquisition and continued by a failure to divest—may also be punished as a crime. But conduct in some form—an act, an omission, or possession—remains everywhere accepted as an essential prerequisite of criminal conviction and punishment.

## 2. RATIONALE FOR THE ACT REQUIREMENT

Justice Black offered a rationale for the act requirement in his concurring opinion in Powell v. Texas, 392 U.S. 514, 543 (1968):

> The reasons for [the] refusal to permit conviction without proof of an act are difficult to spell out, but they are nonetheless perceived and universally expressed in our criminal law. Evidence of propensity can be considered relatively unreliable and more difficult for a defendant to rebut; the requirement of a specific act thus provides some protection against false charges. . . . Perhaps more fundamental is the difficulty of distinguishing, in the absence of any conduct, between desires of the day-dream variety and fixed intentions that may pose a real threat to society; extending the criminal law to cover both types of desire would be unthinkable, since "[t]here can hardly be anyone who has never thought evil. When a desire is inhibited it would be absurd to condemn this natural psychological mechanism as illegal."[c]

Compare the rationale offered in John C. Jeffries, Jr. and Paul Stephan, Defenses, Presumptions, and Burden of Proof in the Criminal Law, 88 Yale L. J. 1325, 1371 n.130 (1979). "The significance of the act requirement should not be understated," they say, for three reasons.

The first is that "it serves a critical evidentiary function in corroborating other proof going to the existence of evil intent." There is a substantial risk of error, they add, if state of mind is judged when "not anchored in evidence of objectively demonstrable conduct." Therefore "proof of conduct" is required "to establish culpability." A jury finding of the mens rea required for a crime is best anchored, in other words, in inferences drawn from the defendant's conduct.

Second, "proof of conduct is necessary to establish dangerousness." Actual conduct is important "in differentiating daydreams from fixed intentions." State of mind may be "evanescent, fluid, and various." If "there is no real prospect that evil thought will be translated into evil deed, there is no legitimate occasion for punishment." Requiring conduct thus "precludes criminal penalty for fantasy, wish, or conjecture." It establishes that the defendant is a genuine threat to public safety because thoughts have been translated into resolution to act.

Third, the act requirement serves an important civil liberties function. It "preserves the liberty of the individual citizen by constraining penal liability within a tolerable sphere." It limits "the coercive power of the state and marks a boundary of individual accountability to the collective will." Jeffries and Stephan illustrated this third point by referring to Herbert Packer's argument that "the act requirement provides a locus

[c] The quote is from Sir William Blackstone, an English jurist of the 18th Century most noted for his authoritative commentaries on the common law.

poenitentiae to enable the law-abiding citizen to avoid criminal liability." Simply put, individual liberty is promoted because people know that they can avoid criminal liability simply by not doing certain things.

In The Limits of the Criminal Sanction 73–75 (1968), Packer argued that there is nothing in the nature of things that requires the criminal law to focus on conduct rather than on thoughts, emotions, personality, and character. If ascertaining these characteristics of the citizen was the justification for punishment, he concluded, conduct would merely be evidence of guilt rather than an independent requirement. Presumably we would then be prepared to punish people for their thoughts and propensities—for who they were—rather than for what they actually did.

One reason we do not do this, Packer surmised, is that "we have not been sufficiently stirred by the danger presented or sufficiently confident of our ability to discern propensities in the absence of conduct." Without conduct we cannot be certain, as Jeffries and Stephan argued, of either danger or culpability. But these reasons alone were not, he thought, sufficient justification for the independent focus of the criminal law on conduct. The criminal law punishes culpable choices that threaten public safety and other basic public interests. A central theoretical premise is that these choices are the product of individual "free will and human autonomy":

> Neither philosophic concepts nor psychological realities are actually at issue in the criminal law. The idea of free will in relation to conduct is not, in the legal system, a statement of fact, but rather a value preference having very little to do with the metaphysics of determinism and free will. . . . Very simply, the law treats man's conduct as autonomous and willed, not because it is, but because it is desirable to proceed as if it were. It is desirable because the capacity of the individual human being to live his life in reasonable freedom from socially imposed external constraints (the only kind with which the law is concerned) would be fatally impaired unless the law provided a locus poenitentiae, a point of no return beyond which external constraints may be imposed but before which the individual is free—not free of whatever compulsions determinists tell us he labors under but free of the very specific social compulsions of the law. . . .

## 3. QUESTIONS AND COMMENTS ON THE CONDUCT REQUIREMENT

Suppose, hypothetically, that scientifically based predictive techniques were sufficiently refined to allow accurate predictions of violent criminal behavior. Suppose, to be specific, that persons extremely likely to engage in violent rape could be identified in advance of such conduct by some scientific test or procedure. If such a procedure were feasible, should it be used as a basis for criminal prosecution? Doing so would prevent rape rather than merely punishing the offender after it occurs. Would this be a sufficient justification for punishment in advance of conduct? Or would it still be preferable to await punishable conduct before coercive state intervention?

## 4. THE REQUIREMENT THAT THE ACT BE VOLUNTARY

The criminal law also requires that the defendant's conduct be "voluntary," that is, in some sense an act of the defendant's free will. The next case and following notes explore the meaning of this requirement.

## Martin v. State

Alabama Court of Appeals, 1944.
4 Div. 805, 17 So.2d 427.

■ SIMPSON, JUDGE.

Appellant was convicted of being drunk on a public highway, and appeals. Officers of the law arrested him at his home and took him onto the highway, where he allegedly committed the proscribed acts, viz., manifested a drunken condition by using loud and profane language.

The pertinent provisions of our statute are: "Any person who, while intoxicated or drunk, appears in any public place where one or more persons are present, . . . and manifests a drunken condition by boisterous or indecent conduct, or loud and profane discourse, shall, on conviction, be fined," etc. Code 1940, tit., 14, § 120.

Under the plain terms of this statute, a voluntary appearance is presupposed. The rule has been declared, and we think it sound, that an accusation of drunkenness in a designated public place cannot be established by proof that the accused, while in an intoxicated condition, was involuntarily and forcibly carried to that place by the arresting officer.

Conviction of appellant was contrary to this announced principle and, in our view, erroneous. It appears that no legal conviction can be sustained under the evidence, so, consonant with the prevailing rule, the judgment of the trial court is reversed and one here rendered discharging appellant. . . .

### NOTES ON THE REQUIREMENT OF A VOLUNTARY ACT

#### 1. THE REQUIREMENT OF A VOLUNTARY ACT

Settled doctrine requires not only that criminal liability be based on conduct, but also that the conduct be voluntary. This is called the requirement of a voluntary "act," but it applies as well to omissions and to possession.[a]

The classic definition of a "voluntary act" is that it must result from an exercise of will.[b] Note the requirement that there be an *exercise* of will. The requirement is not that the exercise of will be free from pressure. Many acts that in some sense are coerced are nevertheless held to satisfy the voluntary act requirement. An example might be the person who steals bread because there is no other way to feed a child. It may seem strained to describe such a theft as voluntary, but it is everywhere agreed that the voluntary act requirement would be met in such a case. The actor may

[a] Criminal liability for omissions and possession is dealt with later in this Chapter.

[b] See J. Austin, Lectures in Jurisprudence 284–91 (4th ed. 1873); J. Salmond, Jurisprudence 367–69 (10th ed. 1947); O. Holmes, The Common Law 53–55 (1881).

have engaged in a coerced choice, but nonetheless a choice was made. Similarly, if a bank is robbed by the victim of the threat, "rob the bank or I will shoot your children," the threat victim would have engaged in a voluntary act. The acts of stealing the bread and robbing the bank in these examples involve decisions, choices to do what was regarded as a lesser evil. In both cases, the threat victims would have engaged in an exercise of will, and hence a voluntary act within the meaning of the law.[c]

How to formulate the voluntary act requirement raises philosophical questions of some difficulty, and theoretical debate over the meaning of the concept continues.[d] The law, however, has largely been content to define by example, which is why most accounts of the voluntary act requirement feature illustrations of acts that are not voluntary. Among the generally accepted instances of involuntary conduct are the following:

**(i) Physically Coerced Movement.** If *A*, without *B*'s assent or cooperation, shoves *B* into *C* and thus knocks *C* into the path of a passing car, *B*'s act is involuntary. Indeed, it may be more idiomatic in this case to say that *B* has engaged in no act at all, for the act is attributed to *A*, not *B*. Under either formulation, *B* is not liable.

**(ii) Reflex Movements.** The usual example is the reaction of a person suddenly attacked by a swarm of bees. According to most authorities, a person so afflicted while, say, driving a car could not be held liable for the resulting loss of control over the vehicle.

**(iii) Muscular Contraction or Paralysis Produced by Disease.** Some disorders of the central nervous system, including epilepsy and chorea, cause muscular contractions beyond the control of the individual. Others, such as a stroke, may suddenly restrict movement or induce partial paralysis. A person who has no control over his or her limbs cannot be said to act voluntarily with respect to their movements.

**(iv) Unconsciousness.** A relatively complete obliteration of consciousness, ranging from coma to normal sleep, ordinarily involves a cessation of most motor functions. In some cases, however, unconscious movements may occur. A sleeping mother may roll over her child and smother it. A person may suffer unconsciousness due to stroke, epilepsy, narcolepsy, or some other neurophysiological disturbance. Physical movements or omissions during these intervals are not, in any meaningful sense, voluntary.

---

[c] This does not mean that the bread stealer and/or the bank robber would have no defense in this situation, only that the voluntary act requirement would be satisfied. One defense that may well be available to the bank robber is called "duress," which is considered in Chapter VII. The bread stealer could perhaps resort to the general defense of "necessity" (or "choice of evils"). This doctrine is also considered in Chapter VII.

There are also many other ways in which mitigation can be accomplished in the criminal justice system. For example, prosecutors can exercise their discretion to decline to prosecute and, in many situations, judges can dismiss the charge, suspend a sentence, or release a convicted offender on probation. See Model Penal Code §§ 2.12, 5.05(2), 6.12.

[d] An early attack on the classical formulation is H.L.A. Hart, Acts of Will and Responsibility, in Punishment and Responsibility at 90 (1968). Hart's views were criticized in Jeffrie G. Murphy, Involuntary Acts and Criminal Responsibility, 81 Ethics 332 (1971), where the author proposes a reformulation of the traditional focus on an exercise of the will. For probing philosophical analysis of this and related questions, see Michael S. Moore, Act and Crime (1993), and the symposium on that book in 142 U. Pa. L. Rev. 1443 (1994).

The common theme in these situations is that the actor's bodily movement or omission is not directed or monitored by conscious mental processes. As H.L.A. Hart once said, what is "missing in such a case is the minimum link between mind and body, indispensable for any form of criminal responsibility."[e]

## 2. CODIFICATION

Because voluntariness was an established feature of common law doctrine, courts have often enforced the voluntary act requirement in the absence of supporting legislation. Older American statutes did sometimes require a "voluntary act" without further explication, e.g., Smith-Hurd Ill. Ann. Stat. § 4–1, or exempt from liability persons who acted "without being conscious thereof," e.g., Cal. Penal Code § 26. A more elaborate formulation was undertaken by the Model Penal Code in § 2.01:

> (1) A person is not guilty of an offense unless his liability is based on conduct which includes a voluntary act or the omission to perform an act of which he is physically capable.
>
> (2) The following are not voluntary acts within the meaning of this Section:
>
> (a) a reflex or convulsion;
>
> (b) a bodily movement during unconsciousness or sleep;
>
> (c) conduct during hypnosis or resulting from hypnotic suggestion;
>
> (d) a bodily movement that otherwise is not a product of the effort or determination of the actor, either conscious or habitual.

Note that the Model Code continues the tradition of definition by example, and that the list of involuntary acts does not purport to be exhaustive. The Model Code provision plainly contemplates that judges will continue case-by-case development of the voluntary act requirement under the rubric of identifying acts that are "not [products] of the effort or determination of the actor, either conscious or habitual."

## 3. CONTENT AND FUNCTION OF THE VOLUNTARY ACT REQUIREMENT

Determining the meaning and scope of the voluntary act requirement poses questions of judgment as well as definition. Ultimately, the law's definition of the concept rests on a normative view of the appropriate reach of penal sanctions. But there is more to it than that. Some situations in which acts are in a sense "involuntary" ought to be resolved by policies that will not be applicable to other situations involving seemingly "involuntary" behavior. For this reason, the law has developed a variety of doctrinal categories to deal with cases which, at bottom, may be thought to raise similar concerns about whether the actor's behavior was the product of free choice.

Consider, for example, the bank robber case hypothesized in Note 1. Plainly the law must take account of the nature of the threat if it is to recognize a defense in such a situation. "Rob the bank or I will shoot your children" is obviously of a different order than "rob the bank or I will

---

[e] H.L.A. Hart, Acts of Will and Responsibility, in Punishment and Responsibility at 92 (1968).

tell everyone you lied about your age in college to buy a drink" or "rob the bank or I will tell your spouse that you are sleeping around." One reason there is a separate doctrinal category for the defense of duress is that the law needs to specify the kind and quality of threats that should count in order for that defense to be successful. And doing so involves very different considerations from those that ought to control whether the actor's conduct is the result of sleepwalking or is in more general terms "a product of the effort or determination of the actor, either conscious or habitual."

It is important also to understand the consequence of a finding that the defendant's conduct is involuntary. Under settled principles, a voluntary act is a necessary, though not sufficient, condition of criminal liability. Holding an act involuntary completely precludes criminal liability for that act. The result is outright acquittal, and a total sacrifice of the public protection objectives that may be implicated by the actor's conduct.

Not surprisingly, the complete exculpation that results from a finding of involuntariness has constrained the interpretation of that concept. Consider the defense of insanity, another doctrinal category that in some contexts might be seen as involving "involuntary" behavior. Determining when a person's mental illness overrides the capacity to conform behavior to social norms involves subtle judgments about what kinds of mental diseases count and when capacity to choose is overridden. These judgments raise policy concerns that are completely different from those raised by the bank robber who acts under duress. And both cases raise completely different concerns from those raised by the person who causes harm because of an epileptic seizure. For this reason alone, different doctrinal categories are used to develop customized limitations appropriate for each situation. But consider also that people whose mental illness impairs their capacity to make rational choices may pose a continuing threat to public safety. Giving them a voluntary act defense would result in simple acquittal. Those who successfully assert an insanity defense, by contrast, are usually subjected to periods of confinement for treatment of their mental condition designed in part to protect the public from future harm. This is another reason for a separate doctrinal category.

It is important to remember, therefore, that finding an act voluntary does not automatically lead to criminal liability. It merely forecloses one of several potential grounds of exculpation. The law deals with behavior that might be "coerced" or "involuntary" in some broad moral sense through a number of different doctrines.

### 4. INVOLUNTARY ACT IN A VOLUNTARY COURSE OF CONDUCT: *PEOPLE V. DECINA*

A recurring problem is the case of an involuntary act embedded in an otherwise voluntary course of conduct. Here the Model Penal Code formulation is instructive. It does not flatly preclude liability based on involuntary conduct; instead, it requires that liability be based on "conduct which includes" a voluntary act. The point of this phrasing is to leave open the possibility of penal sanctions for a voluntary course of conduct that includes some involuntary aspects.

The issue is raised by the famous case of People v. Decina, 2 N.Y.2d 133, 138 N.E.2d 799 (1956). The defendant suffered an epileptic seizure while driving and ran over and killed several children. He was convicted under a statute punishing negligent homicide in a motor vehicle.[f] Everyone agreed that the seizure itself was involuntary and could not support penal liability, but the prosecution proceeded on the theory that the defendant was liable for the negligent and voluntary act of driving a car with knowledge that he was subject to epileptic seizures. The indictment was sustained on the ground that the admittedly involuntary character of the seizure did not vitiate the defendant's responsibility for his voluntary acts prior to losing consciousness:

> To hold otherwise would be to say that a man may freely indulge himself in liquor in the same hope that it will not affect his driving, and if it later develops that ensuing intoxication causes dangerous and reckless driving resulting in death, his unconsciousness or involuntariness at that time would relieve him from prosecution under the statute. His awareness of a condition which he knows may produce such consequences as these, and his disregard of the consequences, [render] him liable for culpable negligence. . . . To have a sudden sleeping spell, an unexpected heart or other disabling attack, without any prior knowledge or warning thereof, is an altogether different situation. . . .

This is not to say that it is necessarily negligent to drive with knowledge of a potentially disabling medical condition, but only that the act of doing so may be serve in an appropriate case as the basis for criminal liability.[g] For another example of such a situation, see Frederick Kunkle, Case Moves Forward in Frederick Fatalities, Wash. Post, Jan. 18, 2004, at C1.

Compare *Decina* to *Martin*. Was Martin prosecuted, in the words of the Model Penal Code, for "conduct which includes" a voluntary act? Most courts, if not all, would not allow the mere fact that Martin was drunk to support the proposition that his behavior after he reached the public highway was involuntary. Given that, why was he entitled to acquittal based on the involuntary act doctrine? His behavior "included" a voluntary act, did it not? Might there have been a reason other than the voluntary act doctrine that motivated the Court to reverse Martin's conviction?

## 5. CONCLUDING PROBLEM: *PEOPLE V. GASTELLO*

Similar problems have arisen when persons arrested for crime had on their persons controlled substances and were later charged with introducing them into a correctional facility. Examples are Oregon v. Tippetts, 180 Or.App. 350, 43 P.3d 455 (2002), and People v. Gastello, 149 Cal.App.4th 943, 57 Cal.Rptr.3d 293 (2007). In the latter case:

> Defendant Tommy Gastello was convicted of bringing drugs into a jail. His case presents one question: Is an accused guilty of bringing drugs into jail if he or she entered the jail only due to being arrested and brought there in custody? The answer has to be

---

[f] N.Y. Penal Law § 1053–a provided punishment for anyone "who operates or drives any vehicle of any kind in a reckless or culpably negligent manner, whereby a human being is killed . . . . ."

[g] While this position seems consistent with the voluntary act requirement, the point is not entirely free from doubt. In particular, debate may arise over whether the specific voluntary act committed by the defendant was the act proscribed by the offense. Essentially, this is an issue of statutory construction. For discussions evidencing concern with this problem, see the dissent in People v. Decina, 2 N.Y.2d at 140, 138 N.E.2d at 804, and the earlier decision in People v. Freeman, 61 Cal.App.2d 110, 142 P.2d 435 (1943).

> no. Before defendant went out and encountered the police, he intentionally put the drugs in his pocket and was guilty of simple possession, but . . . he did not engage in the voluntary act (actus reus) necessary for the crime of *bringing them into the jail*. He was driven to the jail in custody, in a police car, in handcuffs. . . . The conviction of bringing drugs into a jail is reversed.
>
> The case is even stronger for the defendant than Martin v. State, 31 Ala.App. 334, 17 So.2d 427 (1944). *Martin* is a criminal law classic on the subject of actus reus and is a favorite of casebooks and law review articles. Martin was arrested in his house. Police officers then took him out onto the street. There, he "manifested a drunken condition by using loud and profane language." He was convicted of public drunkenness. The Alabama Court of Appeals reversed. . . . Martin at least did the affirmative act of yelling profanities after being arrested and brought into the street. Here defendant did nothing at all after police officers took custody of him; he omitted to confess to having drugs and submitted to being taken to prison. For these reasons, the evidence did not support the essential element of actus reus.

The California Court of Appeal plainly thought that *Gastello* was controlled by *Martin*. Are the two cases really alike? In what sense did Gastello fail to commit a voluntary act? Was he not perfectly free to disclose his possession of drugs and thereby avoid bringing them into the jail? It may be understandable that he did not wish to do so, but does that render his conduct involuntary? Might there be some other explanation for the result?

## SECTION 2: THE REQUIREMENT THAT OFFENSES BE PREVIOUSLY DEFINED

### Rex v. Manley

Court of Criminal Appeal, 1932.
[1933] 1 K.B. 529.

Appeal against conviction, a certificate of fitness for appeal having been granted by the Recorder of London.

On November 18, 1932, the appellant, Elizabeth Manley, was charged at the Central Criminal Court on an indictment containing two counts, the first count being that she "on September 10, 1932, did, by means of certain false statements, to wit that on that day a man whose description she then gave had hit her with his fist and taken from her handbag, six 10*s*. notes, nine 1*l*. notes, 15*s*. in silver, and a receipt, cause officers of the metropolitan police maintained at public expense for the public benefit to devote their time and services to the investigation of false allegations, thereby temporarily depriving the public of the services of these public officers, and rendering liege subjects of the king liable to suspicion, accusation and arrest, and in so doing did unlawfully effect a public mischief"; and the second count being that on September 15, 1932, she made a statement that on September 10, 1932, a man whose description she gave came up behind her and that she then felt a blow in the back and that her bag containing 12*l*. 12*s*. 6*d*. had been taken from under her arm.

*plea*   [ The appellant pleaded not guilty.

On behalf of the prosecution evidence was called to support the allegations in the indictment.

On behalf of the appellant these allegations were not denied and no evidence was called, but the submission was made that the indictment disclosed no offence known to the law, and that there was no cause to go to the jury.

In giving <u>judgment</u> on that submission the <u>Recorder</u> said: "It is my clear view that this act is one which may tend to a public mischief. It would be intolerable that our police force, already hard pressed to preserve law and order in a time of increasing lawlessness, should have their services deflected in order to follow up charges which are entirely bogus to the knowledge of those making them. In my view, taking the times—you must consider the times in which we live—such an act may distinctly tend to the public mischief. . . . I hold <u>as a matter of law</u> that

*holding of*   [ this <u>indictment discloses a common law misdemeanour.</u>"
*lower court*

The jury <u>found</u> on the evidence that the appellant had done the acts

*jury found*   [ which she was alleged to have done and that she was <u>guilty of the of-</u>
*appellant*   <u>fence with which she was charged.</u>
*guilty*

The <u>Recorder postponed sentence</u>, and granted a certificate that the case was fit for an appeal to the Court of Criminal Appeal on the question whether he was right in holding that the indictment disclosed a common law misdemeanour; and he bound <u>the appellant over to come</u>

*result*   [ <u>up for judgment when the Court of Criminal Appeal had decided</u> the

*"bound*   *CCA decides*   question of law. . . .
*over"*   *question of law*

■ <u>LORD HEWART</u>, C.J. The appellant in this case was indicted at the Central Criminal Court before the learned Recorder of London for having effected a public mischief. [His Lordship read the counts of the indictment, and continued:] The appellant was convicted, and was bound over to come up for judgment when called upon to do so after this court had decided the question of law now raised. It was then submitted on her behalf, as it is submitted now, that she had committed no offence; but before that proposition can be assented to it is necessary, as counsel for the prosecution has indicated, to <u>consider two questions.</u>

*1st question*   The <u>first</u> is whether it is true at the present day <u>to say that there</u> is
*court answers*   a <u>misdemeanour of committing an act tending to the public mischief.</u> In our opinion that question ought to be answered in the <u>affirmative</u>. We think that the law remains as it was stated to be by <u>Lawrence</u>, J., in

*the law—*   Rex v. Higgins, [1801] 2 East 5, 21: "<u>All offences of a public nature, that</u>
*Rex v. Higgins*   <u>is, all such acts or attempts as tend to the prejudice of the community,</u> <u>are indictable.</u>" That case was referred to with approval in the case of Rex v. Brailsford, [1905] 2 K.B. 730, and in the still more recent case of Rex v. Porter, [1910] 1 K.B. 369, 372, where Lord Alverstone, C.J., in delivering the judgment of the court, said: "We are of opinion that it is for the court to direct the jury as to whether such an act may tend to the public mischief, and that it is not in such a case an issue of fact upon which evidence can be given."

*2nd*   The <u>second question</u> is whether <u>the appellant did acts which consti-</u>
*question*   <u>tute a public mischief.</u> As counsel has said, the facts stated in the indictment are not in dispute, and it is admitted that what is there alleged to have been done by the appellant was done by her. In

the opinion of the Court the indictment aptly describes two ingredients of public mischief or prejudice to the community, one of these being that officers of the metropolitan police were led to devote their time and services to the investigation of an idle charge, and the other being that members of the public, or at any rate those of them who answered a certain description, were put in peril of suspicion and arrest.

For these reasons the court is of opinion that the conviction should stand and that the appeal should be dismissed.

Appeal dismissed.

## NOTES ON THE PRINCIPLE OF LEGALITY AND THE COMMON LAW

### 1. THE METHODOLOGY OF THE COMMON LAW

*Manley* illustrates an important feature of the methodology of the "common law." That phrase has a variety of meanings but is used chiefly to refer to judge-made law. Most of the ancient English offenses were judicial in origin. By the accession of Elizabeth I (1558), the English courts had created and defined felonies of murder, suicide (which might have been an independent felony or a species of murder), manslaughter, arson, burglary, robbery, mayhem, larceny, sodomy, and rape. Various lesser wrongs were punished as misdemeanors. Offenses in both categories were created by judges who acted without aid of statute to protect societal interests as they saw them. The legacy of the common law, therefore, was an assumption of judicial authority to adapt broad principles to new situations as the occasion arose.

Over time, the exercise of this authority became more constrained. For one thing, with the evolution of the idea of precedent, the common law tradition bred its own limitation. Future decisions were supposed to be constrained by the principles announced in prior ones. As an ever more elaborate body of precedent built up, opportunities for judicial innovation were reduced.

Increasing activity by parliament further lessened the need for activism by the courts. Early legislative efforts were usually addressed to gaps in the common law. As parliament met more often and grew in power and prestige, more and more statutes were enacted to supplement or correct the law as declared by judges. Gradually, the locus of crime creation shifted from the courts to the legislature. As early as 1600, judicial creation of new felonies was a thing of the past. New misdemeanors, on the other hand, continued to be recognized, albeit infrequently, throughout the 17th and 18th centuries. The judges who decided these cases often spoke of the residual authority of courts to punish as criminal any conduct contra bonos mores et decorum—in more modern phrasing, any conduct tending to outrage decency or to corrupt public morals.

A famous early assertion of this power was Rex v. Sidley, 82 E.R. 1036 (1663), where Sir Charles Sidley was found guilty of a common law misdemeanor for standing naked on a balcony at Covent Garden. Others were held liable for such things as blasphemy, publication of an obscene book, public nudity and exhibitionism, and digging up corpses for anatomical inspection. Decisions of this sort were made sporadically at least through 1774, when the underlying claim of continuing common law authority to create new crimes was endorsed by the great Lord Mansfield. "Whatever is contra bonos mores et decorum," said Mansfield, "the principles of our law prohibit, and the king's court, as the general censor and guardian of the public manners, is bound to restrain and punish." Jones v. Randall, [1774] 98 E.R. 706, 707.

By the late 19th century, the power of the courts to punish new kinds of conduct tending to corrupt morals or to create public mischief had fallen into disuse and apparent disrepute, even though prosecutions continued for previously defined offenses. In 1883 the common law authority to create new crimes was denounced by no less an authority than Sir James Fitzjames Stephen, a successor to Mansfield on the Queen's Bench and pre-eminent Victorian historian of the criminal law: "Though the existence of this power as inherent in the judges has been asserted by several high authorities for a great length of time, it is hardly probable that any attempt would be made to exercise it at the present day; and any such attempt would be received with great opposition, and would place the bench in an invidious position." 3 James Stephen, A History of the Criminal Law of England 359–60 (1883). The result was that *Manley*, decided half a century after Stephen's pronouncement, came as a surprise and provoked something of a furor in English legal circles.[a]

## 2. THE PRINCIPLE OF LEGALITY

principle of legality

Today, *Manley* would widely be thought to violate the "principle of legality." The principle of legality is not in any ordinary sense a rule of law. It is more nearly a statement of an ideal. Put simply, the principle of legality forbids retroactive crime definition. Often reduced to the maxim, nulla poena (or nullum crimen) sine lege, this construct condemns judicial crime creation of the sort involved in *Manley*. The essential idea is that no one should be punished for a crime that has not been defined in advance by the appropriate authority. Generally speaking, the appropriate institution for crime definition is the legislature. For most purposes, therefore, the principle of legality may be taken to signify the desirability in principle of advance legislative specification of criminal conduct.

Note at the outset two important features of the principle of legality. First, it is not so much a unitary idea as a cluster of ideas that grew up together historically. Logically, advance specification of crime does not necessarily require that the definition be *legislative*. Courts can also give prospective definitions of conduct to be punished in the future. And, as later materials illustrate, the fact that the legislature has passed a statute does not necessarily mean that there is meaningful advance specification of what conduct is criminal. Legislative statements may be so general as to leave all the real work to the courts. Moreover, all language is to some ex-

[a] For criticism of *Manley*, see Glanville Williams, Criminal Law: The General Part 596–600 (2d ed. 1961), and the authorities cited in id. at 596 n.2. See also Withers v. Director of Public Prosecutions, [1975] A.C. 842, in which *Manley* is expressly repudiated. *Withers* notwithstanding, other modern English cases followed *Manley* in punishing new kinds of misconduct under the broad rubrics of the common law. See, e.g., Shaw v. Director of Public Prosecutions, [1961] 2 All E.R. 446 (upholding conviction for conspiracy to corrupt public morals for publishing a "ladies directory" furnishing contact information for prostitutes); Knuller v. Director of Public Prosecutions, [1972] 2 All E.R. 898 (upholding conviction of the same offense for publishing a magazine containing classified ads by male homosexuals); Regina v. Hamilton, [2007] E.W.C.A. Crim. 2062 (upholding conviction for common law misdemeanor of outraging public decency for "upskirting," i.e., surreptitious filming up women's skirts).

tent ambiguous. Legislative definitions of crimes require interpretation by courts as they are applied to specific situations. In some sense *any* judicial decision that resolves a previously unsettled ambiguity involves an element of retroactivity when the result is applied to the defendant then before the court. This raises a question of some subtlety. Not surprisingly, as illustrated later in this Chapter, a line must be drawn between "interpretation" and "creation" when courts apply statutory language to defendants before them.

Second, it is important to remember that the insistence on advance legislative crime definition has no necessary relation to the content of the offenses so defined. The principle of legality does not speak to the question of what conduct should be declared criminal. Rather, it states a normative expectation regarding how that decision should be made. In other words, the principle concerns the *process* of crime definition rather than the *content* of specific offenses. The issues are *who* makes the decision and, perhaps more importantly, *when* the decision is made. *What* the substance of the prohibition should be and how severely it should be punished are important, to be sure, but raise wholly different issues.

### 3. QUESTIONS AND COMMENTS ON *MANLEY*

One way to test understanding of the point just made is to ask two questions. The first is whether *what* Manley did should be a crime. Is there any doubt that she deserved to be convicted of a (minor) crime? Were not the authors of the Model Penal Code right when they so concluded in § 241.5? Were they also right to divide the offense into different levels of seriousness?

The second question is whether the precedents on which the *Manley* Court relied were sufficiently precise to say that the crime she committed had been defined before she acted. Were they? Should that have mattered? In the end, was the court's decision in *Manley* right or wrong? These questions should be revisited after reading the notes below on the history and rationale of the principle of legality.

### 4. THE CONTINUING SIGNIFICANCE OF THE COMMON LAW

Despite the fact that judicial crime creation is largely a thing of the past, the common law of crimes remains significant. Rejection of common law crime creation does not necessarily mean that the results of that tradition have also been abandoned. Several states occasionally enforce previously recognized non-statutory offenses, even though they do not assert the authority to create new ones.[b] Such prosecutions are not widely perceived

---

[b] As of 1947, fully 31 American jurisdictions recognized the continued viability of the common law insofar as it had not been superseded by legislation. Note, Common Law Crimes in the United States, 47 Colum. L. Rev. 1332 (1947). In succeeding decades, the number of states taking this position declined sharply. The greatest single factor was the widespread adoption of revised criminal codes, virtually all of which follow Section 1.05 of the Model Penal Code in eliminating non-statutory crimes. Nevertheless, in 2014, at least 15 states continued to allow prosecution for non-statutory offenses. See Fla. Stat. Ann. § 775.01(2013); Md. Const. Code Ann. art. 5; Mass. Gen. Laws Ann. Const. pt. 2, ch. 6, art. VI; Mich. Comp. Laws Ann. Const. art. 3, § 7; Miss. Code Ann. § 99–1–3 (2007); N.M. Stat. Ann. § 30–1–3 (West 2003); N.C. Gen. Stat. § 4–1 (2013); R.I. Gen. Laws § 11–1–1 (2002); S.C. Code Ann. § 14–1–50 (1977); Vt. Stat. Ann. tit. 1, § 271 (2010); Va. Code Ann. § 1–200 (2011); Wash. Rev. Code Ann. § 9A.04.060 (2012); W.Va. Code § 2–1–1(LexisNexis 2013); Wyo. Stat. § 8–1–101 (2013). In

as violations of the principle of legality, so long as they are adequately based on prior precedents defining the specific conduct as an offense at common law.

Of far greater consequence than the occasional prosecution for a non-statutory offense is the pervasive role of the common law as an aid to the implementation or interpretation of criminal statutes. In Virginia, for example, the legislature gave the courts the choice of resorting to the common law or starting over from scratch when it assigned penalties for second degree murder by defining it as "all murder other than capital murder and murder in the first degree." Va. Code Ann. § 18.2–32. Similarly, the Virginia legislature provided punishments for voluntary and involuntary manslaughter without any specification of how those offenses should be defined. Va. Code Ann. §§ 18.2–35, 18.2–36. Often a statutory definition of crime will repeat the common law definition or incorporate terms used by the common law. In such cases, gaps or ambiguities in the statutory formulation are often filled in by reference to common law understanding. An illustration is provided by *Keeler v. Superior Court of Amador County*, a main case in Section 3 below.

The common law is important to modern American criminal law for other reasons as well. For one thing, virtually the entire body of what is often called the "general part" of the criminal law—consisting of doctrines applicable to many specific crimes, such as self-defense or the insanity defense—is based in many jurisdictions on principles derived from the common law. The federal insanity defense, for example, was not defined by statute until 1984. Before then, each Circuit Court of Appeals defined insanity for itself using the classic common law methodology and relying on sources based on the common law. Many state and federal defenses remain statutorily undefined, which leaves the courts to develop and apply appropriate principles that often have origins in the common law.[c]

Moreover, the common law developed a distinctive vocabulary and methodology of continuing influence in the analysis of criminal law issues. This is most notable in the mens rea cases considered in Chapters III and IV, but it can also be found, for example, in the law governing what kinds of omissions can constitute a criminal actus reus.

Finally, the substantive content of the common law remains significant. Many states explicitly base their criminal law on common law antecedents. Others base their law on statutes derived from the Model Penal Code, but that code also borrows much of its content from the earlier common law. Thus, the common law remains vitally important to the student of modern American criminal law.

---

Tennessee there is no express statute but case law indicates that prosecution for common law crimes continues. E.g., Gervin v. State, 212 Tenn. 653, 371 S.W.2d 449 (1963).

[c] See, for example, Dixon v. United States, 548 U.S. 1 (2006), which concerned the defense of duress to a federal crime. Neither the content of the defense nor whether the prosecution or the defense had to bear the burden of proof was defined by statute. The Supreme Court therefore had to deal with both issues on its own.

## NOTES ON THE HISTORY AND RATIONALE OF THE PRINCIPLE OF LEGALITY

### 1. ORIGINS OF THE PRINCIPLE OF LEGALITY

Although there may have been ancient antecedents, the categorical insistence on advance legislative crime definition began in late 18th-century Europe. The idea sprang from the intellectual movement known as the Enlightenment, and its origins are deeply embedded in Enlightenment thought.

At the level of individual behavior, Enlightenment thinkers viewed humans as rational and hedonistic. Since individual conduct presumably was based on a utilitarian calculation of pain and pleasure, criminal acts could be deterred by a credible threat of a penalty sufficient to outweigh the expected gain from wrongdoing. In order for this scheme to work, crimes and punishments had to be spelled out in advance.

At the level of societal organization, Enlightenment thought emphasized contractarian notions of the legitimacy of government. The state owed its authority to the aggregate surrenders of individual freedom necessary to the formation of the social compact. Everyone gave up some freedom in order to secure the benefits of an ordered society, and the punishment of individuals was legitimate if based on laws established for the protection of society as a whole. Implicit in this conception is a commitment to representative government. Accordingly, Enlightenment thinkers identified the legislature as the only legitimate institution for assessing the needs of society and for implementing those judgments through penal laws. Thus, Enlightenment ideology insisted not only that crime definition be prospective in nature but also that it be legislative in origin.

Enlightenment thinkers who proved especially influential in the development of criminal law were Montesquieu and Cesare Beccaria. In a republic, according to Montesquieu, "the people should have the sole power to enact laws." Montesquieu, The Spirit of the Laws 13 (T. Nugent, trans., 1897). As the branch of government most directly responsive to the popular will, the legislature had the power to define crimes. Judges were to enforce statutes, not to make law. Beccaria emphasized the notion that advance definition of offenses was essential to crime control. He argued that crime was actually caused, in part, by the obscurity and irrationality of the penal law. By creating clear, precise, and reasonable laws, with penalties proportionate to the gravity of the offense and sufficiently harsh to offset any gain to the offender, the legislature could attack the problem of crime. In Beccaria's view, judicial innovation would lead to arbitrariness and inconsistency. Results would depend on "the good or bad logic of the judge; and this will depend on his good or bad digestion; on the violence of his passion; on the rank and condition of the accused, or on his connections with the judge. . . ." Cesare Beccaria, On Crimes and Punishments 23–24 (E. Ingraham, trans., 1819). The upshot of such disarray would be impairment of the law's capacity to exert a restraining influence on human passions.

### 2. THE AMERICAN EXPERIENCE: ENCOUNTER WITH THE COMMON LAW

In many ways the newly independent American nation was fertile soil for the doctrine of nulla poena sine lege. For one thing, there was the pervasive influence of Enlightenment thought generally.[a] Montesquieu and Beccaria were widely read, and their insistence on a sharp differentiation of legislative, executive, and judicial functions found practical expression in the American scheme of separation of powers. That concept called for a division of responsibilities among three branches of government. The power to make laws was assigned to the legislature. Perhaps most importantly, the insistence on legislative action as essential to the political legitimacy of crime definition was a natural corollary of the American ideal of popular sovereignty through republican government.

In light of these factors, one might have expected nulla poena sine lege quickly to take its place as the first principle of American criminal law. In fact, the story is much more complicated. "English law—as authority, as legitimizing precedent, as embodied principle, and as the framework of historical understanding—stood side by side with Enlightenment rationalism" in influencing the American revolutionaries. Bernard Bailyn, The Ideological Origins of the American Revolution 31 (1967). In the United States, unlike Europe, the theoretical insistence on legislative crime definition ran up against the ancient, familiar, and entrenched tradition of the English common law.

The conflict between the common law heritage and Enlightenment ideals of political organization was nowhere more apparent than in the debate whether to allow criminal prosecution for non-statutory offenses. At the federal level, the answer was "no." Federal courts do not have the authority to create crimes in the common law fashion, and no crime can be prosecuted as a federal offense unless duly enacted by Congress. See United States v. Hudson and Goodwin, 11 U.S. (7 Cranch) 32 (1812).

At the state level, the story was entirely different. Despite the efforts of early law reformers, all of the original states, and most of the later ones, adopted English common law insofar as it was deemed applicable to local conditions. This "reception" of the common law, as it came to be called, usually included English law of a general nature as of a certain date. Many states used 1607, when the first colony was founded, while others used 1775 or 1776, when the break with England occurred. Whatever the date used, the reception of English common law included not only the roster of offenses previously defined by the English courts, but also the familiar and intimately related assumption that the courts had residual authority to adapt old principles to new situations should the need arise. See generally Ford W. Hall, The Common Law: An Account of Its Reception in the United States, 4 Vand. L. Rev. 791 (1951).

An early example of the exercise of this power is Pennsylvania v. Gillespie, 1 Add. 267 (1795), where the defendant was indicted for "unlawfully, forcibly and contemptuously tearing down" an advertisement for a tax sale. This act was held criminal despite the absence of any statute against it. In State v. Buckman, 8 N.H. 203 (1836), the defendant was indicted for putting a dead animal into a well. The court upheld the conviction on the ground that the act was analogous to selling unwholesome food and to poisoning food or drink intended for human consumption, both of which were indictable at common law. The rationale for such innovations

---

[a] See generally Bernard Bailyn, The Ideological Origins of the American Revolution (1967), and Peter Gay, America The Paradoxical, 62 Va. L. Rev. 843 (1976).

was explained by the Supreme Court of Pennsylvania in Commonwealth v. Taylor, 5 Binn. 277, 281 (Pa.1812):

> It is impossible to find precedents for all offenses. The malicious ingenuity of mankind is constantly producing new inventions in the art of disturbing their neighbors. To this invention must be opposed general principles, calculated to meet and punish them.

Respected commentators also endorsed this approach. See Joel Bishop, Commentaries on the Criminal Law 18 (8th ed. 1892).

### 3. RECENT EXPERIENCE

In the United States, judicial crime creation is increasingly hard to find. Judges no longer feel free to respond to new situations as the occasion demands. They increasingly regard themselves as bound to enforce only those offenses previously declared to exist. Partly, this reflects a normative consensus against judicial crime creation. But it also reflects the lack of any practical necessity for such action. Legislatures sit more frequently and for longer sessions than ever before. Penal statutes accumulate over time, and there seems to be little difficulty in focusing legislative sentiment on the need to prohibit anti-social conduct. The result is such a comprehensiveness, not to say redundancy, of penal legislation that judicial crime creation is rendered unnecessary as well as objectionable.

### 4. MODERN RATIONALES

Today, few would take seriously Beccaria's idea that advance legislative crime definition plays a crucial role in the practical business of controlling criminal conduct. It seems far-fetched to believe that crime results in significant degree from the failure of citizens to know what is forbidden. Most criminals know their conduct is illegal but believe they will not be caught. Today, the principle of legality is seldom advanced as an aid to deterrence. Instead, it is defended chiefly as a normative proposition, essential to the ethical integrity of the criminal law but not to its efficiency.

In contrast, the political-legitimacy rationale for insisting on advance legislative crime definition survives, though perhaps with somewhat diminished force. Separation of powers remains a fundamental principle of American government, and lawmaking continues to be primarily the responsibility of the legislative branch. To this extent, Montesquieu's ideas endure.

It is clear, however, that the political-legitimacy rationale for preferring legislative to judicial crime creation does not tell the whole story. Modern explanations of the legality construct also emphasize fairness to the defendant. In particular, modern theorists view the principle of legality as an important prophylaxis against the arbitrary and abusive exercise of discretion in the enforcement of the penal law.

Herbert Packer[b] so concluded when he said that the principle of legality "operates primarily to control the discretion of the police and of prosecutors rather than that of judges." The possibility of arbitrary decision-making by courts is constrained by the fact that they "operate in the open through . . . a process of reasoned elaboration" that relates what happens in each new case to what happened in previous cases. Police and prosecutors,

[b] See Herbert Packer, The Limits of the Criminal Sanction 88–91 (1968).

in contrast, "operate in a setting of secrecy and informality." They never act with the transparency that characterizes the judicial system. Packer continued:

> Does this mean, then, that the conventional focus of the principle of legality, which is on defining the respective roles of legislatures and courts, is distorted? Does it really make no difference whether the operative law is "made" by legislatures, declaring certain kinds of conduct criminal before they occur, or by courts, looking backward at the conduct whose criminality they are called upon to adjudicate? Not at all. The conventional focus is perfectly correct . . . because in a system that lodges the all-important initiating power in the hands of officials who operate, as they must, through informal and secret processes, there must be some devices to insure that the initiating decisions are, to the greatest extent possible, fair, evenhanded, and rational. Most of these devices . . . are in the nature of post-audits on the decisions taken by the police and prosecutors. But the most important single device is the requirement . . . that the police and prosecutors confine their attention to the catalogue of what has already been defined as criminal. . . .
>
> If criminal law can be made a posteriori by judges, rather than a priori, by legislatures, then the enforcement officials are under strong temptation to guess what the judges will do in a particular case. This temptation cannot be eliminated . . . , but it can be minimized through the habits of thought acquired by enforcement officials who work under the principle of legality.

Factors such as political ideology, religion, race, ethnic identity, personal lifestyle, perceived class substructures, and sexual orientation may place one or another individuals or groups outside the mainstream of the culture in which they live. The principle of legality, or as it is often called the "rule of law," provides significant protection, as Packer argued, to people who are perceived to fit these categories, and indeed to all of us from the potential of arbitrary arrest based on the ad hoc judgments of the police. That the institutions of law should be arrayed to protect such diversity may seem obvious in a liberal democracy, but it is far from commonplace, either historically or among some contemporary cultures. Would it be expected, for example, that a Puritan theocracy, some examples of modern Islamic states, or a traditional Marxist dictatorship would have a comparable commitment to such protections? However this question is answered in different times and different places, the principle of legality is a fundamental underlying assumption about the relation of the state to individual citizens in a liberal democracy. It is a well-accepted underpinning of many of the doctrines developed in this Chapter and Chapters to follow.

## 5. THE DOCTRINE OF VAGUENESS

Principle of legality values are embedded in American constitutional law by the doctrine of vagueness. This doctrine performs at least two important functions. The first is what Anthony Amsterdam described in a famous law school student Note as providing a "buffer zone" for specifically

1st Function

protected constitutional rights.[c] In this function, the doctrine requires especially careful drafting of criminal statutes that could potentially threaten First Amendment free speech rights, for example, because people might steer clear of constitutionally protected activity in order to avoid the possibility of criminal prosecution. But as the next case illustrates, the vagueness doctrine independently protects principle of legality or rule of law values in situations where legislation does not adequately constrain the authority of police, prosecutors, and courts to engage in arbitrary, ad hoc, decisionmaking.[d]

## Papachristou v. City of Jacksonville

Supreme Court of the United States, 1972.
405 U.S. 156.

■ JUSTICE DOUGLAS delivered the opinion of the Court.

This case involves eight defendants who were convicted in a Florida municipal court of violating a Jacksonville, Florida, vagrancy ordinance.[1] Their convictions, entailing fines and jail sentences (some of which were suspended), were affirmed by the Florida [state courts]. The case is here on a petition for certiorari . . . . For reasons which will appear, we reverse.

---

[c] Note, The Void-For-Vagueness Doctrine in the Supreme Court, 109 U. Pa. L. Rev. 67, 75 (1960): As the law had evolved to the point in time when he was writing, "the doctrine of unconstitutional indefiniteness has been used by the Supreme Court almost invariably for the creation of an insulating buffer zone of added protection at the peripheries of several of the Bill of Rights freedoms."

[d] For discussion of the relation between the vagueness doctrine and the rule of law, see John C. Jeffries, Jr., Legality, Vagueness, and the Construction of Penal Statutes, 71 Va. L. Rev. 189, 201–19 (1985). Jeffries describes the vagueness doctrine as "the operational arm of legality." Id. at 196.

Amsterdam also recognized that the vagueness doctrine independently served rule of law values. See Note, The Void-For-Vagueness Doctrine in the Supreme Court, 109 U. Pa. L. Rev. 67, 85–87 (1960). He described this use of the vagueness doctrine by adding that his "buffer zone" thesis "does not mean . . . that unconstitutional uncertainty will never be found in a statute all of whose possible applications the enacting legislature would have had constitutional power to prescribe." The example he used—he wrote before *Papachristou* was decided—was Lanzetta v. New Jersey, 306 U.S. 451 (1939), which is described in the notes following *Papachristou*.

For a more recent proposal that the language of the vagueness doctrine be refined, but not its purpose or effect, see Peter W. Low and Joel S. Johnson, Changing the Vocabulary of the Vagueness Doctrine, 101 Va. L. Rev. ___ (2015) (pre-publication draft available on SSRN). *Papachristou* is discussed in detail.

[1] Jacksonville Ordinance Code § 26–57 provided at the time of these arrests and convictions as follows:

> Rogues and vagabonds, or dissolute persons who go about begging, common gamblers, persons who use juggling or unlawful games or plays, common drunkards, common night walkers, thieves, pilferers or pickpockets, traders in stolen property, lewd, wanton and lascivious persons, keepers of gambling places, common railers and brawlers, persons wandering or strolling around from place to place without any lawful purpose or object, habitual loafers, disorderly persons, persons neglecting all lawful business and habitually spending their time by frequenting houses of ill fame, gaming houses, or places where alcoholic beverages are sold or served, persons able to work but habitually living upon the earnings of their wives or minor children shall be deemed vagrants and, upon conviction in the Municipal Court shall be punished as provided for Class D offenses.

Class D offenses at the time of these arrests and convictions were punishable by 90 days' imprisonment, $500 fine, or both. . . .

At issue are five consolidated cases. Margaret Papachristou, Betty Calloway, Eugene Eddie Melton, and Leonard Johnson were all arrested early on a Sunday morning, and charged with vagrancy—"prowling by auto."

Jimmy Lee Smith and Milton Henry were charged with vagrancy—"vagabonds."

Henry Edward Heath and a codefendant were arrested for vagrancy—"loitering" and "common thief."

Thomas Owen Campbell was charged with vagrancy—"common thief."

Hugh Brown was charged with vagrancy—"disorderly loitering on street" and "disorderly conduct—resisting arrest with violence."

The facts are stipulated. Papachristou and Calloway are white females. Melton and Johnson are black males. Papachristou was enrolled in a job-training program sponsored by the State Employment Service at Florida Junior College in Jacksonville. Calloway was a typing and shorthand teacher at a state mental institution located near Jacksonville. She was the owner of the automobile in which the four defendants were arrested. Melton was a Vietnam war veteran who had been released from the Navy after nine months in a veterans' hospital. On the date of his arrest he was a part-time computer helper while attending college as a full-time student in Jacksonville. Johnson was a tow-motor operator in a grocery chain warehouse and was a lifelong resident of Jacksonville.

At the time of their arrest the four of them were riding in Calloway's car on the main thoroughfare in Jacksonville. They had left a restaurant owned by Johnson's uncle where they had eaten and were on their way to a nightclub. The arresting officers denied that the racial mixture in the car played any part in the decision to make the arrest. The arrest, they said, was made because the defendants had stopped near a used-car lot which had been broken into several times. There was, however, no evidence of any breaking and entering on the night in question.

Of these four charged with "prowling by auto" none had been previously arrested except Papachristou who had once been convicted of a municipal offense.

Jimmy Lee Smith and Milton Henry (who is not a petitioner) were arrested between 9 and 10 a.m. on a weekday in downtown Jacksonville, while waiting for a friend who was to lend them a car so they could apply for a job at a produce company. Smith was a part-time produce worker and part-time organizer for a Negro political group. He had a common-law wife and three children supported by him and his wife. He had been arrested several times but convicted only once. Smith's companion, Henry, was an 18-year-old high school student with no previous record of arrest.

This morning it was cold, and Smith had no jacket, so they went briefly into a dry cleaning shop to wait, but left when requested to do so. They thereafter walked back and forth two or three times over a two-block stretch looking for their friend. The store owners, who apparently were wary of Smith and his companion, summoned two police officers who searched the men and found neither had a weapon. But they were arrested because the officers said they had no identification and because the officers did not believe their story.

Heath and a codefendant were arrested for "loitering" and for "common thief." Both were residents of Jacksonville, Heath having lived there all his life and being employed at an automobile body shop. Heath had previously been arrested but his codefendant had no arrest record. Heath and his companion were arrested when they drove up to a residence shared by Heath's girl friend and some other girls. Some police officers were already there in the process of arresting another man. When Heath and his companion started backing out of the driveway, the officers signaled to them to stop and asked them to get out of the car, which they did. Thereupon they and the automobile were searched. Although no contraband or incriminating evidence was found, they were both arrested, Heath being charged with being a "common thief" because he was reputed to be a thief. The codefendant was charged with "loitering" because he was standing in the driveway, an act which the officers admitted was done only at their command.

Campbell was arrested as he reached his home very early one morning and was charged with "common thief." He was stopped by officers because he was traveling at a high rate of speed, yet no speeding charge was placed against him.

Brown was arrested when he was observed leaving a downtown Jacksonville hotel by a police officer seated in a cruiser. The police testified he was reputed to be a thief, narcotics pusher, and generally opprobrious character. The officer called Brown over to the car, intending at that time to arrest him unless he had a good explanation for being on the street. Brown walked over to the police cruiser, as commanded, and the officer began to search him, apparently preparatory to placing him in the car. In the process of the search he came on two small packets which were later found to contain heroin. When the officer touched the pocket where the packets were, Brown began to resist. He was charged with "disorderly loitering on street" and "disorderly conduct—resisting arrest with violence." While he was also charged with a narcotics violation, that charge was nolled.

Jacksonville's ordinance . . . [was derived from early English law and employs archaic language in its definition] of vagrants. The history is an often-told tale. The break-up of feudal estates in England led to labor shortages which in turn resulted in the Statutes of Laborers, designed to stabilize the labor force by prohibiting increases in wages and prohibiting the movement of workers from their home areas in search of improved conditions. Later vagrancy laws became criminal aspects of the poor laws. The series of laws passed in England on the subject became increasingly severe. . . . The conditions which spawned these laws may be gone, but the archaic classifications remain.

This ordinance is void for vagueness, both in the sense that it [fails to give a person of ordinary intelligence fair notice that his contemplated conduct is forbidden by the statute] and because it encourages arbitrary and erratic arrests and convictions.

Living under a rule of law entails various suppositions, one of which is that "[all persons] are entitled to be informed as to what the

State commands or forbids." Lanzetta v. New Jersey, 306 U.S. 451, 453 (1939)

*Lanzetta* is one of a well-recognized group of cases insisting that the law give fair notice of the offending conduct. See [, e.g.,] Connally v. General Construction Co., 269 U.S. 385, 391 (1926). In the field of regulatory statutes governing business activities, where the acts limited are in a narrow category, greater leeway is allowed.

The poor among us, the minorities, the average householder are not in business and not alerted to the regulatory schemes of vagrancy laws; and we assume they would have no understanding of their meaning and impact if they read them. Nor are they protected from being caught in the vagrancy net by the necessity of having a specific intent to commit an unlawful act.

The Jacksonville ordinance makes criminal activities which by modern standards are normally innocent. "Nightwalking" is one. Florida construes the ordinance not to make criminal one night's wandering, only the 'habitual' wanderer or, as the ordinance describes it, "common night walkers." We know, however, from experience that sleepless people often walk at night, perhaps hopeful that sleep-inducing relaxation will result.

Luis Munoz-Marin, former Governor of Puerto Rico, commented once that "loafing" was a national virtue in his Commonwealth and that it should be encouraged. It is, however, a crime in Jacksonville.

"[P]ersons able to work but habitually living upon the earnings of their wives or minor children"—like habitually living "without visible means of support"—might implicate unemployed pillars of the community who have married rich wives.

"[P]ersons able to work but habitually living upon the earnings of their wives or minor children" may also embrace unemployed people out of the labor market, by reason of a recession or disemployed by reason of technological or so-called structural displacements.

Persons "wandering or strolling" from place to place have been extolled by Walt Whitman and Vachel Lindsay. The qualification "without any lawful purpose or object" may be a trap for innocent acts. Persons "neglecting all lawful business and habitually spending their time by frequenting . . . places where alcoholic beverages are sold or served" would literally embrace many members of golf clubs and city clubs.

Walkers and strollers and wanderers may be going to or coming from a burglary. Loafers or loiterers may be "casing" a place for a holdup. Letting one's wife support him is an intra-family matter, and normally of no concern to the police. Yet it may, of course, be the setting for numerous crimes.

The difficulty is that these activities are historically part of the amenities of life as we have known them. They are not mentioned in the Constitution or in the Bill of Rights. These unwritten amenities have been in part responsible for giving our people the feeling of independence and self-confidence, the feeling of creativity. These amenities have dignified the right of dissent and have honored the right to be nonconformists and the right to defy submissiveness. They have encouraged lives of high spirits rather than hushed, suffocating silence. . . .

This aspect of the vagrancy ordinance before us is suggested by what this Court said in 1876 about a broad criminal statute enacted by Congress: "It would certainly be dangerous if the legislature could set a net large enough to catch all possible offenders, and leave it to the courts to step inside and say who could be rightfully detained, and who should be set at large." United States v. Reese, 92 U.S. 214, 221 (1875).

While that was a federal case, the due process implications are equally applicable to the States and to this vagrancy ordinance. Here the net cast is large, not to give the courts the power to pick and choose but to increase the arsenal of the police. In Winters v. New York, 333 U.S. 507, 540 (1948), [Justice Frankfurter said of this class of cases]:

> Only a word needs to be said regarding Lanzetta v. New Jersey, 306 U.S. 451 (1939). The case involved a New Jersey statute of the type that seek to control "vagrancy." These statutes are in a class by themselves, in view of the familiar abuses to which they are put. . . . Definiteness is designedly avoided so as to allow the net to be cast at large, to enable men to be caught who are vaguely undesirable in the eyes of police and prosecution, although not chargeable with any particular offense. In short, these "vagrancy statutes" and laws against "gangs" are not fenced in by the text of the statute or by the subject matter so as to give notice of conduct to be avoided.

Where the list of crimes is so all-inclusive and generalized as the one in this ordinance, those convicted may be punished for no more than vindicating affronts to police authority:

> The common ground which brings such a motley assortment of human troubles before the magistrates in vagrancy-type proceedings is the procedural laxity which permits "conviction" for almost any kind of conduct and the existence of the House of Correction as an easy and convenient dumping-ground for problems that appear to have no other immediate solution.

Caleb Foote, Vagrancy-Type Law and Its Administration, 104 U. Pa. L. Rev. 603, 631 (1956).[11]

Another aspect of the ordinance's vagueness appears when we focus, not on the lack of notice given a potential offender, but on the effect of the unfettered discretion it places in the hands of the Jacksonville police. Caleb Foote, an early student of this subject, has called the vagrancy-type law as offering "punishment by analogy." Id. at 609. Such crimes . . . are not compatible with our constitutional system. We allow our police to make arrests only on "probable cause" [that a specific crime has been committed], a Fourth and Fourteenth Amendment standard applicable to the States as well as to the Federal Government. Arresting a person on suspicion, like arresting a person for investigation, is foreign to our system, even when the arrest is for past criminality. Future criminality, however, is the common justification for the presence of vagrancy statutes. See Foote at 625. Florida

---

[11] Thus, "prowling by auto," which formed the basis for the vagrancy arrests and convictions of four of the petitioners herein, is not even listed in the ordinance as a crime. But see Hanks v. State, 195 So.2d 49, 51 Fla. 1967), in which the Florida District Court of Appeal construed "wandering or strolling from place to place" as including travel by automobile.

has, indeed, construed her vagrancy statute "as necessary regulations . . . to deter vagabondage and prevent crimes." Johnson v. State, 202 So.2d 852 (Fla. 1967); Smith v. State, 239 So.2d 250, 251 (Fla. 1970).

A direction by a legislature to the police to arrest all "suspicious" persons would not pass constitutional muster. A vagrancy prosecution may be merely the cloak for a conviction which could not be obtained on the real but undisclosed grounds for the arrest. But as Chief Justice Hewart said in Frederick Dean, 18 Crim.App. 133, 134 (1924):

> It would be in the highest degree unfortunate if in any part of the country those who are responsible for setting in motion the criminal law should entertain, connive at or coquette with the idea that in a case where there is not enough evidence to charge the prisoner with an attempt to commit a crime, the prosecution may, nevertheless, on such insufficient evidence, succeed in obtaining and upholding a conviction under the Vagrancy Act, 1824.

Those generally implicated by the imprecise terms of the ordinance—poor people, nonconformists, dissenters, idlers—may be required to comport themselves according to the life style deemed appropriate by the Jacksonville police and the courts. Where, as here, there are no standards governing the exercise of the discretion granted by the ordinance, the scheme permits and encourages an arbitrary and discriminatory enforcement of the law. It furnishes a convenient tool for "harsh and discriminatory enforcement by local prosecuting officials, against particular groups deemed to merit their displeasure." Thornhill v. Alabama, 310 U.S. 88, 97–98 (1940). It results in a regime in which the poor and the unpopular are permitted to "stand on a public sidewalk . . . only at the whim of any police officer." Shuttlesworth v. City of Birmingham, 382 U.S. 87, 90 (1965). . . .

A presumption that people who might walk or loaf or loiter or stroll or frequent houses where liquor is sold, or who are supported by their wives or who look suspicious to the police are to become future criminals is too precarious for a rule of law. The implicit presumption in these generalized vagrancy standards—that crime is being nipped in the bud—is too extravagant to deserve extended treatment. Of course, vagrancy statutes are useful to the police. Of course, they are nets making easy the roundup of so-called undesirables. But the rule of law implies equality and justice in its application. Vagrancy laws of the Jacksonville type teach that the scales of justice are so tipped that even-handed administration of the law is not possible. The rule of law, evenly applied to minorities as well as majorities, to the poor as well as the rich, is the great mucilage that holds society together.

The Jacksonville ordinance cannot be squared with our constitutional standards and is plainly unconstitutional.

Reversed.

■ JUSTICE POWELL and JUSTICE REHNQUIST took no part in the consideration or decision of this case.

## NOTES ON THE VAGUENESS DOCTRINE

### 1. INTRODUCTION TO THE VAGUENESS DOCTRINE

As Justice Douglas noted in *Papachristou*, the vagueness doctrine is concerned with two potential flaws in a criminal statute. First, a statute is said to be unconstitutionally vague when it fails to give adequate notice of what is prohibited. As the Court said in Lanzetta v. New Jersey, 306 U.S. 451, 453 (1939), "[n]o one may be required at peril of life, liberty or property to speculate as to the meaning of penal statutes." Similarly, in Connally v. General Construction Co., 269 U.S. 385, 391 (1926), the Court said that, "a statute which either forbids or requires the doing of an act in terms so vague that men of common intelligence must necessarily guess at its meaning and differ as to its application, violates the first essential of due process of law."

A second problem is that an indefinite law invites arbitrary and discriminatory enforcement. The fear is that behavior will be unfairly and unevenly identified as a criminal offense based on day-to-day subjective judgments by street officials, prosecutors, and courts. As the Supreme Court noted over a century ago, "[i]t would certainly be dangerous if the legislature could set a net large enough to catch all possible offenders, and leave it to the courts to step inside and say who could be rightfully detained, and who should be set at large." United States v. Reese, 92 U.S. 214, 221 (1875). A vague law leaves police, prosecutors, and courts unconstrained in the performance of their duties. The result is a drift toward arbitrariness and inequality in the administration of justice.

### 2. THE THEORY IN CONTEXT

Modern decisions focus on fair warning and non-discriminatory enforcement as rationales for invalidating vague laws, but neither justification can be accepted entirely at face value. Consider fair warning. Invalidating some laws because they do not give adequate notice presupposes that other laws provide effective notice. Yet there is something inescapably fictive in the notion that potential criminals learn what is forbidden from the words of a statute. That assumption may hold true for those who seek advice of counsel, but the ordinary citizen is not likely to have such resources or, indeed, any occasion to expend them. Most people do not have access to the statute books or the skill to unravel the legislative language should they find it. And since everyone knows that "ignorance of the law is no excuse," a mistaken interpretation of the meaning of a criminal statute by a lay person or a lawyer is not likely to provide a defense in any event.

The rationale of fair warning is further compromised by the rule that the precision required of a penal statute need not appear on its face. Facial uncertainty can be cured by judicial construction. Thus, review of a state statute for unconstitutional vagueness often turns not on the text of the law as it stands on the books but on its meaning as construed by the state's courts. Where the meaning of a statute depends on prior judicial construction, ascertaining the content of the law becomes all but impossible for the lay person and can often be a challenge for even the most sophisticated lawyer.

The concern for non-discriminatory enforcement of the penal law also has difficulties. It is true that the vagueness doctrine invalidates laws that are especially susceptible to arbitrary enforcement and contributes to evenhandedness in the administration of justice. Yet it is revealing to note how imperfect is the law's commitment to that goal. A vague statute may *invite* arbitrary enforcement, but virtually any law *allows* it. The difference may not be all that great. Even an ideally precise statute is subject to discretionary, and hence potentially discriminatory, administration. The police decide which laws to enforce and whom to arrest. Prosecutors decide whether to bring charges and for which offenses. Prosecutors may accept or reject guilty pleas and make or withhold recommendations of sentence. In all these decisions, the exercise of discretion is virtually uncontrolled. Only in the truly exceptional case where the defendant can prove that the prosecutorial decision was made on some plainly illegitimate basis—such as race or religion—can a prosecution be defeated on grounds of arbitrary or selective enforcement. Otherwise, discretion prevails.

Given what most people know about the text of the criminal law and its interstices, what, then, can it mean to say that the Constitution requires fair warning? Are there meaningful criteria for determining when a statute provides fair warning? And what, if anything, does the prevalence of discretionary authority throughout the criminal justice system say about the arbitrary enforcement rationale of the vagueness doctrine? Again, are there meaningful criteria for determining when this aspect of the vagueness doctrine will be triggered? The notes that follow address these questions, but first some further comments on the nature of the vagueness doctrine are required.

### 3. CRITERIA FOR DETERMINING UNCONSTITUTIONAL VAGUENESS

Whether a criminal statute is unconstitutionally vague is not an on-off switch that can be applied analytically. It involves a judgment about whether the text of a statute provides "sufficient" fair warning and whether it affords "too much" opportunity for arbitrary and discriminatory enforcement. It involves, in other words, application of a standard to judge whether statutory language is sufficiently precise.

A prominent feature of vagueness cases is that the constitutional standard varies with the context. Consider the following from Village of Hoffman Estates v. Flipside, 455 U.S. 489, 498–99 (1982):

> [Vagueness] standards should not, of course, be mechanically applied. The degree of vagueness that the Constitution tolerates—as well as the relative importance of fair notice and fair enforcement—depends in part on the nature of the enactment. Thus, economic regulation is subject to a less strict vagueness test because its subject matter is often more narrow, and because businesses, which face economic demands to plan behavior carefully, can be expected to consult relevant legislation in advance of action. Indeed, the regulated enterprise may have the ability to clarify the meaning of the regulation by its own inquiry, or by resort to an administrative process. . . . And the Court has recognized that a scienter[a] requirement may mitigate a law's

[a] "Scienter" is a generic reference to mens rea. The *Flipside* case itself illustrates how a mens rea requirement can cure potential vagueness. One of the challenged provisions covered the display of goods in a store. The Court concluded that it was not unconstitutionally vague because it also required that the goods be displayed in a manner that was intended to promote the illegal use of drugs.—[Footnote by eds.]

> vagueness, especially with respect to the adequacy of notice to the complainant that his conduct is proscribed.
>
> Finally, perhaps the most important factor affecting the clarity that the Constitution demands of a law is whether it threatens to inhibit the exercise of constitutionally protected rights. If, for example, the law interferes with the right of free speech or of association, a more stringent vagueness test should apply.

As the Court pointed out in *Papachristou*, the case did not involve economic regulation, where "greater leeway" would have been allowed. Nor did it involve what might be called core criminality. Nor did it involve, in the *Papachristou* Court's words, behavior accompanied by "a specific intent to commit an unlawful act." And it did not involve constitutionally protected rights such as free speech or association.

Instead, the case involved the validity of a statute governing behavior in which, as the Court pointed out, ordinary law-abiding citizens would be likely to engage as they went about their everyday activities. Why did the Court hold the *Papachristou* ordinance unconstitutionally vague? What criteria did it use in doing so? Consider the two cases summarized below in connection with these questions.

### 4. *LANZETTA V. NEW JERSEY*

Lanzetta v. New Jersey, 306 U.S. 451 (1939), is prominently featured in Justice Douglas's *Papachristou* opinion. The statute involved in that case read:

> Any person not engaged in any lawful occupation, known to be a member of any gang consisting of two or more persons, who has been convicted at least three times of being a disorderly person, or who has been convicted of any crime, in this or in any other State, is declared to be a gangster . . . .

Violations of this statute were punishable by imprisonment not exceeding 20 years. Lanzetta himself was convicted for committing this offense on four specific days and sentenced to not more than 10 years at hard labor and not less than five.

The Court held the statute unconstitutionally vague. "The applicable rule," it said, "is stated in Connally v. General Construction Co., 269 U.S. 385, 391 (1926)":

> "That the terms of a penal statute creating a new offense must be sufficiently explicit to inform those who are subject to it *what conduct on their part will render them liable to its penalties* is a well-recognized requirement, consonant alike with ordinary notions of fair play and the settled rules of law; and a statute which either forbids or requires the doing of an act in terms so vague that men of common intelligence must necessarily guess at its meaning and differ as to its application violates the first essential of due process of law." [Emphasis added.]

The Court then examined the text of the statute in detail, including its prior interpretation by the New Jersey courts. It concluded that "[t]he challenged provision *condemns no act or omission*; the terms it employs to indicate what it purports to denounce are so vague, indefinite and uncertain that it must be condemned as repugnant to the due process clause of the Fourteenth Amendment." [Emphasis added.]

Note the focus of the phrases italicized above on the traditional requirement that crime be based on conduct. Does the *Lanzetta* statute identify *any* specific contemporaneous conduct in which one must engage in order to violate its terms? Is that its vice? Examine carefully the facts of the various convictions in *Papachristou*. How many were based on specific conduct that fit within a fair construction of the text of the Jacksonville ordinance? Is the failure of a criminal statute to focus on specified behavior in part what the vagueness doctrine is about?

Compare the holding in Robinson v. California, 370 U.S. 660 (1962). Robinson had been convicted under a statute that punished one who was "addicted to the use of" narcotics. The Court held, in effect, that the Constitution required that criminal punishment be based on the *conduct* of drug use and not the *status* of drug addiction. Are *Robinson* and *Lanzetta* kindred spirits?

### 5. *SHUTTLESWORTH V. CITY OF BIRMINGHAM*

Shuttlesworth v. City of Birmingham, 382 U.S. 87, 90 (1965), was also cited in *Papachristou*. Shuttlesworth was convicted of violating a provision of the Birmingham city code providing that "[i]t shall . . . be unlawful for any person to stand or loiter upon any street or sidewalk of the city after having been requested by any police officer to move on."[b] He had been standing on a sidewalk with 10 or 12 companions outside a department store when a police officer ordered the group to move on. The group began to disperse but Shuttlesworth remained. The officer repeated his order three times, the last after Shuttlesworth asked: " 'Do you mean to tell me we can't stand here in front of this store?' " Shuttlesworth was arrested after the last order, by which time all of his companions had left. He was tried, convicted, and sentenced to imprisonment for 180 days at hard labor and an additional 61 days if he did not pay a $100 fine and costs.[c]

The Supreme Court's reasons for overturning the conviction were short and to the point:

> Literally read . . . the . . . ordinance says that a person may stand on a public sidewalk in Birmingham only at the whim of any police officer of that city. The constitutional vice of so broad a provision needs no demonstration. It "does not provide for government by clearly defined laws, but rather for government by the moment-to-moment opinions of a policeman on his beat." Cox v. State of Louisiana, 379 U.S. 536, 579 (1965) (separate opinion of Mr. Justice Black). Instinct with its ever-present potential for ar-

---

[b] The Alabama Court of Appeals had construed this language to authorize police to issue orders to move on only in situations where people were obstructing sidewalk traffic. Middlebrooks v. City of Birmingham, 42 Ala.App. 525, 170 So.2d 424 (1964). But this construction was adopted *after* Shuttlesworth was convicted and therefore could not be used to sustain his conviction. The U.S. Supreme Court understood the conviction itself to be based on the literal language of the ordinance.

[c] Shuttlesworth was a well-known Southern civil rights leader in Birmingham, Alabama, during the 1950s and 1960s. See Andrew M. Manus, A Fire You Can't Put Out: The Civil Rights Life of Birmingham's Reverend Fred Shuttlesworth (1999). Today, the Birmingham International Airport is named for him.

bitrarily suppressing First Amendment liberties, that kind of law bears the hallmark of a police state.[d]

The Court cited a series of First Amendment cases in two footnotes that accompanied this passage, but Shuttlesworth was not engaged in picketing or any other expressive activity when he was arrested. His claim was that he could not be arrested for simply standing on the sidewalk. Be that as it may, the case can be read as adopting a legality-based anti-delegation[e] principle: it is unconstitutional for the state to delegate to police the job of deciding based on their "moment-to-moment opinions" the kinds of behavior that can be punished by criminal sanctions. The *Shuttlesworth* statute authorized "law by cop," not "law by law."

Taken together, did *Lanzetta* and *Shuttlesworth* identify meaningful criteria for determining when a criminal statute is unconstitutionally vague that the Court could (and did) use in *Papachristou*?[f] Note in this connection Justice Frankfurter's comment in *Winters* (quoted in *Papachristou*) that one of the vices of vagueness is that applications of a vague law are not "fenced in by the text of the statute."

## 6. TOLERABLE VAGUENESS AND QUESTIONS OF DEGREE

The law is full of instances where the fact or grade of criminal liability turns on application of a standard that involves an estimate of degree. The widely copied Model Penal Code, for example, uses "recklessness" as a major component of numerous crimes, defining it in part as taking a risk when "its disregard involves a gross deviation from the standard of conduct that a law-abiding person would observe in the actor's situation."[g] Following another person may be punished as stalking if it "would cause a reasonable person to fear for such person's physical safety or the physical safety of a third person."[h] Assault may be a felony or a misdemeanor depending on whether the attack caused "serious" bodily injury.[i] Even the imposition of the death penalty may depend on whether the accused had a "significant" history of prior criminal activity[j] or whether the circumstances of his crime

---

[d] Shuttlesworth was also convicted of violating another ordinance which, as construed by the Alabama Supreme Court, permitted orders to move on in the context of regulating vehicular traffic. The U.S. Supreme Court overturned this conviction on the ground that there was "no evidence whatever" that the police officer was directing vehicular traffic at the time of the arrest. See Thompson v. City of Louisville, 362 U.S. 199 (1960)—[Footnote by eds.]

[e] See Grayned v. City of Rockford, 408 U.S. 104, 108–09 (1972): "A vague law impermissibly delegates basic policy matters to policemen, judges, and juries for resolution on an ad hoc and subjective basis, with the attendant dangers of arbitrary and discriminatory applications."

[f] A proposed answer to this question can be found in Peter W. Low and Joel S. Johnson, Changing the Vocabulary of the Vagueness Doctrine, 101 Va. L. Rev. ___ (2015) (prepublication draft available on SSRN).

[g] Chapter III contains many examples of similar definitions of the mental state of modern crimes.

[h] Conn. Gen. Stat. § 53a–181d.

[i] See, e.g., N.H.Rev.Stat.Ann. §§ 631:1 and 631:2 (1994). The concept of "serious bodily injury" is defined under New Hampshire law to include "harm to the body which causes severe, permanent, or protracted loss of or impairment to the health or the function of any part of the body." N.H.Rev.Stat.Ann. § 625:11(VI) (1986).

[j] The Arkansas, Florida, and Utah death penalty statutes list among relevant mitigating circumstances the fact that the "defendant has no significant history of prior criminal activity." Ark. Code Ann. § 5–4–605(6) (Michie 1993); Fla.Stat.Ann. § 921.141(6)(a) (West 1995); Utah Code Ann. § 76–3–207(4)(a) (1995).

were "especially" heinous.[k] Does the indefiniteness of concepts such as recklessness or words such as "reasonable" and "serious" in the law implicate the rationales of the vagueness doctrine? Why is such uncertainty so widely featured in the criminal law and so widely tolerated?

The answer might be called "law enforcement necessity," by which is meant the need for legislative use of standards in order to establish appropriate norms of behavior by which both the fact and degree of criminality should be measured. Note the Court's rejection near the end of its *Papachristou* opinion of the claim that "crime is being nipped in the bud" by enactments such as the Florida vagrancy law. Law enforcement necessity—nipping crime in the bud—was not a plausible argument, the Court thought, in the *Papachristou* context. There are other, more narrowly tailored, laws that can accomplish this objective.[l]

The Supreme Court had this point in mind when it said, in United States v. Petrillo, 332 U.S. 1, 8 (1947), that "the Constitution does not require impossible standards" of clarity or precision. In the end, the vagueness doctrine has a practical dimension. The language in which crimes are defined plays a critical role in the ability of legislatures to accomplish one of the central purposes of government: maintenance of the social order and protection of citizens from harm. Requiring impractical precision would unacceptably undermine its ability to address that goal. The concern that legislatures not be required to meet impossible standards comes directly into play whenever the criminal law draws lines measured by a matter of degree. One well-known example is Nash v. United States, 229 U.S. 373 (1913). *Nash* involved a vagueness challenge to criminal prosecution under the Sherman Antitrust Act, which had been interpreted to forbid an "*undue* restraint of trade."[m] Nash argued that the judgment of degree called for by the term "undue" rendered the statute unconstitutionally vague but, speaking for the Court, Justice Holmes disagreed:

> [T]he law is full of instances where a man's fate depends on his estimating rightly, that is, as the jury subsequently estimates it, some matter of degree. If his judgment is wrong, not only may he incur a fine or a short imprisonment, as here; he may incur the penalty of death. . . . "The criterion in such cases is to examine whether common social duty would, under the circumstances, have suggested a more circumspect conduct."

Note that *Nash* involved economic regulation, an area where the standards of vagueness are somewhat relaxed. But it is clear nonetheless that Justice Holmes' reference to "whether common social duty

---

[k] See, e.g., Fla .Stat. Ann. § 921.141(5)(h) (West 1995) (identifying as an aggravating circumstance for determination of sentence that the "capital felony was especially heinous, atrocious or cruel"), upheld in Proffitt v. Florida, 428 U.S. 242 (1976).

[l] This topic is addressed in more detail in materials on attempt and conspiracy in Chapters V and VI, respectively.

[m] Section 1 of the Sherman Antitrust Act declared illegal "[e]very contract, combination in the form of trust or otherwise, or conspiracy in restraint of trade or commerce . . . ." Of course, it is the essence of contract to restrain future choice. If read literally, the Sherman Act would forbid any commercial agreement. The Supreme Court avoided this absurdity by declaring, in the context of civil antitrust litigation, that the Sherman Act should be interpreted according to a "rule of reason." See Standard Oil Co. v. United States, 221 U.S. 1 (1911), and United States v. American Tobacco Co., 221 U.S. 106 (1911). By this construction, the Court transformed the condemnation of "every" restraint of trade to one that reached only an *undue* restraint of trade.

would, under the circumstances, have suggested a more circumspect conduct" was meant to be more broadly applicable to laws that involve matters of degree. One cannot complain, he meant to say, about the unfairness of application of a standard to conduct when the average well-adjusted citizen socialized to contemporary moral values is likely to be aware that caution is required. A person who acts in such a context can always choose not to act. It is not unfair in such a situation, Holmes meant to argue, to punish a person for acting irresponsibly. Consider, as an example, the Model Penal Code definition of "recklessness" quoted above. Causing harm to another recklessly involves behavior that is "a gross deviation from the standard of conduct that a law-abiding person would observe in the actor's situation." "Common social duty" would surely suggest in such a context "more circumspect conduct."

Note that the inquiry quoted by Holmes has nothing to do with the *text* of a criminal law. One's "social conscience" is not derived from the text of criminal statutes. To the extent that the vagueness doctrine is about the text of the law, its focus is therefore different. But does this line of thinking suggest yet another meaningful fairness baseline that the criminal law should observe? Might the inquiry quoted by Holmes be considered as part of what the law should mean by "fair notice"? Consider, for example, Heath's codefendant in *Papachristou*. He was arrested for loitering because he was standing in a driveway after having been told to do so by the police. Was it fair for the police to arrest him for that? Would *anyone* suspect that such behavior risks arrest for a crime?

### 7. VAGUENESS AND THE PRESERVATION OF LEGISLATIVE OBJECTIVES

The vagueness doctrine is about *how* the legislature may pursue its legitimate objectives, not *what* those objectives should be. One consequence of "not requir[ing] impossible standards" of clarity or precision is that sometimes the Court must make a choice between foreclosing a legitimate legislative objective and tolerating imprecise language that threatens the values underlying the vagueness doctrine. The Court's typical response in this situation is to hold that the law is not unconstitutionally vague. If it is possible to do better, the Court might require that the legislature do so. If it is not possible to do better in the sense of writing a more precise law, the law is likely to stand.

The law of obscenity provides an example. Recall the Court's observation in the quotation from *Flipside* in Note 3 above that "a more stringent vagueness test should apply" to laws that affect free speech or association. The rationale for heightened scrutiny of laws touching First Amendment freedoms is that vagueness in this context is especially costly. In the traditional terminology of the First Amendment, an imprecise law may have a "chilling effect" on the exercise of protected rights. As the Supreme Court explained in N.A.A.C.P. v. Button, 371 U.S. 415 (1963), the "standards of permissible statutory vagueness are strict in the area of free expression":

> The objectionable quality of vagueness [depends] upon the danger of tolerating, in the area of First Amendment freedoms, the existence of a penal statute susceptible of sweeping and improper application. These freedoms are delicate and vulnerable, as well as supremely precious in our society. The threat of sanctions may deter their exercise almost as potently as the actual application of sanctions. Because First Amendment freedoms need breathing

> space to survive, government may regulate in the area only with narrow specificity. . . .[n]

Thus laws that potentially reach picketing, political protests, civil rights demonstrations, and other forms of constitutionally protected expressive activity are especially likely to be tested by stringent vagueness standards.

The Court held in Roth v. United States, 354 U.S. 476 (1957), that obscenity is not protected speech under the First Amendment:[o]

> [T]he unconditional phrasing of the First Amendment was not intended to protect every utterance. . . . [I]mplicit in the history of the First Amendment is the rejection of obscenity as utterly without redeeming social importance. This rejection . . . is mirrored in the universal judgment that obscenity should be restrained, reflected in the international agreement of over 50 nations, in the obscenity laws of all of the 48 States, and in the 20 obscenity laws enacted by the Congress from 1842 to 1956. . . . We hold that obscenity is not within the area of constitutionally protected speech or press.

This meant that legislatures could pass criminal laws against purveyors of obscenity. And it meant that a line had to be drawn between speech that was obscene and speech that was not obscene. Speech that was not obscene remained protected by the Constitution. Should it follow that laws against obscenity are subject to the "chilling effect" rationale of cases like *N.A.A.C.P. v. Button* and that "a more stringent vagueness test" should therefore be applied?

The problem is that defining "obscenity" with precision seems a hopeless task. Indeed, Justice Stewart famously said in a case involving a highly acclaimed film[p] that the Court in obscenity cases is "faced with the task of trying to define what may be indefinable" and that he would

> not today attempt further to define the kinds of material I understand to be embraced within [the concept of "hard-core pornography"]; and perhaps I could never succeed in intelligibly doing so. But I know it when I see it, and the motion picture involved in this case is not that.[q]

Be this as it may, the Supreme Court has undertaken to define the difference between punishable obscenity and protected speech. Its latest definitional effort includes the terms "appealing to prurient interest," "patently offensive," and "lacking serious literary, artistic, political, or scientific value" and permits jurors applying these concepts to rely on "the standards of their community" in making the judgment whether a particular publication or exhibition is criminally obscene.[r]

---

[n] This idea was mentioned above. See footnote c and its accompanying text in the Note on the Doctrine of Vagueness that immediately precedes *Papachristou*.—[Footnote by eds.]

[o] The First Amendment provides that "Congress shall make no law . . . abridging the freedom of speech. . . ."

[p] The case involved a French film called "Les Amants" ("The Lovers"). Justice Brennan's opinion noted that "[t]he film was favorably reviewed in a number of national publications, although disparaged in others, and was rated by at least two critics of national stature among the best films of the year in which it was produced." It was shown in more than 100 major cities in the United States.

[q] Jacobellis v. Ohio, 378 U.S. 184, 197 (1964)(Stewart, J., concurring).

[r] See Miller v. California, 413 U.S. 15 (1973).

The inability of legislatures and courts to define obscenity with clarity and the vagaries of application of the law based on the standards of local communities leaves constitutionally protected speech on the borderline of obscenity, it can be argued, especially subject to the fair notice and arbitrary enforcement concerns that underlie the vagueness doctrine. This fact led Justice Brennan in a well-known dissent to conclude that obscenity was "incapable of definition with sufficient clarity to withstand attack on vagueness grounds."[s] But this view has not commanded a majority of the Court. Today, obscenity laws defined in the terms quoted above are not unconstitutionally vague.

Why not? How can nationwide publishers of books and films determine whether communities in one locality or another will find their product "prurient," "patently offensive," and lacking "serious value"? Should laws that punish obscenity be held unconstitutionally vague? If so, of course, the doctrine of vagueness would have the substantive effect of denying legislatures permission to punish as a crime behavior that the most applicable provision of the Constitution—the First Amendment—does not protect. Should vagueness in such a context be tolerated because the doctrine should not be used to foreclose valid legislative objectives when neither the legislature nor the Supreme Court can define obscenity with more precision? This seems to be the destination at which the Supreme Court has arrived.

An important qualification should be added as these questions are addressed. The cases quoted above had to do with the exposure of obscene materials to *consenting* adults. The stakes are different when *unconsenting* adults are victimized and, especially so, when children are used as performers in the making of pornographic materials or are exposed to pornography. Most who would credit the vagueness argument in the context of consenting adults would rethink their position, and perhaps change it, as the harms to potential victims escalated.

## SECTION 3: INTERPRETATION OF PROSCRIBED CONDUCT

### INTRODUCTORY NOTES ON THE INTERPRETATION OF CRIMINAL STATUTES

#### 1. PRELIMINARY OBSERVATIONS

Section 1 of this Chapter focused on the traditional requirement that penal sanctions be reserved for conduct, whether in the form of affirmative behavior, an omission in the face of a legal duty to act, or possession. Section 2 introduced the concept of the rule of law, requiring that conduct be proscribed in advance, generally by legislation, if it is to be punished as criminal. This Section takes the inquiry to the next step. Today advance specification of the norms that are enforced by the criminal law typically comes from legislation. The state legislature or the federal Congress describes in a statute the conduct that is to be punished. But the words of statutes are not self-executing. They require interpretation when they are applied by courts to concrete situations, and it is not always clear whether

[s] Paris Adult Theatre I v. Slaton, 413 U.S. 49, 85 n.9 (1973 (Brennan, J., dissenting). Justice Brennan was joined in this dissent by Justices Stewart and Marshall. The dissent reserved decision in situations where children were involved.

they were meant to apply to one or another variation of the stereotype the legislature had in mind when it enacted the law.

Consider, for example, a traditional definition of burglary: "breaking and entering" the dwelling of another at night with the intent to commit a felony therein. Suppose a thief reaches through an open window and steals jewelry from a nearby table. Does "break" mean "cause physical damage to a barrier to entry"? Does "enter" mean "penetrate the premises with one's entire body"? Perhaps, in which case the hypothetical defendant is guilty of theft but not burglary. But perhaps "break" means "break the plane of the household" and "enter" means "penetrate any portion of the premises in any manner." In that case, the defendant is guilty of both theft and burglary.

Whether courts should convict the defendant of burglary in such a situation involves a wide range of considerations: whether the text of the statute can fairly be read to cover such facts, whether the situation is fairly encompassed within the behavioral norm enforced by the statute, whether the legislature is likely to have intended such a case to be covered, how severely the defendant's behavior might be punished by other crimes, and so on. Separation of powers questions can arise as well, as one may be left to wonder if the court convicts whether it is applying the legislative norm or inventing a new one. Courts, it can be argued, should not engage in the latter enterprise when they are purporting to engage in the former. The legislature is the body that should be in charge of creating new norms that are enforced by the criminal law.

It is possible, moreover, for a statute to be narrow and precise but for its words to be construed in such a surprising and unexpected fashion as to invoke the same rule-of-law concerns as those protected by the vagueness doctrine. The case in the next Note is an illustration. But it needs to be recognized that this potential problem has an everyday aspect to it. All words are to some extent imprecise. As illustrated by the burglary hypothetical above, there are borderlands of ambiguity in any legal term used in the description of any criminal offense, no matter how precise it may seem on its face. And there is a sense in which *any* construction of a criminal statute that upholds a conviction by settling an unresolved legal issue constitutes retroactive law-making that could be regarded as inconsistent with the rule of law. Almost by definition, a question of statutory interpretation that requires resolution by an appellate court resolves an ambiguity that was not clearly settled by prior law. Virtually every case in this book that upholds a conviction would therefore be problematic if retroactive application of previously unresolved issues was always impermissible. Some retroactive applications of previously unresolved issues seem essential to effective operation of the legal system.

So there is a tension here. Some judicial constructions are going to be consistent with the rule of law, and others not. How does one tell the difference? The case in the next Note addresses this question.

## 2. *BOUIE V. CITY OF COLUMBIA*

Bouie v. City of Columbia, 376 U.S. 347 (1964), involved a sit-in demonstration in which black defendants were convicted of trespass for refusing to vacate a segregated lunch counter after being ordered by the proprietor and the police to leave. The trespass statute under which they were convicted was a traditional "posting" statute designed to protect livestock from hunters.[a] It punished entry in violation of notice not to enter. No such notice was posted at the lunch counter where the defendants sought service. The South Carolina Supreme Court affirmed their convictions, however, after construing the statute to cover refusal to leave private property after a request to leave. The U.S. Supreme Court carefully examined prior South Carolina law and found no basis in previously decided cases for such a construction. In the course of its opinion reversing the convictions, it said:

> The basic principle that a criminal statute must give fair warning of the conduct that it makes a crime has often been recognized by this Court. As was said in United States v. Harriss, 347 U.S. 612, 617 (1954):
>
> > The constitutional requirement of definiteness is violated by a criminal statute that fails to give a person of ordinary intelligence fair notice that his contemplated conduct is forbidden by the statute. The underlying principle is that no man shall be held criminally responsible for conduct which he could not reasonably understand to be proscribed.
>
> Thus we have struck down a state criminal statute under the Due Process Clause where it was not "sufficiently explicit to inform those who are subject to it what conduct on their part will render them liable to its penalties." Connally v. General Construction Co., 269 U.S. 385, 391 (1926). We have recognized in such cases that "a statute which either forbids or requires the doing of an act in terms so vague that men of common intelligence must necessarily guess at its meaning and differ as to its application violates the first essential of due process of law," id., and that "No one may be required at peril of life, liberty or property to speculate as to the meaning of penal statutes. All are entitled to be informed as to what the State commands or forbids." Lanzetta v. New Jersey, 306 U.S. 451, 453 (1939).
>
> It is true that in the *Connally* and *Lanzetta* cases, and in other typical applications of the principle, the uncertainty as to the statute's prohibition resulted from vague . . . language in the statute itself, and the Court concluded that the statute was "void for vagueness." The instant case seems distinguishable, since on its face the language . . . of the South Carolina Code was admirably narrow and precise; the statute applied only to "entry upon the lands of another . . . after notice . . . prohibiting such entry . . . ." The thrust of the distinction, however, is to produce a potentially greater deprivation of the right to fair notice in this sort of case, where the claim is that a statute precise on its face has been unforeseeably and retroactively expanded by judicial construction,

---

[a] The statute provided:

*Entry on lands of another after notice prohibiting same.* Every entry upon the lands of another where any horse, mule, cow, hog or any other livestock is pastured, or any other lands of another, after notice from the owner or tenant prohibiting such entry, shall be a misdemeanor and be punished by a fine not to exceed one hundred dollars, or by imprisonment with hard labor on the public works of the county for not exceeding thirty days. When any owner or tenant of any lands shall post a notice in four conspicuous places on the borders of such land prohibiting entry thereon, a proof of the posting shall be deemed and taken as notice conclusive against the person making entry as aforesaid for the purpose of trespassing.

> than in the typical "void for vagueness" situation. When a statute on its face is vague or overbroad, it at least gives a potential defendant some notice, by virtue of this very characteristic, that a question may arise as to its coverage, and that it may be held to cover his contemplated conduct. When a statute on its face is narrow and precise, however, it lulls the potential defendant into a false sense of security, giving him no reason even to suspect that conduct clearly outside the scope of the statute as written will be retroactively brought within it by an act of judicial construction. If the Fourteenth Amendment is violated when a person is required "to speculate as to the meaning of penal statutes," as in *Lanzetta*, or to "guess at [the statute's] meaning and differ as to its application," as in *Connally*, the violation is that much greater when, because the uncertainty as to the statute's meaning is itself not revealed until the court's decision, a person is not even afforded an opportunity to engage in such speculation before committing the act in question.
>
> There can be no doubt that a deprivation of the right of fair warning can result not only from vague statutory language but also from an unforeseeable and retroactive judicial expansion of narrow and precise statutory language. . . . Indeed, an unforeseeable judicial enlargement of a criminal statute, applied retroactively, operates precisely like an ex post facto law, such as Art. I, § 10, of the Constitution forbids. An ex post facto law has been defined by this Court as one "that makes an action done before the passing of the law, and which was innocent when done, criminal; and punishes such action," . . . . Calder v. Bull, 3 U.S. (3 Dall.) 386, 390 (1798).[4] If a state legislature is barred by the Ex Post Facto Clause from passing such a law, it must follow that a State Supreme Court is barred by the Due Process Clause from achieving precisely the same result by judicial construction. The fundamental principle that 'the required criminal law must have existed when the conduct in issue occurred,' Jerome Hall, General Principles of Criminal Law (2d ed. 1960), at 58–59, must apply to bar retroactive criminal prohibitions emanating from courts as well as from legislatures. If a judicial construction of a criminal statute is "unexpected and indefensible by reference to the law which had been expressed prior to the conduct in issue," it must not be given retroactive effect. Id. at 61.

At least in most contexts, it is surely fictional to think that a precise statute that is unpredictably broadened "lulls the potential defendant into a false sense of security," just as it is unrealistic to expect the average citizen to know and understand the meaning of criminal statutes as construed by prior precedent. But does the *Bouie* opinion nonetheless give important and meaningful content to the concept of "fair notice"? Does it state a useful criterion that can aid in determining when statutory construction might be regarded as violating the legality principle and when it can be regarded as

---

[4] Thus, it has been said that "No one can be criminally punished in this country, except according to a law prescribed for his government by the sovereign authority before the imputed offence was committed, and which existed as a law at the time." Kring v. Missouri, 107 U.S. 221, 235 (1883).

routine business?[b] This issue is further explored in the next case and following notes.

## Keeler v. Superior Court of Amador County

Supreme Court of California, 1970.
2 Cal.3d 619, 87 Cal.Rptr. 481, 470 P.2d 617.

■ MOSK, J. In this proceeding for [a] writ of prohibition we are called upon to decide whether an unborn but viable fetus is a "human being" within the meaning of the California statute defining murder, Cal.Penal Code § 187. We conclude that the legislature did not intend such a meaning, and that for us to construe the statute to the contrary and apply it to this petitioner would exceed our judicial power and deny petitioner due process of law.

issue

holding

The evidence received at the preliminary examination may be summarized as follows: Petitioner and Teresa Keeler obtained an interlocutory decree of divorce on September 27, 1968. They had been married for 16 years. Unknown to petitioner, Mrs. Keeler was then pregnant by one Ernest Vogt, whom she had met earlier that summer. She subsequently began living with Vogt in Stockton, but concealed the fact from petitioner. Petitioner was given custody of their two daughters, aged 12 and 13 years, and under the decree Mrs. Keeler had the right to take the girls on alternate weekends.

preliminary hearing

On February 23, 1969, Mrs. Keeler was driving on a narrow mountain road in Amador County after delivering the girls to their home. She met petitioner driving in the opposite direction; he blocked the road with his car, and she pulled over to the side. He walked to her vehicle and began speaking to her. He seemed calm, and she rolled down her window to hear him. He said, "I hear you're pregnant. If you are you had better stay away from the girls and from here." She did not reply, and he opened the car door; as she later testified, "He assisted me out of the car. . . . [I]t wasn't roughly at this time." Petitioner then looked at her abdomen and became "extremely upset." He said, "You sure are. I'm going to stomp it out of you." He pushed her against the car, shoved his knee into her abdomen, and struck her in the face with several blows. She fainted, and when she regained consciousness petitioner had departed.

Mrs. Keeler drove back to Stockton, and the police and medical assistance were summoned. She had suffered substantial facial injuries, as well as extensive bruising of the abdominal wall. A caesarian section was performed and the fetus was examined in utero. Its head was found to be severely fractured, and it was delivered stillborn. The pathologist gave as his opinion that the cause of death was skull fracture with con-

---

[b] *Bouie* arose in a politically charged context in which it appears that the Supreme Court decided the case on the ground it chose in order to avoid decision of claims by sit-in demonstrators that they were constitutionally entitled to equal access to places of public accommodation. The Court ducked this constitutional question, it seems obvious, because it was clear that Congress would soon address the issue in the Civil Rights Act of 1964 (as it did). While the Court may for that reason have applied the *Bouie* standard more strictly than it would have in a less charged context, the case remains an important precedent for the principle on which it relied. See, e.g., Rogers v. Tennessee, 532 U.S. 451 (2001); Metrish v. Lancaster, ___ U.S. ___, 133 S.Ct. 1781 (2013).

sequent cerebral hemorrhaging, that death would have been immediate, and that the injury could have been the result of force applied to the mother's abdomen. There was no air in the fetus' lungs, and the umbilical cord was intact.

Upon delivery the fetus weighed five pounds and was 18 inches in length. Both Mrs. Keeler and her obstetrician testified that fetal movements had been observed prior to February 23, 1969. The evidence was in conflict as to the estimated age of the fetus; the expert testimony on the point, however, concluded "with reasonable medical certainty" that the fetus had developed to the stage of viability, i.e., that in the event of premature birth on the date in question it would have had a 75 per cent to 96 per cent chance of survival.

An information was filed charging petitioner, in count I, with committing the crime of murder in that he did "unlawfully kill a human being, to wit Baby Girl Vogt, with malice aforethought." . . . His motion to set aside the information for lack of probable cause was denied, and he now seeks a writ of prohibition. . . .

Penal Code Section 187 provides: "Murder is the unlawful killing of a human being, with malice aforethought." The dispositive question is whether the fetus which petitioner is accused of killing was, on February 23, 1969, a "human being" within the meaning of the statute. If it was not, petitioner cannot be charged with its "murder" and prohibition will lie.

Section 187 was enacted as part of the Penal Code of 1872. Inasmuch as the provision has not been amended since that date, we must determine the intent of the legislature at the time of its enactment. But Section 187 was, in turn, taken verbatim from the first California statute defining murder, part of the Crimes and Punishments Act of 1850. Penal Code Section 5 (also enacted in 1872) declares: "The provisions of this code, so far as they are substantially the same as existing statutes, must be construed as continuations thereof, and not as new enactments." We begin, accordingly, by inquiring into the intent of the legislature in 1850 when it first defined a murder as the unlawful and malicious killing of a "human being."

It will be presumed, of course, that in enacting a statute the legislature was familiar with the relevant rules of the common law, and, when it couches its enactment in common law language, that its intent was to continue those rules in statutory form. This is particularly appropriate in considering the work of the first session of our legislature: its precedents were necessarily drawn from the common law, as modified in certain respects by the Constitution and by legislation of our sister states.

We therefore undertake a brief review of the origins and development of the common law of abortional homicide. [An extensive review of English cases and authorities revealed that an infant could not be the subject of criminal homicide at common law unless it had been born alive.]

By the year 1850 this rule of the common law had long been accepted in the United States. As early as 1797 it was held that proof the child was born alive is necessary to support an indictment for murder. . . .

While it was thus "well settled" in American case law that the killing of an unborn child was not homicide, a number of state legislatures in the first half of the 19th century undertook to modify the common law in this respect. [The court then discussed the enactment in New York and in a few other states, but not in California, of statutes specially directed against feticide.]

We conclude that in declaring murder to be the unlawful and malicious killing of a "human being" the legislature of 1850 intended that term to have the settled common law meaning of a person who had been born alive, and did not intend the act of feticide—as distinguished from abortion—to be an offense under the laws of California.

Nothing occurred between the years 1850 and 1872 to suggest that in adopting the new penal code on the latter date the legislature entertained any different intent. The case law of our sister states, for example, remained consonant with the common law. . . .

Any lingering doubt on this subject must be laid to rest by a consideration of the legislative history of the Penal Code of 1872. The act establishing the California Code Commission required the commissioners to revise all statutes then in force, correct errors and omissions, and "recommend all such enactments as shall, in the judgment of the commission, be necessary to supply the defects of and give completeness to the existing legislation of the state. . . ." In discharging this duty the statutory schemes of our sister states were carefully examined, and we must assume the commissioners had knowledge of the feticide laws noted hereinabove. Yet the commissioners proposed no such law for California, and none has been adopted to this day. . . .

It is the policy of this state to construe a penal statute as favorably to the defendant as its language and the circumstances of its application may reasonably permit; just as in the case of a question of fact, the defendant is entitled to the benefit of every reasonable doubt as to the true interpretation of words or the construction of language used in a statute. We hold that in adopting the definition of murder in Penal Code Section 187 the legislature intended to exclude from its reach the act of killing an unborn fetus.

The People urge, however, that the sciences of obstetrics and pediatrics have greatly progressed since 1872, to the point where with proper medical care a normally developed fetus prematurely born at 28 weeks or more has an excellent chance of survival, i.e., is "viable"; that the common law requirement of live birth to prove the fetus had become a "human being" who may be the victim of murder is no longer in accord with scientific fact, since an unborn but viable fetus is now fully capable of independent life; and that one who unlawfully and maliciously terminated such a life should therefore be liable to prosecution for murder under Section 187. We may grant the premises of this argument; indeed, we neither deny nor denigrate the vast progress of medicine in the century since the enactment of the Penal Code. But we cannot join in the conclusion sought to be deduced: we cannot hold this petitioner to answer for murder by reason of his alleged act of killing an unborn—even though viable—fetus. To such a charge there are two insuperable obstacles, one "jurisdictional" and the other constitutional.

Penal Code Section 6 declares in relevant part that "[n]o act or omission" accomplished after the code has taken effect "is criminal or punishable, except as prescribed or authorized by this code, or by some of the statutes which it specifies as continuing in force and as not affected by its provisions, or by some ordinance, municipal, county, or township regulation. . . ." This section embodies a fundamental principle of our tripartite form of government, i.e., that subject to the constitutional prohibition against cruel and unusual punishment, the power to define crimes and fix penalties is vested exclusively in the legislative branch. Stated differently, there are no common law crimes in California. . . .

Settled rules of construction implement this principle. Although the Penal Code commands us to construe its provisions "according to the fair import of their terms, with a view to effect its objects and to promote justice," Cal.Penal Code § 4, it is clear the courts cannot go so far as to create an offense by enlarging a statute, by inserting or deleting words, or by giving the terms used false or unusual meanings. Penal statutes will not be made to reach beyond their plain intent; they include only those offenses coming clearly within the import of their language. . . .

Applying these rules to the case at bar, we would undoubtedly act in excess of the judicial power if we were to adopt the People's proposed construction of Section 187. As we have shown, the legislature has defined the crime of murder in California to apply only to the unlawful and malicious killing of one who has been born alive. We recognize that the killing of an unborn but viable fetus may be deemed by some to be an offense of similar nature and gravity; but as Chief Justice Marshall warned long ago, "[i]t would be dangerous, indeed, to carry the principle, that a case which is within the reason or mischief of a statute, is within its provisions, so far as to punish a crime not enumerated in the statute, because it is of equal atrocity, or of kindred character, with those which are enumerated." Whether to thus extend liability for murder in California is a determination solely within the province of the legislature. For a court to simply declare, by judicial fiat, that the time has now come to prosecute under Section 187 one who kills an unborn but viable fetus would indeed be to rewrite the statute under the guise of construing it. Nor does a need to fill an asserted "gap" in the law between abortion and homicide—as will appear, no such gap in fact exists—justify judicial legislation of this nature: to make it a "judicial function" to explore such new fields of crime as they may appear from time to time is wholly foreign to the American concept of criminal justice and "raises very serious questions concerning the principle of separation of powers."

The second obstacle to the proposed judicial enlargement of Section 187 is the guarantee of due process of law. Assuming arguendo that we have the power to adopt the new construction of this statute as the law of California, such a ruling, by constitutional command, could operate only prospectively, and thus could not in any event reach the conduct of petitioner on February 23, 1969.

The first essential of due process is fair warning of the act which is made punishable as a crime. "That the terms of a penal statute creating a new offense must be sufficiently explicit to inform those who are subject to it what conduct on their part will render them liable to its penalties, is a well-recognized requirement, consonant alike with ordinary notions of fair play and the settled rules of law." Connally v. Gen. Constr. Co., 269 U.S. 385, 391 (1926). "No one may be required at peril of life, liberty or property to speculate as to the meaning of penal statutes. All are entitled to be informed as to what the state commands or forbids." Lanzetta v. New Jersey, 306 U.S. 451, 453 (1939). . . .

This requirement of fair warning is reflected in the constitutional prohibition against the enactment of ex post facto laws, U.S.Const. art. I, §§ 9, 10; Cal.Const. art. I, § 16. When a new penal statute is applied retrospectively to make punishable an act which was not criminal at the time it was performed, the defendant has been given no advance notice consistent with due process. And precisely the same effect occurs when such an act is made punishable under a pre-existing statute but by means of an unforeseeable *judicial* enlargement thereof. Bouie v. City of Columbia, 378 U.S. 347 (1964).

In *Bouie* two Negroes took seats in the restaurant section of a South Carolina drugstore; no notices were posted restricting the area to whites only. When the defendants refused to leave upon demand, they were arrested and convicted of violating a criminal trespass statute which prohibited entry on the property of another "after notice" forbidding such conduct. Prior South Carolina decisions had emphasized the necessity of proving such notice to support a conviction under the statute. The South Carolina Supreme Court nevertheless affirmed the convictions, construing the statute to prohibit not only the act of entering after notice not to do so but also the wholly different act of remaining on the property after receiving notice to leave.

The United States Supreme Court reversed the convictions, holding that the South Carolina court's ruling was "unforeseeable" and when an "unforeseeable state-court construction of a criminal statute is applied retroactively to subject a person to criminal liability for past conduct, the effect is to deprive him of due process of law in the sense of fair warning that his contemplated conduct constitutes a crime." Analogizing to the prohibition against retrospective penal legislation, the high court reasoned

> Indeed, an unforeseeable judicial enlargement of a criminal statute, applied retroactively, operates precisely like an ex post facto law, such as Art. I, § 10, of the Constitution forbids. An ex post facto law has been defined by this Court as one "that makes an action done before the passing of the law, and which was *innocent* when done, criminal; and punishes such action," or "that *aggravates* a *crime*, or makes it *greater* than it was, when committed." If a state legislature is barred by the ex post facto clause from passing such a law, it must follow that a state supreme court is barred by the due process clause from achieving precisely the same result by judicial construction. The fundamental principle that "the required criminal law must have existed when the conduct in issue occurred," must apply to bar retroactive criminal prohibitions emanating from courts as well as from legislatures. If a judicial construction of a criminal statute is "unexpected and indefensible by reference

to the law which had been expressed prior to the conduct in issue," it must not be given retroactive effect. . . .

It is true that Section 187, on its face, is not as "narrow and precise" as the South Carolina statute involved in *Bouie*; on the other hand, neither is it as vague as the statutes struck down in *Connally* and *Lanzetta*. Rather, Section 187 bears a plain, common-sense meaning, well settled in the common law and fortified by its legislative history in California. In *Bouie*, moreover, the Court stressed that a breach of the peace statute was also in force in South Carolina at the time of the events, and that the defendants were in fact arrested on that ground and prosecuted (but not convicted) for that offense. Here, too, there was another statute on the books which petitioner could well have believed he was violating: Penal Code Section 274 defines the crime of abortion, in relevant part, as the act of "[e]very person who . . . uses or employs any instrument *or any other means whatever*, with intent thereby to procure the miscarriage" of any woman, and does not come within the exceptions provided by law. The gist of the crime is the performance, with the requisite intent, of any of the acts enumerated in the statute. It is therefore no defense to a charge of violating Section 274 that the act was committed unusually late in the woman's pregnancy or by a method not commonly employed for that purpose. . . .

Turning to the case law, we find no reported decisions of the California courts which should have given petitioner notice that the killing of an unborn but viable fetus was prohibited by Section 187. . . .

Properly understood, the often cited case of People v. Chavez, 77 Cal.App.2d 621, 176 P.2d 92 (1947), does not derogate from this rule. There the defendant was charged with the murder of her newborn child, and convicted of manslaughter. She testified that the baby dropped from her womb into the toilet bowl; that she picked it up two or three minutes later, and cut but did not tie the umbilical cord; that the baby was limp and made no cry; and that after 15 minutes she wrapped it in a newspaper and concealed it, where it was found dead the next day. The autopsy surgeon testified that the baby was a full-term, nine-month child, weighing six and one-half pounds and appearing normal in every respect; that the body had very little blood in it, indicating the child had bled to death through the untied umbilical cord; that such a process would have taken about an hour; and that in his opinion "the child was born alive, based on conditions he found and the fact that the lungs contained air and the blood was extravasated or pushed back into the tissues, indicating heart action."

On appeal, the defendant emphasized that a doctor called by the defense had suggested other tests which the autopsy surgeon could have performed to determine the matter of live birth; on this basis, it was contended that the question of whether the infant was born alive "rests entirely on pure speculation." The Court of Appeals found only an insignificant conflict in that regard, and focused its attention instead on testimony of the autopsy surgeon admitting the possibility that the evidence of heart and lung action could have resulted from the child's breathing "after presentation of the head but before the birth was completed."

The court cited [various] mid-19th century English infanticide cases . . . and noted that the decisions had not reached uniformity on whether breathing, heart action, severance of the umbilical cord, or some combination of these or other factors established the status of "human being" for the purposes of the law of homicide. The court then adverted to the state of modern medical knowledge, discussed the phenomenon of viability, and held that "a viable child *in the process of being born* is a human being within the meaning of the homicide statutes, whether or not the process has been fully completed. It should at least be considered a human being where it is a living baby and where in the natural course of events *a birth which is already started* would naturally be successfully completed." (Italics added.) Since the testimony of the autopsy surgeon left no doubt in that case that a live birth had at least begun, the court found "the evidence is sufficient here to support the implied finding of the jury that this child *was born alive and became a human being within the meaning of the homicide statutes*." (Italics added.)

*Chavez* thus stands for the proposition—to which we adhere—that a viable fetus "in the process of being born" is a human being within the meaning of the homicide statutes. But it stands for no more; in particular it does not hold that a fetus, however viable, which is *not* "in the process of being born" is nevertheless a "human being" in the law of homicide. On the contrary, the opinion is replete with references to the common law requirement that the child be "born alive," however that term is defined, and must accordingly be deemed to reaffirm that requirement as part of the law of California. . . .

We conclude that the judicial enlargement of Section 187 now urged upon us by the People would not have been foreseeable to this petitioner, and hence that its adoption at this time would deny him due process of law.

Let a peremptory writ of prohibition issue restraining respondent court from taking any further proceedings on Count I of the information, charging petitioner with the crime of murder.

■ BURKE, ACTING C.J. [dissenting]. The majority hold that "Baby Girl" Vogt, who, according to medical testimony, had reached the 35th week of development, had a 96 percent chance of survival, and was "definitely" alive and viable at the time of her death, nevertheless was not a "human being" under California's homicide statutes. In my view, in so holding, the majority ignore significant common law precedents, frustrate the express intent of the legislature, and defy reason, logic and common sense. . . .

The majority opinion suggests that we are confined to common law concepts, and to the common law definition of murder or manslaughter. However, the legislature, in Penal Code Sections 187 and 192, has defined those offenses: homicide is the unlawful killing of a "human being." These words need not be frozen in place as of any particular time, but must be fairly and reasonably interpreted by this court to promote justice and to carry out the purposes of the legislature in adopting a homicide statute. Thus, Penal Code Section 4, which was enacted in 1872 along with Sections 187 and 192, provides: "The rule of the common law, that penal statutes are to be strictly construed, has no application to this code. All its provisions are to be construed according to the fair import of their terms, with a view to effect its objects and to promote justice." . . .

Penal Code Section 4, which abolishes the common law principle of the strict construction of penal statutes, . . . permits this court fairly to construe the terms of those statutes to serve the ends of justice. Consequently, nothing should prevent this court from holding that Baby Girl Vogt was a human ("belonging or relating to man; characteristic of man")[4] being ("existence, as opp. to nonexistence; specif. life")[5] under California's homicide statutes.

We commonly conceive of human existence as a spectrum stretching from birth to death. However, if this court properly might expand the definition of "human being" at one end of that spectrum, we may do so at the other end. Consider the following examples: All would agree that "shooting or otherwise damaging a corpse is not homicide. . . ." In other words, a corpse is not considered to be a "human being" and thus cannot be the subject of a "killing" as those terms are used in the homicide statutes. However, it is readily apparent that our concepts of what constitutes a "corpse" have been and are being continually modified by advances in the field of medicine, including new techniques for life revival, restoration and resuscitation such as artificial respiration, open heart massage, transfusions, transplants and a variety of life-restoring stimulants, drugs and new surgical methods. Would this court ignore these developments and exonerate the killer of an apparently "drowned" child merely because that child would have been pronounced dead in 1648 or 1850? Obviously not. Whether a homicide occurred in that case would be determined by medical testimony regarding capability of the child to have survived prior to the defendant's act. And that is precisely the test which this court should adopt in the instant case.

*[margin annotation:]* Capability of survival new test

The common law reluctance to characterize the killing of a quickened fetus as a homicide was based solely upon a presumption that the fetus would have been born dead. This presumption seems to have persisted in this country at least as late as 1876. Based upon the state of the medical art in the 17th, 18th and 19th centuries, that presumption may have been well-founded. However, as we approach the 21st century, it has been apparent that "This presumption is not only contrary to common experience and the ordinary course of nature, but it is contrary to the usual rule with respect to presumptions followed in this state." People v. Chavez, 77 Cal.App.2d 621, 176 P.2d 92 (1947).

There are no accurate statistics disclosing fetal death rates in "common law England," although the foregoing presumption of death indicates a significantly high death experience. On the other hand, in California the fetal death rate[6] in 1968 is estimated to be 12 deaths in 1,000, a ratio which would have given Baby Girl Vogt a 98.8 per cent chance of survival. If, as I have contended, the term "human being" in our homicide statutes is a fluid concept to be defined in accordance with present conditions, then there can be no question that the term should include the fully viable fetus.

The majority suggests that to do so would improperly create some new offense. However, the offense of murder is no new offense. Contrary to the majority opinion, the legislature has not "defined the crime of

---

4    Webster's New International Dictionary (2d ed. 1959), page 1211, column 3.

5    Id. at 247.

6    I.e., fetal deaths of 20 weeks or more gestation.

murder in California to apply only to the unlawful and malicious killing of one who has been born alive." Instead, the legislature simply used the term "human being" and directed the courts to construe that term according to its "fair import" with a view to effect the objects of the homicide statutes and promote justice. Cal.Penal Code § 4. What justice will be promoted, what objects effectuated, by construing "human being" as excluding Baby Girl Vogt and her unfortunate successors? Was defendant's brutal act of stomping her to death any less an act of homicide than the murder of a newly born baby? No one doubts that the term "human being" would include the elderly or dying persons whose potential for life has nearly lapsed; their proximity to death is deemed immaterial. There is no sound reason for denying the viable fetus, with its unbounded potential for life, the same status.

The majority also suggest that such an interpretation of our homicide statutes would deny defendant "fair warning" that his act was punishable as a crime. Aside from the absurdity of the underlying premise that defendant consulted Coke, Blackstone or Hale before kicking Baby Girl Vogt to death, it is clear that defendant had adequate notice that his act could constitute homicide. Due process only precludes prosecution under a new statute insufficiently explicit regarding the specific conduct proscribed, or under a pre-existing statute "by means of an unforeseeable *judicial* enlargement thereof."

Our homicide statutes have been in effect in this state since 1850. The fact that the California courts have not been called upon to determine the precise question before us does not render "unforeseeable" a decision which determines that a viable fetus is a "human being" under those statutes. Can defendant really claim surprise that a 5-pound, 18-inch, 34-week-old, living, viable child is considered to be a human being?

The fact is that the foregoing construction of our homicide statutes easily could have been anticipated from strong dicta in *People v. Chavez*, wherein the court reviewed common law precedents but disapproved their requirement that the child be born alive and completely separated from its mother. . . . In dicta, the court discussed the question when an unborn infant becomes a human being under the homicide statutes, as follows: " . . . While it may not be possible to draw an exact line applicable to all cases, the rules of law should recognize and make some attempt to follow the natural and scientific facts to which they relate. . . . [I]t would be a mere fiction to hold that a child is not a human being because the process of birth has not been fully completed, when it has reached that state of viability when the destruction of the life of its mother would not end its existence and when, if separated from the mother naturally or by artificial means, it will live and grow in the normal manner."

Thus the *Chavez* case explodes the majority's premise that a viability test for defining the "human being" under our homicide statutes was unforeseeable. . . . I would conclude that defendant had sufficient notice that the words "human being" could include a viable fetus. . . .

## NOTES ON *KEELER* AND THE INTERPRETATION OF CRIMINAL STATUTES

### 1. QUESTIONS ON *KEELER*

Is the *Keeler* result compelled by considerations underlying the vagueness doctrine? By *Bouie*? What does the court mean when it refers to a "jurisdictional" obstacle to the prosecution? Is that argument compelling? Or does the case turn, in the end, on the construction of the murder statute that is most faithful to the intent of the legislature and the purpose of the murder statute? How, in these terms, should the case have been decided? The notes that follow will help in thinking about these questions.

### 2. AMENDMENT OF THE CALIFORNIA MURDER STATUTE

*Keeler* was denounced by the majority leader of the state Assembly the day after it was decided, and the legislature moved swiftly thereafter to amend the murder statute. The new statute reads:

> Section 187. Murder defined; death of fetus.
>
> (a) Murder is the unlawful killing of a human being, or a fetus, with malice aforethought.
>
> (b) This section shall not apply to any person who commits an act which results in the death of a fetus if any of the following apply:
>
> (1) The act complied with the Therapeutic Abortion Act. . . .
>
> (2) The act was committed by a holder of a physician's and surgeon's certificate . . . in a case where, to a medical certainty, the result of childbirth would be death of the mother of the fetus or where her death from childbirth, although not medically certain, would be substantially certain or more likely than not.
>
> (3) The act was solicited, aided, abetted, or consented to by the mother of the fetus.
>
> (c) Subdivision (b) shall not be construed to prohibit the prosecution of any person under any other provision of law.

This statute was clearly aimed at overturning *Keeler*. It did so not by disapproving the decision, but by stating a new rule of substantive law. Suppose *Keeler* had come out the other way, construing the term "human being" to include "Baby Girl Vogt." How does amended version of § 187 differ from the situation that would then have resulted? Does the difference shed light on why *Keeler* might have been decided the way it was?

### 3. *PEOPLE V. DAVIS*

The question in *Keeler* was whether an unborn but viable fetus should be considered a human being under the murder statute. In People v. Davis, 7 Cal. 4th 797, 872 P.2d 591 (1994), the question was whether § 187 as amended required that the fetus be viable, an issue that the text of the statute did not address.

Robert Davis pulled a gun on Maria Flores as she left a store that cashed her welfare check. When she refused to hand over the money, Davis shot her in the chest. Flores survived, but her unborn child—who likely had not reached the stage of viability—did not. Davis was convicted of assault and robbery of Flores and murder of the fetus. He appealed on the ground that the jury had not been properly instructed on viability, but the California Supreme Court concluded that the statute did not require viability. Instead, quoting a medical dictionary definition of "fetus," the court interpreted the statute to apply to the killing of any "unborn offspring in the postembryonic period, after major structures have been outlined," a development reached seven or eight weeks after conception.

*[handwritten margin note: Convicted assault, robbery & murder]*
*[handwritten margin note: did not require viability]*
*[handwritten margin note: definition of fetus]*

This interpretation contradicted several lower court decisions stating or assuming that § 187 required viability.[a] These and similar decisions had been reached after Roe v. Wade, 410 U.S. 113 (1973), which made viability the critical dividing line between a woman's right to abortion and a state's interest in protecting future human life. The *Davis* court concluded that "*Roe v. Wade* principles are inapplicable to a statute (like § 187(a)) that criminalizes the killing of a fetus without the mother's consent." The point was explained more fully in the concurrence by Justice Kennard:

*[handwritten margin note: Roe v. Wade not applicable (mother's consent)]*

> When the appellate court in *People v. (K.A.) Smith* read a constitutional requirement of viability into the fetal murder statute, it did so in mistaken reliance on *Roe v. Wade*. It appears that the Court of Appeal confused the issue of state authority to interfere with a woman's procreative choice with the quite distinct issue of state authority to punish a third party whose violent conduct against the pregnant woman deprives her of that choice. Although in *Roe* the concept of "fetal viability" was critical to the first of the two issues, it has no application to California's fetal murder statute . . . ."

On this issue, only Justice Mosk (the author of *Keeler*) dissented. He interpreted the amendment to § 187 as a very specific response to *Keeler*, designed only to overrule that decision. For him it "follow[ed] that by enacting the 1970 amendment to § 187 the Legislature extended the crime of murder, as *Keeler* refused to do, to include the malicious killing of a *viable* fetus" and intended to go no further.

The court disagreed with Justice Mosk as to the meaning of the statute, but held that its interpretation of § 187 could not be applied to Davis. Instead, the interpretation could be applied only prospectively. The reasoning was similar to the constitutional justification for *Keeler*:

> [H]olding a defendant criminally responsible for conduct that he could not reasonably anticipate would be proscribed violates due process because the law must give sufficient warning so that individuals "may conduct themselves so as to avoid that which is forbidden." Rose v. Locke, 423 U.S. 48, 50 (1975). . . . [S]everal Courts of Appeal have erroneously implied a viability requirement into § 187(a). . . . [T]he fact that a viability requirement has consistently been read into § 187(a) supports defendant's assertion that our proposed holding creates an unforeseeable judicial en-

---

[a]    See, e.g., People v. (K.A.) Smith, 59 Cal. App.3d 751(1976); People v. (R.P.) Smith, 188 Cal. App.3d 1495 (1987).

largement of a criminal statute. Bouie v. City of Columbia, 378 US. 347, 353 (1964). . . .

Two Justices dissented on this point.

Suppose the court had applied its construction of the murder statute to Davis. Would the principles underlying *Bouie* or the vagueness doctrine have been violated? Consider a somewhat narrower question about the California murder statute. Neither "viability" nor the *Davis* court's understanding of "fetus" is self-defining. Both raise line-drawing problems, although they draw the line in different places. Does that raise a *Bouie* or a vagueness issue? In People v. Henderson, 25 Cal. App.3d 1129 (1990), the California Court of Appeal held that the viability requirement then understood to be implicit in § 187 did not render the statute unconstitutionally vague. Presumably, the same result would apply to the new definition of fetus as an "unborn offspring in the postembryonic period." Is that definition constitutionally acceptable?

## 4. THE DOCTRINE OF STRICT CONSTRUCTION

Recall the statement in *Keeler* that "[i]t is the policy of this state to construe a penal statute as favorably to the defendant as its language and the circumstances of its application may reasonably permit . . . ." This is the doctrine of strict construction, sometimes referred to as the rule of lenity. It requires that ambiguity in the interpretation of criminal statutes be resolved in favor of the accused.

The history of this doctrine is described in Livingston Hall, Strict or Liberal Construction of Penal Statutes, 48 Harv. L. Rev. 748, 749–51 (1935). The doctrine originated in the late 17th and early 18th Century "to meet a very definite situation, and for a very definite purpose," namely as a response by courts to the "unmitigated severity" of increased legislative use of capital punishment.[b] But, as so often happened with the common law, the rule outlived its rationale:

> It was from cases and text writers in the England of this period that the doctrine of strict construction was brought to this country.
>
> The nineteenth century, both here and in England, marked the end of the death penalty as the chief mode of punishment for serious crimes. And with its passing, the factor which had brought the doctrine of strict construction into existence . . . disappeared—yet the doctrine itself lived, the sole relic of what had once been a veritable conspiracy for administrative nullification.

A number of 19th-century American legislatures saw the doctrine of strict construction as an unwarranted limitation on their ability to accomplish statutory purposes. The original suggestion to overrule it came from the Field Code proposed for New York:

> The rule of the common law that penal statutes are to be strictly construed has no application to this Code. All its provi-

---

[b] "Faced with a vast and irrational proliferation of capital offenses, judges invented strict construction to stem the march to the gallows." John C. Jeffries, Jr., Legality, Vagueness, and the Construction of Penal Statutes, 71 Va. L. Rev. 189, 198 (1985). Jeffries points out that there were more than 200 capital offenses by the end of the 17th century, with mandatory death being the penalty for most.

> sions are to be construed according to the fair import of their terms, with a view to effect its objects and to promote justice.

David Field, William Noyes and Alexander Bradford, Draft of a Penal Code for the State of New York § 10 (1864).

As *Keeler* reveals, this proposal was adopted verbatim as § 4 of the California Code of 1872. Additionally, some 18 other states, most of them west of the Mississippi, passed similar statutes in the years before World War I. In a few cases, the enactment of such laws seems immediately to have altered the terms of judicial construction, but in other jurisdictions—as in *Keeler*—the courts continued to invoke the doctrine of strict construction despite the contrary legislative command.

One reason for the persistence of the doctrine, undoubtedly, is its theoretical appeal as an embodiment of important modern values. See, for example, the Supreme Court's fair notice and separation of powers rationale for narrowly construing a federal criminal statute in Bass v. United States, 404 U.S. 336 (1971):

> "[A]mbiguity concerning the ambit of criminal statutes should be resolved in favor of lenity." . . . In various ways over the years, we have stated that "when choice has to be made between two readings of what conduct Congress has made a crime, it is appropriate, before we choose the harsher alternative, to require that Congress should have spoken in language that is clear and definite." . . . This principle is founded on two policies that have long been part of our tradition. First, "a fair warning should be given to the world in language that the common world will understand, of what the law intends to do if a certain line is passed. To make the warning fair, so far as possible the line should be clear." . . . Second, because of the seriousness of criminal penalties, and because criminal punishment usually represents the moral condemnation of the community, legislatures and not courts should define criminal activity. This policy embodies "the instinctive distastes against men languishing in prison unless the lawmaker has clearly said they should." H. Friendly, Mr. Justice Frankfurter and the Reading of Statutes, in Benchmarks 196, 209 (1967). Thus, where there is ambiguity in a criminal statute, doubts are resolved in favor of the defendant.[c]

It is observed in Daniel M. Kahan, Lenity and Federal Common Law Crimes, 1994 Sup. Ct. Rev. 345, 346, however, that this "theory . . . isn't the reality. Judicial enforcement of lenity is notoriously sporadic and unpredictable." The fact is, as Kahan demonstrates, that lenity is most often invoked, at least by the Supreme Court, as an additional rationale once the Court has already determined that a narrow interpretation is preferable. Operationally, its persuasive force is limited to those who are already persuaded.[d]

---

[c] In addition to lenity, the *Bass* Court also relied on a second principle—namely that "unless Congress conveys its purpose clearly, it will not be deemed to have significantly changed the federal-state balance." In the interpretation of federal statutes, in other words, concepts of federalism, i.e., the appropriate role of the federal government vis-à-vis the states, are relevant and sometimes controlling.

[d] See also John C. Jeffries, Jr., Legality, Vagueness, and the Construction of Penal Statutes, 71 Va. L. Rev. 189, 198–99 (1985): "Today, strict construction survives more as a makeweight for results that seem right on other grounds than as a consistent policy of statu-

Modern penal codes typically include some statement on statutory construction. Often, they simply carry forward a variant of the Field Code provision quoted above. See, e.g., N.Y. Penal Law § 5.00 (McKinney 1987). Other states have followed the more elaborate formulation in § 1.02 of the Model Penal Code:

> (1) The general purposes of the provisions governing the definition of offenses are:
>
> (a) to forbid and prevent conduct that unjustifiably and inexcusably inflicts or threatens substantial harm to individual or public interests;
>
> (b) to subject to public control persons whose conduct indicates that they are disposed to commit crimes;
>
> (c) to safeguard conduct that is without fault from condemnation as criminal;
>
> (d) to give fair warning of the nature of the conduct declared to constitute an offense;
>
> (e) to differentiate on reasonable grounds between serious and minor offenses. . . .
>
> (3) The provisions of the Code shall be construed according to the fair import of their terms but when the language is susceptible of differing constructions it shall be interpreted to further the general purposes stated in this Section and the special purposes of the particular provision involved. . . .

Does such a statute provide useful guidance for decisions such as *Keeler*, *Davis*, and *Sobiek*? Is there any useful guidance that can be applied to all criminal statutes, or do these questions depend too much on context? From another perspective, is the reliance of the *Keeler* court on the doctrine of strict construction—even given the enactment of § 4 of the California code—understandable?

## ADDITIONAL NOTES ON THE CONSTRUCTION OF CRIMINAL STATUTES

### 1. *PEOPLE V. SOBIEK*

People v. Sobiek, 30 Cal.App.3d 458, 106 Cal.Rptr. 519 (1973), involved the dismissal of an indictment charging Sobiek with theft. On appeal by the prosecution, a California intermediate appellate court held that the prosecution could proceed.

Sobiek was the president of an investment club in which several friends had put money into a central pot. Over a period of time a substantial portion of the money found its way into Sobiek's pocket. His argument on appeal was that, even though he had helped himself to the money, its conversion did not count as theft because, as prior cases had held, "a partner may not steal nor embezzle the property of his partnership." As the court elaborated:

---

tory interpretation." For a list of federal cases in which the rule of lenity could have turned the tide but did not, see William J. Stuntz, The Pathological Politics of Criminal Law, 100 Mich. L. Rev. 505, 564 (2002).

> The basic thought behind the decisions sustaining the rule that a partner may not steal partnership property seems to be that as each partner is the ultimate owner of an undivided interest in all the partnership property and as no one can be guilty of stealing or embezzling what belongs to him, a general partner cannot be convicted of embezzling partnership property, i.e., the property must be "of another." This rule, when thus broadly stated, goes further than the simple statutory requirement that the property be "of another." When thus stated, the rule requires that the property be wholly that of another because a part interest by the defendant prevents a conviction.

The court found, however, that despite the frequency with which it was repeated, the rule was based on "misinterpretation and dicta":

> The broad rule that a partner cannot embezzle from a partnership has been rejected by the American Law Institute. In Model Penal Code § 223.0(7), "property of another" is defined to include property in which any person other than the actor has an interest which the actor is not privileged to infringe, regardless of the fact that the actor also has an interest in the property. [The rationale for this result is] to nullify the concept that each of the joint owners has complete title to the jointly owned property so that a joint owner cannot misappropriate what already belongs to him.... [W]hatever might be the merits of such notions in the civil law, it is clear they have no relevance to the criminal law's effort to deter deprivations of other people's economic interests. Modern statutes, including those of Minnesota, Wisconsin, and Illinois, either expressly or impliedly reach the same result....
>
> It is both illogical and unreasonable to hold that a partner cannot steal from his partners merely because he has an undivided interest in the partnership property. Fundamentally, stealing that portion of the partners' shares which does not belong to the thief is no different from stealing the property of another person. There is nothing in Penal Code Section 484 which requires an interpretation different from that in Model Penal Code § 223.0(7).

As to whether *Bouie* prohibited Sobiek's prosecution, the court said:

> [*Bouie*] was an entirely different situation from the one at bench where not only is the interpretation of the grand theft [statute] reasonable, but the respondent must have known that his act was immoral and that he was taking the property of another.
>
> In United States v. Rundle, 255 F.Supp. 936 (E.D.Pa.1966), [the court distinguished *Bouie*, observing:]
>
> > It is not always true that where the definition of a crime is extended by judicial construction, a conviction which results therefrom is a denial of due process and, quoting Mr. Justice Holmes, ... "the law is full of instances where a man's fate depends on his estimating rightly, that is, as the jury subsequently estimates it, some matter of degree. If his judgment is wrong, not only may he incur a fine or a short imprisonment, as here; he may incur the penalty of death.... '*The criterion in such cases is to examine whether common so-*

*cial duty would, under the circumstances, have suggested a more circumspect conduct.*' *Nash* v. *United States*. (Emphasis added)."

Similarly, in the case at bar, "common social duty" would have forewarned respondent that "circumspect conduct" prohibited robbing his partners and also would have told him that he was stealing "property of another."

common social duty

Nor did the reasoning in *Keeler* bar the prosecution:

Keeler v. Superior Court, 2 Cal.3d 619, 87 Cal.Rptr. 481, 470 P.2d 617 (1970), at first blush seems to support respondent's contention that the construction of Section 487 placed upon it by this court deprives respondent of due process. However, a study of *Keeler* shows that it is not in point. *Keeler* held that the brutal killing of a fetus did not violate Section 187 of the Penal Code, which defines murder as "the unlawful killing of a human being," because, as the court expends a number of pages to prove, a fetus is not a "human being" and "the legislature intended to exclude from its reach the act of killing an unborn fetus." The court then states that were the court to determine that an infant in utero was a human being within the meaning of the murder statute, such determination would have met jurisdictional and constitutional barriers. That this is dictum cannot be gainsaid, for once the court determined the fetus was not a human being there was nothing more that needed to be determined. Dictum is not binding on this court.

Moreover, the circumstances applying to Section 187 are entirely different from those applying to Section 487. The court in *Keeler* said that, prior to the killing, the defendant had no notice from any cause that destroying a viable fetus might be murder. As to the grand theft statute, Section 487, there is no indication that the legislature did not intend to include in "property of another" the property of partners other than the one stealing such property, or of the partnership itself. . . .

As we have shown, respondent's defense relies upon an interpretation of the law which is improper because it is based upon mere dictum. If respondent, at the time he stole his partner's property, relied on a mistaken dictum of court, traditional notions of fair play and substantial justice are not offended by applying to his act the clear meaning of Sections 484 and 487.

Intermediate appellate courts in California are bound to follow decisions by the California Supreme Court and the United States Supreme Court. Did the court in *Sobiek* do so? Can both *Keeler* and *Sobiek* be right?[a] Consider in this connection a side debate between Justice Black, dissenting in *Bouie*, and the Court's response. Justice Black said:

We cannot believe that either the petitioners or anyone else could have been misled by the language of this statute into believ-

[a] For review of *Keeler* and *Sobiek* and an argument that the cases are consistent and are importantly different from vagueness cases and from *Manley*, see John C. Jeffries, Jr., Legality, Vagueness, and the Construction of Penal Statutes, 71 Va. L. Rev. 189, 223–34 (1985). For a thoughtful analysis of these issues from a British perspective, see A.T.H. Smith, Judicial Law Making in the Criminal Law, 100 Law Q.R. 46 (1984).

> ing that it would permit them to stay on the property of another over the owner's protest without being guilty of trespass.

He appended a footnote in which he added:

> The petitioners testified that they had agreed the day before to "sit in" at the drugstore restaurant. One petitioner said that he had intended to be arrested; the other said that he had the same purpose "if it took that."

The Court responded in a footnote:

> We think it irrelevant that petitioners at one point testified that they had intended to be arrested. The determination whether a criminal statute provides fair warning of its prohibitions must be made on the basis of the statute itself and the other pertinent law, rather than on the basis of an ad hoc appraisal of the subjective expectations of particular defendants.

Was the *Sobiek* court's distinction of *Bouie* consistent with the majority's side of this debate? Is the California court's decision nonetheless consistent with *Bouie*?

### 2. *SHUTTLESWORTH* REVISITED

Recall *Shuttlesworth v. City of Birmingham*, discussed in the Notes on the Vagueness Doctrine following *Papachristou* in Section 2 above. Shuttlesworth had been convicted of violating a statute providing that it was "unlawful for any person to stand or loiter upon any street or sidewalk of the city after having been requested by any police officer to move on." The Alabama Court of Appeals had construed this language to authorize police to issue orders to move on only in situations where people were obstructing sidewalk traffic. But since this construction was not adopted until *after* Shuttlesworth had been convicted, it could not be used to sustain his conviction. This led the Supreme Court to reverse his conviction because it impermissibly authorized arrest "only at the whim" of the police.

The Supreme Court's disposition in *Shuttlesworth* ordered the case "remanded to the Court of Appeals of Alabama for proceedings not inconsistent with this opinion." Assume that there was evidence that Shuttlesworth had been obstructing pedestrian traffic on the sidewalk, evidence that was not used in the initial trial because it was not thought necessary. Would it have been acceptable for the Alabama Court of Appeals to order a new trial following the Supreme Court's remand at which such evidence, if believed, could be the basis for a new conviction? Would a new conviction based on such evidence—and the Alabama court's construction of the statute adopted *after* his conduct—be inconsistent with *Bouie*?

Interestingly, the author of *Bouie* thought a new trial and conviction would be permissible. Justice Brennan's entire separate concurrence in *Shutlesworth* read:

> I join the Court's opinion on my understanding that *Middlebrooks v. City of Birmingham* is being read as holding that [the statute] applies only when a person (a) stands, loiters or walks on a street or sidewalk so as to obstruct free passage, (b) is requested by an officer to move on, and (c) thereafter continues to block passage by loitering or standing on the street. It is only this limiting construction which saves the statute from the constitu-

> tional challenge that it is overly broad. Moreover, because this construction delimits the statute to "the sort of 'hard-core' conduct that would obviously be prohibited under any construction," it may be legitimately applied to such conduct occurring before that construction.

Was Justice Brennan inconsistent with his opinion in *Bouie*?[b]

### 3. *ROGERS V. TENNESSEE*

Rogers was convicted of second degree murder by stabbing. One of the stab wounds penetrated the victim's heart. During surgery to repair the wound, the victim went into cardiac arrest. He survived the surgery but, due to loss of oxygen to the brain, his higher brain functions ceased and he went into a coma. The coma lasted 15 months before he died as a result of ensuing complications. Rogers's conviction was affirmed by the Tennessee Supreme Court in State v. Rogers, 992 S.W.2d 393 (Tenn. 1999).

The traditional definition of murder, as paraphrased from a 17th century source, was:

> When a man of sound memory and of the age of discretion unlawfully kills any reasonable creature in being and under the King's peace, with malice aforethought, either express or implied by the law, the death taking place within a year and a day. [c]

The question before the Tennessee courts was whether the common law "year and a day" rule was part of Tennessee law. Three prior Tennessee cases, one decided by the state supreme court and the others by an intermediate appellate court, had mentioned the rule, but it had not actually been at issue. In 1989 Tennessee had adopted a comprehensive revision of its criminal law based on the Model Penal Code. As in the Model Code, the rule was not mentioned in the new murder or causation provisions.[d]

The intermediate appellate court held that the rule had been abolished by the new Tennessee code. Since Rogers's behavior occurred after the new code went into effect, it said, the rule therefore did not apply to him and the result of his conduct was properly measured by ordinary causation standards. The Tennessee Supreme Court disagreed. It held that the rule had been part of Tennessee law before the new code was written, that it had not been abolished by the new code, and that it remained a part of the law of Tennessee when Rogers acted. But, after a detailed analysis of the historical justifications for the rule, it decided that the time had come for a change:

> Clearly, advances in medical science, improved trial procedure, and sentencing reform have eroded the reasons originally

---

[b] Compare Dombrowski v. Pfister, 380 U.S. 479, 491 n.7 (1965) (Opinion for the Court by Justice Brennan):

> Our cases indicate that once an acceptable limiting construction is obtained, it may be applied to conduct occurring prior to the construction, provided such application affords fair warning to the defendants.

[c] See 3 Coke, Institutes * 47; Royal Comm'n on Capital Punishment, CMND. No. 8932, at 28 (1953).

[d] The commentary to the Model Penal Code says that "the purpose of the year-and-a-day rule was to insure that the defendant's action was the cause of death" and that such a provision is "unnecessary" under appropriate modern rules of causation. ALI, Model Penal Code and Commentaries 9 & n.15 (1980).

supporting the common law year-and-a-day rule. Accordingly, we hereby abolish the common law rule, and by doing so, join the majority of other jurisdictions which have recently considered the issue.

*abolish common law rule of 1 yr and day*

The question then became whether this new Tennessee law could be applied to Rogers, and specifically whether it would be inconsistent with *Bouie* to do so. The court held:

*new question*

> Given the fact that the rule has been abolished by every court which has squarely faced the issue, and given the fact that the validity of the rule has been questioned in this State in light of the passage of the 1989 Act, we conclude that our decision abrogating the rule is not an unexpected and unforeseen judicial construction of a principle of criminal law. Moreover, we emphasize that abolition of the rule does not allow the State to obtain a conviction upon less proof, nor does its abolition impose criminal sanctions for conduct that was heretofore innocent. Accordingly, we apply our decision abolishing the rule retroactively to the facts of this case and affirm the defendant's conviction.

*retroactive application*

*SCOTUS holding affirm*

The United States Supreme Court affirmed. Rogers v. Tennessee, 532 U.S. 451 (2001). Joined by Chief Justice Rehnquist and Justices Kennedy, Souter, and Ginsburg, Justice O'Connor wrote for a five-to-four majority. Her opinion concluded:

> [T]he Tennessee Court's abolition of the year and a day rule was not unexpected and indefensible. The year and a day rule is widely viewed as an outdated relic of the common law. Petitioner does not even so much as hint that good reasons exist for retaining the rule, and so we need not delve too deeply into the rule and its history here. Suffice it to say that . . . the primary and most frequently cited justification for the rule is that 13th century medical science was incapable of establishing causation beyond a reasonable doubt when a great deal of time had elapsed between the injury to the victim and his death; and that, as practically every court recently to have considered the rule has noted, advances in medical and related science have so undermined the usefulness of the rule as to render it without question obsolete.
>
> For this reason, the year and a day rule has been legislatively or judicially abolished in the vast majority of jurisdictions recently to have addressed the issue. Citing *Bouie,* petitioner contends that the judicial abolition of the rule in other jurisdictions is irrelevant to whether he had fair warning that the rule in Tennessee might similarly be abolished and, hence, to whether the Tennessee Court's decision was unexpected and indefensible as applied to him. . . . This case, however, involves not the precise meaning of the words of a particular statute, but rather the continuing viability of a common law rule. Common law courts frequently look to the decisions of other jurisdictions in determining whether to alter or modify a common law rule in light of changed circumstances, increased knowledge, and general logic and experience. Due process, of course, does not require a person to apprise himself of the common law of all 50 States in order to guarantee that his actions will not subject him to punishment in light of a developing trend in the law that has not yet made its way to his State. At the same

*not precise meaning but continuing viability of a law*

time, however, the fact that a vast number of jurisdictions have abolished a rule that has so clearly outlived its purpose is surely relevant to whether the abolition of the rule in a particular case can be said to be unexpected and indefensible by reference to the law as it then existed.

Finally, and perhaps most importantly, at the time of petitioner's crime the year and a day rule had only the most tenuous foothold as part of the criminal law of the State of Tennessee. The rule did not exist as part of Tennessee's statutory criminal code. And while the Supreme Court of Tennessee concluded that the rule persisted at common law, it also pointedly observed that the rule had never once served as a ground of decision in any prosecution for murder in the State. Indeed, in all the reported Tennessee cases, the rule has been mentioned only three times, and each time in dicta. . . .

These [three] cases hardly suggest that the Tennessee Court's decision was "unexpected and indefensible" such that it offended the due process principle of fair warning articulated in *Bouie* and its progeny. This is so despite the fact that, as Justice Scalia correctly points out, the Court viewed the year and a day rule as a "substantive principle" of the common law of Tennessee. As such, however, it was a principle in name only, having never once been enforced in the State. The Supreme Court of Tennessee also emphasized this fact in its opinion, and rightly so, for it is surely relevant to whether the Court's abolition of the rule in petitioner's case violated due process limitations on retroactive judicial decisionmaking. And while we readily agree with Justice Scalia that fundamental due process prohibits the punishment of conduct that cannot fairly be said to have been criminal at the time the conduct occurred, nothing suggests that is what took place here.

There is, in short, nothing to indicate that the Tennessee Court's abolition of the rule in petitioner's case represented an exercise of the sort of unfair and arbitrary judicial action against which the Due Process Clause aims to protect. Far from a marked and unpredictable departure from prior precedent, the Court's decision was a routine exercise of common law decisionmaking in which the Court brought the law into conformity with reason and common sense. It did so by laying to rest an archaic and outdated rule that had never been relied upon as a ground of decision in any reported Tennessee case.

Joined by Justices Stevens, Thomas, and Breyer, Justice Scalia dissented. The Scalia opinion concluded:

[T]he only "fair warning" discussed in our precedents, and the only "fair warning" relevant to the issue before us here, is fair warning *of what the law is.* That warning . . . goes well beyond merely "safeguarding defendants against *unjustified* and *unpredictable* breaks with prior law." It safeguards them against *changes in the law after the fact.* But even accepting the Court's novel substitute, the opinion's conclusion that this watered-down standard has been met seems to me to proceed on the principle that a large number of almost-valid arguments makes a solid case. As far as I can tell, petitioner had nothing that could fairly be called a "warning" that the Supreme Court of Tennessee would retroactively eliminate one of the elements of the crime of murder. . . .

To decide this case, we need only conclude that due process prevents a court from (1) acknowledging the validity, when they were rendered, of prior decisions establishing a particular element of a crime; (2) changing the prior law so as to eliminate that element; and (3) applying that change to conduct that occurred under the prior regime. A court would remain free to apply common law criminal rules to new fact patterns so long as that application is consistent with a fair reading of prior cases. It would remain free to conclude that a prior decision or series of decisions establishing a particular element of a crime was in error, and to apply that conclusion retroactively (so long as the "fair notice" requirement of *Bouie* is satisfied). It would even remain free . . . to "reevaluat[e] and refin[e]" the elements of common law crimes to its heart's content, so long as it does so prospectively. (The majority of state courts that have abolished the year-and- a-day rule have done so in this fashion.) And, of course (as Blackstone and the Framers envisioned), legislatures would be free to eliminate outmoded elements of common law crimes for the future *by law*. But what a court cannot do, consistent with due process, is what the Tennessee Supreme Court did here: avowedly *change* (to the defendant's disadvantage) the criminal law governing past acts.

Which opinion has the better argument? Notice that neither the Court nor Justice Scalia mentioned the possibility that the 1989 recodification of Tennessee criminal law made it predictable that the year-and-a-day rule had been abolished prior to Rogers' behavior, albeit that this was not the ground upon which the Tennessee Supreme Court rested its decision to affirm his conviction. Should it matter to the *Bouie* question *why* a court applies a particular legal rule to a given situation so long as it was predictable that it would?

## 4. POSTSCRIPT: RELEVANCE OF THE EX POST FACTO CLAUSE

There was a substantial side debate in *Rogers* about the relevance of the Ex Post Facto Clause of the Constitution to the *Bouie* issue.[e] All Justices agreed that the Ex Post Facto Clauses provide limits on legislation, not judicial decisions. But Justice Scalia thought that the Due Process limits on judicial action were congruent with the Ex Post Facto limits on the legislature, and that since it was clear that the legislature could not have abolished the year-and-a-day rule retroactively, it followed that courts could not do so either. In a lengthy part of his opinion that Justice Breyer did not join and Justice Stevens expressed doubts about,[f] Scalia read *Bouie* as precedent for the congruence and said, in effect, that the Framers did not include

---

[e] Actually, there are two Ex Post Facto Clauses in the Constitution. The first, in Article I, Section 9, limits the federal Congress by providing that "No . . . ex post facto Law shall be passed." The second, in Article I, Section 10, provides that "No State shall . . . pass any . . . ex post facto Law."

[f] The central difficulty Justice Stevens had with the majority opinion was "the fact that [it] has undervalued the threat to liberty that is posed whenever the criminal law is changed retroactively."

an ex post facto limitation on courts because it never would have occurred to them that courts could *change* law. Their conception of the job of courts, in his view, was to discover and apply law, not to make it or change it.

Justice O'Connor's opinion for the Court, however, held that the Due Process limitation on courts is different from the Ex Post Facto limitation on legislatures:

> Petitioner observes that the Due Process and Ex Post Facto Clauses safeguard common interests—in particular, the interests in fundamental fairness (through notice and fair warning) and the prevention of the arbitrary and vindictive use of the laws. While this is undoubtedly correct, petitioner is mistaken to suggest that these considerations compel extending the strictures of the Ex Post Facto Clause to the context of common law judging. The Ex Post Facto Clause, by its own terms, does not apply to courts. Extending the Clause to courts through the rubric of due process thus would circumvent the clear constitutional text. It also would evince too little regard for the important institutional and contextual differences between legislating, on the one hand, and common law decisionmaking, on the other.
>
> Petitioner contends that state courts acting in their common law capacity act much like legislatures in the exercise of their lawmaking function, and indeed may in some cases even be subject to the same kinds of political influences and pressures that justify ex post facto limitations upon legislatures. A court's "opportunity for discrimination," however, "is more limited than [a] legislature's, in that [it] can only act in construing existing law in actual litigation." James v. United States, 366 U.S. 213, 247, n.3 (1961) (Harlan, J., concurring in part and dissenting in part). Moreover, "[g]iven the divergent pulls of flexibility and precedent in our case law system," id., incorporation of [ex post facto limits] into due process limitations on judicial decisionmaking would place an unworkable and unacceptable restraint on normal judicial processes and would be incompatible with the resolution of uncertainty that marks any evolving legal system.
>
> That is particularly so where, as here, the allegedly impermissible judicial application of a rule of law involves not the interpretation of a statute but an act of common law judging. In the context of common law doctrines (such as the year and a day rule), there often arises a need to clarify or even to reevaluate prior opinions as new circumstances and fact patterns present themselves. Such judicial acts, whether they be characterized as "making" or "finding" the law, are a necessary part of the judicial business in States in which the criminal law retains some of its common law elements. Strict application of ex post facto principles in that context would unduly impair the incremental and reasoned development of precedent that is the foundation of the common law system. The common law, in short, presupposes a measure of evolution that is incompatible with stringent application of ex post facto principles. It was on account of concerns such as these that *Bouie* restricted due process limitations on the retroactive application of judicial interpretations of criminal statutes to those

that are "unexpected and indefensible by reference to the law which had been expressed prior to the conduct in issue."

We believe this limitation adequately serves the common law context as well. It accords common law courts the substantial leeway they must enjoy as they engage in the daily task of formulating and passing upon criminal defenses and interpreting such doctrines as causation and intent, reevaluating and refining them as may be necessary to bring the common law into conformity with logic and common sense. It also adequately respects the due process concern with fundamental fairness and protects against vindictive or arbitrary judicial lawmaking by safeguarding defendants against unjustified and unpredictable breaks with prior law. Accordingly, we conclude that a judicial alteration of a common law doctrine of criminal law violates the principle of fair warning, and hence must not be given retroactive effect, only where it is "unexpected and indefensible by reference to the law which had been expressed prior to the conduct in issue."

As discussed in connection with the vagueness materials in Section 2 of this Chapter, the clarity required of legislation often involves a trade-off between law enforcement necessity on the one hand and unfair imprecision on the other. What are the trade-offs involved in the *Rogers* situation? Note that Justice Scalia would continue to apply the *Bouie* formula to situations where courts were purporting to *apply* the law to a novel factual situation. He would forbid only a retroactive *change* in the law by courts. Is it necessary for courts to have the power retroactively to *change* the law as envisaged by the O'Connor opinion? Would it promote the fairness of the system and its fidelity to the principle of legality if it were required that judicial *changes* in the criminal law be prospective only?[g] But, to argue in favor of the Court's decision, did anything unfair happen to Rogers? Should his conviction be reversed because something unfair might happen to someone else in another case in another context someday if a court were to misuse the power preserved by the majority opinion and if *Bouie*, for one reason or another, was not used to fix it? How likely is it that this might happen?[h]

---

[g] It is likely that Rogers could have been convicted of attempted murder if it were held that the change in Tennessee law could only be prospective. Indeed, he had argued before the intermediate appellate court in Tennessee "that his conviction should be modified to criminal attempt to commit murder because the victim's death had occurred more than a year and one day after the stabbing incident." State v. Rogers, 992 S.W.2d 393, 395 (Tenn. 1999).

[h] For detailed consideration of *Bouie*, *Rogers*, and their relation to statutory vagueness, see Peter W. Low and Joel S. Johnson, Changing the Vocabulary of the Vagueness Doctrine, 101 Va. L. Rev. ___ (2015) (pre-publication draft available on SSRN).

## SECTION 4: OMISSIONS

### Billingslea v. State

Court of Criminal Appeals of Texas, 1989.
780 S.W.2d 271.

■ DUNCAN, JUDGE.

Appellant was charged with the offense of injury to an elderly individual pursuant to V.T.C.A. Penal Code, § 22.04(a)(1). A jury found the appellant guilty as charged and assessed his punishment at 99 years in the Texas Department of Corrections. The appellant's conviction was subsequently reversed and his acquittal ordered. We affirm the judgment of the court of appeals.

The State's petition for discretionary review was granted to consider the following grounds: First, whether the court of appeals erred in holding that the indictment charging the appellant was defective because it did not allege a statutory duty to act; and, second, whether the court of appeals erred in finding the evidence insufficient to support appellant's conviction because he had no statutory duty to act.

We note at the outset that the Legislature recently amended the statute under which the appellant was charged and initially convicted. The amended version . . . is set forth fully in [the appendix to this opinion]. We are compelled, however, to review this case in light of the statute as it existed at the time of this offense.

I

Since the State assails the court of appeals' ruling on the sufficiency of the evidence, a brief review of the facts is in order. Appellant, his wife, and son lived with Hazel Billingslea (also referred to as the decedent), appellant's 94-year-old mother, in a small two-story frame house in Dallas. Hazel Billingslea's home had been her son's residence since approximately 1964. Appellant's only sibling was his sister, Katherine Jefferson, a resident of New Mexico. Virginia Billingslea (the decedent's granddaughter), Katherine Jefferson's daughter, lived approximately 15 blocks from her grandmother's Dallas home. Virginia Billingslea was raised by Hazel Billingslea and had a close relationship with her. Accordingly, she kept in regular contact by telephone and by occasional visits to her grandmother's house.

Unspecified frailties of old age affecting the elder Mrs. Billingslea forced her to become bedridden in March, 1984. Granddaughter Virginia, unaware of her grandmother's condition, made several attempts to visit her during the ensuing weeks. On each occasion her uncle (appellant) "testily" informed her that her grandmother was "asleep." Undaunted, Virginia attempted to reach her grandmother by telephone, only to be threatened by her uncle on at least two occasions to "keep [her] goddamned motherfucking ass out of him and his mother's business or he would kill [her]."

After all attempts to visit her grandmother failed, Virginia contacted her mother (appellant's sister), Katherine Jefferson, in New Mexico. Mrs. Jefferson in turn contacted the Dallas Social Security Office and requested a formal inquiry into her mother's welfare.

Velma Mosley with the Adult Protective Services section of the Texas Department of Human Resources testified that she received a report from the Social Security Office on April 20, 1984, requesting that she check on the elder Mrs. Billingslea. A few days later, Ms. Mosley, accompanied by two Dallas police officers and a police social service employee, proceeded to Mrs. Billingslea's house.

They came upon the appellant in the front yard. After some discussion, he reluctantly allowed them to enter the premises. Upon entering, they were assailed by the strong, offensive odor of rotting flesh permeating the household. While one of the police officers remained downstairs with the appellant, who wanted to know "what these motherfuckers were doing in his house," the social worker and police officer made their way upstairs. Upon entering the bedroom, they found Hazel Billingslea lying in bed, moaning and asking for help. Ms. Mosley testified that the stench was so overwhelming that she was forced to cover her face. Ms. Mosley pulled back the sheets to examine Mrs. Billingslea. Nude from the waist down, Mrs. Billingslea appeared weak and in a great deal of pain.

Ms. Mosley discovered that part of Mrs. Billingslea's heel was eaten away by a large decubitus (bedsore). Other decubiti on her hip and back appeared to have eaten through to the bone. When Ms. Mosley attempted to raise Mrs. Billingslea from the bed to continue her physical examination, "she moaned so much till I didn't look any further." Mrs. Billingslea was immediately transported to Parkland Hospital in Dallas.

Dr. Frase, at that time Chief Medical Resident at Parkland Hospital, examined Mrs. Billingslea. He testified that she was severely cachectic, i.e., that she had suffered severe muscle loss. Her mental state was one of near total disorientation, and she had apparently been unable to feed herself for some time. In addition to the decubiti, second degree burns and blisters were found on her inner thighs, caused by lying in pools of her own urine. Maggots were festering in her open bedsores.

Dr. Frase testified that weeping bedsores as severe as those he found on Hazel Billingslea would have taken anywhere from four to six weeks to develop. He further testified that until her death Mrs. Billingslea required large dosages of narcotics to relieve her pain. In his opinion, the bedsores, burns, blisters, and loss of muscle resulted in serious bodily injury indicative of overall neglect of Mrs. Billingslea in the months prior to her death.

## II

The question of whether criminal liability may be imposed for omissions against elderly individuals is one of first impression in Texas.

The defendant was charged under V.T.C.A. Penal Code, § 22.04. Until September 1, 1981, § 22.04 covered only offenses against children 14 years of age or younger. That year, the Legislature added "elderly individuals 65 years of age or older" to the definition of those protected by § 22.04:

> Injury to a Child or Elderly Individual.
>
> (a) A person commits an offense if he intentionally, knowingly, recklessly, or with criminal negligence, by act or omis-

sion, engages in conduct that causes to a child who is 14 years of age or younger or to an individual who is 65 years of age or older:

(1) serious bodily injury;

(2) serious physical or mental deficiency or impairment;

(3) disfigurement or deformity; or

(4) bodily injury.

Deleting the formal requisites, the indictment is as follows:

> [That the defendant did] then and there intentionally and knowingly engage in conduct that caused serious bodily injury to Hazel Billingslea, an individual over 65 years of age, said conduct being by the following act and omission, to wit: the said defendant failed to obtain medical care for Hazel Billingslea, the natural mother of the said defendant, who lived in the same house as the defendant, and the said Hazel Billingslea was at said time physically unable to secure medical care for herself.[2]

In its petition, the State contends that a duty to act need not be embodied in a statute for § 22.04 to apply. Instead, the State argues that the duty to act in behalf of an elderly person may be derived from legal or common law duties as would arise from the factual, not necessarily familial, relationship of the parties. Limiting § 22.04 to explicit statutory duties, according to the State, "would vitiate the intent of the statute." Relative to the present case, the State contends that the appellant owed a duty of care to the decedent because he voluntarily assumed primary responsibility for caring for his mother who was unable to care for herself and, by assuming that responsibility, prevented others from coming to her aid. According to the State, the indictment is legally sufficient because it alleges facts giving rise to appellant's duty and failure to act pursuant to that duty. Consequently, the State argues that the court of appeals erred in holding that the indictment was fundamentally defective.

While we agree with the State that the 1981 amendments to § 22.04 reflect the Legislature's intention to penalize omissions toward elderly persons, the indictment is nevertheless fundamentally defective for failing to include a statutory duty imposing a punishable omission.

An "omission" is defined in the Penal Code as a failure to act. V.T.C.A. Penal Code, § 1.07(a)(23). The Penal Code's foundation for criminal omissions may be found in § 6.01, which states that a person commits an offense if he "voluntarily engages in conduct, including an act, omission, or possession." Subsection (c) provides that "a person who omits to perform an act does not commit an offense unless a statute provides that the omission is an offense or otherwise provides that he has a duty to perform the act." Stated another way, (1) a statute must

---

[2] Although the indictment was couched in terms of an "act or omission" on the part of the defendant, the offensive conduct was recited as omission: "The defendant failed to obtain medical care [for the decedent]." While § 22.04 unquestionably imposes criminal liability for acts committed against elderly individuals, the allegation that a punishable "act" occurred is absent from this indictment.

provide that an omission is an offense, or (2) a statute otherwise prescribes a duty to act, and a subsequent failure to act pursuant to that duty is an offense. Since § 6.01(c) is stated in the disjunctive, it appears to provide alternative grounds for finding a criminally punishable omission. In reality, however, only the second clause is substantive.

The first ground is obscure because it purports to allow a penal statute to make an omission an offense merely by stating that "an omission is an offense." This simply begs the question of what constitutes an omission. Logic dictates that in order for there to be an omission, there must be a corresponding duty to act. As one commentator noted, "giving legal effect to [the first] portion of § 6.01(c) would abolish the requirement of a legal duty altogether." Deborah H. Goodall, Penal Code Section 22.04: A Duty to Care for the Elderly, 35 Baylor Law.Rev. 589, 596 (1983).

The Practice Commentary to V.T.C.A. Penal Code, § 6.01(c), offers the following interpretation of the first clause of Subsection (c): "many offenses proscribe omissions to act, and when they do the first branch of the rule permits the imposition of criminal responsibility for the omission. Examples of such offenses include Sections 25.03 (interference with child custody), 25.05 (criminal nonsupport), [and] 38.08 (permitting or facilitating escape)."

Notably, each of these provisions provides the duty to act and the omission within the parameters of the specific penal proscription. For example, § 38.08, Permitting or Facilitating Escape, provides that "an official or an employee that is responsible for maintaining persons in custody commits an offense if he intentionally, knowingly, or recklessly permits or facilitates the escape of a person in custody." Similarly, § 25.05, Criminal Nonsupport, provides that "an individual commits an offense if he intentionally or knowingly fails to provide support for his child younger than 18 years of age or for his child who is the subject of a court order requiring the individual to support the child." Thus, each omission is predicated upon a duty to act; both elements of which are found within the same statute.

In neglect cases, the focus has been upon the second ground, which must be read in conjunction with a corresponding statute specifying a duty to act. Since no provisions of the Penal Code at the time of this offense included a duty to provide care for another person, the duties were typically derived from other statutes outside of the Penal Code. The Practice Commentary offers the following illustration:

> If the offense itself does not penalize an omission, "there must be a violation of some duty [to perform the omitted act] imposed by law, directly or impliedly, and with which duty the defendant is especially charged. . . ." The second branch codifies the common law rule, but narrows it to encompass only duties imposed by statute. . . . [A] niece's failure to feed her invalid aunt, who starves to death as a result, is not guilty of criminal homicide because the niece has no statutory duty of support. Contractual duties, or those arising from a special relationship, or fact situation, are thus excluded and will not support the imposition of criminal responsibility.

Analogous to the offense of injury to an elderly person, child abuse and neglect cases demonstrate how the second branch of § 6.01(c) has been applied. For example, in Ronk v. State, 544 S.W.2d 123 (Tex. Cr. App. 1976), this Court held that an indictment charging injury to a child was fundamentally defective because it failed to allege a necessary element to the offense, i.e., it failed to allege a relationship between the defendants and child which would have placed the defendants under a statutory duty to secure medical treatment for the child. The corresponding duty to act was found in V.T.C.A. Family Code, § 12.04(3), which imposes a duty on parents "to support the child, including providing the child with clothing, food, shelter, medical care, and education . . . ."

Similarly, in Smith v. State, 603 S.W.2d 846 (Tex.Cr.App. 1980), the mother and the stepfather were charged under § 22.04 with burning, striking, and denying adequate food and medical care to a young boy. This Court agreed that the allegation "by then and there denying the said Michael Franks of food and nourishment and adequate medical attention" should be construed as alleging omissions, but held the "omissions" portion of the indictment defective in that it failed to allege a statutory duty to act pursuant to the Family Code. As to the allegations of conduct of burning and striking the child, however, the indictment was sufficient because they constituted acts, not omissions. Criminal responsibility for acts does not require an underlying duty of any kind. The Court noted that "parents and non-parents alike may commit the offense of injury to a child by such acts as striking and burning."

And, in Lang v. State, 586 S.W.2d 532 (Tex.Cr.App. 1979), we reversed the defendant's conviction based upon a fundamentally defective indictment because it failed to state, pursuant to § 22.04, that the victim was a child 14 years or younger. The appellant's conviction was overturned on this basis in spite of the defendant's guilty plea and judicial confession. Although §§ 12.04 and 4.02 of the Family Code require parents to care for their minor children, Penal Code § 22.04 limits that duty to children 14 years old or younger.

While the above cases seem to have allowed reprehensible conduct to go unpunished on the basis of a defective indictment, it is indisputable that those accused of an offense are entitled to sufficient notice of the charges against them. While other States may imply duties or derive them from the common law,[5] under the laws of this State notice of an offense must invariably rest on a specific statute. This notion is firmly rooted in the evolution of Texas criminal jurisprudence. Since the days of the Republic and early statehood, Texas courts have been prohibited from allowing common law duties to form the basis of criminal sanctions. That longstanding prohibition is specifically embodied in our Penal Code, which provides that "conduct does not constitute an offense unless it is defined as an offense by statute, municipal ordinance, order of a county commissioners court, or rule authorized by and lawfully adopted under a statute." V.T.C.A. Penal Code, § 1.03(a).

---

[5] [For example], in State v. Mason, 18 N.C.App. 433, 197 S.E.2d 79 (1973), the North Carolina Court of Appeals upheld the manslaughter conviction of parents charged with failing to provide proper care for their child, basing their decision on the ground that the defendants omitted to perform a legal duty owed their child based on a common law relationship.

Moreover, penal provisions which criminalize a failure to act without informing those subject to prosecution that they must perform a duty to avoid punishment are unconstitutionally vague.[6] Where an indictment in Texas fails to allege the deceased child's age, or fails to allege a parent-child relationship, thereby invoking a concomitant statutory duty to act in behalf of the child, a conviction based on that indictment is void. Similarly, although the indictment herein alleged sufficient facts to imply both a duty to act and an omission under the common law, the indictment is fundamentally defective in the absence of an allegation reciting a concomitant statutory duty to care for an elderly person. Accordingly, the indictment could not have alleged a statutory duty for the appellant to act in behalf of his ailing parent because no such duty existed.

As one commentator noted:

> If no one is under a statutory duty to act toward an elderly person, then how can a court choose to prosecute *B* for the death of *A* instead of prosecuting *X*, a neighbor, or *Y*, *A*'s sister, or *Z*, the Governor? In a jurisdiction like Texas which does not allow common law duties to form the basis for criminal actions, the duty to care for *A* must therefore rest either on all persons alive at her death or on no one, since the duty has not been statutorily assigned to any particular person. See Goodall, supra, at 602.

While children may have a moral duty to care for their elderly parents, moral imperatives are not the functional equivalent of legal duties. Since we do not recognize legal duties derived from the common law and since no one was assigned a statutory duty to care for an elderly person, the version of § 22.04 relative to omissions toward elderly individuals under which the appellant was indicted is unenforceable. Consequently, the indictment charging the appellant with "failure to obtain medical care" for his mother is fundamentally defective. The State's first ground for review is overruled.

III

The State's second ground for review contends that the court of appeals erred in holding the evidence insufficient to support the appellant's conviction. In light of the foregoing discussion, it is axiomatic that the State failed to establish an essential element of the offense, namely, the duty to act, because no such duty existed. Accordingly, the State's second ground for review is overruled.

IV

Fortuitously, the Legislature identified the problematical application of § 22.04 as applied to omissions toward elderly persons and recently amended the statute. [See appendix.] If anything, the amendments to § 22.04 clearly suggest that the Legislature perceived

---

[6] See, e.g., Kolender v. Lawson, 461 U.S. 352 (1983) (California statute requiring loiterers to carry "credible and reliable" identification or be subject to penalty unconstitutionally vague for failure to clarify meaning of "credible and reliable"); Lambert v. California, 355 U.S. 225 (1957) (Los Angeles city ordinance requiring those convicted of felony to register with the city held unconstitutionally vague; due process allowed defendant to plead ignorance of the law as a defense where "circumstances which might move one to inquire as to the necessity of [taking affirmative action] are completely lacking.").

the paradoxical futility of applying the former law: there could never be a failure to perform that which no one had a statutory duty to perform in the first place. The recent action taken by the Legislature in amending the statute to correct the previous statute's defect further underscores our conclusion that the version of § 22.04 under which the appellant was convicted was unenforceable. Nevertheless, we must adhere to the law as it existed at the time of the offense. Accordingly, we affirm the judgment of the court of appeals.

## APPENDIX

V.T.C.A. Penal Code, § 22.04, as amended May 29, 1989, S.B. 1154, effective Sept. 1, 1989, is as follows:

Section 22.04. Injury to a Child, Elderly Individual, or Invalid.

(a) A person commits an offense if he intentionally, knowingly, recklessly, or with criminal negligence, by act or intentionally, knowingly, or recklessly by omission, engages in conduct that causes to a child, elderly individual, or invalid individual:

(1) serious bodily injury;

(2) serious physical or mental deficiency or impairment;

(3) disfigurement or deformity; or

(4) bodily injury.

(b) An omission that causes a condition described by Subsections (a)(1) through (a)(4) of this section is conduct constituting an offense under this section if:

(1) the actor has a legal or statutory duty to act; or

(2) the actor has assumed care, custody or control of a child, elderly individual, or invalid individual.

(c) In this section:

(1) "Child" means a person 14 years of age or younger;

(2) "Elderly individual" means a person 65 years of age or older;

(3) "Invalid individual" means a person older than 14 years of age who by reason of age or physical or mental disease, defect, or injury is substantially unable to protect himself from harm or to provide food, shelter, or medical care for himself. . . .

(d) The actor has assumed care, custody, or control if he has by act, words, or course of conduct acted so as to cause a reasonable person to conclude that he has accepted responsibility for protection, food, shelter, and medical care for a child, elderly individual, or invalid individual. . . .

(i) It is an affirmative defense to the prosecution under Subsection (b)(2) of this section that before the offense the actor:

(1) notified in person the child, elderly individual, or invalid individual that he would no longer provide any of the care described by Subsection (d) of this section; and

(2) notified in writing the parents or person other than himself acting in loco parentis to the child, elderly individual, or invalid individual that he would no longer provide any of the care described by Subsection (d) of this section; or

(3) notified in writing the Texas Department of Human Services that he would no longer provide any of the care set forth in Subsection (d) of this section. . . .

(k) (1) It is a defense to prosecution under this section that the conduct engaged in by act or omission consisted of:

(A) reasonable medical care occurring under the direction of or by a licensed physician; or

(B) emergency medical care administered in good faith and with reasonable care by a person not licensed in the healing arts.

(2) It is an affirmative defense to prosecution under this section that the act or omission was based on treatment in accordance with the tenets and practices of a recognized religious method of healing with a generally accepted record of efficacy.

## NOTES ON OMISSIONS

### 1. THE NECESSITY OF A DUTY TO ACT

*Billingslea* starkly illustrates the distinction between the law's treatment of acts, on the one hand, and omissions or failures to act, on the other. As the court remarked when discussing the *Smith* case, a prosecution based on acts, such as "striking and burning," does not require proof of "an underlying duty of any kind." By contrast, a prosecution based on an omission may proceed only where the accused had a duty to perform the omitted act. A moral obligation to perform the act will not do; in the words of *Billingslea*, "moral imperatives are not the functional equivalent of legal duties." In the absence of a legal duty to act, the accused may not be held criminally liable no matter how morally reprehensible the failure to act or how serious the consequences of such failure.

Of course, many criminal statutes expressly punish failures to act. In addition to the statutes mentioned in *Billingslea*, there are other familiar examples, such as laws punishing failure to stop at a red light, failure to file a tax return, failure (by men) to register for the draft, etc. In such cases, the statute defining the crime creates the legal duty to act. The same may be said of the host of penal statutes proscribing some combination of act and omission—e.g., driving without a license. Enforcement of such offenses presents no special difficulty.

Problems arise where the offense in question does not expressly proscribe a particular omission or, for that matter, a particular act, but covers any conduct that causes a forbidden result. The classic example is homicide. Typically, criminal homicide statutes punish one who "causes death of another." A more elaborate formulation might provide that a person is guilty if he or she "does or omits to do anything that causes death of another." Despite the potential breadth of such statutory language, criminal liability for causing the forbidden result is importantly constrained by the rule that an omission suffices only when it breaches a legal duty to act. In other words, courts will interpret statutory language such as "omits to do anything" as if it stated "omits to do anything that the actor has a legal duty to do." Where the legal duty is not found on the face of the statute defining the offense, as is the case with homicide statutes, it must be found in some other source of law that specifies legal obligations among citizens.

Most jurisdictions recognize that legal duties to act may be rooted in a contract or in a common law source, as well as in a statute. The chief categories of legal duty are summarized in Jones v. United States, 308 F.2d 307 (D.C. Cir. 1962). They include:

— duties based on statute, such as the common provision that a driver involved in an automobile accident must stop and render assistance to injured persons;

— duties based on relationship, such as that between a parent and a minor child;

— duties based on contract, such as the employment responsibilities of a lifeguard; and

— duties based on voluntary assumption of responsibility that effectively precludes aid from others, such as the person who takes a foundling home and thus secretes it from the agencies of public assistance.

In some circumstances, legal duties may also be based on control over the conduct of another, as in the obligation of an employer to oversee employees, and sometimes on the existence of a peril for which the actor was in some way responsible. Finally, a landowner or businessman may be found to have a legal duty to provide for the safety of persons invited onto the property. A survey of recognized legal duties may be found in Paul H. Robinson, Criminal Liability for Omissions: A Brief Summary and Critique of the Law in the United States, 29 N.Y.L.S.L.Rev. 101 (1984).

## 2. QUESTIONS AND COMMENTS ON *BILLINGSLEA*

As *Billingslea* explains, Texas law at the time of the offense authorized liability for omissions only in cases where a statute explicitly imposed a duty to perform the omitted act. On what grounds does the court justify this apparently grudging approach to omissions liability? By its verdict, the jury found that Billingslea's neglect had caused his mother to suffer serious bodily injury. And, as the court acknowledged, the Texas legislature intended to penalize omissions committed against elderly persons. Nonetheless, the court throws out Billingslea's conviction. Were there good reasons for doing so?

Notice too that everyone agrees that, if Billingslea had caused his mother's "second-degree burns" by acts of burning, rather than by neglect, his conviction would have been upheld. Is it true that Billingslea committed no "acts" that contributed to his mother's injuries? Did the prosecution have no choice but to pursue this case only on omissions, or might the state have alleged and proved that Billingslea engaged in culpable actions as well?

Consider the amended version of the "elder abuse" statute set forth in the *Billingslea* appendix. If that statute has been in effect at the time of Billingslea's failure to care for his mother, could the state have successfully prosecuted him? Is there any other actor in the case who might have been held liable thereunder?

### 3. FAILURE TO PROVIDE SUSTENANCE

Many omission cases involve failure to provide sustenance to a person who dies of starvation and neglect. Consider these two famous examples.

#### (i) *Regina v. Instan*

In Regina v. Instan, [1893] Cox C.C. 602, the defendant lived with, and was supported by, her aunt. Some 10 days before her death, the aunt contracted gangrene. The defendant continued to live in the aunt's house and to take in food supplied by tradespeople, but she neither procured medical attention nor notified anyone of the aunt's condition. The aunt died of gangrene and neglect, and defendant was found guilty of manslaughter. The court upheld the conviction:

> It is not correct to say that every moral obligation is a legal duty, but every legal duty is founded upon a moral obligation. In this case, as in most cases, the legal duty can be nothing else than taking upon oneself the performance of the moral obligation. There is no question whatever that it was this woman's clear duty to impart to the deceased so much of that food which was taken into the house and paid for by the deceased as was necessary to sustain her life.

Is *Instan* correct? Does it matter that the defendant was supported by the deceased? Would the case have been different if the defendant had been living off her own income? Would liability have attached merely because the defendant was the only person who knew of the aunt's condition? If so, would the same rule apply to a neighbor who happened to discover the situation but did nothing to help?

#### (ii) *Jones v. United States*

The defendant in Jones v. United States, 308 F.2d 307 (D.C. Cir. 1962), was entrusted with the care of two children, Robert Lee Green and Anthony Lee Green. Initially, the mother agreed to pay for the care of the elder child, but the payments stopped after a few months. It was disputed whether any such arrangement was made for the younger child.

Collectors for the local gas company discovered the two children in the defendant's basement. Three days later the police removed the children to the hospital, where Anthony Lee was found to be suffering from malnutrition and lesions caused by diaper rash. He was fed repeatedly but died of malnutrition less than 34 hours after being admitted to the hospital. At birth, he had weighed six pounds, 15 ounces. At his death, 10 months later, he weighed seven pounds, 13 ounces. Normal weight would have been approximately double that figure.

A jury found the defendant guilty of involuntary manslaughter, but the appeals court reversed. The trial court had erred by failing to require the jury to find that defendant had a legal duty to care for Anthony Lee. The appeals court found that the failure to instruct the jury on the necessity of a legal duty left critical factual issues unresolved—specifically, "whether appellant had entered into a contract with the mother for the care of Anthony Lee or, alternatively, whether she assumed the care of the child and secluded him from the care of his mother, his natural protector." The evidence might have been sufficient to support a finding of legal duty on these grounds, but since the instructions had not required the jury to make such a finding, the conviction was reversed.

## 4. FAILURE TO SUMMON MEDICAL ASSISTANCE FOR DRUG OVERDOSE

What duties do people owe to companions who need emergency medical care for a drug or alcohol overdose? These cases raise difficult ethical and practical dilemmas. What role should the criminal law play in creating incentives for behavior in this context or in providing the occasion for the expression of community condemnation? Over the years, courts have struggled with these questions. Consider the following cases:

### *(i) People v. Beardsley*

A famous old chestnut is People v. Beardsley, 150 Mich. 206, 113 N.W. 1128 (1907). Defendant arranged with one Blanche Burns to spend the weekend in his rooms. They drank more or less steadily for two days. Additionally, without his consent and, indeed, over his objections, she obtained and took some morphine. When defendant began to expect the return of his wife, he arranged for Blanche to be moved to the room of a friend, whom he asked to look after her and to let her out the back way when she awoke. Some hours later she died.

Defendant was convicted of manslaughter for failure to render reasonable care, but the Supreme Court of Michigan reversed:

> It is urged by the prosecutor that the [defendant] "stood towards this woman for the time being in the place of her natural guardian and protector, and as such owed her a clear legal duty which he completely failed to perform." The cases cited and digested establish that no such legal duty is created based upon a mere moral obligation. The fact that this woman was in his house created no such legal duty as exists in law and is due from a husband towards his wife, as seems to be intimated by the prosecutor's brief. Such an inference would be very repugnant to our moral sense.... Had this been a case where two men under like circumstances had voluntarily gone on a debauch together, and one had attempted suicide, no one would claim that this doctrine of legal duty could be invoked to hold the other criminally responsible for omitting to make effort to rescue his companion. How can the fact that in this case one of the parties was a woman change the principle of law applicable to it?

Around the middle of the last century, one commentator condemned *Beardsley* as a "savage proclamation that the wages of sin is death." Graham Hughes, Criminal Omissions, 67 Yale L.J. 590, 624 (1958). Do you agree? Is it, as Hughes continued, reflective of a morality which is "smug, ignorant, and vindictive," or is there some other justification for the result?

The quoted passage from *Beardsley* implies that, unlike mere social acquaintances or friends, husbands and wives owe each other duties of care, whose omission may provide the basis for criminal liability. Yet, litigation over the appropriate scope of spousal duties can raise questions of considerable difficulty. It might seem obvious, as the passage from *Beardsley* suggests, that spouses are legally obliged to rescue each other in medical emergencies. But what if one spouse wants to use drugs or drink excessively? Must the other, on pain of criminal punishment, intervene? If so, under what precise circumstances and to what extent? Complicated questions also arise when a spouse decides to forgo medical treatment for a serious health condition or elects one course of treatment rather than another. Does the other spouse have the obligation to question and, possibly, to override that decision? If such an obligation exists, when is it triggered, and how is it satisfied? Some of these questions have been litigated in homicide prosecutions of spouses whose partners have died after choosing to rely on prayer, rather than medicine, to treat their illnesses. See People v. Robbins, 443 N.Y.S.2d 1016 (App. Div. 1981); Commonwealth v. Konz, 265 Pa.Super. 570, 402 A.2d 692 (1979), rev'd, 498 Pa. 639, 450 A.2d 638 (1982).

### *(ii) People v. Oliver*

A modern variation on *Beardsley* arose in People v. Oliver, 210 Cal. App.3d 138, 258 Cal.Rptr. 138 (1989). The defendant returned to her apartment with Carlos Cornejo, whom she had met in a bar. Although already extremely drunk, Cornejo asked for a spoon, which the defendant provided. She then remained in the living room while he "shot up" in the bathroom. Afterward, he collapsed, and she returned to the bar. Later, the defendant's daughter and a friend returned home to find the unconscious Cornejo. On defendant's instructions, they dragged him outside "in case he woke up and became violent" and put him behind a shed so that the neighbors would not see. By the next morning, he had died of heroin overdose.

Defendant moved to dismiss an indictment for involuntary manslaughter on the ground that she owed no legal duty to the deceased, but the court disagreed:

> At the time [defendant] left the bar with Cornejo, she observed that he was extremely drunk, and drove him to her home. In so doing, she took him from a public place where others might have taken care to prevent him from injuring himself, to a private place—her home—where she alone could provide such care. To a certain, if limited, extent, therefore, she took charge of a person unable to prevent harm to himself. She then allowed Cornejo to use her bathroom, without any objection on her part, to inject himself with narcotics, an act involving the definite potential for fatal consequences. When Cornejo collapsed to the floor, [defendant] should have known that her conduct had contributed to creating an unreasonable risk of harm for Cornejo—death. At that

point, she owed Cornejo a duty to prevent that risk from occurring by summoning aid. . . .

## 5. A GENERAL DUTY TO RESCUE?

An underlying issue in all these cases is whether there should be a general duty to rescue. Rather than focusing on particular legal duties based on contract or status, why should not the law simply recognize that each of us has a duty to give reasonable assistance to a person in peril?

Consider, for example, the facts of *Jones*. Why should it be necessary to prove that the defendant had contracted with the boy's mother for maintenance or that she had acted to seclude him from his mother's protection? Why isn't it enough that the defendant, at no special cost or danger to herself, could have saved the life of a child and that she chose not to do so?

A defense of the traditional view against a general duty to rescue was attempted by Lord Macaulay. In his notes on a proposed Indian penal code, Macaulay undertook to assess the extent to which omissions productive of evil consequences should be punished on the same footing as affirmative misconduct leading to those results. After rejecting the categorical alternatives of "always" and "never," Macaulay explained the drafters' choice of a "middle course":

> What we propose is this: that where acts are made punishable on the ground that they have caused, or have been intended to cause, or have been known to be likely to cause, a certain evil effect, omissions which have caused, which have been intended to cause, or which have been known to be likely to cause the same effect, shall be punishable in the same manner, provided that such omissions were, on other grounds, illegal. An omission is illegal if it be an offense, if it be a breach of some direction of law, or if it be such a wrong as would be a good ground for a civil action.
>
> We cannot defend this rule better than by giving a few illustrations of the way in which it will operate. *A* omits to give *Z* food, and by that omission voluntarily causes *Z*'s death. Is this murder? Under our rule it is murder if *A* was *Z*'s jailer, directed by the law to furnish *Z* with food. It is murder if *Z* was the infant child of *A*, and had, therefore, a legal right to sustenance, which right a civil court would enforce against *A*. It is murder if *Z* was a bedridden invalid, and *A* a nurse hired to feed *Z*. . . . It is not murder if *Z* is a beggar, who has no other claim on *A* than that of humanity. . . .
>
> We are sensible that in some of the cases which we have put, our rule may appear too lenient; but we do not think that it can be made more severe without disturbing the whole order of society. It is true that the man who, having abundance of wealth, suffers a fellow-creature to die of hunger at his feet is a bad man—a worse man, probably, than many of those for whom we have provided very severe punishment. But we are unable to see where, if we make such a man legally punishable, we can draw the line. If the rich man who refuses to save a beggar's life at the cost of a little copper is a murderer, is the poor man just one degree above beggary also to be a murderer if he omits to invite the beggar to partake his hard-earned rice? Again, if the rich man is a murderer for

> refusing to save the beggar's life at the cost of a little copper, is he also to be a murderer if he refuses to save the beggar's life at the cost of a thousand rupees? . . . The distinction between a legal and an illegal omission is perfectly plain and intelligible; but the distinction between a large and a small sum of money is very far from being so, not to say that a sum which is small to one man is large to another. . . .
>
> It is, indeed, most highly desirable that men should not merely abstain from doing harm to their neighbors, but should render active services to their neighbors. In general, however, the penal law must content itself with keeping men from doing positive harm, and must leave to public opinion, and to the teachers of morality and religion, the office of furnishing men with motives for doing positive good. . . .

Thomas Macaulay, Notes on the Indian Penal Code, in 4 Miscellaneous Works 251–56 (1880).

Is Macaulay's argument persuasive? Are the line-drawing problems so intractable as to preclude recognition of a general duty to rescue? Might this difficulty be alleviated by drawing the line very far to one side—as, for example, in a rule imposing a duty to rescue only where there is no appreciable risk or expense to the actor?

For trenchant criticism of the traditional view, see Daniel B. Yeager, A Radical Community of Aid: A Rejoinder to Opponents of Affirmative Duties to Help Strangers, 71 Wash. U.L.Q. 1 (1993). See also A.D. Woozley, A Duty to Rescue: Some Thoughts on Criminal Liability, 69 Va. L. Rev. 1273 (1983). For sophisticated philosophic analysis of the significance of action or omission in the criminal law, see Michael S. Moore, Act and Crime (1993), which is the subject of a symposium in 142 U. Penn. L. Rev. 1443 (1994).

## 6. OMISSION OF LIFE-SUSTAINING TREATMENT

A particularly vexing question of liability for omissions concerns the removal of deeply comatose individuals from life-sustaining equipment. Although this practice is fairly common, Barber v. Superior Court of Los Angeles County, 147 Cal.App.3d 1006, 195 Cal.Rptr. 484 (1983), is a very rare reported case of criminal prosecution in such circumstances. In *Barber*, a patient went into cardio-respiratory arrest after undergoing routine surgery. The medical staff revived him and placed him on life-support equipment. Within several days, medical specialists concluded that he had suffered severe brain damage and that his vegetative state was likely to be permanent. Following consultation with the patient's family, the doctors removed him from all life-support equipment, including a respirator and the intravenous tubes that had provided hydration and nourishment. After the patient died, the doctors were prosecuted for murder and conspiracy to commit murder. The California Court of Appeals relied on the distinction between act and omission in throwing out the criminal complaint:

> As a predicate to our analysis of whether the petitioners' conduct amounted to an "unlawful killing," we conclude that the cessation of "heroic" life support measures is not an affirmative act but rather a withdrawal or omission of further treatment.

> Even though these life support devices are, to a degree, "self-propelled," each pulsation of the respirator or each drop of fluid introduced into the patient's body by intravenous feeding devices is comparable to a manually administered injection or item of medication. Hence "disconnecting" of the mechanical devices is comparable to withholding the manually administered injection or medication. . . .

Having analyzed the case as one of omission, the *Barber* court found no legal duty to act once the situation had become medically hopeless and hence no criminal liability for failure to do so.

*Barber* accords with prevailing medical practice, both in upholding the acceptability of terminating life-sustaining treatment and in grounding that result in a distinction between act and omission.[a] But does the distinction make sense? If the physician and/or the patient's family are competent to decide when to end treatment, why are they not equally competent to decide whether there should be an affirmative action to end the patient's suffering? Do the considerations at stake really depend on the distinction between act and omission?

Indeed, even if one accepts that there is a difference in principle between act and omission in terminating medical care, there remains the difficulty of differentiating between them. In some cases the distinction seems clear. If a terminally ill patient experiences spontaneous cardio-respiratory arrest, the physician who foregoes heroic attempts at resuscitation has omitted to act. Less clear is the termination of treatment already underway. Is turning off the respirator an act or an omission? Many physicians, who are ready to *withhold* treatment in appropriate cases, are nevertheless reluctant to *withdraw* treatment once begun. The former conduct seems an acceptable omission, while the latter comes dangerously close to an act.[b]

The *Barber* court obviated this difficulty by construing turning off the respirator and withdrawing intravenous feeding as omissions rather than acts. Is this characterization persuasive? Is there a meaningful distinction to be made between not turning on a respirator and later turning it off? Between turning off the respirator and withdrawing sustenance? Between any of these "omissions" and the undoubted "act" of injecting a lethal dose of morphine?

---

[a] See, e.g., § 2.11 of the Opinions of the Judicial Council of the American Medical Association (1982), where it is stated: "For humane reasons, with informed consent a physician may do what is medically necessary to alleviate severe pain, or cease or omit treatment to let a terminally ill patient die, but he should not intentionally cause death." For a comprehensive but economical treatment of the "right to stop treatment" of incompetent patients, see John A. Robertson, The Rights of the Critically Ill 49–70 (1983).

[b] Ironically, the distinction between withholding and withdrawing treatment may sometimes be medically perverse. A presidential commission on the subject received testimony that the fear that a therapy once begun could not be discontinued has "unduly raised the threshold" for vigorous intervention on behalf of defective newborns. The Commission's view was that, contrary to the usual formulation, the decision to withhold treatment should actually require a *greater* justification than the decision to withdraw treatment. "Whether a particular treatment will have positive effects is often highly uncertain before the therapy has been tried. If a trial of therapy makes clear that it is not helpful to the patient, this is actual evidence (rather than mere surmise) to support stopping because the therapeutic benefit that earlier was a possibility has been found to be clearly unobtainable." The President's Commission for the Study of Ethical Problems in Medicine and Biomedical and Behavioral Research, Deciding to Forego Life-Sustaining Treatment 75–76 (1983).

# SECTION 5: POSSESSION

## INTRODUCTORY NOTE

As the preceding materials indicate, criminal liability may be based on an affirmative act proscribed by law or on failure to perform an act required by law. There is also a third possibility—liability for possession. Possession may be thought of as a status that begins with the act of acquisition and that is continued by a failure to divest. Alternatively, possession may be viewed simply as an indirect way of proving the act of acquisition. In any event, possession is widely employed as a basis of criminal liability, no doubt because it is generally much simpler for the prosecution to prove possession of a forbidden item than to prove purchase or use. In particular, possession prosecutions typically require only police witnesses and therefore do not introduce the difficulty, in some circumstances, of producing civilian witnesses. The Model Penal Code merely confirms existing law when it identifies possession, along with acts and omissions, as possible grounds for criminal liability. Section 2.01(4) provides that, "[p]ossession is an act . . . if the possessor knowingly procured or received the thing possessed or was aware of his control thereof for a sufficient period to have been able to terminate his possession." There seems to be no objection in principle to punishing crimes of possession, but as the next case indicates, problems can and do arise in the administration of such offenses.

## United States v. Nevils

United States Court of Appeals for the Ninth Circuit, 2008.
548 F.3d 802.

■ PAEZ, CIRCUIT JUDGE.

Earl Nevils appeals from a jury conviction for being a felon in possession of firearms and ammunition in violation of 18 U.S.C. § 922(g)(1). We reverse the conviction because the evidence offered at trial was insufficient with regard to the element of knowing possession.

On April 14, 2003, LAPD officers specializing in anti-gang enforcement were investigating unrelated criminal activity at an apartment complex in a high-crime area of Los Angeles when they encountered Earl Nevils asleep on a couch in one of the apartments (Apartment 6). The officers were originally following another man because he ran away when they approached him and his friends on the street. As they followed the man into the courtyard of the apartment complex, he approached Apartment 6, started to enter, and then apparently changed his mind and entered another apartment on the other side of the courtyard. When the officers approached Apartment 6 to investigate, their attention was diverted from the other man to Nevils.

The wooden door of Apartment 6 was off its hinges and leaning against the interior wall, and the metal security door, or screen door, was ajar. Inside, the officers could see Nevils asleep on a couch. Leaning against Nevils's body were two firearms—one on his lap and another leaning against his leg. There was a coffee table approximately one foot from the couch. On the table were several items that the police later determined to be baggies full of marijuana and ecstasy, a cell phone, wrist watches, documents, and U.S. currency.

The police officers entered the apartment with guns drawn, conducted a "sweep," and then began to approach Nevils. As they approached, Nevils began to wake up. At that point, both officers identified themselves and yelled for Nevils to get down on the ground. Nevils either "rolled" or "slid[ ]" onto the ground, and the officers arrested Nevils for drug possession. Both officers testified that Nevils "startled" awake. One officer testified more specifically that, before Nevils rolled or slid onto the ground, "his eyes . . . kind of came full—fully opened and for a brief second he appeared like he was going to, you know, grab towards his lap and then he stopped and put his hands up." The other officer did not mention any brief pause; he stated that the events were "very quick" and "almost immediate," and that Nevils "jumped up as a startled jump and rolled over onto the ground." Some time after the arrest, a sergeant who had arrived on the scene was questioning Nevils to make sure he was not injured, when Nevils stated: "I don't believe this shit. Those motherfuckers left me sleeping and didn't wake me." . . .

Nevils was later charged and tried in federal court on a single count of being a felon in possession of a firearm. . . . The Government's case consisted primarily of the testimony of the two arresting officers setting forth the incriminating circumstances surrounding Nevils's arrest. In his defense, Nevils presented evidence that he had been at a party in a neighboring apartment all day, had become so drunk that he could not stand, and was taken by friends to Apartment 6 and laid on the couch (on his side "[s]o he wouldn't throw up") to sleep it off. Jonnetta Campbell, who helped take Nevils to Apartment 6, testified that at the time she left Nevils on the couch and closed the door behind her, there were no other people in Apartment 6, and no guns or drugs were visible. It was undisputed at trial that Nevils did not live in Apartment 6 and that many other people had access to the vacant apartment, although Nevils was the only person present when the police entered.

At the close of the Government's case and again at the close of all the evidence, Nevils moved under Federal Rule of Criminal Procedure 29 for a judgment of acquittal on the basis of insufficiency of the evidence. The district court denied both motions, and the jury found Nevils guilty. . . .

In considering a challenge to the sufficiency of the evidence, we review the entire record, "[v]iewing the evidence in the light most favorable to the government," and "must determine whether any rational jury could have found [the defendant] guilty of each element of the crime beyond a reasonable doubt." We do not "question [the] jury's assessment of witnesses' credibility, and must presume that the trier of fact resolved any conflicting inferences in favor of the prosecution." . . .

The crime charged, being a felon in possession of a firearm in violation of 18 U.S.C. § 922(g)(1), requires proof of three elements: "(1) that the defendant was a convicted felon; (2) that the defendant was in knowing possession of a firearm; and (3) that the firearm was in or affecting interstate commerce." United States v. Beasley, 346 F.3d 930, 933–34 (9th Cir. 2003). The first element was conceded by stipulation, and the third was not contested. The only disputed element at trial was Nevils's knowing possession of the firearms.

Proof of knowing possession in the context of 18 U.S.C. § 922(g)(1) requires "that the defendant consciously possessed what he knew to be a firearm." Id. at 934. "In general, a person is in possession of something if the person knows of its presence *and* has physical control of it, or has the power and intention to control it." United States v. Cain, 130 F.3d 381, 382 (9th Cir. 1997) (emphasis in original) (internal quotation marks omitted).

"[T]he element of control necessary for possession [is not] satisfied if it [i]s shown that the defendant was merely 'in the presence of the contraband and could reach out and take it' if he so desired." United States v. Chambers, 918 F.2d 1455, 1459 (9th Cir. 1990). . . . "Mere proximity, presence and association go only to the contraband's *accessibility*, not to the dominion or control which must be proved to establish possession." Id. (emphasis in original) (internal quotation marks omitted). . . .

Noting that Nevils was alone in Apartment 6 when he was arrested, the Government argues that "a rational trier of fact could find that the physical location of the firearms on defendant's lap and leaning against his leg, as well as the presence of packaged drugs, a cell phone, and money within a foot from where defendant lay, constituted possession of the firearms. In short, the jury was entitled to rely upon his actual possession of the firearms to infer that his possession was knowing." . . . But the pivotal circumstance in this case is the undisputed fact that *Nevils was asleep* (or passed out). Thus, the fact that the firearms were physically touching him is not sufficient to show that he was conscious of their presence. . . . . That the weapons were touching Nevils is a factor tending to make knowing possession more likely, but without evidence that Nevils was aware of their presence, this fact is not enough. . . . Despite the close physical proximity of the guns to Nevils, the fact remains that the circumstantial evidence of knowledge and intent to control here falls far short of that found sufficient [in prior cases.] The Government did not offer evidence tying Nevils to any of the other personal items in the apartment. . . . The Government did not present any other evidence linking Nevils to the guns or to the other items in Apartment 6 (the drugs, the phones, etc.). Further, Nevils was only slightly linked to the apartment itself, having been there at least one other time. To the contrary, there was every reason to believe that the apartment was open to all comers.

Nor does Nevils's gang affiliation, familiarity with the apartment complex, or Nevils's prior experience with drugs provide sufficient evidence to support an inference *that he was in knowing possession of a firearm on April 14, 2003*. Nevils's mere presence at the scene and his general character and history as a gang member are insufficient evidence of the required mental state. . . .

If the firearms in this case had been found on the coffee table—along with the drugs, cell phone, watches, U.S. currency, and documents—there is no doubt that a judgment of acquittal would be required, as no other evidence tied Nevils to the firearms or the apartment, other than his presence in the apartment on one other occasion. Indeed, the district court here did not hesitate at sentencing to find that the Government had failed to prove—even by a preponderance of the evidence—that Nevils possessed the drugs on the coffee table. In declining to make such a finding, the district court emphasized that Nevils "was asleep at the time."

The sufficiency of the Government's evidence thus depends on the distinction between the guns being found on the coffee table and their being found on and leaning against Nevils's body as he slept. Despite the Government's insistence that the distinction itself is enough to demonstrate Nevils's "actual possession" of the firearms, possession—whether labeled actual or constructive—requires *knowledge* of the object possessed *and intent* to control that object. Knowledge and intent obviously require consciousness, at some point. There was no direct evidence showing that Nevils was ever conscious in Apartment 6 on April 14, 2003. All of the evidence presented indicated that he was asleep and/or passed out. . . .

"When there is an innocent explanation for a defendant's conduct as well as one that suggests that the defendant was engaged in wrongdoing, the government must produce evidence that would allow a rational jury to conclude beyond a reasonable doubt that the latter explanation is the correct one." United States v. Vasquez-Chan, 978 F.2d 546, 549 (9th Cir. 1992). Here, the Government did not produce evidence that would allow a rational jury to conclude beyond a reasonable doubt that Nevils was guarding the drugs or otherwise consciously in possession of the guns, as opposed to being passed out at the wrong place, at the wrong time.

Although Nevils's proffered explanation might seem implausible in many towns and many apartment complexes, it is not implausible given the evidence that *this* neighborhood, *this* apartment complex, and Apartment 6 itself, were neck-deep in gang activity and the illicit drug trade. Further, the presence of several watches, a cell phone, other personal items, and drugs packaged for retail sale—none of which were tied to Nevils—supports the inference that other people were in Apartment 6 before the police arrived.

Finally, we reject the Government's reliance on Nevils's post-arrest statement as supporting a jury inference of knowing possession. The statement "[t]hose motherfuckers left me sleeping and didn't wake me" is ambiguous and is subject to multiple interpretations, and the Government did not produce evidence sufficient to allow a jury to choose an inculpatory interpretation. . . . The Government argues that "the most reasonable inference . . . from this statement was that defendant was angry that his friends failed to warn him . . . something he expected them to do because he knew he was illegally in possession of guns and drugs." To the contrary, the statement merely demonstrates Nevils's mastery of the obvious: some person or persons (1) had been in Apartment 6, and then (2) absconded and left him surrounded by the incriminating evidence. The fact that Nevils realized he had been left high and dry, and was not happy about it, is hardly incompatible with his innocent explanation of his circumstances (i.e., that he was asleep), and it does not show that Nevils had knowledge of the firearms *before being arrested*. . . . On this record, we hold that the Government failed to produce evidence that would have allowed a rational jury to infer knowing possession beyond a reasonable doubt. . . .

■ BYBEE, CIRCUIT JUDGE, dissenting.

It is said that the wife of English lexicographer Samuel Johnson returned home unexpectedly in the middle of the day, to find Dr. Johnson in the kitchen with the chambermaid. She exclaimed, "My dear Dr.

Johnson, I am surprised." To which he reputedly replied, "No my dear, you are amazed. We are surprised."

Earl Nevils was surprised when two LA police officers with guns drawn ordered him not to move. But Nevils was not amazed in the least by the circumstances in which he found himself: he had a loaded, chambered semiautomatic Tec 9 on his lap and a loaded, chambered .40 caliber pistol by his leg. Nor was he astonished by the marijuana, ecstasy, cash and a cellphone on a table a foot away. Although the unoccupied apartment was not his, Nevils wasn't the least bewildered at finding himself in Apartment #6—officers had found drugs and guns in the apartment just three weeks earlier and had arrested Nevils there for parole violation. According to one of the officers, Nevils first impulse was to "grab towards his lap" where the Tec 9 lay and "then he stopped and put his hands up." He later exclaimed to an officer, "I don't believe this s—. Those m—left me sleeping and didn't wake me." The jury found him guilty of being a felon in possession.

The majority overturns his conviction because it finds the evidence insufficient to show that Nevils knowingly possessed the guns. It surmises that it is equally plausible that someone—anyone, actually, since the defense couldn't finger any person in particular—set Nevils up by placing the guns on him while he was in a drunken stupor. Thus, the majority concludes, no reasonable juror—certainly not the twelve who did—could have found that Nevils knowingly possessed the guns. Like Mrs. Johnson, I am both amazed and disappointed. I respectfully dissent.

. . . There was ample circumstantial evidence for a rational jury to conclude that Earl Nevils knew he possessed, at the least, the 9mm Luger semi-automatic handgun (also referred to in the record as a Tec 9) on his lap. The gun was loaded with several live rounds of ammunition, including one in the gun's chamber. The jury heard evidence from which it could easily have inferred that Nevils knew the gun was there. Officer Clauss, one of the two police officers who apprehended Nevils, testified that when they came upon Nevils and announced themselves, "At that point, you know, his eyes, you know, kind of came full—fully opened and for a brief second he appeared like he was going to, you know, grab toward his lap and then he stopped and put his hands up." A rational juror could equally infer from Nevils' behavior that his first instinct was to reach for his weapon—an instinct that was suppressed when Nevils realized the officers had already drawn their guns and one of the officers had flanked him. Nevil's subsequent behavior is consistent with the jury's finding. When he talked to Sergeant Coleman after his arrest, Nevils did not express any consternation over waking up in a strange place, or amazement about finding guns on his person. He didn't say "Hey, how did I get here?" or "Where did those guns come from?" Instead, he simply expressed anger over being left alone, proclaiming, "I can't believe this s—. Those m— left me sleeping and didn't wake me."

The majority rejects these perfectly plausible explanations because it finds another explanation in equipoise with the government's case and relies on the rule that where the evidence presented at trial does not "establish any reason to believe that an innocent explanation of that evidence was any less likely than the incriminating explanation advanced by the government," it cannot establish the defendant's guilt beyond a reasonable doubt. United States v. Vasquez-Chan, 978 F.2d 546, 551 (9th Cir. 1992). The majority's "innocent explanation" in this case, however, is extraordinarily implausible. The defense's theory, adopted by the majority, is that Nevils, after arriving at the apartment complex for a baby shower, became drunk, passed out, and was carried into the notorious Apartment #6 by several female friends. He then remained unconscious for some seven hours (from approximately 4:00 or 5:00 p.m., a few hours after the baby shower ended, until around 11:45 p.m., when the police officers entered the apartment complex). During that period, one or more persons, whose identities and reasons are unknown, entered Apartment #6, placed drugs in small baggies, a cell phone, and cash on the coffee table in front of Nevils and left a loaded semiautomatic handgun on Nevils' lap and another loaded pistol leaning against his leg. This activity, apparently, did not wake the lethargic Nevils. Instead, the majority believes, he continued to sleep soundly until the police arrived, was awakened, and was amazed to find himself surrounded by drugs and guns.

Even more curious than Nevils' behavior under the majority's "innocent explanation" is the behavior of the anonymous drug dealers. What did the drug dealers do? There are a couple of options, none of them very good. . . . These drug dealers, according to one version of the theory, were surprised by the presence of a police car outside the apartment complex, got scared, and ran off. They decided it was best to leave their drugs and weaponry with the sleeping Nevils, and either threw or placed the heavy guns unto Nevils' lap and leg (all without waking him) as they rushed to leave the premises. Although ordinary drug dealers might, with an eye towards profits, stuff the drugs, cash, and cellphones in their pockets while they were leaving, the majority's anonymous constructs are no ordinary drug dealers. Instead, these guys were so frightened of being caught by the police that they left all their loot on the coffee table, ran out the front door of the apartment, and disappeared before the police arrived. Ironically, their haste did not appear to be necessary—the police officers saw no one leaving Apartment #6 and were only drawn to the apartment after noticing a person furtively trying to enter it later.

Alternatively, the drug dealers deliberately decided to leave their paraphernalia in the apartment. But rather than leave one of their number behind to guard the loot, they set up a scarecrow of sorts—arming the unconscious Nevils and propping him up on the couch to look menacing. This plan, of course, was foiled by the arrival of the police, who weren't impressed with the sleeping Nevils. This theory, like the first, is so farfetched that a rational jury could easily have rejected it in favor of the far more plausible conclusion that Nevils simply fell asleep while guarding the drugs.

The majority recognizes that its theory is implausible "in many towns and many apartment complexes." But it finds that its "innocent explanation" is "not implausible given the evidence that *this* neighborhood, *this* apartment complex, and Apartment 6 itself, were neck-deep in gang activity in the illegal drug trade." In other words, the alternate theory would be implausible if Nevils had been found in an ordinary apartment complex, but because this was a notorious drug area, *anything* can happen. The majority's admission that its theory is generally implausible is healthy, but it can't make its implausible theory plausible just because these events took place in a drug-infested area. No one—not even drug dealers, and maybe *especially* drug dealers—are going to go off and abandon their loaded weapons, drugs, cash and cellphones with a man sleeping off a drunken binge. It makes no sense whatsoever. . . .

I would affirm the district court's determination that the evidence was sufficient to convict Nevils of knowing possession of the weapons. Thus, I respectfully dissent.

## NOTES ON POSSESSION

### 1. THE LEGAL DEFINITION OF POSSESSION

In order to convict Nevils of "being a felon in possession of a firearm," the government had to prove what the court calls "three elements," only one of which was disputed. The defendant conceded that the government could prove the first element of the crime—i.e., that he "was a convicted felon"—and he made no effort to contest the third element—i.e., the firearm "was in or affecting interstate commerce." He challenged only that he was "in knowing possession of a firearm." After hearing all the evidence, the jury rejected that claim and convicted him. Nevils appealed, arguing that the evidence was insufficient to support the jury's verdict.

On appeal, the panel divided, but the judges did not disagree over the meaning of "knowing possession." The term requires careful elaboration. Although the majority opinion initially refers to "knowing possession" as "one element" of the crime, it goes on to describe this element in terms that plainly require the jury to make findings on a number of distinct ingredients. These ingredients seem to be as much about the defendant's mental state, as his conduct. As the court explains, a possession case requires the prosecution to establish, first, that the defendant was conscious of the presence of the forbidden item. Second, the prosecution must prove that the defendant knew what the item was. Finally, the prosecution must prove *either* that the defendant had "physical control" of the item *or* that he had "the power and intention to control it." When the item is within the defendant's "physical control," the case involves "actual possession." "Constructive possession" exists when the defendant lacks actual possession, but knowingly has the power and the intention to exercise dominion and control over the item, either directly or through others.

Of course, each of these inquiries presupposes that the prosecution must prove that in fact the item was present (somewhere), but the defendant's knowledge of and mental attitude toward the item are just as crucial. While criminal law classifies "possession" as an actus reus element, it might be fairer to say that the element is a hybrid or compound construct, which includes an inquiry into and findings about the defendant's mens rea as well as actus reus. "Possession" doesn't count for purposes of criminal liability unless, at a minimum, it is "conscious" and "knowing."

### 2. FINDING THE FACTS

The *Nevils* case illustrates the significant role that lawyers, judges, and jurors play in producing and evaluating the factual narratives that support a defendant's guilt or innocence. Consider the basic facts of the case. Two police officers looked through the open door of Apartment 6. There, they saw Nevils sleeping on a couch, with one gun on his lap and another gun leaning on his leg. Upon a nearby coffee table were baggies full of drugs, a phone, watches, papers, and cash. The police entered the apartment and approached Nevils, at which point he began to wake up. The police identified themselves, they ordered Nevils to get down on the ground, he complied with that order, and they arrested him for drug possession. According to both officers, Nevils "startled" awake. One of the officers stated that Nevils seemed briefly to consider grabbing towards his lap before surrendering and putting his hands in the air. A third officer reported that Nevils cursed the people who had left him sleeping in the apartment. Imagine that, when deliberating over the case, the jurors were allowed to consider only the facts contained in this narrow time frame. Would these facts establish, beyond a reasonable doubt, that Nevils was in "knowing possession" of a firearm? On these facts, would some of the ingredients of "knowing possession" be difficult to prove? If so, which ones?

As the panel opinions reveal, the jurors were not required to confine their attention to the basic facts concerning what the police learned during their confrontation with Nevils. They also were entitled to consider the competing narratives offered by the parties to explain how Nevils came to find himself in this pickle. Precisely what are those competing narratives? As important, where do the stories come from? As for the defense side, it called a witness who provided an exculpatory narrative. What about the inculpatory narrative put forward by the government? What was its source? Whatever the answer to these questions, the verdict makes clear that the jury accepted some version of the tale sponsored by the government, while rejecting that of the defense. The jury was not required to offer any explanation—beyond its general verdict—for why it chose the government's story over that of the defendant.

On appeal, Nevils made a "sufficiency of the evidence" argument. This argument is a routine feature of criminal appellate practice, but the standard of appellate review makes it a tough sell for defendants. As the majority opinion explains, when evaluating a challenge to the sufficiency of the evidence to support a criminal conviction, the reviewing court must "view the evidence in the light most favorable to the government" as the verdict winner. Under this standard, the court must "not question [the] jury's assessment of witnesses' credibility," and it must presume that the jury resolved conflicting inferences in the prosecution's favor. After reviewing the entire record, the court is to ask itself one question: Could a rational juror have found the defendant guilty of each element of the crime beyond a reasonable doubt? If the answer to that question is "yes"—and it almost always is "yes"—the appellate court must affirm the conviction.

A majority of the *Nevils* panel decided that the answer to that crucial question was "no," however, and it reversed the conviction. Because the case involved an innocent explanation (Nevils was passed out in the wrong place at the wrong time) as well as a guilty one (Nevils knowingly possessed the gun) the majority concluded that the government was required to produce evidence to rule out or rebut the innocent interpretation. For the majority, "the pivotal circumstance in this case is the undisputed fact that *Nevils was asleep* (or passed out). Thus, the fact that the firearms were physically touching him is not sufficient to show that he was conscious of their presence." Nor did the other proof in the case provide sufficient circumstantial evidence of the "required mental state" to establish "knowing possession." By contrast, the dissenter, Judge Bybee, believed that the record contained "ample circumstantial evidence" that Nevils knowingly possessed a handgun, and he chided the majority for rejecting a number of plausible explanations that supported the jury's guilty verdict, in favor of the "farfetched" innocent theory offered by the defense. What problem did the majority have in mind when it found "not implausible" for Nevils and Apartment 6 a narrative that it conceded would be implausible for other defendants and other homes?

Nevils's appellate triumph was short-lived. The Ninth Circuit granted the government's petition for a rehearing en banc and reversed the panel's decision. United States v. Nevils, 598 F.3d 1158 (9th Cir. 2010). The en banc court acknowledged that, over the years, it had struggled to articulate correctly the standard of review for sufficiency of the evidence claims. After surveying decisions by the United States Supreme Court, as well as its own precedents, the court explained that, contrary to the approach followed by the panel, the reviewing court is not to construe the evidence in the light most favorable to innocence and then require the prosecution to negate the innocent explanation. Instead, the reviewing court is to construe the evidence only in the light most favorable to the prosecution as verdict winner, and then is to ask only whether a rational trier of fact could have found the defendant guilty beyond a reasonable doubt. The Ninth Circuit recognized that, under this standard, reviewing courts rarely will have the occasion to reverse a finding of guilt made by a properly instructed jury. Those "rare occasions" will include cases where there is a "total failure of proof" of one of the elements of the crime, where the verdict is supported by "mere speculation," or where, even when construed in favor of the government, the evidence is still "so supportive of innocence that no rational juror could" convict. Not surprisingly, the en banc court concluded that *Nevils* did not constitute one of these rare occasions and agreed with Judge Bybee that the evidence was sufficient to support the verdict.

By the way, why did everyone agree that the government could not prosecute Nevils for possession of the drugs found on the coffee table in Apartment 6? Would such a case rest on "mere speculation," rather than on "reasonable inferences" from the facts reported by the police witnesses and from the narrative that supported the felon-in-possession conviction?

### 3. *UNITED STATES V. KITCHEN*

In United States v. Kitchen, 57 F.3d 516 (7th Cir. 1995), the defendant was convicted, among other crimes, of possession of cocaine with intent to distribute. On appeal, he argued that the evidence was insufficient to support a finding that he "possessed" the cocaine. The case involved a standard undercover narcotics operation known as a "reverse buy," in which government agents posing as drug traffickers arrange to sell narcotics to an unsuspecting customer. On the day of the transaction, Kitchen and one of his confederates met with the agents to complete the buy. He went with one of the agents to "inspect the merchandise." His confederate, who was holding the cash to purchase the drugs, remained behind with another agent. When Kitchen arrived at the car that contained the cocaine, an agent popped the trunk, opened a garbage bag located there, and showed Kitchen two packages of cocaine. The parties disputed what happened next. Kitchen insisted that "he never touched the cocaine," while the government "suggested" that he picked up one of the packages and held it for "two or three seconds." However, the parties did agree that, at this point, Kitchen voiced some concern about the purity of the drugs. The Seventh Circuit provided an extensive summary of its reasons for concluding that Kitchen had met his "heavy burden" on appeal:

> [T]he doctrine of "possession" contains concepts that can become almost metaphysical. Few would suggest that "possession" of an object should be confined to instances of physical holding. [T]his case raises the opposite, yet related, question: is any physical holding—no matter the circumstances—sufficient to establish possession? . . .
>
> Possession . . . may be either "actual" or "constructive." It is the government's position that actual possession is established if a defendant picks a controlled substance up for "one fleeting moment"—or 2 or 3 seconds, as seems to have occurred here. This position, the government asserts, is supported by cases [in which the courts have refused] to define possession in "a manner that affords [a defendant] an opportunity to escape with the contraband." And in each case, the court rejects the argument that a defendant cannot have possessed the controlled substance in light of the presence of federal agents. But these cases hardly establish that Kitchen's "fleeting moment" of contact with the narcotics demonstrates actual possession.
>
> . . . Instead, in each, the defendant engaged in some act that was clearly consistent with transporting the narcotics away from the scene of the transaction. In [one case], the defendant took the cocaine from the government agent and put it in a briefcase which he then locked. In [another], the defendant loaded bales of marijuana into his van. And, [in a third], the defendant's coconspirator accepted keys to a van containing marijuana, got into the van and attempted to start it. These cases all involve conduct over and above a defendant's momentary handling of a controlled substance.
>
> This conduct—all acts indicating that transportation of narcotics is imminent—is important precisely because it is unequivocal. By taking delivery of the drug and loading it into a briefcase or a van, a defendant clearly demonstrates his assent to the drug transaction. Here, however, we have no indication of assent. The record is devoid of evidence that Kitchen intended to walk away with the narcotics or otherwise transport them. This factual distinction might not be dispositive if the record revealed *any* evidence that Kitchen had completed the sale or indicated some sort of unequivocal agreement to complete the drug transaction. Given that sort of clear evidence, perhaps a momentary holding, without more, would be sufficient to demonstrate actual possession. But that is not the case before us now.
>
> The undisputed evidence in Kitchen's case tells a strikingly different story—different, ultimately, because here, the sale of the drugs remained incomplete at the time of arrest, and the record reveals no other indication that Kitchen would have proceeded with the drug sale. On the day of the proposed transaction, Kitchen and his [confederate] met the government [agents] at a

predetermined location. There, the four men got into Kitchen's car. The stated plan was for Kitchen to pay for one kilogram of cocaine and have the remaining kilogram "fronted" to him for payment at a later date. Kitchen showed [the agents] the money and then handed it to his [confederate. The agent] admitted that at no point did either Kitchen or [his confederate offer the agents] the money or attempt to hand the money over. Instead, Kitchen left the money with [his confederate] and proceeded to another location with [the agent] to examine the drugs.

Both at the initial meeting and en route to the second location, [the agents] repeatedly urged Kitchen to "check out the merchandise" or otherwise inspect the narcotics.... It is clear that Kitchen proceeded to the second location . . . to do just this.

It is also clear, however, that at the second location, no transaction occurred. [The agent] admitted that Kitchen never stated that he would complete the transaction or made a similar affirmative comment to that effect. Instead, Kitchen made a statement expressing doubt about the quality of the cocaine. These factors indicate that the transaction simply had not been completed at the time of Kitchen's arrest. Kitchen had neither tendered any portion of the money nor otherwise agreed to complete the transaction. Absent evidence suggesting that the transaction was in any sense final or certain, we are quite uncomfortable with the notion that momentary contact with narcotics establishes actual possession.

Our discomfort stems from a number of sources. First, the cases upholding convictions for possession do so only in the context of some sort of unequivocal conduct on the part of the defendants. Often, . . . that conduct will consist of actions consistent with transporting the drug away from the site of the deal. [Or] the conduct may be more idiosyncratic. [For example, in one case, the defendant went to purchase a pair of shoes to replace the government informant's shoes, which secreted illegal drugs. In another case, the defendant's performance of tests on each of thirty one-kilo bags of cocaine over a two-hour period sufficed to establish possession.]

By demanding some sort of unequivocal conduct or assent to the transaction we do not invade the jury's province. We remain aware that the jury is entrusted with finding the facts, and we remain bound by the principle that we must view the evidence in the light most favorable to the government. But resort to this principle cannot be used as a substitute for essential proof. The government is still in the position of establishing possession as an element of the crime. And here, the essential proof of possession that we require is *some factor* indicating that Kitchen had the authority or the ability to exercise control over the contraband.

This demand is hardly foreign to the doctrine of possession. Constructive possession, as developed in this circuit, expressly demands this sort of showing. The government suggests that this factor is not relevant in light of Kitchen's momentary holding of the narcotics. Yet the cases discussing actual possession do not support this argument; in each, as demonstrated, some sort of unequivocal conduct indicating acceptance of the drug or assent to the transaction was present. We suspect, in any event, that the notion of control is not absent from the concept of actual possession. In most cases of actual possession, because the defendant physically holds or carries the narcotics, his control over them is presumed. But to state that control is presumed is not to suggest that actual possession can be established when it is completely absent.

The facts suggest that it was absent in this case. . . . Although Kitchen held the cocaine in his hand, he did not yet have a recognized authority to exert control over it. This is so not because the presence of federal agents would have ultimately prevented his success, but because he had not yet assented in any form to the transaction. Had he paid part of the purchase price, verbally assented to the deal, or otherwise unambiguously indicated his agreement to complete the deal, the case would be different. But the government has failed to point to factors that would enable a jury to find that Kitchen accepted the cocaine. It is critical here that, prior to giving some sort of assent to the sale, Kitchen's conduct was consistent only with that of a prospective buyer inspecting goods. He did not yet have the ability to control the contraband, despite the fact that he momentarily held it in his hand.

The government does, however, point to evidence of Kitchen's *intent* to transact a drug deal. And it suggests that the jury concluded that Kitchen *intended* to purchase the cocaine. It further suggests that various indicia of Kitchen's intent should be sufficient to establish possession of the narcotics. In support of this conclusion, the government highlights the repeated phone conversations between Kitchen and Griffin discussing potential transactions; Kitchen's various admissions about unrelated drug dealings; and Kitchen's arrival at the scene with the required cash in hand. Yet these factors establish only that Kitchen intended to purchase cocaine, and Kitchen's intent to purchase, without more, is insufficient to establish possession because it overlooks the required element of dominion or control.

By reading the element of control out of the equation, we risk confusing possession with attempted possession. It is well-established that intent is a key element of the doctrine of attempted possession. Given intent, the jury's focus is directed to whether the defendant engaged in conduct that constituted a "substantial step" toward the commission of the crime. An examination of garden variety attempt cases reveals that Kitchen's conduct is more consistent with that sort of criminal behavior. While these attempt cases hardly establish the absence of possession in Kitchen's case, they do suggest that his case fits more neatly into an attempt paradigm.

The intent to engage in a drug transaction, without more, cannot support a conviction for possession. The missing link in this case is the ability to control the contraband. Had the evidence indicated some sort of unequivocal assent to the transaction, then a momentary holding might have been sufficient to establish the required element of control. But the momentary holding upon which the government relies here simply is not adequate to overcome our concerns. There simply is no evidence—such as payment of the purchase price or verbal agreement—that the drug transaction was in any sense certain or complete. We believe that although Kitchen held the drugs for a moment, he neither controlled them nor had recognized authority over them. His conduct was consistent with inspection—but nothing more. Lack of control is dispositive under both the doctrines of actual and constructive possession. We therefore find the evidence insufficient to support Kitchen's conviction for possession of cocaine.

# CHAPTER III

# THE CRIMINAL MIND

## INTRODUCTORY NOTE

A "guilty mind" is generally regarded as an essential requirement for imposing criminal liability. The concept is often captured in the ancient maxim "actus reus non facit reum nisi mens sit rea," which can be roughly translated as "a criminal act does not make a criminal unless the mind be criminal." The criminal law enforces the "guilty mind" requirement (i.e., measures fault or culpability) in two principal ways. One is through doctrines of mens rea, which are covered in Chapters III and IV. The other is through special defenses, which are covered in subsequent chapters.

Chapter III introduces mens rea concepts. Section 1 covers the basic structure of mens rea as it emerged at common law. Section 2 turns to the Model Penal Code. The very heart of the Model Code is a mens rea structure that has supplanted the common law in many (but far from all) American jurisdictions. It is derived from the common law but is distinctive in its analytical rigor. Any lawyer who expects to understand American criminal law today must study the very different conceptual frameworks of the common law and the Model Penal Code.

Section 3 takes up ignorance or mistake of law, the basic doctrine for which is often captured in the generalization that "ignorance of the law is no excuse." Sections 1 and 2 of the Chapter describe the positive content of mens rea in the criminal law, that is, what mens rea *is*. By contrast, Section 3 deals with an important respect in which a potential fault or culpability inquiry *is not* typically part of the mens rea required for crime. Together, these three Sections set forth the basic rules for determining the meaning of mens rea at common law and under the Model Penal Code.

Chapter III concludes with a Section on intoxication. The voluntary ingestion of drink or drugs frequently accompanies criminal behavior, and can produce effects that are sometimes relevant to the mens rea components of a crime. This Section covers the law's response to this possibility.

Chapter IV offers a series of optional elaborations on the basic issues outlined in Chapter III. All build on the materials in Chapter III, but each is independent of the others and none is necessary to a basic understanding of mens rea. The intent is to allow instructors to assign or omit the individual sections of Chapter IV, to teach them in any order after finishing Chapter III, or to merge them for discussion with appropriate materials in Chapter III.

## SECTION 1: THE FOUNDATIONS OF MENS REA

### INTRODUCTORY NOTES ON THE REQUIREMENT OF MENS REA

#### 1. THE HISTORY

The origins of the criminal law's focus on the defendant's mental state are obscure. It is clear, however, that for most offenses some requirement of mens rea has existed for centuries. The early development of the concept is described in Francis Bowes Sayre, Mens Rea, 45 Harv. L. Rev. 974 (1932), on which the following summary is based.[a]

With respect to some offenses, early criminal law apparently focused on harms caused and not on the motive or intent of the actor. Liability was, in modern parlance, "absolute" or "strict." By the 12th century, the influence of Roman and canon law led to what Sayre calls an inquiry into "general moral blameworthiness." The next stage of development consisted of the conversion of this requirement into more specific questions about the defendant's state of mind that varied with the particular crime involved. In larceny, for example, Sayre observed three stages of evolution: (i) an initial formulation (prior to the legal separation of crime and tort) permitting an action against one in possession of stolen goods without regard to wrongful intent and whether or not that person was the thief; (ii) the later idea that the proper inquiry for the criminal law was whether the actor was morally blameworthy in the sense that the conduct was wicked or evil; (iii) and finally, the modern concept that the mens rea for larceny should focus more precisely on the defendant's state of mind at the time of the taking, as reflected in what became the traditional common law definition of the offense: "taking and carrying away the personal property of another with intent permanently to deprive the other of the property."

Sayre's general conclusion was that the concept of mens rea had "no fixed continuing meaning" over time. Instead:

> The conception of mens rea has varied with the changing underlying conceptions and objectives of criminal justice. . . . Under the dominating influence of the canon law and the penitential books the underlying objective of criminal justice gradually came to be the punishment of evil-doing; as a result the mental factors necessary for criminality were based upon a mind bent on evil-doing in the sense of moral wrong. Our modern objective tends more and more in the direction, not of awarding adequate punishment for moral wrong-doing, but of protecting social and public interests. To the extent that this objective prevails, the mental element requisite for criminality . . . is coming to mean, not so much a mind bent on evil-doing as an intent to do that which unduly endangers social or public interests.

## 2. *MORISSETTE V. UNITED STATES*

The commitment of modern criminal law to a mens rea requirement was summarized by Justice Robert Jackson in a well-known opinion in Morissette v. United States, 342 U.S. 246 (1952):

> The contention that an injury can amount to a crime only when inflicted by intention is no provincial or transient notion. It is as universal and persistent in mature systems of law as belief in freedom of the human will and a consequent ability and duty of the normal individual to choose between good and evil.[4] A relation

[a] For a more recent review of the history, see Martin R. Gardner, The Mens Rea Enigma: Observations on the Role of Motive in the Criminal Law Past and Present, 1993 Utah L. Rev. 635.

[4] . . . "Historically, our substantive criminal law is based upon a theory of punishing the vicious will. It postulates a free agent confronted with a choice between doing right and doing

between some mental element and punishment for a harmful act is almost as instinctive as the child's familiar exculpatory "But I didn't mean to," and has afforded the rational basis for a tardy and unfinished substitution of deterrence and reformation in place of retaliation and vengeance as the motivation for public prosecution. Unqualified acceptance of this doctrine by English common law in the 18th century was indicated by Blackstone's sweeping statement that to constitute any crime there must first be a "vicious will." . . .

Crime, as a compound concept, generally constituted only from concurrence of an evil-meaning mind with an evil-doing hand, was congenial to an intense individualism and took deep and early root in American soil. As the states codified the common law of crimes, even if their enactments were silent on the subject, their courts assumed that the omission did not signify disapproval of the principle but merely recognized that intent was so inherent in the idea of the offense that it required no statutory affirmation. Courts, with little hesitation or division, found an implication of the requirement as to offenses that were taken over from the common law. The unanimity with which they have adhered to the central thought that wrongdoing must be conscious to be criminal is emphasized by the variety, disparity and confusion of their definitions of the requisite but elusive mental element. However, courts of various jurisdictions, and for the purposes of different offenses, have devised working formulae, if not scientific ones, for the instruction of juries around such terms as "felonious intent," "criminal intent," "malice aforethought," "guilty knowledge," "fraudulent intent," "wilfulness," "scienter," to denote guilty knowledge, or "mens rea," to signify an evil purpose or mental culpability. By use or combination of these various tokens, they have sought to protect those who were not blameworthy in mind from conviction of infamous common law crimes. . . .

## 3. THE IMPLICATIONS OF PREVENTION: OLIVER WENDELL HOLMES

In The Rationale of Punishment, published in 1830, Jeremy Bentham argued that "[g]eneral prevention ought to be the chief end of punishment, as it is its real justification." In comments first published in The Common Law in 1881, Oliver Wendell Holmes explained why this view is consistent with the principles of Anglo-American criminal law, including the requirement of mens rea. In debates about the theory of punishment, Holmes observed, "the main struggle lies between" retribution and prevention. He continued:

> It is objected that the preventive theory is immoral because it overlooks the ill-desert of wrong-doing, and furnishes no measure of the amount of punishment, except the lawgiver's subjective opinion in regard to the sufficiency of the amount of preventive suffering. In the language of Kant, it treats the man as a thing, not as a person; as a means and not as an end in himself. It is said

---

wrong and choosing freely to do wrong." Pound, Introduction to Sayre, Cases on Criminal Law (1927).

to conflict with the sense of justice, and to violate the fundamental principle of all free communities, that the members of such communities have equal rights to life, liberty, and personal security.

In spite of all this, probably most English-speaking lawyers would accept the preventive theory without hesitation. As to the violation of equal rights which is charged, it may be replied that the dogma of equality makes an equation between individuals only, not between an individual and the community. No society has ever admitted that it could not sacrifice individual welfare for its own existence. If conscripts are necessary for its army, it seizes them, and marches them, with bayonets in their rear, to death. It runs highways and railroads through old family places in spite of the owner's protest, paying in this instance the market value, to be sure, because no civilized government sacrifices the citizen more than it can help, but still sacrificing his will and his welfare to that of the rest.

[T]here can be no case in which the law-maker makes certain conduct criminal without his thereby showing a wish and purpose to prevent that conduct. Prevention would accordingly seem to be the chief and only universal purpose of punishment. The law threatens certain pains if you do certain things, intending thereby to give you a new motive for not doing them. If you persist in doing them, it has to inflict the pains in order that its threats may continue to be believed.

If this is a true account of the law as it stands, the law does undoubtedly treat the individual as a means to an end, and uses him as a tool to increase the general welfare at his own expense. It has been suggested above, that this course is perfectly proper; but even if it is wrong, our criminal law follows it, and the theory of our criminal law must be shaped accordingly. . . .

If the foregoing arguments are sound, it is already manifest that liability to punishment cannot be finally and absolutely determined by considering the actual personal unworthiness of the criminal alone. That consideration will govern only so far as the public welfare permits or demands.[b] And if we take into account the general result which the criminal law is intended to bring about, we shall see that the actual state of mind accompanying a criminal act plays a different part from what is commonly supposed.

For the most part, the purpose of the criminal law is only to induce external conformity to rule. All law is directed to conditions of things manifest to the senses. And whether it brings those conditions to pass immediately by the use of force, as when it protects a house from a mob by soldiers, or appropriates private property to public use, or hangs a man in pursuance of a judicial sentence, or whether it brings them about mediately through

[b] Holmes had earlier observed that "[i]f punishment stood on the moral grounds which are proposed for it, the first thing to be considered would be those limitations in the capacity for choosing rightly which arise from abnormal instincts, want of education, lack of intelligence, and all the other defects which are most marked" in the vast majority of criminals. Yet, he continued, the criminal law has never been structured to take these elements into account.—[Footnote by eds.]

men's fears, its object is equally an external result. In directing itself against robbery or murder, for instance, its purpose is to put a stop to the actual physical taking and keeping of other men's goods, or the actual poisoning, shooting, stabbing, and otherwise putting to death of other men. If those things are not done, the law forbidding them is equally satisfied, whatever the motive.

Considering this purely external purpose of the law together with the fact that it is ready to sacrifice the individual so far as necessary in order to accomplish that purpose, we can see more readily than before that the actual degree of personal guilt involved in any particular transgression cannot be the only element, if it is an element at all, in the liability incurred. . . .

It is not intended to deny that criminal liability . . . is founded on blameworthiness. Such a denial would shock the moral sense of any civilized community; or, to put it another way, a law which punished conduct which would not be blameworthy in the average member of the community would be too severe for that community to bear. It is only intended to point out that, when we are dealing with that part of the law which aims more directly than any other at establishing standards of conduct, we should expect there more than elsewhere to find that the tests of liability are external, and independent of the degree of evil in the particular person's motives or intentions. The conclusion follows directly from the nature of the standards to which conformity is required. These are not only external, as was shown above, but they are of general application. They do not merely require that every man should get as near as he can to the best conduct possible for him. They require him at his own peril to come up to a certain height. They take no account of incapacities, unless the weakness is so marked as to fall into well-known exceptions, such as infancy or madness. They assume that every man is as able as every other to behave as they command. If they fall on any one class harder than on another, it is on the weakest. For it is precisely to those who are most likely to err by temperament, ignorance, or folly, that the threats of the law are the most dangerous.

The reconciliation of the doctrine that liability is founded on blameworthiness with the existence of liability where the party is not to blame . . . is found in the conception of the average man, the man of ordinary intelligence and reasonable prudence. Liability is said to arise out of such conduct as would be blameworthy in him. But he is an ideal being, represented by the jury when they are appealed to, and his conduct is an external or objective standard when applied to any given individual. That individual may be morally without stain, because he has less than ordinary intelligence or prudence. But he is required to have those qualities at his peril. If he has them, he will not, as a general rule, incur liability without blameworthiness.

## 4. QUESTIONS AND COMMENTS

Is it clear that the criminal law, as a general proposition, ought to focus on the defendant's state of mind when actions are taken? What policies support that result? What consequences would ensue if mens rea in the criminal law were abandoned? Consideration of these questions will be aided by examination of the materials below.

## Regina v. Faulkner

Ireland, Court of Crown Cases Reserved, 1877.
13 Cox C.C. 550.

[The defendant was a seaman on a ship carrying a cargo of rum, sugar, and cotton. He was not permitted in the cargo area where the rum was stored, but ignoring the prohibition in order to satisfy his thirst, he entered the storage hold, poked a hole in a rum cask, and helped himself. In order to plug the hole after he was finished, he lit a match to see. The rum caught fire, which injured him and destroyed the ship. He was indicted for arson, on the charge that he "feloniously, unlawfully, and maliciously did set fire to the said ship, with intent thereby to prejudice" the owners of the ship. It was conceded that he had no actual intention to set fire to the vessel, and no instruction was requested as to his awareness of the probable consequences of his act.

[The prosecutor's theory was that since the defendant was stealing rum when he started the fire, his felonious intent with respect to the arson was established by his intent with respect to the theft. The trial judge accepted this theory in the instructions, and the jury convicted. On appeal, the prosecutor argued that " 'the terms malice and malicious are used in a general sense, as denoting a wicked, perverse, and incorrigible disposition.' Here the felonious act of the prisoner showing a wicked, perverse, and incorrigible disposition supplies the malice required. . . ." One member of the court, Justice Keogh, accepted the theory, noting that he was of the opinion "that the conviction should stand, as I consider all questions of intention and malice are closed by the finding of the jury, that the prisoner committed the act with which he was charged whilst engaged in the commission of a substantive felony. On this broad ground, irrespective of all refinements as to 'recklessness' and 'wilfulness,' I think the conviction is sustained."

[The majority of the appellate court, however, voted to quash the conviction. Excerpts from some of their opinions follow.]

■ FITZGERALD, J. . . . I am . . . of opinion that in order to establish the charge . . . , the intention of the accused forms an element in the crime to the extent that it should appear that the defendant intended to do the very act with which he is charged, or that it was the necessary consequence of some other felonious or criminal act in which he was engaged, or that having a probable result which the defendant foresaw, or ought to have foreseen, he, nevertheless, persevered in such other felonious or criminal act. The prisoner did not intend to set fire to the ship—the fire was not the necessary result of the felony he was attempting; and if it was a probable result, which he ought to have foreseen, of the felonious transaction on which he was engaged, and from which a malicious design to commit the injurious act with which he is charged might have been fairly imputed to him, that view of the case was not submitted to the jury. On the contrary, it was excluded from their consideration on the requisition of the counsel for the prosecution. Counsel for the prosecution in effect insisted that the defendant, being engaged in the commission of, or in an attempt to commit a felony, was criminally responsible for every result that was occasioned thereby, even though it was not a probable consequence of his act or such as he could have reasonably foreseen or intended. No authority has been cited for a proposition so extensive, and I am of opinion that it is not warranted by law. . . .

■ FITZGERALD, B. . . . The utmost which I can conceive the jury to have found over and above the facts stated is, that at the time when the prisoner set fire to this ship he was actuated by a felonious intent, which no doubt is malice; but I must take this not to have been the particular malicious intent of burning the vessel, but the particular felonious intent, which is an element of larceny. Its whole force, therefore, in the present case (if any) is as evidence of malice in general. . . . In my opinion, this general malice might have been sufficiently connected with the overt act in this case, from which the injury resulted, if the jury had found that the injury was a reasonable consequence—that is to say, a consequence which any man of reason might have anticipated as probable of an act or acts. . . . Now, however clearly I may be satisfied that the jury ought, as a matter of fact, if the question had been left to it, to have found that injury was the reasonable consequence of an act or acts done with a felonious intent, I cannot draw the conclusion as a matter of law. . . . I am quite satisfied that in cases like the present, if the overt act from which injury resulted be actuated by any malice, and the injury is the reasonable consequence of such overt act so actuated, malice would be sufficiently established. . . . I am clearly of opinion that there was evidence on which the jury might have found the malice necessary to sustain the indictment . . . , yet I think the question of malice was not left to the jury at all—the conviction cannot be sustained.

■ PALLES, C.B. I concur in the opinion of the majority of the Court. . . . I agree with my brother Keogh that from the facts proved the inference might have been legitimately drawn that the setting fire to the ship was malicious. . . . I am of opinion that that inference was one of fact for the jury, and not a conclusion of law at which we can arrive upon the case before us. There is one fact from which, if found, that inference would, in my opinion, have arisen as matter of law, as that the setting fire to the ship was the probable result of the prisoner's act in having a lighted match in the place in question; and if that had been found I should have concurred in the conclusion at which Mr. Justice Keogh has arrived. In my judgment the law imputes to a person who wilfully commits a criminal act an intention to do everything which is the probable consequence of the act constituting the corpus delicti which actually ensues. In my opinion this inference arises irrespective of the particular consequence which ensued being or not being foreseen by the criminal, and whether his conduct is reckless or the reverse. . . .

## NOTES ON THE EVOLUTION OF MENS REA

### 1. THE LANGUAGE OF MENS REA

The first lesson to be learned about the words used to express common law mens rea requirements is that they often do not signify what one would expect. There is often little correlation between their legal meaning and their meaning in ordinary usage. Before mens rea terms can be understood in their special legal sense, therefore, one must face a problem of translation. Just as one begins the study of a foreign language by learning the English equivalent of the words to be used, and gradually learns to use the foreign vocabulary without the intermediate step of constant translation, it is useful to treat common law mens rea terms, and indeed much of the language of the law, as words that must be translated into ordinary language before one can learn how to use them.

The difficulty of the terminology is compounded by the colorful variety of mens rea terms in common usage. They include "corruptly," "scienter," "wilfully," "maliciously," "fraudulently," "wantonly," "feloniously," "wilful neglect," "recklessly," "negligently," "wanton and wilful," and many more. Learning to use these words would not be too problematic if their meanings were settled. Unfortunately, this is not the case. To return to the foreign language analogy, there are no accepted meanings into which these terms invariably can be translated. Different courts translate them differently, and the same court will use them differently for different crimes. What is required, therefore, is not memorization of accepted definitions, but sensitive assessment and analysis informed by context.

There is at least one further difficulty. It is typical in American legislation based on common law terminology for a collection of mens rea terms to be strung together, without attention to what they mean or how they relate to each other. An example of the origins of the practice is the phrase "feloniously, unlawfully, and maliciously" in the indictment in *Faulkner*. A study of modern federal criminal legislation is also instructive:

> . . . The "mental element" of federal crimes is specified in the definitions of the crimes, which definitions are frequently modified, if not indeed distorted, in judicial decisions. If one looks to the statutes alone, the specifications of mental states form a staggering array: [Here some 78 different combinations of words are extracted from various federal statutes. Examples are "willfully and corruptly," "willfully and maliciously," "willfully or maliciously," "willfully and unlawfully," "willfully and knowingly," "willfully, deliberate, malicious, and premeditated," "unlawfully and willfully," "knowingly and willfully," "knowingly or willfully," "fraudulently or wrongfully," "from a premeditated design unlawfully and maliciously to," "knowingly, willfully, and corruptly," "willfully neglects," and "improperly."]
>
> Unsurprisingly, the courts have been unable to find substantive correlates for all these varied descriptions of mental states, and, in fact, the opinions display far fewer mental states than the statutory language. Not only does the statutory language not reflect accurately or consistently what are the mental elements of the various crimes; there is no discernible pattern or consistent rationale which explains why one crime is defined or understood to require one mental state and another crime another mental state or indeed no mental state at all.

1 National Commission on Reform of Federal Criminal Laws, Working Papers 119–20 (1970). The same study concludes with respect to the word "willfully" that "the courts, including the Supreme Court, have endowed the requirement of willfulness with the capacity to take on whatever meaning seems appropriate in the statutory context." The same comment could be made about many other common law mens rea terms.

Willfully

## 2. MENS REA AND GENERAL MALEVOLENCE

Sayre described the emerging notion of mens rea in the 12th century as a concept of "general moral blameworthiness." By that he appears to have meant what we might call a holistic judgment about the general character and disposition of the actor. The argument advanced by the prosecutor in *Faulkner* was similar: " '[T]he terms malice and malicious are used in a general sense, as denoting a wicked, perverse, and incorrigible disposition.' Here the felonious act of the prisoner [stealing rum] showing a wicked, perverse, and incorrigible disposition supplies the malice required. . . . " Notice that the word "malice" is not being used by the prosecutor in *Faulkner* in an artificial sense. In common usage it means "badness," "wickedness," "active ill-will," or the like. Yet the appellate court, reflecting changes in the law that Sayre recounted, rejected this ordinary language definition and substituted a different measure of the defendant's blameworthiness.

What exactly is the appellate court's definition of "malice"? Assume that Faulkner was a seaman whose job it was periodically to inspect the hold in which the rum was kept. Could he have been convicted if, while performing that duty, he lit a match in order to see and carelessly caused the same destruction? Whatever the answer to this question, it is clear that the judges are using the string of mens rea words in the indictment in a way that is foreign to their normal meaning. Do the opinions by Fitzgerald, Fitzgerald, and Palles reflect serious disagreement about the mens rea that should be required? On what elements of the context and the defendant's behavior do they focus?

Use of the vocabulary of general moral blameworthiness is not confined to 19th century English courts. Such language persists in modern appellate opinions in the federal system and in many states and, significantly, in jury instructions still in use. The law has failed to adjust its vocabulary in many American jurisdictions as the concept of mens rea has evolved.

One of the major contributions of the American Law Institute's Model Penal Code was to standardize and simplify the vocabulary of mens rea. As illustrated below, modern courts and legislatures—supported by modern academic commentary—frequently reject the common law language and describe mens rea concepts in the more readily accessible language proposed by the Model Code.

## 3. *REGINA V. CUNNINGHAM*

In Regina v. Cunningham, 41 Crim.App. 155 (1957), the defendant was convicted and sentenced to five years' imprisonment under the following statute:

> Whosoever shall unlawfully and maliciously administer to or cause to be administered to or taken by any other person any poison or other destructive or noxious thing, so as thereby to endanger the life of such person, or so as thereby to inflict upon such person any grievous bodily harm, shall be guilty of felony.

The facts, as recited by the appellate court, were that:

> [T]he appellant was engaged to be married and his prospective mother-in-law was the tenant of a house, No. 7a, Bakes Street, Bradford, which was unoccupied but which was to be occu-

pied by the appellant after his marriage. Mrs. Wade and her husband, an elderly couple, lived in the house next door. At one time the two houses had been one, but when the building was converted into two houses a wall had been erected to divide the cellars of the two houses, and that wall was composed of rubble loosely cemented. On the evening of January 17 last the appellant went to the cellar of No. 7a, Bakes Street, wrenched the gas meter from the gas pipes and stole it, together with its contents, and in a second indictment he was charged with the larceny of the gas meter and its contents. To that indictment he pleaded guilty and was sentenced to six months' imprisonment. In respect of that matter he does not appeal. The facts were not really in dispute, and in a statement to a police officer the appellant said: "All right I will tell you. I was short of money, I had been off work for three days, I got eight shillings from the gas meter. I tore it off the wall and threw it away." Although there was a stop tap within two feet of the meter, the appellant did not turn off the gas, with the result that a very considerable volume of gas escaped, some of which seeped through the wall of the cellar and partially asphyxiated Mrs. Wade, who was asleep in her bedroom next door, with the result that her life was endangered.

The trial judge instructed the jury as follows:

You will observe that there is nothing [in the statute] about "with intention that that person should take [the noxious substance]." He has not got to intend that it should be taken; it is sufficient that by his unlawful and malicious act he causes it to be taken. What you have to decide here, then, is whether, when he loosed that frightful cloud of coal gas into the house which he shared with this old lady, he caused her to take it by his unlawful and malicious action. "Unlawful" does not need any definition. It is something forbidden by law. What about "malicious"? "Malicious" for this purpose means wicked—something which he has no business to do and perfectly well knows it. "Wicked" is as good a definition as any other which you would get. The facts . . . are these. [T]he prisoner quite deliberately, intending to steal the money that was in the meter, . . . broke the gas mains away from the supply pipes and thus released the main supply of gas at large into that house. When he did that he knew that this old lady and her husband were living next door to him. The gas meter was in a cellar. The wall which divided his cellar from the cellar next door was a kind of honeycomb wall through which gas could very well go, so that when he loosed that cloud of gas into that place he must have known perfectly well that gas would percolate all over the house. If it were part of this offence—which it is not—that he intended to poison the old lady, I should have left it to you to decide, and I should have told you that there was evidence on which you could find that he intended that, since he did an action which he must have known would result in that. As I have already told you, it is not necessary to prove that he intended to do it; it is quite enough that what he did was done unlawfully and maliciously.

The appellate court quashed the conviction. Excerpts from the opinion follow:

> In any statutory definition of a crime, malice must be taken not in the old vague sense of wickedness in general but as requiring either (i) an actual intention to do the particular kind of harm that in fact was done; or (ii) recklessness as to whether such harm should occur or not (i.e., the accused has foreseen that the particular kind of harm might be done and yet has gone on to take the risk of it). It is neither limited to nor does it indeed require any ill will towards the person injured. . . . We think that this is an accurate statement of the law. . . . In our opinion, the word "maliciously" in a statutory crime postulates foresight of consequence. . . .
>
> With the utmost respect to the learned judge, we think it is incorrect to say that the word "malicious" in a statutory offence merely means wicked. We think the learned judge was in effect telling the jury that if they were satisfied that the appellant acted wickedly—and he had clearly acted wickedly in stealing the gas meter and its contents—they ought to find that he had acted maliciously in causing the gas to be taken by Mrs. Wade so as thereby to endanger her life.
>
> In our view, it should have been left to the jury to decide whether, even if the appellant did not intend the injury to Mrs. Wade, he foresaw that the removal of the gas meter might cause injury to someone but nevertheless removed it. We are unable to say that a reasonable jury, properly directed as to the meaning of the word "maliciously" in the [statute], would without doubt have convicted.
>
> In these circumstances this court has no alternative but to allow the appeal and quash the conviction.

## 4. *FAULKNER* AND *CUNNINGHAM* COMPARED

There are important differences between the mental state required by the Irish Court of Crown Cases Reserved in *Faulkner* and the English Court of Criminal Appeals in *Cunningham*, differences that would appear to have little to do with the language used in the definition of the respective offenses. Both courts appear to have been concerned to state the minimum conditions of criminal liability in general terms—terms likely to be applied to other offenses as well as the ones before the court. What accounts for the disagreement between the two courts? Are there practical differences between them? What philosophical differences might explain the different outcomes?

Assume that Cunningham had been a meter repairman who allowed the gas to escape and endanger Mrs. Wade when he dismantled the meter and returned to his shop to get a spare part. Could he then have been convicted under the approach taken in *Faulkner*? In *Cunningham*? How do *Faulkner* and *Cunningham* fit within the evolution of mens rea described by Sayre?

## NOTES ON CRIMINAL NEGLIGENCE

### 1. INTRODUCTION

At a minimum, according to the *Faulkner* court, the offense for which Faulkner was convicted required that he "ought to have foreseen" the fire. Many commentators conclude that most or all crimes should require more culpability than this. But the law today in every American jurisdiction is that, if an element of a crime is to require mens rea at all,[a] some form of negligence is acceptable for some elements of some crimes. The following notes describe what criminal negligence might mean.

"Criminal negligence" usually is said to be an especially egregious sort of callousness, different in kind or degree from the "ordinary" negligence that will warrant recovery in a civil suit for damages. In General Principles of Criminal Law 124 (2d ed. 1960), Jerome Hall summarized early English efforts to define criminal negligence:

> For many years [the judges] relied on adjectives qualifying "negligence" to carry their meaning; and they continued to do this long after the adjectives were regarded as mere "vituperative epithets." Nor has so-called "criminal negligence" been clarified by judicial efforts to distinguish it from civil negligence. The opinions run in terms of "wanton and wilful negligence," "gross negligence," and more illuminating yet, "that degree of negligence that is more than the negligence required to impose tort liability." The apex of this infelicity is "wilful, wanton negligence," which suggests a triple contradiction—"negligence" implying inadvertence; "wilful," intention; and "wanton," recklessness.

There have been efforts, however, to define the term more carefully.

### 2. *DIRECTOR OF PUBLIC PROSECUTIONS V. SMITH*

Smith was convicted of murder. He was stopped at an intersection when a policeman, whom he knew, came to the driver's window and spoke to him. The policeman saw some goods in the back of the car that appeared to have been stolen, and told Smith to pull over. Smith started to do so, but soon rapidly accelerated. The policeman began to run with the car, and grabbed onto it as it sped off. The officer was killed when he was thrown off the car about 130 yards later, into the path of an oncoming vehicle.

Conviction for murder required a mens rea of "malice aforethought," which is a common law term of art that includes a number of different mental states having little to do with the ordinary meaning of either "malice" or "aforethought." The one on which the prosecution relied in *Smith* was that the defendant "intended to inflict grievous bodily harm or knew that such harm would result." In Director of Public Prosecutions v. Smith, [1960] 3 All.E.R. 161, [1961] A.C. 290, the question before the House of Lords was how the jury should be asked to implement this standard. The jury was instructed as follows:

> The intention with which a man did something can usually be determined by a jury only by inference from the surrounding circumstances. . . . If you feel yourselves bound to conclude from

---

[a] Strict liability—that is no mens rea requirement—is a possibility for some elements of some crimes. This possibility is illustrated at numerous points below.

> the evidence that the accused's purpose was to dislodge the officer, then you ask yourselves this question: Could any reasonable person fail to appreciate that the likely result would be at least serious harm to the officer? If you answer that question by saying that the reasonable person would certainly appreciate that, then you may infer that that was the accused's intention, and that would lead to a verdict of guilty on the charge of capital murder. . . .
>
> Now the only part of that evidence of [Police Constable] Weatherill which the accused challenges is the part that incriminates him, namely, "I only wanted to shake him off." He says he did not say that. Well, you may think it is a curious thing to imagine, and further it may well be the truth—he did only want to shake him off; but if the reasonable man would realise that the effect of doing that might well be to cause serious harm to this officer, then, as I say, you would be entitled to impute such an intent to the accused, and, therefore, to sum up the matter as between murder and manslaughter, if you are satisfied that when he drove his car erratically up the street, close to the traffic on the other side, he must as a reasonable man have contemplated that grievous bodily harm was likely to result to that officer still clinging on, and that such harm did happen and the officer died in consequence, then the accused is guilty of capital murder, and you should not shrink from such a verdict because of its possible consequences.
>
> On the other hand, if you are not satisfied that he intended to inflict grievous bodily harm upon the officer—in other words, if you think he could not as a reasonable man have contemplated that grievous bodily harm would result to the officer in consequence of his actions—well, then, the verdict would be guilty of manslaughter.

Smith argued that the trial judge was "applying what is referred to as an objective test, namely, the test of what a reasonable man would contemplate as the probable result of his acts, and therefore, would intend, whereas the question for the jury, it is said, was what the respondent himself intended." The Court of Appeals agreed, and reversed the conviction. It said:

> [T]he present case [is] one in which the degree of likelihood of serious injury to the police officer depended on which of the not always consistent versions of the facts given by witnesses for the prosecution was accepted. It was one in which it could not be said that there was a certainty that such injury would result; and it was one in which there always remained the question whether the appellant really did during the relevant 10 seconds realise what was the degree of likelihood of serious injury. If the jury took the view that the appellant [the present respondent] deliberately tried to drive the body of the police officer against oncoming cars, the obvious inference was open to them that the appellant intended serious injury to result; if, however, they concluded he merely swerved or zigzagged to shake off the officer, or if they concluded that for any reason he may not have realised the degree of danger to which he was exposing the officer, a different situation would arise with regard to the inferences to be drawn.

The House of Lords disagreed, and reinstated the conviction. It stated the operative standard as follows:

> The jury must of course in such a case as the present make up their minds on the evidence whether the accused was unlawfully and voluntarily doing something to someone. The unlawful and voluntary act must clearly be aimed at someone in order to eliminate cases of . . . careless or dangerous driving. Once, however, the jury are satisfied as to that, it matters not what the accused in fact contemplated as the probable result, or whether he ever contemplated at all, provided he was in law responsible and accountable for his actions. . . . On the assumption that he is accountable for his actions, the sole question is whether the unlawful and voluntary act was of such a kind that grievous bodily harm was the natural and probable result. The only test available for this is what the ordinary responsible man would, in all the circumstances of the case, have contemplated as the natural and probable result. . . .
>
> [T]here seems to be no ground on which the approach by the trial judge in the present case can be criticised. [H]e asked the jury to consider what were the exact circumstances at the time as known to the respondent and what were the unlawful and voluntary acts which he did towards the police officer. The learned judge then prefaced the passages of which complaint is made by saying, in effect, that if, in doing what he did, he must as a reasonable man have contemplated that serious harm was likely to occur then he was guilty of murder. . . . [O]nce the accused's knowledge of the circumstances and the nature of his acts have been ascertained, [absent] proof of incapacity to form an intent[, the defendant is responsible for] the natural and probable consequences of his acts. . . .

### 3. THE MODEL PENAL CODE DEFINITION

What were the analytic steps used in *Smith* to determine whether the defendant was culpable? Compare the Model Penal Code definition of negligence in § 2.02(2)(d):

> A person acts negligently with respect to a material element of an offense when he should be aware of a substantial and unjustifiable risk that the material element exists or will result from his conduct. The risk must be of such a nature and degree that the actor's failure to perceive it, considering the nature and purpose of his conduct and the circumstances known to him, involves a gross deviation from the standard of care that a reasonable person would observe in the actor's situation.

Are there substantial differences?

### 4. MODEL PENAL CODE RECKLESSNESS COMPARED

Compare the definition of recklessness in MPC § 2.02(2)(c):

> A person acts recklessly with respect to a material element of an offense when he consciously disregards a substantial and unjustifiable risk that the material element exists or will result from his conduct. The risk must be of such a nature and degree that,

> considering the nature and purpose of the actor's conduct and the circumstances known to him, its disregard involves a gross deviation from the standard of conduct that a law-abiding person would observe in the actor's situation.

What are the differences between Model Penal Code negligence and recklessness? Do they fairly track the difference in culpability standards adopted in *Faulkner* and *Cunningham*?

### 5. NEGLIGENCE AS A BASIS FOR CRIMINAL LIABILITY

There is disagreement in the literature about whether negligence can ever be a proper basis for criminal liability. The argument against the use of negligence proceeds from the premise that personal blameworthiness is the essential ethical predicate for the criminal sanction. H.L.A. Hart discusses this question in Punishment and Responsibility (1968). He starts by observing:

> "I didn't *mean* to do it: I just didn't think." "But you should have thought." Such an exchange, perhaps over the fragments of a broken vase destroyed by some careless action, is not uncommon; and most people would think that, in ordinary circumstances, . . . a rejection of "I didn't think" as an excuse is quite justified. . . . [I]t does not appear unduly harsh, or a sign of archaic or unenlightened conceptions of responsibility, to include gross, unthinking carelessness among the things for which we blame and punish. . . .

It follows that there is a morally significant difference, Hart concludes, between punishing people for unintended results that they thoughtlessly and carelessly caused and punishing them for unintended results that no exercise of reasonable care could have avoided. Most opponents of negligence as a basis for criminal liability concede this much, and respond with a point anticipated in Hart's next paragraph:

> To break your Ming china, deliberately or intentionally, is worse than to knock it over while waltzing wildly round the room and not thinking of what might get knocked over. . . . [S]howing that the damage was not intentional, but the upshot of thoughtlessness or carelessness, has its relevance as a mitigating factor affecting the quantum of blame or punishment.
>
> The question then becomes whether the quantum of moral blame that we assign to thoughtlessness or carelessness is sufficient to justify use of the criminal sanction. This is the fighting issue.

The argument in favor of negligence as an appropriate basis for criminal liability can proceed from two sorts of premises. The first is essentially utilitarian, based on the need for effective social control tempered by limitations based on blameworthiness.[b] The second is that liability for negli-

---

[b] See the argument by Holmes in Note 3 of the Introductory Notes preceding *Regina v. Faulkner*. At another point Holmes said: "[W]hereas . . . the question of knowledge is a question of the actual condition of the defendant's consciousness, the question of what he might have foreseen is determined by the standard of the prudent man, that is, by general experience. For it is to be remembered that the object of the law is [prevention and] the reason for this limitation is simply to make a rule which is not too hard for the average member of the community. As the purpose is to compel men to abstain from dangerous conduct, and not merely to restrain them from evil inclinations, the law requires them at their peril to know the teachings of common experience. . . . "

gence is consistent with other forms of liability based on blame. The argument is that the central characteristic that justifies blame in any case is present when liability is based on negligence. Hart takes this position. Criminal liability is appropriate in cases where the actor intended the harm caused or where there was foresight of consequences and the actor nonetheless took the risk that they would occur. Hart asks whether negligence is importantly different:

> [Consider] the case of a signalman whose duty it is to signal a train. . . . He may say after the disaster, "Yes, I went off to play a game of cards. I just didn't stop to think about the 10:15 when I was asked to play." [*I*]*f* anyone is *ever* responsible for *anything,* there is no general reason why men should not be responsible for such omissions to think, or to consider the situation and its dangers before acting.

Hart sees analytical similarities between liability for negligence and liability where there is foresight of consequences. He concludes that it is appropriate in both cases to assign blame because the defendant knew enough about the context to have behaved differently. The "quantum of blame" may be different for different levels of fault, to be sure, but the differences are of degree not of kind.[c]

## NOTES ON COMMON LAW TREATMENT OF MISTAKE OF FACT

### 1. "SPECIFIC" AND "GENERAL" INTENT

Early common law courts divided crimes into two categories for purposes of determining the relevance of certain defenses, among them the defense of mistake of fact. Modern legislatures in many American jurisdictions have either carried forward these or similar classifications, or by silence have left courts to continue their use.

The easiest category to understand consisted of crimes that required a "specific intent." The other category, basically, was "everything else." Crimes that did not fit into the "specific intent" category were said to require only "general intent." There is, however, an initial difficulty. Crimes do not come with a label of specific or general intent. Sometimes the definitions of crimes are completely silent as to whether the defendant's conduct must be accompanied by a particular state of mind. The rule normally is that such a crime will require mens rea anyway. Silence in the definition does not automatically signal whether the offense fits into the specific intent or the general intent category.

---

[c] Smith was sentenced to death. The case is much criticized for permitting that penalty based on the level of culpability upheld in the decision. The "quantum of blame" for that level of culpability, the argument goes, may well have justified a criminal conviction, but was insufficient to warrant such a severe penalty.

Professor Rhoda Berkowitz of the University of Toledo College of Law informed the editors that, in response to the curiosity of her students, she checked with the Home Office in England to find out whether Smith was actually executed. He was not. His sentence was commuted to life imprisonment. Did that solve the problem?

In any event, it appears that *Smith* no longer reflects English law on the mens rea for murder: "[I]n Franklin and Moore v. R, [1987] A.C. 576, the Privy Council . . . held that in so far as it laid down an objective test, *Smith* did not represent the common law of England. Though the Privy Council cannot formally overrule a decision of the House of Lords, it can probably be taken, for all practical purposes, that *Smith* is overruled." David Ormerod, Smith & Hogan Criminal Law 437 (11th ed. 1992).

Moreover, when a crime does include a specified state of mind requirement, often it is stated in a murky manner that—to borrow a phrase from Justice Cardozo from another context—can only be characterized as a "mystifying cloud of words."[a] *Faulkner* and *Cunningham* are examples. In neither case did the mens rea required by the court have any necessary relation to the words used in the definition of the offense.

But this is not the only potential confusion. A crime may have a perfectly understandable word in its definition—"knowingly," for example—but its legal meaning may have nothing to do with what the word ordinarily connotes.

Illustrations of these complexities are given below.

### *(i) Specific Intent Crimes*

Generally speaking, larceny and other theft crimes require an "intent to steal," that is, an intent to effect a permanent deprivation of another's property. In his 1881 book on The Common Law, Oliver Wendell Holmes defended this result:

> In larceny the consequences immediately flowing from the act are generally exhausted with little or no harm to the owner. Goods are removed from his possession by trespass, and that is all, when the crime is complete. But they must be permanently kept from him before the harm is done which the law seeks to prevent. A momentary loss of possession is not what has been guarded against with such severe penalties. What the law means to prevent is the loss of it wholly and forever, as is shown by the fact that it is not larceny to take for a temporary use without intending to deprive the owner of his property. If then the law punishes the mere act of taking, it punishes an act which will not of itself produce the evil effect sought to be prevented, and punishes it before that effect has in any way come to pass.
>
> The reason is plain enough. The law cannot wait until the property has been used up or destroyed in other hands than the owner's, or until the owner has died, in order to make sure that the harm which it seeks to prevent has been done. And for the same reason it cannot confine itself to acts likely to do that harm. For the harm of permanent loss of property will not follow from the act of taking, but only from the series of acts which constitute removing and keeping the property after it has been taken. After these preliminaries, the bearing of intent upon the crime is easily seen.
>
> According to Mr. Bishop, larceny is "the taking and removing, by trespass, of personal property which the trespasser knows to belong either generally or specially to another, with the intent to deprive such owner of his ownership therein. . . ."
>
> There must be an intent to deprive such owner of his ownership therein, it is said. But why? . . . The true answer is, that the

[a] Benjamin Cardozo, Law and Literature 101 (1931), quoted in context in the discussion of the Pennsylvania deliberation and premeditation formula for murder in Chapter X. Sometimes, it must be noted, the "mystifying cloud of words" might be held to signal a specific intent. Often, however, only "general" criminal intent will be implied.

> intent is an index to the external event which probably would have happened, and that, if the law is to punish at all, it must, in this case, go on probabilities, not on accomplished facts. The analogy to the manner of dealing with attempts is plain. Theft may be called an attempt to permanently deprive a man of his property, which is punished with the same severity whether successful or not. If theft can rightly be considered in this way, intent must play the same part as in other attempts. An act which does not fully accomplish the prohibited result may be made wrongful by evidence that but for some interference it would have been followed by other acts coordinated with it to produce that result. This can only be shown by showing intent. In theft the intent to deprive the owner of his property establishes that the thief would have retained, or would not have taken steps to restore, the stolen goods. . . .

As Holmes says, taking and carrying away the personal property of another, even without permission, does not warrant the severe sanctions of theft—unless the defendant intends to keep the property. Rather than wait until a permanent deprivation of the property has occurred, the criminal law intervenes at a point where possession has been obtained, accompanied by the intent to effect a permanent deprivation. It is this additional "specific intent" that makes the offense serious enough to be classified as theft.

To take a modern example, the specific intent to steal is the difference between car theft and joyriding. The specific intent required for larceny is an essential part of the definition of the offense. The punitive objectives of the law of theft are not implicated unless the offender has the particular state of mind required by the definition of the offense. The offense requires that the defendant engage in specified conduct (taking the car), with the intent to bring about a specified result that will occur in the future (permanent deprivation). The law intervenes before that result actually occurs, and convicts based on the combination of conduct and intent specified in the definition of the offense.

Burglary is another example of a specific intent crime. The common law definition of burglary ran something like this: "breaking and entering the dwelling house of another at night with the intent to commit a crime therein." Here the defendant engages in specified conduct (breaking and entering the dwelling house of another at night), with the specific intent to engage in further conduct (with the intent to commit a crime therein). The law chooses to intervene before that additional conduct has occurred, and measures its likelihood by asking whether the defendant intended its occurrence. Better not to wait until the additional crime is committed, the reasoning goes, but to punish based on the commission of a threatening act in a context where the defendant intends further criminal behavior.[b]

The paradigm example of a specific intent crime, then, is an offense where the definition describes specific behavior in which the defendant must engage, and further specifies a particular state of mind which must accompany that behavior. Examples would be an intention to cause a harmful result in the future (larceny), or an intention to engage in further crimi-

---

[b] It is likely that a given jurisdiction will have one or more lesser offenses (e.g., trespass, breaking and entering a building, breaking and entering a dwelling at night) that are committed if the defendant does not have the additional specific intent. These offenses will then be "graded" along a spectrum of potential punishments with burglary the most severe.

nal behavior (burglary).[c] The defendant who engages in the specified behavior is guilty if that state of mind exists. The defendant is not guilty if that state of mind is absent. The future events contemplated by the defendant, moreover, need not occur in order for the crime to be complete. They are not part of the actus reus of the offense.

### *(ii) General Intent Crimes*

It is much more difficult to specify the meaning of general intent. Typically, the mens rea required for general intent offenses is not spelled out at all, much less with clarity, in the definition of the offense or in any widely applied rule. The mens rea in general intent offenses also has chameleon-like characteristics. The tradition is that courts explicated the meaning of general intent, as they did specific intent, when the defendant raised a particular exculpatory defense. The precise meaning of general intent in connection with any given crime can therefore be determined only by careful reading of opinions that dispose of these exculpatory defenses. Moreover, one must be ever alert to the possibility that the meaning of general intent can change, even for the same crime, based on policies that govern the availability and scope of different defenses. The best that can be said by way of generalization has been said above. Some crimes require a specific intent. General intent crimes are "everything else."

### *(iii) The Mistake of Fact Rules*

A common defense raised in criminal cases concerns the defendant's misperception of factual circumstances that are made relevant by the definition of the crime. These circumstances may be part of the actus reus of the offense—that is, they must actually exist for the crime to be committed. Or they may be a required part of a specific intent, that is, the defendant must believe that they exist in order for a required specific intent to be satisfied. The question to be considered is what happens if the defendant is mistaken about such circumstances. The defendant thinks they do not exist, but in fact they do. The defendant gets the facts wrong.

Over time, the common law developed two default rules for dealing with the defense of mistake of fact. The specific intent rule is simple and logical. A specific intent is a special intent required for the commission of an offense. A mistake of fact is a defense if it shows that the required special intent did not exist. As the common law put it, a mistake of fact is a defense to a specific intent crime if it is honestly (that is, actually) made. A lie won't do, of course, but if the defendant claims that a mistake of fact shows the absence of a specific intent and the jury believes that assertion, the mistake is a defense.

The general intent rule can also be stated simply, but is subject to a number of qualifications. The rule says that a mistake of fact is a defense to a general intent crime if it is "honest and reasonable," that is, if the defendant actually made the mistake *and* if the mistake was reasonable under the circumstances. This approach imposes liability for negligence, and would be fairly simple to administer if it were consistently applied. But as illustrated below, the general intent rule needs to be studied in the context of different kinds of mistakes of fact in order to appreciate the subtleties in its application.

---

[c] As Note 4 below illustrates, this is not the only form that a specific intent can take.

### 2. SPECIFIC INTENT CRIMES: *GREEN V. STATE*

In Green v. State, 153 Tex.Cr.R. 442, 221 S.W.2d 612 (1949), the defendant drove into a woodland and killed several hogs. He loaded them into his car and took them home. The police arrived, identified the hogs as belonging to someone else, and returned them to their owner. The defendant was prosecuted for stealing the hogs. His defense was that he had hogs running on the range at the time and thought the hogs were his.

Larceny was defined as "taking and carrying away the personal property of another with intent permanently to deprive the other of the property." The defendant in *Green* unquestionably committed the actus reus of this offense—he clearly "took and carried away the personal property of another." But his testimony raised the question of whether he had the required "intent permanently to deprive the other of the property." At common law, the question to be put to the jury was one of fact: did Green actually have the intent to appropriate someone else's property? If he honestly thought the hogs were his, he did not have this intent and would be entitled to acquittal. An honest mistake of fact is a defense to a specific intent crime.

### 3. GENERAL INTENT CRIMES: *STATE V. WALKER*

In State v. Walker, 35 N.C.App. 182, 241 S.E.2d 89 (1978), the defendant was charged with child abduction. Prior cases established that the statute was violated only if neither parent consented to the abduction.

The defendant and his son picked up a seven-year-old boy and a five-year-old girl as the children were leaving a school bus in front of the school building. About five minutes later, the girl was found walking back to the school. The boy was still missing at the time of trial. The boy was the defendant's grandson. The appellate court dismissed the case as to his abduction on the ground that the father of the boy had participated in the abduction and had thereby given his consent. The girl, however, was unrelated to the two men. The defendant's contention as to her is revealed in the following excerpt from the court's opinion:

> [D]efendant contends that the trial judge erred in failing to instruct the jury on the defense of mistake of fact. In support of this argument defendant cites evidence tending to show that defendant and his son were operating under the mistaken belief that the female child whom they allegedly abducted was Joy Walker, the granddaughter of defendant.
>
> It is an elementary principle that general criminal intent is an essential component of every malum-in-se criminal offense. [A]n inference of general criminal intent is raised by evidence tending to show that the defendant committed the acts comprising the elements of the offense charged. [But if] an inference that the defendant committed the act without criminal intent is raised by the evidence then the [defendant is entitled to a jury instruction on mistake of fact.]
>
> An examination of the evidence presented by the defendant reveals that the general principles recited above are applicable to the present case. The defendant testified that when he took the little girl, Vickie Irby, he believed that she was his granddaugh-

ter, Joy Walker; that he discerned the true identity of the child after he and his son had driven one-half mile from the school; that upon realizing that the child was not his granddaughter, he returned to the school and let the child out of the automobile. According to this evidence, if the facts had been as the defendant supposed, he would have committed no crime in taking Joy Walker since he was acting under the authority and with the consent of her father. The evidence viewed in this light obviously permits the inference that defendant in taking Vickie Irby was laboring under a mistake as to the identity of the little girl which could negate any criminal intent. In appropriate cases, culpable negligence has been considered the equivalent of criminal intent. Accordingly, in order to negate criminal intent, the mistake under which the defendant was acting must have been made in good faith and with due care.

In accordance with the principles set forth, we hold that the trial judge erred in not declaring and explaining the law on a substantial feature of the case arising from the evidence that the defendant believed that he and his son were taking the latter's daughter, Joy Walker, when they were in fact taking Vickie Irby. . . .

The statute at issue in *Walker* punished a person who abducted a child without the consent of either parent. There was no special mens rea requirement in the language of the offense, indeed, no mens rea requirement at all. As the North Carolina courts had interpreted the statute, the crime of child abduction required only a general intent, which meant that an honest and reasonable mistake of fact was a defense. Since the defendant offered evidence that he had made such a mistake, he was entitled to a jury instruction on the issue. In the court's language, he was entitled to a defense if the mistake was "made in good faith and with due care."

The concept of general intent and its corresponding common law mistake of fact doctrine reflect the default culpability required for crime. Any given offense might require more culpability (a specific intent) or less culpability as to a specific actus reus element (strict liability) depending on its definition and the interpretational policies the courts think applicable. But the requirement of a general criminal intent was the customary starting point for reasoning about the appropriate mens rea for all actus reus elements of all serious crimes at common law.

## 4. "KNOW" AS A MENS REA REQUIREMENT

Variants of the word "know" frequently appear in crime definition.[d] Several points need to be understood about what they might mean.

Of course, they might mean that the defendant actually needs to know. That is, they might carry the meaning that could be found by looking the word up in a dictionary, something like "general awareness or possession of information." This meaning of "know" is not problematic. And this is what "know" means as a mens rea term—most of the time. The problem comes when it means something else.

[d] E.g., "knowing," "knowingly," "with knowledge that," etc.

As is the case with all mens rea words used by the common law, "know" or some variant of the word could be an artificial token that stands for a completely different concept. An example is provided by Pereira v. United States, 347 U.S. 1 (1954). In that case, the United States Supreme Court read the words "knowingly causes to be delivered by mail" in the federal mail fraud statute, 18 U.S.C. § 1341, to mean "where such use can reasonably be foreseen, even though not actually intended." We need not now be concerned with *why* "knowingly" was so read in that case. The lessons now are that "know" and its variants *are* sometimes read in non-intuitive ways and that there is no a priori way of figuring out whether they *will* be read that way (or some other way) by a particular court interpreting a particular crime. The beginning of wisdom is to be alert to the possibility of differing interpretations, and not to be lured into the false assumption that lawyers speak English. Only by being alert to such possibilities can one learn when and why the law means what it says and when and why it means something else.

The complexity does not end here. Sometimes "know" (whatever it means) is an express mens rea term included in the definition of an offense. *Pereira* is an example. Another example is given in the next Note. Sometimes, however, "know" (whatever it means) will be the required level of culpability even though the definition of the offense contains no reference to mens rea. An example of the latter is the crime involved in Staples v. United States, 511 U.S. 600 (1994).[e] The statute in that case, which was silent on mens rea, punished possession of certain unregistered weapons. The weapon involved in the case was a machine gun. The Court held that the defendant had to know (in the sense of actually being aware) that the weapon had the characteristics that made it a machine gun, that is, that it would fire repeatedly with a single pull of the trigger.

So "know" might or might not mean "know," and it might or might not be required when the statute makes no reference to mental state. What can be said to a fair degree of certainty is that when "know" means "know" in the ordinary sense, the crime is one of specific intent. A mistake of fact defense will be handled by applying the specific intent rule that the absence of such knowledge is exculpatory. The defendant must "know" that certain circumstances exist, and it will be a defense if the defendant lacks such "knowledge" due to an honest mistake of fact. The next Note provides an illustration.

### 5. FURTHER ILLUSTRATION OF SPECIFIC AND GENERAL INTENT CRIMES: *UNITED STATES V. OGLIVIE*

In United States v. Oglivie, 29 M.J. 1069 (1990), the United States Army Court of Military Review recited the facts:

> The appellant married his first wife, Amparo, in December 1986, while stationed in Panama. In January 1987, the appellant was reassigned from Panama to Germany, but his wife remained in Panama. While in Germany, the appellant did not know Amparo's address or telephone number, but sent letters to a friend, who passed them on to her. The appellant returned from Germany in March 1988 and was reassigned to Fort Sill, Oklahoma.

---

[e] *Staples* is discussed in Section 2 of Chapter IV in the Notes following *United States v. Freed*.

> In August 1988, the appellant sent his wife a money order with his telephone number written on it. The appellant filed for divorce in Oklahoma and sent a copy of the petition to a friend's post office box in Panama for delivery to his wife. In September or October 1988, Amparo called the appellant from Panama and informed him that she had filed for divorce in Panama, that there was "nothing between the two of us" and that he "didn't have to worry about her anymore." The appellant testified that he thought he was divorced at that point. In November 1988, the Red Cross notified the appellant that Amparo had been hospitalized. The Red Cross referred to Amparo as his "ex-wife." On 9 November 1988, the appellant requested that his basic allowance for quarters (BAQ) at the "with dependents" rate be terminated because he was divorced. . . . In December 1988, the appellant married Jackline, and requested that his BAQ at the "with dependents" rate be reinstated.

Oglivie's divorce from Amparo was not final at the time of his second marriage to Jackline. He was convicted for bigamy. He was also convicted on two counts of making a false official statement. The first statement was on November 9 when he told military officials that he was divorced from Amparo. The second was in December when he told officials that he was married to Jackline. He defended on the ground that he honestly believed that he was divorced from Amparo and that he was therefore legally married to Jackline.

The Court addressed the false statement offenses first:

> Making a false official statement in violation of UCMJ, Article 107, 10 U.S.C. § 907 (1982),[f] is a specific intent crime. An honest mistake of fact regarding the truth of the statement made is a defense. The evidence establishes that Amparo told the appellant she had filed for divorce, that the appellant received correspondence from the Red Cross referring to Amparo as his "ex-wife," and that he attempted to terminate his entitlement to BAQ, on the ground that he was divorced. He then participated in a marriage ceremony and received a marriage certificate indicating that he was married to Jackline. Based upon the entire record, we find that the defense of an honest mistake of fact was raised and not overcome by the government's evidence. Accordingly, we find that the evidence is insufficient to prove appellant's guilt of making false official statements. . . .

But as to the bigamy charge, the result was different:

> Bigamy is a general intent crime.[g] To constitute a defense to bigamy, a mistake of fact must be both honest and reasonable.

---

[f] "Any person subject to this chapter who, with intent to deceive, signs any false record, return, regulation, order, or other official document, knowing it to be false, or makes any other false official statement knowing it to be false, shall be punished as a court-martial may direct."—[Footnote by eds.]

[g] The Court added the following footnote on the definition of bigamy:

> Regarding the definition of bigamy, the Court of Military Appeals noted in United States v. Patrick, 7 C.M.R. 65, 67, 2 USCMA 189, 191 (1953): "There is no definition of bigamy in the punitive articles of the Uniform Code of Military Justice. However, the section on forms contained in the Manual for Courts-Martial, United States, 1951, describes the offense in terms substantially in accord with those of the common

While the appellant may have honestly believed that he was divorced from Amparo, we find that he did not take the steps which a reasonable man would have taken to determine the validity of his honest belief. He was not reasonable in assuming that he was divorced. . . . Accordingly, we find that the evidence is sufficient to prove bigamy.

*holding*

6.  GENERAL INTENT ELEMENTS OF SPECIFIC INTENT CRIMES:
    *UNITED STATES V. YERMIAN* (false statements on security clearance form)

There is an additional wrinkle to the specific intent rule. If a common law crime required a specific intent but the mistake of fact was relevant to an element of the offense other than the specific intent, the courts followed the rule for general intent. The specific intent mistake-of-fact rule, in other words, applied only to the specific intent.

For an example, consider United States v. Yermian, 468 U.S. 63 (1984). That case concerned the federal "false statements" offense, then defined as follows:

> Whoever, in any matter within the jurisdiction of any department or agency of the United States knowingly and willfully . . . makes any false . . . statements . . . shall be fined not more than $10,000 or imprisoned not more than five years, or both.

Everyone agreed that "knowingly and willfully" in this statute meant, in ordinary language, that defendants actually had to know that the statements were false. The offense therefore required a specific intent.

*facts*

Yermian knowingly made false statements on a security clearance form so that his answers would be consistent with false statements he had made in his application for employment. His [defense] was that he did not

*defense he did not know*

realize that his lies on the security clearance form related to a matter "within the jurisdiction of [a] department or agency of the United States." The District Court responded to the asserted defense by instructing the jury that it should convict if it found that the defendant "knew or should have known that the information was to be submitted to a government agency."

The common law methodology supports this result as follows. The false statements offense required a specific intent ("knowingly . . . makes any false . . . statements"). But the mistake of fact offered as a defense was not relevant to that requirement—the defendant admitted that he knowingly made false statements. The mistake was offered with regard to an element of the offense that was not part of the specific intent, i.e., that the false statement involved a "matter within the jurisdiction of" the United States. The general intent rules therefore applied, and the issue for the jury was

*jury instruction issue*

whether the defendant "honestly and reasonably" believed that the lies did not implicate the interests of the federal government. Or, as the District Court instructed, the jury was authorized to convict if it found that the defendant "knew or should have known" that the answers were relevant to the federal government's concerns.[h]

---

law—that is, that the accused entered into marriage, having at the time a lawful spouse then living."—[Footnote by eds.]

[h] Yermian appealed on the ground that the jury should have been told that "knowledge" (in the sense of "actually being aware of") was the required mens rea for the jurisdictional

## 7.   STRICT LIABILITY FOR GRADING ELEMENTS

The common law formulation of the mistake of fact rule for general intent crimes was usually qualified in the following manner:

> If an actor honestly and reasonably, although mistakenly, believed the facts to be other than they were, and if his conduct would not have been criminal had the facts been as he believed them to be, then his mistake is a defense if he is charged with a crime which requires "mens rea". . . .

Jerome Michael and Herbert Wechsler, Criminal Law and Its Administration 756 (1940).[i]

Consider the following hypothetical. Defendant commits a theft of jewelry actually worth $10,000. Defendant thinks the item is costume jewelry and fences it for $50. Assume that the defendant's belief is reasonable under the circumstances. If the dividing line between grand larceny and petty larceny is $500, should evidence of the defendant's "honest and reasonable" mistake of fact be admissible as a basis for reducing the conviction from grand to petty larceny?

The answer at common law was "no." Even though larceny is a specific intent offense, the value of the property relates to elements not included in the specific intent. Therefore the general intent rules apply to this mistake of fact.[j] The general intent rule, as formulated by Michael and Wechsler, would permit a mistake "honestly and reasonably made" to be a defense if, but only if, on the facts as the defendant believed them to be, no crime would have been committed. Here on the facts as the defendant believed them to be, at least petty larceny was being committed. For that reason, the mistake of fact defense as to the value of the property will be denied. In effect, strict liability is applied to the "grading" element of the offense—that is, to an element that differentiates one level of criminality from another. The defendant is punished on the basis of what was done, not what was intended or thought to have been done.

*general intent "no crime would be committed"*

## 8.   STRICT LIABILITY FOR INDEPENDENT MORAL WRONGS: *REGINA V. PRINCE* (statutory rape: taking of a girl under 16)

There were also crimes at common law that applied strict liability to elements that did not differentiate one grade of offense from another, but in which a so-called "independent moral wrong" would have been committed had the facts been as the defendant believed them to be. The most famous early example is Regina v. Prince, L.R. 2 C.C.R. 154 (1875).

---

element. The Supreme Court affirmed the conviction. The District Court's instruction was sufficient, the Court held, but may not have been necessary. This aspect of the case is considered when *Yermian* is revisited in Section 2 of Chapter IV.

[i]   Compare the statement in *State v. Walker* (quoted in context in Note 3 above) that "[a]ccording to [the] evidence, if the facts had been as the defendant supposed, he would have committed no crime in taking Joy Walker since he was acting under the authority and with the consent of her father."

[j]   See the discussion of *Yermian* in the preceding note.

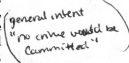

The defendant in *Prince* was indicted under a statute that read:

> Whosoever shall unlawfully take . . . any unmarried girl, being under the age of 16 years, out of the possession and against the will of her father . . . shall be guilty of a misdemeanor. . . .

The defendant committed the acts proscribed by this statute. The girl was 14, but the jury found that the defendant honestly and reasonably believed that she was 18. The question was whether that mistake should be a defense.

Conviction of the defendant was affirmed in four separate opinions. The one of relevance here[k] was written by Judge Bramwell, who reasoned that the conviction should be affirmed because Prince's conduct would have been morally wrong even if the girl had been 18. He explained:

> The act forbidden is wrong in itself, if without lawful cause; I do not say illegal, but wrong. . . . The legislature has enacted that if anyone does this wrong act, he does it at the risk of her turning out to be under 16. This opinion gives full scope to the doctrine of the mens rea. If the taker believed he had the father's consent, though wrongly, he would have no mens rea; so if he did not know she was in anyone's possession, nor in the care or charge of anyone. In those cases he would not know he was doing the *act* forbidden by the statute—an act which, if he knew she was in possession and in care or charge of anyone, he would know was a crime or not, according as she was under 16 or not.

Judge Bramwell's position was that since Prince knew enough about his conduct to make it morally wrongful, his mistake about the age of the girl should be irrelevant. To put the point another way, mens rea should be required for those elements central to the wrongfulness of the act. Liability should be strict as to the remaining elements of the offense.

The specific offense involved in *Prince* is dated, as is the social context in which it was decided. But the principle on which Judge Bramwell relied seems clear enough and, in some situations, assumed a life of its own in the early common law. In Ignorance and Mistake in Criminal Law, 88 U. Pa. L. Rev. 35, 62–65 (1939), Rollin Perkins argued that Judge Bramwell's view in *Prince* is reflected in the common law development of a number of other crimes. These are "extreme situations," he said, where a reasonable mistake has been made about a factual situation that would not have been a crime had the facts been as the defendant believed. The case most likely would have involved "a high degree of moral delinquency even under the supposed facts." The best examples he could give, again quite dated by now, were abduction and adultery:

> A man who has illicit sexual intercourse with a girl under the age of consent is guilty of statutory rape although she consented and he mistakenly believed she was older than the limit thus established. This is true no matter how reasonable his mistaken belief may have been, as in cases in which both her appearance and her positive statement indicated she was older than she was in fact, or in which he had exercised considerable pains in the effort to ascertain her age. One who has illicit intercourse with

---

[k] For a thorough consideration of the various opinions in *Prince,* see Glanville Williams, Criminal Law: The General Part 185–99 (2d ed. 1961).

> a married person is guilty of adultery even if he has no idea that the other is married. . . .

This does not mean, he continued, that these crimes have no mens rea component. It is possible to make an "innocent" mistake of fact even in such cases, an issue that has arisen most frequently in the context of adultery:

> If the intercourse is obviously illicit, the mistaken belief in the unmarried status of the other party is not an *innocent* mistake, however well grounded it may be, since the conduct falls far below the line of social acceptability even under the supposed facts. "In such a case there is a measure of wrong in the act as the defendant understands it, and his ignorance of the fact that makes it a greater wrong will not relieve him from the legal penalty." On the other hand, in spite of some indication to the contrary, it is clearly established that if the intercourse follows a marriage ceremony entered into in good faith, with no thought or reason to believe that the other party is already married, it does not constitute the crime of adultery if it does not occur after the mistake has been discovered.

9. QUESTIONS AND COMMENTS

Do the various common law positions on mistake of fact make sense? Do they follow a coherent set of policies? An appropriate set of policies?

Note that each of the mistake of fact situations described above relates to the defendant's perception of the circumstances in which the alleged offense was committed. Green's mistake was as to who owned the hogs, Walker's was as to the identity of his granddaughter, Yermian's was as to whether the federal government was interested in his truth-telling, etc. Mistake of fact defenses, in other words, arise in situations where the defendant admittedly engaged in the behavior defined as part of the offense, but claims to have been mistaken about the context or circumstances in which that behavior occurred.

Mistake of fact defenses occurence.

## SECTION 2: THE MODEL PENAL CODE

### INTRODUCTORY NOTES ON THE MODEL PENAL CODE

The Model Penal Code introduced a new vocabulary and a new approach to the mental elements of a crime. The approach is new both in analytical structure and in judgments of policy. It builds on the common law tradition, however, and works a skillful blending of the old and the new. By one report, at least 22 States have adopted culpability provisions derived from the Model Code.[a] The federal system and the remainder of the states still ground culpability in the common law, but even in these jurisdictions the Model Code has had an important impact on decisional law.

The Model Code abandons much of the terminology of the common law. It proposes instead a tightly integrated structure built on definitions

---

[a] See Dannye Holley, The Influence of the Model Penal Code's Culpability Provisions on State Legislatures: A Study of Lost Opportunities, Including Abolishing the Mistake of Fact Doctrine, 27 Sw. U. L. Rev. 229, 236–49 (1997).

that are more faithful to ordinary usage of language. The structure is difficult, at first imposingly so, and requires careful study.

## 1. THE CRIMINAL ACT

The starting point is the criminal act. The required criminal act is determined by careful reading of the definition of the offense. As at common law, the criminal act can consist of positive conduct, an omission where there is a duty to act, and possession. The common law voluntary act requirement is retained. See § 2.01.

In the initial analysis, elements of an offense that describe a mental state should temporarily be set aside. The act elements of the offense are characterized by the Model Code as combinations of "conduct," "circumstances," and "results." See § 1.13(9)(a).

"Conduct" elements describe the acts or omissions required to commit an offense. Examples are "takes, or exercises . . . control over" in theft as defined in § 223.2(1) of the Model Code, "enters" in the § 221.1(1) burglary offense, and the like. Every offense must contain some "conduct" as so defined, although sometimes the exact nature of the conduct is not described in the definition of the offense. For example, the act component of murder is any conduct (or omission in the face of a legal duty to act) that "causes" the death of another person. See §§ 210.1, 210.2. For murder, the "conduct" that must occur includes the total universe of behavior that causes the death of another. For offenses such as theft or burglary, by contrast, only conduct properly described as "takes," "exercises control over," "enters," etc., will suffice. In cases where the nature of the conduct elements is specifically designated in the definition of the offense, nice questions can arise as to whether they are satisfied. For example, does reaching through an open window (and breaking the plane fixed by the window) constitute "enters" for purposes of Model Penal Code burglary?

"Circumstance" elements consist of external facts that must exist in order for the crime to be committed. Theft as defined in § 223.2, for example, requires taking the "movable property of another." The circumstance elements are that the object taken must be "movable" property (do growing crops count?) of "another" (is partnership property included?). Sometimes, particularly in jurisdictions that base their criminal law on the Model Penal Code, such questions are answered in a definitional section of the criminal code. See, e.g., § 223.0. Other examples of circumstance elements would be "the dwelling of another at night" (is an occupied tent a dwelling? when does "night" begin?) if included in the definition of burglary, the status of a person as an FBI agent if included in a federal crime of killing an FBI agent, the age of the victim where made relevant by the definition of a crime, and so on.

"Result" elements are any consequences of the defendant's conduct that are incorporated in the definition of the offense. The obvious example is "the death of another human being" in murder. See §§ 210.1, 210.2. Other result elements would include "bodily injury to another," "serious bodily injury to another" or "fear of imminent serious bodily injury" as used in an assault statute. See § 211.1. Note that most offenses are defined only in terms of conduct and circumstances, with no required result. For example, only conduct and circumstance elements are contained in the Model Penal Code definitions of theft and burglary. Note also that, when a crime definition does include a "result" element, an additional requirement of a causal relationship between the defendant's conduct and the prohibited result is necessarily implied.

These three categories are somewhat arbitrary. It is not always clear how a particular element should be classified. For example, in rape as defined in § 213.1(1)(a) of the Model Penal Code, the actor is guilty if "he compels [the victim] to submit by force." Is it intuitively clear how each of these elements should be classified? Does the quoted phrase describe conduct or a result or both?

Fortunately, in most situations nothing turns on the proper classification of a given element. The principal purpose of adopting this structure is to ensure that lawyers, judges, and juries focus separately on each component of the offense rather than (as the common law was wont to do) treat the combination of conduct, circumstances, and results prohibited by a given offense as an undifferentiated whole. Separating the elements of an offense in this manner is an essential analytical step in approaching *every* criminal offense under the Model Code or any statute or definition of crime derived from it.[b]

There are some cases, however, (the crime of attempt is an example) where proper categorization of some elements is crucial. These cases are considered in due course below. For now, it would be wise to experiment with the classification scheme, and be aware of the ambiguities and difficulties that a given classification entails. To this end, a useful exercise is to select a variety of substantive offenses defined by the Model Code and, before reading on, to classify each element that does not prescribe a required state of mind as a conduct element, a result element, or a circumstance element. This exercise should be repeated until it becomes an automatic first step in *every* analysis of a problem under the Model Code or a statute based on the Model Code.

## 2. STATE OF MIND

The next step in the Model Penal Code analysis is to ascertain the state of mind required for commission of the offense. The Model Code is based on the proposition that four concepts are both necessary and sufficient to describe the state of mind required for the array of crimes punished by a penal code. They are "purpose," "knowledge," "recklessness," and "negligence." Each of these terms is carefully defined. A fifth possibility is "none of the above." In rare instances—an example is provided by the combination of § 213.1(1)(d) and § 213.6(1)—the Model Penal Code imposes strict liability for a circumstance element of an offense. The default, absent an explicit statement to the contrary, is that one of the four prescribed mental state requirements will apply.

The state of mind required for a given crime is determined by ascertaining which one of these four concepts applies to *each* of the conduct, circumstance, and result elements of the offense and by adding any other specifically prescribed state of mind requirement that is contained in the definition of the offense. Thus, absent an explicit statement to the contrary, once the crime is broken down into its conduct, circumstance, and result components, one of the four defined culpability concepts will be applied to

[b] It can be a useful exercise in a common law jurisdiction as well. Often translating a common law rule into the Model Code vocabulary—and analyzing it under the Model Code methodology—can lead to clearer understanding of the content of the common law rule.

each in order to determine the state of mind required for that offense. And there may be yet an additional mental element of the offense specifically stated in its definition.

For example, theft under § 223.2(1) of the Model Penal Code applies to one who "unlawfully takes, or exercises unlawful control over, movable property of another with purpose to deprive him thereof." One would first classify "takes" and "exercises control over" as conduct elements, and ask whether that conduct has occurred. One would then ask which of the four state-of-mind terms applies to each of these elements. The same analysis would be followed for the circumstance elements "movable property" and "of another."[c] One could then describe the mental state required for theft as consisting of the sum of all of these requirements *plus* the specified purpose to effect a permanent deprivation.

At this point, careful study of the provisions of § 2.02 is required. The notes following the text of the Code explicate their meaning.

## MODEL PENAL CODE CULPABILITY PROVISIONS

### Section 2.02. General Requirements of Culpability

(1) Minimum Requirements of Culpability. Except as provided in Section 2.05, a person is not guilty of an offense unless he acted purposely, knowingly, recklessly or negligently, as the law may require, with respect to each material element of the offense.

(2) Kinds of Culpability Defined.

(a) Purposely.

A person acts purposely with respect to a material element of an offense when:

(i) if the element involves the nature of his conduct or a result thereof, it is his conscious object to engage in conduct of that nature or to cause such a result; and

(ii) if the element involves the attendant circumstances, he is aware of the existence of such circumstances or he believes or hopes that they exist.

(b) Knowingly.

A person acts knowingly with respect to a material element of an offense when:

---

[c] The word "unlawfully" in the definition of theft defies classification as a "conduct," "result," or "circumstance" element. It is designed to refer to conditions under which it is permissible to "take" or "exercise control over" property of another with intent to keep it. Otherwise, for example, assuming control over a gift would arguably amount to a theft, perhaps depending on when title passed. Compare § 212.3 of the Model Code ("A person commits a misdemeanor if he knowingly restrains another unlawfully so as to interfere substantially with his liberty"). Without the word "unlawfully," a law enforcement officer would violate this provision by making a lawful arrest.

Generally speaking, when used in the definition of a crime, "unlawfully" or a variant is a fair proxy for "without lawful justification." It builds into the definition of the offense a rationale for excluding a variety of circumstances under which innocent behavior would otherwise be criminal. Viewed another way, a word like "unlawfully" builds into the definition of an offense a hook on which the courts can hang justification defenses in situations where the definition of the offense might literally apply but where a criminal conviction would be inappropriate.

(i) if the element involves the nature of his conduct or the attendant circumstances, he is aware that his conduct is of that nature or that such circumstances exist; and

(ii) if the element involves a result of his conduct, he is aware that it is practically certain that his conduct will cause such a result.

(c) Recklessly.

A person acts recklessly with respect to a material element of an offense when he consciously disregards a substantial and unjustifiable risk that the material element exists or will result from his conduct. The risk must be of such a nature and degree that, considering the nature and purpose of the actor's conduct and the circumstances known to him, its disregard involves a gross deviation from the standard of conduct that a law-abiding person would observe in the actor's situation.

(d) Negligently.

A person acts negligently with respect to a material element of an offense when he should be aware of a substantial and unjustifiable risk that the material element exists or will result from his conduct. The risk must be of such a nature and degree that the actor's failure to perceive it, considering the nature and purpose of his conduct and the circumstances known to him, involves a gross deviation from the standard of care that a reasonable person would observe in the actor's situation.

(3) Culpability Required Unless Otherwise Provided. When the culpability sufficient to establish a material element of an offense is not prescribed by law, such element is established if a person acts purposely, knowingly or recklessly with respect thereto.

(4) Prescribed Culpability Requirement Applies to All Material Elements. When the law defining an offense prescribes the kind of culpability that is sufficient for the commission of an offense, without distinguishing among the material elements thereof, such provision shall apply to all the material elements of the offense, unless a contrary purpose plainly appears.

(5) Substitutes for Negligence, Recklessness and Knowledge. When the law provides that negligence suffices to establish an element of an offense, such element also is established if a person acts purposely, knowingly or recklessly. When recklessness suffices to establish an element, such element also is established if a person acts purposely or knowingly. When acting knowingly suffices to establish an element, such element also is established if a person acts purposely. . . .

(7) Requirement of Knowledge Satisfied by Knowledge of High Probability. When knowledge of the existence of a particular fact is an element of an offense, such knowledge is established if a person is aware of a high probability of its existence, unless he actually believes that it does not exist. . . .

### Section 2.04. Ignorance or Mistake

(1) Ignorance or mistake as to a matter of fact or law is a defense if:

(a) the ignorance or mistake negatives the purpose, knowledge, belief, recklessness or negligence required to establish a material element of the offense; or

(b) the law provides that the state of mind established by such ignorance or mistake constitutes a defense. . . .

## NOTES ON THE MODEL PENAL CODE CULPABILITY STRUCTURE

### 1. MINIMUM REQUIREMENTS OF CULPABILITY

Section 2.02(1) is the heart of the Model Penal Code culpability structure. It must be read repeatedly and carefully. The following comments elaborate on its provisions.

#### *(i) Strict Liability*

Section 2.05, to which reference is made in the opening phrase, is the Model Penal Code's response to the "public welfare" offenses described by Justice Jackson in Morissette v. United States, 342 U.S. 246 (1952).[a] These are minor offenses that the Model Code calls "violations." Under § 1.04, violations are not "crimes" and carry only fines, forfeitures, or other civil penalties. The culpability structure does not apply to violations, which means that liability for them may be "strict." For present purposes, these types of offenses can be ignored.

#### *(ii) Types of Culpability*

Section 2.02(1) introduces the four mainstays of the culpability structure—purpose, knowledge, recklessness, and negligence. Each of these terms is defined in § 2.02(2). Common law terms that describe the state of mind for criminality are discarded.

The provision of only four basic levels of culpability—five if you count strict liability—represents an important insight. The Model Code position is that these concepts are both necessary and sufficient—necessary because the distinctions among them are required as a basis for crime definition and grading, and sufficient because additional generalized discriminations would be superfluous. This proposition can be tested by asking whether all of the concepts encountered in previously studied cases decided within the common law tradition can be translated into one or more of these ideas.

#### *(iii) "As the Law May Require"*

The phrase "as the law may require" refers to the analytical process for determining which culpability levels are to be applied to each of the conduct, circumstance, and result elements of an offense. This process is described in detail below.

---

[a] *Morissette* is a main case in Section 1 of Chapter IV.

### *(iv) Material Element*

The term "material element" is defined in § 1.13(9) and § 1.13(10). The important point for present purposes is that the definition explicitly includes "(i) such conduct or (ii) such attendant circumstances or (iii) such a result of conduct as . . . is included . . . in the definition of the offense." Section 1.13 thus establishes the need to divide a criminal offense into its conduct, circumstance, and result components.

### *(v) "Each" Material Element*

"Each" may be the most important word in § 2.02(1). It requires that a level of mens rea—purpose, knowledge, recklessness, or negligence[b]—be applied to "each" conduct, circumstance, and result element of an offense. Each conduct, circumstance, and result element of an offense will thus have its own culpability requirement.

As an analytical matter, this represents one of the most important contributions of the Model Code. Thinking about culpability separately for each element of an offense permits far more precision than was achieved by the common law. This is true both for legislatures as they specify what the law should be and for courts and juries as they implement legislative decisions. Note that this analytical insight does not require the legislature to select any particular level of fault for any particular element of a crime. The legislature is completely free to choose any one of the levels anytime, or indeed to impose strict liability if the policy of the offense calls for it. The structure simply requires that the mens rea question be *asked* for each element. It does not itself give the answer to that question. The answer is provided by the interaction of the remaining provisions of § 2.02 with the definition of the individual offense. By careful drafting and attention to the structure established by § 2.02, the legislature can achieve any result that it desires.

## 2. PURPOSE

"Purpose" is defined in the ordinary-language sense of conscious objective or desire. Many enactments based on the Model Code have used the word "intent" to mean the same thing.

Why has the Model Code defined this term differently for conduct and result elements on the one hand and circumstance elements on the other? The answer lies in common sense. Circumstances cannot be "intended." They concern matters external to the actor that either exist or do not exist (property does or does not belong to another; it is or is not night; the victim is or is not a specified age; the victim is or is not a public officer). The actor can, of course, *believe or hope* that property belongs to another, that it is night, or that the victim is a certain age. And the actor can make a mistake—i.e., can believe or hope for that which is not true. But it strains the ordinary use of language, the Model Code drafters thought, to say that a defendant has a purpose that it now be nighttime.

---

[b] As was pointed out above, occasionally, but only occasionally, the Model Penal Code will impose strict liability for an element, that is, it will not require any level of culpability for a particular element of an offense. In the rare cases where this is done, the definition of the offense is explicit. For an example, see § 213.6(1) (age below 10 in sex offenses). This, then, is "as the law may require" for this particular offense.

### 3. KNOWLEDGE

"Knowledge" is defined as awareness. Why in this case are conduct and circumstances distinguished from results? The answer is that one cannot "know" with certainty that results will flow from conduct. Common experience will indicate a degree of likelihood, but cause and effect are always matters of probability.

For a result element, "knowledge" under the Model Code is satisfied if the actor is "practically certain" that the result will follow. Whether the result is desired is irrelevant to such knowledge, though of course it would be relevant to whether there was a purpose to cause the result. For most offenses, this subtle difference between "purpose" and "knowledge" is unimportant. It is rare for the definition of an offense to distinguish between them.

### 4. RECKLESSNESS

Application of the Model Code concept of recklessness requires careful dissection of the definition in § 2.02(2)(c). Unlike "purpose" and "knowledge," "recklessness" applies in the same terms to conduct, circumstances, and results. It is also unlike "purpose" and "knowledge" in a more important respect. Deciding whether the defendant had a purpose to do something or knew that an external circumstance existed requires the jury to make only a finding of fact—the defendant either had the required purpose or knowledge or did not. Asking a jury to determine whether a defendant was "reckless," by contrast, requires it both to find facts and to make a judgment. In this case, the jury is asked to apply a set of criteria to the defendant's beliefs and actions, and to make a judgment whether the defendant fell sufficiently below community standards of behavior to warrant criminal punishment.

Section 2.02(2)(c) requires that the risk that an element of the offense will occur be "substantial" and "unjustifiable." Obviously relevant to a judgment that a risk should not have been taken are the likelihood or predictability that the risk will be realized and the justifications one might have for taking it. Physicians, for example, are frequently called upon to take very substantial risks, but such risks can be entirely justifiable given the alternatives. What the jury must decide is how "substantial" the risk was and how "justifiable" it might have been to take the risk in the context of the defendant's behavior. To be guilty of an offense that requires recklessness, the defendant must be aware of the facts that make the risk substantial and the facts that make it unjustifiable.

But this is not the end of the inquiry. In effect, the jury must decide that given the context, the defendant should not have taken the risk and should be subject to criminal punishment for having done so. This it does by applying the criteria in the second sentence of the definition. It must consider "the nature and purpose of the actor's conduct and the circumstances known to him," and in that light decide whether disregarding the risk "involves a gross deviation from the standard of conduct that a law-abiding person would observe in the actor's situation."

The word "situation" contains an important and deliberate ambiguity. Suppose, for example, the defendant has a physical condition that impairs perception or judgment. Should that be relevant in deciding whether taking the risk was a "gross deviation" from law-abiding behavior? The drafters of the Model Code opted not to resolve this question in advance, but to leave the matter to judicial evolution. The function of the word "situation" is to permit the courts to personalize the standard where mitigation or exoneration based on individual characteristics of the offender would not undermine the functions of the criminal law. This problem surfaces in many places and raises policy questions of the most fundamental kind.

Some final observations should be added about the relationship between the definitions of knowledge and recklessness. For result elements, there is a fine line between one who is "practically certain" that a result will occur (knowledge) and one who "consciously disregards a substantial and unjustifiable risk" that it will take place (recklessness). Is the line too fine? Maybe it is, but the issue is of limited practical significance. Most cases turning on the occurrence of results involve one or another form of criminal homicide. There are special rules to manage this problem in the law of homicide, even under the Model Penal Code.[c] Few offenses other than homicide turn on results actually caused, and even fewer turn on the difference between results caused knowingly and results caused recklessly. The issue can arise, however, as in the provisions of § 211.1(2)(b) of the Model Code, which defines aggravated assault as occurring, inter alia, when one "knowingly causes bodily injury to another with a deadly weapon."

Another subtlety in the relationship between knowledge and recklessness is raised by § 2.02(7). It is there stated that when knowledge "of the existence of a particular fact" (as opposed to knowledge that a result will follow) is an element of an offense, such knowledge is established if the defendant "is aware of a high probability of its existence, unless he actually believes that it does not exist." This language endorses the concept of "willful blindness," originally developed in English law. The issue would arise, for example, in a case where the defendant is offered $5,000 to drive a car across the Mexican-American border. If the car is found to contain illegal drugs, the defendant might not be heard to assert ignorance of that fact as a defense to a crime that requires that the defendant know that drugs are being transported or possessed.[d]

## 5. NEGLIGENCE

The major difference between recklessness and negligence is that negligence is based on inattention to risk. To be reckless, the defendant must be "consciously aware" of the risk. To be negligent, it is enough that the defendant "should have been aware" of the risk. Otherwise, the analysis is the same. The jury decides whether the risks were substantial and unjustifiable and whether the defendant should have been aware of them. And considering "the nature and purpose of the actor's conduct and the circumstances known to him," the jury must decide whether disregarding the risk "involves a gross deviation from the standard of care that a reasonable person would observe in the actor's situation."[e]

---

[c] These special rules are dealt with in the homicide chapter.

[d] "Willful blindness" is the subject of a main case, *United States v. Heredia*, in Chapter IV, Section 3.

[e] No explanation is offered in the Commentary to the Model Code for why "reasonable person" is used for negligence and "law-abiding person" for recklessness. Nor is it explained why "standard of conduct" is used in the definition of recklessness as opposed to "standard of care" in the definition of negligence.

## 6. HIERARCHY OF MODEL PENAL CODE CULPABILITY TERMS

Section 2.02(5) ranks the four Model Code culpability terms, with purpose as the most culpable and negligence the least. If negligence is the mens rea required for a given element, the prosecution can establish its case by proving purpose, knowledge, recklessness, or negligence. Plainly, if negligence is sufficient, the defendant is *more* culpable, not less, if purpose, knowledge, or recklessness can be proved. Similarly, if recklessness is required by the definition of a particular offense, proof of knowledge or purpose also suffices. Section 2.02(5) thus stands for the common sense proposition that if the prosecutor proves the defendant more blameworthy than is required by the offense charged, the defendant should be convicted.

## 7. OFFENSE SILENT AS TO STATE OF MIND

Section 2.02(3) establishes a drafting convention and an important substantive conclusion. These two points deserve separate consideration.

Section 2.02(3) states that recklessness is the minimum culpability required for every conduct, circumstance, and result element, absent legislative direction to the contrary in a particular offense definition. As a drafting matter, this specification is a great convenience. It establishes a default rule. It eliminates the necessity to spell out the culpability requirement for each separate element of an offense and thus makes the drafting process less cumbersome. It permits implementation of an important analytical insight of the Model Code—that the legislature should establish the required culpability for each conduct, circumstance, and result element of an offense in the definition of the crime—without unnecessary verbiage.

In thinking about the practical implications of this requirement, bear in mind the hierarchy point in the preceding Note. Normally defendants will know perfectly well what they are doing (e.g., they will know they are breaking into a house). A default requirement of recklessness for "breaking" and "house" means only that recklessness is the *minimum* culpability that will satisfy the definition of the offense. A defendant who is *more* culpable—who knows when recklessness will do—is plainly guilty and plainly deserving of conviction.

Section 2.02(3) also expresses an important substantive judgment. In general, those who formulated the Model Code thought that recklessness was the appropriate minimum culpability level for any conduct, circumstance, and result element of any crime. They did not disapprove of liability based on negligence—the proscription of negligent homicide in § 210.4 and the assault provision in § 211.1(1)(b) belie that conclusion—but they thought that liability based on negligence should be the exception rather than the rule and should be the result of specific legislative command.

It should be added that § 2.02(3) is defended in the Commentary to the Code as a statement of the usual common law mens rea default.[f] Whether this assertion is descriptively accurate is doubtful. It certainly does not accurately capture the common law position on mistakes of fact in general intent crimes. Notwithstanding its inadequacy as a description of the common law, § 2.02(3) expresses an important normative proposition, the correctness of which can be debated independently of the common law tradi-

---

[f] ALI, Model Penal Code and Commentaries, § 2.02, p. 244 (1985) (Subsection (3) "accepts as the basic norm what usually is regarded as the common law position").

tion and of the analytical structure established by the Model Code culpability provisions.

## 8. AMBIGUOUS CULPABILITY PROVISIONS

A second drafting convention is established by § 2.02(4). It is intended merely to resolve linguistic ambiguities, but its application is sometimes confusing. Four illustrations are given below: the first two are situations where the application of § 2.02(4) presents little difficulty; the third is a straightforward application of § 2.02(3); the last raises a common point of confusion as to how § 2.02(3) and § 2.02(4) should be applied where the answer intended by the drafters of the Model Code is clear but the text of § 2.02(4) is not.

### *(i) False Imprisonment*

State v. Walker, 35 N.C.App. 182, 241 S.E.2d 89 (1978), is described above in the Notes on Mistake of Fact and the Common Law. The defendant and his son abducted a seven-year-old boy and a five-year-old girl as they were leaving a school bus in front of their school. About five minutes later the girl was found walking back to the school. The boy was still missing at the time of trial. The boy, it turned out, was the defendant's grandson. The court held that his abduction was not criminal because the boy's father participated in the episode and, as the father, was entitled to take custody of his own son. But the girl was unrelated to the two men. The defense in *Walker* was that the two men also thought it was lawful to take the girl because they thought she was the boy's sister. When they found out that she was not, they let her go.

What would be the result if the father and grandfather are prosecuted under § 212.3 of the Model Penal Code, which punishes one who "knowingly restrains another unlawfully so as to interfere substantially with his liberty"? Would they be able to defend on the ground that they thought the girl was their daughter and granddaughter, respectively? The answer, if the jury believes the defendants, is "yes."

The first step in reaching this result is to apply § 2.02(4) to the definition of the offense. The key to understanding § 2.02(4) is to begin, as in all cases, by breaking out the conduct, circumstance, and result elements of the offense. Here, there are four: "restrains," "another [person]," "unlawfully," and "so as to interfere substantially with his liberty." The next step is to ask why the word "knowingly" is included in the definition of the offense. The answer is that it *at least* establishes that the defendant must know that the restraint has occurred.

With respect to the mental element intended for the other three elements, however, § 212.3 is ambiguous. One cannot tell from reading the definition of the offense whether the legislature meant for the word "knowingly" to be confined to the word it immediately modifies ("restrains") or whether it was included as a shorthand way of saying that one must know about the entire transaction, i.e., one must know that another person is being restrained in a substantial manner and must know the facts that make the restraint unlawful. In the ordinary usage of language, either meaning could have been intended.

Section 2.02(4) was included for the purpose of resolving such an ambiguity—*and only for that purpose*. It applies *only* when a culpability term clearly applies to one element of an offense and it is not clear from the wording whether it is also meant to apply to others. It is designed to remove all doubt about how far down a sentence a particular culpability term was meant to travel. Section 2.02(4) says that "unless a contrary purpose plainly appears," a term that clearly applies to one of the conduct, circumstance, and result elements of an offense will also apply to others that follow. Since it is not clear from reading the definition in § 212.3 whether "knowingly" was meant to apply only to "restrains" or whether it was also meant to apply to the elements contained in the rest of the sentence, it should be applied to all of them. A legislature that does not want this result can achieve its purpose by rewording the offense.

Under § 2.02(4), therefore, "knowledge" would apply to "unlawfully." To be guilty in the *Walker* situation posed above, the defendants must "know" the facts that make it "unlawful" for the restraint to occur. Except in unusual circumstances not shown to be present here, it is not unlawful for a father to restrain his own children or for a grandfather to do so in the father's presence and with his consent. So the result under these provisions of the Model Penal Code is that the defendants must have known, respectively, that the girl was not their daughter or granddaughter. If the jury believes the defense assertions about the identity of the girl, they should be acquitted.

The provisions of § 2.04(1)(a) should also be examined in connection with this hypothetical. Notice that § 2.04(1)(a) in effect states the reciprocal of § 2.02. If § 2.02 requires knowledge for a certain element, then § 2.04(1)(a) provides a defense if the defendant does not know that the element exists. In the *Walker* hypothetical, § 2.04(1)(a) provides a mistake of fact defense based on lack of knowledge because the application of § 2.02(4) establishes that the defendants must "know" that the restraint was "unlawful." Mistakes of fact under the common law provide a defense when they satisfy a complex series of doctrinal rules. Mistakes of fact under the Model Penal Code are defenses based on a logical corollary. Once one knows the culpability standard for the relevant element, it is a defense if the defendant lacked that level of culpability because of a mistake of fact.

Consider one more point. On the facts of *Walker* as they actually evolved, is there another defense these defendants might be able to assert to a charge of violating § 212.3 if the jury disbelieves them on this one?

### *(ii) Reckless Burning*

Section 220.1(2)(a) punishes one who "purposely starts a fire . . . and thereby recklessly places another person in danger of death or bodily injury." If Faulkner were charged with this offense, could he defend on the ground that it was not his objective to place other persons in danger of death or bodily injury? Does § 2.02(4) mean that the defendant must "purposely" create the danger of death or bodily injury to another? Plainly not. Here the definition of the offense is clear that "recklessly" modifies the element "places another person in danger of death or bodily injury," and there is no ambiguity with respect to this element for § 2.02(4) to resolve. As applied to the facts of *Faulkner*, the question under § 220.1(2)(a) would be whether Faulkner was reckless in placing others in danger of death or injury.

Again consider one more point. On the facts of *Faulkner* as they actually evolved, is there another defense that Faulkner might be able to assert if charged with a violation of § 220.1(2)(a)?

### *(iii) Escape*

Section 242.6(1) covers one who "fails to return to official detention following temporary leave granted for a . . . limited period." What culpability is established for the "limited period" element of the offense? Must the defendant know that the length of time for which leave was granted has expired? The answer is that "recklessness" applies. No culpability term is included in the definition of the offense, and § 2.02(3) provides that recklessness is required as to all of the conduct, circumstance, and result elements of the offense in such a case.

### *(iv) Hindering Prosecution*

The preceding illustrations are straightforward. This next one is more complicated.

Section 242.3(5) provides that a person commits an offense "if, with purpose to hinder the apprehension, prosecution, conviction or punishment of another for crime, he . . . volunteers false information to a law enforcement officer." Consider a situation where, in order to prevent the apprehension of a fugitive, the defendant tells everyone who asks that the fugitive was seen in California last week. In fact, the defendant knows that the fugitive is still in Chicago. If the defendant said this to a plainclothes police officer and was charged under § 242.3(5), on what basis could the defense that the defendant was unaware that the person lied to was "a law enforcement officer" be successful? The answer is that recklessness is the standard for this element. The defense would fail if the defendant was reckless as to whether the lie was told to a law enforcement officer.

How is this answer derived? Section 2.02(4) could be misunderstood to say that if a culpability term is used anywhere in the definition of the offense, it applies to every element of the offense "unless a contrary purpose plainly appears." Under this reading, purpose would apply to all elements of § 242.3(5) since the defendant must have a "purpose to hinder" and since there is no indication that this purpose need not accompany the commission of each element of the offense. Since "purpose" is the same as "knowledge" when applied to circumstance elements (see § 2.02(2)(a)(ii)), "knowledge" would be required for the circumstance element "law enforcement officer" under this reading of § 2.02(4).

Although this may be a plausible reading of § 2.02(4), it is not what the drafters intended. The intended reading can be derived from the following reasoning. Again, the first step is to isolate the conduct, circumstance, and result elements of the offense. Here, they are "volunteers," "false information," and "law enforcement officer." All of these elements must coexist in order for this crime to occur. The next step is to ask whether there are any words in the offense which indicate that purpose, knowledge, recklessness, or negligence was meant by the legislature to apply to one of these elements. *There are no such words in the definition of this offense.* Here, the culpability phrase in the definition of the offense is not designed to provide that purpose, knowledge, recklessness, or negligence is the culpability standard for any one of the three specific elements isolated in the first step of the analysis. It does not say whether purpose, knowledge, recklessness, or negligence is the culpability level for "volunteers," for "false information," or for "law enforcement officer." What it does, instead, is describe an additional objective or motive that must accompany the defendant's conduct. The defendant must, in effect, hope that the volunteering of false information will have the described impact on law enforcement. That impact need not in fact occur. The defendant is still guilty even if the officer disbelieves the defendant and does nothing in response to the false information. The desire to hinder law enforcement must exist, moreover, independently of any culpability that may or may not be required for each of the other three elements of the offense.

The intent of the drafters of § 2.02(4) is that additional motives or purposes of this sort (which the common law called a specific intent) should be ignored in applying the drafting conventions of § 2.02. Such motives or purposes are independent of the culpability that is required for the remaining elements of the offense. They are simply additional mental states required for the offense to occur. Section 242.3(5) has no culpability words that are designed to supply the required state of mind for the independent requirements that the defendant engage in activity that fits the words "volunteers," "false information," and "law enforcement officer." Independently of a purpose to hinder law enforcement, it is possible for the defendant to have a purpose to do all these things, to know that they are being done, or to be reckless or negligent as to these elements of the offense. Which of these culpability levels is required is not specified in the definition of the offense for any one of these elements, and there is therefore no linguistic ambiguity for § 2.02(4) to resolve. Since the offense is silent as to the required culpability for these elements, the default provisions of § 2.02(3) establish that recklessness applies to the "law enforcement officer" element.[g] Recklessness would also apply to whether the information was false and whether it was volunteered.

Contrast the situation that would occur if the definition of the offense were "if, with purpose to hinder the apprehension, prosecution, conviction or punishment of another for crime, he knowingly volunteers false information to a law enforcement officer." In that case, the function of the word "knowingly" would be at least to prescribe the level of culpability required for the element "volunteers." And the sentence would be ambiguous as to whether "knowingly" was meant to apply only to this element or whether the legislature meant that the defendant must also know both that the information was false and that it was delivered to a law enforcement officer. If this were the definition of the offense, the culpability for "law enforcement officer" would be "knowledge," derived from the provisions of § 2.02(4) as in the false imprisonment example given above.

Compare the definition of falsely incriminating another in § 241.5. The crime is committed if one "knowingly gives false information to any law enforcement officer with purpose to implicate another." By the reasoning

---

[g] The commentary uses a burglary example to make this point, concluding that the "purpose to commit a crime therein" required by § 221.1 does not establish the culpability for the additional elements "dwelling house" and "night." The commentary concludes that § 2.02(4) "is designed to apply . . . only to offenses where a particular culpability requirement is stated in such a way as to make it unclear whether the requirement applies to all of the material elements of an offense or only to the material element it introduces." ALI, Model Penal Code and Commentaries § 2.02, p. 246 (1985). The culpability level for "dwelling house" and "night" would therefore be recklessness, derived by applying § 2.02(3) to those elements.

outlined above, the culpability for the element "law enforcement officer" would be "knowledge" because of the provisions of § 2.02(4).

If the word "knowingly" were omitted from the definition in § 241.5 and it was otherwise worded the same way, the culpability for "law enforcement officer" would be "recklessness." Section 2.02(4) would not apply, and the answer would be derived from § 2.02(3). But suppose the offense definition were changed to read "with purpose to implicate another, gives false information to any law enforcement officer." What culpability for "law enforcement officer" then? The answer is that it would still be "recklessness." Moving the "with purpose to" clause around in the sentence would not change the analysis. The clause would still serve to describe what the common law would call a specific intent, there would be no work for § 2.02(4) to do because there is no relevant ambiguity to be resolved, and the culpability for this element would be supplied by the default provisions of § 2.02(3). If the legislative objective were to make recklessness apply to the falsity of the information and knowledge to the law enforcement officer element, it could rewrite the offense to say "with purpose to implicate another, gives false information to any person known to be a law enforcement officer." It still would not matter for any of these variations whether the "with purpose to" clause were at the beginning or the end of the sentence.

## 9. MISTAKE OF FACT

As illustrated by the false imprisonment example given above, § 2.04(1)(a) states a tautology. If an offense requires a prescribed mental state for a given element, it is a defense if the defendant did not have that mental state.[h] If knowledge is the culpability for a given element, it is a defense if the defendant did not know. If recklessness is the culpability level, it is a defense if the defendant was not reckless. And so on.

The application of § 2.04(1)(a) is therefore totally dependent on an accurate determination of the level of culpability required for the element at issue. If the analysis described above is properly applied and the appropriate culpability level determined for each conduct, circumstance, and result element of the offense, the significance of a mistake of fact automatically follows. Section 2.04(1)(a) merely confirms what logic would dictate.

Notice another aspect of the Model Penal Code treatment of mistakes of fact. The common law default for general intent crimes provides a defense if the mistake is "honest and reasonable." That rule imposes liability for ordinary negligence. By contrast, the Model Penal Code default for mistakes of fact—established by the application of § 2.02(3)—is recklessness. Recklessness not only requires that the defendant actually be aware of the risk that the relevant element exists, but requires also that ignoring the risk involve "a gross deviation from the standard of conduct that a law-abiding person would observe in the actor's situation." This is by any measure a much higher standard of culpability for mistakes of fact than its common law counterpart. Which is the best default position? What normative principles account for the difference?

[h] There are exceptions to this statement, most notably in some cases where the defendant is intoxicated by drink or drugs. These situations are dealt with below, and need not be of concern now.

## 10.  GRADING

Most modern statutes are ambiguous on the effect of mistakes of fact that relate only to grading elements. A new federal code—proposed but not enacted by the Congress—explicitly embraced the common law rule: "Except as otherwise expressly provided, culpability is not required with respect to any fact which is solely a basis . . . for grading." Final Report of the National Commission on Reform of Federal Criminal Laws § 302(3)(c) (1971).

Unusually, the Model Penal Code disagrees. Section 2.04(2) provides:

> Although ignorance or mistake would otherwise afford a defense to the offense charged, the defense is not available if the defendant would be guilty of another offense had the situation been as he supposed. In such case, however, the ignorance or mistake of the defendant shall reduce the grade and degree of the offense of which he may be convicted to those of the offense of which he would be guilty had the situation been as he supposed.

*[margin handwriting: defense not available if still guilty of something]*

Application of the culpability structure to grading elements is confirmed in § 2.02(1). This structure applies to "each material element of the offense." Section 1.13(9) defines "element" to include all of the conduct, circumstance, and result components "included in the description of the forbidden conduct in the definition of the offense." A "material" element, as provided in § 1.13(10), is any element having to do with "the harm or evil, incident to conduct, sought to be prevented by the law defining the offense." There is, to be sure, some ambiguity in these provisions. It is not entirely clear, for example, whether § 223.1(2) is part of "the description of the forbidden conduct in the definition of the offense" punished by § 223.2. But there is no doubt that it was the intention of the drafters of the Model Code to apply ordinary culpability rules to the grading elements of crimes.[i]

This point can be tested by reconsideration of the theft example posited in Note 7 in the Notes on Mistake of Fact and the Common Law. The defendant committed a theft of jewelry actually valued at $10,000, but thought the item stolen was merely costume jewelry and therefore fenced it for $50. By what culpability standard is the defendant's mistake to be judged if prosecuted under § 223.2 of the Model Penal Code? The answer is "recklessness." Section 223.1(2) establishes $500 as the dividing line between felony and misdemeanor theft. No culpability words apply to this element, so the default of "recklessness" would be applied under § 2.02(3). If the defendant was not reckless in the belief that the jewelry was worth less than $500, the conviction would be for the misdemeanor not the felony. At common law on the same facts, the conviction would be for the felony. Which solution is preferable?

## 11.  LESSER MORAL WRONG

Judge Bramwell's opinion in *Regina v. Prince*[j] describes, in effect, a rule of statutory construction. Elements of an offense that are an essential

---

i    See American Law Institute, Model Penal Code and Commentaries § 2.04, pp. 272–74 (1985). Note that "dwelling house" and "night" are grading elements in the example given in footnote g above, and that the commentary treats these identically to all other elements that are included in the definition of the offense.

j    See the discussion of *Prince* in the Notes on Mistake of Fact and the Common Law.

part of the community ethic as measured by current societal standards should require some form of mens rea. But if the defendant would be violating accepted social standards even on a mistaken view of a given element of an offense, strict liability should be imposed for that element and the mistake should not be a defense. This principle is not universally followed, but it has been used by the common law in several contexts.

It is irrelevant under the Model Penal Code—except perhaps on credibility—that a lesser moral wrong was committed on the facts as the defendant believed them to be. But consider § 213.1(1)(d), which provides that a "male who has sexual intercourse with a female not his wife is guilty of rape if . . . the female is less than 10 years old." Section 213.6(1) imposes strict liability on the age element of this offense. It denies a defense if the claim is "I thought she was 11," even if the belief was entirely reasonable on the facts. On what rationale might this provision be defended? Why might it be wrong?

## SECTION 3: IGNORANCE OR MISTAKE OF LAW

### State v. Fox

Supreme Court of Idaho, 1993.
124 Idaho 924, 866 P.2d 181.

■ MCDEVITT, CHIEF JUSTICE.

On January 11, 1991, appellant Milton Fox was charged with . . . possession of ephedrine, a controlled substance. As far as the Court can tell from the record, Fox ordered and received 100,000 tablets of ephedrine from an out-of-state mail order distributor. According to the Physician's Desk Reference, ephedrine has a stimulative effect on the central nervous system and is used to treat asthma symptoms. In some states, ephedrine is a legal over-the-counter drug. In Idaho, ephedrine was listed as a Schedule II substance in the Uniform Controlled Substances Act in 1988. I.C. § 37–2707(g)(1)(b). Compounds containing ephedrine could be sold over-the-counter until November 1990, when the Idaho Board of Pharmacy designated ephedrine as a prescription drug.

. . . During the trial . . . , Fox attempted to introduce [as defense exhibits] magazines carrying mail order advertisements for ephedrine from out-of-state suppliers. The state objected to the exhibits as cumulative (apparently the state introduced a magazine with a similar advertisement) and the court sustained the state's objection. The court then held a hearing outside the presence of the jury. During this hearing, the court held that the proffered exhibits were not relevant because knowledge that possession of ephedrine was illegal was not an element of the offense.

The next day, Fox renewed his argument that the exhibits were relevant. He pointed out that the state's proposed jury instruction required that it prove that "Milton Fox had knowledge of its [i.e., the ephedrine's] presence and nature as a controlled substance." The court responded by ruling that it would not give that instruction, or the similar one which the defense proposed, because these instructions did not accurately state the law.

After that ruling, Fox entered a conditional plea of guilty pursuant to I.C.R. 11(a)(2) which preserved his right to appeal the trial court's rulings. On appeal, Fox states the issues as follows:

*disputes*

> Did the District Court err in holding that intent, general intent or specific intent, "is not a required element for guilt in possession of a controlled substance" and, further, "that mistakes of law or fact are not defenses to the crime of possession of a controlled substance[?]"

We will address each contention in turn.

*holding*

1.    THE MENS REA ELEMENT OF THE OFFENSE OF POSSESSION OF A CONTROLLED SUBSTANCE IS KNOWLEDGE OF POSSESSION, NOT KNOWLEDGE THAT THE SUBSTANCE POSSESSED IS A CONTROLLED SUBSTANCE.

The Uniform Controlled Substances Act, in I.C. § 37–2732(c), states that:

*possesion statute*

> It is unlawful for any person to possess a controlled substance unless the substance was obtained directly from, or pursuant to, a valid prescription or order of a practitioner while acting in the course of his professional practice, or except as otherwise authorized by this chapter.

*reasoning*

The text of the possession statute does not set forth any mental state as an element of the offense. This Court has previously ruled that "whether a criminal intent is a necessary element of a statutory offense is a matter of construction, to be determined from the language of the statute in view of its manifest purpose and design, and where such intent is not made an ingredient of the offense, the intention with which the act is done, or the lack of any criminal intent in the premises, is immaterial." State v. Sterrett, 35 Idaho 580, 583, 207 P. 1071, 1072 (1922).

*π argues general intent*
*Δ argues specific intent*

Fox therefore turns to I.C. § 18–114, which provides that "[i]n every crime or public offense there must exist a union, or joint operation, of act and intent, or criminal negligence." Fox argues that this statute means that conviction under the possession statute requires specific intent. The state argues that only a general intent is required. This Court has explained the difference between specific and general intent as follows: A general criminal intent requirement is satisfied if it is shown that the defendant knowingly performed the proscribed acts, but a specific intent requirement refers to that state of mind which in part defines the crime and is an element thereof.

*reasoning?*

This Court has previously determined, however, that the intent required by I.C. § 18–114 is "not the intent to commit a crime, but is merely the intent to knowingly perform the interdicted act, or by criminal negligence the failure to perform the required act." State v. Parish, 79 Idaho 75, 78, 310 P.2d 1082, 1083 (1957).

*mistake of fact defense*

Fox then argues that a mistake of fact is available to him, pursuant to I.C. § 18–201. Idaho Code § 18–201 provides a defense for "[p]ersons who committed the act or made the omission charged, under an ignorance or mistake of fact which disproves any criminal intent." Our review of the record does not support this contention. Fox does not claim that he did not know he possessed ephedrine. His claim is that he did not know ephedrine was illegal. In short, Fox asserts a mistake of law claim rather than a mistake of fact claim.

*mistake of law claim?*

Thus, as I.C. § 37–2732(c) does not expressly require any mental element and I.C. § 18–114 only requires a general intent, we conclude that the offense only requires a general intent, that is, the knowledge that one is in possession of the substance. Consequently, we also conclude that the trial court was correct in refusing Fox's proffered exhibits because any evidence tending to establish Fox's lack of knowledge that ephedrine was illegal is irrelevant. Evidence that is not relevant is not admissible. I.R.E. 402. We also affirm the district court's refusal to give the proposed jury instructions because they were not accurate statements of the law.

*] holding general intent*

*] holding refusal of exhibits*

*] holding refusal of jury instructions*

2.    FOX CANNOT CLAIM A GOOD FAITH MISTAKE OF LAW DEFENSE UPON THE RECORD IN THIS CASE.

Fox also argues that a good faith mistake of law excuses his possession of the ephedrine. As far as we can tell, Fox's attempted defense at trial on this issue was that he did not know or reasonably could not have known that ephedrine was a controlled substance.

Ignorance of the law is not a defense. See e.g., Hale v. Morgan, 22 Cal.3d 388, 149 Cal.Rptr. 375, 380, 584 P.2d 512, 517 (1978) ("[I]n the absence of specific language to the contrary, ignorance of a law is not a defense to a charge of its violation"); State v. Einhorn, 213 Kan. 271, 515 P.2d 1036, 1039 (1973) ("The general rule is that ignorance of the law does not disprove criminal intent"). There is no indication in the record, nor is any argument made, that the defendant could not have discovered what substances were listed in the schedules of controlled substances. Ephedrine had in fact been added to the list in 1988, several years prior to Fox's possession of the substance in 1991.

*Ignorance*

*§2.04 MPC, p.168*

This is simply a case where Fox possessed a substance, knowing full well what the substance was, but claiming now that he did not know it was listed in the statutes as a controlled substance. There is nothing in that argument which would rise to the level of a viable defense.

*] holding no viable defense*

The district court is affirmed.

■ JOHNSON, TROUT and SILAK, JJ., concur.

■ BISTLINE, JUSTICE, conceding that the applicable statute is controlling as the state contends, but dissenting from the result.

That the other members of the Court have readily joined an opinion which affirms the trial court is not a great surprise. As the brief prepared in the office of the Attorney General of the State of Idaho informs its readers, the law as presently structured makes it impossible to do other than affirm the trial court; the hands of the trial judge were equally tied. Reluctantly I concede that convicting Fox under I.C. § 37–2732(c) was the correct procedure in this case. I write separately to register my concerns regarding the potential application of I.C. § 37–2732(c) to other Idaho citizens who possess far smaller amounts of ephedrine than did Fox, who purchase [the] ephedrine validly, but who may subsequently be convicted as felons.

*correct procedure*

Fox ordered the ephedrine by calling the toll-free number of a national outlet. Apparently, some of the ephedrine advertisements that are available to Idaho citizens contain warnings that the offer is void where prohibited by law, but some do not; ordering from the wrong catalog may therefore be a defendant's biggest mistake. In another potential scenario, an Idaho citizen might travel to another state for business or pleasure, purchase ephedrine while there to alleviate his or her bronchial or other health-related symptoms, and return home again, bearing the ephedrine, only to be possibly convicted under I.C. § 37–2732(c).

Ephedrine is a drug used for medical purposes. Surely persons who make out-of-state purchases of ephedrine for medical reasons pose no more of a threat to Idaho's safety and freedom from drug traffickers than persons who purchase ephedrine pursuant to a valid prescription or practitioner order while in Idaho. The Idaho Legislature is to be commended in its effort to reduce the trade of drugs, but I.C. § 37–2732(c) is truly too blunt an instrument. Moreover, at the least, the statute should provide a defense to Idaho citizens who did not know about the statute, did not comprehend its import, and were not alert enough to see that they should comply, even though they knew naught.

It is often stated that ignorance of the law is no excuse. The responsibility of the legislative branch in drafting the laws that govern society, then, is weighty. A law that imposes a felony for potentially very innocent behavior must be carefully worded; I.C. § 37–2732 is not.

## NOTES ON IGNORANCE OR MISTAKE OF CRIMINALITY

### 1. THE MODEL PENAL CODE

*Fox* illustrates the maxim, ignorantia juris neminem excusat.[a] As will be seen, the maxim is susceptible to misapplication and increasingly subject to exceptions. It is nevertheless descriptive of the dominant policy of the penal law with respect to awareness of illegality. Generally speaking, criminal liability does not depend on the actor's awareness of the criminality of conduct. Thus, ignorance or mistake regarding the criminality of one's act is ordinarily no defense to criminal prosecution. In more familiar phrasing, "ignorance of the law is no excuse."

Section 2.02(9) of the Model Code continues this tradition:

> Neither knowledge or recklessness or negligence as to whether conduct constitutes an offense or as to the existence, meaning or application of the law determining the elements of an offense is an element of such offense, unless the definition of the offense or the Code so provides.

### 2. APPLICATION OF THE MAXIM

The idea that mistake or ignorance as to criminality should not have defensive significance is deeply embedded in the law. Some idea of the law's commitment to this policy may be illustrated by the following cases:

[a] Sometimes given as ignorantia legis neminem excusat or as ignorantia juris non excusat.

*(i)   People v. Marrero* (possession of a pistol)

The problem in *People v. Marrero* was stated by an intermediate appellate court:

> Defendant, employed as a federal corrections officer in Danbury, Connecticut, was found to be in possession of a loaded .38 caliber pistol on December 19, 1977, while in a social club located at 207 Madison Street, New York City. This resulted in an indictment charging defendant with criminal possession of a weapon in the third degree pursuant to Penal Law § 265.02. The sole issue on appeal is whether the defendant is exempt from prosecution pursuant to Penal Law § 265.20(a)(1)(a) which in pertinent part provides that the offense for which defendant was indicted shall not apply to ". . . peace officers as defined in . . . section 1.20 of the criminal procedure law." Relevant to defendant's status, CPL § 1.20 enumerates as being peace officers "[a]n attendant, or an official, or guard of any state prison or of any penal correctional institution." In dismissing the indictment on defendant's motion to dismiss, the [trial court] found CPL § 1.20 to be ambiguous in that the adjective "state" may be construed as modifying only the term "prison" and not the term "any penal correctional institution." Having found such ambiguity, the court chose to resolve it in defendant's favor by concluding that as defendant was a federal corrections officer, he was entitled to the statutory exemption.

*[margin: dispute]*
*[margin: holding]*

A divided (three-to-two) intermediate appellate court read the statute differently, holding "that the clear intent of Penal Law § 265.20 [when other provisions were taken into account] was to provide persons in the service of the United States (as is defendant) immunity from prosecution for weapon possession [only] when that possession is duty-related or duly authorized by federal law, regulation or order." It accordingly reversed the dismissal of the indictment and remanded the case for trial.

*[margin: appellate court different]*
*[margin: holding/procedure]*

At trial, the defendant argued that his "personal misunderstanding of the statutory definition of a peace officer is enough to excuse him from criminal liability." Evidence was offered that other federal officers had so construed the statute, as had the merchant who sold defendant the gun. The trial judge refused to charge the jury on this defense, and the resulting conviction was affirmed by the intermediate appellate court. In People v. Marrero, 69 N.Y.2d 382, 507 N.E.2d 1068 (1987), the New York Court of Appeals affirmed.

*[margin: procedure/holding]*

*(ii)   Hopkins v. State* (wedding signs)

The Reverend William F. Hopkins specialized in weddings. In an attempt to discourage this enterprise, the legislature made it unlawful to erect or maintain any sign intended to aid in the solicitation or performance of marriages. Hopkins then sought the advice of the local state's attorney as to the legality of certain signs he proposed to erect. After receiving assurances that they would not violate the law, Hopkins put up one sign with the words, "Rev. W. F. Hopkins" and another with the legend, "W. F. Hopkins, Notary Public, Information."

Three years later, Hopkins was indicted for violating the anti-sign law. His offer of proof regarding the assurances by the state's attorney was excluded from evidence, and his conviction followed. In Hopkins v.

*[margin: issue]*

*procedure* State, 193 Md. 489, 499, 69 A.2d 456, 460 (1949), the state supreme court affirmed:

> If the right of a person to erect a sign of a certain type and size depends upon the construction and application of a penal statute, and the right is somewhat doubtful, he erects the sign at his peril. In other words, a person who commits an act which the law declares to be criminal cannot be excused from punishment upon the theory that he misconstrued or misapplied the law.

*misconstruction or misapplication not excused*

The fact that the misconstruction was confirmed by the state's attorney was thought inconsequential.

### (iii) State v. Striggles (gambling machine) or not

The facts of State v. Striggles, 202 Iowa 1318, 210 N.W. 137 (1926), were stated by the court as follows:

> On August 1, 1923, in several proceedings then pending in the municipal court of the city of Des Moines, a decision was rendered holding that [a particular] machine was not a gambling device. The distributors of the machine in question thereupon secured a certified copy of said decree, and equipped themselves with a letter from the county attorney, and also one from the mayor of the city, stating that such machine was not a gambling device. Thus equipped they presented themselves to appellant, Striggles, who conducted a restaurant in the city of Des Moines, and induced him to allow them to install a machine in his place of business.

*issue*
*procedure*

Two years later, the Supreme Court of Iowa held that the machine in question was indeed a gambling device. Striggles was convicted for permitting such a machine to be used for gambling on his premises. The Iowa Supreme Court upheld his conviction:

> There is no case cited, nor can we find one on diligent search, holding that the decision of an inferior court can be relied upon to justify the defendant in a criminal case in the commission of the act which is alleged to be a crime. We are disposed to hold ... that, when the highest court of a jurisdiction passes on any given proposition, all citizens are entitled to rely upon such decision; but we refuse to hold that the decisions of any court below, inferior to the supreme court, are available as a defense under similar circumstances.

*no decision of lower court is a defense*

The letters from the county attorney and the mayor were given no further mention.

### 3.   PROBLEMS WITH THE MAXIM

Is it obvious that the claims of Fox, Marrero, Hopkins, and Striggles should have been rejected? Or is there something wrong with criminal conviction in some or all of these cases?

Some have argued that criminal punishment without regard to awareness of illegality is objectionable because it is ineffective. See Ron Cass, Ignorance of the Law: A Maxim Reexamined, 17 Wm & M.L. Rev. 671, 684–85 (1976). The argument seems to be that the threat of penal sanctions can have no deterrent effect if the actor reasonably believes conduct to be lawful. The infliction of punishment in such cases is therefore seen as gratuitous and hence unjustified. Is this right? Does a reasonable belief in the legality of one's conduct vitiate the deterrent function of the law? Consider in this connection the following observations by Livingston Hall and Selig J. Seligman, in Mistake of Law and Mens Rea, 8 U. Chi. L. Rev. 641, 648 (1941):

> This problem of educating the community by law is a practical one. A conviction for doing that which violates a new law, although not regarded as wrong in the community, is a matter of considerable interest and does a great deal to educate the community; an acquittal for violation of such a law, on the ground of a mistake of law, would scarcely cause a ripple in the current of community thought. As de Saint-Exupery has his airline manager say, to justify cutting pilots' punctuality bonuses whenever their planes started late, even where it was due to the weather and was not their fault: "If you only punish men enough, the weather will improve." It is a hard doctrine, but an effective one.

A different contention is that punishment on these facts is objectionable because it is unfair. In what sense might it be unfair to punish without regard to awareness of illegality? Is the element of unfairness (if any) the same in each of the cases referred to above? In connection with these questions, consider the following possible justifications for adherence to the traditional policy regarding ignorance of the law.

## 4. JUSTIFICATIONS FOR THE MAXIM

Ignorantia juris neminem excusat is often associated with the proposition that "everyone is presumed to know the law." At one time this "presumption" may have been a fair approximation of reality. Certainly, awareness of illegality would be overwhelmingly likely in a legal system where the penal law was used almost exclusively to redress depredations against the person or property of another. It was with respect to such offenses, sometimes called mala in se, that one court commented that "every one has an innate sense of right and wrong, which enables him to know when he violates the law, and it is of no consequence, if he be not able to give the name, by which the offence is known in the law books, or to point out the nice distinctions between the different grades of offence." State v. Boyett, 32 N.C. 336, 343–44 (1849).

"everyone knows the law"

However plausible this view may have been at one time, it is hardly true today. Modern laws define a great many crimes that are not mala in se but only mala prohibita. For such offenses, no "innate sense of right and wrong" suffices, and the presumption that everyone knows the law seems an obvious fiction. Not surprisingly, it is precisely in the context of modern regulatory offenses that plausible claims of ignorance of the law most commonly arise. In such cases, the policy of ignorantia legis must be explained as something other than an attempt to describe reality.

Consider the following efforts to provide a rationale for the ignorantia legis concept:

(i) 1 J. Austin, Lectures on Jurisprudence 498–99 (3d ed. 1869):

> The only *sufficient* reason for the rule in question, seems to be this: that if ignorance of law were admitted as a ground of exemption, the courts would be involved in questions which it were

scarcely possible to solve, and which would render the administration of justice next to impracticable. If ignorance of law were admitted as a ground of exemption, ignorance of law would always be alleged by the party, and the court, in every case, would be bound to decide the point.

But, in order that the court might decide the point, it [is] incumbent upon the court to examine the following questions of fact: First, was the party ignorant of the law at the time of the alleged wrong? Second, assuming that he was ignorant of the law at the time of the wrong alleged, was his ignorance of the law *inevitable* ignorance, or had he been previously placed in such a position that he might have known the law, if he had duly tried?

*2 questions to decide ignorance of the law*

It is manifest that the latter question is not less material than the former. If he might have known the law in case he had duly tried . . . the conduct in question [is] imputable, in the last result, to his *negligence*.

Now either of these questions [is] next to insoluble. Whether the party was *really* ignorant of the law, and was *so* ignorant of the law that he had no *surmise* of its provisions, could scarcely be determined by any evidence accessible to others. And for the purpose of determining the *cause* of his ignorance (its *reality* being ascertained), it [would be] incumbent upon the tribunal to unravel his previous history, and to search his whole life for the elements of a just solution.

(ii) O. Holmes, The Common Law 47–48 (1881):

Ignorance of the law is no excuse for breaking it. This substantive principle is sometimes put in the form of a rule of evidence, that every one is presumed to know the law. It has accordingly been defended by Austin and others, on the ground of difficulty of proof. If justice requires the fact to be ascertained, the difficulty of doing so is no ground for refusing to try. But every one must feel that ignorance of the law could never be admitted as an excuse, even if the fact could be proved by sight and hearing in every case. Furthermore, now that parties can testify, it may be doubted whether a man's knowledge of the law is any harder to investigate than many questions which are gone into. The difficulty, such as it is, would be met by throwing the burden of proving ignorance on the law-breaker.

*burden of proof shift*

*reasoning principle*

The principle cannot be explained by saying that we are not only commanded to abstain from certain acts, but also to find out that we are commanded. For if there were such a second command, it is very clear that the guilt of failing to obey it would bear no proportion to that of disobeying the principal command if known, yet the failure to know would receive the same punishment as the failure to obey the principal law.

*sacrifice the individual*

The true explanation of the rule is the same as that which accounts for the law's indifference to a man's particular temperament, faculties, and so forth. Public policy sacrifices the individual to the general good. It is desirable that the burden of all should be equal, but it is still more desirable to put an end to robbery and murder. It is no doubt true that there are many cases in which the

> criminal could not have known that he was breaking the law, but to admit the excuse at all would be to encourage ignorance where the law-maker has determined to make men know and obey, and justice to the individual is rightly outweighed by the larger interests on the other side of the scale.

(iii) J. Hall, General Principles of Criminal Law 380–83 (2d ed. 1960):

According to Jerome Hall, Holmes's thesis "is surely questionable." The object of penal policy, Hall argued, "is not to make men know the law, as such, but to help them inhibit harmful conduct." Hall placed the justification for ignorantia juris on entirely different grounds, grounds having to do with the essential character of the adjudicatory system:

> The meaning of the rules of substantive penal law is unavoidably vague, the degree of vagueness increasing as one proceeds from the core of the rules to their periphery. It is therefore possible to disagree indefinitely regarding the meaning of these words. But in adjudication, such indefinite disputation is barred because that is opposed to the character and requirements of a legal order, as is implied in the principle of legality. Accordingly, a basic axiom of legal semantics is that legal rules do or do not include certain behavior; and the linguistic problem must be definitely solved one way or the other, on that premise. These characteristics of legal adjudication imply a degree of necessary reliance upon authority.

To that end, decisions of competent tribunals must be accepted as authoritative. The law *is* whatever the officially authorized judicial body declares it to be. A defendant who claims that he did not know that his conduct was criminal—either because he did not know of the existence of the prohibition or because he interpreted it not to apply to his conduct—is essentially opposing his view of the law to the officially sanctioned declaration of its meaning. If such a claim were accepted, said Hall, "the consequence would be: Whenever a defendant in a criminal case thought the law was thus and so, he is to be treated as though the law were thus and so, i.e., *the law actually is thus and so.*" In Hall's view, accepting such a defense would "contradict the essential requisites of a legal system":

> To permit an individual to plead successfully that he had a different opinion or interpretation of the law would contradict the . . . postulates of a legal order. For there is a basic incompatibility between asserting that the law is what certain officials declare it to be after a prescribed analysis, and asserting also, that those officials *must* declare it to be, i.e. that the law is, what defendants or their lawyers believed it to be. A legal order implies the rejection of such contradiction. It opposes objectivity to subjectivity, judicial process to individual opinion, official to lay, and authoritative to non-authoritative declarations of what the law is. This is the rationale of ignorantia juris neminem excusat.

## 5. PROPOSALS FOR REFORM

There have been proposals to ameliorate the ignorantia juris concept. The revised New Jersey penal code, for example, provides that a belief that one's conduct does not constitute a crime is a defense if the mistake is reasonable and if the actor "diligently pursues all means available to ascertain

*(2) honestly and good faith*

the meaning and application of the offense to his conduct and honestly and in good faith concludes his conduct is not an offense in circumstances in which a law-abiding and prudent person would also so conclude." N.J.Stat.Ann. § 2C:2–4(c)(3). A similar proposal was advanced earlier in Rollin M. Perkins, Ignorance and Mistake in Criminal Law, 88 U. Pa. L. Rev. 35, 45 (1939):

> If the meaning of a statute is not clear, and has not been judicially determined, one who has acted in "good faith" should not be held guilty of crime if his conduct would have been proper had the statute meant what he "reasonably believed" it to mean, even if the court should decide later that the proper construction is otherwise.

Do these provisions identify the most sympathetic cases for granting a defense? One could argue that a defendant who knows that a statute *might* be applicable, but makes a reasonable mistake as to its meaning, has a fair opportunity to avoid breaking the law simply by not engaging in the conduct. But what of the defendant who has no idea that proposed conduct might violate the criminal law? In contrast to the New Jersey provision quoted above, might it be rational to deny a defense for a reasonable *mistake* about the meaning of the criminal law but grant it for reasonable *ignorance* that proposed conduct might be punished as a crime? Consider Justice Bistline's dissent in *Fox* in connection with the preceding questions. What was his concern with the Idaho statute? Consider also the next case.

### 6.   *LAMBERT V. CALIFORNIA* (failure to register, felon of forgery)

*facts*

Ms. Lambert had been convicted in Los Angeles of forgery. Unknown to her, a Los Angeles ordinance required all convicted felons to register if they remained in Los Angeles for a period longer than five days. Another ordinance made each day's failure to register a misdemeanor, punishable by a fine of up to $500 and/or up to six months in jail. She lived in Los Angeles. She was arrested on suspicion of committing another offense, but was convicted of violating the registration law, was fined $250, and was placed on probation for three years.

*dispute*

She argued that not allowing her a defense that she was unaware of the registration requirement violated her rights under the due process clause of the 14th amendment to the federal Constitution.[b]

*holding procedure*

In Lambert v. California, 355 U.S. 225 (1957), the Supreme Court reversed her conviction. Justice Douglas wrote for the Court:

> Registration laws are common and their range is wide. Many such laws are akin to licensing statutes in that they pertain to the regulation of business activities. But the present ordinance is entirely different. Violation of its provisions is unaccompanied by any activity whatever, mere presence in the city being the test. Moreover, circumstances which might move one to inquire as to the necessity of registration are completely lacking. At most the ordinance is but a law-enforcement technique designed for the convenience of law-enforcement agencies through which a list of the names and addresses of felons then residing in a given community is compiled. The disclosure is merely a compilation

---

[b]   Section 1 of the 14th Amendment provides that no state shall "deprive any person of life, liberty, or property, without due process of law. . . ."

of former convictions already publicly recorded in the jurisdiction where obtained. Nevertheless, this appellant on first becoming aware of her duty to register was given no opportunity to comply with the law and avoid its penalty, even though her default was entirely innocent. She could but suffer the consequences of the ordinance, namely, conviction with the imposition of heavy criminal penalties thereunder. We believe that actual knowledge of the duty to register or proof of the probability of such knowledge and subsequent failure to comply are necessary before a conviction under the ordinance can stand. As Holmes wrote in The Common Law, "A law which punished conduct which would not be blameworthy in the average member of the community would be too severe for that community to bear." Its severity lies in the absence of an opportunity either to avoid the consequences of the law or to defend any prosecution brought under it. Where a person did not know of the duty to register and where there was no proof of the probability of such knowledge, he may not be convicted consistently with due process. Were it otherwise, the evil would be as great as it is when the law is written in print too fine to read or in a language foreign to the community.

In Mens Rea and the Supreme Court, 1962 Sup.Ct.Rev. 107, Herbert Packer summarized *Lambert* by saying that the mental element of crime "is an important requirement, but it is not a constitutional requirement, except sometimes." Is it possible to be more precise about the scope of *Lambert*? Is *Lambert* merely a rare exception to the ignoranti legis principle, or does it address a more fundamental concern about the minimum acceptable conditions for the imposition of criminal liability? Consider the following hypotheticals in connection with these questions:

(i) Defendant is prosecuted for murder. He deliberately allowed his infant son to starve to death, and defends on the ground that he did not know of his duty of care in such a situation or that such behavior could be murder.

(ii) Defendant, a manufacturer of sulphuric acid, shipped its product by common carrier. Federal regulations require such shipments to be labeled "Corrosive Liquid." Defendant did not so label the shipment, and defends prosecution for violation of the regulation on the ground that it did not know of its existence.

(iii) Defendant purchased a bottle labeled "aspirin" in a drug store and she believed the label. She is arrested as she leaves the store and is prosecuted for possession of narcotics, which tests prove the bottle contained. Her defense is that she believed the label on the bottle.

Would *Lambert* forbid conviction in any of these cases?[c] Would it forbid prosecution in *Fox*? In the variation of *Fox* suggested in Justice Bistline's dissent?[d] In any of the other cases in the notes following *Fox*?

---

[c] For an analysis of *Lambert* that locates the decision in both constitutional law and deeply embedded fault principles of the criminal law, see Peter W. Low & Benjamin Charles Wood, *Lambert* Revisited, 100 Va. L. Rev. 1603 (2014).

[d] For consideration of an interesting Florida narcotics statute that requires knowledge of the nature of the substance and also provides an affirmative defense based on lack of knowledge of the illicit nature of the transaction, see State v. Adkins, 96 So. 3d 412 (Fla. 2012). For a discussion of *Adkins* calling it a "judicial train wreck, see Robert Batey, Mens Rea

## 7. OFFICIAL MISSTATEMENT OF CRIMINAL LAW

There are two situations in which there is emerging statutory agreement that an exception to ignoranti legis is warranted. Section 2.04 of the Model Penal Code is illustrative:

> (3) A belief that conduct does not legally constitute an offense is a defense to a prosecution for that offense based upon such conduct when:
>
> (a) the statute or other enactment defining the offense is not known to the actor and has not been published or otherwise reasonably made available prior to the conduct alleged; or
>
> (b) he acts in reasonable reliance upon an official statement of the law, afterward determined to be invalid or erroneous, contained in (i) a statute or other enactment; (ii) a judicial decision, opinion or judgment; (iii) an administrative order or grant of permission; or (iv) an official interpretation of the public officer or body charged by law with responsibility for the interpretation, administration or enforcement of the law defining the offense.
>
> (4) The defendant must prove a defense arising under Subsection (3) of this Section by a preponderance of the evidence.

This provision can be defended on several grounds. First, persons who fall within the exceptions will have engaged in behavior that is consistent with a law-abiding character, the likelihood of collusion between the defendant and those upon whom she or he might rely is small, and it will not be difficult to determine whether the statute has "reasonably [been] made available" or whether the defendant acted "in reasonable reliance" upon the named official sources. Second, and more broadly, the exceptions are most likely to apply in regulatory contexts, where there are no significant moral overtones to the defendant's conduct. In such cases, only deliberate and repeated violations are appropriately punished by criminal sanctions. Might Striggles or Reverend Hopkins have fared differently if such provisions had been in effect in the jurisdictions in which they were convicted? Does § 2.04(3)(a) codify *Lambert*?

Provisions based on the Model Code proposal have been enacted in at least 17 states, though several restrict the defense more than does the Model Code. An example is Article 8.03 of the Texas Penal Code:

> (a) It is no defense to prosecution that the actor was ignorant of the provisions of any law after the law has taken effect.
>
> (b) It is an affirmative defense to prosecution that the actor reasonably believed the conduct charged did not constitute a crime and that he acted in reasonable reliance upon:
>
>> (1) an official statement of the law contained in a written order or grant of permission by an administrative agency charged by law with responsibility for interpreting the law in question; or
>>
>> (2) a written interpretation of the law contained in an opinion of a court of record or made by a public official

---

and Constitutional Law: A Report Card for the Florida Supreme Court in *State v. Adkins*, 43 Stetson L. Rev. 3, 4, 15 (2013).

charged by law with responsibility for interpreting the law in question.

(c) Although an actor's mistake of law may constitute a defense to the offense charged, he may nevertheless be convicted of a lesser included offense of which he would be guilty if the law were as he believed.

## 8.   ENTRAPMENT: *COX V. LOUISIANA*

Compare § 2.13 of the Model Penal Code, which defines one form of entrapment as follows:

(1) A public law enforcement official or a person acting in cooperation with such an official perpetrates an entrapment if for the purpose of obtaining evidence of the commission of an offense, he induces or encourages another person to engage in conduct constituting such offense by . . . :

(a) making knowingly false representations designed to induce the belief that such conduct is not prohibited. . . .

In Cox v. Louisiana, 379 U.S. 559 (1965), the Court found a violation of Due Process in a similar situation. The defendant was convicted of violating a statute punishing one who "pickets or parades . . . near a building housing a [state] court." The Court's assessment of the situation was as follows:

*[handwritten margin note: (violation of picketing statute by state court) bldg]*

[T]he highest police officials of the city, in the presence of the sheriff and mayor, in effect told the demonstrators that they could meet where they did, 101 feet from the courthouse steps, but could not meet closer to the courthouse. In effect, appellant was advised that a demonstration at the place it was held would not be one "near" the courthouse within the terms of the statute.

In Raley v. Ohio, 360 U.S. 423 (1959), this Court held that the Due Process Clause prevented conviction of persons refusing to answer questions of a state investigating commission when they relied upon assurances of the commission, either express or implied, that they had a privilege under state law to refuse to answer, though in fact this privilege was not available to them. The situation presented here is analogous to that in *Raley*, which we deem to be controlling. As in *Raley*, under all the circumstances of this case, after the public officials acted as they did, to sustain appellant's later conviction for demonstrating where they told him he could "would be to sanction an indefensible sort of entrapment by the state—convicting a citizen for exercising a privilege which the state had clearly told him was available to him." The Due Process Clause does not permit convictions to be obtained under such circumstances.[e]

*[handwritten margin note: entrapment (holding)]*

---

e  For general discussion of *Cox* and related cases, see Sean Connelly, Bad Advice: The Entrapment by Estoppel Doctrine in Criminal Law, 48 U. Miami L. Rev. 627 (1994).—[Footnote by eds.]

## NOTES ON IGNORANCE OR MISTAKE OF NON-CRIMINAL LAW

### 1.   INTRODUCTION

The materials studied thus far support two broad generalizations. First, ignorance or mistake as to the existence, scope, or meaning of the criminal law is not a defense. Second, a mistake of fact that negates a required element of mens rea is a defense. The issue now to be considered concerns a third kind of mistake.

The situation arises when the defendant makes a mistake of non-criminal law relevant to the criminality of conduct. Many crimes—larceny and burglary, for example—involve invasions of the property rights of others. The criminal law is not the source of property rights. These rights are created by a body of private law that defines the content of the rights and the extent to which ordinary civil remedies can be invoked for their protection. The question to be considered is this: If the defendant makes a mistake as to the relevant law of property and wrongly comes to the conclusion that she or he "owns" certain property, is it a defense if the actor then does things with or to the property that would otherwise constitute larceny or burglary? The problem is a pervasive one. Can a mistake as to the validity of a divorce be offered as a defense to a charge of bigamy? Can a mistake as to child custody rights be a defense to abduction? The following notes deal with the response of the criminal law to these questions.

*[margin note: mistake of non-criminal law relevant to the criminality of conduct]*

*[margin note: defense?]*

### 2.   THE COMMON LAW

The common law, at least as it has emerged in modern times, was very clear on one aspect of this problem. If the offense required a specific intent or some other special mental element, a mistake of the non-criminal law that negated that intent was a defense. Thus, for example, a mistake as to ownership of property resulting from an error of property law was a defense to larceny because the requisite intent to deprive another of the property would be lacking. It follows that in a prosecution for larceny, it does not matter whether a mistake as to ownership is a mistake of fact or a mistake of property law.

The offense of persistent non-support as defined in § 230.5 of the Model Penal Code provides another illustration: "A person commits a misdemeanor if he persistently fails to provide support which he can provide and which he knows he is legally obliged to provide to a spouse, child or other dependent." The legal obligation to provide support arises from the general provisions of family law and, in particular cases, may be governed by a support decree or some other court order. Since the definition of the offense requires that one "know" of the legal obligation to provide support, any mistake as to the scope of the legal duty would be a defense if a common law jurisdiction created a similarly defined offense, as it would be under the Model Penal Code itself.

General intent crimes, however, were sometimes treated differently. The usual rule was that no mistakes of law were exculpatory, and the courts rarely offered reasons for this conclusion . Sometimes the result was said to be required by the policies underlying the particular offense. More often, it was explained by a reflexive invocation of the principle that "ignorance of the law is no excuse."

*[margin note: General intent usually was different]*

### 3. GENERAL INTENT RULE IN OPERATION: *LONG V. STATE*

Operation of the general intent rule is illustrated by Long v. State, 44 Del. 262, 65 A.2d 489 (1949). The defendant, a resident of Delaware, obtained a divorce in Arkansas and moved back to Delaware. He subsequently wished to remarry, but was concerned about whether he was free to do so. He had consulted a Delaware attorney before he obtained the divorce and was assured that it would be valid. He consulted the same attorney before he remarried, and again was assured that his divorce was valid and that he was free to marry. He made arrangements with a minister to perform the ceremony. The minister was concerned about the legal situation, so he too went to the defendant's lawyer to make sure the divorce was valid. He was assured that it was. The defendant then returned to the attorney one more time to make sure, after which he went through with the second marriage.

He was subsequently prosecuted for bigamy. The court held that the prior divorce was invalid in Delaware and that he was therefore in fact not free to remarry. He argued that he had been assured that the applicable family law rules in Delaware recognized the dissolution of his first marriage, that he honestly believed he was free to marry again, that his belief was reasonable, and that his belief should afford him a defense even if mistaken. The court began its analysis of this issue by resolving the question of whether bigamy was a strict liability crime that did not recognize a mistake of fact defense:[a]

> Of course, the mere specification of certain defenses in [the bigamy statute] does not exclude all other defenses. We can think of no sound reason why defenses of coercion and insanity, for instance, should not be available. A recognition of mistake of fact as a defense is found in Regina v. Tolson, 23 Q.B.D. 168 (1889). There, the defense of absence of a spouse for seven years, specified in a bigamy statute, was held not to exclude a defense of reasonable mistake of fact where the accused, believing erroneously but on reasonable grounds that her husband was dead, had remarried after his absence for less than seven years. The defense of mistake of fact is important only because it negatives a "criminal mind," general criminal intent. Upon considering the particular behavior defined as criminal . . . , the specified defenses themselves, and the seriousness of the punishment provided, we accept the view that the [bigamy] statute does not exclude as a defense the absence of general criminal intent. . . .

The question then was whether the defendant's mistake was a defense to a crime of general criminal intent. The court summarized the applicable rules as follows:

> We turn now to the ground that this is a case to which the ignorance of law maxim applies. In many crimes involving a *specific* criminal intent, an honest mistake of law constitutes a defense if it negatives the specific intent. [Citing cases involving

[a] Most bigamy statutes of the day (including Delaware's) listed a series of available defenses, none of which were applicable to the defendant's behavior. Many courts held that this list was exclusive, and no other defenses should be permitted. The *Long* court adopted the minority view that the list was not exclusive, and that the elements of bigamy should be treated under the ordinary general intent rules.

*[margin: reasoning]*

larceny and embezzlement]. As to crimes not involving a specific intent, an honest mistake of law is usually . . . held not to excuse conduct otherwise criminal.

At first pass, therefore, the defense was to be denied. *[margin: holding]*

## 4.    THE MODEL PENAL CODE

Re-examine § 2.04(1)(a) of the Model Penal Code. Notice that it reads "[i]gnorance or mistake as to a matter of fact *or law* is a defense if. . . ." What is the function of the words "or law"? Under what circumstances are mistakes of "law" intended to be a defense under the Model Penal Code?

Section 2.04(1)(a) must be read in conjunction § 2.02 in general and in particular with § 2.02(9). The effect of § 2.02(9) in the ordinary case—as explained above—is to deny a defense for ignorance or mistake of the criminal law. It was intended by the Model Penal Code drafters that § 2.02 and the "or law" provision in § 2.04(1)(a) would provide a defense for ignorance or mistake of non-criminal law if a similar mistake as to a matter of fact would be exculpatory. In contrast to the common law, the Model Penal Code treats mistakes of non-criminal law the same as mistakes of fact throughout all levels of culpability. Both are a defense if they negate a required culpability element. And, to complete the circle, a culpability element required by § 2.02 extends not only to the defendant's perceptions of the facts but also to the defendant's understanding of how the facts are characterized by the non-criminal law.[b] On the facts of *Long*, therefore, the Model Penal Code would treat a mistake of family law ("I thought I was divorced") the same as a mistake of fact ("I thought my spouse was dead").

*[margin: provision of defense for mistake of non-criminal law]*

Consider another example. Assume that *A* lived with *B* long enough and under such conditions that under the law of the relevant jurisdiction their relationship amounted to a common law marriage. *A,* unaware that the law has attached this conclusion to her relationship with *B,* marries *C.* *B* complains to the police and *A* is prosecuted for bigamy under § 230.1 of the Model Code. Is *A*'s evidence of ignorance of law admissible, and if so, under what jury instruction?

---

[b]    See ALI, Model Penal Code and Commentaries, § 2.04, p. 270 & n.2 (1985). The words "or law" need not have this meaning. Section 2.02(9) states a default rule that knowledge, recklessness, or negligence is not required as to whether conduct constitutes an offense or as to the law governing the meaning of its elements. But there is an exception. The provision concludes with the phrase "unless the definition of the offense or the Code so provides." Thus knowledge, recklessness, or negligence as to the criminal law *is* required if affirmatively made an element of an offense by its definition or some other provision of the Code, and § 2.04(1)(a) will provide a defense in cases where a mistake negates such an element. Thus, it is not *required* that the words "or law" in that section refer to non-criminal law in order to recognize that sometimes a mistake of law will be a defense. And it follows that the "law" referred to in § 2.02(9) could mean non-criminal as well as criminal law. Section 2.02(9) could mean that no mistakes of law—criminal or non-criminal—are a defense unless the code or the definition of the offense specifically so provides. See Gerald Leonard, Rape, Murder, and Formalism: What Happens if We Define Mistake of Law, 72 Colo. L. Rev. 507, 546 h.133 (2001).

Think of it another way. On any view of the meaning of "or law," § 2.04(1)(a) states a tautology. If § 2.02 establishes a required culpability element, § 2.04(1)(a) provides a defense when that element is missing. What the Model Penal Code drafters intended is that the culpability levels of § 2.02 apply in the same manner to perceptions of non-criminal law as they apply to perceptions of observable fact. Alternatively, they could have meant for the culpability levels to apply only to perceptions of observable fact, and for § 2.02(9) to say that perceptions of any kind of law are included only where specifically provided by the definition of a crime or some special provision of the Code. The commentary makes clear that the drafters meant the former, not the latter.

### 5. CATEGORIZATION OF MISTAKES OF FACT AND LAW

Can it be argued that the defendant's mistake in *Long* was one of fact? Can the same argument be made in the common law marriage example in the previous note? What is the difference between a mistake of law and a mistake of fact in situations like these?

#### (i) *Long v. State Revisited*

In the end, the *Long* court recognized the asserted defense. It began with a comment:

> A mistake of law, where not a defense, may nevertheless negative a general criminal intent as effectively as would an exculpatory mistake of fact. Thus, mistake of law is disallowed as a defense in spite of the fact that it may show an absence of the criminal mind.

Having recognized that, just like a mistake of fact, a mistake of divorce law could function to negate Long's culpability, the court turned to the rationale for the common law rule that nonetheless denied the defense. The reasons for the rule, the court noted, "are practical considerations dictated by deterrent effects upon the administration and enforcement of the criminal law, which are deemed likely to result if it were allowed as a general defense." The court then rehearsed the reasons, discussed above, for why ignorance or mistake of the criminal law is generally not recognized as a defense. In the end, it adopted an exception to the ignorantia juris concept similar to the statute later enacted in New Jersey:[c]

> Any deterrent effects upon the administration of the criminal law which might result from allowing [the] defense seem greatly outweighed by considerations which favor allowing it. To hold a person punishable as a criminal transgressor where the conditions of [this case] are present would be palpably unjust and arbitrary. Most of the important reasons which support the prohibition of ex post facto legislation are opposed to such a holding. It is difficult to conceive what more could be reasonably expected of a "model citizen" than that he guide his conduct by "the law" ascertained in good faith, not merely by efforts which might seem adequate to a person in his situation, but by efforts as well designed to accomplish ascertainment as any available under our system. We are not impressed with the suggestion that a mistake under such circumstances should aid the defendant only in inducing more lenient punishment by a court, or executive clemency after conviction. The circumstances seem so directly related to the defendant's behavior upon which the criminal charge is based as to constitute an integral part of that behavior, for purposes of evaluating it. No excuse appears for dealing with it piecemeal. We think such circumstances should entitle a defendant to full exoneration as a matter of right, rather than to something less, as a matter of grace.

[c] See Note 5, Proposals for Reform, in the Notes following *State v. Fox*, above.

*(ii)  People v. Bray* (convicted felon in possession of a concealable firearm)

In People v. Bray, 52 Cal.App.3d 494, 124 Cal.Rptr. 913 (1975), the defendant was convicted on two counts of being a felon in possession of a concealable firearm. There was no doubt that he had possessed two concealable firearms. The question was whether he knew he was a convicted felon. His only prior conviction had occurred some years before in Kansas, where he had pleaded guilty to being an accessory after the fact and had been sentenced to, and successfully served, a period of probation. The California prosecutor, not being sure that the offense involved was a felony under Kansas law, sought to introduce expert testimony at the trial to the effect that it was. On several occasions, the defendant had been required to fill out forms asking if he had a prior felony conviction. On most, he had answered that he did not know and made full disclosure of the situation. California officials had permitted him to vote in the face of such disclosures.

*procedure* [ The court reversed Bray's conviction on the ground that the jury had not been properly instructed on the doctrine of mistake of fact:

*reasoning* [ Although the district attorney had great difficulty in determining whether the Kansas offense was a felony or a misdemeanor, he expects the layman Bray to know his status easily. There was no doubt Bray knew he had committed an offense; there was, however, evidence to the effect he did not know the offense was a felony. Without this knowledge Bray would be ignorant of the facts necessary for him to come within the proscription of [the statute].

*holding* [ Under these circumstances the requested instructions on mistake or ignorance of fact and knowledge of the facts which make the act unlawful should have been given.

Presumably the instruction to which Bray was entitled would state the typical common law rule on mistake of fact for general intent offenses.

### (iii) Questions and Comments

The court in *Long* treated the defendant's claim as though it was a mistake of the criminal law. That is, it treated mistakes of the criminal law and non-criminal law alike, and created an exception to the general principle that ignorance of the law is no excuse. Is the premise of the court's reasoning correct? Should mistakes of criminal law and mistakes of non-criminal law be treated the same? Or are mistakes of the non-criminal law more like mistakes of fact?

Compare the reasoning in *Long* to the reasoning in *Oglivie*, summarized in Note 5 of the Notes on Mistakes of Fact, above. Oglivie was convicted of bigamy because his mistake of "fact" concerning whether he was divorced was unreasonable. Is it clear why Oglivie made a mistake of "fact" and Long made a mistake of "law"? Now consider *Bray*. The California court never mentioned the possibility that Bray might have made a mistake of law. Why not? How could a mistake about whether a crime is a felony *not* be a mistake of law? If the mistake was one of law, was it a mistake of criminal law or non-criminal law? How can the result in *Bray* be explained?

The Model Penal Code does not contain an offense comparable to the one charged in *Bray*. If it did, how would the *Bray* situation be analyzed?

## SECTION 4: INTOXICATION

### INTRODUCTORY NOTE

There are many circumstances and situations that can affect a person's state of mind and potentially demonstrate that the mens rea required for a criminal offense does not exist. Factual ignorance or mistake is the most obvious. The effect of drugs and alcohol is another. Assaultive behavior and various kinds of risk-taking activities are strongly associated with the ingestion of intoxicants, many of which can and do affect state of mind in ways relevant to mens rea. It is important that the law formulate an appropriate response to the voluntary ingestion of intoxicants. The case that follows deals with this issue.

## Director of Public Prosecutions v. Majewski

*(intoxication defense when committing assault in bar)*

House of Lords, 1976.
[1976] 2 All E.R. 142.

■ LORD ELWYN-JONES, L.C. My Lords, Robert Stefan Majewski appeals against his conviction [for] assault occasioning actual bodily harm. [H]e was placed on probation for three years. . . .

*] procedure*

The appellant's case was that when the assaults were committed he was acting under the influence of a combination of drugs (not medically prescribed) and alcohol, to such an extent that he did not know what he was doing and that he remembered nothing of the incidents that had occurred. After medical evidence had been called by the defence as to the effect of the drugs and drink the appellant had taken, the learned judge . . . ruled that he would direct the jury in due course that . . . the question whether [the defendant] had taken drink or drugs was immaterial. The learned judge directed the jury that in relation to an offence not requiring a specific intent, the fact that a man has induced in himself a state in which he is under the influence of drink and drugs, is no defence. . . .

*] dispute*

*immaterial*

*] jury charge*

In view of the conclusion to which I have come that the appeal should be dismissed . . . , it is desirable that I should refer in some detail to the facts, which were largely undisputed. During the evening of 19th February 1973 the appellant and his friend, Leonard Stace, who had also taken drugs and drink, went to the Bull public house in Basildon. The appellant obtained a drink and sat down in the lounge bar at a table by the door. Stace became involved in a disturbance. Glasses were broken. The landlord asked Stace to leave and escorted him to the door. As he did so, Stace called to the appellant: "He's putting me out." The appellant got up and prevented the landlord from getting Stace out and abused him. The landlord told them both to go. They refused. The appellant butted the landlord in the face and bruised it, and punched a customer. The customers in the bar and the landlord forced the two out through the bar doors. They re-entered by forcing the outer door, a glass panel of which was broken by Stace. The appellant punched the landlord and pulled a piece of broken glass from the frame and started swinging it at the landlord and a customer, cutting the landlord slightly on his arm. The appellant then burst through the inner door of the bar with such force that he fell on the floor. The

*] holding*

landlord held him there until the police arrived. The appellant was violent and abusive and spat in the landlord's face. When the police came, a fierce struggle took place to get him out. He shouted at the police: "You pigs, I'll kill you all, you f . . . pigs, you bastards." P[olice] C[onstable] Barkway said the appellant looked at him and kicked him deliberately. . . .

Cross-examined as to the appellant's condition that evening the publican said he seemed to have gone berserk, his eyes were a bit glazed and protruding. A customer said he was "glarey-eyed," and went "berserk" when the publican asked Stace to leave. He was screaming and shouting. A policeman said he was in a fearful temper.

The appellant gave evidence and said that on Saturday, 17th February 1973, he bought, not on prescription, about 440 Dexadrine tablets ("speeds") and early on Sunday morning consumed about half of them. That gave him plenty of energy until he "started coming down." He did not sleep throughout Sunday. On Monday evening at about 6:00 p.m. he acquired a bottle full of sodium nembutal tablets which he said were tranquillisers—"downers," "barbs"—and took about eight of them at about 6:30 p.m. He and his friends went to the Bull. He said he could remember nothing of what took place there save for a flash of recollection of Stace kicking a window. All he recollected of the police cell was asking the police to remove his handcuffs and then being injected.

In cross-examination he admitted he had been taking amphetamines and barbiturates, not on prescription, for two years, in large quantities. On occasions he drank barley wine or Scotch. He had sometimes "gone paranoid." This was the first time he had "completely blanked out."

Dr. Bird, called for the defence, said that the appellant had been treated for drug addiction since November 1971. There was no history in his case of psychiatric disorder or diagnosable mental illness, but the appellant had a personality disorder. Dr. Bird said that barbiturates and alcohol are known to potentiate each other and to produce rapid intoxication and affect a person's awareness of what was going on. In the last analysis one could be rendered unconscious and a condition known as pathological intoxication can occur, but it is uncommon and there are usually well-marked episodes. It would be possible, but unlikely, to achieve a state of automatism as a result of intoxication with barbiturates and alcohol or amphetamines and alcohol. Aggressive behavior is greater. After a concentration of alcohol and barbiturates it was not uncommon for "an amnesic patch" to ensue.

In cross-examination, Dr. Bird said he had never in practice come across a case of "pathological intoxication" and it is an unusual condition. It is quite possible that a person under the influence of barbiturates, amphetamines or alcohol or all three in combination may be able to form certain intentions and execute them, punching and kicking people, and yet afterwards be unable to remember anything about it. During such "disinhibited behaviour" he may do things which he would not do if he was not under the influence of the various sorts of drink and drugs about which evidence has been given.

In a statement Dr. Mitchell expressed the opinion that at the police station on the morning of 20th February, the appellant was completely out of control mentally and physically, which might have been due to "withdrawal symptoms."

The Court of Appeal dismissed the appeal against conviction but granted leave to appeal to your Lordships' House . . . . The appeal raises issues of considerable public importance. . . . Self-induced alcoholic intoxication has been a factor in crimes of violence, like assault, throughout the history of crime in this country. But voluntary drug taking with the potential and actual dangers to others it may cause has added a new dimension to the old problem with which the courts have had to deal in their endeavour to maintain order and to keep public and private violence under control. To achieve this is the prime purpose of the criminal law. I have said "the courts," for most of the relevant law has been made by the judges. A good deal of the argument in the hearing of this appeal turned on that judicial history, for the crux of the case for the Crown was that, illogical as the outcome may be said to be, the judges have evolved for the purpose of protecting the community a substantive rule of law that, in crimes of basic intent as distinct from crimes of specific intent, self-induced intoxication provides no defence and is irrelevant to offences of basic intent, such as assault.

The case of counsel for the appellant was that there was no such substantive rule of law and that if there was, it did violence to logic and ethics and to fundamental principles of the criminal law which had been evolved to determine when and where criminal responsibility should arise. [Lord Elwyn-Jones began his consideration of this argument with a general discussion of the meaning of mens rea and the definition of assault. He concluded that assault was a crime of "basic intent" and that recklessness was the minimum culpability ordinarily required. He then continued by asking:]

How does the factor of self-induced intoxication fit into [this] analysis? If a man consciously and deliberately takes alcohol and drugs not on medical prescription, but in order to escape from reality, to go "on a trip," to become hallucinated, whatever the description may be, and thereby disables himself from taking the care he might otherwise take and as a result by his subsequent actions causes injury to another—does our criminal law enable him to say that because he did not know what he was doing he lacked both intention and recklessness and accordingly is entitled to an acquittal?

Originally the common law would not and did not recognise self-induced intoxication as an excuse. . . . The authority which for the last half century has been relied on in this context has been the speech of Lord Birkenhead, L.C. in Director of Public Prosecutions v. Beard, [1920] A.C. 479, 494, [1920] All E.R. 21, 25:

> Under the law of England as it prevailed until early in the 19th century voluntary drunkenness was never an excuse for criminal misconduct; and indeed the classic authorities broadly assert that voluntary drunkenness must be considered rather an aggravation than a defence. This view was in terms based upon the principle that a man who by his own voluntary act debauches and destroys his will power shall be no better situated in regard to criminal acts than a sober man.

Lord Birkenhead, L.C. made an historical survey of the way the common law from the 16th century on dealt with the effect of self-induced intoxication on criminal responsibility. [He] concluded that . . . the decisions . . .

> establish where a specific intent is an essential element in the offence, evidence of a state of drunkenness rendering the accused incapable of forming such an intent should be taken into consideration in order to determine whether he had in fact formed the intent necessary to constitute the particular crime. If he was so drunk that he was incapable of forming the intent required he could not be convicted of a crime which was committed only if the intent was proved. . . .

From this it seemed clear—and this is the interpretation which the judges have placed on the decision during the ensuing half-century—that it is only in the limited class of cases requiring proof of specific intent that drunkenness can exculpate. Otherwise in no case can it exempt completely from criminal liability. . . .

I do not for my part regard that general principle as either unethical or contrary to the principles of natural justice. If a man of his own volition takes a substance which causes him to cast off the restraints of reason and conscience, no wrong is done to him by holding him answerable criminally for any injury he may do while in that condition. His course of conduct in reducing himself by drugs and drink to that condition in my view supplies the evidence of mens rea, of guilty mind certainly sufficient for crimes of basic intent. It is a reckless course of conduct and recklessness is enough to constitute the necessary mens rea in assault cases. . . . The drunkenness is itself an intrinsic, an integral part of the crime, the other part being the evidence of the unlawful use of force against the victim. Together they add up to criminal recklessness. . . . This approach is in line with the American Model Code [Section 2.08(2)]:

> When recklessness establishes an element of the offence, if the actor, due to self-induced intoxication, is unaware of a risk of which he would have been aware had he been sober, such unawareness is immaterial.

Acceptance generally of intoxication as a defence (as distinct from the exceptional cases where some additional mental element above that of ordinary mens rea has to be proved) would in my view undermine the criminal law and I do not think that it is enough to say, as did counsel for the appellant, that we can rely on the good sense of the jury . . . to ensure that the guilty are convicted. . . .

■ LORD SIMON OF GLAISDALE. . . . One of the prime purposes of the criminal law, with its penal sanctions, is the protection from certain proscribed conduct of persons who are pursuing their lawful lives. Unprovoked violence has, from time immemorial, been a significant part of such proscribed conduct. To accede to the argument on behalf of the appellant would leave the citizen legally unprotected from unprovoked violence, where such violence was the consequence of drink or drugs having obliterated the capacity of the perpetrator to know what he was doing or what were its consequences.

. . . Though the problem of violent conduct by intoxicated persons is not new to society, it has been rendered more acute and menacing by the more widespread use of hallucinatory drugs. For example, in Regina v. Lipman, [1969] All E.R. 410, [1970] 1 Q.B. 152, the accused committed his act of mortal violence under the hallucination (induced by drugs) that he was wrestling with serpents.[a] He was convicted of manslaughter. But, on the logic of the appellant's argument, he was innocent of any crime.

[T]here is nothing unreasonable or illogical in the law holding that a mind rendered self-inducedly insensible . . . , through drink or drugs, to the nature of a prohibited act or to its probable consequences is as wrongful a mind as one which consciously contemplates the prohibited act and foresees its probable consequences (or is reckless whether they ensue). The latter is all that is required by way of mens rea in a crime of basic intent. But a crime of specific intent requires something more than contemplation of the prohibited act and foresight of its probable consequences. The mens rea in a crime of specific intent requires proof of a purposive element. This purposive element either exists or not; it cannot be supplied by saying that the impairment of mental powers by self-induced intoxication is its equivalent, for it is not. So . . . the 19th century development of the law as to the effect of self-induced intoxication on criminal responsibility is juristically entirely acceptable. . . .

■ LORD SALMON. . . . A number of distinguished academic writers support [the defendant's] contention on the ground of logic. As I understand it, the argument runs like this. Intention, whether special or basic (or whatever fancy name you choose to give it), is still intention. If voluntary intoxication by drink or drugs can, as it admittedly can, negative the special or specific intention necessary for the commission of crimes such as murder and theft, how can you justify in strict logic the view that it cannot negative a basic intention, e.g., the intention to commit offences such as assault and unlawful wounding? The answer is that in strict logic this view cannot be justified. But this is the view that has been adopted by the common law of England, which is founded on common sense and experience rather than strict logic. There is no case in the 19th century when the courts were relaxing the harshness of the law in relation to the effect of drunkenness on criminal liability in which the courts ever went so far as to suggest that drunkenness, short of drunkenness producing insanity, could ever exculpate a man from any offence other than one which required some special or specific intent to be proved.

. . . I accept that there is a degree of illogicality in the rule that intoxication may excuse or expunge one type of intention and not another. This illogicality is, however, acceptable to me because the benevolent part of the rule removes undue harshness without imperilling safety and the stricter part of the rule works without imperilling justice. It would be just as ridiculous to remove the benevolent part of the rule (which no one suggests) as it would be to adopt the alternative of removing the stricter part of [the] rule for the sake of preserving absolute logic. . . .

---

[a] Lipman killed his companion by stuffing bedclothes down her throat under the delusion, induced by hallucinatory drugs, that he was fighting for his life against snakes.—[Footnote by eds.]

■ LORD EDMUND-DAVIES. . . . Illogical though the present law may be, it represents a compromise between the imposition of liability on inebriates in complete disregard of their condition (on the alleged ground that it was brought on voluntarily), and the total exculpation required by the defendant's actual state of mind at the time he committed the harm in issue. . . . As to the complaint that it is unethical to punish a man for a crime when his physical behaviour was not controlled by a conscious mind, I have long regarded as a convincing theory in support of penal liability for harms committed by voluntary inebriates, the view of Austin, who argued that a person who voluntarily became intoxicated is to be regarded as acting recklessly, for he made himself dangerous in disregard of public safety. . . . It may be that Parliament should look at [the situation], and devise a new way of dealing with drunken or drugged offenders. But, until it does, the continued application of the existing law is far better calculated to preserve order than [acceptance of the argument] that he and all who act similarly should leave the dock as free men. . . .

■ LORD RUSSELL OF KILLOWEN. . . . That the facts of the case give rise to the question [raised], I doubt. The appellant's participation in the events of the evening begin when he is told by the other man that the latter is to be ejected: whereupon the appellant stationed himself before the door to prevent that, which shows comprehension and intention on his part. When the police arrived the appellant called them adjectival pigs, a word which has of recent years been revived as a reference to law enforcement officers, having been current in the early 19th century. . . . This . . . negatives lack of understanding. Nevertheless, the question requires to be answered, and I agree with the answer proposed. . . .

Appeal dismissed.

## NOTES ON MENS REA AND INTOXICATION

### 1. INTRODUCTION

In *Majewski*, the House of Lords considered the significance of a claim that the defendant's conscious mental functioning at the time of the offense was impaired as a result of intoxication. In rare cases, a defendant might claim, as Majewski did, that he or she was so intoxicated as to lack any conscious awareness of, or control over, behavior. This claim may be legally significant if it shows that the defendant's conduct was not produced by a "voluntary act." More typically, a defendant who was consciously aware of some aspects of conduct may claim to have lacked the mens rea required for conviction because of unawareness or misperception of legally pertinent circumstances or risks, or may claim to have lacked the type of conscious objective (e.g., purpose to kill) prescribed for the offense. All of these claims may be logically relevant to the elements of the offense. However, as the *Majewski* opinions indicate, there has been broad consensus that evidence of voluntary intoxication should be restricted considerably short of its logical import.[a] How far short has been the question on which the authorities disagree.

---

[a] As *Majewski* indicates, the law does not distinguish between drugs and alcohol in this context. It should also be noted that the doctrine applied in *Majewski* pertains only to volun-

## 2. GENERAL INTENT CRIMES

There is a consensus in American law that the result in *Majewski* is correct, i.e., that intoxication evidence is inadmissible to negate mens rea for general or "basic" intent offenses. If general intent is equated to negligence, this result is not surprising. It is clear enough that the standard for negligence is not the "reasonable intoxicated" person. It is therefore never "reasonable" for a mistake to be induced by intoxication. Logically, however, intoxication might be relevant where recklessness is required, as the condition might negate conscious awareness of risk. But even under the Model Penal Code, the rule of logical relevance is modified when the actual awareness of risk is sought to be rebutted by evidence of intoxication.

The Model Code position has been defended on four grounds: (i) the weight of authority, which is virtually unanimous; (ii) the fairness of postulating a moral equivalence between the act of getting drunk as a risk-taking venture and the harms subsequently caused by drunken conduct; (iii) the difficulty of measuring actual foresight when the actor is drunk; and (iv) the rarity of cases in which drunkenness leads to unawareness as opposed to imprudence.[b] Are these reasons persuasive as applied to alcohol? As applied to the types of substances ingested by Majewski? As applied to all drugs? What of Glanville Williams' point, in Criminal Law: The General Part 564 (2d ed. 1961), that "[i]f a man is punished for doing something when drunk that he would not have done when sober, is he not in plain truth punished for getting drunk?"

## 3. SPECIFIC INTENT CRIMES

*Majewski* says that evidence of intoxication is admissible to negate a specific intent. There is disagreement on that proposition in American law. The cases fall into three groups.

### *(i) Restrictive Positions*

In at least 11 states, evidence of intoxication is not admissible in any (or most) specific intent crimes. Virginia is an example.[c] In Chittum v. Commonwealth, 211 Va. 12, 174 S.E.2d 779 (1970), the defendant was convicted of attempted rape. The defendant's argument on appeal, and the

---

tary ingestion of intoxicating substances; involuntary or otherwise non-culpable intoxication is governed by other doctrines, considered elsewhere in these materials. Finally, the restrictive doctrine illustrated by *Majewski* and the notes to follow is qualified by the possibility that a person who ingests alcohol or drugs may become legally insane. The relation between intoxication and the insanity defense is also considered elsewhere in these materials.

[b] Compare Monrad Paulsen, Intoxication as a Defense to Crime, 1961 U.Ill.L.F. 1: "Drinking alcohol impairs judgment, releases inhibitions, and thus permits the drinker to engage in behavior quite different from the normal pattern. 'Alcohol is an anesthetic or depressant, and its action is approximately the same on all human central nervous systems: it is usually described as reducing the speed and accuracy of perception, slowing down reaction time, and diminishing tensions, anxieties and inhibitions.' Drinking 'stimulates' the drinker, but does so by 'loosening the brakes,' not by 'stepping on the gas.'"

[c] Citations to cases and statutes in 10 other states that adopt a version of the Virginia position are contained in Montana v. Egelhoff, 518 U.S. 37, 48 n.2 (1996). *Egelhoff* upheld the constitutionality over four dissents of a Montana rule that excluded evidence of intoxication offered to show that the defendant lacked "purpose" or "knowledge" (both defined similarly to the Model Penal Code) in a murder prosecution.

terms in which it was rejected, are revealed in the following excerpt from the affirmance of his conviction:

> The issue presented . . . is whether a defendant is entitled to have the jury instructed to the effect that when a specific intent is a necessary element of the crime charged, the drunkenness of defendant, although voluntary, may be considered in determining whether he was capable of forming or entertaining that requisite intent.
>
> Although a majority of jurisdictions would allow such an instruction, we have held . . . that "[v]oluntary drunkenness, where it has not produced permanent insanity, is *never* an excuse for crime; *except,* where a party is charged with murder, if it appear that the accused was too drunk to be capable of deliberating and premeditating, then he can be convicted only of murder in the second degree." . . . We think this to be the better rule.
>
> In [another case involving] a prosecution for robbery, an instruction was offered on the theory that if defendant was too drunk to entertain the specific intent to rob he could not be found guilty. We agreed with the trial court that there was no evidence to support the instruction and said, "Even if there had been evidence of drunkenness, under the decisions of this court, it would have been no excuse for the crime."

If it is right to reject evidence of intoxication offered to negate the awareness required for recklessness, is it not also right to reject its use in all cases? Consider in this connection the following excerpt from Monrad Paulsen, Intoxication as a Defense to Crime, 1961 U.Ill.L.F. 1, 11:

> The present policy of the law which permits the disproof of knowledge or purpose by evidence of extreme intoxication is sound enough. If a crime (or a degree of crime) requires a showing of one of these elements, it is because the conduct involved presents a special danger, if done with purpose or knowledge or the actor presents a special cause for alarm. A burglar, one who breaks in with a purpose to commit a felony, is more dangerous than the simple housebreaker. The aggravated assaults are punished more severely precisely because of the danger presented by the actor's state of mind. He who passes counterfeit money with knowledge is a greater threat than the actor who transfers it without understanding. If purpose or knowledge [is] not present, the cause for the lack is not important. The policy served by requiring these elements of culpability will obtain whether or not their absence is established by proof of extreme intoxication or any other evidence.

Contrast to this line of argument the following comments from Montana v. Egelhoff, 518 U.S. 37 (1996), where the Supreme Court upheld the constitutionality of a Montana rule excluding evidence of intoxication on the issues of "purpose" and "knowledge" in a murder prosecution. Writing for a plurality of the Court, Justice Scalia reviewed the history, noting that initially the common law embodied a "stern rejection of inebriation as a defense" in all cases, but that "by the end of the 19th century, in most American jurisdictions, intoxication could be considered in determining whether a defendant was capable of forming the specific intent necessary to commit the crime charged." Nonetheless, he upheld the restrictive

Montana rule, in part because it conformed to "a lengthy common-law tradition which remains supported by valid justifications today." He added:

> It is not surprising that many states have held fast to or resurrected the common-law rule prohibiting consideration of voluntary intoxication in the determination of mens rea, because that rule has considerable justification. . . . A large number of crimes, especially violent crimes, are committed by intoxicated offenders; modern studies put the numbers as high as half of all homicides, for example. Disallowing consideration of voluntary intoxication has the effect of increasing the punishment for all unlawful acts committed in that state, and thereby deters drunkenness or irresponsible behavior while drunk. The rule also serves as a specific deterrent, ensuring that those who prove incapable of controlling violent impulses while voluntarily intoxicated go to prison. And finally, the rule comports with and implements society's moral perception that one who has voluntarily impaired his own faculties should be responsible for the consequences.

> There is, in modern times, even more justification for [such] laws . . . than there used to be. Some recent studies suggest that the connection between drunkenness and crime is as much cultural as pharmacological—that is, that drunks are violent not simply because alcohol makes them that way, but because they are behaving in accord with their learned belief that drunks are violent. See, e.g., James J. Collins, Suggested Explanatory Frameworks to Clarify the Alcohol Use/Violence Relationship, 15 Contemp. Drug Prob. 107, 115 (1988); Barbara Critchlow, The Powers of John Barleycorn, 41 Am. Psychologist 751, 754–55 (July 1986). This not only adds additional support to the traditional view that an intoxicated criminal is not deserving of exoneration, but it suggests that juries—who possess the same learned belief as the intoxicated offender—will be too quick to accept the claim that the defendant was biologically incapable of forming the requisite mens rea. Treating the matter as one of excluding misleading evidence therefore makes some sense.

## (ii) Lack of Capacity vs. Factual Relevance

Modern cases also reflect a division—originating in 19th century English decisions—as to how the rule relating to intoxication and specific intent should be stated. Some jurisdictions apply a rule of logical relevance. Evidence of intoxication is admitted on mens rea issues for what it is worth. If the jury believes the mens rea was lacking, because the defendant was too drunk to form mens rea or for any other reason, it is told to acquit. The prosecution is required to prove mens rea beyond a reasonable doubt in any event. The Model Penal Code adopts this position in the combination of § 2.08(1) and § 2.08(2). [handwritten margin note: rule of logical relevance]

Other jurisdictions admit intoxication evidence on mens rea, but limit its impact in two ways: the jury is instructed to acquit only if the intoxication was so severe that the defendant was *incapable* of forming mens rea; and the defendant must prove this effect by a preponderance of the evidence. This position is defended in Arthur A. Murphy, The Intoxication Defense: An Introduction to Mr. Smith's Article, 76 Dick. L. Rev. 1, 12–13 (1971–72). Unless instructed otherwise, Murphy observes, "a juror might [handwritten margin note: Δ must prove incapacity] believe that an inebriate who acts on impulse never acts with specific intent or that specific intent requires relatively clearheaded thought processes." When jurors hear evidence that a defendant who denies the relevant mens rea was intoxicated at the time, the jury may require "a higher quality of specific intent—a more culpable state of mind—than required by generally accepted legal doctrine." Requiring the defendant to prove "incapacity" to form specific intent "conveys the idea that only extreme intoxication precludes intent. It focuses the inquiry on the defendant's *potential* for forming the required intent and implies that any intent will serve (impulsive or at a low level of awareness?) so long as the defendant is *capable* of the kind of intent required by law." This approach may be "more likely to avoid improper verdicts," Murphy concludes, because "specific intent crimes can be committed by stupid, unstable and quite peculiar people and . . . intent or conscious purpose does not require a cool head, clear thinking or, indeed, very much in the way of mental activity."

Is Murphy right? Or should the prosecution be required to prove specific intent for intoxicated defendants as it must for sober ones?

Murphy also focuses on a logical difficulty with the incapacity position. The jury is instructed that it must find mens rea beyond a reasonable doubt, but is also told that intoxication is not relevant to the mens rea finding if the defendant has not proved incapacity by a preponderance of the evidence. What is the jury to do if it believes that there is a substantial chance that the defendant was incapable of forming mens rea? It cannot convict, because its belief is inconsistent with a finding of mens rea beyond a reasonable doubt. It cannot acquit, because the defendant has not met the preponderance burden. Is this a serious problem?

## NOTE ON MENTAL ABNORMALITY AND MENS REA

Evidence of mental abnormality can be relevant to the mens rea determinations previously explored. As in the case of intoxication, however, the law has always treated a claim of ignorance or mistake based on mental abnormality as presenting a special problem. The long-standing tradition has been to recognize a separate defense of insanity that, if established, excuses the actor even though the formal elements of actus reus and mens rea have been proved. Whether, apart from the defense of insanity, evidence of mental abnormality can also be considered on mens rea issues is a question of considerable difficulty and debate.

It is helpful in understanding why this is so to recognize that the common law courts saw sanity and insanity as categorical concepts. Insane persons—those who acted in a frenzy induced by madness, in the language of the early days—were said to lack the capacity to entertain a "criminal intent." They were incapable of having "guilty minds." However, a defendant who did not claim to be insane was conclusively presumed to have the capacity to form a criminal intent. There was no middle ground. As a result, evidence of mental abnormality was inadmissible unless it was offered in support of an insanity defense.

This categorical approach to evidence of mental abnormality began to break down during the late 19th and early 20th centuries. One important factor was the emergence of psychiatry as a recognized scientific discipline, a development that was accompanied by efforts to relate advances in psychological understanding to the doctrines of the criminal law. A central theme in the forensic literature of the period was the variety and complexity of mental dysfunction and the difficulty of relating emerging psychiatric concepts to the sane-insane model of the law. Another important influence was the emergence during the same period of integrated approaches to the culpability requirements of the criminal law, including an increased focus on subjective components of mens rea.

Today, there is considerable support for the proposition that evidence of mental abnormality, including expert testimony, should be admissible whenever it is relevant to any issue of culpability in the criminal law. However, some jurisdictions adhere rigorously to the notion that evidence of mental abnormality may be considered only in connection with the insanity defense. Others admit the evidence only on some mens rea issues, and still others admit it whenever relevant to any mens rea issue. There is disagreement too—as in the case of intoxication—on how its relevance should be stated in cases where it is admissible. Some jurisdictions, for example, insist that evidence of mental abnormality must show lack of capacity to formulate the required mens rea and that such evidence must be confined to cases where the defendant was afflicted with some recognized disease or illness.

Full explication and evaluation of these issues cannot usefully be undertaken until the separate defense of insanity is considered, an enterprise that is postponed to Chapter VIII in these materials. Chapter VIII deals with insanity and then returns to the problems of mens rea and evidence of mental abnormality. Additionally, Chapter X explores some related problems in the law of criminal homicide.

# CHAPTER IV

# MENS REA STRUCTURE: ILLUSTRATIONS FROM FEDERAL LAW

## INTRODUCTORY NOTE

This Chapter consists of a moveable feast, to be digested in its entirety, sampled to taste, or omitted in favor of other topics. It elaborates on the mens rea structure developed in Chapter III, using illustrations from federal law. Each Section stands alone. Once the basic mens rea structure of Chapter III is understood, any or all of the materials in this Chapter can be examined, and in any order.

Section 1 begins with important background principles stated in *Morissette v. United States*, which also provides an occasion to explore the difference between "public welfare" or "regulatory" offenses and real crimes. *Morissette* makes clear that common law principles will inform the construction of serious federal crimes based on the common law. But it leaves open the possibility that the same principles may not apply to "new" crimes lacking a common law heritage. Section 2 addresses this possibility in a variety of contexts. It provides occasion for study of the current principles used by the Supreme Court to determine the mens rea applicable to federal crimes, no matter their relation to ancient crimes. Sections 1 and 2 would likely be studied together, but Section 2 could be covered alone if necessary.

Section 3 explores the concept of willful blindness, a variation on the meaning of the mens rea term "knowledge." It does so in the traditional context of a drug possession crime, in this instance through an en banc decision by the Ninth Circuit.

Section 4 concludes the Chapter by revisiting the proposition that ignorance of the law is no excuse. It is arguably unfair to apply that proposition to situations where an ordinary person would have no idea that proposed behavior might be a crime. Section 4 consists of federal cases addressing that concern.

## SECTION 1: INTERPRETATIONS WITHIN THE COMMON LAW TRADITION

### Morissette v. United States

Supreme Court ofUnited States, 1952.
342 U.S. 246.

■ MR. JUSTICE JACKSON delivered the opinion of the Court.

This would have remained a profoundly insignificant case to all except its immediate parties had it not been so tried and submitted to the jury as to raise questions both fundamental and far-reaching in federal criminal law, for which reason we granted certiorari.

On a large tract of uninhabited and untilled land in a wooded and sparsely populated area of Michigan, the government established a practice bombing range over which the Air Force dropped simulated bombs at ground targets. These bombs consisted of a metal cylinder about 40 inches long and eight inches across, filled with sand and enough black powder to cause a smoke puff by which the strike could be located. At various places about the range signs read "Danger—Keep Out—Bombing Range." Nevertheless, the range was known as good deer country and was extensively hunted.

Spent bomb casings were cleared from the targets and thrown into piles "so that they will be out of the way." They were not stacked or piled in any order but were dumped in heaps, some of which had been accumulating for four years or upwards, were exposed to the weather and rusting away.

Morissette, in December of 1948, went hunting in this area but did not get a deer. He thought to meet expenses of the trip by salvaging some of these casings. He loaded three tons of them on his truck and took them to a nearby farm, where they were flattened by driving a tractor over them. After expending this labor and trucking them to market in Flint, he realized $84.

Morissette, by occupation, is a fruit stand operator in summer and a trucker and scrap iron collector in winter. An honorably discharged veteran of World War II, he enjoys a good name among his neighbors and has had no blemish on his record more disreputable than a conviction for reckless driving.

The loading, crushing and transporting of these casings were all in broad daylight, in full view of passers-by, without the slightest effort at concealment. When an investigation was started, Morissette voluntarily, promptly and candidly told the whole story to the authorities, saying that he had no intention of stealing but thought the property was abandoned, unwanted and considered of no value to the government. He was indicted, however, on the charge that he "did unlawfully, wilfully and knowingly steal and convert" property of the United States of the value of $84, in violation of 18 U.S.C. § 641[2]. . . . Morissette was convicted and sentenced to imprisonment for two months or to pay a fine of $200. The Court of Appeals affirmed, one judge dissenting.

On his trial, Morissette, as he had at all times told investigating officers, testified that from appearances he believed the casings were cast-off and abandoned, that he did not intend to steal the property, and took it with no wrongful or criminal intent. The trial court, however, was unimpressed, and ruled:

> [H]e took it because he thought it was abandoned and he knew he was on government property. . . . That is no defense. . . . I don't think anybody can have the defense [that]

---

[2] Section 641, so far as pertinent, reads:

Whoever embezzles, steals, purloins, or knowingly converts to his use or the use of another . . . any . . . thing of value of the United States [s]hall be fined not more than $10,000 or imprisoned not more than ten years, or both; but if the value of such property does not exceed the sum of $100, he shall be fined not more than $1,000 or imprisoned not more than one year, or both.

they thought the property was abandoned on another man's piece of property.

The court stated:

> I will not permit you to show this man thought it was abandoned. . . . I hold in this case that there is no question of abandoned property.

The court refused to submit or to allow counsel to argue to the jury whether Morissette acted with innocent intention. It charged:

> And I instruct you that if you believe the testimony of the government in this case, he intended to take it. . . . He had no right to take this property. [A]nd it is no defense to claim that it was abandoned, because it was on private property. . . . And I instruct you to this effect: That if this young man took this property (and he says he did), without any permission (he says he did), that was on the property of the United States Government (he says it was), that it was of the value of one cent or more (and evidently it was), that he is guilty of the offense charged here. If you believe the government, he is guilty. . . . The question on intent is whether or not he intended to take the property. He says he did. Therefore, if you believe either side, he is guilty. . . .

The Court of Appeals suggested that "greater restraint in expression should have been exercised," but affirmed the conviction because, "[a]s we have interpreted the statute, appellant was guilty of its violation beyond a shadow of doubt, as evidenced even by his own admissions." Its construction of the statute is that it creates several separate and distinct offenses, one being knowing conversion of government property. The court ruled that this particular offense requires no element of criminal intent. This conclusion was thought to be required by the failure of Congress to express such a requisite and this Court's decisions in United States v. Behrman, 258 U.S. 280 (1922), and United States v. Balint, 258 U.S. 250 (1922).

I.

In those cases this Court did construe mere omission from a criminal enactment of any mention of criminal intent as dispensing with it. If they be deemed precedents for principles of construction generally applicable to federal penal statutes, they authorize this conviction. Indeed, such adoption of the literal reasoning announced in those cases would do this and more—it would sweep out of all federal crimes, except when expressly preserved, the ancient requirement of a culpable state of mind. We think a resume of their historical background is convincing that an effect has been ascribed to them more comprehensive than was contemplated and one inconsistent with our philosophy of criminal law.

The contention that an injury can amount to a crime only when inflicted by intention is no provincial or transient notion. It is as universal and persistent in mature systems of law as belief in freedom of the human will and a consequent ability and duty of the normal individual to choose between good and evil. A relation between some mental element and punishment for a harmful act is almost as instinctive as the child's familiar exculpatory "But I didn't mean to," and has afforded the rational basis for a tardy and unfinished substitution of deterrence and reformation in place of retaliation and vengeance as the motivation for public prosecution. Unqualified acceptance of this doctrine by English common law in the eighteenth century was indicated by Blackstone's sweeping statement that to constitute any crime there must first be a "vicious will." . . .

Crime, as a compound concept, generally constituted only from concurrence of an evil-meaning mind with an evil-doing hand, was congenial to an intense individualism and took deep and early root in American soil.[9] As the states codified the common law of crimes, even if their enactments were silent on the subject, their courts assumed that the omission did not signify disapproval of the principle but merely recognized that intent was so inherent in the idea of the offense that it required no statutory affirmation. Courts, with little hesitation or division, found an implication of the requirement as to offenses that were taken over from the common law. The unanimity with which they have adhered to the central thought that wrongdoing must be conscious to be criminal is emphasized by the variety, disparity and confusion of their definitions of the requisite but elusive mental element. However, courts of various jurisdictions, and for the purposes of different offenses, have devised working formulae, if not scientific ones, for the instruction of juries around such terms as "felonious intent," "criminal intent," "malice aforethought," "guilty knowledge," "fraudulent intent," "wilfulness," "scienter," to denote guilty knowledge, or "mens rea," to signify an evil purpose or mental culpability. By use or combination of these various tokens, they have sought to protect those who were not blameworthy in mind from conviction of infamous common-law crimes.

However, the *Balint* and *Behrman* offenses belong to a category of another character, with very different antecedents and origins. The crimes there involved depend on no mental element but consist only of forbidden acts or omissions. This . . . is made clear from examination of a century-old but accelerating tendency, discernible both here and in England,[11] to call into existence new duties and crimes which disregard any ingredient of intent. The industrial revolution multiplied the number of workmen exposed to injury from increasingly powerful and complex mechanisms, driven by freshly discovered sources of energy, requiring higher precautions by employers. Traffic of velocities, volumes and varieties unheard of came to subject the wayfarer to intolerable casualty risks if owners and drivers were not to observe new cares and uniformities of conduct. Congestion of cities and crowding of quarters called for health and welfare regulations undreamed of in simpler times. Wide distribution of goods became an instrument of wide distribution of harm when those who dispersed food, drink, drugs, and even

---

[9] Holmes, The Common Law, considers intent in the chapter on The Criminal Law, and earlier makes the pithy observation: "Even a dog distinguishes between being stumbled over and being kicked."

[11] The changes in English law are illustrated by 19th Century English cases. [For example,] in an action to enforce a statutory forfeiture for possession of adulterated tobacco, the respondent was held liable even though he had no knowledge of, or cause to suspect, the adulteration. Countering respondent's arguments, Baron Parke said, "It is very true that in particular instances it may produce mischief, because an innocent man may suffer from his want of care in not examining the tobacco he has received, and not taking a warranty; but the public inconvenience would be much greater, if in every case the officers were obliged to prove knowledge. They would be very seldom able to do so." Regina v. Woodrow, 15 M. & W. 404, 417 (Exch. 1846). Convenience of the prosecution thus emerged as a rationale. . . .

securities, did not comply with reasonable standards of quality, integrity, disclosure and care. Such dangers have engendered increasingly numerous and detailed regulations which heighten the duties of those in control of particular industries, trades, properties or activities that affect public health, safety or welfare.

While many of these duties are sanctioned by a more strict civil liability, lawmakers, whether wisely or not, have sought to make such regulations more effective by invoking criminal sanctions to be applied by the familiar technique of criminal prosecutions and convictions. This has confronted the courts with a multitude of prosecutions, for what have been aptly called "public welfare offenses." These cases do not fit neatly into any of such accepted classifications of common-law offenses, such as those against the state, the person, property, or public morals. Many of these offenses are not in the nature of positive aggressions or invasions, with which the common law so often dealt, but are in the nature of neglect where the law requires care, or inaction where it imposes a duty. Many violations of such regulations result in no direct or immediate injury to person or property but merely create the danger or probability of it which the law seeks to minimize. While such offenses do not threaten the security of the state in the manner of treason, they may be regarded as offenses against its authority, for their occurrence impairs the efficiency of controls deemed essential to the social order as presently constituted. In this respect, whatever the intent of the violator, the injury is the same, and the consequences are injurious or not according to fortuity. Hence, legislation applicable to such offenses, as a matter of policy, does not specify intent as a necessary element. The accused, if he does not will the violation, usually is in a position to prevent it with no more care than society might reasonably expect and no more exertion than it might reasonably exact from one who assumed his responsibilities. Also, penalties commonly are relatively small, and conviction does no grave damage to an offender's reputation. Under such considerations, courts have turned to construing statutes and regulations which make no mention of intent as dispensing with it and holding that the guilty act alone makes out the crime. This has not, however, been without expressions of misgiving.

The pilot of the movement in this country appears to be a holding that a tavernkeeper could be convicted for selling liquor to an habitual drunkard even if he did not know the buyer to be such. Barnes v. State, 19 Conn. 398 (1849). Later came Massachusetts holdings that convictions for selling adulterated milk in violation of statutes forbidding such sales require no allegation or proof that defendant knew of the adulteration. Commonwealth v. Farren, 9 Allen 489 (1864); Commonwealth v. Nichols, 10 Allen 199 (1865); Commonwealth v. Waite, 11 Allen 264 (1865). Departures from the common-law tradition, mainly of these general classes, were reviewed and their rationale appraised by Chief Justice Cooley, as follows: "I agree that as a rule there can be no crime without a criminal intent, but this is not by any means a universal rule. . . . Many statutes which are in the nature of police regulations, as this is, impose criminal penalties irrespective of any intent to violate them, the purpose being to require a degree of diligence for the protection of the public which shall render violation impossible." People v. Roby, 52 Mich. 577, 579, 18 N.W. 365, 366 (1884).

After the turn of the Century, a new use for crimes without intent appeared when New York enacted numerous and novel regulations of tenement houses, sanctioned by money penalties. Landlords contended that a guilty intent was essential to establish a violation. Judge Cardozo wrote the answer: "The defendant asks us to test the meaning of this statute by standards applicable to statutes that govern infamous crimes. The analogy, however, is deceptive. The element of conscious wrongdoing, the guilty mind accompanying the guilty act, is associated with the concept of crimes that are punished as infamous. . . . Even there it is not an invariable element. But in the prosecution of minor offenses there is a wider range of practice and of power. Prosecutions for petty penalties have always constituted in our law a class by themselves. . . . That is true, though the prosecution is criminal in form." Tenement House Department of City of New York v. McDevitt, 215 N.Y. 160, 168, 109 N.E. 88, 90 (1915).

*minor offenses; class of their own*

Soon, employers advanced the same contention as to violations of regulations prescribed by a new labor law. Judge Cardozo, again for the court, pointed out, as a basis for penalizing violations whether intentional or not, that they were punishable only by fine "moderate in amount," but cautiously added that in sustaining the power so to fine unintended violations "we are not to be understood as sustaining to a like length the power to imprison. We leave that question open." People ex rel. Price v. Sheffield Farms-Slawson-Decker Co., 225 N.Y. 25, 32–33, 121 N.E. 474, 476, 477 (1918).

Thus, for diverse but reconcilable reasons, state courts converged on the same result, discontinuing inquiry into intent in a limited class of offenses against such statutory regulations.

*Statutory regulations*

Before long, similar questions growing out of federal legislation reached this Court. Its judgments were in harmony with this consensus of state judicial opinion, the existence of which may have led the Court to overlook the need for full exposition of their rationale in the context of federal law. In overruling a contention that there can be no conviction on an indictment which makes no charge of criminal intent but alleges only making of a sale of a narcotic forbidden by law, Chief Justice Taft, wrote: "While the general rule at common law was that the scienter was a necessary element in the indictment and proof of every crime, and this was followed in regard to statutory crimes even where the statutory definition did not in terms include it . . ., there has been a modification of this view in respect to prosecutions under statutes the purpose of which would be obstructed by such a requirement. It is a question of legislative intent to be construed by the court. . . ." *United States v. Balint*, 258 U.S. at 251–52.

*Taft: modification*

He referred, however, to "regulatory measures in the exercise of what is called the police power where the emphasis of the statute is evidently upon achievement of some social betterment rather than the punishment of the crimes as in cases of mala in se," and drew his citation of supporting authority chiefly from state court cases dealing with regulatory offenses.

On the same day, the Court determined that an offense under the Narcotic Drug Act does not require intent, saying, "If the offense be a statutory one, and intent or knowledge is not made an element of it, the indictment need not charge such knowledge or intent." *United States v. Behrman*, 258 U.S. at 288.

Of course, the purpose of every statute would be "obstructed" by requiring a finding of intent, if we assume that it had a purpose to convict without it. Therefore, the obstruction rationale does not help us to learn the purpose of the omission by Congress. And since no federal crime can exist except by force of statute, the reasoning of the Behrman opinion, if read literally, would work far-reaching changes in the composition of all federal crimes. Had such a result been contemplated, it could hardly have escaped mention by a Court which numbered among its members one especially interested and informed concerning the importance of intent in common-law crimes [Justice Holmes]. This might be the more expected since the *Behrman* holding did call forth his dissent, in which Mr. Justice McReynolds and Mr. Justice Brandeis joined, omitting any such mention.

It was not until recently that the Court took occasion more explicitly to relate abandonment of the ingredient of intent, not merely with considerations of expediency in obtaining convictions, nor with the malum prohibitum classification of the crime, but with the peculiar nature and quality of the offense. We referred to ". . . a now familiar type of legislation whereby penalties serve as effective means of regulation," and continued, "such legislation dispenses with the conventional requirement for criminal conduct—awareness of some wrongdoing. In the interest of the larger good it puts the burden of acting at hazard upon a person otherwise innocent but standing in responsible relation to a public danger." But we warned: "Hardship there doubtless may be under a statute which thus penalizes the transaction though consciousness of wrongdoing be totally wanting." United States v. Dotterweich, 320 U.S. 277, 280–81, 284 (1943)

Neither this Court nor, so far as we are aware, any other has undertaken to delineate a precise line or set forth comprehensive criteria for distinguishing between crimes that require a mental element and crimes that do not. We attempt no closed definition, for the law on the subject is neither settled nor static. The conclusion reached in the Balint and Behrman cases has our approval and adherence for the circumstances to which it was there applied. A quite different question here is whether we will expand the doctrine of crimes without intent to include those charged here.

Stealing, larceny, and its variants and equivalents, were among the earliest offenses known to the law that existed before legislation; they are invasions of rights of property which stir a sense of insecurity in the whole community and arouse public demand for retribution, the penalty is high and, when a sufficient amount is involved, the infamy is that of a felony, which, says Maitland, is ". . . as bad a word as you can give to man or thing." State courts of last resort, on whom fall the heaviest burden of interpreting criminal law in this country, have consistently retained the requirement of intent in larceny-type offenses. If any state has deviated, the exception has neither been called to our attention nor disclosed by our research.

Congress, therefore, omitted any express prescription of criminal intent from the enactment before us in the light of an unbroken course of judicial decision in all constituent states of the Union holding intent inherent in this class of offense, even when not expressed in a statute. Congressional silence as to mental elements in an Act merely adopting into federal statutory law a concept of crime already so well defined in common law and statutory interpretation by the states may warrant quite contrary inferences than the same silence in creating an offense new to general law, for whose definition the courts have no guidance except the Act. Because the offenses before this Court in the *Balint* and *Behrman* cases were of this latter class, we cannot accept them as authority for eliminating intent from offenses incorporated from the common law. Nor do exhaustive studies of state court cases disclose any well-considered decisions applying the doctrine of crime without intent to such enacted common-law offenses.[20] . . .

*[margin note: reasoning]*

The Government asks us by a feat of construction radically to change the weights and balances in the scales of justice. The purpose and obvious effect of doing away with the requirement of a guilty intent is to ease the prosecution's path to conviction, to strip the defendant of such benefit as he derived at common law from innocence of evil purpose, and to circumscribe the freedom heretofore allowed juries. Such a manifest impairment of the immunities of the individual should not be extended to common-law crimes on judicial initiative.

The spirit of the doctrine which denies to the federal judiciary power to create crimes forthrightly admonishes that we should not enlarge the reach of enacted crimes by constituting them from anything less than the incriminating components contemplated by the words used in the statute. And where Congress borrows terms of art in which are accumulated the legal tradition and meaning of centuries of practice, it presumably knows and adopts the cluster of ideas that were attached to each borrowed word in the body of learning from which it was taken and the meaning its use will convey to the judicial mind unless otherwise instructed. In such case, absence of contrary direction may be taken as satisfaction with widely accepted definitions, not as a departure from them.

*[margin note: holding]*

We hold that mere omission from § 641 of any mention of intent will not be construed as eliminating that element from the crimes denounced.

## II.

It is suggested, however, that the history and purposes of § 641 imply something more affirmative as to elimination of intent from at least one of the offenses charged under it in this case. The argument does not contest that criminal intent is retained in the offenses of embezzlement, stealing and purloining, as incorporated into this section. But it is urged that Congress joined with those, as a new, separate and distinct offense, knowingly to convert government property, under circumstances which imply that it is an offense in which the mental element of intent is not necessary.

*[margin note: Knowingly convert gov't property]*

---

[20] Francis Bowes Sayre, Public Welfare Offenses, 33 Colum. L. Rev. 55, 73, 84 (1933), cites and classifies a large number of cases and concludes that they fall roughly into subdivisions of (1) illegal sales of intoxicating liquor, (2) sales of impure or adulterated food or drugs, (3) sales of misbranded articles, (4) violations of anti-narcotic Acts, (5) criminal nuisances, (6) violations of traffic regulations, (7) violations of motor-vehicle laws, and (8) violations of general police regulations, passed for the safety, health or well-being of the community.

Congress has been alert to what often is a decisive function of some mental element in crime. It has seen fit to prescribe that an evil state of mind, described variously in one or more such terms as "intentional," "wilful," "knowing," "fraudulent" or "malicious," will make criminal an otherwise indifferent act, or increase the degree of the offense or its punishment. Also, it has at times required a specific intent or purpose which will require some specialized knowledge or design for some evil beyond the common law intent to do injury. . . . In view of the care that has been bestowed upon the subject, it is significant that we have not found, nor has our attention been directed to, any instance in which Congress has expressly eliminated the mental element from a crime taken over from the common law.

The section with which we are here concerned was enacted in 1948, as a consolidation of four former sections of Title 18. . . . We find no other purpose in the 1948 re-enactment than to collect from scattered sources crimes so kindred as to belong in one category. Not one of these had been interpreted to be a crime without intention and no purpose to differentiate between them in the matter of intent is disclosed. No inference that some were and some were not crimes of intention can be drawn from any difference in classification or punishment. [E]ach is, at its least, a misdemeanor, and if the amount involved is $100 or more each is a felony. If one crime without intent has been smuggled into a section whose dominant offenses do require intent, it was put in ill-fitting and compromising company. The government apparently did not believe that conversion stood so alone when it drew this one-count indictment to charge that Morissette "did unlawfully, wilfully and knowingly steal and convert to his own use."

Congress, by the language of this section, has been at pains to incriminate only "knowing" conversions. But, at common law, there are unwitting acts which constitute conversions. In the civil tort, except for recovery of exemplary damages, the defendant's knowledge, intent, motive, mistake, and good faith are generally irrelevant.[31] If one takes property which turns out to belong to another, his innocent intent will not shield him from making restitution or indemnity, for his well-meaning may not be allowed to deprive another of his own.

Had the statute applied to conversions without qualification, it would have made crimes of all unwitting, inadvertent and unintended conversions. Knowledge, of course, is not identical with intent and may not have been the most apt words of limitation. But knowing conversion requires more than knowledge that defendant was taking the property into his possession. He must have had knowledge of the facts, though not necessarily the law, that made the taking a conversion. In the case before us, whether the mental element that Congress required be spoken of as knowledge or as intent, would not seem to alter its bearing on guilt. For it is not apparent how Morissette could have knowingly or

[31] The rationale underlying [this rule] is that when one clearly assumes the rights of ownership over property of another no proof of intent to convert is necessary. It has even been held that one may be held liable in conversion even though he reasonably supposed that he had a legal right to the property in question. [Such cases] leave no doubt that Morissette could be held liable for a civil conversion for his taking of the property here involved, and the instructions to the jury might have been appropriate in such a civil action. This assumes of course that actual abandonment was not proven, a matter which petitioner should be allowed to prove if he can.

intentionally converted property that he did not know could be converted, as would be the case if it was in fact abandoned or if he truly believed it to be abandoned and unwanted property.

It is said, and at first blush the claim has plausibility, that, if we construe the statute to require a mental element as part of criminal conversion, it becomes a meaningless duplication of the offense of stealing, and that conversion can be given meaning only by interpreting it to disregard intention. But here again a broader view of the evolution of these crimes throws a different light on the legislation.

It is not surprising if there is considerable overlapping in the embezzlement, stealing, purloining and knowing conversion grouped in this statute. What has concerned codifiers of the larceny-type offense is that gaps or crevices have separated particular crimes of this general class and guilty men have escaped through the breaches. The books contain a surfeit of cases drawing fine distinctions between slightly different circumstances under which one may obtain wrongful advantages from another's property. The codifiers wanted to reach all such instances. Probably every stealing is a conversion, but certainly not every knowing conversion is a stealing. "To steal means to take away from one in lawful possession without right with the intention to keep wrongfully." Conversion, however, may be consummated without any intent to keep and without any wrongful taking, where the initial possession by the converter was entirely lawful. Conversion may include misuse or abuse of property. It may reach use in an unauthorized manner or to an unauthorized extent of property placed in one's custody for limited use. Money rightfully taken into one's custody may be converted without any intent to keep or embezzle it merely by commingling it with the custodian's own, if he was under a duty to keep it separate and intact. It is not difficult to think of intentional and knowing abuses and unauthorized uses of government property that might be knowing conversions but which could not be reached as embezzlement, stealing or purloining. Knowing conversion adds significantly to the range of protection of government property without interpreting it to punish unwitting conversions.

The purpose which we here attribute to Congress parallels that of codifiers of common law in England and in the states and demonstrates that the serious problem in drafting such a statute is to avoid gaps and loopholes between offenses. It is significant that the English and state codifiers have tried to cover the same type of conduct that we are suggesting as the purpose of Congress here, without, however, departing from the common law tradition that these are crimes of intendment.

We find no grounds for inferring any affirmative instruction from Congress to eliminate intent from any offense with which this defendant was charged.

III.

. . . The [trial] court thought the only question was, "Did he intend to take the property?" That the removal of them was a conscious and intentional act was admitted. But that isolated fact is not an adequate basis on which the jury should find the criminal intent to steal or knowingly convert, that is, wrongfully to deprive another of possession of property. Whether that intent existed, the jury must determine, not only from the act of taking, but from that together with defendant's testimony and all of the surrounding circumstances.

Of course, the jury, considering Morissette's awareness that these casings were on government property, his failure to seek any permission for their removal and his self-interest as a witness, might have disbelieved his profession of innocent intent and concluded that his assertion of a belief that the casings were abandoned was an afterthought. Had the jury convicted on proper instructions it would be the end of the matter. But juries are not bound by what seems inescapable logic to judges. They might have concluded that the heaps of spent casings left in the hinterland to rust away presented an appearance of unwanted and abandoned junk, and that lack of any conscious deprivation of property or intentional injury was indicated by Morissette's good character, the openness of the taking, crushing and transporting of the casings, and the candor with which it was all admitted. They might have refused to brand Morissette as a thief. Had they done so, that too would have been the end of the matter.

*holding/reasoning*

*juries not bound by inescapable logic to judges*

*holding/reasoning*

Reversed.

■ MR. JUSTICE DOUGLAS concurs in the result.

■ MR. JUSTICE MINTON took no part in the consideration or decision of this case.

## NOTES ON *MORISSETTE*

### 1. INTRODUCTION

Justice Jackson set out to reconcile two lines of doctrine in *Morissette*. One, traditionally involving so-called "regulatory" or "public welfare" offenses, typically dispensed with the common law mens rea tradition by employing strict liability on a central element, and sometimes vicarious liability as well. Often, though not always, these were not offenses of high moral stigma, and they usually did not result in significant imprisonment. The other line involved modern statutory formulations of traditional common law crimes. Typically, they concerned serious offenses such as murder, rape, and various forms of theft, offenses involving high stigma and carrying heavy penalties. The tradition here, reflecting the common law focus on personal responsibility and blame, was to require mens rea. As Jackson framed the question in *Morissette*, his task was to ascertain which of the two lines of cases controlled the issue before the Court.

### 2. "PUBLIC WELFARE" OFFENSES

Although United States v. Behrman, 258 U.S. 280 (1922), and United States v. Balint, 258 U.S. 250 (1922), traditionally have been placed in the "public welfare" category and were so viewed by Justice Jackson, whether they belong there is a matter of debate. The two cases summarized below, one cited by Justice Jackson and the other more modern, are more typical illustrations of the "public welfare" concept.

*(i) United States v. Dotterweich* (conviction of misbranding and adulterated drugs into interstate commerce)

Dotterweich was president and general manager of a company that purchased drugs from the manufacturer, repackaged them, and shipped them under a new label. He was convicted of a misdemeanor for company shipments of adulterated and misbranded drugs in interstate commerce, even though he had no personal involvement in the shipments. He was sentenced to pay a fine and to 60 days on probation. In United States v. Dotterweich, 320 U.S. 277 (1943), the Supreme Court upheld his conviction. For the Court, Justice Frankfurter wrote:

> The Food and Drugs Act of 1906 was an exertion by Congress of its power to keep impure and adulterated food and drugs out of the channels of commerce. By the Act of 1938, Congress extended the range of its control over illicit and noxious articles and stiffened the penalties for disobedience. The purposes of this legislation thus touch phases of the lives and health of people which, in the circumstances of modern industrialism, are largely beyond self-protection. Regard for these purposes should infuse construction of the legislation if it is to be treated as a working instrument of government and not merely as a collection of English words. The prosecution to which Dotterweich was subjected is based on a now familiar type of legislation whereby penalties serve as effective means of regulation. Such legislation dispenses with the conventional requirement for criminal conduct—awareness of some wrongdoing. In the interest of the larger good it puts the burden of acting at hazard upon a person otherwise innocent but standing in responsible relation to a public danger. . . .
>
> Whether an accused shares responsibility in the business process resulting in unlawful distribution depends on the evidence produced at the trial and its submission—assuming the evidence warrants it—to the jury under appropriate guidance. The offense is committed, unless the enterprise which they are serving enjoys the immunity of a guaranty, by all who do have such a responsible share in the furtherance of the transaction which the statute outlaws, namely, to put into the stream of interstate commerce adulterated or misbranded drugs. Hardship there doubtless may be under a statute which thus penalizes the transaction though consciousness of wrongdoing be totally wanting. Balancing relative hardships, Congress has preferred to place it upon those who have at least the opportunity of informing themselves of the existence of conditions imposed for the protection of consumers before sharing in illicit commerce, rather than to throw the hazard on the innocent public who are wholly helpless.
>
> It would be too treacherous to define or even to indicate by way of illustration the class of employees which stands in such a responsible relation. To attempt a formula embracing the variety of conduct whereby persons may responsibly contribute in furthering a transaction forbidden by an Act of Congress, to wit, to send illicit goods across state lines, would be mischievous futility. In such matters the good sense of prosecutors, the wise guidance of trial judges, and the ultimate judgment of juries must be trusted. Our system of criminal justice necessarily depends on "conscience and circumspection in prosecuting officers," Nash v. United States, 229 U.S. 373, 378 (1913), even when the consequences are far more drastic than they are under the provision of law before us. . . . For present purpose it suffices to say that in what the de-

fense characterized as "a very fair charge" the District Court properly left the question of the responsibility of Dotterweich for the shipment to the jury, and there was sufficient evidence to support its verdict. *[holding]*

### (ii)  United States v. Park *(CEO charged [with] violations of FDA Act of contamination by rodents)*

Park was the chief executive officer of Acme Markets, a national retail food chain with 874 retail outlets, 16 warehouses, and 36,000 employees. He was charged with five violations of the Federal Food, Drug, and Cosmetic Act based on shipments of food that had been exposed to contamination by rodents in an Acme warehouse. *[charged with 5 violations]* The company had been repeatedly warned that FDA inspections had discovered evidence of rodent infestation and other insanitary conditions in specified Acme warehouses. A subsequent inspection of one of the warehouses found that "there was still evidence of rodent activity in the building and in the warehouses and . . . some rodent-contaminated lots of food items."

Park maintained in his defense that he had been assured that appropriate company officials responsible for sanitation were dealing with the problems and that he did not "believe there was anything [he] could have done more constructively than what [he] found was being done." *[Park's Defense]* On cross examination he admitted that "providing sanitary conditions for food offered for sale to the public was something that he was 'responsible for in the entire operation of the company.'" He also admitted that the repeat offenses "indicated the system for handling sanitation 'wasn't working perfectly' and that as Acme's chief executive officer he was responsible for 'any result which occurs in our company.'" Park was convicted and sentenced to pay a fine of $50 for each of the five offenses.[a] *[Procedure]* In United States v. Park, 421 U.S. 658 (1975), the Supreme Court affirmed. Chief Justice Burger spoke for the Court:

> The rule that corporate employees who have "a responsible share in the furtherance of the transaction which the statute outlaws" are subject to the criminal provisions of the Act was not formulated in a vacuum. Cases under the Federal Food and Drugs Act of 1906 reflected the view both that knowledge or intent were not required to be proved in prosecutions under its criminal provisions, and that responsible corporate agents could be subjected to the liability thereby imposed. *[knowledge or intent not required corporate agents]* Moreover, the principle had been recognized that a corporate agent, through whose act, default, or omission the corporation committed a crime, was himself guilty individually of that crime. The principle had been applied whether or not the crime required "consciousness of wrongdoing," and it had been applied not only to those corporate agents who themselves committed the criminal act, but also to those who by virtue of their managerial positions or other similar relation to the actor could be deemed responsible for its commission.

> In the latter class of cases, the liability of managerial officers did not depend on their knowledge of, or personal participation in, the act made criminal by the statute. Rather, where the statute

---

[a]  The maximum penalty for a first violation of the statute under which Park was convicted was one year and/or a fine of not more than $1,000. A second or subsequent offense carried a maximum of three years and/or a fine of $10,000.

under which they were prosecuted dispensed with "consciousness of wrongdoing," an omission or failure to act was deemed a sufficient basis for a responsible corporate agent's liability. It was enough in such cases that, by virtue of the relationship he bore to the corporation, the agent had the power to prevent the act complained of.

The rationale of the interpretation given the Act in United States v. Dotterweich, 320 U.S. 277 (1943), as holding criminally accountable the persons whose failure to exercise the authority and supervisory responsibility reposed in them by the business organization resulted in the violation complained of, has been confirmed in our subsequent cases. Thus, the Court has reaffirmed the proposition that "the public interest in the purity of its food is so great as to warrant the imposition of the highest standard of care on distributors." Smith v. California, 361 U.S. 147, 152 (1959). In order to make "distributors of food the strictest censors of their merchandise," id, the Act punishes "neglect where the law requires care, or inaction where it imposes a duty." Morissette v. United States, 342 U.S. 246, 255 (1952). "The accused, if he does not will the violation, usually is in a position to prevent it with no more care than society might reasonably expect and no more exertion than it might reasonably exact from one who assumed his responsibilities." Id. at 256. Similarly, in cases decided after *Dotterweich*, the Courts of Appeals have recognized that those corporate agents vested with the responsibility, and power commensurate with that responsibility, to devise whatever measures are necessary to ensure compliance with the Act bear a "responsible relationship" to, or have a "responsible share" in, violations.

Thus *Dotterweich* and the cases which have followed reveal that in providing sanctions which reach and touch the individuals who execute the corporate mission—and this is by no means necessarily confined to a single corporate agent or employee—the Act imposes not only a positive duty to seek out and remedy violations when they occur but also, and primarily, a duty to implement measures that will insure that violations will not occur. The requirements of foresight and vigilance imposed on responsible corporate agents are beyond question demanding, and perhaps onerous, but they are no more stringent than the public has a right to expect of those who voluntarily assume positions of authority in business enterprises whose services and products affect the health and well-being of the public that supports them.

The Act does not, as we observed in *Dotterweich*, make criminal liability turn on "awareness of some wrongdoing" or "conscious fraud." The duty imposed by Congress on responsible corporate agents is, we emphasize, one that requires the highest standard of foresight and vigilance, but the Act, in its criminal aspect, does not require that which is objectively impossible. The theory upon which responsible corporate agents are held criminally accountable for "causing" violations of the Act permits a claim that a defendant was "powerless" to prevent or correct the violation to "be raised defensively at a trial on the merits." United States v. Wiesenfeld Warehouse Co., 376 U.S. 86, 91 (1964). If such a claim is made, the defendant has the burden of coming forward with evidence, but this does not alter the Government's ultimate burden of proving beyond a reasonable doubt the defendant's guilt, including his power, in light of the duty imposed by the Act, to prevent or correct the prohibited condition. Congress has seen fit to enforce the accountability of responsible corporate agents dealing with products which may affect the health of consumers by penal sanctions cast in rigorous terms, and the obligation of the courts is to give them effect so long as they do not violate the Constitution.

## 3. BACKGROUND ON THE LAW OF THEFT

The crime involved in *Morissette* is best understood against the background of the law of theft. The common law crime of larceny required a trespassory taking of the personal property of another with intent to appropriate. The taking was said to be "trespassory" when the initial acquisition of the property violated rights of possession. For this reason, larceny was often said to be an offense against possession.

It is clear, however, that theft can occur in contexts where the actor does not "trespass" on the possessory rights of others in obtaining the property. Bank tellers, servants, and agents, for example, lawfully possess property that belongs to others. They are not, however, entitled to treat such property as their own. When they deprive owners of their property, such persons should be guilty of theft even though their initial possession was lawful.

The Anglo-American legal system reached this conclusion very slowly. The earliest forms of larceny were concerned with misappropriations by violence or stealth. Over the years, and often through legal fictions, the concept of trespassory taking was expanded to encompass other means of misappropriating the property of another. For example, "larceny by trick" covered cases where a "constructive" trespass was said to have occurred if the property was obtained under specified fraudulent circumstances. Generally speaking, "larceny by trick" occurred when the actor had the intent to steal property at the time its temporary use was lawfully obtained from the owner. To take a modern example, one who intended to steal a car at the time it was rented would be guilty of larceny by trick. But if one rented the car and only later decided to steal it, the law's ability to perceive a fictional trespass would have been exceeded and no larceny would have occurred. Indeed, for a substantial period of common law history, no crime at all would have been committed if property were stolen in this manner.

The most important effort to close this gap was begun in England in 1799 by the enactment of the statutory offense of embezzlement. Originally, embezzlement dealt with situations where a master's property was received from a third person by a servant, who then proceeded to steal it. Subsequently, the offense was expanded by additional statutes, both in England and in this country, to cover most variations of the situation where a lawful custodian misappropriated custodial property. In separate developments, offenses also emerged to deal with obtaining property by false pretenses, extortion, and the like.[b]

---

[b] For a more detailed review of the history of larceny, embezzlement, and related offenses, see Jerome Hall, Theft, Law and Society (2d ed. 1952); Wayne LaFave & Austin Scott,

*does it matter much any more?*

The technical distinctions among these various theft offenses were extremely complicated. Moreover, it mattered a great deal that the prosecutor charged the right offense. If the prosecutor charged larceny by trick, the defendant could defend on the ground that what really happened was embezzlement. The defendant might then be charged with embezzlement, but could defend the second charge on the ground that the crime really was larceny by trick.[c]

Statutes such as the one in *Morissette* were enacted to avoid such technicalities and to make sure, as the Court says, that gaps between the various theft offenses were filled. More comprehensive consolidation of theft offenses was proposed by the Model Penal Code, and most modern statutes have followed its approach. Article 223 of the Model Code consolidates the law of theft into a single, comprehensive offense.[d] Its principal thrust is to eliminate the procedural consequences of distinctions between separately defined theft offenses. As can be seen from the detail of Article 223, however, this approach does not eliminate the need for statutes and implementing decisions to focus on differences in the ways in which one can appropriate the property of another.[e]

## 4. QUESTIONS AND COMMENTS

There was no doubt on the facts that Morissette meant permanently to appropriate to himself the value of the bomb casings. He sold them and pocketed the money. Assume, however, a different scenario. Suppose he spotted an Army truck on the property, used it to take the casings home, and then returned it. Or suppose he was a government employee who, in violation of office policy, took an office computer home for the weekend and brought it back on Monday. Would he be guilty of "knowing conversion" of the truck or the computer in these situations? Is the Court reading Congress as having significantly extended the crime of theft? If so, is the extension justified?

Justice Jackson said at one point in his opinion that "Congressional silence as to mental elements in an act merely adopting into federal statutory law a concept of crime already so well defined in common law and statutory interpretation by the states may warrant quite contrary inferences than the same silence in creating an offense new to general law, for whose definition the courts have no guidance except the act." Does this mean that

---

Criminal Law 618–712 (1972); Rollin Perkins & Ronald Boyce, Criminal Law 292–452 (3d ed. 1982).

   c   The example may sound fanciful but, as reported in Jerome Michael & Herbert Wechsler, Criminal Law and Its Administration 545 (1940), the "books are replete with dismissals and reversals on the ground that the indictment or the conviction was for the wrong crime." They cite Commonwealth v. O'Malley, 97 Mass. 584 (1867), as an illustration. In that case the defendant was acquitted of larceny and later convicted of embezzlement. The conviction was then set aside on the ground that the evidence proved larceny.

*Commonwealth v. O'Malley*

   d   For a general discussion of the purpose of consolidation and some of the problems of implementation, see ALI, Model Penal Code and Commentaries § 223.1, pp. 127–38 (1980). At least 30 states have adopted consolidated theft provisions since the promulgation of the Model Penal Code in 1962. The Model Code was not the first effort at consolidation, though it has been by far the most influential. An earlier treatment of the consolidation issue can be found in Jerome Michael & Herbert Wechsler, Criminal Law and Its Administration 545–52 (1940).

   e   For example, theft by deception requires definition of what counts as obtaining property by "deception" and theft by extortion what counts as obtaining property by "threat." See Model Penal Code §§ 223.3, 223.4.

different mens rea principles ought to apply to offenses that are not derived from common law antecedents but are "new to general law"? The next Section addresses this question.

## SECTION 2: THE LEGACY OF *MORISSETTE*

### United States v. Freed

Supreme Court of the United States, 1971.
401 U.S. 601.

*(indictment for possession of hand grenades)*

■ MR. JUSTICE DOUGLAS delivered the opinion of the Court.

[The defendants were indicted for possession of unregistered hand grenades in violation of a federal statute that carried a 10-year maximum sentence. The district court dismissed the indictments on the ground, inter alia, that due process was violated by the failure to allege mens rea. The government appealed.]

*dispute / procedure*

We . . . conclude that the district court erred in dismissing the indictment for absence of an allegation of scienter.

*holding*

The act requires no specific intent or knowledge that the hand grenades were unregistered. It makes it unlawful for any person "to receive or possess a firearm which is not registered to him." By the lower court decisions at the time that requirement was written into the Act the only knowledge required to be proved was knowledge that the instrument possessed was a firearm.

*reasoning no specific intent about registration*

*knowledge was a firearm*

The presence of a "vicious will" or mens rea was long a requirement of criminal responsibility. But the list of exceptions grew, especially in the expanding regulatory area involving activities affecting public health, safety, and welfare. The statutory offense of embezzlement, borrowed from the common law where scienter was historically required, was in a different category:

> [W]here Congress borrows terms of art in which are accumulated the legal tradition and meaning of centuries of practice, it presumably knows and adopts the cluster of ideas that were attached to each borrowed word in the body of learning from which it was taken and the meaning its use will convey to the judicial mind unless otherwise instructed.

*When Congress adopts old common law it adopts all w/ it.*

Morissette v. United States, 342 U.S. 246, 263 (1952).

At the other extreme is Lambert v. California, 355 U.S. 225 (1957), in which a municipal code made it a crime to remain in Los Angeles for more than five days without registering if a person had been convicted of a felony. Being in Los Angeles is not per se blameworthy. The mere failure to register, we held, was quite "unlike the commission of acts, or the failure to act under circumstances that should alert the doer to the consequences of his deed." The fact that the ordinance was a convenient law enforcement technique did not save it:

> Where a person did not know of the duty to register and where there was no proof of the probability of such knowledge, he may not be convicted consistently with due process. Were it otherwise, the evil would be as great as it is when the law is

written in print too fine to read or in a language foreign to the community.

In United States v. Dotterweich, 320 U.S. 277 (1943), a case dealing with the imposition of a penalty on a corporate officer whose firm shipped adulterated and misbranded drugs in violation of the Food and Drug Act, we approved the penalty "though consciousness of wrongdoing be totally wanting."

The present case is in the category neither of *Lambert* nor *Morissette*, but is closer to *Dotterweich*. This is a regulatory measure in the interest of the public safety, which may well be premised on the theory that one would hardly be surprised to learn that possession of hand grenades is not an innocent act. They are highly dangerous offensive weapons, no less dangerous than the narcotics involved in United States v. Balint, 258 U.S. 250 (1922), where a defendant was convicted of sale of narcotics against his claim that he did not know the drugs were covered by a federal act. We say with Chief Justice Taft in that case:

> It is very evident from a reading of it that the emphasis of the section is in securing a close supervision of the business of dealing in these dangerous drugs by the taxing officers of the government and that it merely uses a criminal penalty to secure recorded evidence of the disposition of such drugs as a means of taxing and restraining the traffic. Its manifest purpose is to require every person dealing in drugs to ascertain at his peril whether that which he sells comes within the inhibition of the statute, and if he sells the inhibited drug in ignorance of its character, to penalize him. Congress weighed the possible injustice of subjecting an innocent seller to a penalty against the evil of exposing innocent purchasers to danger from the drug, and concluded that the latter was the result preferably to be avoided.

Reversed.

■ MR. JUSTICE BRENNAN, concurring in the judgment of reversal.

[A]lthough I reach the same result as the Court on the intent the government must prove to convict, I do so by another route. . . .

The Court's discussion of the intent the government must prove . . . does not dispel the confusion surrounding a difficult, but vitally important, area of the law. This case does not raise questions of "consciousness of wrongdoing" or "blameworthiness." If the ancient maxim that "ignorance of the law is no excuse" has any residual validity, it indicates that the ordinary intent requirement—mens rea—of the criminal law does not require knowledge that an act is illegal, wrong, or blameworthy. Nor is it possible to decide this case by a simple process of classifying the statute involved as a "regulatory" or a "public welfare" measure. To convict appellees of possession of unregistered hand grenades, the government must prove three material elements: (i) that appellees possessed certain items; (ii) that the items possessed were hand grenades; and (iii) that the hand grenades were not registered. The government and the Court agree that the prosecutor must prove knowing possession of the items and also knowledge that the items possessed were hand grenades. Thus, while the Court does hold that no intent at all need be proved in regard to one element of the offense—the unregistered status of the grenades—knowledge must still be proved as to the other two elements. Consequently, the National Firearms Act does not create a crime of strict liability as to all its elements. It is no help in deciding what level of intent must be proved as to the third element to declare that the offense falls within the "regulatory" category.

*no intent for unregistered · knowledge for two other elements*

Following the analysis of the Model Penal Code, I think we must recognize, first, that "[t]he existence of a mens rea is the rule of, rather than the exception to, the principles of Anglo-American criminal jurisprudence;" second, that mens rea is not a unitary concept, but may vary as to each element of a crime; and third, that Anglo-American law has developed several identifiable and analytically distinct levels of intent, e.g., negligence, recklessness, knowledge, and purpose. To determine the mental element required for conviction, each material element of the offense must be examined and the determination made what level of intent Congress intended the government to prove, taking into account constitutional considerations, . . . as well as the common law background, if any, of the crime involved. See Morissette v. United States, 342 U.S. 246 (1952).

*① mens rea is the rule*
*② mens rea not a unitary concept*
*③ several distinct levels of intent*
*what level of intent of each material element?*

Although the legislative history of the amendments to the National Firearms Act is silent on the level of intent to be proved in connection with each element of the offense, we are not without some guideposts. I begin with the proposition stated in *Morissette* that the requirement of mens rea "is no provincial or transient notion. It is as universal and persistent in mature systems of law as belief in freedom of the human will and a consequent ability and duty of the normal individual to choose between good and evil." In regard to the first two elements of the offense, (i) possession of items that (ii) are hand grenades, the general rule in favor of some intent requirement finds confirmation in the case law . . . . [W]e may therefore properly infer that Congress meant that the government must prove knowledge with regard to the first two elements of the offense under the amended statute.

*Knowledge for first 2 elements*

The third element—the unregistered status of the grenades—presents more difficulty. Proof of intent with regard to this element would require the government to show that the appellees knew that the grenades were unregistered or negligently or recklessly failed to ascertain whether the weapons were registered. It is true that such a requirement would involve knowledge of law, but it does not involve "consciousness of wrongdoing" in the sense of knowledge that one's actions were prohibited or illegal. Rather, the definition of the crime, as written by Congress, requires proof of circumstances that involve a legal element, namely whether the grenades were registered in accordance with federal law. The knowledge involved is solely knowledge of the circumstances that the law has defined as material to the offense. The Model Penal Code illustrates the distinction:

> It should be noted that the general principle that ignorance or mistake of law is no excuse is usually greatly overstated; it has no application when the circumstances made material by the definition of the offense include a legal element. So, for example, it is immaterial in theft, when claim of right is adduced in defense, that the claim involves a legal judgment as to the right of property. It is a defense because knowledge that

*ignorance or mistake of law greatly overstated*

> the property belongs to someone else is a material element of the crime and such knowledge may involve matter of law as well as fact. . . . The law involved is not the law defining the offense; it is some other legal rule that characterizes the attendant circumstances that are material to the offense. Model Penal Code § 2.02, Comment 131 (Tent. Draft No. 4, 1955).

Therefore, as with the first two elements, the question is solely one of congressional intent. And while the question is not an easy one, two factors persuade me that proof of mens rea as to the unregistered status of the grenades is not required. First, . . . the case law under the provisions replaced by the current law dispensed with proof of intent in connection with this element. Second, the firearms covered by the act are major weapons such as machine guns and sawed-off shotguns; deceptive weapons such as flashlight guns and fountain-pen guns; and major destructive devices such as bombs, grenades, mines, rockets, and large caliber weapons including mortars, anti-tank guns, and bazookas. Without exception, the likelihood of governmental regulation of the distribution of such weapons is so great that anyone must be presumed to be aware of it. In the context of a . . . registration scheme, I therefore think it reasonable to conclude that Congress dispensed with the requirement of intent in regard to the unregistered status of the weapon, as necessary to effective administration of the statute.

## NOTES ON MENS REA ELEMENTS IN FEDERAL CRIMES

### 1. *STAPLES V. UNITED STATES*

Compare the Douglas and Brennan opinions in *Freed*. And consider the last paragraph of Section 1. Does the *Freed* statute create an offense "new to general law" to which ordinary common law mens rea principles do not apply? Does it create a "public welfare" offense? Or does it create an addition to the federal criminal law to which ordinary common law principles should apply? At the end of the day, how do the answers to these questions bear on the approach one takes to the level of mens rea required for a federal crime?

The Supreme Court returned to these issues in Staples v. United States, 511 U.S. 600 (1994). That case involved the failure to register a machine gun under the same statute at issue in *Freed*. The facts were these:

> Upon executing a search warrant at petitioner's home, local police and agents of the Bureau of Alcohol, Tobacco and Firearms (BATF) recovered, among other things, an AR-15 rifle.[a] . . . Suspecting that the AR-15 had been modified to be capable of fully

---

[a] As the Court explained:

> The AR-15 is the civilian version of the military's M-16 rifle, and is, unless modified, a semiautomatic weapon. The M-16, in contrast, is a selective fire rifle that allows the operator, by rotating a selector switch, to choose semiautomatic or automatic fire. Many M-16 parts are interchangeable with those in the AR-15 and can be used to convert the AR-15 into an automatic weapon. No doubt to inhibit such conversions, the AR-15 is manufactured with a metal stop on its receiver that will prevent an M-16 selector switch, if installed, from rotating to the fully automatic position. The metal stop on petitioner's rifle, however, had been filed away, and the rifle had been assembled with an M-16 selector switch and several other M-16 internal parts, including a hammer, disconnector, and trigger.

automatic fire, BATF agents seized the weapon. Petitioner subsequently was indicted for unlawful possession of an unregistered machinegun in violation of § 5861(d).

At trial, BATF agents testified that when the AR-15 was tested, it fired more than one shot with a single pull of the trigger. It was undisputed that the weapon was not registered as required by § 5861(d). Petitioner testified that the rifle had never fired automatically when it was in his possession. He insisted that the AR-15 had operated only semiautomatically, and even then imperfectly, often requiring manual ejection of the spent casing and chambering of the next round. According to petitioner, his alleged ignorance of any automatic firing capability should have shielded him from criminal liability for his failure to register the weapon. He requested the District Court to instruct the jury that . . . the Government must prove beyond a reasonable doubt that the defendant "knew that the gun would fire fully automatically." The District Court rejected petitioner's proposed instruction and instead charged the jury as follows:

> The Government need not prove the defendant knows he's dealing with a weapon possessing every last characteristic [which subjects it] to the regulation. It would be enough to prove he knows that he is dealing with a dangerous device of a type as would alert one to the likelihood of regulation.

Petitioner was convicted and sentenced to five years' probation and a $5,000 fine.

### (i) *Majority Opinion*

The Court agreed with Staples. It held the statute to require that the defendant know of the characteristics requiring classification of the weapon as a machine gun, namely, that it was capable of being fired repeatedly with a single pull of the trigger. For the Court, Justice Thomas began as follows:

> Whether or not § 5861(d) requires proof that a defendant knew of the characteristics of his weapon that made it a "firearm" under the Act is a question of statutory construction. . . . The language of the statute, the starting place in our inquiry, provides little explicit guidance in this case. Section 5861(d) is silent concerning the mens rea required for a violation. It states simply that "[i]t shall be unlawful for any person . . . to receive or possess a firearm which is not registered to him in the National Firearms Registration and Transfer Record." 26 U.S.C. § 5861(d). Nevertheless, silence on this point by itself does not necessarily suggest that Congress intended to dispense with a conventional mens rea element, which would require that the defendant know the facts that make his conduct illegal. . . . On the contrary, we must construe the statute in light of the background rules of the common law, in which the requirement of some mens rea for a crime is firmly embedded. As we have observed, "[t]he existence of a mens rea is the rule of, rather than the exception to, the principles of Anglo-American criminal jurisprudence." United States v. United States Gypsum Co., 438 U.S. 422, 436 (1978). See also Morissette v. United States, 342 U.S. 246, 250 (1952). . . . Relying on the

strength of the traditional rule, we have stated that offenses that require no mens rea generally are disfavored, and have suggested that some indication of congressional intent, express or implied, is required to dispense with mens rea as an element of a crime.

*reasoning*

As to the relevance of *Freed*, Thomas added:

> *Freed* did not address the issue presented here. In *Freed*, we decided only that § 5861(d) does not require proof of knowledge that a firearm is *unregistered*. The question presented by a defendant who possesses a weapon that is a "firearm" for purposes of the Act, but who knows only that he has a "firearm" in the general sense of the term, was not raised or considered. And our determination that a defendant need not know that his weapon is unregistered suggests no conclusion concerning whether § 5861(d) requires the defendant to know of the features that make his weapon a statutory "firearm"; different elements of the same offense can require different mental states. Moreover, our analysis in *Freed* likening the Act to the public welfare statute in *Balint* rested entirely on the assumption that the defendant knew that he was dealing with hand grenades—that is, that he knew he possessed a particularly dangerous type of weapon (one within the statutory definition of a "firearm"), possession of which was not entirely "innocent" in and of itself. The predicate for that analysis is eliminated when, as in this case, the very question to be decided is *whether* the defendant must know of the particular characteristics that make his weapon a statutory firearm. . . .

*Knowledge that weapon is a "firearm"*

*question*

> [D]espite their potential for harm, guns generally can be owned in perfect innocence. Of course, we might surely classify certain categories of guns—no doubt including the machineguns, sawed-off shotguns, and artillery pieces that Congress has subjected to regulation—as items the ownership of which would have the same quasi-suspect character we attributed to owning hand grenades in *Freed*. But precisely because guns falling outside those categories traditionally have been widely accepted as lawful possessions, their destructive potential . . . cannot be said to put gun owners sufficiently on notice of the likelihood of regulation to justify interpreting § 5861(d) as not requiring proof of knowledge of a weapon's characteristics.

*reasoning*

Justice Thomas also made the following general comments about the category of public welfare offenses:

> According to the Government, . . . the nature and purpose of the Act suggest that the presumption favoring mens rea does not apply to this case. The Government argues that Congress intended the Act to regulate and restrict the circulation of dangerous weapons. Consequently, in the Government's view, this case fits in a line of precedent concerning what we have termed "public welfare" or "regulatory" offenses, in which we have understood Congress to impose a form of strict criminal liability through statutes that do not require the defendant to know the facts that make his conduct illegal. In construing such statutes, we have inferred from silence that Congress did not intend to require proof of mens rea to establish an offense. . . .

*strict criminal liability*

> The potentially harsh penalty attached to violation of § 5861(d)—up to 10 years' imprisonment—confirms our reading of the Act. Historically, the penalty imposed under a statute has been a significant consideration in determining whether the statute should be construed as dispensing with mens rea. Certainly, the cases that first defined the concept of the public welfare offense almost uniformly involved statutes that provided for only light penalties such as fines or short jail sentences, not imprisonment in the state penitentiary.
>
> As commentators have pointed out, the small penalties attached to such offenses logically complemented the absence of a mens rea requirement: in a system that generally requires a "vicious will" to establish a crime, 4 William Blackstone, Commentaries *21, imposing severe punishments for offenses that require no mens rea would seem incongruous Indeed, some courts justified the absence of mens rea in part on the basis that the offenses did not bear the same punishments as "infamous crimes," and questioned whether imprisonment was compatible with the reduced culpability required for such regulatory offenses. Similarly, commentators collecting the early cases have argued that offenses punishable by imprisonment cannot be understood to be public welfare offenses, but must require mens rea. See Rollin Perkins, Criminal Law 793–98 (2d ed. 1969) (suggesting that the penalty should be the starting point in determining whether a statute describes a public welfare offense); Sayre, supra, at 72 ("Crimes punishable with prison sentences . . . ordinarily require proof of a guilty intent").
>
> In rehearsing the characteristics of the public welfare offense, we, too, have included in our consideration the punishments imposed and have noted that "penalties commonly are relatively small, and conviction does no grave damage to an offender's reputation." Morissette v. United States, 342 U.S. 246, 256 (1952). . . .
>
> Our characterization of the public welfare offense in *Morissette* hardly seems apt, however, for a crime that is a felony, as is violation of § 5861(d). After all, "felony" is, as we noted in distinguishing certain common law crimes from public welfare offenses, " 'as bad a word as you can give to man or thing.' " *Morissette*, supra, at 260. Close adherence to the early cases described above might suggest that punishing a violation as a felony is simply incompatible with the theory of the public welfare offense. In this view, absent a clear statement from Congress that mens rea is not required, we should not apply the public welfare offense rationale to interpret any statute defining a felony offense as dispensing with mens rea. . . .

The Court declined, however, to "adopt such a definitive rule of construction to decide this case . . . ." It held instead that "a severe penalty is a further factor tending to suggest that Congress did not intend to eliminate a mens rea requirement" for violation of the firearm registration statute before the Court. Therefore, "the usual presumption that a defendant must know the facts that make his conduct illegal should apply." "[W]e conclude that the background rule of the common law favoring mens rea should govern . . . in this case. Silence does not suggest that Congress dispensed with mens rea for the element . . . at issue here. Thus, to obtain a conviction, the Government should have been required to prove that petitioner knew of the features of his AR-15 that brought it within the scope of the Act."

### *(ii) The Ginsburg Concurrence*

Joined by Justice O'Connor, Justice Ginsburg concurred in the judgment. She started by observing in a footnote that "[c]ontrary to the dissent's suggestion, we have not confined the presumption of mens rea to statutes codifying traditional common-law offenses, but have also applied the presumption to offenses that are 'entirely a creature of statute'. . . ." Later she said:

> Conviction under § 5861(d), the Government . . . concedes, requires proof that Staples "knowingly" possessed the machinegun. The question before us is not *whether* knowledge of possession is required, but what level of knowledge suffices: (1) knowledge simply of possession of the object; (2) knowledge, in addition, that the object is a dangerous weapon; (3) knowledge, beyond dangerousness, of the characteristics that render the object subject to regulation, for example, awareness that the weapon is a machinegun. Recognizing that the first reading effectively dispenses with mens rea, the Government adopts the second, contending [in its brief] that it avoids criminalizing "apparently innocent conduct," because under the second reading, "a defendant who possessed what he thought was a toy or a violin case, but which in fact was a machinegun, could not be convicted."

She responded to the Government argument as follows:

> The Government, however, does not take adequate account of the "widespread lawful gun ownership" Congress and the States have allowed to persist in this country. . . . The Nation's legislators chose to place under a registration requirement only a very limited class of firearms, those they considered especially dangerous. The generally "dangerous" character of all guns . . . did not suffice to give individuals in Staples' situation cause to inquire about the need for registration. Only the third reading, then, suits the purpose of the mens rea requirement—to shield people against punishment for apparently innocent activity.[3]
>
> The indictment in Staples' case charges that he "knowingly received and possessed firearms." "Firearms" has a circumscribed statutory definition. The "firear[m]" the Government contends Staples possessed in violation of § 5861(d) is a machinegun. The

---

[3] The mens rea presumption requires knowledge only of the facts that make the defendant's conduct illegal, lest it conflict with the related presumption, "deeply rooted in the American legal system," that, ordinarily, "ignorance of the law or a mistake of law is no defense to criminal prosecution." Cheek v. United States, 498 U.S. 192, 199 (1991). The maxim explains why some "innocent" actors—for example, a defendant who knows he possesses a weapon with all of the characteristics that subject it to registration, but was unaware of the registration requirement, or thought the gun was registered—may be convicted under § 5861(d). Knowledge of whether the gun was registered is so closely related to knowledge of the registration requirement that requiring the Government to prove the former would in effect require it to prove knowledge of the law.

indictment thus effectively charged that Staples *knowingly possessed a machinegun.* "Knowingly possessed" logically means "possessed and knew that he possessed." The Government can reconcile the jury instruction with the indictment only on the implausible assumption that the term "firear[m]" has two different meanings when used once in the same charge—simply "gun" when referring to what petitioner knew, and "machinegun" when referring to what he possessed.

*Knowingly possessed*

For these reasons, I conclude that conviction under § 5861(d) requires proof that the defendant knew he possessed not simply a gun, but a machinegun. The indictment in this case, but not the jury instruction, properly described this knowledge requirement. I therefore concur in the Court's judgment.

*holding*

## (iii) The Stevens Dissent

Joined by Justice Blackmun, Justice Stevens dissented. In his view, "[b]ecause the offense involved in this case is entirely a creature of statute . . . 'the background rules of the common law' do not require a particular construction, and critically different rules of construction apply."[b] Justice Stevens continued:

> An examination of § 5861(d) in light of our precedent dictates that the crime of possession of an unregistered machinegun is in a category of offenses described as "public welfare" crimes.[9] Our decisions interpreting such offenses clearly require affirmance of petitioner's conviction. . . . Public welfare statutes render criminal "a type of conduct that a reasonable person should know is subject to stringent public regulation and may seriously threaten the community's health or safety." *Liparota v. United States,* 471 U.S. 419, 433 (1985). . . . We . . . have read a knowledge requirement into public welfare crimes, but not a requirement that the defendant know all the facts that make his conduct illegal. . . . Petitioner knowingly possessed a semiautomatic weapon that was readily convertible into a machinegun. The "character and nature" of such a weapon is sufficiently hazardous to place the possessor on notice of the possibility of regulation. No significant difference exists between imposing upon the possessor a duty to determine whether such a weapon is registered, and imposing a duty to determine whether that weapon has been converted into a machinegun. . . .

*public welfare offense*

*character and nature*

> The enforcement of public welfare offenses always entails some possibility of injustice. Congress nevertheless has repeatedly decided that an overriding public interest in health or safety may outweigh that risk when a person is dealing with products that

*possible injustice*

---

[b]  As authority for this conclusion, he quoted the passage in *Morissette* in which Justice Jackson said: "Congressional silence as to mental elements in an Act merely adopting into federal statutory law a concept of crime already . . . well defined in common law and statutory interpretation by the states may warrant quite contrary inferences than the same silence in creating an offense new to general law, for whose definition the courts have no guidance except the Act."

[9]  These statutes are sometimes referred to as "strict liability" offenses. [B]ecause the defendant must know that he is engaged in the type of dangerous conduct that is likely to be regulated, the use of the term "strict liability" to describe these offenses is inaccurate. I therefore use the term "public welfare offense" to describe this type of statute.

> are sufficiently dangerous or deleterious to make it reasonable to presume that he either knows, or should know, whether those products conform to special regulatory requirements. The dangerous character of the product is reasonably presumed to provide sufficient notice of the probability of regulation to justify strict enforcement against those who are merely guilty of negligent, rather than willful, misconduct.
>
> . . . In the National Firearms Act, Congress determined that the serious threat to health and safety posed by the private ownership of such firearms warranted the imposition of a duty on the owners of dangerous weapons to determine whether their possession is lawful. Semiautomatic weapons that are readily convertible into machineguns are sufficiently dangerous to alert persons who knowingly possess them to the probability of stringent public regulation. The jury's finding that petitioner knowingly possessed "a dangerous device of a type as would alert one to the likelihood of regulation" adequately supports the conviction.

## 2. QUESTIONS AND COMMENTS ON *FREED*

After *Staples*, does the applicability of ordinary common law mens rea principles turn on whether an offense carrying serious criminal penalties is "new to general law"? Or has the suggestion in *Morissette* to this effect been rejected? Can the result in *Freed* be defended as an *application* of ordinary common law mens rea principles?

Strict liability promotes preventive goals at the expense of liability based on blame. One way of putting the argument in favor of the *Freed* result is that it is appropriate to use strict liability where the potential social harm is great and the context as known to the defendant should give adequate notice that the behavior is wrong. Is this a persuasive rationale for the imposition of strict liability? Was this, in the end, the reason for the result in *Freed*?

How do "public welfare" offenses differ from crimes carrying serious penalties? Does it matter in the end how the crime is classified? Consider the following comments by Justice Thomas in *Staples*:

> [P]ublic welfare offenses have been created by Congress, and recognized by this Court, in "limited circumstances." United States v. United States Gypsum, 438 U.S. 422, 437 (1978). Typically, our cases recognizing such offenses involve statutes that regulate potentially harmful or injurious items. Cf. United States v. International Minerals & Chemical Corp., 402 U.S. 558, 564–65 (1971) (characterizing [such] cases as involving statutes regulating "dangerous or deleterious devices or products or obnoxious waste materials"). In such situations, we have reasoned that as long as a defendant knows that he is dealing with a dangerous device of a character that places him "in responsible relation to a public danger," United States v. Dotterweich, 320 U.S. 277, 281 (1943), he should be alerted to the probability of strict regulation, and we have assumed that in such cases Congress intended to place the burden on the defendant to "ascertain at his peril whether [his conduct] comes within the inhibition of the statute." United States v. Balint, 258 U.S. 250, 254 (1922). Thus, we essentially have relied on the nature of the statute and the particular

character of the items regulated to determine whether congres- *[nature of the statute + particular character]* sional silence concerning the mental element of the offense should be interpreted as dispensing with conventional mens rea require-ments.[3]

Is the rationale for strict liability in a public welfare offense similar to the rationale for strict liability in *Freed*? Of what consequence is the higher penalty in *Freed*?

3.    *UNITED STATES V. YERMIAN*   *(lied about employment history and criminal record to employer)*

One way to think about *Freed* and *Staples* is that strict liability for the registration element is required in order to promote preventive goals, while a mens rea of knowledge for the possession and nature of the firearm ele-ments helps to make this approach fair by limiting the extent to which the crime will ensnare "innocent conduct." Looking at it from the perspective of the costs to law enforcement, the burdens on the prosecutor, and the diffi-culty of obtaining appropriate convictions, the strict liability part elimi-nates potential loopholes and makes case-by-case litigation more efficient. The mens rea requirements make it less likely that "innocent" behavior will be punished, but do so in a manner that does not substantially increase the burdens on the prosecutor. It will be easy in most cases for the prosecutor to show that defendants "know" that the weapons they are possessing are mortars, anti-tank guns, and bazookas.

It is interesting in this connection to compare the tradeoffs along these lines in United States v. Yermian, 468 U.S. 63 (1984). The defendant lied about his employment history and criminal record on a security question-naire[c] that his employer, a defense contractor, required him to complete *[facts]* because he would have access to classified information. He was convicted of violating 18 U.S.C. § 1001, which then provided:

> Whoever, in any matter within the jurisdiction of any de-partment or agency of the United States knowingly and willfully . . . makes any false . . . statements . . . shall be fined not more than $10,000 or imprisoned not more than five years, or both.

*[§ 18 U.S.C § 1001 ("false statements")]*

Yermian admitted at his trial that he had intentionally made false statements on the form so that the information it contained would *[intentionally made false statements]*

---

[3]   By interpreting such public welfare offenses to require at least that the defendant know that he is dealing with some dangerous or deleterious substance, we have avoided con-struing criminal statutes to impose a rigorous form of strict liability. See, e.g., United States v. International Minerals & Chemical Corp., 402 U.S. 558, 563–64 (1971) (suggesting that if a person shipping acid mistakenly thought that he was shipping distilled water, he would not violate a statute criminalizing undocumented shipping of acids). True strict liability might suggest that the defendant need not know even that he was dealing with a dangerous item. Nevertheless, we have referred to public welfare offenses as "dispensing with" or "eliminating" a mens rea requirement or "mental element" and have described them as strict liability crimes. While use of the term "strict liability" is really a misnomer, we have interpreted stat-utes defining public welfare offenses to eliminate the requirement of mens rea; that is, the requirement of a "guilty mind" with respect to an element of a crime. Under such statutes we have not required that the defendant know the facts that make his conduct fit the definition of the offense. Generally speaking, such knowledge is necessary to establish mens rea. . . .

[c]   The form was entitled "Department of Defense Personnel Security Questionnaire." The document contained a reference to the "Defense Industrial Security Clearance Office," stated that Yermian's work would require access to "secret" material, and stated explicitly that sign-ing it would grant the "Department of Defense" permission to conduct an investigation. A warning that any false answers would subject him to prosecution under "§ 1001 of the United States Criminal Code" was printed right above the place where Yermian signed the form.

be consistent with similar false statements he had made on his employment application. His sole defense was that he had no knowledge that his false statements would be transmitted to a federal agency. His attorney requested an instruction to the effect that the jury could not convict unless it found that he knew that the statements were made in a matter within the jurisdiction of a federal agency. The trial judge rejected this request, but instructed the jury that it should convict if it found that the defendant "knew or should have known that the information was to be submitted to a government agency."

The Court of Appeals reversed, but the Supreme Court reinstated the conviction. Justice Powell's opinion for the Court classified the language "in any matter within the jurisdiction of any department or agency of the United States" as a "jurisdictional element," that is, an element "whose primary purpose is to identify the factor that makes the false statement an appropriate subject for federal concern." "Jurisdictional language," Justice Powell continued, "need not contain the same culpability requirement as other elements of the offense." He then noted that the statutory language was clear in this case, since the

> jurisdictional language appears in a phrase separate from the prohibited conduct modified by the terms "knowingly and willfully." Any natural reading of § 1001, therefore, establishes that the terms "knowingly and willfully" modify only the making of "false . . . statements" and not the predicate circumstance that those statements be made in a matter within the jurisdiction of a federal agency. Once this is clear, there is no basis for requiring proof that the defendant had actual knowledge of federal agency jurisdiction. The statute contains no language suggesting any additional element of intent . . . . On its face, therefore, § 1001 requires that the government prove that false statements were made knowingly and willfully, and it unambiguously dispenses with any requirement that the government also prove that those statements were made with actual knowledge of federal agency jurisdiction.

Justice Powell's reading of the legislative history of the statute confirmed this conclusion. He then turned to the defendant's argument that construed in this manner § 1001 becomes a " 'trap for the unwary' imposing criminal sanctions on 'wholly innocent conduct.' " He responded:

> Whether or not respondent fairly may characterize the intentional and deliberate lies prohibited by the statute (and manifest in this case) as "wholly innocent conduct," this argument is not sufficient to overcome the express statutory language of § 1001. Respondent does not argue that Congress lacks the power to impose criminal sanctions for deliberately false statements submitted to a federal agency, regardless whether the person who made such statements actually knew that they were being submitted to the federal government. That is precisely what Congress has done here. In the unlikely event that § 1001 could be the basis for imposing an unduly harsh result on those who intentionally make false

statements to the federal government, it is for Congress and not this Court to amend the criminal statute.[14]

Justice Rehnquist dissented, joined by Justices Brennan, Stevens, and O'Connor. He argued that the statute was ambiguous and that the legislative history confirmed that actual knowledge as to the jurisdictional element should be required. He also argued that it should not lightly be inferred that Congress

> intended to criminalize the making of even the most casual false statements so long as they turned out, unbeknownst to their maker, to be material to some federal agency function. The latter interpretation would substantially extend the scope of the statute even to reach, for example, false statements privately made to a neighbor if the neighbor then uses those statements in connection with his work for a federal agency.

He also criticized the Court for not resolving the question whether some lesser culpability was required for the jurisdictional element.

Was *Yermian* correctly decided? When the issue returns, should the Court choose strict liability or negligence as the mens rea for the jurisdictional element? Recklessness? Or should it have agreed with Rehnquist and opted for a mens rea of knowledge?

4.  *DEAN V. UNITED STATES* (robbing bank at gunpoint but seem surprized shot went off)

Does the approach to mens rea for serious crimes reflected in *Morissette* and *Staples* apply to sentencing factors that authorize increased punishment? That issue came before the Court in Dean v. United States, 556 U.S. 568 (2009).[d] Wearing a mask, Dean entered a bank, waved a gun, and told everyone to get down. He went behind the counter and helped himself to money from the teller stations. He grabbed the money with one hand while holding the gun in the other. As he reached over a teller to get some money, the gun discharged, resulting in a bullet hole in a partition in between two teller stations but no personal injury. He cursed, and ran from the bank. Witnesses testified that he seemed surprised when the gun went off.

---

[14] In the context of this case, respondent's argument that § 1001 is a 'trap for the unwary' is particularly misplaced. It is worth noting that the jury was instructed, without objection from the prosecution, that the government must prove that respondent 'knew or should have known' that his false statements were made within the jurisdiction of a federal agency.

As the government did not object to the reasonable foreseeability instruction, it is unnecessary for us to decide whether that instruction erroneously read a culpability requirement into the jurisdictional phrase. Moreover, the only question presented in this case is whether the government must prove that the false statement was made with *actual* knowledge of federal agency jurisdiction. The jury's finding that federal agency jurisdiction was reasonably foreseeable by the defendant, combined with the requirement that the defendant had actual knowledge of the falsity of those statements, precludes the possibility that criminal penalties were imposed on the basis of innocent conduct.

[d] Recall the common law rule for mistakes of fact that relate to grading elements: "If an actor honestly and reasonably, although mistakenly, believed the facts to be other than they were, and if his conduct would not have been criminal had the facts been as he believed them to be, then his mistake is a defense if he is charged with a crime which requires 'mens rea' . . . ." Jerome Michael and Herbert Wechsler, Criminal Law and Its Administration 756 (1940). *Dean* did not involve a mistake of fact, but a problem that arguably raised similar questions of policy.

Section 924(c)(1)(A) of title 18 of the United States Code provides:

> [A]ny person who, during and in relation to any crime of violence or drug trafficking crime . . . uses or carries a firearm, or who, in furtherance of any such crime, possesses a firearm, shall, in addition to the punishment provided for such crime of violence or drug trafficking crime—
>
> (i) be sentenced to a term of imprisonment of not less than 5 years;
>
> (ii) if the firearm is brandished, be sentenced to a term of imprisonment of not less than 7 years; and
>
> (iii) if the firearm is discharged, be sentenced to a term of imprisonment of not less than 10 years.

Dean argued that the sentencing enhancement required by subsection (iii) should only be invoked if the gun was intentionally discharged. The District Court disagreed, and imposed the 10-year mandatory minimum sentence. The Court of Appeals affirmed, as did the Supreme Court.

Chief Justice Roberts wrote for the Court. He began with this observation:

> Accidents happen. Sometimes they happen to individuals committing crimes with loaded guns. The question here is whether extra punishment Congress imposed for the discharge of a gun during certain crimes applies when the gun goes off accidentally.

Starting with the text of the statute, he noted that it "does not require that the discharge be done knowingly or intentionally, or otherwise contain words of limitation." He made several other textual points. One was that the use by Congress of the passive voice indicated that proof of intent was not required. "It is whether something happened—not how or why it happened—that matters." Another was that Congress had defined "brandishing" to require an intent to intimidate. "Congress did not, however, separately define 'discharge' to include an intent requirement." This difference in treatment of the two terms supported the inference that no mens rea requirement was intended when the weapon was discharged. A third was that the words "during and in relation to" in the introductory phrase of subsection (A), which the Court had previously held to require that the firearm had "some purpose or effect" with respect to the underlying crime, did not establish an intent requirement for subsection (iii). "There is no basis for reading 'in relation to' to extend all the way down to modify 'is discharged.' The better reading of the statute is that the adverbial phrases in the opening paragraph—'in relation to' and 'in furtherance of'—modify their respective nearby verbs, and that neither phrase extends to the sentencing factors."

The Chief Justice then addressed the relevance of the *Morissette-Staples* line of cases:

> Dean further argues that even if the statute is viewed as silent on the intent question, that silence compels a ruling in his favor. There is, he notes, a presumption that criminal prohibitions include a requirement that the Government prove the defendant intended the conduct made criminal. In light of this presumption, we have "on a number of occasions read a state-of-mind component into an offense even when the statutory definition did not in

terms so provide." United States v. United States Gypsum Co., 438 U.S. 422, 437 (1978). "[S]ome indication of congressional intent, express or implied, is required to dispense with mens rea as an element of a crime." Staples v. United States, 511 U.S. 600, 606 (1994).

Dean argues that the presumption is especially strong in this case, given the structure and purpose of the statute. In his view, the three subsections are intended to provide harsher penalties for increasingly culpable conduct: a 5-year minimum for using, carrying, or possessing a firearm; a 7-year minimum for brandishing a firearm; and a 10-year minimum for discharging a firearm. Incorporating an intent requirement into the discharge provision is necessary to give effect to that progression, because an accidental discharge is less culpable than intentional brandishment.

It is unusual to impose criminal punishment for the consequences of purely accidental conduct. But it is not unusual to punish individuals for the unintended consequences of their *unlawful* acts. The felony-murder rule is a familiar example: If a defendant commits an unintended homicide while committing another felony, the defendant can be convicted of murder. The Sentencing Guidelines reflect the same principle. See United States Sentencing Commission, Guidelines Manual § 2A2.2(b)(3) (Nov.2008) (USSG) (increasing offense level for aggravated assault according to the seriousness of the injury); § 2D2.3 (increasing offense level for operating or directing the operation of a common carrier under the influence of alcohol or drugs if death or serious bodily injury results).

Blackstone expressed the idea in the following terms:

> [I]f any accidental mischief happens to follow from the performance of a *lawful* act, the party stands excused from all guilt: but if a man be doing any thing *unlawful*, and a consequence ensues which he did not foresee or intend, as the death of a man or the like, his want of foresight shall be no excuse; for, being guilty of one offence, in doing antecedently what is in itself unlawful, he is criminally guilty of whatever consequence may follow the first misbehaviour. 4 W. Blackstone, Commentaries on the Laws of England 26–27 (1769).

Here the defendant is already guilty of unlawful conduct twice over: a violent or drug trafficking offense and the use, carrying, or possession of a firearm in the course of that offense. That unlawful conduct was not an accident.

The fact that the actual discharge of a gun covered under § 924(c)(1)(A)(iii) may be accidental does not mean that the defendant is blameless. The sentencing enhancement in subsection (iii) accounts for the risk of harm resulting from the manner in which the crime is carried out, for which the defendant is responsible. An individual who brings a loaded weapon to commit a crime runs the risk that the gun will discharge accidentally. A gunshot in such circumstances—whether accidental or intended—increases the risk that others will be injured, that people will panic, or that violence (with its own danger to those nearby) will be used in response. Those criminals wishing to avoid the penalty for an inadvertent discharge can lock or unload the firearm, handle it with care during the underlying violent or drug trafficking crime, leave the gun at home, or—best yet—avoid committing the felony in the first place. . . . [A]lthough the point is not relevant under the correct reading of the statute, it is wrong to assert that the gunshot here "caused no harm." By pure luck, no one was killed or wounded. But the gunshot plainly added to the trauma experienced by those held during the armed robbery. See, e.g., App. 22 (the gunshot "shook us all"); ibid. ("Melissa in the lobby popped up and said, 'oh, my God, has he shot Nora?' ").

Justices Stevens dissented.[e] He argued first that "the structure of § 924(c)(1)(A) suggests that Congress intended to provide escalating sentences for increasingly culpable conduct and that the discharge provision therefore applies only to intentional discharges." Second, he asserted that "the common-law presumption that provisions imposing criminal penalties require proof of mens rea [should] lead to the same conclusion." On the latter point, he argued:

Although mandatory minimum sentencing provisions are of too recent genesis to have any common-law pedigree, there is no sensible reason for treating them differently from offense elements for purposes of the presumption of mens rea. Sentencing provisions of this type have substantially the same effect on a defendant's liberty as aggravated offense provisions. Although a sentencing judge has discretion to issue sentences under § 924(c)(1)(A) within the substantial range bounded on one end by the 5–, 7–, or 10-year mandatory minimum sentence and on the other by the statutory maximum sentence, judges in practice rarely exercise that discretion. As Justice Thomas noted in Harris v. United States, 536 U.S. 545, 578 (2002), "the sentence imposed when a defendant is found only to have 'carried' a firearm 'in relation to' a drug trafficking offense appears to be, almost uniformly, if not invariably, five years," and "those found to have brandished a firearm typically, if not always, are sentenced only to 7 years in prison while those found to have discharged a firearm are sentenced only to 10 years." If anything, imposition of a mandatory minimum sentence under § 924(c)(1)(A) will likely have a greater effect on a defendant's liberty than will conviction for another offense because, unlike sentences for most federal offenses, sentences imposed pursuant to that section must be served consecutively to any other sentence. See § 924(c)(1)(D)(ii).

As the foregoing shows, mandatory minimum sentencing provisions are in effect no different from aggravated offense provisions. The common-law tradition of requiring proof of mens rea to establish criminal culpability should thus apply equally to such sentencing factors. Absent a clear indication that Congress intended to create a strict liability enhancement, courts should presume that a provision that mandates enhanced criminal penalties requires proof of intent. . . . I would apply the presumption in this case and avoid the strange result of imposing a substantially

[e] Justice Breyer wrote a separate dissent.

harsher penalty for an act caused not by an "evil-meaning mind" but by a clumsy hand.

The *Dean* situation is more complex today. Harris v. United States, 536 U.S. 545 (2002), held that the brandishing and discharge provisions in § 924(c)(1)(A) were factors to be taken into account at sentencing and were not elements of the offense that were required to be proved to a jury beyond a reasonable doubt. Whether the discharge occurred and whatever mens rea was required for the discharge was therefore determined in *Dean* by the judge under the less formal procedural rules that governed the sentencing stage of the case.

The Court overruled *Harris* in Alleyne v. United States, 570 U.S. ___, 133 S. Ct. 2151 (2013). It held that the Constitution did not permit judges to sentence offenders based on the factors identified in subsections (ii) and (iii) of § 924(c)(1)(A) unless the prosecution proved them beyond a reasonable doubt to a jury. Effectively, therefore, these factors became elements of the offense in the same sense as all of its other actus reus and mens rea ingredients.

Will this development change the result in *Dean* in the future? Most likely not, one could argue, because the *Dean* result was primarily based on a close textual analysis of the statute and on substantive policy concerns that are independent of the procedural issues involved in *Harris* and *Alleyne*. But it could be argued in response that the textual clues and policy concerns are not strong enough to overcome the mens rea presumption that otherwise applies to the elements of a federal crime. Stay tuned.

5. *CARTER V. UNITED STATES*

The next main case also involves the interpretive principles the Supreme Court brings to bear on federal mens rea issues. After *Carter* and *Dean*, is the legacy of *Morissette* fairly clear?

## Carter v. United States

Supreme Court of the United States, 2000
530 U.S. 255.

■ JUSTICE THOMAS delivered the opinion of the Court. . . .

I

On September 9, 1997, petitioner Floyd J. Carter donned a ski mask and entered the Collective Federal Savings Bank in Hamilton Township, New Jersey. Carter confronted a customer who was exiting the bank and pushed her back inside. She screamed, startling others in the bank. Undeterred, Carter ran into the bank and leaped over the customer service counter and through one of the teller windows. One of the tellers rushed into the manager's office. Meanwhile, Carter opened several teller drawers and emptied the money into a bag. After having removed almost $16,000 in currency, Carter jumped back over the counter and fled from the scene. Later that day, the police apprehended him.

A grand jury indicted Carter, charging him with violating § 2113(a). While not contesting the basic facts of the episode, Carter pleaded not guilty on the theory that he had not taken the bank's money "by force and violence, or by intimidation," as § 2113(a) requires. Before trial, Carter moved that the court instruct the jury on the offense described by § 2113(b) as a lesser included offense of the offense described by § 2113(a). The District Court . . . denied the motion in a preliminary ruling. At the close of the Government's case, the District Court denied Carter's motion for a judgment of acquittal and indicated that the preliminary ruling denying the lesser included offense instruction would stand. The jury, instructed on § 2113(a) alone, returned a guilty verdict, and the District Court entered judgment pursuant to that verdict.

The Court of Appeals . . . affirmed. . . . We granted certiorari . . . and now affirm.

II

In Schmuck v. United States, 489 U.S. 705 (1989), we were called upon to interpret Federal Rule of Criminal Procedure 31(c)'s provision that "[t]he defendant may be found guilty of an offense necessarily included in the offense charged." We held that this provision requires application of an elements test, under which "one offense is not 'necessarily included' in another unless the elements of the lesser offense are a subset of the elements of the charged offense."[2] The elements test requires "a textual comparison of criminal statutes," an approach that, we explained, lends itself to "certain and predictable" outcomes.[3] . . .

[T]he Government contends that three elements required by § 2113(b)'s first paragraph are not required by § 2113(a): (1) specific intent to steal; (2) asportation; and (3) valuation exceeding $1,000. The statute provides:

> § 2113. Bank robbery and incidental crimes
>
> (a) Whoever, by force and violence, or by intimidation, takes, or attempts to take, from the person or presence of another, or obtains or attempts to obtain by extortion any property or money or any other thing of value belonging to, or in the care, custody, control, management, or possession of, any bank, credit union, or any savings and loan association . . . [s]hall be fined under this title or imprisoned not more than twenty years, or both.
>
> (b) Whoever takes and carries away, with intent to steal or purloin, any property or money or any other thing of value exceeding $1,000 belonging to, or in the care, custody, control, management, or possession of any bank, credit union, or any savings and loan association, shall be fined under this title or imprisoned not more than ten years, or both; or
>
> Whoever takes and carries away, with intent to steal or purloin, any property or money or any other thing of value not exceeding $1,000 belonging to, or in the care, custody, control, management, or possession of any bank, credit union, or any

---

[2] By "lesser offense," *Schmuck* meant lesser in terms of magnitude of punishment. When the elements of such a "lesser offense" are a subset of the elements of the charged offense, the "lesser offense" attains the status of a "lesser *included* offense."

[3] A defendant must also satisfy the "independent prerequisite . . . that the evidence at trial . . . be such that a jury could rationally find the defendant guilty of the lesser offense, yet acquit him of the greater." *Schmuck,* 489 U.S. at 716. In light of our holding that petitioner fails to satisfy the elements test, we need not address the latter requirement in this case.

> savings and loan association, shall be fined not more than $1,000 or imprisoned not more than one year, or both.

A "textual comparison" of the elements of these offenses suggests that the Government is correct. First, whereas subsection (b) requires that the defendant act "with intent to steal or purloin," subsection (a) contains no similar requirement. Second, whereas subsection (b) requires that the defendant "tak[e] and carr[y] away" the property, subsection (a) only requires that the defendant "tak[e]" the property. Third, whereas the first paragraph of subsection (b) requires that the property have a "value exceeding $1,000," subsection (a) contains no valuation requirement. . . .

Carter urges that the foregoing application of *Schmuck*'s elements test is too rigid and submits that ordinary principles of statutory interpretation are relevant to the *Schmuck* inquiry. We do not dispute the latter proposition. The *Schmuck* test, after all, requires an exercise in statutory interpretation before the comparison of elements may be made, and it is only sensible that normal principles of statutory construction apply. We disagree, however, with petitioner's conclusion that such principles counsel a departure in this case from what is indicated by a straightforward reading of the text.

III

Carter . . . submits that, insofar as subsections (a) and (b) are similar to the common-law crimes of robbery and larceny, we must assume that subsections (a) and (b) require the *same* elements as their common-law predecessors, at least absent Congress' affirmative indication (whether in text or legislative history) of an intent to displace the common-law scheme. While we (and the Government) agree that the statutory crimes at issue here bear a close resemblance to the common-law crimes of robbery and larceny, that observation is beside the point. The canon on imputing common-law meaning applies only when Congress makes use of a statutory *term* with established meaning at common law, and Carter does not point to any such term in the text of the statute.

This limited scope of the canon on imputing common-law meaning has long been understood. In Morissette v. United States, 342 U.S. 246, 263 (1952), for example, we articulated the canon in this way:

> [W]here Congress borrows *terms* of art in which are accumulated the legal tradition and meaning of centuries of practice, it presumably knows and adopts the cluster of ideas that were attached to each borrowed *word* in the body of learning from which it was taken and the meaning its use will convey to the judicial mind unless otherwise instructed. In such case, absence of contrary direction may be taken as satisfaction with widely accepted definitions, not as a departure from them. (Emphasis added.)

In other words, a "cluster of ideas" from the common law should be imported into statutory text only when Congress employs a common-law *term*, and not when, as here, Congress simply describes an offense analogous to a common-law crime without using common-law terms. . . .

Here, it is undisputed that "robbery" and "larceny" are terms with established meanings at common law. But neither term appears in the text of § 2113(a) or § 2113(b).[5] While the term "robbery" does appear in § 2113's title, the title of a statute " '[is] of use only when [it] shed[s] light on some ambiguous word or phrase' " in the statute itself. Pennsylvania Dept. of Corrections v. Yeskey, 524 U.S. 206, 212 (1998). And Carter does not claim that this title illuminates any such ambiguous language. Accordingly, the canon on imputing common-law meaning has no bearing on this case.

IV

We turn now to Carter's more specific arguments concerning the "extra" elements of § 2113(b). . . .

As to "intent to steal or purloin," it will be recalled that the text of subsection (b) requires a specific "intent to steal or purloin," whereas subsection (a) contains no explicit mens rea requirement of any kind. Carter nevertheless argues that such a *specific intent* requirement must be deemed implicitly present in § 2113(a) by virtue of "our cases interpreting criminal statutes to include broadly applicable scienter requirements, even where the statute by its terms does not contain them." United States v. X-Citement Video, Inc., 513 U.S. 64, 70 (1994).[6] Properly applied to § 2113, however, the presumption in favor of scienter demands only that we read subsection (a) as requiring proof of *general intent*—that is, that the defendant possessed knowledge with respect to the actus reus of the crime (here, the taking of property of another by force and violence or intimidation).

Before explaining why this is so under our cases, an example, United States v. Lewis, 628 F.2d 1276, 1279 (10th Cir. 1980), will help to make the distinction between "general" and "specific" intent less esoteric. In Lewis, a person entered a bank and took money from a teller at gunpoint, but deliberately failed to make a quick getaway from the bank in the hope of being arrested so that he would be returned to prison and treated for alcoholism. Though this defendant knowingly engaged in the acts of using force and taking money (satisfying "general intent"), he did not intend permanently to deprive the bank of its possession of the money (failing to satisfy "specific intent").[7]

The presumption in favor of scienter requires a court to read into a statute only that mens rea which is necessary to separate wrongful conduct from "otherwise innocent conduct." *X-Citement Video*, 513 U.S.

---

[5] Congress could have simply punished "robbery" or "larceny" as some States have done (and as Congress itself has done elsewhere, see, e.g., 18 U.S.C. §§ 2112, 2114, 2115), thereby leaving the definition of these terms to the common law, but Congress instead followed the more prevalent legislative practice of spelling out elements of these crimes.

[6] This interpretive principle exists quite apart from the canon on imputing common-law meaning. See, e.g., X-Citement Video, 513 U.S. at 70 (applying presumption in favor of scienter to statute proscribing the shipping or receiving of visual depictions of minors engaging in sexually explicit conduct, without first inquiring as to the existence of a common-law antecedent to this offense); Staples v. United States, 511 U.S. 600 (1994) (similar).

[7] The dissent claims that the *Lewis* court determined that the jury could have found specific intent to steal on the facts presented, and thus disputes our characterization of the case as illustrating a situation where a defendant acts only with general intent. The dissent fails to acknowledge, however, that the *Lewis* court made this determination only because some evidence suggested that, if the defendant had not been arrested, he would have kept the stolen money. The *Lewis* court, implicitly acknowledging the possibility that some defendant (if not Lewis) might unconditionally intend to turn himself in after completing a bank theft, proceeded to hold, in the alternative, that § 2113(a) covers a defendant who acts only with general intent.

at 72. In Staples v. United States, 511 U.S. 600 (1994), for example, to avoid criminalizing the innocent activity of gun ownership, we interpreted a federal firearms statute to require proof that the defendant knew that the weapon he possessed had the characteristics bringing it within the scope of the statute. By contrast, some situations may call for implying a specific intent requirement into statutory text. Suppose, for example, a statute identical to § 2113(b) but without the words "intent to steal or purloin." Such a statute would run the risk of punishing seemingly innocent conduct in the case of a defendant who peaceably takes money believing it to be his. Reading the statute to require that the defendant possess general intent with respect to the actus reus—i.e., that he know that he is physically taking the money—would fail to protect the innocent actor. The statute therefore would need to be read to require not only general intent, but also specific intent—i.e., that the defendant take the money with "intent to steal or purloin."

In this case, as in *Staples*, a general intent requirement suffices to separate wrongful from "otherwise innocent" conduct. . . . And once this mental state and actus reus are shown, the concerns underlying the presumption in favor of scienter are fully satisfied, for a forceful taking—even by a defendant who takes under a good-faith claim of right—falls outside the realm of the "otherwise innocent." Thus, the presumption in favor of scienter does not justify reading a specific intent requirement—"intent to steal or purloin"—into § 2113(a).

Independent of his reliance upon the presumption in favor of scienter, Carter argues that the legislative history of § 2113 supports the notion that an "intent to steal" requirement should be read into § 2113(a). Carter points out that, in 1934, Congress enacted what is now § 2113(a), but with the adverb "feloniously" (which all agree is equivalent to "intent to steal") modifying the verb "takes." Act of May 18, 1934, ch. 304, § 2(a), 48 Stat. 783. In 1937, Congress added what is now § 2113(b). Act of Aug. 24, 1937, ch. 747, 50 Stat. 749. Finally, in 1948, Congress made two changes to § 2113, deleting "feloniously" from what is now § 2113(a) and dividing the "robbery" and "larceny" offenses into their own separate subsections. 62 Stat. 796.

Carter concludes that the 1948 deletion of "feloniously" was merely a stylistic change, and that Congress had no intention, in deleting that word, to drop the requirement that the defendant "feloniously" take the property—that is, with intent to steal. Such reasoning, however, misunderstands our approach to statutory interpretation. In analyzing a statute, we begin by examining the text, not by "psychoanalyzing those who enacted it," Bank One Chicago, N.A. v. Midwest Bank & Trust Co., 516 U.S. 264, 279 (1996) (Scalia, J., concurring in part and concurring in judgment). While "feloniously" no doubt would be sufficient to convey a specific intent requirement akin to the one spelled out in subsection (b), the word simply does not appear in subsection (a).

Contrary to the dissent's suggestion, this reading is not a fanciful one. The absence of a specific intent requirement from subsection (a), for example, permits the statute to reach cases like Lewis, where an ex-convict robs a bank because he wants to be apprehended and returned to prison. (The Government represents that indictments on this same fact pattern (which invariably plead out and hence do not result in reported decisions) are brought "as often as every year," Brief for United

States 22, n. 13.) It can hardly be said, therefore, that it would have been absurd to delete "feloniously" in order to reach such defendants. And once we have made that determination, our inquiry into legislative motivation is at an end.

[Justice Thomas then turned to the second and third ways in which the two provisions differed. As to the second, "Carter contends that the 'takes' in subsection (a) is equivalent to 'takes and carries away' in subsection (b)." Thomas answered that "our inquiry focuses on an analysis of the textual product of Congress' efforts, not on speculation as to the internal thought processes of its Members." As to the "exceeding $1,000" language in subsection (b), Thomas concluded that it was enough that this was plainly an element of subsection (b) and not subsection (a):

> The structure of subsection (b) strongly suggests that its two paragraphs—the first of which requires that the property taken have "value exceeding $1,000," the second of which refers to property of "value not exceeding $1,000"—describe distinct offenses. Each begins with the word "[w]hoever," proceeds to describe identically (apart from the differing valuation requirements) the elements of the offense, and concludes by stating the prescribed punishment. That these provisions "stand on their own grammatical feet" strongly suggests that Congress intended the valuation requirement to be an element of each paragraph's offense. . . .]

We hold that § 2113(b) is not a lesser included offense of § 2113(a), and therefore that petitioner is not entitled to a jury instruction on § 2113(b). The judgment of the Third Circuit is affirmed. . . .

■ JUSTICE GINSBURG, with whom JUSTICE STEVENS, JUSTICE SOUTER, and JUSTICE BREYER join, dissenting.

At common law, robbery meant larceny *plus* force, violence, or putting in fear. Because robbery was an aggravated form of larceny at common law, larceny was a lesser included offense of robbery. Congress, I conclude, did not depart from that traditional understanding when it rendered "Bank robbery and incidental crimes" federal offenses. . . . I emphasize . . . the title of § 2113. . . . This Court has repeatedly recognized that " 'the title of a statute and the heading of a section' are 'tools available for the resolution of a doubt' about the meaning of a statute." Almendarez-Torres v. United States, 523 U.S. 224, 234 (1998).[2] Robbery, all agree, was an offense at common law, and this Court has consistently instructed that courts should ordinarily read federal criminal laws in accordance with their common-law origins, if Congress has not directed otherwise. . . . In interpreting § 2113, then, I am guided by the common-law understanding of "robbery and incidental crimes." At common law, as the Government concedes, robbery was an aggravated form of larceny. Specifically, the common law defined larceny as "the felonious taking, and carrying away, of the personal goods of another." 4 W. Blackstone, Commentaries on the Laws of England 230 (1769)

[2] The majority says that courts may use a statutory title or heading only to "shed light on some ambiguous word or phrase," but not as a guide to a statute's overall meaning. Our cases have never before imposed such a wooden and arbitrary limitation, and for good reason: A statute's meaning can be elusive, and its title illuminating, even where a court cannot pinpoint a discrete word or phrase as the source of the ambiguity.

(Blackstone). Robbery, in turn, was larceny effected by taking property from the person or presence of another by means of force or putting in fear. Brief for United States 29–30 (citing 2 W. LaFave & A. Scott, Substantive Criminal Law § 8.11, pp. 437–438 (1986) (LaFave & Scott)). Larceny was therefore a lesser included offense of robbery at common law. See 4 Blackstone 241 (robbery is "[o]pen and violent larceny from the person"); 2 E. East, Pleas of the Crown § 124, p. 707 (1803) (robbery is a species of "aggravated larceny"); 2 W. Russell & C. Greaves, Crimes and Misdemeanors *101 ("robbery is an aggravated species of larceny").

Closer inspection of the common-law elements of both crimes confirms the relationship. The elements of common-law larceny were also elements of robbery. First and most essentially, robbery, like larceny, entailed an intentional taking. Second, . . . the taking in a robbery had to be "felonious," a common-law term of art signifying an intent to steal. And third, again like larceny, robbery contained an asportation requirement. Unlike larceny, however, robbery included one further essential component: an element of force, violence, or intimidation. Precedent thus instructs us to presume that Congress has adhered to the altogether clear common-law understanding that larceny is a lesser included offense of robbery, unless Congress has affirmatively indicated its design, in codifying the crimes of robbery and larceny, to displace their common-law meanings and relationship.

Far from signaling an intent to depart from the common law, the codification of § 2113's predecessor statute suggests that Congress intended to adhere to the traditional ranking of larceny as a lesser included offense of robbery. There is no indication at any point during the codification of the two crimes that Congress meant to install new conceptions of larceny and robbery severed from their common-law foundations.

Prior to 1934, federal law did not criminalize bank robbery or larceny; these crimes were punishable only under state law. Congress enacted the precursor to § 2113(a) in response to an outbreak of bank robberies committed by John Dillinger and others who evaded capture by state authorities by moving from State to State. In bringing federal law into this area, Congress did not aim to reshape robbery by altering the common-law definition of that crime. On the contrary, Congress chose language that practically jumped out of Blackstone's Commentaries:

> Whoever, by force and violence, or by putting in fear, feloniously takes, or feloniously attempts to take, from the person or presence of another any property or money or any other thing of value belonging to, or in the care, custody, control, management, or possession of, any bank shall be fined not more than $5,000 or imprisoned not more than twenty years, or both. Act of May 18, 1934, ch. 304, § 2(a), 48 Stat. 783.

It soon became apparent, however, that this legislation left a gap: It did not reach the thief who intentionally, though not violently, stole money from a bank. Within a few years, federal law enforcers endeavored to close the gap. In a letter to the Speaker of the House, the Attorney General conveyed the Executive Branch's official position: "The fact that the statute is limited to robbery and does not include larceny and burglary has led to some incongruous results." In particular, the Attorney General cited the example of a thief apprehended after taking

$11,000 from a bank while a teller was temporarily absent. He therefore asked Congress to amend the bank robbery statute, specifically to add a larceny provision shorn of any force, violence, or fear requirement. Congress responded by passing an Act "[t]o amend the bank robbery statute to include burglary and larceny." Act of Aug. 24, 1937, ch. 747, 50 Stat. 749. The Act's new larceny provision, which Congress placed in the very same section as the robbery provision, punished "whoever shall take and carry away, with intent to steal or purloin," property, money, or anything of value from a bank. There is not the slightest sign that, when this new larceny provision was proposed in terms tracking the common-law formulation, the Attorney General advocated any change in the definition of robbery from larceny plus to something less. Nor is there any sign that Congress meant to order such a change. The Act left in place the 1934 Act's definition of bank robbery, which continued to include the word "feloniously," requiring (as the Court concedes) proof by the Government of an intent to steal.

In its 1948 codification of federal crimes, Congress delineated the bank robbery and larceny provisions of §§ 2113(a) and 2113(b) and placed these provisions under the title "Bank robbery and incidental crimes." Act of June 25, 1948, § 2113, 62 Stat. 796–797. In this codification, Congress deleted the word "feloniously" from the robbery provision, leaving the statute in substantially its present form. . . . That 1948 deletion forms the basis of the Government's prime argument against characterizing § 2113(b) as a lesser included offense of § 2113(a), namely, that robbery, unlike larceny, no longer requires a specific intent to steal. The Government concedes that to gain a conviction for robbery at common law, the prosecutor had to prove the perpetrator's intent to steal. The Government therefore acknowledges that when Congress uses the terms "rob" or "robbery" "without further elaboration," Congress intends to retain the common-law meaning of robbery. But the Government contends that the 1948 removal of "feloniously" from § 2113(a) showed Congress' purpose to dispense with any requirement of intent to steal.

It is true that the larceny provision contains the words "intent to steal" while the current robbery provision does not.[4] But the element-based comparison called for by *Schmuck* is not so rigid as to require that the compared statutes contain identical words. Nor does *Schmuck* counsel deviation from our traditional practice of interpreting federal criminal statutes consistently with their common-law origins in the absence of affirmative congressional indication to the contrary. Guided by the historical understanding of the relationship between robbery and larceny both at common law and as brought into the federal criminal code, I conclude that the offense of bank robbery under § 2113(a), like the offense of bank larceny under § 2113(b), has always included and continues to include a requirement of intent to steal.

This traditional reading of the robbery statute makes common sense. The Government agrees that to be convicted of robbery, the defendant must resort to force and violence, or intimidation, to accomplish his purpose. But what purpose could this be other than to steal? The Government describes two scenarios in which, it maintains, a person

---

[4] Notably, the Court would read a requirement of intent to steal into § 2113(b) even if that provision did not contain such words.

could commit bank robbery while nonetheless lacking intent to steal. One scenario involves a terrorist who temporarily takes a bank's money or property aiming only to disrupt the bank's business; the other involves an ex-convict, unable to cope with life in a free society, who robs a bank because he wants to be apprehended and returned to prison.

The Government does not point to any cases involving its terrorist scenario, and I know of none. To illustrate its ex-convict scenario, the Government cites United States v. Lewis, 628 F.2d 1276 (10th Cir. 1980), which appears to be the only reported federal case presenting this staged situation. The facts of *Lewis*—a case on which the Court relies heavily—were strange, to say the least. Hoping to be sent back to prison where he could receive treatment for his alcoholism and have time to pursue his writing hobby, Lewis called a local detective and informed him of his intention to rob a bank. He also discussed his felonious little plans with the police chief, undercover police officers, and a psychologist. He even allowed his picture to be taken so that it could be posted in local banks for identification. Following his much-awaited heist, Lewis was arrested in the bank's outer foyer by officers who had him under surveillance.

I am not sure whether a defendant exhibiting this kind of "bizarre behavior" should in fact be deemed to lack a specific intent to steal. (The Tenth Circuit, I note, determined that specific intent was present in Lewis, for "[t]he jury, charged with the duty to infer from conflicting evidence the defendant's intent, could have concluded that if Lewis was not arrested he would have kept the money and spent it.") But whatever its proper disposition, this sort of case is extremely rare—the Government represents that, nationwide, such indictments are brought no more than once per year. Moreover, unlike a John Dillinger who foils state enforcers by robbing banks in Chicago and lying low in South Bend, the thief who orchestrates his own capture at the hands of the local constable hardly poses the kind of problem that one would normally expect to trigger a federal statutory response. In sum, I resist the notion—apparently embraced by the Court—that Congress' purpose in deleting the word "feloniously" from § 2113(a) was to grant homesick ex-convicts like Lewis their wish to return to prison. Nor can I credit the suggestion that Congress' concern was to cover the Government's fictional terrorist, or the frustrated account holder who "withdraws" $100 by force or violence, believing the money to be rightfully his, or the thrill seeker who holds up a bank with the intent of driving around the block in a getaway car and then returning the loot, or any other defendant whose exploits are seldom encountered outside the pages of law school exams.

Indeed, there is no cause to suspect that the 1948 deletion of "feloniously" was intended to effect any substantive change at all. Nothing indicates that Congress removed that word in response to any assertion or perception of prosecutorial need. Nor is there any other reason to believe that it was Congress' design to alter the elements of the offense of robbery. Rather, the legislative history suggests that Congress intended only to make "changes in phraseology." . . . As the Third Circuit has recognized, "it seems that the deletion of 'feloniously' was a result of Congress' effort to delete references to felonies and misdemeanors from the code, inasmuch as both terms were defined in 18 U.S.C. § 1," a statute that has since been repealed.[5] I would not attribute to Congress a design to create a robbery offense stripped of the requirement of larcenous intent in the absence of any affirmative indication of such a design.[6]. . .

Having accepted the Government's argument concerning intent to steal, the Court goes on to agree with the Government that robbery, unlike larceny, does not require that the defendant carry away the property. As with intent to steal, the historical linkage of the two crimes reveals the Court's error. It is true that § 2113(b) includes the phrase "takes and carries away" while § 2113(a) says only "takes." Both crimes, however, included an asportation requirement at common law. Indeed, the text of §§ 2113(a) and (b)—which the Court maintains must be the primary focus of lesser included offense analysis—mirrors the language of the common law quite precisely. At common law, larceny was typically described as a crime involving both a "taking" and a "carrying away." See 4 Blackstone 231. Robbery, on the other hand, was often defined in "somewhat undetailed language," LaFave & Scott § 8.11, at 438, n. 6, that made no mention of "carrying away," see 4 Blackstone 231, but was nevertheless consistently interpreted to encompass an element of asportation. The Court overlooks completely this feature of the common-law terminology. I note, moreover, that the asportation requirement, both at common law and under § 2113, is an extremely modest one: even a slight movement will do. See LaFave & Scott § 8.11, at 439. The text of §§ 2113(a) and (b) thus tracks the common law. The Court's conclusory statement notwithstanding, nothing in the evolution of the statute suggests that "Congress adopted a different view in § 2113(a), deliberately doing away with the minimal asportation requirement in prosecutions for bank robbery. I would hold, therefore, that both crimes continue to contain an asportation requirement.

Finally, the Court concludes that the "value exceeding $1,000" requirement of the first paragraph of § 2113(b) is an element of the offense described in that paragraph. I agree with this conclusion and with the reasoning in support of it. It bears emphasis, however, that the lesser degree of bank larceny defined in § 2113(b)'s second paragraph contains no dollar value element even arguably impeding its classification as a lesser included offense of bank robbery. The Government does not contend that the "value not exceeding $1,000" component of that paragraph is an element of the misdemeanor offense, and such a contention would make scant sense. Surely Congress did not intend that a defendant charged only with the lower grade of bank larceny could successfully defend against that charge by showing that he stole *more* than $1,000. In other words, if a defendant commits larceny without exhibiting the distinguishing characteristics of robbery (force and violence, or intimidation), he has necessarily committed at least the lesser degree of larceny, whether he has taken $500 or $5,000. Under *Schmuck*, then, a defendant charged with bank robbery in violation of § 2113(a) is not

---

[5] The various classes of federal felonies and misdemeanors are now defined at 18 U.S.C. § 3559.

[6] Congress could have provided such an affirmative indication in any number of ways. The simplest would have been to say so in the statute, e.g.: "It shall not be a defense that the accused person lacked an intent to steal." Cf. 18 U.S.C. § 645 (criminalizing embezzlement by judicial officers, and providing that "[i]t shall not be a defense that the accused person had any interest in [the embezzled] moneys or fund").

barred as a matter of law from obtaining a jury instruction on bank larceny as defined in the second paragraph of § 2113(b).

I see no reason why a defendant charged with bank robbery, which securely encompasses as a lesser included offense the statutory equivalent of petit larceny, should automatically be denied an instruction on the statutory equivalent of grand larceny if he wants one. It is clear that petit and grand larceny were two grades of the same offense at common law. And, as earlier explained, robbery at common law was an aggravated form of that single offense. One of the key purposes of *Schmuck's* elements test is to allow easy comparison between two discrete crimes. That purpose would be frustrated if an element that exists only to distinguish a more culpable from a less culpable grade of the same crime were sufficient to prevent the defendant from getting a lesser included offense instruction as to the more culpable grade. I would therefore hold that a defendant charged with the felony of bank robbery is not barred as a matter of law from requesting and receiving an instruction describing as a lesser included offense the felony grade of bank larceny.[7] . . .

In sum, I would hold that a defendant charged with bank robbery as defined in 18 U.S.C. § 2113(a) is not barred as a matter of law from obtaining a jury instruction on bank larceny as defined in 18 U.S.C. § 2113(b). In reaching the opposite conclusion, the Court gives short shrift to the common-law origin and statutory evolution of § 2113. The Court's woodenly literal construction . . . effectively shrinks the jury's choices while enlarging the prosecutor's options. I dissent.

## SECTION 3: WILLFUL BLINDNESS

### United States v. Heredia

United States Court of Appeals for the Ninth Circuit, en banc, 2007.
483 F.3d 913.

Before MARY M. SCHROEDER, CHIEF JUDGE, HARRY PREGERSON, ALEX KOZINSKI, PAMELA ANN RYMER, ANDREW J. KLEINFELD, MICHAEL DALY HAWKINS, SIDNEY R. THOMAS, BARRY G. SILVERMAN, SUSAN P. GRABER, M. MARGARET MCKEOWN, RICHARD A. PAEZ, RICHARD C. TALLMAN, RICHARD R. CLIFTON, CONSUELO M. CALLAHAN, and CARLOS T. BEA, CIRCUIT JUDGES.

■ KOZINSKI, CIRCUIT JUDGE. . . .

We revisit United States v. Jewell, 532 F.2d 697 (9th Cir.1976) (en banc), and the body of caselaw applying it.

I

Defendant Carmen Heredia was stopped at an inland Border Patrol checkpoint while driving from Nogales to Tucson, Arizona. Heredia was at the wheel and her two children, mother and one of her aunts were passengers. The border agent at the scene noticed what he described as a "very strong perfume odor" emanating from the car. A second agent

---

[7] The court could instruct the jury as to the common elements of both grades of bank larceny, and then add that in order to return a conviction of the higher grade, the jury must also find that the value of the stolen property exceeded $1,000.

searched the trunk and found 349.2 pounds of marijuana surrounded by dryer sheets, apparently used to mask the odor. Heredia was arrested and charged with possessing a controlled substance with intent to distribute under 21 U.S.C. § 841(a)(1).[a]

At trial, Heredia testified that on the day of her arrest she had accompanied her mother on a bus trip from Tucson to Nogales, where her mother had a dentist's appointment. After the appointment, she borrowed her Aunt Belia's car to transport her mother back to Tucson.[1] Heredia told DEA Agent Travis Birney at the time of her arrest that, while still in Nogales, she had noticed a "detergent" smell in the car as she prepared for the trip and asked Belia to explain. Belia told her that she had spilled Downey fabric softener in the car a few days earlier, but Heredia found this explanation incredible.

Heredia admitted on the stand that she suspected there might be drugs in the car, based on the fact that her mother was visibly nervous during the trip and carried a large amount of cash, even though she wasn't working at the time. However, Heredia claimed that her suspicions were not aroused until she had passed the last freeway exit before the checkpoint, by which time it was too dangerous to pull over and investigate.

The government requested a deliberate ignorance instruction, and the judge obliged, overruling Heredia's objection. The instruction, cribbed from our circuit's Model Jury Instruction 5.7, read as follows:

> You may find that the defendant acted knowingly if you find beyond a reasonable doubt that the defendant was aware of a high probability that drugs were in the vehicle driven by the defendant and deliberately avoided learning the truth. You may not find such knowledge, however, if you find that the defendant actually believed that no drugs were in the vehicle driven by the defendant, or if you find that the defendant was simply careless.

On appeal, defendant asks us to overrule *Jewell* and hold that § 841(a)(1) extends liability only to individuals who act with actual knowledge. Should *Jewell* remain good law, she asks us to reverse her conviction because the instruction given to the jury was defective and because there was an insufficient factual basis for issuing the instruction in the first place.

II

While *Jewell* has spawned a great deal of commentary and a somewhat perplexing body of caselaw, its core holding was a rather straightforward matter of statutory interpretation: "[K]nowingly in criminal statutes is not limited to positive knowledge, but includes the state of mind of one who does not possess positive knowledge only because he consciously avoided it." In other words, when Congress made it a crime to "knowingly . . . possess with intent to manufacture, distrib-

---

[a] Section 841(1)(a) provides: "[I]t shall be unlawful for any person knowingly or intentionally . . . to manufacture, distribute, or dispense, or possess with intent to manufacture, distribute, or dispense, a controlled substance."—[Footnote by eds.]

[1] Belia was not the aunt in the car with Heredia at the time she was stopped at the checkpoint. Belia was traveling on the same interstate at about the same time, but in a separate car.

ute, or dispense, a controlled substance," 21 U.S.C. § 841(a)(1), it meant to punish not only those who know they possess a controlled substance, but also those who don't know because they don't want to know.[4]

. . . Since *Jewell* was decided in 1976, every regional circuit—with the exception of the D.C. Circuit—has adopted its central holding. Indeed, many colloquially refer to the deliberate ignorance instruction as the "*Jewell* instruction." Congress has amended § 841 many times since *Jewell* was handed down, but not in a way that would cast doubt on our ruling. Given the widespread acceptance of *Jewell* across the federal judiciary, of which Congress must surely have been aware, we construe Congress's inaction as acquiescence.[6]

That said, there are circumstances when a precedent becomes so unworkable that keeping it on the books actually undermines the values of evenhandedness and predictability that the doctrine of stare decisis aims to advance. Here, we recognize that many of our post-*Jewell* cases have created a vexing thicket of precedent that has been difficult for litigants to follow and for district courts—and ourselves—to apply with consistency. But, rather than overturn *Jewell,* we conclude that the better course is to clear away the underbrush that surrounds it.

III

The parties have pointed out one area where our cases have not been consistent: Whether the jury must be instructed that defendant's motive in deliberately failing to learn the truth was to give himself a defense in case he should be charged with the crime.[8] *Jewell* itself speculated that defendant's motive for failing to learn the truth in that case was to "avoid responsibility in the event of discovery."[9] Yet the opinion did not define motive as a separate prong of the deliberate ignorance instruction. And we affirmed, even though the instruction given

---

[4] As our cases have recognized, deliberate ignorance, otherwise known as willful blindness, is categorically different from negligence or recklessness. A willfully blind defendant is one who took deliberate actions to avoid confirming suspicions of criminality. A reckless defendant is one who merely knew of a substantial and unjustifiable risk that his conduct was criminal; a negligent defendant is one who should have had similar suspicions but, in fact, did not.

[6] Our dissenting colleague seeks support for her position from the fact that Congress has, on occasion, defined the scienter requirement in some criminal statutes as "knows, or has reasonable grounds to believe." But "has reasonable grounds to believe" defines a mental state that is less than actual knowledge. By contrast, *Jewell* defines willful blindness as knowledge—and sets a much higher standard for satisfying it. Thus, under *Jewell,* the prosecution must prove that defendant was aware of a "high probability" that he is in the possession of contraband, and that he "deliberately avoided learning the truth." This standard focuses on defendant's actual beliefs and actions, whereas "has reasonable grounds to believe" is an objective standard that could be satisfied by showing what a reasonable person would believe, regardless of defendant's actual beliefs. That Congress chose to set a lower scienter requirement in some criminal statutes tells us nothing about our interpretation of "knowledge" in *Jewell.* It certainly provides an insufficient basis for rejecting an interpretation that Congress has left undisturbed for three decades and that has since been adopted by 10 of our sister circuits.

[8] The motive prong usually requires the jury to find that defendant was deliberately ignorant "in order to provide himself with a defense in the event of prosecution." United States v. Baron, 94 F.3d 1312, 1317 (9th Cir.1996).

[9] The concurrence makes much out of this phrase, but it cuts entirely the other way because (as noted in the text) *Jewell* approved an instruction that did not contain the motive prong. Even though the *Jewell* court believed this was defendant's likely motive, it did not choose to make it an independent element of deliberate indifference.

at Jewell's trial made no mention of motive. Since then, we've upheld two-pronged instructions, similar to the one given here, in at least four other published opinions.

The first mention of the motive prong came in a dissent by then-Judge Kennedy, who also authored the dissent in *Jewell*. See United States v. Murrieta-Bejarano, 552 F.2d 1323, 1326 (9th Cir.1977) (Kennedy, J., dissenting). Judge Kennedy's chief concern was with what he viewed as the absence of *deliberate* avoidance on the part of the defendant in that case. At any rate, he was not writing for the court. Yet some of our opinions seem to have adopted the motive prong, providing little justification for doing so other than citation to Judge Kennedy's dissent.

Heredia argues that the motive prong is necessary to avoid punishing individuals who fail to investigate because circumstances render it unsafe or impractical to do so. She claims that she is within this group, because her suspicions did not arise until she was driving on an open highway where it would have been too dangerous to pull over. She thus claims that she had a motive *other* than avoiding criminal culpability for failing to discover the contraband concealed in the trunk.

We believe, however, that the second prong of the instruction, the requirement that defendant have *deliberately* avoided learning the truth, provides sufficient protections for defendants in these situations. A deliberate action is one that is "[i]ntentional; premeditated; fully considered." Black's Law Dictionary 459 (8th ed. 2004). A decision influenced by coercion, exigent circumstances or lack of meaningful choice is, perforce, not deliberate. A defendant who fails to investigate for these reasons has not deliberately chosen to avoid learning the truth.[10] . . .

We conclude, therefore, that the two-pronged instruction given at defendant's trial met the requirements of *Jewell* and, to the extent some of our cases have suggested more is required, they are overruled. A district judge, in the exercise of his discretion, may say more to tailor the instruction to the particular facts of the case. Here, for example, the judge might have instructed the jury that it could find Heredia did not act deliberately if it believed that her failure to investigate was motivated by safety concerns. Heredia did not ask for such an instruction and the district judge had no obligation to give it sua sponte. Even when defendant asks for such a supplemental instruction, it is within the district court's broad discretion whether to comply.

IV

Defendant also claims there was insufficient foundation to give the *Jewell* instruction. . . . A district court should approach the government's request to give a *Jewell* instruction in the same way it deals with any other proposed jury instruction. In general, a party is entitled

---

[10] The concurrence would add the third prong to the *Jewell* instruction in order to protect defendants who have "innocent" motives for deliberately avoiding the truth. But the deliberate ignorance instruction defines when an individual has sufficient information so that he can be deemed to "know" something, even though he does not take the final step to confirm that knowledge. The *reason* the individual fails to take that final step has no bearing on whether he has sufficient information so he can properly be deemed to "know" the fact. An innocent motive for being deliberately ignorant no more vitiates the knowledge element of a crime than does an innocent motive vitiate any other element. . . .

to an instruction to help it prove its theory of the case, if the instruction is "supported by law and has foundation in the evidence."

In deciding whether to give a particular instruction, the district court must view the evidence in the light most favorable to the party requesting it. When a party requests instructions on alternative theories, the district judge must consider the instructions separately and determine if the evidence could support a verdict on either ground. When knowledge is at issue in a criminal case, the court must first determine whether the evidence of defendant's mental state, if viewed in the light most favorable to the government, will support a finding of actual knowledge.[13] If so, the court must instruct the jury on this theory. Actual knowledge, of course, is inconsistent with willful blindness. The deliberate ignorance instruction only comes into play, therefore, if the jury rejects the government's case as to actual knowledge. In deciding whether to give a willful blindness instruction, in addition to an actual knowledge instruction, the district court must determine whether the jury could rationally find willful blindness even though it has rejected the government's evidence of actual knowledge. If so, the court may also give a *Jewell* instruction.

This case well illustrates the point. Taking the evidence in the light most favorable to the government, a reasonable jury could certainly have found that Heredia actually knew about the drugs. Not only was she driving a car with several hundred pounds of marijuana in the trunk, but everyone else who might have put the drugs there—her mother, her aunt, her husband—had a close personal relationship with Heredia. Moreover, there was evidence that Heredia and her husband had sole possession of the car for about an hour prior to setting out on the trip to Tucson. Based on this evidence, a jury could easily have inferred that Heredia actually knew about the drugs in the car because she was involved in putting them there.

The analysis in the foregoing paragraph presupposes that the jury believed the government's case in its entirety, and disbelieved all of Heredia's exculpatory statements. While this would have been *a* rational course for the jury to take, it was not the only one. For example, a rational jury might have bought Heredia's basic claim that she didn't know about the drugs in the trunk, yet disbelieved other aspects of her story. The jury could, for example, have disbelieved Heredia's story about *when* she first began to suspect she was transporting drugs. The jury could have found that her suspicions were aroused when Belia gave her the unsatisfactory explanation for the "detergent" scent, or while she drove to Tucson but before the last exit preceding the checkpoint. Or, the jury might have believed Heredia that she became suspicious only after she had passed the last exit before the checkpoint but disbelieved that concerns about safety motivated her failure to stop.

All of these are scenarios the jury could rationally have drawn from the evidence presented, depending on how credible they deemed Heredia's testimony in relation to the other evidence presented. The government has no way of knowing which version of the facts the jury will believe, and it is entitled (like any other litigant) to have the jury in-

[13] As previously noted, willful blindness is tantamount to knowledge. We use the phrase "actual knowledge" to describe the state of mind when defendant, in fact, knows of the existence of the contraband rather than being willfully blind to its existence.

structed in conformity with each of these rational possibilities. That these possibilities are mutually exclusive is of no consequence. A party may present alternative factual theories, and is entitled to instructions supporting all rational inferences the jury might draw from the evidence.

We do not share the worry, expressed in some of our cases, that giving both an actual knowledge and a deliberate ignorance instruction is likely to confuse the jury. A jury is presumed to follow the instructions given to it, and we see no reason to fear that juries will be less able to do so when trying to sort out a criminal defendant's state of mind than any other issue. Nor do we agree that the *Jewell* instruction risks lessening the state of mind that a jury must find to something akin to recklessness or negligence. The instruction requires the jury to find beyond a reasonable doubt that defendant "was aware of a high probability" of criminality and "deliberately avoided learning the truth." Indeed, the instruction actually given in this case told the jurors to acquit if they believed defendant was "simply careless." Recklessness or negligence never comes into play, and there is little reason to suspect that juries will import these concepts, as to which they are not instructed, into their deliberations. . . .

V

We decline the invitation to overrule *Jewell,* and further hold that district judges are owed the usual degree of deference in deciding when a deliberate ignorance instruction is warranted. While the particular form of the instruction can vary, it must, at a minimum, contain the two prongs of suspicion and deliberate avoidance. The district judge may say more, if he deems it advisable to do so, or deny the instruction altogether. We review such decisions for abuse of discretion. The instruction given at defendant's trial met these requirements, and the district judge did not abuse his discretion in issuing it.

Affirmed.

■ KLEINFELD, CIRCUIT JUDGE, concurring in the result:

Because the evidence in this case justified a wilful blindness instruction, and the instruction's form (to which no objection was made below) was not *plainly* erroneous, I would affirm Heredia's conviction. But the majority errs in concluding that motivation to avoid criminal responsibility need not be an element of a wilful blindness instruction. . . . To avoid injustice, the jury needs to be instructed that they must find a motivation to avoid criminal responsibility to be the reason for lack of knowledge.[3] . . .

[Quoting Glanville Williams, Criminal Law: The General Part, § 57 at 159 (2d ed. 1961), we said in United States v. Jewell, 532 F.2d 697, 700 n.7 (9th Cir, 1976) (en banc):]

> A court can properly find wilful blindness only where it can almost be said that the defendant actually knew. He suspected the fact; he realized its probability; but he refrained from obtaining the final confirmation *because he wanted in the*

[3] See United States v. Jewell, 532 F.2d 697, 700 (9th Cir.1976) (en banc) ("The substantive justification for the rule [that wilful blindness is equivalent to knowledge] is that deliberate ignorance and positive knowledge are equally culpable.")

> *event to be able to deny knowledge. This, and this alone, is wilful blindness. It requires in effect a finding that the defendant intended to cheat the administration of justice. Any wider definition would make the doctrine of wilful blindness indistinguishable from the civil doctrine of negligence in not obtaining knowledge.* [Emphasis added.] . . .

The majority converts the statutory element that the possession be "knowing" into something much less—a requirement that the defendant be suspicious and deliberately avoid investigating. The imposition on people who intend no crime of a duty to investigate has no statutory basis. The majority says that its requirement is enough to protect defendants who cannot investigate because of "coercion, exigent circumstances or lack of meaningful choice." . . . The majority seems to mean that if someone can investigate, they must. A criminal duty to investigate the wrongdoing of others to avoid wrongdoing of one's own is a novelty in the criminal law. . . .

A *Jewell* instruction ought to incorporate what our case law has developed, that the wilful blindness doctrine is meant to punish a defendant who "all but knew" the truth—a defendant who "suspects a fact, realizes its [high] probability, but refrains from obtaining final confirmation in order to be able to deny knowledge if apprehended." "This, and this alone, is wilful blindness." The jury instruction in this case told the jury that Heredia had "knowing" possession of the marijuana in the trunk if she "was aware of a high probability" that drugs were in the car and "deliberately avoided learning the truth." That mental state would fit . . . the child of an aging hippy, as well as a drug mule. A *Jewell* instruction ought to require (1) a belief that drugs are present, (2) avoidance of confirmation of the belief, and (3) wilfulness in that avoidance—that is, choosing not to confirm the belief in order to "be able to deny knowledge if apprehended." The instruction should expressly exclude recklessness, negligence and mistake (the one given only excluded "simpl[e] careless[ness]" and an "actual[ ] belie[f] that no drugs were in the vehicle"). Anything less supports convictions of persons whom Congress excluded from statutory coverage with the word "knowingly." People who possess drugs, but do not do so "knowingly," are what we traditionally refer to as "innocent." . . .

■ GRABER, CIRCUIT JUDGE, with whom PREGERSON, THOMAS, and PAEZ, CIRCUIT JUDGES, join, dissenting:

. . . [A]s a matter of statutory construction, I believe that the *Jewell* instruction is not proper because it misconstrues, and misleads the jury about, the mens rea required by 21 U.S.C. § 841(a)(1). Because the legal error of giving a *Jewell* instruction in this case was not harmless beyond a reasonable doubt, I respectfully dissent.

Under 21 U.S.C. § 841(a)(1), it is a crime to "*knowingly or intentionally* . . . manufacture, distribute, or dispense, or possess with intent to manufacture, distribute, or dispense, a controlled substance." (Emphasis added.) The plain text of the statute does not make it a crime to have a high probability of awareness of possession—knowledge or intention is required.

The majority recognizes that willful blindness is a mens rea separate and distinct from knowledge. [It recognizes that:] "Actual knowledge, of course, is inconsistent with willful blindness." [Similarly, Judge Kennedy's opinion in *Jewell* said:] "The majority opinion justifies the conscious purpose jury instruction as an application of the wilful blindness doctrine recognized primarily by English authorities. . . . [T]he English authorities seem to consider wilful blindness a state of mind *distinct from, but equally culpable as,* actual knowledge" (emphasis added). Similarly, if not even more obviously, willful blindness is at least one step removed from intention.

Instead of justifying its sleight-of-hand directly, the majority points to the fact that *Jewell* has been on the books for 30 years and that Congress has not amended the statute in a way that repudiates *Jewell* expressly. I find this reasoning unpersuasive. "[C]ongressional inaction lacks persuasive significance because several equally tenable inferences may be drawn from such inaction. . . . " United States v. Craft, 535 U.S. 274, 287 (2002). . . .

Whatever relevance congressional *inaction* holds in this case is outweighed by actual congressional *action.* Under 21 U.S.C. § 841(a)(1), a person is guilty of a crime only if the requisite act is performed "knowingly or intentionally." By contrast, both before and after *Jewell,* Congress has defined several other crimes in which the mens rea involves a high probability of awareness—but it has done so in phrases dramatically different than the one here, which lists only knowledge and intent. See, e.g., 18 U.S.C. §§ 175b(b)(1)("knows or has reasonable cause to believe"), . . . 792 ("knows, or has reasonable grounds to believe or suspect"), . . . 2424(a) ("knowing or in reckless disregard of the fact"). Most importantly, Congress has done so in adjacent sections of the same statute, the Controlled Substances Act, 21 U.S.C. §§ 801–971, and even within the same section of the same statute. See 21 U.S.C. §§ 841(c)(2)("knowing, or having reasonable cause to believe"), 843(a)(6) ("knowing, intending, or having reasonable cause to believe"), 843(a)(7) (same). "It is axiomatic that when Congress uses different text in adjacent statutes it intends that the different terms carry a different meaning." White v. Lambert, 370 F.3d 1002, 1011 (9th Cir.2004). Thus, "[i]f we do our job of reading the statute whole, we have to give effect to [its] plain command, even if doing that will reverse the longstanding practice under the statute and the rule." Lexecon Inc. v. Milberg Weiss Bershad Hynes & Lerach, 523 U.S. 26, 35 (1998).

The majority recognizes that the *Jewell* instruction embodies a substantive decision that those who possess a controlled substance and "don't know because they don't want to know" are just as culpable as those who knowingly or intentionally possess a controlled substance. [See] Model Penal Code § 2.02 comment 9, at 248 ("Whether such cases [of wilful blindness] should be viewed as instances of acting recklessly or knowingly presents a subtle but important question."). But Congress never made this substantive decision about levels of culpability—the *Jewell* court did. [T]he majority chooses to reaffirm this judge-made substantive decision. In so doing, the majority directly contravenes the principle that "[i]t is the legislature, not the Court, which is to define a crime, and ordain its punishment." United States v. Wiltberger, 18 U.S. (5 Wheat.) 76, 95 (1820). "The spirit of the doctrine which denies to the federal judiciary power to create crimes forthrightly admonishes that we should not enlarge the reach of enacted crimes by constituting them from anything less than the incriminating components contemplated by the words used in the statute." Morissette v. United States, 342 U.S. 246, 263 (1952). The majority creates a duty to investigate for drugs that appears nowhere in the text of the statute, transforming knowledge into a mens rea more closely akin to negligence or recklessness.

I agree with the *Jewell* court that "one 'knows' facts of which he is less than absolutely certain." That being so, the mens rea-reducing *Jewell* instruction not only is wrong, it also is unnecessary in the face of the kind of proof that a prosecutor is likely to produce. For example, if your husband comes home at 1:00 a.m. every Friday (after having left work at 5:00 p.m. the day before as usual), never reveals where he has been, won't look you in the eye on Fridays, and puts Thursday's shirts in the hamper bearing lipstick stains, your friends will agree that you "know" he is having an affair even if you refuse to seek confirmation. The role of a jury is to apply common sense to the facts of a given case. A sensible jury will be persuaded that a drug mule "knows" what she is carrying when confronted with evidence of how mules typically operate and how this mule acted—all without reference to a *Jewell* instruction.

Thus, I would overrule *Jewell* and interpret 21 U.S.C. § 841(a) to require exactly what its text requires—a knowing or intentional mens rea. If Congress wants to criminalize willful ignorance, it is free to amend the statute to say so and, in view of the several examples quoted above, it clearly knows how.

## NOTES ON WILLFUL BLINDNESS

### 1. THE MODEL PENAL CODE

Section 2.02(7) of the Model Penal Code codifies the concept of willful blindness as follows: "When knowledge of the existence of a particular fact is an element of an offense, such knowledge is established if a person is aware of a high probability of its existence, unless he actually believes that it does not exist." The Commentary explains:

> Subsection (7) deals with the situation that British commentators have denominated "wilful blindness" or "connivance," the case of the actor who is aware of the probable existence of a material fact but does not determine whether it exists or does not exist. Whether such cases should be viewed as instances of acting recklessly or knowingly presents a subtle but important question.
>
> The Code proposes that the case be viewed as one of acting knowingly when what is involved is a matter of existing fact, but not when what is involved is the result of the defendant's conduct, necessarily a matter of the future at the time of acting. The position reflects what was believed to be the normal policy of criminal enactments that rest liability on acting "knowingly." The inference of "knowledge" of an existing fact is usually drawn from proof of notice of high probability of its existence, unless the defendant establishes an honest, contrary belief. Subsection 7 solidifies this usual result and clarifies the terms in which the issue is submitted to the jury.

ALI, Model Penal Code and Commentaries § 2.02, p. 248 (1985). The commentary then cites comparable statutes in Delaware, Illinois, Montana, New Jersey, Alaska, South Carolina, West Virginia, and Indiana. It also refers to an Ohio statute defining "knowingly" as "any awareness that something is 'probable.' "

## 2. QUESTIONS AND COMMENTS

The *Heredia* opinions isolate four potential elements of a willful blindness instruction: (1) that the defendant was aware of a high probability that the fact existed; (2) that the defendant deliberately avoided learning the truth; (3) that the defendant did not actually believe that the fact did not exist; and (4) that the defendant avoided learning the truth out of desire to escape criminal responsibility.

The majority opinion embraced the first three elements, the concurrence the fourth. Which opinion has the better of it? Note that the Model Penal Code includes only the first and third of these requirements. Is that a better view? The Model Code commentary seems to assert that, absent an affirmative belief that the fact does not exist, it is acceptable to rely on proof of a high probability of knowledge because the "inference of 'knowledge' of an existing fact is usually drawn from proof of notice of high probability of its existence." Does this approach confuse how one proves something with what must be proved? Does it reduce the standard of proof for knowledge to the point that it is difficult to distinguish from recklessness? What is the difference between one who is "aware of a high probability" and one who "consciously disregards a substantial and unjustifiable risk"? This question, the commentary asserts, is "subtle but important." Subtle to be sure, but "important"? Is the difference intelligible?

The majority in *Heredia* adds the second of the four elements listed above. It says in footnote 3, therefore, that a "willfully blind defendant is one who took deliberate actions to avoid confirming suspicions of criminality. A reckless defendant is one who merely knew of a substantial and unjustifiable risk that his conduct was criminal. . . . " Does this coherently explain the difference between willful blindness and recklessness? And does it establish that willful blindness is the moral equivalent of knowledge? Is it necessary, as the concurrence would have it, to add the fourth element in order to establish moral equivalence?

The majority opinion states that "[a]ctual knowledge, of course, is inconsistent with willful blindness. The deliberate ignorance instruction only comes into play, therefore, if the jury rejects the government's case as to actual knowledge." Does this mean that Judge Graber is right? Congress required "knowledge," she argues, not something that, in the majority's words is "tantamount to knowledge." Is it appropriate for the courts to substitute a different culpability standard than the one Congress provided because they regard it as morally equivalent?

The point in the end may be one of practical enforcement. Would it be much more difficult to enforce the drug laws if the government could not get a willful blindness instruction?

# SECTION 4: IGNORANCE OR MISTAKE OF LAW AND MENS REA

## Bryan v. United States

Supreme Court of the United States, 1998.
524 U.S. 184.

■ JUSTICE STEVENS delivered the opinion of the Court.

Petitioner was convicted of "willfully" dealing in firearms without a federal license. The question presented is whether the term "willfully" in 18 U.S.C. § 924(a)(1)(D) requires proof that the defendant knew that his conduct was unlawful, or whether it also requires proof that he knew of the federal licensing requirement.

I

In 1968 Congress enacted the Omnibus Crime Control and Safe Streets Act. In Title IV of that Act Congress . . . amended the Criminal Code to include detailed provisions regulating the use and sale of firearms. As amended, 18 U.S.C. § 922 defined a number of "unlawful acts"; subsection (a)(1) made it unlawful for any person except a licensed dealer to engage in the business of dealing in firearms.[2] Section 923 established the federal licensing program and repeated the prohibition against dealing in firearms without a license, and § 924 specified the penalties for violating "any provision of this chapter," [authorizing] the imposition of a fine of up to $5,000 or a prison sentence of not more than five years, "or both," on any person who dealt in firearms without a license. . . .

In 1986 Congress enacted the Firearms Owners' Protection Act (FOPA). . . . The findings in that statute explained that additional legislation was necessary to protect law-abiding citizens with respect to the acquisition, possession, or use of firearms for lawful purposes. FOPA therefore amended § 921 to include a definition of the term "engaged in the business,"[4] and amended § 924 to add a scienter requirement as a condition to the imposition of penalties for most of the unlawful acts defined in § 922. For three categories of offenses the intent required is that the defendant acted "knowingly;" for the fourth category, which

---

[2] The current version of this provision, which is substantially the same as the 1968 version, is codified at 18 U.S.C. § 922(a)(1)(A). It states:

(a) It shall be unlawful—

(1) for any person—

(A) except a licensed importer, licensed manufacturer, or licensed dealer, to engage in the business of importing, manufacturing, or dealing in firearms, or in the course of such business to ship, transport, or receive any firearm in interstate or foreign commerce.

[4] Section 921 of title 18, United States Code, is amended— . . . . .

(21) The term 'engaged in the business' means— . . . . .

(C) as applied to a dealer in firearms, as defined in section 921(a)(11)(A), a person who devotes time, attention, and labor to dealing in firearms as a regular course of trade or business with the principal objective of livelihood and profit through the repetitive purchase and resale of firearms, but such term shall not include a person who makes occasional sales, exchanges, or purchases of firearms for the enhancement of a personal collection or for a hobby, or who sells all or part of his personal collection of firearms. . . .

includes "any other provision of this chapter," the required intent is that the defendant acted "willfully." The . . . offense at issue in this case is an "other provision" in the "willfully" category.

II

The jury having found petitioner guilty, we accept the government's version of the evidence. That evidence proved that petitioner did not have a federal license to deal in firearms; that he used so-called "straw purchasers" in Ohio to acquire pistols that he could not have purchased himself; that the straw purchasers made false statements when purchasing the guns; that petitioner assured the straw purchasers that he would file the serial numbers off the guns; and that he resold the guns on Brooklyn street corners known for drug dealing. The evidence was unquestionably adequate to prove that petitioner was dealing in firearms, and that he knew that his conduct was unlawful.[8] There was, however, no evidence that he was aware of the federal law that prohibits dealing in firearms without a federal license.

. . . After the close of evidence, petitioner requested that the trial judge instruct the jury that petitioner could be convicted only if he knew of the federal licensing requirement, but the judge rejected this request. Instead, the trial judge gave this explanation of the term "willfully":

> A person acts willfully if he acts intentionally and purposely and with the intent to do something the law forbids, that is, with the bad purpose to disobey or to disregard the law. Now, the person need not be aware of the specific law or rule that his conduct may be violating. But he must act with the intent to do something that the law forbids.

Petitioner was found guilty. . . . On appeal he argued that the evidence was insufficient because there was no proof that he had knowledge of the federal licensing requirement, and that the trial judge had erred by failing to instruct the jury that such knowledge was an essential element of the offense. The Court of Appeals affirmed. It concluded that the instructions were proper and that the government had elicited "ample proof" that petitioner had acted willfully. . . .

III

The word "willfully" is sometimes said to be "a word of many meanings" whose construction is often dependent on the context in which it appears. Most obviously it differentiates between deliberate and unwitting conduct, but in the criminal law it also typically refers to a culpable state of mind. . . . As a general matter, when used in the criminal context, a "willful" act is one undertaken with a "bad purpose." In other words, in order to establish a "willful" violation of a statute, "the government must prove that the defendant acted with knowledge that his conduct was unlawful." Ratzlaf v. United States, 510 U.S. 135, 137 (1994).

Petitioner argues that a more particularized showing is required in this case for two principal reasons. First, he argues that the fact that

---

[8] Why else would he make use of straw purchasers and assure them that he would shave the serial numbers off the guns? Moreover, the street corner sales are not consistent with a good-faith belief in the legality of the enterprise.

Congress used the adverb "knowingly" to authorize punishment of three categories of acts made unlawful by § 922 and the word "willfully" when it referred to unlicensed dealing in firearms demonstrates that the government must shoulder a special burden in cases like this. This argument is not persuasive because the term "knowingly" does not necessarily have any reference to a culpable state of mind or to knowledge of the law. As Justice Jackson correctly observed, "the knowledge requisite to knowing violation of a statute is factual knowledge as distinguished from knowledge of the law."[14] Thus, in United States v. Bailey, 444 U.S. 394, 408 (1980), we held that the prosecution fulfills its burden of proving a knowing violation of the escape statute "if it demonstrates that an escapee knew his actions would result in his leaving physical confinement without permission." And in Staples v. United States, 511 U.S. 600, 602 (1994), we held that a charge that the defendant's possession of an unregistered machinegun was unlawful required proof "that he knew the weapon he possessed had the characteristics that brought it within the statutory definition of a machinegun." It was not, however, necessary to prove that the defendant knew that his possession was unlawful. Thus, unless the text of the statute dictates a different result,[15] the term "knowingly" merely requires proof of knowledge of the facts that constitute the offense.

With respect to the three categories of conduct that are made punishable by § 924 if performed "knowingly," the background presumption that every citizen knows the law makes it unnecessary to adduce specific evidence to prove that "an evil-meaning mind" directed the "evil-doing hand." More is required, however, with respect to the conduct in the fourth category that is only criminal when done "willfully." The jury must find that the defendant acted with an evil-meaning mind, that is to say, that he acted with knowledge that his conduct was unlawful.

Petitioner next argues that we must read [the statute] to require knowledge of the law because of our interpretation of "willfully" in two other contexts. In certain cases involving willful violations of the tax laws, we have concluded that the jury must find that the defendant was aware of the specific provision of the tax code that he was charged with violating. See, e.g., Cheek v. United States, 498 U.S. 192, 201 (1991). Similarly, in order to satisfy a willful violation in *Ratzlaf*, we concluded that the jury had to find that the defendant knew that his structuring of cash transactions to avoid a reporting requirement was unlawful. Those cases, however, are readily distinguishable. Both the tax cases and *Ratzlaf* involved highly technical statutes that presented the danger of ensnaring individuals engaged in apparently innocent conduct. As a result, we held that these statutes "carv[e] out an exception to the traditional rule" that ignorance of the law is no excuse and require that the defendant have knowledge of the law.[22] The danger of convicting

[14] . . . Boyce Motor Lines, Inc. v. United States, 342 U.S. 337, 345 (1952) (dissenting opinion).

[15] Liparota v. United States, 471 U.S. 419 (1985), was such a case. We there concluded that both the term "knowing" in § 2024(c) and the term "knowingly" in § 2024(b)(1) of Title 7 literally referred to knowledge of the law as well as knowledge of the relevant facts.

[22] Even before *Ratzlaf* was decided, then Chief Judge Breyer explained why there was a need for specificity under those statutes that is inapplicable when there is no danger of conviction of a defendant with an innocent state of mind. He wrote:

individuals engaged in apparently innocent activity that motivated our decisions in the tax cases and *Ratzlaf* is not present here because the jury found that this petitioner knew that his conduct was unlawful.[23]

Thus, the willfulness requirement of [the statute] does not carve out an exception to the traditional rule that ignorance of the law is no excuse; knowledge that the conduct is unlawful is all that is required. . . .

[Part IV of the Court's opinion, dealing with additional arguments made by the petitioner, is omitted.]

V

One sentence in the trial court's instructions to the jury, read by itself, contained a misstatement of the law. In a portion of the instructions that were given after the correct statement that we have already quoted, the judge stated: "In this case, the government is not required to prove that the defendant knew that a license was required, *nor is the government required to prove that he had knowledge that he was breaking the law*." If the judge had added the words "that required a license," the sentence would have been accurate, but as given it was not.

Nevertheless, that error does not provide a basis for reversal for four reasons. First, petitioner did not object to that sentence, except insofar as he had argued that the jury should have been instructed that the Government had the burden of proving that he had knowledge of the federal licensing requirement. Second, in the context of the entire instructions, it seems unlikely that the jury was misled. Third, petitioner failed to raise this argument in the Court of Appeals. Finally, our grant of certiorari was limited to the narrow legal question whether knowledge of the licensing requirement is an essential element of the offense.

Accordingly, the judgment of the Court of Appeals is affirmed.

It is so ordered.[a]

■ JUSTICE SCALIA, with whom . . . CHIEF JUSTICE [REHNQUIST] and JUSTICE GINSBURG join, dissenting.

Petitioner Sillasse Bryan was convicted of "willfully" violating the federal licensing requirement for firearms dealers. The jury apparently found, and the evidence clearly shows, that Bryan was aware in a general way that some aspect of his conduct was unlawful. The issue is

---

> I believe that criminal prosecutions for "currency law" violations, of the sort at issue here, very much resemble criminal prosecutions for tax law violations. Both sets of laws are technical; and both sets of laws sometimes criminalize conduct that would not strike an ordinary citizen as immoral or likely unlawful. Thus, both sets of laws may lead to the unfair result of criminally prosecuting individuals who subjectively and honestly believe they have not acted criminally. Cheek v. United States, 498 U.S. 192 (1991), sets forth a legal standard that, by requiring proof that the defendant was subjectively aware of the duty at issue, would avoid such unfair results.

United States v. Aversa, 984 F.2d 493, 502 (1st Cir. 1993) (concurring opinion). He therefore concluded that the "same standards should apply in both" the tax cases and in cases such as *Ratzlaf*.

[23] Moreover, requiring only knowledge that the conduct is unlawful is fully consistent with the purpose of FOPA, as FOPA was enacted to protect law-abiding citizens who might inadvertently violate the law. See n. 4, supra.

[a] Justice Souter's concurring opinion is omitted.—[Footnote by eds.]

whether that general knowledge of illegality is enough to sustain the conviction, or whether a "willful" violation of the licensing provision requires proof that the defendant knew that his conduct was unlawful specifically because he lacked the necessary license. On that point the statute is, in my view, genuinely ambiguous. . . .

Section 922(a)(1)(A) . . . makes it unlawful for any person to engage in the business of dealing in firearms without a federal license. That provision is enforced criminally [by imposing] criminal penalties on [persons who act "willfully"]. The word "willfully" has a wide range of meanings, and "its construction [is] often . . . influenced by its context." Ratzlaf v. United States, 510 U.S. 135, 141 (1994). In some contexts it connotes nothing more than "an act which is intentional, or knowing, or voluntary, as distinguished from accidental." United States v. Murdock, 290 U.S. 389, 394 (1933). In the present context, however, inasmuch as the preceding three subparagraphs of § 924 specify a mens rea of "knowingly" for other firearms offenses, a "willful" violation . . . must require some mental state more culpable than mere intent to perform the forbidden act. The United States concedes (and the Court apparently agrees) that the violation is not "willful" unless the defendant knows in a general way that his conduct is unlawful. ("The jury must find that the defendant acted with an evil-meaning mind, that is to say, that he acted with knowledge that his conduct was unlawful.")

That concession takes this case beyond any useful application of the maxim that ignorance of the law is no excuse. Everyone agrees that [the statute] requires some knowledge of the law; the only real question is which law? The Court's answer is that knowledge of any law is enough—or, put another way, that the defendant must be ignorant of every law violated by his course of conduct to be innocent of willfully violating the licensing requirement. The Court points to no textual basis for that conclusion other than the notoriously malleable word "willfully" itself. Instead, it seems to fall back on a presumption (apparently derived from the rule that ignorance of the law is no excuse) that even where ignorance of the law is an excuse, that excuse should be construed as narrowly as the statutory language permits.

I do not believe that the Court's approach makes sense of the statute that Congress enacted. I have no quarrel with the Court's assertion that "willfully" in [this statute] requires only "general" knowledge of illegality—in the sense that the defendant need not be able to recite chapter and verse from Title 18 of the United States Code. It is enough, in my view, if the defendant is generally aware that the actus reus punished by the statute—dealing in firearms without a license—is illegal. But the Court is willing to accept a mens rea so "general" that it is entirely divorced from the actus reus this statute was enacted to punish. That approach turns [the statute] into a strange and unlikely creature. Bryan would be guilty of "willfully" dealing in firearms without a federal license even if, for example, he had never heard of the licensing requirement but was aware that he had violated the law by using straw purchasers or filing the serial numbers off the pistols. The Court does not even limit (for there is no rational basis to limit) the universe of relevant laws to federal firearms statutes. Bryan would also be "act[ing] with an evil-meaning mind," and hence presumably be guilty of "willfully" dealing in firearms without a license, if he knew that his street-corner transactions violated New York City's business licensing or sales tax ordinances. (For that matter, it ought to suffice if Bryan knew that the car out of which he sold the guns was illegally double-parked, or if, in order to meet the appointed time for the sale, he intentionally violated Pennsylvania's speed limit on the drive back from the gun purchase in Ohio.) Once we stop focusing on the conduct the defendant is actually charged with (i.e., selling guns without a license), I see no principled way to determine what law the defendant must be conscious of violating.

Congress is free, of course, to make criminal liability under one statute turn on knowledge of another, to use its firearms dealer statutes to encourage compliance with New York City's tax collection efforts, and to put judges and juries through the kind of mental gymnastics described above. But these are strange results, and I would not lightly assume that Congress intended to make liability under a federal criminal statute depend so heavily upon the vagaries of local law—particularly local law dealing with completely unrelated subjects. . . . I think it would be more reasonable to [conclude] that, when Congress makes ignorance of the law a defense to a criminal prohibition, it ordinarily means ignorance of the unlawfulness of the specific conduct punished by that criminal prohibition.

That is the meaning we have given the word "willfully" in other contexts where we have concluded it requires knowledge of the law. See, e.g., *Ratzlaf*, 510 U.S. at 149 ("To convict Ratzlaf of the crime with which he was charged, . . . the jury had to find he knew the structuring in which he engaged was unlawful"); Cheek v. United States, 498 U.S. 192, 201 (1991) ("[T]he standard for the statutory willfullness requirement is the 'voluntary, intentional violation of a known legal duty.' . . . [T]he issue is whether the defendant knew of the duty purportedly imposed by the provision of the statute or regulation he is accused of violating"). The Court explains these cases on the ground that they involved "highly technical statutes that presented the danger of ensnaring individuals engaged in apparently innocent conduct." That is no explanation at all. The complexity of the tax and currency laws may explain why the Court interpreted "willful" to require some awareness of illegality, as opposed to merely "an act which is intentional, or knowing, or voluntary, as distinguished from accidental." *Murdock*, 290 U.S. at 394. But it in no way justifies the distinction the Court seeks to draw today between knowledge of the law the defendant is actually charged with violating and knowledge of any law the defendant could conceivably be charged with violating. . . .

. . . It is common ground that the statutory context here requires some awareness of the law . . . , but the statute is simply ambiguous, or silent, as to the precise contours of that mens rea requirement. In the face of that ambiguity, I would invoke the rule that " 'ambiguity concerning the ambit of criminal statutes should be resolved in favor of lenity,' " *United States v. Bass*, 404 U.S. at 347.

> The rule that penal laws are to be construed strictly, is, perhaps, not much less old than construction itself. It is founded on the tenderness of the law for the rights of individuals; and on the plain principle that the power of punishment is vested in the legislative, not in the judicial department.

United States v. Wiltberger, 18 U.S. (5 Wheat.) 76 (1820).

In our era of multiplying new federal crimes, there is more reason than ever to give this ancient canon of construction consistent application: by fostering uniformity in the interpretation of criminal statutes, it will reduce the occasions on which this Court will have to produce judicial havoc by resolving in defendants' favor a circuit conflict regarding the substantive elements of a federal crime.

I respectfully dissent.

## NOTES ON IGNORANCE OR MISTAKE OF LAW

### 1. *LIPAROTA V. UNITED STATES*

Liparota was convicted of acquiring and possessing food stamps in violation of 7 U.S.C. § 2024(b), which provides that "whoever knowingly uses, transfers, acquires, alters, or possesses [food stamps] in any manner not authorized by [applicable] regulations" is punishable by a maximum fine of $10,000 and/or imprisonment for up to five years if the value of the stamps exceeds $100. Liparota co-owned a restaurant that was not authorized to accept food stamps. On three occasions he purchased food stamps from an undercover agent with a face value totaling $1195, for which he paid only $800. His argument that the statute applied only to "people who knew that they were acting unlawfully" was rejected by the lower courts. In Liparota v. United States, 471 U.S. 419 (1985), the Supreme Court reversed. Justice Brennan wrote for the Court:

> The controversy between the parties concerns the mental state, if any, that the government must show in proving that petitioner acted "in any manner not authorized by [applicable] regulations." The government argues that petitioner violated the statute if he knew that he acquired or possessed food stamps and if in fact that acquisition or possession was in a manner not authorized by [the] regulations. . . . Petitioner claims that the government's interpretation . . . dispenses with the only morally blameworthy element in the definition of the crime. To avoid this allegedly untoward result, he claims that an individual violates the statute if he knows that he has acquired or possessed food stamps and if he also knows that he has done so in an unauthorized manner.

The Court found nothing helpful in the language of the statute or its legislative history, and concluded:

> Absent indication of contrary purpose in the language or legislative history of the statute, we believe that § 2024(b) requires a showing that the defendant knew his conduct to be unauthorized by statute or regulations.[9] . . . This construction is particularly

[9] The dissent repeatedly claims that our holding today creates a defense of "mistake of law." Our holding today no more creates a "mistake of law" defense than does a statute making knowing receipt of stolen goods unlawful. In both cases, there is a legal element in the definition of the offense. In the case of a receipt of stolen goods statute, the legal element is that the goods were stolen; in this case, the legal element is that the "use, transfer, acquisition," etc., were in a manner not authorized by statute or regulations. It is not a defense to a charge of receipt of stolen goods that one did not know that such receipt was illegal, and it is not a defense to a charge of a § 2024(b) violation that one did not know that possessing food stamps in a manner unauthorized by statute or regulations was illegal. It is, however, a defense to a charge of knowing receipt of stolen goods that one did not know that the goods were

appropriate where, as here, to interpret the statute otherwise would be to criminalize a broad range of apparently innocent conduct. For instance, § 2024(b) declares it criminal to use, transfer, acquire, alter, or possess food stamps in any manner not authorized by statute or regulations. The statute provides further that "[c]oupons issued to eligible households shall be used by them only to purchase food in retail food stores which have been approved for participation in the food stamp program *at prices prevailing in such stores*." 7 U.S.C. § 2016(b) (emphasis added). This seems to be the only authorized use. A strict reading of the statute with no knowledge of illegality requirement would thus render criminal a food stamp recipient who, for example, used stamps to purchase food from a store that, unknown to him, charged higher than normal prices to food stamp program participants. Such a reading would also render criminal a nonrecipient of food stamps who "possessed" stamps because he was mistakenly sent them through the mail due to administrative error, "altered" them by tearing them up, and "transferred" them by throwing them away. Of course, Congress could have intended that this broad range of conduct be made illegal, perhaps with the understanding that prosecutors would exercise their discretion to avoid such harsh results. However, given the paucity of material suggesting that Congress did so intend, we are reluctant to adopt such a sweeping interpretation.

In addition, requiring mens rea is in keeping with our longstanding recognition of the principle that "ambiguity concerning the ambit of criminal statutes should be resolved in favor of lenity." Rewis v. United States, 401 U.S. 808, 812 (1971). Application of the rule of lenity ensures that criminal statutes will provide fair warning concerning conduct rendered illegal and strikes the appropriate balance between the legislature, the prosecutor, and the court in defining criminal liability. . . .

We hold that in a prosecution for violation of § 2024(b), the government must prove that the defendant knew that his acquisition or possession of food stamps was in a manner unauthorized by statute or regulations. This holding does not put an unduly heavy burden on the government in prosecuting violators of § 2024(b). To prove that petitioner knew that his acquisition or possession of food stamps was unauthorized, for example, the government need not show that he had knowledge of specific regulations governing food stamp acquisition or possession. Nor must the government introduce any extraordinary evidence that would conclusively demonstrate petitioner's state of mind. Rather, as in any other criminal prosecution requiring mens rea, the government may prove by reference to facts and circumstances surrounding the case that petitioner knew that his conduct was unauthorized or illegal.[17]

---

stolen, just as it is a defense to a charge of a § 2024(b) violation that one did not know that one's possession was unauthorized.

[17] In this case, for instance, the government introduced evidence that petitioner bought food stamps at a substantial discount from face value and that he conducted part of the trans-

Joined by Chief Justice Burger, Justice White dissented. His conclusion was that "the statute does not mean what the Court says it does":

> Rather, it requires only that the defendant be aware of the relevant aspects of his conduct. A requirement that the defendant know that he is acting in a particular manner, coupled with the fact that that manner is forbidden, does not establish a defense of ignorance of the law. It creates only a defense of ignorance or mistake of fact. Knowingly to do something that is unauthorized by law is not the same as doing something knowing that it is unauthorized by law. . . .
>
> [I]nstead of detailing the various legal requirements, [§ 2024(b)] incorporates them by proscribing use of coupons "in any manner not authorized" by law. This shorthand approach to drafting does not transform knowledge of illegality into an element of the crime. As written, § 2024(b) is substantively no different than if it had been broken down into a collection of specific provisions making crimes of particular improper uses. For example, food stamps cannot be used to purchase tobacco. The statute might have said, inter alia, that anyone "who knowingly uses coupons to purchase cigarettes" commits a crime. Under no plausible reading could a defendant then be acquitted because he did not know cigarettes are not "eligible food." But in fact, that is exactly what § 2024(b) does say, it just does not write it out longhand.
>
> The Court's opinion provides another illustration of the general point: someone who used food stamps to purchase groceries at inflated prices without realizing he was overcharged. I agree that such a person may not be convicted, but not for the reason given by the majority. The purchaser did not "knowingly" use the stamps in the proscribed manner, for he was unaware of the circumstances of the transaction that made it illegal.
>
> The majority and I would part company in result as well as rationale if the purchaser knew he was charged higher than normal prices but not that overcharging is prohibited. In such a case, he would have been aware of the nature of his actions, and therefore the purchase would have been "knowing." I would hold that such a mental state satisfies the statute. Under the Court's holding, as I understand it, that person could not be convicted because he did not know that his conduct was illegal.[3] . . .

---

action in a back room of his restaurant to avoid the presence of the other patrons. Moreover, the government asserts that food stamps themselves are stamped "nontransferable." A jury could have inferred from this evidence that petitioner knew that his acquisition and possession of the stamps was unauthorized.

[3] The appropriate prosecutorial target in such a situation would of course be the seller rather than the purchaser. I have no doubt that every prosecutor in the country would agree. The discussion of this hypothetical is wholly academic.

For similar reasons, I am unmoved by the spectre of criminal liability for someone who is mistakenly mailed food stamps and throws them out, and do not think the hypothetical offers much of a guide to congressional intent. We should proceed on the assumption that Congress had in mind the run-of-the-mill situation, not its most bizarre mutation. Arguments that presume wildly unreasonable conduct by government officials are by their nature unconvincing, and reliance on them is likely to do more harm than good. No rule, including that adopted by the Court today, is immune from such contrived defects.

## 2. *UNITED STATES V. INTERNATIONAL MINERALS*

United States v. International Minerals & Chemical Corp., 402 U.S. 558 (1971), involved a corporation that shipped sulfuric acid and hydrofluosilicic acid in interstate commerce without the label "Corrosive Liquid" on the shipping papers. Federal regulations required such a label. Title 18 U.S.C. § 834(f) made it a misdemeanor punishable by up to a year in prison to "knowingly violate[ ] any such regulation."

Justice Douglas wrote for the Court, stating the question as "whether 'knowledge' of the regulation is . . . required." His answer was "no":

> We . . . see no reason why the word "regulations" should not be construed as a shorthand designation for specific acts or omissions which violate the Act. The Act, so viewed, does not signal an exception to the rule that ignorance of the law is no excuse and is wholly consistent with the legislative history. . . .
>
> The principle that ignorance of the law is no defense applies whether the law be a statute or a duly promulgated and published regulation. [W]e decline to attribute to Congress the inaccurate view that [the] Act requires proof of knowledge of the law, as well as the facts. . . . We conclude that the meager legislative history of the 1960 amendments makes unwarranted the conclusion that Congress abandoned the general rule and required knowledge of both the facts and the pertinent law before a criminal conviction could be sustained under this Act.
>
> So far as possession, say, of sulfuric acid is concerned the requirement of "mens rea" has been made a requirement of the Act as evidenced by the use of the word "knowingly." A person thinking in good faith that he was shipping distilled water when in fact he was shipping some dangerous acid would not be covered. . . . Pencils, dental floss, paper clips may also be regulated. But they may be the type of products which might raise substantial due process questions if Congress did not require "mens rea" as to each ingredient of the offense. But where . . . dangerous or deleterious devices or products or obnoxious waste materials are involved, the probability of regulation is so great that anyone who is aware that he is in possession of them or dealing with them must be presumed to be aware of the regulation.

Justice Stewart, joined by Justices Harlan and Brennan, dissented. For him, knowledge meant knowledge: "That is what the law quite clearly says, what the federal courts have held, and what the legislative history confirms." He elaborated on these themes, and added a concluding paragraph:

> A final word is in order. Today's decision will have little practical impact upon the prosecution of interstate motor carriers or institutional shippers. For interstate motor carriers are members of a regulated industry, and their officers, agents, and employees are required by law to be conversant with the regulations in question. . . . The only real impact of this decision will be upon the casual shipper, who might be any man, woman, or child in the Nation. A person who had never heard of the regulation might make a single shipment of an article covered by it in the course of a lifetime. . . . Yet today's decision holds that [such] a person . . . is

> guilty of a criminal offense punishable by a year in prison. This seems to me a perversion of the purpose of criminal law.

## 3. *UNITED STATES V. WILSON*

Wilson pulled to the side of a highway, and a police officer stopped to assist. A routine check of his driver's license revealed an outstanding arrest warrant for failing to appear in court. Wilson was arrested, and a shotgun, a rifle, and a handgun were found in an inventory search of his vehicle. Wilson was subject to an order of protection initiated by his wife in divorce proceedings. Enforced by criminal provisions requiring a "knowing" violation, 18 U.S.C. § 922(g)(8) provided that it was unlawful for a person who was subject to such an order to possess a firearm. Wilson was convicted for violating this statute.

On appeal, the court held in United States v. Wilson, 159 F.3d 280 (7th Cir. 1998), that "[u]nless the text of the statute at issue dictates a different result, establishing a 'knowing' violation of the statute only requires proof of knowledge by the defendant of the facts that constitute the offense." This knowledge he had. He knew that he possessed a firearm. And he knew that he was subject to an order of protection. Wilson argued that the statute also required that he "know" that it was a crime for him to possess firearms. The court responded:

> To the extent that Wilson is arguing that he was unaware of the law and that his conviction therefore cannot stand, he is also incorrect. The traditional rule in American jurisprudence is that ignorance of the law is no defense to a criminal prosecution. Wilson has not shown that the present statute falls into an exception to this general rule, and the fact that he was unaware of the existence of § 922(g)(8) does not render his conviction erroneous.

Judge Posner dissented:

> It is wrong to convict a person of a crime if he had no reason to believe that the act for which he was convicted *was* a crime, or even that it was wrongful. This is one of the bedrock principles of American law. It lies at the heart of any civilized system of law. Yet like most legal generalizations, it can be maintained only with careful qualification. We generally do not require prosecutors to prove that the defendant *knew* that he was violating the law, even in cases in which the law is sufficiently remote from the moral code of the society that such knowledge cannot be presumed or its absence taken as evidence of culpable moral obtuseness. We say instead that "ignorance of the law is no defense," and do not pause to consider the consistency of this maxim with what we elsewhere affirm to be a fundamental constituent of the rule of law and the Constitution of the United States. In the unusual circumstances of this case, the maxim of expedience should yield to the bedrock principle; and there is enough room in the statutory language to achieve this end without having to trundle out the heavy artillery of constitutional law.
>
> Congress created, and the Department of Justice sprang, a trap on Carlton Wilson as a result of which he will serve more than three years in federal prison for an act (actually an omission to act) that he could not have suspected was a crime or even a civil

wrong. We can release him from the trap by interpreting the statute under which he was convicted to require the government to prove that the violator knew that he was committing a crime. This is the standard device by which the courts avoid having to explore the outer boundaries of the constitutional requirement of fair notice of potential criminal liability.

Section 922(g)(8) of the federal criminal code . . . , when read in conjunction with section 924(a)(2), makes it a crime punishable by up to 10 years in prison for any person to possess a gun if he is subject to a domestic-relations restraining order against stalking or otherwise threatening a spouse or child. The first of these sections, 18 U.S.C. § 922(g)(8), contains no reference to the defendant's knowledge. But this section merely makes the conduct (the possession of a gun by a person subject to a stalking order) unlawful; it imposes no penalty for a violation. The penalty provision is section 924(a)(2), and it requires that the defendant have "knowingly" violated section 922(g).

The stalking provision was enacted in 1994 and the number of prosecutions for violating it has been minuscule (perhaps fewer than 10, though I have not been able to discover the exact number, which is not a reported statistic) in relation to the probable number of violations. I estimate that every year the law has been in effect almost one hundred *thousand* restraining orders against domestic violence have been issued. . . . Since 40 percent of U.S. households own guns . . . , there can be very little doubt that a large percentage of those orders were issued against gun owners.

How many of these gun owners, when they got notice of the restraining order, dispossessed themselves of their guns? I doubt that any did. The law is malum prohibitum, not malum in se; that is, it is not the kind of law that a lay person would intuit existed because the conduct it forbade was contrary to the moral code of his society. . . . Yet the Department of Justice took no steps to publicize the existence of the law until long after Wilson violated it, even to the extent of advising the state judiciaries of it so that judges could warn defendants in domestic-relations disputes. At argument the prosecutor told us that the Office of the U.S. Attorney for the Southern District of Illinois has made no effort to advise the local judiciary of the law. Later he sent us two bulletins from Department of Justice headquarters in Washington to the U.S. Attorneys' Offices throughout the country directing the U.S. Attorneys to "educate your state and local counterparts on these provisions. Their assistance, *particularly in working with local judges to fashion domestic violence protective orders,* is essential to the effective implementation of the [provisions]" (emphasis added). But these bulletins—a tacit admission that four years after the enactment of the law, the word hadn't gotten out even to judges—were not circulated until after Wilson's trial.

The federal criminal code contains thousands of separate prohibitions, many ridiculously obscure, such as the one against using the coat of arms of Switzerland in advertising, 18 U.S.C. § 708, or using "Johnny Horizon" as a trade name without the authorization of the Department of the Interior. 18 U.S.C. § 714. The prohibition in section 922(g)(8) is one of the most obscure. A person owns a hunting rifle. He knows or should know that if he is convicted of a felony he will have to get rid of the gun; if he doesn't know, the judge or the probation service will tell him. But should he be made subject to a restraining order telling him to keep away from his ex-wife, whom he has *not* ever threatened with his hunting rifle (the judge who issued the restraining order could but did not issue an order forbidding Wilson to possess a firearm as long as the order was in force), it will not occur to him that he must give up the gun unless the judge issuing the order tells him. The judge didn't tell Wilson; so far as appears, the judge was unaware of the law. Wilson's lawyer didn't tell him either—Wilson didn't have a lawyer. No one told him. And there is no reason that he should have guessed, for while he had beaten his wife and threatened to kill her, there is no indication that guns played any part in the beating or the threats. The fact that the restraining order contained no reference to guns may have lulled him into thinking that, as long as he complied with the order and stayed away from his wife, he could carry on as before.

When a defendant is morally culpable for failing to know or guess that he is violating *some* law (as would be the case of someone who committed a burglary without thinking—so warped was his moral sense—that burglary might be a crime), we rely on conscience to provide all the notice that is required. Sometimes the existence of the law is common knowledge, as in the case of laws forbidding people to own hand grenades (see United States v. Freed, 401 U.S. 601, 609 (1971)), forbidding convicted felons to own any firearms, and requiring a license to carry a handgun. And sometimes, though the law is obscure to the population at large and nonintuitive, the defendant had a reasonable opportunity to learn about it, as in the case of persons engaged in the shipment of pharmaceuticals who run afoul of the criminal prohibitions in the federal food and drug laws. See United States v. Dotterweich, 320 U.S. 277 (1943). We want people to familiarize themselves with the laws bearing on their activities. But a reasonable opportunity doesn't mean being able to go to the local law library and read Title 18. It would be preposterous to suppose that someone from Wilson's milieu is able to take advantage of such an opportunity. If none of the conditions that make it reasonable to dispense with proof of knowledge of the law is present, then to intone "ignorance of the law is no defense" is to condone a violation of fundamental principles for the sake of a modest economy in the administration of criminal justice.

Actually a false economy. The purpose of criminal laws is to bring about compliance with desired norms of behavior. In the present case it is to reduce domestic violence by getting guns out of the hands of people who are behaving menacingly toward (in the usual case) an estranged or former spouse. This purpose is ill served by keeping the law a secret, which has been the practical upshot of the Department of Justice's failure—until too late, at least for Wilson—either to enforce the law vigorously or to notify the relevant state officials of the law's existence. In such circumstances the law is not a deterrent. It is a trap.

All the Department of Justice had to do in order to preserve the rule of law was to notify all state courts that have a domestic-relations jurisdiction of the existence and terms of 18 U.S.C. § 922(g)(8) and to suggest that every domestic-relations restraining order contain a printed warning that the defendant is violating federal criminal law unless he immediately divests himself of any firearms and ammunition that he owns. Domestic-relations judges would be happy to include such a warning because it would give added teeth to their orders. At slight cost—negative, really, when one considers how compliance with the law would soar—the administration of the law would be brought into conformity with the rule of law. The bulletins that the home office of the Department of Justice has sent the U.S. Attorneys is a belated but welcome recognition of my point but came too late to help Wilson avoid becoming a federal felon.

We thus have an example of those "highly technical statutes that present . . . the danger of ensnaring individuals engaged in apparently innocent conduct" of which the Supreme Court spoke in Bryan v. United States, 524 U.S. 184 (1998). This case differs from *Bryan* because the statute here is easy to understand; but it is hard to discover, and that comes to the same thing, as we know from Lambert v. California, 355 U.S. 225 (1957). The law challenged in that case required a felon to register with the police. Lambert, a felon, failed to do so. She "had no actual knowledge of the requirement"; there was no showing of "the probability of such knowledge"; "violation of [the law's] provisions [was] unaccompanied by any activity whatever"; and "circumstances which might move one to inquire as to the necessity of registration [were] completely lacking." The Court voided Lambert's conviction. We should do the same for Wilson's conviction.

*Bryan*'s reference to "apparently innocent conduct" describes the ownership of rifles and handguns, for personal use and not for sale, by nonfelons in this nation's gun-friendly culture. "[T]here is a long tradition of widespread lawful gun ownership by private individuals in this country." Staples v. United States, 511 U.S. 600, 610 (1994). Such ownership is as innocent as making huge cash deposits, or having a large professional income but not filing income tax returns—activities that the Supreme Court has held do not subject a person to criminal liability if he is ignorant of the law. Ratzlaf v. United States, 510 U.S. 135 (1994); Cheek v. United States, 498 U.S. 192 (1991); see also Liparota v. United States, 471 U.S. 419 (1985).

It is true that strict liability, of which convicting a person for conduct that he could not, realistically, have known was criminal is an example, is not unknown to the criminal law. There are strict-liability crimes, which is to say crimes that can be committed without any culpable state of mind whatever. And many crimes have an element of strict liability, the classic example being statutory rape in jurisdictions in which the girl's apparent maturity is not a defense. But the existence and content of the criminal prohibition in these cases are not hidden; the defendant is warned to steer well clear of the core of the offense (as in the statutory-rape case . . .), or to take the utmost care (the food and drug cases), or to familiarize himself with the laws relating to his business. . . . None of these rationales applies to Wilson. His is the classic case of the unwarned defendant. He is entitled to a new trial at which the government would have to prove that he knew that continued possession of guns after the restraining order was entered was a crime. This conclusion is a linguistically permissible interpretation of the statute because only the *knowing* violation of section 922(g)(8) carries a criminal penalty; the interpretation avoids a constitutional issue; and it is supported by *Lambert, Ratzlaf, Cheek*, and other decisions.

## 4. QUESTIONS AND COMMENTS

The system is comfortable with the notion that, when the elements of murder, rape, burglary, or robbery have been proved, it is not unfair to deny a defense based on the assertion "I did not know it was a crime to do these things." The nature of the underlying conduct itself, it is assumed, gives "fair notice" of the illegality of the behavior. The doctrine that "ignorance of the law is no excuse" is acceptable in such a case because it is fair to assume that one who commits all of the elements of the offense ought to know and is likely to know that the conduct is illegal.

In *Bryan*, however, the Court permits conviction only if the defendant "knew" that his conduct was "unlawful." Why? Is there a case to be made for such an instruction in *any* situation where there are concerns that the average citizen who has mens rea in the ordinary sense may not know that the conduct is illegal? Would a similar instruction have cured Judge Posner's problem in *Wilson*? The Supreme Court thought *Liparota* was a case where such an instruction was warranted, but that *International Minerals* was not. Were these cases correctly decided?

Consider *Bryan* from another perspective. In summary, the elements of the offense were (a) engaging in the business of dealing in firearms (b) without a federal license. Bryan clearly engaged in this actus reus. As for the required mens rea, the Court holds that Bryan did *not* need to know about the second element, i.e., Bryan did not need to know (in the sense of consciously adverting to the fact) that he did not have a federal license or that he was acting in violation of a duty to obtain one. Without saying so explicitly, it imposed strict liability on that element, as Part V of its opinion attests. It did require, however, that the defendant know that the behavior was "unlawful." That is, although the Court did not put it this way, the imposition of strict liability on the second element of the offense was acceptable because the jury was asked to find that, based on what the defendant did know about his behavior, he knew enough to know not to do it. He knew enough to make his conviction fair.[a]

If this analysis is correct, might the case have adopted a solution that may make sense in some prosecutions—perhaps even some future prosecutions under this statute—but not in the particular context before the Court? It was a crime to "engage in the business" of dealing in firearms. By

---

[a] For discussion of *International Minerals, Wilson, Liparota*, and *Bryan* along these lines, see Peter W. Low and Benjamin Charles Wood, *Lambert* Revisited, 100 Va. L. Rev. 1603, 1628–30, 1632–35, 1640–46 (2014). For an analysis of *Cheek* (discussed in Note 5(i) below), see id. at 1611 n.32, 1643 n.178.

definition, this prohibition applied only to one "who devotes time, attention, and labor to dealing in firearms as a regular course of trade or business with the principal objective of livelihood and profit through the repetitive purchase and resale of firearms." Specifically excluded was "a person who makes occasional sales, exchanges, or purchases of firearms for the enhancement of a personal collection or for a hobby, or who sells all or part of his personal collection of firearms." If a mens rea of "knowledge" is applied to element (a) as listed in the preceding paragraph and strict liability to element (b), is more needed to protect against an unfair conviction? Is the case then comparable to *International Minerals*? Or is it more like *Wilson*? Why should it also be required that the defendant "know" the behavior is "unlawful"? From another perspective, if mens rea should be required for the unlawfulness of the behavior, why require knowledge? Why not recklessness or negligence?

### 5. *CHEEK* AND *RATZLAF*

*Bryan* distinguished Cheek v. United States, 498 U.S. 192 (1991), and Ratzlaf v. United States, 510 U.S. 135 (1994). The following notes summarize those cases. Were they correctly decided? Are they distinguishable from *Bryan*, as Justice Stevens argued? Or are they at bottom based on a similar principle, i.e., that *some* knowledge of at least *some* aspect of the lawfulness of one's behavior is necessary in *some* contexts in order to be fair to potentially innocent people?

#### *(i) Cheek v. United States*

Cheek v. United States, 498 U.S. 192 (1991), involved the meaning of "willfully" in 26 U.S.C. § 7201, which makes it a felony if a person "willfully attempts in any manner to evade or defeat any tax imposed by this title or the payment thereof," and 26 U.S.C. § 7203, which makes it a misdemeanor if any "person required under this title . . . or by regulations made under authority thereof to make a return . . . willfully fails to . . . make such return." Cheek was an airline pilot. He did not file a tax return for a number of years and limited withholdings from his paycheck by claiming 60 allowances. He claimed that he did so in the beliefs, among others, that his wages were not income, that he was not a taxpayer within the meaning of the tax laws, and that the federal tax laws were unconstitutional:

> Cheek represented himself at trial and testified in his defense. He admitted that he had not filed personal income tax returns during the years in question. He testified that as early as 1978, he had begun attending seminars sponsored by, and following the advice of, a group that believes, among other things, that the federal tax system is unconstitutional. Some of the speakers at these meetings were lawyers who purported to give professional opinions about the invalidity of the federal income tax laws. Cheek produced a letter from an attorney stating that the 16th Amendment did not authorize a tax on wages and salaries but only on gain or profit. Petitioner's defense was that, based on the indoctrination he received from this group and from his own study, he sincerely believed that the tax laws were being unconstitutionally enforced and that his actions during the 1980–86 period were lawful. He therefore argued that he had acted without

the willfulness required for conviction of the various offenses with which he was charged.

The Supreme Court set the stage for its analysis as follows:

> The general rule that ignorance of the law or a mistake of law is no defense to criminal prosecution is deeply rooted in the American legal system. Based on the notion that the law is definite and knowable, the common law presumed that every person knew the law. This common law rule has been applied by the Court in numerous cases construing criminal statutes.
>
> The proliferation of statutes and regulations has sometimes made it difficult for the average citizen to know and comprehend the extent of the duties and obligations imposed by the tax laws. Congress has accordingly softened the impact of the common law presumption by making specific intent to violate the law an element of certain federal criminal tax offenses. Thus, the Court almost 60 years ago interpreted the statutory term "willfully" as used in the federal criminal tax statutes as carving out an exception to the traditional rule. This special treatment of criminal tax offenses is largely due to the complexity of the tax laws.

The Court then turned to the content of the exception:

> Willfulness, as construed by our prior decisions in criminal tax cases, requires the government to prove that the law imposed a duty on the defendant, that the defendant knew of this duty, and that he voluntarily and intentionally violated that duty. We deal first with the case where the issue is whether the defendant knew of the duty purportedly imposed by the provision of the statute or regulation he is accused of violating, a case in which there is no claim that the provision at issue is invalid. In such a case, if the government proves actual knowledge of the pertinent legal duty, the prosecution, without more, has satisfied the knowledge component of the willfulness requirement. But carrying this burden requires negating a defendant's claim of ignorance of the law or a claim that because of a misunderstanding of the law, he had a good-faith belief that he was not violating any of the provisions of the tax laws. This is so because one cannot be aware that the law imposes a duty upon him and yet be ignorant of it, misunderstand the law, or believe that the duty does not exist. In the end, the issue is whether, based on all the evidence, the government has proved that the defendant was aware of the duty at issue, which cannot be true if the jury credits a good-faith misunderstanding and belief submission, whether or not the claimed belief or misunderstanding is objectively reasonable.
>
> In this case, if Cheek asserted that he truly believed that the Internal Revenue Code did not purport to treat wages as income, and the jury believed him, the government would not have carried its burden to prove willfulness, however unreasonable a court might deem such a belief. Of course, in deciding whether to credit Cheek's good-faith belief claim, the jury would be free to consider any admissible evidence from any source showing that Cheek was aware of his duty to file a return and to treat wages as income, including evidence showing his awareness of the relevant provisions

of the Code or regulations, of court decisions rejecting his interpretation of the tax law, of authoritative rulings of the Internal Revenue Service, or of any contents of the personal income tax return forms and accompanying instructions that made it plain that wages should be returned as income. . . .

It was therefore error to instruct the jury to disregard evidence of Cheek's understanding that, within the meaning of the tax laws, he was not a person required to file a return or to pay income taxes and that wages are not taxable income, as incredible as such misunderstandings of and beliefs about the law might be. Of course, the more unreasonable the asserted beliefs or misunderstandings are, the more likely the jury will consider them to be nothing more than simple disagreement with known legal duties imposed by the tax laws and will find that the government has carried its burden of proving knowledge.

The Court next turned to the effect of believing the law invalid:

Cheek asserted in the trial court that he should be acquitted because he believed in good faith that the income tax law is unconstitutional as applied to him and thus could not legally impose any duty upon him of which he should have been aware. Such a submission is unsound, not because Cheek's constitutional arguments are not objectively reasonable or frivolous, which they surely are, but because the . . . cases [do] not support such a position. . . .

Claims that some of the provisions of the tax code are unconstitutional . . . do not arise from innocent mistakes caused by the complexity of the Internal Revenue Code. Rather, they reveal full knowledge of the provisions at issue and a studied conclusion, however wrong, that those provisions are invalid and unenforceable. Thus in this case, Cheek paid his taxes for years, but after attending various seminars and based on his own study, he concluded that the income tax laws could not constitutionally require him to pay a tax.

We do not believe that Congress contemplated that such a taxpayer, without risking criminal prosecution, could ignore the duties imposed upon him by the Internal Revenue Code and refuse to utilize the mechanisms provided by Congress to present his claims of invalidity to the courts and to abide by their decisions. There is no doubt that Cheek, from year to year, was free to pay the tax that the law purported to require, file for a refund and, if denied, present his claims of invalidity, constitutional or otherwise, to the courts. Also, without paying the tax, he could have challenged claims of tax deficiencies in the Tax Court, with the right to appeal to a higher court if unsuccessful. Cheek took neither course in some years, and when he did was unwilling to accept the outcome. As we see it, he is in no position to claim that his good-faith belief about the validity of the Internal Revenue Code negates willfulness or provides a defense to criminal prosecution under §§ 7201 and 7203. Of course, Cheek was free in this very case to present his claims of invalidity and have them adjudicated, but like defendants in criminal cases in other contexts, who "willfully" refuse to comply with the duties placed upon them by the law, he must take the risk of being wrong.

We thus hold that in a case like this, a defendant's views about the validity of the tax statutes are irrelevant to the issue of willfulness and need not be heard by the jury, and, if they are, an instruction to disregard them would be proper. For this purpose, it makes no difference whether the claims of invalidity are frivolous or have substance. . . .

### *(ii) Ratzlaf v. United States*

In Ratzlaf v. United States, 510 U.S. 135 (1994), the Court set forth the problem and its solution as follows:

> Federal law requires banks and other financial institutions to file reports with the Secretary of the Treasury whenever they are involved in a cash transaction that exceeds $10,000. It is illegal to "structure" transactions—i.e., to break up a single transaction above the reporting threshold into two or more separate transactions—for the purpose of evading a financial institution's reporting requirement. "A person willfully violating" this antistructuring provision is subject to criminal penalties. . . . Does a defendant's purpose to circumvent a bank's reporting obligation suffice to sustain a conviction for "willfully violating" the antistructuring provision? We hold that the "willfulness" requirement mandates something more. To establish that a defendant "willfully violat[ed]" the antistructuring law, the government must prove that the defendant acted with knowledge that his conduct was unlawful.

The language of the applicable statutes required both that the defendant act "for the purpose of evading the reporting requirement" and that the defendant "willfully" violate the statutory requirements. The government argued that those who "purposely evaded" necessarily acted with knowledge that they were violating the law and that this should be enough. But the Court disagreed:

> Undoubtedly there are bad men who attempt to elude official reporting requirements in order to hide from government inspectors such criminal activity as laundering drug money or tax evasion. But currency structuring is not inevitably nefarious. Consider, for example, the small business operator who knows that reports filed under 31 U.S.C. § 5313(a) are available to the Internal Revenue Service. To reduce the risk of an IRS audit, she brings $9,500 in cash to the bank twice each week, in lieu of transporting over $10,000 once each week. That person, if the United States is right, has committed a criminal offense. . . . Nor is a person who structures a currency transaction invariably motivated by a desire to keep the government in the dark. But under the government's construction an individual would commit a felony against the United States by making cash deposits in small doses, fearful that the bank's reports would increase the likelyhood of burglary, or in an endeavor to keep a former spouse unaware of his wealth.
>
> Courts have noted "many occasions" on which persons, without violating any law, may structure transactions "in order to

avoid the impact of some regulation or tax." [Citation omitted.] This Court, over a century ago, supplied an illustration:

> The Stamp Act of 1862 imposed a duty of two cents upon a bank-check, when drawn for an amount not less than twenty dollars. A careful individual, having the amount of twenty dollars to pay, pays the same by handing to his creditor two checks of ten dollars each. He thus draws checks in payment of his debt to the amount of twenty dollars, and yet pays no stamp duty. . . . While his operations deprive the government of the duties it might reasonably expect to receive, it is not perceived that the practice is open to the charge of fraud. He resorts to devices to avoid the payment of duties, but they are not illegal. He has the legal right to split up his evidences of payment, and thus to avoid the tax.

United States v. Isham, 84 U.S. (17 Wall.) 496, 506 (1873). In current days, as an amicus noted, countless taxpayers each year give a gift of $10,000 on December 31 and an identical gift the next day, thereby legitimately avoiding the taxable gifts reporting required by 26 U.S.C. § 2503(b).

In light of these examples, we are unpersuaded by the argument that structuring is so obviously "evil" or inherently "bad" that the "willfulness" requirement is satisfied irrespective of the defendant's knowledge of the illegality of structuring. Had Congress wished to dispense with the requirement, it could have furnished the appropriate instruction.[b]

We do not dishonor the venerable principle that ignorance of the law generally is no defense to a criminal charge. In particular contexts, however, Congress may decree otherwise. That, we hold, is what Congress has done. . . . To convict Ratzlaf of the crime with which he was charged, . . . the jury had to find he knew the structuring in which he engaged was unlawful.

[b] Congress responded to *Ratzlaf* in the Money Laundering Suppression Act of 1994, P.L. No. 103–325, by amending the applicable statutes to eliminate the "willfulness" requirement.—[Footnote by ed.]

# CHAPTER V

# ATTEMPT

## INTRODUCTORY NOTE ON THE CRIME OF ATTEMPT

Rex v. Scofield, Cald. 397 (1784), written by Lord Mansfield, was the seminal decision in the evolution of the crime of attempt. The case involved an attempt to commit arson, and conviction was based on the doctrine, as subsequently stated in Rex v. Higgins, 2 East 5, 102 Eng. Rep. 269 (1801), that "all offenses of a public nature, that is, all such acts or attempts as tend to the prejudice of the community, are indictable."[a] This development occurred too late to be received as part of the common law in the United States. But in both England (by decision) and America (by statute), it had become settled by the mid-1830s that an attempt to commit any offense was itself punishable.[b]

There were crimes in the early law covering certain forms of analytically similar conduct. Indeed, it seems clear that the pressure to create a generic attempt offense emerged so late because many of the more serious forms of attempt had already been recognized as substantive crimes. Larceny, for example, was defined in terms that fell short of requiring a permanent deprivation of property. Assault, defined as an attempt to commit a battery, dealt with efforts to attack a person. Robbery in effect was an aggravated combination of the two—an effort to obtain property by means of assault. Burglary combined an attempt to commit a felony with trespass in a dwelling. Early American statutes supplemented these offenses with many crimes of the "assault with intent" variety, as in "assault with intent to kill," "assault with intent to rape," etc.

The crime of attempt punishes conduct preliminary to other crimes, including those that themselves address inchoate behavior. Thus, for example, it is a crime to attempt to commit larceny, which is itself defined in inchoate terms. The effect is to push back toward more preliminary conduct the point at which criminal liability attaches.

## SECTION 1: THE REQUIRED CONDUCT

### INTRODUCTORY NOTES ON THE CONDUCT REQUIRED FOR ATTEMPT

#### 1. THE ACT REQUIREMENT

It would be appropriate at this point to revisit the discussion in Chapter II, Section 1, addressing the conduct requirement in the criminal law.

---

[a] Compare *Rex v. Manley* in Chapter II.

[b] The history is summarized in Jerome Hall, General Principles of the Criminal Law 558–74 (2d ed. 1960), and in Francis Bowes Sayre, Criminal Attempts, 41 Harv. L. Rev. 821 (1928). Attempts carry penalties that are usually a proportion of the penalty for the completed offense. For a discussion of American grading patterns, see ALI, Model Penal Code and Commentaries § 5.05, pp. 485–87 (1985); Herbert Wechsler, William Kenneth Jones & Harold L. Korn, The Treatment of Inchoate Crimes in the Model Penal Code of the American Law Institute: Attempt, Solicitation, and Conspiracy II, 61 Colum. L. Rev. 957, 1022–24 (1961).

As the following materials demonstrate, the law of attempt tests the rationale for the conduct requirement. One question in every attempt case is whether there has been enough conduct to justify criminal punishment. Thinking about that question must begin with why the criminal law requires conduct in the first place.

## 2.    MINIMUM CONDUCT AND THE LAW OF ATTEMPT

Although minimum conduct requirements are a matter of pervasive importance in the penal law, the issue has received doctrinal attention chiefly in the law of attempt. Attempt is defined in reference to the object offense. Thus, there can be no attempt standing alone. There must be an attempt to commit murder, rape, larceny, or some other substantive offense. In each instance, the actor takes steps toward completion of the underlying crime. The question is: How many steps are enough? How far must the actor proceed towards completion of the underlying offense for attempt liability to attach? Doctrinally, this question is put as the distinction between preparation and attempt. The latter is punishable, while the former is not. The line between preparation and attempt thus marks the point at which the actor's conduct triggers criminal liability.

In order to isolate the question of how much conduct is enough, one should assume that all other requirements of the law of attempt have been met. In particular, one should take as given that the actor has been shown to have the state of mind required for the crime of attempt. For present purposes, one should assume (and this turns out to be very nearly correct) that the state of mind required for attempt is purpose. The actor must have a conscious objective or desire to complete a course of conduct proscribed as criminal. In each of the situations discussed below, the trier of fact is prepared to conclude, beyond a reasonable doubt, that the actor had such a purpose. The question is whether actions taken toward that purpose were sufficient to support criminal liability.

*mens rea = purpose* [handwritten margin note]

## People v. Bowen and Rouse

*( attempted larceny in a building )* [handwritten margin note]

Court of Appeals of Michigan, 1968.
10 Mich.App. 1, 158 N.W.2d 794.

■ LEVIN, JUDGE. Defendants, Sherrel Bowen and William Rouse, appeal their convictions of attempted larceny in a building.

On January 19, 1965, at approximately eight o'clock p.m., the defendants and two female companions were admitted to the home of one Matilda Gatzmeyer, an 80-year-old woman. The defendants' car was observed parked in front of Miss Gatzmeyer's residence and a neighbor, believing the defendants to have designs upon her property, called the police. Two police officers arrived and entered the home along with the neighbor. The defendants were found in the rear of the house near or on the basement steps. The two female companions were seated on either side of Miss Gatzmeyer, apparently engaged with her in conversation. The bedroom of the house was in a state of disarray.

The police ordered defendants to come to the front of the house and sit in the living room. Defendant Rouse seated himself within a foot of the TV, and some time thereafter one of the police officers spotted under the TV set two rings belonging to Miss Gatzmeyer. The neighbor testified she found a necklace on the staircase near where defendant

Bowen had been standing when he was first sighted by the police. When the neighbor's discovery was called to the attention of one of the police officers, he and Miss Gatzmeyer went to the staircase and found the necklace in that location.

After interrogation, the defendants were arrested and charged with larceny of "rings and necklace" in a building in violation of Mich. Comp. Laws Ann. § 28.592.[a]

Bowen had been to the Gatzmeyer home on a number of prior occasions, ostensibly as a handyman, the same reason he gave Miss Gatzmeyer for appearing on the night in question. Miss Gatzmeyer testified that on this occasion the defendants sought to hire themselves out to clean and to do some masonry work on the chimney. She complained about the high prices charged by Bowen and his failure to do work as agreed, and that Bowen's helper (the role allegedly filled by Rouse at the time of the incident) generally helped himself to things that belonged to her.

The neighbor testified that she had met Bowen on three occasions prior to the one in question and that on one occasion Bowen had induced Miss Gatzmeyer to go with him to the bank, but it was not clear whether the visit to the bank was to withdraw money to pay Bowen that which was due him or unlawfully to separate Miss Gatzmeyer from her money.

The neighbor testified that she visited with Miss Gatzmeyer daily and assisted her in various chores and generally in getting around. She stated that when she and the police officers arrived on the night in question the dresser drawers in the bedroom were all pulled out and everything thrown all over the bed. This was not the way Miss Gatzmeyer generally kept the house according to the neighbor: "she has a very neat house, everything is in its place." The neighbor further testified that "after Miss Gatzmeyer cleaned up (presumably after the police left) she found more jewelry back of the pillows" on the couch Bowen sat on during his interrogation by the police.

Miss Gatzmeyer testified that the defendants removed the jewelry from her bedroom without her consent.

At the beginning of his charge to the jury, the trial judge stated that because he doubted whether the case properly could be submitted to the jury on the original charge of larceny in a building he had decided to submit it to the jury solely on the included offense of attempt to commit larceny in a building.

## I

There was sufficient evidence to support the defendants' conviction of attempt to commit larceny. The jury could properly infer from the testimony that the defendants did in fact ransack Miss Gatzmeyer's bedroom and furniture without her permission, remove the two rings which were found under the TV set and the necklace found on the staircase. Such a finding would justify conviction of attempted larceny, the elements of which are a felonious intent to commit larceny and an overt

[a] The statute provides, in pertinent part, that "[a]ny person who shall commit the crime of larceny by stealing in any dwelling house . . . or any building used by the public shall be guilty of a felony."—[Footnote by eds.]

act going beyond mere preparation towards the commission of the crime. It is the jury's function to weigh the evidence and to determine therefrom whether such intent is manifest and in doing so the jury may draw reasonable inferences from the facts.

II

We do find error in the judge's failure properly to charge the jury on the necessity of finding an overt act [towards commission of larceny in a building]. It has been said that the overt act "is the essence of the offense" or the "gravamen of the offense." Not only did the trial judge fail to charge the jury at all concerning the necessity of finding an overt act, but he also incorrectly charged that the jury could convict if it found that the defendants came to or entered Miss Gatzmeyer's house with the intention of committing larceny.

During the charge, the trial judge stated:

> The theory of the People is that the evidence in this case, that is, the age of the complainant, Mrs. Gatzmeyer, the lateness of the visit to the house, the presence of two women to talk to the complainant, and the condition of the bedroom which it is claimed indicated ransacking and the attempt of the defendants to hide when the police were called, bear upon and indicate that the two defendants *came there with the intention* of committing larceny in the dwelling. The offense of larceny isn't clear but the attempt to commit larceny it is charged by the People . . . is clear.
>
> Now, the defense is rather brief and that is that the testimony given here does not tend to prove beyond a reasonable doubt that the defendants *entered the place with the intent* or for the purpose of attempting to commit larceny. In other words, the defense is that the testimony that is shown here is not sufficient to convict the defendants beyond a reasonable doubt of *coming* into that building or *going into the building* on the night in question *with the intent* to commit larceny. (Emphasis supplied.)

There was ample evidence from which the jury could have found felonious intent. There are the circumstances related by the judge in his charge, as well as the other evidence previously set forth in this opinion. We must assume that, in convicting the defendants, the jury followed the judge's instructions and found the requisite felonious intent.

[T]he trial judge's failure to charge the jury on the necessity of finding commission of an overt act, as a separate ingredient or element, might not be error if he were correct in charging the jury that if it found defendants "came" to or "entered" Miss Gatzmeyer's house with intent to commit larceny it could bring in a verdict of guilty. If defendants' coming to, or entering, Miss Gatzmeyer's house with felonious intent was an "overt act", the jury verdict of guilty could be viewed as a finding of the requisite overt act.

Thus, the narrow question before us is whether the defendants when they came to or entered Miss Gatzmeyer's house with the intent to commit larceny committed an overt act that would support their conviction of attempted larceny. In our opinion, their mere coming to or entry of Miss Gatzmeyer's house was not an overt act, under the circumstances that Mr. Bowen and other helpers had rightfully been in the house on prior occasions and were admitted to the house by Miss Gatzmeyer on the night in question. . . .

In People v. Coleman, 350 Mich. 268, 86 N.W.2d 281 (1957), the Supreme Court stated that a defendant may not be convicted of an attempt unless he has "gone beyond acts of an ambiguous nature" or those that are "equivocal,"[7] and that a "thoughtful test" for the resolution of the equivocal act has been phrased by Turner in his article, Attempts to Commit Crimes in 5 Camb. L.J. 230, 237–38 (1933), in these words:

*tests for attempt*

> If the acts of the accused, taken by themselves, are unambiguous, and cannot, in reason, be regarded as pointing to any other end than the commission of the specific crime in question, then they constitute a sufficient actus reus. In other words, his acts must be *unequivocally referable* to the commission of the specific crime. They must, as the late Sir John Salmond said, "speak for themselves." If the example may be permitted, it is as though a cinematograph film, which has so far depicted merely the accused person's acts without stating what was his intention, had been suddenly stopped, and the audience were asked to say to what end those acts were directed. If there is only one reasonable answer to this question then the accused has done what amounts to an "attempt" to attain that end. If there is more than one reasonably possible answer, then the accused has not yet done enough. . . .

*unequivocally referable*

*only one reasonable answer*

It has been suggested that the basic function of the overt act is corroboration of the felonious intent. However, that analysis can become somewhat circular if we permit intent to be gleaned from the overt act itself.

The testimony in this case was that defendant Bowen had, on a number of prior occasions, been in Miss Gatzmeyer's house with helpers. With that in mind and even if it be assumed (on the basis of the jury finding) that the defendants entered her house with a felonious intent, their mere presence there did not indicate, let alone "corroborate," that intention. The defendants did not break into Miss Gatzmeyer's house—they were voluntarily admitted by her. At the time of defendants' admission to Miss Gatzmeyer's house their *acts* were entirely "ambiguous" and "equivocal." It is the acts thereafter allegedly committed (but as to which we have no finding from the jury)[10] that were neither ambiguous nor equivocal.

---

[7]  . . . Other courts have said much the same thing in describing the overt act as one that can have "no other purpose" or "apparent result" than the commission of the principal crime—the "natural and probable" effect test is of the same genre; and then there are the judicial and text statements which speak of the overt act as an act that "commences" or has a "direct tendency" or "sufficient proximity" or "sufficient nearness" to the commission of the principal offense that (some add, having in mind the seriousness and enormity of the principal offense), in the opinion of the court, the actor's purpose is clear. Whether the differences in language used by the courts bring about different results or merely permit the courts that speak in terms of proximity or nearness or the like to explain their results with greater ease is beyond the scope of this opinion. On the question before us, we found substantial uniformity in results, if not in their explanation.

[10] The only jury finding before us is a finding that the defendants came to Miss Gatzmeyer's house with a felonious intent. While we proceed on the assumption that in convicting the defendants the jury concluded that the defendants came to or entered Miss

Our analysis of the authorities convinces us that the function of the overt act is not to "corroborate," but rather to demonstrate that the defendant has converted resolution into action. Man being what he is, evil thoughts and intentions are easily formed. Fortunately, for society, most felonious thoughts are not fulfilled. The law does not punish evil intent or even every act done with the intent to commit a crime. The requirement that the jury find an overt act proceeds on the assumption that the devil may lose the contest, albeit late in the hour.

The overt act is not any act. In this connection, "overt" is used in the sense of "manifest" or symbolic. The act must manifest, or be symbolic of, the crime. Considering that Bowen and helpers had been in Miss Gatzmeyer's house on previous occasions (and, whatever her differences with Bowen may have been, she nevertheless admitted him on the night in question), the fact that the defendants came to and entered Miss Gatzmeyer's house would not manifest or symbolize the crime . . . which they were convicted of attempting to commit. . . .

Attempt patterns vary widely. No rule can be laid down applicable to all cases. Most cases will in the end turn on their own facts.

> It is a question of degree. . . . [T]he degree of proximity held sufficient may vary with the circumstances, including among other things the apprehension which the particular crime is calculated to excite.

Commonwealth v. Peaslee, 177 Mass. 267, 272, 59 N.E. 55, 56 (1901) [per Holmes, J.].

In the last cited case the defendant arranged combustibles in a building, then left the building. Later he set out for the building with the intention of lighting it, but changed his mind and turned back. Held not to be an attempt.

In People v. Pippin, 316 Mich. 191, 25 N.W.2d 164 (1946), defendant, who had on a prior occasion been convicted of gross indecency, was found guilty of parole violation on evidence that he had invited a 13-year-old boy to enter his automobile. The Supreme Court said the question was whether the defendant could be convicted of attempt to commit the crime of gross indecency. The court assumed arguendo that intent had been established (just as we assume in this case that the jury found the defendants here before us harbored a felonious intent) but ruled that an overt act had not been established—"the act [committed by Pippin], at most can be considered no more than preparation for the attempt."

In People v. Youngs, 122 Mich. 292, 81 N.W. 114 (1899), the defendant armed himself with a revolver, purchased cartridges, obtained an armed accomplice, carried slippers to perpetrate a silent entry of the intended victim's house, purchased chloroform to be used in

---

Gatzmeyer's house with a felonious intent, we cannot similarly assume that the jury found that the defendant ransacked Miss Gatzmeyer's room or removed her personal belongings from her bedroom or were responsible for the fact that they were found under the TV set or on the staircase, where the only issue submitted to the jury was whether the "defendants *came there* with intention of committing larceny." The jury could have found such *intention* on the basis of evidence other than the ransacking and the atypical locations of her personal belongings.

the commission of the crime, and had already set out for the selected scene of the crime when he was arrested. Our Supreme Court reversed the conviction, holding that the defendant had not gone beyond preparation. . . .

Where entry or attempted entry upon the victim's premises has been held in itself sufficient to constitute an overt act, such entry or attempted entry has been without permission, or the defendant came armed or with burglary tools or other means of committing the crime. . . .

Reversed and remanded for a new trial.

## NOTES ON PREPARATION AND ATTEMPT

### 1. PROXIMITY TESTS

The drafters of the Model Penal Code referred to the distinction between preparation and attempt as "the most difficult problem in defining criminal attempt." Model Penal Code and Commentaries § 5.01, at 321 (1985). This judgment is confirmed by the cases.

Many courts have emphasized the physical proximity of the actor's conduct to the completed offense. The focus here is not on what has already been done but on what yet remains to be done to complete the crime. Under this view, the actor's separation from the criminal objective—whether in terms of time, distance, or necessary steps not yet taken—becomes the critical factor.

The physical-proximity test is illustrated by the well-known case of People v. Rizzo, 246 N.Y. 334, 158 N.E. 888 (1927). Defendant and three others planned to rob Charles Rao, a payroll clerk for a construction company. The men armed themselves and set off in a car to find their intended victim. They went to the bank from which he was supposed to draw the money and to the company's construction sites, but they located neither the clerk nor the money. They succeeded, however, in attracting the attention of the police, with the result that the defendants were convicted of attempt to commit robbery. The courts construed New York law to require that the actor come "*very near* to the accomplishment of the crime" in order to be liable for attempt. Applying this standard, the Court of Appeals reversed the convictions:

> To constitute the crime of robbery, the money must have been taken from Rao by means of force or violence, or through fear. The crime of attempt to commit robbery was committed, if these defendants did an act tending to the commission of this robbery. Did the acts above described come dangerously near to the taking of Rao's property? Did the acts come so near the commission of robbery that there was reasonable likelihood of its accomplishment but for the interference [of the police]? Rao was not found; the defendants were still looking for him; no attempt to rob him could be made, at least until he came in sight. . . . Men would not be guilty of an attempt at burglary if they had planned to break into a building and were arrested while they were hunting about the streets for the building not knowing where it was. Neither would a man be guilty of an attempt to commit murder if he armed himself and started out to find the person whom he had planned to

> kill but could not find him. So here these defendants were not guilty of an attempt to commit robbery . . . when they had not found or reached the presence of the person they intended to rob.

An expanded version of the proximity test was advanced by Justice Holmes. Under his approach, the issue of the actor's physical nearness to completion of the offense is subsumed in a broader inquiry that also encompasses the gravity of the harm threatened, the degree of apprehension aroused, and the probability that the conduct would result in the intended offense. Evaluating all these factors, the courts should ask whether there was a "dangerous proximity to success" in the actor's conduct. Hyde v. United States, 225 U.S. 347, 388 (1912) (Holmes, J., dissenting). See also Commonwealth v. Peaslee, 177 Mass. 267, 59 N.E. 55 (1901).

This approach—in common with other variations on the proximity doctrine—reflects the view that the essential purpose of the law of attempt is to punish dangerous conduct. The ultimate harms to be avoided are those identified by substantive crimes. Where the substantive offense is complete, the danger has been realized and punishment is warranted. Where the offense is not complete, the danger has not been realized and the case for punishment is weaker. Only where the anticipatory conduct comes dangerously close to accomplishing the harm ultimately feared is there sufficient justification for punishment of the actor, even though best efforts may have been made to commit the completed crime.

## 2. RES IPSA LOQUITUR

An entirely different approach was first suggested by Justice Salmond of New Zealand in King v. Barker, [1924] N.Z.L.R. 865, 874:

> An act done with intent to commit a crime is not a criminal attempt unless it is of such a nature as to be in itself sufficient evidence of the criminal intent with which it is done. A criminal attempt is an act which shows criminal intent on the face of it. The case must be one in which res ipsa loquitur.

See also J. Salmond, Jurisprudence 350–52 (3d ed. 1910).

Unlike the various proximity doctrines, Salmond's inquiry looks to what the actor has already done rather than to what remains to be done. The object of this inquiry is not to assess the dangerousness of the anticipatory conduct itself, but to focus on the dangerousness of the actor who engaged in it. The premise is that the individual who has demonstrated a resolute commitment to a criminal endeavor poses a threat to the social order and therefore may properly be subject to criminal punishment. The argument is that the objectives of the criminal law are well served by focusing on the actor's demonstrated propensity toward criminal misbehavior rather than solely on the dangerousness of completed conduct.

The difficulty with this approach is that it requires a prediction. Where an individual is judged dangerous on some basis other than the demonstrated dangerousness of completed conduct (as the proximity tests would require), the possibility of error seems great. The problem is the potential for over-prediction, and the question is whether a focus on the dangerous propensities of individuals can separate those who are truly intent on criminal misconduct from those who may not complete the offense.

The res ipsa loquitur test responds to these concerns in two ways. First, the requirement that the actor's criminal purpose be evident on the face of the conduct precludes criminal liability based solely on confessions or other representations of purpose. In other words, the requirement of unequivocal conduct demands manifest evidence of the actor's blameworthiness. It protects against conviction based on inadequate or unreliable proof of criminal purpose. Second, the res ipsa loquitur test may also be justified on the closely related ground of ensuring adequate evidence of the actor's commitment to the criminal purpose. Requiring conduct that speaks for itself differentiates daydream from fixed intention and limits liability for attempt to persons firmly resolved to violate societal interests.

Critics of the res ipsa test question its feasibility. Does any conduct truly speak for itself? Consider, for example, the hypotheticals offered in Salmond's *Barker* opinion, [1924] N.Z.L.R. at 875–76:

> To buy a box of matches with intent to use them in burning a haystack is not an attempt to commit arson, for it is in itself and in appearance an innocent act, there being many other reasons than arson for buying matches. The act does not speak for itself of any guilty design. The criminal intent is not manifested by any overt act sufficient for that purpose. But he who takes matches to a haystack and there lights one of them, and blows it out on finding that he is observed, has done an act which speaks for itself, and he is guilty of a criminal attempt accordingly.

Does the latter conduct really speak for itself? Does it show criminal intent on the face of it, or are there other possible explanations for lighting a match near a haystack? Strict adherence to the res ipsa loquitur test would disable the law in cases where liability should obtain. Glanville Williams used a variation of Salmond's hypothetical in support of his view that conviction should be permitted in at least some instances where unequivocality cannot be shown:

> D goes up to a haystack, fills his pipe, and lights a match. The act of lighting the match, even to a suspicious-minded person, is ambiguous. It may indicate only that *D* is going to light his pipe; but perhaps, on the other hand, the pipe is only a "blind" and *D* is really bent on setting fire to the stack. We do not know. Therefore, on the equivocality test, the act is not proximate. But suppose that as a matter of actual fact *D*, after his arrest, confesses to the guilty intent, and suppose that that confession is believed. We are now certain of the intent and the only question is as to proximity. It becomes clear that the act satisfies all the requirements for a criminal attempt.

Glanville Williams, Criminal Law: The General Part 630 (2d ed. 1961). Is Williams right in relying on subjective indicia of intent? Or is Salmond right in insisting on conduct which is "in itself sufficient evidence of the intent with which it is done"?

## 3. THE MODEL PENAL CODE

The Model Penal Code standard for distinguishing preparation from attempt is stated in § 5.01(1)(c). Conviction for attempt is allowed where the actor engages in "an act or omission constituting a substantial step in a

course of conduct planned to culminate in his commission of the crime."
Section 5.01(2) elaborates on the meaning of "substantial step":

*Substantial step*

*Strongly corroborative*

*§5.01(2)*

> Conduct shall not be held to constitute a substantial step under Subsection (1)(c) of this Section unless it is strongly corroborative of the actor's criminal purpose. Without negativing the sufficiency of other conduct, the following, if strongly corroborative of the actor's criminal purpose, shall not be held insufficient as a matter of law:

> (a) lying in wait, searching for or following the contemplated victim of the crime;

> (b) enticing or seeking to entice the contemplated victim of the crime to go to the place contemplated for its commission;

> (c) reconnoitering the place contemplated for the commission of the crime;

> (d) unlawful entry of a structure, vehicle or enclosure in which it is contemplated that the crime will be committed;

> (e) possession of materials to be employed in the commission of the crime, which are specially designed for such unlawful use or which can serve no lawful purpose of the actor under the circumstances;

> (f) possession, collection or fabrication of materials to be employed in the commission of the crime, at or near the place contemplated for its commission, where such possession, collection or fabrication serves no lawful purpose of the actor under the circumstances;

> (g) soliciting an innocent agent to engage in conduct constituting an element of the crime.

The Model Code significantly broadens liability for attempt. The fact that the actor has not come dangerously close to completing the crime would not bar conviction—provided that the completed conduct constitutes a substantial step strongly corroborative of criminal purpose. In focusing on what has been done rather than on what remains to be done, the Model Code reflects the conclusion that the proximity tests unduly compromise the social control function of the penal law. The rationales for the Model Code conduct requirement are the same as for the res ipsa loquitur test. Both standards seek to avoid speculative and undisciplined inquiry into state of mind, and both seek to ensure that the existence and firmness of the actor's criminal purpose are substantiated by objectively demonstrable conduct. Unlike the res ipsa test, however, the Model Code does not demand that the actor's conduct be *in itself* sufficient evidence of criminal purpose (if that is indeed possible). Instead, it demands only that the actor's conduct *strongly corroborate* the existence of a criminal purpose that may be shown by other means. In essence, therefore, the Model Code recasts the conceptual focus of the res ipsa loquitur test into a more manageable standard for imposing liability. The ultimate objectives are to protect individuals against free-wheeling inquiries into criminal purpose and at the same time to broaden the scope of attempt so as to facilitate early police intervention and the effective neutralization of dangerous persons.

### 4. TESTING CASE: *UNITED STATES V. HARPER*

*Rizzo* provides a testing case for how one should approach the sufficiency of acts to support an attempt conviction. Consider the factual variations on this theme discussed in United States v. Harper, 33 F.3d 1143 (9th Cir. 1994). *Harper* itself involved the following situation:

> Police officers in Buena Park, California, found [Harper and two other defendants] sitting in a rented car in the parking lot of the Home Savings Bank shortly after 10:00 p.m. on the evening of September 21, 1992. The officers searched the defendants, the vehicle and the surrounding area. They found two loaded handguns—a .44 caliber Charter Arms Bulldog and a .357 magnum Smith and Wesson—under a bush located five or six feet from the car, where a witness had earlier seen one of the car's occupants bending over. In the car, the police discovered a roll of duct tape in a plastic bag, a stun gun, and a pair of latex surgical gloves. They found another pair of latex surgical gloves in the pocket of [one of the defendant's] sweat pants. They also found six rounds of .357 magnum ammunition in the pocket of his shorts, which he wore under his sweat pants. Some of this ammunition came from either the same box or the same lot as the ammunition in the loaded .357 magnum handgun. The defendants had a total of approximately $182 in cash among them and [another defendant] was carrying an automated teller machine (ATM) card which bore the name of Kimberly Ellis.
>
> Harper had used the ATM card belonging to Kimberly Ellis shortly before 9:00 p.m. that evening in an ATM at the Buena Park branch of the Bank of America, which was located adjacent to the Home Savings parking lot in which the defendants were parked. The ATM's camera photographed Harper. Harper had requested a $20 withdrawal from the ATM, but had not removed the cash from the cash drawer. This omission had created what is known as a "bill trap." When a bill trap occurs, the ATM shuts itself down and the ATM supply company that monitors the ATM contacts its ATM service technicians to come and repair the ATM. These facts were known to Harper, who had previously worked for both Bank of America and one of its ATM service companies. . . . The prosecution's theory was that Harper had intentionally caused the bill trap to summon the ATM service technicians who would have to open the ATM vault to clear the trap. At that time, the theory went, the defendants planned to rob the technicians of the money in the ATM.

The three defendants were convicted of attempted bank robbery. The Court of Appeals agreed that there was sufficient evidence to find that the defendants intended to rob the Bank of America. But it concluded that they had not taken a "substantial step" towards commission of the offense:

> Our primary authorities are United States v. Buffington, 815 F.2d 1292, 1301 (9th Cir.1987), and United States v. Still, 850 F.2d 607, 608 (9th Cir.1988). In *Buffington*, the defendants had driven past the supposed target bank twice. One of the three male defendants then entered a store near the bank and observed the bank. The two other defendants, one dressed as a woman, exited

their vehicle in the bank parking lot, stood near the vehicle and focused their attention on the bank. They were armed. We held that the evidence was insufficient . . . as to the existence of conduct constituting a substantial step towards the commission of the crime. With regard to the latter element, we observed:

> Not only did appellants not take a single step toward the bank, they displayed no weapons and no indication that they were about to make an entry. Standing alone, their conduct did not constitute that requisite "appreciable fragment" of a bank robbery, nor a step toward commission of the crime of such substantiality that, unless frustrated, the crime would have occurred.

The same may be said of the defendants in this case. True, Harper had left money in the ATM, causing a bill trap that would eventually bring service personnel to the ATM. That act, however, is equivocal in itself. The robbery was in the future and, like the defendants in *Buffington*, the defendants never made a move toward the victims or the Bank to accomplish the criminal portion of their intended mission. They had not taken a step of "such substantiality that, unless frustrated, the crime would have occurred." Id. Their situation is therefore distinguishable from that of the defendant in United States v. Moore, 921 F.2d 207 (9th Cir.1990), upon which the government relies. In *Moore*, the defendant was apprehended "walking toward the bank, wearing a ski mask, and carrying gloves, pillowcases and a concealed, loaded gun." These actions were a true commitment toward the robbery, which would be in progress the moment the would-be robber entered the bank thus attired and equipped. That stage of the crime had not been reached by [the defendants here]; their actual embarkation on the robbery lay as much as 90 minutes [the normal response time for the ATM service technicians] away from the time when Harper left money in the ATM, and that time had not expired when they were apprehended.

*Still* provides further support for our conclusion. There, we relied upon *Buffington* to reverse a similar conviction for attempted bank robbery. The defendant in that case was seen sitting in a van approximately 200 feet from the supposed target bank. In the van he had a fake bomb, a red pouch with note demanding money attached to it, a police scanner, and a notebook containing drafts of the note. He also had been seen putting on a blonde wig while sitting in the van. The defendant's intent was clear; he told police that he had been about to rob the bank and "[t]hat's what [he] was putting the wig on for." We concluded, however, that the evidence was insufficient to establish that the defendant had taken a substantial step toward commission of the offense. "Our facts do not establish either actual movement toward the bank or actions that are analytically similar to such movement." Defendant Still, like the defendants here, was sitting in his vehicle when the police approached. As in *Still*, we conclude that the crime was too inchoate to constitute an attempt.

When criminal intent is clear, identifying the point at which the defendants' activities ripen into an attempt is not an analytically satisfying enterprise. There is, however, a substantial difference between causing a bill trap, which will result in the appearance of potential victims, and moving toward such victims with gun and mask, as in *Moore*. Making an appointment with a potential victim is not of itself such a commitment to an intended crime as to constitute an attempt, even though it may make a later attempt possible. Little more happened here; this case is more like *Buffington* and *Still* than it is like *Moore*. Accordingly, we reverse the appellants' convictions for attempted bank robbery.

In how many of these cases did the court get the right answer? How would the cases have been decided under the Model Penal Code? Under the approach of *Bowen and Rouse*?[a]

### 5. TESTING CASE: *UNITED STATES V. GLADISH*

A jury convicted Brian Gladish under 18 U.S.C. § 2422(b), which includes knowingly attempting to persuade, induce, entice, or coerce a person under 18 to engage in prostitution or other criminal sexual activity. The Seventh Circuit reversed in United States v. Gladish, 536 F.3d 646 (7th Cir. 2006). Speaking for the court, Judge Posner reasoned as follows:

> The defendant, a 35-year-old man, was caught in a sting operation in which a government agent impersonated a 14-year-old girl in an Internet chat room called "Indiana regional romance." The defendant visited the chat room and solicited "Abagail" (as the agent called herself) to have sex with him. The defendant lived in southern Indiana; "Abagail" purported to live in the northern part of the state. She agreed to have sex with the defendant and in a subsequent chat he discussed the possibility of traveling to meet her in a couple of weeks, but no arrangements were made. He was then arrested.
>
> The defendant of course did not succeed in getting "Abagail" to have sex with him, and if he had, he would not have been guilty of a completed violation of section 2422(b) because the agent who called herself "Abagail" was not a minor. The question (the only one we need answer to resolve the appeal) is whether the defendant is guilty of having *attempted* to get an underage girl to have sex with him. To be guilty of an attempt you must intend the completed crime and take a "substantial step" toward its completion. . . . The "substantial step" toward completion is the demonstration of dangerousness, and has been usefully described as "some overt act adapted to, approximating, and which in the ordinary and likely course of things will result in, the commission of the particular crime." . . . You have to do something that makes it reasonably clear that had you not been interrupted or made a mistake—for example, the person you thought you were shooting was actually a clothier's manikin—you would have completed the crime. That something marks you as genuinely dangerous—a doer

---

[a] Often, it should be noted, it will be possible to convict the defendant of some other offense even if it is determined that an attempt did not occur. In *Harper*, for example, the defendants were also convicted of a conspiracy to rob the bank and of carrying a firearm during and in relation to a crime of violence (namely, the conspiracy). See 18 U.S.C. §§ 371, 924(c). These convictions were affirmed.

and not just one of the "hollow men" of T. S. Eliot's poem, incapacitated from action because

> Between the conception
> And the creation
> Between the emotion
> And the response
> Falls the Shadow.

Hollow Men

In the usual prosecution based on a sting operation for attempting to have sex with an underage girl, the defendant after obtaining the pretend girl's consent goes to meet her and is arrested upon arrival. . . . It is always possible that had the intended victim been a real girl the defendant would have gotten cold feet at the last minute and not completed the crime even though he was in position to do so. But there is a sufficient likelihood that he would have completed it to allow a jury to deem the visit to meet the pretend girl a substantial step toward completion, and so the visit is conduct enough to make him guilty of an attempt and not merely an intent.

reasoning

Travel is not a sine qua non of finding a substantial step in a section 2422(b) case. The substantial step can be making arrangements for meeting the girl, as by agreeing on a time and place for the meeting. It can be taking other preparatory steps, such as making a hotel reservation, purchasing a gift, or buying a bus or train ticket, especially one that is nonrefundable. "[T]he defendant's initiation of sexual conversation, writing insistent messages, and attempting to make arrangements to meet" were described as a substantial step in United States v. Goetzke, 494 F.3d 1231, 1237 (9th Cir. 2007). "Child sexual abuse is often effectuated following a period of 'grooming' and the sexualization of the relationship." Sana Loue, Legal and Epidemiological Aspects of Child Maltreatment, 19 J. Legal Med. 471, 479 (1998). We won't try to give an exhaustive list of the possibilities.

reasoning

But we disagree with the government's suggestion that the line runs between "harmless banter" and a conversation in which the defendant unmistakably proposes sex. In all the cases cited to us by the government or found by our independent research there was more than the explicit sex talk that the government quotes from the defendant's chats with "Abagail." The *Goetzke* decision, from which we quoted, goes the furthest in the direction of the government's position, but is distinguishable. The court noted that

> Goetzke made advances of a sexual nature—telling W that he was a "cute young man," suggesting an exchange of pictures, describing how he liked giving W a backrub and wanted to rub his "nice butt," advising W how to stimulate himself, and expressing the desire to see W naked and to "put your peter in my mouth." Redolent of the fun they had together riding horses, fishing, and being massaged, the letters were crafted to appeal to W, flatter him, impress him, and encourage him to come back to Montana "maybe this summer" when school was out, by promising the same kind of fun and a motorcycle of W's own. The letters essentially began to

"groom" W for a sexual encounter in the event he returned to Montana. . . . Because of the allure of the recreational activities and the prospect of a motorcycle, the letters fit neatly within the common understanding of persuade, induce, or entice. . . . [Goetzke] sent W letters replete with compliments, efforts to impress, affectionate emotion, sexual advances, and dazzling incentives to return to Montana, and proposed that W return during the upcoming summer. In short, Goetzke made his move. Indeed, given their prior relationship and what Goetzke knew of W and their circumstances, the most substantial steps he realistically could take were to communicate his affections and carefully-crafted incentives to W by telephone and mail, which he did.

Because Goetzke and his intended victim had a prior relationship, his effort to lure the victim back to Montana for sex could not be thought idle chatter. But the fact that the defendant in the present case said to a stranger whom he thought a young girl things like "ill suck yoru titties" and "ill kiss yrou inner thighs" and "ill let ya suck me and learn about how to do that," while not "harmless banter," did not indicate that he would travel to northern Indiana to do these things to her in person; nor did he invite her to meet him in southern Indiana or elsewhere. His talk and his sending her a video of himself masturbating . . . are equally consistent with his having intended to obtain sexual satisfaction vicariously. There is no indication that he has ever had sex with an underage girl. Indeed, since she furnished no proof of her age, he could not have been sure and may indeed have doubted that she was a girl, or even a woman. He may have thought (this is common in Internet relationships) that they were both enacting a fantasy.

We are surprised that the government prosecuted him under section 2422(b). Treating speech (even obscene speech) as the "substantial step" would abolish any requirement of a substantial step. It would imply that if *X* says to *Y*, "I'm planning to rob a bank," *X* has committed the crime of attempted bank robbery, even though *X* says such things often and never acts. The requirement of proving a substantial step serves to distinguish people who pose real threats from those who are all hot air; in the case of Gladish, hot air is all the record shows. . . . The defendant's conviction of violating 18 U.S.C. § 2422(b) is reversed with instructions to acquit.

## SECTION 2: MENS REA

### People v. Thomas

Supreme Court of Colorado, 1986.
729 P.2d 972.

■ LOHR, JUSTICE. The defendant, John Leago Thomas, Jr., was convicted of attempted reckless manslaughter and first degree assault as the result of a jury trial in Adams County District Court. On appeal, the defendant argued, among other things, that attempted reckless manslaughter is not a cognizable crime in Colorado. The court of appeals agreed with the defendant's argument and reversed the conviction for attempted reckless manslaughter, but affirmed the conviction for first degree assault. We granted certiorari to determine whether attempted reckless manslaughter is a cognizable crime in the state of Colorado. We conclude that it is, and hold that the court of appeals erred in reversing the defendant's conviction for that crime.

I.

On the evening of February 4, 1981, the defendant received a telephone call from a former girlfriend informing him that she had been raped in her apartment by a man who lived in an apartment upstairs. The defendant arrived at the woman's apartment shortly thereafter, armed with a pistol. He went upstairs and gained entrance into the apartment occupied by the alleged assailant by identifying himself as a policeman. The defendant pointed his gun at the man who, believing the defendant was a police officer, accompanied him back down to the woman's apartment. The woman identified the man as the rapist, and the defendant instructed her to call the police. At that time, the man started to flee to his own apartment, and the defendant gave chase. The defendant fired three shots, two of which struck the fleeing man. The defendant testified that he fired the first shot as a warning when the man was going up the stairs, that he fired a second shot accidentally when the man kicked him while on the stairs, and that the third shot was also a warning shot, fired from the outside of the building near the window of the apartment occupied by the alleged rapist. When the police arrived, they found the defendant still waiting outside, holding the gun.

The jury was instructed on the crimes of attempted first degree murder, first degree assault, and the lesser included offenses of attempted second degree murder, attempted reckless manslaughter, attempted heat of passion manslaughter, and second degree assault.[a] The jury returned verdicts of guilty to the charges of first degree assault and attempted reckless manslaughter, and the trial court entered judgment accordingly.

Upon appeal, the court of appeals sustained the conviction for first degree assault, but reversed the attempted reckless manslaughter conviction on the basis that attempted reckless manslaughter is not a legally cognizable offense in Colorado. We granted certiorari to review that latter conclusion and the resulting reversal of the defendant's conviction for attempted reckless manslaughter.

II.

A.

The language of the relevant statutes provides the framework for our analysis. The crime of reckless manslaughter is defined in § 18–3–104(1)(a), 8B C.R.S. (1986), as follows:

> (1) A person commits the crime of manslaughter if: (a) He recklessly causes the death of another person;. . .

---

[a] The relevant Colorado statutes are reproduced in Appendix B.—[Footnote by eds.]

"Recklessly," the relevant culpable mental state for this crime, is defined in § 18–1–501(8):

> A person acts recklessly when he consciously disregards a substantial and unjustifiable risk that a result will occur or that a circumstance exists.

As applied to the offense of reckless manslaughter, the requisite conscious disregard of a substantial and unjustifiable risk relates to a result, the death of another person.

The inchoate offense of criminal attempt is defined as follows in § 18–2–101(1):

> A person commits criminal attempt if, acting with the kind of culpability otherwise required for commission of an offense, he engages in conduct constituting a substantial step toward the commission of the offense. A substantial step is any conduct, whether act, omission, or possession, which is strongly corroborative of the firmness of the actor's purpose to complete the commission of the offense. . . .

The court of appeals held that "[r]ecklessness is . . . a mental culpability which is incompatible with the concept of an intentional act." This is so, the court held, because the "conscious disregard" with respect to risk of death that is essential to reckless manslaughter cannot be equated with the conscious intent to cause death which the court of appeals implicitly determined to be a necessary element of the offense of criminal attempt in this context. On certiorari review, the defendant supports this analysis, contending that "[o]ne cannot intend to cause a specific result . . . by consciously disregarding the risk that the result will occur." A careful analysis of the elements of criminal attempt and of reckless manslaughter demonstrates, however, that the court of appeals' analysis and the defendant's supporting arguments are misconceived.

In People v. Frysig, 628 P.2d 1004 (Colo.1981), we construed the criminal attempt statute in the context of a charge of attempted first degree sexual assault. We held that the intent to commit the underlying offense is an essential element of the crime. More precisely, in order to be guilty of criminal attempt, the actor must act with the kind of culpability otherwise required for commission of the underlying offense and must engage in the conduct which constitutes the substantial step with the further intent to perform acts which, if completed, would constitute the underlying offense. In order to complete the offense of reckless manslaughter, it is necessary that the actor cause the death of another person by acting in a manner that involves a substantial and unjustifiable risk of death of that other person and that the actor be conscious of that risk and of its nature when electing to act. Attempted reckless manslaughter requires that the accused have the intent to commit the underlying offense of reckless manslaughter. The "intent to commit the underlying offense" of which *People v. Frysig* speaks is the intent to engage in and complete the risk-producing act or conduct. It does not include an intent that death occur even though the underlying crime, reckless manslaughter, has death as an essential element.

The crime of attempted reckless manslaughter also requires that the risk-producing act or conduct be commenced and sufficiently pursued to constitute a "substantial step toward the commission of the offense." § 18–2–101(1). That is, the act or conduct must proceed far enough to be "strongly corroborative of the firmness of the actor's purpose" to complete those acts that will produce a substantial and unjustifiable risk of death of another.

Finally, in order to be guilty of attempted reckless manslaughter the actor must engage in the requisite acts or conduct "with the kind of culpability otherwise required for the commission of the underlying offense," that is, with a conscious disregard of a substantial and unjustifiable risk that the acts or conduct will cause the death of another person. Based upon this analysis, and contrary to the defendant's argument, there is no logical or legal inconsistency involved in the recognition of attempted reckless manslaughter as a crime under the Colorado Criminal Code.

Our analysis of the crime of attempted reckless manslaughter is buttressed by the case of People v. Castro, 657 P.2d 932 (Colo. 1983), in which we held that attempted extreme indifference murder is a cognizable crime under the Colorado Criminal Code. In that case, the defendant urged that extreme indifference murder involves an unintentional and inchoate act—apparently referring to the required element of the death of another, which can more accurately be characterized as a result than as an act—and that criminal attempt requires an intent to complete the underlying offense. The latter intent, the argument proceeded, necessarily involves an intent that the death of another result from the actor's conduct. The defendant argued that to intend an unintentional and inchoate act defies logic, so there can be no such crime as attempted extreme indifference murder. We concluded that an essential premise of this argument was fatally flawed. [W]e noted that "[t]he crime of extreme indifference murder, . . . while not requiring a conscious object to kill, necessitates a conscious object to engage in conduct that creates a grave risk of death to another. . . . In this sense the culpability element of extreme indifference murder is akin to what traditionally has been known as 'general intent.'" Therefore, since the intentional state of mind required by the crime of attempted extreme indifference murder relates to the proscribed conduct and not the proscribed result, death of another person, we concluded that there is no logical inconsistency inherent in charging an attempt to commit extreme indifference murder. This parallels the foregoing analysis and conclusion with respect to the crime of attempted reckless manslaughter to which the present case relates.

Stated somewhat differently, *People v. Castro* makes clear that the intent requirement for extreme indifference murder does not involve a conscious object to kill, but instead necessitates a conscious object to engage in conduct that in fact creates a grave risk of death to another. This is not the specific intent encompassed within the Colorado Criminal Code's definition of the terms "intentionally" or "with intent" which requires a conscious object to cause a proscribed result. Rather, it is "akin to what traditionally has been known as 'general intent,'" which is described by the terms "knowingly" or "willfully," defined in § 18–1–501(6) as those terms relate to conduct. Therefore, since the underlying crime of extreme indifference murder does not involve unintentional conduct, the attempt to commit that crime does not involve an attempt to commit an unintentional act. So it is as well with the crime of reckless manslaughter.

## B.

In People v. Krovarz, 697 P.2d 378 (Colo. 1985), we employed a new mode of analysis to determine whether a particular substantive crime can provide a foundation for criminal attempt liability. There, we examined the rationale for imposition of criminal penalties for attempts falling short of accomplishment of a completed substantive crime. We concluded that "culpability for criminal attempt rests primarily upon the actor's purpose to cause harmful consequences," and that "[p]unishment is justified where the actor intends harm because there exists a high likelihood that his 'unspent' intent will flower into harmful conduct at any moment." We held, however, that our criminal attempt statute does not require a conscious purpose to achieve proscribed results as a condition to criminal liability. That is, criminal attempt is not a specific intent offense. . . . Rather, the probability of future dangerousness that has given rise to the justified legislative judgment that criminal attempt liability should be imposed "is equally present when one acts knowingly." . . .

*[margin note: unspent intent]*

One acts recklessly with respect to result when he consciously disregards a substantial and unjustified risk that a result will occur. When one engages in conduct that involves a risk of death that is both substantial and unjustified, and is conscious of the nature and extent of the risk, the actor demonstrates such a disregard for the likelihood that another will die as to evince a degree of dangerousness hardly less threatening to society than if the actor had chosen to cause death. . . . [5]

. . . The critical inquiry under *Krovarz* is potential for future danger. For this purpose, the awareness of a practical certainty of the prohibited result that is required for knowing conduct cannot be viewed as more dangerous, in any important degree, than the conscious disregard of a substantial and unjustifiable risk that the proscribed result will occur—the hallmark of reckless action. Although a difference in the degree of moral culpability of the actor might be perceived between knowingly achieving a proscribed result and recklessly accomplishing it, we now conclude that the difference in potential for future danger inherent in those two culpable mental states is not significant enough to justify a different result under the *Krovarz* test.

*[margin note: potential for future danger]*

*[margin note: Krovarz test]*

We conclude that the index of dangerousness analysis utilized in *People v. Krovarz* leads to the same result achieved by examining and construing the statutory language under the standards of *People v. Castro* and *People v. Frysig*. Accordingly, we hold that attempted reckless manslaughter is a crime proscribed by the Colorado Criminal Code.

*[margin note: holding]*

We reverse that part of the court of appeals' judgment overturning the defendant's conviction for attempted reckless manslaughter.

*[margin note: disposition]*

---

[5] In People v. Hernandez, 44 Colo.App. 161, 614 P.2d 900 (1980), the court of appeals held that attempted criminally negligent homicide is not a cognizable crime. The analysis in that case parallels that of the court of appeals in the present case. Although we have rejected this analysis, we express no opinion concerning the correctness of the result reached by the court of appeals in *People v. Hernandez*.

■ DUBOFSKY, J., specially concurs. I join the majority opinion under the facts of this case. People v. Krovarz, 697 P.2d 378, 381 n.9 (Colo. 1985), suggests that the analysis employed in that case should not be extended to attempted reckless conduct. The footnote in Krovarz reflected the concern of a commentator who observed that allowing one to be charged with attempted murder under the wide range of conduct encompassed within "reckless," without a resulting death, may extend criminal liability for harmful conduct to situations such as driving very fast on the wrong side of the road while going around a curve. Arnold Enker, Mens Rea and Criminal Attempt, 1977 Am.Bar Found.Res.J. 845, 854. The conduct is not in fact harmful if there is no traffic coming in the opposite direction. The commentator suggested that where the actor risks harm, rather than intending harm, the conduct should be penalized under a legislative definition of a substantive crime instead of the common law definition of attempt. Given the facts in this case, however, I am convinced that the defendant came close enough to intending harm that he can be convicted of attempted reckless manslaughter.

## NOTES ON THE MENS REA OF ATTEMPT

1. THE TRADITIONAL VIEW: *THACKER V. COMMONWEALTH*

The result in *Thomas* is unusual.[a] The traditional view is that attempt requires a specific intent "to do the entire evil thing. The intent in the mind covers the thing in full; the act covers it only in part." Merritt v. Commonwealth, 164 Va. 653, 661, 180 S.E. 395, 399 (1935). Thacker v. Commonwealth, 134 Va. 767, 114 S.E. 504 (1922), illustrates the traditional approach. The facts were:

> The accused, in company with two other young men, . . . was attending a church festival in Alleghany County, at which all three became intoxicated. They left the church between 10 and 11 o'clock at night, and walked down the country road about one and one-half miles, when they came to a sharp curve. Located in this curve was a tent in which . . . Mrs. J.A. Ratrie, her husband, four children, and a servant were camping for the summer. The husband, though absent, was expected home that night, and Mrs. Ratrie, upon retiring, had placed a lighted lamp on a trunk by the head of her bed. After 11 o'clock she was awakened by the shots of a pistol and loud talking in the road near by, and heard a man say, "I am going to shoot that Goddamned light out"; and another voice said, "Don't shoot the light out." The accused and his friends then appeared at the back of the tent, where the flaps of the tent were open, and said they were from Bath County and had lost their way, and asked Mrs. Ratrie if she could take care of

[a] But it is not unique. Compare Gentry v. State, 437 So.2d 1097 (Fla. 1983):

> In the instant case, the appellant . . . swore at his father, choked him, snapped a pistol several times to his head and when the weapon failed to fire, struck his father in the head with the gun. Had a homicide occurred, there can be no doubt that the appellant could have been successfully prosecuted for second-degree murder without the state adducing proof of a specific intent to kill. The fact that the father survived was not the result of any design on the part of the appellant not to effect death but was simply fortuitous. We can think of no good reason to reward the appellant for such fortuity by imposing upon the state the added burden of showing a specific intent to kill in order to successfully prosecute the attempted offense.

them all night. She informed them she was camping for the summer, and had no room for them. One of the three thanked her, and they turned away, but after passing around the tent the accused used some vulgar language and did some cursing and singing. When they got back in the road, the accused said again he was going to shoot the light out, and fired three shots, two of which went through the tent, one passing through the head of the bed in which Mrs. Ratrie was lying, just missing her head and the head of her baby, who was sleeping with her. The accused did not know Mrs. Ratrie, and had never seen her before. He testified he did not know any of the parties in the tent, and had no ill will against either of them; that he simply shot at the light, without any intent to harm Mrs. Ratrie or any one else; that he would not have shot had he been sober, and regretted his action.

The defendant was convicted of attempted murder, but the Supreme Court of Appeals of Virginia reversed:

> In discussing the law of attempts, W. Clark, Criminal Law 111–12 (1894), says:
>
> > The act must be done with the specific intent to commit a particular crime. This specific intent at the time the act is done is essential. To do an act from general malevolence is not an attempt to commit a crime because there is no specific intent, though the act according to its consequences may amount to a substantive crime. . . . A man actuated by general malevolence may commit murder, though there is not actual intention to kill; to be guilty of an attempt to murder there must be a specific intent to kill.
>
> 1 J. Bishop, Criminal Law 731–36 (8th ed. 1892), says:
>
> . . . When we say that a man attempted to do a given wrong, we mean that he intended to do specifically it, and proceeded a certain way in the doing. The intent in the mind covers the thing in full; the act covers it only in part. Thus to commit murder, one need not intend to take life, but to be guilty of an attempt to murder, he must so intend. It is not sufficient that his act, had it proved fatal, would have been murder. We have seen that the unintended taking of life may be murder, yet there can be no attempt to murder without the specific intent to commit it. . . . For example, if one from a housetop recklessly throws down a billet of wood upon the sidewalk where persons are constantly passing, and it falls upon a person passing by and kills him, this would be common law murder, but if, instead of killing, it inflicts only a slight injury, the party could not be convicted of an assault with intent to commit murder since, in fact, the murder was not intended.
>
> The application of the foregoing principles to the facts of the instant case shows clearly, as we think, that the judgment complained of is erroneous. While it might possibly be said that the firing of the shot into the head of Mrs. Ratrie's bed was an act done towards the commission of the offense charged, the evidence

falls far short of proving that it was fired with the intent to murder her. . . . [b]

## 2. THE MODEL PENAL CODE

The Model Penal Code accepts the *Thacker* result, but departs from the common law position that a specific intent is required as to *all* elements of the offense attempted. Section 5.01 of the Model Code provides:

> (1) . . . A person is guilty of an attempt to commit a crime if, acting with the kind of culpability otherwise required for commission of the crime, he:
>
> (a) purposely engages in conduct which would constitute the crime if the attendant circumstances were as he believes them to be; or
>
> (b) when causing a particular result is an element of the crime, does or omits to do anything with the purpose of causing or with the belief that it will cause such result without further conduct on his part; or
>
> (c) purposely does or omits to do anything which, under the circumstances as he believes them to be, is an act or omission constituting a substantial step in a course of conduct planned to culminate in his commission of the crime.

This is one of the more inartfully drafted provisions of the Model Code. Its intended meaning is clear, although how one gets there from the statutory language is uncharacteristically obscure. The intended meaning is explained in elaborate commentary by its drafters in Herbert Wechsler, William Kenneth Jones & Harold L. Korn, The Treatment of Inchoate Crimes in the Model Penal Code of the American Law Institute: Attempt, Solicitation, and Conspiracy, 61 Colum. L. Rev. 571, 957 (1961). The Model Code means to require a purpose to engage in the conduct and to achieve the result elements of the object offense,[c] but the mens rea for the circumstance elements of an attempt would be the same as would be required by the underlying offense.[d] The Model Code does, however, add a substantive

[b] People v. Acevedo, 32 N.Y.2d 807, 345 N.Y.S.2d 555 (1973), reached the same result. The defendant fired a rifle from a rooftop and seriously wounded several people. The applicable murder statute covered "[t]he killing of a human being [by] an act imminently dangerous to others, and evincing a depraved mind, regardless of human life, although without a premeditated design to effect the death of any individual." Acevedo's conviction of attempted murder was reversed because the jury instruction did not require the finding of a specific intent to kill.

A situation comparable to *Thacker* and *Acevedo* arose under the revised Oregon statutes reproduced in Appendix B. In State v. Smith, 21 Or.App. 270, 534 P.2d 1180 (1975), the court held that a charge of attempted reckless murder could not be sustained. For discussion of an interesting series of Illinois decisions coming eventually to the same result, see People v. Harris, 72 Ill.2d 16, 17 Ill.Dec. 838, 377 N.E.2d 28 (1978).

[c] There is a minor exception for result elements intended by the language "or with the belief that it will cause such result without further conduct on his part" in subsection (1)(b). These words are designed to permit an attempt charge against actors who believe that a forbidden result will occur, though they may be indifferent to its occurrence. An example would be a case where a business rival rigs a competitor's airplane so that it will crash, in order to cause a prospective customer to believe that it is defectively designed. The actor in such a case may believe that the pilot will be killed, but either not care or hope that the pilot is skillful enough to escape in some manner. Such a case, in the view of the Model Code drafters, should be assimilated to one where the actor intends to kill.

[d] Section 5.01 thus is one of the rare instances under the Model Code where proper classification of an element as a "circumstance" as opposed to "conduct" or "result" is crucial.

offense designed to cover the *Thomas* and *Thacker* situations. Section 211.2 (recklessly endangering another person) provides:

> A person commits a misdemeanor if he recklessly engages in conduct which places or may place another person in danger of death or serious bodily injury. Recklessness and danger shall be presumed where a person knowingly points a firearm at or in the direction of another, whether or not the actor believed the firearm to be loaded.

*§ 211.2 (recklessly endangering another person)*

## 3. RATIONALE FOR REQUIRING SPECIFIC INTENT

One reason for requiring specific intent for attempts was offered in J.C. Smith, Two Problems in Criminal Attempts, 70 Harv. L. Rev. 422, 434 (1957):

*J.C. Smith*

> The conception of attempt seems necessarily to involve the notion of an intended consequence. Thus the word "attempt" is defined in the Shorter Oxford English Dictionary as "a putting forth of effort to accomplish what is uncertain or difficult." When a man attempts to do something he is "endeavoring" or "trying" to do it. All these ways of describing an attempt seem to require a desired, or at least an intended, consequence. Recklessness and negligence are incompatible with desire or intention. [T]herefore, in a crime which by definition may be committed recklessly or negligently . . . , it is impossible to conceive of an attempt.[e]

*attempt requires a desired or intended consequence*

*recklessness and negligence no conceiving of attempt.*

Oliver Wendell Holmes, in The Common Law 65–68 (1881), preferred a different rationale. He argued:

*Oliver W. Holmes rationale*

> There is [a] class of cases in which intent plays an important part. . . . The most obvious examples of this class are criminal attempts. . . .
>
> Some acts may be attempts . . . which could not have effected the crime unless followed by other acts on the part of the wrongdoer. For instance, lighting a match with intent to set fire to a haystack has been held to amount to a criminal attempt to burn it, although the defendant blew out the match on seeing that he was watched. . . .
>
> In such cases the law goes on a new principle, different from that governing most substantive crimes. The reason for punishing any act must generally be to prevent some harm which is foreseen as likely to follow that act under the circumstances in which it is done. In most substantive crimes the ground on which that likelihood stands is the common working of natural causes as shown by experience. But when an act is punished the natural effect of which is not harmful under the circumstances, that ground alone will not suffice. The probability does not exist unless there are grounds for expecting that the act done will be followed by other acts in connection with which its effect will be harmful, although not so otherwise. But as in fact no such acts have followed, it cannot, in general, be assumed, from the mere doing of what has been

*new principle*

*foreseeable harm likely to follow*

---

[e]   Cf. Rollin Perkins & Ronald Boyce, Criminal Law 637 (3d ed. 1982): "The word 'attempt' means to try; it implies an effort to bring about a desired result. Hence an attempt to commit any crime requires a specific intent to commit that particular offense."

done, that they would have followed if the actor had not been interrupted. They would not have followed it unless the actor had
chosen, and the only way generally available to show that he
would have chosen to do them is by showing that he intended to
do them when he did what he did. The accompanying intent in
that case renders the otherwise innocent act harmful, because it
raises a probability that it will be followed by such other acts and
events as will all together result in harm. The importance of the
intent is not to show that the act was wicked, but to show that it
was likely to be followed by hurtful consequences. . . .

*Probability that hurtful consequences or harm will follow/result*

Are there other reasons for the specific intent requirement? Should the
specific intent apply to all elements of the object offense? The next two
notes explore these questions in more detail.

4.   CIRCUMSTANCE ELEMENTS

Consider the following cases:

*attempted statutory rape example*

The crime of statutory rape is usually defined as sexual intercourse with a person below a certain age, irrespective of consent. Typically, liability is strict as to the age of the victim. A mistake by the defendant as to the other person's age, no matter how
reasonable, is not a defense. Assume that the age of consent is 16
and that the defendant has passed beyond mere preparation and
is interrupted just prior to actual intercourse. Assume further
that the defendant intended intercourse, that the defendant's
conduct fully corroborates this intent, and that the victim was 15.
Should a belief that the victim was 17 be a defense to an attempt
charge even if the underlying offense is defined to impose strict liability? The answer would be "yes" if specific intent is required for
*all* of the elements of the completed offense—if, indeed, the defendant must intend "to do the entire evil thing." Is this the right
answer? How would the *Thomas* court analyze this problem?
What result under the Model Penal Code?

Assume that burglary is defined in the traditional common
law manner as breaking and entering the dwelling house of another at night with the intent to commit a felony therein. Assume
that 7 p.m. is when "night" begins. If the defendant completed the
offense at 7:30 p.m., the defendant's belief that it was only 6:30
would not be a valid defense. If the defendant was caught before
the offense was completed, would the belief that it was only 6:30
constitute a defense to attempted burglary? Should it?

*attempt mens rea same for all elements as completed offense*

J.C. Smith has argued that no special policy of the law of attempt
should displace the mens rea otherwise required for the completed offense
in the situation illustrated by these two hypotheticals. He believes that the
mens rea as to circumstance elements should be the same for the attempt
as it would be for the completed offense. In Two Problems in Criminal Attempts, 70 Harv. L. Rev. 422, 434–35 (1957), he explained that an "attempt
is . . . essentially connected with consequences [and] the only essential intention is an intention to bring about those consequences." If "recklessness,
or negligence, or even blameless inadvertence" is sufficient for the circumstance elements of the substantive crime, he continued, they "will suffice

also for the attempt." He admitted that there was no authority that supported this conclusion,[f] but argued that there was no contrary authority and that it

> achieve[s] a common-sense result and [is] in accordance with principle. . . If *D*'s state of mind is sufficiently blameworthy to ground liability for the complete crime, it is surely sufficiently blameworthy to ground liability for the attempt.

Is Smith right?

## 5.  COMPLETED CONDUCT BUT NO RESULT

Does *Thomas* likewise present a situation where there should be no special policy of the law of attempt elevating the mens rea above what would be required for the completed offense? Consider the following line of argument.

The law of attempt proceeds on the premise that the deterrent or social control functions of the criminal law require punishment of those who come dangerously close to the commission of crime or who manifest a dangerous propensity to engage in criminal behavior. Thomas completed conduct that created a serious risk of fatality and, for all that appears, was saved from a manslaughter conviction only by fortuitous circumstances. He appears to have been no less culpable and no less dangerous than he would have been had a death occurred.

*dangerous propensity*

Consider also the arguments in favor of requiring a specific intent for attempts. Holmes contended that specific intent is required in attempt offenses in order to show that the defendant was likely to engage in additional conduct that would complete the crime. This rationale explains some cases, but seems clearly inapplicable to situations like that presented in *Thomas*. Thomas completed his planned course of behavior, and no further conduct would have been required to justify convicting him of manslaughter had a death resulted.

*additional conduct*

If a specific intent is to be required in the *Thomas* situation, therefore, some other rationale must be advanced. One possibility is that the requirement of specific intent serves the function of protecting the innocent from unwarranted conviction. However, this interest, which arises frequently in attempt prosecutions, is of serious concern only when the defendant's conduct is ambiguous and there is genuine doubt whether the defendant actually presented the dangers at which the law of attempt is aimed. There is little basis for such concern in *Thomas*.

*other rationale needed for specific intent requirement*

*① protection of innocent from unwarranted conviction*
*- assumes: serious concern but only when Δ conduct is ambiguous; genuine doubt whether Δ actually presented the dangers*

---

[f]   The English Court of Appeal subsequently adopted Smith's view in Regina v. Pigg, [1982] 2 All. E.R. 591, holding that recklessness was sufficient for the "consent" element in a charge of attempted rape. See also Glanville Williams, The Problem of Reckless Attempts, [1983] Crim. L. Rev. 365, which defends *Pigg* as the right result even under the subsequently enacted English attempt statute that requires an "intent to commit an offence" without differentiating among the elements thereof.

There seem to be few American authorities that speak to this point. But see State v. Davis, 108 N.H. 158, 160–61, 229 A.2d 842, 844 (1967), where the court said without elaboration: "The fact that defendant was ignorant of the age of the female or that he did not intend the intercourse to be with a girl of non-age would not prevent his act from constituting [statutory] rape if completed, or an attempt, if it failed." In People v. Krovarz, 697 P.2d 378, 383 n.11 (Colo.1985), the court adverted to the issue but found it not presented by the facts of the case.—[Footnote by eds.]

How, then, can one explain the traditional view to the contrary and its endorsement in the Model Penal Code? How would one answer the line of argument recited above?

### 6. QUESTIONS AND COMMENTS ON *THOMAS*

Thomas was convicted of assault in the first degree (a class 3 felony) and attempted reckless manslaughter (manslaughter is a class 4 felony; an attempt to commit a class 4 felony is a class 5 felony).[g] Consider the following provisions of Colorado law in connection with *Thomas*:

> § 18–3–206. Menacing. A person commits the crime of menacing if, by any threat or physical action, he knowingly places or attempts to place another person in fear of imminent serious bodily injury. Menacing is a class 3 misdemeanor, but, if committed by the use of a deadly weapon, it is a class 5 felony.
>
> § 18–3–208. Reckless endangerment. A person who recklessly engages in conduct which creates a substantial risk of serious bodily injury to another person commits reckless endangerment, which is a class 3 misdemeanor.

What is the function in Colorado of the offense of attempted reckless manslaughter? Is there any violation of § 18–3–206 or § 18–3–208 that would not also be an attempted manslaughter? Has the court in *Thomas* undermined the grading structure adopted by the Colorado legislature? On what principles does that grading structure appear to be based? Compare *People v. Castro* (described in *Thomas*). Does that case present the same problems?

Notice that there is no offense of "negligent endangering" in the Model Penal Code or in Colorado law. Should there be one?[h] When the question decided in *People v. Hernandez* (described in a footnote in *Thomas*) reaches the Colorado Supreme Court, how should it be decided?

## SECTION 3: IMPOSSIBILITY

### People v. Dlugash

Court of Appeals of New York, 1977.
41 N.Y.2d 725, 363 N.E.2d 1155, 395 N.Y.S.2d 419.

■ JASEN, JUDGE.

The criminal law is of ancient origin, but criminal liability for attempt to commit a crime is comparatively recent. At the root of the concept of attempt liability are the very aims and purposes of penal law. The ultimate issue is whether an individual's intentions and actions, though failing to achieve a manifest and malevolent criminal purpose, constitute a danger to organized society of sufficient magnitude to war-

---

[g] The sentencing provisions of Colorado law are complex, but in rough terms the maxima in 1995 were 16 years for a class 3 felony, eight years for a class 4 felony, and four years for a class 5 felony. The maximum penalties in effect at the time of Thomas' offense for each class were half of the 1995 levels.

[h] At least one state punishes negligent endangerment: "A person who negligently engages in conduct that creates a substantial risk of death or serious bodily injury to another commits the offense of negligent endangerment." Mont. Code Ann. § 45–5–208. The maximum penalty is a fine "not to exceed $1,000 or imprison[ment] in the county jail for a term not to exceed 1 year, or both."

rant the imposition of criminal sanctions. Difficulties in theoretical analysis and concomitant debate over very pragmatic questions of blameworthiness appear dramatically in reference to situations where the criminal attempt failed to achieve its purpose solely because the factual or legal context in which the individual acted was not as the actor supposed them to be. Phrased somewhat differently, the concern centers on whether an individual should be liable for an attempt to commit a crime when, unknown to him, it was impossible to successfully complete the crime attempted. For years, serious studies have been made on the subject in an effort to resolve the continuing controversy when, if at all, the impossibility of successfully completing the criminal act should preclude liability for even making the futile attempt. The 1967 revision of the Penal Law approached the impossibility defense to the inchoate crime of attempt in a novel fashion. The statute provides that, if a person engages in conduct which would otherwise constitute an attempt to commit a crime, "it is no defense to a prosecution for such attempt that the crime charged to have been attempted was, under the attendant circumstances, factually or legally impossible of commission, if such crime could have been committed had the attendant circumstances been as such person believed them to be." (Penal Law, § 110.10.) This appeal presents to us, for the first time, a case involving the application of the modern statute. We hold that, under the proof presented by the People at trial, defendant Melvin Dlugash may be held for attempted murder, though the target of the attempt may have already been slain, by the hand of another, when Dlugash made his felonious attempt.

On December 22, 1973, Michael Geller, 25 years old, was found shot to death in the bedroom of his Brooklyn apartment. The body, which had literally been riddled by bullets, was found lying face up on the floor. An autopsy revealed that the victim had been shot in the face and head no less than seven times. Powder burns on the face indicated that the shots had been fired from within one foot of the victim. Four small caliber bullets were recovered from the victim's skull. The victim had also been critically wounded in the chest. One heavy caliber bullet passed through the left lung, penetrated the heart chamber, pierced the left ventricle of the heart upon entrance and again upon exit, and lodged in the victim's torso. A second bullet entered the left lung and passed through to the chest, but without reaching the heart area. Although the second bullet was damaged beyond identification, the bullet tracks indicated that these wounds were also inflicted by a bullet of heavy caliber. A tenth bullet, of unknown caliber, passed through the thumb of the victim's left hand. The autopsy report listed the cause of death as "[m]ultiple bullet wounds of head and chest with brain injury and massive bilateral hemothorax with penetration of [the] heart." Subsequent ballistics examination established that the four bullets recovered from the victim's head were .25 caliber bullets and that the heart-piercing bullet was of .38 caliber. [The evidence revealed that Joe Bush had fired as many as five shots with a .38 caliber weapon and that "a few minutes [later], perhaps two, perhaps as much as five," the defendant "walked over to the fallen Geller, drew his .25 caliber pistol, and fired approximately five shots in the victim's head and face."]

Defendant was indicted by the Grand Jury of Kings County on a single count of murder in that, acting in concert with another person actually present, he intentionally caused the death of Michael Geller. . . . From [two] physicians, the prosecution sought to establish that Geller was still alive at the time defendant shot at him. Both physicians testified that each of the two chest wounds, for which defendant alleged Bush to be responsible, would have caused death without prompt medical attention. Moreover, the victim would have remained alive until such time as his chest cavity became fully filled with blood. Depending on the circumstances, it might take five to 10 minutes for the chest cavity to fill. Neither prosecution witness could state, with medical certainty, that the victim was still alive when, perhaps five minutes after the initial chest wounds were inflicted, the defendant fired at the victim's head.

The defense produced but a single witness, the former Chief Medical Examiner of New York City. This expert stated that, in his view, Geller might have died of the chest wounds "very rapidly" since, in addition to the bleeding, a large bullet going through a lung and the heart would have other adverse medical effects. "Those wounds can be almost immediately or rapidly fatal or they may be delayed in there, in the time it would take for death to occur. But I would say that wounds like that which are described here as having gone through the lungs and the heart would be fatal wounds and in most cases they're rapidly fatal."

The trial court . . . submitted . . . two theories to the jury: that defendant had either intentionally murdered Geller or had attempted to murder Geller. The jury found the defendant guilty of murder. . . . [9] On appeal, the Appellate Division reversed. . . . The court ruled that "the People failed to prove beyond a reasonable doubt that Geller had been alive at the time he was shot by defendant; defendant's conviction of murder thus cannot stand. Further, the court held that the judgment could not be modified to reflect a conviction for attempted murder because "the uncontradicted evidence is that the defendant, at the time that he fired the five shots into the body of the decedent, believed him to be dead. . . ."

Preliminarily, we state our agreement with the Appellate Division that the evidence did not establish, beyond a reasonable doubt, that Geller was alive at the time defendant fired into his body. To sustain a homicide conviction, it must be established, beyond a reasonable doubt, that the defendant caused the death of another person. The People were required to establish that the shots fired by defendant Dlugash were a sufficiently direct cause of Geller's death. While the defendant admitted firing five shots at the victim approximately two to five minutes after Bush had fired three times, all three medical expert witnesses testified that they could not, with any degree of medical certainty, state whether the victim had been alive at the time the latter shots were fired by the defendant. Thus, the People failed to prove beyond a reasonable doubt that the victim had been alive at the time he was shot by the defendant.

---

[9] It should be noted that Joe Bush pleaded guilty to a charge of manslaughter in the first degree. At the time he entered his plea, Bush detailed his version of the homicide. According to Bush, defendant Dlugash was a dealer in narcotic drugs and Dlugash claimed that Geller owed him a large sum of money from drug purchases. Bush was in the kitchen alone when Geller entered and threatened him with a shotgun. Bush pulled out his .38 caliber pistol and fired five times at Geller. Geller slumped to the floor. Dlugash then entered, withdrew his .25 caliber pistol and fired five shots into the deceased's face. Bush, however, never testified at Dlugash's trial.

Whatever else it may be, it is not murder to shoot a dead body. Man dies but once.

. . . The most intriguing attempt cases are those where the attempt to commit a crime was unsuccessful due to mistakes of fact or law on the part of the would-be criminal. A general rule developed in most American jurisdictions that legal impossibility is a good defense but factual impossibility is not. Thus, for example, it was held that defendants who shot at a stuffed deer did not attempt to take a deer out of season, even though they believed the dummy to be a live animal. The court stated that there was no criminal attempt because it was no crime to "take" a stuffed deer, and it is no crime to attempt to do that which is legal. (State v. Guffey, 262 S.W.2d 152 (Mo. App. 1953); see, also, State v. Taylor, 345 Mo. 325, 133 S.W.2d 336 (1939) (no liability for attempt to bribe a juror where person bribed was not, in fact, a juror).) These cases are illustrative of legal impossibility. A further example is Francis Wharton's classic hypothetical involving Lady Eldon and her French lace. Lady Eldon, traveling in Europe, purchased a quantity of French lace at a high price, intending to smuggle it into England without payment of the duty. When discovered in a customs search, the lace turned out to be of English origin, of little value and not subject to duty. The traditional view is that Lady Eldon is not liable for an attempt to smuggle. (1 F. Wharton, Criminal Law (12th ed.), § 225, p. 304, n.9 (1932); for variations on the hypothetical see Graham Hughes, One Further Footnote on Attempting the Impossible, 42 N.Y.U.L. Rev. 1005 (1967).)

On the other hand, factual impossibility was no defense. For example, a man was held liable for attempted murder when he shot into the room in which his target usually slept and, fortuitously, the target was sleeping elsewhere in the house that night. (State v. Mitchell, 170 Mo. 633, 71 S.W. 175 (1902)) Although one bullet struck the target's customary pillow, attainment of the criminal objective was factually impossible. State v. Moretti, 52 N.J. 182, 244 A.2d 499 (1968) presents a similar instance of factual impossibility. The defendant agreed to perform an abortion, then a criminal act, upon a female undercover police investigator who was not, in fact, pregnant. The court sustained the conviction, ruling that "when the consequences sought by a defendant are forbidden by the law as criminal, it is no defense that the defendant could not succeed in reaching his goal because of circumstances unknown to him." On the same view, it was held that men who had sexual intercourse with a woman, with the belief that she was alive and did not consent to the intercourse, could be charged for attempted rape when the woman had, in fact, died from an unrelated ailment prior to the acts of intercourse. (United States v. Thomas, 13 U.S.C.M.A. 278 (1962))

The New York cases can be parsed out along similar lines. One of the leading cases on legal impossibility is People v. Jaffe, 185 N.Y. 497, 78 N.E. 169 (1906), in which we held that there was no liability for the attempted receipt of stolen property when the property received by the defendant in the belief that it was stolen was, in fact under the control of the true owner. Similarly, in People v. Teal, 196 N.Y. 372, 89 N.E. 1086 (1909), a conviction for attempted subornation of perjury was overturned on the theory that the testimony attempted to be suborned was irrelevant to the merits of the case. Since it was not subornation of perjury to solicit false, but irrelevant, testimony, "the person through whose procuration the testimony is given cannot be guilty of subornation of perjury and, by the same rule, an unsuccessful attempt to that which is not a crime when effectuated, cannot be held to be an attempt to commit the crime specified." Factual impossibility, however, was no defense. Thus, a man could be held for attempted grand larceny when he picked an empty pocket. (People v. Moran, 123 N.Y. 254, 25 N.E. 412 (1890))

As can be seen from even this abbreviated discussion, the distinction between "factual" and "legal" impossibility was a nice one indeed and the courts tended to place a greater value on legal form than on any substantive danger the defendant's actions posed for society. The approach of the draftsmen of the Model Penal Code was to eliminate the defense of impossibility in virtually all situations. Under the [Model Penal Code] provision, to constitute an attempt, it is still necessary that the result intended or desired by the actor constitute a crime. However, the [Model Penal Code] suggested a fundamental change to shift the locus of analysis to the actor's mental frame of reference and away from undue dependence upon external considerations. The basic premise of the [Model Penal Code] provision is that what was in the actor's own mind should be the standard for determining his dangerousness to society and, hence, his liability for attempted criminal conduct.

In the belief that neither of the two branches of the traditional impossibility arguments detracts from the offender's moral culpability, the Legislature substantially carried the [Model Penal Code's] treatment of impossibility into the 1967 revision of the Penal Law. Thus, a person is guilty of an attempt when, with intent to commit a crime, he engages in conduct which tends to effect the commission of such crime. (Penal Law, § 110.00.) It is no defense that, under the attendant circumstances, the crime was factually or legally impossible of commission, "if such crime could have been committed had the attendant circumstances been as such person believed them to be." (Penal Law, § 110.10.) Thus, if defendant believed the victim to be alive at the time of the shooting, it is no defense to the charge of attempted murder that the victim may have been dead.

Turning to the facts of the case before us, we believe that there is sufficient evidence in the record from which the jury could conclude that the defendant believed Geller to be alive at the time defendant fired shots into Geller's head. Defendant admitted firing five shots at a most vital part of the victim's anatomy from virtually point blank range. Although defendant contended that the victim had already been grievously wounded by another, from the defendant's admitted actions, the jury could conclude that the defendant's purpose and intention was to administer the coup de grace. . . .

Defendant argues that the jury was bound to accept, at face value, . . . indications in his admissions [to the police] that he believed Geller dead [when he shot him.] Certainly, it is true that the defendant was entitled to have the entirety of the admissions, both the inculpatory and the exculpatory portions, placed in evidence before the trier of facts. . . . However, the jury was not required to automatically credit the exculpatory portions of the admissions. . . . In this case, there is ample other evidence to contradict the defendant's assertion that he believed Geller dead. There were five bullet wounds inflicted with stunning accuracy in a vital part of the victim's anatomy. The medical testimony indicated that Geller may have been alive at the time defendant fired at him. The defendant voluntarily left the jurisdiction immediately after the crime with his coperpetrator. Defendant did not report the crime to the police when left on his own by Bush. Instead, he attempted to conceal his and Bush's involvement with the homicide. In addition, the other portions of defendant's admissions make his contended belief that Geller was dead extremely improbable. Defendant, without a word of instruction from Bush, voluntarily got up from his seat after the passage of just a few minutes and fired five times point blank into the victim's face, snuffing out any remaining chance of life that Geller possessed. Certainly, this alone indicates a callous indifference to the taking of a human life. His admissions are barren of any claim of duress and reflect, instead, an unstinting co-operation in [subsequent] efforts to dispose of vital in-criminating evidence [the guns]. Indeed, defendant maintained a false version of the occurrence until such time as the police informed him that they had evidence that he lately possessed a gun of the same cali-ber as one of the weapons involved in the shooting. From all of this, the jury was certainly warranted in concluding that the defendant acted in the belief that Geller was yet alive when shot by defendant.

*jury gave murder conviction*

The jury convicted the defendant of murder. Necessarily, they found that defendant intended to kill a live human being. Subsumed within this finding is the conclusion that defendant acted in the belief that Geller was alive. . . . Although it was not established beyond a rea-sonable doubt that Geller was, in fact, alive, such is no defense to at-tempted murder since a murder would have been committed "had the attendant circumstances been as (defendant) believed them to be." (Pe-nal Law, § 110.10.) The jury necessarily found that defendant believed Geller to be alive when defendant shot at him.

*reasoning*

The Appellate Division erred in not modifying the judgment to re-flect a conviction for the lesser included offense of attempted murder. An attempt to commit a murder is a lesser included offense of murder and the Appellate Division has the authority, where the trial evidence is not legally sufficient to establish the offense of which the defendant was convicted, to modify the judgment to one of conviction for a lesser included offense which is legally established by the evidence. . . .

*holding modify judgment to attempted murder.*

## NOTES ON IMPOSSIBILITY AND ATTEMPT

### 1.   "LEGAL" AND "FACTUAL" IMPOSSIBILITY

Cases such as *Dlugash* have bedeviled the courts throughout the histo-ry of the law of attempt. Indeed, the "impossibility" problem has been more widely discussed in the cases and the literature than any other aspect of the offense.

*Dlugash* describes the traditional approach. Situations are classified as involving "legal" or "factual" impossibility. "Factual" impossibility cases can be prosecuted as attempts. "Legal" impossibility cases cannot. How can one tell the difference?

In Booth v. State, 398 P.2d 863, 870–71 (Okla. Crim. App.1964), the distinction was defined as follows:

> The reason for the "impossibility" of completing the substantive crime ordinarily falls into one of two categories: (i) where the act if completed would not be criminal, a situation which is usually described as a "legal impossibility," and (ii) where the basic or substantive crime is impossible of completion, simply because of some physical or factual condition unknown to the defendant, a situation which is usually described as a "factual impossibility."

Does this help?

## 2. An Alternative Common Law Approach

Rollin Perkins and Ronald Boyce, in Criminal Law 624 (3d ed. 1982),* have argued that in at least some of the situations illustrated in *Dlugash*, the actor properly can be viewed as having passed beyond preparation and completed an attempt before any impossibility problem arose. Thus, as to *People v. Jaffe* (discussed in *Dlugash*), they reasoned:

> [M]uch could be said for [acquittal] if nothing was involved except the purchase of property under such circumstances that the buyer firmly, but mistakenly, believed it to be stolen. More was involved, however . . . .Property had in fact been stolen, the thief and [the defendant] had made arrangements for [the defendant] to receive it and [the defendant] did receive it. In the meantime the thief had been apprehended and the property recovered. After it had thus lost its stolen character it was returned to the thief to carry out the original plan [and it was then sold to the defendant for about half its value]. The courts overlooked everything except the very last step by which the property was actually handed over. [The defendant] had gone beyond preparation and moved in the direction of receiving stolen property before that last step and should have been convicted. . . .

Other factual patterns, Perkins and Boyce continue, should be analyzed differently:

> Deeply intrenched in the common law is the principle that conviction of crime cannot be based upon intent alone. . . . This raises the question of "inconsistent intents." At times one has two different intents which seem only one to him but are so inconsistent that only one is possible of achievement. . . . In such a situation the law regards one intent as primary and the other as secondary and only the primary intent controls [a]. . . .
>
> It has been said that if *D* takes his own umbrella, thinking it belongs to another and with intent to steal, this does not constitute an attempt to commit larceny. Here . . . we find utterly inconsistent intents unrealized by the actor. He intends to take a particular umbrella (which actually belongs to him). He also has in

---



[a] For more elaborate statements of this position, see Edwin R. Keedy, Criminal Attempts at Common Law, 102 U. Pa. L. Rev. 464 (1954); Rollin Perkins, Criminal Attempt and Related Problems, 2 U.C.L.A.L. Rev. 319 (1955).—[Footnote by eds.]

mind the intent to steal the umbrella of another. His primary intent is to take the umbrella he actually seizes and hence there is nothing wrongful in what is actually done but only in his secondary, inconsistent intent. Hence in such a situation, if there is nothing in his conduct either preceding or following the taking, which manifests a criminal purpose he should not be held guilty of attempted larceny. To convict him merely because he admitted his mistaken notion at a later time would be to convict him on intent alone. But this does not mean that he should not be convicted of attempt to steal if his conduct at the time of the transaction clearly manifested a criminal purpose.

*nothing in his conduct that manifests*

*conduct manifests criminal purpose*

How helpful is the primary-secondary intent distinction? Does it guide analysis, or does it rationalize a result reached for other reasons? Suppose *A* aims a gun at *B* and pulls the trigger with intent to kill. If the bullet misses, what is *A*'s primary intent? Is this case different from the umbrella situation? From *Jaffe*?

## 3.   THE MODEL PENAL CODE

The Model Penal Code approach to the impossibility issue can be extracted from three separate sources.

*MPC impossibility*

First, all three versions of attempt in § 5.01(1) mandate that criminality should be judged from the circumstances as the defendant perceived them. This is accomplished in Subsection (1)(a) by the language "if the attendant circumstances were as he believes them to be." Thus, the defendant would be guilty in the umbrella case hypothesized by Perkins. Similar language in Subsection (1)(c) applies where the actor's conduct is incomplete but has passed beyond mere preparation. And the same result would also follow under Subsection (1)(b) in the case where the defendant shot a stuffed deer believing it to be alive. The actor in that case would have fired at the dummy "with the purpose of causing [the death of the deer] without further conduct on his part."

*§5.01(1) circumstances as defendant perceived them*
*(a) attendant circumstances as he believes them to be*
*(c) beyond mere preparation*
*(b) purpose of causing w/out further conduct*

Second, the provisions of §§ 5.05(2) and 2.12 permit the grade of the offense to be reduced, or in extreme cases the prosecution to be dismissed, when the actor's conduct "is so inherently unlikely to result or culminate in the commission of a crime that neither such conduct nor the actor presents a public danger" or where the actor's conduct "did not actually cause or threaten the harm or evil sought to be prevented by the law defining the offense or did so only to an extent too trivial to warrant the condemnation of conviction." Thus, in a case involving a toy pistol, incantation, or voodoo, the court would have the authority to reduce the charges or dismiss them altogether, based on its evaluation of the dangers presented by the defendant.

*§5.05(2)*
*§2.12*
*(grade of offense can be reduced OR prosecution can be dismissed)*

Third, certain substantive offenses, most particularly § 223.6 (receiving stolen property), have been defined to eliminate the possibility of acquittal on the basis of impossibility. Section 223.6 provides that an actor is guilty who has received property "believing that it has probably been stolen." On the facts of *Jaffe*, the defendant would be guilty of the completed substantive offense, making resort to a charge of attempt unnecessary.

*§223.6*
*"certain offenses eliminate the possibility of acquittal on basis of impossibility"*

These results are defended[b] on the rationale that most defendants who attempt impossible crimes have demonstrated their readiness to violate the criminal law, have manifested the required culpability, and have posed sufficient social danger to warrant criminal sanctions. Three functions are seen to have been served by the impossibility defense. First, it has functioned as a surrogate for uncertainties on the facts about whether the defendant had the required criminal purpose. Second, it also has functioned as a surrogate for the entrapment defense, allowing courts to express their displeasure at certain law enforcement techniques involving the use of traps or decoys. Third, it has eliminated from the ambit of the criminal law certain cases where the defendant does not threaten the interests the law is designed to serve. Each of these functions is said to have been sufficiently taken into account elsewhere in the Model Code provisions, and accordingly impossibility as such is no defense.

## 4. *UNITED STATES V. FARNER*

*Dlugash* involved a missing result element. The court applied the Model Penal Code approach to a missing circumstance element in United States v. Farner, 251 F.3d 510 (5th Cir. 2001). Farner, an adult male who lived in Dallas, met a 14-year-old girl named "Cindy" through an internet service. He asked her whether she was looking for an older man. When she responded "yes," he engaged in a three month internet romance in which he tried to persuade Cindy to meet him so they could engage in sexual relations. He also sent her four pornographic pictures showing adults participating in various sexual acts. Cindy finally agreed to meet him at a local restaurant in Houston, where Farner was to attend a conference. When he drove to the restaurant to meet her, he was arrested by Kathy Crawford, an FBI agent who had posed as "Cindy" in an undercover sting operation.

Farner was convicted of attempting to violate 18 U.S.C. § 2422(b).[c] He appealed on the ground that "it was legally impossible for him to have committed the crime since the 'minor' involved . . . was actually an adult." The court responded:

> The distinction between factual and legal impossibility is elusive at best. Most federal courts have repudiated the distinction or have at least openly questioned its usefulness.
>
> The illusory distinction between the two defenses is evident in the instant case. Thus, Farner says this is a case of legal impossibility because Kathy Crawford was an adult, and the statute does not address attempted sexual activity between adults. On the other hand, the district court viewed the impossibility as factual, because the defendant unquestionably intended to engage in

---

[b] See Herbert Wechsler, William Kenneth Jones & Harold L. Korn, The Treatment of Inchoate Crimes in the Model Penal Code of the American Law Institute: Attempt, Solicitation, and Conspiracy, 61 Colum. L. Rev. 571, 578–84 (1961). See also ALI, Model Penal Code and Commentaries § 5.01, pp. 315–17 (1985).

[c] That statute reads: "Whoever, using the mail or any facility or means of interstate or foreign commerce, or within the special maritime and territorial jurisdiction of the United States knowingly persuades, induces, entices or coerces any individual who has not attained the age of 18 years, to engage in prostitution or any sexual activity for which any person can be charged with a criminal offense, or attempts to do so, shall be fined under this title, imprisoned not more than 15 years or both." Sexual activity between an adult and a person under the age of 18 is a felony in Texas.

the conduct proscribed by law but failed only because of circum- *[district court holding; circuit holding]*
stances unknown to him. We think the latter view is correct.

In any event, this circuit has properly eschewed the semanti- *[2 elements in criminal attempt:]*
cal thicket of the impossibility defense in criminal attempt cases
and has instead required proof of two elements: first, that the de- *[① Kind of culpability otherwise required]*
fendant acted with the kind of culpability otherwise required for
the commission of the underlying substantive offense, and, sec-
ond, that the defendant had engaged in conduct which constitutes *[② substantial step which strongly corroborates]*
a substantial step toward commission of the crime. The substan-
tial step must be conduct which strongly corroborates the firmness of defendant's criminal attempt. The Model Penal Code endorses this approach. In this case, the district court correctly concluded from the stipulated evidence, beyond a reasonable doubt, *[holding]*
that Farner intended to engage in sexual acts with a 14-year-old
girl and that he took substantial steps toward committing the
crime.

## 5. THE IMPORTANCE OF THE ACTUS REUS: *UNITED STATES V. OVIEDO*

*[Oviedo sold a pound of substance to undercover agent he said was heroin but was procaine, not a controlled substance]*

The *Farner* court discarded the impossibility inquiry and instead required *both* that the defendant have the appropriate mens rea *and* that the
defendant engage in behavior that constituted a substantial step towards
the criminal objective. An earlier Fifth Circuit case, United States
v. Oviedo, 525 F.2d 881 (5th Cir. 1976), illustrates the importance of the
second requirement.

By prior arrangement, Oviedo sold to an undercover agent a pound of a
substance he identified as heroin. A field test for heroin performed by the
agent was positive. Oviedo was then arrested. A subsequent search of his
residence yielded two pounds of a similar substance hidden in a television *[facts]*
set. Further analysis of both substances revealed that they were not in fact
heroin, but procaine hydrochloride. Procaine hydrochloride gives a positive
reaction to the field test used by the agent, but is not an opium derivative
and is not a controlled substance.

Oviedo was charged with attempting to sell heroin. He testified that he *[charged w/ attempt to sell heroin]*
knew he was not selling heroin and that he was merely trying to "rip off"
his proposed buyer. He was a thief, he told the jury, not a drug distributor. *[procedure]*
The jury was instructed that it could find Oviedo guilty of an attempt to
distribute heroin if, contrary to his testimony, he believed that he was sell- *[reversed on appeal]*
ing heroin. His subsequent conviction was reversed on appeal.

The court first rejected Oviedo's argument that there was insufficient
evidence that he meant to sell heroin. It then said:

> We thus take as fact Oviedo's belief that the substance was hero-
> in. The facts before us are therefore simple—Oviedo sold a sub-
> stance he thought to be heroin, which in reality was an uncon-
> trolled substance. The legal question before us is likewise sim- *[issue/question]*
> ple—are these combined acts and intent cognizable as a criminal
> attempt . . . . The answer, however, is not so simple.

The reason the answer was not simple, the court continued, was that it
turned on the elusive distinction between legal and factual impossibility. *[elusive distinction btwen 'legal and factual impossibility]*
Oviedo's conduct could readily be characterized as either. It could be legal
because what he actually did was not a crime. It could be factual because it

was a crime on the facts as he thought them to be. Both of these possibilities, said the Court, "miss the mark, but in opposite directions." If one takes the legal impossibility approach, "impossibility would always be a valid defense." If one takes the factual impossibility approach, it would turn "the attempt statute into a new substantive criminal statute where the critical element to be proved is mens rea simpliciter. It would allow us to punish one's thoughts, desires, or motives, through indirect evidence, without reference to any objective fact." The court resolved the case on the following rationale:

> We reject the notion . . . adopted by the district court . . . that the conviction in the present case can be sustained since there is sufficient proof of intent, not because of any doubt as to the sufficiency of the evidence in that regard, but because of the inherent dangers such a precedent would pose in the future.
>
> When the question before the court is whether certain conduct constitutes mere preparation which is not punishable, or an attempt which is, the possibility of error is mitigated by the requirement that the objective acts of the defendant evidence commitment to the criminal venture and corroborate the mens rea. To the extent that this requirement is preserved it prevents the conviction of persons engaged in innocent acts on the basis of a mens rea proved through speculative inferences, unreliable forms of testimony, and past criminal conduct.
>
> Courts could have approached the preparation-attempt determination in another fashion, eliminating any notion of particular objective facts, and simply could have asked whether the evidence at hand was sufficient to prove the necessary intent. But this approach has been rejected for precisely the reasons set out above, for conviction upon proof of mere intent provides too great a possibility of speculation and abuse. . . .
>
> When the defendant sells a substance which is actually heroin, it is reasonable to infer that he knew the physical nature of the substance, and to place on him the burden of dispelling that inference.[10] However, if we convict the defendant of attempting to sell heroin for the sale of a non-narcotic substance, we eliminate an objective element that has major evidentiary significance and we increase the risk of mistaken conclusions that the defendant believed the goods were narcotics.[11]

---

[10] A similar inference obtains when possession is established, but the defendant contends that he did not know of the presence of the controlled substance.

[11] Arnold Enker, Impossibility in Criminal Attempts-Legality and the Legal Process, 53 Minn. L. Rev. 665, 680, 688 (1969):

> Mens rea is within one's control but, as already seen, it is not subject to direct proof. More importantly, perhaps, it is not subject to direct refutation either. It is the subject of inference and speculation. The act requirement with its relative fixedness, its greater visibility and difficulty of fabrication, serves to provide additional security and predictability by limiting the scope of the criminal law to those who have engaged in conduct that is itself objectively forbidden and objectively verifiable. Security from officially imposed harm comes now only from the knowledge that one's thoughts are pure but that one's acts are similarly pure. So long as a citizen does not engage in forbidden conduct, he has little need to worry about possible erroneous official conclusions about his guilty mind.

Thus, we demand that in order for a defendant to be guilty of a criminal attempt, the objective acts performed, without any reliance on the accompanying mens rea, mark the defendant's conduct as criminal in nature. The acts should be unique rather than so commonplace that they are engaged in by persons not in violation of the law.

*must be objective*

Here we have only two objective facts. First, Oviedo told the agent that the substance he was selling was heroin, and second, portions of the substance were concealed [at his home] in a television set. If another objective fact were present, if the substance were heroin, we would have a strong objective basis for the determination of criminal intent and conduct consistent and supportive of that intent. The test set out above would be met, and, absent a delivery, the criminal attempt would be established. But when this objective basis for the determination of intent is removed, when the substance is not heroin, the conduct becomes [ambiguous], and we are left with a sufficiency-of-the-evidence determination of intent rejected in the preparation-attempt dichotomy. We cannot conclude that the objective acts of Oviedo apart from any indirect evidence of intent mark his conduct as criminal in nature. Rather, those acts are consistent with a noncriminal enterprise. Therefore, we will not allow the jury's determination of Oviedo's intent to form the sole basis of a criminal offense.

*holding*

The government . . . argues that United States v. Mandujano, 499 F.2d 370 (5th Cir 1974) . . . compels a contrary result. In *Mandujano*, the defendant negotiated a sale of heroin with an undercover agent. After taking the agent's money, the defendant set about to find his source. He was unsuccessful, and returned a few hours later with the money and without the heroin. We found the evidence sufficient to take the case beyond preparation, and to support his conviction for attempted distribution.

*US v. Mandujano (convicted for attempted distribution when he negotiated a sale of heroin w/ undercover agent but was unsuccessful in finding it but took the money)*

In making that determination, we recognized that in order to be guilty of an attempt, the objective conduct of the defendant must strongly corroborate the firmness of the defendant's criminal intent. The objective acts must not be equivocal in nature. In that case, we had as objective facts defendant's act of taking money and his personal statements that he would purchase heroin with that money. Importantly, there were no objective facts which made these acts equivocal.

*objective must not be equivocal*

The situation in *Mandujano* is distinguishable from that now before us. Just as it is reasonable to infer a person's knowledge and criminal intent from the possession of a substance which is in fact narcotics, it is also reasonable to infer that same knowledge and intent from an individual's statements of future intention. However, just as it is impossible to infer that intent when the substance possessed is not in fact narcotics, it is also impossible to infer that intent when objective facts indicate that the person did not carry out his self-proclaimed intention.

*distinguishable*

Thus, when Mandujano stated that he would purchase heroin, we could infer that he intended to purchase heroin since there were no objective facts to the contrary. But here, Oviedo stated he would sell heroin and then sold procaine. Based on these objective facts, we cannot infer that he intended to do that which he said he was going to do, because he in fact did something else.

### 6. QUESTIONS AND COMMENTS ON *OVIEDO* AND THE MODEL PENAL CODE

Did the court ask the right questions in *Oviedo*? Did it reach the right result? The court distinguished its earlier decision in *Mandujano*. Was that case correctly decided? Was it, as the court thought, distinguishable?

Consider also how *Oviedo* would be decided under the Model Penal Code. Does the Code take into account the concerns that motivated the *Oviedo* result? Notice that the "substantial step" requirement in the Code applies only to § 5.01(1)(c) and that Oviedo would apparently be decided under § 5.01(1)(a). Does subsection (1)(a) require, in the *Oviedo* court's words, that the "objective acts of Oviedo apart from any indirect evidence of intent mark his conduct as criminal in nature"? Should it?

Consider in connection with these questions the comments in Arnold Enker, Impossibility in Criminal Attempts—Legality and the Legal Process, 53 Minn. L. Rev. 665, 682–83 (1969). Enker criticized the Model Code attempt provisions:

> [T]he Model Penal Code's requirement that the act corroborate the mens rea applies only to cases in the preparation-attempt continuum. Cases such as *Jaffe* and Lady Eldon are covered by a separate provision which provides that where the defendant does any act which would constitute a crime under the circumstances as he thought them to be, he is guilty of an attempt. The corroboration requirement of § 5.01(2) does not apply to this section.[40] . . . [What the drafters of the Code] failed to see is that the act in its narrow sense of the defendant's physical movements can be perfectly innocent in itself—possession of goods, bringing goods into the country—and that what gives the act character as corroborative of mens rea is often the objective element or the attendant circumstances that the goods possessed are in fact stolen, or that the goods brought into the country are in fact dutiable, or that the goods possessed are in fact narcotics.

The Model Code is defended in the face of these criticisms in ALI, Model Penal Code and Commentaries § 5.01, pp. 319–20 (1985). Three reasons are advanced in support of the Model Code as drafted: first, that the issue is "more theoretical than practical" because it is unlikely that persons will be prosecuted for innocuous behavior solely on the basis of their admissions; second, that a requirement of corroboration in the context of completed conduct may lead to the acquittal of persons whose behavior alone is insufficiently corroborative, but whose behavior in light of contemporaneous statements and later admissions, provides a sufficient case for guilt; and third, that contemporaneous statements and later admissions might be

---

[40] "Impossibility cases are dealt with in Subsections (1)(a) . . . and (1)(b) . . . of Section 5.01. Subsection (1)(c) deals with attempt-preparation cases. The corroboration requirement is contained in the first sentence of Section 5.01(2) which is limited to defining the term 'substantial step' under Subsection (1)(c). Indeed, Subsections (1)(a) and (1)(b) do not require a 'substantial step.' And while some impossibility cases will fit under Section (1)(c), the requirement of substantiality is judged there, too, by reference to 'the circumstances as [the defendant] believes them to be. . . .' "

thought to be a more reliable indicator of guilt in a case of completed conduct than in a case where the actor has yet to complete proposed behavior.

Is this response persuasive? Or is Enker right that the Model Code does not adequately protect against the risk in a case like *Oviedo* of convicting innocent persons?

### 7. TRUE LEGAL IMPOSSIBILITY

There is one variation of the impossibility situation on which everyone agrees. Consider the following case. The defendant smokes a marijuana cigarette, believing that it is a crime to do so. If such behavior is not a crime in the jurisdiction in question, and if the Model Penal Code approach to impossibility were to be taken, could this person be convicted of attempting to violate the law? The answer is "no." A defendant cannot be convicted of an attempt if, on the facts as he or she believed them to be, no crime would have been committed. As the court said in *Dlugash*, "it is still necessary that the result intended or desired by the actor constitute a crime."

The court in *United States v. Farner* also noted this possibility. It said:

> We need not hold that there can never be a case of true legal impossibility, although such a case would be rare. The typical definition of that defense is a situation "when the actions which the defendant performs or sets in motion, even if fully carried out *as he desires,* would not constitute a crime." United States v. Oviedo, 525 F.2d 881, 883 (5th Cir. 1976) (emphasis added). . . . The situation in the instant case is quite different. Defendant Farner's scheme, if fully carried out as he "desired" or "planned," was not to engage in sexual relations with an adult FBI officer. By his own [admission], the person whom he desired to entice was a 14-year-old girl. The only reason he failed was because the true facts were not as he believed them to be.

The court added in a footnote that "[a]nother label that could describe the [true legal impossibility situation] is the 'principle of legality.'" It cited United States v. Lanier, 520 U.S. 259 (1997), for the proposition that "conduct may not be treated as criminal unless it has been so defined by a competent authority."

### 8. COMPLETED OFFENSES: *BRONSTON V. UNITED STATES*

To what extent should the proper analysis of impossibility cases in the law of attempt apply to "completed" crimes? Consider, in this connection, Bronston v. United States, 409 U.S. 352 (1973). Bronston was the president and sole owner of Bronston Productions. The company petitioned for an arrangement with creditors under the federal Bankruptcy Act. At a hearing to determine the extent and location of the company's assets, Bronston gave the following testimony:

> Q. Do you have any bank accounts in Swiss banks, Mr. Bronston?
>
> A. No, sir.
>
> Q. Have you ever?
>
> A. The company had an account there for about six months, in Zurich.

> Q. Have you any nominees who have bank accounts in Swiss banks?
>
> A. No, sir.
>
> Q. Have you ever?
>
> A. No, sir.

The facts, as described by the Court, were as follows:

> It is undisputed that for a period of nearly five years, between October 1959 and June 1964, petitioner had a personal bank account at the International Credit Bank in Geneva, Switzerland, into which he made deposits and upon which he drew checks totaling more than $180,000. It is likewise undisputed that petitioner's answers were literally truthful. (i) Petitioner did not at the time of questioning have a Swiss bank account. (ii) Bronston Productions, Inc., did have the account in Zurich described by petitioner. (iii) Neither at the time of questioning nor before did petitioner have nominees who had Swiss accounts. The government's prosecution for perjury went forward on the theory that in order to mislead his questioner, petitioner answered the second question with literal truthfulness but unresponsively addressed his answer to the company's assets and not to his own—thereby implying that he had no personal Swiss bank account at the relevant time.

Bronston was convicted of perjury, but the Supreme Court unanimously reversed. It reasoned:

> Beyond question, petitioner's answer to the crucial question was not responsive if we assume, as we do, that the first question was directed at personal bank accounts. There is, indeed, an implication in the answer to the second question that there was never a personal bank account; in casual conversation this interpretation might reasonably be drawn. But we are not dealing with casual conversation. . . . [W]e perceive no reason why Congress would intend the drastic sanction of a perjury prosecution to cure a testimonial mishap that could readily have been reached with a single additional question by counsel alert—as every examiner ought to be—to the incongruity of petitioner's unresponsive answer. Under the pressures and tensions of interrogation, it is not uncommon for the most earnest witnesses to give answers that are not entirely responsive. Sometimes the witness does not understand the question, or may in an excess of caution or apprehension read too much or too little into it. It should come as no surprise that a participant in a bankruptcy proceeding may have something to conceal and consciously tries to do so, or that a debtor may be embarrassed at his plight and yield information reluctantly. It is the responsibility of the lawyer to probe; testimonial interrogation, and cross-examination in particular, is a probing, prying, pressing form of inquiry. If a witness evades, it is the lawyer's responsibility to recognize the evasion and to bring the witness back to the mark, to flush out the whole truth with the tools of adversary examination.
>
> It is no answer to say that here the jury found that petitioner intended to mislead his examiner. A jury should not be permitted

to engage in conjecture whether an unresponsive answer, true and complete on its face, was intended to mislead or divert the examiner. . . . It may well be that petitioner's answers were not guileless but were shrewdly calculated to evade. Nevertheless, we [conclude] that any special problems arising from the literally true but unresponsive answer are to be remedied through the "questioner's acuity" and not by a federal perjury prosecution.

What was the basis for the reversal of Bronston's conviction? Should the result be the same if Bronston had been charged with perjury under § 241.1 of the Model Penal Code? Would the situation be any different if he was charged with attempted perjury? More broadly, is the impossibility-attempt situation symptomatic of a larger and more pervasive problem in the criminal law, one that really has little to do with "impossibility" as a concept or even the crime of attempt?

## SECTION 4: OTHER INCHOATE OFFENSES

### INTRODUCTORY NOTE

This Section considers additional problems that arise when the law of attempt intersects with solicitation, complicity, and conspiracy. Chapter VI contains additional materials on complicity and conspiracy. Instructors who do not wish to consider complicity and conspiracy in detail can use this Section as an introduction to those concepts and then move on to other topics. Those who plan to cover most or all of Chapter VI may wish to postpone this Section for now and assign it after Section 2 of Chapter VI. Another option would be to assign individual segments of Chapter VI. The subsection of Chapter VI on natural and probable consequences, for example, could be taught as a stand-alone addition to the materials in this Section.

### People v. Superior Court

Supreme Court of California, 2007.
41 Cal.4th 1, 157 P.3d 1017.

■ BAXTER, J.

Defendant and real party in interest Ronald Decker has been charged with the attempted willful, deliberate, and premeditated murder of his sister, Donna Decker, and her friend, Hermine Riley Bafiera. . . . Decker does not dispute that the . . . evidence was sufficient to hold him to answer to the charge of solicitation of the murder of Donna and Hermine but argues that this evidence was insufficient to support a charge of their attempted murder. The magistrate and the trial court, believing themselves bound by People v. Adami, 36 Cal.App. 3d 452, 111 Cal.Rptr. 544 (1973) (*Adami*), reluctantly agreed with Decker and dismissed the attempted murder charges. The Court of Appeal disagreed with *Adami* and issued a writ of mandate directing the respondent court to reinstate the dismissed counts. We granted review to address the conflict and now affirm. . . .

Ronald Decker was charged by felony complaint with the attempted willful, deliberate, and premeditated murder of his sister, Donna Decker, and her friend, Hermine Riley Bafiera; the solicitation of Detective Wayne Holston to commit these murders; and the solicitation of Russell Wafer to murder Donna Decker. The undisputed evidence presented at the preliminary hearing revealed the following:

On August 20, 2003, Ronald Decker (identifying himself only as "Ron") placed a telephone call to Russell Wafer, a gunsmith at Lock, Stock and Barrel in Temple City (Los Angeles County). Decker said he was looking for someone to do some "work" for him and arranged to meet privately with Wafer the following week. During that meeting, Decker explained that he had been in contact with Soldier of Fortune magazine, had done some research, and came up with Wafer's name as a possible "contractor" for a local "job"—"basically it was that he wanted someone taken care of." Decker added that he could not kill the victim himself because he would be a prime suspect. Wafer advised that while he could not handle the job, his friend "John" from Detroit might be interested. After Decker offered to pay the killer $35,000 and an additional $3,000 to Wafer as a finder's fee, Wafer said he would try to contact John. He instructed Decker to call him back the following week.

In reality, however, Wafer did not know a "John" in Detroit who would be interested in a contract murder. Wafer instead called the Los Angeles County Sheriff's Department, spoke to Detective Wayne Holston, and agreed to assist in a sting operation. When Decker called Wafer on September 2, Wafer claimed he had been in contact with "John," who was coming to town shortly. Wafer asked Decker for his phone number and promised to arrange a meeting with "John." Based on the physical description Wafer had provided and on the phone number Decker had supplied, Holston located a photograph of Decker. Wafer immediately recognized Decker as "Ron," the man he had met the previous week. At Holston's request, Wafer arranged a meeting with Decker for the evening of September 5 at a golf course parking lot in Arcadia. Holston accompanied Wafer to the meeting and was introduced as "John" from Detroit. Holston was wearing a "wire," and the encounter was both videotaped and recorded.

After Wafer left the two men alone, Decker explained that a "lady" owed him a lot of money and that the only way for him to get it back was "to take her out." Decker subsequently identified the target as his sister, Donna Decker, and provided descriptions of her person, her mode of dress, her residence, her office, her car, and her daily habits. Decker offered Holston $25,000 to perform the execution, with a $10,000 bonus if it were a "nice, neat, clean job." Decker reiterated that he could not do it himself, as "he would be the prime suspect," and might "slip up" somewhere. When Decker proposed that Holston kill Donna in an automobile accident, Holston warned him that she might survive such an accident. Decker agreed that this might not be the best method, since he wanted her "totally expired," and said he appreciated Holston's advice: "I want a professional—someone that's gonna do the job, and do it right—and do it right." When Holston then proposed killing Donna during a staged robbery or carjacking, Decker said that would be "great" and urged Holston to "shoot her in the heart and head both, just to make sure." Decker added that Donna spent a lot of time with her friend and coworker, Hermine Riley Bafiera, and that Holston might need to "take out" Hermine as well to avoid having a witness. Decker did not care for Hermine, either.

When Holston said he could complete the job within a week, Decker replied, "Marvelous. . . . The sooner the better." Holston also asked for some money up front, and Decker said he could supply him with $5,000 in cash as a downpayment in a couple of days "so you can start right away." The downpayment was also designed to prove Decker's sincerity, since "once this goes into effect—she's gonna be killed." Decker could barely contain his eagerness: "Well that's what I want[.] I don't want go to the hospital then come home. I want absolutely positively expired. Totally expired."

*[margin note: $5000 downpayment sincerity]*

Decker and Holston met again at the golf course on September 7. This meeting was also videotaped and recorded. Decker gave Holston $5,000 in cash, wrapped in two plastic bundles. He reiterated that Holston, after Donna had been murdered, should use a pay phone to leave him a voicemail message—Holston was to say that "the paint job has been completed"—and that Holston would get the rest of the money about a month later. Decker also reiterated that "if Hermine is in the car, with her, you cannot, I understand if I were in your business, I would never leave a witness. You have to take her out too. Whoever's with her you gotta take the other person out too. But don't charge me double."

*[margin note: take out any witnesses]*

Holston told Decker that he had already performed some intelligence work, that he was "convinced" he would see the victim the next day, and that he could get this "job" done quickly—eliciting another "marvelous" from Decker—and explained that "once I leave here, it's done. So, you sure you want to go through with it?" Decker replied, "I am absolutely, positively, 100 percent sure, that I want to go through with it. I've never been so sure of anything in my entire life. . . . [D]o it very fast . . . as fast as you can." At the end of the conversation, Decker seemed "very pleased" and thanked Holston and Wafer. A short time after Holston and Wafer drove off, Decker was arrested.

*[margin note: 100% sure "go through with it"]*

*[margin note: arrested]*

. . . Attempted murder requires the specific intent to kill and the commission of a direct but ineffectual act toward accomplishing the intended killing. The uncontradicted evidence that Decker harbored the specific intent to kill his sister (and, if necessary, her friend Hermine) was overwhelming. Decker expressed to both Wafer and Holston his desire to have Donna killed. He researched how to find a hired assassin. He spent months accumulating cash in small denominations to provide the hired assassin with a downpayment and had also worked out a method by which to pay the balance. He knew the layout of his sister's condominium and how one might enter it surreptitiously. He had tested the level of surveillance in the vicinity of her home and determined it was "not really that sharp." He chronicled his sister's daily routine at both her home and her office. He offered Holston recommendations on how his sister should be killed and what materials would be necessary. And, at both meetings with Holston, he insisted that Hermine, if she were present, be killed as well, so as to prevent her from being a witness.

*[margin note: attempted murder 2 elements]*

The controversy in this case, as the parties readily concede, is whether there was also a direct but ineffectual act toward accomplishing the intended killings. For an attempt, the overt act must go beyond mere preparation and show that the killer is putting his or her plan into action; it need not be the last proximate or ultimate step toward

*[margin note: question was there a direct but ineffectual act towards accomplishing the intended killings?]*

commission of the crime or crimes, nor need it satisfy any element of the crime. However, as we have explained, "[b]etween preparation for the attempt and the attempt itself, there is a wide difference. The preparation consists in devising or arranging the means or measures necessary for the commission of the offense; the attempt is the direct movement toward the commission after the preparations are made." People v. Murray, 14 Cal. 159, 159 (1859).

As simple as it is to state the terminology for the law of attempt, it is not always clear in practice how to apply it. . . . Although a definitive test has proved elusive, we have long recognized that "whenever the design of a person to commit crime is clearly shown, slight acts in furtherance of the design will constitute an attempt." People v. Anderson, 1 Cal.2d 687, 690, 37 P.2d 67, 68 (1934). Viewing the entirety of Decker's conduct in light of his clearly expressed intent, we find sufficient evidence under the slight-acts rule to hold him to answer to the charges of attempted murder.

Decker's plan was to get rid of his sister so that he could recover money that she owed him. He was concerned, however, that he would be considered an obvious suspect in her murder, so he sought out someone else to carry out his plan. To that end, he conducted research into the underworld of professional killers, he budgeted to pay for those services, he evaluated how and where the murder should be done, he tested the level of security around his sister's condominium, and he considered the possibility that there might be a witness and what should be done in that event. Once he met Detective Holston, who he believed was a professional assassin, they agreed Holston would kill Donna and (if necessary) her friend Hermine, they agreed on a price, and they agreed it would be done within the week. Decker provided Holston with all of the necessary information concerning his sister, her home and office, and her habits and demeanor. He also gave Holston the agreed-on downpayment of $5,000 cash. Before he did, Holston warned him, "I want you to know, once I leave here, it's done. So, you sure you want to go through with it?" Decker replied, "I am absolutely, positively, 100 percent sure, that I want to go through with it. I've never been so sure of anything in my entire life."

Accordingly, at the time Decker handed Holston the downpayment on the murder, Decker's intention was clear. It was equally clear that he was "actually putting his plan into action." People v. Dillon, 34 Cal. 3d 441, 453, 668 P.2d 697, 702 (1983). Decker had secured an agreement with Holston to murder Donna (and, if necessary, her friend Hermine); had provided Holston with all the information necessary to commit the crimes; had given Holston the $5,000 downpayment; and had understood that "it's done" once Holston left with the money. These facts would lead a reasonable person to "believe a crime is about to be consummated absent an intervening force"—and thus that "the attempt is underway." Id. at 455, 668 P.2d at 703. Indeed, as Justice Epstein noted for the Court of Appeal, "[t]here was nothing more for Decker to do to bring about the murder of his sister." Although Decker did not himself point a gun at his sister, he did aim at her an armed professional who had agreed to commit the murder.

As contrary authority, Decker relies on *Adami,* which affirmed the dismissal of an attempted murder charge on similar facts, and relies also on the small number of out-of-state majority and minority opinions that have followed *Adami.* [Citing cases from Alaska, Idaho, and South Dakota.] In *Adami,* the defendant sought to have his wife killed because she had stolen money from him. He agreed on a price with an undercover police agent posing as an assassin and supplied the agent with a photograph of the victim, a description of the victim and her residence and vehicles, and other pertinent information. The defendant gave the police agent $500 as a downpayment and announced he was not going to change his mind. *Adami* declared that these acts "consisted solely of solicitation or mere preparation" and concluded, in accordance with the "weight of authority," that "solicitation alone is not an attempt."

We perceive several flaws in *Adami's* analysis.

First, the opinion makes no mention of the slight-acts rule, which has long been the rule for attempted crimes in California. Indeed, *Adami*'s progeny make no pretense of reconciling their analysis with the slight-acts rule and instead explicitly reject it. . . . These cases thus conflict with well-established California law and with the law concerning attempted crimes in most jurisdictions.

Decker argues that the slight-acts rule should not be applied to the crime of attempted murder, but his argument lacks legal or logical support. Our adoption of the slight-acts rule in *People v. Anderson* was supported by a citation to Stokes v. State, 92 Miss. 415, 46 So. 627 (1908), which is "[o]ne of the leading cases in the United States on attempt to commit a crime" Duke v. State, 340 So.2d 727, 729 (Miss. 1976), and which (like the present case) involved a defendant who hired another to perform a murder. The cases on which Decker relies thus conflict not only with California law, but also with the "fairly general agreement . . . that slight acts are enough when the intent to murder is clearly shown." Annot., What Constitutes Attempted Murder 54 A.L.R. 3d 612, 617–18 (1974). Indeed, where (as here) the crime involves concerted action—and hence a greater likelihood that the criminal objective will be accomplished—there is a *greater* urgency for intervention by the state at an *earlier* stage in the course of that conduct. Had Decker struck an agreement with and paid earnest money to a real hired killer, he could have been prosecuted for conspiracy to commit murder, which is punishable to the same extent as the completed crime of first degree murder. Because of the fortuity that Decker's hired killer was actually an undercover detective, Decker faces the much less serious charge of attempted murder. Neither Decker nor the dissent has offered any reason for us create an exception to the slight-acts rule for attempted murder, especially in *Stokes*'s classic formulation where the attempt involves concerted action with others, merely so that Decker's maximum potential punishment may be further reduced.

Second, *Adami* has misconceived the issue under these circumstances to be "whether the solicitation itself was sufficient to establish probable cause to believe that defendant attempted the murder." (*Adami*, 36 Cal.App.3d at 455, 111 Cal.Rptr. at 545. Decker similarly expends considerable effort to convince us that "solicitation of another to commit a crime is an attempt to commit that crime if, but only if, it takes the form of urging the other to join with the solicitor in perpetrating that offense, not at some future time or distant place, but here and now, and the crime is such that it cannot be committed by one without the cooperation and submission of another." Rollin Perkins, Criminal Law 519 (1957). But a solicitation requires only that a person invite another to commit or join in an enumerated crime (including murder) with the intent that the crime be committed. The solicitation is complete once the request is made and is punishable "irrespective of the reaction of the person solicited." In re Ryan N., 92 Cal.App.4th 1359, 1377, 112 Cal.Rptr.2d 620, 635 (2001). In this case, the solicitation was complete early in Decker's first conversation with Holston, when he asked Holston to kill Donna. But the People do not contend that this request was sufficient to prosecute Decker for attempted murder. They argue instead that the solicitation, in combination with Decker's subsequent conduct, revealed his plan to have Holston murder Donna (and, if necessary, her friend Hermine) and that Decker put this plan into operation no later than the point at which he completed the agreement with Holston, finalized the details surrounding the murders, and paid Holston $5,000 in earnest money.

The issue, then, is not whether "solicitation alone" is sufficient to establish an attempt (*Adami*, 36 Cal.App.3d at 457, 111 Cal.Rptr. at 547, but whether a solicitation to commit murder, combined with a completed agreement to hire a professional killer and the making of a downpayment under that agreement, can establish probable cause to believe Decker attempted to murder these victims. A substantial number of our sister states have held that it can. [Citations to cases from nine states, the Second Circuit, and the Court of Military Appeals omitted.] Additional jurisdictions have held that a solicitation to murder, in combination with a completed agreement to hire a professional killer and further conduct implementing the agreement, can similarly constitute an attempted murder. [Citations to cases from two states omitted.] We find these authorities persuasive.

Third, *Adami* mistakenly assumes that there can be no overlap between the evidence that would tend to prove solicitation to murder and that which would tend to prove attempted murder. Indeed, Decker asserts that these are "mutually exclusive crimes." But it could not be plainer, as Chief Justice Holmes put it, that while "preparation is not an attempt," nonetheless "*some* preparations may amount to an attempt." Commonwealth v. Peaslee, 177 Mass. 267, 272, 59 N.E. 55, 56 (1901) (italics added). Conduct that qualifies as mere preparation and conduct that qualifies as a direct but ineffectual act toward commission of the crime exist on a continuum, "since all acts leading up to the ultimate consummation of a crime are by their very nature preparatory." State v. Sunzar, 331 N.J.Super. 248, 254, 751 A.2d 627, 630 (Law Div.1999). The difference between them "is a question of degree." *Peaslee*, 177 Mass. at 272, 59 N.E. at 56. There is thus no error in resting a finding of attempted murder in part on evidence that *also* tends to establish solicitation to commit murder and vice versa. After all, even under Decker's analysis, evidence of a solicitation to commit murder can tend to support a finding of attempted murder if the defendant then "provides the hit man the instrument or other means to procure the death." Decker offers no principled basis for a different result when the hit man already has a weapon and the defendant instead begins payment under the contract to kill.

Fourth, we reject the contention, endorsed by Decker and by *Adami's* progeny, that there is "no persuasive reason" why a solicitation to commit murder "should be treated differently under the law merely because part of the agreed upon fee has passed hands. There is no greater proximity, no significantly greater likelihood of consummation, and no act of a nature other than incitement or preparation inherent in the solicitation itself." State v. Otto, 102 Idaho 250, 254, 629 P.2d 646, 650 (1981). As the People point out, though, a downpayment on a contract to murder serves the same purpose as a downpayment on any other type of contract. It evidences the solicitor's "seriousness of purpose" and makes the object of the contract "closer to fruition." State v. Molasky, 765 S.W.2d 597, 602 (Mo.1989). It blinks reality to equate the threat posed by an individual who has merely invited another, perhaps unsuccessfully, to commit murder with the threat posed by an individual who has already reached an agreement with a hired killer to commit murder, finalized the plans, and made the downpayment under the contract to kill. But for Holston's status as an undercover detective, it is likely that Decker's conduct would have resulted in the murder of these victims. Where, as here, the defendant's intent is unmistakable, "the courts should not destroy the practical and common-sense administration of the law with subtleties as to what constitutes preparation and what constitutes an act done toward the commission of a crime." People v. Memro, 38 Cal.3d 658, 698, 700 P.2d 446, 474 (1985).

The purpose of requiring an overt act is that until such act occurs, one is uncertain whether the intended design will be carried out. When, by reason of the defendant's conduct, the situation is "without any equivocality," and it appears the design will be carried out if not interrupted, the defendant's conduct satisfies the test for an overt act. People v. Miller, 2 Cal.2d 527, 532, 42 P.2d 308, 310 (1935). Here, the record supported at least a strong suspicion that Decker's intent to have his sister (and, if necessary, her friend) murdered was unambiguous and that he had commenced the commission of the crime by doing all that he needed to do to accomplish the murders.

In finding the record sufficient to hold Decker to answer to the charges of attempted murder here, we do not decide whether an agreement to kill followed by a downpayment is *always* sufficient to support a charge of attempted murder. Whether acts done in contemplation of the commission of a crime are merely preparatory or whether they are instead sufficiently close to the consummation of the crime is a question of degree and depends upon the facts and circumstances of a particular case. A different situation may exist, for example, when the assassin has been hired and paid but the victims have not yet been identified. In this case, however, Decker had effectively done all that he needed to do to ensure that Donna and her friend be executed. Accordingly, he should have been held to answer to the charges of attempted murder. We disapprove *Adami* to the extent it is inconsistent with this opinion. . . .

The judgment of the Court of Appeal is affirmed.

We Concur: GEORGE, C.J., KENNARD, CHIN, MORENO and CORRIGAN, JJ.

■ Dissenting Opinion by WERDEGAR, J.

My colleagues hold that defendant's conduct in soliciting the murder of his sister, reaching an agreement with a hired assassin to do the killing, and making a downpayment under the agreement establishes probable cause to believe defendant himself attempted the murder. I respectfully dissent. "An attempt to commit a crime consists of two elements: a specific intent to commit the crime, and a direct but ineffectual act done toward its commission." Penal Code § 21a. Defendant's conduct in this case does not include "a direct but ineffectual act" done toward the murder's commission. Accordingly, he cannot be guilty of attempted murder.

As we have long recognized, the required act for an attempt under California law must be "directed towards immediate consummation," People v. Dillon, 34 Cal.3d 441, 454, 668 P.2d 697, 703 (1983), of the crime attempted. As the majority details, defendant's conduct included numerous *indirect* acts toward accomplishing the murder of his sister: he sought the services of a hired assassin; he located a person (actually an undercover police detective) he thought would act as such; he furnished the supposed assassin with a description of his sister, her home, her car and her workplace, as well as specific information concerning her daily habits; he discussed how the murder would be done and how and when he would pay for the work, agreeing to furnish $5,000 in cash as a downpayment; and, finally, just before he was arrested, he stated he was "absolutely, positively, 100 percent sure, that I want to go through with it" and urged the supposed assassin to do it "as fast as you can."

I agree with the majority that as evidence defendant harbored the specific intent to kill his sister, these facts are overwhelming. None of them, however, constitutes a *direct* but ineffectual act done toward the murder's commission. As the majority states, defendant "did not himself point a gun at his sister"; neither did he otherwise directly menace her. Instead, he relied on the person he thought had agreed to commit the murder to do the actual deed.[1] The direct object of defendant's preparatory acts was the person he sought to engage as his agent—not the ultimate, intended victim of the scheme.

We previously have stated that for attempt, it must be "clear from a suspect's acts what *he* intends to do. . . ." *Dillon*, 34 Cal.3d at 455, 668 P.2d at 703 (italics added). In this case, what defendant intended to do was have his sister killed *by someone else*. Defendant's own conduct did not include even "slight" acts toward actual commission of the murder. That he hired another, supplied him with information, and paid him a downpayment only highlights his intention not to perform the act himself.

The California cases the majority purports to rely on generally involve single actors, i.e., defendants who acted directly on their victims. These cases simply confirm that for attempt a defendant must have

---

[1] Although the majority asserts defendant "did aim at [his sister] an armed professional who had agreed to commit the murder," the armed professional referred to (i.e., the detective) only *pretended* to agree so that in fact there was no agreement, though defendant thought there was. This absence of actual agreement presumably is why the case was not prosecuted as a conspiracy. . . .

committed a direct act toward commission of the crime. Defendant here committed no direct act toward commission of the murder, since his scheme interposed a third party between himself and his intended victim, and the third party never acted. The majority goes astray in applying to this solicitation-of-murder case, where action by another person was required to effectuate (or attempt) the intended killing, principles applicable when an offense is intended and attempted by a single individual.

Although defendant's conduct went beyond the minimum required for solicitation, for purposes of attempt law his arrangements constitute mere preparation. Reprehensible as they were, his acts "did not amount to any more than the mere arrangement of the proposed measures for [the] accomplishment" of the crime. People v. Adami, 36 Cal.App.3d at 457–58, 111 Cal.Rptr. 544, 547 (1973). This is because, as a logical matter, they did no more than "leave the intended assailant only in the condition to commence the first direct act toward consummation of the defendant's design." Id. at 458, 111 Cal.Rptr. at 547. To do all one can to motivate and encourage another to accomplish a killing—even to make a downpayment on a contract to kill—while blameworthy and punishable, is neither logically nor legally equivalent to attempting the killing oneself. In concluding to the contrary, the majority blurs the distinction between preparation and perpetration the Legislature intended by requiring that an attempt include a direct act. The majority's supportive reasoning likewise conflates the two separate elements of attempt, specific intent and direct act: "Viewing the entirety of [defendant's] conduct *in light of his clearly expressed intent,* we find sufficient evidence under the slight-acts rule to hold him to answer to the charges of attempted murder." As a court, we are not authorized to ignore the statutory requirements.

The majority's criticisms of *Adami* are unpersuasive. The majority faults *Adami* for not mentioning the slight acts rule, but since the *Adami* court concluded no "appreciable fragment of the crime charged was accomplished," the rule had no application. Nor, contrary to the majority's account, did *Adami* assume that evidence of solicitation cannot also be evidence of attempt. *Adami* simply held that hiring a murderer, planning the murder, and making a downpayment logically constitute "solicitation or mere preparation," not attempted murder.

Confronted with statutory language and judicial precedent contrary to its conclusion, the majority relies on out-of-state cases. Several of these interpret attempt statutes distinguishable from our own. Others involve more than a completed agreement with a hired killer, including a direct act toward the victim. The remaining cases are in my view mistaken for the same reason the majority is mistaken: they implicitly allow that a defendant may be guilty of attempt when no direct act toward the commission of the crime has been done. Courts in some other jurisdictions have, as the majority fails to acknowledge, maintained the distinction between preparation and attempt in cases similar to this.

Had the supposed assassin hired to kill defendant's sister actually attempted to kill her, defendant would be punishable under Penal Code section 31 as a principal in the offense, either as an aider and abettor or as a coconspirator. But in this case, neither defendant nor the supposed assassin took a direct act toward commission of the offense. Defendant's conduct was confined to encouraging and enabling his intended agent to kill (or attempt to kill), but the detective with whom he dealt took no such action. There was no attempt.

For the foregoing reasons, I dissent.

## NOTES ON THE RELATION OF ATTEMPT TO SOLICITATION, COMPLICITY, AND CONSPIRACY

### 1.  SOLICITATION AS AN INDEPENDENT OFFENSE

A recurring challenge for the common law concerned persons who hired others to commit homicide, only to discover that the supposed assassins were undercover police. At one time, courts held that such conduct could not constitute attempt because the person solicited to commit the offense had no intention of going through with it. People v. Adami, 36 Cal.App.3d 452, 111 Cal.Rptr. 544 (1973), is illustrative of many of the older decisions. The difficulty of securing attempt convictions in such situations led to the fairly widespread enactment of an independent offense of criminal solicitation. The prototype is § 5.02 of the Model Penal Code:

*no attempt*

*Criminal solicitation*

*§5.02 MPC*

> A person is guilty of solicitation to commit a crime if with the purpose of promoting or facilitating its commission he commands, encourages or requests another to engage in specific conduct which would constitute such crime or an attempt to commit such crime. . . .

*Solicitation as independent offense*

Such provisions reflect the view that purposeful solicitation of criminal conduct by another warrants preventive intervention by the police and is sufficiently indicative of criminality to support penal sanctions. Recognizing solicitation as an independent offense renders immaterial the fact that the person solicited may not actually intend to commit the crime. The guilt or innocence of the person solicited has no bearing on the liability of the initiating party.[a]

Should there be an independent offense of criminal solicitation? If so, is the Model Code definition successful? Does every solicitation involve sufficient conduct to justify criminal liability?[b]

### 2.  QUESTIONS AND COMMENTS ON *PEOPLE V. SUPERIOR COURT*

The Model Penal Code punishes attempt and solicitation as crimes of the same grade, and they cannot be the basis for cumulative punishment. See MPC § 5.05. Under that structure, the creation of an independent offense of solicitation completely obviates the question whether hiring an undercover agent to commit murder can constitute criminal attempt. In most jurisdictions, however, attempt and solicitation are graded differently, with solicitation often a much less serious offense. In California, for example, attempt to commit willful, deliberate and premeditated murder can result

---

[a]  For a more detailed exposition of this view, along with a useful review of the common law history of criminal solicitation, see Herbert Wechsler, William Kenneth Jones & Harold L. Korn, The Treatment of Inchoate Crimes in the Model Penal Code of the American Law Institute: Attempt, Solicitation, and Conspiracy, Part I, 61 Colum. L. Rev. 571, 621–28 (1961).

[b]  For a discussion of some of these issues and an argument that solicitation should be limited to cases where the underlying offense is serious, see Note, Reforming the Law of Inchoate Crimes, 59 Va. L. Rev. 1235, 1260–68 (1973).

imprisonment for no less than 15 years and a maximum of life. See Cal. Penal Code § 664(f). Solicitation to commit murder, however, triggers a term of years that is capped at nine. See Cal. Penal Code § 653f.

This disparity led prosecutors to challenge the rule of *Adami*, and ultimately to the decision in *People v. Superior Court*. Did the California Supreme Court get the right answer? Is the dissent persuasive? Note that the majority appears to relax the preparation-attempt standard in favor of its "slight-acts rule" in cases where intent is clear. Is this approach defensible?

## 3. RELATION OF ATTEMPT AND COMPLICITY

Multi-party crimes are managed by the criminal law in a number of different ways, each of which intersects with the law of attempt. Solicitation, addressed in the preceding notes, is one of them. Another is the law of conspiracy, which is addressed in the next note. The present note explores the relationship between accomplice liability—sometimes referred to as complicity—and the crime of attempt. Note first the vocabulary: the primary actor—the person whose job it is to commit the crime—is usually called the "principal"; secondary actors—the helpers—are called "aiders and abettors" or "accomplices."

### *(i) Requirement That Crime Be Committed by Principal*

Note the observation in the last substantive paragraph of the dissent in *People v. Superior Court* that Decker would have been guilty of murder (or attempted murder) had the supposed assassin actually killed either of the two women (or attempted to do so). This statement describes conventional complicity principles, under which secondary parties who aid primary actors in the commission of a crime are guilty of the offense committed by the primary actor if they act with a purpose to bring that crime about. The implication of the last paragraph of the dissent is that there is no liability as an accomplice if the primary actor does not commit the object offense.

This is the usual rule. Accomplice liability is based on commission of an offense by the primary actor. Secondary parties are not liable as accomplices unless the primary actor commits the object crime or attempts to commit it.[c] The Model Penal Code adheres to this position. See ALI, Model Penal Code and Commentaries, § 2.06, p. 314 n.46 (1985):

> Section 2.06(3) of the Model Code is predicated . . . on the actual commission of the offense by the person aided. Assuming the requisite culpability, one who aids, attempts to aid, or agrees to aid, is thus liable under this section only if the principal actor actually commits an offense.

---

[c] For example, the Court said in Dusenbery v. Commonwealth, 220 Va. 770, 771–72, 263 S.E.2d 392, 393 (1980), that "by definition, there can be no accessory without a principal. Although conviction of a principal in the first degree is not a condition precedent to conviction of an accessory, 'before the accessory to a crime can be convicted . . . , it must be shown that the crime has been committed by the principal.' Snyder v. Commonwealth, 202 Va. 1009, 1017, 121 S.E.2d 452, 458 (1961)." See also State v. Montanez, 277 Conn. 735, 756, 894 A.2d 928, 941 (2006) ("[A]nother person's commission of an offense is a condition precedent to the imposition of accessorial liability."); United States v. Ruffin, 613 F.2d 408, 412 (2d Cir. 1979) ("It is hornbook law that a defendant charged with aiding and abetting the commission of a crime by another cannot be convicted in the absence of proof that the crime was actually committed.").

It therefore follows under ordinary principles of accomplice liability that Decker could be convicted as an accomplice only if the person he solicited to kill his sister actually killed her or attempted to do so. Since Holston did not kill Decker's sister and had no intention of doing so, the law of complicity appears to provide no basis for punishing Decker.

### (ii)  Principal Does Not Commit Offense

The Model Penal Code proposes a logical and creative solution for people like Decker—it treats him as though he was attempting to commit the object crime. Section 5.01(3) of the Code provides:

> (3) Conduct Designed to Aid Another in Commission of a Crime. A person who engages in conduct designed to aid another to commit a crime which would establish his complicity under Section 2.06 if the crime were committed by such other person, is guilty of an attempt to commit the crime, although the crime is not committed or attempted by such other person.

*[handwritten margin note: §5.01(3) Aid in commission = attempt]*

Thus Decker would be guilty of attempted murder under the Model Penal Code because he plainly engaged in sufficient conduct to have been an accomplice had the purported assassin completed his task. This solution, which has been copied in a number of legislative revisions that were inspired by the Model Code,[d] fills the gap that concerned the California Supreme Court in *People v. Superior Court.*

### (iii)  Principal Commits Actus Reus but Lacks Mens Rea

Section 5.01(3) of the Model Code would also permit conviction as an accomplice in a case where the principal engaged in the actus reus of the offense but lacked the mens rea. This was the situation in *Regina v. Cogan and Leak,* [1976] 1 Q.B. 217:

> [On July 10, 1974] Leak came home at about 6 p.m. with Cogan. Both had been drinking. Leak told his wife Cogan wanted to have sexual intercourse with her and that he, Leak, was going to see she did. She was frightened of him and what he might do. . . . He made her go upstairs where he took her clothes off and lowered her on to a bed. Cogan then came into the room. Leak asked him twice whether he wanted sexual intercourse with her. On both occasions he said he did not. Leak then had sexual intercourse with her in the presence of Cogan. When he had finished, Leak again asked Cogan if he wanted sexual intercourse with his wife. This time Cogan said he did. He asked Leak to leave the room but he refused to do so. Cogan then had sexual intercourse with Mrs. Leak. Her husband watched. While all this was going on for most of the time, if not all, Mrs. Leak was sobbing. She did not struggle while Cogan was on top of her but she did try to turn away from him. When he had finished, he left the room. Leak then had intercourse with her again and behaved in a revolting fashion to her. When he had finished he joined Cogan and the pair of them left the house to renew their drinking. Mrs. Leak dressed. She went to a neighbour's house and then to the police.

---

d   See ALI, Model Penal Code and Commentaries § 5.01, p. 356 n.266 (1985), which list 13 states with comparable provisions.

The jury found that Cogan believed, albeit unreasonably, that Leak's wife had consented to the sexual intercourse. His rape conviction was therefore quashed on the ground that he lacked the required mens rea.[e] The Court of Appeal nonetheless upheld Leak's conviction for aiding and abetting a rape:

> [T]he wife had been raped. Cogan had had sexual intercourse with her without her consent. The fact that Cogan was innocent of rape because he believed that she was consenting does not affect the position that she was raped.
>
> Her ravishment had come about because Leak had wanted it to happen and had taken action to see that it did by persuading Cogan to use his body as the instrument for the necessary physical act. In the language of the law the act of sexual intercourse without the wife's consent was the actus reus: it had been procured by Leak who had the appropriate mens rea, namely, his intention that Cogan should have sexual intercourse with her without her consent. In our judgment it is irrelevant that the man whom Leak had procured to do the physical act himself did not intend to have sexual intercourse with the wife without her consent.

As stated above, the result in *Cogan and Leak* is unusual—normally guilt of the principal is a prerequisite to one's guilt as an accessory.[f] The Model Penal Code provides the different solution in such a case of convicting the accomplice for an attempt to commit the object offense. Note that the Model Code grades attempts at the same level as the completed offense. If attempts are graded at a lesser level, as will be the case in most jurisdictions, would § 5.01(3) be the best approach to Leak's liability for rape? Or should he be convicted of the completed offense in such a jurisdiction?

### *(iv) Principal Commits Offense but Aid Ineffective*

Suppose the principal commits the object offense and the purported accessory tries to render aid but fails because the aid was unnecessary, ineffective, or otherwise had no impact on the behavior of the primary actor. The Model Penal Code solution to this scenario is to treat the accomplice as though the aid had been effective. See § 2.06(3)(a)(ii): "A person is an accomplice of another person in the commission of an offense if . . . with the purpose of promoting or facilitating the commission of the offense, he . . . aids or agrees or *attempts to aid* such other person in planning or committing it." (Emphasis added.) This is consistent with the MPC position that

[e] Regina v. Morgan, [1976] A.C. 182, was the source of Cogan's mens rea defense. The issue raised by *Morgan* is addressed in Chapter IX, Section I-B. For a detailed criticism of the *Morgan* result and a short discussion of *Cogan and Leak*, see Dolly F. Alexander, Twenty Years of *Morgan*: A Criticism of the Subjectivist View of Mens Rea and Rape in Great Britain, 7 Pace Int'l L. Rev. 207 (1995). Parliament has since codified a new definition of rape, which rejects the mens rea level set by *Morgan*. Under the new provision, a mistake as to the victim's consent is exculpatory only if it is "reasonable." The statute also provides that, in deciding whether such a mistake is reasonable, the factfinder must take account of "all the circumstances, including any steps" taken by the defendant to ascertain whether the victim consented. See Sexual Offenses Act, 2003, c. 42, § 1.

[f] See footnote c, supra. There is support in the literature for the *Cogan and Leak* result. See, e.g., J. C. Smith & Brian Hogan, Criminal Law 140 (5th ed. 1983) ("The true principle . . . is that where the principal has caused an actus reus, the liability of each of the secondary parties should be assessed according to his own mens rea."). The successor volume to this treatise asserts that this position "seems the best available," but has backed away from the assertion that it is descriptive of the prevailing caselaw. See David Ormerod, Smith and Hogan, Criminal Law 206 (11th ed. 2005).

an attempt should be graded at the same level as the completed offense that was its object. Would the Model Code solution on this issue be appropriate in a jurisdiction that punished attempts at a lower level than the completed offense? How should that situation be handled?

## 4. RELATION OF ATTEMPT AND CONSPIRACY

One of the principal functions of the law of conspiracy is to punish anticipatory or inchoate behavior. In this respect, conspiracy supplements attempt. The two offenses are closely parallel. Both confront a similar range of problems in assigning criminal liability for uncompleted conduct.

One major difference must be emphasized. The crime of attempt occurs at some point between conception and consummation. The attempt merges into the completed offense upon commission of the object offense, with the result that one can be guilty of a crime or an attempt to commit it but not both. This is not ordinarily the case with conspiracy. Traditionally, one can be convicted of *both* a conspiracy to commit an offense *and* the commission of that offense. The Model Penal Code disagrees with this result. See §§ 1.07(1)(b), 5.05(3). But the federal government and most states do not follow the MPC in this respect.[g]

### *(i) The Necessity and Sufficiency of Agreement*

The traditional definition of conspiracy is an agreement between two or more persons to do an unlawful act or to do a lawful act by unlawful means. Modern formulations restrict the offense to agreement to do an act which is itself a crime. The objective need not be achieved for the offense to be made out. The essence of conspiracy is the agreement itself.

At common law, no additional conduct was needed. Many statutes, however, also require that there be an overt act in furtherance of the conspiracy. Under the prevailing view, an act done by any one of the conspirators suffices for all. The significance of the overt-act requirement, however, may well be doubted. Unlike the law of attempt, the law of conspiracy has never elaborated doctrinal tests to determine what kind of act suffices. Instead, the courts have held that virtually any act committed by a conspirator in furtherance of the conspiracy will do. The result is that the independent requirement of an overt act, even where imposed, tends not to be very important. The actus reus of the offense is essentially the act of agreement.

By focusing on the formation of an agreement, the law of conspiracy allows intervention and punishment at a very early stage of misconduct. Indeed, one justification for the offense of conspiracy is that it punishes some instances of inchoate misconduct that could not be reached under the law of attempt. The question therefore arises: Is the act of agreeing to commit a

---

[g] The rationale for this outcome is considered in Note 4(ii) below as well as in Chapter VI. The Model Penal Code grades attempt and conspiracy at the same level as the object offenses. See § 5.05(1). This provision is unusual. Normally attempt is graded as some fraction of the offense attempted, whereas the generic conspiracy offense is often graded at a fixed level irrespective of the object offenses. See, e.g., 18 U.S.C. § 371 (five-year maximum for conspiracy to commit a felony). There are, not surprisingly, multiple exceptions to these generalizations. Recall, for example, the court's observation in *People v. Superior Court* that "[h]ad Decker struck an agreement with and paid earnest money to a real hired killer, he could have been prosecuted for conspiracy to commit murder, which is punishable to the same extent as the completed crime of first degree murder."

crime, standing alone or in connection with an overt act in furtherance of the agreement, a sufficient basis in conduct to support penal liability? Are the underlying concerns of the act requirement adequately protected by this rule?

The drafters of the Model Penal Code defended criminal liability based on an agreement in the following terms:

> The act of agreeing with another to commit a crime, like the act of soliciting, is concrete and unambiguous; it does not present the infinite degrees and variations possible in the general category of attempts. The danger that truly equivocal behavior may be misinterpreted as preparation to commit a crime is minimized; purpose must be relatively firm before the commitment involved in agreement is assumed. . . .
>
> In the course of preparation to commit a crime, the act of combining with another is significant both psychologically and practically, the former because it crosses a clear threshold in arousing expectations, the latter because it increases the likelihood that the offense will be committed. Sharing lends fortitude to purpose. The actor knows, moreover, that the future is no longer governed by his will alone; others may complete what he has had a hand in starting, even if he has a change of heart.

ALI, Model Penal Code and Commentaries § 5.03, p. 388 (1985).[h] A few American jurisdictions have supplemented the requirement of an overt act in conspiracy by analogy to the law of attempt. In Maine, Ohio, and Washington, conspiracy statutes explicitly require a "substantial step" in furtherance of the conspiracy.[i]

### *(ii) Bilateral or Unilateral Agreement*

Both the majority and the dissent in *People v. Superior Court* observe that Decker would have been guilty of a conspiracy to commit murder if he and the putative assassin had actually consummated an agreement to kill Decker's sister and her friend. Decker may have thought he had an agreement, but the absence of a true meeting of the minds would have prevented prosecution for conspiracy in California as it would have in many other states.

Under traditional conspiracy law, it takes two to tango. The definition of conspiracy as an agreement between two or more persons has led to a requirement of bilateralism.[j] Some courts have disagreed with this

---

[h] For criticism of this position, see Phillip E. Johnson, The Unnecessary Crime of Conspiracy, 61 Calif.L.Rev. 1137, 1161–64 (1973). Johnson concludes that "insofar as conspiracy adds anything to [modern] attempt provisions . . . , it adds only overly broad criminal liability. . . . [T]he use of an independent crime of conspiracy to punish inchoate crimes turns out to be unnecessary."

[i] 17–A Me.Rev.Stat.Ann. § 151(4); Ohio Rev.Code § 2923.01; Rev.Code Wash.Ann. § 9A.28.040. The Maine provision goes on to define "substantial step" in terms strongly reminiscent of the Model Penal Code standard for distinguishing preparation from attempt. Under Maine law, there must be "conduct which, under the circumstances in which it occurs, is strongly corroborative of the firmness of the actor's intent to complete commission of the crime."

[j] See, e.g., Regle v. Maryland, 9 Md.App. 346, 351, 264 A.2d 119, 122 (1970) ("[I]t must be shown that at least two persons had a meeting of the minds—a unity of design and purpose—to have an agreement.").

approach,[k] as does the Model Penal Code.[l] The Model Code position is often called the "unilateral" view of conspiracy. Under this view, Decker could be convicted of conspiracy to murder his sister and her friend because he "unilaterally" believed that he had reached an agreement with a person who would undertake the killing. It would not matter that the assassin he was attempting to hire had no intention of agreeing to the killings.

The modern trend is to follow the Model Code. Yet the unilateral approach is not without its critics. For a sustained and elaborate rebuttal of the Model Code solution, see Paul Marcus, Prosecution and Defense of Criminal Conspiracy Cases, pp. 2–9 to 14 (1978). Marcus argues that the requirement of bilateralism reflects the essential rationale for punishing conspiracy in the first place:

> The strongest proponents of conspiracy law argue that the reason the inchoate conspiracy offense is legitimate, and the reason the conspiracy offense can be punished wholly apart from the substantive offense, is that conspirators acting together are dangerous. Group activities, it is said, are more likely to lead to serious anti-social acts than the acts of a single criminal. Reasonable people may disagree on such a rationale, but it is the rationale which has been accepted by the courts and commentators. With the unilateral approach, however, this grave risk will likely be lessened considerably, or actually wholly eliminated. Under such circumstances the rationale for the crime is destroyed, for there is no group danger.

Is this right? Does the "special danger of group criminality" rationale for the inchoate offense of conspiracy necessarily require bilateral agreement? Or could the unilateral approach be viewed as also consistent with that rationale? Recall that as a general matter one can be convicted of both a conspiracy and the offense that is its object. What is the justification for this result if the unilateral approach is taken?

### *(iii) Mens Rea for Conspiracy*

The mens rea of the inchoate offense of conspiracy parallels that of attempt. Both are, in the words of the common law, specific-intent offenses. There is the additional requirement for conspiracy that there must be an intent to agree, but both offenses require an intent to accomplish an objective that the law has designated as a crime. As with attempt, the actor must have *at least* the level of culpability required by the object offense. And again as with attempt, the more difficult issue is whether conspiracy requires *additional* mens-rea elements beyond that of the underlying offense.

The only real issue in this area is whether the inchoate offense of conspiracy imposes special mens-rea requirements with respect to the attendant circumstances of an actor's conduct. Recall the statutory rape and burglary examples in Note 4 of the Notes on the Mens Rea of Attempt in Section 2 of this Chapter. Assume an age of consent of 16 and a conspiracy

---

[k] See, e.g., State v. St. Christopher, 305 Minn. 226, 232 N.W.2d 798 (1975).

[l] Section 5.03 of the Model Code does not explicitly say that it is taking a "unilateral" view of the agreement, but the commentary affirms that the words "agrees with such other person" are meant to be so interpreted. See ALI, Model Penal Code and Commentaries § 5.03, pp. 398–402 (1985).

to engage in sex with an identified victim who is actually 15 but reasonably believed to be 17. Should that belief be a defense to a conspiracy charge when it would not be for the completed offense?

The Model Penal Code answer for the crime of attempt suggests a similar answer here. The Code commentary on conspiracy recognizes the parallel, but concludes that the issue is best "left . . . to interpretation in the context in which . . . [it] is presented."[m] The Supreme Court held in United States v. Feola, 420 U.S. 671 (1975), that where a substantive offense requires no mens rea with respect to facts giving rise to federal jurisdiction, conspiracy to commit that offense also requires no mens rea with respect to such facts. It may be that this result is explained by the peculiarities of jurisdictional elements in federal crimes, but the principle seems sound as a generalization. A contrary answer is suggested by Judge Learned Hand's famous comment in United States v. Crimmins, 123 F.2d 271, 273 (2d Cir. 1941):

> While one may, for instance, be guilty of running past a traffic light of whose existence one is ignorant, one cannot be guilty of conspiring to run past such a light, for one cannot agree to run past a light unless one supposes that there is a light to run past.

Is there enough force to Judge Hand's observation to warrant distinguishing conspiracy from attempt on this issue?

## 5. CONCLUDING HYPOTHETICALS

A good way to test understanding of the materials in this Section is to consider the following problems.[n] For each situation, assume that *A* initiated the criminal endeavor by suggesting to *B* that they cooperate in the burglary of a store. *B,* who is related to the store owner, fakes acquiescence in order to trap *A,* and the following variations occur.

> (i) *A* and *B* go to the store at midnight. *A* helps *B* enter the store and waits outside for *B* to hand out the loot. As B has arranged, the police intervene, and *A* is arrested.
>
> (ii) *A* and *B* go to the store at midnight. *A* brings to the store various implements designed to facilitate surreptitious entry. *A* assists *B* to use these implements to pick the lock of the store's back door. Before either *A* or *B* gain entry to the store, the police intervene, and *A* is arrested.
>
> (iii) Finally, suppose that *B* purports to agree with *A*'s scheme but goes directly to the police without taking any action toward fulfillment of the plan. The police find *A* at home, and *A* is arrested.

What should *A*'s liability be in each of these situations under the doctrinal variations considered in the preceding Notes?

---

[m] ALI, Model Penal Code and Commentaries § 5.03, p. 414 (1985).

[n] The fact situation is based on State v. Hayes, 105 Mo. 76, 16 S.W. 514 (1891).

## SECTION 5: ABANDONMENT

### Ross v. Mississippi

Supreme Court of Mississippi, 1992.
601 So.2d 872.

■ PRATHER, JUSTICE, for the Court. . . .

This attempted-rape case arose on the appeal of Sammy Joe Ross from the 10-year sentence imposed . . . by the Circuit Court of Union County. The appellant timely filed a notice of appeal and dispositively raises the issue: Whether the trial court erred in denying the defendant's motion for directed verdict on the charge of attempted rape. This Court reverses . . . the conviction for attempted rape. . . .

On September 16, 1987, sometime around 2:15 in the afternoon, Deputy Sheriff Edwards of the Union County Sheriff's Department was driving on Highway 30 heading east. Before he turned south onto Highway 9, he saw an oncoming truck, a white, late-model Ford pickup, turn left onto the first gravel road. Because the truck had out-of-county tags and turned down a road on which several crimes had occurred, Edwards jotted down the tag number, which action he described as routine practice.

Dorothy Henley[1] and her seven-year-old daughter lived in a trailer on the gravel road. Henley was alone at home and answered a knock at the door to find Sammy Joe Ross asking directions. Henley had never seen Ross before. She stepped out of the house and pointed out the house of a neighbor who might be able help him. When she turned back around, Ross pointed a handgun at her. He ordered her into the house, told her to undress, and shoved her onto the couch. Three or four times Ross ordered Henley to undress and once threatened to kill her. Henley described herself as frightened and crying. She attempted to escape from Ross and told him that her daughter would be home from school at any time. She testified: "I started crying and talking about my daughter, that I was all she had because her daddy was dead, and he said if I had a little girl he wouldn't do anything, for me just to go outside and turn my back." As instructed by Ross, Henley walked outside behind her trailer. Ross followed and told her to keep her back to the road until he had departed. She complied. . . .

On December 21, 1987, a Union County grand jury indicted Sammy Joe Ross for the attempted rape of Henley, charging that Ross "did unlawfully and feloniously attempt to rape and forcibly ravish" the complaining witness, an adult female. On January 25, 1988, Ross waived arraignment and pled not guilty.

On June 23, 1988, the jury found Ross guilty. On July 7, the court sentenced Ross to a 10-year term. When Ross moved for a judgment notwithstanding the verdict or, in the alternative, for a new trial, the court denied the motion. Ross timely filed a notice of appeal.

[T]he . . . issue . . . is whether sufficient evidence presents a question of fact as to whether Ross abandoned his attack as a result of outside intervention. . . . Ross asserts that "it was not . . . Henley's

---

[1] The complainant's name has been changed.

resistance that prevented her rape nor any independent intervening cause or third person, but the voluntary and independent decision by her assailant to abandon his attack." The state, on the other hand, claims that Ross "panicked" and "drove away hastily."

As recited above, Henley told Ross that her daughter would soon be home from school. She also testified that Ross stated if Henley had a little girl, he wouldn't do anything to her and to go outside [the house] and turn her back [to him]. Ross moved that the court direct a verdict in his favor on the charge of attempted rape, which motion the court denied.

*motion denied*

The trial court instructed the jury that if it found that Ross did "any overt act with the intent to have unlawful sexual relations with [the complainant] without her consent and against her will" then the jury should find Ross guilty of attempted rape. The court further instructed the jury that:

*jury instruction*

> before you can return a verdict against the defendant for attempted rape, that you must be convinced from the evidence and beyond a reasonable doubt, that the defendant was prevented from completing the act of rape or failed to complete the act of rape by intervening, extraneous causes. If you find that the act of rape was not completed due to a voluntary stopping short of the act, then you must find the defendant not guilty.

*Jury instruction*
*intervening extraneous causes*
*vs.*
*voluntary stopping*

Ross did not request, and the court did not give, any lesser included offense instructions.

Review of a directed verdict made at the close of the defendant's case consists of this court's applying a reasonable doubt standard to the verdict, while viewing the evidence in a light most favorable to the verdict. Stever v. State, 503 So.2d 227, 230 (Miss.1987). This court may not then discharge the defendant unless the court concludes that no reasonable, hypothetical juror could have found the defendant guilty. Pearson v. State, 428 So.2d 1361, 1364 (Miss.1983). . . .

The crime of attempt to commit an offense occurs when a person "shall design and endeavor to commit an offense, and shall do any overt act toward the commission thereof, but shall fail therein, or shall be prevented from committing the same." Miss. Code Ann. § 97–1–7 (1972). Put otherwise, attempt consists of "1) an intent to commit a particular crime; 2) a direct ineffectual act done toward its commission; and 3) failure to consummate its commission." Pruitt v. State, 528 So.2d 828, 830 (Miss.1988) (attempted rape was voluntarily abandoned by defendant when he told victim she was free to leave).

*Miss. attempt elements*

The Mississippi attempt statute requires that the third element, failure to consummate, result from extraneous causes. Thus, a defendant's voluntary abandonment may negate a crime of attempt. Where a defendant, with no other impetus but the victim's urging, voluntarily ceases his assault, he has not committed attempted rape. In *Pruitt*, where the assailant released his throathold on the unresisting victim and told her she could go, after which a third party happened on the scene, the court held that the jury could not have reasonably ruled out abandonment.

*Mississippi 3rd element*
*voluntary*

In comparison, this court has held that where the appellant's rape attempt failed because of the victim's resistance and ability to sound the alarm, the appellant cannot establish an abandonment defense. Alexander v. State, 520 So.2d 127, 130 (Miss.1988). In the *Alexander* case, the evidence sufficiently established a question of attempt for the jury. The defendant did not voluntarily abandon his attempt, but instead fled after the victim, a hospital patient, pressed the nurse's buzzer; a nurse responded and the victim spoke the word "help." The court concluded, "[T]he appellant ceased his actions only after the victim managed to press the buzzer alerting the nurse." In another case, the court properly sent the issue of attempt to the jury where the attacker failed because the victim resisted and freed herself. Harden v. State, 465 So.2d 321, 325 (Miss.1985).

Thus, abandonment occurs where, through the verbal urging of the victim, but with no physical resistance or external intervention, the perpetrator changes his mind. At the other end of the scale, a perpetrator cannot claim that he abandoned his attempt when, in fact, he ceased his efforts because the victim or a third party intervened or prevented him from furthering the attempt. Somewhere in the middle lies a case such as *Alexander*, where the victim successfully sounded an alarm, presenting no immediate physical obstacle to the perpetrator's continuing the attack, but sufficiently intervening to cause the perpetrator to cease his attack.

In this case, Ross appeals the denial of his motion for directed verdict; thus, he challenges only the sufficiency of the evidence, that is, whether it raised a sufficient factual issue to warrant a jury determination. Even under this rigorous standard of review, Ross's appeal should succeed on this issue. The evidence does not sufficiently raise a fact question as to whether he attempted rape. The evidence uncontrovertibly shows that he did not, but instead abandoned the attempt.

The key inquiry is a subjective one: what made Ross leave? According to the undisputed evidence, he left because he responded sympathetically to the victim's statement that she had a little girl. He did not fail in his attack. No one prevented him from completing it. Henley did not sound an alarm. She successfully persuaded Ross, of his own free will, to abandon his attempt. No evidence shows that Ross panicked and hastily drove away, but rather, the record shows that he walked the complainant out to the back of her trailer before he left. Thus, the trial court's failure to grant a directed verdict on the attempted rape charge constituted reversible error. As this court stated in *Pruitt*, this is not to say that Ross committed no criminal act, but "our only inquiry is whether there was sufficient evidence to support a jury finding that [Ross] did not abandon his attempt to rape [Henley]." This Court holds that there was not. . . .

Reversed and appellant discharged.

## NOTES ON ABANDONMENT

### 1. THE TRADITIONAL POSITION ON ABANDONMENT OF ATTEMPTS

Analytically, *Ross* presents two distinct questions. The first is whether the defendant progressed sufficiently beyond "mere preparation" to attempted rape. The second is whether, if he did (and did so with the required specific intent), he is nevertheless entitled to acquittal if he "voluntarily" abandoned his criminal plan. How should the second issue be treated? Should it matter whether Ross changed his mind before he completed the crime?

In Criminal Attempts, 41 Harv. L. Rev. 821, 847 (1928), Francis Beale Sayre states the usual position of the courts on this question:

> So far as the defendant's criminality is concerned, it would seem to make little or no difference whether the interruption of the defendant's intended acts is due to another's interference or to his own repentance or change of mind. Once the defendant's acts have gone far enough to make him liable for a criminal attempt, no subsequent repentance or change of mind or abstention from further crime can possibly wipe away liability for the crime already committed. Genuine repentance may cause a reduction of sentence, but it cannot free from criminal liability. In the cases where the defendant voluntarily abandons his intended course of conduct, therefore, the problem reduces itself to whether or not the defendant's conduct before the abandonment had gone so far as to constitute an indictable attempt. The burglar who, while trying to force the lock on the front door, decides to abandon the attempt is equally guilty whether his change of mind is due to the voice of his own conscience or the voice of an approaching policeman. Present virtue never wipes away past crimes.

## 2. QUESTIONS AND COMMENTS ON THE TRADITIONAL POSITION

What purposes are served by punishing a person who abandons a criminal intention before committing a completed offense? Does the abandonment raise doubt about the firmness of the actor's original criminal purpose, suggesting that it was only "half-formed or provisional"?[a] Does it suggest that the defendant has not, in fact, "gone far enough to show that he has broken through the psychological barrier to crime?"[b] In this sense, is an abandonment defense a desirable complement to a modern reformulation of the actus reus of attempt?

It has been argued that a voluntary renunciation of criminal intentions should be regarded as a praiseworthy act that erases the defendant's original blameworthiness and therefore removes the ethical predicate for criminal liability.[c] Others have claimed that recognition of an abandonment defense would offer an incentive to inchoate offenders to desist from their plan to commit a criminal offense.[d] Are these positions plausible?[e]

---

[a] G. Williams, Criminal Law: The General Part 620–21 (2d ed. 1961).

[b] Id. at 379–80.

[c] G. Fletcher, Rethinking the Criminal Law 190 (1978).

[d] "In our view, the most persuasive argument in favour of the provision of a withdrawal defence is that, since the object of the criminal law is to prevent crime, it is equally important to give reasonable encouragement to a conspirator, attempter or inciter to withdraw before a substantive offence is committed as it is to encourage an accomplice to end his participation in that offence. The absence of such a defence may operate to dissuade an individual who might otherwise decide to cease participating in the planning of a crime from taking that decision, since, having become a party to the inchoate offence, there is no inducement for him to cease his activities before commission of the substantive offence takes place. It may well be that the type of criminal who is liable to change his mind in this way is a relative newcomer to crime and would, in any event, be given the opportunity to give evidence for the prosecution. But provision of the defence would make it quite clear that the criminal in these circumstances

3.   THE MODEL PENAL CODE ON ABANDONMENT OF ATTEMPTS

Section 5.01(4) of the Model Penal Code reads as follows:

*§ 5.01(4)*
*Abandonment of*
*Attempts*

> When the actor's conduct would otherwise constitute an attempt under Subsection (1)(b) or (1)(c) of this Section, it is an affirmative defense that he abandoned his effort to commit the crime or otherwise prevented its commission, under circumstances manifesting a complete and voluntary renunciation of his criminal purpose. . . .

> Within the meaning of this Article, renunciation of criminal purpose is not voluntary if it is motivated, in whole or in part, by circumstances, not present or apparent at the inception of the actor's course of conduct, which increase the probability of detection or apprehension or which make more difficult the accomplishment of the criminal purpose. Renunciation is not complete if it is motivated by a decision to postpone the criminal conduct until a more advantageous time or to transfer the criminal effort to another but similar objective or victim.

Although the Model Code proposal has been adopted in several states, it has not met with widespread approval in recent American penal code revisions. Why might this be so? Is there a relationship between the grading of attempt and the case for an abandonment defense?

4.   COMPLICITY

*§ 2.06(6)*
*defense of*
*withdrawal or*
*abandonment*

Note also that § 2.06(6) of the Model Penal Code codifies the defense of withdrawal or abandonment as it applies to complicity. Specifically, the provision states that a person is not liable as an accomplice to the offense of another if "he terminates his complicity prior to the commission of the offense and (i) wholly deprives it of effectiveness in the commission of the offense; or (ii) gives timely warning to the law-enforcement authorities or otherwise makes proper effort to prevent commission of the offense." The role of withdrawal or abandonment in the law of complicity is analogous to the similar issue in the law of attempt. The chief differences are, first, that the defense is more widely recognized in the context of complicity, and, second, that most formulations of withdrawal from complicity require that the

*differences*
*w/ attempt*

accomplice make affirmative efforts to give timely warning or otherwise prevent the commission of the offense.

5.   CONSPIRACY

The role of conspiracy as an inchoate offense raises the question whether renunciation or abandonment should be a defense. The traditional position is that once agreement (or agreement plus an overt act) is reached,

*traditional*
*position*

a criminal conspiracy is complete and no subsequent abandonment is a de-

---

would not be liable to be charged at all." The Law Commission, Working Paper No. 50, Inchoate Offences 102 (1973).

e   "How likely is it that a man who is sufficiently far along the path towards committing a criminal offense, that he would be guilty of an attempt if he stopped, and who then decided not to commit it, would change his mind again and decide to carry on, since he realizes he is guilty of the attempt anyway? The argument is farfetched." M. Wasik, Abandoning Criminal Intent, [1980] Crim. L. Rev. 785, 793.

fense. As it has in the analogous situation with attempts, the Model Penal Code proposed in § 5.03(6) that renunciation be recognized as a defense if "the actor, after conspiring to commit a crime, thwarted the success of the conspiracy, under circumstances manifesting a complete and voluntary renunciation of his criminal purpose."

*§ 5.03(6)*
*Renunciation can be defense for conspiracy*

Renunciation as a defense to liability for conspiracy should be distinguished from the related issue of withdrawal as a means of terminating one's involvement in a conspiracy. Withdrawal does not exculpate the actor from liability for the conspiracy, but it would limit liability for substantive offenses committed by co-conspirators after the actor's participation had ceased. Additionally, withdrawal of an individual from an on-going criminal enterprise starts the statute of limitations for that individual. For a discussion of both withdrawal and true renunciation, see Note, Conspiracy: Statutory Reform Since the Model Penal Code, 75 Colum.L.Rev. 1122 (1975).

*withdrawal distinguished*

## 6. REACH OF THE ABANDONMENT DEFENSE

If an abandonment defense makes sense for attempt, complicity, and conspiracy, are there other offenses to which it should also be applicable? Not surprisingly, the Model Code includes a comparable defense for solicitation. See § 5.02(3). And it also includes a similar defense for perjury. See § 241.1(4). But no similar provision is made, for example, for larceny. If the actor "exercise[d] unlawful control over . . . property of another with purpose to deprive" (§ 223.2(1)) and at the next instant had a change of heart, would the situation be any different from a case where the actor tried to exercise unlawful control and voluntarily desisted after committing an attempt? Should the abandonment defense be applicable, if it is to be recognized at all, to all offenses defined in terms that fall short of ultimate harm? If not, by what criteria should such offenses be distinguished?[f]

*how far should abandonment defense go?*

---

[f]     For discussion of these issues, see Paul R. Hoeber, The Abandonment Defense to Criminal Attempt and Other Problems of Temporal Individuation, 74 Calif. L. Rev. 377 (1986).

# CHAPTER VI

# LIABILITY FOR THE CONDUCT OF ANOTHER

## SECTION 1: COMPLICITY

### INTRODUCTORY NOTES ON PARTIES TO CRIME

#### 1. THE COMMON LAW

By long tradition, the common law authorized punishment in specified circumstances for crimes committed by someone else. Typically, it accomplished this result by application of one or more of three different theories. The first was liability as an accomplice. The second was liability of a member of a conspiracy for crimes committed by a co-conspirator. The third was the felony murder doctrine, under which each person participating in a felony was liable for a homicide committed by any one of the felons.[a]

At common law, parties to a felony were described as principals in the first and second degree and accessories before and after the fact. The principal in the first degree was the primary actor, the person who personally engaged in the criminal conduct. A principal in the second degree aided or abetted the primary actor in the commission of a felony and was present at the perpetration thereof. Presence was essential, but it could be constructive in nature. A typical example was the lookout who stood guard some distance from a robbery. In general, a person was constructively present at a felony whenever he or she was situated to assist the primary actor during commission of the crime. A person who aided, counseled, commanded, solicited, or encouraged the commission of a felony, but who was not present at its perpetration, was designated an accessory before the fact. Finally, one whose assistance came after the felony and who assisted a known felon to avoid apprehension, trial, or punishment became an accessory after the fact.

Even at common law, the distinction among principals rarely mattered. Principals in the first and second degree received the same punishment. Since both had to be present at the scene of the crime, both were subject to the jurisdiction of the same court. Furthermore, it was not necessary, as a matter of pleading, to specify the degree of a principal's participation; conviction in either capacity could be had upon the same indictment. Finally, liability of one principal did not depend upon the liability of the other. A principal in the second degree could be tried before or after the principal in the first degree and could be convicted even if the primary actor was acquitted.

In contrast, the distinction between principals and accessories was critically important. Jurisdiction over principals lay where the crime was committed, but an accessory could be tried only where the act of assistance

---

[a] The felony murder rule is addressed briefly below but is covered more extensively in Chapter X.

was performed. Moreover, the indictment had to specify the defendant's role as principal or accessory. A person charged as an accessory before the fact could not be convicted if the evidence demonstrated liability as a principal, or vice versa. Most striking of all was the requirement of conviction of the principal as a prerequisite to liability of an accessory. Anything that defeated conviction of the primary actor also barred punishment of an accessory. If the principal escaped apprehension, or died before trial, or for any reason was found not guilty, the accessory had to go free.

This scheme invited evasion of justice. Suppose a person tricked an unsuspecting child or servant to poison the victim's coffee. Would the evildoer have to go free because the immediate actor was innocent? The common-law answer to this problem was the doctrine of innocent agency. Under this view, the guiltless actor was deemed a mere instrumentality of the ultimate wrongdoer. Thus, a person apparently in the posture of an accessory before the fact could be tried and convicted as a principal in the first degree for acting through an innocent agent.[b] But the primary actor had to be truly innocent, not just not convicted or beyond the reach of the law.

## 2. MODERN STATUTES

### (i) *Accessories After the Fact*

A universal characteristic of modern statutory treatment of the law of accessories is that accessories after the fact are dealt with separately. For one thing, they are punished differently. The common law made all parties to crime equally liable. One who helped a murderer escape became subject to the penalties for murder. Today, the liability of an accessory after the fact is fixed, usually at the level of a misdemeanor or junior felony. More radically, many modern statutes abandon altogether the fiction that one who aids a felon to avoid justice somehow becomes a retroactive participant in the original crime. These statutes punish such misconduct as a form of obstruction of justice.

Section 242.3 of the Model Penal Code is illustrative. It does not deal with parties to crime but defines an independent offense of hindering apprehension of another. The gist of the offense is the purposeful hindering of the apprehension, prosecution, conviction, or punishment of another by any of a number of specified activities—e.g., harboring a fugitive; providing a weapon, transportation, disguise, or other means of effecting escape; or concealing evidence. The focus of this offense is on interference with law enforcement rather than on the obvious fiction that one who aids a fugitive thereby becomes a party to the original crime. In line with this approach, the Model Code provision is not limited to aiding persons known to be guilty of crime; it also applies to persons merely charged with, or sought for, criminal activity. The core of the offense is obstructive conduct done with the purpose "to hinder the apprehension, prosecution, conviction or punishment of another for crime." Penalties for this offense are similar to those assigned to other forms of obstruction of justice and in no case approach the very serious sanctions provided for major felonies.

---

[b] See § 2.06(2)(a) of the Model Penal Code for a modern statement of the innocent agent rule.

### *(ii) Principals and Accessories Before the Fact*

The common law regarded the liability of an accessory before the fact as derivative in nature. Since the liability of the secondary party derived from that of the principal offender, establishing the guilt of the latter was an indispensable precondition to punishing the former. Today, every American jurisdiction has modified this scheme by legislation. These statutes abrogate procedural distinctions between principals and accessories before the fact and allow prosecution of all such parties as principals. The statutes specifically reject the rule that conviction of the principal is a precondition for conviction of an accessory before the fact.

The federal provision is fairly typical. It provides that "[w]hoever commits an offense against the United States or aids, abets, counsels, commands, induces or procures its commission, is punishable as a principal." 18 U.S.C. § 2(a). Since it is no longer necessary to distinguish between principals in the second degree and accessories before the fact, all such parties are designated by the generic term "accomplice." Today, the term "accomplice" is widely used to describe anyone other than the primary actor who participates in a crime prior to or during its commission. Accessories after the fact continue to be treated separately, as described above.

The federal aiding and abetting statute carries forward the common-law tradition in the profusion of terms defining (or describing) the actus reus of complicity. Note that it does not contain formal actus reus elements of the offense in the normal sense. It does not, as with the terms "breaking and entering" in burglary, identify a particular form of behavior that must be committed in order for a crime to occur. Rather, it defines the required conduct generically. *Any* form of aid or assistance rendered with the requisite intent will suffice. The New York statute is another illustration. It provides that one person is criminally liable for the conduct of another when, acting with the required culpability, he or she "solicits, requests, commands, importunes, or intentionally aids such person to engage in such conduct." N.Y. Penal Code § 20.00. The verbal formulas of the federal and New York statutes are different, but the difference does not matter. Both are designed to say that helping another commit a crime is an offense when accompanied by the required intent, no matter how that help is given.

It must not be supposed, however, that the statutory abrogation of common law procedural technicalities has rendered that tradition entirely irrelevant. Common law terminology is still used in many jurisdictions, as the statutes quoted above reflect. And even though the common law has been everywhere curtailed, bits and pieces of that legacy continue to turn up. Most importantly, the requirement that the principal actually commit an offense continues to influence the substantive conditions for liability as an accomplice. Thus, although *conviction* of the principal actor is no longer a procedural prerequisite to trial of an accessory, it is typically necessary to prove in the prosecution of a secondary party that the primary actor committed the crime sought to be attributed to the secondary party.

The Model Penal Code is drafted on this premise. It contains an especially elaborate provision on accomplice liability that is atypical in its detail, but that—with exceptions to be noted below—carries forward the solutions embraced in statutes and decisions nationwide. Section 2.06(1) provides that a person is guilty of an offense "if *it* is committed by his own conduct or by the conduct of another person for which he is legally accountable." Section 2.06(2) provides for several situations where one can be "legally accountable" for the conduct of another, the important one for present purpose being that "he is an accomplice of such other person *in the commission of the offense*." Section 2.06(3) then gets to the meat of the matter:

> A person is an accomplice of another person *in the commission of an offense* if:
>
> (a) with the purpose of promoting or facilitating the commission of the offense, he
>
> (i) solicits such other person *to commit it*; or
>
> (ii) aids or agrees or attempts to aid such other person in *planning or committing it*; or
>
> (iii) having a legal duty to prevent the commission of the offense, fails to make proper effort so to do . . . .

The italicized portions of the Model Code implement the requirement that the principle actor actually commit an offense.[c] The commentary to the Code cements the point:

> Section 2.06(3) of the Model Code is predicated . . . on the actual commission of the offense by the person aided. Assuming the requisite culpability, one who aids, attempts to aid, or agrees to aid, is thus liable under this section only if the principal actor actually commits an offense.

ALI, Model Penal Code and Commentaries, § 2.06, p. 314 n.46 (1985).

The most commonly litigated issue to which § 2.06(3) speaks is the affirmative assistance covered by subsection (ii). The preconditions for liability on this basis are covered in detail in the next main case and following notes. But § 2.06(3) also covers the potential liability of an accomplice for both omissions and soliciting another to commit a crime.

State v. Walden, 306 N.C. 466, 293 S.E.2d 780 (1982), illustrates accomplice liability based on an omission. Walden was charged with aiding and abetting a felonious assault on her one-year-old son. The child was beaten with a leather belt by "Bishop" Hoskins. The belt had a metal buckle, and the child was seriously injured. The mother was present during the beating. She did not join in, but neither did she do anything to prevent the assault. The trial court ruled that no affirmative action by the mother was necessary to her liability. Specifically, the jury was instructed that the defendant should be found guilty if she "was present with the reasonable opportunity and duty to prevent the crime and failed to take reasonable steps to do so." The resulting conviction was affirmed by the North Carolina Supreme Court, which stated:

> It remains the law that one may not be found to be an aider and abettor, and thus guilty as a principal, solely because he is present when a crime is committed. It will still be necessary, in order to have that effect, that it be shown that the defendant said

---

[c] One of the complexities of the law of complicity is its intersection with problems also addressed by the laws of attempt and conspiracy. It may be possible, for example, for a person who tries to become an accomplice but fails—either because the aid was ineffective or because the principal did not commit any or all of the elements of the offense—to be prosecuted for an attempt to commit the offense or a conspiracy to commit it. This possibility is considered in Section 4 of Chapter V.

> or did something showing his consent to the criminal purpose and contribution to its execution. But we hold that the failure of a parent who is present to take all steps reasonably possible to protect the parent's child from an attack by another person constitutes an act of omission by the parent showing the parent's consent and contribution to the crime being committed.

McGhee v. Virginia, 221 Va. 422, 270 S.E.2d 729 (1980), is a typical illustration of solicitation leading to accomplice liability. McGhee's husband and two co-workers were killed by her lover and his brother. McGhee urged the lover to kill her husband and informed him of the logging site where the husband could be found. There was no evidence that the defendant was involved in planning the details of the killing or that she knew the precise date when it would occur. McGhee was convicted as an accessory before the fact to murder and sentenced to a term of 20 years.

The Supreme Court of Virginia affirmed. The court noted that Virginia law defined an accessory as "one not present at the commission of the offense, but who is in some way concerned therein, either before or after, as [a] contriver, instigator or advisor, or as a receiver or protector of the perpetrator." Applying this definition, the court said:

> In the trial of an accessory before the fact, the Commonwealth must establish the accused was a "contriver, instigator *or* advisor" of the crime committed by the principal. An instigator of a crime is an accessory before the fact even though he or she did not participate in the planning of the crime or even though unaware of the precise time or place of the crime's commission or of the precise method employed by the principal. A contrary holding would allow instigators to escape liability for their actions by removing themselves from the planning of crimes they have incited.

## Rosemond v. United States

Supreme Court of the United States, 2014.
572 U.S. ___, 134 S. Ct. 1240.

■ JUSTICE KAGAN delivered the opinion of the Court.*

A federal criminal statute, § 924(c) of Title 18, prohibits "us[ing] or carr[ying]" a firearm "during and in relation to any crime of violence or drug trafficking crime." In this case, we consider what the Government must show when it accuses a defendant of aiding or abetting that offense. We hold that the Government makes its case by proving that the defendant actively participated in the underlying drug trafficking or violent crime with advance knowledge that a confederate would use or carry a gun during the crime's commission. We also conclude that the jury instructions given below were erroneous because they failed to require that the defendant knew in advance that one of his cohorts would be armed.

### I

This case arises from a drug deal gone bad. Vashti Perez arranged to sell a pound of marijuana to Ricardo Gonzales and Coby Painter. She drove to a local park to make the exchange, accompanied by two

* Justice Scalia joins all but footnotes 7 and 8 of this opinion.

confederates, Ronald Joseph and petitioner Justus Rosemond. One of those men apparently took the front passenger seat and the other sat in the back, but witnesses dispute who was where. At the designated meeting place, Gonzales climbed into the car's backseat while Painter waited outside. The backseat passenger allowed Gonzales to inspect the marijuana. But rather than handing over money, Gonzales punched that man in the face and fled with the drugs. As Gonzales and Painter ran away, one of the male passengers—but again, which one is contested—exited the car and fired several shots from a semiautomatic handgun. The shooter then re-entered the vehicle, and all three would-be drug dealers gave chase after the buyers-turned-robbers. But before the three could catch their quarry, a police officer, responding to a dispatcher's alert, pulled their car over. This federal prosecution of Rosemond followed.[1]

The Government charged Rosemond with, inter alia, violating § 924(c) by using a gun in connection with a drug trafficking crime, or aiding and abetting that offense under § 2 of Title 18. Section 924(c) provides that "any person who, during and in relation to any crime of violence or drug trafficking crime[,] . . . uses or carries a firearm," shall receive a five-year mandatory-minimum sentence, with seven- and ten-year minimums applicable, respectively, if the firearm is also brandished or discharged. 18 U.S.C. § 924(c)(1)(A). Section 2, for its part, is the federal aiding and abetting statute: It provides that "[w]hoever commits an offense against the United States or aids, abets, counsels, commands, induces or procures its commission is punishable as a principal."

Consistent with the indictment, the Government prosecuted the § 924(c) charge on two alternative theories. The Government's primary contention was that Rosemond himself used the firearm during the aborted drug transaction. But recognizing that the identity of the shooter was disputed, the Government also offered a back-up argument: Even if it was Joseph who fired the gun as the drug deal fell apart, Rosemond aided and abetted the § 924(c) violation.

The District Judge accordingly instructed the jury on aiding and abetting law. He first explained, in a way challenged by neither party, the rudiments of § 2. Under that statute, the judge stated, "[a] person who aids or abets another to commit an offense is just as guilty of that offense as if he committed it himself." And in order to aid or abet, the defendant must "willfully and knowingly associate[ ] himself in some way with the crime, and . . . seek[ ] by some act to help make the crime succeed." The judge then turned to applying those general principles to § 924(c)—and there, he deviated from an instruction Rosemond had proposed. According to Rosemond, a defendant could be found guilty of aiding or abetting a § 924(c) violation only if he "intentionally took some action to facilitate or encourage the use of the firearm," as opposed to the predicate drug offense. But the District Judge disagreed, instead telling the jury that it could convict if "(1) the defendant knew his cohort used a firearm in the drug trafficking crime, and (2) the defendant knowingly and actively participated in the drug trafficking crime." In closing argument, the prosecutor contended that Rosemond easily

[1] The Government agreed not to bring charges against the other four participants in the narcotics deal in exchange for their giving truthful testimony against Rosemond.

satisfied that standard, so that even if he had not "fired the gun, he's still guilty of the crime." After all, the prosecutor stated, Rosemond "certainly knew [of] and actively participated in" the drug transaction. "And with regards to the other element," the prosecutor urged, "the fact is a person cannot be present and active at a drug deal when shots are fired and not know their cohort is using a gun. You simply can't do it."

The jury convicted Rosemond of violating § 924(c) (as well as all other offenses charged). The verdict form was general: It did not reveal whether the jury found that Rosemond himself had used the gun or instead had aided and abetted a confederate's use during the marijuana deal. As required by § 924(c), the trial court imposed a consecutive sentence of 120 months of imprisonment for the statute's violation.

The Tenth Circuit affirmed, rejecting Rosemond's argument that the District Court's aiding and abetting instructions were erroneous.[2] The Court of Appeals acknowledged that some other Circuits agreed with Rosemond that a defendant aids and abets a § 924(c) offense only if he intentionally takes "some action to facilitate or encourage his cohort's use of the firearm." But the Tenth Circuit had already adopted a different standard, which it thought consonant with the District Court's instructions[, which required] that the defendant "actively participated in the" underlying crime and "knew [his confederate] was carrying [a] firearm"). And the Court of Appeals held that Rosemond had presented no sufficient reason for departing from that precedent.

We granted certiorari to resolve the Circuit conflict over what it takes to aid and abet a § 924(c) offense. Although we disagree with Rosemond's principal arguments, we find that the trial court erred in instructing the jury. We therefore vacate the judgment below.

## II

The federal aiding and abetting statute, 18 U.S.C. § 2, states that a person who furthers—more specifically, who "aids, abets, counsels, commands, induces or procures"—the commission of a federal offense "is punishable as a principal." That provision derives from (though simplifies) common-law standards for accomplice liability. And in so doing, § 2 reflects a centuries-old view of culpability: that a person may be responsible for a crime he has not personally carried out if he helps another to complete its commission.

We have previously held that under § 2 "those who provide knowing aid to persons committing federal crimes, with the intent to facilitate the crime, are themselves committing a crime." Central Bank of Denver, N.A. v. First Interstate Bank of Denver, N. A., 511 U.S. 164, 181 (1994). Both parties here embrace that formulation, and agree as well that it has two components. As at common law, a person is liable under § 2 for aiding and abetting a crime if (and only if) he (1) takes an affirmative act in furtherance of that offense, (2) with the intent of facilitating the offense's commission. . . .

The questions that the parties dispute, and we here address, concern how those two requirements—affirmative act and intent—apply in

[2] The Court of Appeals stated that it had to address that argument even if the jury could have found that Rosemond himself fired the gun, because "a conviction based on a general verdict is subject to challenge if the jury was instructed on alternative theories of guilt and may have relied on an invalid one."

a prosecution for aiding and abetting a § 924(c) offense. Those questions arise from the compound nature of that provision. Recall that § 924(c) forbids "us[ing] or carr[ying] a firearm" when engaged in a "crime of violence or drug trafficking crime." The prosecutor must show the use or carriage of a gun; so too he must prove the commission of a predicate (violent or drug trafficking) offense. For purposes of ascertaining aiding and abetting liability, we therefore must consider: When does a person act to further this double-barreled crime? And when does he intend to facilitate its commission? We address each issue in turn.

A

Consider first Rosemond's account of his conduct (divorced from any issues of intent). Rosemond actively participated in a drug transaction, accompanying two others to a site where money was to be exchanged for a pound of marijuana. But as he tells it, he took no action with respect to any firearm. He did not buy or borrow a gun to facilitate the narcotics deal; he did not carry a gun to the scene; he did not use a gun during the subsequent events constituting this criminal misadventure. His acts thus advanced one part (the drug part) of a two-part incident—or to speak a bit more technically, one element (the drug element) of a two-element crime. Is that enough to satisfy the conduct requirement of this aiding and abetting charge, or must Rosemond, as he claims, have taken some act to assist the commission of the other (firearm) component of § 924(c)?

The common law imposed aiding and abetting liability on a person (possessing the requisite intent) who facilitated any part—even though not every part—of a criminal venture. As a leading treatise, published around the time of § 2's enactment, put the point: Accomplice liability attached upon proof of "*[a]ny* participation in a general felonious plan" carried out by confederates. 1 F. Wharton, Criminal Law § 251, p. 322 (11th ed. 1912) (hereinafter Wharton) (emphasis added). Or in the words of another standard reference: If a person was "present abetting while *any* act necessary to constitute the offense [was] being performed through another," he could be charged as a principal—even "though [that act was] *not the whole thing necessary*." 1 J. Bishop, Commentaries on the Criminal Law § 649, p. 392 (7th ed. 1882) (emphasis added). . . . Indeed, as yet a third treatise underscored, a person's involvement in the crime could be not merely partial but minimal too: "The quantity [of assistance was] immaterial," so long as the accomplice did "*something*" to aid the crime. R. Desty, A Compendium of American Criminal Law § 37a, p. 106 (1882) (emphasis added). After all, the common law maintained, every little bit helps—and a contribution to some part of a crime aids the whole.

That principle continues to govern aiding and abetting law under § 2: As almost every court of appeals has held, "[a] defendant can be convicted as an aider and abettor without proof that he participated in each and every element of the offense." United States v. Sigalow, 812 F.2d 783, 785 (2d Cir. 1987). In proscribing aiding and abetting, Congress used language that "comprehends all assistance rendered by words, acts, encouragement, support, or presence," Reves v. Ernst & Young, 507 U.S. 170, 178 (1993)—even if that aid relates to only one (or some) of a crime's phases or elements. So, for example, . . . we approved a conviction for abetting mail fraud even though the defendant had played no part in mailing the fraudulent documents; it was enough to satisfy the law's conduct requirement that he had in other ways aided the deception. See *Pereira v. United States,* 347 U.S. 1, 8–11 (1954). The division of labor between two (or more) confederates thus has no significance: A strategy of "you take that element, I'll take this one" would free neither party from liability.[6]

*[margin note: division of labor]*

Under that established approach, Rosemond's participation in the drug deal here satisfies the affirmative-act requirement for aiding and abetting a § 924(c) violation. As we have previously described, the commission of a drug trafficking (or violent) crime is—no less than the use of a firearm—an "essential conduct element of the § 924(c) offense." United States v. Rodriguez-Moreno, 526 U.S. 275, 280 (1999). In enacting the statute, "Congress proscribed both the use of the firearm *and* the commission of acts that constitute" a drug trafficking crime. *Rodriguez-Moreno,* 526 U.S. at 281. Rosemond therefore could assist in § 924(c)'s violation by facilitating either the drug transaction or the firearm use (or of course both). In helping to bring about one part of the offense (whether trafficking drugs or using a gun), he necessarily helped to complete the whole. And that ends the analysis as to his conduct. It is inconsequential, as courts applying both the common law and § 2 have held, that his acts did not advance each element of the offense; all that matters is that they facilitated one component.

*[margin note: affirmative-act requirement satisfied]*

Rosemond argues, to the contrary, that the requisite act here "must be directed at the use of the firearm," because that element is § 924(c)'s most essential feature. But Rosemond can provide no authority for demanding that an affirmative act go toward an element considered peculiarly significant; rather, as just noted, courts have never thought relevant the importance of the aid rendered. And in any event, we reject Rosemond's premise that § 924(c) is somehow more about using guns than selling narcotics. It is true enough, as Rosemond says in support of that theory, that § 924(c) "establishes a separate, freestanding offense that is 'distinct from the underlying [drug trafficking crime].'" But it is just as true that § 924(c) establishes a freestanding offense distinct from any that might apply just to using a gun—say, for discharging a firearm in a public park. That is because § 924(c) is, to coin a term, a combination crime. It punishes the temporal and relational conjunction of two separate acts, on the ground that together they pose an extreme risk of harm. And so, an act relating to drugs, just as much as an act relating to guns, facilitates a § 924(c) violation.

*[margin note: § 924(c) combination crime]*

Rosemond's related argument that our approach would conflate two distinct offenses—allowing a conviction for abetting a § 924(c) violation whenever the prosecution shows that the defendant abetted the underlying drug trafficking crime—fares no better. That is because, as we will describe, an aiding and abetting conviction requires not just an act facilitating one or another element, but also a state of mind extending to the entire crime. And under that rule, a defendant may be convicted of

---

6   Consider a hypothetical similar to . . . *Pereira.* . . . Suppose that as part of a kidnapping scheme, one accomplice lures the victim into a car under false pretenses; another drives the vehicle; a third allows the use of her house to hold the victim captive; and still a fourth keeps watch outside to divert potential witnesses. None would have personally completed, or even assisted with, all elements of the offense. But (if they had the requisite intent) all would be liable under § 2.

abetting a § 924(c) violation only if his intent reaches beyond a simple drug sale, to an armed one. Aiding and abetting law's intent component—to which we now turn—thus preserves the distinction between assisting the predicate drug trafficking crime and assisting the broader § 924(c) offense.

B

Begin with (or return to) some basics about aiding and abetting law's intent requirement, which no party here disputes. As previously explained, a person aids and abets a crime when (in addition to taking the requisite act) he intends to facilitate that offense's commission. An intent to advance some different or lesser offense is not, or at least not usually, sufficient: Instead, the intent must go to the specific and entire crime charged—so here, to the full scope (predicate crime plus gun use) of § 924(c).[7] And the canonical formulation of that needed state of mind—later appropriated by this Court and oft-quoted in both parties' briefs—is Judge Learned Hand's: To aid and abet a crime, a defendant must not just "in some sort associate himself with the venture," but also "participate in it as in something that he wishes to bring about" and "seek by his action to make it succeed." Nye & Nissen v. United States, 336 U.S. 613, 619 (1949) (quoting United States v. Peoni, 100 F.2d 401, 402 (2d Cir. 1938)).

We have previously found that intent requirement satisfied when a person actively participates in a criminal venture with full knowledge of the circumstances constituting the charged offense. In *Pereira,* the mail fraud case discussed above, we found the requisite intent for aiding and abetting because the defendant took part in a fraud "know[ing]" that his confederate would take care of the mailing. 347 U.S., at 12. Likewise, in Bozza v. United States, 330 U.S. 160, 165 (1947), we upheld a conviction for aiding and abetting the evasion of liquor taxes because the defendant helped operate a clandestine distillery "know[ing]" the business was set up "to violate Government revenue laws." And several Courts of Appeals have similarly held—addressing a fact pattern much like this one—that the unarmed driver of a getaway car had the requisite intent to aid and abet armed bank robbery if he "knew" that his confederates would use weapons in carrying out the crime. See, e.g., United States v. Akiti, 701 F.3d 883, 887 (8th 2012); United States v. Easter, 66 F.3d 1018, 1024 (9th Cir. 1995). So for purposes of aiding and abetting law, a person who actively participates in a criminal scheme knowing its extent and character intends that scheme's commission.[8]

The same principle holds here: An active participant in a drug transaction has the intent needed to aid and abet a § 924(c) violation

---

[7] Some authorities suggest an exception to the general rule when another crime is the "natural and probable consequence" of the crime the defendant intended to abet. See, e.g., 2 W. LaFave § 13.3(b), at 356 (2003) (citing cases); but see id., § 13.3 ("Under the better view, one is not an accomplice to a crime merely because . . . that crime was a natural and probable consequence of another offense as to which he is an accomplice"). That question is not implicated here, because no one contends that a § 924(c) violation is a natural and probable consequence of simple drug trafficking. We therefore express no view on the issue.

[8] We did not deal in these cases, nor do we here, with defendants who incidentally facilitate a criminal venture rather than actively participate in it. A hypothetical case is the owner of a gun store who sells a firearm to a criminal, knowing but not caring how the gun will be used. We express no view about what sort of facts, if any, would suffice to show that such a third party has the intent necessary to be convicted of aiding and abetting.

when he knows that one of his confederates will carry a gun. In such a case, the accomplice has decided to join in the criminal venture, and share in its benefits, with full awareness of its scope—that the plan calls not just for a drug sale, but for an armed one. In so doing, he has chosen (like the abettors in *Pereira* and *Bozza* or the driver in an armed robbery) to align himself with the illegal scheme in its entirety—including its use of a firearm. And he has determined (again like those other abettors) to do what he can to "make [that scheme] succeed." *Nye & Nissen,* 336 U.S. at 619. He thus becomes responsible, in the typical way of aiders and abettors, for the conduct of others. He may not have brought the gun to the drug deal himself, but because he took part in that deal knowing a confederate would do so, he intended the commission of a § 924(c) offense—i.e., an armed drug sale.

For all that to be true, though, the § 924(c) defendant's knowledge of a firearm must be advance knowledge—or otherwise said, knowledge that enables him to make the relevant legal (and indeed, moral) choice. When an accomplice knows beforehand of a confederate's design to carry a gun, he can attempt to alter that plan or, if unsuccessful, withdraw from the enterprise; it is deciding instead to go ahead with his role in the venture that shows his intent to aid an *armed* offense. But when an accomplice knows nothing of a gun until it appears at the scene, he may already have completed his acts of assistance; or even if not, he may at that late point have no realistic opportunity to quit the crime. And when that is so, the defendant has not shown the requisite intent to assist a crime involving a gun. . . . For the reasons just given, we think that means knowledge at a time the accomplice can do something with it—most notably, opt to walk away.[9]

Both parties here find something to dislike in our view of this issue. Rosemond argues that a participant in a drug deal intends to assist a § 924(c) violation only if he affirmatively desires one of his confederates to use a gun. The jury, Rosemond concedes, could infer that state of mind from the defendant's advance knowledge that the plan included a firearm. But according to Rosemond, the instructions must also permit the jury to draw the opposite conclusion—that although the defendant participated in a drug deal knowing a gun would be involved, he did not specifically want its carriage or use. That higher standard, Rosemond claims, is necessary to avoid subjecting persons of different culpability to the same punishment. Rosemond offers as an example an unarmed driver assisting in the heist of a store: If that person spent the drive "trying to persuade [his confederate] to leave [the] gun behind," then he should be convicted of abetting shoplifting, but not armed robbery.

We think not. What matters for purposes of gauging intent, and so what jury instructions should convey, is that the defendant has chosen, with full knowledge, to participate in the illegal scheme—not that, if all had been left to him, he would have planned the identical crime. . . . The law does not, nor should it, care whether he participates with a happy heart or a sense of foreboding. Either way, he has the same

[9] Of course, if a defendant continues to participate in a crime after a gun was displayed or used by a confederate, the jury can permissibly infer from his failure to object or withdraw that he had such knowledge. In any criminal case, after all, the factfinder can draw inferences about a defendant's intent based on all the facts and circumstances of a crime's commission.

culpability, because either way he has knowingly elected to aid in the commission of a peculiarly risky form of offense.

A final, metaphorical way of making the point: By virtue of § 924(c), using a firearm at a drug deal ups the ante. A would-be accomplice might decide to play at those perilous stakes. Or he might grasp that the better course is to fold his hand. What he should not expect is the capacity to hedge his bets, joining in a dangerous criminal scheme but evading its penalties by leaving use of the gun to someone else. Aiding and abetting law prevents that outcome, so long as the player knew the heightened stakes when he decided to stay in the game.

The Government, for its part, thinks we take too strict a view of when a defendant charged with abetting a § 924(c) violation must acquire that knowledge. . . . [T]he Government recognizes that the accused accomplice must have "foreknowledge" of a gun's presence. But the Government views that standard as met whenever the accomplice, having learned of the firearm, continues any act of assisting the drug transaction. According to the Government, the jury should convict such a defendant even if he became aware of the gun only after he realistically could have opted out of the crime.

But that approach, we think, would diminish too far the requirement that a defendant in a § 924(c) prosecution must intend to further an *armed* drug deal. Assume, for example, that an accomplice agrees to participate in a drug sale on the express condition that no one brings a gun to the place of exchange. But just as the parties are making the trade, the accomplice notices that one of his confederates has a (poorly) concealed firearm in his jacket. The Government would convict the accomplice of aiding and abetting a § 924(c) offense if he assists in completing the deal without incident, rather than running away or otherwise aborting the sale. But behaving as the Government suggests might increase the risk of gun violence—to the accomplice himself, other participants, or bystanders; and conversely, finishing the sale might be the best or only way to avoid that danger. In such a circumstance, a jury is entitled to find that the defendant intended only a drug sale—that he never intended to facilitate, and so does not bear responsibility for, a drug deal carried out with a gun. A defendant manifests that greater intent, and incurs the greater liability of § 924(c), when he chooses to participate in a drug transaction knowing it will involve a firearm; but he makes no such choice when that knowledge comes too late for him to be reasonably able to act upon it.

## III

Under these principles, the District Court erred in instructing the jury, because it did not explain that Rosemond needed advance knowledge of a firearm's presence. Recall that the court stated that Rosemond was guilty of aiding and abetting if "(1) [he] knew his cohort used a firearm in the drug trafficking crime, and (2) [he] knowingly and actively participated in the drug trafficking crime." We agree with that instruction's second half: As we have explained, active participation in a drug sale is sufficient for § 924(c) liability (even if the conduct does not extend to the firearm), so long as the defendant had prior knowledge of the gun's involvement. The problem with the court's instruction came in its description of that knowledge requirement. In telling the jury to consider merely whether Rosemond "knew his cohort used a firearm," the court did not direct the jury to determine *when* Rosemond obtained the requisite knowledge. So, for example, the jury could have convicted even if Rosemond first learned of the gun when it was fired and he took no further action to advance the crime. . . . The court's statement failed to convey that Rosemond had to have advance knowledge, of the kind we have described, that a confederate would be armed. . . . Accordingly, we vacate the judgment below and remand the case for further proceedings consistent with this opinion.

It is so ordered.

■ JUSTICE ALITO, with whom JUSTICE THOMAS joins, concurring in part and dissenting in part.

[Justice Alito dissented "from that portion of the Court's opinion which places on the Government the burden of proving that the alleged aider and abettor of a § 924(c) offense had what the Court terms 'a realistic opportunity' to refrain from engaging in the conduct at issue." He thought this part of the Court's analysis confused motive and intent, and invaded the province of affirmative defenses such as necessity and duress that the defendant should be required to prove. He added in a footnote:

> I am also concerned that the Court's use, without clarification, of the phrase "advance knowledge" will lead readers astray. Viewed by itself, the phrase most naturally means knowledge acquired in advance of the commission of the drug trafficking offense, but this is not what the Court means. Rather, "advance knowledge," as used by the Court, may include knowledge acquired while the drug trafficking offense is in progress. Specifically, a defendant has such knowledge, the Court says, if he or she first learns of the gun while the drug offense is in progress and at that time "realistically could have opted out of the crime."]

## NOTES ON THE CONDUCT REQUIRED FOR COMPLICITY

### 1. QUESTIONS AND COMMENTS ON *ROSEMOND*

In *Rosemond*, the defendant was present at the scene and clearly involved in promoting and assisting the drug transaction. But he did not, he claimed, play any role in the firearm aspect of the offense.

The full text of 18 U.S.C. § 924(c)(1)(A) provides:

> Except to the extent that a greater minimum sentence is otherwise provided by this subsection or by any other provision of law, any person who, during and in relation to any crime of violence or drug trafficking crime (including a crime of violence or drug trafficking crime that provides for an enhanced punishment if committed by the use of a deadly or dangerous weapon or device) for which the person may be prosecuted in a court of the United States, uses or carries a firearm, or who, in furtherance of any such crime, possesses a firearm, shall, in addition to the punishment provided for such crime of violence or drug trafficking crime—

> (i) be sentenced to a term of imprisonment of not less than 5 years;
>
> (ii) if the firearm is brandished, be sentenced to a term of imprisonment of not less than 7 years; and
>
> (iii) if the firearm is discharged, be sentenced to a term of imprisonment of not less than 10 years.

It was clear at the time of Rosemond's trial and conviction that the elements of the offense were as quoted at the beginning of Justice Kagan's opinion: " 'us[ing] or carr[ying]' a firearm 'during and in relation to any crime of violence or drug trafficking crime.' " At the time of Rosemond's prosecution, the provisions of § 924(c)(1)(A)(ii) and (iii) ("brandishing" and "discharging") were considered sentencing factors that could be determined by a preponderance of the evidence by the trial judge after conviction. They did not need to be proved by the prosecutor beyond a reasonable doubt to the jury as elements of the offense.[a]

On his version of the facts, Rosemond's assistance aided only one element (the drug transaction) of a two element (drugs plus firearm) offense. The Court unanimously holds this immaterial. It endorsed the common law rule that "imposed aiding and abetting liability on a person (possessing the requisite intent) who facilitated any part—even though not every part—of a criminal venture." Was it right to do so? Should it be required that Rosemond also assist the gun-use element of the offense?

## 2. AMOUNT OF CONDUCT

Whatever the answers to the preceding questions, there is no doubt that Rosemond actively participated in a substantial part of the criminal transaction. He clearly aided and abetted the drug offense. A question that commonly arises in other complicity prosecutions, however, is how much aid is enough.

Consider, for example, the facts of Creek v. United States, 324 A.2d 688 (D.C. App. 1974) (per curiam):

> The evidence shows that on a late winter afternoon, a married woman, who lived in the Capitol Hill section, was returning with her son from a shopping trip. As she parked her car on a side street near her house, she noticed three young men walking together on the sidewalk in her direction. She waited until they had passed her car and then walked behind them around the corner to her home, a rowhouse with a front gate and stairs leading up to the door.
>
> When she reached her gate the trio were ahead of her on the sidewalk and still walking. After closing the gate behind her and starting to unlock the door, one of the youths suddenly materialized on the doorstep, pulled her pocketbook from under her arm, ran down the stairs and jumped over the gate. She turned and saw his two companions watching just outside the gate, slightly crouched. As the purse-snatcher made his exit, they ran with him down the street.

---

[a] See Harris v. United States, 536 U.S. 545 (2002).

> The woman reported the incident to a reserve police officer who happened to be passing and had seen the group run in front of his car. He pursued them on foot but lost them as they rounded a corner. Soon thereafter, a police officer in a scout car, pursuant to a radio message, saw three persons running together a few blocks from the scene. He was able to catch only one, appellant. The latter was arrested and identified by the victim almost immediately thereafter as one of the two standing beside the gate when her pocketbook was grabbed.

A subsequent conviction of robbery on an aiding and abetting theory was affirmed on appeal:

> Presence at the scene of the crime, while insufficient without more to prove criminal complicity will nevertheless, constitute aiding and abetting if it "designedly encourages the perpetrator, facilitates the unlawful deed . . . or . . . stimulates others to render assistance to the criminal act." Bailey v. United States, 135 U.S. App. D.C. 95, 98–99, 416 F.2d 1110, 1113–14 (1969). . . .
>
> Appellant was no innocent bystander. He was walking in the company of the actual robber immediately prior to the offense, retraced his steps with him when the latter turned back to complainant's house and stationed himself at the front gate while the purse was being seized. He fled with the thief and he was still with him when they were confronted by the police. The inference that appellant's presence by the gate "designedly encouraged" or "facilitated" the robbery is clearly warranted.

Is it clear that Creek engaged in sufficient conduct to justify a robbery conviction?

Compare the facts of State v. Vaillancourt, 122 N.H. 1153, 453 A.2d 1327 (1982):

> The factual backdrop of the case involves an attempted burglary on the morning of December 8, 1980, at the O'Connor residence in Manchester. On that day, a neighbor observed two young men, allegedly the defendant, David W. Vaillancourt, and one Richard Burhoe, standing together on the O'Connors' front porch. The men were ringing the doorbell and conversing with one another. Because they remained on the porch for approximately ten minutes, the neighbor became suspicious and began to watch them more closely. She saw them walk around to the side of the house where Burhoe allegedly attempted to break into a basement window. The defendant allegedly stood by and watched his companion, talking to him intermittently while the companion tried to pry open the window. The neighbor notified the police, who apprehended the defendant and Burhoe as they were fleeing the scene.

The Court dismissed the ensuing indictment:

> The crime of accomplice liability . . . necessitates some active participation by the accomplice. We have held that . . . mere presence at the scene of a crime could not support a conviction for accomplice liability because [it is not a] sufficient affirmative act[ ] to satisfy the actus reus requirement of the accomplice liability statute.

*[margin note: accomplice liability needs active participation mere presence not enough]*

> In the instant case, other than the requisite mens rea, the State alleged only that the defendant aided Burhoe "by accompanying him to the location of the crime and watching . . ." Consistent with our rulings with respect to "mere presence," we hold that accompaniment and observation are not sufficient acts to constitute "aid" under [our statute]. We conclude that the trial court erred in upholding the defendant's indictment.

Is it clear that Vaillancourt did not engage in sufficient conduct to justify an attempted burglary conviction? Is his case distinguishable from Creek's?

### 3. A PROBLEM AND AN ANALOGY

As the preceding note illustrates, the traditional words used to describe the conduct required for accomplice liability—e.g., "aids, abets, counsels, commands, induces or procures" in 18 U.S.C. § 2—are not very limiting. On the contrary, they are exceedingly broad. The reach of such language has been justified on the grounds that so long as a purpose to promote or facilitate the offense "is proved, there is, it would seem, little risk of innocence; nor does there seem to be occasion to inquire into the precise extent of influence exerted on the ultimate commission of the crime." ALI, Model Penal Code and Commentaries, § 2.06, p. 314 (1985). Is this persuasive? Is it clear that so long as proof of a purpose to facilitate is required, there is no risk of unwarranted conviction?

Compare the law of attempt. Attempt requires proof of the actor's purpose to complete the underlying offense. Yet the law does not rest liability entirely on proof of purpose. It also mandates an independent inquiry into the sufficiency of the actor's conduct. In the phraseology of the common law, this is the distinction between a criminal attempt and mere preparation. Under the Model Penal Code and derivative statutes, this issue is addressed through the requirement of "an act or omission constituting a substantial step in a course of conduct planned to culminate in [the] commission of the crime." MPC § 5.01(1)(c). This standard is elaborated further by examples and by the general specification that it must be conduct "strongly corroborative of the actor's criminal purpose." MPC § 5.01(2). Why is the same concern not present in the context of accomplice liability? Should the approach to this question in the law of attempt be adapted for inclusion in the law of complicity? Would it have helped in a case like *Creek* or *Vaillancourt* if the issue was put in terms of whether the defendant took a "substantial step" to aid or encourage commission of the offense and if on review the question was whether there was sufficient evidence on which such a conclusion could be reached?

One answer under the language of the Model Code itself ("aids . . . or attempts to aid") might be that either actual (substantial?) aid is required, in which case the actor's culpability is corroborated by the fact of assistance in a criminal endeavor, or an attempt to aid is required, in which case the standards of § 5.01 apply. Is this a sufficient response? Should the Model Penal Code be interpreted to require a "substantial step" in all accomplice liability cases?

## NOTES ON THE INTENT REQUIRED FOR COMPLICITY

### 1. QUESTIONS AND COMMENTS ON *ROSEMOND*

The Court held in *Rosemond* that the mens rea required for complicity was derived from the well-known formulation by Judge Learned Hand that the defendant "must not just 'in some sort associate himself with the venture,' but also 'participate in it as in something that he wishes to bring about' and 'seek by his action to make it succeed.'" United States v. Peoni, 100 F.2d 401, 402 (2d Cir. 1938). This standard is often reduced to the shorthand that the accomplice must have a "stake in the venture." On the facts of *Rosemond* this translated into a requirement that the defendant know in advance that one of his companions was armed, knowledge that would "enable[ ] him to make the relevant legal (and indeed, moral) choice" and that would confirm his choice "to align himself with the illegal scheme in its entirety."

In other words, Rosemond had to know about the weapon early enough to have formed the intent to "align himself" with the crime of using a firearm in a drug transaction. For the Court, this meant that he had to have this "knowledge at a time the accomplice can do something with it—most notably, opt to walk away." Is this the right focus? If the jury found that Rosemond had learned that his companion was armed at a point when it was too late to walk away but nonetheless that he still actively helped to complete the drug offense, would it be inappropriate to uphold a conviction for the drug-plus-firearm offense?

### 2. CULPABILITY REQUIRED FOR RESULTS

As a textual matter, one might conclude that the purpose required by *Rosemond* extends at least to the *conduct* elements of the offense committed by the principal actor. Might the answer be different as to *result* elements?

There is little in the language of *Rosemond* to suggest that such a classification would matter. But the Model Penal Code has a specific provision that distinguishes the accomplice's mens rea as to the *conduct* of the principal from the mens rea as to *results* of that conduct. Section 2.06(4) states:

> When causing a particular result is an element of an offense, an accomplice in the conduct causing such result is an accomplice in the commission of that offense, if he acts with the kind of culpability, if any, with respect to that result that is sufficient for the commission of the crime.

An illustration of how this provision might be applied is provided by the Alaska Court of Appeals decision in Riley v. State, 60 P.3d 204, 221 (2002). Riley had been convicted on two counts of first-degree assault, defined as recklessly causing serious physical injury by means of a dangerous instrument. He and a companion had fired weapons into an unsuspecting crowd and seriously injured two persons. The prosecutor could easily prove that the injuries were caused by one of the two but, as often happens in such situations, lacked physical or other evidence as to which one. The court approved instructions permitting Riley's conviction as a principal or, if the jury could not find that he fired the wounding shots, as an accomplice. He was convicted as an accomplice. The court said:

> The rule at common law is that when a person purposely assists or encourages another person to engage in conduct that is dangerous to human life or safety, and unintended injury or death results, it does not matter which person actually caused the injury or death by their personal conduct. Any participant can be convicted of assault or manslaughter (or any similar crime involving proof of an unintended result) so long as the government can prove that the participant acted with the culpable mental state required for the underlying crime—"recklessness," "criminal negligence," "extreme indifference to the value of human life," etc.

common law rule

The Alaska complicity statute was based on § 2.06(3) of the Model Penal Code, but did not include a counterpart to § 2.06(4). The court nonetheless said that the "intent to promote or facilitate the commission of the offense" required by the Alaska wording

> means that the accomplice must act with the intent to promote or facilitate the *conduct* that constitutes the actus reus of the offense. With respect to offenses that require proof of a particular result, the government must prove that the accomplice acted with the culpable mental state that applies to that result, as specified in the underlying statute.

In *People v. Thomas*, a main case in Section 2 of Chapter V above, the court concluded that result elements in the crime of attempt should be handled the same way. The required purpose in an attempt prosecution, the *Thomas* court held, is an intent to "complete the risk-producing act or conduct." The mens rea for ensuing results, it continued, would be controlled by the mens rea for the object offense.

*Thomas*, as the Notes following the case make clear, states a distinctly minority position with respect to the crime of attempt. *Riley*, on the other hand, states the prevailing position for complicity. Why the difference? Why did the Model Penal Code require purpose with respect to results for attempt but use the mens rea for the target offense when dealing with an accomplice? Was it right to do so?

## 3. CULPABILITY REQUIRED FOR CIRCUMSTANCES

In contrast to the explicit differentiation of conduct and results, even modern penal codes fail to specify the state of mind required of an accomplice with respect to the attendant *circumstances* of the criminal conduct. There are two obvious possibilities. One is to require that the accomplice know that the circumstance element exists. The alternative is to require of the accomplice the same culpability required of the primary actor by the definition of the underlying offense. The difference between these formulations is posed by the following hypothetical:

> *A* is asked by his friend *B* to assist in the latter's seduction of *C*, a mutual acquaintance. Specifically, *B* wants to borrow *A*'s apartment. *A* agrees, and the seduction is accomplished. To the surprise of both *A* and *B*, *C* turns out to be underage.

Under traditional laws against statutory rape, *B* is strictly liable with respect to the age of the sexual partner. Thus, criminal punishment of *B* for consensual sexual intercourse with an underage person is authorized even if *B* honestly and reasonably believed *C* to be over the age of consent. The issue here is whether *A* may be held liable on the same basis or whether a special mens-rea requirement of knowledge should be imposed for complicity.

Current law on this question is unclear. Some statutes can be read to say that no special mens rea is required,[a] but most are ambiguous. How should the Model Penal Code be read on this question? Does the word "offense" in § 2.06(3)(a) refer to all elements of the object offense (including result elements?) or just to the offending conduct? The Model Code commentary says that:

> There is a deliberate ambiguity as to whether the purpose requirement extends to circumstance elements of the contemplated offense or whether, as in the case of attempts, the policy of the substantive offense on this point should control.

ALI, Model Penal Code and Commentaries § 2.06, p. 311 n.37 (1985). What language is ambiguous?

The absence of any settled common-law understanding is probably due to the infrequency with which the question arises. Perhaps for that reason, there seems to be no clear rule. If the issue arises, how should it be resolved? Is the discussion of the analogous issue in the law of attempt helpful?

## NOTES ON ADDITIONAL COMPLEXITIES IN THE *ROSEMOND* SITUATION

### 1. CONDUCT

Recall that the elements of the crime for which Rosemond was convicted were " 'us[ing] or carr[ying]' a firearm 'during and in relation to any crime of violence or drug trafficking crime.' " At the time of his prosecution, the "brandishing" and "dischargeing" provisions of the offense were treated as sentencing factors and as such could be found by a preponderance of the evidence by the trial judge after conviction. They did not need to be proved by the prosecutor beyond a reasonable doubt to the jury as elements of the offense.

The situation is different today. In Alleyne v. United States, 570 U.S. ___, 133 S. Ct. 2151 (2013), the Court held that, by constitutional compulsion, the provisions of § 924(c)(1)(A)(ii) and (iii) can be invoked only if they are treated as elements of the offense. So today the prosecutor would have to prove brandishing or discharge of the firearm beyond a reasonable doubt to the jury in order to justify a mandatory minimum sentence of seven or 10 years.

It is unlikely that this development would matter for the *conduct* component for complicity in a case like *Rosemond*. Presumably, participation in "any part—even though not every part—of [the] criminal venture" would still suffice, so long as the requisite intent was present. The impact of *Alleyne* on the mens rea issue, however, may be a different matter.

---

[a] See, e.g., N.Y. Penal Code § 20.00, which reads in its entirety as follows:

> When one person engages in conduct which constitutes an offense, another person is criminally liable for such conduct when, *acting with the mental culpability required for the commission thereof*, he solicits, requests, commands, importunes or intentionally aids such person to engage in such conduct. [Emphasis added.]

## 2. MENS REA

At the time of Rosemond's trial, the Court's mens rea standard meant that he had to have a stake in the drug venture and also know well enough in advance to do something about it that one of his companions would be armed. Today, the armed companion could be sentenced to a 10-year mandatory minimum only if the prosecutor proved beyond a reasonable doubt to the jury that the firearm was discharged. Does this mean that a person in Rosemond's situation today could be sentenced to the same 10-year mandatory minimum only if he knew in advance, in time to do something about it, that his companion would discharge the gun and also have a "wish" to bring the discharge about? Is it likely that a prosecutor could meet this burden? Is it sensible to require it?[a]

Whether the prosecutor should be required to prove knowledge or purpose with respect to the discharge element turns out to be a knotty problem. A logical place to start thinking about it is to isolate the mens rea for the discharge that would be required for the person who actually fired the weapon. The answer is strict liability. The defendant in Dean v. United States, 556 U.S. 568 (2009), discharged a gun accidentally during a bank robbery. His 10-year mandatory minimum sentence under § 924(c)(1)(A)(iii) was affirmed by the Supreme Court. It was appropriate in this instance, the Court held, to punish Dean for the unintended consequences of his unlawful act. He could readily have avoided discharge of the gun, the Court said, by leaving the gun at home or—better yet—by not committing the bank robbery in the first place.[b]

Given that no mens rea would be required on this component of the offense for the principal actor, would it make sense to come to the same conclusion for the accomplice? If so, is there any language in the Court's *Rosemond* opinion that would support this result? Would a person in Rosemond's situation have "align[ed] himself with the illegal scheme in its entirety" if the companion was known to be carrying a gun but its accidental discharge was a surprise?

Consider also how this situation would be handled under the Model Penal Code. Section 2.06(3) says that a person is an accomplice if the requisite assistance is accompanied by "the purpose of promoting or facilitating the commission of the offense." Is there any room in this language for strict liability for the accomplice if strict liability is applied to the principal actor's conduct in discharging the weapon? Consider also the Model Penal Code provision with respect to result elements. Might it be possible

---

[a] Rosemond's offense occurred in August of 2007 and the Court of Appeals affirmed his conviction in September of 2012. See Brief for the United States, *Rosemond v. United States*, at 1–2. *Alleyne* was decided in June of 2013 and *Rosemond* in March of 2014. Whether *Alleyne* should be held retroactively applicable to Rosemond's case presents a complex question that was not presented in *Rosemond* itself and that has not yet been resolved. The likelihood is that *Alleyne* will not be applied retroactively to convictions that were final at the time it was decided. See Schriro v. Summerlin, 542 U.S. 348 (2004). But since Rosemond's case was still in the direct appeal process, it may well be that he would be entitled to raise an *Alleyne* issue in a collateral attack on his conviction.

[b] *Dean* is excerpted in Note 4 of the Notes on Mens Rea Elements in Federal Crimes in Chapter IV. *Alleyne* was decided after *Dean*, and it is possible, as discussed in the Chapter IV Note, that this will change the mens rea for the discharge element to something more demanding than strict liability. But for present purposes it is best to assume that strict liability will still prevail on this element of the offense, and it is likely that this assumption will turn out to be correct.

to classify discharge of the weapon as a result element and therefore to measure each participant based on their own culpability as to that element? If so, and if the Supreme Court could be persuaded to follow the Model Penal Code on this point, would the courts then be free to apply strict liability to both the principal actor and the accomplice? If they could, then presumably it would only have to be proved that the accomplice knew about the weapon early enough to have formed the intent to "align himself" with the crime of using a firearm in a drug transaction. If not, then perhaps the prosecutor would be required to assume the far more difficult burden of proving in addition that he "aligned himself" with its discharge.

## SECTION 2: TWO ISSUES COMMON TO COMPLICITY AND CONSPIRACY

### PRELIMINARY NOTE ON THE RELATIONSHIP BETWEEN COMPLICITY AND CONSPIRACY

The crime of conspiracy often functions as an alternative to complicity. Formally, the two concepts are distinct. The law of complicity applies where one person's assistance in the commission of a crime justifies holding that person responsible for the crime even though the criminal act is committed by another. The law of conspiracy criminalizes agreement with another to commit a crime in the future. It functions analogously to the crime of attempt by imposing liability for a preliminary step in a course of conduct that is designed to result in the commission of an offense. Parties to such an agreement may also be criminally responsible for completed offenses that are the object of the conspiracy even though they do not personally commit the crimes themselves. This aspect of the law of conspiracy functions much like the law of complicity. It holds one conspirator responsible for crimes committed by another. In many situations, these two approaches to liability for the conduct of another can be functionally interchangeable.

Subsections A and B below illustrate this potential overlap by exploring two issues that arise in both the law of conspiracy and the law of complicity.

Subsection A deals with an ambiguity about the level of intent required for both complicity and conspiracy. Most cases hold that a true purpose to promote the object offense is required, a "stake in the venture" as Learned Hand suggested in *Peoni*. Some, however, require only that the secondary party provide substantial aid knowing that it will assist in the commission of a crime.

Subsection B covers the "natural and probable consequences" doctrine. When applicable, this doctrine holds one person responsible for additional crimes that are the "natural and probable consequences" of the crime for which responsibility as an accomplice or a co-conspirator has already been established.

## SUBSECTION A: KNOWING FACILITATION

### People v. Lauria

California Court of Appeal, Second District, 1967.
251 Cal.App.2d 471, 59 Cal.Rptr. 628.

■ FLEMING, ASSOCIATE JUSTICE. In an investigation of call-girl activity the police focused their attention on three prostitutes actively plying their trade on call, each of whom was using Lauria's telephone answering service, presumably for business purposes.

On January 8, 1965, Stella Weeks, a policewoman, signed up for telephone service with Lauria's answering service. Mrs. Weeks, in the course of her conversation with Lauria's office manager, hinted broadly that she was a prostitute concerned with the secrecy of her activities and their concealment from the police. She was assured that the operation of the service was discreet and "about as safe as you can get." It was arranged that Mrs. Weeks need not leave her address with the answering service, but could pick up her calls and pay her bills in person.

On February 11, Mrs. Weeks talked to Lauria on the telephone and told him her business was modelling and she had been referred to the answering service by Terry, one of the three prostitutes under investigation. She complained that because of the operation of the service she had lost two valuable customers, referred to as tricks. Lauria defended his service and said that her friends had probably lied to her about having left calls for her. But he did not respond to Mrs. Weeks' hints that she needed customers in order to make money, other than to invite her to his house for a personal visit in order to get better acquainted. In the course of his talk he said "his business was taking messages."

On February 15, Mrs. Weeks talked on the telephone to Lauria's office manager and again complained of two lost calls, which she described as a $50 and a $100 trick. On investigation the office manager could find nothing wrong, but she said she would alert the switchboard operators about slip-ups on calls.

On April 1 Lauria and the three prostitutes were arrested. Lauria complained to the police that this attention was undeserved, stating that Hollywood Call Board had 60 to 70 prostitutes on its board while his own service had only nine or 10, that he kept separate records for known or suspected prostitutes for the convenience of himself and the police. When asked if his records were available to police who might come to the office to investigate call girls, Lauria replied that they were whenever the police had a specific name. However, his service didn't "arbitrarily tell the police about prostitutes on our board. As long as they pay their bills we tolerate them." In a subsequent voluntary appearance before the grand jury Lauria testified he had always cooperated with the police. But he admitted he knew some of his customers were prostitutes, and he knew Terry was a prostitute because he had personally used her services, and he knew she was paying for 500 calls a month.

Lauria and the three prostitutes were indicted for conspiracy to commit prostitution, and nine overt acts were specified. Subsequently the trial court set aside the indictment as having been brought without reasonable or probable cause. The People have appealed, claiming that a sufficient showing of an unlawful agreement to further prostitution was made.

To establish agreement, the People need show no more than a tacit, mutual understanding between conspirators to accomplish an unlawful act. Here the People attempted to establish a conspiracy by showing that Lauria, well aware that his co-defendants were prostitutes who received business calls from customers through his telephone answering service, continued to furnish them with such service. This approach attempts to equate knowledge of another's criminal activity with conspiracy to further such criminal activity, and poses the question of the criminal responsibility of a furnisher of goods or services who knows his product is being used to assist the operation of an illegal business. Under what circumstances does a supplier become part of a conspiracy to further an illegal enterprise by furnishing goods or services which he knows are to be used by the buyer for criminal purposes?

The two leading cases on this point face in opposite directions. In United States v. Falcone, 311 U.S. 205 (1940), the sellers of large quantities of sugar, yeast, and cans were absolved from participation in a moonshining conspiracy among distillers who bought from them, while in Direct Sales Co. v. United States, 319 U.S. 703 (1943), a wholesaler of drugs was convicted of conspiracy to violate the federal narcotic laws by selling drugs in quantity to a co-defendant physician who was supplying them to addicts. The distinction between these two cases appears primarily based on the proposition that distributors of such dangerous products as drugs are required to exercise greater discrimination in the conduct of their business than are distributors of innocuous substances like sugar and yeast.

In the earlier case, *Falcone*, the sellers' knowledge of the illegal use of the goods was insufficient by itself to make the sellers participants in a conspiracy with the distillers who bought from them. Such knowledge fell short of proof of a conspiracy, and evidence on the volume of sales was too vague to support a jury finding that respondents knew of the conspiracy from the size of the sales alone.

In the later case of *Direct Sales*, the conviction of a drug wholesaler for conspiracy to violate federal narcotic laws was affirmed on a showing that it had actively promoted the sale of morphine sulphate in quantity and had sold codefendant physician, who practiced in a small town in South Carolina, more than 300 times his normal requirements of the drug, even though it had been repeatedly warned of the dangers of unrestricted sales of the drug. The court contrasted the restricted goods involved in *Direct Sales* with the articles of free commerce involved in *Falcone*:

> All articles of commerce may be put to illegal ends .... But all do not have inherently the same susceptibility to harmful and illegal use.... This difference is important for two purposes. One is for making certain that the seller knows the buyer's intended illegal use. The other is to show that by the sale he intends to further, promote and cooperate in it. This intent, when given effect by overt act, is the gist of conspiracy. While it is not identical with mere knowledge that another purposes unlawful action, it is not unrelated to such knowledge.... The

> step from knowledge to intent and agreement may be taken. There is more than suspicion, more than knowledge, acquiescence, carelessness, indifference, lack of concern. There is informed and interested cooperation, stimulation, instigation. And there is also a "stake in the venture" which, even if it may not be essential, is not irrelevant to the question of conspiracy.

While *Falcone* and *Direct Sales* may not be entirely consistent with each other in their full implications, they do provide us with a framework for the criminal liability of a supplier of lawful goods or services put to unlawful use. Both the element of *knowledge* of the illegal use of the goods or services and the element of *intent* to further that use must be present in order to make the supplier a participant in a criminal conspiracy.

Proof of *knowledge* is ordinarily a question of fact and requires no extended discussion in the present case. The knowledge of the supplier was sufficiently established when Lauria admitted he knew some of his customers were prostitutes and admitted he knew that Terry, an active subscriber of his service, was a prostitute. In the face of these admissions he could scarcely claim to have relied on the normal assumption an operator of a business or service is entitled to make, that his customers are behaving themselves in the eyes of the law. Because Lauria knew in fact that some of his customers were prostitutes, it is a legitimate inference he knew they were subscribing to his answering service for illegal business purposes and were using his service to make assignations for prostitution. On this record we think the prosecution is entitled to claim positive knowledge by Lauria of the use of his service to facilitate the business of prostitution.

The more perplexing issue in the case is the sufficiency of proof of *intent* to further the criminal enterprise. The element of intent may be proved either by direct evidence, or by evidence of circumstances from which an intent to further a criminal enterprise by supplying lawful goods or services may be inferred. . . . [I]n cases where direct proof of complicity is lacking, intent to further the conspiracy must be derived from the sale itself and its surrounding circumstances in order to establish the supplier's express or tacit agreement to join the conspiracy.

In the case at bench the prosecution argues that since Lauria knew his customers were using his service for illegal purposes but nevertheless continued to furnish it to them, he must have intended to assist them in carrying out their illegal activities. Thus through a union of knowledge and intent he became a participant in a criminal conspiracy. Essentially, the People argue that knowledge alone of the continuing use of his telephone facilities for criminal purposes provided a sufficient basis from which his intent to participate in those criminal activities could be inferred.

In examining precedents in this field we find that sometimes, but not always, the criminal intent of the supplier may be inferred from his knowledge of the unlawful use made of the product he supplies. Some consideration of characteristic patterns may be helpful.

(i) Intent may be inferred from knowledge, when the purveyor of legal goods for illegal use has acquired a stake in the venture. (United States v. Falcone, 109 F.2d 579, 581 (2d Cir., 1940)). For example, in Regina v. Thomas, 2 All E.R. 181, 342 (1957), a prosecution for living off the earnings of prostitution, the evidence showed that the accused, knowing the woman to be a convicted prostitute, agreed to let her have the use of his room between the hours of 9 p. m. and 2 a. m. for a charge of £3 a night. The Court of Criminal Appeal refused an appeal from the conviction, holding that when the accused rented a room at a grossly inflated rent to a prostitute for the purpose of carrying on her trade, a jury could find he was living on the earnings of prostitution.

In the present case, no proof was offered of inflated charges for the telephone answering services furnished the co-defendants.

(ii) Intent may be inferred from knowledge, when no legitimate use for the goods or services exists. The leading California case is People v. McLaughlin, 111 Cal.App.2d 781, 245 P.2d 1076 (1952), in which the court upheld a conviction of the suppliers of horse-racing information by wire for conspiracy to promote bookmaking, when it had been established that wire-service information had no other use than to supply information needed by bookmakers to conduct illegal gambling operations. . . . In such cases the supplier must necessarily have an intent to further the illegal enterprise since there is no known honest use for his goods.

However, there is nothing in the furnishing of telephone answering service which would necessarily imply assistance in the performance of illegal activities. Nor is any inference to be derived from the use of an answering service by women, either in any particular volume of calls, or outside normal working hours. Night-club entertainers, registered nurses, faith healers, public stenographers, photographic models, and free-lance substitute employees, provide examples of women in legitimate occupations whose employment might cause them to receive a volume of telephone calls at irregular hours.

(iii) Intent may be inferred from knowledge, when the volume of business with the buyer is grossly disproportionate to any legitimate demand, or when sales for illegal use amount to a high proportion of the seller's total business. In such cases an intent to participate in the illegal enterprise may be inferred from the quantity of the business done. For example, in *Direct Sales*, supra, the sale of narcotics to a rural physician in quantities 300 times greater than he would have normal use for provided potent evidence of an intent to further the illegal activity. In the same case the court also found significant the fact that the wholesaler had attracted as customers a disproportionately large group of physicians who had been convicted of violating the Harrison Act. . . .

No evidence of any unusual volume of business with prostitutes was presented by the prosecution against Lauria.

Inflated charges, the sale of goods with no legitimate use, sales in inflated amounts, each may provide a fact of sufficient moment from which the intent of the seller to participate in the criminal enterprise may be inferred. In such instances participation by the supplier of legal goods to the illegal enterprise may be inferred because in one way or another the supplier has acquired a special interest in the operation of the illegal [enterprise]. His intent to participate in the crime of which he has knowledge may be inferred from the existence of his special interest.

Yet there are cases in which it cannot reasonably be said that the supplier has a stake in the venture or has acquired a special interest in the enterprise, but in which he has been held liable as a participant on the basis of knowledge alone. Some suggestion of this appears in *Direct Sales*, where both the knowledge of the illegal use of the drugs and the intent of the supplier to aid that use were inferred. In Regina v. Bainbridge, 3 W.L.R. 656 (C.C.A.1959), a supplier of oxygen-cutting equipment to one known to intend to use it to break into a bank was convicted as an accessory to the crime. In Sykes v. Director of Public Prosecutions, [1962] A.C. 528, one having knowledge of the theft of 100 pistols, four submachine guns, and 1960 rounds of ammunition was convicted of misprision of felony for failure to disclose the theft to the public authorities. It seems apparent from these cases that a supplier who furnishes equipment which he *knows* will be used to commit a serious crime may be deemed from that knowledge alone to have intended to produce the result. Such proof may justify an inference that the furnisher intended to aid the execution of the crime and that he thereby became a participant. For instance, we think the operator of a telephone answering service with positive knowledge that his service was being used to facilitate the extortion of ransom, the distribution of heroin, or the passing of counterfeit money who continued to furnish the service with knowledge of its use, might be chargeable on knowledge alone with participation in a scheme to extort money, to distribute narcotics, or to pass counterfeit money. The same result would follow the seller of gasoline who knew the buyer was using his product to make Molotov cocktails for terroristic use.

Logically, the same reasoning could be extended to crimes of every description. Yet we do not believe an inference of intent drawn from knowledge of criminal use properly applies to the less serious crimes classified as misdemeanors. The duty to take positive action to dissociate oneself from activities helpful to violations of the criminal law is far stronger and more compelling for felonies than it is for misdemeanors or petty offenses. In this respect, as in others, the distinction between felonies and misdemeanors, between more serious and less serious crime, retains continuing vitality. In historically the most serious felony, treason, an individual with knowledge of the treason can be prosecuted for concealing and failing to disclose it. In other felonies, both at common law and under the criminal laws of the United States, an individual knowing of the commission of a felony is criminally liable for concealing it and failing to make it known to proper authority. But this crime, known as misprision of felony, has always been limited to knowledge and concealment of felony and has never extended to misdemeanor. A similar limitation is found in the criminal liability of an accessory after the fact, which is restricted to aid in the escape of a principal who has committed or been charged with a *felony*. We believe the distinction between the obligations arising from knowledge of a felony and those arising from knowledge of a misdemeanor continues to reflect basic human feelings about the duties owed by individuals to society. Heinous crime must be stamped out, and its suppression is the responsibility of all. Venial crime and crime not evil in itself present less of a danger to society, and perhaps the benefits of their suppression through the modern equivalent of the posse, the hue and cry, the informant, and the citizen's arrest, are outweighed by the disruption to everyday life brought about by amateur law enforcement and private officiousness in relatively inconsequential delicts which do not threaten our basic security. . . .

With respect to misdemeanors, we conclude that positive knowledge of the supplier that his products or services are being used for criminal purposes does not, without more, establish an intent of the supplier to participate in the misdemeanors. With respect to felonies, we do not decide the converse, viz. that in all cases of felony knowledge of criminal use alone may justify an inference of the supplier's intent to participate in the crime. The implications of *Falcone* make the matter uncertain with respect to those felonies which are merely prohibited wrongs. But decision on this point is not compelled, and we leave the matter open.

*[margin: misdemeanors needs more]*

*[margin: felony: knowledge suffices]*

From this analysis of precedent we deduce the following rule: the intent of a supplier who knows of the criminal use to which his supplies are put to participate in the criminal activity connected with the use of his supplies may be established by (i) direct evidence that he intends to participate, or (ii) through an inference that he intends to participate based on, (a) his special interest in the activity, or (b) the aggravated nature of the crime itself.

*[margin: rule]*

When we review Lauria's activities in the light of this analysis, we find no proof that Lauria took any direct action to further, encourage, or direct the call-girl activities of his codefendants and we find an absence of circumstances from which his special interest in their activities could be inferred. Neither excessive charges for standardized services, nor the furnishing of services without a legitimate use, nor an unusual quantity of business with call girls, are present. The offense which he is charged with furthering is a misdemeanor, a category of crime which has never been made a required subject of positive disclosure to public authority. Under these circumstances, although proof of Lauria's knowledge of the criminal activities of his patrons was sufficient to charge him with that fact, there was insufficient evidence that he intended to further their criminal activities, and hence insufficient proof of his participation in a criminal conspiracy with his codefendants to further prostitution. Since the conspiracy centered around the activities of Lauria's telephone answering service, the charges against his codefendants likewise fail for want of proof.

*[margin: holding]*

*[margin: holding insufficient evidence]*

*[margin: want of proof]*

In absolving Lauria of complicity in a criminal conspiracy we do not wish to imply that the public authorities are without remedies to combat modern manifestations of the world's oldest profession. Licensing of telephone answering services under the police power, together with the revocation of licenses for the toleration of prostitution, is a possible civil remedy. The furnishing of telephone answering service in aid of prostitution could be made a crime. Other solutions will doubtless occur to vigilant public authorities if the problem of call-girl activity needs further suppression.

*[margin: possible civil remedy]*

The order is affirmed. *[margin: disposition]*

## NOTES ON KNOWING FACILITATION

### 1. *BACKUN V. UNITED STATES*

As discussed in, *Rosemond v. United States*, Learned Hand's opinion in United States v. Peoni, 100 F.2d 401 (2d Cir. 1938), stated what is today accepted as the mens rea standard for liability as an accomplice. Most federal and state courts agree with this conclusion.

An early competitor to Hand's position in *Peoni* was Judge John J. Parker's opinion in Backun v. United States, 112 F.2d 635 (4th Cir. 1940). Backun sold stolen silverware to Zucker, and was convicted as an accomplice to Zucker's crime of transporting stolen goods in interstate commerce. Zucker testified for the prosecution after pleading guilty. Judge Parker said:

> . . . [I]t is to be noted that the case presented is not that of a mere seller of merchandise, who knows that the buyer intends to put it to an unlawful use, but who cannot be said in anywise to will the unlawful use by the buyer. It is the case of a sale of stolen property by a guilty possessor who knows that the buyer will transport it in interstate commerce in violation of law and who desires to sell it to him for that reason. The stolen property was not salable in New York. Backun knew that Zucker could dispose of it on his visits to the Southern pawnbrokers and would take it with him on his trips to the South. The sale was made at a grossly inadequate price and Zucker was credited for a part even of that. While there was no express contract that Zucker was to carry the property out of the state, Backun knew that he would do so; and, by making the sale to him, caused the transportation in interstate commerce just as certainly as if that transportation had been a term of the contract of sale. As his will thus contributed to the commission of the felony by Zucker, he would have been guilty at common law as an accessory before the fact to the commission of the felony. His guilt as a principal is fixed by 18 U.S.C. § 550, which provides that one who "aids, abets, counsels, commands, induces, or procures" the commission of an offense is guilty as a principal. . . .
>
> Whether one who sells property to another knowing that the buyer intends to use it for the commission of a felony renders himself criminally liable as aiding and abetting in its commission, is a question as to which there is some conflict of authority. It must be remembered, however, that guilt as accessory before the fact has application only in cases of felony; and since it is elementary that every citizen is under moral obligation to prevent the commission of felony, if possible, and has the legal right to use force to prevent its commission and to arrest the perpetrator without warrant, it is difficult to see why, in selling goods which he knows will make its perpetration possible with knowledge that they are to be used for that purpose, he is not aiding and abetting in its commission within any fair meaning of those terms. Undoubtedly he would be guilty, were he to give to the felon the goods which make the perpetration of the felony possible with knowledge that they would be used for that purpose; and we cannot see that his guilt is purged or his breach of social duty excused

because he receives a price for them. In either case, he knowingly aids and assists in the perpetration of the felony.

*Knowingly aids and assists*

Guilt as an accessory depends, not on "having a stake" in the outcome of the crime . . . but on aiding and assisting the perpetrators; and those who make a profit by furnishing to criminals, whether by sale or otherwise, the means to carry on their nefarious undertakings aid them just as truly as if they were actual partners with them, having a stake in the fruits of their enterprise. To say that the sale of goods is a normally lawful transaction is beside the point. The seller may not ignore the purpose for which the purchase is made if he is advised of that purpose, or wash his hands of the aid that he has given the perpetrator of a felony by the plea that he has merely made a sale of merchandise. One who sells a gun to another knowing that he is buying it to commit a murder, would hardly escape conviction as an accessory to the murder by showing that he received full price for the gun; and no difference in principle can be drawn between such a case and any other case of a seller who knows that the purchaser intends to use the goods which he is purchasing in the commission of felony. In any such case, not only does the act of the seller assist in the commission of the felony, but his will assents to its commission, since he could refuse to give the assistance by refusing to make the sale. . . .

*guilt depends on aiding and assisting the perps.*

*act of seller assists & his will assents*

But even if the view be taken that aiding and abetting is not to be predicated [on] an ordinary sale made with knowledge that the purchaser intends to use the goods purchased in the commission of felony, we think that the circumstances relied on by the government here are sufficient to establish the guilt of Backun. The sale here was not of a mere instrumentality to be used in the commission of felony, but of the very goods which were to be feloniously transported. Backun knew not only that the commission of felony was contemplated by Zucker with respect to such goods, but also that the felony could not be committed by Zucker unless the sale were made to him. The sale thus made possible the commission of the felony by Zucker; and, if Zucker is to be believed, the commission of the felony was one of the purposes which Backun had in mind in making the sale. After testifying that he had told Backun that he wished to go on the road with the silverware (i.e., transport it in interstate commerce), he says "He (Backun) knew that. That is the reason he wanted to sell it to me." There can be no question, therefore, but that the evidence sustains the view that the felony committed by Zucker flowed from the will of Backun as well as from his own will, and that Backun aided its commission by making the sale. There was thus evidence of direct participation of Backun in the criminal purpose of Zucker; and whatever view be taken as to the case of a mere sale, certainly such evidence is sufficient to establish guilt. . . .

*Feloniously transported*

*sale had to be made*

*one of the purposes*

*holding*

*- sufficient*

## 2.   KNOWLEDGE VS. STAKE IN THE VENTURE

*Peoni* and *Backun* are the most famous entries in debate about the culpability required for complicity. *Lauria* illustrates the same controversy in the law of conspiracy. The dispute is about the required culpability of the *required culpability of 2nd party*

secondary party with respect to the conduct of the primary actor. Must the accomplice or co-conspirator actually intend to promote the criminal venture in the sense of being interested in its success? Or should it suffice that the accomplice knowingly assisted criminal activity by another?

Recall footnote 8 in the Supreme Court's *Rosemond* opinion. The Court said there that it was not dealing with a case where defendants "incidentally facilitate a criminal venture rather than actively participate in it" and that it meant to "express no view about what sort of facts, if any, would suffice to show that such a third party has the intent necessary to be convicted of aiding and abetting." Resolution of this question matters in cases such as *Backun* and *Lauria* when a vendor sells something with knowledge that it will be used in the commission of a crime. Many other examples readily come to mind. Should a landlord be liable for crimes committed by a lessee if the landlord knows about use of the premises for illegal activity? Should one who knowingly but indifferently aids a terrorist act or a would-be assassin be immune from the consequences of those acts? In spite of the Court's disclaimer, does *Rosemond* have anything to say about how such cases should be resolved?

The drafters of the Model Penal Code had trouble coming to rest on these questions. The tentative draft on complicity read:

> A person is an accomplice of another person in commission of a crime if . . . acting with knowledge that such other person was committing or had the purpose of committing the crime, he knowingly, substantially facilitated its commission.

*MPC tentative draft §2.04*

MPC § 2.04 (Tent. Draft No. 1, 1953). This proposal was defended on the ground that knowing assistance should suffice for liability whenever such assistance *substantially* facilitated the criminal scheme. A vendor who sold goods in the ordinary course of business would not be liable as an accomplice to a customer's crime, even if the criminal purpose were known at the time of sale. On the other hand, a vendor of highly specialized goods (e.g., unregistered firearms or an obscure poison) or one who sold outside the ordinary course of business (e.g., through special credit arrangements to an otherwise uncreditworthy purchaser) likely would be covered.

*purpose of promoting or facilitating*

The wisdom of this approach came to be doubted. The quoted provisions were deleted by vote of the American Law Institute after a floor debate in which both Judge Hand and Judge Parker participated. As finally approved, the Model Penal Code imposes liability as an accomplice only where the aider has "the purpose of promoting or facilitating the commission of the offense." Is the change justified? Are there situations where the Tentative Draft approach would be preferable? Or is it too encompassing if applicable to all crimes?[a]

## 3.   COMPROMISE SOLUTIONS AND THE OFFENSE OF FACILITATION

*Split diff. btwn "Knowledge" and a "stake in the venture"*

Some have sought to split the difference between knowledge and a stake in the venture. One such effort was the original Model Penal Code proposal to punish knowing assistance as complicity, but only where

---

[a]   For a general treatment of this issue, see Louis Westerfield, The Mens Rea Requirement of Accomplice Liability in American Criminal Law—Knowledge or Intent, 51 Miss.L.J. 155 (1980). The involved but interesting history of the issue in California is analyzed in Catherine L. Carpenter, Should the Court Aid and Abet the Unintending Accomplice: The Status of Complicity in California, 24 Santa Clara L.Rev. 343 (1984).

it *substantially* facilitated commission of the offense. Another idea is to punish knowing assistance for serious offenses, but to require a stake in the venture for minor crimes. Although the courts seldom articulate a distinction of this sort, a review of the cases suggests that the gravity of the offense affects the readiness to base accomplice liability on knowing aid. *Lauria* follows this approach in suggesting that courts should be more generous in allowing jury inferences of intent from knowing assistance in the case of serious crimes than for minor offenses.

The most interesting compromise comes from the revised penal code of New York. The New York provision on complicity requires that the accomplice "intentionally aid" the criminal conduct of another. N.Y. Penal Code § 20.00. As the accompanying commentary explains, this formulation was intended to preclude liability as an accomplice for knowing aid rendered "without having any specific intent . . . to commit or profit from the crime." N.Y. Penal Code § 20.00, Practice Commentaries at 44. Additionally, however, the New York Code includes an entirely new series of offenses called "criminal facilitation," which are graded according to the seriousness of the facilitated offense. N.Y. Penal Code § 115.00 creates a Class A misdemeanor:

> A person is guilty of criminal facilitation in the fourth degree when, believing it probable that he is rendering aid
>
> 1. to a person who intends to commit a crime, he engages in conduct which provides such person with means or opportunity for the commission thereof and which in fact aids such person to commit a felony; or
>
> 2. to a person under sixteen years of age who intends to engage in conduct which would constitute a crime, he, being over eighteen years of age, engages in conduct which provides such person with means or opportunity for the commission thereof and which in fact aids such person to commit a crime.

Related provisions use similar language to grade criminal facilitation at various felony levels if committed under aggravating circumstances.

These provisions punish some, but not all, instances of knowing assistance to criminal activity by another. For one thing, the facilitation offenses require that the aid or assistance provide the principal actor "with means or opportunity for the commission" of the crime. This specification of the required quantum of assistance has no parallel in the New York complicity provision. It is reminiscent of the original Model Code proposal, which emphasized the substantiality of the facilitation as a criterion of liability. Moreover, most of the New York facilitation offenses are limited to conduct that aids others to commit a *felony*. With the exception quoted above in § 115.00(2), knowing assistance to misdemeanors is excluded. And finally, in each of the provisions the facilitation crime is graded less severely than the object offense.

For an argument in favor of a facilitation offense and analysis of its application in particular cases, see Catherine L. Carpenter, Should the Court Aid and Abet the Unintending Accomplice: The Status of Complicity in California, 24 Santa Clara L. Rev. 353, 363–70 (1984).

## SUBSECTION B: NATURAL AND PROBABLE CONSEQUENCES

### INTRODUCTORY NOTES ON THE RULE OF NATURAL AND PROBABLE CONSEQUENCES

#### 1. INTRODUCTION

The California Supreme Court said in People v. McCoy, 25 Cal.4th 1111, 1117, 24 P.3d 1210, 1213 (2001), that there are two different ways to measure the culpability of aiders and abettors:

> First, an aider and abettor with the necessary mental state is guilty of the intended crime. Second, under the natural and probable consequences doctrine, an aider and abettor is guilty not only of the intended crime, but also "for any other offense that was a 'natural and probable consequence' of the crime aided and abetted."

As applied to accomplice liability, the natural and probable consequences doctrine has origins that are deeply embedded in the common law and continues to have force in many jurisdictions—California is an example—even though not mentioned in the generic aiding and abetting statutes.[a] Some states, however, have explicitly codified the rule. For example, Kan Stat. Ann. § 21–5210 provides:

> (a) A person is criminally responsible for a crime committed by another if such person, acting with the mental culpability required for the commission thereof, advises, hires, counsels or procures the other to commit the crime or intentionally aids the other in committing the conduct constituting the crime.
>
> (b) A person liable under subsection (a) is also liable for any other crime committed in pursuance of the intended crime if reasonably foreseeable by such person as a probable consequence of committing or attempting to commit the crime intended.

To the same effect is Wis.Stat.Ann. § 939.05:

> (1) Whoever is concerned in the commission of a crime is a principal and may be charged with and convicted of the commission of the crime although the person did not directly commit it and although the person who directly committed it has not been convicted or has been convicted of some other degree of the crime or of some other crime based on the same act.
>
> (2) A person is concerned in the commission of the crime if the person:
>
> (a) Directly commits the crime; or
>
> (b) Intentionally aids and abets the commission of it; or
>
> (c) Is a party to a conspiracy with another to commit it or advises, hires, counsels or otherwise procures another to

---

[a] The generic California aiding and abetting statute, for example, provides:

> All persons concerned in the commission of a crime, whether it be felony or misdemeanor, and whether they directly commit the act constituting the offense, or aid and abet in its commission, or, not being present, have advised and encouraged its commission . . . are principals in any crime so committed.

> commit it. Such a party is also concerned in the commission of any other crime which is committed in pursuance of the intended crime and which under the circumstances is a natural and probable consequence of the intended crime. This paragraph does not apply to a person who voluntarily changes his or her mind and no longer desires that the crime be committed and notifies the other parties concerned of his or her withdrawal within a reasonable time before the commission of the crime so as to allow the others also to withdraw.

## 2. HOW THE RULE FUNCTIONS

Section 187 of the California Penal Code defines murder as "the unlawful killing of a human being . . . with malice aforethought." Section 188 adds (in typically colorful common law terminology) that malice can be express "when there is manifested a deliberate intention unlawfully to take away the life of a fellow creature" or it can be implied "when the circumstances attending the killing show an abandoned and malignant heart." Section 189 then divides murder into degrees. First degree murder includes any kind of "willful, deliberate, and premeditated killing." Second degree murder is "all other kinds of murders." Leaving aside the death penalty, first degree murder is punishable by life without parole or a prison term of 25 years to life. And leaving aside certain special categories of second degree murder, the default punishment for second degree murder is 15 years to life.

As developed in more detail in Chapter X, the phrase "willful, deliberate, and premeditated" is derived from a 1794 Pennsylvania statute that was widely copied throughout the United States. In some jurisdictions—Pennsylvania is one of them—it means no more than an intent to kill. But in California, the terms are taken literally. In People v. Anderson, 70 Cal.2d 15, 73 Cal.Rptr. 550, 447 P.2d 942 (1968), the court quoted other cases in describing their meaning:

> " '[t]he intent to kill must be . . . formed upon a *pre-existing* reflection' [and must have] been the subject of actual deliberation or *forethought*." We have therefore [required that the killer act] "as a result of careful thought and weighing of considerations; as a *deliberate* judgment or plan; carried on coolly and steadily, [especially] according to a *preconceived design*."

Second degree murder in California—"all other kinds of murder" according to the statute quoted above—thus would include an intent to kill that is not formed in this manner, as well as other types of murder that fit within the common law term "malice aforethought." Again the full meaning of "malice aforethought" is developed in more detail in Chapter X, but for present purposes it can be taken to encompass homicides committed with a level of culpability that is at least an egregious form of recklessness.[b]

So in summary, the principal actor in a homicide in California can be convicted of first degree murder only if the decision to kill was formed after

---

[b] In *People v. Chiu*, the next main case, the court paraphrased another California decision that described the required culpability for second degree murder as "the intentional killing without premeditation and deliberation or an unlawful killing proximately caused by an intentional act, the natural consequences of which are dangerous to life, performed with knowledge of the danger and with conscious disregard for human life."

careful planning and reflection and can be convicted of second degree murder if the actor intended to kill or was extremely reckless as to death. Consider now how the natural and probable consequences rule would operate if applied to this grading scheme. Liability of the accomplice for *either* first or second degree murder (depending, presumably, on which level of homicide was committed by the principal) could be based, essentially, on ordinary negligence.[c]

*accomplice liability "ordinary ~~responsibility~~ negligence"*

The two actors—the principal and the accomplice—are thus measured by dramatically different culpability standards. The question to be considered in connection with the materials that follow is whether this conclusion can be justified. Does it make sense to continue the natural and probable consequences rule in the various contexts in which it is applied below?

## 3. STATUS OF THE RULE

*rule of natural and probable consequences good law in accomplice liability*

The rule of natural and probable consequences is still good law as applied to accomplice liability in some jurisdictions. It has been abandoned, however, in most states that have adopted comprehensive revisions of their penal laws. This, at least, is the implication of those statutes, such as Model Penal Code § 2.06(3)(a), that expressly require that the accomplice have "the purpose of promoting or facilitating the commission of the offense" by the principal actor. See, e.g., Haw. Rev. Stat. § 702–222; Cons. Penn. Stat. Ann. tit. 18, § 306(c); Or. Rev. Stat. § 161.155. Such provisions presumably adopt the *Peoni* mens rea principle and preclude liability as an accomplice where the particular purpose to promote or facilitate the crimes committed by the principal's conduct cannot be proved.

*MPC §2.06(3)*

Recall, however, the discussion of result elements in the Notes on the Intent Required for Complicity following *Rosemond v. United States*, the main case in Section 1 above. Under § 2.06(4) of the Model Penal Code, the liability of both primary and secondary actors is measured by their own culpability as to results:

*§2.06(4)*

> When causing a particular result is an element of an offense, an accomplice in the conduct causing such result is an accomplice in the commission of that offense, if he acts with the kind of culpability, if any, with respect to that result that is sufficient for the commission of the crime.

*accomplice mens rea*

The Model Penal Code would therefore handle an accomplice's liability for homicide based on the *accomplice*'s mens rea for the result of death if the requisite purpose to promote or facilitate the principal's conduct could be proved. Under the natural and probable consequences rule, on the other hand, the liability of the principal actor is measured by the culpability required for the offense committed but the liability of secondary participants is measured by a standard of reasonable foreseeability. Section 2.06(4) rejects an independent natural and probable consequences rule for result offenses and instead measures each of the actors based on his or her own culpability as to the death.

*not for result offenses*  [his or hew own culpability]

---

c   As expressed in *People v. Chiu*, the accomplice is liable if the death was "reasonably foreseeable." As the court elaborated, "[i]t only requires that under all of the circumstances presented, a reasonable person in the defendant's position would have or should have known that the . . . offense was a reasonably foreseeable consequence of the act aided and abetted by the defendant."

## 4. *WILSON-BEY V. UNITED STATES*

Wilson-Bey v. United States, 903 A.2d 818 (D.C. 2006) (en banc), illustrates judicial acceptance of the Model Penal Code approach, at least for first degree murder, without the aid of codification. Wilson-Bey killed her victim after a violent confrontation in which Marbury, her sister, had provided assistance. Both were convicted of first degree murder. In reversing Marbury's conviction, the court held that "in any prosecution for premeditated murder, whether the defendant is charged as a principal or as an aider or abettor, the government must prove all of the elements of the offense, including premeditation, deliberation, and intent to kill."

The court based its conclusion on precedent and policy. As for precedent, it noted that *Peoni* "remains the prevailing authority defining accomplice liability" and that every U.S. Court of Appeals follows it, as do a "majority of state courts." Courts in only "a minority of jurisdictions have applied a 'natural and probable consequences' approach to accomplice liability." As for the policy of the matter, the court noted its agreement with the observations of a Maryland judge:

> When two or more persons are joint participants in a crime, they are joint participants only with respect to a single and common actus reus. Where, however, a single criminal act has different levels of blameworthiness contingent upon the particular mens rea with which it is perpetrated, multiple participants in that crime do not necessarily share the same mens rea. Although joint participation ultimately depends upon a mutual tie to the same criminal act, the individual mentes reae or levels of guilt of the joint participants are permitted to float free and are not tied to each other in any way. If their mentes reae are different, their independent levels of guilt, reflected by nondependent verdicts, will necessarily be different as well. . . .
>
> The mens rea or level of blameworthiness of a principal in the first degree by no means controls the mens rea or level of blameworthiness of a principal in the second degree or of an accessory before the fact. If three codefendants burst into a motel room and discover the wife of one of them in an act of adultery, what is the crime if the two adulterers are then shot and killed? If the triggerman (the principal in the first degree) is the cuckolded husband, the rule of provocation may mitigate his guilt downward to the manslaughter level. The accomplice who hands him the gun, however, will be guilty at least of murder in the second degree, notwithstanding the fact that he is aiding and abetting a mere manslayer. If the third codefendant, who led the suspicious husband to the motel room in the first place, knew full well what would there be found and had been scheming for some time thereby to get rid of the adulterous lover, his premeditated intent to kill would raise his guilt to the first degree notwithstanding the guilt of his fellow participants at lower levels. Conversely, the principal in the first degree (the triggerman) could have possessed a premeditated intent to kill and his aider and abettor, who handed him the gun in a fit of jealous rage, might be the beneficiary of the rule of provocation.

The court added its concurrence with the statements in the Model Penal Code commentary that "[t]o say that the accomplice is liable if the offense . . . is 'reasonably foreseeable' or the 'probable consequence' of another crime is to make him liable for negligence, even though more is required in order to convict the principal actor. This is both incongruous and unjust."[d] The court concluded that it served "neither the ends of justice nor the purposes of the criminal law" to permit Marbury's conviction on a natural and probable consequences theory.

## People v. Chiu

Supreme Court of California, June 2, 2014.
59 Cal.4th 155, 325 P.3d 972.

■ CHIN, J.

. . . [A] jury found defendant, Bobby Chiu, guilty of first degree willful, deliberate and premeditated murder (premeditated murder) . . . . [There was conflicting testimony about Chiu's part in a homicide that occurred during a gang-related brawl outside a pizzeria. One participant testified that he heard Chiu tell his friend Rickie Che during the melee to "[g]rab the gun." There was also testimony that Chiu said "shoot him, shoot him" before Che shot and killed Roberto Treadway. Another participant testified that he did not hear anything about a gun while he was fighting with Chiu. And Chiu testified that he never said anything about a gun, did not know that Che had a gun, and did not want Che to shoot Treadway nor expect that he would.]

The . . . prosecution set forth two alternate theories of liability. First, defendant was guilty of murder because he directly aided and abetted Che in the shooting death of Treadway. Second, defendant was guilty of murder because he aided and abetted Che in the target offense of assault or of disturbing the peace, the natural and probable consequence of which was murder.

Regarding the natural and probable consequences theory, the trial court instructed that before it determined whether defendant was guilty of murder, the jury had to decide (1) whether he was guilty of the target offense (either assault or disturbing the peace); (2) whether a coparticipant committed a murder during the commission of the target offense; and (3) whether a reasonable person in defendant's position would have known that the commission of the *murder* was a natural and probable consequence of the commission of either target offense.

The trial court instructed that to find defendant guilty of murder, the People had to prove that the perpetrator committed an act that caused the death of another person, that the perpetrator acted with malice aforethought, and that he killed without lawful justification. The trial court further instructed that if the jury found defendant guilty of murder as an aider and abettor, it had to determine whether the murder was in the first or second degree. It then instructed that to find defendant guilty of first degree murder, the People had to prove that the

[d] This passage continues: "[I]f anything, the culpability level for the accomplice should be higher than that of the principal actor, because there is generally more ambiguity in the overt conduct engaged in by the accomplice, and thus a higher risk of convicting the innocent." ALI, Model Penal Code and Commentaries § 2.06, p. 312 n.42 (1985).

perpetrator acted willfully, deliberately, and with premeditation, and that all other murders were of the second degree.

The jury found defendant guilty of first degree murder . . . .

[T]he Court of Appeal reversed the first degree murder conviction. It held that the trial court erred in failing to instruct sua sponte that the jury must determine not only that the murder was a natural and probable consequence of the target crime, but also that the perpetrator's willfulness, deliberation, and premeditation were natural and probable consequences.

*procedure*

We granted the People's petition for review. . . .

Penal Code section 31, which governs aider and abettor liability, provides in relevant part: "All persons concerned in the commission of a crime, whether it be felony or misdemeanor, and whether they directly commit the act constituting the offense, or aid and abet in its commission . . . are principals in any crime so committed." An aider and abettor is one who acts "with knowledge of the criminal purpose of the perpetrator *and* with an intent or purpose either of committing, or of encouraging or facilitating commission of, the offense." People v. Beeman, 35 Cal.3d 547, 560, 674 P.2d 1318, 1325 (1984).

*directly commit the act or aid and abet are principals*

*§2.06(4)*

"'A person who knowingly aids and abets criminal conduct is guilty of not only the intended crime [target offense] but also of any other crime the perpetrator actually commits [nontarget offense] that is a natural and probable consequence of the intended crime.'" People v. Medina, 46 Cal.4th 913, 920, 209 P.3d 105, 110 (2009). "Thus, for example, if a person aids and abets only an intended assault, but a murder results, that person may be guilty of that murder, even if unintended, if it is a natural and probable consequence of the intended assault." People v. McCoy, 25 Cal.4th 1111, 1117, 24 P.3d 1210, 1213 (2001).

*guilty of target offense and natural and probable consequence of intended crimes*

A nontarget offense is a "natural and probable consequence" of the target offense if, judged objectively, the additional offense was reasonably foreseeable. The inquiry does not depend on whether the aider and abettor actually foresaw the nontarget offense. Rather, liability "'is measured by whether a reasonable person in the defendant's position would have or should have known that the charged offense was a reasonably foreseeable consequence of the act aided and abetted.'" *Medina*, 46 Cal. 4th at 920, 209 P.3d at 110. Reasonable foreseeability "is a factual issue to be resolved by the jury." Id.

*reasonably foreseeable*

*reasonable person in the Δ's position would have or should have known*

. . . The natural and probable consequences doctrine was recognized at common law and is firmly entrenched in California law as a theory of criminal liability. . . . We may, as a court, determine the extent of aiding and abetting liability for a particular offense, keeping in mind the rational function that the doctrine is designed to serve and with the goal of avoiding any unfairness which might redound from too broad an application.[1]

Aider and abettor culpability under the natural and probable consequences doctrine is vicarious in nature. . . .

---

[1]  [A]iding and abetting is one means under which derivative liability for the commission of a criminal offense is imposed. It is not a separate criminal offense." People v. Francisco, 22 Cal.App.4th 1180, 1190 (1994).

> By its very nature, aider and abettor culpability under the natural and probable consequences doctrine is not premised upon the intention of the aider and abettor to commit the non-target offense because the nontarget offense was not intended at all. It imposes vicarious liability for any offense committed by the direct perpetrator that is a natural and probable consequence of the target offense. Because the nontarget offense is unintended, the mens rea of the aider and abettor with respect to that offense is irrelevant and culpability is imposed simply because a reasonable person could have foreseen the commission of the nontarget crime.

People v. Canizalez, 197 Cal.App.4th 832, 852, 128 Cal.Rptr.3d 565, 583 (2011).

The natural and probable consequences doctrine is based on the principle that liability extends to reach "the actual, rather than the planned or 'intended' crime, committed on the *policy* [that] . . . aiders and abettors should be responsible for the criminal *harms* they have naturally, probably, and foreseeably put in motion." People v. Luparello, 187 Cal.App.3d 410, 439 (1986). We have never held that the application of the natural and probable consequences doctrine depends on the foreseeability of every element of the nontarget offense. Rather, in the context of murder under the natural and probable consequences doctrine, cases have focused on the reasonable foreseeability of the actual resulting harm or the criminal act that caused that harm.

In the context of murder, the natural and probable consequences doctrine serves the legitimate public policy concern of deterring aiders and abettors from aiding or encouraging the commission of offenses that would naturally, probably, and foreseeably result in an unlawful killing. A primary rationale for punishing such aiders and abettors—to deter them from aiding or encouraging the commission of offenses—is served by holding them culpable for the perpetrator's commission of the nontarget offense of second degree murder. People v. Knoller, 41 Cal.4th 139, 143, 151–52, 158 P.3d 731, 732, 738–39 (2007) (second degree murder is the intentional killing without premeditation and deliberation or an unlawful killing proximately caused by an intentional act, the natural consequences of which are dangerous to life, performed with knowledge of the danger and with conscious disregard for human life). It is also consistent with reasonable concepts of culpability. Aider and abettor liability under the natural and probable consequences doctrine does not require assistance with or actual knowledge and intent relating to the nontarget offense, nor subjective foreseeability of either that offense or the perpetrator's state of mind in committing it. People v. Nguyen, 21 Cal.App.4th 518, 531, 26 Cal.Rptr.2d 323, 331 (1993) (inquiry is strictly objective and does not depend on defendant's subjective state of mind). It only requires that under all of the circumstances presented, a reasonable person in the defendant's position would have or should have known that the nontarget offense was a reasonably foreseeable consequence of the act aided and abetted by the defendant.

However, this same public policy concern loses its force in the context of a defendant's liability as an aider and abettor of a first degree premeditated murder. First degree murder, like second degree murder, is the unlawful killing of a human being with malice aforethought, but

has the additional elements of willfulness, premeditation, and delibera- *mental state is uniquely subjective and personal*
tion which trigger a heightened penalty. That mental state is uniquely
subjective and personal. It requires more than a showing of intent to
kill; the killer must act deliberately, carefully weighing the considerations for and against a choice to kill before he or she completes the acts
that caused the death. People v. Anderson. 70 Cal.2d 15, 447 P.2d 942
(1968). Additionally, whether a direct perpetrator commits a nontarget
offense of murder with or without premeditation and deliberation has
no effect on the resultant harm. The victim has been killed regardless of
the perpetrator's premeditative mental state. Although we have stated
that an aider and abettor's "punishment need not be finely calibrated to
the criminal's mens rea," People v. Favor, 54 Cal.4th 868, 878, 279 P.3d
1131, 1136 (2012), the connection between the defendant's culpability
and the perpetrator's premeditative state is too attenuated to impose *holding*
aider and abettor liability for first degree murder under the natural and
probable consequences doctrine, especially in light of the severe penalty
involved and the above-stated public policy concern of deterrence.

Accordingly, we hold that punishment for second degree murder is
commensurate with a defendant's culpability for aiding and abetting a
target crime that would naturally, probably, and foreseeably result in a *holding*
murder under the natural and probable consequences doctrine. We further hold that where the direct perpetrator is guilty of first degree premeditated murder, the legitimate public policy considerations of deter- *holding*
rence and culpability would not be served by allowing a defendant to be
convicted of that greater offense under the natural and probable consequences doctrine. . . . .

Aiders and abettors may still be convicted of first degree premeditated murder based on direct aiding and abetting principles. Under
those principles, the prosecution must show that the defendant aided or
encouraged the commission of the murder with knowledge of the unlawful purpose of the perpetrator and with the intent or purpose of committing, encouraging, or facilitating its commission. Because the mental *preserves distinction*
state component—consisting of intent and knowledge—extends to the
entire crime, it preserves the distinction between assisting the predicate crime of second degree murder and assisting the greater offense of
first degree premeditated murder. *McCoy*, 25 Cal.4th at 1118, 24 P.3d
at 1214 ("an aider and abettor's mental state must be at least that required of the direct perpetrator"); cf. Rosemond v. United States 572 *Rosemond*
U.S. ___, 134 S. Ct. 1240 (2014). An aider and abettor who knowingly
and intentionally assists a confederate to kill someone could be found to
have acted willfully, deliberately, and with premeditation, having
formed his own culpable intent. Such an aider and abettor, then, acts
with the mens rea required for first degree murder. . . .

The record shows that the jury may have based its verdict of first
degree premeditated murder on the natural and probable consequences
theory. . . . Regarding the remedy, the . . . People [may] accept a reduction of the conviction to second degree murder or . . . retry the greater *holding*
offense. . . . If the People choose to retry the case, they may seek a first
degree murder conviction under a direct aiding and abetting theory. . . .

Accordingly, we affirm the judgment of the Court of Appeal.

■ We Concur: BAXTER, WERDEGAR, and CORRIGAN, JJ.

■ Concurring and Dissenting Opinion by KENNARD, J.

I agree with the majority's affirmance of the Court of Appeal's decision, which reverses the judgment convicting defendant of first degree murder. I disagree, however, with the majority's reasons for the affirmance. . . . I would hold, as did the Court of Appeal, that the trial court committed prejudicial error by instructing the jury that it could convict defendant as an accomplice to *first degree murder* under the natural and probable consequences rule without any need to determine whether the particular circumstances that elevated the murder to first degree were reasonably foreseeable. . . .

*[margin note: disagree w/ reasoning]*

*[margin note: holding]*

The trial court gave the jury this instruction on the natural and probable consequences rule:

> Before you may decide whether the defendant is guilty of murder under a theory of natural and probable consequences, you must decide whether he is guilty of the crime of assault or disturbing the peace. To prove the defendant is guilty of murder, the People must prove that: 1. The defendant is guilty of assault or disturbing the peace; 2. During the commission of assault or disturbing the peace, a co-participant in that assault or disturbing the peace committed the crime of murder; and 3. Under all of the circumstances, a reasonable person in the defendant's position would have known that the *commission of the murder* was a natural and probable consequence of the commission of the assault or disturbing the peace. (Italics added.)

The court also instructed the jury that to prove defendant guilty of first degree murder the prosecution had to prove that the *perpetrator* acted willfully, deliberately, and with premeditation, but it did not tell the jury that it must find that a willful, deliberate, and premeditated act of murder was a natural and probable consequence of assault or disturbing the peace. . . .

[T]o convict an accomplice defendant under the natural and probable consequences rule, the jury must find that "the *offense*" committed by the perpetrator was "a natural and probable consequence of the target crime that the defendant aided and abetted." People v. Prettyman, 14 Cal.4th 248, 262, 926 P.2d 1013, 1020 (1996). Every offense is made up of factual elements, each of which must be proven by the prosecution to establish the commission of the offense. Thus, under the natural and probable consequences rule, *every element* of the offense must be foreseeable to a reasonable person in the accomplice defendant's position. If *any* element is not reasonably foreseeable, the commission of the offense is not reasonably foreseeable.

*[margin note: natural and probable consequences rule]*

*[margin note: every element must be foreseeable]*

Here, the jury convicted defendant of *first degree murder,* which, as pertinent here, is statutorily defined as a willful, deliberate, and premeditated killing with malice aforethought. But the trial court did not instruct the jury that to convict defendant accomplice of first degree murder the jury must find that it was reasonably foreseeable that the actual perpetrator, Che, would commit a *premeditated* murder. Instead, the court essentially instructed the jury that it could convict defendant of *first degree* murder if *any* murder was reasonably foreseeable. Murder includes not only premeditated (first degree) murder, but also unpremeditated (second degree) murder. Thus, the trial court's instructions here permitted the jury, applying the natural and probable consequences rule, to convict defendant of premeditated first degree murder based on a conclusion that only second degree murder was a reasonably foreseeable consequence of the target crimes of either assault or disturbing the peace. . . .

The majority sidesteps the question . . . whether under the natural and probable consequences rule the jury here had to find that *each element* of premeditated first degree murder was reasonably foreseeable, or whether . . . only the actual perpetrator's homicidal *act* was reasonably foreseeable. Instead, the majority creates an exception to the natural and probable consequences rule, declaring that it can *never* be the basis for a first degree murder conviction. . . . The majority's justifications for its newly created exception are unpersuasive. . . .

*[margin note: majority creates an exception]*

The majority says that imposing liability for *first degree* murder under the natural and probable consequences rule does not serve the purpose of that rule, which, according to the majority, is to "deter[ ] aiders and abettors from aiding or encouraging the commission of offenses that would naturally, probably, and foreseeably result in an unlawful killing." Noting that an unlawful killing is first degree murder only if it is premeditated, the majority observes:

> That mental state is *uniquely subjective* and personal. It requires more than a showing of intent to kill; the killer must act deliberately, carefully weighing the considerations for and against a choice to kill before he or she completes the acts that caused the death. Additionally, whether a direct perpetrator commits a nontarget offense with or without premeditation and deliberation has *no effect on the resultant harm.*

Thus, the majority concludes, "the connection between the defendant's culpability and the perpetrator's premeditative state is too attenuated to impose aider and abettor liability for first degree murder under the natural and probable consequences doctrine."

The essence of the majority's reasoning is that premeditation is "uniquely subjective" and does not affect the "resultant harm." But the majority does not explain why malice is any less subjective, or has any greater effect on the resultant harm. Therefore, the majority's reasoning proves too much. It precludes not only a first degree murder conviction based on the natural and probable consequences rule, but also a second degree murder conviction based on that rule.

*[margin note: majority reasoning precludes liability for murder]*

Yet the majority insists that holding defendants liable for second degree murder under the natural and probable consequences rule "serves the legitimate public policy concern of deterring aiders and abettors from aiding or encouraging the commission of offenses that would naturally, probably, and foreseeably result in an unlawful killing." Why is the mental state of malice foreseeable, but not the mental state of premeditation? The majority does not say. And why are the deterrent purposes of the natural and probable consequences rule served by applying it to second degree murder, but not to first degree murder? Again, the majority does not say.

When the California Legislature enacted the Penal Code in 1872, it said in section 31 that persons who "aid and abet" the commission of a crime are punishable as principals, but it left undefined the words "aid and abet." Because the natural and probable consequences rule has long been "an 'established rule' of American jurisprudence," *Prettyman*, 14 Cal.4th at 260, 926 P.2d at 1019, and was part of English common law (id.), it is reasonable to infer that the 1872 Legislature intended to include that rule within the meaning of "aid and abet" as that phrase is used in section 31. But it is *not* reasonable to infer, as the majority impliedly does here, that the 1872 Legislature intended to apply the rule to every crime *except* first degree murder. The majority makes no effort to tether that inference to anything in the common law, in this court's decisions preceding the Legislature's enactment of the Penal Code in 1872, or in the legislative history of section 31 to show a legislative intent to create a "first degree murder exception" to the applicability of the natural and probable consequences rule. What research *does* reveal is that for more than 40 years this court has upheld *first degree* murder convictions by juries instructed on the natural and probable consequences rule, without any hint that this might be legally problematic. [Citations omitted.]

In the majority's view here, the punishment for second degree murder (imprisonment for 15 years to life) is "commensurate with a defendant's culpability for aiding and abetting a target crime that would naturally, probably, and foreseeably result in a murder." But as this court has repeatedly stated, "in our tripartite system of government it is the function of the legislative branch to define crimes and prescribe punishments, and . . . such questions are in the first instance for the judgment of the Legislature alone," not the judiciary. In re Lynch, 8 Cal.3d 410, 414, 503 P.2d 921, 923 (1972). It is thus for the Legislature, not this court, to determine whether a defendant who aids a target crime that naturally and probably results in first degree murder deserves a prison sentence of 25 years to life (the punishment for first degree murder) or 15 years to life (the punishment for second degree murder). . . .

I would affirm the Court of Appeal's judgment.

■ We Concur: CANTIL-SAKAUYE, C.J., and LIU, J.

## NOTES ON THE RULE OF NATURAL AND PROBABLE CONSEQUENCES FOR ACCOMPLICE LIABILITY

### 1. QUESTIONS AND COMMENTS ON *PEOPLE V. CHIU*

Three approaches to Chiu's potential liability for murder were taken by various judges in the *Chiu* litigation. The trial judge thought a conviction of first degree murder was appropriate if any form of murder was the natural and probable consequence of Chiu's intentional assistance to the assault. The intermediate appellate court and the California Supreme Court dissenters disagreed. Their view was that Chiu could be convicted of first degree murder on the natural and probable consequences theory only if a *premeditated* murder was a reasonably foreseeable result of the assistance. The majority of the California Supreme Court rejected the natural and probable consequences theory altogether for first degree murder, but thought it acceptable for second degree murder. Which is the better position?

Is the majority position in *Chiu* internally consistent? It holds both the principal and the accomplice to the same culpability standards for the first degree offense. Chiu cannot be an accomplice to Che's premeditated murder, the court said, unless he too acted with premeditation and deliberation. As it quoted from another case near the end of its opinion, "an aider and abettor's mental state must be at least that required of the direct perpetrator." But the court sanctions differential culpability between the principal and the accomplice for murder in the second degree. Che was guilty of first degree murder based on a finding of premeditation, or he could have been convicted of second degree murder or manslaughter only if he was found to have acted with the culpability required for those offenses. Yet Chiu as an accomplice to the assault can be guilty of second degree murder based only on a finding of ordinary negligence as to the death. Does this make any sense? Why is the natural and probable consequences theory acceptable for second degree murder and not first degree? Why is it acceptable at all?

Revisit footnote 7 of the United States Supreme Court's opinion in *Rosemond v. United States*, the first main case in this Chapter. The Court said there that "[s]ome authorities suggest an exception to the general rule when another crime is the 'natural and probable consequence' of the crime the defendant intended to abet. . . . That question is not implicated here. . . . We therefore express no view on the issue." Since *Rosemond* involved only questions of federal criminal law, it of course has no binding effect on how California might choose to interpret its own criminal law. But could the natural and probable consequences doctrine be applied to an accomplice in a federal murder prosecution based on federal law consistently with the rationale in *Rosemond*?[a]

## 2. THE NATURAL AND PROBABLE CONSEQUENCES DOCTRINE IN OTHER CONTEXTS

After holding in agreement with Chiu that the natural and probable consequences doctrine could not be applied in a prosecution for first degree murder, the court in Wilson-Bey v. United States, 903 A.2d 818 (D.C. 2006) (en banc), added that "District of Columbia law treats a killing as first-degree murder, without requiring proof of intent to kill, only under two carefully circumscribed doctrines: felony murder and conspiracy." It added that "[e]ach of the two special doctrines has a unique rationale that does not exist in the markedly different context of accomplice liability."

---

[a] The traditionally worded federal murder statute, applicable within the special maritime and territorial jurisdiction of the United States, provides:

> Murder is the unlawful killing of a human being with malice aforethought. Every murder perpetrated by poison, lying in wait, or any other kind of willful, deliberate, malicious, and premeditated killing; or committed in the perpetration of, or attempt to perpetrate, any arson, escape, murder, kidnapping, treason, espionage, sabotage, aggravated sexual abuse or sexual abuse, child abuse, burglary, or robbery; or perpetrated as part of a pattern or practice of assault or torture against a child or children; or perpetrated from a premeditated design unlawfully and maliciously to effect the death of any human being other than him who is killed, is murder in the first degree.
>
> Any other murder is murder in the second degree.

18 U.S.C. § 1111. The federal accomplice liability statute, like its California counterpart, says nothing about the natural and probable consequences doctrine. See 18 U.S.C. § 2, quoted in Note 2(ii) in the Introductory Notes at the beginning of this Chapter.

Application of the natural and probable consequence doctrine in these two arenas is considered in separate sets of Notes below.

## NOTES ON THE *PINKERTON* DOCTRINE

### 1. INTRODUCTION TO THE LAW OF CONSPIRACY

The court in *Wilson-Bey* contrasted aiding and abetting liability to the conspiracy doctrine associated with *Pinkerton v. United States*. It seemed to accept the conclusion that the natural and probable consequences doctrine was appropriate in conspiracy prosecutions even if it would not be acceptable on the same facts if aiding and abetting were charged. The reasons for this conclusion are not clear, but that view probably prevails. *Pinkerton* has spawned an expansive and widely used theory of conspiracy law that provides an independent ground for holding one person liable for the conduct of another. There are several other aspects of conspiracy law that must be understood as background for consideration of the *Pinkerton* doctrine.

First, unlike the crime of attempt and liability as an accessory, conspiracy is typically an independent crime for which one can be prosecuted and convicted *in addition to* any crimes that are its object. The Model Penal Code rejects this position, providing in § 5.05(3)—a section that applies to both attempt and conspiracy—that "[a] person may not be convicted of more than one offense defined by this Article for conduct designed to commit or to culminate in the commission of the same crime." Most jurisdictions, however, authorize conviction for both a conspiracy and any object crimes that are committed in pursuance of the conspiracy. In no jurisdiction, however, can one be convicted for both an attempt and the completed crime that is its object. Nor is "being an accessory" anywhere a separate crime independently of conviction for the crime to which one is an accomplice.[a]

The rationale for cumulative convictions for a conspiracy and its object offense is murky. The standard explanation, advanced by the Supreme Court in Callanan v. United States, 364 U.S. 587 (1961), is that the special danger of concerted criminal activity warrants independent punishment. The Model Penal Code commentary responds:

> When a conspiracy is declared criminal because its object is a crime, it is entirely meaningless to say that the preliminary combination is more dangerous than the forbidden consummation; the measure of its danger is the risk of such a culmination. On the other hand, the combination may and often does have criminal objectives that transcend any particular offenses that have been committed in pursuance of its goals. In the latter case, cumulative sentences for conspiracy and substantive offenses ought to be permissible . . . .[b]

---

[a] See, e.g., footnote 1 of the majority opinion in *People v. Chiu*.

[b] ALI, Model Penal Code and Commentary § 5.03, p. 390 (1985). Thus, for example, if two people conspire to commit a bank robbery and then commit the robbery, there is only one crime under the Model Code (but two in most jurisdictions). But if two people agree to commit a series of bank robberies and are caught after the first one, all jurisdictions—and the Model Penal Code as well—would permit two convictions: one for the completed bank robbery and another for a conspiracy to commit other bank robberies in the future. The "special danger" associated with conspiracies, the Code drafters concluded, lies only in cases where there is a threat to commit future crimes that have not yet been consummated.

Second, there are significant trial advantages to the prosecution when a conspiracy is charged. Hearsay statements, normally inadmissible under the rules of evidence, are admissible in a conspiracy prosecution if offered by one conspirator to incriminate another. Conspiracy prosecutions also afford opportunities for joint trial of multiple defendants who are part of the same conspiratorial arrangement. This creates the possibility of incriminating finger-pointing among defendants who are represented by different lawyers and encourages the jury to draw a "birds of a feather" conclusion when at least some of the defendants are proved to be really bad actors. As Justice Jackson observed in a concurring opinion in Krulewitch v. United States, 336 U.S. 440, 454 (1949):

*(margin: ② conspiracy provides trial advantages to it)*

*(margin: birds of a feather)*

> A co-defendant in a conspiracy trial occupies an uneasy seat. There generally will be evidence of wrongdoing by somebody. It is difficult for the individual to make his own case stand on its own merits in the minds of jurors who are ready to believe that birds of a feather are flocked together. If he is silent, he is taken to admit it and if, as often happens, co-defendants can be prodded into accusing or contradicting each other, they convict each other.

Normally, the venue in a criminal case lies where the criminal act occurred. But in a conspiracy trial, venue is appropriate in the place where the agreement was made as well as where any act in furtherance of the agreement was performed. As Jackson added:

*(margin: venue)*

> [T]he crime is considered so vagrant as to have been committed in any district where any one of the conspirators did any one of the acts, however innocent, intended to accomplish its object. The government may, and often does, compel one to defend at a great distance from any place he ever did any act because some accused confederate did some trivial and by itself innocent act in the chosen district.

## 2. *PINKERTON V. UNITED STATES*

*(margin: Pinkerton brothers each convicted of conspiracy and additional crimes question could Daniel be liable for his partnership? (agreement) thus other offenses when he did not participate directly)*

Walter and Daniel Pinkerton were brothers engaged in moonshining. They were convicted of a conspiracy to violate tax provisions of the Internal Revenue Code. Walter was convicted of nine additional substantive crimes, and Daniel six. The convictions were affirmed in Pinkerton v. United States, 328 U.S. 640 (1946). There was, as Justice Douglas said for the Court, "no evidence to show that Daniel participated directly in the commission of the substantive offenses on which his conviction has been sustained." Indeed, as the dissent by Justice Rutledge pointed out, "Daniel in fact was in the penitentiary, under sentence for other crimes, when some of Walter's crimes were done." But the Court had no difficulty in affirming Daniel's convictions on the substantive counts:

*(margin: procedure dispute)*

> [S]o long as the partnership in crime continues, the partners act for each other in carrying it forward. It is settled that "an overt act of one partner may be the act of all without any new agreement specifically directed to that act." Motive or intent may be proved by the acts or declarations of some of the conspirators in furtherance of the common objective. A scheme to use the mails to defraud, which is joined in by more than one person, is a conspiracy. Yet all members are responsible, though only one did the mailing. The governing principle is the same when the substantive offense is committed by one of the conspirators in furtherance of the

*(margin: holding)*

unlawful project. The criminal intent to do the act is established by the formation of the conspiracy. Each conspirator instigated the commission of the crime. The unlawful agreement contemplated precisely what was done. It was formed for the purpose. The act done was in execution of the enterprise. The rule which holds responsible one who counsels, procures, or commands another to commit a crime is founded on the same principle. That principle is recognized in the law of conspiracy when the overt act of one partner in crime is attributable to all. An overt act is an essential ingredient of the crime of conspiracy under [18 U.S.C. § 371]. If that can be supplied by the act of one conspirator, we fail to see why the same or other acts in furtherance of the conspiracy are likewise not attributable to the others for the purpose of holding them responsible for the substantive offense.

A different case would arise if the substantive offense committed by one of the conspirators was not in fact done in furtherance of the conspiracy, did not fall within the scope of the unlawful project, or was merely a part of the ramifications of the plan which could not be reasonably foreseen as a necessary or natural consequence of the unlawful agreement. But as we read this record, that is not this case.

The operation of the *Pinkerton* rule was described in State v. Coward, 292 Conn. 296, 972 A.2d 691 (2009), as follows:

> [T]he focus in determining whether a defendant is liable under the *Pinkerton* doctrine is whether the coconspirator's commission of the subsequent crime was *reasonably foreseeable,* and not whether the defendant could or did *intend* for that particular crime to be committed. In other words, the only mental states that are relevant with respect to *Pinkerton* liability are that of the defendant in relation to the conspiracy itself, and that of the coconspirator in relation to the offense charged. If the state can prove that the *coconspirator*'s conduct and mental state satisfied each of the elements of the subsequent crime at the time that the crime was committed, then the defendant may be held liable for the commission of that crime under the *Pinkerton* doctrine if it was reasonably foreseeable that the coconspirator would commit that crime within the scope of and in furtherance of the conspiracy.

### 3. PERVASIVENESS OF THE *PINKERTON* RULE

Several modern codes do not adopt a natural and probable consequences theory for accomplices and limit the liability of co-conspirators to crimes for which generally applicable accomplice liability principles are satisfied. See, e.g., Code of Ala., §§ 13A–4–3(f), 13A–2–23; N.D.Cent. Code § 12.1–03–01(1)(c); 17–A Me.Rev. Stat.Ann. §§ 57, 151(5). These statutes are derived from the Model Penal Code. Section 5.03 of the Code punishes conspiracy itself, but individual conspirators are liable for crimes committed by their co-conspirators only under the accomplice liability principles contained in § 2.06. There is no independent basis in the Model Code conspiracy provisions for the prosecution of secondary parties for crimes committed pursuant to the conspiracy, and no incorporation of *Pinkerton* liability for either accomplices or conspirators.

The *Pinkerton* rule is probably the law, however, in a majority of American jurisdictions. Typically, it is enforced without explicit statutory support. Some modern statutes, however, do codify the rule, generally in the provision on complicity rather than in the section on conspiracy. Section 7.02 of the Texas Penal Code, entitled "Criminal Responsibility for the Conduct of Another," is an illustration. Subsection (a) sets forth the general requirements for complicity. Subsection (b) adds the following:

> If, in the attempt to carry out a conspiracy to commit one felony, another felony is committed by one of the conspirators, all conspirators are guilty of the felony actually committed, though having no intent to commit it, if the offense was committed in furtherance of the unlawful purpose and was one that should have been anticipated as a result of the carrying out of the conspiracy.[c]

One does not have to look far to find illustrations of the *Pinkerton* doctrine in practice. United States v. Zachery, 494 F.3d 644 (8th Cir. 2006), for example, involved a pre-*Rosemond* conviction for attempted bank robbery and brandishing a weapon in violation of 18 U.S.C. § 924(c). Zachery was one of two persons who attempted the bank robbery. The robber who brandished the firearm was never caught. The Court of Appeals described the District Court findings after a bench trial:

> Zackery did not possess the firearm and did not commit any overt act "to aid Robber No. 1 in the possession of the gun." However, the court found that "it was reasonably foreseeable to Mr. Zackery that a participant in the robbery would possess a weapon . . . based upon the complex planning that went into the commission of the robbery." Therefore, Zackery was guilty of the substantive § 924(c) offense based upon a *Pinkerton* theory of liability, namely, it was reasonably foreseeable to Zackery that his accomplice would use a firearm in furtherance of their conspiracy to commit a violent crime, attempted bank robbery.

The Court of Appeals held:

> Zackery argues that his conviction under the *Pinkerton* theory of liability impermissibly lessened the government's burden of proof of an aiding and abetting offense—from whether he knowingly aided commission of the offense to whether the offense was reasonably foreseeable and in furtherance of the conspiracy. We disagree. Zackery was charged with violating 18 U.S.C. § 924(c). Aiding and abetting, not itself an offense, was simply one way to prove him guilty of that charge. As the Supreme Court made clear in Nye & Nissen v. United States, 336 U.S. 613, 618–20 (1949), aiding and abetting and *Pinkerton* are *alternative theories* by which the government may prove joint criminal liability for a substantive offense. That the standards of proof are different is irrelevant. Thus, it is well settled that, "[e]ven in the absence of evidence supporting an aiding and

---

[c] See also Wis.Stat.Ann. § 939.05, quoted above in Note 2 of the Notes on the Rule of Natural and Probable Consequences for Accomplice Liability. The revised New Jersey Code appears to be even broader: "A person is legally accountable for the conduct of another person when . . . [h]e is engaged in a conspiracy with such other person." N.J.Stat.Ann. § 2C:2–6(b)(4). But the Supreme Court of New Jersey has held that this language was intended to constrain the liability of co-conspirators by the *Pinkerton* limitation. See State v. Bridges, 133 N.J. 447, 628 A.2d 270 (1993).—[Footnote by eds.]

abetting conviction, persons indicted as aiders and abettors may be convicted pursuant to a *Pinkerton* instruction." United States v. Comeaux, 955 F.2d 586, 591 (8th Cir. 1992).

An extreme example of the application of *Pinkerton* is found in State v. Coltherst, 263 Conn. 478, 820 A.2d 1024 (2003). Coltherst was convicted of capital murder and sentenced to life without parole. The murder occurred during a carjacking on the same day that Coltherst was released from a youth correctional facility for another offense. Coltherst and Johnson stole a car, kidnapped the driver, and forced him to help them withdraw money from an ATM. Johnson then drove to an interstate entrance ramp, ordered the driver out of the car, and shot him execution style. Coltherst knew Johnson had a gun, and indeed possessed it himself for part of the escapade. He gave it back to Johnson shortly before the killing. He was apparently surprised that Johnson shot the driver. He asked Johnson why he did so, and Johnson responded that he did not want any witnesses. Coltherst objected to instructions which "allowed the jury to convict him of intentional murder without finding that he had intended to kill the victim." The Court rejected the argument, holding that the conviction could be upheld because of *Pinkerton*:

*[marginalia: State v. Coltherst]*

> We conclude that the *Pinkerton* doctrine . . . should be applied in cases in which the defendant did not have the level of intent required by the substantive offense with which he was charged. The rationale for the doctrine is to deter collective criminal agreement and to protect the public from its inherent dangers by holding conspirators responsible for the natural and probable— not just the intended—results of their conspiracy. "[T]he danger which a conspiracy generates is not confined to the substantive offense which is the immediate aim of the enterprise." In other words, one natural and probable result of a criminal conspiracy is the commission of originally unintended crimes. When the defendant has "played a necessary part in setting in motion a discrete course of criminal conduct," he cannot reasonably complain that it is unfair to hold him vicariously liable, under the *Pinkerton* doctrine, for the natural and probable results of that conduct that, although he did not intend, he should have foreseen. The defendant in this case makes no claim that the nexus between his involvement in the conspiracy and Johnson's murder of the victim was "so attenuated or remote . . . that it would be unjust to hold the defendant responsible for the criminal conduct of his coconspirator." Accordingly, we conclude that the trial court properly instructed the jury that it could convict the defendant of intentional murder under the *Pinkerton* doctrine.

*[marginalia: apply Pinkerton when level of intent not there]*

*[marginalia: liable for natural and probable results of criminal conspiracy]*

*[marginalia: unless so attenuated or remote]*

The next to last sentence in the quotation above referred to a passage in State v. Diaz, 237 Conn. 518, 530, 679 A.2d 902, 911 (1996), where the court said that

*[marginalia: State v. Diaz]*

> there may be occasions when it would be unreasonable to hold a defendant criminally liable for offenses committed by his coconspirators even though the state has demonstrated technical compliance with the *Pinkerton* rule. . . . For example, a factual scenario may be envisioned in which the nexus between the defendant's role in the conspiracy and the illegal conduct of a coconspirator is so attenuated or remote, notwithstanding the fact that the latter's

*[marginalia: unreasonable]*

*[marginalia: nexus is so attenuated or remote]*

> actions were a natural consequence of the unlawful agreement, that it would be unjust to hold the defendant responsible for the criminal conduct of his coconspirator. In such a case, a *Pinkerton* charge would not be appropriate.

Is this an adequate escape hatch? Is it even sensible? How can something be attenuated and remote but natural and probable? Or is this simply a "mystifying cloud of words"[d] used to mask a compromise allowing a court to reject extreme applications of *Pinkerton* when its sense of justice is offended?

More broadly, is the natural and probable consequences rule a more acceptable basis for conspiracy liability than it is for liability as an accomplice? Or should the standards for liability be the same for both? The next Note considers potential rationales for holding that conspiracy is different. Are they persuasive?

### 4. RATIONALES FOR THE *PINKERTON* RULE

State v. Coward, 292 Conn. 296, 972 A.2d 691 (2009), offered the following rationale for the *Pinkerton* rule:

> In analyzing vicarious liability under the *Pinkerton* doctrine, we have stated that the *Pinkerton* doctrine . . . should be applied in cases in which the defendant did not have the level of intent required by the substantive offense with which he was charged. The rationale for the doctrine is to deter collective criminal agreement and to protect the public from its inherent dangers by holding conspirators responsible for the natural and probable—not just the intended—results of their conspiracy. . . . This court previously has recognized that [c]ombination in crime makes more likely the commission of crimes unrelated to the original purpose for which the group was formed. In sum, the danger which a conspiracy generates is not confined to the substantive offense which is the immediate aim of the enterprise. . . . In other words, one natural and probable result of a criminal conspiracy is the commission of originally unintended crimes. Indeed, we specifically have contrasted *Pinkerton* liability, "which is predicated on an agreement to participate in the conspiracy, and requires the substantive offense to be a reasonably foreseeable product of that conspiracy" State v. Martinez, 278 Conn. 598, 615, 900 A.2d 485, 495 (2006), with accessorial liability, which "requires the defendant to have the specific mental state required for the commission of the substantive crime." Id.

In Wilson-Bey v. United States, 903 A.2d 818 (D.C. 2006) (en banc), the Court limited the operation of the natural and probable consequences rule in the context of accomplice liability but defended it for conspiracies:

> The rationale of *Pinkerton,* which imposes liability on members of a conspiracy for certain acts of co-conspirators, turns on the existence of a criminal agreement. "[T]he agreement is

[d] The phrase is borrowed from a lecture given by Judge Cardozo to the Academy of Medicine in 1928 and published in Law and Literature (1931). He used it in connection with the "mystifying" language in which New York distinguished between first and second degree murder. The phrase is quoted in context in Note 1(i) of the Notes on First-Degree Murder in Section 2 of Chapter X.

the 'essence' or 'gist' of the crime of conspiracy." Wayne R. LaFave, Substantive Criminal Law § 12.2(a) at 266 (2d ed.2003). A criminal conspiracy is an offense "of the gravest character" that implicates concerns beyond the commission of the substantive crime which is the object of the conspiracy:

> A conspiracy is a partnership in crime. It has ingredients, as well as implications, distinct from the completion of the unlawful project. . . . "For two or more to confederate and combine together to commit or cause to be committed a breach of the criminal laws, is an offense of the gravest character, sometimes quite outweighing, in injury to the public, the mere commission of the contemplated crime. It involves deliberate plotting to subvert the laws, educating and preparing the conspirators for further and habitual criminal practices. And it is characterized by secrecy, rendering it difficult of detection, requiring more time for its discovery, and adding to the importance of punishing it when discovered."

Pinkerton v. United States, 328 U.S. 640, 644 (1946) (quoting United States v. Rabinowich, 238 U.S. 78, 88 (1915)).

Foreseeable acts of co-conspirators in furtherance of a conspiracy are imputed to the conspirator-defendant because the co-conspirators are deemed by the law to be his agents. In principle, the law treats the co-conspirator as the conspirator-defendant's alter ego, and presumes him to be bound by the pre-existing conspiracy to achieve his fellow co-conspirators' shared objectives. This court has recognized the uncommon character of this aspect of conspiracy law:

> Conspiracy is a unique theory of liability that renders individual defendants guilty of any offense committed by co-conspirators in furtherance of the conspiracy. . . . Special evidentiary rules apply where a conspiracy is charged or alleged, and hearsay evidence . . . may be introduced against a co-conspirator under the exception for admissions or statements of party opponent on the theory that one co-conspirator is the agent of another. [*B*]*ecause the agency theory underlies conspiracy liability*, the only admissions of party opponent admissible in a trial where the government seeks to assign vicarious liability to co-conspirators are those statements and acts of a co-conspirator *made during and in furtherance of the conspiracy*.

Akins v. United States, 679 A.2d 1017, 1028 (D.C. 1996) (emphasis added).

## NOTE ON FELONY MURDER AND THE NATURAL AND PROBABLE CONSEQUENCES DOCTRINE

The court in *People v. Chiu* said, "An aider and abettor's liability for murder under the natural and probable consequences doctrine operates independently of the felony-murder rule. Our holding in this case does not affect or limit an aider and abettor's liability for first degree felony murder." And recall that *Wilson-Bey* said that the felony murder doctrine is a second special situation where the natural and probable consequences idea is still used in District of Columbia law.

Debate about the justifications for and content of the felony murder rule is postponed to the Chapter X materials on homicide. It should be noted here, however, that application of the natural and probable consequences concept has completely different implications for felony murder than it does for complicity and conspiracy.

One difference is that the felony murder doctrine applies the same mens rea standard to *both* the principal actor *and* the accomplice. However that doctrine is defined and whatever its ultimate scope, one of its important functions is to reduce the mens rea for the primary actor. Statutes that define first degree murder as a deliberate and premeditated killing also commonly provide that any conduct that causes a death during the commission of certain listed felonies constitutes first degree murder. See, for example, the federal murder statute quoted in the footnote in the Notes following *People v. Chiu* above. The person who causes the death in such a situation can be convicted of first degree murder no matter whether the death was caused deliberately and with premeditation, whether it was caused recklessly or negligently, or whether it was merely accidental. Strict liability is applied to homicides that occur during the course of an included felony.

*If* this is the right result for the principal actor—and whether it is right is best considered in the context of cases to be read in Chapter X—it is a small step to say that accomplices in the felony should be liable for murder under the same standard. If the culpability of the principal actor and the accomplice is the same with respect to the death, the reasoning would go, they should both be treated the same way.

There is a second important difference. The traditional statement of the felony murder rule is that the actors are responsible for deaths that occur during the commission of a felony whether or not the death was intended, recklessly or negligently caused, or accidental. When the principal actor is made liable for felony murder only for deaths that are the natural and probable result of the commission of the felony, however, the natural and probable consequences concept is acting as a *limitation* on the reach of the felony murder doctrine. Under this rule, an accidental killing during the course of a listed felony would be *excluded* from felony murder if it were not a natural and probable result of the felony. *Both* the principal actor *and* the accomplice would be entitled to take advantage of this limitation on the reach of the doctrine.

The operation of the natural and probable consequences doctrine in the felony murder context is therefore quite different from its operation in the context of complicity and conspiracy. When used for complicity and conspiracy, its effect is to *extend* the liability of secondary parties by applying to them a *lesser* mens rea standard than would be applicable to the principal actor. If Wilson-Bey can only be liable for murder by proof of premeditation and deliberation, to use that situation as an example, a lesser standard of culpability would be applied to her sister if her sister could be convicted on the theory that she was an accomplice to an assault and the death was a natural and probable consequence of the assault. This, the *Wilson-Bey* court held, would be unfair to the sister.

The point at this stage is not to say anything about whether the law should contain a felony murder rule or, if so, what its content should be. The point is that the acceptability of the natural and probable consequences doctrine in the context of accomplice and conspiracy liability raises completely different concerns than does the same idea in the context of felony murder. The focus now should be on use of the doctrine in the laws of complicity and conspiracy. Debate about its use in felony murder—and indeed about whether the felony murder rule should be recognized at all—raises different issues and is best postponed.

## SECTION 3: SCOPE AND DURATION OF CONSPIRACY

### Albernaz v. United States

Supreme Court of the United States, 1981.
450 U.S. 333.

■ JUSTICE REHNQUIST delivered the opinion of the Court.

Petitioners were convicted of conspiracy to import marihuana (Count I), in violation of 21 U.S.C. § 963, and conspiracy to distribute marihuana (Count II), in violation of 21 U.S.C. § 846. Petitioners received consecutive sentences on each count. . . . We granted certiorari to consider whether Congress intended consecutive sentences to be imposed for the violation of these two conspiracy statutes and, if so, whether such cumulative punishment violates the Double Jeopardy Clause of the Fifth Amendment of the United States Constitution.

The facts forming the basis of petitioners' convictions . . . need not be repeated in detail here. For our purposes, we need only relate that the petitioners were involved in an agreement, the objectives of which were to import marihuana and then to distribute it domestically. Petitioners were charged and convicted under two separate statutory provisions and received consecutive sentences. The length of each of their combined sentences exceeded the maximum five-year sentence which could have been imposed either for a conviction of conspiracy to import or for a conviction of conspiracy to distribute.

The statutes involved in this case are part of the Comprehensive Drug Abuse Prevention and Control Act of 1970, 21 U.S.C. § 801 et seq. Section 846 is in Subchapter I of the Act and provides:

> Any person who attempts or conspires to commit any offense defined in this subchapter is punishable by imprisonment or fine or both which may not exceed the maximum punishment prescribed for the offense, the commission of which was the object of the attempt or conspiracy.

This provision [includes] conspiracy to distribute marihuana . . . .

Section 963, which is part of Subchapter II of the Act, contains a provision identical to § 846 and proscribes . . . conspiracy to import marihuana . . . . Thus, a conspiratorial agreement which envisages both the importation and distribution of marihuana violates both statutory provisions, each of which authorizes a separate punishment.

Petitioners do not dispute that their conspiracy to import and distribute marihuana violated both § 846 and § 963. Rather, petitioners contend it is not clear whether Congress intended to authorize multiple punishment for violation of these two statutes in a case involving only a single agreement or conspiracy, even though that isolated agreement had dual objectives. Petitioners argue that because Congress has not spoken with the clarity required for this Court to find an "unambiguous intent to impose multiple punishment," we should invoke the rule of lenity and hold that the statutory ambiguity on this issue prevents the imposition of multiple punishment. Petitioners further contend that even if cumulative punishment was authorized by Congress, such punishment is barred by the Double Jeopardy Clause of the Fifth Amendment.

In resolving petitioners' initial contention that Congress did not intend to authorize multiple punishment for violations of §§ 846 and 963, our starting point must be the language of the statutes. Absent a "clearly expressed legislative intention to the contrary, that language must ordinarily be regarded as conclusive." Consumers Product Safety Comm'n v. GTE Sylvania, Inc., 447 U.S. 102, 108 (1980). Here, we confront separate offenses with separate penalty provisions that are contained in distinct Subchapters of the Act. The provisions are unambiguous on their face and each authorizes punishment for a violation of its terms. Petitioners contend, however, that the question presented is not whether the statutes are facially ambiguous, but whether consecutive sentences may be imposed when convictions under those statutes arise from participation in a single conspiracy with multiple objectives—a question raised, rather than resolved, by the existence of both provisions.

The answer to petitioners' contention is found, we believe, in application of the rule announced by this Court in Blockburger v. United States, 284 U.S. 299 (1932), and most recently applied . . . in Whalen v. United States, 445 U.S. 684 (1980). In *Whalen*, the Court explained that the "rule of statutory construction" stated in *Blockburger* is to be used "to determine whether Congress has in a given situation provided that two statutory offenses may be punished cumulatively." The Court then referenced the following test set forth in *Blockburger:*

> The applicable rule is that where the same act or transaction constitutes a violation of two distinct statutory provisions, the test to be applied to determine whether there are two offenses or only one, is whether each provision requires proof of a fact which the other does not.

*Blockburger*, 284 U.S. at 304. . . .

The statutory provisions at issue here clearly satisfy the rule announced in *Blockburger* and petitioners do not seriously contend otherwise. Sections 846 and 963 specify different ends as the proscribed object of the conspiracy—distribution as opposed to importation—and it is beyond peradventure that "each provision requires proof of a fact [that] the other does not." Thus, application of the *Blockburger* rule to determine whether Congress has provided that these two statutory offenses be punished cumulatively results in the unequivocal determination that §§ 846 and 963 . . . proscribe separate statutory offenses the violations of which can result in the imposition of consecutive sentences.

*Braverman v. United States*

Our conclusion in this regard is not inconsistent with our earlier decision in Braverman v. United States, 317 U.S. 49 (1942), on which petitioners rely . . . . Petitioners argue that *Blockburger* cannot be used for divining legislative intent when the statutes at issue are conspiracy statutes. Quoting *Braverman*, they argue that whether the objective of a single agreement is to commit one or many crimes, it is in either case the agreement which constitutes the conspiracy which the statute punishes.

*one agreement can't be stretched*

"The one agreement cannot be taken to be several agreements and hence several conspiracies because it envisages the violation of several statutes rather than one." *Braverman*, 317 U.S. at 53. *Braverman*, however, does not support petitioners' position. Unlike the instant case . . . , the conspiratorial agreement in *Braverman*, although it had many objectives, violated but a single statute. The *Braverman* Court specifically noted:

> Since the single continuing agreement, which is the conspiracy here, thus embraces its criminal objects, it differs from successive acts which violate a single penal statute and *from a single act which violates two statutes*. See Blockburger v. United States, 284 U.S. 299, 301–04 (1932). The single agreement is the prohibited conspiracy, and however diverse its objects it violates but a single statute . . . . For such a violation, only the single penalty prescribed by the statute can be imposed.

317 U.S. at 54 (emphasis added). . . .

*Blockburger not controlling*

*contrary legislative intent*

The *Blockburger* test is a "rule of statutory construction," and because it serves as a means of discerning congressional purpose the rule should not be controlling where, for example, there is a clear indication of contrary legislative intent. Nothing, however, in the legislative history which has been brought to our attention discloses an intent contrary to the presumption which should be accorded to these statutes after application of the *Blockburger* test. In fact, the legislative history is silent on the question of whether consecutive sentences can be imposed for conspiracy to import and distribute drugs. Petitioners read this silence as an "ambiguity" over whether Congress intended to authorize multiple punishment. Petitioners, however, read much into nothing. Congress cannot be expected to specifically address each issue of statutory construction which may arise. But, as we have previously noted, Congress is "predominantly a lawyer's body," Callanan v. United States, 364 U.S. 587, 594 (1961), and it is appropriate for us "to assume that our elected representatives . . . know the law." Cannon v. University of Chicago, 441 U.S. 677, 696–97 (1979). As a result, if anything is to be assumed from the congressional silence on this point, it is that Congress was aware of the *Blockburger* rule and legislated with it in mind. It is not a function of this Court to presume that "Congress was unaware of what it accomplished. . . ." Railroad Retirement Bd. v. Fritz, 449 U.S. 166, 179 (1980).

*not specifically address every issue*

Finally, petitioners contend that because the legislative history is "ambiguous" on the question of multiple punishment, we should apply the rule of lenity so as not to allow consecutive sentences in this situation. . . . [T]he rule of lenity is a principle of statutory construction which applies not only to interpretations of the substantive ambit of criminal prohibitions, but also to the penalties they impose. . . . [As we

*application of rule of lenity*

said in Bifulco v. United States, 447 U.S. 381, 387 (1980),] the "touchstone" of the rule of lenity "is statutory ambiguity." And we stated: "Where Congress has manifested its intention, we may not manufacture ambiguity in order to defeat that intent." Id. Lenity thus serves only as an aid for resolving an ambiguity; it is not to be used to beget one. The rule comes into operation "at the end of the process of construing what Congress has expressed, not at the beginning as an overriding consideration of being lenient to wrongdoers." *Callanan*, 364 U.S. at 596.

In light of these principles, the rule of lenity simply has no application in this case; we are not confronted with any statutory ambiguity. To the contrary, we are presented with statutory provisions which are unambiguous on their face and a legislative history which gives us no reason to pause over the manner in which these provisions should be interpreted.

The conclusion we reach today regarding the intent of Congress is reinforced by the fact that the two conspiracy statutes are directed to separate evils presented by drug trafficking. "Importation" and "distribution" of marihuana impose diverse societal harms, and . . . Congress has in effect determined that a conspiracy to import drugs and to distribute them is twice as serious as a conspiracy to do either object singly. This result is not surprising for, as we observed many years ago, the history of the narcotics legislation in this country "reveals the determination of Congress to turn the screw of the criminal machinery—detection, prosecution and punishment—tighter and tighter." Gore v. United States, 357 U.S. 386, 390 (1958).

Having found that Congress intended to permit the imposition of consecutive sentences for violations of § 846 and § 963, we are brought to petitioners' argument that notwithstanding this fact, the Double Jeopardy Clause of the Fifth Amendment of the United States Constitution precludes the imposition of such punishment. . . . [T]he question of what punishments are constitutionally permissible is not different from the question of what punishments the Legislative Branch intended to be imposed. Where Congress intended, as it did here, to impose multiple punishments, imposition of such sentences does not violate the Constitution. The judgment of the Court of Appeals is accordingly

Affirmed.[a]

## NOTES ON THE SCOPE OF A CONSPIRACY

### 1. *BRAVERMAN V. UNITED STATES*

Conspiracy is a continuing offense, beginning when the agreement is formed and ending either when its objects are accomplished or when its participants withdraw from the agreement or abandon its objectives. A number of issues arise in the implementation of these ideas.

The one addressed by *Albernaz* is how many crimes have been committed by a confederation that has multiple objectives. To be contrasted with the holding in *Albernaz* is Braverman v. United States, 317 U.S. 49 (1942).

---

[a] Joined by Justices Marshall and Stevens, Justice Stewart wrote a short opinion—omitted here—in which he concurred in the judgment.—[Footnote by eds.]

*Braverman* involved the predecessor to general federal conspiracy statute, now codified at 18 U.S.C. § 371, which provides:

> If two or more persons conspire either to commit any offense against the United States, or to defraud the United States, or any agency thereof in any manner or for any purpose, and one or more of such persons do any act to effect the object of the conspiracy, each shall be fined under this title or imprisoned not more than five years, or both.
>
> If, however, the offense, the commission of which is the object of the conspiracy, is a misdemeanor only, the punishment for such conspiracy shall not exceed the maximum punishment provided for such misdemeanor.

The petitioners were charged with seven conspiracy counts based on different violations of the internal revenue laws.[a] The question was whether they had committed one crime or seven. The Court held that one crime was committed:

> [W]hen a single agreement to commit one or more substantive crimes is evidenced by an overt act, as the statute requires, the precise nature and extent of the conspiracy must be determined by reference to the agreement which embraces and defines its objects. Whether the object of a single agreement is to commit one or many crimes, it is in either case that agreement which constitutes the conspiracy which the statute punishes. The one agreement cannot be taken to be several agreements and hence several conspiracies because it envisages the violation of several statutes rather than one. . . .
>
> The single agreement is the prohibited conspiracy, and however diverse its objects it violates but a single statute . . . . For such a violation, only the single penalty prescribed by the statute can be imposed.

### 2. QUESTIONS AND COMMENTS ON *ALBERNAZ* AND *BRAVERMAN*

The reaction of courts to the *Braverman* issue is not always consistent.[b] Does *Braverman* set the right standard? Section 5.03 of the Model Penal Code addresses this issue differently:

> If a person conspires to commit a number of crimes, he is guilty of only one conspiracy so long as such multiple crimes are the object of the same agreement or continuous conspiratorial relationship.

[a] The seven counts charged them with conspiracy: (i) to engage in the wholesale and retail liquor business without obtaining occupational tax stamps; (ii) to possess liquor on which tax stamps had not been affixed; (iii) to transport liquor on which tax stamps had not been affixed; (iv) to engage in the distilling business without posting a required bond; (v) to defraud the government of liquor taxes; (vi) to possess unregistered stills; and (vii) to make and ferment mash on unauthorized premises.

[b] Compare Lievers v. State, 3 Md.App. 597, 241 A.2d 147 (1968), where the defendant was ringleader of a bad-check operation. Prosecution was based on an effort by Lievers and several cohorts to cash a forged check made out in a fictitious name. The Maryland Court of Appeals upheld separate convictions for conspiracy to forge the check, conspiracy to obtain money by false pretenses from the party who cashed the forged check, and conspiracy to use a counterfeit Maryland chauffeur's license in the name of the fictitious payee.

Does the concept of "continuous conspiratorial relationship" improve on *Braverman*? From a different perspective, why should conspiracy to commit several crimes be only one conspiracy, while attempt to commit several crimes is several attempts?

*attempt to committ several crimes is severa attempts*

Neither *Braverman* nor the Model Penal Code addresses the question of how many crimes are committed when the defendants violate several different conspiracy statutes. This was the situation in *Albernaz*. Did the Court get the right answer? Is there a substantive difference between the *Braverman* and *Albernaz* situations? Could it plausibly be said that the *Braverman* defendants agreed to commit "separate evils presented by" the various tax provisions violated by their illegal distilling business? Or that *Albernaz* involved a "single agreement" with multiple objectives?

Reconsider the federal conspiracy statute quoted in the Note on *Braverman*. It punishes persons who "conspire either to commit any offense against the United States, or to defraud the United States." A dissenting opinion in United States v. Rigas, 605 F.3d 194 (3d Cir. 2010) (en banc), argued that this language creates two offenses:

> Congressional intent to impose separate punishments is "reinforced" where . . . two conspiracy provisions address separate evils. Clearly, these provisions do. The "defraud" clause focuses narrowly on conspiracies targeting the federal government. The "offense" clause aims to protect the public generally.

*Rigas* involved separate prosecutions for an ongoing conspiracy that engaged in multiple acts of securities fraud that harmed the general public and multiple acts of tax evasion that defrauded the federal treasury. Is this two conspiracies or one?

## ADDITIONAL NOTES ON THE SCOPE AND DURATION OF A CONSPIRACY

### 1.    SCOPE OF CONSPIRACY: THE PARTY DIMENSION

The preceding Notes illustrate a situation where it is to the prosecutor's advantage to multiply the number of conspiracies that can be found in a related transaction and where the defense will contend that there was only one conspiracy with multiple objectives. Sometimes, however, the incentives are reversed, and the prosecutor will want to argue for one large conspiracy, while the defense will wish to claim there were several small ones.

*advantages and disadvantages of several small multiple conspiracies vs. one large conspiracy*

This is likely to be the case when the defendant is charged with various substantive offenses committed by co-conspirators. In that circumstance, the prosecutor will try to enlarge the conspiracy in order to increase the number of offenses for which each co-conspirator is responsible. The defense will want exactly the opposite.

*various substantive offenses*

There are a number of other questions that turn on the issue of one or several conspiracies. One is the running of the statute of limitations. Under settled doctrine, a member of a single, continuing conspiracy may be prosecuted for that offense, even though prosecution for his or her personal participation in the criminal enterprise would be barred by the statute of limitations. Other examples that turn on whether there is one conspiracy or several are various procedural questions, such as which defendants can be

*statute of limitations*

*procedural questions*

tried jointly or the scope of the co-conspirator's exception to the hearsay rule.

Resolving questions like these can get very complex. Consider a drug ring,[a] consisting of importers who smuggle drugs into the country, distributors who buy from the importers, and one or more groups of dealers who operate in different areas. The importers and the retail dealers may never have direct contact or communication, yet each is likely to know of, and depend on, the existence of the other. Are all these persons involved in one large conspiracy, or is there one conspiracy between the importers and the distributors and another between the distributors and (each group of?) dealers? Even at the retail level, the question of scope can be difficult. Is each street-level drug dealer involved in one large conspiracy with all other dealers who work for the same boss? Even though they may have no contact or communication with each other? If so, the scope of liability for the substantive offenses committed by co-conspirators may reach very far indeed.

Traditionally, this issue is dealt with by superimposing on the evidence of conspiracy some visualization of its structure. The two most prominent shapes accorded to conspiracies are the chain and the wheel. The chain conspiracy focuses on successive stages of cooperation, as, for example, between *A* and *B, B* and *C, C* and *D*, and so forth. A person at one end of the chain may be found to have conspired with others with whom that person had no direct dealing. The wheel conspiracy is based on a central figure (the hub) who deals separately with various peripheral figures (the spokes) in a common undertaking. Each of the spokes may be judged a member of the same conspiracy, even though they have no direct relations with one another. Both types are illustrated in the drug hypothetical recited above. The progression from importers to distributors to dealers is a classic chain, while the various street-level dealers who buy from the same source can be seen as separate spokes of a wheel.

The chain and wheel conceptions are frequently used, but rarely determinative. In fact, the number of conspiracies is not something that either exists or does not exist out there in the real world. It is, instead, a product of the evidence available to the prosecutor, the number of statutes that may have been violated, and the narrative that the prosecutor can tell to weave the defendants together in single or multiple webs.

The Model Penal Code suggests a method for resolving this issue. Subsection (1) of § 5.03 declares a person guilty of conspiracy with another to commit a crime if, *with purpose to promote that crime*, he or she "agrees with such other person or persons that they or one or more of them will engage in conduct which constitutes such crime or an attempt or solicitation to commit such crime" or "agrees to aid such other person or persons in the planning or commission of such crime or of an attempt or solicitation to commit such crime." The key to the Model Code, therefore, is for the prosecutor to find a specific crime to which all parties sought to be prosecuted can be said to have agreed. Subsection (2) expands the party dimension of this liability as follows:

> If a person guilty of conspiracy, as defined by Subsection (1) of this Section, knows that a person with whom he conspires to

[a] The facts of this illustration are taken from a famous old case, United States v. Bruno, 105 F.2d 921 (2d Cir. 1939), but there are many examples.

commit a crime has conspired with another person or persons to commit *the same crime*, he is guilty of conspiring with such other person or persons, whether or not he knows their identity, to commit such crime. (Emphasis added.)

What are the various narratives the prosecutor could present in the drug ring hypothetical posed above? How could the "conspiracy" be expanded or contracted by the ways in which the prosecution chose to proceed?

## 2. SCOPE OF CONSPIRACY: DURATION

Another dimension of the scope of a conspiracy is its duration. This may control the statute of limitations, the admissibility of evidence under the co-conspirator's exception to the hearsay rule, and the reach of an individual's liability under *Pinkerton* for the crimes of co-conspirators. The basic propositions in this area are set forth in Model Penal Code § 5.03(7), which essentially codifies prior law. Paragraph (a) states the general rule that conspiracy is a continuing offense; it does not terminate with the agreement but continues until the objective is either accomplished or abandoned. Paragraph (b) imposes a limit on the continuing nature of a conspiracy by creating a presumption of abandonment where no overt act was committed during the applicable period of limitations. Thus, in most cases the defense will simply point to the prosecution's failure to prove an overt act occurring during the relevant time frame as proof that the conspiracy is over. Paragraph (c) deals with the somewhat special case of the individual who claims that an ongoing criminal enterprise is terminated as to that individual by withdrawal from participation. The Code makes such abandonment effective only where it is confirmed by notice to the other participants or by report to the authorities.

*[margin note: MPC § 5.03(7) Limits scope of conspiracy]*

Prosecutors have tried to extend the life of a conspiracy by focusing on the subsidiary objective, which surely must be implicit in every criminal agreement, to conceal the activities from the authorities, but the courts have not been sympathetic. See, e.g., Grunewald v. United States, 353 U.S. 391 (1957), and the cases cited therein.

# SECTION 4: LIMITS ON ACCOMPLICE AND CONSPIRACY LIABILITY

## City of Auburn v. Hedlund

Supreme Court of Washington, 2009.
165 Wn.2d 645, 201 P.3d 315.

*[margin note: Hedlund and friends got drunk at her house got in the car and had fatal accident everyone killed except Hedlund question can she be an accomplice to a crime she was victim of]*

■ CHAMBERS, J. Under Washington statutes, a person is not an accomplice to a crime if she is a victim of that same crime. Teresa Hedlund hosted a party where the liquor flowed freely. Following the party, Hedlund was the only survivor of a single car accident. Hedlund was seriously injured herself. She was charged in Auburn Municipal Court with (among other things) being an accomplice to driving under the influence (DUI) and reckless driving. At the close of the city of Auburn's case in chief, the trial court dismissed the DUI and reckless driving charges because a victim may not be charged as an accomplice under RCW 9A.08.020. We recognize that the legislature may have intended a more limited application of the statute, but based upon the

*[margin notes: WA Law / charged w/ accomplice DUI and reckless driving / procedure]*

plain language of the law, we agree with the municipal court judge and the Court of Appeals that Hedlund cannot be prosecuted as an accomplice.

*procedure/holding*

## Facts and Procedural History

*accident*

On July 16, 2001, a Ford Escort smashed into a concrete pillar in Auburn, killing the driver and five of the six passengers. Earlier in the evening, all the occupants of the car had been at a party at the apartment Hedlund shared with her mother, fiancé, and daughter. Hedlund was 28 at the time; the guests were between 17 and 22. Hedlund's four-year-old daughter was also present. One of the guests had brought a video camera, which was passed around to record the festivities. Most of those present, including the 17-year-old, were drinking alcohol and performing for the video camera. Hedlund's four-year-old daughter is also on camera with a lighted cigarette, dancing and performing at her mother's encouragement. Hedlund is heard asking her daughter to get the cigarettes, telling everyone to look at her daughter, and telling the girl to "shake your moneymaker." At one point on the video, the four-year-old turns around, pulls down her pajamas, and bares her buttocks for the camera.

*underage drinking*

*7 ppl in the car*

When Hedlund's mother came home, she threw the partyers out. Seven people squeezed into the two-door Ford Escort with four seat belts and the back window broken out. Jayme, the owner of the car and the only sober guest, was one of the two smallest people. She sat on someone's lap in the backseat. Also in the backseat were Hedlund's fiancé, Tim, and their friends Marcus, Brandon, and April, the 17-year-old who was carried unconscious into the car. At the wheel was Tim's twin brother Tom, who was heard earlier on the videotape declaring how "liquored up" he was.

*on video camera*

*death*

No one saw the collision, but the events inside the car were preserved on the video camera. During the drive, Hedlund was in the front passenger seat, on her knees, facing the rear of the car, filming. The sober Jayme repeatedly screamed at Tom to slow down. When Hedlund asked Jayme if she wanted her (Hedlund) to drive instead of Tom, Jayme replied that she wanted Tom to stop the car. Hedlund said that Tom was only being funny. Tom then declared, "I'm going to kill us all right now." Seconds later, everyone but Hedlund was dead. Yaw marks on the pavement, together with the video, suggested that Tom put the car into a slide to scare his passengers, lost control, and hit the concrete pillar. The police determined the crash was caused by excessive speed and recklessness. Postmortem blood alcohol tests showed everyone but Jayme had been drinking and the driver's blood alcohol was at nearly twice the legal limit. Hedlund spent months in hospitals and rehabilitation as a result of the wreck.

*city charged Hedlund*

The King County prosecutor declined to charge Hedlund and instead referred the case to the Auburn city attorney. The city charged Hedlund with DUI and reckless driving as an accomplice . . . After reviewing the videotape, the city added a charge of furnishing tobacco to a minor. The city's theory was that all evening, the camera was used to encourage inappropriate behavior and "showboating," which continued in the car because Hedlund kept filming. . . .

The case was tried to a jury. At the end of the city's case in chief, the trial judge reluctantly granted Hedlund's motion to dismiss the reckless driving and DUI charges because "there's no way [the jury] could conclude that she was not also a victim." The city sought a writ of review to the superior court. Judge Cayce concluded that the statute, preventing a victim from being prosecuted as an accomplice, applied only to crimes that required a victim. He further concluded that because DUI and reckless driving do not require an injured victim, Hedlund was a victim of vehicular assault, not DUI or reckless driving. . . . Hedlund's appeal was stayed pending the lower court's proceedings. *[margin: procedure]* *[margin: ] appeal stayed]*

The Auburn Municipal Court trial proceeded, and the jury found Hedlund guilty of all charges except reckless driving. Hedlund [appealed, and] Superior Court Judge Roberts reversed all of the convictions because of cumulative errors. The city's appeal of that decision was consolidated with Hedlund's earlier appeal of the writ of review. Division One of the Court of Appeals affirmed the reversal of the DUI conviction, concluding Hedlund was a victim of that crime. . . . *[margin: procedure]* *[margin: ]victim]*

## Accomplice Liability

We review questions of statutory interpretation de novo. Under Washington law, "[u]nless otherwise provided by this title or by the law defining the crime, a person is not an accomplice in a crime committed by another person if: (a) He is a victim of that crime." RCW 9A.08.020(5). The word "victim" is not specifically defined anywhere in the Washington Criminal Code or in Washington motor vehicle statutes. Unrelated laws, such as the . . . crime victims' compensation act are in accord with the common understanding that a "victim" is a person who suffers injury as a direct result of a crime.[3] See Webster's II New Riverside University Dictionary 1286 (1984) ("One harmed or killed by another."); cf. Black's Law Dictionary 1598 (8th ed. 2004) ("[a] person harmed by a crime, tort, or other wrong"). *[margin: de novo]* *[margin: the word "victim"]*

The city argues the legislature simply could not have intended that anyone injured in a crime is absolved of accomplice liability. The city argues the statute does not apply because Hedlund was not yet a victim at the time she committed the acts, making her an accomplice to DUI. It notes the statute reads, "*is a victim*" not "*LATER BECOMES A VICTIM.*" We decline the city's invitation to so define "victim." This interpretation would render the statute meaningless because many accomplices provide assistance before a crime and many victims cannot be defined as such until the crime is complete. Additionally, Hedlund's alleged encouragement of the DUI (the filming) continued up until moments before the crash that made her a victim. *[margin: Statutory meaning/ interpretation]*

---

[3]    We respectfully disagree with our dissenting colleague's characterization of our opinion as choosing the definition from the crime victims' compensation act. We also respectfully disagree that our approach is inconsistent with that act. That act defines a "victim" as "a person who suffers bodily injury or death as a proximate result of a criminal act of another person." This . . . definition accords with [our] approach and would clearly include Hedlund. [The act also] exempts from eligibility for benefits several categories of persons and injuries, including, as the dissent notes, injuries "[s]ustained while the crime victim was engaged in the attempt to commit, or the commission of, a felony." No similar exemption appears in the victim/accomplice statute. Instead, the exemption effectively acknowledges that a person can be both criminally liable and a victim. While the legislature could have . . . excluded accomplices from the definition of "victim" for the victim accomplice rule, it did not and neither shall we.

*Common law rule codified*

The statute appears to be a codification of a much older common law rule dating at least back to an 1893 English statutory rape case, where the court reasoned that a law intended to protect young girls could not also hold them responsible as accomplices. The Queen

*The Quee v. Tyrell (statutor rape)*

v. Tyrell, 1 Q.B. 710, 711–12 (1894). The United States Supreme Court first applied the rule in Gebardi v. United States, 287 U.S. 112 (1932).

*Gebardi v. United States (prostitution) consent transporting*

The Court held that a prostitute could not be an accomplice to the crime of transporting herself across state lines. Similarly, there are cases applying the rule to protect victims of criminal abortions and, more recently, battered women who invite their abusers to violate protection orders. The history of the rule does not support the city's contention because in any of the examples above, the alleged accomplice/victim could

*Statutory rape context*

easily have committed acts of encouragement well before becoming a victim, just as Hedlund is alleged to have done. This history does not indicate the rule applied only to those whose complicit acts occurred at the same time as their victimization.

The city also argues that Hedlund was not a victim of DUI but of vehicular assault. While DUI liability does not depend on the existence of a victim, the law does contemplate the existence of victims. See RCW 46.61.5055(7)(a) (the court in a DUI case must consider whether the defendant "was responsible for injury or damage to another or another's property"). We do not believe that DUI is a victimless crime.

It well may be that Judge Cayce was correct, and the rule should be limited to crimes that require a victim. Broadly applied, the statute protecting victims could lead to strange results. For example, one who knowingly provides fuel to an arsonist could be trapped in the fire. Or one who receives relatively minor injuries during a crime could be considered a victim. But the legislature has been quite clear: "a person is

*holding*

not an accomplice in a crime committed by another person if: (a) He is a victim of that crime."[4] We resist the urge to essentially rewrite such a plainly written statute. Should the legislature intend a more limited definition of "victim," it, not this court, should amend that statute. . . .

*Dissent*

■ MADSEN, J. (dissenting) . . . The majority wanders unnecessarily from the criminal statutes. Instead of reaching for a definition of "victim" outside the criminal and motor vehicle codes, I would hold that RCW

*holding*

9A.08.020(5) applies only when the elements of the charged offense includes injury to a person or a person's property. In other words, when the statute includes a victim as an element of the crime, it is appropriate to relieve that victim from culpability as an accomplice. Therefore, I would look no further than the definition of the crime charged to deter-

*look at definition of the crime*

mine the meaning of "victim." Because DUI does not include an element of injury to persons or property, I would hold that RCW 9A.08.020(5) does not preclude the prosecution of Ms. Hedlund as an accomplice in

*holding*

this case.

In attempting to show that it is adhering to RCW 9A.08.020(5) and that my reading is incorrect, the majority declares that use of the word "a" in the statute ("*a* victim of that crime") shows that the statute

---

[4] We respectfully contend that the dissent would have more force if the accomplice liability statute had said that "the" victim of a crime could not be liable as an accomplice rather than "a" victim. The exemption of "a" victim is expansive and seems to reasonably contemplate broad application. An exemption of "the" victim, by contrast, might point to a more restrictive scope.

should be given broad application. The legislature did not use the word
"a" so that the statute would be applied to achieve indefensible results.
Instead, it did so simply because some crimes have a single victim while
others have multiple victims. "A" is grammatically proper when there
are multiple victims and reference is being made to one of them. . . .

The majority recognizes that its construction will result in
"strange" results. In fact, the majority gives its own examples.[7] But, the
majority says the legislature must have intended absurd results and
this court should not "rewrite such a plainly written statute." I disagree. It is a well-settled principle that "[i]n undertaking a plain language analysis, . . . [a]bsurd results should be avoided because it will
not be presumed that the legislature intended absurd results." . . .

*Strange results*

*well-settled principle avoid absurd results*

Finally, the majority takes some pains to review the origins of the
rule. . . . However, the history actually supports the city's argument
that "victim" should be defined by the elements of the charged crime. As
the majority notes, the statute has its roots in a statutory rape case
where the court reasoned that a law intended to protect young girls
could not also hold them responsible as accomplices. The Queen
v. Tyrrell, 1 Q.B. 710, 711–12 (1894). Similarly, the rule was first applied in the United States in Gebardi v. United States, 287 U.S. 112
(1932), where the court held a prostitute could not be an accomplice to
the crime of transporting herself across state lines. In each of these applications of the rule, the crime charged involved a victim in its elements. The courts in these cases were not faced with and did not have
to consider whether the rule should apply if the elements of the charged
crime did not identify a victim of the crime. The same is true of a more
modern application of the rule in cases involving victims of criminal
abortions and battered women who invite their abusers to violate protection orders.

A forthright application of the rules of statutory construction, the
historical underpinnings of RCW 9A.08.020(5), and common sense lead
me to conclude that Ms. Hedlund was properly tried as an accomplice to
the crime of DUI.

*properly tried as accomplice*

## NOTES ON THE LIMITS ON ACCOMPLICE AND CONSPIRACY LIABILITY

### 1. THE VICTIM EXEMPTION TO COMPLICITY LIABILITY

In *Hedlund*, the Supreme Court of Washington construed a provision
from the Washington Criminal Code that is based on § 2.06(6)(a) of the
Model Penal Code. When describing the origins of this section, the drafters
of the Model Code referred to the *Tyrrel* case, which is also cited
in *Hedlund*. In *Tyrell*, an underage girl was convicted for having aided and
abetted one Thomas Froud to commit statutory rape "upon herself." The
court quashed the conviction on the ground that the legislature could not
have intended for the statutory rape victim herself to be convicted as an

*MPC § 2.06(6)(a)*

*Tyrrel case statutory rape victim*

---

[7]    Although the majority lists examples, it fails to acknowledge the enormous impact of
its decision. The getaway driver wounded in a robbery; the accomplice who is injured by the
true victim defending himself against an assault; the accomplice injured by his crime partners
in a dispute over "loot"—just a few examples of those who will escape prosecution because they
are "victims" of the crime.

accomplice to the carnal act. In the view of Lord Coleridge, the legislature "intended . . . to protect girls against themselves, and it cannot be said that an act which says nothing at all about the girl inciting . . . , and the whole object of which is to protect women against men, is to be construed so as to render the girl against whom an offense is committed equally liable with the man by whom the offense is committed." In their Commentaries, the drafters of the Model Penal Code offered these remarks to support their codification of the victim exemption implied in *Tyrell*:

> . . . It seems clear that a victim of a crime should not be held as an accomplice in its perpetration, even though his conduct in a sense may have assisted in the commission of the crime and the elements of complicity . . . may technically exist. The businessman who yields to the extortion of a racketeer, the parent who pays ransom to the kidnapper, may be unwise or may even be thought immoral. To view them as involved in the commission of the crime confounds the policy embodied in the prohibition; it is laid down, wholly or in part, for their protection. So, too, to hold the female an accomplice in a statutory rape upon her person would be inconsistent with the legislative purpose to protect her against her own weakness in consenting, the very theory of the crime.

ALI, Model Penal Code and Commentaries § 2.06, pp. 323–24 (1985).

In *Hedlund*, the majority and dissent divide over the meaning of the phrase "a victim of that crime." The majority appears to read the phrase so as to exempt from accessorial liability any person who is injured by the crime with which she is charged, no matter how active she may have been in aiding or promoting that crime. By contrast, the dissent would limit the exemption to accessories who are the victims of crimes whose elements include a specific victim and the accessory qualifies as such a victim. The Model Code Commentaries provide no direct assistance in resolving this dispute. Which interpretation does *Tyrell* best support?

Note that Model Penal Code § 2.06(6)(b) provides that an actor is not an accomplice in an offense committed by another person if "the offense is so defined that his conduct is inevitably incident to its commission." Is this a helpful addition?

## 2. CONSPIRACY

Not surprisingly, the law of conspiracy also includes a victim exemption. A good example is Gebardi v. United States, 287 U.S. 112 (1932), which involved prosecution for conspiracy to violate the Mann Act. That statute punished "any person" who knowingly transported in interstate commerce any "any woman or girl for the purpose of prostitution or debauchery. . . ." The defendant was a man, and the person with whom he conspired was the woman to be transported. The Supreme Court disapproved the conviction on the ground that since the Mann Act did not condemn the woman's participation in these interstate transportations, her assent could not form the basis of liability for conspiracy.

Much the same reasoning lies behind the hoary doctrine known as Wharton's rule. Basically, Wharton's rule deals with offenses that are defined to require the participation of more than one person. Classic examples are adultery, incest, bigamy, and dueling. Wharton's rule declares that the agreement between the essential participants to commit such a crime should ordinarily not be prosecuted as conspiracy. As Wharton himself explained, "[w]hen to the idea of an offense plurality of agents is logically necessary, conspiracy, which assumes the voluntary accession of a person to a crime of such a character that it is aggravated by a plurality of agents, cannot be maintained." 2 Francis Wharton, Criminal Law 1862 (12th ed. 1932). The Supreme Court has made clear that this "rule" is actually only a "judicial presumption, to be applied in the absence of legislative intent to the contrary." Iannelli v. United States, 420 U.S. 770, 782 (1975). On that basis, the *Iannelli* Court refused to apply Wharton's rule to a prosecution for conspiracy to violate 18 U.S.C. § 1955, which punished as a federal crime managing or owning an illegal gambling business involving five or more persons. Relying on the history of the statute, the Court found that the imposition of liability for illegal gambling involving five or more persons was not designed to preclude liability for conspiracy to commit that offense.

# SECTION 5: RICO

## INTRODUCTORY NOTES ON RICO

### 1. BACKGROUND

The Racketeer Influenced and Corrupt Organizations Act[a] (RICO) was enacted as title IX of the Organized Crime Control Act of 1970. It is codified in 18 U.S.C. §§ 1961–68. In conception, RICO had a narrow but important objective, namely to protect the legitimate business marketplace from the competitive distortions that occurred when organized crime infiltrated ordinary businesses.[b] To do so, it employed three key concepts.

The first was the "enterprise," which was broadly defined to include virtually any form of doing business. The second was "racketeering activity," which was broadly defined to include virtually any kind of state or federal crime that organized criminals could commit. The third was a "pattern" of racketeering activity, which was again was broadly defined, in this case to express the idea of repetitive criminality.

These three ideas were used to define three basic crimes. The first prohibited the use of funds generated by repetitive criminality to establish, operate, or purchase an interest in an enterprise. The second prohibited acquiring or maintaining an interest in an enterprise through repetitive criminality (e.g., extortion). The first, in a nutshell, was "buying in" with dirty money; the second "muscling in" with dirty tactics. In both cases, bad

[a] No one could have come up with this name unless the acronym "RICO" was the objective. Why pick "RICO"? The lore is that the author of the statute was a fan of old movies and the name was selected because the title character in the first movie on organized crime—"Little Caesar" starring Edward G. Robinson—was named "Rico." For discussion of the point by a person who was there at the beginning, see G. Robert Blakey and Thomas A. Perry, An Analysis of the Myths that Bolster Efforts to Rewrite RICO and the Various Proposals for Reform: "Mother of God—Is this the End of Rico?", 43 Vand. L. Rev. 851, 982–87 (1990). For a penetrating and comprehensive analysis of RICO in the early days, see Gerard E. Lynch, RICO: The Crime of Being a Criminal, Parts I & II, 87 Colum. L. Rev. 661, Parts III & IV, 87 Colum. L. Rev. 920 (1987).

[b] RICO was "neatly designed to deal with . . . congressional concern with organized criminal infiltration of legitimate business." Id., 87 Colum. L. Rev. at 681.

effects on legitimate competition were likely to occur once organized crime secured a foothold in ongoing and otherwise ordinary business activity.

The third offense focused on the actual operation of an otherwise legitimate business by using the methods of organized crime. One way to look at it is to view the first two offenses as inchoate crimes designed to punish various forms of entry by organized crime into the legitimate marketplace. The third was designed to punish what organized criminals do once they are there. It is a crime if they operate an otherwise legitimate business by doing what organized criminals do.

The text of RICO should be examined carefully. It is reproduced in the next note. Section 1961 establishes the three basic concepts: "enterprise," "racketeering activity," and "pattern." Section 1962 establishes the three crimes described above, and adds a fourth: a conspiracy to commit any of the three. Section 1963 establishes serious criminal penalties for violating any of the four RICO provisions: a 20-year maximum sentence and forfeiture of anything a convicted defendant might have gained by participating in a RICO offense. Section 1964 establishes various civil remedies, the most important of which is triple damages and attorney's fees for persons injured in their business or property by a RICO violation.

## 2. THE STATUTE

RICO is an extremely elaborate statute, which reads, in part, as follows:

§ 1961. Definitions

As used in this chapter—

(1) "racketeering activity" means

(A) any act or threat involving murder, kidnaping, gambling, arson, robbery, bribery, extortion, dealing in obscene matter, or dealing in narcotic or other dangerous drugs, which is chargeable under State law and punishable by imprisonment for more than one year;

(B) any act which is indictable under any of the following provisions of title 18, United States Code: [Here are cited sections covering, inter alia, bribery, sports bribery, counterfeiting, felonious theft from interstate shipment, embezzlement from pension and welfare funds, extortionate credit transactions, fraud, transmission of gambling information, mail fraud, wire fraud, obscene matter, obstruction of justice, interference with commerce, robbery, or extortion, racketeering, interstate transportation of wagering paraphernalia, illegal gambling businesses, laundering of monetary instruments, use of interstate commerce facilities in the commission of murder-for-hire, sexual exploitation of children, interstate transportation of stolen motor vehicles, interstate transportation of stolen property, trafficking in contraband cigarettes, white slave traffic. Subsection (C) adds certain labor offenses, and subsection (D) adds securities fraud or "the felonious manufacture, importation, receiving, concealment, buying, selling, or otherwise dealing in narcotic or other dangerous drugs, punishable under any law of the United States." Finally, subsection (E) adds certain currency offenses involving the reporting of foreign transactions.]; . . .

(4) "enterprise" includes any individual, partnership, corporation, association, or other legal entity, and any union or group of individuals associated in fact although not a legal entity;

(5) "pattern of racketeering activity" requires at least two acts of racketeering activity, one of which occurred after the effective date of this chapter and the last of which occurred within ten years (excluding any period of imprisonment) after the commission of a prior act of racketeering activity;

(6) "unlawful debt" means a debt

(A) incurred or contracted in gambling activity which was in violation of the law of the United States, a State or political subdivision thereof, or which is unenforceable under State or Federal law in whole or in part as to principal or interest because of the laws relating to usury, and

(B) which was incurred in connection with the business of gambling in violation of the law of the United States, a State or political subdivision thereof, or the business of lending money or a thing of value at a rate usurious under State or Federal law, where the usurious rate is at least twice the enforceable rate;. . . .

§ 1962. Prohibited activities

(a) It shall be unlawful for any person who has received any income derived, directly or indirectly, from a pattern of racketeering activity or through collection of an unlawful debt in which such person has participated as a principal within the meaning of section 2, title 18, United States Code, to use or invest, directly or indirectly, any part of such income, or the proceeds of such income, in acquisition of any interest in, or the establishment or operation of, any enterprise which is engaged in, or the activities of which affect, interstate or foreign commerce. A purchase of securities on the open market for purposes of investment, and without the intention of controlling or participating in the control of the issuer, or of assisting another to do so, shall not be unlawful under this subsection if the securities of the issuer held by the purchaser, the members of his immediate family, and his or their accomplices in any pattern or racketeering activity or the collection of an unlawful debt after such purchase do not amount in the aggregate to one percent of the outstanding securities of any one class, and do not confer, either in law or in fact, the power to elect one or more directors of the issuer.

(b) It shall be unlawful for any person through a pattern of racketeering activity or through collection of an unlawful debt to acquire or maintain, directly or indirectly, any interest in or control of any enterprise which is engaged in, or the activities of which affect, interstate or foreign commerce.

(c) It shall be unlawful for any person employed by or associated with any enterprise engaged in, or the activities of which affect, interstate or foreign commerce, to conduct or participate, directly or indirectly, in the conduct of such enterprise's affairs through a pattern of racketeering activity or collection of unlawful debt.

(d) It shall be unlawful for any person to conspire to violate any of the provisions of subsection (a), (b), or (c) of this section.

§ 1963. Criminal penalties

(a) Whoever violates any provision of section 1962 of this chapter shall be fined under this title or imprisoned not more than 20 years (or for life if the violation is based on a racketeering activity for which the maximum penalty includes life imprisonment), or both, and shall forfeit to the United States, irrespective of any provision of State law—

(1) any interest the person has acquired or maintained in violation of section 1962;

(2) any—

(A) interest in;

(B) security of;

(C) claim against; or

(D) property or contractual right of any kind affording a source of influence over;

any enterprise which the person has established, operated, controlled, conducted, or participated in the conduct of, in violation of section 1962; and

(3) any property constituting, or derived from, any proceeds which the person obtained, directly or indirectly, from racketeering activity or unlawful debt collection in violation of section 1962.

The court, in imposing sentence on such person shall order, in addition to any other sentence imposed pursuant to this section, that the person forfeit to the United States all property described in this subsection. In lieu of a fine otherwise authorized by this section, a defendant who derives profits or other proceeds from an offense may be fined not more than twice the gross profits or other proceeds. . . .

§ 1964. Civil remedies . . .

(c) Any person injured in his business or property by reason of a violation of section 1962 of this chapter may sue therefor in any appropriate United States district court and shall recover threefold the damages he sustains and the cost of the suit, including a reasonable attorney's fee. . . .

## 3. THE ISSUE IN *TURKETTE*

RICO has become the most important weapon against organized crime ever developed. But this did not happen because of successful prosecutions against organized crime for infiltrating or operating legitimate businesses. It happened because the Justice Department undertook the prosecution of organized crime based on a theory that never occurred to Congress. The government argued that the term "enterprise" should be interpreted to mean the very organization that held organized crime together. If it was a crime for people to establish an organization for the purpose of committing crimes and then to commit the crimes for which the organization was created, the Department would be able to prosecute organized criminals for doing what organized criminals do.

As a textual matter, this argument was not difficult. An "enterprise" is a "union or group of individuals associated in fact," whether or not it is a legal entity. This language fits the government's theory by encompassing, if taken literally, the "organization" underlying organized crime. And § 1962(c) punishes people associated with an "enterprise" who "conduct or participate" in the affairs of the enterprise by engaging in a "pattern of racketeering activity." This language fits the theory too—it punishes members of the "organization" for committing a series of crimes, for doing what organized criminals do. On this reading, RICO punishes anyone who engages in repetitive criminality on behalf of a group devoted to that purpose or who conspires with others to achieve that end.

*enterprise*
*"legal or not" entities*

*§1962(c) people associated*

*repetitive criminality*

This approach to RICO fit the text of the statute, but not the idea behind it. The Circuit Courts split on whether prosecutions of organized criminals should be allowed to proceed on this basis. In *United States v. Turkette*, the Supreme Court resolved the Circuit split.

## United States v. Turkette

Supreme Court of the United States, 1981.
452 U.S. 576.

*Turkette charged as leader of criminal enterprise under Rico question became are illegitimate enterprises covered under Rico*

■ JUSTICE WHITE delivered the opinion of the Court.

... The question in this case is whether the term "enterprise" as used in [the Racketeer Influenced and Corrupt Organizations Act (RICO)] encompasses both legitimate and illegitimate enterprises or is limited in application to the former. The Court of Appeals ... held that Congress did not intend to include within the definition of "enterprise" those organizations which are exclusively criminal. ...

*question*

*procedure*

### I

Count nine of a nine-count indictment charged respondent and 12 others with conspiracy to conduct and participate in the affairs of an enterprise engaged in interstate commerce through a pattern of racketeering activities, in violation of 18 U.S.C. § 1962(d). The indictment described the enterprise as "a group of individuals associated in fact for the purpose of illegally trafficking in narcotics and other dangerous drugs, committing arsons, utilizing the United States mails to defraud insurance companies, bribing and attempting to bribe local police officers, and corruptly influencing and attempting to corruptly influence the

*charge*

outcome of state court proceedings. . . ." The other eight counts of the indictment charged the commission of various substantive criminal acts by those engaged in and associated with the criminal enterprise, including possession with intent to distribute and distribution of controlled substances, and several counts of insurance fraud by arson and other means. The common thread to all counts was respondent's alleged leadership of this criminal organization through which he orchestrated and participated in the commission of the various crimes delineated in the RICO count or charged in the eight preceding counts.

*common thread*

After a six-week jury trial, in which the evidence focused upon both the professional nature of this organization and the execution of a number of distinct criminal acts, respondent was convicted on all nine counts. He was sentenced to a term of 20 years on the substantive counts, as well as a two-year special parole term on the drug count. On the RICO conspiracy count he was sentenced to a 20-year concurrent term and fined $20,000.

*jury trial*

*conviction*

On appeal, respondent argued that RICO was intended solely to protect legitimate business enterprises from infiltration by racketeers and that RICO does not make criminal the participation in an association which performs only illegal acts and which has not infiltrated or attempted to infiltrate a legitimate enterprise. The Court of Appeals agreed. We reverse.

*appeal Δ argues*

*procedure*

## II

. . . Section 1962(c) makes it unlawful "for any person employed by or associated with any enterprise engaged in, or the activities of which affect, interstate or foreign commerce, to conduct or participate, directly or indirectly, in the conduct of such enterprise's affairs through a pattern of racketeering activity or collection of unlawful debt." The term "enterprise" is defined as including "any individual, partnership, corporation, association, or other legal entity, and any union or group of individuals associated in fact although not a legal entity." § 1961(4). There is no restriction upon the associations embraced by the definition: an enterprise includes any union or group of individuals associated in fact. On its face, the definition appears to include both legitimate and illegitimate enterprises within its scope; it no more excludes criminal enterprises than it does legitimate ones. Had Congress not intended to reach criminal associations, it could easily have narrowed the sweep of the definition by inserting a single word, "legitimate." But it did nothing to indicate that an enterprise consisting of a group of individuals was not covered by RICO if the purpose of the enterprise was exclusively criminal.

*enterprise*

*on its face*

The Court of Appeals, however, clearly departed from and limited the statutory language. It gave several reasons for doing so, none of which is adequate. First, it relied in part on the rule of ejusdem generis, an aid to statutory construction problems suggesting that where general words follow a specific enumeration of persons or things, the general words should be limited to persons or things similar to those specifically enumerated. The Court of Appeals ruled that because each of the specific enterprises enumerated in § 1961(4) is a "legitimate" one, the final catchall phrase—"any union or group of individuals associated in fact"—should also be limited to legitimate enterprises. There are at least two flaws in this reasoning. The rule of ejusdem generis is no more

*Ctr. of Appeals said no*

*rule of ejusdem generis*

than an aid to construction and comes into play only when there is some uncertainty as to the meaning of a particular clause in a statute. Considering the language and structure of § 1961(4), however, we not only perceive no uncertainty in the meaning to be attributed to the phrase, "any union or group of individuals associated in fact" but we are convinced for another reason that ejusdem generis is wholly inapplicable in this context.

Section 1961(4) describes two categories of associations that come within the purview of the "enterprise" definition. The first encompasses organizations such as corporations and partnerships, and other "legal entities." The second covers "any union or group of individuals associated in fact although not a legal entity." The Court of Appeals assumed that the second category was merely a more general description of the first. Having made that assumption, the court concluded that the more generalized description in the second category should be limited by the specific examples enumerated in the first. But that assumption is untenable. Each category describes a separate type of enterprise to be covered by the statute—those that are recognized as legal entities and those that are not. The latter is not a more general description of the former. The second category itself not containing any specific enumeration that is followed by a general description, ejusdem generis has no bearing on the meaning to be attributed to that part of § 1961(4).[4]

A second reason offered by the Court of Appeals in support of its judgment was that giving the definition of "enterprise" its ordinary meaning would create several internal inconsistencies in the act. With respect to § 1962(c), it was said: "If 'a pattern of racketeering' can itself be an 'enterprise' for purposes of § 1962(c), then the two phrases 'employed by or associated with any enterprise' and 'the conduct of such enterprise's affairs through [a pattern of racketeering activity]' add nothing to the meaning of the section. The words of the statute are coherent and logical only if they are read as applying to legitimate enterprises." This conclusion is based on a faulty premise. That a wholly criminal enterprise comes within the ambit of the statute does not mean that a "pattern of racketeering activity" is an "enterprise." In order to secure a conviction under RICO, the government must prove both the existence of an "enterprise" and the connected "pattern of racketeering activity." The enterprise is an entity, for present purposes a group of persons associated together for a common purpose of engaging in a course of conduct. The pattern of racketeering activity is, on the other hand, a series of criminal acts as defined by the statute. The former is proved by evidence of an ongoing organization, formal or informal, and by evidence that the various associates function as a continuing unit. The latter is proved by evidence of the requisite number of acts of racketeering committed by the participants in the enterprise. While the proof used to establish these separate elements may in particular cases coalesce, proof of one does not necessarily establish the other.

[4] The Court of Appeals' application of ejusdem generis is further flawed by the assumption that "any individual, partnership, corporation, association or other legal entity" could not act totally beyond the pale of the law. The mere fact that a given enterprise is favored with a legal existence does not prevent that enterprise from proceeding along a wholly illegal course of conduct. Therefore, since legitimacy of purpose is not a universal characteristic of the specifically listed enterprises, it would be improper to engraft this characteristic upon the second category of enterprises.

The "enterprise" is not the "pattern of racketeering activity"; it is an entity separate and apart from the pattern of activity in which it engages. The existence of an enterprise at all times remains a separate element which must be proved by the government.[5]

Apart from § 1962(c)'s proscription against participating in an enterprise through a pattern of racketeering activities, RICO also proscribes the investment of income derived from racketeering activity in an enterprise engaged in or which affects interstate commerce as well as the acquisition of an interest in or control of any such enterprise through a pattern of racketeering activity. 18 U.S.C. §§ 1962(a) and (b). The Court of Appeals concluded that these provisions of RICO should be interpreted so as to apply only to legitimate enterprises. If these two sections are so limited, the Court of Appeals held that the proscription in § 1962(c), at issue here, must be similarly limited. Again, we do not accept the premise from which the Court of Appeals derived its conclusion. It is obvious that § 1962(a) and (b) address the infiltration by organized crime of legitimate businesses, but we cannot agree that these sections were not also aimed at preventing racketeers from investing or reinvesting in wholly illegal enterprises and from acquiring through a pattern of racketeering activity wholly illegitimate enterprises such as an illegal gambling business or a loan-sharking operation. There is no inconsistency or anomaly in recognizing that § 1962 applies to both legitimate and illegitimate enterprises. Certainly the language of the statute does not warrant the Court of Appeals' conclusion to the contrary.

Similarly, the Court of Appeals noted that various civil remedies were provided by § 1964, including divestiture, dissolution, reorganization, restrictions on future activities by violators of RICO, and treble damages. These remedies it thought would have utility only with respect to legitimate enterprises. As a general proposition, however, the civil remedies could be useful in eradicating organized crime from the social fabric, whether the enterprise be ostensibly legitimate or admittedly criminal. The aim is to divest the association of the fruits of its ill-gotten gains. Even if one or more of the civil remedies might be inapplicable to a particular illegitimate enterprise, this fact would not serve to limit the enterprise concept. Congress has provided civil remedies for use when the circumstances so warrant. It is untenable to argue that their existence limits the scope of the criminal provisions.

Finally, it is urged that the interpretation of RICO to include both legitimate and illegitimate enterprises will substantially alter the balance between federal and state enforcement of criminal law. This is particularly true, so the argument goes, since included within the definition of racketeering activity are a significant number of acts made criminal under state law. But even assuming that the more inclusive

---

[5] The government takes the position that proof of a pattern of racketeering activity in itself would not be sufficient to establish the existence of an enterprise: "We do not suggest that any two sporadic and isolated offenses by the same actor or actors ipso facto constitute an 'illegitimate' enterprise; rather, the existence of the enterprise as an independent entity must also be shown." But even if that were not the case, the Court of Appeals' position on this point is of little force. Language in a statute is not rendered superfluous merely because in some contexts that language may not be pertinent.

definition of enterprise will have the effect suggested,[9] the language of the statute and its legislative history indicate that Congress was well aware that it was entering a new domain of federal involvement through the enactment of this measure. Indeed, the very purpose of the Organized Crime Control Act of 1970 was to enable the federal government to address a large and seemingly neglected problem. The view was that existing law, state and federal, was not adequate to address the problem, which was of national dimensions. That Congress included within the definition of racketeering activities a number of state crimes strongly indicates that RICO criminalized conduct that was also criminal under state law, at least when the requisite elements of a RICO offense are present. As the hearings and legislative debates reveal, Congress was well aware of the fear that RICO would "mov[e] large substantive areas formerly totally within the police power of the state into the federal realm." 116 Cong.Rec. 35217 (1970) (remarks of Rep. Eckhardt). In the face of these objections, Congress nonetheless proceeded to enact the measure, knowing that it would alter somewhat the role of the federal government in the war against organized crime and that the alteration would entail prosecutions involving acts of racketeering that are also crimes under state law. There is no argument that Congress acted beyond its power in so doing. That being the case, the courts are without authority to restrict the application of the statute.

Contrary to the judgment below, neither the language nor structure of RICO limits its application to legitimate "enterprises." Applying it also to criminal organizations does not render any portion of the statute superfluous nor does it create any structural incongruities within the framework of the act. The result is neither absurd nor surprising. On the contrary, insulating the wholly criminal enterprise from prosecution under RICO is the more incongruous position.

Section 904(a) of RICO, 84 Stat. 947, directs that "[t]he provisions of this Title shall be liberally construed to effectuate its remedial purposes." With or without this admonition, we could not agree with the Court of Appeals that illegitimate enterprises should be excluded from coverage. We are also quite sure that nothing in the legislative history of RICO requires a contrary conclusion.

### III

The statement of findings that prefaces the Organized Crime Control Act of 1970 reveals the pervasiveness of the problem that Congress was addressing by this enactment:

> The Congress finds that (1) organized crime in the United States is a highly sophisticated, diversified, and widespread activity that annually drains billions of dollars from America's economy by unlawful conduct and the illegal use of force, fraud, and corruption; (2) organized crime derives a major

---

[9] RICO imposes no restrictions upon the criminal justice systems of the states. See 84 Stat. 947 ("Nothing in this title shall supersede any provision of Federal, State, or other law imposing criminal penalties or affording civil remedies in addition to those provided for in this title"). Thus, under RICO, the states, remain free to exercise their police powers to the fullest constitutional extent in defining and prosecuting crimes within their respective jurisdictions. That some of those crimes may also constitute predicate acts of racketeering under RICO, is no restriction on the separate administration of criminal justice by the states.

> portion of its power through money obtained from such illegal endeavors as syndicated gambling, loan sharking, the theft and fencing of property, the importation and distribution of narcotics and other dangerous drugs, and other forms of social exploitation; (3) this money and power are increasingly used to infiltrate and corrupt legitimate business and labor unions and to subvert and corrupt our democratic processes; (4) organized crime activities in the United States weaken the stability of the nation's economic system, harm innocent investors and competing organizations, interfere with free competition, seriously burden interstate and foreign commerce, threaten the domestic security, and undermine the general welfare of the nation and its citizens; and (5) organized crime continues to grow because of defects in the evidence-gathering process of the law inhibiting the development of the legally admissible evidence necessary to bring criminal and other sanctions or remedies to bear on the unlawful activities of those engaged in organized crime and because the sanctions and remedies available to the government are unnecessarily limited in scope and impact.

84 Stat. 922–23.

In light of the above findings, it was the declared purpose of Congress "to seek the eradication of organized crime in the United States by strengthening the legal tools in the evidence-gathering process, by establishing new penal prohibitions, and by providing enhanced sanctions and new remedies to deal with the unlawful activities of those engaged in organized crime." Id., at 923. The various titles of the act provide the tools through which this goal is to be accomplished. Only three of those titles create substantive offenses, Title VIII, which is directed at illegal gambling operations, Title IX, at issue here, and Title XI, which addresses the importation, distribution, and storage of explosive materials. The other titles provide various procedural and remedial devices to aid in the prosecution and incarceration of persons involved in organized crime.

Considering this statement of the act's broad purposes, the construction of RICO suggested by respondent and the court below is unacceptable. Whole areas of organized criminal activity would be placed beyond the substantive reach of the enactment. For example, associations of persons engaged solely in "loan sharking, the theft and fencing of property, the importation and distribution of narcotics and other dangerous drugs," id., at 922–23, would be immune from prosecution under RICO so long as the association did not deviate from the criminal path. Yet these are among the very crimes that Congress specifically found to be typical of the crimes committed by persons involved in organized crime, and as a major source of revenue and power for such organizations. Along these same lines, Senator McClellan, the principal sponsor of the bill, gave two examples of types of problems RICO was designed to address. Neither is consistent with the view that substantive offenses under RICO would be limited to legitimate enterprises: "Organized criminals, too, have flooded the market with cheap reproductions of hit records and affixed counterfeit popular labels. They are heavily engaged in the illicit prescription drug industry." 116 Cong.Rec.

592 (1970). In view of the purposes and goals of the act, as well as the language of the statute, we are unpersuaded that Congress nevertheless confined the reach of the law to only narrow aspects of organized crime, and, in particular, under RICO, only the infiltration of legitimate business.

This is not to gainsay that the legislative history forcefully supports the view that the major purpose of Title IX is to address the infiltration of legitimate business by organized crime. The point is made time and again during the debates and in the hearings before the House and Senate. But none of these statements requires the negative inference that Title IX did not reach the activities of enterprises organized and existing for criminal purposes.

On the contrary, these statements are in full accord with the proposition that RICO is equally applicable to a criminal enterprise that has no legitimate dimension or has yet to acquire one. Accepting that the primary purpose of RICO is to cope with the infiltration of legitimate businesses, applying the statute in accordance with its terms, so as to reach criminal enterprises, would seek to deal with the problem at its very source. . . .

As a measure to deal with the infiltration of legitimate businesses by organized crime, RICO was both preventive and remedial. Respondent's view would ignore the preventive function of the statute. If Congress had intended the more circumscribed approach espoused by the Court of Appeals, there would have been some positive sign that the law was not to reach organized criminal activities that give rise to the concerns about infiltration. The language of the statute, however—the most reliable evidence of its intent—reveals that Congress opted for a far broader definition of the word "enterprise," and we are unconvinced by anything in the legislative history that this definition should be given less than its full effect.

The judgment of the Court of Appeals is accordingly

Reversed.

■ JUSTICE STEWART agrees with the reasoning and conclusion of the Court of Appeals as to the meaning of the term "enterprise" in this statute. Accordingly, he respectfully dissents.

## NOTES ON THE IMPACT OF *TURKETTE*

### 1. INTRODUCTION

*Turkette* solved one problem and created another. The problem it solved was how to maximize the effectiveness of RICO as a weapon against organized crime. The way it did so was to allow the law of conspiracy to be put to a new use.

Classically, a conspiracy requires two or more persons to agree to the commission of a specific crime. Section 5.03(1)(a) of the Model Penal Code, for example, provides that a person is guilty of conspiracy "to commit *a crime*" who, with the purpose "of promoting or facilitating *its* commission," agrees that "conduct which constitutes *such crime*" will be committed by one or more of the parties to the conspiracy. One problem when applying this definition to the leaders of organized crime is that it is difficult to tie the Michael Corleones or Tony Sopranos of the world to an agreement to commit the specific crimes undertaken by their underlings. The next note on *United States v. Elliott* describes how post-*Turkette* RICO addressed this difficulty and why it matters.

The problem *Turkette* created was how (or indeed whether) to limit the reach of the concept of "enterprise." Literally, an "enterprise" is "*any*" union or group of individuals. Suppose two people agree to commit a series of bank robberies, and they are caught before committing or attempting any of them. Clearly they can be prosecuted for conspiracy under 18 U.S.C. § 371 (five-year maximum sentence).[a] But are they conspiring to conduct the affairs of a criminal "enterprise" and therefore subject to a conviction for violating RICO (20-year maximum sentence and significant forfeiture penalties)? If not, how big and how complex does their organization have to be and how many different types of crime must they have in mind to commit before their activity crosses the line distinguishing a § 371 conspiracy from an "enterprise" that violates RICO? This question is dealt with in the notes following *Elliott* and in the next main case.

## 2. RICO CONSPIRACY VS. ORDINARY CONSPIRACY: *UNITED STATES V. ELLIOTT*

The facts in United States v. Elliott, 571 F.2d 880 (5th Cir. 1978), were summarized by the court as follows:

> In this case we deal with the question of whether and, if so, how a free society can protect itself when groups of people, through division of labor, specialization, diversification, complexity of organization, and the accumulation of capital, turn crime into an ongoing business. . . . Today we review the convictions of six persons accused of conspiring to violate the RICO statute, two of whom were also accused and convicted of substantive RICO violations. . . . Predictably, the government and the defendants differ as to what this case is about. According to the defendants, what we are dealing with is a leg, a tail, a trunk, an ear—separate entities unaffected by RICO proscriptions. The government, on the other hand, asserts that we have come eyeball to eyeball with a single creature of behemoth proportions, securely within RICO's grasp. After a careful, if laborious study of the facts and the law, we accept, with minor exceptions, the government's view. . . .
>
> Here, the government proved beyond a reasonable doubt the existence of an enterprise comprised of at least five of the defendants. This enterprise can best be analogized to a large business conglomerate. Metaphorically speaking, J.C. Hawkins was the chairman of the board, functioning as the chief executive officer and overseeing the operations of many separate branches of the corporation. An executive committee in charge of the "Counterfeit Title, Stolen Car, and Amphetamine Sales Department"

---

[a] Section 371 provides:

If two or more persons conspire either to commit any offense against the United States, or to defraud the United States, or any agency thereof in any manner or for any purpose, and one or more of such persons do any act to effect the object of the conspiracy, each shall be fined under this title or imprisoned not more than five years, or both.

> was comprised of J.C., Delph, and Taylor, who supervised the operations of lower level employees such as Farr, the printer, and Green, Boyd, and Jackson, the car thieves. Another executive committee, comprised of J.C., Recea and Foster, controlled the "Thefts From Interstate Commerce Department", arranging the purchase, concealment, and distribution of such commodities as meat, dairy products, "Career Club" shirts, and heavy construction equipment. An offshoot of this department handled subsidiary activities, such as murder and obstruction of justice, intended to facilitate the smooth operation of its primary activities. Each member of the conglomerate, with the exception of Foster, was responsible for procuring and wholesaling whatever narcotics could be obtained. The thread tying all of these departments, activities, and individuals together was the desire to make money.[b]

In the course of its opinion, the court discussed the differences between a charge of conspiracy under pre-RICO law and under § 1962(d):

> All six defendants were convicted under 18 U.S.C. § 1962(d) of having conspired to violate a substantive RICO provision, § 1962(c). In this appeal, [the] defendants . . . argue that while the indictment alleged but one conspiracy, the government's evidence at trial proved the existence of several conspiracies, resulting in a variance which substantially prejudiced their rights and requires reversal. . . . Prior to the enactment of the RICO statute, this argument would have been more persuasive. However, as we explain below, RICO has displaced many of the legal precepts traditionally applied to concerted criminal activity. Its effect in this case is to free the government from the strictures of the multiple conspiracy doctrine and to allow the joint trial of many persons accused of diversified crimes.
>
> [Traditional conspiracy doctrine] applies only insofar as the alleged agreement has "a common end or single unified purpose." Generally, where the government has shown that a number of otherwise diverse activities were performed to achieve a single goal, courts have been willing to find a single conspiracy. This "common objective" test has most often been used to connect the many facets of drug importation and distribution schemes. The rationale falls apart, however, where the remote members of the alleged conspiracy are not truly interdependent or where the vari-

[b] The court affirmed the conviction of five of the six defendants for conspiring to violate RICO. The conspiracy conviction of the sixth defendant—Elliott, whose name adorns the case in the Federal Reporter—was reversed. Elliott was plainly a marginal player. The court was convinced that he " 'associated with the wrong people and was convicted because of guilt by association only.' " Of the other five defendants, J.C. Hawkins and Recea Hawkins (his brother) were convicted both of a substantive RICO count and the count charging conspiracy to violate RICO. Various combinations of the defendants were also convicted of separately stated predicate offenses. Twenty-five overt acts were recited in the conspiracy count, ranging from arson to drug crimes. The "pattern" of racketeering activity alleged in the substantive RICO count (grounded on § 1962(c)) was based on four violations of federal law alleged in separate counts (three involving thefts from interstate shipments and the fourth a counterfeit security), as well as a series of federal drug crimes, an arson in violation of state law, and a murder in violation of state law. J.C. was the ringleader. He was sentenced to 80 years imprisonment. Recea got 50 years. Two other defendants were sentenced to 10 years in prison, and the fifth defendant was sentenced to one year plus five years probation.—[Footnote by eds.]

ous activities sought to be tied together cannot reasonably be said to constitute a unified scheme. . . .

Applying pre-RICO conspiracy concepts to the facts of this case, we doubt that a single conspiracy could be demonstrated. Foster had no contact with Delph and Taylor during the life of the alleged conspiracy. Delph and Taylor, so far as the evidence revealed, had no contact with Recea Hawkins. The activities allegedly embraced by the illegal agreement in this case are simply too diverse to be tied together on the theory that participation in one activity necessarily implied awareness of others. Even viewing the "common objective" of the conspiracy as the raising of revenue through criminal activity, we could not say, for example, that Foster, when he helped to conceal stolen meat, had to know that J.C. was selling drugs to persons unknown to Foster, or that Delph and Taylor, when they furnished counterfeit titles to a car theft ring, had to know that the man supplying the titles was also stealing goods out of interstate commerce. The enterprise involved in this case probably could not have been successfully prosecuted as a single conspiracy under the general federal conspiracy statute, 18 U.S.C. § 371.

. . . In the context of organized crime, [traditional conspiracy doctrine] inhibited mass prosecutions because a single agreement or "common objective" cannot be inferred from the commission of highly diverse crimes by apparently unrelated individuals. RICO helps to eliminate this problem by creating a substantive offense which ties together these diverse parties and crimes. Thus, the object of a RICO conspiracy is to violate a substantive RICO provision—here, to conduct or participate in the affairs of an enterprise through a pattern of racketeering activity. The gravamen of the conspiracy charge in this case is not that each defendant agreed to commit arson, to steal goods from interstate commerce, to obstruct justice, and to sell narcotics; rather, it is that each agreed to participate, directly and indirectly, in the affairs of the enterprise by committing two or more predicate crimes. Under the statute, it is irrelevant that each defendant participated in the enterprise's affairs through different, even unrelated crimes, so long as we may reasonably infer that each crime was intended to further the enterprise's affairs. To find a single conspiracy, we still must look for agreement on an overall objective. What Congress did was to define that objective through the substantive provisions of the act. . . .

In the instant case, it is clear that "the essential nature of the plan" was to associate for the purpose of making money from repeated criminal activity. Defendant Foster, for example, hired J.C. Hawkins to commit arson, helped him to conceal large quantities of meat and shirts stolen from interstate commerce, and bought a stolen forklift from him. It would be "a perversion of natural thought and of natural language" to deny that these facts give rise to the inference that Foster knew he was directly involved in an enterprise whose purpose was to profit from crime. . . . Foster also had to know that the enterprise was bigger than his role in it, and that others unknown to him were participating in its affairs. He may have been unaware that others who had agreed to participate in the enterprise's affairs did so by selling drugs and murdering a key witness. That, however, is irrelevant to his own liability, for he is charged with agreeing *to participate* in the enterprise through his own crimes, not with agreeing *to commit* each of the crimes through which the overall affairs of the enterprise were conducted. . . . [31]

We do not lightly dismiss the fact that under this statute four defendants who did not commit murder have been forced to stand trial jointly with, and as confederates of, two others who did. Prejudice inheres in such a trial; great Neptune's ocean could not purge its taint.[33] But the Constitution does not guarantee a trial free from the prejudice that inevitably accompanies any charge of heinous group crime; it demands only that the potential for transference of guilt be minimized to the extent possible under the circumstances in order "to individualize each defendant in his relation to the mass." Kotteakos v. United States, 328 U.S. 750, 773 (1946). The RICO statute does not offend this principle. Congress, in a proper exercise of its legislative power, has decided that murder, like thefts from interstate commerce and the counterfeiting of securities, qualifies as racketeering activity. This, of course, ups the ante for RICO violators who personally would not contemplate taking a human life. Whether there is a moral imbalance in the

const. rights

[31] Although the evidence here supports the inference that each remote member of this enterprise knew he was a part of a much larger criminal venture, we do not wish to imply that each "department" of the enterprise was wholly independent of the others. A close look at the modus operandi of the enterprise reveals a pattern of interdependence which bolsters our conclusion that the functions of each "department" directly contributed to the success of the overall operation. Many of the enterprise's practices were analogous to those common in legitimate businesses:

—*Investment Capital*: Most of the enterprise's activities depended upon the ready availability of investment capital, or "front money", to finance the purchase of stolen goods and narcotics for eventual resale at a profit. In this sense, money brought in from one project could be used to purchase goods in another unrelated project.

—*"Good Will"*: Part of the value of a business is the reputation it has established in the community, its "good will." The enterprise here benefitted from a negative form of "good will." For example, Foster and J.C. exploited their cooperation in the Sparta nursing home arson to gain the confidence of James Gunnells when they needed his help in concealing stolen meat; that earlier endeavor furnished proof that Foster and J.C. could be trusted in criminal pursuits. Similarly, J.C.'s threats of physical harm to many of those involved with the enterprise helped to build a fear in the community which deterred potential witnesses from going to the police. In this way, each successful criminal act and each threat contributed to the success of the enterprise as a whole.

—*Arrangements to Limit Liability*: Like most large business organizations, this enterprise conducted its affairs in a manner calculated to limit its liability for the acts of its agents. J.C. erroneously believed that he could limit each person's liability by keeping him as isolated from the others as possible—in other words, that it would be safer to have the affairs of the enterprise conducted through chains composed of many persons playing limited roles than through a small circle of individuals performing many functions. Where overlap was unavoidable, the enterprise's ongoing operations depended upon each member's confidence that the others would remain silent. When J.C. spoke to Joe Fuchs in January, 1976, for example, he expressed confidence that the government could never make a case against his enterprise. He was certain that James Elliott would not talk because "James is scared." He also assured Fuchs that he, J.C., and Scooter Herring would say nothing: as for Recea, "that's plum out of the question, you can eliminate that." Thus, he concluded, the only other persons who might implicate Fuchs could provide only uncorroborated accounts which would "mean nothing" in court.

[33] Cf. Shakespeare, Macbeth, Act III, Scene I.

> equation of thieves and counterfeiters with murderers is a question whose answer lies in the halls of Congress, not in the judicial conscience. . . .
>
> Through RICO, Congress defined a new separate crime to help snare those who make careers of crime. Participation in the affairs of an enterprise through the commission of two or more predicate crimes is now an offense separate and distinct from those predicate crimes. So too is conspiracy to commit this new offense a crime separate and distinct from conspiracy to commit the predicate crimes. The necessity which mothered this statutory invention was caused by the inability of the traditional criminal law to punish and deter organized crime.

Is it clear after *Elliott* why RICO has become a significant prosecutorial weapon in the fight against organized crime? What features make it so valuable?

### 3. INTRODUCTORY COMMENTS ON THE DEFINITION OF "ENTERPRISE"

As mentioned in Note 1, a major problem created by *Turkette* was the reach of the term "enterprise." It is the perpetration of crime through the vehicle of an "enterprise" that serves to distinguish "ordinary" criminal conspiracies from the "organized" crime that triggers RICO penalties. What kinds of criminal activity are large enough or "organized" enough to warrant the severe sanctions authorized by RICO? Are two (or three or four or ten?) people who plan a series of similar crimes (or a variety of different types of crimes) engaged in an ordinary conspiracy (five-year maximum) or are they conspiring to conduct the affairs of a RICO "enterprise" through a pattern of racketeering activity (20-year maximum plus an important array of forfeiture sanctions)? Where is the line between these two conspiracy offenses to be drawn?[c]

*Turkette* alluded to this question, but did not carry the analysis very far. It seemed to imply, though, that the concept of "enterprise" did not incorporate an ordinary conspiracy:

> [An] enterprise is an entity, for present purposes a group of persons associated together for a common purpose of engaging in a course of conduct. [It] is proved by evidence of an ongoing organization, formal or informal, and by evidence that the various associates function as a continuing unit. . . . The "enterprise" . . . is an entity separate and apart from the pattern of activity in which it engages.

Although the Supreme Court had held there need not be an economic motive,[d] it was not until *Boyle v. United States* (the next main case) that the Court identified the characteristics that would make group criminal activity a RICO "enterprise."

---

[c] The term "pattern" can also help draw the line between ordinary crime and RICO crime. How it might do so is dealt with later in this Section. For now, the focus should remain on the meaning of "enterprise."

[d] See National Organization for Women, Inc. v. Scheidler, 510 U.S. 249 (1994) (the objective of the "enterprise" was to close down abortion clinics).

## 4.   NARROW DEFINITIONS OF "ENTERPRISE"

After *Turkette* and prior to *Boyle*, some Circuit Courts sought to limit the application of RICO to activities that looked like the product of organized crime. United States v. Bledsoe, 674 F.2d. 647 (8th Cir. 1982), is a well-known early example:

> The primary intent of Congress in enacting 18 U.S.C. § 1962(c) was to prevent organized crime from infiltrating businesses and other legitimate economic entities. . . . When directed against infiltration of legitimate enterprises, the provisions have a relatively well defined scope of application. Legitimate businesses and other legitimate organizations tend to have a definite structure and clear boundaries which limit the applicability of a criminal statute aimed at the infiltration of criminal elements into these entities. Infiltration of legitimate entities also warrants the act's severe sanctions. The act's drafters perceived a distinct threat to the free market in organized criminal groups gaining control of enterprises operating in that market. These congressmen thought that organized criminal elements exert a monopoly-like power in the legitimate economic sphere. The bill's sponsors also believed that such infiltration was a source of power and protection for organized crime and gave it a permanent base from which it was more likely to perpetrate a continuing pattern of criminal acts.
>
> But Congress did not draft the statute to apply solely to infiltration of legitimate enterprises. The statute also reaches wholly criminal organizations. However, the act was not intended to reach any criminals who merely associate together and perpetrate two of the specified crimes, rather it was aimed at "organized crime." . . . Obviously, no statute could and this statute was not intended to require direct proof that individuals are engaged in something as ill defined as "organized crime." The statute is an attack on organized crime, but it utilizes a per se approach. . . . Each element of the crime, that is, the predicate acts, the pattern of such acts, and the enterprise requirement, was designed to limit the applicability of the statute and separate individuals engaged in organized crime from ordinary criminals. The enterprise requirement must be interpreted in this light.
>
> [T]he enterprise must be more than an informal group created to perpetrate the acts of racketeering. [It] cannot simply be the undertaking of the acts of racketeering, neither can it be the minimal association which surrounds these acts. Any two criminal acts will necessarily be surrounded by some degree of organization and no two individuals will ever jointly perpetrate a crime without some degree of association apart from the commission of the crime itself. Thus unless the inclusion of the enterprise element requires proof of some structure separate from the racketeering activity and distinct from the organization which is a necessary incident to the racketeering, the act simply punishes the commission of two of the specified crimes within a 10-year period. Congress clearly did not intend such an application of the act.

*[handwritten margin notes:]*
*United States v. Bledsoe*
*limit app. of RICO to activities that are product of organized crime.*

*Aimed at organized crime not any mere associates*

*utilizes a per se approach*
*limit applicability to organize crime not just ordinary criminals*

Although commonality of purpose may be the sine qua non of a criminal enterprise, in many cases this singular test fails to distinguish enterprises from individuals merely associated together for the commission of sporadic crime. Any two wrongdoers who through concerted action commit two or more crimes share a purpose. This suggests that an enterprise must exhibit each of three basic characteristics.

In addition to having a common or shared purpose which animates those associated with it, it is fundamental that the enterprise "function as a continuing unit." In *Turkette*, the Supreme Court stated that an enterprise "is proved by evidence of an *ongoing* organization, formal or informal, and by evidence that the various associates function as a *continuing* unit." (Emphasis added.) This does not mean the scope of the enterprise cannot change as it engages in diverse forms of activity nor does it mean that the participants in the enterprise cannot vary with different individuals managing its affairs at different times and in different places. What is essential, however, is that there is some continuity of both structure and personality. For example, the operatives in a prostitution ring may change through time, but the various roles which the old and new individuals perform remain the same. But if an entirely new set of people begin to operate the ring, it is not the same enterprise as it was before.

Finally, an enterprise must have an "ascertainable structure" distinct from that inherent in the conduct of a pattern of racketeering activity. This distinct structure might be demonstrated by proof that a group engaged in a diverse pattern of crimes or that it has an organizational pattern or system of authority beyond what was necessary to perpetrate the predicate crimes. The command system of a Mafia family is an example of this type of structure as is the hierarchy, planning, and division of profits within a prostitution ring.

In *Boyle v. United States*, the Supreme Court—by a vote of seven to two—approached the issue quite differently.

## Boyle v. United States

Supreme Court of the United States, 2009.
556 U.S. 938.

■ JUSTICE ALITO delivered the opinion of the Court.

We are asked in this case to decide whether an association-in-fact enterprise under the Racketeer Influenced and Corrupt Organizations Act (RICO), 18 U.S.C. § 1961 et seq., must have "an ascertainable structure beyond that inherent in the pattern of racketeering activity in which it engages." We hold that such an enterprise must have a "structure" but that an instruction framed in this precise language is not necessary. The District Court properly instructed the jury in this case. We therefore affirm the judgment of the Court of Appeals.

I

A

The evidence at petitioner's trial was sufficient to prove the following: Petitioner and others participated in a series of bank thefts in New York, New Jersey, Ohio, and Wisconsin during the 1990's. The participants in these crimes included a core group, along with others who were recruited from time to time. Although the participants sometimes attempted bank-vault burglaries and bank robberies, the group usually targeted cash-laden night-deposit boxes, which are often found in banks in retail areas.

Each theft was typically carried out by a group of participants who met beforehand to plan the crime, gather tools (such as crowbars, fishing gaffs, and walkie-talkies), and assign the roles that each participant would play (such as lookout and driver). The participants generally split the proceeds from the thefts. The group was loosely and informally organized. It does not appear to have had a leader or hierarchy; nor does it appear that the participants ever formulated any long-term master plan or agreement.

From 1991 to 1994, the core group was responsible for more than 30 night-deposit-box thefts. By 1994, petitioner had joined the group, and over the next five years, he participated in numerous attempted night-deposit-box thefts and at least two attempted bank-vault burglaries.

In 2003, petitioner was indicted for participation in the conduct of the affairs of an enterprise through a pattern of racketeering activity, in violation of 18 U.S.C. § 1962(c); conspiracy to commit that offense, in violation of § 1962(d); conspiracy to commit bank burglary, in violation of § 371; and nine counts of bank burglary and attempted bank burglary, in violation of § 2113(a).

B

In instructing the jury on the meaning of a RICO "enterprise," the District Court relied largely on language in United States v. Turkette, 452 U.S. 576 (1981). The court told the jurors that, in order to establish the existence of such an enterprise, the Government had to prove that: "(1) There [was] an ongoing organization with some sort of framework, formal or informal, for carrying out its objectives; and (2) the various members and associates of the association function[ed] as a continuing unit to achieve a common purpose." Over petitioner's objection, the court also told the jury that it could "find an enterprise where an association of individuals, without structural hierarchy, form[ed] solely for the purpose of carrying out a pattern of racketeering acts" and that "[c]ommon sense suggests that the existence of an association-in-fact is oftentimes more readily proven by what it does, rather than by abstract analysis of its structure."[1]

---

1 The relevant portion of the instructions was as follows:

The term "enterprise" as used in these instructions may also include a group of people associated in fact, even though this association is not recognized as a legal entity. Indeed, an enterprise need not have a name. Thus, an enterprise need not be a form[al] business entity such as a corporation, but may be merely an informal association of individuals. A group or association of people can be an "enterprise" if, among other requirements, these individuals "associate" together for a purpose of engaging

Petitioner requested an instruction that the Government was required to prove that the enterprise "had an ongoing organization, a core membership that functioned as a continuing unit, and an ascertainable structural hierarchy distinct from the charged predicate acts." The District Court refused to give that instruction.

Petitioner was convicted on 11 of the 12 counts against him, including the RICO counts, and was sentenced to 151 months' imprisonment. In a summary order, the Court of Appeals for the Second Circuit affirmed his conviction but vacated the sentence on a ground not relevant to the issues before us. The Court of Appeals did not specifically address the RICO jury instructions, stating only that the arguments not discussed in the order were "without merit." Petitioner was then resentenced, and we granted certiorari to resolve conflicts among the Courts of Appeals concerning the meaning of a RICO enterprise.

## II

### A

RICO makes it "unlawful for any person employed by or *associated with any enterprise* engaged in, or the activities of which affect, interstate or foreign commerce, to conduct or participate, directly or indirectly, in the conduct of such enterprise's affairs through a pattern of racketeering activity or collection of unlawful debt." 18 U.S.C. § 1962(c) (emphasis added).

The statute does not specifically define the outer boundaries of the "enterprise" concept but states that the term "includes any individual, partnership, corporation, association, or other legal entity, and any union or group of individuals associated in fact although not a legal entity." § 1961(4).[2] This enumeration of included enterprises is obviously broad, encompassing "*any* . . . group of individuals associated in fact" (emphasis added). The term "any" ensures that the definition has a wide reach, and the very concept of an association in fact is expansive. In addition, the RICO statute provides that its terms are to be "liberally

---

in a course of conduct. Common sense suggests that the existence of an association-in-fact is oftentimes more readily proven by what it does, rather than by abstract analysis of its structure.

Moreover, you may find an enterprise where an association of individuals, *without structural hierarchy,* forms solely for the purpose of carrying out a pattern of racketeering acts. Such an association of persons may be established by evidence showing an ongoing organization, formal or informal, and . . . by evidence that the people making up the association functioned as a continuing unit. Therefore, in order to establish the existence of such an enterprise, the government must prove that: (1) There is an ongoing organization with some sort of framework, formal or informal, for carrying out its objectives; and (2) the various members and associates of the association function as a continuing unit to achieve a common purpose.

Regarding "organization," *it is not necessary that the enterprise have any particular or formal structure,* but it must have sufficient organization that its members functioned and operated in a coordinated manner in order to carry out the alleged common purpose or purposes of the enterprise. (Emphasis added.)

[2] This provision does not purport to set out an exhaustive definition of the term "enterprise." Compare §§ 1961(1)–(2) (defining what the terms "racketeering activity" and "State" *mean*) with §§ 1961(3)–(4) (defining what the terms "person" and "enterprise" *include*). Accordingly, this provision does not foreclose the possibility that the term might include, in addition to the specifically enumerated entities, others that fall within the ordinary meaning of the term "enterprise."

construed to effectuate its remedial purposes." § 904(a), note following 18 U.S.C. § 1961; see also, e.g., National Organization for Women, Inc. v. Scheidler, 510 U.S. 249, 257 (1994) ("RICO broadly defines 'enterprise' "); Sedima, S.P.R.L. v. Imrex Co., 473 U.S. 479, 497 (1985) ("RICO is to be read broadly"); Russello v. United States, 464 U.S. 16, 21 (1983) (noting "the pattern of the RICO statute in utilizing terms and concepts of breadth").

In light of these statutory features, we explained in *Turkette* that "an enterprise includes any union or group of individuals associated in fact" and that RICO reaches "a group of persons associated together for a common purpose of engaging in a course of conduct." Such an enterprise, we said, "is proved by evidence of an ongoing organization, formal or informal, and by evidence that the various associates function as a continuing unit."

Notwithstanding these precedents, the dissent asserts that the definition of a RICO enterprise is limited to "business-like entities." We see no basis to impose such an extratextual requirement.

B

As noted, the specific question on which we granted certiorari is whether an association-in-fact enterprise must have "an ascertainable structure beyond that inherent in the pattern of racketeering activity in which it engages." We will break this question into three parts. First, must an association-in-fact enterprise have a "structure"? Second, must the structure be "ascertainable"? Third, must the "structure" go "beyond that inherent in the pattern of racketeering activity" in which its members engage?

"*Structure*." We agree with petitioner that an association-in-fact enterprise must have a structure. In the sense relevant here, the term "structure" means "[t]he way in which parts are arranged or put together to form a whole" and "[t]he interrelation or arrangement of parts in a complex entity." American Heritage Dictionary 1718 (4th ed. 2000); see also Random House Dictionary of the English Language 1410 (1967) (defining structure to mean, among other things, "the pattern of relationships, as of status or friendship, existing among the members of a group or society").

From the terms of RICO, it is apparent that an association-in-fact enterprise must have at least three structural features: a purpose, relationships among those associated with the enterprise, and longevity sufficient to permit these associates to pursue the enterprise's purpose. As we succinctly put it in *Turkette,* an association-in-fact enterprise is "a group of persons associated together for a common purpose of engaging in a course of conduct."

That an "enterprise" must have a purpose is apparent from meaning of the term in ordinary usage, i.e., a "venture," "undertaking," or "project." Webster's Third New International Dictionary 757 (1976). The concept of "associat[ion]" requires both interpersonal relationships and a common interest. See *id.*, at 132 (defining "association" as "an organization of persons having a common interest"); Black's Law Dictionary 156 (rev. 4th ed.1968) (defining "association" as a "collection of persons who have joined together for a certain object"). Section 1962(c) reinforces this conclusion and also shows that an "enterprise" must have some longevity, since the offense proscribed by that provision demands proof that the enterprise had "affairs" of sufficient duration to permit an associate to "participate" in those affairs through "a pattern of racketeering activity."

Although an association-in-fact enterprise must have these structural features, it does not follow that a district court must use the term "structure" in its jury instructions. A trial judge has considerable discretion in choosing the language of an instruction so long as the substance of the relevant point is adequately expressed.

"*Ascertainable.*" Whenever a jury is told that it must find the existence of an element beyond a reasonable doubt, that element must be "ascertainable" or else the jury could not find that it was proved. Therefore, telling the members of the jury that they had to ascertain the existence of an "ascertainable structure" would have been redundant and potentially misleading.

"*Beyond that inherent in the pattern of racketeering activity.*" This phrase may be interpreted in least two different ways, and its correctness depends on the particular sense in which the phrase is used. If the phrase is interpreted to mean that the existence of an enterprise is a separate element that must be proved, it is of course correct. As we explained in *Turkette,* the existence of an enterprise is an element distinct from the pattern of racketeering activity and "proof of one does not necessarily establish the other."[4]

On the other hand, if the phrase is used to mean that the existence of an enterprise may never be inferred from the evidence showing that persons associated with the enterprise engaged in a pattern of racketeering activity, it is incorrect. We recognized in *Turkette* that the evidence used to prove the pattern of racketeering activity and the evidence establishing an enterprise "may in particular cases coalesce."

C

The crux of petitioner's argument is that a RICO enterprise must have structural features in addition to those that we think can be fairly inferred from the language of the statute. Although petitioner concedes that an association-in-fact enterprise may be an " 'informal' " group and that "not 'much' " structure is needed, he contends that such an enterprise must have at least some additional structural attributes, such as a structural "hierarchy," "role differentiation," a "unique modus operandi," a "chain of command," "professionalism and sophistication of organization," "diversity and complexity of crimes," "membership dues, rules and regulations," "uncharged or additional crimes aside from predicate acts," an "internal discipline mechanism," "regular meetings regarding enterprise affairs," an "enterprise 'name,' " and "induction or initiation ceremonies and rituals."

We see no basis in the language of RICO for the structural requirements that petitioner asks us to recognize. As we said in *Turkette,* an association-in-fact enterprise is simply a continuing unit

[4] It is easy to envision situations in which proof that individuals engaged in a pattern of racketeering activity would not establish the existence of an enterprise. For example, suppose that several individuals, independently and without coordination, engaged in a pattern of crimes listed as RICO predicates—for example, bribery or extortion. Proof of these patterns would not be enough to show that the individuals were members of an enterprise.

that functions with a common purpose. Such a group need not have a hierarchical structure or a "chain of command"; decisions may be made on an ad hoc basis and by any number of methods—by majority vote, consensus, a show of strength, etc. Members of the group need not have fixed roles; different members may perform different roles at different times. The group need not have a name, regular meetings, dues, established rules and regulations, disciplinary procedures, or induction or initiation ceremonies. While the group must function as a continuing unit and remain in existence long enough to pursue a course of conduct, nothing in RICO exempts an enterprise whose associates engage in spurts of activity punctuated by periods of quiescence. Nor is the statute limited to groups whose crimes are sophisticated, diverse, complex, or unique; for example, a group that does nothing but engage in extortion through old-fashioned, unsophisticated, and brutal means may fall squarely within the statute's reach. . . .

III

A

Contrary to petitioner's claims, rejection of his argument regarding these structural characteristics does not lead to a merger of the crime proscribed by 18 U.S.C. § 1962(c) (participating in the affairs of an enterprise through a pattern of racketeering activity) and . . . conspiring to commit one or more crimes that are listed as RICO predicate offenses, § 371; or conspiring to violate the RICO statute, § 1962(d). . . .

[P]roof that a defendant conspired to commit a RICO predicate offense—for example, arson—does not necessarily establish that the defendant participated in the affairs of an arson enterprise through a pattern of arson crimes. Under § 371, a conspiracy is an inchoate crime that may be completed in the brief period needed for the formation of the agreement and the commission of a single overt act in furtherance of the conspiracy.[a] See United States v. Feola, 420 U.S. 671, 694 (1975). Section 1962(c) demands much more: the creation of an "enterprise"—a group with a common purpose and course of conduct—and the actual commission of a pattern of predicate offenses.[5]

Finally, while in practice the elements of a violation of §§ 1962(c) and (d) are similar, this overlap would persist even if petitioner's conception of an association-in-fact enterprise were accepted.

---

[a] Section 371 provides:

> If two or more persons conspire either to commit any offense against the United States, or to defraud the United States, or any agency thereof in any manner or for any purpose, and one or more of such persons do any act to effect the object of the conspiracy, each shall be fined under this title or imprisoned not more than five years, or both.
>
> If, however, the offense, the commission of which is the object of the conspiracy, is a misdemeanor only, the punishment for such conspiracy shall not exceed the maximum punishment provided for such misdemeanor.—[Footnote by eds.]

[5] The dissent states that "[o]nly if proof of the enterprise element . . . requires evidence of activity or organization beyond that inherent in the pattern of predicate acts will RICO offenses retain an identity distinct from § 371 offenses." This is incorrect: Even if the same evidence may prove two separate elements, this does not mean that the two elements collapse into one.

B

Because the statutory language is clear, there is no need to reach petitioner's remaining arguments based on statutory purpose, legislative history, or the rule of lenity. In prior cases, we have rejected similar arguments in favor of the clear but expansive text of the statute. See National Organization for Women, 510 U.S., at 262 ("The fact that RICO has been applied in situations not expressly anticipated by Congress does not demonstrate ambiguity. It demonstrates breadth"). . . .

IV

The instructions the District Court judge gave to the jury in this case were correct and adequate. These instructions explicitly told the jurors that they could not convict on the RICO charges unless they found that the Government had proved the existence of an enterprise. The instructions made clear that this was a separate element from the pattern of racketeering activity.

The instructions also adequately told the jury that the enterprise needed to have the structural attributes that may be inferred from the statutory language. As noted, the trial judge told the jury that the Government was required to prove that there was "an ongoing organization with some sort of framework, formal or informal, for carrying out its objectives" and that "the various members and associates of the association function[ed] as a continuing unit to achieve a common purpose."

Finally, the trial judge did not err in instructing the jury that "the existence of an association-in-fact is oftentimes more readily proven by what it does, rather than by abstract analysis of its structure." This instruction properly conveyed the point we made in *Turkette* that proof of a pattern of racketeering activity may be sufficient in a particular case to permit a jury to infer the existence of an association-in-fact enterprise.

We therefore affirm the judgment of the Court of Appeals.

It is so ordered.

■ JUSTICE STEVENS, with whom JUSTICE BREYER joins, dissenting.

In my view, Congress intended the term "enterprise" as it is used in the Racketeer Influenced and Corrupt Organizations Act (RICO), 18 U.S.C. § 1961 et seq., to refer only to business-like entities that have an existence apart from the predicate acts committed by their employees or associates. The trial judge in this case committed two significant errors relating to the meaning of that term. First, he instructed the jury that "an association of individuals, without structural hierarchy, form[ed] solely for the purpose of carrying out a pattern of racketeering acts" can constitute an enterprise. And he allowed the jury to find that element satisfied by evidence showing a group of criminals with no existence beyond its intermittent commission of racketeering acts and related offenses. Because the Court's decision affirming petitioner's conviction is inconsistent with the statutory meaning of the term enterprise and serves to expand RICO liability far beyond the bounds Congress intended, I respectfully dissent.

I

. . . It is clear from the statute and our earlier decisions construing the term that Congress used "enterprise" in these provisions in the sense of "a business organization," Webster's Third New International Dictionary 757 (1976), rather than "a 'venture,' 'undertaking,' or 'project,' "(quoting Webster's Third New International Dictionary, at 757). First, the terms "individual, partnership, corporation, association, or other legal entity" describe entities with formal legal structures most commonly established for business purposes. § 1961(4). In context, the subsequent reference to any "union or group of individuals associated in fact *although not a legal entity*" reflects an intended commonality between the legal and nonlegal entities included in the provision (emphasis added). "The juxtaposition of the two phrases suggests that 'associated in fact' just means structured without the aid of legally defined structural forms such as the business corporation." Limestone Development Corp. v. Lemont, 520 F.3d 797, 804–05 (7th Cir. 2008).[1] . . .

Our cases . . . make clear that an enterprise "is an entity separate and apart from the pattern of activity in which it engages." United States v. Turkette, 452 U.S. 576, 583 (1981). As with the requirement that an enterprise have business-like characteristics, that an enterprise must have a separate existence is confirmed by § 1962(c) . . . . If an entity's existence consisted solely of its members' performance of a pattern of racketeering acts, the "enterprise's affairs" would be synonymous with the "pattern of racketeering activity." Section 1962(c) would then prohibit an individual from conducting or participating in "the conduct of [a pattern of racketeering activity] through a pattern of racketeering activity"—a reading that is unbearably redundant, particularly in a case like this one in which a single pattern of activity is alleged. The only way to avoid that result is to require that an "enterprise's affairs" be something other than the pattern of racketeering activity undertaken by its members.[2]

---

[1] To be sure, we have read RICO's enterprise term broadly to include entities with exclusively noneconomic motives or wholly unlawful purposes. See National Organization for Women, Inc. v. Scheidler, 510 U.S. 249, 252 (1994) (*NOW*); United States v. Turkette, 452 U.S. 576, 580–81 (1981). But those holdings are consistent with the conclusion that an enterprise is a business-like entity. Indeed, the examples of qualifying associations cited in *Turkette*—including loan-sharking, property-fencing, drug-trafficking, and counterfeiting operations—satisfy that criterion, as each describes an organization with continuing operations directed toward providing goods or services to its customers. Similarly, the enterprise at issue in *NOW* was a nationwide network of antiabortion groups that had a leadership counsel and regular conferences and whose members undertook an extensive pattern of extortion, arson, and other racketeering activity for the purpose of "shut[ting] down abortion clinics."

[2] The other subsections of 18 U.S.C. § 1962 further demonstrate the business-like nature of the enterprise element and its necessary distinctness from the pattern of racketeering activity. Subsection (a) prohibits anyone who receives income derived from a pattern of racketeering activity from "us[ing] or invest[ing], directly or indirectly, any part of such income . . . in acquisition of any interest in, or the establishment or operation of, any enterprise." And subsection (b) prohibits anyone from "acquir[ing] or maintain[ing]" any interest in or control of an enterprise through a pattern of racketeering activity. We noted in *NOW* that the term enterprise "plays a different role in the structure" of those subsections than it does in subsection (c) because the enterprise in those subsections is the victim. We did not, however, suggest that the term has a substantially different meaning in each subsection. To the contrary, our observation that the enterprise in subsection (c) is "the vehicle through which the unlawful pattern of racketeering activity is committed" indicates that, as in subsections (a) and (b), the enterprise must have an existence apart from the pattern of racketeering activity.

Recognizing an enterprise's business-like nature and its distinctness from the pattern of predicate acts, however, does not answer the question of what proof each element requires. In cases involving a legal entity, the matter of proving the enterprise element is straightforward, as the entity's legal existence will always be something apart from the pattern of activity performed by the defendant or his associates. But in the case of an association-in-fact enterprise, the Government must adduce other evidence of the entity's "separate" existence and "ongoing organization." There may be cases in which a jury can infer that existence and continuity from the evidence used to establish the pattern of racketeering activity. But that will be true only when the pattern of activity is so complex that it could not be performed in the absence of structures or processes for planning or concealing the illegal conduct beyond those inherent in performing the predicate acts. More often, proof of an enterprise's separate existence will require different evidence from that used to establish the pattern of predicate acts.

Precisely what proof is required in each case is a more difficult question, largely due to the abundant variety of RICO predicates and enterprises. Because covered enterprises are necessarily business-like in nature, however, proof of an association-in-fact enterprise's separate existence will generally require evidence of rules, routines, or processes through which the entity maintains its continuing operations and seeks to conceal its illegal acts. As petitioner suggests, this requirement will usually be satisfied by evidence that the association has an "ascertainable structure beyond that inherent in the pattern of racketeering activity in which it engages." Examples of such structure include an organizational hierarchy, a "framework for making decisions," an "internal discipline mechanism," "regular meetings," or a practice of "reinvest[ing] proceeds to promote and expand the enterprise." In other cases, the enterprise's existence might be established through evidence that it provides goods or services to third parties, as such an undertaking will require organizational elements more comprehensive than those necessary to perform a pattern of predicate acts. Thus, the evidence needed to establish an enterprise will vary from case to case, but in every case the Government must carry its burden of proving that an alleged enterprise has an existence separate from the pattern of racketeering activity undertaken by its constituents.

II

In some respects, my reading of the statute is not very different from that adopted by the Court. We agree that "an association-in-fact enterprise must have at least three structural features: a purpose, relationships among those associated with the enterprise, and longevity sufficient to permit these associates to pursue the enterprise's purpose." But the Court stops short of giving content to that requirement. It states only that RICO "demands proof that the enterprise had 'affairs' of sufficient duration to permit an associate to 'participate' in those affairs through 'a pattern of racketeering activity,'" before concluding that "[a] trial judge has considerable discretion in choosing the language of an instruction" and need not use the term "structure." While I agree the word structure is not talismanic, I would hold that the instructtions must convey the requirement that the alleged enterprise have an existence apart from the alleged pattern of predicate acts. The

Court's decision, by contrast, will allow juries to infer the existence of an enterprise in every case involving a pattern of racketeering activity undertaken by two or more associates.

By permitting the Government to prove both elements with the same evidence, the Court renders the enterprise requirement essentially meaningless in association-in-fact cases. It also threatens to make that category of § 1962(c) offenses indistinguishable from conspiracies to commit predicate acts, see § 371, as the only remaining difference is § 1962(c)'s pattern requirement. The Court resists this criticism, arguing that § 1962(c) "demands much more" than the inchoate offense defined in § 371. It states that the latter "may be completed in the brief period needed for the formation of the agreement and the commission of a single overt act in furtherance of the conspiracy," whereas the former requires the creation of "a group with a common purpose and course of conduct—and the actual commission of a pattern of predicate offenses." Given that it is also unlawful to conspire to violate § 1962(c), see § 1962(d), this comment provides no assurance that RICO and § 371 offenses remain distinct. Only if proof of the enterprise element—the "group with a common purpose and course of conduct"—requires evidence of activity or organization beyond that inherent in the pattern of predicate acts will RICO offenses retain an identity distinct from § 371 offenses.

This case illustrates these concerns. The trial judge instructed the jury that an enterprise need have only the degree of organization necessary "for carrying out its objectives" and that it could "find an enterprise where an association of individuals, without structural hierarchy, forms solely for the purpose of carrying out a pattern of racketeering acts." These instructions were plainly deficient, as they did not require the Government to prove that the alleged enterprise had an existence apart from the pattern of predicate acts. Instead, they permitted the Government's proof of the enterprise's structure and continuing nature—requirements on which all agree—to consist only of evidence that petitioner and his associates performed a pattern of racketeering activity.

Petitioner's requested instruction would have required the jury to find that the alleged enterprise "had an ongoing organization, a core membership that functioned as a continuing unit, and an ascertainable structural hierarchy distinct from the charged predicate acts." That instruction does not precisely track my understanding of the statute; although evidence of "structural hierarchy" can evidence an enterprise, it is not necessary to establish that element. Nevertheless, the proposed instruction would have better directed the jury to consider whether the alleged enterprise possessed the separate existence necessary to expose petitioner to liability under § 1962(c), and the trial judge should have considered an instruction along those lines.

The trial judge also erred in finding the Government's evidence in this case sufficient to support petitioner's RICO convictions. Petitioner was alleged to have participated and conspired to participate in the conduct of an enterprise's affairs through a pattern of racketeering activity consisting of one act of bank robbery and three acts of interstate transportation of stolen funds. The "primary goals" of the alleged enterprise "included generating money for its members and associates through the commission of criminal activity, including bank robberies, bank burglaries and interstate transportation of stolen money." And its modus operandi was to congregate periodically when an associate had a lead on a night-deposit box that the group could break into. Whoever among the associates was available would bring screwdrivers, crowbars, and walkie-talkies to the location. Some acted as lookouts, while others retrieved the money. When the endeavor was successful, the participants would split the proceeds. Thus, the group's purpose and activities, and petitioner's participation therein, were limited to sporadic acts of taking money from bank deposit boxes. There is no evidence in RICO's text or history that Congress intended it to reach such ad hoc associations of thieves.

*holding*

## III

*dissent*

Because the instructions and evidence in this case did not satisfy the requirement that an alleged enterprise have an existence separate and apart from the pattern of activity in which it engages, I respectfully dissent.

## NOTE ON *BOYLE V. UNITED STATES*

Can *Boyle* be read to hold that RICO applies to any ordinary conspiracy that remains in operation long enough to commit or conspire to commit a "pattern of racketeering activity"? Is there anything in *Boyle* to suggest that the Court will take the statutory language of RICO other than literally? Is the Court right to take this position?

Note the separation-of-powers implications of a contrary decision in *Boyle*. Assume the Court was right in *Turkette* in concluding that a wholly criminal organization should be punishable as a RICO "enterprise." That conclusion certainly makes sense both as a literal application of the text and as a means of furthering the intent of Congress to strike a serious blow against organized crime. Assume also that Justice Stevens was right in *Boyle* in concluding that RICO should be limited to "business-like entities" and should not cover "ordinary" conspiracies. That conclusion makes sense as well as a means of limiting the severe sanctions of RICO more or less to the target Congress clearly had in mind. But who, then, is to define the characteristics of "business-like entities"? Which is better: for the Court to apply RICO literally to situations clearly beyond any conceivable Congressional objective or for the Court to limit RICO to its clear objectives by doing a job Congress should have done?

*Stevens limiting to business-like entities*

From another perspective, does it matter in making the "enterprise" determination how many people are involved? Can two people be an "enterprise"? If a "group" of people more than two is required, who decides how many it takes? In the implementation of RICO, in other words, it may not be possible for the Court entirely to escape a lawmaking role. By what criteria should the Court determine how much lawmaking is too much when the issue is how to interpret and apply a criminal statute that is as open-ended as RICO? As *Boyle* illustrates, the Supreme Court is divided on this issue.

*Court in lawmaking role*

*United States v. Bass*

Consider the following from United States v. Bass, 404 U.S. 336, 347–50 (1971), in thinking about these questions. In choosing the narrower of two interpretations of a criminal statute, the Court referred to "two wise principles this Court has long followed":

> First, . . . "ambiguity concerning the ambit of criminal statutes should be resolved in favor of lenity." In various ways over the years, we have stated that "when choice has to be made between two readings of what conduct Congress has made a crime, it is appropriate, before we choose the harsher alternative, to require that Congress should have spoken in language that is clear and definite." This principle is founded on two policies that have long been part of our tradition. First, "a fair warning should be given to the world in language that the common world will understand, of what the law intends to do if a certain line is passed. To make the warning fair, so far as possible the line should be clear." Second, because of the seriousness of criminal penalties, and because criminal punishment usually represents the moral condemnation of the community, legislatures and not courts should define criminal activity. This policy embodies "the instinctive distastes against men languishing in prison unless the lawmaker has clearly said they should." Thus, where there is ambiguity in a criminal statute, doubts are resolved in favor of the defendant. . . .
>
> There is a second principle supporting today's result: unless Congress conveys its purpose clearly, it will not be deemed to have significantly changed the federal-state balance. Congress has traditionally been reluctant to define as a federal crime conduct readily denounced as criminal by the States. This congressional policy is rooted in the same concepts of American federalism that have provided the basis for judge-made doctrines. As this Court [has] emphasized, we will not be quick to assume that Congress has meant to effect a significant change in the sensitive relation between federal and state criminal jurisdiction. In traditionally sensitive areas, such as legislation affecting the federal balance, the requirement of clear statement assures that the legislature has in fact faced, and intended to bring into issue, the critical matters involved in the judicial decision. . . . In the instant case, the broad construction urged by the Government renders traditionally local criminal conduct a matter for federal enforcement and would also involve a substantial extension of federal police resources. . . .

Do these factors counsel against the result in *Turkette*? In a footnote at the end of Part II of its opinion in *Turkette*, the Court said "no":

> We find no occasion to apply the rule of lenity to this statute. "[T]hat 'rule,' as is true of any guide to statutory construction, only serves as an aid for resolving an ambiguity; it is not to be used to beget one. . . . The rule comes into operation at the end of the process of construing what Congress has expressed, not at the beginning as an overriding consideration of being lenient to wrongdoers." Callanan v. United States, 364 U.S. 587, 596 (1961). There being no ambiguity in the RICO provisions at issue here, the rule of lenity does not come into play. See United States v. Moore, 423 U.S. 122, 145 (1975) . . . (The canon in favor of strict construction [of criminal statutes] is not an inexorable command to override common sense and evident statutory purpose. . . . Nor does it demand that a statute be given the "narrowest meaning"; it is satisfied if the words are given their fair meaning in accord with the manifest intent of the lawmakers).

Is the Court's response persuasive? Question-begging? Now consider how the *Bass* factors might apply to *Boyle*. Was the Court right to construe RICO broadly in both *Turkette* and *Boyle*?

*conspiracy vs. RICO determination made by the Justice Dept.*

One effect of *Boyle* is that the operational difference between a violation of RICO and a violation of ordinary conspiracy law—between a 20-year maximum with forfeiture of assets and a five-year maximum—is determined by the charging decisions of the Justice Department. One suspects that most of the time the Department will use RICO to pursue the primary targets at which it was aimed. But *Boyle* does not require that it do so. This is typical of federal crimes. The federal criminal law consists of an exceedingly broad series of nets that federal prosecutors can use to pick and choose the fish they wish to catch in which nets. Cases like *Boyle* also ease the path to conviction even in "real" organized crime cases by substantially reducing the proof required to establish an "enterprise." Is it sensible to put such power in the hands of the prosecutor? In effect the Supreme Court's choice not to place serious limitations on the reach of RICO is a delegation of that authority to the Justice Department. Is that better?

*ease the path to conviction*

## NOTES ON "PATTERN OF RACKETEERING ACTIVITY"

### 1.   THE RICO "PATTERN OF RACKETEERING ACTIVITY"

Each of the substantive offenses punished by RICO requires that the defendants engage in a "pattern of racketeering activity." Crimes that constitute "racketeering activity" are listed at length in § 1961(1). A "pattern" is defined in § 1961(5) as requiring "at least two acts of racketeering activity."

Further elaboration of this concept is not too important where the "enterprise" being pursued is the organized criminal activity itself. A different situation is presented where a *legitimate* enterprise is the target of the organized criminal activity or the means through which the organized criminal activity is conducted. If it is alleged that a legitimate business has been infiltrated by a pattern of racketeering activity or that the affairs of a legitimate business have been conducted by a pattern of racketeering activity, the need to distinguish "ordinary" criminality from "organized" crime once again emerges. Are two acts of mail fraud in conducting an otherwise legitimate business a "pattern of racketeering activity"? Three? In this kind of case, the "pattern" of criminality is the only factor separating ordinary criminal sanctions from the elevated sanctions available under RICO.

The primary context in which this issue has arisen is civil litigation under § 1964(c). Mail fraud and wire fraud are potential "racketeering acts" under § 1961(1), and these crimes are so broadly defined that it is often quite plausible to characterize ordinary commercial disputes as involving one or both of these offenses. Since treble damages and attorney's fees are available to a civil plaintiff if a violation of RICO can be made out, there is a powerful incentive for private plaintiffs to add a RICO count to what might ordinarily be a typical common law suit for breach of contract of for some kind of business tort. The allegation in such cases is that § 1962(c) has been violated because the "enterprise" (the defendant's otherwise legitimate business entity) has been conducted by a "pattern of racketeering activity" (breaches of contract that amount to mail or wire fraud).

## 2. *SEDIMA, S.P.R.L. V. IMREX CO., INC.*

The Supreme Court's first attempt to define "pattern of racketeering activity" occurred in a footnote in Sedima, S.P.R.L. v. Imrex Co., Inc., 473 U.S. 479, 497 n.14 (1985). The facts of *Sedima*, fairly typical of such suits, were as follows:

> In 1979, petitioner Sedima, a Belgian corporation, entered into a joint venture with respondent Imrex Co. to provide electronic components to a Belgian firm. The buyer was to order parts through Sedima; Imrex was to obtain the parts in this country and ship them to Europe. The agreement called for Sedima and Imrex to split the net proceeds. Imrex filled roughly $8 million in orders placed with it through Sedima. Sedima became convinced, however, that Imrex was presenting inflated bills, cheating Sedima out of a portion of its proceeds by collecting for nonexistent expenses.
>
> In 1982, Sedima filed this action. . . . The complaint set out common law claims of unjust enrichment, conversion, and breach of contract, fiduciary duty, and a constructive trust. In addition, it asserted RICO claims under § 1964(c) against Imrex and two of its officers. Two counts alleged violations of § 1962(c) based on predicate acts of mail and wire fraud. . . . Sedima sought treble damages and attorney's fees.

The Court was asked in *Sedima* to adopt several limitations on civil RICO actions that are not material for present purposes.[a] In declining to do so, it held that "Sedima may maintain this action if the defendants conducted the enterprise through a pattern of racketeering activity. The questions whether the defendants committed the requisite predicate acts, and whether the commission of those acts fell into a pattern, are not before us." It did, however, add a footnote on what might constitute a pattern:

> As many commentators have pointed out, the definition of a "pattern of racketeering activity" differs from the other provisions in § 1961 in that it states that a pattern "*requires* at least two acts of racketeering activity," (emphasis added), not that it "means" two such acts. The implication is that while two acts are necessary, they may not be sufficient. Indeed, in common parlance two of anything do not generally form a "pattern." The legislative history supports the view that two isolated acts of racketeering activity do not constitute a pattern. As the Senate Report explained: "The target of [RICO] is thus not sporadic activity. The infiltration of legitimate business normally requires more than one 'racketeering activity' and the threat of continuing activity to be effective. It is this factor of *continuity plus relationship* which combines to produce a pattern." S.Rep. No. 91–617, p. 158 (1969) (emphasis added). Similarly, the sponsor of the Senate bill, after quoting this portion of the Report, pointed out to his colleagues that "[t]he term 'pattern' itself requires the showing of a relationship. . . . So, therefore, proof of two acts of racketeering activity, without more, does not establish a pattern. . . ." 116 Cong.Rec.

[a] Specifically, it was asked to require a special "racketeering injury" as a prerequisite to civil suit under RICO and to hold that a civil RICO claim could not be filed unless there was a prior criminal conviction.

18940 (1970) (statement of Sen. McClellan). See also id., at 35193 (statement of Rep. Poff) (RICO "not aimed at the isolated offender"); House Hearings, at 665. Significantly, in defining "pattern" in a later provision of the same bill, Congress was more enlightening: "[C]riminal conduct forms a pattern if it embraces criminal acts that have the same or similar purposes, results, participants, victims, or methods of commission, or otherwise are interrelated by distinguishing characteristics and are not isolated events." 18 U.S.C. § 3575(e). This language may be useful in interpreting other sections of the act.

### 3. *H.J. INC. V. NORTHWESTERN BELL TELEPHONE COMPANY*

A more elaborate definition of "pattern" was offered in H.J. Inc. v. Northwestern Bell Telephone Company, 492 U.S. 229 (1989). *H.J. Inc.* was also a civil suit. It involved a class action brought by customers of a telephone company who alleged that excessive rates were authorized by the regulatory authorities because they were bribed by officers of the company. The lower courts dismissed the suit because they thought RICO required "multiple illegal schemes" before a "pattern" could be found, whereas what the plaintiffs alleged was a "single fraudulent effort" to obtain higher rates. The Supreme Court reversed. It was unanimous in its conclusion that a series of acts in support of a single scheme or episode could, on appropriate facts, constitute a RICO "pattern."

#### *(i) Justice Brennan's Opinion*

For the Court, Justice Brennan admitted that "developing a meaningful concept of 'pattern' . . . has proved to be no easy task," but made the effort as follows:

> We find no support . . . for the proposition . . . that predicate acts of racketeering may form a pattern only when they are part of separate illegal schemes. Nor can we agree . . . that a pattern is established merely by proving two predicate acts . . . or . . . that the word "pattern" refers only to predicates that are indicative of a perpetrator involved in organized crime or its functional equivalent. In our view, Congress had a more natural and commonsense approach to RICO's pattern element in mind, intending a more stringent requirement than proof simply of two predicates, but also envisioning a concept of sufficient breadth that it might encompass multiple predicates within a single scheme that were related and that amounted to, or threatened the likelihood of, continued criminal activity.
>
> . . . In normal usage, [a] "pattern" is an "arrangement or order of things or activity," 11 Oxford English Dictionary 357 (2d ed. 1989). . . . It is not the number of predicates but the relationship that they bear to each other or to some external organizing principle that renders them "ordered" or "arranged." . . . It is reasonable to infer . . . that Congress intended to take a flexible approach, and envisaged that a pattern might be demonstrated by reference to a range of different ordering principles or relationships between predicates, within the expansive bounds set. . . . The legislative history . . . shows that "[t]he term 'pattern' itself requires the showing of a relationship" between the predicates, 116 Cong. Rec.,

at 18940 (1970) (Sen. McClellan), and of "the threat of continuing activity," ibid. "It is this factor of *continuity plus relationship* which combines to produce a pattern." Ibid. (emphasis added). RICO's legislative history reveals Congress' intent that to prove a pattern of racketeering activity a plaintiff or prosecutor must show that the racketeering predicates are related, and that they amount to or pose a threat of continued criminal activity.

For analytic purposes these two constituents of RICO's pattern requirement must be stated separately, though in practice their proof will often overlap. The element of relatedness is the easier to define, for we may take guidance from a provision [in another portion of the statute of which RICO formed a part. That section provides:] "[C]riminal conduct forms a pattern if it embraces criminal acts that have the same or similar purposes, results, participants, victims, or methods of commission, or otherwise are interrelated by distinguishing characteristics and are not isolated events." We have no reason to suppose that Congress had in mind for RICO's pattern of racketeering component any more constrained a notion of the relationships between predicates that would suffice.

"Continuity" is both a closed-and open-ended concept, referring either to a closed period of repeated conduct, or to past conduct that by its nature projects into the future with a threat of repetition. It is, in either case, centrally a temporal concept—and particularly so in the RICO context, where what must be continuous, RICO's predicate acts or offenses, and the relationship these predicates must bear one to another, are distinct requirements. A party alleging a RICO violation may demonstrate continuity over a closed period by proving a series of related predicates extending over a substantial period of time. Predicate acts extending over a few weeks or months and threatening no future criminal conduct do not satisfy this requirement: Congress was concerned in RICO with long-term criminal conduct. Often a RICO action will be brought before continuity can be established in this way. In such cases, liability depends on whether the threat of continuity is demonstrated.

Whether the predicates proved establish a threat of continued racketeering activity depends on the specific facts of each case. Without making any claim to cover the field of possibilities—preferring to deal with this issue in the context of concrete factual situations presented for decision—we offer some examples of how this element might be satisfied. A RICO pattern may surely be established if the related predicates themselves involve a distinct threat of long-term racketeering activity, either implicit or explicit. Suppose a hoodlum were to sell "insurance" to a neighborhood's storekeepers to cover them against breakage of their windows, telling his victims he would be reappearing each month to collect the "premium" that would continue their "coverage." Though the number of related predicates involved may be small and they may occur close together in time, the racketeering acts themselves include a specific threat of repetition extending indefinitely into the future, and thus supply the requisite threat of continuity. In other cases, the threat of continuity may be established by showing that the predicate acts or offenses are part of an ongoing entity's regular way of doing business. Thus, the threat of continuity is sufficiently established where the predicates can be attributed to a defendant operating as part of a long-term association that exists for criminal purposes. Such associations include, but extend well beyond, those traditionally grouped under the phrase "organized crime." The continuity requirement is likewise satisfied where it is shown that the predicates are a regular way of conducting defendant's ongoing legitimate business (in the sense that it is not a business that exists for criminal purposes), or of conducting or participating in an ongoing and legitimate RICO "enterprise."

### (ii) *Justice Scalia's Opinion*

Justice Scalia, joined by Chief Justice Rehnquist and by Justices O'Connor and Kennedy, wrote separately. His critique was scathing:

> Four terms ago, in Sedima, S.P.R.L. v. Imrex Co., 473 U.S. 479, 497 n.14 (1985), we gave lower courts [some] clues concerning the meaning of the enigmatic term "pattern of racketeering activity". . . . Thus enlightened, the District Courts and Courts of Appeals . . . promptly produced the widest and most persistent Circuit split on an issue of federal law in recent memory. Today, four years and countless millions in damages and attorney's fees later (not to mention prison sentences under the criminal provisions of RICO), the Court does little more than repromulgate those hints as to what RICO means, though with the caveat that Congress intended that they be applied using a "flexible approach."
>
> Elevating to the level of statutory text a phrase taken from the legislative history, the Court counsels the lower courts: "continuity plus relationship." This seems to me about as helpful to the conduct of their affairs as "life is a fountain." Of the two parts of this talismanic phrase, the relatedness requirement is said to be the "easier to define,". . . . [T]he Court's definition . . . has the feel of being solidly rooted in law, since it is a direct quotation of [another statute]. Unfortunately, if normal (and sensible) rules of statutory construction were followed, the existence of [the other statute]—which is the definition contained in another title of the act that was explicitly not rendered applicable to RICO—suggests that whatever "pattern" might mean in RICO, it assuredly does not mean that. . . . But that does not really matter, since [the Court's language] is utterly uninformative anyway. It hardly closes in on the target to know that "relatedness" refers to acts that are related by "purposes, results, participants, victims, . . . methods of commission, or [just in case that is not vague enough] otherwise." Is the fact that the victims of both predicate acts were women enough? Or that both acts had the purpose of enriching the defendant? Or that the different coparticipants of the defendant in both acts were his coemployees? I doubt that the lower courts will find the Court's instructions much more helpful than telling them to look for a "pattern"—which is what the statute already says.

> The Court finds "continuity" more difficult to define precisely. "Continuity," it says, "is both a closed-and open-ended concept, referring either to a closed period of repeated conduct, or to past conduct that by its nature projects into the future with a threat of repetition." I have no idea what this concept of a "closed period of repeated conduct" means. Virtually all allegations of racketeering activity, in both civil and criminal suits, will relate to past periods that are "closed" (unless one expects plaintiff or the prosecutor to establish that the defendant not only committed the crimes he did, but is still committing them), and all of them must relate to conduct that is "repeated," because of RICO's multiple-act requirement. . . . Since the Court has rejected the concept of separate criminal "schemes" or "episodes" as a criterion of "threatening future criminal conduct," I think it must be saying that at least a few months of racketeering activity (and who knows how much more?) is generally for free, as far as RICO is concerned. The "closed period" concept is a sort of safe harbor for racketeering activity that does not last too long, no matter how many different crimes and different schemes are involved, so long as it does not otherwise "establish a threat of continued racketeering activity." A gang of hoodlums that commits one act of extortion on Monday in New York, a second in Chicago on Tuesday, a third in San Francisco on Wednesday, and so on through an entire week, and then finally and completely disbands, cannot be reached under RICO. I am sure that is not what the statute intends, but I cannot imagine what else the Court's murky discussion can possibly mean.

But Justice Scalia relented a bit:

> It is, however, unfair to be so critical of the Court's effort, because I would be unable to provide an interpretation of RICO that gives significantly more guidance concerning its application. It is clear to me . . . that the word "pattern" in the phrase "pattern of racketeering activity" was meant to import some requirement beyond the mere existence of multiple predicate acts. . . . But what that something more is, is beyond me. As I have suggested, it is also beyond the Court. . . . Today's opinion has added nothing to improve our prior guidance, which has created a kaleidoscope of Circuit positions, except to clarify that RICO may in addition be violated when there is a "threat of continuity." It seems to me this increases rather than removes the vagueness. There is no reason to believe that the Courts of Appeals will be any more unified in the future, than they have in the past, regarding the content of this law.
>
> That situation is bad enough with respect to any statute, but it is intolerable with respect to RICO. For it is not only true, as Justice Marshall commented in *Sedima* that our interpretation of RICO has "quite simply revolutionize[d] private litigation" and "validate[d] the federalization of broad areas of state common law of frauds," so that clarity and predictability in RICO's civil applications are particularly important; but it is also true that RICO, since it has criminal applications as well, must, even in its civil applications, possess the degree of certainty required for criminal

laws. No constitutional challenge to this law has been raised in the present case, and so that issue is not before us. That the highest Court in the land has been unable to derive from this statute anything more than today's meager guidance bodes ill for the day when that challenge is presented.

### 4. QUESTIONS AND COMMENTS

Although most litigation of the "pattern" requirement has arisen in civil suits under RICO, there are occasions when it becomes crucial in criminal RICO as well. It is possible, for example, for government entities (a governor's or attorney general's office, a mayor's office, a police department) to be the RICO "enterprise" through which corrupt behavior occurs. And although most RICO prosecutions are based on *Turkette*-theory charges of violating § 1962(c), there are scattered prosecutions for criminal activity committed through an otherwise legitimate "enterprise" and for the illegitimate acquisition of legitimate enterprises. In those instances, it is the "pattern of racketeering activity" that determines the applicability of RICO sanctions rather than just the sanctions otherwise available for the crimes committed. Has the Court adequately defined "pattern of racketeering activity" in this context? Has it adequately distinguished RICO crime from ordinary crime?

Justice Brennan's objective in *H.J. Inc.* appears to have been to limit the reach of RICO in civil cases involving otherwise legitimate businesses but to permit its broad application in criminal cases that target organized crime. Did he succeed? Consider the facts of United States v. Indelicato, 865 F.2d 1370 (2d Cir. 1989) (en banc). Indelicato was a member of the "Bonanno family," one of the five La Cosa Nostra families in New York City. He and two other men shot and killed the boss of the Bonanno family and two others as part of a leadership realignment ordered by the "Commission," which was alleged to be the national ruling body of organized crime families. He was convicted of a substantive RICO count and of a RICO conspiracy. His "principal argument on appeal [was] that proof of his commission of, or agreement to commit, three murders as part of a single criminal transaction is insufficient to establish a 'pattern of racketeering activity' within the meaning of RICO." The Court affirmed his conviction. Is this outcome consistent with *H.J. Inc.*?

The Supreme Court has not revisited the "pattern" issue since *Boyle*, and philosophically the two cases are inconsistent.[b] Is it likely that the *H.J. Inc.* limitations will stand the test of time? If one were to take the *Boyle* approach to the *H.J. Inc.* issue, what would "pattern of racketeering activity" mean? Recall the separation of powers questions asked in the Note on *Boyle*. There are similar issues here. If "pattern" is going to mean anything other than "at least two" acts of racketeering activity, the choice as an operational matter will be made either by the Supreme Court or the Justice Department and major sentencing consequences will follow. Where should this choice be made? The ideal answer might be Congress. But how likely is it that Congress will act to *restrict* the reach of RICO? Since the major effect of an "enterprise" limitation is likely to be felt by serious criminals and a limitation of "pattern" along the lines of *H.J. Inc.* is likely to be felt by

---

[b] The *H.J. Inc.* majority consisted of Justices Brennan, Blackmun, Stevens, White, and Marshall. The *Boyle* majority was Alito, Roberts, Scalia, Kennedy, Souter, Thomas, and Ginsburg.

legitimate businesses that are potential defendants in a civil suit, one might think that Congress would have every incentive to leave "enterprise" alone but could perhaps be persuaded by the business lobby to redefine "pattern" more narrowly. But such efforts have failed. How should "pattern of racketeering activity" be read by the Supreme Court in the meantime?

# CHAPTER VII

# JUSTIFICATION AND EXCUSE

## INTRODUCTORY NOTE ON JUSTIFICATION AND EXCUSE

The preceding chapters cover the central doctrines that shape the definition of criminal offenses. This chapter explores a body of defenses that are extrinsic to the definitions of specific crimes but that further elaborate the conditions of criminal liability. These defenses are usually grouped into the two general categories of justification and excuse.[a]

Justification defenses state exceptions to the prohibitions laid down by specific offenses. Thus, for example, an intentional homicide that would otherwise be murder is no crime at all if committed in self-defense. Similarly, conduct that would otherwise constitute criminal assault may be justified by a policeman's obligation to enforce the law. Self-defense and law enforcement are typical defenses of justification. They qualify and refine the proscriptions of the penal law. The considerations determining the scope of justification defenses are essentially the same as those governing the contours of particular offenses; both define the prohibitory content of the criminal law. Section 1 of this chapter elaborates the concept of justification, both generally and in selected specific contexts.

The law also includes doctrines of excuse. These defenses recognize claims that particular individuals cannot fairly be blamed for admittedly wrongful conduct. The defendant is excused not because his or her conduct was socially desirable, but rather because the circumstances of the offense evoke the societal judgment that criminal conviction and punishment would be morally inappropriate. As Francis Bowes Sayre explained in Mens Rea, 45 Harv.L.Rev. 974, 1021 (1932), doctrines of excuse were a natural outgrowth of the early common law insistence on moral guilt as the basis of criminal liability:

> [T]he strong tendency of the early days to link criminal liability with moral guilt made it necessary to free from punishment those who perhaps satisfied the requirements of specific intent for particular crimes but who, because of some personal mental defect or restraint, should not be convicted of any crime. The person who lacked a normal intelligence because of mental disease, or who lacked discretion because of tender years, or who through fear of death lacked the power to choose his conduct—all these must escape punishment if criminality was to be based upon moral guilt.

---

[a] For analysis of the doctrinal structure of exculpatory defenses, see Paul Robinson, Criminal Law Defenses: A Systematic Analysis, 83 Colum.L.Rev. 199 (1982), and Glanville Williams, Offences and Defences, 2 Leg.Stud. 233 (1982). For specific coverage of defensive doctrines, see Paul Robinson, Criminal Law Defenses (1984) (2 vols.). For discussion of the significance of the distinction between justification and situational excuse, see Mitchell N. Berman, Justification and Excuse, Law and Morality, 53 Duke L.J. 1 (2003); George P. Fletcher, Rethinking the Criminal Law, 759 et seq. (1978); Joshua Dressler, New Thoughts About the Concept of Justification in the Criminal Law: A Critique of Fletcher's Thinking and *Rethinking,* 32 UCLA L.Rev. 61 (1984); Kent Greenawalt, The Perplexing Borders of Justification and Excuse, 84 Colum.L.Rev. 1897 (1984); Glanville Williams, The Theory of Excuses, [1982] Crim.L.Rev. 732.

Thus, there developed certain well-recognized defenses in criminal law, affecting one's general capacity to commit crime. . . .

At one time, theoretical coherence was attempted by characterizing all the various doctrines of excuse as defects of capacity. Insane persons, infants, and those acting under duress were all said to lack the capacity for criminal mens rea. Today, this unifying rubric has dissolved in the face of recognition that the various defects of "capacity" raise very different kinds of issues. In these materials, therefore, the topics of excuse are sorted into two categories. Section 2 of this chapter explores "situational excuse." This label is designed to suggest that offenders may be excused if the situations in which they find themselves overbear their otherwise normal abilities to conform their conduct to the requirements of law. In other words, the doctrines of situational excuse make allowance for abnormal situations, not abnormal persons. In such cases, the focus, as in the defenses of justification, is on the external realities of the actor's situation and the attitude of the actor concerning those realities. The problems of abnormal individuals—most notably immaturity and insanity—are covered in Chapter VIII under the rubric of "criminal responsibility."

## SECTION 1: JUSTIFICATION

### SUBSECTION A: THE GENERAL PRINCIPLE OF JUSTIFICATION

#### Commonwealth v. Markum

Superior Court of Pennsylvania, 1988.
373 Pa.Super. 341, 541 A.2d 347.

■ CIRILLO, PRESIDENT JUDGE. Appellants take this appeal from a judgment of sentence of one day to three months imprisonment imposed by . . . the Court of Common Pleas of Philadelphia County following their conviction for defiant trespass. We affirm.

On August 10, 1985, as part of an anti-abortion demonstration, appellants pushed their way into the Northeast Women's Center on Roosevelt Boulevard in Philadelphia, and occupied several rooms there. Once inside, they damaged two aspirator machines and other medical instruments, threw equipment out of a third floor window, and placed "pro-life" stickers on the doors, walls, and ceilings. Appellants refused to leave, even after several requests by the Center's staff, and were ultimately removed when police arrived and carried them from the scene. . . .

During a hearing on a motion in limine, appellants made an offer of proof in support of . . . a defense of justification. [The trial judge] ruled that justification did not lie. [The jury convicted all appellants.] . . .

Following sentencing, the appellants were immediately paroled on the condition that they each perform fifty hours of community service, not to be served in any pro-life agencies, and refrain from trespassing on medical facilities that perform abortions. . . .

Appellants raise one issue on appeal: whether the trial judge erred in not allowing appellants to present the defense of justification to the jury. . . .

[In Pennsylvania, the defense of justification is recognized by statute.] Section 503 states:

> (a) General rule.—Conduct which the actor believes to be necessary to avoid a harm or evil to himself or to another is justifiable if:
>
> > (1) the harm or evil sought to be avoided by such conduct is greater than that sought to be prevented by the law defining the offense charged;
> >
> > (2) neither this title nor other law defining the offense provides exceptions or defenses dealing with the specific situation involved; and
> >
> > (3) a legislative purpose to exclude the justification claimed does not otherwise plainly appear.
>
> (b) Choice of evils.—When the actor was reckless or negligent in bringing about the situation requiring a choice of harms or evils or in appraising the necessity for his conduct, the justification afforded by this section is unavailable in a prosecution for any offense for which recklessness or negligence, as the case may be, suffices to establish culpability. . . .

The Pennsylvania Supreme Court, in Commonwealth v. Capitolo, 508 Pa. 372, 498 A.2d 806 (1985), and Commonwealth v. Berrigan, 509 Pa. 118, 501 A.2d 226 (1985), addressed the applicability of the justification provisions. . . .

In *Capitolo*, Patricia Capitolo and four others crept under a fence enclosing the Shippingsport Nuclear Power Plant. Once through, they sat down about ten to twelve feet inside of the fence and held hands. They were placed under arrest after refusing requests of plant representatives that they leave the premises. The five sought to present a justification defense under § 503, . . . but . . . the trial judge [rejected the defense on the ground that the defendants] would not have been able to prove that their trespass was justified. They were subsequently convicted of trespass. . . .

On appeal, a majority of this court reversed the decision of the trial court, concluding that appellants' offer of proof met the requirements of § 503 and that they should have been able to present to the jury evidence in support of the defense.

Our supreme court reversed and reinstated the convictions, holding that the defense of justification is available only when the [defendant] is able to make an offer of proof which establishes:

> (1) that the actor was faced with a clear and imminent harm, not one which is debatable or speculative;
>
> (2) that the actor could reasonably expect that the actor's actions would be effective in avoiding this greater harm;
>
> (3) there was no legal alternative which will be effective in abating the harm; and
>
> (4) the Legislature had not acted to preclude the defense by a clear and deliberate choice regarding the matter at issue. . . .

Capitolo Test

After applying these basic principles, [the *Capitolo*] court concluded that the danger at the nuclear plant was not imminent and that the appellees "could not establish that their criminal conduct was necessary to avoid harm or evil to themselves or others."

In *Berrigan*, the Berrigan brothers and six others entered the General Electric plant in King of Prussia, Pennsylvania, where they damaged hydrogen bomb missile components and poured human blood on the premises. Property damage exceeded $28,000. The eight involved were charged and convicted of burglary, criminal mischief, and criminal conspiracy. An offer of proof was made . . . to present the defense of justification. The trial judge permitted them to offer their own testimony in support of the defense, but refused to permit them to present expert testimony.

On appeal, this court held that appellants should have been able to present the defense, and present expert testimony in support of the defense.

Once again, our supreme court reversed. . . . The court . . . reiterated the four-part test used in *Capitolo* and determined that the trial court had properly ruled that the offer of proof was insufficient to establish that the nuclear holocaust that appellees sought to avert was a clear and imminent public disaster.

The court in *Berrigan* went even further, however, and held additionally that the defense of justification was not available "in situations where the conduct some perceive to engender public disaster has been specifically approved of by legislation making it legal conduct . . . ".

Abortion has been specifically approved by the Pennsylvania Legislature in the Abortion Control Act. . . . Were it not protected by such legislation, the justification defense would continue to remain unavailable because a woman's right to abortion is protected by the Constitution of the United States. Roe v. Wade, 410 U.S. 113 (1973). The *Berrigan* mandate that a justification defense may not be raised if the asserted "harm" is legal is not dependent upon whether such conduct has been made legal through legislative choice or judicial fiat. . . . We are each bound by the law no matter what its source. Were we free to pick and choose which laws we wished to obey, the result would be a society of strife and chaos. . . . Democracy allows the citizenry to protest laws of which they disapprove. But they must nonetheless obey such laws or face the legal consequences. To allow the defense of justification to those who willingly and intentionally break the law would encourage criminality cloaked in the guise of conscience. . . .

Appellants wish to produce testimony to establish that life begins at conception. They wish to show scientifically that a fetus as young as eight weeks of age has measurable brain-wave activity. Because Pennsylvania's Determination of Death Act, provides that death occurs when all brain activity ceases, appellants assert that their evidence would demonstrate that abortion is the taking of a human life, and hence, a "public disaster." They also claim that the disaster was imminent, not speculative, and that their actions were effective in averting the disaster. Finally, they assert that there was no legal alternative for their actions.

Appellants' first argument, that abortion constitutes a public disaster, fails. As we have noted, pre-viability abortion is lawful by virtue of state statute and federal constitutional law. The United States Supreme Court has consistently held that the state's interest in protecting fetal life does not become compelling, and cannot infringe on a woman's right to choose abortion, until the fetus is viable. Appellants do not suggest that viability and conception are simultaneous occurrences. We find that a legally sanctioned activity cannot be termed a public disaster.

Appellants' second argument, that the disaster was imminent and that their actions were effective in averting it, similarly must fail. It is unreasonable for appellants to believe that their brief occupation of one center would effectively put an end to the practice of abortion. Appellants' occupation of the Women's Center did not stop its operation. Legal abortions continued to be performed in the Center and were available in other medical facilities throughout Pennsylvania.

Appellants' third contention, that there was no legal alternative to their actions, is misguided. As [the trial court] noted, "[t]here are obviously numerous means in a democratic society to express a point of view or to attempt to prevent a perceived harm without resorting to criminal behavior." Appellants were free to peacefully demonstrate outside of the center in an effort to prevent the harm that they perceived from occurring.

Finally, appellants' offer of proof was insufficient to show that no legislative purpose exists to exclude the justification defense, nor could they, because Pennsylvania law is to the contrary. . . . Clearly, to permit private citizens the right to prevent women from exercising their right to abortion would be a violation of both state statute and federal constitutional law. . . .

The appellants are actually requesting that this court countenance civil disobedience, which is defined as: A form of lawbreaking employed to demonstrate the injustice or unfairness of a particular law and indulged in deliberately to focus attention on the allegedly undesirable law.

Though our nation has a long and proud history of civil disobedience, appellants are not in that tradition. From the Boston Tea Party to the abolitionists to conscientious objectors to the sit-ins of Martin Luther King, civil disobedience has often stirred our nation's collective conscience and spurred us to change or repeal unjust laws. Often, juries refused to convict good men of conscience whose love of justice had motivated them to violate the law. On some occasions, a jury would convict but the judge in recognition of the righteousness of the underlying cause would suspend sentence or issue a nominal fine. Abortion demonstrators argue that they are in this tradition and should be treated accordingly. They overlook the key distinction between their actions and the behavior of those cited above.

The true conscientious objector refuses to obey the very law which he claims is unjust. Rosa Parks refused to sit in the back of the bus and "draft dodgers" refused to register for the draft. When prosecuted, they challenged the wisdom, morality and constitutionality of the law in question.[2] They did not employ their objections to that law as an excuse to engage in general or targeted violence. But that is what the demonstrators in this case have done. On this appeal, the demonstrators challenge the applicability of our criminal trespass laws to their activities. But they do not assert that those laws are unconstitutional or unjust. Rather they believe that because they disagree with the practice of abortion they are entitled to deface and occupy property belonging to other persons. How sad that their sense of justice and outrage is so narrowly focused. . . .

■ MCEWEN, JUDGE, concurring and dissenting. . . . I write . . . to express the view that appellants have surmounted three of the four obstacles to presentation of the defense. . . .

While the defense of justification has a number of synonyms, it is " 'often expressed in terms of choice of evils: When the pressure of circumstances presents one with a choice of evils, the law prefers that he avoid the greater evil by bringing about the lesser evil.' " "Determination of the issues of competing values and, therefore, the availability of the defense of necessity is precluded, however, when there has been a deliberate legislative choice as to the values at issue." . . .

The disaster which appellants sought to prevent was the abortions that would be completed in a very brief time after the women entered the building. . . . The danger perceived by appellants was, therefore, clear and imminent. Further, were appellants able to prevent the women from entering into the building, their action would have been quite effective in thwarting the immediate disaster appellants perceived as awaiting the women and their unborn children in the clinic. And, of course, appellants had no legal alternative available. Therefore, I conclude that appellants complied with three of the conditions precedent to presentation of the defense of justification.

[However, I agree with the majority that] the appellants here did not—in fact, could not—establish the absence of a legislative purpose to exclude the defense of justification. . . .

■ TAMILIA, JUDGE, dissenting. I follow and support the reasoning of the majority in its analysis of the justification defense to the point where it holds that [the] defense . . . is precluded by legislative and constitutional protection. Abortion is constitutionally protected but it [receives] qualified protection. The significant distinction between this case and [*Berrigan*] is that there was no imminent danger in constructing atomic warheads. Abortion stands on an entirely different footing. I believe the defense is available in two respects despite statutory and constitutional limitations. First, if the clinic was processing abortions beyond the time of viability, as established by *Roe*, the right to protect the life of a fetus in those circumstances would exist within the present legislative and constitutional parameters. [Second,] the Supreme Court, in fixing viability at a point supported by medical knowledge as it existed at [the time *Roe* was decided], has left open the question of when the state may intervene, [and the answer to that question is] dependent on medical

---

[2] Of course, some civil disobedience such as the Boston Tea Party or the work of the abolitionists calls into question the very moral authority of the government. Obviously, this is not what the appellants intended as on this appeal they seek the protection of a statutory defense promulgated by our government.

evidence as to viability at the time at issue. *Roe v. Wade* was promulgated in 1973. In the intervening years, enormous strides have been made in sustaining [fetal] life outside the womb. . . .

[In *Roe*, the Supreme Court observed that medical experts accepted a fetal age of 28 weeks as the appropriate criterion of viability at that time. In subsequent cases, the Supreme Court acknowledged that *Roe* left the point of viability "flexible for anticipated advancements in medical skill." Today, viability has been reduced to below 24 weeks. Thus, while viability, and not conception, determines when the state interest may be invoked on behalf of the fetus, the viability criterion of 28 weeks applied in *Roe* is no longer valid given the developments in medical technology. Indeed, fetal viability in the first trimester of pregnancy may be possible in the not too distant future.]

If viability has significantly been advanced and abortion services continue to apply the *Roe* standards, then a state interest in protecting fetal life is likely implicated in some cases. Fetal life is, therefore, protected in those instances and the defense of justification would be available to persons attempting to protect or save a fetus capable of surviving under the advanced medical standards. Unquestionably, clinics and hospitals can and do establish standards and controls to assure that no abortions are performed except in cases in which the fetus could not be viable under advanced medical technology. This may not, however, be presumed in the face of an offer of proof on the defense of justification. . . .

In this case, the appellants conceivably could have produced evidence that . . . a viable fetus, who would survive under the advanced medical technology available, would be terminated and that the actions of the appellants would be effective in avoiding the greater harm. . . . It is also clear that no legal alternative would have been effective in abating the harm. Thus, the denial of the right to pursue the justification defense precluded the appellants from attempting to establish the proof of viability and the inherent right to protect life under the circumstances of this case. . . .

## NOTES ON THE DEFENSE OF NECESSITY

### 1. COMMON LAW NECESSITY

In his concurring and dissenting opinion, Judge McEwen notes that the "general defense of justification" is a codification of the common law defense of necessity. At one level, the proposition that the common law recognized a general defense of necessity is unexceptional, for the unifying theme of the specific defenses of justification is the necessity for making a choice among evils. Defense of self and others, defense of property, the exercise of public authority, and law enforcement are doctrinal particularizations of the necessity principle.

Whether there remains a residual and otherwise undefined defense of necessity apart from such specific doctrines is not entirely clear. Most courts and commentators seem to agree that a general necessity defense did exist at common law.[a] The uncertainty is no doubt due to

---

[a] See, e.g., 2 Wayne R. LaFave, Substantive Criminal Law 121–24 (2003), and the authorities cited therein.

the infrequency with which the issue is presented. Most claims of justification are handled under the more specific doctrines of self-defense, defense of others, etc. Only rarely is there need to consider whether any more general doctrine should be recognized. *Markum* provides an unusual occasion for exploring necessity and its place in the structure of justification defenses.

In jurisdictions that have not codified a general defense of justification or necessity, modern decisions tend to assume the existence of such defense at common law, often while holding that the defendant's evidence is legally insufficient to raise it. As *Markum* illustrates, claims of necessity or choice of evils have often been raised, almost always unsuccessfully, by persons protesting politically controversial issues, including U.S. participation in the Vietnam War,[b] the construction or operation of nuclear power plants,[c] and abortion.[d]

## 2. MODERN STATUTORY FORMULATIONS

The Pennsylvania justification statute applied in *Markum* is identical to the general choice-of-evils defense in the Model Penal Code. This provision was one of the significant innovations of the Model Code, and it has been adopted in substance by approximately 10 American jurisdictions.

New York also has codified the defense of justification, and its provision has served as the model for legislation in about 10 additional states. Section 35.05 of the New York Penal Code states, in pertinent part:

> Unless otherwise limited by the ensuing provisions of this article defining justifiable use of physical force, conduct which would otherwise constitute an offense is justifiable and not criminal when . . .
>
> (2) Such conduct is necessary as an emergency measure to avoid an imminent public or private injury which is about to occur by reason of a situation occasioned or developed through no fault of the actor, and which is of such gravity that, according to ordinary standards of intelligence and morality, the desirability and urgency of avoiding such injury clearly outweigh the desirability of avoiding the injury sought to be prevented by the statute defining the offense in issue. The necessity and justifiability of such conduct may not rest upon considerations pertaining only to the morality and advisability of the statute, either in its general application or with respect to its application to a particular class of cases arising thereunder. Whenever evidence relating to the defense of justification under this [provision] is offered by the defendant, the court shall rule as a matter of law whether the

---

[b] See, e.g., United States v. Simpson, 460 F.2d 515 (9th Cir.1972); United States v. Kroncke, 459 F.2d 697 (8th Cir.1972).

[c] See, e.g., Commonwealth v. Capitolo, 508 Pa. 372, 498 A.2d 806 (1985); State v. Warshow, 138 Vt. 22, 410 A.2d 1000 (1979); State v. Dorsey, 118 N.H. 844, 395 A.2d 855 (1978).

[d] See, e.g., State v. O'Brien, 784 S.W.2d 187 (Mo.App.1989); Sigma Reproductive Health Center v. State, 297 Md. 660, 467 A.2d 483 (1983); Cleveland v. Municipality of Anchorage, 631 P.2d 1073 (Alaska 1981); People v. Krizka, 92 Ill.App.3d 288, 48 Ill.Dec. 141, 416 N.E.2d 36 (1980); Gaetano v. United States, 406 A.2d 1291 (D.C.App.1979).

claimed facts and circumstances would, if established, constitute a defense.

On facts similar to those of *Markum*, a New York court concluded that the New York provision and the Model Penal Code section embody different definitions of what constitutes an evil or "injury to be avoided" for purposes of the necessity defense. In People v. Archer, 537 N.Y.S.2d 726 (1988), the City Court of Rochester compared the alternative approaches:

> [The Model Penal Code eliminates the necessity defense whenever the legislature has specifically spoken on the topic.] Under the Model Penal Code, whatever [is] legal, therefore, could not be evil. The Model Code, in other words, precluded the necessity defense whenever the legislature had legalized conduct.
>
> But what this court must observe is that [New York adopted] a different standard. [The New York statute provides] that the "injury . . . to be avoided must . . . *according to ordinary standards of intelligence and morality*, clearly outweigh the injury" the criminal law(s) in question were designed to prevent. The [legislature] deliberately chose to enlarge the categories of possible evils to include not simply illegal behavior, but any injury which existed "according to ordinary standards of intelligence and morality." . . .
>
> What is obvious here is that [the New York legislature has recognized] a different standard of judgment for determining what is an "injury to be avoided," which standard is broader, and more encompassing, than the legal/illegal classifications within the Penal Law itself. Granted what is criminally illegal is, *ipso facto*, an injury to be avoided. But the contrary of that proposition—namely, "what is legal is therefore *not* an injury to be avoided" does not follow. In the former case, behavior which is criminally forbidden always violates "ordinary standards of intelligence and morality." But in the latter case, behavior which is permissively legal, does not always comport with ordinary standards of intelligence and morality.
>
> In Nevada, for example, prostitution is legal, but still, immoral. Some type of gambling is almost everywhere legal, but many persons of ordinary intelligence and morality still consider it immoral. Traffic in alcoholic beverages is legal, but its byproduct, drunkenness, remains immoral. Divorce is legal, but, in many cases, it is immoral, especially when it affects innocent children of the marriage. Thus . . . morality and legality . . . are not the same. Morality is the standard of conduct to which, as good and decent people, we all aspire. Legality is the standard of conduct to which, as members of a civilized society, and under penalty of the criminal sanction, we must all adhere. . . .
>
> Thus, in cases of moral indignation, the flexibility of the New York statute avoids the chafing attrition of the eternal struggle between what is legal and what is moral. The statute allows a jury to ventilate its displeasure at morally reprehensible conduct regardless of its legality by approving, in a verdict of not guilty, the behavior of those who try, even illegally, to prevent that conduct from happening.

According to *Archer*, the New York justification defense authorizes jurors to reject the legislative "choice among evils," embodied in a statute legalizing abortions, and to decide that abortions inflict injuries that outweigh those sought to be prevented by the trespass laws. However, the court also concluded that first-trimester abortions do not qualify as "injuries to be avoided" for purposes of this defense. Since such abortions are constitutionally protected under *Roe v. Wade*, "neither the [justification] statute, nor the Court, nor the Jury itself, can intrude upon that constitutionally protected area of privacy."

Does *Archer* properly construe the New York justification statute? Why does a judicial choice of evils, such as that endorsed by *Roe v. Wade*, preclude the necessity defense if a legislative choice of evils does not?

## 3. ECONOMIC NECESSITY

An often cited choice-of-evils case is State v. Moe, 174 Wash. 303, 24 P.2d 638 (1933), which arose during the Depression. The defendants tried, unsuccessfully, to persuade the chairman of the local Red Cross relief committee to increase their allowance of flour. Having been advised that their demands would not be met, the defendants entered a local grocery store and helped themselves. The Washington Supreme Court affirmed their convictions for grand larceny and riot and upheld the trial court's rejection of defendants' offer to prove their poverty in justification of their actions. The court stated:

> Economic necessity has never been accepted as a defense to a criminal charge. The reason is that, were it ever countenanced, it would leave to the individual the right to take the law into his own hands. In larceny cases, economic necessity is frequently invoked in mitigation of punishment, but has never been recognized as a defense.

The reach of this language has frequently been criticized on the ground that a defense might be appropriate in a case involving theft by a mother to feed her starving child, but no such case appears in the books. However, an analogous claim of economic necessity was raised in Mayfield v. State, 585 S.W.2d 693 (Tex. Crim. App. 1979).[e] Mayfield was charged with fraudulently obtaining welfare assistance. She admitted that she had falsely stated that she was unemployed and that she had failed to report her earned income to her caseworker as she was legally required to do. She claimed that she needed the additional money to prevent irreparable harm to her children. In support of her claim, she proffered the testimony of a physician and nurse who testified that the Mayfield children were suffering from nutritional deficiencies amounting to "starvation" in the medical sense. Welfare department employees testified that the level of benefits granted to recipients was only 75 percent of that computed in 1969 to be needed by a family of her size for a subsistence level of living. She also proffered testimony by an economist who stated that the failure of the welfare department to adjust benefit levels between 1969 and 1974 (when the offenses occurred) had resulted in a 30 per cent loss of purchasing power. Is this evidence legally sufficient to raise a necessity defense at common law?

---

[e] *Mayfield* is discussed in J. Thomas Sullivan, The Defense of Necessity in Texas: Legislative Invention Comes of Age, 16 Houston L.Rev. 333 (1979). Mayfield's conviction was reversed on other grounds in Mayfield v. State, 585 S.W.2d 693 (Tex.Crim.App.1979).

Would Mayfield be entitled to a jury instruction under the Model Code? Under the New York statute?

## 4. MEDICAL NECESSITY

One of the issues discussed in *Markum* is the effect of prior judicial and legislative resolution of the abortion issue. A comparable issue arises in cases where an accused argues that a violation of the drug laws is justifiable by reason of medical necessity.

Medical necessity sometimes is used to defend against marijuana possession charges. In such cases, the accused claims that he or she suffers from a physical infirmity for which there is no effective conventional treatment, but for which ingestion of marijuana provides relief. These claims have met with varying success in the courts. State v. Tate, 102 N.J. 64 (1986), represents one reaction. The defendant in *Tate* was a quadriplegic. According to the Supreme Court of New Jersey, "[t]he spasticity associated with that condition is sometimes so severe as to render defendant completely disabled." When he was charged with unlawful possession of marijuana, defendant argued that his conduct was justified because, unlike conventional treatments, marijuana eased the spastic contractions. The court held that the legislature intended to preclude such a defense. In particular, the court pointed out that the legislature had passed a Therapeutic Research Act, which authorized the study of medical uses of controlled substances and allowed marijuana to be prescribed to patients in some circumstances. By making available this "specific exception," the legislature intended to exclude claims based on medical necessity in all other cases of marijuana possession. Should the outcome be different in states whose legislatures have not enacted laws allowing the use of controlled substances in therapeutic research? What if a federal therapeutic research program is available?

Other courts have allowed defendants to defend drug possession charges on grounds of medical necessity.[f] For example, in State v. Diana, 24 Wash.App. 908, 604 P.2d 1312 (1979), the defendant suffered from multiple sclerosis, and he claimed that marijuana relieved disabling symptoms for which lawful treatments were ineffective. Although the defendant had not offered a medical necessity defense at trial, the Court of Appeals of Washington concluded that the interests of justice required that the case be remanded for the trial court to consider such a defense. The state legislature recently had enacted a Controlled Substances Therapeutic Act, which authorized the dispensing of marijuana to persons suffering from the effects of glaucoma and cancer chemotherapy. According to the court, the legislature thus had recognized that in some cases marijuana possesses medicinal benefits that outweigh any harms its use inflicts, and the defendant should be given the opportunity to demonstrate that multiple sclerosis is another such case:

> . . . To summarize, medical necessity exists in this case if the court finds that (1) the defendant reasonably believed his use of marijuana was necessary to minimize the effects of multiple

[f] Beginning with California's Compassionate Use Act in 1996, at least 20 state legislatures have legalized access to marijuana for specific medical uses recommended by a physician even if the person is not participating in a clinical trial and even though cultivation, distribution, and possession of the drug remain unlawful under federal law.

> sclerosis; (2) the benefits derived from its use are greater than the harm sought to be prevented by the controlled substances law; and (3) no drug is as effective in minimizing the effects of the disease. [C]orroborating medical testimony is required. In reaching this decision, the court must balance the defendant's interest in preserving his health against the state's interest in regulating the drug involved. Defendant bears the burden of proving the existence of necessity, an affirmative defense, by a preponderance of the evidence. . . .

Finally, consider the threat by the federal Food and Drug Administration to crack down on illegal sales of thalidomide. Thalidomide was first produced and widely marketed in Europe in the late 1950's. At that time, the drug was prescribed for pregnant women as a medication to relieve morning sickness. The consequences were tragic: in the early 1960's, researchers discovered that thalidomide caused severe birth defects. Thousands of the women who took thalidomide gave birth to babies with missing or deformed limbs, or damaged internal organs; some of the babies were born dead. The drug was banned worldwide in 1962.[g] However, in recent years, some scientists have concluded that thalidomide may be beneficial to persons afflicted with serious illnesses, including AIDS, cancer, leprosy, and tuberculosis. In 1995, the FDA approved the experimental use of thalidomide in clinical studies involving persons suffering from severe AIDS-related maladies, but the agency continues to prohibit broader distribution of the drug. Because some early studies suggest that thalidomide may prolong the lives of persons in the late stages of AIDS, the drug is being sold illegally by AIDS activists. Could the sale of thalidomide be justified by medical necessity? Does such sale raise the same issues as *Markum* or the marijuana possession cases?

## 5. NECESSITY AS A JUSTIFICATION FOR HOMICIDE: *DUDLEY AND STEPHENS*

The claim of necessity as a justification for intentional homicide arguably presents a special case. At common law, self-defense and other specific doctrines of justification authorized the necessary use of deadly force against a wrongdoer. The common law did not, however, permit a general plea of necessity to justify killing an innocent person in order to avoid some other evil. In contrast, most modern statutes, including both the Model Penal Code and the New York provision, seem to contemplate that a defense of necessity or choice of evils may be raised where one innocent person is killed in order to save others. This position was defended by the drafters of the Model Penal Code on the ground that "[i]t would be particularly unfortunate to exclude homicidal conduct from the scope of the defense," because "recognizing that the sanctity of life has a supreme place in the hierarchy of values, it is nonetheless true that conduct that results in taking life may promote the very value sought to be protected by the law of homicide."[h]

---

[g] Sale of thalidomide never has been lawful in the United States because the FDA refused to approve the drug until research demonstrated that it was safe and effective. To date, in the view of the FDA, such research has not been forthcoming.

[h] ALI, Model Penal Code and Commentaries, § 3.02, p. 14 (1985). Several jurisdictions reject this position and withdraw the necessity defense in murder cases. See 2 Paul H. Robinson, Criminal Law Defenses 63 (1984).

The question of whether necessity may justify intentional homicide is considered in the famous case of Regina v. Dudley and Stephens, 14 Q.B.D. 273 (1884).[i] The facts were found by the jury in a special verdict:

> [T]hat on July 5, 1884, the prisoners, Thomas Dudley and Edward Stephens, with one Brooks, all able-bodied English seamen, and the deceased also an English boy between 17 and 18 years of age, the crew of an English yacht, a registered English vessel, were cast away in a storm on the high seas 1600 miles from the Cape of Good Hope, and were compelled to put into an open boat belonging to the said yacht. That in this boat they had no supply of water and no supply of food, except two one lb. tins of turnips, and for three days they had nothing else to subsist upon. That on the fourth day they caught a small turtle, upon which they subsided for a few days, and this was the only food they had up to the 20th day when the act now in question was committed. That on the 12th day the remains of the turtle were entirely consumed, and for the next eight days they had nothing to eat. That they had no fresh water, except such rain as they from time to time caught in their oilskin capes. That the boat was drifting on the ocean, and was probably more than 1000 miles away from land. That on the 18th day, when they had been seven days without food and five without water, the prisoners spoke to Brooks as to what should be done if no succour came, and suggested that some one should be sacrificed to save the rest, but Brooks dissented, and the boy, to whom they were understood to refer, was not consulted. That on the 24th of July, the day before the act now in question, the prisoner Dudley proposed to Stephens and Brooks that lots should be cast who should be put to death to save the rest, but Brooks refused to consent, and it was not put to the boy, and in point of fact there was no drawing of lots. That on that day the prisoners spoke of their having families, and suggested it would be better to kill the boy that their lives should be saved, and Dudley proposed that if there was no vessel in sight by the morrow morning the boy should be killed. That next day, the 25th of July, no vessel appearing, Dudley told Brooks that he had better go and have a sleep, and made signs to Stephens and Brooks that the boy had better be killed. The prisoner Stephens agreed to the act, but Brooks dissented from it. That the boy was then lying at the bottom of the boat quite helpless, and extremely weakened by famine and by drinking sea water, and unable to make any resistance, nor did he ever assent to his being killed. The prisoner Dudley offered a prayer asking forgiveness for them all if either of them should be tempted to commit a rash act, and that their souls might be saved. That Dudley, with the assent of Stephens, went to the boy, and telling him that his time was come, put a knife into his throat and killed him then and there; that the three fed upon the body and blood of the boy for four days; that on the fourth day after the act had been committed the boat was picked up by a passing vessel, and the prisoners were rescued, still alive, but in the lowest state of prostration. That they were carried to the port

[i] For a superb historical account of this case, see A.W.B. Simpson, Cannibalism and the Common Law: The Story of the Tragic Last Voyage of the *Mignonette* and the Strange Legal Proceedings to Which It Gave Rise (1984).

> of Falmouth, and committed for trial at Exeter. That if the men had not fed upon the body of the boy they would probably not have survived to be so picked up and rescued, but would within the four days have died of famine. That the boy, being in a much weaker condition, was likely to have died before them. That at the time of the act in question there was no sail in sight, nor any reasonable prospect of relief. That under these circumstances there appeared to the prisoners every probability that unless they then fed or very soon fed upon the boy or one of themselves they would die of starvation. That there was no appreciable chance of saving life except by killing someone for the others to eat. That assuming any necessity to kill anybody, there was no greater necessity for killing the boy than any of the other three men.

On these facts, the court found the defendants guilty of murder. The court rejected the defendants' necessity defense. The following excerpt from the opinion of Lord Coleridge explains why:

> . . . Now, it is admitted that the deliberate killing of this unoffending and unresisting boy was clearly murder, unless the killing can be justified by some well-recognised excuse admitted by the law. It is further admitted that there was in this case no such excuse, unless the killing was justified by what has been called "necessity." But the temptation to the act which existed here was not what the law has ever called necessity. Nor is this to be regretted. Though law and morality are not the same, and many things may be immoral which are not necessarily illegal, yet the absolute divorce of law from morality would be of fatal consequence; and such divorce would follow if the temptation to murder in this case were to be held by law an absolute defence of it. It is not so. To preserve one's life is generally speaking a duty, but it may be the plainest and the highest duty to sacrifice it. War is full of instances in which it is a man's duty not to live, but to die. The duty, in case of shipwreck, of a captain to his crew, of the crew to the passengers, of soldiers to women and children, . . . these duties impose on men the moral necessity, not of the preservation, but of the sacrifice of their lives for others, from which in no country, least of all, it is to be hoped, in England, will men ever shrink, as indeed, they have not shrunk. It is not correct, therefore, to say that there is any absolute or unqualified necessity to preserve one's life. . . . It would be a very easy and cheap display of commonplace learning to quote from Greek and Latin authors, from Horace, from Juvenal, from Cicero, from Euripides, passage after passage, in which the duty of dying for others has been laid down in glowing and emphatic language as resulting from the principles of heathen ethics; it is enough in a Christian country to remind ourselves of the Great Example whom we profess to follow. It is not needful to point out the awful danger of admitting the principle which has been contended for. Who is to be the judge of this sort of necessity? By what measure is the comparative value of lives to be measured? Is it to be strength, or intellect, or what? It is plain that the principle leaves to him who is to profit by it to determine the necessity which will justify him in deliberately taking another's life to save his own. In this case the weakest, the youngest, the most unresisting, was chosen. Was it more necessary to

kill him than one of the grown men? The answer must be "No"— . . . It is not suggested that in this particular case the deeds were "devilish," but it is quite plain that such a principle once admitted might be made the legal cloak for unbridled passion and atrocious crime. There is no safe path for judges to tread but to ascertain the law to the best of their ability and to declare it according to their judgment; and if in any case the law appears to be too severe on individuals, to leave it to the sovereign to exercise that prerogative of mercy which the constitution has intrusted to the hands fittest to dispense it.

It must not be supposed that in refusing to admit temptation to be an excuse for crime it is forgotten how terrible the temptation was; how awful the suffering; how hard in such trials to keep the judgment straight and the conduct pure. We are often compelled to set up standards we cannot reach ourselves, and to lay down rules which we could not ourselves satisfy. But a man has no right to declare temptation to be an excuse, though he might himself have yielded to it, nor allow compassion for the criminal to change or weaken in any manner the legal definition of the crime. It is therefore our duty to declare that the prisoners' act in this case was wilful murder, that the facts as stated in the verdict are no legal justification of the homicide; and to say that in our unanimous opinion the prisoners are upon this special verdict guilty of murder.[j]

Should choice of evils never be allowed to justify intentional homicide, or is there some narrower principle on which the result in *Dudley and Stephens* can be defended?

## 6. NECESSITY CREATED BY FAULT OF THE ACTOR

The New York statute construed in *Archer* expressly limits the choice-of-evils defense to cases where the necessity is "occasioned or developed through no fault of the actor." Most state statutes on the subject impose a similar limitation, as does the Model Penal Code.[k] The application of this limitation is typically illustrated by the following hypothetical: *A* becomes voluntarily intoxicated and, in an impaired condition, seriously injures *B*. Because *B* needs immediate medical assistance, *A* drives *B* to the hospital. If *A* is arrested for driving while intoxicated, *A* could not justify doing so by the necessity to seek help for *B*. The defect in the claim is that the situation requiring a choice of evils arose from *A*'s own fault. Is there logic to this position? Might there be cases in which denial of a necessity defense on this ground (assuming that the actor was aware of the law and acted accordingly) would encourage socially undesirable behavior? If there is to be a middle ground, in what kinds of situations should the necessity defense be denied because of the actor's fault in creating the occasion for his conduct?

---

[j] The court sentenced the defendants to death; however, this sentence was afterwards commuted by the Crown to six months' imprisonment.—[Footnote by eds.]

[k] For a thorough discussion of this limitation, see Paul H. Robinson, Causing the Conditions of One's Own Defense: A Study in the Limits of Theory in Criminal Law Doctrine, 71 Va.L.Rev. 1 (1985).

## SUBSECTION B: DEFENSE AGAINST AGGRESSION

### People v. Goetz

Court of Appeals of New York, 1986.
68 N.Y.2d 96, 497 N.E.2d 41, 506 N.Y.S.2d 18.

■ WACHTLER, CHIEF JUDGE. A grand jury has indicted defendant on attempted murder, assault, and other charges for having shot and wounded four youths on a New York City subway train after one or two of the youths approached him and asked for $5. The lower courts, concluding that the prosecutor's charge to the grand jury on the defense of justification was erroneous, have dismissed the attempted murder, assault and weapons possession charges. We now reverse and reinstate all counts of the indictment.

I.

The precise circumstances of the incident giving rise to the charges against defendant are disputed, and ultimately it will be for a trial jury to determine what occurred. We feel it necessary, however, to provide some factual background to properly frame the legal issues before us. Accordingly, we have summarized the facts as they appear from the evidence before the grand jury. We stress, however, that we do not purport to reach any conclusions or holding as to exactly what transpired or whether defendant is blameworthy. The credibility of witnesses and the reasonableness of defendant's conduct are to be resolved by the trial jury.

On Saturday afternoon, December 22, 1984, Troy Canty, Darryl Cabey, James Ramseur, and Barry Allen boarded an IRT express subway train in the Bronx and headed south toward lower Manhattan. The four youths rode together in the rear portion of the seventh car of the train. Two of the four, Ramseur and Cabey, had screwdrivers inside their coats, which they said were to be used to break into the coin boxes of video machines.

Defendant Bernhard Goetz boarded this subway train at 14th Street in Manhattan and sat down on a bench towards the rear section of the same car occupied by the four youths. Goetz was carrying an unlicensed .38 caliber pistol loaded with five rounds of ammunition in a waistband holster. The train left the 14th Street station and headed towards Chambers Street.

It appears from the evidence before the Grand Jury that Canty approached Goetz, possibly with Allen beside him, and stated "give me five dollars." Neither Canty nor any of the other youths displayed a weapon. Goetz responded by standing up, pulling out his handgun and firing four shots in rapid succession. The first shot hit Canty in the chest; the second struck Allen in the back; the third went through Ramseur's arm and into his left side; the fourth was fired at Cabey, who apparently was then standing in the corner of the car, but missed, deflecting instead off of a wall of the conductor's cab. After Goetz briefly surveyed the scene around him, he fired another shot at Cabey, who then was sitting on the end bench of the car. The bullet entered the rear of Cabey's side and severed his spinal cord.

... The conductor, who had been in the next car, heard the shots and instructed the motorman to radio for emergency assistance. The conductor then went into the car where the shooting occurred and saw Goetz sitting on a bench, the injured youths lying on the floor or slumped against a seat, and two women who had apparently taken cover, also lying on the floor. Goetz told the conductor that the four youths had tried to rob him.

While the conductor was aiding the youths, Goetz headed towards the front of the car. The train had stopped just before the Chambers Street station and Goetz went between two of the cars, jumped onto the tracks and fled. Police and ambulance crews arrived at the scene shortly thereafter. Ramseur and Canty, initially listed in critical condition, have fully recovered. Cabey remains paralyzed, and has suffered some degree of brain damage.

On December 31, 1984, Goetz surrendered to police.... Later that day, after receiving *Miranda* warnings, he made two lengthy statements, both of which were tape recorded with his permission. In the statements, ... Goetz admitted that he had been illegally carrying a handgun in New York City for three years. He stated that he had first purchased a gun in 1981 after he had been injured in a mugging. Goetz also revealed that twice ... he had successfully warded off assailants simply by displaying the pistol.

[T]he first contact [Goetz] had with the four youths came when Canty, sitting or lying on the bench across from him, asked "how are you," to which he replied "fine." Shortly thereafter, Canty, followed by one of the other youths, walked over to the defendant and stood to his left, while the other two youths remained to his right, in the corner of the subway car. Canty then said "give me five dollars." Goetz stated that he knew from the smile on Canty's face that they wanted to "play with me." Although he was certain that none of the youths had a gun, he had a fear, based on prior experiences, of being "maimed."

Goetz then established "a pattern of fire," deciding specifically to fire from left to right. His stated intention at that point was to "murder [the four youths], to hurt them, to make them suffer as much as possible." When Canty again requested money, Goetz stood up, drew his weapon, and began firing, aiming for the center of the body of each of the four. Goetz recalled that the first two he shot "tried to run through the crowd [but] they had nowhere to run." Goetz then turned to his right to "go after the other two." One of these two "tried to run through the wall of the train, but ... he had nowhere to go." The other youth (Cabey) "tried pretending that he wasn't with [the others]" by standing still, holding on to one of the subway hand straps, and not looking at Goetz. Goetz nonetheless fired his fourth shot at him. He then ran back to the first two youths to make sure they had been "taken care of." Seeing that they had both been shot, he spun back to check on the latter two. Goetz noticed that the youth who had been standing still was now sitting on a bench and seemed unhurt. As Goetz told the police, "I said '[you] seem to be all right, here's another,'" and he then fired the shot which severed Cabey's spinal cord. Goetz added that "if I was a little more under self-control ... I would have put the barrel against his forehead and fired." He also admitted that "if I had had more [bullets], I would have shot them again, and again, and again."

II.

On March 27, 1985, the . . . grand jury filed a 10-count indictment, containing four charges of attempted murder, four charges of assault in the first degree, one charge of reckless endangerment in the first degree, and one charge of criminal possession of a weapon in the second degree. . . .

. . . Goetz moved to dismiss the charges . . . alleging, among other things, that the evidence before the . . . grand jury was not legally sufficient to establish the offenses charged, and that the prosecutor's instructions to [the] grand jury on the defense of justification were erroneous and prejudicial to the defendant so as to render its proceedings defective.

[W]hile the motion to dismiss was pending . . . the New York Daily News [published a column in] which the columnist . . . claimed that Cabey had told him . . . that the other three youths had all approached Goetz with the intention of robbing him. The day after the column was published, a . . . police officer informed the prosecutor that he had been one of the first police officers to enter the subway car after the shootings, and that Canty had said to him "we were going to rob [Goetz]." . . .

[The] Criminal Term . . . dismissed all counts of the . . . indictment, other than the reckless endangerment charge. . . . The court . . . rejected Goetz's contention that there was not legally sufficient evidence to support the charges. It held, however, that the prosecutor, in a supplemental charge elaborating upon the justification defense, had erroneously introduced an objective element into this defense by instructing the grand jurors to consider whether Goetz's conduct was that of a "reasonable man in [Goetz's] situation." The court . . . concluded that the statutory test for whether the use of deadly force is justified to protect a person should be wholly subjective, focusing entirely on the defendant's state of mind when he used such force. It concluded that dismissal was required for this error because the justification issue was at the heart of the case. . . .

On appeal by the People, a divided Appellate Division affirmed Criminal Term's dismissal of the charges. . . .

III.

Penal Law article 35 recognizes the defense of justification, which "permits the use of force under certain circumstances." One such set of circumstances pertains to the use of force in defense of a person, encompassing both self-defense and defense of a third person. Penal Law § 35.15(1) sets forth the general principles governing all such uses of force: "[a] person may . . . use physical force upon another person when and to the extent he reasonably believes such to be necessary to defend himself or a third person from what he reasonably believes to be the use or imminent use of unlawful physical force by such other person."[3]

Section 35.15(2) sets forth further limitations on these general principles with respect to the use of "deadly physical force:" "A person may not use deadly physical force upon another person under circumstances specified in subdivision one unless (a) He reasonably believes

[3] Subdivision (1) contains certain exceptions to this general authorization to use force, such as where the actor himself was the initial aggressor.

that such other person is using or about to use deadly physical force . . .[4] or (b) He reasonably believes that such other person is committing or attempting to commit a kidnapping, forcible rape, forcible sodomy or robbery."

Thus, . . . Penal Law § 35.15 permits the use of deadly physical force only where requirements as to triggering conditions and the necessity of a particular response are met. As to the triggering conditions, the statute requires that the actor "reasonably believes" that another person either is using or about to use deadly physical force or is committing or attempting to commit one of certain enumerated felonies, including robbery. As to the need for the use of deadly physical force as a response, the statute requires that the actor "reasonably believes" that such force is necessary to avert the perceived threat.[5]

Because the evidence before the . . . grand jury included statements by Goetz that he acted to protect himself from being maimed or to avert a robbery, the prosecutor correctly chose to charge the justification defense. . . . The prosecutor properly instructed the grand jurors to consider whether the use of deadly physical force was justified to prevent either serious physical injury or a robbery, and, in doing so, to separately analyze the defense with respect to each of the charges. He elaborated . . . by . . . paraphrasing . . . Penal Law § 35.15. . . .

When the prosecutor had completed his charge, one of the grand jurors asked for clarification of the term "reasonably believes." The prosecutor responded by instructing the grand jurors that they were to consider the circumstances of the incident and determine "whether the defendant's conduct was that of a reasonable man in the defendant's situation." It is this response by the prosecutor—and specifically his use of "a reasonable man"—which is the basis for the dismissal of the charges by the lower courts. As expressed repeatedly in the Appellate Division's plurality opinion, because § 35.15 uses the term "he reasonably believes," the appropriate test, according to that court, is whether a defendant's beliefs and reactions were "reasonable to him." Under that reading of the statute, a jury which believed a defendant's testimony that he felt that his own actions were warranted and were reasonable would have to acquit him, regardless of what anyone else in defendant's situation might have concluded. . . .

Penal statutes in New York have long codified the right recognized at common law to use deadly physical force, under appropriate circumstances, in self-defense. These provisions have never required that an actor's belief as to the intention of another person to inflict serious injury be correct in order for the use of deadly force to be justified, but they have uniformly required that the belief comport with an objective notion of reasonableness. . . .

---

[4] Section 35.15(2)(a) further provides, however, that even under these circumstances a person ordinarily must retreat "if he knows that he can with complete safety as to himself and others avoid the necessity of [using deadly physical force] by retreating."

[5] While the [provision] pertaining to the use of deadly physical force to avert a felony such as robbery does not contain a separate "retreat" requirement, it is clear from reading subdivisions (1) and (2) of § 35.15 together, as the statute requires, that the general "necessity" requirement in subdivision (1) applies to all uses of force under § 35.15, including the use of deadly physical force under subdivision (2)(b).

In Shorter v. People, 2 N.Y. 193 (1849), we emphasized that deadly force could be justified . . . even if the actor's beliefs as to the intentions of another turned out to be wrong, but noted there had to be a reasonable basis, viewed objectively, for the beliefs. We explicitly rejected the position that the defendant's own belief that the use of deadly force was necessary sufficed to justify such force regardless of the reasonableness of the beliefs. . . .

In 1961 the Legislature established a Commission to undertake a complete revision of the Penal Law. . . . The impetus for the decision to update the Penal Law came in part from the drafting of the Model Penal Code by the American Law Institute, as well as from the fact that the existing law was poorly organized and in many aspects antiquated. . . . The drafting of the general provisions of the new Penal Law, including the article on justification, was particularly influenced by the Model Penal Code. While using the Model Penal Code provisions on justification as general guidelines, however, the drafters of the new Penal Law did not simply adopt them verbatim.

The provisions of the Model Penal Code with respect to the use of deadly force in self-defense reflect the position of its drafters that any culpability which arises from a mistaken belief in the need to use such force should be no greater than the culpability such a mistake would give rise to if it were made with respect to an element of a crime. Accordingly, under Model Penal Code § 3.04(2)(b), a defendant charged with murder (or attempted murder) need only show that he "[believed] that [the use of deadly force] was necessary to protect himself against death, serious bodily injury, kidnapping or [forcible] sexual intercourse" to prevail on a self-defense claim. If the defendant's belief was wrong, and was recklessly, or negligently formed, however, he may be convicted of the type of homicide charge requiring only a reckless or negligent, as the case may be, criminal intent.

The drafters of the Model Penal Code recognized that the wholly subjective test set forth in § 3.04 differed from the existing law in most states by its omission of any requirement of reasonableness. The drafters were also keenly aware that requiring that the actor have a "reasonable belief" rather than just a "belief" would alter the wholly subjective test. . . .

New York did not follow the Model Penal Code's equation of a mistake as to the need to use deadly force with a mistake negating an element of a crime, choosing instead to use a single statutory section which would provide either a complete defense or no defense at all to a defendant charged with any crime involving the use of deadly force. The drafters of the new Penal Law adopted in large part the structure and content of Model Penal Code § 3.04, but, crucially, inserted the word "reasonably" before "believes."

The plurality below [held] that the change in the statutory language from "reasonable ground," used prior to 1965, to "he reasonably believes" in Penal Law § 35.15 evinced a legislative intent to conform to the subjective standard contained in Model Penal Code § 3.04. This argument, however, ignores the plain significance of the insertion of "reasonably." Had the drafters of § 35.15 wanted to adopt a subjective standard, they could have simply used the language of § 3.04. "Believes" by itself requires an honest or genuine belief by a defendant as to the need to use deadly force. Interpreting the statute to require only that the defendant's belief was "reasonable to him," as done by the plurality below, would hardly be different from requiring only a genuine belief; in either case, the defendant's own perceptions could completely exonerate him from any criminal liability.

We cannot lightly impute to the legislature an intent to fundamentally alter the principles of justification to allow the perpetrator of a serious crime to go free simply because that person believed his actions were reasonable and necessary to prevent some perceived harm. To completely exonerate such an individual, no matter how aberrational or bizarre his thought patterns, would allow citizens to set their own standards for the permissible use of force. It would also allow a legally competent defendant suffering from delusions to kill or perform acts of violence with impunity, contrary to fundamental principles of justice and criminal law.

We can only conclude that the legislature retained a reasonableness requirement to avoid giving a license for such actions. The plurality's interpretation, as the dissenters below recognized, excises the impact of the word "reasonably." . . .

Goetz also argues that the introduction of an objective element will preclude a jury from considering factors such as the prior experiences of a given actor and thus, require it to make a determination of "reasonableness" without regard to the actual circumstances of a particular incident. This argument, however, falsely presupposes that an objective standard means that the background and other relevant characteristics of a particular actor must be ignored. To the contrary, . . . a determination of reasonableness must be based on the "circumstances" facing a defendant or his "situation." Such terms encompass more than the physical movements of the potential assailant. [T]hese terms include any relevant knowledge the defendant had about that person. They also necessarily bring in the physical attributes of all persons involved, including the defendant. Furthermore, the defendant's circumstances encompass any prior experiences he had which could provide a reasonable basis for a belief that another person's intentions were to injure or rob him or that the use of deadly force was necessary under the circumstances. . . .

. . . The grand jury has indicted Goetz. It will now be for the petit jury to decide whether the prosecutor can prove beyond a reasonable doubt that Goetz's reactions were unreasonable and therefore excessive. . . .

Accordingly, the order of the Appellate Division should be reversed, and the dismissed counts of the indictment reinstated.

## NOTES ON DEADLY FORCE IN DEFENSE OF SELF AND PROPERTY

### 1. INTRODUCTION

In general, one who is free from fault may use force to defend his or her person or property against harm threatened by the unlawful act of another if: (i) the person cannot avoid the threatened harm without using defensive force or giving up some right or privilege; and (ii) the force used for this purpose is not excessive in view of the harm which it is intended to prevent. This general principle has acquired contextual specificity through centuries of judicial development. Separate defenses are usually provided for use of force in defense of person, habitation, and property, and in aid of law enforcement. Cutting across these doctrines is a set of limitations regarding the use of deadly force (force intended or likely to cause death or great bodily harm) as distinguished from non-deadly, or moderate, force. It is in this context, where one person kills another in defense of his or her own interests, that the most controversial issues arise.

The common law and many codes recognize several situations in which the use of deadly force might be privileged. Each of these privileges implicates difficult questions. What are the permissible occasions for defensive use of deadly force? What interests (if any) other than the preservation of life should justify killing an aggressor?

According to Sanford Kadish, the doctrines governing the use of deadly force represent an evolving accommodation of values of personal autonomy and proportionality. Kadish argues that personal autonomy presupposes that "no one may be used as the mere instrument of another." Sanford L. Kadish, Respect for Life and Regard for Rights in the Criminal Law, 64 Cal.L.Rev. 871, 886–88 (1976). Therefore, people have the "right to resist threats to [themselves] or interests closely identified therewith." As Kadish emphasizes, an autonomy-based right to resist aggression has no intrinsic limitation; the victim of aggression may use whatever force is necessary, including deadly force, to protect any of his or her "interests of personality." However, he argues, the principle of autonomy should be limited by a concept of proportionality: "[T]he moral right to resist threats is subject to the qualification that the actions necessary to resist the threat must not be out of proportion to the nature of the threat." It is the tension between these two principles, Kadish concludes, that "underlies the perennial controversy and changing shape of the law with respect to defining the interests for whose protection one may kill."

## 2. SELF-DEFENSE

As the New York Court of Appeals observed in *Goetz*, the prosecutor properly instructed on the justification defense because the evidence before the grand jury "included statements by Goetz that he acted to protect himself from being maimed." All jurisdictions and commentators agree that an actor's interest in preserving his life or protecting himself from serious bodily harm justifies the use of deadly force to repel an aggressor. If the self-defense privilege rests on a balance of the competing harms, why does the preservation of one life (that of Goetz) outweigh the (potential) loss of four lives? Does the balance of evils take account of some interests or values other than the protection of life and physical integrity?

## 3. PREVENTION OF DANGEROUS FELONIES

Goetz's statement to the police also suggested that he shot the youths "to avert a robbery." At common law, every citizen was entitled to prevent any felony from being committed, regardless of whether he or she was the intended victim. Today, for several reasons, the privilege of crime-prevention has an uncertain status. First, many of the situations covered by this common law defense are now covered by separate privileges concerning defense of person, habitation, and property against unprovoked attack. Second, the penal law now punishes as felonies a range of misconduct far wider than the major predatory crimes so classified at common law. Third, at common law all felonies were punishable by death; today only the most serious homicides are subject to the capital sanction. Where crime prevention is still recognized as a separate defense, it usually justifies deadly force only to prevent "dangerous" felonies. Statutory formulations typically provide that innocent victims may use deadly force to protect against forcible sexual assault, kidnapping, or robbery.

Media reports about the *Goetz* case suggest that the public is ambivalent about the status of the crime prevention privilege. At the time of the subway shootings, many people apparently believed that the shootings were justified even if Goetz's life was not in danger. Assuming that Goetz was confronted with a demand that he hand over his money—but not with a threat of death or serious bodily harm—should his use of lethal force nonetheless be justified? If justification defenses require that the actor avoid the greater evil, what arguments might Goetz's lawyers offer to suggest that the shootings averted a more serious injury than they inflicted?

## 4. PREVENTION OF ESCAPE

Consider the following variation of the facts of *Goetz*. Suppose that after Goetz entered the subway car, the four men robbed him and exited the subway at the next stop, threatening to kill him if he went to the police. Suppose further that Goetz followed them onto the subway platform and shouted at them to stop. When they failed to comply, Goetz shot one of the men as he ran away.

On these facts, the use of force would no longer be necessary for Goetz to defend himself or his property against any present threat, since the harm already would have occurred. Although Goetz would be privileged to use reasonable force to recapture his property in fresh pursuit of the thief, it is clear that he would not be justified in using deadly force merely to recover his property. Nor would the assailant's threat to harm him in the future create a present necessity to defend himself.

However, another justification might be available in this situation. Although deadly force was never permitted for the purpose of apprehending a misdemeanant or preventing his escape from custody, the common law was clearly otherwise for fleeing felons:

> If a felony be committed and the felon fly from justice . . . it is the duty of every man to use his best endeavours for preventing an escape; and if in the pursuit the felon be killed, where he cannot otherwise be overtaken, the homicide is justifiable.

1 E. East, Pleas of the Crown 298 (1806). Although some states continue to authorize private citizens to use deadly force to prevent the escape of a person believed to have committed a violent felony, the modern trend is to permit deadly force to be used in such circumstances only by law-enforcement officers and those aiding them. Moreover, police department regulations permit officers to use deadly force only when apprehending offenders who pose a threat of serious harm to others.[a]

[a] This policy judgment represents a constitutional limitation. In Tennessee v. Garner, 471 U.S. 1 (1985), the Supreme Court held that the Fourth Amendment limits police officers' use of deadly force in making arrests to those cases where the force is necessary to prevent the escape of one who poses a threat of death or serious bodily harm.

Should this hypothetical use of deadly force be justified on the ground that it was necessary to arrest the attackers or to prevent their escape? If not, should the victim ever be permitted to use deadly force to prevent the escape of a felonious attacker? What if the attacker had just killed or raped a family member?

How would this hypothetical be analyzed under the Model Penal Code? Would Goetz be entitled to acquittal under § 3.07(1) and (2), governing use of deadly force to effect an arrest? Under § 3.07(5), governing use of deadly force to prevent the "consummation" of a crime? Under § 3.06(3)(d), governing use of deadly force to prevent "consummation" of robbery? Are the Model Penal Code provisions consistent?

### 5. DEFENSE OF HABITATION

Under another traditional common law doctrine, a person was permitted to use deadly force to prevent an entry into his or her home based on the reasonable belief that such force was necessary to prevent robbery, burglary, arson, or felonious assault. This defense applied even if the actor did not fear death or great bodily injury. As a practical matter, of course, circumstances that would arouse a reasonable fear of such dangers often would also arouse fear of death or serious injury. The trend appears to be in the direction of reaffirming a distinct "defense of habitation," which is available even where the fact-finder concludes that deadly force was not reasonably necessary to defend life. See Rollin M. Perkins and Ronald N. Boyce, Criminal Law 1148–54 (3d ed.1982). For example, although most jurisdictions disallow the use of deadly force to prevent a mere trespass or non-felonious attack, the Colorado legislature recently proclaimed that "citizens . . . have a right to expect absolute safety within their own homes," and it enacted a law known as the "make my day statute." Section 18–1–704.5(2) of the Colorado Revised Statutes provides:

> [A]ny occupant of a dwelling is justified in using any degree of physical force, including deadly physical force, against another person when that other person has made an unlawful entry into the dwelling, and when the occupant has a reasonable belief that such other person has committed a crime in the dwelling in addition to the uninvited entry, or is committing or intends to commit a crime against a person or property in addition to the uninvited entry, and when the occupant reasonably believes that such other person might use any physical force, no matter how slight, against any occupant.

## NOTES ON THE EFFECT OF MISTAKE IN CLAIMS OF SELF-DEFENSE

### 1. INTRODUCTION

The court in *Goetz* emphasized that the self-defense statute does not require that the "actor's belief as to the intention of another person to inflict serious injury be correct in order for the use of deadly force to be justified." Rather, deadly force may be "justified" even if the actor's beliefs as to the need for lethal force "turned out to be wrong." As the discussion in *Goetz* reflects, courts assume that juries are capable of predicting what the alleged attacker ultimately would have done had the defendant not resisted. Assuming that a jury engages in this predictive exercise and concludes that the defendant's belief in the need to use deadly force was wrong, the question arises: Under what circumstances, if any, should such mistaken belief support a self-defense claim?

### 2. REASONABLE MISTAKE

Under *Goetz*, the right to kill another in self-defense is triggered in cases where the actor honestly and reasonably believes in the need to use deadly force, even if hindsight reveals that such belief was not correct. The common law and modern statutes concur in this view. An honest and reasonable belief in the existence of justificatory facts is ordinarily a defense, even if the belief turns to have been mistaken.[a] Since one of the most crucial and difficult issues in the law of self-defense is the meaning of the term "reasonable belief," that issue is discussed in separate notes below.

### 3. UNREASONABLE MISTAKE

Assume that jurors determined that Goetz's apprehension of harm was unreasonable. The youths did not display a weapon, and their conduct—asking Goetz "how are you" and requesting that he give them five dollars—was not life-threatening. Even if Goetz genuinely feared that they planned to maim him, he was wrong, and his fear was not reasonable. What would be the effect of such a mistake under the New York self-defense provision?

### 4. MISTAKE AND THE MODEL PENAL CODE

In *Goetz*, the New York Court of Appeals contrasts New York's approach to the use of defensive force—which "provide[s] either a complete defense or no defense at all"—to the approach offered by the drafters of the Model Penal Code. The Model Code endorses the doctrine of "imperfect justification." The common law developed this doctrine in response to the following problem. A person who intentionally kills another ordinarily is guilty of murder. If an actor intentionally kills another in the honest and reasonable, but mistaken, belief that deadly force is essential to the actor's self-defense, the actor is guilty of no crime. But if the actor's belief in the necessity of deadly force is unreasonable, the actor has no defense and is guilty of murder, even though liability for murder generally requires more than negligence. Under the doctrine of "imperfect justification," an unreasonable belief in the existence of justificatory facts negates the mens rea required for murder. The unreasonable mistake, however, provides no defense to the lesser charge of manslaughter. The effect is that unreasonable mistake is a mitigation but not a complete defense.

The Model Penal Code generalizes the idea of imperfect justification. This is done by linking the kind of mistake deemed exculpatory with the kind of culpability required by the definition of the offense. Conceptually, the scheme is quite simple. A person who believes, however unreasonably, in the existence of justificatory facts has a defense to any crime requiring a culpability of purpose or knowledge. For a crime requiring recklessness, the

---

[a] It is not clear that the common law uniformly recognized reasonable mistake as a defense for all doctrines of justification. The position stated above seems to have been firmly established for self-defense, however, which is the paradigm doctrine of justification and the principal context for litigation of such questions. For an illuminating description and criticism of the literature on mistaken justification, see Mitchell N. Berman, Justification and Excuse, Law and Morality, 53 Duke L.J. 1, 39–58 (2003).

mistaken belief must be not only sincere but also non-reckless. And for a crime requiring only negligence, the mistaken belief is exculpatory if non-negligent.

Implementation of this scheme is technically elaborate. It is accomplished in two steps. First, each of the several justification defenses is defined in purely subjective terms. For example, § 3.04(1) provides that "the use of force upon or toward another person is justifiable when the actor *believes* that such force is immediately necessary for the purpose of protecting himself against the use of unlawful force by such other person on the present occasion" (emphasis added). Section 3.04(2)(b) provides that the use of deadly force in self-defense is not justified "unless the actor *believes* that such force is necessary to protect himself against death, serious bodily harm, kidnapping or sexual intercourse compelled by force or threat . . . " (emphasis added). If these provisions were left unqualified, an honest belief in the necessity of using deadly force would be a defense to any charge of assault or homicide, no matter how reckless or negligent the actor might have been in forming that belief.

Section 3.09(2) provides the second step:

> When the actor believes that the use of force upon or toward the person of another is necessary for any of the purposes for which such belief would establish a justification . . . but the actor is reckless or negligent in having such belief or in acquiring or failing to acquire any knowledge or belief which is material to the justifiability of his use of force, the justification . . . is unavailable in a prosecution for an offense for which recklessness or negligence, as the case may be, suffices to establish culpability.

This scheme achieves a symmetry between the kind of belief recognized as a defense and the kind of culpability required by the definition of the crime. The rationale for this approach, however, is not merely aesthetic. The Model Code treatment of mistaken belief in the existence of justificatory facts is an essential feature of its general commitment to the proposition that criminal punishment should be proportional to the culpability manifested by the defendant.

## 5. EXCESSIVE USE OF DEFENSIVE FORCE

In general, a person who responds to unlawful aggression with excessive force is guilty of the assaultive offense applicable to his or her conduct. Although the provoking circumstances undoubtedly will influence prosecutorial charging and plea-bargaining decisions, the fact that a person who uses excessive force was defending against unlawful aggression is technically immaterial to the grade of the offense. However, a person who kills an aggressor whose conduct justified only moderate force would not be liable for murder in most jurisdictions. Instead, the conviction would be for manslaughter. In most cases, this would be because the actor responded in the "heat of passion" to the aggressor's provocation and therefore would be said to lack the "malice aforethought" required for a murder conviction.[b]

---

[b] The concept of provocation is explored in Chapter X.

## NOTES ON THE MEANING OF "REASONABLE" BELIEF

### 1. OBJECTIVE REASONABLENESS

In *Goetz*, the New York Court of Appeals rejected the standard employed by the intermediate appellate court for evaluating whether the accused had a reasonable belief in the need to use deadly force. The courts disagreed over the perspective to be used to evaluate the reasonableness of the defendant's belief.

The intermediate appellate court concluded that the test "is whether a defendant's beliefs and reactions were 'reasonable to him.'" The New York Court of Appeals rejected this standard on the ground that it was "wholly subjective," effectively requiring jurors to acquit a defendant who honestly believed "that his own actions were warranted and were reasonable . . . , regardless of what anyone else in defendant's situation might have concluded." According to the Court of Appeals, the defendant's belief must comport with an "objective" standard of reasonableness. Under this "objective" inquiry, jurors must decide whether the defendant's beliefs would be held by a reasonable person in the defendant's "situation." This standard depends on precisely what factors or circumstances are encompassed by the defendant's "situation." What factors does the Court of Appeals mention?

From the time of the subway shooting through the trial and its aftermath, the *Goetz* case has raised explosive questions concerning racism in the criminal justice system. Goetz is white, and the four men he shot are black. For purposes of the present discussion, the question is whether race should have any bearing on the reasonableness of Goetz's belief that the men intended to maim or rob him. Although the Court of Appeals did not mention this issue, its description of the defendant's "situation" might be interpreted to include inferences about a person's dangerousness arising from his or her race in this particular social context. Is the race of the alleged attackers "relevant knowledge" that Goetz possessed "which could provide a reasonable basis" for a belief that their intentions were to injure or rob him?

When the case went to trial, the evidence included statements Goetz made to police and prosecutors in which he mentioned that in 1981 he had been mugged and seriously injured by three men. As George Fletcher explained, Goetz's defense did not bring out the fact that the men who attacked Goetz in 1981 were black or otherwise explicitly appeal to racist bias. However, Fletcher contended that Goetz's defense team made a powerful indirect appeal to racist assumptions. Its "strategy of relentlessly attacking the 'gang of four,' 'the predators' on society, calling them 'vultures' and 'savages,'" he said, "carried undeniable racial overtones." George P. Fletcher, A Crime of Self Defense: Bernhard Goetz and the Law on Trial 206 (1988). He continued:

> The question whether a reasonable person considers race in assessing the danger that four youths on the subway might represent goes to the heart of what the law demands of us. The statistically ordinary New Yorker would be more apprehensive of the "kind of people" who mugged him once, and it is difficult to expect the ordinary person in our time not to perceive race as one—just one—of the factors defining the "kind" of person who poses a danger. The law, however, may demand that we surmount racially

> based intuitions of danger. Though . . . there is no settled law on this issue, the standard of reasonableness may require us to be better than we really are.

Fletcher concluded that the defense strategy was effective precisely because it "remained hidden behind innuendo and suggestion." An open conversation about racial fear might have assisted the jurors to consider rationally and to reject their own racial biases. In any event, the petit jury acquitted Goetz on all four charges of attempted murder, and, as Fletcher pointed out, many members of the public seem to have interpreted the verdict as a declaration that Goetz's use of deadly force was reasonable.

State v. Brown, 91 N.M. 320, 573 P.2d 675 (1977), raises additional questions about the relationship between race and the reasonableness of an actor's belief that he needs to use deadly force. Brown was a black man who was convicted of two counts of assault upon a police officer with intent to kill. Brown conceded that he shot the officers, but he argued that he did so in self-defense. At trial, Brown testified that he feared the officers because the police "hassled" him and other black persons in his neighborhood. The trial court allowed Brown and other defense witnesses to describe specific encounters between Brown and police officers, in which the officers harassed and threatened Brown. However, the trial court refused the defense's proffer of testimony by a social psychologist concerning "police conduct toward minority groups and the perception by minority groups, particularly blacks, that the police are a threat to minority group members." On appeal, the Court of Appeals of New Mexico held that exclusion of the expert's testimony was reversible error. Such testimony was relevant to an element of self-defense, namely, whether Brown feared that he was in immediate danger of bodily harm. Moreover, the psychologist's testimony may have rebutted an inference that Brown acted not out of fear, but out "of anger and . . . rejection of authority." Does the expert testimony also support the conclusion that Brown's fear was "objectively" reasonable under the *Goetz* standard? Do Fletcher's concerns about the invidious implications of the defense strategy in *Goetz* apply with equal force to the defense theory in *Brown*?

## 2. SUBJECTIVE REASONABLENESS

The court in *Goetz* remarked that some states apply a subjective standard of reasonableness " 'and judge from the standpoint of the very defendant concerned.' "[a] In State v. Leidholm, 334 N.W.2d 811 (1983), the Supreme Court of North Dakota adopted a subjective definition of reasonableness and endeavored to explain the distinction between the objective and subjective approaches:

> Courts have traditionally distinguished between standards of reasonableness by characterizing them as either "objective" or "subjective." An objective standard of reasonableness requires the factfinder to view the circumstances surrounding the accused at the time he used force from the standpoint of a hypothetical reasonable and prudent person. Ordinarily, under such a view, the unique physical and psychological characteristics of the accused are not taken into consideration in judging the reasonableness of the accused's belief.

[a] Ohio appears to employ a purely subjective perspective. See Nelson v. State, 42 Ohio App. 252, 181 N.E. 448 (1932).

> This is not the case, however, where a subjective standard of reasonableness is employed. Under the subjective standard the issue is not whether the circumstances attending the accused's use of force would be sufficient to create in the mind of a reasonable and prudent person the belief that the use of force is necessary . . . , but rather whether the circumstances are sufficient to induce in *the accused* an honest and reasonable belief that he must use force to defend himself against imminent harm. . . .
>
> Because . . . we agree . . . that a subjective standard is the more just, we [adopt such standard.]
>
> The practical and logical consequence of this interpretation is that an accused's actions are to be viewed from the standpoint of a person whose mental and physical characteristics are like the accused's and who sees what the accused sees and knows what the accused knows. For example, if the accused is a timid, diminutive male, the factfinder must consider these characteristics in assessing the reasonableness of his belief. If, on the other hand, the accused is a strong, courageous, and capable female, the factfinder must consider these characteristics in judging the reasonableness of her belief.

Is the standard endorsed by the New York Court of Appeals in *Goetz* all that different from the "subjective standard of reasonableness" adopted in *Leidholm*? Is *Leidholm* a wholly "subjective" standard? What is the difference between (a) a standard that asks whether the reasonable person in the defendant's situation would have believed deadly force was necessary and (b) a standard that asks whether the accused reasonably believed that deadly force was necessary?

The court in *Leidholm* asserts that a subjective standard of reasonableness is "more just" than an objective standard.[b] Perhaps the judges believed that individuals differ markedly in their reactions to stress and in their susceptibility to panic. If that is the case, it may be difficult, if not impossible, to identify a community standard to which actors who subjectively perceive a deadly peril should be required to conform. Glanville Williams defends a subjective approach in his Textbook of Criminal Law 452 (1978). He argues that the reasonableness requirement is designed to encourage people to verify their beliefs before acting and to compel compliance with well-known rules of prudence. However, persons who are convinced they are about to be attacked tend to act instantly and instinctively. In such cases, he argues, punishment serves no utilitarian purpose:

> . . . No rule of prudence decides the question whether another person is about to launch a fierce attack on you. Generally there will be no way in which the defender can check the validity of his belief, and such a situation is so unlikely to be repeated that he will probably not benefit from experience. Also, a defender is subject to the strong emotion of fear, which may well warp his judgment. If the law is to allow self-defence at all, must it now allow it on the facts as they appear to the defender whether reasonably or unreasonably?

---

[b] For an illuminating discussion of why a self-defense theory that incorporates some subjective criteria is preferable for purposes of both moral philosophy and criminal law, see Russell Christopher, Self-Defense and Defense of Others, 27 Phil. & Pub. Affairs 123 (1998).

### 3. WHAT DIFFERENCE DOES IT MAKE?

In order to identify and evaluate the difference between the objective and subjective standards, consider the following case.[c]

In June 1994 in Nashville, Tennessee, Charles Langley shot and killed Harry Woods. At his trial for first-degree murder, Langley argued that the killing was justified because he had acted in self-defense. Just before the killing, Langley and his father were refinishing hardwood floors at a mansion that was undergoing renovation. Woods arrived at the mansion to fix the plumbing; he was accompanied by his son and nephew. Ignoring signs warning them to stay off the floors, the three plumbers walked across a floor that Langley had just finished sanding. Woods's son and Langley exchanged harsh words. Langley picked up a linoleum knife and said that he would cut the plumber's throat if he walked on the floor again. Upon hearing about Langley's threat, Woods became very angry and tried to hit Langley with a lead pipe. The job foreman intervened and separated the men, but Woods managed to kick Langley in the side. Langley went outside the mansion to his truck, retrieved a semiautomatic pistol, and placed the gun in the back of his waistband. He then stood in the yard talking with the job foreman. At this point, Woods came running towards them. Woods was not armed, but he shoved the foreman out of the way in an attempt to get at Langley. Langley opened fire and shot Woods four or five times, with two shots hitting Woods in the back. Langley was 30 years old, stood five feet, six inches tall, and weighed 130 pounds. Woods was 48 years old, six feet tall, and 220 pounds.

Before the trial, Langley was examined by a clinical psychologist and a psychiatrist. The experts concluded that Langley was an insecure and usually passive man. He was much more likely than the average person to become frightened quickly when he felt threatened. He felt vulnerable because of his small size and because he was tormented by bullies when he was in school. Langley was not an angry person; if given the chance, he would run away from confrontations. At the time he shot Woods, Langley was scared to death.

What would the result be under the "objective" standard employed by *Goetz*? Under the "objective" standard described and rejected by the court in *Leidholm*? Under the "subjective" standard endorsed by *Leidholm*? In applying these standards, which of the foregoing facts about the confrontation, about Langley, and about Woods would jurors be permitted to consider?

## INTRODUCTORY NOTES ON THE RETREAT REQUIREMENT

### 1. THE RETREAT RULE

Suppose *A*, who is free from fault, is placed in actual peril of deadly attack by *B*, who is wielding a knife. Should *A* be privileged "to stand his ground and resort to deadly force *there* merely because he is where he has a right to be, or must he take advantage of an obviously safe retreat if one is

---

[c] The following description of the *Langley* case is based on Kirk Loggins, Suspect "Scared to Death" Doctor Says, The Tennessean, Sept. 28, 1995, at B1; Kirk Loggins, Floor Finisher Found Not Guilty of Murder, The Tennessean, Sept. 29, 1995, at A1; Toni Dew, Self-Defense, Not Murder Verdict, For Man Who Shot, Killed Plumber, The Nashville Banner, Sept. 29, 1995, at B3.

available"? Rollin Perkins, Self-Defense Re-examined, 1 U.C.L.A.L.Rev. 133, 145 (1954). This has been one of the most hotly contested questions in the law of self-defense.

The history was summarized by the New Jersey Supreme Court in State v. Abbott, 36 N.J. 63, 69–72, 174 A.2d 881, 884–86 (1961), as a prelude to embracing a retreat requirement:

> The question whether one who is neither the aggressor nor a party to a mutual combat must retreat has divided the authorities. Self-defense is measured against necessity. From that premise one could readily say there was no necessity to kill in self-defense if the use of deadly force could have been avoided by retreat. The critics of the retreat rule do not quarrel with the theoretical validity of this conclusion, but rather condemn it as unrealistic. The law of course should not denounce conduct as criminal when it accords with the behavior of reasonable men. Upon this level, the advocates of no-retreat say the manly thing is to hold one's ground, and hence society should not demand what smacks of cowardice. Adherents of the retreat rule reply it is better that the assailed shall retreat than that the life of another be needlessly spent. They add that not only do right-thinking men agree, but further a rule so requiring may well induce others to adhere to that worthy standard of behavior. There is much dispute as to which view commands the support of ancient precedents. . . .
>
> Other jurisdictions are closely divided upon the retreat doctrine. . . . The Model Penal Code embraces the retreat rule while acknowledging that on numerical balance a majority of the precedents oppose it.
>
> We are not persuaded to depart from the principle of retreat. We think it salutary if reasonably limited. Much of the criticism goes not to its inherent validity but rather to unwarranted applications of the rule. For example, it is correctly observed that one can hardly retreat from a rifle shot at close range. But if the weapon were a knife, a lead of a city block might be well enough. Again, the rule cannot be stated baldly, with indifference to the excitement of the occasion. As Mr. Justice Holmes cryptically put it, "[d]etached reflection cannot be demanded in the presence of an uplifted knife." Brown v. United States, 256 U.S. 335, 343 (1921). Such considerations, however, do not demand that a man should have the absolute right to stand his ground and kill in any and all situations. Rather, they call for a fair and guarded statement of appropriate principles. . . .
>
> We believe the following principles are sound:
>
> 1. The issue of retreat arises only if the defendant resorted to a deadly force. It is deadly force which is not justifiable when an opportunity to retreat is at hand. . . .
>
> Hence it is not the nature of the force defended against which raises the issue of retreat, but rather the nature of the force which the accused employed in his defense. If he does not resort to a deadly force, one who is assailed may hold his ground whether the attack upon him be of a deadly or some lesser character.

> 2. What constitutes an opportunity to retreat which will defeat the right of self-defense? As [§ 3.04(2)(b)(ii)] of the Model Penal Code states, deadly force is not justifiable "if the actor *knows* that he can avoid the necessity of using such force *with complete safety* by retreating. . . ." We emphasize "knows" and "with complete safety." One who is wrongfully attacked need not risk injury by retreating, even though he could escape with something less than serious bodily injury. It would be unreal to require nice calculations as to the amount of hurt, or to ask him to endure any at all. And the issue is not whether in retrospect it can be found the defendant could have retreated unharmed. Rather the question is whether he knew the opportunity was there, and of course in that inquiry the total circumstances including the attendant excitement must be considered. . . .

Glanville Williams has argued, contrary to the view taken in *Abbott* and the Model Penal Code, that there should be no retreat rule. Glanville Williams, Textbook of Criminal Law 462–63 (1978). Although Williams concedes that the privilege of self-defense should ordinarily be "limited to circumstances of necessity," he argues that the requirement of necessity is not unqualified. He illustrates his point with the following hypothetical: If *A* says to *B*, "If you don't do as I tell you, I will kill you," *B* is entitled to refuse to obey the order and to resist any attack thereafter initiated by *A* even though *B* could have avoided the necessity of self-defense by complying with the order in the first instance. Similarly, Williams argues, the requirement of necessity should "not generally imply a duty to run away." Even though "many courageous people would rather run away than shed blood," the law should not impose such a duty. To the contrary, he concludes, "one who prefers to stand his ground and then act in necessary self-defence should be allowed to do so, unless he was the initial aggressor."

## 2. THE WISDOM OF RULES

As the *Abbott* court notes, the majority of states have rejected the retreat rule. Until recently, as developed further below, they also rejected the "right to stand one's ground" preferred by Professor Williams. Instead, the preponderant 20th century view was the one endorsed by the United States Supreme Court in Brown v. United States, 256 U.S. 335, 343 (1921), that "the failure to retreat is a circumstance to be considered with all the others in order to determine whether the defendant went farther than he was justified in doing; not a categorical proof of guilt."

Debate regarding a retreat rule illustrates one of the generic issues in the formulation of doctrines of personal defense: To what extent should the norms governing the use of defensive force, especially deadly force, be specified by rule rather than be left to particularized applications of standards of "reasonableness" and "necessity." The typical formulation of a retreat rule has been criticized because of its inflexibility: "For the law to attempt a detailed formulation of rights and duties in cases of self-defence would be both futile and unjust—futile because no one can foresee all the possible circumstances in which self-defence might be raised, and unjust insofar as the result of failure to legislate for a particular type of situation might be the absence of rights on a most worthy occasion." A.J. Ashworth, Self-Defence and the Right to Life, 34 Camb.L.J. 282, 292 (1975). On the other hand, the open-textured standard of reasonableness—reflected in the majority view that the availability of an avenue of retreat is merely one of the circumstances to be taken into account in assessing the reasonableness of the defendant's use of deadly force—may be criticized on the grounds that it gives inadequate protection to human life and that it leaves too much room for inconsistent administration of the law.

Are the outcomes of jury deliberations on self-defense claims likely to depend on which of these instructions is given? Are there operational differences—in ruling on sufficiency of the evidence, in framing jury instructions, and in the role of appellate courts—between these two approaches to the retreat problem?

### 3. THE "CASTLE" EXCEPTION

Even jurisdictions that have adopted a retreat requirement typically recognize an exception for a person attacked in his or her own home. In Weiland v. State, 732 So.2d 1044 (Fla. 1999), a woman claimed self-defense after she killed her husband during a violent argument in the apartment where they were living with their infant daughter. The question was whether she had a duty to retreat before using deadly force. The court said "no":

> Under Florida statutory and common law, a person may use deadly force in self-defense if he or she reasonably believes that deadly force is necessary to prevent imminent death or great bodily harm. Even under those circumstances, however, a person may not resort to deadly force without first using every reasonable means within his or her power to avoid the danger, including retreat. The duty to retreat emanates from common law, rather than from our statutes.
>
> There is an exception to this common law duty to retreat "to the wall," which applies when an individual claims self-defense in his or her own residence. An individual is not required to retreat from the residence before resorting to deadly force in self-defense, so long as the deadly force is necessary to prevent death or great bodily harm.
>
> The privilege of nonretreat from the home, part of the "castle doctrine," has early common law origins. [In New York v. Tomlins, 213 N.Y. 240, 107 N.E. 496 (1914),] Justice Cardozo explained the historical basis of the privilege of nonretreat from the home:
>
>> It is not now and never has been the law that a man assailed in his own dwelling is bound to retreat. If assailed there, he may stand his ground and resist the attack. He is under no duty to take to the fields and the highways, a fugitive from his own home. More than 200 years ago it was said by Lord Chief Justice Hale: In case a man "is assailed in his own house, he need not flee as far as he can, as in other cases of se defendendo, for he hath the protection of his house to excuse him from flying, as that would be to give up the protection of his house to his adversary by flight." *Flight is for sanctuary and shelter, and shelter, if not sanctuary, is in the home.... The rule is the same whether the attack proceeds from some other occupant or from an intruder.*

The Florida Supreme Court decided in *Weiland* to "join the majority of jurisdictions that do not impose a duty to retreat from the residence when a defendant uses deadly force in self-defense, if that force is necessary to prevent death or great bodily harm from a co-occupant."

Where such a doctrine is embraced, questions arise as to what constitutes a "castle" and whether any places other than one's home should qualify. The Model Penal Code, which requires retreat if it can be accomplished "with complete safety," incorporates the traditional exception and does not require retreat from a person's "dwelling or place of work, unless [the actor] was the initial aggressor or is assailed in his place of work by another person whose place of work the actor knows it to be." Section 3.04(2)(b)(ii)(1). Are these exceptions to the retreat rule appropriate? Why did the drafters fail to require retreat in the workplace if it can be accomplished with complete safety? Why should it make any difference that the assailant and the victim work in the same place? If it makes a difference in the workplace, why did the drafters fail to require a person to retreat from his home when the assailant also lives there? Is it wise to prescribe rules of this detail in legislation?

### 4. "STAND YOUR GROUND" LEGISLATION

When George Zimmerman shot and killed a young black man, Trayvon Martin, in Sanford, Florida, on the night if February 26, 2012, a national furor erupted, with sharp racial overtones, over Florida's so-called "stand your ground" law. Adopted in 2005 and soon thereafter followed to one extent or another by a majority of American jurisdictions,[a] the Florida law significantly expanded the no-retreat obligation that had prevailed up to that point in most jurisdictions.

As described in Mary Anne Franks, Real Men Advance, Real Women Retreat: Stand Your Ground, Battered Women's Syndrome, and Violence As Male Privilege, 68 U. Miami L. Rev. 1099 (2014), "the majority" of the Florida law "should not be seen as particularly controversial." But she points out four respects in which the law significantly extends the no-retreat principle.[b]

---

[a] An ABA Report states that "[a]s of 2014, 33 states have Stand Your Ground laws," 24 by statute and the rest by decision. ABA National Task Force on Stand Your Ground Laws, Preliminary Report and Recommendations 19 (August 8, 2014). The Report contains an extensive bibliography.

[b] The text of the 2005 Florida law is reproduced in Appendix B. Amendments adopted in 2014 can also be found there. The primary purpose of the amendments was to *extend* coverage of the stand your ground provisions to threats to use deadly force as well as the use of such force. Efforts to repeal the Florida law following the Trayvon Martin incident failed. See ABA National Task Force on Stand Your Ground Laws, Preliminary Report and Recommendations 35 (August 8, 2014).

The NRA has lobbied extensively throughout the country for adoption and expansion of stand your ground laws. See, e.g., Mary Anne Franks, Real Men Advance, Real Women Retreat: Stand Your Ground, Battered Women's Syndrome, And Violence As Male Privilege, 68 U. Miami L. Rev. 1099, 1101 & n.6 (2014); Tamara Rice Lave, Shoot to Kill: A Critical Look at Stand Your Ground Laws, 67 U. Miami L. Rev. 827, 836 (2013) ("According to a wide variety of sources, the NRA was instrumental in getting *stand your ground* passed."); Jeannie Suk, The True Woman: Scenes from the Law of Self-Defense, 31 Harv. J. Law & Gender 237, 260 (2008).

First, the law does not require retreat if deadly force is used to "prevent the commission of a forcible felony." "Forcible felony" is defined to include robbery and burglary.[c] Franks criticizes this provision as

> a significant departure from the long-held belief that the use of deadly force should not be used to protect mere property. Inasmuch as this [long-held] belief reflects the principle that life is precious and should not be taken except under extraordinary circumstances, this is an innovation that fosters disrespect for human life.

Second, the law "greatly expands" the "castle doctrine." The innovation here, Franks says, is stark:

> Under Stand Your Ground, one is allowed to use deadly force even when one could retreat in complete safety not only in homes (the traditional view) but in any "dwelling," which is expansively defined as "a building or conveyance of any kind, including any attached porch, whether the building or conveyance is temporary or permanent, mobile or immobile, which has a roof over it, including a tent, and is designed to be occupied by people lodging therein at night" as well as in "occupied vehicles."

Indeed, the label "castle doctrine" is often used to describe the expansion of no-retreat rules accomplished by stand your ground laws.[d]

Third, the law contains presumptions about what constitutes "reasonable fear" that can justify use of deadly force in a dwelling. The presumption applies, in its 2014 version, if:

> (a) The person against whom the defensive force was used or threatened was in the process of unlawfully and forcefully entering, or had unlawfully and forcibly entered, a dwelling, residence, or occupied vehicle, or if that person had removed or was attempting to remove another against that person's will from the dwelling, residence, or occupied vehicle; and
>
> (b) The person who uses or threatens to use defensive force knew or had reason to believe that an unlawful and forcible entry or unlawful and forcible act was occurring or had occurred.

Fla. Stat. § 776.013(1).

Fourth, "the most unsettling innovation," Franks continues, and "the one that arguably does the most to shift social norms away from a default position of respecting human life," is the provision that provides immunity from criminal prosecution and civil liability. The 2014 version of that section of the law states:

> (1) A person who uses or threatens to use force as permitted in [the statutes governing self-defense, home protection, and

---

[c] Section 776.08 of the Florida Statutes Annotated provides:

> "Forcible felony" means treason; murder; manslaughter; sexual battery; carjacking; home-invasion robbery; robbery; burglary; arson; kidnapping; aggravated assault; aggravated battery; aggravated stalking; aircraft piracy; unlawful throwing, placing, or discharging of a destructive device or bomb; and any other felony which involves the use or threat of physical force or violence against any individual.

[d] See, e.g., http://www.nraila.org/news-issues/issues/self-defense-castle-doctrine.aspx, in which National Rifle Association discussions of issues related to stand your ground laws are presented under the heading "Self Defense/Castle Doctrine."

> defense of property] is justified in such conduct and is immune from criminal prosecution and civil action for the use or threatened use of such force by the person, personal representative, or heirs of the person against whom the force was used or threatened . . . .
>
> (2) A law enforcement agency may use standard procedures for investigating the use or threatened use of force as described in subsection (1), but the agency may not arrest the person for using or threatening to use force unless it determines that there is probable cause that the force that was used or threatened was unlawful.
>
> (3) The court shall award reasonable attorney's fees, court costs, compensation for loss of income, and all expenses incurred by the defendant in defense of any civil action brought by a plaintiff if the court finds that the defendant is immune from prosecution as provided in subsection (1).

Fla. Stat. § 776.032.

"In sum," Franks concludes, "the significant alterations that Stand Your Ground makes to self-defense law are the authorization of the use of deadly force to protect property; the extension of the castle doctrine to a broad category of 'dwellings' as well as 'occupied vehicles'; presumptions about the reasonableness of the use of deadly force; and immunity from arrest and prosecution." The following case involves an application of the immunity provision.

## Mobley v. State

District Court of Appeal of Florida, Third District, 2014.
132 So.3d 1160.

■ WELLS, JUDGE.

We have jurisdiction to review the instant petition for writ of prohibition seeking to preclude the court below from proceeding further in adjudicating criminal charges against petitioner, Gabriel Mobley, on the grounds that Mobley is immune from prosecution under the provisions of Chapter 776 of the Florida Statutes (Florida's Stand Your Ground Law). . . .

The standard of review applicable to this case is the same as that which is applied to the denial of a motion to suppress. . . . Under this standard, the trial court's findings of fact are "presumed correct and can be reversed only if they are not supported by competent substantial evidence," while the trial court's legal conclusions are reviewed de novo. For the reasons that follow, we grant the petition but withhold issuance of our writ confident that the court below will comply with this court's order.

*Facts*

Gabriel Mobley, the petitioner here, was charged with two counts of second degree murder following a shooting which took place outside a local Chili's restaurant on February 27, 2008. The day of the fatal shooting, Mobley finished work around 3:00 pm at his pressure cleaning business, and after going home to shower and change, went to work at the tax preparation office of high school friend, Jose (Chico) Correa. After working several hours at Chico's business, Mobley was invited by Chico to join him and his staff at a local Chili's to unwind. Mobley agreed to join them but drove his own car intending to go home from the restaurant. When Mobley arrived at the restaurant, he removed the handgun that he was carrying and stowed the gun in the glove compartment of his car. He did so because he believed from the training that he had received to secure a concealed carry license that firearms could not be brought into any establishment where food and alcohol are served. By the time Mobley got to the restaurant, a number of Chico's female employees had arrived and were sitting at a booth located near one end of the restaurant's bar. Because the booth was crowded, Mobley, Chico, and another of Chico's employees (another man) sat at the bar nearest the booth.

Sometime after food and drinks were ordered, Mobley and Chico went outside to smoke. They returned to the bar where they ate, drank and conversed without incident. However, things changed after Mobley and Chico went outside a second time for a smoke. This time when they reentered the restaurant, they found two men, later identified as Jason Gonzalez and Rolando (Roly) Carrazana, talking to Chico's female employees. According to Chico, the women seemed to be uncomfortable so he told the men to leave. This sparked a verbal altercation between Chico and the two men which continued until the two men returned to their table at the other end of the bar. The altercation, which lasted only a few minutes, was loud enough to attract the attention of the restaurant's security guard and its manager, who asked the guard to keep an eye on Jason and Roly.

Mobley was not involved in the argument but acted as peacemaker instead, going to Jason's and Roly's table to ask them to forget what he described as a petty misunderstanding. He even shook Jason's hand and gave him a friendly pat on the back. Mobley also spoke to a third person seated at the bar who appeared to be with Jason and Roly about forgetting this petty disagreement.

Although the altercation appeared to have ended, Mobley testified that he began to feel uncomfortable after he noticed Roly staring in the direction of Chico's party with a "mean, cold [look] on his face."[5] He decided it was time to leave. But before he left, he and Chico went to the restroom where he expressed his concerns to his friend. As Mobley and Chico were returning from the bathroom, they passed the front of the restaurant where Mobley saw Jason, with Roly nearby, banging aggressively on the restaurant's window and pointing toward them. When Mobley and Chico reached their seats, Mobley suggested that after Jason and Roly left, they should all go home. Approximately ten to fifteen minutes later, after Jason and Roly appeared to have left, Mobley left the restaurant alone while Chico settled the check.

The events that transpired next were captured on a security camera recording made outside the restaurant, and, for the most part, are beyond dispute. The recording shows that at 23:52:15, Mobley, wearing only a sleeveless tee shirt, exited the Chili's front door and went to his

[5] Alexandra Martinez, a server at the restaurant called by the State to testify, confirmed that Jason and Roly continued to be angry after the initial shouting match had ended and appeared to become angrier as the evening wore on.

vehicle parked only feet away, but mostly outside the security camera's viewing range. There, Mobley, as subsequent footage confirms, donned a sweat shirt, because, according to Mobley, it was chilly that night.[7] He also retrieved his gun and put it in a holster that he wore around his waist. Less than a minute after Mobley left the restaurant, Chico and the third man in their party exited the front door. Chico was joined by Mobley who walked with Chico to his nearby car.[8] There the two remained for approximately thirty seconds until, at 23:53:38, Mobley stepped onto the sidewalk near the front fender of Chico's car. Approximately twenty seconds later, Chico joined him on the sidewalk where the two smoked a cigarette.

Four seconds after Chico joined Mobley on the sidewalk, Jason Gonzalez can be seen rapidly approaching from Mobley's and Chico's right. Four seconds after that, Jason delivered a vicious punch to Chico's face which fractured Chico's eye socket. Jason then can be seen to dance backward, hands raised in a fighter's pose, and within four seconds of landing the punch on Chico advance forward toward Mobley. Mobley reacted by raising his arm and hand to ward Jason off. Two seconds later, as Jason steps back from Mobley, Roly can be seen rushing up from the rear of the restaurant to join Jason in what Mobley testified he believed to be a renewed attack on both himself and Chico. At this juncture, as Roly neared Jason, who was only feet from both Mobley and Chico, Mobley testified that he saw Roly reach under his long, baggy shirt. Believing that Roly was reaching for a weapon to use in an attack, Mobley drew his gun and shot at Roly hitting both Roly and Jason.

This entire series of events, from the time Jason first comes into view on the sidewalk until the first shot was fired, took only twelve seconds. After being shot, Jason turned and fled toward his (or Roly's) car to collapse with a gunshot wound to the chest and die. Roly, hit four times, fell to the ground near the restaurant's door where he was assisted by the third man in their party who had been sitting at the bar. Roly later died at a local hospital. Although no weapons were found on Roly's body, two knives were found on the ground near where he fell.[9]

Following the shooting, Mobley remained at the scene and had the other members of his party, who by then were leaving in their cars, return to wait for the authorities. When police officers arrived only minutes later, Mobley told them that he was armed and otherwise fully cooperated with them. After being held in a police car for a number of hours, he was transported to the police station where he was read and waived his *Miranda* rights. While there, he gave both an unsworn and a sworn statement. He was then released but not charged.

Several weeks later, after a new lead investigator had been assigned to the case, Mobley agreed to be and was re-interviewed. While there is no indication that his version of the events changed in any manner during this interview, he subsequently was arrested and

---

[7] The video recording confirms that Chico was wearing a coat and that most everyone else who appears on the recording was wearing either a sweat shirt or a long sleeved shirt.

[8] The third man walked to his car parked next to Chico's and remained there until after the shooting occurred.

[9] According to Ms. Martinez, the man who went to Roly's aid after he was shot took a knife with him when he left the restaurant.

charged with two counts of second degree murder. Mobley claimed below and now claims here that these facts are undisputed and demonstrate that he is immune from prosecution as provided by sections 776.012 and 776.032 of the Florida Statutes. We agree in part that the pertinent facts are not in dispute and that Mobley is entitled to immunity from prosecution.

*Analysis*

Florida law confers immunity from criminal prosecution and civil liability, without the obligation to retreat, on those who use deadly force reasonably believing that the use of such force is necessary to either prevent imminent death or great bodily harm to self or others or to prevent the imminent commission of a forcible felony. See § 776.032, Fla. Stat. (2013) (providing that a "person who uses force as permitted in s. 776.012, s. 776.013, or s. 776.031 is justified in using such force and is immune from criminal prosecution and civil action for the use of such force"); see also § 776.012(1), (2), Fla. Stat. (2013) (providing that a "person is justified in the use of deadly force . . . and does not have a duty to retreat if: (1) [h]e or she reasonably believes that such force is necessary to prevent imminent death or great bodily harm to himself or herself or another or to prevent the imminent commission of a forcible felony; or (2) [u]nder those circumstances permitted pursuant to s. 776.013").

An objective standard is applied to determine whether the immunity provided by these provisions attaches. . . . That standard requires the court to determine whether, based on circumstances as they appeared to the defendant when he or she acted, a reasonable and prudent person situated in the same circumstances and knowing what the defendant knew would have used the same force as did the defendant. . . .

Here, the court below determined that Mobley did not "reasonably" believe that deadly force was "necessary" to prevent "imminent" death, great bodily harm, or commission of a forcible felony. In doing so, the court discounted the totality of the circumstances facing Mobley and concluded that the use of deadly force was not reasonable, first, because Mobley "never saw a weapon and did not know anything about the possibility of a weapon," with him only seeing "the second attacker appear to be reaching for something under his shirt," and second, because Mobley should have brandished his gun, fired a warning shot or told the attackers to stop because he had a gun. We disagree for the following reasons.

As a preliminary matter, Mobley was not required to warn that he had a gun. Section 776.012(1), (2), clearly states where the danger of death, great bodily harm or the commission of a forcible felony is "imminent," *the use* of deadly force is justified. The statute contains no warning requirement. See T.P. v. State, 117 So.3d 864, 866 (Fla. 4th DCA 2013) ("[U]nder section 776.013, a person who is attacked is allowed to stand his or her ground and 'meet force with force.' It appears that the new law places no duty on the person to avoid or retreat from danger, so long as that person is not engaged in an unlawful activity and is located in a place where he or she has a right to be.").

As to the primary reason given by the court for rejecting Mobley's "Stand Your Ground" defense—that Mobley did not see a weapon, this likewise cannot be deemed determinative. The record reflects that Mobley observed Jason viciously attack his friend Chico outside the Chili's. Mobley then saw Jason's friend Roly approach and reach under his shirt. It was then that Mobley became afraid for his safety and life and for that of his friend and he pulled his gun:

Q. Okay. So, as soon as he [Roly] was coming towards you, you shot?

A. Yes.

Q. Why did you first pull your firearm?

A. Why[?]

Q. Yes.

A. By this time, you know, I didn't know what they had done—I didn't know what Chico had got hit with, and it was so much blood, I freaked, I was scared and I seen [sic] this other guy coming up from the back. And he reached up under his shirt. So, I was scared, I thought, they were going to shoot or kill us or stab us or something. So I was scared.

The shooting at issue did not occur in a vacuum. Mobley did not shoot two innocent bystanders who just happened upon him on a sidewalk. The record—as corroborated by a video of the events—is that (1) Mobley found himself in the middle of a violent, unprovoked attack on a companion who was standing right next to him, by one of two men who earlier had engaged in an altercation to which he was a witness; (2) after the initial violent attack on Mobley's friend, the attacker immediately turned his attention to Mobley; (3) less than four seconds after that, the first attacker was joined by the second man involved in the altercation inside the restaurant; and (4) when the second man reached under his shirt after rushing up to join his companion who had not abandoned the field, Mobley believed the second man was reaching for a weapon to continue the attack. With these facts at hand, and with Mobley's knowledge of these two assailants, the issue for determination was not whether Mobley knew a weapon was possible or whether he actually saw one, but whether a reasonably prudent person in those same circumstances and with the same knowledge would have used the force Mobley used.

Rather than applying the objective standard required, the court below instead focused on the events that transpired inside the Chili's to entirely discount Mobley's "expressed beliefs or intentions" about what occurred outside the Chili's. The court found that because Mobley was not directly involved in the earlier altercation inside the restaurant between Chico and Jason/Roly, but had acted as peacemaker, he could not have feared for his own life during the events which happened later outside the restaurant. However the events that occurred inside the Chili's are relevant only insofar as they provide the context for Mobley's actions when the attack outside the restaurant occurred.

It may have been more prudent for Mobley and Chico to skitter to their cars and hightail it out of there when they had the chance; however, as even the State concedes and the court below recognized, Mobley and Chico had every right to be where they were, doing what they were doing and they did nothing to precipitate this violent attack. The only relevant inquiry was whether, given the totality of the circumstances leading up to the attack, the appearance of danger was so real that a reasonably cautious and prudent person under the same circumstances would have believed that the danger could be avoided only through the use of deadly force.

Because the preponderance of the evidence demonstrates that had the proper standard been applied, Mobley's use of deadly force was justified, the motion to dismiss should have been granted. See Dennis v. State, 51 So.3d 456, 460 (Fla.2010) (confirming that, where a defendant claims immunity from prosecution under sections 776.012, 776.013 and 776.032, the court below must determine whether that defendant has shown by a preponderance of the evidence that the immunity attaches).

In so holding, we are mindful that, under our standard of review which is akin to that applied to the trial court's ruling on a motion to suppress, the trial court's ruling comes to this court "clothed with a presumption of correctness and the court must interpret the evidence and reasonable inferences and deductions derived therefrom in a manner most favorable to sustaining the trial court's ruling." Terry v. State, 668 So.2d 954, 958 (Fla.1996). Nevertheless, considering the entire record and reasonable inferences derived therefrom in a manner most favorable to the trial court's ruling, we nonetheless find there is no basis to support the trial court's decision to deny immunity in this case.

Petition granted.

Shepherd, C.J., concurs.

■ SALTER, J. (dissenting).

I respectfully dissent. Under the Stand Your Ground (SYG) immunity statute and applicable case law, the trial court is the initial fact finder regarding a defendant's claim of immunity. The SYG hearing is nothing more or less than a mini-trial conducted by the court without a jury on the fact-intensive issues framed by the statute: in the present case, did the defendant *reasonably* believe that *deadly force* was *necessary* to prevent *imminent death* or *great bodily harm* to himself or another or to prevent the *imminent commission of a forcible felony*? The defendant bears the burden of proving these elements by a preponderance of the evidence, and the trial court's findings of fact are presumptively correct for purposes of our review. Those findings can be reversed here only if they are not supported by competent substantial evidence. The trial court's legal conclusions are reviewed de novo.

Regarding the facts, four judges have now split evenly on whether the defendant's decisions to 1) take his Glock .45 out of the glove compartment of his truck, following a verbal altercation within the restaurant, and 2) fire five shots into the two decedents, after a single punch was thrown outside the restaurant, met the requirements for SYG immunity. One was the trial judge who actually heard and observed thirteen witnesses under oath and subjected to cross-examination. This Court was of course required to conduct its review of the testimony by reading it and without observing the witnesses as they testified.

The facts are also ambiguous when it comes to the surveillance video recorded by the camera affixed to the outside of the restaurant. Did deceased victim Carrazana appear to be reaching for a weapon, as the defendant testified? The video has only two frames per second (human vision is equivalent to 60 frames per second), and the camera caught the action from above and behind the incident. As described below, the few video freeze-frames of the incident seem to me to disprove, rather than prove the defendant's testimony. These uncertainties confirm that the defendant's claim is a classic, fact-based issue for the jury at trial.

Nor do I agree that the trial court committed any error of law in ruling on the defendant's motion. The trial court's reference to the defendant's conflicting statements regarding the fear that purportedly caused him to shoot both decedents—whether a fear of imminent death or great bodily harm to (a) himself, (b) Chico Correa, or (c) both of them—is a reflection (and not the only one) on the defendant's disparate accounts of the incident, going to credibility, and not a legal error (application of a "subjective" standard regarding the defendant's state of mind as opposed to an "objective" standard regarding a reasonably prudent person's state of mind), as characterized by the majority. For these reasons, we should deny the defendant's petition without prejudice to his right to present SYG immunity and self-defense as affirmative defenses at trial.

*Additional Facts*

A number of additional facts in the record before us warrant specific consideration. The first is that the defendant and his friend Mr. Correa went outside to smoke cigarettes three times during their visit to the restaurant on the evening in question. During the first and second of those cigarette breaks, the defendant was unarmed—his firearm was inside the glove compartment of his truck—and he was wearing a sun shirt. Only at the time of his third exit from the restaurant (after the verbal exchanges inside the restaurant, and after the defendant had told others that he planned to return home to his pregnant wife), did he instead unlock his truck, put on a sweatshirt, retrieve his firearm and holster from the glove compartment, and tuck the holstered firearm into his belt under the sweatshirt. Instead of going home to his wife as he had said, the defendant lingered on the sidewalk with Mr. Correa for a third, fateful smoke.

It was a cool February evening in Miami when the defendant had first arrived at the restaurant (well after 9:00 p.m.), but he had not put on his sweatshirt for the first and second cigarette breaks. He did not unlock his truck and put on his sweatshirt until the sweatshirt was used to cover his holster and Glock .45.

A second factual point for consideration is the punch thrown by Mr. Gonzalez at Mr. Correa's right eye. The testimony established that: Mr. Correa did not fall to the ground; his injury was treated with an ice pack at the scene; his vital signs were normal when he was checked by a fire rescue lieutenant at the scene after the incident; and he declined to be transported to an emergency room or other medical provider for treatment that night. Mr. Gonzalez's blow drew blood and, according to Mr. Correa's description of a later diagnosis, fractured his eye socket, but ordinarily an assessment of "great bodily harm" is a jury issue. Classification of Mr. Correa's injury as a forcible felony would also turn on whether the single punch intentionally or knowingly caused "great bodily harm, permanent disability, or permanent disfigurement."[14]

A third factual consideration involves the surveillance video of the incident and freeze-frame images from that video. The images do not corroborate the testimony by Mr. Correa and the defendant that the second decedent, Mr. Carrazana, seemed to be reaching under a jacket as if for a weapon. To the contrary, Mr. Carrazana is not fully visible in the images until time stamp label 23:54:09. In that image, the defendant was off the sidewalk, three feet or so into a vacant parking place, and Mr. Carrazana had both hands well away from his waistline, extended as in a normal gait. Both hands were visible and neither held a weapon. His sleeves were rolled up.

In the next frame, stamped 23:54:10, the defendant's line of sight to Mr. Carrazana was blocked by Mr. Gonzalez. In the very next frame, 23:54:11, both Mr. Gonzalez and Mr. Carrazana are staggering from the first gunshot or gunshots that hit them.[15] The evidence at the SYG hearing did not establish that either decedent carried a knife, displayed a knife, or that Mr. Correa or the defendant ever saw a knife before the defendant opened fire. The two restaurant knives later found outside the door (after the incident) were not shown by the defense to have been obtained, displayed, or held by either decedent at any time.

The fourth and final factual point warranting additional discussion is also pertinent in self-defense and SYG cases—the relative size and weight of the parties involved in an attack claimed to justify the use of deadly force. In the present case, the decedents were five feet, eight inches, and 217 pounds (Mr. Gonzalez), and five feet, six inches, and 156 pounds (Mr. Carrazana). Mr. Correa, punched by Mr. Gonzalez, was six feet, one inch, and 285 pounds, while the defendant was six feet, two inches, and weighed 285 pounds.

Having addressed these four additional factual points that were part of the record before the trial court, I next turn to the majority's conclusion that the trial court applied the incorrect legal standard to the evidence. As noted at the outset, the trial court's rulings on matters of law are subject to de novo review here.

*Montanez and the "Objective, Reasonable Person" Standard*

While I agree with the majority that the "objective, reasonable person" standard applies to an assessment of whether the use of deadly force is justifiable (under Montanez v. State, 24 So.3d 799, 803 (Fla. 2d

---

[14] Compare § 784.03(1), Fla. Stat. (2008) (misdemeanor battery) to § 784.041(1), Fla. Stat. (2008) (felony battery) and § 784.045, Fla. Stat. (2008) (aggravated battery, also a felony).

[Section 784.03(1) provides that a battery occurs when a person "[a]ctually and intentionally touches or strikes another person against the will of the other; or [i]ntentionally causes bodily harm to another person." Section 784.041(1) says that a felony battery occurs when a person "[a]ctually and intentionally touches or strikes another person against the will of the other; and [c]auses great bodily harm, permanent disability, or permanent disfigurement." Section 784.045 provides in relevant part that an aggravated battery occurs when a person "[i]ntentionally or knowingly causes great bodily harm, permanent disability, or permanent disfigurement; or [u]ses a deadly weapon."]—Addition to footnote by eds.

[15] The forensic evidence confirmed that one gunshot, fired from several feet away, hit Mr. Gonzalez (who had been in front of Mr. Carrazana and was closest to the defendant), who then turned and staggered several steps away from Mr. Mobley before collapsing and dying. Additional gunshots (also fired from several feet away) hit, and ultimately killed, Mr. Carrazana.

DCA 2010), and Fla. Std. Jury Instr. (Crim.) 3.6(f)), I disagree with the majority's further conclusions regarding the trial court's adherence to that standard and the remedy applicable to the alleged failure to apply that standard.

As to the argument that the trial court erroneously applied a subjective, state-of-the-defendant's mind standard, it must be remembered that the "objective, reasonable person" is not a hypothetical, unknowing stranger dropped into the altercation and the defendant's shoes a microsecond before Mr. Gonzalez punched Mr. Correa. The "objective, reasonable person" is a person situated in the same circumstances as the defendant and knowing what the defendant knew. *Montanez* at 803 n.6.

In the present case, the trial court correctly assessed those circumstances and the defendant's state of knowledge; the trial court did not otherwise dwell on the defendant's subjective state of mind or intentions. The fact-intensive determination of whether a reasonable and prudent person in the defendant's shoes might have perceived that Mr. Carrazana was reaching for a deadly weapon turned on the court's assessment of the defendant's credibility. The defendant and his friend of 17 years were the only living eyewitnesses to that important fact. The video and freeze-frame images did not definitively prove or disprove the reasonableness of that alleged perception—an alleged perception which turned out to be erroneous.

Simply stated, the justifiability of this defendant's use of force, or of a hypothetical "reasonably prudent person's" use of force, turns on a fact dependent on the defendant's credibility. The majority disagrees with the trial court regarding the trial court's assessment of the defendant's credibility, but that is an assessment to which we should defer. There is competent, substantial evidence in this record to support the trial court's determination that the defendant failed to prove his entitlement to immunity. In such a case, the petition should be denied.

My second departure from the majority's analysis involves the remedy that would be appropriate if it were established (though it has not been) that the trial court committed legal error by applying the wrong standard. The majority would grant the petition and thereby mandate the discharge of the defendant on grounds of immunity. However, since jeopardy never attached—the SYG hearing is a mini-bench trial on a jurisdictional issue—the correct remedy based on the majority's conclusion would be a remand to the trial court to apply the allegedly-correct legal standard and rule accordingly. That is the result when, for example, the trial court erroneously grants a motion to dismiss in a criminal case and we reverse and remand for reinstatement of the information.

*Conclusion*

For these reasons, I respectfully dissent. I would deny the defendant's petition for prohibition without prejudice to his rights to raise self-defense and SYG immunity as affirmative defenses and issues for resolution by a jury. I would also vacate this Court's order of August 15,

2013, which stayed criminal trial proceedings in this case pending further order of this Court.[a]

## NOTES ON THE FLORIDA STAND YOUR GROUND LAW

### 1. QUESTIONS AND COMMENTS

Not surprisingly, the Florida stand your ground law has its defenders and its critics. The Tampa Bay Times has published numerous articles on the topic. It keeps an on-line up-to-date case-by-case summary of the stand your ground cases that have arisen in Florida since 2005—well over 200 by now—introduced with the statements that "[c]ritics say 'stand your ground' turned Florida into the Wild West. Supporters say it has helped keep innocents out of jail."[a] The Times has written that:

> Florida's "stand your ground' " law has allowed drug dealers to avoid murder charges and gang members to walk free. It has stymied prosecutors and confused judges. It has also served its intended purpose, exonerating dozens of people who were deemed to be legitimately acting in self-defense. Among them: a woman who was choked and beaten by an irate tenant and a man who was threatened in his driveway by a felon.[b]

The same article quotes a defender of the law as follows:

> Donald Day is a Naples defense lawyer who has handled three "stand your ground" cases and believes the law is working "remarkably well."
>
> Day said the immunity hearings are a critical backstop in self-defense cases that should never go to a jury. Of the cases in the Times' database that have been resolved, 23 percent were dismissed by a judge after an immunity hearing. That means 38 defendants facing the prospect of a jury trial were set free by a judge who ruled the evidence leaned in their favor.
>
> "Where the defendant is clearly in the right and gets arrested, should you have to take your chance with what six people believe or don't believe?" Day said. "Judges are denying these motions where they should be denied and granting them in the limited number of cases statewide where they should be granted."

On the other side of the debate, an ABA Report recommends that stand your ground laws should be repealed for a number of reasons, among them because they lead to increased homicide rates and because implicit

---

[a] The Florida Supreme Court denied a petition for review, adding that "[n]o petition for rehearing will be entertained by the Court." State v. Mobley, 147 So.3d 527 (2014).—[Footnote by eds.]

[a] See http://www.tampabay.com/stand-your-ground-law/fatal-cases. See also http://www.tampabay.com/stand-your-ground-law/ for a chart as of June 2012 showing that about two-thirds of the people who raised self-defense claims after the adoption of the 2005 law were ultimately not punished (35% were not charged or their cases were dismissed by prosecutors; 23% were granted immunity by a judge; and 10% were acquitted by a jury). Of those convicted, 16% were found guilty by a jury and 16% accepted a plea bargain.

[b] http://www.tampabay.com/news/publicsafety/crime/florida-stand-your-ground-law-yields-some-shocking-outcomes-depending-on/1233133.

racial bias has been a significant factor in causing inconsistent outcomes.[c] The Report adds:

> Supporters of Stand Your Ground laws maintain that these laws afford law-abiding individuals fundamental self-defense rights. A [principal] legislative purpose of Stand Your Ground laws is to allow law abiding individuals to defend themselves without the fear of prosecution. Durell Peaden, the former Florida senator who initially sponsored Florida's Stand Your Ground law, explained that the legislature never intended for people who put themselves in harm's way to benefit from their use deadly force.
>
> Yet, anecdotal evidence suggests otherwise; it is habitual criminal offenders who are exploiting Stand Your Ground laws to avoid liability for their criminal offenses. On this issue, the Tampa Bay Times study reveals that of the 235 cases it examined, one-in-three defendants had been previously accused of violent crimes. For example, one defendant successfully invoked Florida's Stand Your Ground law in connection with drug charges on two separate occasions.

How should the stand your ground controversy be resolved? At the macro level, three issues must be considered.

The first is whether to have a retreat rule at all. The law of self-defense could be defined in terms of reasonable necessity to use deadly force without a statement of elaborate rules about when one is obligated to retreat and whether special considerations should govern retreat obligations that turn on the place where the defendant was attacked. The jury could simply be asked to consider the context and all of the circumstances as part of its judgment about whether deadly force was a reasonable response to the dangers presented.

The second is how to address the subject of retreat if the law is to speak specifically to the topic. One could, as the Model Penal Code has proposed, adopt a retreat rule that is narrowly confined to situations where deadly force is contemplated and the actor knows that retreat "with complete safety" is possible. And one could adopt a "castle" doctrine that is narrowly limited to one's home. Or one could go to the opposite extreme by adopting a rule, like Florida's, which expansively states that a person "does not have a duty to retreat and has the right to stand his or her ground" if the belief in the necessity of using deadly force is reasonable. One could also broadly define, again as Florida does, the places where the "castle" doctrine will apply. If the law is to address the topic, in other words, there are substantial questions about whether to place a thumb on the scale that favors retreat or a thumb that favors the use of defensive force. And once the overall philosophy has been determined, there are substantial questions of detail, specifically how much detail there should be and where lines in the sand should be drawn.

The third is raised by the Florida immunity rule. It would be possible, of course, to adopt a broad "stand your ground" philosophy and leave the issues to a properly instructed jury at the criminal trial. Or, as Florida and a number of other states have done, the law could go further and provide an opportunity to avoid criminal prosecution, as well perhaps as potential

---

[c] ABA National Task Force on Stand Your Ground Laws, Preliminary Report and Recommendations 11 (August 8, 2014).

civil liability, based on a pre-trial hearing before a judge.[d] An immunity hearing such as was involved in *Mobley* is virtually unknown in the criminal law. Normally, a defense is a defense and it is litigated along with all of the other issues in a criminal trial. But perhaps, as the Florida law reflects, the use of force in self-defense is justifiably different.

How should these various questions be addressed? At the micro level, what is the appropriate content of the law of self-defense as it relates to the use of deadly force? At an even more fine-grained level, did the court get the right answer in *Mobley*? Should that case have gone to trial? If it should have gone to trial, is the defect in the stand your ground law or in its application to the particular facts?

## 2. BURDEN OF PROOF

Everyone agrees that the defendant must bear the initial burden of production on the issue of self-defense in a criminal trial. But upon whom should the ultimate burden of persuasion be placed? The burden of persuasion in Florida on a self-defense claim at trial remains with the prosecutor beyond a reasonable doubt.[e] About a third of the states require the defendant to establish self-defense by a preponderance of the evidence or some similar standard.[f]

Now consider the immunity hearing involved in *Mobley*. In Dennis v. State, 51 So.3d 456, 460 (Fla.2010), as the majority says in *Mobley*, the Florida Supreme Court held that a defendant seeking immunity from trial under the stand your ground law is required to prove the facts necessary to establish the claim by a preponderance of the evidence at a pre-trial hearing devoted to that purpose. In a per curiam opinion in Bretherick v. State, 135 So.3d 337 (Fla. 5th DCA), a lower Florida appellate court paved the way for reconsideration of that question. It concluded:

> The issue of who bears the burden of proof may well be significant where the case is an extremely close one, or where only limited evidence is presented for the trial court's consideration. Because, as observed in Judge Schumann's thoughtful concurring opinion, the burden of proof issue was not the primary focus of the *Dennis* opinion, we certify the following question for consideration by the Florida Supreme Court:
>
> > Once the defense satisfies the initial burden of raising the issue, does the state have the burden of disproving a defendant's entitlement to self-defense immunity at a pretrial hearing as it does at trial?

The Florida Supreme Court accepted jurisdiction, indicating its willingness to reconsider the issue. See Bretherick v. State, 145 So.3d 821 (Fla. 2014).

Although she acknowledged that she was bound by the Supreme Court's ruling in *Dennis*, Judge Schumann's *Bretherick* concurrence argued

---

[d] The ABA National Task Force on Stand Your Ground Laws, Preliminary Report and Recommendations 50–51 (August 8, 2014), contains a chart showing that, of the 33 states that adhere to the stand your ground philosophy, seven allow for immunity from both criminal trial and civil liability—Alabama, Florida, Georgia, Kansas. Kentucky, North Carolina, and South Carolina—and 11 more authorize civil immunity only.

[e] See Jenkins v. State, 942 So.2d 910 (Fla. 2d DCA 2006).

[f] For an example, see Martin v. Ohio, 480 U.S. 228 (1987), where the Supreme Court upheld the constitutionality of such a rule.

that the burden of proof at the pre-trial hearing should be placed on the prosecution. She found persuasive two opinions from other states with laws derived from the Florida immunity provision.[g] She added that "[i]f the State is unable to sustain its lesser burden of proof at a pretrial hearing, then it would be unable to prove its case beyond a reasonable doubt at trial." And placing the burden of proof on the state at the pre-trial hearing

> creates a better procedural vehicle to test the State's case at the earliest possible stage of a criminal proceeding. Self-defense immunity statutes are designed to relieve a defendant from the burdens of criminal prosecution from arrest through trial. Placing the burden of proof on the State throughout each phase of criminal prosecution best fulfills the legislative intent to create a broad grant of immunity.

Judge Schumann seemed to assume, if the burden were to be placed on the prosecution, that a preponderance standard stated the right level of proof that should be required. Is this right? Would it not better "fulfill[ ] the legislative intent to create a broad grant of immunity" to require the prosecutor to rebut the claim of immunity, as it would have to do at trial, by proof beyond a reasonable doubt? On the other hand, is it best to leave the burden on the defendant? Whatever the level of proof required, does it disserve the public interest, not to speak of the value of human life, to require the prosecutor to run the gauntlet twice, once before the judge as fact-finder and again before the jury?

### 3. STAND YOUR GROUND VS. SELF-DEFENSE FOR BATTERED WOMEN

The next case considers the law of self-defense as it applies to battered women who kill their abusive husbands. Consider the following comment as the case is read:

> Battered Women's Syndrome remains the chief narrative available to women who fight back, and it is a narrative that forces women to plead for mercy, requiring them to subject their behavior to extensive scrutiny and evaluation by experts, lawyers, and juries. Stand Your Ground, the chief narrative by which men can now justify provoking deadly fights, allows men in some cases to escape evaluation altogether by granting them immunity from prosecution and even from arrest. This two-track system of self-defense—Battered Women's Syndrome for women and Stand Your Ground for men—has far-reaching implications outside of the courtroom. The use of Battered Women's Syndrome frequently sends the legal and social message that women should retreat even from their own homes in the face of objective, repeated harm to their bodies; Stand Your Ground sends the legal and social message that men can advance against strangers anywhere on the basis of vague, subjective perceptions of threats. Male violence is not only tolerated, but celebrated, whereas women's violence is not only discouraged, but stigmatized. Invoking the image of vulnerable women to promote aggressive self-defense rhetoric serves

[g] Rodgers v. Commonwealth, 285 S.W.3d 740 (Ky. 2009); State v. Ultreras, 296 Kan. 828, 295 P.3d 1020 (2013).

to distract from the reality that violence remains chiefly a male privilege.[h]

## State v. Kelly

Supreme Court of New Jersey, 1984.
97 N.J. 178, 478 A.2d 364.

■ WILENTZ, C.J. . . . On May 24, 1980, defendant, Gladys Kelly, stabbed her husband, Ernest, with a pair of scissors. He died shortly thereafter. . . .

Ms. Kelly was indicted for murder. At trial, she did not deny stabbing her husband, but asserted that her action was in self-defense. To establish the requisite state of mind for her self-defense claim, Ms. Kelly called Dr. Lois Veronen as an expert witness to testify about the battered-woman's syndrome. After hearing a lengthy voir dire examination of Dr. Veronen, the trial court ruled that expert testimony concerning the syndrome was inadmissible on the self-defense issue. . . . Apparently the court believed that the sole purpose of this testimony was to explain and justify defendant's perception of the danger rather than to show the objective reasonableness of that perception. Ms. Kelly was convicted of reckless manslaughter. . . .

The Kellys had a stormy [seven-year] marriage. Some of the details of their relationship, especially the stabbing, are disputed. The following is Ms. Kelly's version of what happened—a version that the jury could have accepted and, if they had, a version that would make the proffered expert testimony not only relevant, but critical.

The day after the marriage, Mr. Kelly got drunk and knocked Ms. Kelly down. Although a period of calm followed the initial attack, the next seven years were accompanied by periodic and frequent beatings, sometimes as often as once a week. During the attacks, which generally occurred when Mr. Kelly was drunk, he threatened to kill Ms. Kelly and to cut off parts of her body if she tried to leave him. Mr. Kelly often moved out of the house after an attack, later returning with a promise that he would change his ways. Until the day of the homicide, only one of the attacks had taken place in public.

[On the morning of the stabbing, Mr. Kelly] left for work. Ms. Kelly next saw her husband late that afternoon at a friend's house. She had gone there with her daughter, Annette, to ask Ernest for money to buy food. He told her to wait until they got home, and shortly thereafter the Kellys left. After walking past several houses, Mr. Kelly, who was drunk, angrily asked "What the hell did you come around here for?" He then grabbed the collar of her dress, and the two fell to the ground. He choked her by pushing his fingers against her throat, punched or hit her face, and bit her leg.

---

[h] Mary Anne Franks, Real Men Advance, Real Women Retreat: Stand Your Ground, Battered Women's Syndrome, And Violence As Male Privilege, 68 U. Miami L. Rev. 1099, 1102–03 (2014). The "image" referred to in the last sentence of the quotation was invoked by Marion Hammer, a former President of the National Rifle Association who is said to have written part of the 2005 Florida law or at the least was an influential lobbyist for it, when she said that the previous law required potential rape victims to retreat: "It required her to try to get away and run and be chased down by the perpetrator before she could then use force to protect herself." See id. at 1105. Franks attacks this argument as disingenuous hyperbole.—[Footnote by eds.]

A crowd gathered on the street. Two men from the crowd separated them, just as Gladys felt that she was "passing out" from being choked. Fearing that Annette had been pushed around in the crowd, Gladys then left to look for her. . . .

After finding her daughter, Ms. Kelly then observed Mr. Kelly running toward her with his hands raised. Within seconds he was right next to her. Unsure of whether he had armed himself while she was looking for their daughter, and thinking that he had come back to kill her, she grabbed a pair of scissors from her pocketbook. She tried to scare him away, but instead stabbed him.[1] . . .

In the past decade social scientists and the legal community began to examine the forces that generate and perpetuate wife beating and violence in the family.[2] What has been revealed is that the problem affects many more people than had been thought. . . .

Due to the high incidence of unreported abuse (the FBI and other law enforcement experts believe that wife abuse is the most unreported crime in the United States), estimates vary of the number of American women who are beaten regularly by their husband, boyfriend, or the dominant male figure in their lives. One recent estimate puts the number of women beaten yearly at over one million. The state police statistics show more than 18,000 *reported* cases of domestic violence in New Jersey during the first nine months of 1983, in 83% of which the victim was female. It is clear that the American home, once assumed to be the cornerstone of our society, is often a violent place.

While common law notions that assigned an inferior status to women, and to wives in particular, no longer represent the state of the law as reflected in statutes and cases, many commentators assert that a bias against battered women still exists, institutionalized in the attitudes of law enforcement agencies unwilling to pursue or uninterested in pursuing wife-beating cases. See Comment, The Battered Wife's Dilemma: Kill or be Killed, 32 Hastings L.J., 895, 897–911 (1981). . . .

As the problem of battered women has begun to receive more attention, sociologists and psychologists have begun to focus on the effects a sustained pattern of physical and psychological abuse can have on a woman. The effects of such abuse are what some scientific observers have termed "the battered-woman's syndrome," a series of common characteristics that appear in women who are abused physically and psychologically over an extended period of time by the dominant male figure in their lives. . . .

---

1 This version of the homicide—with a drunk Mr. Kelly as the aggressor both in pushing Ms. Kelly to the ground and again in rushing at her with his hands in a threatening position after the two had been separated—is sharply disputed by the state. The prosecution presented testimony intended to show that the initial scuffle was started by Gladys; that upon disentanglement, while she was restrained by bystanders, she stated that she intended to kill Ernest; that she then chased after him, and upon catching up with him stabbed him. . . .

2 The works that comprise the basic study of the problem of battered women are all relatively recent. See, e.g., Roger Langley & Richard C. Levy, Wife Beating: The Silent Crisis (1979); Del Martin, Battered Wives (1976); Lenore E. Walker, The Battered Woman (1979); Richard J. Gelles, The Violent Home: A Study of Physical Aggression Between Husbands and Wives (1971); Battered Women: A Psychosociological Study of Domestic Violence (Maria Roy ed. 1977).

According to Dr. [Lenore] Walker, relationships characterized by physical abuse tend to develop battering cycles. Violent behavior directed at the woman occurs in three distinct and repetitive stages that vary both in duration and intensity depending on the individuals involved.

Phase one of the battering cycle is referred to as the "tension-building stage," during which the battering male engages in minor battering incidents and verbal abuse while the woman, beset by fear and tension, attempts to be as placating and passive as possible in order to stave off more serious violence.

Phase two of the battering cycle is the "acute battering incident." At some point during phase one, the tension between the battered woman and the batterer becomes intolerable and more serious violence inevitable. The triggering event that initiates phase two is most often an internal or external event in the life of the battering male, but provocation for more severe violence is sometimes provided by the woman who can no longer tolerate or control her phase-one anger and anxiety.

Phase three of the battering cycle is characterized by extreme contrition and loving behavior on the part of the battering male. During this period the man will often mix his pleas for forgiveness and protestations of devotion with promises to seek professional help, to stop drinking,[5] and to refrain from further violence. For some couples, this period of relative calm may last as long as several months, but in a battering relationship the affection and contrition of the man will eventually fade and phase one of the cycle will start anew.

The cyclical nature of battering behavior helps explain why more women simply do not leave their abusers. The loving behavior demonstrated by the batterer during phase three reinforces whatever hopes these women might have for their mate's reform and keeps them bound to the relationship. Roger Langley & Richard C. Levy, Wife Beating: The Silent Crisis 112–14 (1977).

Some women may even perceive the battering cycle as normal, especially if they grew up in a violent household. Battered Women, A Psychosociological Study of Domestic Violence 60 (Maria Roy ed. 1977); Del Martin, Battered Wives, 60 (1981). Or they may simply not wish to acknowledge the reality of their situation. Terry Davidson, Conjugal Crime, at 50 (1978) ("The middle-class battered wife's response to her situation tends to be withdrawal, silence and denial . . . ").

Other women, however, become so demoralized and degraded by the fact that they cannot predict or control the violence that they sink into a state of psychological paralysis and become unable to take any action at all to improve or alter the situation. There is a tendency in battered women to believe in the omnipotence or strength of their battering husbands and thus to feel that any attempt to resist them is hopeless.

In addition to these psychological impacts, external social and economic factors often make it difficult for some women to extricate

---

[5] Alcohol is often an important component of violence toward women. Evidence points to a correlation between alcohol and violent acts between family members. In one British study, 44 of 100 cases of wife abuse occurred when the husband was drunk. John J. Gayford, Wife Battering: A Preliminary Survey of 100 Cases, 1 Brit. Med. J. 194–97 (1975). . . .

themselves from battering relationships. A woman without independent financial resources who wishes to leave her husband often finds it difficult to do so because of a lack of material and social resources.

Even with the progress of the last decade, women typically make less money and hold less prestigious jobs than men, and are more responsible for child care. Thus, in a violent confrontation where the first reaction might be to flee, women realize soon that there may be no place to go. Moreover, the stigma that attaches to a woman who leaves the family unit without her children undoubtedly acts as a further deterrent to moving out.

In addition, battered women, when they want to leave the relationship, are typically unwilling to reach out and confide in their friends, family, or the police, either out of shame and humiliation, fear of reprisal by their husband, or the feeling they will not be believed.

Dr. Walker and other commentators have identified several common personality traits of the battered woman: low self-esteem, traditional beliefs about the home, the family, and the female sex role, tremendous feelings of guilt that their marriages are failing, and the tendency to accept responsibility for the batterer's actions.

Finally, battered women are often hesitant to leave a battering relationship because, in addition to their hope of reform on the part of their spouse, they harbor a deep concern about the possible response leaving might provoke in their mates. They literally become trapped by their own fear. Case histories are replete with instances in which a battered wife left her husband only to have him pursue her and subject her to an even more brutal attack.

The combination of all these symptoms—resulting from sustained psychological and physical trauma compounded by aggravating social and economic factors—constitutes the battered-woman's syndrome. Only by understanding these unique pressures that force battered women to remain with their mates, despite their long-standing and reasonable fear of severe bodily harm and the isolation that being a battered woman creates, can a battered woman's state of mind be accurately and fairly understood.

The voir dire testimony of Dr. Veronen . . . conformed essentially to this outline of the battered-woman's syndrome. Dr. Veronen . . . documented, based on her own considerable experience in counseling, treating, and studying battered women, and her familiarity with the work of others in the field, the feelings of anxiety, self-blame, isolation, and, above all, fear that plagues these women and leaves them prey to a psychological paralysis that hinders their ability to break free or seek help. . . .

Dr. Veronen described the various psychological tests and examinations she had performed in connection with her independent research. These tests and their methodology, including their interpretation, are, according to Dr. Veronen, widely accepted by clinical psychologists. Applying this methodology to defendant (who was subjected to all of the tests, including a five-hour interview), Dr. Veronen concluded that defendant was a battered woman and subject to the battered-woman's syndrome.

In addition, Dr. Veronen was prepared to testify as to how, as a battered woman, Gladys Kelly perceived her situation at the time of the stabbing, and why, in her opinion, defendant did not leave her husband despite the constant beatings she endured.

Whether expert testimony on the battered-woman's syndrome should be admitted in this case depends on whether it is relevant to defendant's claim of self-defense, and, in any event, on whether the proffer meets the standards for admission of expert testimony in this state. We examine first the law of self-defense and consider whether the expert testimony is relevant. . . .

While it is not imperative that *actual* necessity exist, a valid plea of self-defense will not lie absent an actual (that is, honest) belief on the part of the defendant in the necessity of using force. [Further,] even when the defendant's belief in the need to kill in self-defense is conceded to be sincere, if it is found to have been unreasonable under the circumstances, such a belief cannot be held to constitute complete justification for a homicide. As with the determination of the existence of the defendant's belief, the question of the reasonableness of this belief "is to be determined by the jury, not the defendant, in light of the circumstances existing at the time of the homicide." . . .

Gladys Kelly claims that she stabbed her husband in self-defense, believing he was about to kill her. The gist of the state's case was that Gladys Kelly was the aggressor, that she consciously intended to kill her husband, and that she certainly was not acting in self-defense.

The credibility of Gladys Kelly is a critical issue in this case. If the jury does not believe Gladys Kelly's account, it cannot find she acted in self-defense. The expert testimony offered was directly relevant to one of the critical elements of that account, namely, what Gladys Kelly believed at the time of the stabbing, and was thus material to establish the honesty of her stated belief that she was in imminent danger of death.[10] . . .

As can be seen from our discussion of the expert testimony, Dr. Veronen would have bolstered Gladys Kelly's credibility. Specifically, by showing that her experience, although concededly difficult to comprehend, was common to that of other women who had been in similarly abusive relationships, Dr. Veronen would have helped the jury understand that Gladys Kelly could have honestly feared that she would suffer serious bodily harm from her husband's attacks, yet still remain with him. This, in turn, would support Ms. Kelly's testimony about her state of mind (that is, that she honestly feared serious bodily harm) at the time of the stabbing. . . .

We also find the expert testimony relevant to the reasonableness of defendant's belief that she was in imminent danger of death or serious injury. We do not mean that the expert's testimony could be used to

---

[10] The factual contentions of the parties eliminated any issue concerning the duty to retreat. If the state's version is accepted, defendant is the aggressor; if defendant's version is accepted, the possibility of retreat is excluded by virtue of the nature of the attack that defendant claims took place. We do not understand that the state claims defendant breached that duty under any version of the facts. If, however, the duty becomes an issue on retrial, the trial court will have to determine the relevancy of the battered-woman's syndrome to that issue. Without passing on that question, it appears to us to be a different question from whether the syndrome is relevant to defendant's failure to leave her husband in the past.

show that it was understandable that a battered woman might believe that her life was in danger when indeed it was not and when a reasonable person would not have so believed. . . . . Expert testimony in that direction would be relevant solely to the honesty of defendant's belief, not its objective reasonableness. Rather, our conclusion is that the expert's testimony, if accepted by the jury, would have aided it in determining whether, under the circumstances, a reasonable person would have believed there was imminent danger to her life.

At the heart of the claim of self-defense was defendant's story that she had been repeatedly subjected to "beatings" over the course of her marriage. While defendant's testimony was somewhat lacking in detail, a juror could infer from the use of the word "beatings," as well as the detail given concerning some of these events (the choking, the biting, the use of fists), that these physical assaults posed a risk of serious injury or death. When that regular pattern of serious physical abuse is combined with defendant's claim that the decedent sometimes threatened to kill her, defendant's statement that on this occasion she thought she might be killed when she saw Mr. Kelly running toward her could be found to reflect a reasonable fear; that is, it could so be found if the jury believed Gladys Kelly's story of the prior beatings, if it believed her story of the prior threats, and, of course, if it believed her story of the events of that particular day.

The crucial issue of fact on which this expert's testimony would bear is why, given such allegedly severe and constant beatings, combined with threats to kill, defendant had not long ago left decedent. Whether raised by the prosecutor as a factual issue or not, our own common knowledge tells us that most of us, including the ordinary juror, would ask himself or herself just such a question. And our knowledge is bolstered by the experts' knowledge, for the experts point out that one of the common myths, apparently believed by most people, is that battered wives are free to leave. To some, this misconception is followed by the observation that the battered wife is masochistic, proven by her refusal to leave despite the severe beatings; to others, however, the fact that the battered wife stays on unquestionably suggests that the "beatings" could not have been too bad for if they had been, she certainly would have left. The expert could clear up these myths, by explaining that one of the common characteristics of a battered wife is her *inability* to leave despite such constant beatings; her "learned helplessness"; her lack of anywhere to go; her feeling that if she tried to leave, she would be subjected to even more merciless treatment; her belief in the omnipotence of her battering husband; and sometimes her hope that her husband will change his ways.

Unfortunately, in this case the state reinforced the myths about battered women. On cross-examination, when discussing an occasion when Mr. Kelly temporarily moved out of the house, the state repeatedly asked Ms. Kelly: "You wanted him back, didn't you?" The implication was clear: domestic life could not have been too bad if she wanted him back. In its closing argument, the state trivialized the severity of the beatings, saying:

> I'm not going to say they happened or they didn't happen, but life isn't pretty. Life is not a bowl of cherries. [E]ach and every person who takes a breath has problems. Defense

counsel says bruised and battered. Is there any one of us who hasn't been battered by life in some manner or means?

Even had the state not taken this approach, however, expert testimony would be essential to rebut the general misconceptions regarding battered women. . . .

Since a retrial is necessary, we think it advisable to indicate the limit of the expert's testimony on this issue of reasonableness. It would not be proper for the expert to express the opinion that defendant's belief on that day was reasonable, not because this is the ultimate issue, but because the area of *expert* knowledge relates, in this regard, to the reasons for defendant's failure to leave her husband. Either the jury accepts or rejects that explanation and, based on that, credits defendant's stories about the beatings she suffered. No expert is needed, however, once the jury has made up its mind on those issues, to tell the jury the logical conclusion, namely, that a person who has in fact been severely and continuously beaten might very well reasonably fear that the imminent beating she was about to suffer could be either life-threatening or pose a risk of serious injury. What the expert could state was that defendant had the battered-woman's syndrome, and could explain that syndrome in detail, relating its characteristics to defendant, but only to enable the jury better to determine the honesty and reasonableness of defendant's belief. Depending on its content, the expert's testimony might also enable the jury to find that the battered wife, because of the prior beatings, numerous beatings, as often as once a week, for seven years, from the day they were married to the day he died, is particularly able to predict accurately the likely extent of violence in any attack on her. That conclusion could significantly affect the jury's evaluation of the reasonableness of defendant's fear for her life.[13]

Having determined that testimony about the battered-woman's syndrome is relevant, we now consider whether Dr. Veronen's testimony satisfies the limitations placed on expert testimony by Evidence Rule 56(2) and by applicable case law. . . .

As previously discussed, a battering relationship embodies psychological and societal features that are not well understood by lay observers. Indeed, these features are subject to a large group of myths and

---

[13] At least two other courts agree that expert testimony about the battered-woman's syndrome is relevant to show the reasonableness as well as the honesty of defendant's fear of serious bodily harm. . . .

Defendant's counsel at oral argument made it clear that defendant's basic contention was that her belief in the immediate need to use deadly force was both honest and reasonable; and that the evidence concerning the battered-woman's syndrome was being offered solely on that issue. We therefore are not faced with any claim that a battered woman's honest belief in the need to use deadly force, even if objectively unreasonable, constitutes justification so long as its unreasonableness results from the psychological impact of the beatings. The effect of cases like State v. Sikora, 44 N.J. 453, 210 A.2d 193 (1965) (opinion of psychiatrist that acts of defendant, admittedly sane, were predetermined by interaction of events and his abnormal character held inadmissible on issue of premeditation), and State v. Bess, 53 N.J. 10, 247 A.2d 669 (1968) (reasonableness of belief in need for deadly force not measured by what would appear "reasonable" to abnormal defendant) is not before us. Nor is there any claim that the battering provocation might have some legal effect beyond the potential reduction of defendant's culpability to manslaughter, or that something other than an "immediate" need for deadly force will suffice. See State v. Felton, 110 Wis.2d 485, 329 N.W.2d 161 (1983) (battered wife stabs sleeping husband).

stereotypes. It is clear that this subject is beyond the ken of the average juror and thus is suitable for explanation through expert testimony.

The second requirement that must be met before expert testimony is permitted is a showing that the proposed expert's testimony would be reliable. The rationale for this requirement is that expert testimony seeks to assist the trier of fact. An expert opinion that is not reliable is of no assistance to anyone.

[J]udicial opinions thus far have been split concerning the scientific acceptability of the syndrome and the methodology used by the researchers in this area. [T]he record before us reveals that the battered woman's syndrome has a sufficient scientific basis to produce uniform and reasonably reliable results. . . . The numerous books, articles and papers referred to earlier indicate the presence of a growing field of study and research about the battered woman's syndrome and recognition of the syndrome in the scientific field. However, while the record before us could require such a ruling, we refrain from conclusively ruling that Dr. Veronen's proffered testimony about the battered-woman's syndrome would satisfy New Jersey's standard of acceptability for scientific evidence. This is because the state was not given a full opportunity in the trial court to question Dr. Veronen's methodology in studying battered women or her implicit assertion that the battered-woman's syndrome has been accepted by the relevant scientific community. . . . [23]

[The Court reversed the conviction and remanded for a new trial.]

■ HANDLER, J., concurring in part and dissenting in part. . . . The court in this case takes a major stride in recognizing the scientific authenticity of battered women's syndrome and its legal and factual significance in the trial of certain criminal cases. My difference with the court is quite narrow. I believe that defendant Gladys Kelly has demonstrated at her trial by sufficient expert evidence her entitlement to the use of the battered women's syndrome in connection with her defense of self-defense. I would therefore not require this issue—the admissibility of the battered women's syndrome—to be tried again. . . .

---

[23] We note that under the Code even if it is certain that the actor's life will soon be threatened, the actor may not use deadly defensive force until that threat is imminent. . . . The requirement that the use of deadly force, in order to be justifiable, must be immediately necessary, has as its purpose the preservation of life by preventing the use of deadly force except when its need is beyond debate. The rule's presumed effect on an actor who reasonably fears that her life will soon be endangered by an imminent threat is to cause her to leave the danger zone, especially if, because of the circumstances, she knows she will be defenseless when that threat becomes imminent. The rule, in effect, tends to protect the life of both the potential aggressor and victim. If, however, the actor is unable to remove herself from the zone of danger (a psychological phenomenon common to battered women, according to the literature), the effect of the rule may be to prevent her from exercising the right of self-defense at the only time it would be effective. Instead she is required by the rule to wait until the threat against her life is imminent before she responds, at which time she may be completely defenseless.

There is, of course, some danger that any attempt to mitigate what may be undeserved punishment in these cases (by some further statutory differentiation of criminal responsibility) might weaken the general deterrent effect of our homicide laws. That is a matter the legislature might wish to examine.

## NOTES ON DOMESTIC VIOLENCE AND THE LAW OF SELF-DEFENSE

### 1.   QUESTIONS AND COMMENTS ON *KELLY*

The issue raised in *Kelly* has been widely litigated in the last two decades. Most courts have allowed testimony concerning the battered woman syndrome to be admitted in this context if offered by a qualified expert. See *Most courts allow* Laurie Kratky Dore, Downward Adjustment and the Slippery Slope: The Use of Duress in Defense of Battered Offenders, 56 Ohio St. L. J. 665, 683–84 n.77 (1995) ("Today, courts uniformly regard the battered woman syndrome as generally accepted scientific evidence, and, subject to case-specific relevance and expert qualifications, admissible in support of self-defense."). The Court of Criminal Appeals of Oklahoma has remarked, "[t]o date, 31 states and the District of Columbia allow the use of expert testimony on the subject. Five states [have] acknowledged its validity, but held the testimony inadmissible based on the facts of the particular case." Bechtel v. State, 840 P.2d 1 (Okla.Crim.App.1992).

One of the disputes regarding testimony on the battered woman syndrome has focused on its scientific merit.[a] Once that debate is resolved in favor of the scientific validity of such evidence, the critical question is whether the testimony is relevant to a self-defense claim. According to *Kelly*, the syndrome describes "a series of common characteristics that appear in women" who are the victims of domestic abuse. What are those characteristics? To which elements of the self-defense claim are the characteristics relevant? Why does the expert testimony (assuming that the jury accepts it) tend to support a finding that Kelly's fear of her husband was "objectively reasonable," as the court asserts?

James Acker and Hans Toch argue that the probative value of testimony concerning battered woman syndrome is outweighed by its tendency to expand the scope of self-defense beyond the bounds of lawful justification:

*Acker + Toch expand scope of self-defense*

> When the prior bad acts (the repeated beatings) and the bad character ("battering husband") of the deceased are made principal issues, this through the supportive testimony of an expert witness, the classic defense stratagem of "blaming the victim" for his own demise has been interjected before the jury. This "defense" has been dignified by the "syndrome" concept which draws attention to the prevalence of domestic victimization in society, and which makes the victim and the deceased examples of this problem. The killing of a battering husband could be "justified" in the jurors' minds not because it was necessary that a battered woman act with responsive deadly force when she was threatened with death or serious bodily injury by her mate but because it was a fitting act of retribution directed at a member of a sadistic fraternity who had finally reaped his just deserts.

*worry is that retribution is taken over into court instead of threat*

James Acker and Hans Toch, Battered Women, Straw Men, and Expert Testimony: A Comment on State v. Kelly, 21 Crim.L.Bull. 125 (1985). Is this argument persuasive? The risk of distortion described by Acker and Toch appears to exist even without the expert testimony. Kelly was entitled to testify, and introduce corroborative evidence, about her husband's prior

---

[a]   See generally John Monahan & Laurens Walker, Social Science in Law: Cases and Materials 465–73 (2002).

acts of violence against her. Moreover, on the facts presented, she was entitled to an instruction on self-defense. Does the expert testimony enhance the risk of distortion?

## 2. BATTERED WOMAN SYNDROME AND IMMINENCE

Unlike Acker and Toch, some commentators argue that the battered woman syndrome is valuable precisely because it may lead lawmakers to relax the requirements of self-defense. One such requirement is that the threat of harm confronting the actor be "imminent." In *Kelly*, the court mentioned that this requirement might not be satisfied in some cases where women kill abusive men. As the court explained, the imminence requirement is designed to protect both "the potential aggressor and victim" from deadly harm: "The rule's presumed effect on an actor who reasonably fears that her life will soon be endangered by an imminent threat is to cause her to leave the danger zone. . . ." However, the court questioned whether the imminence requirement achieves a just result in cases involving battered women. "If . . . the actor is unable to remove herself from the zone of danger (a psychological phenomenon common to battered women, according to the literature), the effect of the rule may be to prevent her from exercising the right of self-defense at the only time it would be effective. Instead she is required by the rule to wait until the threat against her life is imminent before she responds, at which time she may be completely defenseless."

Responding to these concerns, some commentators have asserted that it may be necessary for a woman to kill her abuser even though at the time she does so he presents no imminent harm because "he has already finished beating her, has only threatened to attack her at some time in the future, or has even fallen asleep." Kit Kinports, Defending Battered Women's Self-Defense Claims, 67 Or. L. Rev. 393, 425 (1988). Kinports argues:

> [T]he battered woman may reasonably believe that any other efforts to avoid her husband's violence are futile. For a variety of reasons, she may reasonably feel that she cannot escape from her husband and that she cannot rely on the police for meaningful help. Moreover, any attempt to defend herself while her husband is beating her is likely to be useless because of the substantial disparity in their size and strength and because efforts to resist typically further infuriate the attacker. Thus, the battered woman may come to believe that her only options are killing herself, letting her husband kill her, or killing him—and, in addition, that her only opportunity to kill him is in a nonconfrontational setting.

According to psychologist Julie Blackman, battered women sometimes perceive that they must use deadly force to repel threats of future harm. Based on the previous pattern of violence, battered women "can detect changes or signs of novelty in the pattern of normal violence that connote increased danger." She recounts the case of Madelyn Diaz, a 24-year-old who was married to a policeman who had frequently beaten her, had often coerced compliance with his wishes by threatening her with his gun, and had used his gun once to compel her to have sex with a stranger. She described the final provocation as follows:

> The night before she killed him, Madelyn and her husband had an argument. He was drunk and wanted to have sex with her. She refused. . . . He said that if she did not change [her attitude]

> by the following day, he would "blow the baby's brains out." He took his gun and placed it against the head of their six month old daughter as he made this threat. . . . Following this exchange, they both went to sleep. In the morning, Madelyn woke up before her husband. She dressed her children and took them outside to the car to go grocery shopping. She then realized she had forgotten her money. She went back into the apartment and went to the drawer where they kept their money. Her husband's gun was in the same drawer. She took the gun from the drawer; as she did, she relived the moment of his threat against their daughter. She later reported that she could see him holding his gun to the baby's head—something he had never done before, a novel form of violence for him. She fired twice into his sleeping body. . . . .

Julie Blackman, Potential Uses for Expert Testimony: Ideas Toward the Representation of Battered Women Who Kill, 9 Women's Rts. L. Rptr. 227, 236–37 (1986). At Diaz's trial for second-degree murder, Blackman provided expert testimony on behalf of the defense, and Diaz "was acquitted on the grounds of self-defense." In Blackman's estimation, the verdict reflected the jurors' "acceptance . . . of the idea that a perception of future, inescapable danger could provide sufficient grounds for reasonable, self-defensive, life-taking action—even when the source of the danger was asleep."

Should the imminence requirement be replaced by a standard that authorizes the use of deadly force to repel a "future, inescapable danger"? Under what circumstances is a future danger "inescapable"? Was the danger "inescapable" in *Diaz*?

Most appellate courts that have considered the question have held that the imminence element is not satisfied by a showing that the actor faced threats of future physical violence or harm. In particular, the courts have been inclined to rebuff self-defense claims made by battered women who killed their mates when the men were asleep. According to the Kansas Supreme Court, for example, "a battered woman cannot reasonably fear imminent life-threatening danger from her sleeping spouse." State v. Stewart, 243 Kan. 639, 763 P.2d 572 (1988). *Stewart* emphasized that "the existence of the battered woman syndrome in and of itself" does not provide a defense to homicide, and it refused to relax the imminence requirement in the context of domestic abuse.

One of the most often-cited battered woman cases, State v. Norman, 324 N.C. 253, 378 S.E.2d 8 (1989), is to the same effect. In *Norman*, the defendant shot her husband three times in the back of his head while he was sleeping in his bed. She was indicted for first-degree murder. The trial judge refused to charge the jury on self-defense, and Ms. Norman was convicted of voluntary manslaughter. On appeal, the Court of Appeals of North Carolina reversed the conviction on the ground that the trial judge had erred in failing to give a self-defense instruction. The Supreme Court of North Carolina reversed and reinstated the verdict. To support its judgment that no self-defense charge was warranted, the court provided an extensive summary of the evidence, which chronicled the brutal abuse and degradation inflicted by the decedent on his wife. Some of the facts in evidence were these:

> [After she shot and killed her husband, the defendant made a statement to a deputy sheriff in which she described the events that took place immediately before the shooting.] The defendant

[said] that her husband had been beating her all day and had made her lie down on the floor while he slept on the bed. After her husband fell asleep, the defendant carried her grandchild to the defendant's mother's house. The defendant took a pistol from her mother's purse and walked the short distance back to her home. She pointed the pistol at the back of her sleeping husband's head, but it jammed the first time she tried to shoot him. She fixed the gun and then shot her husband in the back of the head as he lay sleeping. After one shot, she felt her husband's chest and determined that he was still breathing and making sounds. She then shot him twice more in the back of the head. The defendant [stated] that she killed her husband because "she took all she was going to take from him so she shot him."

The defendant [also] presented evidence tending to show a long history of physical and mental abuse by her husband due to his alcoholism. At the time of the killing, the 39-year-old defendant and her husband had been married almost 25 years and had several children. The defendant testified that her husband had started drinking and abusing her about five years after they were married. His physical abuse of her consisted of frequent assaults that included slapping, punching and kicking her, striking her with various objects, and throwing glasses, beer bottles and other objects at her. The defendant described other specific incidents of abuse, such as her husband putting her cigarettes out on her, throwing hot coffee on her, breaking glass against her face and crushing food on her face. Although the defendant did not present evidence of ever having received medical treatment for any physical injuries inflicted by her husband, she displayed several scars about her face which she attributed to her husband's assaults.

The defendant's evidence also tended to show other indignities inflicted upon her by her husband. Her . . . husband did not work and forced her to make money by prostitution, and he made humor of that fact to family and friends. He would beat her if she resisted going out to prostitute herself or if he was unsatisfied with the amounts of money she made. He routinely called the defendant "dog," "bitch" and "whore," and on a few occasions made her eat pet food out of the pets' bowls and bark like a dog. He often made her sleep on the floor. At times, he deprived her of food and refused to let her get food for the family. During those years of abuse, the defendant's husband threatened numerous times to kill her and to maim her in various ways.

The defendant said her husband's abuse occurred only when he was intoxicated, but that he would not give up drinking. She . . . and her husband "got along very well when he was sober," and . . . he was "a good guy" when he was not drunk. She had accompanied her husband to the local mental health center for sporadic counseling sessions for his problem, but he continued to drink.

In the early morning hours on the day before his death, the defendant's husband, who was intoxicated, went to a rest area off I–85 near Kings Mountain where the defendant was engaging in prostitution and assaulted her. While driving home, he was stopped by a patrolman and jailed on a charge of driving while impaired. After the defendant's mother got him out of jail at the defendant's request later that morning, he resumed his drinking and abuse of the defendant.

The defendant's . . . husband seemed angrier than ever after he was released from jail and . . . his abuse of the defendant was more frequent. That evening, sheriff's deputies were called to the Norman residence, and the defendant complained that her husband had been beating her all day and she could not take it anymore. The defendant was advised to file a complaint, but she said she was afraid her husband would kill her if she had him arrested. The deputies told her they needed a warrant before they could arrest her husband, and they left the scene.

The deputies were called back less than an hour later after the defendant had taken a bottle of pills. The defendant's husband cursed her and called her names as she was attended by paramedics, and he told them to let her die. A sheriff's deputy finally chased him back into his house as the defendant was put into an ambulance. The defendant's stomach was pumped at the local hospital, and she was sent home with her mother.

While in the hospital, the defendant was visited by a therapist with whom she discussed filing charges against her husband and having him committed for treatment. [The] defendant agreed to go to the mental health center the next day to discuss those possibilities. The therapist testified at trial that the defendant seemed depressed in the hospital, and that she expressed considerable anger toward her husband. He testified that the defendant threatened a number of times that night to kill her husband and that she said she should kill him "because of the things he had done to her."

The next day, the day she shot her husband, the defendant went to the mental health center to talk about charges and possible commitment, and she confronted her husband with that possibility. She testified that she told her husband later that day: "J. T., straighten up. Quit drinking. I'm going to have you committed to help you." She said her husband then told her he would "see them coming" and would cut her throat before they got to him.

The defendant also went to the social services office that day to seek welfare benefits, but her husband followed her there, interrupted her interview and made her go home with him. He continued his abuse of her, threatening to kill and to maim her, slapping her, kicking her, and throwing objects at her. At one point, he took her cigarette and put it out on her, causing a small burn on her upper torso. He would not let her eat or bring food into the house for their children.

That evening, the defendant and her husband went into their bedroom to lie down, and he called her a "dog" and made her lie on the floor when he lay down on the bed. Their daughter brought in her baby to leave with the defendant, and the defendant's husband agreed to let her baby-sit. After the defendant's husband fell asleep, the baby started crying and the defendant took it to her

> mother's house so it would not wake up her husband. She returned shortly with the pistol and killed her husband.
>
> The defendant testified . . . that she was too afraid of her husband to press charges against him or to leave him. She said that she had temporarily left their home on several previous occasions, but he had always found her, brought her home and beaten her. Asked why she killed her husband, the defendant replied: "Because I was scared of him and I knowed when he woke up, it was going to be the same thing, and I was scared when he took me to the truck stop that night it was going to be worse than he had ever been. I just couldn't take it no more. There ain't no way, even if it means going to prison. It's better than living in that. That's worse hell than anything."
>
> The defendant and other witnesses testified that for years her husband had frequently threatened to kill her and to maim her. When asked if she believed those threats, the defendant replied: "Yes. I believed him; he would, he would kill me if he got a chance. If he thought he wouldn't a had to went to jail, he would a done it."

The Court of Appeals of North Carolina held that the foregoing evidence supported a jury instruction on self-defense. In effect, the court reasoned that the criminal law's commitment to the preservation of human life, which is embodied in the imminence requirement, must take account of the "realities" of the defendant's condition, including her "learned helplessness," her terror of seeking help from authorities, and her vulnerability to her husband. In that court's view, "[g]iven the characteristics of battered spouse syndrome, we do not believe that a battered person must wait until a deadly attack occurs or that the victim must in all cases be actually attacking or threatening to attack at the very moment defendant commits the unlawful act for the battered person to act in self-defense." Thus, it would be proper for jurors to hold that the killing was a justified act of self-defense if they found "that decedent's sleep was but a momentary hiatus in a continuous reign of terror by the decedent and that defendant merely took advantage of her first opportunity to protect herself."

Over a sharp dissent by Justice Martin, the Supreme Court of North Carolina reversed. The court explicitly rejected the Court of Appeals' effort to revise the elements of self-defense in cases involving battered persons. Moreover, it concluded that the evidence "would not support a finding that the defendant killed her husband due to a reasonable fear of imminent death or great bodily harm, as is required before a defendant is entitled to jury instructions concerning . . . self-defense."

> [The defendant's expert witness testified that] defendant "believed herself to be doomed . . . to a life of the worst kind of torture and abuse, degradation that she had experienced over the years in a progressive way; that it would only get worse, and that death was inevitable." Such evidence of the defendant's speculative beliefs concerning her remote and indefinite future, while indicating she had felt generally threatened, did not tend to show that she killed in the belief—reasonable or otherwise—that her husband presented a threat of *imminent* death or great bodily harm. Under our law of self-defense, a defendant's subjective belief of what might be "inevitable" at some indefinite point in the future does

not equate to what she believes to be "imminent." Dr. Tyson's opinion that the defendant believed it was necessary to kill her husband for "the protection of herself and her family" was similarly indefinite and devoid of time frame and did not tend to show a threat or fear of *imminent* harm.

The defendant testified that, "I knowed when he woke up, it was going to be the same thing, and I was scared when he took me to the truck stop that night it was going to be worse than he had ever been." She also testified, when asked if she believed her husband's threats: "Yes. . . . [H]e would kill me if he got a chance. If he thought he wouldn't a had to went to jail, he would a done it." Testimony about such indefinite fears concerning what her sleeping husband might do at some time in the future did not tend to establish a fear—reasonable or otherwise—of *imminent death or great bodily harm* at the time of the killing.

We are not persuaded by the reasoning of our Court of Appeals in this case that when there is evidence of battered wife syndrome, neither an actual attack nor threat of attack by the husband at the moment the wife uses deadly force is required to justify the wife's killing of him in perfect self-defense. The Court of Appeals concluded that to impose such requirements would ignore the "learned helplessness," meekness and other realities of battered wife syndrome and would effectively preclude such women from exercising their right of self-defense.

The reasoning of our Court of Appeals . . . proposes to change the established law of self-defense by giving the term "imminent" a meaning substantially more indefinite and all-encompassing than its present meaning. This would result in a substantial relaxation of the requirement of real or apparent necessity to justify homicide. Such reasoning proposes justifying the taking of human life not upon the reasonable belief it is necessary to prevent death or great bodily harm—which the imminence requirement ensures—but upon purely subjective speculation that the decedent probably would present a threat to life at a future time and that the defendant would not be able to avoid the predicted threat.

. . . Such predictions of future assaults to justify the defendant's use of deadly force in this case would be entirely speculative because there was no evidence that her husband had ever inflicted any harm upon her that approached life-threatening injury, even during the "reign of terror." It is far from clear in the defendant's poignant evidence that any abuse by the decedent had ever involved the degree of physical threat required to justify the defendant in using deadly force, even when those threats were imminent. The use of deadly force in self-defense to prevent harm other than death or great bodily harm is excessive as a matter of law.

[We decline to stretch] the law of self-defense to fit the facts of this case [because doing so] would weaken our assurances that justification for the taking of human life remains firmly rooted in real or apparent necessity. [The] result in principle could not be limited to a few cases decided on evidence as poignant as this. The relaxed requirements for perfect self-defense proposed by our

Court of Appeals would tend to categorically legalize the opportune killing of abusive husbands by their wives solely on the basis of the wives' testimony concerning their subjective speculation as to the probability of future felonious assaults by their husbands. Homicidal self-help would then become a lawful solution, and perhaps the easiest and most effective solution, to this problem.

Martha Mahoney criticizes *Stewart* and *Norman* for ignoring the fact that both defendants attempted to leave their violent marriages and that their husbands responded by escalating the abuse. Rather than engaging in vigilante action, as the courts implied, the women were "hostages" who resisted death at their "captors' " hands. Mahoney concludes, "We believe the danger to a hostage is imminent *both* because the force used to hold them there is apparent *and* because our cultural knowledge includes the memory of the many hostages who have been harmed in the past." Martha R. Mahoney, Legal Images of Battered Women: Redefining the Issue of Separation, 90 Mich. L. Rev. 1, 92–93 (1991).

Does Mahoney's "hostage" metaphor answer the concerns raised by *Stewart* and *Norman*? Consider a hypothetical offered by Paul Robinson:

> Suppose *A* kidnaps and confines *D* with the announced intention of killing him one week later. *D* has an opportunity to kill *A* and escape each morning as A brings him his daily ration. Taken literally, the imminence requirement would prevent *D* from using deadly force in self-defense until *A* is standing over him with a knife, but that outcome seems inappropriate. . . . The proper inquiry is not the immediacy of the threat but the immediacy of the response necessary in defense. If a threatened harm is such that it cannot be avoided if the intended victim waits until the last moment, the principle of self-defense must permit him to act earlier—as early as is required to defend himself effectively.

2 Paul H. Robinson, Criminal Law Defenses 78 (1984). Is the battered woman's predicament analogous to the case Robinson describes?

### 3. FEMINIST PERSPECTIVES ON THE BATTERED WOMAN SYNDROME

As *Kelly* recounts, commentators from a variety of disciplines claim that testimony concerning battered woman syndrome assists in rebutting sexist "myths and misconceptions" about women who are victims of domestic abuse. Feminist lawyers first encountered these "myths and misconceptions" when defending women charged with murdering abusive men. In Representation of Women Who Defend Themselves in Response to Physical or Sexual Assault, 4 Women's Rts. L. Rptr. 149, 153–57 (1978), Elizabeth M. Schneider and Susan B. Jordan observed more than 35 years ago that the law of self-defense developed in response to "male models and expectations" and that it therefore fails to reflect the circumstances under which women resort to lethal force. The stereotype is a man protecting his home, his family, the chastity of his wife, or repelling a violent attack and his violent response "conforms to the expectation that a real man would fight to the death to protect his pride and property." The stereotypical woman on which the law was based was "viewed as responding hysterically and inappropriately to physical threat" with the result that women were "relegated . . . to a position of second-class status with respect to their abilities to defend themselves." The solution is that

> the special circumstances which may require a woman to use a weapon must be fully explained in the trial, [for example, disparities in size and strength, differential socialization experiences, the fact that a women might perceive the male's fist or body to be a deadly weapon]. The jury must be allowed to consider the [woman's] possible need to resort to a weapon when faced with an unarmed assailant. This approach equalizes the application of the law to women by incorporating the woman's perspective into the deadly force standard and other standards of self-defense.

Elizabeth M. Schneider and Susan B. Jordan, Representation of Women Who Defend Themselves in Response to Physical or Sexual Assault, 4 Women's Rts. L. Rptr. 149, 153–57 (1978). Building on these observations, feminist lawyers began to promote the syndrome testimony as one method for educating judges and jurors about women's perceptions and experiences of violence.

For example, Kit Kinports asserts that the syndrome testimony helps jurors to understand that the woman's lethal conduct was "reasonable" because the expert witness "describes the emotions and reactions that any woman who has experienced spousal abuse for an extended period of time is likely to exhibit." Kit Kinports, Defending Battered Women's Self-Defense Claims, 67 Or. L. Rev. 393, 417 (1988). Kinports also argues that the testimony establishes that the "emotions and reactions" that prompt the woman to kill do not support the imposition of criminal blame:

> . . . Unlike traits such as hotheadedness, drunkenness, or cowardice, the traits characteristic of the battered woman are not attributes that the woman can reasonably be expected to control, that evidence some sort of moral failure for which she can fairly be blamed, or that the criminal law is designed to alter. The battered woman typically has done nothing to bring on her husband's abuse. Therefore, she cannot justly be blamed for her status as a battered woman.

Other feminists point out that appellate opinions authorizing admission of the syndrome testimony tend to "resonate with familiar stereotypes of female incapacity." Elizabeth M. Schneider, Describing and Changing: Women's Self-Defense Work and the Problem of Expert Testimony on Battering, 9 Women's Rts. L. Rptr. 195, 199 (1986). Schneider argues that judges have misinterpreted the syndrome testimony. While the testimony describes a context within which the woman's acts are reasonable, the courts tend to represent battered women as "suffering from a psychological disability [that] prevents them from acting normally." Mahoney agrees that the courts primarily focus on those aspects of the testimony that suggest that battered women are "dysfunctional." Martha R. Mahoney, Legal Images of Battered Women: Redefining the Issue of Separation, 90 Mich. L. Rev. 1, 38–43 (1991). Thus, Mahoney argues that defense lawyers should supplement the syndrome testimony with evidence that the woman was barred from leaving the abusive relationship by a lack of resources, by the apathetic responses of the police, and/or by increased violence by the man.

### 4. SELF-DEFENSE BY A BATTERED CHILD

Analogous issues have been raised in cases involving defendants charged with patricide who seek to introduce expert testimony regarding "battered child syndrome." The relation between this evidentiary question

and the substantive doctrine of self-defense was discussed at length in
Jahnke v. State, 682 P.2d 991 (Wyo.1984). Richard John Jahnke, then 16,
killed his father with a shotgun in the driveway of their home as his mother and father were returning from dinner. The court described the killing
as follows:

*Jahnke v. State*

> [Earlier in the evening defendant] had been involved in a vio-
> lent altercation with his father, and he had been warned not to be
> at the home when the father and mother returned. During the ab-
> sence of his parents the [defendant] made elaborate preparation
> for the final confrontation with his father. He changed into dark
> clothing and prepared a number of weapons which he positioned
> at various places throughout the family home that he selected to
> serve as "backup" positions in case he was not successful in his
> first effort to kill his father. These weapons included two shot-
> guns, three rifles, a .38 caliber pistol and a Marine knife. In addi-
> tion, he armed his sister, Deborah, with a .30 caliber M–1 carbine
> which he taught her how to operate so that she could protect her-
> self in the event that he failed in his efforts. . . . He then waited
> inside the darkened garage in a position where he could not be
> seen but which permitted him to view the lighted driveway on the
> other side of the garage door. Shortly before 6:30 p.m. the parents
> returned, and the [defendant's] father got out of the vehicle and
> came to the garage door. The [defendant] was armed with a 12-
> gauge shotgun loaded with slugs, and when he could see the head
> and shoulders of his father through the spacing of the slats of the
> shade covering the windows of the garage door, he blew his
> R.O.T.C. command-sergeant-major's whistle for courage, and he
> opened fire. All six cartridges in the shotgun were expended, and
> four of them in one way or another struck the father. . . .

*details*

Jahnke was charged with first-degree murder. In support of his self-
defense plea, he sought to introduce evidence that his father had beaten
him, his sister, and his mother over many years, and proffered psychiatric
testimony that he was a battered child who believed himself to be in immediate danger of death or serious harm when he shot his father. Although
the jury was instructed on the law of self-defense, the expert testimony was
excluded. Jahnke was convicted of voluntary manslaughter and sentenced
to a 5-to-15 year term of imprisonment. The Wyoming Supreme Court affirmed the conviction and sentence. The majority explained its ruling on
the evidentiary issue as follows:

*abusive father*

*convicted no self-defense*

> It is clear that self-defense is circumscribed by circumstances
> involving a confrontation, usually encompassing some overt act or
> acts by the deceased, which would induce a reasonable person to
> fear that his life was in danger or that at least he was threatened
> with great bodily harm. . . . Although many people, and the public
> media, seem to be prepared to espouse the notion that a victim of
> abuse is entitled to kill the abuser, that special justification de-
> fense is antithetical to the mores of modern civilized society. It is
> difficult enough to justify capital punishment as an appropriate
> response of society to criminal acts even after the circumstances
> have been carefully evaluated by a number of people. To permit
> capital punishment to be imposed upon the subjective conclusion
> of the individual that prior acts and conduct of the deceased justi-

*must be an imminent confrontation*

fied the killing would amount to a leap into the abyss of anarchy. [If expert testimony] has any role at all, it is in assisting the jury to evaluate the reasonableness of the defendant's fear in a case involving the recognized circumstances of self-defense which include a confrontation or conflict with the deceased not of the defendant's instigation. . . .

*role of expert testimony*

[The] record contained no evidence that [defendant] was under either actual or threatened assault by his father at the time of the shooting. Reliance upon the justification of self-defense requires a showing of an actual or threatened imminent attack by the deceased. Absent [such a showing] the reasonableness of [the defendant's] conduct at the time was not an issue in the case, and the trial court, at the time it made its ruling, properly excluded the testimony sought to be elicited from the forensic psychiatrist.

*actual or threatened imminent attack*

On facts similar to those of *Jahnke*, the Court of Appeals of Washington reversed the conviction of a man who, at age 17, shot and killed his stepfather as the stepfather was returning home from work. See State v. Janes, 64 Wash.App. 134, 822 P.2d 1238 (1992). The court concluded that the trial court erred by excluding expert testimony concerning the "battered child syndrome":

*State v. Janes*

While the "imminent danger" prong requires the jury to find that the victim honestly and reasonably believed that the aggressor intended to inflict serious bodily injury in the near future, there need be no evidence of an actual physical assault to demonstrate the immediacy of the danger. . . .

*no need of evidence of an actual physical assault*

. . . Washington uses a subjective standard to evaluate the imminence of the danger a defendant faced at the time of the act. This requires the court and the jury to evaluate the reasonableness of the defendant's perception of the imminence of that danger in light of all the facts and circumstances known to the defendant at the time he acted, including the facts and circumstances as he perceived them before the crime. Because battering itself can alter the defendant's perceptions, Washington courts have held that expert testimony with respect to the battered woman syndrome is admissible to explain a woman's perception that she had no alternative but to act in the manner that she did. . . .

*WA subjective standard*

Neither law nor logic suggests any reason to limit to women recognition of the impact a battering relationship may have on the victim's actions or perceptions. [C]hildren are both objectively and subjectively more vulnerable to the effects of violence than are adults. For that reason, the rationale underlying the admissibility of testimony regarding the battered woman syndrome is at least as compelling, if not more so, when applied to children. [Until they reach the age of majority, children] have virtually no independent ability to support themselves, thus preventing them from escaping the abusive atmosphere. Further, unlike an adult who may come into a battering relationship with at least some basis on which to make comparisons between current and past experiences, a child has no such equivalent life experience on which to draw to put the battering into perspective. There is therefore every reason to believe that a child's entire world view and sense of self may be conditioned by reaction to that abuse.

*compelling evidence*

Which of these analyses is preferable? By emphasizing children's unique vulnerability to domestic violence, does the court in *Janes* undercut the rationale supporting the battered woman syndrome?

## NOTE ON THE URBAN SURVIVAL SYNDROME

The success of the battered woman syndrome has encouraged defense lawyers to offer testimony concerning other kinds of syndromes in an effort to bolster self-defense claims. One such syndrome is known as "urban survival syndrome." The following case describes the theory underlying urban survival syndrome, as well as one context in which the syndrome is likely to be raised.[a]

On April 18, 1993, Daimian Osby, an 18-year-old black man, shot and killed Willie and Marcus Brooks, who also were black men. The shootings took place in Fort Worth, Texas. Both victims were shot in the side of the head. At his trial on two counts of first-degree murder, Osby claimed that his use of deadly force was justifiable self-defense. According to Osby, during the year that preceded the shootings, the two men had harassed him repeatedly for payment of a gambling debt. The harassment included threats of violence against Osby and members of his family. On at least one occasion, the two men had stalked Osby and threatened him with shotguns. At the time that Osby shot the men, they were unarmed, but Osby believed that the only way for him to avoid death or serious bodily injury at their hands was for him to kill them first. A sociologist testifying on behalf of the defense explained to the jury that Osby lived in an inner city neighborhood with one of the highest rates of violent crime in the country, and he explained that young men raised in these neighborhoods quickly learn that the greatest danger they face is being killed "by one of their own." Based on this testimony, defense counsel argued that Osby's belief that he needed to use lethal force was reasonable. The jury deadlocked eleven to one in favor of conviction. According to defense counsel, the one juror who held out for acquittal was a black man from Osby's neighborhood who agreed that the neighborhood was a "war zone." When Osby was tried a second time on murder charges, his attorneys sought to introduce testimony from a psychologist, as well as the sociologist, concerning the psychological characteristics of persons who live in violent, poor, urban neighborhoods. The trial judge refused to allow the psychologist to testify. Osby was convicted of two counts of murder and sentenced to life in prison.

Should the trial court have excluded the psychologist's testimony concerning urban survival syndrome? Does the answer depend on the standard of reasonableness (objective or subjective) employed by Texas in evaluating claims of self-defense? Recall the arguments offered to support admission of testimony concerning the battered woman syndrome. Can the same kinds of arguments be made to support admission of urban survival syndrome? Do blacks and whites have different perceptions of confrontational situations? If so, must evidence of those differences nonetheless be excluded in order to avoid reinforcing racist stereotypes concerning black men and violence?

---

[a] The following description of the *Osby* case is based on Jacquielynn Floyd, Double-Murder Case Is Declared Mistrial, The Dallas Morning News, April 21, 1994, at A25; Selwyn Crawford, Teen Guilty in Slayings of Two in Fort Worth, The Dallas Morning News, Nov. 11, 1994, at A29.

In this connection, consider again the facts of <u>State v. Brown</u>, 91 N.M. 320, 573 P.2d 675 (1977). Brown was convicted of two counts of assault upon a police officer with intent to kill. Brown was a black man who lived in an inner-city neighborhood, and he claimed that he "<u>feared the officers and shot them in self-defense</u>." Defense witnesses were <u>permitted to describe</u> instances in which police officers physically and verbally harassed Brown and other black persons from his neighborhood. However, the trial court refused to allow a social psychologist to testify about "police conduct toward minority groups and the perception by minority groups, particularly blacks, that the police are a threat to minority group members." Nor did the court allow the psychologist to testify that, in his opinion, Brown "would be likely to fear the police" if he encountered them on the street. The Court of Appeals of New Mexico decided that <u>exclusion of the expert's testimony was erroneous</u>, and it reversed <u>and remanded for a new trial</u>. Such testimony supported <u>Brown's claim that he feared he was in immediate danger of bodily harm when he shot the officers</u>, and it may have rebutted an inference created by other evidence that Brown acted out "of anger and . . . rejection of authority." Did Brown (or, for that matter, Osby) suffer from a "syndrome" in the sense that term is employed by the court in *Kelly*? Is Brown's predicament factually and ethically distinguishable from that of Osby? From that of Kelly?

*[handwritten margin notes: "State v. Brwn ] action" and "] expert testimony allowed"]*

# SECTION 2: SITUATIONAL EXCUSE

## INTRODUCTORY NOTE ON THE DEFENSE OF DURESS

<u>The law has traditionally recognized a defense of duress</u>, as in a case where *A* commits a crime because *B* holds a gun to *A*'s head and forces *A* to do so. Usually, this defense has been restrictively defined. Moreover, the <u>defendant typically bears the burden of proving the elements of the defense to the satisfaction of the jury</u>.

The materials in this section explore the nature of the duress defense. At the outset, it is helpful to note the analytical distinction between the defense of duress and the "voluntary act" doctrine considered in Chapter II. It would do no violence to the English language to characterize as "<u>involuntary</u>" *A*'s act of committing a crime under duress. Indeed, *A*'s claim might appear, at first blush, to be functionally similar to the claim that could be raised by *A* if, with intent to injure *C*, *B* shoved *A* into *C*, thereby knocking *C* into the path of an oncoming car. However, the law draws a distinction between bodily movements that are within the conscious control of the actor and those that are not.

In 2 A History of the Criminal Law of England 102 (1883), Sir James Fitzjames Stephen described this distinction as follows:

> A criminal walking to execution is under compulsion if any man can be said to be so, but his motions are just as much voluntary actions as if he [were] going to leave his place of confinement and regain his liberty. He walks to his death because he prefers it to being carried.

As a matter of legal definition, <u>an act which the actor feels constrained to commit is regarded as "voluntary"</u> for purposes of establishing that the actus reus of the offense has been committed. The <u>involuntary-act doctrine</u>

covers cases where the actor makes no choice at all, not those where he or she is forced by circumstances to make a "hard choice."

Traditionally, the duress defense has been the main device by which the law takes into account external constraints on a person's capacity to choose to comply with the law.[a] Of course, the task of determining when a "hard choice" should have exculpatory significance requires a judgment of degree. As Glanville Williams has noted, "[f]ear of violence does not differ in kind from fear of economic ills, fear of displeasing others, or any other determinant of choice." Criminal Law: The General Part 751 (2d ed. 1961). Under what circumstances should it be said that a person was "compelled" to commit a crime and that he or she should not be punished for failing to do otherwise? Stephen concluded that the law should never give exculpatory significance to hard choices, even those produced by threats of death. In a famous passage opposing the duress defense, 2 A History of the Criminal Law of England 107–08 (1883), Stephen argued as follows:

> Criminal law is itself a system of compulsion on the widest scale. It is a collection of threats of injury to life, liberty, and property if people do commit crimes. Are such threats to be withdrawn as soon as they are encountered by opposing threats? The law says to a man intending to commit murder, if you do it I will hang you. Is the law to withdraw its threat if someone else says, if you do not do it, I will shoot you?
>
> Surely it is at the moment when temptation to crime is strongest that the law should speak most clearly and emphatically to the contrary. It is, of course, a misfortune for a man that he should be placed between two fires, but it would be a much greater misfortune for society at large if criminals could confer impunity upon their agents by threatening them with death or violence if they refused to execute their commands. If impunity could be so secured a wide door would be opened to collusion, and encouragement would be given to associations of malefactors, secret or otherwise. No doubt the moral guilt of a person who commits a crime under compulsion is less than that of a person who commits it freely, but any effect which is thought proper may be given to this circumstance by a proportional mitigation of the offender's punishment.
>
> These reasons lead me to think that compulsion by threats ought in no case whatever to be admitted as an excuse for crime, though it may and ought to operate in mitigation of punishment in most though not in all cases. . . .

Glanville Williams has observed that Stephen's view "would now be regarded as over-severe." In some cases, he continues, "justice demand[s] not merely a mitigation of punishment but no punishment at all. . . ." Glanville Williams, Criminal Law: The General Part 755 (2d ed. 1961). The drafters of the Model Penal Code responded to Stephen's argument as follows:

> [L]aw is ineffective in the deepest sense, indeed . . . it is hypocritical, if it imposes on the actor who has the misfortune to confront a dilemmatic choice, a standard that his judges are not

[a] The impact of a person's abnormal mental condition on his or her capacity to conform to the law is explored in connection with the insanity defense in Chapter VIII.

> prepared to affirm that they should and could comply with if their turn to face the problem should arise. Condemnation in such a case is bound to be an ineffective threat; what is, however, more significant is that it is divorced from any moral base and is unjust. Where it would be both "personally and socially debilitating" to accept the actor's cowardice as a defense, it would be equally debilitating to demand that heroism should be the standard of legality.[b]

Other authors have criticized Stephen's opposition to the duress defense, and a few have suggested that it is a fundamental mistake to characterize duress as an "excuse" rather than as a "justification." Most courts and commentators treat duress as a species of excuse, "rather than a justification, because the community prefers that actors not offend, even under the pressure of serious threats, but will withhold blame where the threats are sufficiently grievous."[c] Still, as the United States Supreme Court has observed, the distinction between duress and necessity is a blurry one.[d] In connection with these observations, consider the following case.

## United States v. Haney

United States Court of Appeals, Tenth Circuit, 2002.
287 F.3d 1266.

■ HENRY, CIRCUIT JUDGE. Robert M. Haney appeals his conviction and sentence for violation of 18 U.S.C. § 1791(a)(2) (possession of escape paraphernalia in prison). Mr. Haney asserts that the district court erred in . . . not permitting him to raise a defense of duress, a defense the jury accepted, on a related count, as to Mr. Haney's co-defendant. [We] vacate Mr. Haney's conviction for possession of escape paraphernalia. . . .

### I. BACKGROUND

Following his escape from prison, the television show "America's Most Wanted" incorrectly described Tony S. Francis, friend and co-defendant of Mr. Haney, as a leader of the Aryan Brotherhood, a prison gang preaching white supremacy. Once recaptured, Mr. Francis found himself housed in the federal penitentiary in Florence, Colorado; Mr. Francis developed anxiety about his incarceration in this facility for at least two reasons. First, Mr. Francis feared the reaction of African-American prisoners because at least some of those prisoners had, in all likelihood, heard the claim of Aryan Brotherhood membership made by "America's Most Wanted." Second, Mr. Francis feared the reaction of members of the Aryan Brotherhood because, in reality, Mr. Francis was not a member of that prison gang.

In 1997, prison authorities became concerned about growing racial tension in the Florence penitentiary; beginning on September 3, 1997, prison authorities "locked down" the penitentiary for ten days. Immediately after prison authorities lifted the lock-down, three African-American inmates threatened Mr. Francis. The inmates approached

---

[b] ALI, Model Penal Code and Commentaries, § 2.09, pp. 374–75 (1985).

[c] Anne M. Coughlin, Excusing Women, 82 Cal. L. Rev. 1, 29–30 & n.143 (1994); see also Mitchell N. Berman, Justification and Excuse, Law and Morality, 53 Duke L.J. 1, 69–73 (2003).

[d] See United States v. Bailey, 444 U.S. 394 (1980).

Mr. Francis, told him that they had seen him on "America's Most Wanted," and offered a warning to the effect that: "When the shit jumps off, you know what time it is"—i.e., a race war was brewing and Mr. Francis was a target.

Mr. Francis concluded that his only option was to attempt a prison escape. In their respective testimonies, Mr. Francis and Mr. Haney each explained this implicit decision not to seek the aid of the prison authorities as resting on the alleged fact that seeking such aid did not constitute a reasonable alternative. Mr. Francis and Mr. Haney testified that, had Mr. Francis sought such assistance, Mr. Francis and Mr. Haney's fellow inmates would have labeled Mr. Francis a snitch, thereby placing Mr. Francis in further danger. Additionally, according to the testimony of Mr. Francis and Mr. Haney, because the special housing units were far from free from violence, placing Mr. Francis in protective custody would also have proven of limited benefit.

Mr. Haney agreed to help Mr. Francis in Mr. Francis' attempted escape. Mr. Haney used his position as an employee in the prison laundry to collect a variety of escape paraphernalia. On September 26, 1997—approximately two weeks after the initial threat—Mr. Francis was shown a "kite" (a note) in which an inmate commented that Mr. Francis was still considered a target. This threat provided renewed impetus for the escape attempt.

On the night of October 3, 1997, Mr. Francis and Mr. Haney gathered the collected escape paraphernalia and hid in the prison yard. As they hid, however, Mr. Haney endeavored to convince Mr. Francis that an escape attempt was, in fact, imprudent; Mr. Haney argued, in effect: "The best possible solution would be to get caught trying to escape, thereby getting placed into disciplinary segregation without having to report the death threats to prison officials." Mr. Francis ultimately agreed. After two hours of strewing the yard with the escape paraphernalia, the two inmates were finally caught.

The United States charged both Mr. Francis and Mr. Haney with (1) violation of 18 U.S.C. § 1791(a)(2) (possession of escape paraphernalia in prison) and (2) violation of 18 U.S.C. § 751(a) (attempted escape). As to Mr. Francis, the district court instructed the jury on the duress defense in regard to both counts; as to Mr. Haney, however, the court refused to give a duress instruction on either count. The jury convicted both Mr. Francis and Mr. Haney of possessing escape paraphernalia but acquitted both Mr. Francis and Mr. Haney of attempting to escape. In acquitting Mr. Francis of the attempted escape, the jury expressly invoked the duress defense.

II. DISCUSSION: Applicability of the Duress Defense

Mr. Haney argues that he was entitled to present a duress defense to the jury.[3] In order to have a theory of defense submitted to the jury, a defendant must present sufficient evidence, on each element of the defense, by which the jury could find in the defendant's favor. Indeed, a "defendant is entitled to jury instructions on any theory of defense finding support in the evidence and the law. Failure to so instruct

[3] Interestingly, Mr. Haney's counsel offered, at least once, to abandon pursuit of the duress defense if the government would agree not to pursue an "aiding and abetting" theory as to the charged attempted escape; the government, however, declined to accept the offer.

is reversible error." . . . The district court concluded that Mr. Haney failed to present sufficient evidence as to the elements of the duress defense and thus that the duress defense was, as a matter of law, inapplicable to Mr. Haney.

[The] duress defense typically consists of three elements:

> (1) The threat of immediate infliction, upon the defendant, of death or bodily harm;
>
> (2) The defendant's well-grounded fear that the threat will be carried out; and
>
> (3) The defendant's lack of a reasonable opportunity to otherwise avert the threatened harm.

By his own admission, Mr. Haney cannot meet the elements of the duress defense, as described above. Quite basically, Mr. Haney makes no allegation that he ever feared for his own safety. Mr. Haney seeks to overcome this obstacle by proposing an extension of the duress defense; Mr. Haney argues that the duress defense should encompass defendants who correctly recognize that another individual's safety is at risk. Thus, Mr. Haney would describe the elements of the duress defense as requiring:[4]

> (1) The threat of immediate infliction, upon the defendant or a third person, of death or bodily harm;
>
> (2) The defendant's well-grounded fear that the threat will be carried out; and
>
> (3) The defendant's, and third person's, lack of a reasonable opportunity to otherwise avert the threatened harm.

The government presents no argument that the duress defense should not extend, in at least certain circumstances, to third parties, thereby essentially conceding the point. Rather, the government presses two grounds on which we might nevertheless conclude, as a matter of law, that the duress defense is here unavailable to Mr. Haney. The government first suggests that the duress defense should be extended to third parties only where the defendant enjoys a familial relationship with the threatened individual. Second, the government suggests that Mr. Haney produced inadequate evidence to create a jury question as to either the first or third element of the duress defense. We address these arguments in turn.

A. Third Party Duress

1. Whether the duress defense should ever extend to third parties

Despite the fact that the government essentially abandons this position (presenting no argument and citing no cases or other legal authority), we begin our discussion of third party duress by considering whether the duress defense should ever be available when a third party (a party other than the defendant) is threatened with death or bodily harm. Logic and overwhelming legal authority conjoin in establishing that the duress defense should, indeed, extend to third parties.

---

[4] The defense of duress, as formulated by Mr. Haney, remains distinct from the "defense of another" in that "defense of another" scenarios feature the defendant taking action directly against the threatening individual(s), while a "third party duress" scenario would involve the defendant taking any other course of action.

The principle underlying the duress defense is one of hard-nosed practicality: sometimes social welfare is maximized by forgiving a relatively minor offense in order to avoid a greater social harm. . . . Where *A*, with apparent credibility, threatens to shoot *B* unless *B* jaywalks (and where *B*, in fear of the threat, possesses no reasonable opportunity to otherwise avert the shooting), the law excuses *B*'s relatively minor offense in order to avoid the greater social harm threatened by *A*. The same logic dictates that so, too, where *A*, again with apparent credibility, threatens to shoot *B* unless *C* jaywalks, the defense of third party duress should excuse *C*'s relatively minor offense (at least so long as (1) *C* actually feared that *A* would execute the shooting and (2) neither *B* nor *C* possessed a reasonable alternative to otherwise avert the shooting).

Commentators and the case law agree that the duress defense should extend to the defense of third parties. . . .

2. Whether the duress defense, once extended to third parties, should be limited to third parties with a familial relationship to the defendant

It is true that, as the government observes, most cases of third-party duress involve familial relationships between the defendant and the threatened individual; however, neither logic nor practicality supports such a "family relationship" limitation. Returning to our basic illustration of the duress defense above, why should it matter whether *C* (who jaywalks in order to prevent *A* from shooting *B*) enjoys a family relationship with *B*; in either case, permitting *C* to jaywalk avoids the greater social harm. Professors Scott and LaFave agree: "As a matter of principle, the threatened harm need not be directed at the defendant himself; it may be aimed at a member of his family or a friend (or, it would seem, even a stranger)." 1 Wayne R. LaFave & Austin W. Scott, Jr., Substantive Criminal Law § 5.3, at 624 (1986); see also, e.g., Model Penal Code § 2.09(1) (declining to limit the duress defense to parties enjoying a familial relationship: "It is an affirmative defense that the actor engaged in the conduct charged to constitute an offense because he was coerced to do so by the use of, or a threat to use, unlawful force against his person or the person of another."); cf. LaFave & Scott, supra, § 5.8(a), at 664 (noting, in the context of the "defense of another" defense, that, while "some early English cases suggested that force may not be used in defense of another unless the defender stands in some personal relationship to the one in need of protection[,] . . . the modern and better rule is that there need be no such relationship").

Indeed, as Professor Hill has written, the applicability of the duress defense may be particularly important precisely where *B* and *C* are not related because it is in this circumstance that *C* may need greater reassurance before risking criminal punishment in order to improve the well-being of *B*.

> Third parties are in special need of protection in situations where the defendant may have no great incentive to protect the third party [i.e., where the defendant and the threatened party are not bonded by familial ties]. Permitting the defense [of duress] in these situations allows the defendant to succumb to the threat without fear of punishment, rather than risk the safety of the third party. In sum, the law should extend the defense to this situation precisely because the actor might not be

> sufficiently coerced to act in a situation where we should encourage such an act.

John Lawrence Hill, A Utilitarian Theory of Duress, 84 Iowa L. Rev. 275, 325 (1999).

Not only is the government's "family members only" limitation unprincipled, it is unworkable. Under the government's proposed limitation, the duress defense would presumably remain available where *B* and *C* enjoy a mother-son or husband-wife relationship but not where *B* and *C* merely find themselves seated next to each other on a public bus. A family relationship, however, is somewhat difficult to identify: what of a couple engaged to be married, an aunt and nephew, in-laws, distant cousins who know each other well, siblings who have never met, unmarried co-habitants, etc.?[5] The government's failure to offer guidance on these issues is surely a product of the unprincipled line drawn by the "family relationship" test.

It is, then, hardly surprising that, in the only federal case . . . to explicitly address the duress defense in the context of an unrelated defendant and threatened party, the Ninth Circuit did not even pause to consider whether the duress defense might not apply in such a situation. United States v. Lopez, 885 F.2d 1428 (9th Cir. 1989), involved a defendant invoking the duress defense after flying a helicopter into a federal prison in order to avert a threatened harm to his "girlfriend," an inmate in that prison. Rather than struggle over whether a non-marital romantic attachment may constitute a "family relationship," the Ninth Circuit moved directly to consideration of whether the defendant had established the substantive elements of the duress defense. Just as we know of no federal case categorically declining to apply the duress defense in the third-party context, we know of no federal case categorically limiting the third party duress defense to defendants who happen to enjoy a family relationship to the threatened individual.

In sum, we see no principled justification for limiting the duress defense to defendants whose own safety is threatened. Nor do we see any justification for limiting the duress defense to defendants in a familial relationship with the threatened individual. Such distinctions would be arbitrary and unjust. As Mr. Haney correctly observes, the duress defense is appropriately defined not by "the nature of the relationship between the alleged law-breaker and the beneficiary third party" but by the "nature of the crime committed and the benefit conferred upon the third party."[6]

---

[5] And, again, how are any of these relationships meaningfully distinct, for purposes of application of the duress defense, from the relationship between two close friends, long-time roommates, work colleagues, a teacher and student, etc.?

[6] While the government has not explicitly argued the point, we briefly consider, and reject, the notion that the prison context . . . should control the applicability of the duress defense. The prison environment does present unique circumstances; these unique circumstances, however, have never before justified a departure from general legal principles. The defenses of insanity and self-defense, for instance, apply both inside and outside the prison walls . . . ; indeed, we know of no defense made unavailable by the fact that the alleged crime occurred within a prison. The same principles that ordinarily underlie the duress defense persist within the prison context: there will be some circumstances, even within a prison, where social utility is maximized by the commission of a relatively minor offense. . . .

B. Sufficiency of the Evidence

Nor can we accept the government's argument that Mr. Haney failed to produce adequate evidence to create a jury issue on either the first or third element of the duress defense. Here, of course, the government's position is weakened (though not logically foreclosed) by the fact that the jury explicitly invoked the duress defense to acquit Mr. Francis of the charged attempted escape. The fact that the jury, hearing much of the same evidence that Mr. Haney would have applied toward his own duress defense, accepted the duress defense in a related context suggests that Mr. Haney did, indeed, offer sufficient evidence.

1. Whether Mr. Haney presented sufficient evidence as to the first element of the duress defense

The first element of the duress defense requires a threat of immediate infliction of death or bodily harm. The government argues that Mr. Haney's testimony that he was "not a hundred percent sure that [Mr. Francis] was going to try to follow through" with the escape, establishes, as a matter of law, that the relevant threat could not have been an immediate one. We reject this notion. Mr. Francis testified to racially motivated threats upon his life in the context of simmering racial tension. [As he stated], "Most everyone in the joint and even in the staff . . . believed that there was going to be a racial war on a riot type of scale. . . . I was going to be one of the first ones hit, killed." Numerous witnesses substantiated the severe racial tension in the prison and the fact that, as a consequence of that tension, Mr. Francis had received a specific and credible threat upon his life. . . .

Certainly the testimony of Mr. Francis, Mr. Haney, prison officials, and fellow inmates created a jury issue regarding the imminence of the threat against Mr. Francis' life. Mr. Haney's admission of some degree of uncertainty regarding whether Mr. Francis would execute the escape attempt creates, at best, some doubt regarding that imminence; Mr. Haney's admission in no way establishes, as a matter of law, that Mr. Francis faced no immediate threat of death or bodily harm.

2. Whether Mr. Haney presented sufficient evidence as to the third element of the duress defense

The third element of the duress defense requires that Mr. Haney and Mr. Francis have each lacked a reasonable legal opportunity to avert the threatened harm. The government notes that "evidence was presented that an inmate could get placed in protective custody through a variety of means, including with the assistance of another inmate." The government points to the testimony of Mr. Francis and Paul Chartier, another inmate at the Florence Penitentiary. On cross-examination and re-cross-examination, respectively, both Mr. Francis and Mr. Chartier answered "yeah" in regard to a question as to whether Mr. Haney might have passed an anonymous note to the prison guards in order to have Mr. Francis involuntarily isolated. In the government's view, Mr. Haney's exercise of that alternative would have averted the threatened harm to Mr. Francis (while also avoiding adverse collateral consequences [inmate-on-inmate violence]); thus, the proposed course of action was a reasonable alternative to the possession of escape paraphernalia.

Again, however, the government confuses evidence that suggests the existence of such a reasonable alternative with evidence establishing, as a matter of law, the existence of such a reasonable alternative. Mr. Francis testified extensively regarding the risks inherent in engineering one's own check-in. [Indeed, he put it bluntly,] "You can be killed when you're labeled [as a check-in]." Further, immediately following Mr. Chartier's "yeah" response noted above, Mr. Chartier added: "It's not an option, though, when you live that life." Other inmates testified along similar lines. . . .

Given the opportunity, a jury certainly might have concluded that Mr. Haney could not claim the duress defense because either he or Mr. Francis possessed a reasonable alternative to the possession of escape paraphernalia. On the other hand, however, a jury could also have concluded that (1) if Mr. Francis had simply checked himself in, he would have exposed himself to an unreasonable risk and likewise (2) if Mr. Haney were to have engineered Mr. Francis' check-in, Mr. Haney would have exposed Mr. Francis to an unreasonable risk that fellow inmates would perceive Mr. Haney's actions to be at the behest of his friend Mr. Francis. In short, the jury could have concluded that neither Mr. Haney nor Mr. Francis in fact possessed any reasonable alternative to the possession of escape paraphernalia.

Because a jury could have concluded (1) that the threat against Mr. Francis was immediate in nature, (2) that Mr. Haney actually possessed a well-grounded fear that the threat would be executed, and (3) that neither Mr. Haney nor Mr. Francis, in order to avert the threatened harm, maintained any reasonable alternative to possessing escape paraphernalia, the district court should have granted Mr. Haney's request for jury instructions on the duress defense.

## III. CONCLUSION

For the reasons set forth above, we decline to limit the duress defense to defendants related by familial ties to a threatened individual and we further conclude that Mr. Haney presented adequate evidence to create a jury issue as to the applicability of that defense to his alleged possession of escape paraphernalia. Obviously we express no further opinion as to the likely merits of Mr. Haney's duress defense. Should the government choose to retry this case, the government, with the duress issue now in play, may well produce overwhelming evidence as to either the non-immediacy of the threat against Mr. Francis or the existence of reasonable alternatives to the possession of escape paraphernalia. These, however, are considerations for a jury: we vacate Mr. Haney's conviction and sentence and remand for further proceedings consistent with this opinion.

## NOTES ON DURESS AND SITUATIONAL EXCUSE

### 1. QUESTIONS AND COMMENTS ON *HANEY*

*Haney* offers a description of duress doctrine with which the vast majority of jurisdictions would agree. Some courts may provide a somewhat more elaborate treatment of the defense, but most statements of doctrine resemble closely the three elements cited in *Haney*. But *Haney*'s account of the principles underlying duress is controversial. According to *Haney*, the theoretical basis for the defense "is one of hard-nosed practicality: sometimes social welfare is maximized by forgiving a relatively minor offense in order to avoid a greater social harm." Here, the court invokes the rhetoric of necessity rather than that of excuse. With this rhetoric, together with its illustrative "jaywalking" example, the court implies that a properly instructed jury might have acquitted Haney on the ground that he did the right thing. It was proper for him to commit a trivial wrong in order to save his friend's life; indeed, because he correctly balanced the evils confronting him, he committed no crime at all. By contrast, if the court had treated duress as an excuse, it would have valued Haney's conduct quite differently. According to the theoretical rationale for excuse, it is unjust to punish a person who committed his crime under the compulsion of threats that other members of the community would not have had the fortitude to resist. On this theory, a jury might have acquitted Haney, but not on the ground that he did the right thing. Rather, the judgment would be that he did the wrong thing, but he should not be punished for it because his options were so excruciating.

Does Haney or any other defendant care if the jury decides that his or her crime should merely be excused rather than justified? In either case, the accused is spared the pain of punishment, and it may be that he or she never notices the normative nuances implied by one judgment as opposed to the other. But, as Chapter I shows when describing the purposes of punishment, the criminal law speaks to more than one audience. Actual offenders are far from the only, or even the principal, targets of the messages that criminal punishment is designed to convey. So it is that commentators and lawmakers continue to believe that members of the community, including the law-abiding as well as potential wrongdoers, do hear and respond to the different evaluative judgments conveyed by the doctrines of excuse and of justification. As Anne Coughlin observes, the community is encouraged to emulate actors whose conduct is justified but not those who are excused: "By finding that a defendant's conduct was justified, the decisionmaker not only announces that no wrong was committed, it also expresses its confidence in the actor's capacity to behave responsibly in the future. In sharp contrast to the justified actor, who is adjudged to have governed himself in an exemplary fashion, the excused defendant achieves leniency only by showing that, at the time he offended, his capacity to choose lawful over unlawful conduct was grossly distorted."[a] Of course, these nuances may not be lost on individual offenders, but even if they are, the system remains committed to making them.

In *Haney*, the court decided that the duress defense should be extended to cases where the target of the threat was not the offender himself, but a third party. The court concluded that there was no principled basis for refusing to allow the defense in such cases. Indeed, the court argued that extending the defense to cases involving threats against third parties would create good incentives for behavior, as actors otherwise might hesitate to violate the law in order to protect the safety of others. If the court's analysis had been informed by principles of excuse rather than necessity, would it have reached the same outcome? If duress is an excuse, is there a principled reason to refuse to allow the defense in cases involving threats against others? To limit it to cases involving threats against family members?

---

[a] Anne M. Coughlin, Excusing Women, 82 Cal. L. Rev. 1, 14 (1994).

## 2. ELEMENTS OF DURESS

As *Haney* reports, the duress defense requires the defendant to show that he was under a "threat of immediate infliction . . . of death or bodily harm" and that he lacked "a reasonable legal opportunity to avert the threatened harm." The court does not explain why, if the defense indeed is a species of necessity, it is defined so narrowly. Why would threats to destroy property or reputation not suffice, as long as the actor correctly chose the lesser of two evils? Does the grudging scope of the defense suggest that it is an excuse, rather than a justification?

A frequently litigated aspect of duress is the requirement that the death threat be "imminent" or "immediate." An example is State v. Toscano, 74 N.J. 421, 378 A.2d 755 (1977). Dr. Toscano, a chiropractor, was convicted of conspiring with one William Leonardo and others to obtain money by false pretenses. Specifically, Toscano signed a false medical report for use by Leonardo in an insurance fraud scheme. Toscano claimed that he "just had to do it" in order to protect himself and his family from bodily harm threatened by Leonardo. Leonardo allegedly made several phone calls insisting that Toscano file the false report and sounded "vicious" and "desperate." Leonardo said, among other things: "Remember you just moved into a place that has a very dark entrance and you live there with your wife. . . . You and your wife are going to jump at shadows when you leave that dark entrance." Defendant finally agreed to Leonardo's demand and made out a single false medical report. He later moved to another house and changed his telephone number to avoid future contact with Leonardo. What he did not do was call the police.

The trial court refused to instruct on duress. The court reasoned that defendant's evidence, even if believed, would not show a "present, imminent and impending" threat of harm. Because Leonardo was not in a position to act immediately, Toscano had ample opportunity to call the police.

The Supreme Court of New Jersey held the evidence of duress sufficient to go to the jury and reversed Toscano's conviction. That court relied on § 2.09 of the Model Penal Code and the then proposed (and subsequently enacted) New Jersey statute, both of which explicitly reject the common law requirement of a threat of imminent harm. Under these provisions, the immediacy of the danger is merely one of the circumstances to be considered in determining whether the threatened use of force was such that "a person of reasonable firmness in [the defendant's] situation would have been unable to resist."

Which approach is preferable? Is it fair to expect a person in Toscano's situation to contact the police rather than commit the crime? Even if he or she believes the police will be unable to provide effective protection? Does the Model Penal Code approach unduly compromise the deterrent effect of the law? Does it permit a terrorist to confer standing immunity on others to do his or her bidding?

## 3. DURESS AND BATTERED WOMAN SYNDROME

The elements of duress bear more than a superficial resemblance to those of self-defense. For either defense to succeed, the actor must establish that she faced a threat of serious bodily harm and that she lacked other reasonable legal alternatives to her own use of force or her commission of another crime. Over the past couple of decades, defense lawyers have started to argue that evidence that the actor suffered from battered woman syndrome should be admissible to help support a claim of duress, just as it is allowed for self-defense. Courts have not been wholly receptive to these claims.

For example, in State v. B.H., 183 N.J. 171, 870 A.2d 273 (2005), the Supreme Court of New Jersey held that evidence of battered woman syndrome may be used to support some—but not all—of the elements of a duress defense put forward by a woman who claimed that she should not be held responsible for a crime because her abusive husband had coerced her into committing it. The facts of *B.H.* are vivid and distressing, even when succinctly summarized in judicial prose:

> In March of 2001, B.H. left her husband, S.H., and took their two young daughters to a women's shelter. While there, she informed a counselor that in 1999 her husband had forced her to have sexual intercourse with her then seven-year-old stepson, L.H. At the counselor's urging, she reported the incident to the Division of Youth and Family Services (DYFS); however, she reunited with her husband when she left the shelter.
>
> DYFS promptly conducted an investigation of the home, and an investigator from the Ocean County Prosecutor's Office contacted B.H. At the investigator's request, B.H. agreed to be interviewed. She appeared voluntarily at police headquarters and was administered *Miranda* warnings. She then talked with investigators for approximately an hour before making a taped statement in which she admitted to having engaged in sexual intercourse with her stepson while her husband watched.
>
> In her statement, B.H. told the investigators that her husband, S.H., had physically and sexually assaulted her on other occasions but she denied that he had threatened her with any violence on the day that the incident with her stepson took place. . . . According to B.H., S.H. justified the intercourse as something that would be "good" for her to do with L.H., "that it would help [them] get along better." B.H. was arrested and charged with first-degree aggravated sexual assault and second-degree endangering the welfare of a child.
>
> . . . However, in her trial testimony, [B.H.'s] description of what had happened that afternoon differed from her prior statement to police. She now claimed that S.H. had threatened her.
>
>> He had his hand at my throat. He wouldn't let me off the bed. And I told him that I didn't want to do this, that I was not going to do this. And he said that if I didn't go through with this, that he would make me pay and that I would never see my daughter again.
>
> B.H. said that she lied in her earlier statement about S.H. because "at that point [S.H.] had already gotten into [her] head again," and he had instructed her not to reveal his role in the incident.
>
> B.H. also testified about earlier incidents of physical, sexual, and emotional abuse that S.H. inflicted on her. She described a relationship with S.H. that involved physical violence (she claimed to be beaten about her breasts where bruises would not be visible

to others, and choked until she would almost pass out) and sexually violent practices that involved recurrent incidents of rape in various forms (described by one expert who interviewed her as "bizarre" sexual practices). The violence began early in the relationship. B.H. was nineteen years of age when she met S.H. She claimed that the first abusive incident occurred not long thereafter, when the two began to live together. In that encounter, S.H. held an ax to B.H.'s throat and, over an extended period of time, repeatedly raped her and performed other acts of a humiliating nature on her. Other incidents that need not be detailed similarly involved threats, physical violence, and violent sexual practices that B.H. also claimed to have endured from S.H. According to B.H., the abuse continued throughout their relationship, except for a short period of time when S.H. was on medication and in therapy.

Based on the foregoing testimony, defense counsel argued that B.H. had engaged in sex with her stepson under duress. As further support for this defense, counsel offered testimony by a forensic psychologist, who described the basic features of the battered woman syndrome and opined that B.H. suffered from it. On rebuttal, the prosecution called its own expert witness, who testified that "the syndrome was not useful in situations in which the woman harms a third person" and rejected the "conclusion that B.H. was a 'battered woman' at the time" of the crime.

The jury convicted B.H. of first-degree aggravated sexual assault and third-degree endangering the welfare of a child,[b] and, on appeal, the Supreme Court of New Jersey considered a question of first impression: may expert testimony concerning battered woman syndrome be used to support the affirmative defense of duress? Following the judgment in *State v. Toscano*, the New Jersey legislature had codified the defense in a statute that tracks the Model Penal Code's duress provision. The New Jersey statute provides:

a. Subject to subsection b. of this section, it is an affirmative defense that the actor engaged in the conduct charged to constitute an offense because he was coerced to do so by the use of, or a threat to use, unlawful force against his person or the person of another, which a person of reasonable firmness in his situation would have been unable to resist.

b. The defense provided by this section is unavailable if the actor recklessly placed himself in a situation in which it was probable that he would be subjected to duress. The defense is also unavailable if he was criminally negligent in placing himself in such a situation, whenever criminal negligence suffices to establish culpability for the offense charged. In a prosecution for murder, the defense is only available to reduce the degree of the crime to manslaughter.

c. It is not a defense that a woman acted on the command of her husband, unless she acted under such coercion as would establish a defense under this section. The presumption that a

[b] S.H., the defendant's husband, was indicted for complicity to commit aggravated sexual assault and for endangering the welfare of a child. Rather than going to trial, he elected to plead guilty pursuant to a plea bargain and was sentenced to serve seven years in prison.

woman, acting in the presence of her husband, is coerced is abolished.

Before evaluating the appropriate scope of battered woman syndrome evidence, the court emphasized that duress is and must be "kept exceptional because of the moral implications inherent in excusing a defendant who 'rationally and intentionally' chooses to commit an unlawful act that may actually include harming an innocent third party." As the court put it, "[d]uress is, at its core, a normative defense," and the exculpatory value of the excuse in any given case depends on both the severity of the coercion the actor faced and the heinousness of the harm she inflicted. The court then described the basic doctrinal components of a successful duress claim, as well as the theory underlying the defense and the kinds of factors that would support it:

> . . . The first [component] of duress [requires that the] defendant actually . . . believe in and be frightened by the likelihood of the threatened harm because the defense rests on principles of necessity. In effect, for duress to be present, "[the] defendant [must] claim[ ] to be psychically incapable of not acting, and therefore excused." Stated conversely, the subjective aspect becomes more apparent—even if a coercive threat may be deemed to be beyond the power of resistance for an ordinary reasonable person, the threat, nonetheless, may be insufficient to coerce the particular defendant and, when that happens, duress is not present for that defendant. The jury, therefore, must assess the sincerity of the defendant's asserted perception of an imminent threat of harm.
>
> The second component of the defense is objective in nature: a defendant's level of resistance to the particular threat must meet community standards of reasonableness. The jury must evaluate a defendant's response to the threat by applying the standard of the "person of reasonable firmness." The norm presupposes an ordinary person without "serious mental and emotional defects." It is an objective standard against which to measure the defendant's response to the "threat."
>
> This normative aspect of duress is essential to the defense's coexistence with society's duty to protect innocent third parties from harm. The defense does not excuse easily criminal conduct that could, or does, present harm to innocent persons. "[T]he normative component of duress assures that the coerced actor demonstrated the degree of fortitude expected of a member of the morally responsible community. In other words, even though the legally coerced actor failed to do the right thing, [his or] her act is nevertheless tolerated because [he or] she attained society's legitimate expectations of moral strength."
>
> In making this assessment, the jury must consider objectively such factors as the gravity of the threat, the proximity of the impending harm being threatened, opportunities for escape, likely execution of the threat, and the seriousness of the crime defendant committed. A defendant's personal timidity or lack of firmness in the face of intimidation does not serve as the measure for his or her conduct. Community expectations prevail in judging a defendant's response to a threat when that response involves engaging

> in criminal action toward, or affecting, an innocent third person—not the one who posed the threat to the defendant. With the defense of duress, a defendant is neither held to a standard of heroism, nor is defendant allowed to rely on his or her idiosyncratic mental and emotional weaknesses.
>
> Finally, before one can even claim to satisfy the components of duress set forth in subsection a of the statute, the defendant must satisfy a threshold requirement set forth in subsection b. The defendant must not have "recklessly placed himself [or herself] in a situation in which it was probable that he [or she] would be subjected to duress." If the defendant has acted so, the duress defense is unavailable.

The court then considered the question of whether expert testimony concerning battered woman syndrome was admissible to support the defendant's claim that she should be excused for having sex with her stepson. In a prior decision, State v. Kelly, 97 N.J. 178, 478 A.2d 364 (1984),[c] the court had considered whether such testimony was admissible to support a self-defense claim made by a woman who had stabbed her allegedly abusive husband to death. There, the court surveyed the social science literature describing the battered woman syndrome, which is "a series of common characteristics that appear in women who are abused physically and psychologically over an extended period of time by the dominant male figure in their lives." These characteristics include "psychological paralysis" that hinders the women from leaving their abusive mates and a belief that separation would be futile because their husband is "omnipotent." Frequently, the psychological "symptoms" are aggravated by social and economic obstacles—i.e., women tend to make less money than men and usually are "more responsible for child care"—that "make it difficult for women to extricate themselves from battering relationships." Ultimately, the court in *Kelly* decided that expert testimony about the syndrome was admissible to support the defendant's claim that the homicide was justified. In the court's view, the testimony would aid the jury in evaluating the basic elements of self-defense, which required the defendant to establish that she honestly and reasonably believed that it was necessary for her to use lethal force to defend herself against her husband.

In *B.H.*, the court cited *Kelly* for the proposition that the syndrome testimony is sufficiently reliable to be admitted "specifically for the purpose of assisting the jury 'to overcome common myths or misconceptions that a woman who had been the victim of battering would have surely have left the batterer.' " The more difficult question was whether the expert evidence also was "relevant in connection with the components of duress [set forth in the New Jersey statute], or to the threshold recklessness assessment that a defendant must vault." Turning first to the threshold question, the court decided that the testimony "was admissible and relevant to the recklessness aspect of the duress defense. . . . Syndrome evidence directly addresses any lay misperception that a defendant is reckless simply because she remained in the abusive relationship by explaining why a battered woman may be unable to leave."

Likewise, the court ruled that the expert testimony was relevant to the subjective question of whether the defendant honestly had believed that

---

[c] *State v. Kelly* is a main case in the self-defense materials in this chapter.

she confronted an imminent threat of danger. Testimony about the syndrome "was found helpful for a similar . . . purpose in respect of self-defense and has been used repeatedly in self-defense contexts when a jury must assess the credibility of a defendant claiming fear of perceived imminent danger from her abuser." The court could identify no reason why the evidence would be less informative for this purpose in the context of duress than in that of self-defense. In the specific circumstances presented in *B.H.*, for example, the court noted that the expert testimony would have bolstered the defendant's credibility by offering an explanation for "why a battered woman would conceal her abuser's role when reporting her own criminal act to police or other officials."

However, the court concluded that battered woman syndrome could not be used to support the second component of duress, which is the "ultimate determination" by the jury of "the reasonableness of a defendant's conduct." The court offered these observations to support this crucial holding:

> Because [the New Jersey duress statute] embodies an objective standard for the evaluation of a defendant's conduct in response to a threat by another, we can discern no place for battered woman syndrome evidence in that assessment. In applying [this] objective measure, it is a person of reasonable firmness that the jury must consider. The jury must evaluate objectively the defendant's criminal conduct toward a third person, and whether a person of ordinary strength and willpower would refuse to do the criminal act even in the face of the harm threatened. The idiosyncratic fact that the defendant may be susceptible to the demands of her abuser because she suffers from battered woman syndrome becomes irrelevant in that assessment. The issue is whether a person of reasonable firmness in her situation would have been able to resist the threat from her abuser. Expert testimony on the syndrome is inconsistent with the objective standard. Other jurisdictions also have held such evidence not relevant to an objective "person of reasonable firmness" standard, reasoning that the evidence simply explains why a particular defendant would succumb to coercion when a person without a background of being battered would not.

Commentators similarly have noted the inapplicability of the syndrome evidence to the objective standard.

> The battered woman defense, as currently formulated, runs contrary to this normative aspect of duress. . . . [T]he battered woman defense typically focuses on how the individual perceptions and psychological capacities of battered women, in fact, differ from those of the person of "reasonable firmness." The more that defense resembles a plea of diminished capacity or insanity, the less the battered offender resembles the morally responsible agent for whom the defense of duress was constructed. In short, the behavioral and psychological characteristics that currently comprise the battered woman defense and that render battered offenders more susceptible to threats and less capable of resistance cannot be imported into the objective standard without gutting duress of its normative function. Laura K. Dore, Downward

Adjustment and the Slippery Slope: The Use of Duress in Defense of Battered Offenders, 56 Ohio St. L.J. 665, 743–44 (1995).

It is not clear that the reasoning of *B.H.* is entirely consistent with that of *State v. Kelly* and the other precedents that have allowed testimony about battered woman syndrome to support claims of self-defense. In *Kelly*, it is important to notice that the court took pains to emphasize that the testimony was relevant not merely to the question of whether the accused woman honestly feared for her life, but also to the "objective reasonableness" of her belief that her life was in danger. As the court put it there, "our conclusion is that the expert's testimony, if accepted by the jury, would have aided it in determining whether, under the circumstances, a reasonable person would have believed there was imminent danger to her life." Does this portion of *Kelly* survive *B.H.*? Or do the two cases stand for the proposition that it is reasonable for a battered woman, when faced with threats of serious bodily harm by her abuser, to defend herself by using lethal force against him but not by following his command to commit an offense against a third party? In other words, do we hold actors to different standards of reasonableness in these two contexts? In *B.H.*, the court emphasizes that duress has a "normative aspect." Of course, self-defense has a "normative aspect" as well. Do the norms governing each context differ? Notice that the New Jersey duress statute, which follows the Model Penal Code, requires the jury to evaluate the compelling character of the alleged unlawful force not from the perspective of "a reasonable person" in the actor's situation but from that of "a person of reasonable firmness" in her situation. Is the "reasonable person" the same as the "person of reasonable firmness"? Is a history of being battered by the threatener relevant to the actor's "situation" in either context?

## 4. DURESS AS A DEFENSE TO MURDER

A controversial issue is whether duress should be recognized as a defense to intentional homicide. The common law rejected such a claim, and many modern codes adhere to this common law position. The drafters of the Model Penal Code, on the other hand, swept away this limitation. Which position should the law favor?[d]

For a brief period, British authorities supported the proposition that the duress defense should be available to a person charged with being an accomplice to murder but not to the principal actor in the homicide. In Director of Public Prosecutions for Northern Ireland v. Lynch, [1975] A.C. 653, the defendant drove several members of the Irish Republican Army on an expedition in which they shot and killed a Belfast policeman. In his defense, he claimed that he was not a member of the I.R.A. and that he drove the vehicle only because he feared that the leader of the group would shoot him if he disobeyed. The Appellate Committee of the House of Lords held, by a three-to-two majority, that an accomplice to murder could rely on a duress defense. However, in Abbott v. The Queen, [1976] 3 All E.R. 140, the Judicial Committee of the Privy Council, sitting on an appeal from Trinidad, refused to extend *Lynch* to a "principal in the first degree."

The defendant in *Abbott* was pressed into the service of a man named Malik who had a reputation for violence. Malik had established a commune

[d] In some jurisdictions an otherwise valid duress claim can reduce murder to manslaughter.

in Trinidad and insisted that Abbott join it. A week later, Malik directed Abbott and others to kill the mistress of another member of the commune and outlined the plan for doing so. When Abbott objected, Malik said that if he did anything to endanger the others, Abbott and his mother would be killed. After Malik left, Abbott and the others began to dig a hole as they had been instructed. When the victim arrived, appellant pushed her into the hole and held her while another person stabbed her. Because she was struggling, only minor wounds were inflicted and Abbott called to another of the group for help. This person jumped into the hole and inflicted a major wound in the victim's lung. The four men, including Abbott, then buried her while she was still alive and struggling. The Lords sitting in *Abbott* distinguished *Lynch* on the ground that this evidence supported the conclusion that Abbott was guilty as "a principal in the first degree in that he took an active and indeed leading part in the killing."

Regina v. Howe

In Regina v. Howe, [1987] 1 All ER 771, the House of Lords revisited this question and decided that the duress defense should be available to neither accomplices nor principals to murder. The facts of *Howe* suggest that the line between accomplice and principal is not a clear one. The appellants in *Howe* were two young men (aged 19 and 20) who assisted two other men in committing two homicides. One of the other men was the "dominant figure" in the group. He was 35 years old and "was dishonest, powerful, violent and sadistic. Through acts of actual violence or threats of violence, [he] gained control of each of the appellants, who became fearful of him." On successive days in October 1983, the four men kidnapped a man and killed him, after raping and torturing him. The appellants participated in beating the first victim, but the "coup de grace was delivered by" one of the other men. The second victim died when the appellants "strangl[ed] him with [a] shoelace, each holding one end." The appellants alleged that they committed these acts "in fear of their own lives;" indeed, they claimed that they believed that their companion "would treat them in the same way as [the victims] had been treated if they did not comply with his directions." Concluding that the appellants had acted as accomplices to the first homicide and as principals to the second, the trial court instructed the jury that the defense of duress was available in connection with the first, but not the second, murder.

The appellants challenged their convictions on the ground that, among other things, the trial court erred in charging the jurors that duress could not be raised by a principal to murder. The House of Lords rejected this argument and took the occasion to overrule *Lynch*. As Lord Mackay remarked in his opinion:

> The argument for the appellants essentially is that, . . . there being no practical distinction available between *Lynch's* case and the present case, this case should be decided in the same way. The opposite point of view is that, since *Lynch's* case was concerned not with the actual killer but with a person who was made guilty . . . by the doctrine of accession, the correct starting point for this matter is the case of the actual killer. In my opinion this latter is the correct approach. The law has extended the liability to trial and punishment faced by the actual killer to those who are participants with him in the crime and it seems to me, therefore, that, where there is a question as important as this in issue, the correct starting point is the case of the actual killer. [W]riters of authority

> [have long agreed] that the defence of duress was not available in a charge of murder . . . because of the supreme importance that the law afforded to the protection of human life and . . . it seemed repugnant that the law should recognize in any individual in any circumstances, however extreme, the right to choose that one innocent person should be killed rather than another. In my opinion that is the question which we still must face. Is it right that the law should confer this right in any circumstances, however extreme? [The House should return to the answer that Hale gave to this question, namely, that a person "ought rather to die himself than kill an innocent."]

The Lords agreed with the proposition that different killers might bear different levels of culpability, but they concluded that the distinction between accomplice and principal did not provide a principled way to distinguish between those who should be permitted to plead duress and those who should not. Lord Brandon explained the dilemma:

> [A]s a matter of common sense one participant in a murder may be considered less morally at fault than another. The youth who hero-worships the gang leader and acts as a look-out man whilst the gang enter a jeweller's shop and kill the owner in order to steal is an obvious example. In the eyes of the law they are all guilty of murder, but justice will be served by requiring those who did the killing to serve a longer period in prison before being released . . . than the youth who acted as look-out. However, it is not difficult to give examples where more moral fault may be thought to attach to a participant in murder who was not the actual killer; I have already mentioned the example of a contract killing. . . . Another example would be an intelligent man goading a weak-minded individual into a killing he would not otherwise commit.
>
> It is therefore neither rational nor fair to make the defence dependent on whether the accused is the actual killer or took some other part in the murder. I have toyed with the idea that it might be possible to leave it to the discretion of the trial judge to decide whether the defence should be available to one who was not the killer, but I have rejected this as introducing too great a degree of uncertainty into the availability of the defence. I am not troubled by some of the extreme examples cited in favour of allowing the defence to those who are not the killer, such as a woman motorist being highjacked and forced to act as getaway driver, or a pedestrian being forced to give misleading information to the police to protect robbery and murder in a shop. The short, practical answer is that it is inconceivable that such persons would be prosecuted; they would be called as the principal witnesses for the prosecution.

## 5. CONTRIBUTORY ACTIONS BY THE DEFENDANT

*State v. B.H.* identifies another significant constraint on the availability of the duress defense. As the court put it there, the defense is not available at all unless the defendant satisfies "a threshold requirement" by showing that she did not "recklessly" place herself "in a situation in which it was probable that [she] would be subjected to duress." The portion of the New Jersey duress statute imposing this limitation, which is quoted in

*B.H.*, is taken verbatim from § 2.09(2) of the Model Penal Code. What policy judgments support this provision? Is the provision consistent with the general grading principles underlying the Model Code? Recall, for example, that a person who mistakenly believes in the necessity of self-defense can be convicted only of an offense for which recklessness is the required culpability if the mistake was made recklessly, and only of an offense for which negligence is the required culpability if the mistake was made negligently.[e] Compare also § 3.02(2). Does the duress defense present a special situation justifying departure from this principle?

Williams v. State, 101 Md.App. 408, 646 A.2d 1101 (1994), presents one context in which this limitation on the defense may apply. In *Williams*, the Court of Special Appeals of Maryland concluded that the duress defense was not available because the "compulsion arose by the defendant's own fault." Williams was convicted for attempted robbery and other crimes after he and three other men pushed their way into the home of Reverend Hale, threatened Hale with a gun, and searched Hale's home for money and "dope." Testifying at trial, Williams explained how he came to participate in this episode:

> [Williams stated] that he was abducted by the three men because they believed that he knew the whereabouts of the drug stash of one Chuckie Eubanks, a reputed drug dealer. Williams had borrowed money from Chuckie's brother . . . and had been induced to make a drug run to New York in order to help repay his debt. The Eubanks organization required Williams to make a second trip to New York, during which Williams cooperated with the police .... Apparently, the three abductors, who were former members of Eubanks's drug organization, knew of Williams's relationship with Eubanks and believed that he would know the location of the stash house. When Williams was abducted by the men, he told them that he did not know its location. Williams led the men to Hale's apartment, told them it was the stash house, and knocked on the door. Once inside Hale's apartment, Williams testified that he pretended to participate in the search of the premises.

After surveying the authorities, the court decided to endorse the Model Code's approach, under which the duress defense is not available to an accused who "recklessly . . . places himself or herself in a situation where it is probable that he or she would be subjected to duress." The court also adopted the reasoning articulated by the drafters of the Model Code in support of this approach. Although this limitation "may have the effect of sanctioning conviction of a crime of purpose when the actor's culpability was limited to recklessness, we think the substitution is permissible in view of the exceptional nature of the defense. The [limitation] will have its main room for operation in the case of persons who connect themselves with criminal activities, in which case too fine a line need not be drawn." Finally, the court concluded that the duress defense was not available to Williams because "his prior conduct contributed mightily to the predicament in which he later found himself:"

---

[e] The Model Code provides in § 2.09(2) that the defense "is also unavailable if he was negligent in placing himself in such a situation, whenever negligence suffices to establish culpability for the offense charged." Section 2.09(2) is thus consistent with the grading judgments expressed elsewhere in the Model Code.

> . . . Williams voluntarily became involved with the Eubanks's drug organization. . . . Williams borrowed money from Rodney Eubanks. Because of his inability to repay promptly, Williams [made two drug runs.] [T]he evidence does not suggest that he was forced to make these runs[;] he did this of his own volition to help pay off his debt. By becoming involved with this drug ring, Williams through his own recklessness made others aware of his connection with Eubanks, including his abductors. . . . This was a situation that would not have occurred but for Williams's association with the drug organization.

Paul Robinson has criticized the Model Code approach on the ground that it "simply does not generate liability proportionate to the actor's culpability." For example, "[o]ne who is reckless as to placing himself in a situation where he will be subjected to coercion is not necessarily reckless as to being coerced *into injuring another*." Paul H. Robinson, Causing the Conditions of One's Own Defense: A Study in the Limits of Theory in Criminal Law Doctrine, 71 Va. L. Rev. 1, 20 (1985). Accordingly, Robinson argues that an actor such as Williams should be punished where he "is not only culpable as to causing the defense conditions, but also has a culpable state of mind *as to causing himself to engage in the conduct constituting the offense*." Would the defendant in *Williams* be liable under Robinson's proposal? Is Robinson's approach preferable to the Model Code's position?

### 6. BRAINWASHING OR COERCIVE PERSUASION

Patricia Hearst was kidnapped and held in captivity by the Symbionese Liberation Army. She reported that she was confined in a closet—tied and blindfolded—for almost two months, and was subjected to persistent interrogation, and to physical, emotional, and sexual abuse, by her captors. See United States v. Hearst, 563 F.2d 1331 (9th Cir. 1977). Two-and-one-half months after her capture, she participated in a bank robbery with her abductors and was subsequently arrested and charged with bank robbery and weapons offenses. She raised two related defensive claims. On the one hand, she claimed that she was forced to participate in the robbery by threats of death—a traditional duress claim; on the other hand, she claimed that after the robbery, her involvement in other criminal activity and her continuing relationship with her captors was attributable to the "brainwashing" or "coercive persuasion" to which she had been subjected. In essence, her claim was that her captors had succeeded in inducing a profound alteration in her character, displacing her attitudes, beliefs, and values with their own.

"Coercive persuasion" was first raised as a defense, unsuccessfully, by American prisoners of war in Korea who were charged in the 1950's with collaborating with the enemy. See, e.g., United States v. Batchelor, 19 C.M.R. 452 (1955). The phenomenon attracted considerable clinical and scientific interest, which was revived in the wake of the Hearst trial. Legal scholars have disagreed over whether the law should recognize "coercive persuasion" as a ground of exculpation. Compare Richard Delgado, Assumption of Criminal States of Mind: Towards a Defense Theory for the Coercively Persuaded ("Brainwashed") Defendant, 63 Minn. L. Rev. 1 (1978), with Joshua Dressler, Professor Delgado's "Brainwashing" Defense: Courting a Determinist Legal System, 63 Minn. L. Rev. 335 (1979). Assuming that sensory deprivation, social isolation, and persistent indoctrination actually can induce a drastic alteration of a captive's character and values, is it morally appropriate to punish the defendant for conduct engaged in while "brainwashed?" Would recognition of the defense undermine the social control functions of the law? Consider, in this connection, the argument that the brainwashed individual's claim is morally indistinguishable from that of a defendant whose attitudes and values were shaped by the experience of growing up in a deviant subculture. If the two claims are morally indistinguishable, should both or neither be recognized as excuses for criminal misconduct? Should one claim be allowed, but not the other?

## 7. A GENERAL PRINCIPLE OF SITUATIONAL COMPULSION?

There appears to be a moral gap between the traditional defenses of duress and necessity. Neither the common law nor most modern codes provide a defense in situations where the defendant's choice is constrained, however severely, by circumstances other than personal threats of harm—unless the harm caused by the offense is less than that which would have occurred in its absence. It has been suggested that the law should close this gap by recognizing a general principle of situational compulsion. The notion is that the law should afford an excuse to defendants whose conduct was responsive to coercive situational pressures rather than to defects of character.

Would such an excuse be appropriate in *Regina* v. *Dudley and Stephens*? In that case two members of a starving, shipwrecked crew were charged with murder for killing and eating a dying cabin boy in order to preserve their own lives. Assuming that the killing of an innocent person under these circumstances is not morally justified as a choice of evils, is it nonetheless appropriate to recognize that the homicide should be excused? Even if Dudley and Stephens acted wrongfully, can they fairly be blamed for having succumbed to the overwhelming pressures that confronted them? Surely, the threshold for giving in to the pressure—and taking an innocent life—should be high, but is it fair to say that there is no point at which such action should be excused? How much fortitude can fairly be demanded of persons in that situation?

Should the principle of situational compulsion be generalized beyond coercive circumstances involving demonstrable threats to the actor's life and safety? Are there other unusual circumstances that can propel the ordinary person toward criminal conduct, even though they may not be as coercive as those involved in *Dudley and Stephens*?

Consider, for example, the recurrent cases of mercy killings. In one publicized case, a 23-year-old man shot his dearly-loved elder brother who had been paralyzed, irreversibly, below the neck in a motorcycle accident. The victim, who was in severe pain, begged his brother to kill him. Three days after the accident, the defendant walked into the hospital and asked his brother if he was still in pain, and his brother nodded that he was. The defendant then said: "Well, I'm here today to end your pain. Is that all right with you?" His brother nodded and the defendant said: "Close your eyes, George. I'm going to kill you." He then placed his shotgun against his brother's temple and pulled the trigger.[f] Should the law recognize a claim of situational excuse in such a case?

---

[f] This case is described in Paige Mitchell, Act of Love: The Killing of George Zygmanik (1976).

## NOTES ON THE DEFENSE OF ENTRAPMENT

### 1. THE ENTRAPMENT DEFENSE

The defense of entrapment, which is recognized in every United States jurisdiction, usually is covered in courses in criminal procedure. The theory for studying the defense under the rubric of criminal procedure is that the defense functions as a limitation on police investigative practices. The idea is that, by making such a defense available, the criminal law will discourage the police from using tactics that improperly induce citizens to commit crimes for which they are then arrested. Under this view, the defense of entrapment, though it is not constitutionally based, is similar to other rules—many of them constitutional in origin—that are designed to limit the zeal with which the police enforce the law. However, there is a competing view of entrapment that holds that the scope of the defense should be determined in part by principles of situational excuse. The two approaches are explored in the following case.

#### *(i) People v. Barraza*

In People v. Barraza, 23 Cal.3d 675, 153 Cal.Rptr. 459, 591 P.2d 947 (1979), the defendant was charged with two counts of selling heroin to a female undercover agent. He denied that the first sale had occurred and claimed he had been entrapped into committing the second. The court summarized the evidence concerning the second transaction:

> [Both the] agent and the defendant testified that the agent tried to contact defendant by telephoning the [drug abuse detoxification center] where he worked as a patient-care technician, several times during the three weeks between the dates of the two alleged heroin sale transactions. On September 11, the agent finally succeeded in speaking to defendant and asked him if he had "anything"; defendant asked her to come to the detoxification center. The two then met at the center and talked for some time—a few minutes according to the agent, more than an hour by the defendant's account.
>
> The agent's version of this encounter described defendant as hesitant to deal because "he had done a lot of time in jail and he couldn't afford to go back to jail and . . . he had to be careful about what he was doing." She further testified that after she convinced defendant she "wasn't a cop," he gave her a note, to present to a woman named Stella, which read: "Saw Cheryl [the agent]. Give her a pair of pants [argot for heroin]. [signed] Cal." The agent concluded her testimony by stating that she then left defendant, used the note to introduce herself to the dealer Stella, and purchased an orange balloon containing heroin.
>
> Defendant described a somewhat different pattern of interaction with the agent at their September 11th meeting. He related that he had asked her to come and see him because he was "fed up with her" and wanted her to quit calling him at the hospital where he worked because he was afraid she would cause him to lose his job. He insisted he told her during their conversation that he did not have anything; that he had spent more than 23 years in prison but now he had held a job at the detoxification center for four

> years, was on methadone and was clean, and wanted the agent to stop "bugging" him. He testified that the agent persisted in her efforts to enlist his aid in purchasing heroin, and that finally—after more than an hour of conversation—when the agent asked for a note to introduce her to a source of heroin he agreed to give her a note to "get her off . . . [his] back." According to the defendant, he told the agent that he did not know if Stella had anything, and gave her a note which read: "Saw Cheryl. If you have a pair of pants, let her have them." . . .

The trial judge refused to instruct the jury on entrapment, and Barraza was convicted. His conviction was reversed by the California Supreme Court.

### *(ii) Approaches to the Defense*

The *Barraza* court's opinion summarized the competing approaches to the entrapment defense as follows:

> Though long recognized by the courts of almost every United States jurisdiction,[1] the defense of entrapment has produced a deep schism concerning its proper theoretical basis and mode of application. The opposing views have been delineated in a series of United States Supreme Court decisions. The Court first considered the entrapment defense in Sorrells v. United States, 287 U.S. 435 (1932). The majority held that entrapment tended to establish innocence, reasoning that Congress in enacting the criminal statute there at issue could not have intended to punish persons otherwise innocent who were lured into committing the proscribed conduct by governmental instigation. This focus on whether persons were "otherwise innocent" led the majority to adopt what has become known as the subjective or origin-of-intent test under which entrapment is established only if (i) governmental instigation and inducement overstep the bounds of permissibility, and (ii) the defendant did not harbor a pre-existing criminal intent. Under the subjective test a finding that the defendant was predisposed to commit the offense would negate innocence and therefore defeat the defense. Finally, because entrapment was viewed as bearing on the guilt or innocence of the accused, the issue was deemed proper for submission to the jury.
>
> Justice Roberts wrote an eloquent concurring opinion, joined by Justices Brandeis and Stone, in which he argued that the purpose of the entrapment defense is to deter police misconduct. He emphatically rejected the notion that the defendant's conduct or predisposition had any relevance: "The applicable principle is that courts must be closed to the trial of a crime instigated by the government's own agents. No other issue, no comparison of equities as between the guilty official and the guilty defendant, has any place in the enforcement of this overruling principle of public poli-

[1] "The defense appears to have first been asserted by Eve, who complained, when charged with eating fruit of the tree of knowledge of good and evil: 'The serpent beguiled me, and I did eat.' Genesis 3:13. Though Eve was unsuccessful in asserting the defense, it has been suggested that the defense was unavailable to her because the entrapping party was not an agent of the punishing authority. Roger D. Groot, The Serpent Beguiled Me and I (Without Scienter) Did Eat—Denial of Crime and the Entrapment Defense, 1973 U.Ill.L.F. 254."

cy." Because he viewed deterrence of impermissible law enforcement activity as the proper rationale for the entrapment defense, Justice Roberts concluded that the defense was inappropriate for jury consideration: "It is the province of the court and of the court alone to protect itself and the government from such prostitution of the criminal law."

In Sherman v. United States, 356 U.S. 369 (1958), the majority refused to adopt the "objective" theory of entrapment urged by Justice Roberts, choosing rather to continue recognizing as relevant the defendant's own conduct and predisposition. The court held that "a line must be drawn between the trap for the unwary innocent and the trap for the unwary criminal." Justice Frankfurter, writing for four members of the Court in a concurring opinion, argued forcefully for Justice Roberts' objective theory: "The courts refuse to convict an entrapped defendant, not because his conduct falls outside the proscription of the statute, but because, even if his guilt be admitted, the methods employed on behalf of the government to bring about conviction cannot be countenanced." He reasoned that "a test that looks to the character and predisposition of the defendant rather than the conduct of the police loses sight of the underlying reason for the defense of entrapment. No matter what the defendant's past record and present inclinations to criminality, or the depths to which he has sunk in the estimation of society, certain police conduct to ensnare him into further crime is not to be tolerated by an advanced society. . . . Permissible police activity does not vary according to the particular defendant concerned. . . ." "Human nature is weak enough," he wrote, "and sufficiently beset by temptations without government adding to them and generating crime." Justice Frankfurter concluded that guidance as to appropriate official conduct could only be provided if the court reviewed police conduct and decided the entrapment issue.

The United States Supreme Court recently reviewed the theoretical basis of the entrapment defense in United States v. Russell, 411 U.S. 423 (1973), and once again the court split five votes to four in declining to overrule the subjective theory adopted in *Sorrells*.

A dissenting opinion in *Barraza* noted that the test in the federal courts and in all but seven states is the "predisposition" or subjective standard. The *Barraza* court nonetheless adopted the minority view on the ground that the defense should be granted in order to deter objectionable police behavior even if the defendant was predisposed to commit the crime. This is also the approach codified in § 2.13 of the Model Penal Code.[a]

### *(iii) Questions on the Defense*

Traditionally, the entrapment defense has been limited to cases involving inducements by the police. In other words, there is no defense of "private entrapment." To the extent that entrapment implies a lack of blameworthiness, why should it matter whether the defendant was entrapped by

[a] The two approaches to entrapment are skillfully contrasted in Roger Park, The Entrapment Controversy, 60 Minn.L.Rev. 163 (1976).

the police? On the other hand, the law's failure to recognize private entrapment tends to confirm the idea that the defense is designed mainly to deter unacceptable police behavior. If so, does it follow that the subjective test should be abandoned in favor of a test focusing squarely on the propriety of the official conduct? Does it follow, in other words, that considerations of individual blameworthiness should be irrelevant to the application of the defense? If so, why should a defendant who was predisposed to commit the crime be acquitted simply because the "ordinary" law-abiding person would also have been induced by the police tactics? Conversely, should a defendant who proves that *he or she* was induced by the police, and would not otherwise have committed the crime, be deprived of the defense because the jury concludes that a hypothetical law-abiding person would not have been induced?

On the other hand, is the entrapment defense consistent with the substantive policies of the penal law? Can it be sensibly argued that the ordinary law-abiding citizen should have the fortitude to resist inducements to criminal behavior, whether by the police or by anyone else? Is a person induced to commit a criminal act by the clever manipulations of undercover agents or informants any less blameworthy than a person who is induced to provide criminal assistance to an employer who threatens to fire him or disclose a sorry episode from his past? Or a person who is induced to provide illegal aid to a loved one who has become enmeshed in criminal activity? Short of duress, does sympathy, friendship, or fear provide an excuse for criminal behavior? Even if a jury were to find that Barraza was not otherwise predisposed to deal heroin and wanted to return to a law-abiding path, is it unfair to hold him criminally liable for giving in to Cheryl's persistent entreaties? Laying aside the question of deterring undesirable police practices, would it be sensible to abolish the entrapment defense?

### 2. *COX V. LOUISIANA*

In Cox v. Louisiana, 379 U.S. 559 (1965), the defendant was convicted of violating a statute punishing one who "pickets or parades . . . near a building housing a [state] court." The defendant's contention is revealed in the following excerpt from the decision reversing the conviction:

> Thus, the highest police officials of the city, in the presence of the sheriff and mayor, in effect told the demonstrators that they could meet where they did, 101 feet from the courthouse steps, but could not meet closer to the courthouse. In effect, appellant was advised that a demonstration at the place it was held would not be one "near" the courthouse within the terms of the statute.
>
> In Raley v. Ohio, 360 U.S. 423 (1959), this Court held that the due process clause prevented conviction of persons refusing to answer questions of a state investigating commission when they relied upon assurances of the commission, either express or implied, that they had a privilege under state law to refuse to answer, though in fact this privilege was not available to them. The situation presented here is analogous to that in *Raley*, which we deem to be controlling. As in *Raley*, under all the circumstances of this case, after the public officials acted as they did, to sustain appellant's later conviction for demonstrating where they told him he could "would be to sanction an indefensible sort of entrapment by the state—convicting a citizen for exercising a privilege which

the state had clearly told him was available to him." The due-process clause does not permit convictions to be obtained under such circumstances.

What was the basis for the *Cox* decision? Is "entrapment" the best description for the idea the Court had in mind? Was the Court aiming to deter objectionable police behavior? Or did the Court conclude that the defendants could not fairly be blamed for violating the law under these circumstances? On the other hand, if *Cox* is a case of situational excuse, is it consistent with the ignorantia-juris principle studied in Chapter III?

How would *Cox* be decided under the Model Penal Code? Would the defendants be entitled to a defense based on official misstatement of the law under § 2.04(3)(b)(iv)? Should the existence of the defense depend upon whether the "highest police officials" were present? Consider also § 2.13(1)(a). Should the existence of the defense depend upon whether the police made "knowingly false" statements designed to induce the defendants to violate the law?

In connection with *Cox*, consider *United States* v. *Barker*. That case involved the "foot-soldiers" of the burglary of the office of Daniel Ellsberg's psychiatrist. The defendants claimed that they believed the break-in had been legally authorized by top White House aides. It turned out, however, that the aides did not have the authority to order a warrantless search. Can the defendants fairly be blamed for unquestioning obedience in this situation? Should a citizen's reasonable reliance on apparent official authority constitute a defense when it turns out that the officials exceeded their authority? Does *Cox* have any bearing on these questions?

# CHAPTER VIII

# CRIMINAL RESPONSIBILITY

## INTRODUCTORY NOTE ON CRIMINAL RESPONSIBILITY

In contemporary usage, the term "mens rea" usually denotes the specific states of mind defined as "elements" of particular criminal offenses. The language is no longer meant to convey the idea of general malevolence characteristic of early common law usage. However, the idea of a "guilty mind," in a more generalized moral sense, has continuing significance in relation to what the commentators have called "the general conditions of criminal responsibility." The two most important of these conditions are maturity and sanity. Early on, the common law courts developed the "defenses" of infancy and insanity (including "idiocy" and "lunacy") to exclude from criminal punishment those who lacked the "capacity" to have a "morally accountable and punishable mind."[a]

This concept of "responsibility" is not congruent with the technical requirements of culpability studied in Chapter III. As Sanford Kadish has noted:[b]

> In requiring mens rea in [its] special sense the law [absolves a person who] has shown himself . . . to be no different than the rest of us, or not different enough to justify the criminal sanction. In requiring . . . legal responsibility, the law absolves a person precisely because his deficiencies of temperament, personality or maturity distinguish him so utterly from the rest of us to whom the law's threats are addressed that we do not expect him to comply.

It is sometimes said that the "tests" of responsibility aim to identify those persons whose immaturity or mental aberration deprives them of the capacity to have criminal intent or mens rea. However, this is not accurate. It is true, of course, that small infants lack the capacity to form a conscious purpose, to have a conscious awareness of the environment, or even to be conscious of making any choices at all. Elderly adults suffering from severe deterioration of brain function also might lack such capacities. However, the defenses of infancy and insanity have never been limited to such persons; the law has also withheld criminal liability from children and mentally disordered adults who clearly had the capacity to entertain the purposes, intentions, beliefs, or perceptions that would establish mens rea in its technical sense. As one commentator observed, "insane persons . . . may have intent to kill, to set fire to houses, to steal, to rape, to defraud; but the great question is whether [such a person] is a responsible moral agent."[c]

The materials in this chapter explore the factors that determine whether children and mentally disordered adults are "responsible moral agents" subject to criminal liability and punishment. Section 1 covers the

---

[a] Henry W. Ballentine, Criminal Responsibility of the Insane and Feebleminded, 9 J. Crim.L. & Criminology 485, 493 (1919).

[b] Sanford Kadish, The Decline of Innocence, 26 Camb.L.J. 273, 275 (1968).

[c] Henry W. Ballentine, Criminal Responsibility of the Insane and Feebleminded, 9 J. Crim.L. & Criminology 485, 492 (1919).

common law defense of infancy and its contemporary applications in the context of juvenile justice. Section 2 covers the defense of insanity and other doctrines dealing with mental abnormality.

## SECTION 1: IMMATURITY

### INTRODUCTORY NOTES ON THE INFANCY DEFENSE AND THE JUVENILE COURT

#### 1. THE COMMON LAW PRESUMPTIONS

As the requirement of blameworthiness began to take shape in the criminal law, the idea soon developed—by the end of the 13th century—that children of tender years could not have a guilty mind and, accordingly, were not punishable. Although older children could be convicted if the circumstances of the offense demonstrated an "understanding discretion," royal pardons apparently spared many such children from execution. Professor Sayre notes that the defense of infancy had "taken definite form" by the 16th century:

> . . . An infant's guilt depended upon his mental state; but in a day when the defendant accused of felony was not allowed to take the stand, the determination of his mental capacity and discretion was naturally sought through legal presumptions and through the consequent drawing of somewhat arbitrary age lines when infants would be conclusively presumed to possess or to lack the necessary "discretion."[a]

The lines marking the operation of these presumptions were somewhat unsettled until the 17th century, when the works of Coke and Hale fixed seven and 14 as the critical ages for determining the criminal responsibility of children. According to Lord Matthew Hale,[b] an infant younger than seven could not "be guilty of felony" because "for them a felonious discretion is almost an impossibility in nature"; the presumption of incapacity was irrebuttable. However, adolescents older than 14 were subject to criminal liability on the same terms as adults, for it was presumed that "they are doli capaces and can discern between good and evil." A child between seven and 14 could be convicted only if it was proved by "strong and pregnant evidence" that "he understood what he did." In these cases the presumption of incapacity applied, but it was rebuttable. These common law presumptions were received intact in the United States.

#### 2. ANTECEDENTS OF THE JUVENILE COURT

The determination that a youth was criminally liable did not necessarily mean that she or he was punished on the same terms as an adult. Historians who have researched early English records and colonial American practices have concluded that the death penalty generally was not imposed on youthful offenders. Also, during the colonial and post-colonial era, convicted children often were bound to masters for lengthy

[a] Francis Bowes Sayre, Mens Rea, 45 Harv.L.Rev. 974, 1009 (1932).

[b] Matthew Hale, The History of the Pleas of the Crown 25–27 (Philadelphia 1847) (1st ed. 1736). On the development of the common law presumptions, see generally A.W.G. Kean, The History of the Criminal Liability of Children, 53 L.Q.Rev. 364 (1937).

apprenticeships instead of suffering the normal penal consequences of conviction. Nonetheless, many youthful offenders were confined with adults in local jails or almshouses and, eventually, in the penitentiaries that most states established during the first half of the 19th century.

A major 19th-century development was the creation of separate "houses of refuge," or reformatories, for children charged with, or convicted of, criminal offenses. One of the first such institutions was established in Pennsylvania in 1826 with statutory authority to "receive . . . such children who shall be taken up or committed as vagrants, or upon any criminal charge, or duly convicted of criminal offenses, as may . . . be deemed proper objects."[c] By the turn of the century, most states had established such institutions. Although some states prohibited confinement of youthful offenders in penitentiaries, assignment to the reformatories usually was discretionary. As a result, juvenile offenders frequently were confined in local jails with adults, both before trial and after conviction. Also, juveniles convicted of serious crimes—usually those punishable by life imprisonment—customarily were regarded as unfit subjects for correction in the houses of refuge and were imprisoned in the penitentiary.

The placement of juvenile offenders in reformatories was an important dispositional reform, but it left the substantive criminal law unchanged. Children older than seven were still subject to conviction and punishment for criminal offenses. However, a concurrent statutory development had more far-reaching substantive significance. Nine years after establishing its House of Refuge, the Pennsylvania legislature authorized the institution to admit children who had not been charged with or convicted of crime, but who had been found by justices of the peace to be incorrigible or beyond parental authority.[d] In so doing, the state was invoking its power as parens patriae or "common guardian of the community." In the course of rejecting a constitutional challenge to the commitment procedure, the Supreme Court of Pennsylvania observed:

> The House of Refuge is not a prison, but a school. . . . The object of the charity is reformation, by training its inmates to industry; by imbuing their minds with principles of morality and religion; by furnishing them with means to earn a living; and, above all, by separating them from the corrupting influence of improper associates. To this end may not the natural parents, when unequal to the task of education, or unworthy of it, be superseded by the parens patriae, or common guardian of the community? . . . The [child] has been snatched from a course which must have ended in confirmed depravity; and, not only is the restraint of her person lawful, but it would be an act of extreme cruelty to release her from it.[e]

Following Pennsylvania's lead, most states authorized summary commitment of incorrigible, ungovernable, or neglected children to the reformatories, and this practice was routinely upheld by the courts. Although data are not available, it seems likely that those youths who lacked criminal responsibility for otherwise criminal acts by operation of the common law

---

[c] Act of March 23, 1826, quoted in Ex parte Crouse, 4 Whart. 9, 10 (Pa.1839).

[d] Act of April 10, 1835, quoted in Ex parte Crouse, 4 Whart. 9, 10 (Pa.1839).

[e] Ex parte Crouse, 4 Whart. 9, 11 (Pa. 1839).

infancy defense were committed to reformatories through this separate "civil" process.[f]

### 3. THE JUVENILE COURT MOVEMENT

The next step was the creation of the juvenile court, a reform reflecting a wholesale repudiation of the premises and methods of the criminal law and an equally sweeping assertion of the state's parens-patriae authority. Jurisdiction over "delinquent" children below a designated age—usually 16 or 18—was vested exclusively in the juvenile court. The declared purpose of the intervention was therapeutic rather than punitive; the judge's task was to diagnose the child's problem and to order appropriate treatment. Illinois generally is credited with enacting the first juvenile-court law in 1899, and by 1917 all but three states had passed such laws. The attitudes and beliefs leading to creation of the juvenile court have been much discussed by legal and social historians. It "represents the most important and ambitious effort yet undertaken by our law to give practical expression to the rehabilitative ideal."[g] The philosophy underlying the new court was enthusiastically described by Herbert H. Lou, Juvenile Courts in the United States 2 (1927):

> [The] principles upon which the juvenile court acts are radically different from those of the criminal courts. In place of judicial tribunals, restrained by antiquated procedure, saturated in an atmosphere of hostility, trying cases for determining guilt and inflicting punishment according to inflexible rules of law, we have now juvenile courts, in which the relations of the child to his parents or other adults and to the state or society are defined and are adjusted summarily according to the scientific findings about the child and his environments. In place of magistrates, limited by the outgrown custom and compelled to walk in the paths fixed by the law of the realm, we have now socially-minded judges, who hear and adjust cases according not to rigid rules of law but to what the interests of society and the interests of the child or good conscience demand. In place of juries, prosecutors, and lawyers, trained in the old conception of law and staging dramatically, but often amusingly, legal battles, as the necessary paraphernalia of a criminal court, we have now probation officers, physicians, psychologists and psychiatrists, who search for the social, physiological, psychological, and mental backgrounds of the child in order to arrive at reasonable and just solutions of individual cases. In other words, in this new court we tear down primitive prejudice, hatred, and hostility toward the lawbreaker . . . and we attempt, as far as possible, to administer justice in the name of truth, love, and understanding.

Challenges to the constitutionality of the procedures employed in juvenile proceedings were quickly and uniformly rejected. The courts typically emphasized the benevolent purposes of the intervention, as did the Supreme Court of Pennsylvania in 1905:

---

[f] The development of the juvenile court is traced in Anthony M. Platt, The Child Savers (1960).

[g] Francis Allen, The Borderland of Criminal Justice 48–49 (1964).

> To save a child from becoming a criminal, or from continuing in a career of crime, to end in maturer years in public punishment and disgrace, the legislature surely may provide for the salvation of such a child . . . by bringing it into one of the courts of the state without any process at all. . . . [T]he act is not for the trial of a child charged with a crime but is mercifully to save it from such an ordeal, with the prison or penitentiary in its wake, if the child's own good and the best interests of the state justify such salvation. . . . The design is not punishment nor the restraint imprisonment any more than is the wholesome restraint which a parent exercises over his child.[h]

## 4. PROCEDURAL REFORM OF JUVENILE JUSTICE

By the 1960s, it was widely recognized that the juvenile-justice system had fallen far short of the aspirations of the child savers described by Lou. The criticisms, which extended both to the premises and methods of the juvenile court, were summarized in 1967 by an influential government report:

> [T]he great hopes originally held for the juvenile court have not been fulfilled. It has not succeeded significantly in rehabilitating delinquent youth, in reducing or even stemming the tide of juvenile criminality, or in bringing justice and compassion to the child offender. . . .
>
> One reason for the failure of the juvenile courts has been the community's continuing unwillingness to provide the resources—the people and facilities and concern—necessary to permit them to realize their potential and prevent them from taking on some of the undesirable features typical of lower criminal courts in this country. . . .
>
> While statutes, judges, and commentators still talk the language of compassion, help, and treatment, it has become clear that in fact the same purposes that characterize the use of the criminal law for adult offenders—retribution, condemnation, deterrence, incapacitation—are involved in the disposition of juvenile offenders too. These are society's ultimate techniques for protection against threatening conduct; it is inevitable that they should be used against threats from the young as well as the old when other resources appear unavailing. . . .
>
> The difficulty is not that this compromise with the rehabilitative ideal has occurred, but that it has not been acknowledged. Juvenile-court laws and procedures that can be defended and rationalized solely on the basis of the original optimistic theories endure as if the vitality of those theories were undiluted. . . . Delinquency is adjudicated in informal proceedings that often lack safeguards fundamental for protecting the individual and for assuring reliable determinations, as if the court were a hospital clinic and its only objective were to discover the child's malady and to cure him. As observed by Mr. Justice Fortas, speaking for

[h] Commonwealth v. Fisher, 213 Pa. 48, 53–56, 62 A. 198, 200–01 (1905). For a review of the early judicial decisions upholding the juvenile court procedures, see Julian Mack, The Juvenile Court, 23 Harv.L.Rev. 104 (1909).—[Footnote by eds.]

the Supreme Court in Kent v. United States, 383 U.S. 541, 546 (1966), "there may be grounds for concern that the child receives the worst of both worlds: that he gets neither the protections accorded to adults nor the solicitous care and regenerative treatment postulated for children."

What emerges then, is this: In theory the juvenile court was to be helpful and rehabilitative rather than punitive. In fact the distinction often disappears, not only because of the absence of facilities and personnel but also because of the limits of knowledge and technique. In theory the court's action was to affix no stigmatizing label. In fact a delinquent is generally viewed by employers, schools, the armed services—by society generally—as a criminal. In theory the court was to treat children guilty of criminal acts in non-criminal ways. In fact it labels truants and runaways as junior criminals.

. . . What is required is . . . a revised philosophy of the juvenile court based on the recognition that in the past our reach exceeded our grasp. The spirit that animated the juvenile-court movement was fed in part by a humanitarian compassion for offenders who were children. That willingness to understand and treat people who threaten public safety and security should be nurtured, not turned aside as hopeless sentimentality, both because it is civilized and because social protection itself demands constant search for alternatives to the crude and limited expedient of condemnation and punishment. But neither should it be allowed to outrun reality. The juvenile court is a court of law, charged like other agencies of criminal justice with protecting the community against threatening conduct. Rehabilitating offenders through individualized handling is one way of providing protection, and appropriately the primary way in dealing with children. But the guiding consideration for a court of law that deals with threatening conduct is nonetheless protection of the community. The juvenile court, like other courts, is therefore obliged to employ all the means at hand, not excluding incapacitation, for achieving that protection. What should distinguish the juvenile from the criminal courts is greater emphasis on rehabilitation, not exclusive preoccupation with it.[i]

Doubts about the benevolent purposes and effects of delinquency adjudication led to sweeping reforms designed to conform the juvenile-justice process more closely to the criminal process. Generally speaking, the doctrines governing the definition of criminal conduct and the procedures required for its proof now apply fully to the definition and proof of delinquent acts. In a series of decisions beginning with In re Gault, 387 U.S. 1 (1967), the Supreme Court held that, aside from trial by jury, a juvenile charged with a delinquent act is constitutionally entitled to virtually all of the procedural protections afforded to a defendant in a criminal prosecution. As the following materials make apparent, however, no consensus has emerged regarding the theoretical underpinnings of delinquency adjudication. Ultimately, the question remains whether juvenile justice should be framed on a model of control and treatment or on a model of punishment.

---

[i] The President's Commission on Law Enforcement and Administration of Justice, Task Force Report: Juvenile Delinquency and Youth Crime 7–9 (1967).

## 5. GET TOUGH POLICIES TOWARD ADOLESCENT OFFENDERS

The erosion, if not complete abandonment, of the "rehabilitative ideal" for juvenile offenders during the 1980s and 1990s was reflected in legislative efforts to assure incapacitative sentences for "super predator" juveniles and others found to have committed violent offenses. These "get tough" reforms, characterized by critics as "dramatic departure from nearly a century of American juvenile justice policy,"[j] included transferring youths charged with violent offenses to the criminal courts, lengthening sentences in the juvenile courts, and allowing split sentences under which older juveniles serve part of their extended terms in adult correctional facilities. Proponents of these changes argued that youth crime policy should emphasize public protection rather than failed policies of rehabilitation and that dangerous adolescents should "serve adult time for adult crime." Critics of "get tough" policies saw them as an overreaction to an upswing in violent crime associated largely with a major epidemic of "crack" use, and argued that the incapacitative approach was ruining the life chances of many youngsters whose criminality was associated with their impulsive and immature responses to the risks and challenges of adolescence and would not have continued into adulthood.

## 6. JUVENILE JUSTICE REFORM AND ADOLESCENT DEVELOPMENT

A new wave of juvenile justice system reform emerged in the 21st century based squarely on scientific knowledge of adolescent development. The scientific foundation of the new approach was summarized by the National Research Council in a 2013 report: Reforming Juvenile Justice: A Developmental Approach, 1–7:

> Recent research on adolescent development has underscored important behavioral differences between adults and adolescents with direct bearing on the design and operation of the justice system, raising doubts about the core assumptions driving the criminalization of juvenile justice policy in the last decades of the 20th century. . . . Adolescence is a distinct, yet transient, period of development between childhood and adulthood characterized by increased experimentation and risk-taking, a tendency to discount long-term consequences, and heightened sensitivity to peers and other social influences. . . . Research indicates that for most youth, the period of risky experimentation does not extend beyond adolescence, ceasing as identity becomes settled with maturity. . . .
>
> Evidence of significant changes in brain structure and function during adolescence strongly suggests that these cognitive tendencies characteristic of adolescents are associated with biological immaturity of the brain and with an imbalance among developing brain systems. This imbalance model implies dual systems: one involved in cognitive and behavioral control and one involved in socioemotional processes. Accordingly, adolescents lack mature capacity for self-regulation because the brain system that influences pleasure-seeking and emotional reactivity develops more rapidly than the brain system that supports self-control. . . .

---

[j] Elizabeth S. Scott and Laurence Steinberg, Rethinking Juvenile Justice 5 (2008).

[T]he brain plays an enormous role in determining behavior, but individual development is affected strongly by the interplay between the brain and an adolescent's environment. In particular, the likelihood and seriousness of offending, as well as the effects of interventions, are strongly affected by the adolescent's interactions with parents, peers, schools, communities and other elements of their social environment. . . . The scientific literature shows that three conditions are critically important to healthy psychological development in adolescence: the presence of a parent or parent figure who is involved with the adolescent and concerned about his or her successful development, inclusion in a peer group that values and models prosocial behavior and academic success, and activities that contribute to autonomous decision making and critical thinking. Schools, extracurricular activities, and work settings can provide opportunities for adolescents to learn to think for themselves, develop self-reliance and self-efficacy, and improve reasoning skills.

Yet the juvenile justice system's heavy reliance on containment, confinement, and control removes youth from their families, peer groups, and neighborhoods—the social context of their future lives—and deprives them of the opportunity to learn to deal with life's challenges. For many youth, the lack of a positive social context during this important developmental period is further compounded by collateral consequences of justice system involvement, such as the public release of juvenile records that follow them throughout their lives and limit future educational and employment opportunities. . . .

The overarching goal of the juvenile justice system is to support prosocial development of youth who become involved in the system and thereby ensure the safety of communities. The specific aims of juvenile courts and affiliated agencies are to hold youth accountable for wrongdoing, prevent further offending, and treat them fairly. It is often thought that these specific aims are in tension with one another. However, when these aims and the actions taken to achieve them are viewed from a developmental point of view, the evidence shows that they are compatible with one another.

Holding adolescents accountable for their offending vindicates the just expectation of society that responsible offenders will be answerable for wrongdoing, particularly for conduct that causes harm to identifiable victims, and that corrective action will be taken. It does not follow, however, that the mechanisms of accountability for juveniles should mimic criminal punishments. Condemnation, control and lengthy confinement ("serving time"), the identifying attributes of criminal punishment, are not necessary features of accountability for juveniles. The research demonstrates that, if designed and implemented in a developmentally informed way, procedures specifically designed for holding adolescents accountable for their offending can promote positive legal socialization, reinforce a prosocial identity, and facilitate compliance with the law. However, unduly harsh interventions and negative interactions between youth and justice system officials can

> undermine respect for the law and legal authority and reinforce a deviant identity and social disaffection. A developmentally informed juvenile justice system can promote accountability by providing a setting and an opportunity for juveniles to accept responsibility for their actions, make amends to individual victims and the community for any harm caused, and to participate in community service or other kinds of programs. Restorative justice programs involving victims and adjudication programs that involve restitution and peers are examples of developmentally appropriate instruments of accountability.
>
> [With respect to preventing reoffending,] assessing the risk of rearrest and the intervention needs of each youth is the necessary first step .... No single risk marker is very strongly associated with serious delinquency.... Whether conducted in institutions or in communities, programs are more likely to have a positive impact when they focus on high-risk offenders, connect sound risk/need assessment with the treatment approach taken, use a clearly specific program rooted in a theory of how adolescents change and tailored to the particular offender, demonstrate program integrity, involve the adolescent's family, and take into account community context. If implemented well, evidence-based programs in both institutions and residential and nonresidential community placement reduce reoffending and produce remarkably large economic returns relative to their costs. ... In general, multifaceted community-based interventions show greater reductions in rearrests than institutional programs. Once in institutional care, adequate time (arguably up to about six months) is needed to provide sufficiently intense services for adolescents to benefit from this experience. There is no convincing evidence, however, that confinement of juvenile offenders beyond the minimum amount needed for this purpose, either in adult prisons or juvenile correctional institutions, appreciably reduces the likelihood of subsequent offending.
>
> Treating youth fairly and ensuring that they perceive that they have been treated fairly and with dignity contribute to positive outcomes in the normal processes of social learning, moral development, and legal socialization during adolescence.

The history of juvenile justice reflects ambivalent policy responses to adolescent deviance, ranging from compassion to impatience and mitigation to incapacitation, all intertwined with suppositions about normal and abnormal trajectories of adolescent development. These themes are explored in the following materials, focusing initially on the purpose of juvenile delinquency adjudication and then on the boundary between the jurisdiction of juvenile courts and the criminal courts.

## In re Tyvonne

Supreme Court of Connecticut, 1989.
211 Conn. 151, 558 A.2d 661.

■ GLASS, ASSOCIATE JUSTICE. In this case we decide whether the common law defense of infancy applies to juvenile delinquency proceedings. . . .

The relevant facts are not in dispute. The respondent was born on July 28, 1978. He lived with his mother, grandmother and two younger siblings in Hartford and attended the Clark Street School. On March 1, 1987, the respondent, who was eight years old, found a small pistol while he was playing in the school yard. He took the pistol and hid it under some papers in a hallway in building 38 of Bellevue Square. The following day he took the pistol to school and put it by a fence. He then went into the school and told another child about the pistol. Other children, including the victim, heard about the pistol. The victim told Tyvonne that she thought the pistol was a fake. After school, the respondent and the victim began arguing over whether the pistol was real. Several children examined the pistol and decided that it was a toy. The victim challenged the respondent again by saying, "Shoot me, shoot me." The respondent exclaimed, "I'll show you it's real." He then pointed the pistol at the victim, pulled the trigger, and fired one shot, which struck and injured her. The respondent then swore at the victim, shouted that he had been telling the truth, and ran from the scene. Shortly thereafter he was apprehended and taken into police custody.

[T]he state filed a petition alleging five counts of delinquent[1] behavior arising from the shooting. The trial court found that Tyvonne had committed assault in the second degree in violation of General Statutes § 53a–60(a)(2).[3] . . . It dismissed the other counts [and] committed the respondent to the department of children and youth services (DCYS) for a period not to exceed four years.[4]

On appeal, the respondent assigns as error the trial court's denial of his motion for judgment of acquittal. He asserts that Connecticut's juvenile justice legislation does not expressly or implicitly eliminate the common law infancy defense from delinquency proceedings. He further argues that because the original goals of rehabilitation and remediation in the juvenile justice system have not been attained, there is no justification for excluding the infancy defense from juvenile delinquency proceedings. Consequently, he claims, the trial court erred in not requiring the state to rebut the presumption that he was incapable of committing

---

[1] General Statutes § 46b–120 provides in pertinent part: "[A] child may be found 'delinquent' (1) who has violated any . . . state law. . . . "

[3] General Statutes § 53a–60(a)(2) provides in pertinent part: "A person is guilty of assault in the second degree when . . . (2) with intent to cause physical injury to another person, he causes such injury to such person . . . by means of a deadly weapon or a dangerous instrument." Under General Statutes § 46b–120, assault in the second degree in violation of § 53a–60 is included in the category of offenses designated as a "serious juvenile offense."

[4] The respondent's attorney filed a petition with the trial court seeking an adjudication that the respondent was an "uncared for" child. See General Statutes § 46b–120 (uncared for child defined as one "who is homeless or whose home cannot provide the specialized care which his physical, emotional or mental condition requires"). The trial court found that the respondent was an uncared for child. In addition to the four year commitment based on the delinquency adjudication, the trial court ordered a commitment of eighteen months based on the adjudication that the respondent was an uncared for child.

the offense underlying the delinquency adjudication. We are not persuaded.

I

The respondent argues that . . . because the juvenile justice legislation is silent with respect to the common law infancy defense, the common law presumptions must apply to delinquency proceedings. The state argues, however, that Connecticut's juvenile justice legislation implicitly abolishes the defense and, further, that application of the defense in delinquency proceedings would frustrate the legislation's remedial objectives. . . .

The common law defense of infancy, like the defense of insanity, differs from the criminal law's requirement of "mens rea" or criminal intent. The law recognized that while a child may have actually intended to perform a criminal act, children in general could not reasonably be presumed capable of differentiating right from wrong. The presumptions of incapacity were created to avoid punishing those who, because of age, could not appreciate the moral dimensions of their behavior, and for whom the threat of punishment would not act as a deterrent. . . .

The concept of juvenile delinquency did not exist at common law. In most states, including Connecticut, legislation was enacted that rendered children under a certain age liable as "delinquents" for committing acts that, if committed by an adult, would be criminal. . . .

Shortly after the creation of the juvenile justice system, we addressed the issue whether a delinquency proceeding is tantamount to a criminal prosecution. Cinque v. Boyd, 99 Conn. 70, 121 A. 678 (1923). In that case, we stated that "the Act [creating the juvenile justice system] . . . is not of a criminal nature. . . ." "The Act is but an exercise by the state of its . . . power over the welfare of its children," and a juvenile subjected to delinquency proceedings "[is] tried for no offense," but "[comes] under the operation of the law in order that he might not be tried for any offense." . . .

The rehabilitative nature of our juvenile justice system is most saliently evidenced by the statutory provisions pertaining to the disposition of delinquent juveniles. Under General Statutes § 46b–134, the trial court may not render a disposition of the case of any delinquent child until the trial court receives from the probation officer assigned to the case a comprehensive background report on the child's characteristics, history and home life. The disposition of a child found delinquent for a serious juvenile offense may be made only after the court receives a complete evaluation of the child's physical and psychological health. . . .

Significantly, commitment of the child to DCYS may be made only if the court finds that "its probation services or other services available to the court are not adequate for such child. . . ." Prior to any such commitment, however, the court must "consult with [DCYS] to determine the placement which will be in the best interest of such child." When the trial court determines that a commitment must be made, it may commit the child to DCYS for an indeterminate period not to exceed two years, or in the case of a child found delinquent for committing a serious juvenile offense, for an indeterminate period not to exceed four years. General Statutes § 46b–141(a).[7] DCYS may petition for an extension of the commitment of a child originally committed for two years. An extension may not exceed an additional two years, and may only be ordered when, after a hearing, it is found to be in the best interests of the child. . . .

It is clear from our analysis that the purpose of the comprehensive statutory treatment of "juvenile delinquents" is clinical and rehabilitative, rather than retributive or punitive. As we recently observed, "[t]he objective of juvenile court proceedings is to 'determin[e] the needs of the child and of society rather than adjudicat[e] criminal conduct. The objectives are to provide measures of guidance and rehabilitation . . . not to fix criminal responsibility, guilt and punishment.' Thus the child found delinquent is not perceived as a criminal guilty of one or more offenses, but rather as a child in need of guidance and rehabilitative services." In effect, the statutes regulating juvenile misconduct represent a system-wide displacement of the common law.

With the enactment of juvenile justice legislation nationwide, several courts have addressed the issue whether the infancy defense applies to delinquency proceedings. Most have held that, in the absence of legislation codifying or adopting the defense, incapacity is not a defense in delinquency proceedings. These courts observe that because a delinquency adjudication is not a criminal conviction, it is unnecessary to determine whether the juvenile understood the moral implications of his or her behavior. In addition, some decisions recognize that the defense would frustrate the remedial purposes of juvenile justice legislation.

Because Connecticut's juvenile justice system is designed to provide delinquent minors with guidance and rehabilitation; we agree with the courts that hold that the common law infancy defense, created to protect children from being punished as criminals, has no place in delinquency proceedings. We also agree that the legislature could decide that the infancy defense would unnecessarily interfere with the state's legitimate efforts to provide structured forms of guidance for children who have committed acts of delinquency. It could conclude that the defense inevitably would exclude those children most in need of guidance from a system designed to instill socially responsible behavior. To construe the legislature's silence as indicating an intent to preserve the infancy defense in delinquency proceedings is unwarranted in light of the legislation's obvious and singular remedial objectives. We are not persuaded that recognition of the defense would advance the interests of either child or society.[9]

## II

Relying on a number of decisions in other states, however, the respondent argues that the rehabilitative objectives of juvenile justice

---

[7] In the present case, the respondent has not challenged the trial court's factual basis for committing the respondent to DCYS for four years.

[9] Nothing in this opinion should be construed to deter the legislature from considering the desirability of a floor for such juvenile proceedings in recognition of the fact that the clinical and rehabilitative needs of a four or eight year old are different from those of a fourteen or fifteen year old.

have become defunct, and cannot justify excluding the infancy defense from delinquency proceedings. . . .

We acknowledge that the United States Supreme Court has opined that the rehabilitative goals of the various state juvenile courts have often not been attained. The Court has made it quite clear that states may not deny juveniles fundamental due process rights simply by labeling delinquency proceedings "civil," or by asserting that the purpose of delinquency proceedings is rehabilitative. *In re Gault*. Thus, the parens patriae doctrine does not support inroads on basic constitutional guarantees simply because a state claims that its juvenile justice system is "rehabilitative" rather than "punitive." The United States Supreme Court, however, has expressly refused to hold that the rehabilitative goals of the various systems of juvenile justice may under no circumstances justify appropriate differential treatment of a child adjudicated a delinquent. . . .

We do not discern in [the Court's decisions] an abandonment of the rehabilitative focus of juvenile justice. The respondent has not presented us with any grounds for concluding that the rehabilitative objectives of Connecticut's juvenile justice system are contradicted in practice. We therefore decline to adopt the somewhat cynical view expressed by some writers that the ideals of the juvenile justice system are now bankrupt, and have necessarily succumbed to the corrosive effects of institutionalization.

Further, we are not persuaded by the respondent's argument that the statutory treatment of juveniles who commit "serious juvenile offenses" requires a conclusion that there is no genuine difference between juvenile and criminal proceedings. The four-year maximum commitment term for serious juvenile offenders certainly contemplates the possibility of a serious restriction on the juvenile's liberty. But as we have already observed, any commitment order must be predicated on a determination that other options not involving commitment are inadequate to address the child's needs. In addition, placement of the child in a program or facility must be based on the child's best interests. We cannot infer from these provisions a legislative intent to inflict retribution on the serious juvenile offender.

Finally, we reject the respondent's argument that the common law presumption should apply in this case because the offense charged was a serious juvenile offense. We acknowledge that the commission of a serious juvenile offense is a prerequisite to the transfer of a juvenile case to the superior court criminal docket. Another prerequisite to such a transfer, however, is that the child must have committed the offense after attaining the age of fourteen. In the present case, the respondent was eight years of age at the time of the predicate offense.

There is no error.

## NOTES ON RESPONSIBILITY IN DELINQUENCY PROCEEDINGS

### 1. THE RELEVANCE OF STATUTORY PURPOSE

*Tyvonne* states the prevailing view that the common law infancy defense does not apply to delinquency proceedings. Should delinquency adjudication require proof that the offender appreciated the wrongfulness of his or her conduct? Do the benevolent purposes of the juvenile-justice system provide a persuasive rationale for not doing so?

Consider whether the result would be different if the Connecticut legislature had explicitly abandoned the rehabilitative model of juvenile justice. In Minnesota, for example, the juvenile-court legislation provides that "[t]he purpose of the laws relating to children alleged or adjudicated to be delinquent is to promote the public safety and reduce juvenile delinquency by maintaining the integrity of the substantive law prohibiting certain behavior and by developing individual responsibility for lawful behavior."[a] Similarly the Washington legislature declared that the purposes of delinquency adjudication included "mak[ing] the juvenile offender accountable for his or her criminal behavior; [and] provid[ing] for punishment commensurate with the age, crime, and criminal history of the juvenile offender."[b] How should *Tyvonne* be decided by a judge in Minnesota or Washington?[c]

## 2. *IN RE GLADYS R.*

In recent years, several courts have held that the infancy defense applies in delinquency adjudication, emphasizing the changing character of juvenile justice. One of the first of these decisions was In re Gladys R., 1 Cal.3d 855, 83 Cal.Rptr. 671, 464 P.2d 127 (1970).[d] In that case a juvenile court found that Gladys R., a 12-year-old girl, had committed an act proscribed by the penal code (annoying or molesting a child under 18) and declared her to be a ward of the court under the delinquency provision (§ 602) of the juvenile-court law. The Supreme Court of California reversed the decision, holding that "in order to become a ward of the court under [the delinquency provision], clear proof must show that a child under the age of 14 years at the time of committing the act appreciated its wrongfulness." The court explained that the common law infancy defense, which had been codified in Section 26 of the California Penal Code, "provides the kind of fundamental protection to children charged under Section 602 which this court should not lightly discard." The court continued:

> If a juvenile court finds a lack of clear proof that a child under 14 years at the time of committing the act possessed knowledge of its wrongfulness . . . the court might well declare the child a ward under § 600 [dependent children] or 601 [ungovernable children]. These latter provisions carry far less severe consequences for the liberty and life of the child. After all, it is the purpose of the Welfare and Institutions Code to "insure that the rights or physical, mental or moral welfare of children are not violated or threatened by their present circumstances or environment." Strong policy reasons cast doubt upon the placement of a

[a] Minn.Stat.Ann. § 260.011. Before the amendment the sole declared purpose of the juvenile code had been to secure "for each minor . . . the care and guidance, preferably in his own home, as will serve the . . . welfare of the minor and the best interests of the state . . . and when the minor is removed from his own family, to secure for him custody, care and discipline as nearly as possible equivalent to that which should have been given by his parents." No distinction in purpose was drawn before the amendment between delinquency proceedings and "dependency-and-neglect" proceedings. As a result of the 1980 amendment, the declaration of exclusively benevolent purposes applies only to dependency-and-neglect jurisdiction.

[b] Rev.Wash.Code Ann. § 13.40.010(2)(c), (d).

[c] See Rev.Wash.Code Ann § 9A.04.050, interpreted and applied in State v. J.P.S., 135 Wash.2d 34, 954 P.2d 894 (1998).

[d] See also In re William A., 313 Md. 690, 548 A.2d 130 (1988).

> child who is unable to appreciate the wrongfulness of his conduct [in] an institution where he will come into contact with many youths who are well versed in criminality. . . . We cannot condone a decision which would expose the child to consequences possibly disastrous to himself and society as a whole.
>
> Other sections may possibly be invoked to provide for a wardship for this child with no injurious potentials. Section 601 provides that a child who disobeys the lawful orders of his parents or school authorities, who is beyond the control of such persons, or who is in danger of leading an immoral life may be adjudged a ward of the court. Section 601 might clearly cover younger children who lacked the age or experience to understand the wrongfulness of their conduct. If the juvenile court considers § 601 inappropriate for the particular child, he may be covered by the even broader provisions of § 600.
>
> Section 602 should apply only to those who are over 14 and may be presumed to understand the wrongfulness of their acts and to those under the age of 14 who clearly appreciate the wrongfulness of their conduct. In the instant case we are confronted with a 12-year-old girl of the social and mental age of a seven-year-old. Section 26 stands to protect her and other young people like her from the harsh strictures of § 602. Only if the age, experience, knowledge, and conduct of the child demonstrate by clear proof that he has violated a criminal law should he be declared a ward of the court under § 602.

Although Gladys R. may not be subject to control as a delinquent, the court strongly hints that she would be committable under the less precise dependency and ungovernability provisions. How would the Supreme Court of California characterize the justifying purposes of intervention under §§ 600 and 601 on the one hand and § 602 on the other? Is it likely to matter to Gladys R. whether she was committed under one section or another? Does anything turn on the distinction?

### 3. MINIMUM AGE FOR DELINQUENCY JURISDICTION

Even if the common law infancy presumptions do not apply to delinquency proceedings, should there be a minimum age for delinquency jurisdiction? A few states specify minimum ages ranging from seven to 10 years of age, and the Juvenile Justice Standards promulgated by the Institute of Judicial Administration and the American Bar Association recommend that delinquency liability be precluded for children younger than 10.[e] However, one commentator has noted that "even in the absence of a minimum age in the statute, there are no reported cases involving an attempt to charge delinquency against a child under the common law immunity age of seven."[f]

On November 5, 2008, an eight-year-old Arizona boy shot and killed his father and a man who was boarding at their house after he came home from school. Each man was shot several times with a .22 caliber rifle, a gun that needs to be reloaded after every shot. The boy, who was allegedly angry about receiving spankings, admitted to police that he had shot both men. The prosecutor charged the child with two counts of first-degree

[e] IJA–ABA, Standards Relating to Juvenile Delinquency and Sanctions § 2.1(A) (1980).

[f] Sanford Fox, Juvenile Courts in a Nutshell 29 (1984).

murder.[g] In February 2009, the prosecution dropped the two counts of first-degree murder, and the then-nine-year-old defendant pled guilty to one count of negligent homicide The plea agreement did not specify jail time but left detention up to the discretion of the juvenile court. He was placed on probation until age 18. Mental health evaluations were ordered at three-year intervals. The boy was not allowed to enroll in any school outside a secure facility in the absence of a judicial determination that he was not a threat to others. The state reserved the right to withdraw from the agreement "if the juvenile is charged with any additional delinquent or incorrigible offenses."[h] Was this an appropriate disposition? Should the child have been subject to the jurisdiction of the juvenile court at all?

Should there be a minimum age or delinquency adjudication? What considerations should it based on? Should the judgment turn on what interventions would most likely reduce the risk of further offending? Perhaps it could be thought that any of the available juvenile justice dispositions for a 9-year-old would be more detrimental to the child's development than leaving his or her discipline and care to parents, schools, and other non-governmental institutions of social control. However, the desert-based rationale for the common law immunity, which is endorsed by the IJA–ABA standards, is that children below some level of maturity cannot fairly be blamed for their wrongful acts. What hypotheses about cognitive, social, and moral development underlie this judgment? Would it be important to know when children conform to social norms because they understand the reasons for the norms rather than because they fear the hand of authority figures? Researchers appear to agree that this phase of moral development rarely occurs until nine or ten. Before that age, their reasoning is considered "preconventional" in the sense that they not yet grasp the idea that there are agreed-upon norms.[i] What other factors should be taken into account in determining when a person is sufficiently mature to be held responsible as a delinquent for wrongful acts?

## INTRODUCTORY NOTE ON TRANSFER OF JUVENILES TO CRIMINAL COURT

*In re Tyvonne* and the previous notes dealt with the minimum level of maturity necessary for the imposition of delinquency liability. As *In re Gladys R.* suggests, the issue may also be characterized as the definition of the boundary between delinquency liability and "non-punitive" methods of coercive intervention for children. The following materials address the other boundary of juvenile-court jurisdiction—the boundary between juvenile delinquency and criminal conviction.

At the extremes, the offender's age is the sole determinant of the jurisdictional question.[a] On the one hand, criminal prosecution of a person

---

[g] *Boy Charged in Slayings Offered Deal*, Phoenix News Story, KPHO.com. Nov. 30, 2008. http://www.kpho.com/news/18170747/detail.html.

[h] *Arizona Boy Pleads Guilty in deaths of father, other man*, CNN.com, Feb. 20, 2009, http://www.cnn.com/2009/CRIME/02/19/arizona.boy.homicide/index.html.

[i] See generally Melanie Killen & Judith Smetana (eds.), Handbook of Moral Development (2d ed, 2013).

[a] The statutes are summarized in Patrick Griffin, Sean Addie, Benjamin Adams & Kathy Firestine, *Trying Juveniles as Adults: An Analysis of State Transfer Laws and Reporting*, Washington DC: U.S. Department of Justice, Office of Juvenile Justice and Delinquency Programs, 2011.

younger than 14 is absolutely barred in a substantial number of states; the juvenile court's jurisdiction over such offenders is exclusive regardless of the offense charged. On the other hand, most states set the outer limit of juvenile-court jurisdiction at the 18th birthday; if the act charged occurred after that date, the criminal court's jurisdiction is exclusive.

The offender's age is not the sole jurisdictional criterion if the offender was older than the minimum (usually 14 or 15) and younger than the maximum (usually 18) at the time of the alleged offense. If the older adolescent is charged with a serious offense, all states require or permit the case to be transferred to or filed in the criminal court. The statutes reflect three general approaches to transfer. Under the individualized approach, the juvenile-court judge retains or waives jurisdiction according to whether, after a transfer hearing, the offender is found "amenable to treatment" in the juvenile system or presents a danger to the community. A second approach is a statute requiring transfer of a juvenile older than the designated age if the court finds probable cause to believe that the offender committed one of several specified serious offenses (or that the offender had a prior record of serious delinquency). These statutes are sometimes characterized as "legislative-waiver" provisions, as contrasted with the "judicial-waiver" provisions described above. It should be noted, however, that even in "legislative-waiver" states, the prosecutor's charging decision may determine which court has jurisdiction. In fact, there has been a recent trend towards implementing a third approach to transfer, under which the law explicitly confers discretionary authority on the prosecutor to initiate either juvenile or criminal proceedings. This approach, which is predicated upon conferring concurrent jurisdiction on juvenile and criminal courts, is known as "prosecutorial waiver."

Various arguments have been made supporting and criticizing the "prosecutorial waiver" approach, also known as "direct file." Its supporters argue that some discretion is needed (as opposed to a categorical legislative offense classification), but that giving such discretion to prosecutors is preferable to giving it to juvenile judges, who tend to be have a bias in favor of retaining jurisdiction. Critics argue that prosecutors tend to be biased toward criminal prosecution, and also that vesting transfer power in prosecutors eventually leads to more subjective and inconsistent transfer decisions than under the judicial transfer process. Proponents of "prosecutorial waiver" also argue that under the approach, transfer determinations are made more quickly and efficiently than under "judicial waiver" because the decision is not subject to the traditional routes of review that could elongate the "judicial waiver" process, and that efficiency leads to more effective justice. But many opponents of "prosecutorial waiver" criticize the approach precisely because the prosecutor's decisions are essentially unreviewable. Some states are considering whether prosecutorial transfer decisions should remain unreviewable, or if they should be subject to the same appellate scrutiny as "judicial waiver" decisions.

At least one state supreme court has declared the "prosecutorial waiver" approach unconstitutional. In large part because of the unbridled discretion given to prosecutors, the Utah Supreme Court found that the state's "direct file" statute denied juvenile defendants equal protection in State v. Mohi, 901 P.2d 991 (Utah 1995), because individual offenders accused of the same offenses were treated differently. However, most state courts have upheld the constitutionality of "prosecutorial waiver," stating that the power to make the transfer decision rests firmly within the charging authority of the executive branch and that such prosecutorial power does not usurp any exclusively judicial power. See, e.g., Manduley v. Superior Court, 27 Cal.4th 537, 41 P.3d 3, 117 Cal.Rptr.2d 168 (2002); People v. Conat, 238 Mich.App. 134, 605 N.W.2d 49 (1999).

The individualized judicial approach to transfer has also been subject to many criticisms. Some critics say that 15–, 16–, or 17-year-olds who commit serious offenses are no less deserving of punishment than older offenders; the transfer decision, they argue, should be governed by the policies of the criminal law rather than the therapeutic assumptions of the juvenile court. Other critics argue that the individualized approach is objectionable on practical grounds. The problem, they argue, is that the question whether a particular juvenile is dangerous or amenable to treatment cannot be answered reliably. The jurisdictional decision, therefore, should be based on the application of more objective criteria. Another common concern in cases involving serious offenses is that the gap between the sanctions available to the juvenile court and those available in the criminal court is often very large, thereby exacerbating the problems of discretionary decisionmaking.

Despite these objections, the traditional individualized approach was endorsed by the Joint Commission on Juvenile Justice Standards of the Institute of Judicial Administration and the American Bar Association.[b] The Commission took the position that persons under 18 should be presumptively subject to juvenile-court jurisdiction; transfer is appropriate, the Commission said, only when a juvenile charged with a serious "class one" juvenile offense[c] "has demonstrated a propensity for violent attacks against other persons and, on the basis of personal background, appears unlikely to benefit from any disposition available in juvenile court." The Commission did not endorse any single rationale in support of its presumption in favor of juvenile-court jurisdiction. While it claimed that the "rehabilitative argument for the juvenile court" has "great moral force," the Commission nonetheless acknowledged that "recent research urges skepticism about the efficacy of existing rehabilitative methods." The Commission also noted the argument that persons below 18 are "in some moral sense less responsible for their acts and more deserving of compassion than are adults." In the final analysis, however, the Commission relied on the argument that delinquency intervention represents the lesser of two evils:

> [T]he criminal justice system is so inhumane, so poorly financed and staffed and so generally destructive that the juvenile court cannot do worse. Perhaps it can do better.[d]

Since the mid-1980s, a strong trend has favored displacing juvenile court jurisdiction in the most serious cases involving adolescents—sometimes even those younger than 14. Evidence of this can be seen in the tendency of legislatures to embrace legislative and prosecutorial waiver statutes, both of which aim to curtail juvenile court jurisdiction. However, because the decision to proceed against youthful offenders as adults carries

---

[b] IJA–ABA, Standards Relating to Transfer Between Courts 3–7, 37 (1980).

[c] The Commission defined a class one juvenile offense as: "Those criminal offenses for which the maximum sentence for adults would be death or imprisonment for life or a term in excess of 20 years."

[d] For a criticism of the Commission's position, see In re Seven Minors, 99 Nev. 427, 664 P.2d 947 (1983).—[Footnote by eds.]

such significant sentencing consequences, the longstanding debate about waiver, and about juvenile justice in general, has intensified.[e] Key themes in the controversy are revealed in the sequence of Minnesota cases that follows.

## In re the Welfare of Dahl

Supreme Court of Minnesota, 1979.
278 N.W.2d 316.

■ SCOTT, JUSTICE. This is an appeal from an order of a three-judge panel of the Ninth Judicial District affirming the Beltrami County Court's referral of a juvenile to district court for adult prosecution. . . .

On April 8, 1978, the dead body of Ricky Alan McGuire, who had been missing since November 17, 1977, was found in a remote area of Beltrami County. A witness described the frontal section of his head as "just disappeared, gone." A cap found near the body had a hole in it about the size of a half dollar. Three expended shotgun cartridges were also found lying near the body. In a petition filed on April 10, 1978, in Beltrami County Court, appellant was charged with delinquency for the first-degree murder of Ricky Alan McGuire. The petition alleged that appellant admitted that he shot McGuire on November 17, 1977, and planned to return to the scene in the spring to conceal the body; that witnesses are fearful of their safety and lives if appellant is freed during the pendency of the proceedings; that appellant was using a considerable amount of marijuana; and that appellant had recently authored a note stating that certain local persons must be "terminated." In addition, the petition requested that the court enter an order referring appellant for prosecution as an adult pursuant to Minn.Stat. Ann. § 260.125.[a]

Appellant was born on March 2, 1960, and therefore was 17 years old at the time of the alleged offense and 18 years old at the time the delinquency petition was filed. His parents described him as a respectful, obedient, and trustworthy child. Appellant stated that he had good

---

[e] See generally Elizabeth S. Scott and Laurence Steinberg, Essay—Blaming Youth, 81 Texas L Rev. 799 (2003); Thomas Grisso and Robert G. Schwartz, eds., Youth on Trial (2000); Jeffrey Fagan and Franklin E. Zimring, eds., The Changing Borders of Juvenile Justice (2000); Darnell Hawkins and Kimberly Kempf-Leonard, eds., Race, Development and Juvenile Justice (2002); Lisa S. Beresford, Is Lowering The Age At Which Juveniles Can Be Transferred To Adult Criminal Court The Answer To Juvenile Crime? A State-By-State Assessment, 37 San Diego L. Rev. 783 (2000).

[a] Section 260.125 then provided:

"(1) When a child is alleged to have violated a state or local law or ordinance after becoming 14 years of age the juvenile court may enter an order referring the alleged violation to the appropriate prosecuting authority for action under laws in force governing the commission of and punishment for violations of statutes or local laws or ordinances. . . .

"(2) The juvenile court may order a reference only if

(a) A petition has been filed . . .

(b) Notice has been given . . .

(c) A hearing has been held . . .

(d) The court finds that the child is not suitable to treatment or that the public safety is not served under the provisions of the law relating to juvenile courts."—[Footnote by eds.]

relationships with his parents and younger brothers, and denied that he had any emotional problems.

At the time of the alleged wrongful conduct, appellant was a senior in high school, maintaining about a B average. He plans to attend Bemidji State University upon his graduation from high school. He participated in interscholastic track and cross-country running and in intramural basketball. He once received a two day in-school suspension for swearing and kicking his locker. This conduct apparently occurred upon appellant's discovery that his expensive watch had been stolen. Appellant was employed since the fall of 1976 by a local restaurant. Prior to that time he worked as a stock boy and carryout boy at a local grocery store and as a trap setter at a local gun club. He was a steady and industrious worker.

Appellant's only prior contact with the juvenile court involved a charge of reckless driving which was eventually dismissed at the completion of a 45-day suspension of his driver's license. Accordingly, the county court observed that:

> [I]t is clearly apparent that the juvenile is not the typical delinquent seen by the juvenile court. This offense [first-degree murder], if he is guilty of it, appears to be an isolated delinquent act rather than an outcropping pattern of behavior normally associated with the classification of juvenile delinquent.

. . . A reference study by the county probation officer at the order of the court . . . recommended that appellant be referred for prosecution as an adult because of the lack of treatment programs for the serious juvenile offender who has reached the age of 18, and because the public safety is not served by the security measures taken at juvenile treatment centers. No psychological or psychiatric information concerning appellant was obtained.

[After a hearing] the [juvenile] court rendered its decision, referring appellant for prosecution as an adult for both non-amenability to treatment and public safety grounds. [A] three-judge panel of the Ninth Judicial District Court affirmed the decision of the [juvenile] court. . . .

The question before us is whether the . . . juvenile court, has met the required standards in ordering this juvenile referred to the adult authorities for prosecution. . . . Since § 2(d) is phrased in the alternative, a finding of either non-amenability to treatment or harm to public safety is sufficient to refer a juvenile for prosecution as an adult. . . . In the instant case, the juvenile court found that both criteria . . . were satisfied, and thus referred appellant for prosecution as an adult.

The decision to refer a juvenile for prosecution as an adult, of course, is of tremendous consequence to both the involved juvenile and society in general. Unfortunately, the standards for referral adopted by present legislation are not very effective in making this important determination. . . .

[The opinion at this point refers to studies indicating that behavioral scientists are unable to predict future behavior and tend to overpredict future violence. It continues:]

Due to these difficulties in making the waiver decision, many juvenile-court judges have tended to be over-cautious, resulting in the referral of delinquent children for criminal prosecution on the erroneous, albeit good-faith, belief that the juveniles pose a danger to the public. Accordingly, a re-evaluation of the existing certification process may be in order. . . .

[However,] until changed, the statutory scheme for reference must be followed.

In this case, appellant was referred for prosecution as an adult primarily because the juvenile court determined that appellant could not be successfully treated within the period of time remaining before the juvenile court's jurisdiction of this matter is terminated.[2] This is a proper basis for concluding that a juvenile is unsuitable for treatment; however, the court's finding is not reasonably supported by the evidence. Although requested by the juvenile, no mental testing of appellant was performed, and consequently the record is devoid of any psychological or psychiatric data which could conceivably support the juvenile court's observation. Nor does the evidence disclose any negative information regarding the juvenile's background prior to the present act. On the contrary, the record shows that appellant has an exemplary background and is not the typical chronic offender who is usually subject to reference. In making its decision the juvenile court relied on the serious nature of the offense involved, appellant's age, "social adjustment," and maturity level. These considerations, in the absence of supporting psychological data or a history of misconduct, are insufficient to support the court's finding that appellant could not be successfully treated within the remaining three years the juvenile could be under the control of the juvenile-court system.

. . . The [juvenile and district] courts, in making their decisions, may very well have been using equitable reasoning and common sense based upon complete and sound logic in viewing a factual situation where an individual shot another three times, killing him; where . . . an adult jury would probably convict; and where in the eyes of the public, if he is convicted, a sentence for more than three years should be served. This attitude seems to be reflected by the record. But no matter how pragmatic such reasoning may be, it is a mistaken interpretation of the statutory intent of the legislature.

The legislature did not single out certain crimes for reference to adult prosecution, although it had that specific opportunity. The law does not say that all petitions filed in juvenile court alleging first-degree murder are automatically subject to certification, nor does the statute provide that 17-year-old violators are automatically referred for adult prosecution. . . . It appears in this case that reference was made because of age and seriousness of the crime, neither of which meets the statutory requirements.

The state argues that the juvenile court's determination, relative to public safety, is reasonable when the considerations set out in State v. Hogan, 297 Minn. 430, 438, 212 N.W.2d 664, 669 (1973),[6] are applied to

---

[2] Minn.Stat.Ann. § 260.181(4) states that the juvenile court's jurisdiction continues until the child reaches the age of 21, unless the court terminates its jurisdiction before that time. Thus, at the time of the court's decision, appellant could have been under the jurisdiction of the juvenile court for a little less than three years.

[6] In *Hogan*, we stated that: "[I]n determining if the public safety would be threatened, among the relevant factors to be considered are: (i) the seriousness of the offense in terms of

the facts of this case. Although this contention has some superficial appeal, when we apply all of the relevant evidence there is nothing in the record to show that the public safety will suffer in the future, or has done so in the time between the act and the arrest. No psychological information is contained in the record which might support this finding, nor does the juvenile's exemplary background indicate that he is a threat to the public safety. The record must reflect more reasons portending future danger; otherwise appellant would be referred solely on the basis of the offense in question. As discussed above, the existing statutory framework does not authorize referral based on the specific crime charged. Accordingly, this court did not intend the application of the *Hogan* factors to result in the referral of a juvenile solely because of the alleged offense. Rather, as stated in *Hogan*, the criteria we listed in that decision are only "*among* the relevant factors to be considered." . . . The record must contain direct evidence that the juvenile endangers the public safety for the statutory reference standard to be satisfied.

The present [delinquency] petition may make one shudder in reflecting upon the alleged event, but the record fails to show that this juvenile is "not suitable" to treatment or that the "public safety" will suffer. We therefore remand to the [juvenile] court with instructions to examine properly admissible evidence to be submitted at a further hearing for the purpose of determining whether, in light of this opinion, the statutory reference criteria are satisfied. If the record's substance is not materially altered as a result of this additional evidence, reference to adult court is not justified and thus the proceedings should continue in juvenile court.

The reference order is vacated and the matter is remanded for further proceedings consistent with this opinion.

## NOTES ON *IN RE THE WELFARE OF DAHL*

### 1. QUESTIONS ON *IN RE THE WELFARE OF DAHL*

The *Dahl* court noted its uneasiness with the individualized predictive approach to the transfer decision and invited the Minnesota legislature to reconsider the statutory criteria for transfer. What are the proper criteria for determining the boundary between delinquency and criminal liability? Should jurisdiction be based on age alone? On some combination of age, offense charged, and prior record of delinquency? Or on the traditional individualized assessment of amenability to treatment? To what extent does the choice depend upon ideological assumptions about the respective purposes of juvenile and criminal processes? Or on dispositional considerations?

---

community protection; (ii) the circumstances surrounding the offense; (iii) whether the offense was committed in an aggressive, violent, premeditated, or willful manner; (iv) whether the offense was directed against persons or property; (v) the reasonably foreseeable consequences of the act; and (vi) the absence of adequate protective and security facilities available to the juvenile treatment system."

## 2. THE LEGISLATIVE RESPONSE

Consider the Minnesota legislature's response to *Dahl*. Although the legislature retained the criteria specified in § 260.125(2)(d) to govern the transfer decision, a 1980 amendment provided that the prosecutor establishes a "prima-facie case that the public safety is not served or that the child is not suitable for treatment" if the child was at least 16 years of age at the time of the alleged offense and if the child:

> (1) Is alleged by delinquency petition to have committed an aggravated felony against the person and (a) in committing the offense, the child acted with particular cruelty or disregard for the life or safety of another; or (b) the offense involved a high degree of sophistication or planning by the juvenile; or
>
> (2) Is alleged by delinquency petition to have committed murder in the first degree; or
>
> (3) Has been found by the court . . . to have committed an offense within the preceding 24 months, which would be a felony if committed by an adult, and is alleged by delinquency petition to have committed murder in the second or third degree, manslaughter in the first degree, criminal sexual conduct in the first degree or assault in the first degree; or
>
> (4) Has been found by the court . . . to have committed two offenses, not in the same behavioral incident, within the preceding 24 months which would be felonies if committed by an adult, and is alleged by delinquency petition to have committed manslaughter in the second degree, kidnapping, criminal sexual conduct in the second degree, arson in the first degree, aggravated robbery, or assault in the second degree; or
>
> (5) Has been found by the court . . . to have committed two offenses, not in the same behavioral incident, within the preceding 24 months, one or both of which would be the felony of burglary of a dwelling if committed by an adult, and the child is alleged by the delinquency petition to have committed another burglary of a dwelling . . . ; or
>
> (6) Has been found by the court . . . to have committed three offenses, none in the same behavioral incident, within the preceding 24 months which would be felonies if committed by an adult, and is alleged by delinquency petition to have committed any felony other than those described in clauses (2), (3) or (4).

Is this a better approach? What is its underlying rationale concerning the respective purposes of the juvenile and criminal processes? Is it likely that transfer practices would change?[a] Would the 1980 amendment have required a different result in *Dahl*?

---

[a] For an empirical study of the impact of these amendments on transfer practices, see Lee Ann Osbun and Peter A. Rode, Prosecuting Juveniles as Adults: The Quest for Objective Decisions, 22 Criminology 187 (1984).

## In re the Welfare of D.F.B.

Supreme Court of Minnesota, 1988.
433 N.W.2d 79.

[Sixteen-year-old D.F.B. was a high-school sophomore with a B+ average who appeared to his peers and teachers to be a well-adjusted teenager. He had no history of illegal misconduct, drug abuse, or aggressive behavior. However, on February 18, 1988, D.F.B. killed both of his parents and younger brother and sister with an axe. According to extensive psychiatric testimony (by a court-appointed expert and by a psychiatrist retained by the defense) at the waiver hearing, D.F.B. was experiencing a severe depressive disorder arising out of persistent conflict with his parents. This progressively worsening problem was manifested by several undetected suicide attempts and eventually led to the homicides. On the basis of this evidence, the trial judge concluded that the state had not proven, by clear and convincing evidence either that D.F.B. posed a threat to public safety[a] or that he "cannot be successfully treated by his 19th birthday."[b] He further commented that, although "it does not make much sense" that a person "convicted of the crime alleged in this case should serve a sentence of less than three years," he was not authorized to decide the case based on his own "feeling of justice." After the court of appeals reversed and ordered the case to be certified to the criminal court, the Minnesota Supreme Court granted D.F.B.'s petition for review.]

■ OPINION BY THE COURT. [T]he court of appeals reversed a decision of the district court denying a motion by the state pursuant to Minn. Stat. § 260.125 (1986) to refer D.F.B., a juvenile, for prosecution as an adult. We granted D.F.B.'s petition for review not because we disagree with the ultimate decision of the court of appeals but in order to provide a different analysis as to why reference is required.

D.F.B., age 16, used an axe to kill his parents and a younger brother and younger sister. The experts seem to agree that D.F.B. had been depressed for a number of years, that he was experiencing severe depression at the time he committed the murders, and that his feeling that he was trapped in a family situation not to his liking somehow led him to the conclusion that the only remedy was to kill the parents. (D.F.B. has said that he killed the younger siblings not because he was angry with them but to spare them further pain.) The experts, however, disagree over the ultimate issue of whether D.F.B. is unamenable to treatment in the juvenile court system consistent with the public safety. Dr. Carl Malmquist, the psychiatrist consulted by the court, reported to the court that he has "serious reservations" as to whether D.F.B. can be treated appropriately and effectively in the juvenile court system before he reaches age 19. He recommended "long term" treatment with the

---

[a] The trial judge relied on undisputed clinical opinion that the offense arose out of an explosive family situation and that D.F.B. did not present a risk to the general public.—[Footnote by eds.]

[b] The judge observed that placement of the burden of proof was significant:

> I do not believe the child could prove suitability for treatment if the burden were placed on him. However, the prosecution has been unable to prove the contrary. Each of the experts [said] that it is possible to complete the treatment in the time available; certainly no one said he could not. Since the evidence cannot be said to be clear and convincing proof that he cannot be treated, the [state] has failed to carry the burden of proof on this issue.—[Footnote by eds.]

aim of "a whole reconstruction of how [D.F.B.] deals with aggression." James Gilbertson, Ph.D., opined that D.F.B. can be treated successfully in 2–1/2 years, and probably in considerably less time. However, he acknowledged that many such depressed people fail in treatment and/or have recurrences after treatment. It appears that the treatment programs for depression available in Minnesota generally provide security only as an initial component of the program.

After thoughtful and careful consideration, the district court concluded that the facts were analogous to those in Matter of Welfare of Dahl, 278 N.W.2d 316 (Minn. 1979), and that—given its conclusion that *Dahl* is still good law in a case such as this where the juvenile has produced substantial evidence of amenability to treatment in the juvenile court system consistent with the public safety—it had no choice but to deny the reference petition, much as it was otherwise inclined to grant the petition.

The court of appeals in a thoughtful opinion concluded that the district court misinterpreted the effect and the intent of the 1980 legislation enacted in response to our decision in *Dahl*. It concluded that keeping D.F.B. in the juvenile court system is inconsistent with the intent of the legislature expressed in those amendments and it therefore reversed the district court. . . . [c]

We have decided a number of post-amendment reference cases. For example, we have made it clear that when the defendant produces "significant" or "substantial" evidence rebutting a prima facie case for reference under the statute, then the role for the juvenile court is to decide on the basis of the entire record, without reference to the prima facie case, whether the state has met its burden of proving by clear and convincing evidence that the juvenile is unamenable to treatment in the juvenile court system consistent with the public safety. Matter of Welfare of J.F.K., 316 N.W.2d 563, 564 (Minn. 1982); Matter of Welfare of Givens, 307 N.W.2d 489, 490 (Minn. 1981). We used the word "substantial" evidence in *J.F.K.* and the word "significant" in *Givens*. We regard the words to be interchangeable. Furthermore, it was our intent that the quantum of evidence connoted by these terms is that which is required to rebut a prima facie case in other civil matters. See Barry C. Feld, Juvenile Court Legislative Reform and the Serious Young Offender: Dismantling the "Rehabilitative Ideal", 65 Minn. L. Rev. 167, 209–10 (1981). Minn. R. Juv. Ct. 32.05, subdivision 2, adopts the prima facie standard of the statute and uses the phrase "rebutted by significant evidence."

In this case the juvenile, D.F.B., came forward with evidence bearing both on amenability to treatment and on public safety. At least, in

---

[c] The court of appeals reasoned that the language of the waiver provision should be interpreted in light of the legislature's simultaneous amendment of the purpose clause of the juvenile code, declaring that the purpose of delinquency adjudication is "to promote the public safety by maintaining the integrity of the substantive law prohibiting certain behavior and by developing individual responsibility for lawful behavior." According to the court of appeals, the legislature intended to prevent "an excessively minimal response to an offense which had a major impact on society" and "to protect the strong and legitimate interest of the public in a fair response by the criminal justice system to a heinous crime." As a result, the "state's interest in the integrity of the substantive law, under the facts of this case, overcomes any consideration, however weighty, given by the trial court to the absence of anti-social or violent behavior in D.F.B.'s past."—[Footnote by eds.]

our opinion, the clear implication of the testimony of the defense expert, Gilbertson, is that he was not just of the opinion that D.F.B. could be treated successfully but was also of the opinion that he could be treated in the juvenile court system consistent with the public safety.

The issue then becomes whether it can be said that the state met its burden of proof without regard to the presumption. In our view, once the district court concludes that the juvenile has rebutted the presumption, then the district court has to analyze the entire record, using the same basic multi-factor analysis discussed in *Dahl*, to see if it may be said that the state has proved by clear and convincing evidence that the juvenile is unamenable to treatment in the juvenile court system consistent with the public safety. Minn. R. Juv. Ct. 32.05, which sets forth the various circumstances that may be involved in the totality of the circumstances, supports this conclusion. Employing the multi-factor analysis in this case—which is what the trial court in *Dahl* was directed to do on remand—would justify a reference decision in this case even if the legislature's 1980 amendment of the purpose section was without significance. While we agree with the court of appeals' conclusion that the amendment of the purpose section makes it easier to conclude that reference is justified in this case, we do not agree with the implication that reference is justified any time a juvenile commits a heinous offense. Rather, reference in this case is justified because—bearing in mind the legislature's revised statement of purpose and looking at all the factors listed in R. 32.05, including the offense with which D.F.B. is charged, the manner in which he committed the offense, the interests of society in the outcome of this case, the testimony of Dr. Malmquist suggesting that treatment of D.F.B. might be unsuccessful, and the weakness of Dr. Gilbertson's testimony—the state met its burden of proving by clear and convincing evidence that D.F.B. is unamenable to treatment in the juvenile court system consistent with the public safety. . . .

In summary, we affirm the decision of the court of appeals reversing the decision of the district court denying the motion to refer D.F.B. for prosecution as an adult.

Affirmed.

## NOTES ON *IN RE THE WELFARE OF D.F.B.* AND PROSECUTION OF JUVENILES AS ADULTS

### 1. QUESTIONS AND COMMENTS ON *IN RE THE WELFARE OF D.F.B*

As the Minnesota Supreme Court acknowledged, the 1980 amendment to the waiver provision did not alter the clinical certification criteria. Moreover, the Supreme Court agreed with the trial judge that the prima facie case favoring certification (based on the murder charges and D.F.B.'s age) had been rebutted by the psychiatric evidence offered in D.F.B.'s behalf. As a result, the criteria governing D.F.B's case were the same as those applied in Dahl's case. Is *D.F.B.* distinguishable from *Dahl*? Did the court offer a persuasive reason for displacing the trial court's findings with its own? In connection with these questions, consider the following critique of *D.F.B.* by Barry Feld, Bad Law Makes Hard Cases: Reflections on Teen Aged Axe-Murderers, Judicial Activism, and Legislative Default, 8 Law and Inequality 1, 85–86 (1989):

> The [court] confronted the problem posed by the legislature's continued emphasis on the characteristics of the offender coupled with the trial courts' virtually unrestricted discretion to make waiver decisions. The problem became critical when a conscientious trial judge followed the legislature's mandate in an extraordinarily difficult and troubling case. *D.F.B.* laid bare the fundamental tension between the principle of individualized justice and the principle of offense. Unfortunately, the supreme court's resolution of *D.F.B.* undermined the integrity of the trial process and did violence to its own appellate function. Although the court may be satisfied that it reached the "right result," it did so by misrepresenting the trial court factual record and the legal issues before it.
>
> In reaching its result, the supreme court may have concluded that it was preferable for one case—*D.F.B.*—to be decided 'wrongly', i.e. contrary to the offender-oriented legislative mandate, in order to avoid a precedent, such as that of the court of appeals, that would create more problems for juveniles and for the administration of the waiver process. Assuring that [D.F.B.] was tried as an adult would provide juvenile courts with the political elbow room to continue exercising sentencing discretion for more routine cases. Thus, the court's strategy supports discretionary, offender-oriented sentencing over retributive, offense-based sentencing, albeit at [D.F.B.'s] expense. As a matter of sentencing policy, the court may have concluded that, despite substantial individual variations, the indeterminacy of discretionary sentencing is likely to result in shorter sentences for most offenders, even though occasional highly visible or career offenders may receive disproportionately severe sentences. This trade-off between discretionary leniency for most juveniles, coupled with severity for a few, is consistent with the view of the waiver process as a 'symbolic gesture' which requires occasional 'sacrificial lambs' as a strategy for maintaining juvenile court jurisdiction over the vast majority of youths and deflecting more fundamental critiques of juvenile justice administration.

### 2. THE LEGISLATIVE RESPONSE

In 1994, the Minnesota legislature substantially revised the waiver statute in several respects. First, it required certification of any case involving a child 16 or older charged with first-degree murder. Second, it eliminated the "amenability to treatment" prong of the certification criteria, leaving as the exclusive standard whether "retaining the proceeding in juvenile court serves the public safety." Third, in determining whether the public safety is served, the court is directed "to give greater weight to the seriousness of the alleged offense and the child's prior record of delinquency than to" the other factors specified as being relevant. Finally, the statute established a presumption in favor of certification in cases involving children 16 or older alleged to have committed "an offense that would result in a presumptive commitment to prison under the sentencing guidelines and applicable statutes" or a felony involving a firearm. When the presumption applies, the case must be certified unless the child proves by clear and convincing evidence that retaining the case in the juvenile court would serve the public safety. Was this a satisfactory response to the problems revealed by *Dahl* and *D.F.B.*?

In 2011, the Minnesota legislature made two additional changes to the certification statute. First it required certification in any felony case in which the youth had been previously certified on a felony charge and convicted of that charge or a lesser-included felony. Second, the legislature further specified the factors that the courts are required to take into account in determining whether the public safety would be served by certification:

> In determining whether the public safety is served by certifying the matter, the court shall consider the following factors:
>
> (1) the seriousness of the alleged offense in terms of community protection, including the existence of any aggravating factors recognized by the Sentencing Guidelines, the use of a firearm, and the impact on any victim;
>
> (2) the culpability of the child in committing the alleged offense, including the level of the child's participation in planning and carrying out the offense and the existence of any mitigating factors recognized by the Sentencing Guidelines;
>
> (3) the child's prior record of delinquency;
>
> (4) the child's programming history, including the child's past willingness to participate meaningfully in available programming;
>
> (5) the adequacy of the punishment or programming available in the juvenile justice system; and
>
> (6) the dispositional options available for the child.
>
> In considering these factors, the court shall give greater weight to the seriousness of the alleged offense and the child's prior record of delinquency than to the other factors listed in this subdivision.[a]

This new provision was applied in the following case.

## In re the Welfare of J.H.

Supreme Court of Minnesota, 2014.
844 N.W.2d 28.

■ DIETZEN, JUSTICE. . . .

On November 23, 2011, the victim G.K., who was 14 years old at the time, told a sexual assault nurse at a children's hospital that she had been raped by gang members. G.K. told police investigators that she and a friend, A.Y., rode in a car driven by Mang Yang to a party . . . at an abandoned house . . . . G.K. recognized six of the individuals at the party as True Blood 22 (TB22)[1] gang members. When G.K. decided to leave the party, she and A.Y. went to Yang's car. Two gang members,

---

[a] Minn. Stat. Ann. § 260B.125, subd. 4

[1] According to the juvenile petition, the TB22 gang is a documented criminal street gang that has been involved in crimes of violence including rapes, assaults, drive-by shootings, possession of stolen guns, auto thefts, burglaries, and drug-related crimes.

however, followed them and forcibly removed G.K. from the car and carried her into a bedroom in the house. G.K. was screaming and resisted going into the bedroom. G.K. was pushed down onto a mattress, her clothing was removed, and then she was held down by several of the gang members and raped by another gang member. Someone in the room yelled "police," and everybody ran out of the bedroom and the house. G.K. told police that there were between six and eight individuals in the bedroom, including J.H., during the rape. . . .

J.H. admitted to police that he was a TB22 gang member . . . . J.H. stated that he was in the room when the rape occurred, that he heard someone "slam" G.K. onto the mattress, that two "big dudes" held G.K. down, and that at least two men raped G.K. J.H. admitted that the rape stopped because someone said the police were coming.

The State filed a juvenile petition alleging J.H. was delinquent based on first-degree criminal sexual conduct . . . , conspiracy to commit first-degree criminal sexual conduct . . . , kidnapping, and committing a crime for the benefit of a gang. J.H. was charged as both a principal and as an accomplice. . . .

[One gang member testified at his own guilty plea hearing that J.H. participated in the plan to rape G.K., and that J.H. intended to rape G.K. He also testified that the gang's method of operation when they party with girls is to get the girls drunk and then rape them.]

At J.H.'s certification hearing, the State presented evidence consistent with the police investigation. The juvenile court heard testimony from 12 people, including Kao Dua Chi Moua, a juvenile probation officer, and Dr. Gary Hertog, a clinical psychologist[, both of whom recommended that J.H. be retained in the juvenile court under the court's "extended jurisdiction" for older juveniles (an "EJJ designation").[a] Moua concluded] that only the seriousness of the offense and J.H.'s culpability favored certification. [Dr. Hertog concluded] that only the seriousness of the offense clearly supported certification . . . .

Following the certification hearing, the juvenile court issued . . . an order certifying J.H. to stand trial as an adult in district court. The court concluded that J.H. had not demonstrated by clear and convincing evidence that retaining the proceeding in the juvenile court would serve public safety. The court determined that five of the six public safety factors [in the Minnesota statute] favored certification, with only J.H.'s lack of a prior record of delinquency favoring [retention in the juvenile court under an] EJJ designation. In doing so, the court rejected Moua's and Dr. Hertog's opinions that public safety would be served by retaining [juvenile court jurisdiction] because, among other reasons, they were unable to testify that even with the available programming it was likely that J.H. would not pose a threat to public safety.

A divided court of appeals reversed. [A key concern expressed by the majority of the court of appeals was that the trial judge appeared to

---

[a] If J.H.'s case had been retained in the juvenile court, it would automatically have been designated as an "extended jurisdiction juvenile prosecution" ("EJJ designation"). In such cases, the juvenile court would have been required to impose, in addition to the appropriate juvenile dispositions, "an adult criminal sentence, the execution of which shall be stayed on the condition that the offender not violate the provisions of the disposition order and not commit a new offense." Minn. Stat. Ann. § 260B.125, subd. 4(a)(2).—[Footnote by eds.]

have given determinative weight to the seriousness of the offense, while failing to give particularized and focused consideration to the fact that J.H. had no prior record of delinquency. In re Welfare of J.H., 829 N.W.2d 607, 617–18 (Ct. App. 2013):

> [Underlying the district court's analysis of the statutory factors here, as evidenced by repeated references to the seriousness of the offense in the findings, is the belief that some offenses are so serious that [EJJ designation] is inappropriate. Yet the legislature and the current statutory scheme provide otherwise. First, Minnesota law designates only one offense so serious that, if alleged to be committed by a juvenile 16 years of age or older, results in immediate transfer to the adult system: murder in the first degree. Reasonable minds may differ as to whether that list should include other offenses, but as of now it does not. Second, for all other offenses, public safety is determined through a consideration of six factors, with the court directed to "give greater weight to the seriousness of the alleged offense and the child's prior record of delinquency."
>
> [Appellant argues that seriousness of the offense should not automatically tip the balance in favor of certification and that, while both the certification study and the psychological evaluation weighed this factor more heavily, they also weighed the lack of a prior record of delinquency more heavily, and they both ultimately recommend EJJ designation.
>
> [While the district court acknowledged that the lack of a prior record weighs in favor of EJJ designation, it did not expressly weigh the factor any heavier than the other factors, while giving great weight to the seriousness of the offense. . . . To state it another way, unless and until the legislature either . . . provide[s] that alleged offenses other than murder in the first degree result in immediate transfer of a juvenile over the age of 16 to the adult system, or provide[s] that only the seriousness of the alleged offense is to be given greater weight when determining whether public safety is best served by certification, it is incumbent upon the district court to specifically delineate the impact of both of the factors to be given greater weight under the statute. The language of the statute suggests that the more serious the alleged offense is, the more significant the lack of a prior record of delinquency becomes for a juvenile seeking EJJ designation. Arguably, under this statutory framework, the presence of a serious offense is offset by no prior record of delinquency, leaving a consideration of the other four factors as the framework for a decision as to whether EJJ designation is proper. Here, the only other factor that favors adult certification is the culpability of appellant. The remaining three factors, appellant's programming history, the adequacy of the punishment or programming available, and the dispositional options, all favor EJJ designation. We therefore conclude that the district court incorrectly determined that the seriousness of the offense and appellant's culpability outweigh all of the other factors.]

It is undisputed that the presumption in favor of certification is applicable to this proceeding. J.H. was 17 years old at the time the alleged offense was committed; the delinquency petition alleges that J.H. committed an offense that would result in a presumptive commitment to prison under the Sentencing Guidelines and applicable statutes; and the juvenile court determined that probable cause exists that J.H. committed the alleged offense. Therefore, the burden was on J.H. to overcome the presumption by demonstrating by clear and convincing evidence that retaining the proceeding in juvenile court would serve public safety. [At this point the court quoted the six "public safety" factors in the statute and the requirement that the juvenile court must "give greater weight to the seriousness of the alleged offense and the child's prior record of delinquency than to the other factors listed." It continued:]

We first address the seriousness of the alleged offense and J.H.'s prior record of delinquency. The juvenile court found that the seriousness of the alleged offense weighs in favor of certification. The court's finding is amply supported in the record. J.H. was charged with first-degree criminal sexual conduct, conspiracy to commit first-degree criminal sexual conduct, kidnapping, and committing a crime for the benefit of a gang. All of these offenses are serious crimes. Cf. State v. Gant, 305 N.W.2d 790, 791 (Minn.1981) (stating that the crimes of unlawfully entering the victim's home at night and violently sexually assaulting the victim were "serious crimes"); see also Coker v. Georgia, 433 U.S. 584, 597–98 (1977) (discussing the "highly reprehensible" nature of rape and stating that "[s]hort of homicide, it is the ultimate violation of self") (internal quotation marks omitted). The record demonstrates that the offenses were especially violent because G.K. was forcibly removed from a car by several men, thrown onto a mattress, held down by several men, and then raped by a gang member. Moreover, the rape had a significant impact on G.K.

Regarding the prior-record-of-delinquency factor, the juvenile court determined that J.H. has no prior record of delinquency, and that therefore the third factor favors EJJ designation. The State does not challenge this finding.

The court of appeals acknowledged the juvenile court gave "great weight to the seriousness of the alleged offense," but determined that the juvenile court abused its discretion because it "did not expressly weigh the [prior record of delinquency] factor any heavier than the other factors." . . .

We conclude that [the statute] does not require the juvenile court to either expressly weigh the seriousness of the offense and the prior record of delinquency separately from the other public safety factors, or specifically delineate how these two factors impacted its certification determination. The juvenile court is required, however, to give greater weight to those two factors than the other factors listed in the statute. The juvenile court must also identify the statutory basis upon which it relied, and demonstrate that it carefully considered its decision.

Here, the juvenile court's order explicitly states that it gave greater weight to the seriousness of the alleged offense and J.H.'s prior record of delinquency than to the other four public safety factors. The order also demonstrates that the court relied on the presumption in favor of certification and that the court thoroughly considered whether J.H. rebutted the presumption in favor of certification. Consequently, the juvenile court satisfied the requirements of the statute.

Turning to the remaining public safety factors, J.H. argues that the culpability-of-the-child factor favors EJJ designation. Specifically, J.H. argues that he played a passive role in the offenses because he did not drag G.K. from the car, hold her down, or sexually assault her. For purposes of a certification determination, the charges against the child and the factual allegations of the petition are presumed true. To determine whether a child is culpable, we examine the alleged offenses. J.H. was charged as a principal and accomplice for first-degree criminal sexual conduct, conspiracy to commit first-degree criminal sexual conduct, kidnapping, and committing a crime for the benefit of a gang. To prove J.H.'s criminal liability as an aider and abettor, the State must prove that J.H. knew that his accomplices were going to commit a crime and that he intended his presence or actions to further the commission of that crime. But "active participation in the overt act which constitutes the substantive offense is not required."

The juvenile court found that the culpability of J.H. weighed in favor of certification. The juvenile court concluded that J.H.'s actions "were part of a horrific concerted effort to rape" G.K., and he was therefore "equally culpable" as the individuals who held G.K. down and raped her. The evidence in the record is sufficient to support the finding of the juvenile court. There is evidence that J.H. and the other gang members planned to get G.K. drunk and then take turns raping her. The gang members, including J.H., executed the plan, and J.H.'s presence in the bedroom during the rape, coupled with his failure to object to the rape, may be viewed as evidence of his support of what occurred. *See State v. Hawes,* 801 N.W.2d 659, 668 (Minn.2011) (stating that a jury may infer a defendant intended his actions to aid the commission of a crime by, among other things, his presence at the crime scene and lack of objection to the crime). At this stage of the proceeding, the juvenile court's finding that J.H. is culpable as an aider and abettor based on the facts alleged in the delinquency petition was not clearly erroneous. . . .

[W]e conclude that a child's programming history in subdivision 4(4) . . . is directed at a specialized system of services, opportunities, or projects designed to meet the relevant behavioral or social needs of the child. Thus, a specialized program provided either through the juvenile justice system, or through a non-juvenile justice system setting, that is designed to address a relevant behavioral or social need of the child may be considered by the court in assessing a child's programming history in subdivision 4(4).

The juvenile court's finding that J.H.'s programming history favored certification is not supported by the record. Specifically, J.H.'s failure to attend a school that provides basic education, and his failure to follow his father's rules do not establish a lack of willingness to participate in a system of services, opportunities, or projects designed to address a relevant behavioral or social need of J.H. We therefore conclude that this factor does not weigh in favor of adult certification.

With respect to the fifth factor, the juvenile court found that the adequacy of the punishment or programming available in the juvenile justice system favored certification. The court found that 42 months of EJJ supervision would not sufficiently address the seriousness of the offense or ensure public safety. The court of appeals, however, credited the testimony of Moua and Dr. Hertog and found that this factor favored EJJ designation. On matters of credibility and the weight to be given the testimony of witnesses, we defer to the juvenile court. Here, Moua admitted, assuming the allegations are true, that J.H. was an untreated sex offender and was a long-standing member of a violent street gang, and Moua did not know whether the available programming could address J.H.'s needs. Dr. Hertog admitted that J.H. may not embrace treatment or change while in the juvenile system. The juvenile court's finding is supported by the record and not clearly erroneous.

Under the sixth factor, the two dispositional options available to J.H. were certification to stand trial as an adult or EJJ designation. The juvenile court concluded EJJ was not an appropriate dispositional option in this case because of J.H.'s long-term gang involvement and the nature of the gang's criminal activities. The court noted that if J.H. were designated for EJJ prosecution, he would be "placed in programming, returned to the community within the next year or two, and supervised to age 21." But if J.H. were certified to adult court and convicted, he faces a term of incarceration anywhere from 204 months to 336 months, followed by intensive supervised release with strict conditions including not associating with gang members for an extended period of time.

The court of appeals relied upon the expert testimony of Moua to conclude that the juvenile court's finding that this factor favors certification is clearly erroneous. But Moua and Dr. Hertog admitted that J.H.'s gang involvement is an obstacle to his successful EJJ participation. And, as with the previous factor, we defer to the juvenile court's determination on the credibility and weight to be given witnesses' testimony. We therefore conclude there is ample evidentiary support in the record for the juvenile court's conclusion that this factor favors certification.

We conclude that the juvenile court did not abuse its discretion when it determined that J.H. had not rebutted the presumption in favor of certification by demonstrating by clear and convincing evidence that public safety would be served by retaining the proceeding in juvenile court. The juvenile court analyzed all six of the statutory public safety factors, made written findings regarding each factor even though it was not required to do so, and expressly stated that it gave greater weight to the seriousness of the offense and J.H.'s prior record of delinquency in making its decision. Because the district court's findings on four of the public safety factors, including the seriousness of the offense, are not clearly erroneous and favor certification, the juvenile court did not abuse its discretion when it certified J.H. for adult prosecution.

Reversed.

## NOTES ON *IN RE THE WELFARE OF J.H.* AND PROSECUTION OF JUVENILES AS ADULTS

### 1. QUESTIONS AND COMMENTS ON *IN RE THE WELFARE OF J.H.*

Would the result in *In re the Welfare of J.H.* have been different under the statutory criteria that preceded the 1994 and 2011 amendments? Since 1994, the sole governing criterion is public safety. Does the result in *J.H.* rest on a judgment that criminal prosecution was necessary to assure protection of public safety? Did J.H's record of offending, the circumstances of the instant offense, and the psychological evidence reveal a high risk of reoffending? What role did gang membership play in the court's analysis? Both experts recommended retention of jurisdiction by the juvenile court. What weight should have been given to the opinion of the experts in reaching a judgment about J.H.'s risk of reoffending and his potential for successful clinical intervention? What is the purpose of considering the dispositional options (factor 6)? One possibility is to ascertain whether the sanctions available to the juvenile court are sufficiently severe to reflect the seriousness of the offense. Is the juvenile court supposed to take this factor into account? Conversely, should the juvenile court consider whether the likely sanction in criminal court (between 17 and 28 years in prison in this case) is unduly severe?

### 2. MITIGATION OF CRIMINAL PUNISHMENT

As illustrated by *In re Welfare of J.H.*, the stakes are high for juveniles in transfer adjudications because the authorized punishments are typically so much more severe in criminal court than in juvenile court. Once the case has been certified for criminal prosecution, what role should the offender's immaturity play in sentencing? To the extent that criminal sentencing is based on considerations of proportionality, should otherwise applicable sentences be mitigated for adolescent offenders tried as adults? To the extent that incapacitative considerations are relevant, should a juvenile's capacity for change be taken into account?

The U.S. Supreme Court has held that the eighth amendment's ban against "cruel and unusual punishments" forbids a sentence of death for offenders who were under 18 at the time of their offenses,[a] prohibits life imprisonment without parole (LWOP) for juveniles who have committed offenses other than homicide,[b] and bans mandatory LWOP sentences for juvenile homicide offenders.[c] The offenders' constitutional claims in this litigation have rested on evidence that juveniles—including older adolescents—are less able to restrain their impulses and exercise self-control; less capable than adults of considering alternative courses of action and maturely weighing risks and rewards; and less oriented to the future and thus less capable of apprehending the consequences of their often impulsive actions.

Within whatever limits are set by the Constitution, how should claims of diminished responsibility associated with developmental immaturity be

---

[a] Roper v. Simmons, 543 U.S. 551 (2005)(death sentences), discussed in Chapter XI.

[b] Graham v. Florida, 560 U.S. 48 (2010)

[c] Miller v. Alabama, 132 S.Ct. 2455 (2012)

taken into account in prescribing and applying criminal sentences?[d] Should potential for rehabilitation be given more weight in sentencing juveniles than in sentencing adults? Should there be a "youth discount" on proportionality grounds? Recent evidence indicates that the maturation of the brain during "adolescence" continues through the early 20s. At what age should such a youth discount be phased out?

# SECTION 2: MENTAL ABNORMALITY

## INTRODUCTORY NOTES ON THE INSANITY DEFENSE

### 1. INTRODUCTION

No area of the substantive criminal law has received more scholarly attention during the 20th century than the relation between mental abnormality and criminal responsibility. Although insanity has been an acknowledged ground of acquittal for several centuries, contemporary opinion reflects continuing disagreement about the type of mental incapacity that should suffice and, indeed, about the desirability of any insanity defense at all. The dimensions of the dispute can readily be seen in any representative sample of commentary on the subject.[a] The reader will find proposals to broaden the exculpatory reach of the defense side-by-side with proposals to abolish it. While proponents of the defense argue that humanitarian morality demands exculpation of the mentally ill, abolitionists assert that a decent respect for the dignity of such persons requires that they be held accountable for their wrongdoing.

The insanity defense is a difficult subject. In large measure this is because the causal links between body, mind, and behavior continue to defy scientific understanding. Most of the clinician's operating assumptions about mental abnormality are not currently susceptible to empirical validation. Moreover, the prevailing clinical understanding is not easily translated into concepts of interest to the criminal law, mainly because scientific study of the human mind is fundamentally unconcerned with questions of blameworthiness and responsibility.

Another difficulty arises from the diversity of perspectives employed by the mental health disciplines in the study of human behavior and in the treatment of mental, emotional, and behavioral problems. One draws on the traditional medical concept of "disease" to describe and explain abnormal mental phenomena. This view rests on the assumption that there are categorical differences, with probable biological underpinnings, between individuals having and not having the "disease." Another approach is taken by behavioral scientists who have tried to identify and measure various dimensions of the human personality that differentiate one person from another—features that fall along a spectrum of degree and, at some point, can be characterized as abnormal. Yet another approach is taken by

---

[d] The developmental evidence is summarized in Elizabeth Scott and Laurence Steinberg, Rethinking Juvenile Justice (2008).

[a] E.g., Abraham Goldstein, The Insanity Defense (1967); Joel Feinberg, Doing and Deserving: Essays in the Theory of Responsibility (1970); Herbert Fingarette and Ann F. Hasse, Mental Disabilities and Criminal Responsibility (1979); Norval Morris, Madness and the Criminal Law (1982); Donald H.J. Hermann, The Insanity Defense: Philosophical, Historical and Legal Perspectives (1983); Michael Moore, Law and Psychiatry: Rethinking the Relationship (1984).

clinicians who study human motivation, aiming to identify the biological, psychological, and social forces that shape behavior, both normal and abnormal.

Although each of these three perspectives is undoubtedly required for a complete understanding of abnormal behavior, the heterogeneous and often conflicting approaches employed by mental health practitioners can befuddle the law's efforts to shape and administer a doctrine of responsibility. Of particular concern are fluid and often imprecise clinical concepts of abnormality. Lines are not easily drawn between mental "illness" or "disease" and other conditions characterized by maladaptive behavior or emotional distress. Yet the law is in an important sense faced with an either/or choice. Questions of degree can be taken into account in grading and sentencing, but the defendant either is guilty or is not guilty of committing a crime.

There is yet another overarching problem. The criminal law's response to the mentally disordered offender is shaped by preventive concerns as well as retributive ones. The imposition of criminal punishment on culpable offenders serves the preventive ends of the penal law, including incapacitation of the dangerous. If abnormal offenders are beyond the reach of the penal law, the preventive function must be performed by alternative mechanisms of social control, such as civil commitment.

The subject of mental abnormality and criminal responsibility is further complicated by questions of implementation. In much of the contemporary commentary, evidentiary questions about the proper scope of expert testimony by psychiatrists and other mental-health professionals[b] are superimposed on the substantive questions regarding the legal significance of mental abnormality. Although the limits of psychiatric expertise and the special risks associated with expert testimony merit independent attention, the materials in this book focus primarily on the substantive issues concerning the exculpatory or mitigating significance of mental abnormality rather than on the evidentiary questions associated with the proof of such conditions.

Despite these many difficulties, the criminal law traditionally has included special doctrines for mentally disordered offenders. From the earliest times, the courts and legislatures have coupled unique dispositional provisions with exculpatory "tests" of criminal responsibility. The following notes introduce the major tests of responsibility. They focus on the criteria of responsibility stated by various "tests" and ask: (i) how the specified criteria relate to other doctrines of exculpation previously studied; (ii) whether it seems appropriate to exculpate mentally disordered offenders who fit these criteria; and (iii) why it seems appropriate to do so. These notes are followed by a series of problems, notes, and cases designed to highlight the clinical realities of mental disorder and to identify the major policy questions that must be addressed by contemporary courts and legislators.

---

[b] In most jurisdictions, opinion testimony concerning a person's mental condition may be offered by psychologists as well as psychiatrists. For convenience of reference, these materials will use "psychiatric testimony" to refer to testimony by any qualified mental-health professional.

## 2. EARLY HISTORY

Before the 12th century, mental disease, as such, apparently had no legal significance.[c] However, as criminal liability came to be predicated upon general notions of moral blameworthiness, "madness" was recognized as an excusing condition. At first, insanity (like self-defense) was not a bar to criminal liability but only a recognized ground for granting a royal pardon; while the records are fragmentary, it appears that the king would remand the person to some form of indefinite custody in lieu of execution. The first recorded case of outright acquittal by reason of insanity occurred in 1505.[d]

The only early commentator to give sustained attention to the subject was Lord Hale, whose treatise was published posthumously in 1736. According to Hale:[e]

> Man is naturally endowed with these two great faculties, understanding and liberty of will. . . . The consent of the will is that which renders human actions either commendable or culpable. . . . And because the liberty or choice of the will presupposeth an act of understanding to know the thing or action chosen by the will, it follows that, where there is a total defect of the understanding, there is no free act of the will. . . .

Hale distinguished between "total defect of understanding" due to insanity and partial madness involving those who "discover their defect in excessive fears and griefs and yet are not wholly destitute of the use of reason." Conceding that "it is very difficult to define the indivisible line that divides perfect and partial insanity," Hale sought to identify that level of "understanding" necessary for criminal liability by assimilating insanity to infancy: "Such a person as labouring under melancholy distempers hath yet ordinarily as great understanding, as ordinarily a child of 14 years hath, is such a person as may be guilty of . . . felony."

Hale's approach failed to take hold.[f] Instead, as Sayre notes, 18th century courts "hark[ed] back strongly to the old ethical basis of criminal responsibility and [made] the test one of capacity to intend evil. Could the defendant at the time of the offense 'distinguish good from evil'?"[g] An often-cited example is Justice Tracy's charge to the jury in Arnold's Case, 16 How.St.Tr. 695, 764 (1724), which involved a known madman who killed a nobleman in the delusion that the victim had "bewitched him" and was "the occasion of all the troubles in the nation." After summarizing the evidence, Justice Tracy said that the only question was "whether this man had the use of his reason and senses." He continued:

---

[c] For general background on the common law history of the insanity defense, see Nigel Walker, Crime and Insanity in England (1968); Homer Crotty, The History of Insanity as a Defense to Crime in English Criminal Law, 12 Calif.L.Rev. 105 (1924); Anthony Platt and Bernard Diamond, The Origins of the "Right and Wrong" Test of Criminal Responsibility and Its Subsequent Development in the United States: An Historical Survey, 54 Calif.L.Rev. 1227 (1966).

[d] Nigel Walker, Crime and Insanity in England 26 (1968). Apparently the offender was set free.

[e] Matthew Hale, The History of Pleas of the Crown 14–15 (Philadelphia 1847) (1st ed. 1736).

[f] Sir James Stephen criticized Hale's comparison of infancy and insanity: "The one is healthy immaturity, the other diseased maturity and between these there is no sort of resemblance." 2 A History of the Criminal Law of England 150–51 (1883).

[g] Francis Bowes Sayre, Mens Rea, 45 Harv.L.Rev. 974, 1006 (1932).

> [I]t is not every kind of frantic humour or something unaccountable in a man's actions, that points him out to be such a madman as is to be exempted from punishment; it must be a man that is totally deprived of his understanding and memory, and doth not know what he is doing, no more than an infant, than a brute, or a wild beast, such a one is never the object of punishment; therefore I must leave it to your consideration, whether the condition this man was in . . . doth shew a man, who knew what he was doing, and was able to distinguish whether he was doing good or evil, and understood what he did. . . .

As late as 1840, no appellate court in England or the United States had occasion to state the law on the defense of insanity. However, the subject received a great deal of attention on both sides of the Atlantic during the middle third of the century. One important development was the publication of Isaac Ray's treatise on the Medical Jurisprudence of Insanity in 1838, signifying the first efforts of the infant science of psychiatry to influence the development of the law. Another major development was the trial, in 1843, of Daniel M'Naghten.

### 3. *M'NAGHTEN'S* CASE

The modern formulations of the insanity defense derive from the "rules" stated by the House of Lords in Daniel M'Naghten's Case, 10 Cl. & F. 200, 8 Eng. Rep. 718 (H.L.1843).[h] M'Naghten was indicted for shooting Edward Drummond, secretary to Robert Peel, the Prime Minister of England. According to M'Naghten's statements to the police, he came to London for the purpose of shooting Peel. However, Drummond was riding in Peel's carriage that day, and M'Naghten shot Drummond in error. M'Naghten described his motive as follows:

> The tories in my native city have compelled me to do this. They follow and persecute me wherever I go, and have entirely destroyed my peace of mind. . . . I cannot sleep at night in consequence of the course they pursue towards me. . . . They have accused me of crimes of which I am not guilty; they do everything in their power to harass and persecute me; in fact they wish to murder me.

The thrust of the medical testimony was that M'Naghten was suffering from what would today be described as delusions of persecution symptomatic of paranoid schizophrenia. One of the medical witnesses concluded that:

> The act with which he is charged, coupled with the history of his past life, leaves not the remotest doubt on my mind of the presence of insanity sufficient to deprive the prisoner of all self-control. I consider the act of the prisoner in killing Mr. Drummond to have been committed whilst under a delusion; the

---

[h] The history of the *M'Naghten* case is reviewed, and the relevant documents collected, in Donald West and Andrew Walk, Daniel McNaughton: His Trial and the Aftermath (1977), and Richard Moran, Knowing Right from Wrong (1981).

M'Naghten's name has been spelled at least 12 different ways. Apparently, the traditional spelling—the one used in this book—is the only one that cannot be reconciled with the defendant's own signature. See Bernard Diamond, On the Spelling of Daniel M'Naghten's Name, 25 Ohio St. L.J. 84 (1964). According to Moran, the correct spelling is probably "McNaughtan."

act itself I look upon as the crowning act of the whole matter—as the climax—as a carrying out of the pre-existing idea which had haunted him for years.

The expert testimony was summarized in the official reports as follows:

> That persons of otherwise sound mind, might be affected by morbid delusions; that the prisoner was in that condition; that a person so labouring under a morbid delusion might have a moral perception of right and wrong, but that in the case of the prisoner it was a delusion which carried him away beyond the power of his own control, and left him no such perception; and that he was not capable of exercising any control over acts which had connexion with his delusion; that it was of the nature of the disease with which the prisoner was affected, to go on gradually until it had reached a climax, when it burst forth with irresistible intensity; that a man might go on for years quietly, though at the same time under its influence, but would all at once break out into the most extravagant and violent paroxysms.

In his charge to the jury, Chief Justice Tindal practically directed a verdict of not guilty by reason of insanity. He observed "that the whole of the medical evidence is on one side and that there is no part of it which leaves any doubt on the mind," and then instructed the jury that the verdict should turn on the answer to the following question:

> [W]hether . . . at the time the act was committed [M'Naghten] had that competent use of his understanding as that he knew that he was doing, by the very act itself, a wicked and a wrong thing. If he was not sensible at the time he committed that act, that it was a violation of the law of God or of man, undoubtedly he was not responsible for that act, or liable to any punishment whatever flowing from that act. . . . But if . . . you think the prisoner capable of distinguishing between right and wrong, then he was a responsible agent. . . .

The jury returned a verdict of not guilty by reason of insanity.[i] This verdict became the subject of "popular alarm," and was regarded with particular concern by Queen Victoria.[j] As a result, the House of Lords asked the judges of that body to give an advisory opinion regarding the answers to five questions "on the law governing such cases." The combined answers to two of these questions have come to be known as *M'Naghten's* rules:

> [E]very man is to be presumed to be sane. . . . [T]o establish a defence on the ground of insanity, it must be clearly proved that, at the time of the committing of the act, the party accused was labouring under such a defect of reason, from disease of the mind, as not to know the nature and quality of the act he was doing; or if

---

[i] Most commentary on the *M'Naghten* case proceeds on the assumption that he was mentally ill and that his crime was related to his delusions. However, a book by Richard Moran presents strong evidence in support of the proposition that M'Naghten was not delusional and that his attempt to assassinate the Tory Prime Minister was "a purposeful act of political criminality." Richard Moran, Knowing Right From Wrong (1981).

[j] She had been the target of assassination attempts three times in the preceding two years, and one of her attackers, Oxford, had also had won an insanity acquittal.

he did know it, that he did not know he was doing what was wrong.

### 4. OTHER COMMON LAW FORMULATIONS

*M'Naghten* quickly became the prevailing approach to the insanity defense in England and in the United States. However, the test was criticized almost as soon as it was uttered. Nineteenth-century critics offered two alternative formulations:

#### *(i) The Product Test*

The "intellectualist" approach of the 18th- and 19th-century English judges was criticized by Isaac Ray[k] and his followers because it failed to comprehend the more subtle forms of mental illness. The prevailing judicial ideas about idiocy and lunacy were derived, Ray argued, from "those wretched inmates of the madhouses whom chains and stripes, cold and filth, had reduced to the stupidity of the idiot or exasperated to the fury of a demon." The law failed to recognize "those nice shades of the disease" which can influence behavior and ought to have exculpatory significance. Accordingly, Ray argued, the insanity defense should turn on whether "the mental unsoundness . . . embraced the act within the sphere of its influence."

The New Hampshire Supreme Court accepted Ray's view. In State v. Pike, 49 N.H. 399 (1870), the court severely criticized the *M'Naghten* rules; the next year, in State v. Jones, 50 N.H. 369 (1871), the court stated its own rule, commonly known as the "product" test:

> No man shall be held accountable, criminally, for an act which was the offspring and product of mental disease. Of the soundness of this proposition there can be no doubt. . . . No argument is needed to show that to hold that a man may be punished for what is the offspring of disease would be to hold that he may be punished for disease. Any rule which makes that possible cannot be law.

Although the New Hampshire formulation was applauded by many medical and legal commentators during the early 20th century, it failed to win support in the courts.[l]

#### *(ii) The Control Test*

Although the notion of "irresistible impulse" was much discussed during the decades after the *M'Naghten* rules were announced,[m] it is not altogether clear whether the early proponents viewed it as an elaboration of *M'Naghten* or as an independent ground of exculpation. Some state courts employed the concept simply to acknowledge that an "insane impulse" could be so strong as to "dethrone reason" and thereby deprive the offender of the capacity to know right from wrong.[n] However, the phrase ultimately

---

[k] Isaac Ray, A Treatise on the Medical Jurisprudence of Insanity (1838).

[l] The product test was adopted by the United States Court of Appeals for the D.C. Circuit in Durham v. United States, 214 F.2d 862 (D.C. Cir. 1954), but was abandoned in favor of the Model Penal Code test in United States v. Brawner, 471 F.2d 969 (D.C. Cir. 1972).

[m] See generally Sheldon Glueck, Mental Disorder and the Criminal Law (1925); John Barker Waite, Irresistible Impulse and Criminal Liability, 23 Mich.L.Rev. 443 (1925).

[n] See, e.g., Commonwealth v. Rogers, 48 Mass. (7 Metc.) 500, 41 Am.Dec. 458 (1844). For a review of the early decisions, see Jerome Hall, Psychiatry and Criminal Responsibility, 65

came to denote an independent exculpatory doctrine. The central proposition was that a person's inability to control behavior as a result of mental disease ought to be exculpatory even though the offender might be aware that the act was wrong. The focus of this doctrine is on mental disease that deprives the individual of the capacity to exercise will, the capacity to choose whether or not to engage in proscribed behavior. It is therefore frequently referred to as a "volitional" or "control" inquiry, in contrast to the focus of the *M'Naghten* rules on the "cognitive" capacities of the defendant.

Sir James Stephen became a leading proponent of a control test. In 1883 he stated: "If it is not, it ought to be the law of England that no act is a crime if the person who does it is at the time . . . prevented either by defective mental power or by any disease affecting his mind from controlling his own conduct, unless the absence of the power of control has been produced by his own default."[o] The first unequivocal appellate endorsement of the control formulation as a supplement to *M'Naghten* is found in Parsons v. State, 81 Ala. 577, 596, 2 So. 854 (1886):

> [D]id he know right from wrong, as applied to the particular act in question? . . . If he did have such knowledge, he may nevertheless not be legally responsible if the two following conditions concur: (i) If, by reason of the duress of such mental disease, he had so far lost the *power to choose* between the right and wrong, and to avoid doing the act in question, as that his free agency was at the time destroyed; (ii) and if, at the same time, the alleged crime was so connected with such mental disease, in the relation of cause and effect, as to have been the product of it *solely*.

Although several other courts endorsed this view during the next decade, most states rejected it. The predominant attitude of the common law judges was graphically stated by a Canadian judge in 1908:

> The law says to men who say they are afflicted with irresistible impulses: "If you cannot resist an impulse in any other way, we will hang a rope in front of your eyes, and perhaps that will help." No man has a right under our law to come before a jury and say to them, "I did commit that act, but I did it under an uncontrollable impulse," leave it at that and then say, "now acquit me."[p]

The formative era of the modern insanity defense was completed by the end of the 19th century. Notwithstanding the persistent barrage of unfavorable commentary by forensic psychiatrists and academic lawyers, the law remained essentially unchanged for the first half of the 20th century. At the time the Model Penal Code was being drafted in 1955, the *M'Naghten* test still constituted the exclusive criterion of exculpation on ground of insanity in about two-thirds of the states.

---

Yale L.J. 761 (1956); Edwin Keedy, Irresistible Impulse as a Defense in the Criminal Law, 100 U.Pa.L.Rev. 956 (1952).

[o] 2 James F. Stephen, A History of the Criminal Law of England 168 (1883).

[p] King v. Creighton, 14 Can. Cr. Cases 349, 350 (1908) (Riddell, J.).

## 5. THE MODEL PENAL CODE

Section 4.01 of the Model Code provides:

> A person is not responsible for criminal conduct if at the time of such conduct as a result of mental disease or defect he lacks substantial capacity either to appreciate the criminality [wrongfulness] of his conduct or to conform his conduct to the requirements of law.

Two points should be noted about this formulation of the insanity defense. First, in its joint focus on the capacity to appreciate criminality and the capacity to conform one's conduct to the requirements of law, the Model Code formulation includes both cognitive and volitional criteria. The drafters thus accepted the major criticism of *M'Naghten* that the exclusive focus on cognitive capacity was too narrow. The Model Code formulation accords *independent* exculpatory significance to volitional impairment.[q] Second, the Model Code "substantial capacity" formulation explicitly acknowledges that there is no bright line between the sane and the insane. Herbert Wechsler, who inspired the Model Code language, explained that "our judgment was that no test is workable that calls for the complete impairment of ability to know or to control." He continued:

> Disorientation, we were told, might be extreme and still might not be total; what clinical experience revealed was closer to a graded scale with marks along the way. Hence, an examiner confronting a person who had performed a seemingly purposive act might helpfully address himself to the extent of awareness, understanding and control. If, on the other hand, he must speak to utter incapacity vel non, he could testify meaningfully only as to delusional psychosis, when the act would not be criminal if the facts were as they deludedly were thought to be, although he knew that there were other situations in which the disorder was extreme.

To meet this aspect of the difficulty, the drafters concluded that the law should pose the question in terms of lack of "substantial capacity" to know or to control, "meaning thereby the reduction of capacity to the vagrant and trivial dimensions characteristic of the most severe afflictions of the mind."[r]

The Model Penal Code test was very influential. By 1980, it had been adopted—by legislation or judicial ruling—in more than half the states. In the absence of congressional action, formulations based on the Model Code were also adopted by all the federal courts of appeal.

---

[q] It should also be noted that the cognitive branch of the Model Code formulation asks only one of the *M'Naghten* questions. Section 4.01 omits reference to the capacity of the defendant to "know the nature and quality" of the act. One reason is that the significance of a person's mistake regarding the nature of an act lies, ultimately, in the fact that it prevents knowledge that it was wrong. Thus, this prong of the test is theoretically superfluous. Another reason is that this aspect of the *M'Naghten* formula is primarily directed to the capacity of the defendant to form mens rea. As addressed in Subsection E below, the admissibility of evidence of mental abnormality on mens rea issues is itself a controversial question. Since the Model Code resolves the controversy in § 4.02 in favor of admissibility, there is no need to include cognition as to the nature of the defendant's behavior as part of the insanity formulation. The effect of Section 4.01, therefore, is to supplement what remains of the *M'Naghten* formula with the volitional or control inquiry.

[r] Herbert Wechsler, Codification of the Criminal Law in the United States: The Model Penal Code, 68 Colum.L.Rev. 1425, 1443 (1968).

## 6. THE *HINCKLEY* CASE

Signs of dissatisfaction with the prevailing approach to insanity began to emerge in the late 1970s. One major factor was public concern about premature release of dangerous defendants acquitted by reason of insanity. During this period, several states narrowed the insanity criteria or introduced a new verdict of "guilty but mentally ill" to supplement the traditional alternatives of conviction or acquittal. One state, Montana, abolished the insanity defense in 1979. The simmering debate about the law of insanity took on national proportions in the aftermath of the trial of John W. Hinckley, Jr.

On March 30, 1981, Hinckley shot and wounded President Ronald Reagan and three other people as the President was walking from the Washington Hilton to his waiting limousine. The shooting was observed by scores of eyewitnesses and seen by millions on television. Hinckley was indicted for 13 offenses, including an attempt to assassinate the President. His claim of insanity was adjudicated under the Model Penal Code test then used in the federal courts for the District of Columbia. Hinckley's trial began on May 4, 1982, and lasted seven weeks. The prosecution and defense experts disagreed on the nature and severity of Hinckley's mental disorder and on his ability to appreciate the wrongfulness of his behavior and conform to the requirements of the law. On June 21, after deliberating for three days, the jury returned a verdict of not guilty by reason of insanity on each of the 13 counts.[s]

According to media accounts and opinion surveys, the Hinckley acquittal shocked and angered the American public. Three days after the verdict, the New York Times referred to a "national reaction of stunned surprise" and a "cascade of public outrage." The verdict catalyzed latent public discomfort with the insanity defense and its administration, and triggered legislative activity throughout the country. The American Bar Association, the American Psychiatric Association, and the National Conference of Commissioners on Uniform State Laws recommended a narrowing of the insanity defense by eliminating its volitional prong. The American Medical Association recommended abolition of the defense entirely. During the ensuing three years, Congress and half of the states modified the law of insanity in some significant respect.

## 7. CURRENT LAW

As a result of the post-*Hinckley* reforms, the Model Code no longer represents the prevailing approach in the United States. The sole criterion in about half the states is whether the defendant was unable to "know" or "appreciate" the nature or wrongfulness of the conduct. In these states volitional impairment is not an independent basis of exculpation. About 20 states retain the Model Code formula, and a few states use *M'Naghten* together with some variation of the "irresistible impulse" test. Only New Hampshire uses the "product" test. Four states—Montana, Idaho, Kansas, and Utah—have abolished the insanity defense.[t]

---

[s] See Richard J. Bonnie, Peter W. Low, and John C. Jeffries, Jr., The Trial of John W. Hinckley, Jr.: A Case Study in the Insanity Defense (3d. ed. 2008).

[t] The statutes in these states are discussed in the notes on abolition of the insanity defense at the end of this Chapter. Twelve states have supplemented the insanity defense with a

Another feature of the law of insanity prominently featured in public discussion after *Hinckley* was the burden of proof. All states place the burden of producing sufficient evidence to raise the defense on the defendant. In two-thirds of the states, the defendant also bears the burden of persuasion, usually by a preponderance of the evidence.[u] In the remaining states, the prosecution bears the burden of disproving the defendant's claim of insanity beyond a reasonable doubt.[v]

Moreover, Congress has modified the federal law on the insanity defense. Until 1984, no statute governed the subject. Although the Supreme Court had ruled in 1895 that the government bore the burden of persuasion on insanity claims in federal prosecutions, the Court had never prescribed a substantive test of insanity for the federal courts. As noted above, each of the federal circuits had adopted tests based on the Model Penal Code. The 1984 legislation eliminated the volitional prong of the defense and required the defendant to establish an insanity claim by clear and convincing evidence. The new federal statute, codified at 18 U.S.C. § 17, provides:

> (a) Affirmative Defense.—It is an affirmative defense to a prosecution under any federal statute that, at the time of the commission of the acts constituting the offense, the defendant as a result of a severe mental disease or defect, was unable to appreciate the nature and quality or the wrongfulness of his acts. Mental disease or defect does not otherwise constitute a defense.[w]
>
> (b) Burden of Proof.—The defendant has the burden of proving the defense of insanity by clear and convincing evidence.

## 8. DISPOSITION OF INSANITY ACQUITTEES

Disposition of insanity acquittees and other mentally disordered offenders is considered in depth in Section 3 of this chapter. However, a brief summary of current dispositional arrangements provides a necessary context for studying the substantive content of the insanity defense because judgments about the proper scope of the defense are likely to be influenced by one's confidence that society will be adequately protected from repeated offending by persons who have been found legally insane. From this perspective, it is important to note that the insanity defense is raised in less than 1% of felony cases and is successful in only a only fraction of those. Every state authorizes indeterminate civil commitment of insanity acquittees to a secure mental hospital for treatment. Under a large majority of these statutes, a committed NGRI patient may be released from the hospital only if a court has found that the person can be safely managed in the

---

separate verdict of "guilty but mentally ill." These statutes are considered in notes at the end of Section 3, Subsection A.

[u] The constitutionality of placing the burden of persuasion on the defendant has been upheld in Leland v. Oregon, 343 U.S. 790 (1952), and Rivera v. Delaware, 429 U.S. 877 (1976). The constitutionality of burden-shifting defenses is considered in Chapter XII.

[v] For empirical assessments of the impact of the post-*Hinckley* changes, see Henry J. Steadman et al, Before and After Hinckley (1993); and Rita J. Simon and David J. Aaronson, The Insanity Defense: A Critical Assessment of Law and Policy in the Post-Hinckley Era (1988).

[w] In United States v. Lyons, 731 F.2d 243, 739 F.2d 994 (5th Cir. 1984) (en banc), the Fifth Circuit anticipated the eventual congressional action by abandoning the volitional prong of the Model Penal Code test.

community under a program of conditional discharge under which a community mental health agency closely monitors the person's condition and behavior, and rehospitalizes those who have not been compliant with the conditions of release or whose condition deteriorates. Studies of these conditional discharge programs have shown that the mental health agencies tend to take a highly precautionary approach, revoking community status upon any showing of material noncompliance, and that the re-arrest rate (both for all crimes and for violent offenses) is substantially lower than comparable rates for prisoners under correctional supervision. See, e.g., Michael Vitacco, Rebecca Vauter, Steven K. Erickson & Laurie Ragatz, Evaluating Conditional Release in Not Guilty by Reason of Insanity Acquittees: A Prospective Follow-Up Study in Virginia, 38 Law & Human Behavior 346 (2014).

## SUBSECTION A: THE INSANITY DEFENSE AND MAJOR MENTAL DISORDER

### The Case of Joy Baker

[The following material presents the facts from a real case involving Joy Baker, a 31-year-old woman who was indicted for the murder of her aunt (Trevah) and pleaded not guilty by reason of insanity. It is designed to provide a basis for exploring the relationship between criminal responsibility and major mental disorder and for analyzing the meanings of the various "tests" of insanity reviewed in the preceding notes. After a summary of Joy Baker's background, the material includes a transcript of her own statements concerning the offense. As this material is read, consider how the various tests of insanity could be applied to her case. The notes following the case will explore the issues raised and will include relevant excerpts from expert opinion supporting her insanity claim.]

Mrs. Baker's mother had a history of psychiatric hospitalization and, due to her mother's emotional instability, she was raised by her grandparents until the age of 10. She then lived with her mother for three years and with Aunt Trevah for two. After an unsuccessful attempt to rejoin her mother, she lived briefly in a foster home before returning to her grandparents.

Upon graduation from high school at 18, Mrs. Baker married. The marriage ended in divorce six years later with Mrs. Baker retaining custody of the two children. A year later she married her present husband, Curtis Baker. According to Mrs. Baker's account, the marriage was a stressful one from the outset. Her husband was often violent, especially when he had been drinking, and frequently assaulted her; the most recent episode was about a month before the offense. She stated that her husband told her that she was "jinxed" and that she brought him bad luck. He also frequently accused her of having extramarital affairs, allegations that she denied.

Mrs. Baker's description of the offense and the preceding three-day period is excerpted below. A transcription of her words obviously cannot convey the intensity with which she delivered this account; however, the transcript does fairly reflect the coherence and detail of her presentation, qualities which are atypical in such cases. During the course of this testimony, Mrs. Baker refers to her two children—Danny (age 11) and Betty (age 9).

Q: What do you remember about the night of the shooting?

A: I know that about three days before that . . . I had gone out to take care of my cats and I noticed that the dog outside had a rope wrapped around her paw, and her paw was swollen and out like this and I put her on the back porch. I took the kitten that had an infected ear to the vet and I drove back. . . . When I got home, for some reason I felt . . . I had to dump all the dirty things in the house outside the house—anything that was bad, like alcohol, or stale food, leftover foods. I put it all in garbage bags and I got rid of the garbage and—

Q: You said you felt you had to do that?

A: I felt like I *had* to, that I *had* to get these things out because something bad was going to happen.

Q: If you didn't take them out.

A: Yes, take all these things out. And I felt like I had to get the house clean, the house had to be very, very clean. Then—I can't keep the days straight, I think it was the next day—my husband decided to stay home, was going to stay home with me for a while.

Q: Why was he going to stay home?

A: He was just going to go in to work late that day for some reason. And over a long period of time—we've been living there about five and one-half years—he'd been asking me who I'd been with, who'd I seen, and where did I go, what did I do. He would accuse me of running around and I went ahead and told him about this one guy that I have talked to before, gave him his name, where he worked and he got angry; he said to write his name down. I wrote his name down on a card and he stormed out of the house. He said he was going to find him and he was going to kill him.

Q: Do you remember when that happened in relationship to the night of the shooting.

A: I think that was the day before the shooting. . . .

Q: Let me repeat this and correct me if I'm wrong. It's my understanding that you had had feelings that something bad was going to happen to you that day. That's why you didn't want to go down the highway [to pick the children up at school]. Is that right?

A: I went down. . . .

Q: But you went anyway.

A: Yes. Well I left the dog out at the school grounds and then I felt like if I leave the dog there she's going to bite the children. I was trying to get the dog in, but I didn't want to put the dog back in the car because I was afraid she'd bite me, but my son started hollering and crying that he wanted his dog Brownie.

Q: Does the dog bite?

A: No, but she didn't want to come to me and I had trouble getting her in so I drove on up the road. I thought that maybe if I drove slow she would follow us.

Q: You say she didn't want to come to you? Is that not like her, or usually she comes to you?

A: Usually she comes to me, but she didn't want to come to me that day.

Q: Wonder why that was?

A: I don't know, but I drove on down to the main highway and I parked the car and I told the children to stay in the car and I felt like that I had to walk down the highway. I felt that sometime during my walk through that field Brownie was going to come up behind me or in front of me and just grab me around the throat and kill me and I stood out there waiting for her to do this and she never came and I turned around for her to do this and she never came and I turned around and started walking back. I remember I was scared and I started walking back to the car and when I got to the door I just jerked the door real quick and jumped in and I started taking off. Danny started hollering that he wanted Brownie and sometime on the way down the road towards the house, Brownie was following us, so I let Brownie in the car from the other side and I told Betty to hold her. I didn't want her near me because I was afraid she'd bite me.

I got home. That afternoon the children were upstairs in their room playing checkers and I was up there and Curtis came up there and he was angry and he had a gun in his hand and he said, "Come with me," and I said, "Well, what about the children?" He said "Leave the children here, they'll be all right." He told me to get in the truck and it was about 4:30, sometime in the afternoon. And I said "Where will we be going?" He says "We're going for a drive."

We drove all over the place, Centerville and everywhere possible. We went to that man's mother's house and several other places. Somebody else's house, I don't know whose and every time we stopped somewhere he'd say "I want you to meet my wife, the adulteress." And we stopped at this store. Curtis got out and was talking to this elderly man who ran the store and when he got ready to get back into the truck I asked the man if he had a telephone. I wanted to call somebody and tell them that Curtis was acting silly, you know, because he kept the gun between us on the truck seat and kept screaming at me about who I went with and what I had done, that I should be ashamed of myself and God is going to get me for this. He demanded I throw my rings out of the window and I threw them out because he was getting angry.

It was late when I got home and we had to knock on the door several times and my daughter came to the door and opened it. The whole time that I was riding around in the truck I thought the dog was going to bite my kids before I could get back home. When I got home I felt sick. I was tired, I hadn't eaten, the children hadn't eaten. I had to get them up at three and I was trying to fix something for them to eat at three o'clock in the morning.

And Brownie was in the house and it looked like everywhere I went, that dog was following me. If I had any food in my hand, she kept trying to get it out of my hands. Then, I fixed bacon. I figured I would throw the bacon real quick to the dog so she'd eat that and be busy eating that so I could give my children something to eat because I felt that she was going to bother them.

And that black dog of Curtis's—when we got back from the ride, that truck ride, he sat down at the table and we were arguing and I saw Curtis make sort of a sneer with his mouth and when he did that then that dog of his growled each time he pulled his lip up. The dog would growl, the black dog. And then Curtis got up, he kind of kicked the chair over and he says, "Make up the bed, I'm going to bed." And he made up the bed. He put the gun on the nightstand and that worried me. I took the gun. He asked me where I was going with it and I put it under the bed. I couldn't sleep. I was upset. I felt like if I went to sleep he was going to kill me. That night I just felt like Curtis didn't act right and I thought well I can't trust him and nobody. So I stayed up and it was about 7:30 when I went to bed because I was just too tired.

Q: 7:30?

A: The next morning. And I guess I slept 'til around 10.

Q: That was the morning of the shooting, is that right?

A: Yes.

Q: What happened that day. You got up?

A: I had a headache again. I felt bad, I was tired and when I got up Curtis wasn't there. I didn't see Curtis and I walked around the house three times and I called him three times and I didn't get any answer. The last time, after I walked through the bedroom and I got right into the living room, he says, "Yeah, what do you want?" I turned around and he was sitting on the bed. That kind of scared me because I hadn't seen him.

And I went ahead and took a bath. I thought maybe that would make me feel better. And I took a bath and then I tried to fix breakfast and everything I did that morning went wrong. I burned the bacon. I tried to clean the house. It seemed like when I cleaned the house I was making more of a mess than I was doing anything else. I tried to wash the dishes and I didn't feel like washing dishes cause when I did it, it just looked like there were that many more dishes to wash.

I tried to clean out my rabbit cage and I felt like if I put my hand in there that rabbit's going to bite me. I felt like my rabbit and my dog had rabies and my yellow cat. As I was putting the dog outside later that morning, she had, well, I don't know, she just looked like she had foam all around her mouth and when I saw that I thought "Oh my God, that dog's got rabies," and I wouldn't let her in and I looked at my yellow cat and he was panting and I said, well the dog has probably bitten the cat and I can't let him in.

Q: Were they vaccinated?

A: Yes.

Q: So even though they were vaccinated you had that feeling they had rabies.

A: Then, Curtis said he was going to the grocery store. I asked him not to leave me in the house in the first place because I was scared and that I was afraid something was going to happen, and he said nothing is going to happen.

Q: What did you think was going to happen?

A: I just felt like somebody was out to get me or those animals were going to attack me or something. When he left I shut the doors and well, really, I thought that the neighborhood—what they call it is God's country, they call that area God's country and for some reason I kind of thought it was funny because I thought to myself this is not God's country, this is Devil's land or something—and I thought like those people round there are witches and I felt like sooner or later they're going to get me. They're either going to kill me or they're going to do something to me and if they don't get to me, my dogs are going to break into the house and they are going to tear me to pieces and for a few minutes, I even thought my children were possessed by demons or a devil, or something.

Q: Had you ever had feelings like this before that day?

A: No, I have never been through anything like this before. I have never felt like I was going to be—[pause]—"slaughtered" is the word for it. I just felt like they were going to do anything and everything they could to destroy me. And my animals—I've never been afraid of my animals except for Midnight. Now I don't particularly like Midnight, the black dog.

Q: That's Curtis's dog.

A: Yeah, he has taught her to jump up and she'd put her teeth around your arm, like this, and she plays rough and when I came back from that ride the day I went to the school, I heard her barking on the back porch and she started growling. Well I was scared to go in there . . . but I had to in order to get in the house because the front door was shut. And to keep the dog from biting me I kept watching her and holding my pocketbook in front of her face because I just felt like she would bite me. And I even asked Curtis several times to get her off the back porch and take and put her back outside because I couldn't get out on the back porch to hang up clothes or anything else because she was out there.

Q: So then what happened?

A: So anyway, sometime or other I found the gun under the bed where I had laid it.

Q: Whose gun was it?

A: It's Curtis's gun.

Q: Does he have a lot of guns at home?

A: Well, he had another one that was hidden, that my aunt had hidden in the trunk, and he wanted that back so I got it back and gave it to him. He used to have a German type gun and he's bought another one since then, I don't know what type it is, it's a smaller one, and this one is a Western style. It's about so long and got a handle on it like this.

Q: Are you experienced with firearms? Do you shoot a lot?

A: No, he said sometime before this happened he said I ought to learn how to load a gun, and he had loaded it and then he says, "Now you try it." And I put the bullet in the slot but I was afraid to push this thing that slides out because I was afraid if I pushed it in and then turned it I might go too far and it might go off or something, so he said, "Well, here let me do it and I'll do it." So he put the two bullets back in the gun.

Q: So there were only the two bullets in the gun?

A: That's all he put in there.

Q: Was there anything special about keeping two bullets in the gun?

A: No, it was just bullets and . . .

Q: So he had that loaded, that gun was loaded then all the time in the house with the two bullets.

A: Yes, it was loaded with those two and he had mentioned something about he had ordered me a gun cause he thought I needed one to protect myself at the house at night and I might need it, being there by myself. Well I don't know anything about guns. The only gun I ever shot was a .22 rifle of my brother's when I was 17 and I just took two shots at a target out on the farm and from then on I had never bothered with guns.

Q: So this day you said you found the gun. It was under the bed. Is that right? You had put it under—

A: It's where I put it the night before and I got scared and I ran into the bedroom and I pulled the gun out and my children, I don't know, I kept telling my children that I felt something was going to happen. Something was wrong and that somebody was going to kill me and I upset them and they were sitting on the couch and I kept thinking "Are you against me too?"

Q: These feelings that everyone was against you were stronger as the day went on; they got worse?

A: Yes, I even demanded my children to tell me which one was against me and if they knew what was going on, that they better tell me. And finally I felt upset because I felt like I was getting so close to shooting my children—you know, I felt that I was going to kill my children—that I told both of them to get up real quick and go in the other room and get a Bible apiece and then go back to the sofa and sit down and turn to the 23rd Psalm and just keep reading it and reading it and not stop reading, because I felt like as long as they were reading that

Bible—I said, "God would protect you from me because I am sick and I'm scared and I don't know what's going on and somebody is going to hurt me."

And I held that gun just like this because I didn't want to use it on my children. And I was just like this and while I was standing there I could see through my living room curtains and my aunt's car came flying down the hill. She looked like she was speeding. Well I didn't expect Trevah. I hadn't even called Trevah and she came up to the front porch and started knocking and calling me and I didn't answer her. I just figured she would go away and she'll leave me alone. But I felt like somebody was going to kill me, or was trying to hurt me and I wouldn't answer that door for her because I felt like, well, she's the one, it's going to be her. So she left the steps and she went around the house and I went through the living room to the back.

Q: Did you see her physically?

A: I could see her shadow through the curtains and I could hear her voice.

Q: You couldn't see her face clearly or you could see her face clearly?

A: Not at the front door.

Q: Not at the front. Okay.

A: And she went around the back and I had to go out and that black dog was there and that dog bothered me cause I thought, "Well if I get out there that thing is going to jump on me." So I took my foot and was kind of kicking the dog away and pushing the dog away with my other hand, and Trevah came around the corner of the back screen door and I told her to stay away and just stay right where she was and to leave me alone, that I didn't want to be bothered.

Q: When you said that to her through the screen door did you see her?

A: I could see her face.

Q: You could see her, and did it look like her or did it look different?

A: She didn't look happy. I mean she looked angry, was how she looked to me. She just looked angry and I said "Trevah get away from me and leave me alone." I said, "You're not going to hurt me, you're the devil, you're a demon or something is wrong, but you stay away from me and don't you come near me."

Q: Have you ever seen her look like that before?

A: Yes, when she's been angry.

Q: Does she look exactly like she looks when she looked angry or did she look different?

A: She looked angry. The expression on her face looked like she was angry and yet I kept telling her to leave me alone. I thought she'd just go on and leave me alone, get away from me.

Q: Were you hearing voices at this time, do you remember?

A: I wasn't hearing any voices. I felt like, right then I felt like "Okay, you're here and if you get your hands on me, you're going to kill me, or those kids are going to kill me, or that dog in front of me is going to jump me," and I was worried about Midnight and my aunt. I had my aunt over there and this black dog over here, and both of them were bothering me and I didn't know what to do with either one of them and I thought well maybe if I could holler at Trevah or get her away from me, she'd leave me alone, and she said, "No, I'm not leaving you alone." She says, "I'm coming in that door," and I said, "You better not, you better get away from me" and she says, "No, I'm not," and she took her hands and she started opening the door knobs off the screen, I think. She took her hands to get the edge of the door and started opening it, and that got on my nerves because I told her to leave me alone. And then I had that black dog in front of me and she turned around and I was trying to kick the dog and Trevah was coming in the door and I just took my hands and I just went like this—right through the screen.

Q: What happened?

A: I shot her.

Q: Then what happened after you shot her?

A: When I shot her she went backwards and she fell in the mud on her back and the dog kept coming near me and I pushed the door open real quick and got the dog out of the way and I, just—I don't know—I just stood there. I started crying and I felt like tearing up, I felt like tearing up everything in that back porch. I felt like taking something heavy and just smashing that red washing machine all to pieces. That's how I felt like. I just felt like I hated everybody and everything that minute, and I was hurting and I was mixed up and I felt sick and I was angry at Curtis for leaving me and I was angry because I had shot my aunt and I just felt like—

Q: Did you know that was your aunt when she came?

A: I know it was Trevah.

Q: Other times, you have said you had feelings that it was something else.

A: No, I knew that that was Trevah, but I felt like she and Curtis, and several of the people in the neighborhood were witches or had given their souls to the devil and they were all out to do some harm to me because they were against me. I just, that's how I felt and I felt like if Trevah got hold of me she was going to kill me because she was with everybody else. And I felt like Curtis was against me because he told me himself when he started taking me around in that truck ride—he says "I'm going to teach you a lesson you'll never forget." And . . .

Q: It was a pretty upsetting experience. . . .

A: So, I talked to my aunt a few minutes, right after I shot her and she said "Joy why?" and I said, "Trevah," I said, "You're the devil," and I said, "You came here to hurt me didn't you?" and she said, "Honey, no, I came to help you." And I started crying and then she said she was hurting and I don't know why I did this—but I guess because I felt that I was the reason for her bleeding to death—I took the gun and shot her again just to relieve the pain she was having because she said she hurt. And that was it. [Witness cries]

Q: What are you feeling now, Mrs. Baker?

A: Hurt. [Witness cries] [Long pause]

You know, sometimes you wonder, I've wondered, if I was going to do something like that, why did I have to hit her to kill her? You know, some people you read about, they shoot people and they hurt them in the arm. I feel like why in the world couldn't I have hit her in the arm and I know I hit her here [in the head] because I saw all that blood coming out of her chest.

Mrs. Baker's husband and children corroborated those portions of her account about which they had direct knowledge.

## NOTES ON THE INSANITY DEFENSE AND MAJOR MENTAL DISORDER

### 1. JOY BAKER'S CREDIBILITY

Because an insanity claim is based largely on what a defendant says was going on in his or her mind—mental events that cannot be verified by, or tested against, the experiences of ordinary people in the same circumstances—administration of the defense involves a considerable risk of fabrication. Does Joy Baker's account give any reason to doubt her veracity or the accuracy of her description of her feelings and thoughts at the time of the offense? Is it relevant that she had no previous history of disordered behavior or psychiatric treatment? Would your assessment of her credibility depend on whether the prosecution introduced any evidence suggesting a "motive" for the killing other than the one described by the defendant? Would your assessment be different if she had shot her husband instead of her aunt?

### 2. THE EXISTENCE OF MENTAL DISEASE

Assume that Joy Baker's account is credible and that she has accurately described the feelings and thoughts that she experienced before and during the shooting. (In fact, everyone who interviewed her believed she was telling the truth.) Does this evidence demonstrate that she had a "defect of reason from disease of the mind," as *M'Naghten* requires, or the "mental disease or defect" required under the Model Penal Code formulation?

The purpose and scope of the "mental-disease" requirement is explored in some detail in the materials that follow; however, several points should be noted here. First, the concept of mental disease is a threshold condition; abnormal psychological functioning at the time of a crime has exculpatory significance only if it can be attributed to the effects of a "mental disease." Obviously this excludes those aberrations in human behavior that are attributable to defects of character, intoxication, or emotional upheaval due to anger, panic, or grief. Second, while the boundaries of the concept are unclear, it plainly comprehends "psychotic" disorders such as schizophrenia that are characterized by "gross impairment of reality testing" and often evidenced by hallucinations or delusions.[a] Indeed, a psychosis is widely regarded as the only manifestation of mental disorder that can have exculpatory significance under *M'Naghten*.[b] Third, mental disease is *not* confined to those abnormalities associated with injured brain tissue, customarily labeled organic brain syndromes—for example, dementia attributable to trauma, cerebrovascular disease or Alzheimer's disease. If the concept were restricted to "organic" disorders, it would exclude a substantial proportion of persons whose contact with reality is severely impaired by what clinicians have traditionally called "functional" psychoses—those for which the presence of a specific organic cause has not yet been established, but which are associated with abnormal functioning of the brain. The major types of "functional" psychoses are the schizophrenic and paranoid disorders and the major affective disorders (e.g., bipolar disorder, also known as manic depressive disorder).

In Joy Baker's case, "direct evidence" of psychotic mental phenomena, including delusions, was presented in her own statements. Should the defendant also be required to introduce expert psychiatric testimony to carry her burden of producing evidence that she was suffering from a "mental disease"? Most courts have said "no," ruling that, in a jury trial, testimony by the defendant or by lay witnesses who have observed the defendant's behavior can be sufficient to raise a jury question on the issue of insanity. In practice, of course, almost all insanity claims are predicated chiefly, if not entirely, on expert testimony. Consider the significance of the following excerpt from the expert opinion on whether Mrs. Baker had a "mental disease" at the time of the offense:

Q: Doctor, in your professional opinion, was the defendant suffering from a mental disease at the time of the offense?

A: When Mrs. Baker killed Trevah she was, in my professional opinion, suffering from an acute episode of paranoid schizophrenia.

---

[a] According to the fifth edition of the Diagnostic and Statistical Manual of the American Psychiatric Association (DSM–5), page 87, schizophrenia and other psychotic disorders "are defined by abnormalities in one or more of the following five domains: delusions, hallucinations, disorganized thinking (speech), grossly disorganized or abnormal motor behavior (including catatonia) and negative symptoms." Clearly the meaning of the term "psychotic" varies somewhat in relation to particular disorders. The following amplifying language, which appeared in the glossary of DSM–IV, is helpful:

> When there is gross impairment in reality testing, the individual incorrectly evaluates the accuracy of his or her perceptions and thoughts and makes incorrect inferences about external reality, even in the face of contrary evidence. The term psychotic does not apply to minor distortions of reality that involve matters of relative judgment. For example, a depressed person who underestimated his achievements would not be described as a psychotic, whereas one who believed he had caused a natural catastrophe would be so described.

[b] Many commentators—whether they support *M'Naghten* or oppose it—have taken the position that the phrase "defect of reason" is substantially equivalent to psychosis. According to Robert Waelder, for example, the threshold condition for an insanity claim is one "in which the sense of reality is crudely impaired, and inaccessible to the corrective influence of experience—for example, when people are confused or disoriented or suffer from hallucinations or delusions." Robert Waelder, Psychiatry and the Problem of Criminal Responsibility, 101 U. Pa.L.Rev. 378, 384 (1952). See also Joseph Livermore & Paul Meehl, The Virtues of *M'Naghten*, 51 Minn.L.Rev. 789, 802–04 (1967).

This is an example of a major psychotic disorder; that is, a condition during which the person loses the ability to distinguish between what is outside herself, or what is "real," and what is inside herself, and in that sense, "not real."

Q: Doctor, could you explain how a person who has no previous history of mental illness would suddenly have an acute psychotic episode?

A: Mrs. Baker has a predisposition for psychiatric disease not only hereditarily via her mother's history of schizophrenia, but also with the chaotic nature of her early home environment. It appears that prior to the shooting, there was a great deal of domestic stress in the Baker home. The stresses which most of us can normally tolerate may become psychologically intolerable for a person with a predisposition for psychiatric disease. The stress precipitates a disintegration of the personality, a deterioration which affects the person's thinking and emotions. Any of us could become acutely psychotic under enough stress. In Mrs. Baker's case, the stress to which she was exposed is readily apparent and this was enough to tip the psychic balance.

## 3. MENTAL DISORDER AND CRIMINAL RESPONSIBILITY

Even if Mrs. Baker was psychotic—was suffering from a major form of mental illness—at the time of the offense, she nonetheless might be found to have been criminally responsible for the homicide. This is because mental disease is a necessary condition, but not a sufficient one, for exculpation on grounds of insanity. Each of the prevailing insanity tests requires proof of two "elements": The defendant must have had (i) a mental disease (ii) that had specified incapacitating effects at the time of the offense. The various tests differ, of course, in their definitions of those incapacities that have exculpatory significance. Should the test ask simply whether the defendant was mentally ill (or "insane") at the time of the offense?

A partial answer to this question is that the criminal act may have been entirely unrelated to a person's sickness. Thus, even a psychotic person usually has some grasp of reality. For example, a person whose interactions with other people are shaped by clearly paranoid thinking and other psychotic symptoms may nonetheless take a radio known to belong to someone else simply out of a desire to have it while hoping that he or she will not be caught. The psychotic symptoms may be entirely unrelated to the "reasons" for engaging in the criminal act. It should be noted, however, that this observation does not provide a complete answer to the question posed above. It demonstrates only that the question should be reformulated to ask whether the symptoms of the defendant's mental illness (or "insanity") were related to the offense. This is precisely what the New Hampshire Supreme Court said when it endorsed the so-called "product" test in State v. Jones, 50 N.H. 369, 398 (1871):

> Whether the defendant had a mental disease . . . seems to be as much a question of fact as whether he had a bodily disease; and whether the killing of his wife was the product of that disease, [is] also as clearly a matter of fact as whether thirst and a quickened pulse are the product of fever. That it is a difficult question does not change the matter at all. [Various] symptoms, phases, or man-

> ifestations of the disease . . . are all clearly matters of evidence to be weighed by the jury upon the question whether the act was the offspring of insanity: if it was, a criminal intent did not produce it; if it was not, a criminal intent did produce it, and it was crime. . . .

Is this a sensible approach? Is it preferable to the other tests described earlier? Consider, in this connection the New Hampshire Supreme Court's criticism of the *M'Naghten* and "irresistible-impulse" tests. These tests, the court said, are misguided because they give conclusive significance to particular "symptoms, phases or manifestations of the disease," such as the capacity to distinguish right from wrong or to resist an insane impulse, instead of looking at the full impact of the disease as a clinical phenomenon. This observation was echoed 80 years later by Judge David Bazelon in a short-lived decision adopting the New Hampshire test: "In attempting to define insanity in terms of a symptom, the courts have assumed an impossible role, not merely one for which they have no special competence." Durham v. United States, 214 F.2d 862, 872 (D.C.Cir. 1954).

Do the tests of criminal responsibility purport to identify "symptoms" of insanity and therefore to establish a legal "test" for what is really a medical question? Sir James Stephen insisted, to the contrary, that definition of "[t]he mental elements of responsibility . . . is and must be a legal question. It cannot be anything else, for the meaning of responsibility is liability to punishment; and if criminal law does not determine who are to be punished under given circumstances, it determines nothing." 2 A History of the Criminal Law of England 183 (1883). Is Stephen's response satisfactory?

### 4. APPLYING THE *M'NAGHTEN* TEST TO JOY BAKER

Application of the *M'Naghten* test requires the fact-finder to reconstruct the defendant's "knowledge" at the time of the offense. The test has two prongs—knowledge of the "nature and quality" of the act and knowledge of its wrongfulness. The task of probing the defendant's psyche and applying these tests—difficult enough in any case—is complicated in Joy Baker's case by the apparent difference in her motivation for the two shots.

#### *(i) Knowledge of the Act*

The first prong of *M'Naghten* overlaps analytically the technical concept of mens rea. Did Mrs. Baker have the mens rea for some form of criminal homicide? It could be argued that she lacked the mens rea for murder at the time of her first shot because she did not intend to kill a "human being." At common law, this claim would probably be characterized as a mistake of fact. Since the mistake was obviously an unreasonable one, however, Mrs. Baker most likely would be guilty of some form of homicide if ordinary mens rea principles were applied. It might also be argued that Mrs. Baker's first shot would have been justified if her delusional beliefs had been true since she would have been acting in self-defense. Again, the application of ordinary common law culpability principles would indicate that she was unreasonably mistaken as to the existence of justificatory facts (the necessity for killing to protect herself) and her defense would fail, although the grade of the offense might be reduced to manslaughter. For present purposes, therefore, it can be assumed that Mrs. Baker would be guilty of some form of homicide—at least manslaughter—unless she is entitled to exculpation on grounds of insanity.[c]

It seems clear that Mrs. Baker was aware that she was pulling the trigger of a gun and that the bullet would kill or seriously injure the victim. But did she "know" that the intended victim was a "human being" when she fired the first shot? In this sense, did she know the nature and quality of her act?

In any event, Mrs. Baker's account shows that she "knew" at the time of the second shot that her aunt was not demonically possessed; her perceptual capacities appear to have been intact at this point. Remember that she observed that her aunt "hurt" and that killing her would put her out of her pain. Does this imply that she "knew" the nature and quality of the act of pulling the trigger the second time? What does "quality" mean?

### *(ii) Knowledge of Wrongfulness*

Even if Joy Baker was sufficiently aware of the physical characteristics of her conduct to be said to have "known" the "nature and quality" of her act, did she "know" that it was wrong? Undoubtedly, she knew, as an abstract matter, that killing another person without justification is both legally and morally wrong. However, Mrs. Baker claimed to have believed at the time of the first shot that she was in imminent peril of annihilation at the hands of the devil. Would such a "defect of reason" prevent her from knowing that her act was wrong? Is it wrong, legally or morally, to shoot the devil?[d]

The second shot, unlike the first, does not appear to have been motivated by Mrs. Baker's delusion. One possible motive was simply to relieve her aunt's suffering. Was the second shot legally justified? If not, did her mental disease prevent her from "knowing" that her act was "wrong"? In what way?

The meaning of the word "wrong" in the *M'Naghten* test has often been in dispute. Some courts permit exculpation only if, as a result of mental disease, the defendant was disabled from knowing that the act was *legally* wrong. Under this approach, a defendant who knew that her conduct was a crime is legally sane regardless of her motivation or reasons for thinking it

---

[c] The general relationship between mens rea and mental abnormality is explored at the end of this section and is explored again in the specific context of homicide offenses in Chapter X.

[d] The *M'Naghten* decision contained another "rule" that might have been applicable to the first shot fired by Mrs. Baker. One of the questions posed by the House of Lords was: "If a person under an insane delusion as to existing facts commits an offense in consequence thereof, is he thereby excused?" The judges responded:

> [M]aking the assumption . . . that he labours under such partial delusion only, and is not in other respects insane, we think he must be considered in the same situation as to responsibility as if the facts with respect to which the delusion exists were real. For example, if, under the influence of his delusion, he supposes another man to be in the act of attempting to take away his life, and he kills that man, as he supposes, in self-defense, he would be exempt from punishment. If his delusion was that the deceased had inflicted a serious injury to his character and fortune, and he killed him in revenge for such supposed injury, he would be liable to punishment. . . .

This "insane delusion" ground of exculpation has been discarded as a separate test in modern formulations of *M'Naghten* on the theory that it is but a specific application of the "nature-and-quality" and "right-wrong" branches of the *M'Naghten* test and is thus redundant as a separate rule.

justified. The trial of Andrea Yates in Texas in 2002 is illustrative.[e] Ms. Yates killed her 5 children, ranging in ages from six months to eight years. At her trial for killing three of the children, she presented uncontested evidence that she had experienced post-partum depression with psychotic features after the birth of her fourth child in 1999 (from which she recovered after treatment with anti-psychotic and anti-depressant medication), and that these symptoms had recurred after the birth of her fifth child but did not respond well to medication. She claimed that she believed her children were "stumbling" into the throes of the devil and were going to burn in the fires of hell for eternity, and that by killing them, she would save them from this fate, she would be executed, and Satan would be vanquished. While the prosecution conceded that she was suffering from a severe mental illness, it insisted that she knew that killing her children was a crime and that she would be punished (indeed, that was part of her motivation). Her efforts to prevent anyone from finding out what she was planning to do, as well as her confession, amply showed that she knew her conduct was "wrong"—"I know what I have done," she acknowledged. In her initial trial, the jury convicted Ms. Yates, although it did not recommend a death sentence. After the conviction was reversed due to erroneous testimony by the prosecution's expert witness, a second jury found her insane.

Many courts take a broader view of what it means to be unable to know that one's conduct is wrong. Under this view, knowing that one's conduct is illegal does not amount to knowing that it is wrong. A famous early case setting forth this view is People v. Schmidt, 216 N.Y. 324, 110 N.E. 945 (1915), involving a defendant who claimed that he killed a woman after hearing the voice of God calling upon him to do so as a sacrifice and atonement. In an opinion by Judge Cardozo, the Court of Appeals held "that there are times and circumstances in which the word 'wrong' . . . ought not to be limited to legal wrong." In particular, if a person has "an insane delusion that God has appeared to [him] and ordained the commission of a crime, we think it cannot be said of the offender that he knows the act to be wrong." More recently, the Connecticut Supreme Court took a similar view in interpreting the word "wrongfulness" to refer to the defendant's understanding of the moral wrongfulness of his actions. State v. Wilson, 242 Conn. 605, 700 A.2d 633 (1997).[f] Wilson killed a man believing that the victim was a mastermind of a large organization designed to control the minds of people worldwide, including his own. The court said that the legislature had purposely decided not to limit the insanity test to legal wrongfulness by rejecting the word "criminality" in favor of the word "wrongfulness" when it adopted the Model Code formulation of the insanity test.[g]

What is left of the right-wrong "test" under the "moral wrongfulness" approach? Does this mean that if a mentally ill person thinks, according to

---

[e] See Deborah W. Denno, Who is Andrea Yates? A Short Story About Insanity, 2 Duke J. Of Gender Law and Policy 1 (2003).

[f] See also State v. Cameron, 100 Wn.2d 520, 674 P.2d 650 (en banc 1983). Cameron stabbed and killed his stepmother, believing that she was a satanic agent and that he was doing God's will, even though he knew that he was committing a crime. The jury was instructed that "the terms 'right and wrong' refer to knowledge of a person at the time of committing an act that he was acting contrary to law." The Washington Supreme Court overturned the conviction, holding that this instruction was erroneous.

[g] The drafters of the Model Penal Code took no position on this question, leaving it to the courts and legislatures to choose whether the test should include the term "wrongfulness" or "criminality." Jurisdictions adopting the Model Code test have divided evenly on the question.

his own lights, that he is doing the "right" thing, then he is not criminally responsible even if he "knew" that his act was a crime and that it would be condemned by others? Courts adopting the "moral wrongfulness" position have resisted a "purely subjective" approach. In *Wilson*, for example, the Connecticut Supreme Court said that a defendant is legally insane if, as a result of mental disease, "he substantially misperceived reality and harbored a delusional belief that society, under the circumstances as the defendant honestly but mistakenly perceived them to be, would not have morally condemned his actions." How would this test apply to Joy Baker? To Andrea Yates and the other defendants mentioned above? Is there any other possible meaning of "wrong"?

### *(iii) The Value of Expert Testimony*

Is the task of applying either branch of *M'Naghten* materially aided by expert psychiatric testimony? Consider the following psychiatric evaluation:

Q: At the time of the offense, did the defendant know she was shooting her aunt?

A: In her psychotic state she was not able to draw the boundary between her internal chaotic reality (her fear of annihilation) and the external reality of her environment, and the two became fused. As she talks about that evening she states that she saw her aunt coming towards the back door and she "knew" that this person was her aunt. It is essential here to understand what the word "know" means in the context of Mrs. Baker's psychiatric illness. It is true that Mrs. Baker was able to recognize the form which approached her home as that of her aunt. This particular perceptual mechanism seemed to remain intact. However, Mrs. Baker's interpretation of this perception is what was so profoundly affected by her psychotic state. Her interpretation of her aunt approaching her home was entirely out of touch with the reality of the situation. Mrs. Baker firmly believed that her aunt was a witch and was afraid her aunt would annihilate her. It was this affective state, or emotional tone, which set the stage for Mrs. Baker's actions. She was unable at the time of the shooting, with her abnormal intellectual functions, to recognize how invalid her interpretations were. This is, of course, a result of her psychotic state. In other words, at the time of the shooting, Mrs. Baker was unable, in my professional opinion, to understand the difference between her own feelings and the events occurring in the world around her. She did not appreciate the nature and consequences of her acts and acted purely from the instinct of self-preservation.

Q: What about the second shot, Doctor?

A: Persons in a psychotic state have extreme polarization of emotions. One moment they may feel intense love, the next moment intense hate. One moment they may feel intensely threatened and the next moment they may feel intensely secure and so forth. In addition these polar feelings may switch very rapidly and will not appear to be connected to one another because of the chaotic state of that person's thinking. In

> Mrs. Baker's psychotic state she experienced these rapid disjointed changes in feelings. This enabled her to feel threatened and fearful in one moment and yet to feel concern and desire to help her wounded aunt in the next.
>
> Thus, the first shot removed the threat of her own imminent destruction and generated feelings of relief. This, in turn "shocked" her and triggered a "jump" in her perceptual modalities. Her perceptive focus shifted from her preoccupation with the threats to herself to a recognition of her aunt's condition. Now she was preoccupied with her desire to "stop the suffering." To Mrs. Baker the immediate way to do this was to shoot her aunt again. In her "regressed" state, she was still not sufficiently in touch with reality to call into play mature, normal responses to her aunt's condition. A person in a psychotic state cannot connect logically chains of events. Hence she did not make the rational connection between the act of shooting her aunt to stop her suffering and the finality of death. Thus, it is my professional opinion that a full appreciation of the nature and consequences of the second shot could not have existed in Mrs. Baker's mind.

Does this opinion help? Should Mrs. Baker be convicted in a *M'Naghten* jurisdiction?

## 5. THE MEANING OF "KNOWING"

The *M'Naghten* formulation has been subject to the persistent criticism that it requires conviction of psychotic offenders who are not blameworthy. According to the critics, only a handful of seriously ill offenders fail to "know" in a purely intellectual sense enough about what they are doing to know that it is punishable. Yet, because a mentally ill person's "intellectual" knowledge may not be assimilated by the whole personality, such a person may lack an emotional appreciation of the significance of conduct. In other words, the term "knowledge" is clinically meaningful, the critics say, only if it is given an "affective" or emotional meaning. The expert opinion quoted above illustrates this clinical interpretation of "knowledge."

Perhaps the most famous statement of the clinical objection to *M'Naghten* language appeared in Gregory Zilboorg, Misconceptions of Legal Insanity, 9 Am.J. Orthopsychiat. 540, 552–53 (1939):

> The fundamental difference between verbal or purely intellectual knowledge and the mysterious other kind of knowledge is familiar to every clinical psychiatrist; it is the difference between knowledge divorced from affect and knowledge so fused with affect that it becomes a human reality. . . . [E]motional appreciation is a very complex phenomenon. It is based on a series of intricate psychological mechanisms, the most potent of which is that of identification. What makes it possible for a civilized, mentally healthy human being to resist a murderous impulse is not the cold detached reasoning that it is wrong and dangerous but the automatic emotional, mostly unconscious identification with the prospective victim, an identification which automatically inhibits the impulse to kill and causes anxiety ("It is dangerous") which in turn produces the reflection: "It is wrong, the same may and should happen to me." Unless this identification is present the

> impulse breaks through and fear of the law and sense of wrong is paled, devoid of its affective component; it becomes a verbal, coldly intellectual, formal, childish, infantile psychological presentation.

In his classic book, The Insanity Defense 49–51 (1967), Abraham Goldstein concluded that, in practice, the *M'Naghten* formula has been interpreted and applied in a much less restrictive fashion than its critics have assumed. Upon close examination, he concluded, very few appellate courts have imposed the restrictive interpretation and most of the pertinent decisions "have favored a rather broad construction." For example, the jury is typically told that an accused "knows" only if he "understands" enough to enable him to judge of "the nature, character and consequence of the act charged against him," or if he has the "capacity to appreciate the character and to comprehend the probable or possible consequences of his act." Under this formulation, Goldstein observed, "the word 'appreciate' draws most psychoses under the *M'Naghten* rules, because it addresses itself to the defendant's awareness of "the true significance of his conduct."

Similarly, Goldstein observed that the phrase "nature and quality of the act" is typically either stated to the jury without explanation or treated as adding nothing to the requirement that the accused know his act was wrong. However, he highlighted one court's observation that "nature and quality" gives "important emphasis" to the realization of the wrongfulness of an act and marks the distinction between "vaguely [realizing] that particular conduct is forbidden" and "real insight into the conduct." He continued:

> This construction illustrates the close connection between the definition of "know" and that of "nature and quality." The broader meaning of "nature and quality" carries with it the broader construction of "know" and vice versa. To know the quality of an act, with all its social and emotional implications, requires more than an abstract purely intellectual knowledge. Likewise, to talk of appreciating the full significance of an act means that "nature and quality" must be understood as including more than the physical nature of the act.

This broader reading of the word "knowledge" as it appears in the *M'Naghten* formulation is, as Goldstein indicated, typically achieved by emphasizing that the actor must "appreciate" the nature and quality of the conduct and that it was wrong in a moral sense. Indeed, "appreciate" has become a kind of code-word for this "affective" reading of "knowledge." The defendant must have sufficient understanding of the nature and consequences of the conduct to be said to "appreciate" its social and moral significance. Without such understanding, the defendant lacks the rudimentary tools by which "normal" responsible people govern their conduct. Use of the word "appreciate" in the reformulation of the *M'Naghten* test in Section 4.01 of the Model Penal Code is intended to embrace this broader notion of what it means to "know" something is wrong.

The trend in favor of an "affective" meaning of knowledge, however, has not been without its critics. Glanville Williams is one of them. In Criminal Law: The General Part 491–92 (2d ed. 1961), he stated:

> The tendency to widen the exemption . . . by referring it to some deeper kind of metaphysical insight is . . . found among

> American psychiatrists. The question, on this view, is not merely . . . whether the accused knew he was killing a human being, but whether he had any "real appreciation" or "understanding" of his act, or of its "enormity, its significance or its implications." This is metaphysical rather than scientific language and it may be permissible to doubt whether any citizen, sane or not, can be credited with the transcendental insight of the mystic. The formula of "real nature" is used indulgently to give a general exemption on the ground of [mental illness].

Does Williams have a point? Should a mere "intellectual knowledge" be sufficient to establish criminal responsibility even if the defendant lacked a "true appreciation" of the significance of his conduct?

### 6. THE SIGNIFICANCE OF COGNITIVE IMPAIRMENT

The preceding notes have used the facts of the Joy Baker case to explore the meaning of the *M'Naghten* test and the analogous language in the Model Penal Code. Now, it is useful to return to the fundamental question raised at the outset, i.e., whether these tests identify proper criteria for assessing criminal responsibility.

To the extent that "nature and quality" of the act refers only to its physical character, the first prong of *M'Naghten* is, in the words of Lord Patrick Devlin, "practically obsolete."[h] No one who squeezes a person's neck really thinks he is squeezing a lemon.[i] Also, as Goldstein noted, an emphasis on the moral "quality" of the act makes this prong of the test functionally equivalent to its right-wrong prong. Thus, under either *M'Naghten* or the analogous language in the Model Penal Code, the real significance of cognitive impairment lies in whether the defendant knew or appreciated the "wrongfulness" of the act. Is this the right question to ask? The liability of a sane person does not turn on having a "mind bent on wrongdoing" or full appreciation or understanding of the legal or moral significance of conduct. Why should the liability of an "insane" person turn on such an inquiry?

Glanville Williams discussed this issue in Criminal Law: The General Part 495–96 (2d ed. 1961):

> Why, precisely, does knowledge of wrong enter into a consideration of responsibility? . . . The exemption . . . may perhaps be regarded as dictated by the object of punishment [because] a psychotic who does not know that his act is wrong is not likely to be deterred by the legal prohibition. Yet the same is true of a sane person who does not know that his act is wrong. Why is not the rule ignorantia juris non excusat applied to the insane? Perhaps it is because the rule presupposes a mind capable of knowing right. But on this interpretation the question should be not: "Did the accused know it was wrong" but "Was he capable of knowing that it was wrong?" For if it once be admitted that some psychotics know

---

[h] Patrick Devlin, Criminal Responsibility and Punishment: Functions of Judge and Jury, [1954] Crim.L.Rev. 661, 678–79.

[i] The hypothetical case of a person who strangles someone in the mistaken belief that he is squeezing a lemon was first used in the early 1970s to illustrate the effect of abolishing the insanity defense while admitting evidence of mental abnormality to negate mens rea. See Heathcoate Wales, An Analysis of the Proposal to "Abolish" the Insanity Defense in S.1: Squeezing a Lemon, 124 U. Pa. L Rev 687 (1976).

> right from wrong, it may be a mere accident of education (such as may befall a sane person) that this particular psychotic did not know the particular act to be wrong. What must be shown is that his ignorance was the result of his mental disease. . . .

Williams' point can be illustrated by the second shot in Joy Baker's case. This shot was not motivated by her delusional beliefs. Under the circumstances as she correctly perceived them, her conduct constitutes murder, for euthanasia has never been recognized as justifiable or excusable homicide under Anglo-American law. Perhaps Joy Baker did not know this, although it is more likely that she acted spontaneously and gave no thought to the legality of her conduct. Yet, if a sane person had shot an injured and suffering Aunt Trevah under similar circumstances, ignorance of (or emotional indifference to) the governing law of homicide would be legally irrelevant. Why should a different rule obtain for Joy Baker?

Questions of this nature have led some commentators to suggest that the *M'Naghten* formulation should be discarded altogether. The real basis for exculpation of the insane, they argue, lies not in a lack of a capacity to know or appreciate the wrongfulness of the conduct, but in a lack of capacity for rational control of behavior in relation to the criminal act.[j] Should irrationality be the test?

### 7. APPLYING CONTROL TESTS TO PSYCHOTIC DEFENDANTS

The control test provides an independent basis for exculpation in more than a third of the states. Proponents of such a test traditionally have claimed that a psychotic person who is "driven" by pathological delusions or hallucinations may be unable to restrain his behavior despite knowing that it is wrong. This "loss of control" is therefore thought to be a morally relevant feature of severe mental disorder. Recall the expert testimony in *M'Naghten*'s case that "he was not capable of exercising any control over acts which had connection with his delusion" and that the natural progression of his disease was "to burst forth with irresistible intensity."

How would the control formulas apply to Joy Baker? Did she act on an "irresistible impulse"? Did she lack "substantial capacity to conform her conduct to the requirements of law"? Is further information needed to apply these tests?

Obviously, the task of applying control tests to Joy Baker requires speculation about whether she "could" have acted otherwise than she did, and whether her mental illness prevented her from having the power of choice that she "normally" would have had. Since the only evidence available is her actual behavior—the defendant shot her aunt (twice)—how can one determine whether she "could" have acted otherwise? Would expert testimony help? Consider these expert observations about Mrs. Baker's case:

> Q: Doesn't Mrs. Baker's effort to protect her children, only moments before the killing, indicate that she had the mental power to resist her homicidal impulses?

---

[j] See, e.g., Stephen Morse, Rationality and Responsibility, 74 S. Cal. L Rev. 251 (2000); Michael Moore, Law and Psychiatry: Rethinking the Relationship (1984); Henry Fingarette and Ann F. Haase, Mental Disabilities and Criminal Responsibility (1979); Joel Feinberg, Doing and Deserving: Essays in the Theory of Responsibility 272–92 (1970).

A: No, I don't think so. When Mrs. Baker ordered the children to read the 23rd Psalm, she was trying to assure that they would not be the ones to attack her; in this sense, putting the Bible in their hands was an act of self-defense. When the victim drove up, Mrs. Baker did everything she could to prevent her aunt from coming in the house. However, once her aunt put her hand through the door, Mrs. Baker had no options left, psychologically speaking. She was in a state of extreme anxiety and was fearful of imminent attack. The impulse for protective action was, if you will, irresistible.

Q: Defendant's own testimony would suggest that she did not feel threatened at the time of the second shot; indeed, her testimony indicates that she was acting from a rational motive—to stop her aunt's suffering. Doesn't this suggest that her capacity to make choices had returned?

A: It is probably true that she was less influenced by her delusional thinking; because her level of intense anxiety had been reduced, she was able to see the victim as her aunt. Her perceptual and interpretive capacities had been restored to some extent. But this doesn't mean her functioning was intact by any means. She still lacked insight and judgment. She was probably very confused. It is possible, as she later recounted, that she saw that her aunt was in pain and that she responded in a regressed, child-like way. She acted impulsively.

Q: Suppose a policeman, or perhaps the rescue squad, had pulled into the driveway after the first shot. As you understand her condition, what do you think she would have done?

A: This is speculation, of course. But I think she would have taken advantage of the alternative way to get help for her aunt. The problem, in fact, was that there were no visible options and in her compromised psychological condition she was unable to think about alternatives that were not visibly apparent.

The desirability of a control test of responsibility has been one of the most hotly debated issues in the criminal law for more than a century. In recent years the debate has focused chiefly on disorders other than psychoses. This dimension of the controversy is covered in the next section, immediately below. However, it should be emphasized that the early proponents of the "irresistible impulse" test argued that the *M'Naghten* formula was an inadequate measure of the morally significant features of psychotic deterioration. Moreover, many psychiatrists have opposed recent efforts to eliminate the volitional criterion on the same basis. In response, many of the commentators who support proposals to narrow the defense have argued that a broad, affective reading of the "knowledge" or "appreciation" test makes the control test superfluous in cases involving psychotic defendants.[k] Is this right? Is Joy Baker's case for exculpation any stronger under a test of volitional impairment than it would be if cognitive impairment were the only inquiry?

---

[k] See, e.g., Jerome Hall, General Principles of Criminal Law 486–500 (1960).

## SUBSECTION B: THE INSANITY DEFENSE AND THE CONTROL INQUIRY

### INTRODUCTORY NOTE ON VOLITIONAL CRITERIA OF RESPONSIBILITY

The central issue in the contemporary debate about the insanity defense is whether volitional incapacity should have independent exculpatory significance. It is important to bear in mind that the volitional inquiry in the insanity defense intersects two other doctrines of the penal law. The first is the requirement of the voluntary act, discussed in Chapter II. According to this doctrine, some acts are regarded as involuntary because they are not within the conscious, physical control of the actor. An opportunity for choosing to act or not to act establishes the minimum link between body and mind necessary for criminal liability. Although a mentally abnormal offender may be said to be driven to act by intra-psychic forces, the technical requirement of a voluntary act is virtually always met if the person is conscious at the time of the offense.[a]

The second intersecting doctrine might be called situational compulsion. Sometimes, people may have conscious, physical control over their bodily movements, but nonetheless feel that they have no "real" choice at all. The classic case is duress: *A* takes *B*'s money because *C* holds a gun to *A*'s head and threatens to shoot if *A* does not do so. The reach of the concept of situational compulsion is explored in Chapter VII. For present purposes, the important point is that a person with normal strength of character who is confronted with such coercive circumstances will not be held criminally liable for "choosing" to violate the penal law. Even if the choice is not justifiable, the actor may be excused if blame would be unfair for conduct that is, morally speaking, "beyond control."

The case for the volitional prong of the insanity defense rests on the empirical proposition that mental abnormalities can impair a person's capacity to choose to comply with the penal law and on the moral proposition that such a person cannot fairly be blamed for criminal acts that are psychologically "compelled". It should be noted, however, that acts "compelled" by internal pathology stand on a very different footing from those "compelled" by external pressure. In the latter case, the incapacity is simply the frailty of the ordinary person; in the former, the defendant's claim to exculpation is pressed precisely because the strengths of the ordinary person are lacking.

## ILLUSTRATIVE CASES OF VOLITIONAL IMPAIRMENT

A full appreciation of the complexities of the volitional inquiry requires familiarity with the variety of clinical explanations that can be given for criminal behavior. The following cases are representative of the range of

[a] Indeed, evidence of mental abnormality is routinely rejected when offered to support an involuntary-act defense. The historical reason for this result, and for the continued conceptual separation of the voluntary-act doctrine and the insanity defense, undoubtedly is closely tied to the dispositional consequences of the two doctrines. Typically, an acquittal by reason of insanity leads to some form of commitment of the defendant for treatment of the underlying mental disorder. An involuntary-act acquittal, on the other hand, has no such consequence. This factor has considerable explanatory power as to why the voluntary-act doctrine is generally conceived in relatively narrow terms.

claims that have been raised. The factual summaries also summarize the expert testimony presented on the defendant's behalf.

## 1. *BARNES*[a]

James Barnes, age 18, was charged with six counts of arson and three counts of murder in connection with one of the fires, which had been set in an apartment building. He pleaded not guilty by reason of insanity. The expert witness testified that the defendant was suffering from a disorder of impulse control (pyromania) and schizoid personality disorder. According to the expert, Barnes' earliest childhood memory was watching a neighbor burn trash in the backyard. He began setting fires around his own home at the age of eight. During high school he set fires to student lockers on four occasions and periodically set fires at his part-time jobs, usually in trash containers in alleys. Despite the frequency of his firesetting, he was rarely caught and never punished for his actions.

Barnes' father was absent from home for extended periods until Barnes was 12. During adolescence, he and his father argued frequently; he felt his father viewed him as an ineffectual person, someone who "could not make it on his own."

At 16, Barnes began calling for emergency assistance from rescue squads in each of the surrounding counties by pretending to be suffocating. This practice continued for more than a year and occurred about 30 times. Barnes described a great sense of satisfaction from being cared for by the emergency crews on these occasions. Soon he became a member of his local rescue squad and felt secure as being part of a "team." He felt especially close to Carson, an older member of the squad. Along with other men of the rescue squad, Barnes and Carson spent their off-hours together.

Within a few months however, Carson married and left the rescue squad to become a fireman. During the same period, Barnes left home and moved into an apartment because of increasing tension with his father. His sense of isolation and loneliness increased soon thereafter, and he had fantasies of being rescued by Carson during a fire. In this fantasy Carson would carry him out of a burning building and would take care of him and ensure his continued safety. He also described feelings of sexual arousal in seeing firemen, particularly Carson, in their rubberized firefighting clothes.

Barnes soon began to set fires, reporting them in the hope that Carson would arrive. In this manner he would see Carson and would be either praised for his assistance in fighting the fire or would be "rescued." It was during this period that he committed the acts for which he was indicted. The last involved an apartment building.

The expert testified that, in his opinion, Barnes' drives and needs were so strong that they were able to override his generally intact judgment and his sense of social responsibility. Acknowledging that Barnes was able to delay his impulse to start a fire until the circumstances were favorable and the likelihood of detection was reduced, the expert nonetheless concluded that Barnes exhibited an "extremely strong need to bring himself into close contact with Carson even though that required him to commit socially irresponsible and illegal actions." Moreover, the expert testified, Barnes' "need

---

[a] This fact situation is based on an unreported case. For a similar case, see Briscoe v. United States, 248 F.2d 640 (D.C.Cir. 1957).

to start the fire in order to bring himself and Carson together was so strong that he unconsciously was able to keep from his awareness the possibility that others might be hurt or that extensive property damage might occur."

## 2. *CHESTER*[b]

Jack Chester was charged with the murder of Beatrice Fishman and pleaded not guilty by reason of insanity. The defendant and the victim met as teenagers and became engaged while he was in the armed forces. Upon being discharged, he obtained a job in a factory in another state and plans were made for the wedding in July of that year. For a variety of reasons, the wedding was repeatedly postponed over the next four months. In October the defendant was "very perturbed" and decided that he and Beatrice "were through." He told her she could keep all that he had given her except the wedding ring.

Between October and the following April, the defendant was depressed. Although he dated other girls, none of them could replace Beatrice. He tried to bring about a reconciliation, but Beatrice seemed indifferent, although she still failed to return the wedding ring. He started to drink heavily and to use marijuana. Sometime before April, he bought a pistol.

The defendant decided to visit Beatrice one April weekend. When packing his bag for the trip he put in the pistol. Upon arriving, he went directly to the Fishman home and was told by her parents that she was "out on a date." After talking with them for a while, he left. On the following day the defendant went to the Fishman home and talked with Beatrice and her mother. Beatrice told him that he had been away so long "she didn't know [him] any more," but if he returned to Boston to live they "could get reacquainted." The defendant asked Beatrice to return the ring, and she told him it was in a safe deposit vault, and he could have it Monday. After further conversation, he became very upset; he later said that he felt that he had become entangled in an "utterly hopeless and impossible situation" and that he wanted to kill Beatrice. But he "fought this emotion down," kissed her goodbye, and walked out of the house.

The defendant, according to his testimony at the trial, went to a bar, had "two shots of bourbon," and smoked two marijuana cigarettes, becoming slightly "high." But he said that this had no effect on his behavior; he admitted that he knew what he was doing. In about half an hour he returned to the Fishman house in an angry mood. He "figured it out [that he] couldn't live with her and [he] couldn't live without her and it did not make any difference." His intent was to "blow her head off." He went to the front door with his pistol in his pocket and rang the doorbell. As Beatrice opened the door he had the pistol in his hand. Seeing it, she hesitated and then closed the door. Thereupon the defendant started pulling the trigger and kept pulling it until he had fired nine shots through the door. Three of these entered the victim's body causing wounds from which she died within an hour. Shortly thereafter the defendant asked a policeman to arrest him as he had "just murdered someone."

According to the expert testimony introduced in support of Chester's insanity defense, his father died when the defendant was about five years old. His father's death was due to a head injury caused by a fall on the ice,

---

[b] This case is based on Commonwealth v. Chester, 337 Mass. 702, 150 N.E.2d 914 (1958).

suffered while running after Chester after he left the house without a hat. The defendant thereafter had guilt feelings because he thought he had caused his father's death. During his boyhood, without a father, he was difficult to control and there was considerable friction between him and his mother. As a result of one dispute with his mother, the defendant, then aged 12, drank a bottle of iodine. At 15 he sustained a serious injury to his eye from an air rifle. The injury affected his appearance, and as a consequence he became self-conscious.

While in the service, the defendant became despondent because of his relations with Beatrice and at one time considered suicide. He was unusually combative and frequently got into fights with other soldiers. Because two airplane pilots lost their lives in the crash of planes on which he had done mechanical work, he felt responsible for their deaths. He felt that he was "no good," that everything he did would turn out badly, and that he would die young.

The defendant's experts concluded that defendant had suffered since the age of 12 from a "personality disorder characterized by passive obstructionism and by a tendency toward overt, aggressive, uncontrolled outbursts or giving vent to one's feelings with vigorous physical action toward others." He also had an obsession with guilt and strong feelings of worthlessness. While conceding that many people have such traits, the expert stated that Chester had them to a marked degree. "Most of the time the defendant has been able to repress his strong feelings of anger. However, when these feelings have become more intense due to an intolerably frustrating situation, he swings into impulsive violent action over which he momentarily has no conscious control." At the time of the offense, according to the expert, Chester was driven by twin motivations: uncontrollable anger at both himself and the victim, and strong feelings of guilt and worthlessness.

### 3. *ELLINGWOOD*[c]

Sonny Ellingwood, a carpenter with no history of criminal behavior, was charged with criminal homicide in the second degree. The testimony adduced at trial revealed that the defendant shot two people with virtually no provocation and with no discernible motive. He pleaded not guilty by reason of insanity.

The evidence shows that on the day of the shooting the defendant was upset about various minor problems arising at home and on the job. During the morning he had corrected an erroneous estimate he had made on a construction project. Apparently his work had deteriorated in the weeks preceding the shooting.

At about noon of this day he returned home with two six-packs of beer. He drank some at that time. His wife chided him for drinking during the day. He complained about being pushed around by people and declared he wanted to quit his job and leave the state. Later he left his house trailer, taking with him his rifle and two bottles of beer. One of these bottles he put down and shot with his rifle. His wife came out of the trailer and reprimanded him for his action. He walked away toward a nearby gravel pit.

At the pit the defendant found James Hunter and his daughter, Jacqueline, removing some loam from the pit. The owner of the pit had

---

[c] This case is based on State v. Ellingwood, 409 A.2d 641 (Me.1979).

requested that the defendant keep watch over it. The defendant confronted this pair demanding to know by what right they were removing soil from the pit. James Hunter countered by asking what business it was to the defendant. After this brief interchange the defendant turned his back to them, put down the remaining beer bottle, and turned again, aiming the rifle at James Hunter.

He sighted the rifle on James Hunter for a few seconds. The victim pointed at the defendant and ordered him to put down the gun. The defendant then shot, hitting James Hunter in the chest. Jacqueline Hunter heard the defendant prepare his rifle for a second shot. She looked at him and ordered him to put down the gun. He shot her in the face.

The defendant's wife drove into the pit and picked up the defendant, who then told her his life was over, that he should shoot himself because he had just killed two people. They then drove to a nearby house where the police were called at the defendant's request.

Police officers described the defendant as blubbering, babbling, and crying. Although he admitted the shooting in general terms at that time, he was never able to recall the events in detail.

The defendant introduced expert testimony to support his insanity plea. The psychiatrist testified that the defendant had an underlying obsessive-compulsive and hysterical personality disorder. Symptoms of this condition include "failure to admit feelings; being overly conscientious; being over-controlled; an inability to relax easily; a feeling of personal inadequacy; a chronic tendency to swallow difficulties without objection." The witness testified that during the days before the offense, the defendant was experiencing substantial anxiety as a result of accumulating stress and that he could not control his exaggerated retributive feelings when confronted with the intruders in the pit. According to the expert, the defendant was probably aware of his actions at the time of the shooting but probably believed, "at some primitive level of psychological functioning, that he was acting in self-defense."

## 4. *MURDOCK*[d]

Murdock was one of three black patrons at a hamburger shop called the Little Tavern. At about 3:00 a.m., a white woman and five white U.S. Marine lieutenants, in dress white uniforms, entered the shop and ordered food. After Murdock had walked out, an argument developed between one of the whites and Alexander, one of Murdock's associates. Apparently one of the whites used a racial epithet, and Alexander drew a gun. Murdock then came back into the shop with his own gun drawn and fired, killing several of the Marines. Alexander and Murdock were charged with murder. Murdock pleaded not guilty by reason of insanity.

Murdock testified that he pulled his gun as a reflex and fired because he thought the Marines, who he said were moving toward him, would kill him. On cross-examination, he admitted that he did not see any weapons, that he emptied his fully loaded revolver at them in the restaurant and that he fired three shots from Alexander's gun from the window of the car as they drove away. In support of his insanity claim Murdock introduced

[d] This case is based on United States v. Alexander and Murdock, 471 F.2d 923 (D.C.Cir. 1972).

psychiatric testimony that he is "strongly delusional, though not hallucinating or psychotic." In particular, he is "greatly preoccupied with the unfair treatment of negroes in this country and believes that racial war is inevitable." The witness stated that this behavior reflects compulsiveness, emotional immaturity and some psychopathic traits, and that his emotional disorder had its roots in his childhood. His father had deserted his mother and he grew up in the Watts section of Los Angeles in a large family with little love or attention. (As his attorney put it in the closing argument, Murdock had a "rotten social background.") Since Murdock's emotional difficulties are strongly tied to his sense of racial oppression, the witness said, "it is probable that when the Marine called him a 'black bastard,' Murdock had an irresistible impulse to shoot."

## NOTES ON THE CONTROL INQUIRY

### 1. QUESTIONS ON BARNES, CHESTER, ELLINGWOOD, AND MURDOCK

It is helpful to reflect on these cases at two levels. First, consider issues connected with applying the tests. In a jurisdiction that uses a control test, is an insanity instruction warranted or required in each case? If not, on what basis would the instruction be denied? Is there sufficient clinical information for a factfinder to decide whether any of these defendants lacked "substantial capacity" to conform his behavior to the requirements of the law? What more information would be useful?

Now consider the underlying policy issue: Does any of these cases present a morally compelling claim of non-responsibility? Should the test of insanity include a volitional prong? Or should claims of this nature be foreclosed?

### 2. THE CONTROL TESTS: CRITICISM AND DEFENSE

Few would dispute the moral basis for the control test—that persons who really "cannot help" doing what they did are not blameworthy. As Herbert Wechsler and Jerome Michael observed in their classic article, A Rationale of the Law of Homicide I, 37 Colum.L.Rev. 701, 754 (1937), a cognitive formulation cannot cover the whole population of those who are beyond the deterrent influence of the penal law "*if* there are persons who, even though they are aware of the potentialities of their acts and of the threat of punishment, are nevertheless incapable of choosing to avoid the act in order to avoid the punishment. There is no reason to doubt that such persons exist." Although some skeptics do, in fact, doubt that "such persons exist," most opponents of the control formulation have concentrated their criticism on the difficulty of administering such a test in light of present knowledge.

The opponents of volitional criteria of responsibility argue that there is no scientific basis for measuring a person's capacity for self-control or for calibrating the impairment of such capacity. There is, in short, no objective basis for distinguishing between offenders who were undeterrable and those who were merely undeterred, between the impulse that was irresistible and the impulse not resisted, or between substantial impairment of capacity and some lesser impairment. Whatever the precise terms of the volitional test, the critics assert that the question is unanswerable—or can be answered only by "moral guesses." To ask it at all, they say, invites fabricated claims, undermines equal administration of the penal law, and compromises its deterrent effect.

Sheldon Glueck observed in Mental Disorder and the Criminal Law 233, 430, 433 (1925), that the 19th-century effort to establish irresistible impulse as a defense met judicial resistance because "much less than we know today was known of mental disease." He predicted "that with the advent of a more scientific administration of the law—especially with the placing of expert testimony upon a neutral, unbiased basis and in the hands of well-qualified experts—much of the opposition to judicial recognition of the effect of disorders of the . . . impulses should disappear." Further, he said, "expert, unbiased study of the individual case will aid judge and jury to distinguish cases of pathological irresistible impulse from those in which the impulse was merely unresisted."

Despite these optimistic sentiments, Wechsler and Michael observed, in 1937, that "except in the clearest cases, such as kleptomania, any effort to distinguish deterrable from non-deterrable persons must obviously encounter tremendous difficulty in the present state of knowledge." Advances in clinical understanding of mental illness in the 1940s inspired a new era of optimism about a "modern" doctrine of responsibility, including a control dimension. One example was the evolution of the Model Penal Code, which was drafted during the 1950s. Another was the Report of the Royal Commission on Capital Punishment, issued in 1953, which recommended that *M'Naghten* be abandoned in favor of a broadened formulation also permitting claims of volitional impairment. Many commentators, however, expressed doubt that medical science had progressed far enough to overcome the difficulties of administration. Lord Patrick Devlin observed, in Criminal Responsibility and Punishment: Functions of Judge and Jury, [1954] Crim. L.Rev. 661, 682–84:

> I think that this is a problem that ought to be solved empirically rather than theoretically. If the door is opened, a multitude will try to enter through it. Many will be cases in which men and women, abnormal, but not in any ordinary sense mad, have failed to exercise proper control over their emotions. There will be many cases of gross mental abnormality where nevertheless it cannot be said that the prisoner was wholly irresponsible. . . . If a sharp dividing line could be drawn between complete and partial irresponsibility, it would be right both in theory and practice that the question should be submitted to the jury. . . . Medical science has advanced far enough to say that there ought to be an addition to the *McNaghten* rules, but not, I think, to formulate a satisfactory one.

Lord Devlin's observations are echoed in the comments of contemporary critics of the control test.[a] Richard Bonnie's views are illustrative. In The Moral Basis of the Insanity Defense, 69 A.B.A.J. 194, 196–97 (1983), he said:

> The Model Penal Code has had an extraordinary impact on criminal law. For this we should be thankful, but I believe the Code approach to criminal responsibility should be rejected.

[a] See, e.g., Stephen Morse, Culpability and Control, 142 Penn. L Rev. 1587 (1994); Donald H.J. Hermann, The Insanity Defense: Philosophical, Historical and Legal Perspectives (1983).

Psychiatric concepts of mental abnormality remain fluid and imprecise, and most academic commentary within the last ten years continues to question the scientific basis for assessment of volitional incapacity.

The volitional inquiry probably would be manageable if the insanity defense were permitted only in cases involving psychotic disorders. When the control test is combined with a loose or broad interpretation of the term "mental disease," however, the inevitable result is unstructured clinical speculation regarding the "causes" of criminal behavior in any case in which a defendant can be said to have a personality disorder, an impulse disorder, or any other diagnosable abnormality.

For example, it is clear enough in theory that the insanity defense is not supposed to be a ground for acquittal of persons with weak behavior controls who misbehave because of anger, jealousy, fear, or some other strong emotion. These emotions may account for a large proportion of all homicides and other assaultive crimes. Many crimes are committed by persons who are not acting "normally" and who are emotionally disturbed at the time. It is not uncommon to say that they are temporarily "out of their minds." But this is not what the law means or should mean by "insanity." Because the control test, as now construed in most states, entitles defendants to insanity instructions on the basis of these claims, I am convinced that the test involves an unacceptable risk of abuse and mistake.

It might be argued, of course, that the risk of mistake should be tolerated if the volitional prong of the defense is morally necessary. The question may be put this way: Are there clinically identifiable cases involving defendants whose behavior controls were so pathologically impaired that they ought to be acquitted although their ability to appreciate the wrongfulness of their actions was unimpaired? I do not think so. The most clinically compelling cases of volitional impairment involve the so-called impulse disorders—pyromania, kleptomania, and the like. These disorders involve severely abnormal compulsions that ought to be taken into account in sentencing, but the exculpation of pyromaniacs would be out of touch with commonly shared moral intuitions.

Not surprisingly, many of the same objections have been raised against the cognitive prong of the insanity defense. However, most opponents of the volitional test do not favor abolition of the cognitive test of responsibility. They argue that the institutional risks are considerably different in the two contexts. Lady Barbara Wootton's observations are illustrative, Book Review of A. Goldstein, The Insanity Defense (1967), 77 Yale L.J. 1019, 1026–27 (1968). While conceding that the *M'Naghten* test is not "free from ambiguities" and may not be "an adequate instrument for distinguishing between the sane and the mentally disordered," Lady Wootton observes that it "has been insufficiently appreciated" that a volitional test raises practical difficulties far more formidable even than those involved in a purely cognitive formula":

Thus, if I am asked to translate a passage from Japanese into English it is indisputable that this is beyond my powers: everyone knows that merely trying harder will not make me any more

> successful. But if I assert that I have an uncontrollable impulse to break shop windows, in the nature of the case no proof of uncontrollability can be adduced. All that is known is that the impulse was not in fact controlled; and it is perfectly legitimate to hold the opinion that, had I tried a little harder, I might have conquered it. It is indeed apparent that some people, such as sadistic sexual perverts, suffer from temptations from which others are immune. But the fact that an impulse is unusual is no proof that it is irresistible. In short, it is not only difficult to devise a test of volitional competence the validity of which can be objectively established: it is impossible.

A similar assessment of the utility of clinical expertise was presented by the American Psychiatric Association in the course of an official statement on the insanity defense:[b]

> . . . Many psychiatrists . . . believe that psychiatric information relevant to determining whether a defendant understood the nature of his act, and whether he appreciated its wrongfulness, is more reliable and has a stronger scientific basis than, for example, does psychiatric information relevant to whether a defendant was able to control his behavior. The line between an irresistible impulse and an impulse not resisted is probably no sharper than that between twilight and dusk. Psychiatry is a deterministic discipline that views all human behavior as, to a good extent, "caused." The concept of volition is the subject of some disagreement among psychiatrists. Many psychiatrists therefore believe that psychiatric testimony (particularly that of a conclusory nature) about volition is more likely to produce confusion for jurors than is psychiatric testimony relevant to a defendant's appreciation or understanding.

Even if Lady Wootton and the other critics are right about the imprecise and speculative nature of the inquiry into volitional impairment, there is nevertheless an argument that the inquiry should be retained. In The Limits of the Criminal Sanction 132–33 (1968), Herbert Packer said:

> We must put up with the bother of the insanity defense because to exclude it is to deprive the criminal law of its chief paradigm of free will. . . . There must be some recognition of the generally held assumption that some people are, by reason of mental illness, significantly impaired in their volitional capacity. [I]t is not too important whether this is in fact the case. Nor is it too important how discriminating we are about drawing some kind of line to separate those suffering volitional impairment from the rest of us. The point is that some kind of line must be drawn in the face of our intuition, however wrongheaded it may be, that mental illness contributes to volitional impairment.

Should the volitional inquiry be retained? Would exclusion of claims of volitional impairment deprive the criminal law of its "chief paradigm of free will" or undermine its "moral integrity," so long as it recognizes claims of cognitive impairment? Should the difficulty of administering the control test be decisive?

---

[b] American Psychiatric Association, Statement on the Insanity Defense (December, 1982).

## 3. RESPONSIBILITY AND UNCONSCIOUS MOTIVATION

The ongoing debate about the control inquiry has been carried on against the backdrop of changing scientific ideas about the human mind. One of the distinctive schools of contemporary clinical psychology emphasizes the role of unconscious motivational processes in shaping human behavior—a person's behavior may "really" be explained and "caused" by unconscious motivations even though the person "thinks," at a conscious level, that action is being taken for other reasons. Many examples may be drawn from normal events in everyday life—e.g., slips of the tongue, sudden lapses of memory, etc. Psychiatrists and other mental-health professionals who find clinical value in a psychodynamic perspective also believe that some types of abnormal behavior may be rooted unconscious mental processes.

Consider the testimony in the cases presented above. Barnes' psychiatric expert described a cluster of psychosexual motivations for his fire-setting behavior that were not accessible to Barnes on a conscious level. Similarly, Chester's homicidal conduct toward Beatrice was said to be produced by repressed feelings of anger toward himself and strong feelings of guilt and worthlessness rooted in his traumatic childhood. If the behavior of these defendants was, in fact, governed or propelled by unconscious forces, as the experts concluded, the question arises whether this explanation should have any legal significance. More generally, the question is whether psychodynamic explanations of criminal behavior should be considered in assessments of criminal responsibility.

The view that responsibility should be assessed at the conscious level was put forcefully by Chief Justice Weintraub of the New Jersey Supreme Court in State v. Sikora, 44 N.J. 453, 475–79, 210 A.2d 193, 205–07 (1965):

> [The] cause-and-effect thesis dominates the psychiatrist's view of his patient. He traces a man's every deed to some cause truly beyond the actor's own making, and says that although the man was aware of his action, he was unaware of assembled forces in his unconscious which decided his course. Thus the conscious is a puppet, and the unconscious the puppeteer. . . .
>
> Under this psychiatric concept no man could be convicted of anything if the law were to accept the impulses of the unconscious as an excuse for conscious misbehavior. . . .
>
> What then shall we do with our fellow automaton whose unconscious directs such anti-social deeds? For one thing, we could say it makes no difference. We could say that in punishing an evil deed accompanied by an evil-meaning mind, the law is concerned only with the existence of a will to do the evil act and it does not matter precisely where within the mind the evil drive resides.
>
> Or we could . . . require an evil-meaning unconscious. The possibilities here are rich. It would be quite a thing to identify the unconscious drive and then decide whether it is evil for the purpose of criminal liability. For example, if we somehow were satisfied that a man murdered another as an alternative to an unconscious demand for suicide or because the unconscious believed it had to kill to avoid a full-blown psychosis, shall we say there was or was not a good defense? Shall we indict for murder a motorist who kills another because, although objectively he was negligent at the worst, the psychoanalyst assures us that the conscious man

> acted automatically to fulfill an unconscious desire for self-destruction? All of this is fascinating but much too frothy to support a structure of criminal law.
>
> Finally, we could amend our concept of criminal responsibility by eliminating the requirement of an evil-meaning mind. That is the true thrust of this psychiatric view of human behavior, for while our criminal law seeks to punish only those who act with a sense of wrongdoing and hence excuses those who because of sickness were bereft of that awareness, the psychiatrist rejects a distinction between the sick and the bad. To him no one is personally blameworthy for his make-up or for his acts. To him the law's distinction between a defect of the mind and a defect of character is an absurd invention. . . .
>
> The subject of criminal blameworthiness is so obscure that there is an understandable disposition to let anything in for whatever use the jury may wish to make of it. But it will not do merely to receive testimony upon the automaton thesis, for the jury must be told what its legal effect may be. Specifically, the jury must be told whether a man is chargeable with his unconscious drives.
>
> It seems clear to me that the psychiatric view . . . is simply irreconcilable with the basic thesis of our criminal law, for while the law requires proof of an evil-meaning mind, this psychiatric thesis denies there is any such thing. To grant a role in our existing structure to the theme that the conscious is just the innocent puppet of a non-culpable unconscious is to make a mishmash of the criminal law, permitting—indeed requiring—each trier of the facts to choose between the automaton thesis and the law's existing concept of criminal accountability. It would be absurd to decide criminal blameworthiness upon a psychiatric thesis which can find no basis for personal blame. [Criminal blameworthiness] must be sought and decided at the level of conscious behavior.

Chief Justice Weintraub implies that the law should take an all-or-nothing view of unconscious motivation. Is he right? Is it possible to formulate a "control" test of responsibility that would permit the fact-finder to absolve Barnes or Chester but would not open the gates to unbounded psychological determinism?

In an article on Responsibility and the Unconscious, 53 So.Cal.L.Rev. 1563 (1980), Michael Moore argues that Weintraub's concern is misplaced; the problem, he suggests, is not the deterministic premise of psychodynamic psychology but rather the meaning of the concept of compulsion, as applied to specific cases. Moore acknowledges at the outset that many psychiatrists think that "unconscious [motivations] cause bad behavior and that causation is an excuse." Moreover, he agrees with Chief Justice Weintraub that the " 'puppeteer' view of human beings" has unacceptable implications for ideas of responsibility:

> [I]f [a defendant] is to be excused simply because his behavior was caused by unconscious mental states, why are all actions not similarly excused? If all conscious mental life is determined by unconscious mental states, as many psychoanalysts believe, why is everyone not excused for all of his actions, seemingly the

product of his conscious decisions but in fact determined by his unconscious mental states?

Moore's answer is that compulsion, not causation, is the legally relevant concept: an action is not "compelled" simply because it is "caused" by unconscious forces; this, he says, "makes it sound as if one's unconscious, in effect, orders one around in the same way as does a gunman with a gun at one's head; both compel one to do what they demand." However, the analogy is not apt, Moore says, because saying that actions are caused, for example, by an unhappy childhood, a chemical imbalance, or a belief that it is raining, is not to say the actions are compelled in a legal sense. What is needed, he says, is the conscious experience of compulsion:

> An unconscious emotion in general, or an unconscious but passionately felt sense of guilt in particular, can be understood in the sense in which an actor does consciously experience or feel something, but does not know the object of his emotion. One may feel angry or afraid without knowing the object of such anger or fear; one may experience the uneasy and tensed craving characteristic of compulsive desires without knowing what one craves. . . . The kleptomaniac feels compelled and knows that he yields to compulsion when he steals; yet he does not know the object of his passionate desire. He knows only that he feels that he must steal. He is compelled by an indefinite craving for some unknown object or objective. A few thefts readily tell him it is not the stolen objects themselves.

Moore goes on to emphasize that compulsion is experienced as a matter of degree and that a person "can be more or less compelled depending upon the severity of the constraints upon choice or upon the strength of the emotions on which one acts."

Where does this discussion lead? Should the law recognize that pathologically strong emotions, perhaps rooted in deep psychological "causes" can compromise or constrain conscious choices. If so, how much constraint is enough to warrant exculpation? Does the clinical evidence demonstrate—in Model Penal Code terms—that Barnes or Chester lacked "substantial capacity" to conform their conduct to the laws against arson and murder?

## NOTES ON THE BOUNDARIES OF CRIMINAL RESPONSIBILITY

### 1. THE SIGNIFICANCE OF MENTAL DISEASE

The concept of "mental disease or defect" is a necessary threshold for the insanity defense under all of the existing tests. Since the concept of irresistible impulse was first recognized, the courts have said the defense is limited to persons whose volition is impaired by mental disease. It has never covered a "normal" person who acts under the influence of strong emotion, nor a person whose weakness of will is attributable to a defect of character.[a] Should a jury question be raised whenever a mental-health

[a] E.g., Parsons v. State, 81 Ala. 577, 594, 2 So. 854, 865 (1886) ("[a] mere moral or emotional insanity, so-called, unconnected with disease of the mind, or irresistible impulse resulting from mere moral obliquity, or wicked propensities and habits, is not recognized as a defense to crime in our courts"); Bell v. State, 120 Ark. 530, 555, 180 S.W. 186, 196 (1915), ("[it] must be remembered that one who is otherwise sane will not be excused from a crime he has committed while his reason is temporarily dethroned not by disease, but by anger, jealousy, or other passion").

professional testifies that the defendant had a diagnosable mental disorder?[b] Would it make sense to rule as a matter of law that any of the defendants in the cases previously discussed did not have a "mental disease" and thereby close the door to their insanity claims? Consider the following approaches to the issue:

### *(i) Restrictive Definition*

Those who are dubious about volitional impairment as an independent ground of exculpation naturally insist on a narrow definition of mental disease, one limited to psychoses. See, e.g., Joseph Livermore and Paul Meehl, The Virtues of *M'Naghten*, 51 Minn.L.Rev. 789, 831–32 (1967). However, even some advocates of the volitional inquiry have regarded a narrow definition of mental disease as an essential feature of the test. For example, the Royal Commission on Capital Punishment recommended revision of the "intellectualist" approach of *M'Naghten* in order to encompass affective and volitional considerations in a responsibility defense. The Commission also recommended that mental disease be defined restrictively, Royal Commission on Capital Punishment, Report 73 (1953):

> [M]ental disease . . . broadly corresponds to what are often called major diseases of the mind, or psychoses; although it may also arise in cases, such as those of epilepsy and cerebral tumour, which are not ordinarily regarded by doctors as psychotic. Among the psychoses are the conditions known as schizophrenia, manic-depressive psychoses, and organic disease of the brain. Other conditions, not included under this term, are the minor forms of mental disorder—the neurotic reactions, such as neurasthenia, anxiety states and hysteria—and the disorders of development of the personality.

A similar approach has been recommended by the American Psychiatric Association:[c]

> Another major consideration in articulating standards for the insanity defense is the definition of mental disease or defect. . . . Allowing insanity acquittals in cases involving persons who manifest primarily "personality disorders" such as antisocial personality disorder (sociopathy) does not accord with modern psychiatric knowledge or psychiatric beliefs concerning the extent to which such persons do have control over their behavior. Persons with antisocial personality disorders should, at least for heuristic reasons, be held accountable for their behavior. The American

---

[b] The definition of "mental disorder" in the American Psychiatric Association's diagnostic manual, DSM–5, provides:

> A mental disorder is a syndrome characterized by clinically significant disturbance in an individual's cognition, emotion regulation, or behavior that reflects a dysfunction in the psychological, biological or developmental processes underlying mental functioning. Mental disorders are usually associated with significant distress or disability in social, occupational or other important activities. An expectable or culturally approved response to a common stressor or loss, such as the death of a loved one, is not a mental disorder. Socially deviant behavior (e.g., political, religious, or sexual) and conflicts that are primarily between the individual and society are not mental disorders unless the deviance or conflict results from a dysfunction in the individual as described above.

[c] American Psychiatric Association, Statement on the Insanity Defense (December, 1982).

Psychiatric Association, therefore, suggests that any revision of the insanity defense standards should indicate that mental disorders potentially leading to exculpation must be *serious*. Such disorders should usually be of the severity (if not always of the quality) of conditions that psychiatrists diagnose as psychoses.

The APA went on to endorse the definition of insanity proposed by Richard Bonnie in The Moral Basis of the Insanity Defense, 69 A.B.A.J. 194, 197 (1983). Bonnie recommended that mental disease should be defined to "include only those severely abnormal mental conditions that grossly and demonstrably impair a person's perception or understanding of reality. . . ."[d]

### *(ii) Intermediate Position*

The drafters of the Model Penal Code rejected the idea that mental disease should be limited to psychoses; they clearly intended to permit neuroses or impulse disorders (kleptomania was the example always used) to have exculpatory significance if they "substantially" affected the defendant's volitional capacity. On the other hand, the drafters contemplated that the courts would exclude some disorders of character or personality even though clinicians might regard these conditions as "mental disorders." This intention is reflected in § 4.01(2): "As used in this Article, the terms 'mental disease or defect' do not include an abnormality manifested only by repeated criminal or otherwise anti-social conduct." It is clear that the drafters meant specifically to exclude offenders who were characterized by clinicians as "psychopaths." The diagnostic label for such a condition has since been changed to "sociopathy" and later to "anti-social personality disorder."

In McDonald v. United States, 312 F.2d 847, 851 (D.C.Cir. 1962), the Court of Appeals for the District of Columbia Circuit defined mental disease or defect as "any abnormal condition of the mind which substantially affects mental or emotional processes and substantially impairs behavior controls." At the time, the court used the "product" test of insanity. However, when the court adopted the Model Penal Code test in United States v. Brawner, 471 F.2d 969 (D.C.Cir. 1972), it retained this definition and endorsed the so-called "caveat paragraph" of Section 4.01(2) as a guideline for the judge rather than as a basis for instructing the jury.[e]

---

[d] See also Stephen Morse, Excusing the Crazy: The Insanity Defense Reconsidered, 58 So.Cal.L.Rev. 777 (1985).

[e] United States v. Brawner, 471 F.2d 969, 994 (D.C.Cir. 1972):

> The judge will be aware that the criminal and antisocial conduct of a person—on the street, in the home, in the ward—is necessarily material information for assessment by the psychiatrist. On the other hand, rarely if ever would a psychiatrist base a conclusion of mental disease solely on criminal and anti-social acts. Our pragmatic solution provides for reshaping the rule, for application by the court, as follows: The introduction or proffer of past criminal and anti-social actions is not admissible as evidence of mental disease unless accompanied by expert testimony, supported by a showing of the concordance of a responsible segment of professional opinion, that the particular characteristics of these actions constitute convincing evidence of an underlying mental disease that substantially impairs behavioral controls.

### *(iii) Abandonment of the Requirement*

In a concurring opinion in *United States* v. *Brawner*, Judge Bazelon took the view that the mental-disease requirement should be abandoned:

> At no point in its opinion does the court explain why the boundary of a legal concept—criminal responsibility—should be marked by medical concepts, especially when the validity of the "medical model" is seriously questioned by some eminent psychiatrists. . . . How many psychiatrists must be convinced that a particular condition is "medical" in nature before a defendant will be permitted, within the confines of the "medical model," to predicate a responsibility defense on such a condition?. . . .
>
> Our instruction to the jury should provide that a defendant is not responsible *if at the time of his unlawful conduct his mental or emotional processes or behavior controls were impaired to such an extent that he cannot justly be held responsible for his act.* This test would ask the psychiatrist a single question: What is the nature of the impairment of the defendant's mental and emotional processes and behavior controls? It would leave for the jury the question whether that impairment is sufficient to relieve the defendant of responsibility for the particular act charged.

### *(iv) Questions on the Mental-Disease Requirement*

Which of these is the better approach? Should the mental-disease concept be limited to psychoses? Or should the law follow Judge Bazelon's approach and abandon the requirement altogether? Does his approach invite unstructured inquiries regarding the determinants of every defendant's criminal behavior? Would the courtroom experience under the Bazelon approach differ substantially from the existing practice under the Model Penal Code or *Brawner* formulations? What is likely to happen in the federal courts under the 1984 statute, which makes the insanity defense available only if the defendant has a "severe" mental disease or defect?

## 2. COMPULSIVE GAMBLING

Claims that defendants were "compelled" to commit their offenses due to disorders of volition such a pathological gambling disorder or compulsive shopping disorder have been raised with increasing frequency, not only as a basis for exculpation (under the "insanity defense"), but also as a basis for mitigation in sentencing as a form of "diminished capacity." Although courts have been skeptical about the exculpatory claims, they have been more receptive to the mitigating claims. As the following materials are read, consider whether this type of claim should have more or less legal significance.

### *(i) Exculpatory Claims: United States v. Torniero*

Torniero, a jewelry store manager, was charged with 10 counts of interstate transportation of jewelry allegedly stolen from his employer. He filed notice of his intent to rely on the insanity defense and to introduce expert testimony showing that he suffered from "pathological gambling disorder,"[f] which led him to accumulate debts that led him to steal. The government's motion to "exclude any expert testimony regarding the defendant's alleged mental disorder 'compulsive gambling' " was granted by Judge Cabranes in United States v. Torniero, 570 F.Supp. 721 (D.Conn. 1983). Judge Cabranes concluded that Torniero's compulsion to gamble, even if it existed, did not have a sufficiently "direct bearing" on the charged criminal acts to establish the legal predicate for an insanity defense.

A. The individual is chronically and progressively unable to resist impulses to gamble.

B. Gambling compromises, disrupts, or damages family, personal, and vocational pursuits, as indicated by at least three of the following:

C. The gambling is not due to antisocial personality disorder.

Judge Cabranes also noted his doubts "whether compulsive gambling disorder ought even to be the basis for an insanity defense when the offense charged is gambling." He thought it "questionable whether [this] disorder, characterized more by repeated engagement in a particular activity than by any derangement of one's mental faculties, amounts to a mental disease as that concept has long been understood by the criminal law." In a more general observation, Judge Cabranes suggested that the insanity defense "can and should be limited to instances where a jury could find that the defendant's mind was truly alienated from ordinary human experience at the time of the commission of the acts with which he is charged and where that mental condition had a direct bearing on the commission of those acts."

At Torniero's subsequent trial, the government showed that he took jewelry valued at approximately $750,000 from New Haven to the "diamond district" of Manhattan and sold it for cash. Notwithstanding the exclusion of the expert testimony concerning "compulsive gambling disorder," Torniero relied on the insanity defense. In support of his claim, he

---

[f] At the time of the *Torniero* decision, "pathological gambling disorder" was described in DSM–III as follows:

> [A] chronic and progressive failure to resist impulses to gamble and gambling behavior that compromises, disrupts, or damages personal, family, or vocational pursuits. The gambling preoccupation, urge, and activity increase during periods of stress. Problems that arise as a result of the gambling lead to an intensification of the gambling behavior. Characteristic problems include loss of work due to absences in order to gamble, defaulting on debts and other financial responsibilities, disrupted family relationships, borrowing money from illegal sources, forgery, fraud, embezzlement, and income tax evasion.
>
> Commonly these individuals have the attitude that money causes and is also the solution to all their problems. As the gambling increases, the individual is usually forced to lie in order to obtain money and to continue gambling, but hides the extent of the gambling. There is no serious attempt to budget or save money. When borrowing resources are strained, antisocial behavior in order to obtain money for more gambling is likely. Any criminal behavior—e.g., forgery, embezzlement, or fraud—is typically nonviolent. There is a conscious intent to return or repay the money.

DSM–III also specified criteria for diagnosing pathological gambling. These included:

A. The individual is chronically and progressively unable to resist impulse to gamble.

B. Gambling compromises, disrupts, or damages family, personal, and volitional pursuits, as indicated by at least three of the following:

> [Here the criteria mention seven effects of excessive gambling, including "arrest for forgery, fraud, embezzlement, or income tax evasion due to attempts to obtain money for gambling."]

C. The gambling is not due to antisocial personality disorder.

presented two psychiatrists who testified that he suffered from paranoia, depression, and a narcissistic personality as a result of which he lacked responsibility under the then-applicable Model Penal Code insanity test. After deliberating for less than one hour, the jury convicted Torniero and the judge sentenced him to a three-year prison term, to be followed by five years' probation and an ongoing duty to pay restitution to his former employer.

On appeal, the Second Circuit affirmed the conviction. United States v. Torniero, 735 F.2d 725 (2d Cir.1984). After reviewing the evolution of the insanity defense in the federal courts, and taking note of the controversy aroused by the *Hinckley* acquittal two years earlier, Judge Kaufman turned to the question raised by Torniero's appeal:

> To put in issue the defense of criminal insanity under the prevailing [Model Code] test in effect in this Circuit, Torniero must make a showing that compulsive gambling is a mental disease or defect. He must also demonstrate that the infirmity could have prevented him from appreciating that theft was wrongful, or could have deprived him of the ability to restrain himself from the criminal act. Torniero does not urge that his condition could have rendered him incapable of appreciating the illegality of transporting stolen goods. He contends only that under the volitional prong of the [Model Code] test, the compulsion to gamble rendered him unable to resist becoming a thief and stealing to support his habit. . . .
>
> This principle on which Torniero relies is a novel one. The disorder of pathological gambling was not included in the American Psychiatric Association Diagnostic and Statistical Manual of Mental Disorders until publication in 1980 of the third edition. . . . Where, as here, a defendant contends that evidence of a newly-recognized disorder would be relevant to an insanity defense, there must be a showing that respected authorities in the field share the view that the disorder is a mental disease or defect that could have impaired the defendant's ability to desist from the offense charged or to appreciate the wrongfulness of his conduct. We state no iron-clad mathematical rule, but we do not believe that an hypothesis subscribed to by only a small number of professionals establishes that a proposed defense can carry the day on relevance.
>
> At the same time, we recognize that unanimity on mental health issues is rare and we suggest no requirement of universal or even majority professional acceptance. In fashioning its preliminary decision on relevance, a court must make a discretionary determination that the hypotheses relied upon have substantial acceptance in the discipline, as a basis for a finding that the disorder is relevant to the insanity defense.

The first hurdle Torniero's proposed insanity defense must traverse is that the alleged disorder constitutes a mental disease or defect as the term is used in the [Model Code] definition. We are convinced that persuasive evidence was adduced at the pretrial hearing to justify a conclusion that members of the mental health profession hold seriously contradicting views in this regard. [A psychiatrist] who helped draft DSM–III testified that the clinical definition of compulsive gambling as a "failure to resist" rather than an "inability to resist" the urge to wager was a deliberate effort to distinguish this disorder from those defects of the mind appropriate for an insanity defense. Another psychiatrist testified before Judge Cabranes in support of the argument that compulsive gambling is not a mental disease or defect as defined by the [Model Code] rule. Several mental health and social work professionals testified on the debilitating effects of the compulsion to gamble and stated for the record that they believed the pathology should be considered a mental disease or defect. One of these witnesses, however, conceded that "pathological gambling has not ever been considered a serious disorder" within the profession.

The trial court stated no conclusion on the issue, nor are we called upon to rule that compulsive gambling can never constitute a mental disease or defect. We need not rest, however, on the ground that the proffered gambling defense was not shown to be a mental disease or defect. Assuming without deciding, that it did cross that threshold of the [Model Code] test, there is still ample basis for the trial court's conclusion that Torniero's compulsive gambling disorder is not relevant to the insanity defense. The trial judge correctly noted that the relevance standard requires that the pathology alleged have "a direct bearing on [the] commission of the acts with which [the defendant] is charged." In sum, a compulsion to gamble, even if a mental disease or defect, is not, ipso facto, relevant to the issue whether the defendant was unable to restrain himself from non-gambling offenses such as transporting stolen property.

Although several of Torniero's witnesses expressed the opinion that compulsive gamblers they have treated or observed were unable to resist the impulse to steal as a result of the gambling pathology, this view was vigorously contradicted by the government's experts. Moreover, not one of the experts stated that the connection between compulsive gambling and the impulse to steal for purposes of the insanity defense has substantial acceptance in the profession. While we cannot agree with the trial court that no evidence whatsoever on the volitional nexus between gambling and stealing was adduced, we are of the view that there is ample basis in the record to warrant the conclusion that the trial judge did not abuse his discretion in finding the connection between the two was not satisfactorily established. In the absence of such evidence the proffered defense cannot be deemed relevant to the insanity defense. . . .

As the psychiatric and psychological professions refine their understanding of impulse disorders such as pathological gambling, courts are called upon to make difficult and delicate decisions under the volitional prong of the insanity test. We rule today that when evidence of an impulse disorder is offered in support of an insanity defense, the trial judge must first determine that the evidence is relevant. We do not foreclose admissibility of compulsive gambling in all circumstances, nor do we speculate on the desirability of the [proposals to eliminate the volitional prong] now being considered by Congress.

The insanity defense has never been free from controversy, criticism, and revision. No rule designed to embody societal values will ever be sacrosanct. As our understanding of the intricacies of the fathomless human mind continues to evolve, legal rules must respond to changed conceptions of the nature of moral culpability, and to advances in the science of mental illness. The fundamental question will always be an inquiry into how best to embody society's sense of what conduct is appropriate for punishment by criminal sanctions. The district court's exclusion of the compulsive gambling defense proposed here accords with accepted notions of criminal responsibility. . . . Accordingly, we affirm the judgment of conviction.

Although it affirmed the district court's decision to exclude the evidence proffered by Torniero, the circuit court refused to foreclose the admissibility of such evidence "in all circumstances." Should similar evidence be admissible in a prosecution for illegal gambling? Recall that chronic and progressive inability to resist impulses to gamble was one of the diagnostic criteria under DSM–III. Of what significance is that fact that the DSM–5 criteria include being "often preoccupied with gambling" and "need[ing] to gamble" instead of "inability to resist"? If the expert testimony would be admitted in a prosecution for illegal gambling, why should it be excluded in a theft prosecution if the defendant's experts are prepared to testify that the defendant's capacity to refrain from stealing was substantially impaired? Is the circuit court decision right? Judge Kaufman's rationale?[g]

### *(ii) Mitigating Claims Under the Federal Sentencing Guidelines*

Section 5K2.13 of the federal sentencing guidelines permits "downward departures" from presumptive sentences for non-violent offenses if the offender had a "significantly reduced mental capacity" at the time of the offense. In United States v. McBroom, 124 F.3d 533 (3d Cir. 1997), the court ruled that the phrase "significantly reduced mental capacity" includes a volitional component and that a defendant's "ability to control his or her own conduct is a relevant consideration when determining the defendant's eligibility for a downward departure."[h] This decision, in effect, said that defenses such as compulsive gambling, while not worthy of complete exculpation, could have a mitigating effect during sentencing.

Although the Third Circuit acknowledged that this ruling was in tension with the 1984 Insanity Defense Reform Act, through which the Congress had eliminated the volitional component of the insanity defense,[i] the court concluded that the "principles of lenity" that underlie downward departures for cognitive impairments "apply with equal force . . . to those who cannot control their behavior." In 1998, the Federal Sentencing

---

[g] For decisions reaching the same result on similar grounds, see United States v. Gould, 741 F.2d 45 (4th Cir.1984), and United States v. Lewellyn, 723 F.2d 615 (8th Cir.1983).

At least one defendant has successfully relied upon pathological gambling disorder in a theft prosecution. In State v. Lafferty, 192 Conn. 571, 472 A.2d 1275 (1984), the defendant was acquitted by reason of insanity, despite having embezzled more than $300,000 from his employer. The Connecticut General Assembly subsequently amended its insanity statute to preclude exculpation in such cases by excluding "pathological or compulsive gambling" from the definition of "mental disease or defect." Conn. Penal Code § 53a–13(c) (1994).

[h] The defendant in McBroom pled guilty to possessing child pornography, and sought a downward departure based on psychological disorders arising out of sexual abuse he suffered as a child that compelled him to commit the offenses.

[i] 18 U.S.C. § 17(a) (1994).

Commission embraced the Third Circuit's view by defining the term "significantly reduced mental capacity" as follows:

> "Significantly reduced mental capacity" means the defendant, although convicted, has a significantly impaired ability to (A) understand the wrongfulness of the behavior comprising the offense or to exercise the power of reason; or (B) control behavior that the defendant knows is wrongful.

In United States v. Sandolsky, 234 F.3d 938 (6th Cir. 2000), the court applied § 5K2.13 to a claim by a defendant convicted of computer fraud that he was compelled to commit these theft offenses to pay debts incurred due to pathological gambling disorder. As in *Torniero*, the government argued that a direct causal link between the reduced capacity and the offense was required. The Sixth Circuit disagreed. In recognizing the expansion of the Federal Sentencing Guidelines to include volitional impairments such as compulsive gambling, the court explained how compulsive gambling could warrant a downgraded sentence even though the compulsive gambling did not directly constitute the offense changed:

> Section 5K2.13 does not distinguish between [significantly reduced mental capacities] that explain the behavior that *constituted* the crime charged and [significantly reduced mental capacities] that explain the behavior that *motivated* the crime. In other words, § 5K2.13 does not require a direct causal link between the [significantly reduced mental capacity] and the crime charged. . . . Thus, because Sandolsky's gambling disorder is a likely cause of his criminal behavior, given that he had already "maxed out" his own credit line before resorting to fraud, the two-point reduction is not inconsistent with the guideline provision.
>
> A rule distinguishing between [significantly reduced mental capacities] that *cause* the behavior that constitutes the crime and [significantly reduced mental capacities] that *motivate* the behavior that constitutes the crime could lead to arbitrary results. For example, under the Government's theory [which requires a direct causal link similar to Judge Kaufman's argument in *Torniero*], if someone with an eating disorder stole food, he or she would be entitled to a downward departure under § 5K2.13. If, however, that same person stole money to buy food, he or she would not be entitled to a downward departure. In the latter situation, the link between the crime, stealing money to buy food, and the [significantly reduced mental capacity], an eating disorder, is no longer technically direct. Nonetheless, no one can dispute that the eating disorder is the driving force behind the crime. Yet under the Government's theory, the two individuals would be treated differently based on a nebulous distinction between a volitional impairment that causes the conduct that constitutes the crime and a volitional impairment that explains the motive for the ultimate crime. This treatment is at odds with the Sentencing Guideline's goal of uniformity of sentencing. More importantly, a bright line rule would undermine not only the district court's discretion, but also the very purpose of § 5K2.13—to mitigate the sentence of one who suffers from a diminished mental capacity.

Would Torniero have been able to use his compulsive gambling to effect a downgrade in his sentence under the reasoning in *Sandolsky*?[j] Should this type of disorder be regarded as a legitimate ground for diminishing responsibility for theft offenses? If so, should it also be regarded as a legitimate basis for negating responsibility?

### 3. DRUG DEPENDENCE: *UNITED STATES V. MOORE*

The boundaries of criminal responsibility in the related context of drug dependence were explored in United States v. Moore, 486 F.2d 1139 (D.C. Cir. 1973). Raymond Moore was charged with possession of heroin. He claimed, in defense, that he was an opiate-dependent person with an overpowering need to use heroin. He sought to introduce supporting testimony on the ground that, due to his abnormal psychological condition, he lacked substantial capacity to conform his behavior to the laws prohibiting possession of heroin. The government, though conceding that Moore was dependent on heroin, objected to the admissibility of this evidence on the ground that it was insufficient, as a matter of law, to establish that Moore lacked criminal responsibility for his acts. Moore was convicted and sentenced to prison. A closely divided (five to four) court of appeals, sitting en banc, affirmed the conviction, rejecting Moore's claim that he was entitled to raise a "common law defense" of addiction. The court also rejected Moore's argument that his conviction was barred by the eighth amendment.[k]

Judge Wright's dissenting opinion observed that the eighth amendment "provides only the floor and not the ceiling for development of common law notions of criminal responsibility" and argued that Moore's claim should be reached by evolving doctrines of volitional impairment:

> The concept of criminal responsibility is, by its very nature, "an expression of the moral sense of the community." . . . [T]here has historically been a strong conviction in our jurisprudence that to hold a man criminally responsible, his actions must have been the product of a "free will." . . . Thus criminal responsibility is assessed only when through "free will" a man elects to do evil, and if he is not a free agent, or is unable to choose or to act voluntarily, or to avoid the conduct which constitutes the crime, he is outside the postulate of the law of punishment.
>
> Despite this general principle, however, it is clear that our legal system does not exculpate all persons whose capacity for control is impaired, for whatever cause or reason. Rather, in determining responsibility for crime, the law assumes "free will" and then recognizes known deviations "where there is a broad consensus that free will does not exist" with respect to the particular condition at issue. The evolving nature of this process is amply

---

[j] For decisions reaching similar results, see United States v. Checoura, 176 F.Supp.2d 310 (D.N.J. 2001); United States v. Ming, 2001 WL 1631874 (N.D.Ill. 2001); United States v. Scholl, 959 F.Supp. 1189 (D.Ariz. 1997).

[k] Moore's eighth amendment argument was based on ***Robinson v. California***, 370 U.S. 660 (1962), which held that punishment for the status of addiction constituted "cruel and unusual punishment" proscribed by the eighth amendment. He argued that punishing an addict for possessing drugs was tantamount to punishing him for his addiction. The court rejected the argument, relying on the Supreme Court's five-four decision in *Powell v. Texas*, 392 U.S. 514 (1968), which held that punishment of an alcoholic for public drunkenness did not violate the eighth amendment.

> demonstrated in the gradual development of such defenses as infancy, duress, insanity, somnambulism and other forms of automatism, epilepsy and unconsciousness, involuntary intoxication, delirium tremens, and chronic alcoholism.
>
> A similar consensus exists today in the area of narcotics addiction. . . . The World Health Organization has ranked heroin addiction as the most intensive form of drug dependence, far more severe than alcoholism. Indeed, the primary element of the most widely accepted definition of opiate addiction is "an *overpowering* desire or need to continue taking the drug," and Congress has repeatedly defined as an addict any individual who is "so far addicted to the use of narcotic drugs as to have *lost the power of self-control* with reference to his addiction." Thus it can no longer seriously be questioned that for at least some addicts the "overpowering" psychological and physiological need to possess and inject narcotics cannot be overcome by mere exercise of "free will." . . .
>
> The genius of the common law has long been its responsiveness to changing times, its ability to reflect new knowledge and developing social and moral values. . . . I conclude that imposition of criminal liability on the non-trafficking addict possessor is contrary to our historic common law traditions of criminal responsibility. This being so, it is clear that a defense of "addiction" must exist for these individuals unless Congress has expressly and unequivocally manifested its intent to preclude such a defense. [Judge Wright concluded that recognition of the defense had not been precluded by congressional action.]

The majority of the court rejected this view. Judge Leventhal responded directly to Judge Wright in his concurring opinion:

> Appellant's key defense concepts are impairment of behavioral control and loss of self-control. These have been considered by this court most fully in discussion of the insanity defense, and the philosophy of those opinions is invoked, although appellant disclaims the insanity defense as such. . . .
>
> Appellant's presentation rests, in essence, on the premise that the "mental disease or defect" requirement of *McDonald* and *Brawner* is superfluous. He discerns a broad principle that excuses from criminal responsibility when conduct results from a condition that impairs behavior control. . . .
>
> It does not follow that because one condition (mental disease) yields an exculpatory defense if it results in impairment of and lack of behavioral controls the same result follows when some other condition impairs behavior controls. . . .
>
> The legal conception of criminal capacity cannot be limited to those of unusual endowment or even average powers. A few may be recognized as so far from normal as to be entirely beyond the reach of criminal justice, but in general the criminal law is a means of social control that must be potentially capable of reaching the vast bulk of the population. Criminal responsibility is a concept that not only extends to the bulk of those below the median line of responsibility, but specifically extends to those who have a realistic problem of substantial impairment and lack

of capacity due, say, to weakness of intellect that establishes susceptibility to suggestion; or to a loss of control of the mind as a result of passion, whether the passion is of an amorous nature or the result of hate, prejudice or vengeance; or to a depravity that blocks out conscience as an influence on conduct.

The criminal law cannot "vary legal norms with the individual's capacity to meet the standards they prescribe, absent a disability that is both gross and verifiable, such as the mental disease or defect that may establish irresponsibility. The most that it is feasible to do with lesser disabilities is to accord them proper weight in sentencing."

Only in limited areas have the courts recognized a defense to criminal responsibility, on the basis that a described condition establishes a psychic incapacity negativing free will in the broader sense. These are areas where the courts have been able to respond to a deep call on elemental justice, and to discern a demarcation of doctrine that keeps the defense within verifiable bounds that do not tear the fabric of the criminal law as an instrument of social control. . . .

[A]ppellant disclaims any direct reliance on the insanity defense. He agrees with our rulings that heroin dependence may have probative value, along with other evidence of mental disease, but is not by itself evidence of "mental disease or defect" sufficient to raise the insanity issue, unless so protracted and extensive as to result in unusual deterioration of controls.

Our opinion in *Brawner* declined to accept the suggestion that it "announce" a standard exculpating anyone whose capacity for control is insubstantial, for whatever cause or reason, and said, disclaiming an "all-embracing unified field theory," that we would discern the appropriate rule "as the cases arise in regard to other conditions."

In our view, the rule for drug addiction should not be modeled on the rule for mental disease because of crucial distinctions between conditions. The subject of mental disease, though subject to some indeterminacy, and difficulty of diagnosis when extended to volitional impairment as well as cognitive incapacity, has long been the subject of systematic study, and in that framework it is considered manageable to ask psychiatrists to address the distinction, all-important and crucial to the law, between incapacity and indisposition, between those who can't and those who won't, between the impulse irresistible and the impulse not resisted. These are matters as to which the court has accepted the analysis of medicine, medical conditions and symptoms, and on the premise that they can be considered on a verifiable basis, and with reasonable dispatch, the courts have recognized a defense even in conditions not as obvious and verifiable as those covered in the older and limited test of capacity to know right from wrong.

[T]here is considerable difficulty of verification of the claim of a drug user that he is unable to refrain from use. . . .

The difficulty of the verification problem of lack of capacity to refrain from use is sharpened on taking into account that

> the issue comprehends the addict's failure to participate in treatment programs. This raises problems of the addict's personal knowledge, disposition, motivation, as well as extent of community programs, that may usefully be assessed by someone considering what program to try now or next, but would irretrievably tangle a trial.
>
> The feature that narcotic addiction is not a stable condition undercuts any approach patterned on the mental disease, where there is a reasonable projection that subsequent analysis of particular incidents over time may delineate an ascertainable condition. It is unrealistic to expect the addict himself to supply accurate information on the nature and extent of addiction at the time of the offense, particularly as to "psychic dependence."
>
> The difficulty is sharpened by the appreciable number of narcotic "addicts" who do abandon their habits permanently, and much larger number who reflect their capacity to refrain by ceasing use for varying periods of time. The reasons are not clear but the phenomenon is indisputable. . . .
>
> There is need for reasonable verifiability as a condition to opening a defense to criminal responsibility. The criminal law cannot gear its standards to the individual's capacity "absent a disability that is both gross and verifiable, such as the mental disease or defect that may establish irresponsibility." . . .
>
> Reliability and validity of a legal defense require that it can be tested by criteria external to the actions which it is invoked to excuse. And so the Model Penal Code's caveat paragraph rejects an insanity defense based on an abnormality manifested only by repeated criminal or otherwise anti-social conduct. This approach was followed in *Brawner*. The defense of drug dependence to a charge of drug use cannot clear the hurdle of circularity.

Does Judge Leventhal or Judge Wright have the better view? Are the reasons given by Judge Leventhal for rejecting the addiction defense also applicable to the volitional prong of the insanity defense? Does the "mental-disease" requirement really limit the defense to conditions that are "gross and verifiable"?

## SUBSECTION C: THE INSANITY DEFENSE, INTOXICATION, AND MEDICAL CONDITIONS THAT IMPAIR CONSCIOUSNESS

### State v. Sexton

Supreme Court of Vermont, 2006.
904 A.2d 1092.

■ REIBER, J. We accepted this interlocutory appeal to consider whether a defendant charged with murder may assert [the insanity defense] where the voluntary use of illegal drugs was an essential causal factor in the defendant's psychotic state at the time of the offense. Consistent with the law of this and other states, we conclude that defendant in these circumstances . . . may not be relieved entirely of responsibility for his or her criminal acts.

[T]he material facts are largely undisputed. On the night of September 27, 2000, police found a Japanese exchange student, Atsuko Ikeda, lying in the street in Winooski. Ikeda had suffered serious injuries, and died shortly after transport to the hospital. During the ensuing investigation, defendant walked onto the crime scene and lay down on the street in front of a police cruiser. Upon questioning by the police, defendant reportedly said, "Just cuff me, I know I did something bad, I just don't know what." Defendant was charged with Ikeda's murder.

While in custody, defendant informed the police that, on the day in question, he had killed his cat and then gone outside intending to kill a person. He recalled lunging at a woman passing on a bicycle (later identified as Ikeda) and then beating her repeatedly until she stopped moving. Defendant later told psychiatrists that he had taken a variety of illegal drugs during the six months preceding the incident. Defendant recounted that for about two months, in July and August 2000, he took many "hits" of LSD, and that his last reported use of LSD was two to three weeks before the September killing. Defendant explained that on the night of the incident he felt that he needed to kill people and "gather their souls."

At defendant's arraignment on a charge of second-degree murder, the court ordered a psychiatric evaluation of defendant's competency and sanity. In December 2000, Dr. Robert Linder, the court-appointed psychiatrist, filed a lengthy report with the court, ultimately concluding that defendant was insane at the time of the offense. The conclusion was based on a series of interviews with defendant and others, defendant's psychiatric and family history, and a battery of psychological tests from which Dr. Linder inferred that defendant was in a florid psychotic state at the time of the crime that prevented him from appreciating the wrongfulness of his conduct or conforming his conduct to the requirements of law. Dr. Linder's preliminary diagnosis was that defendant suffered from either a previously undiagnosed mental disease involving a schizophrenic disorder, or a substance-induced psychosis. At a later deposition in 2002, Dr. Linder noted that defendant's psychotic thoughts had largely resolved and that he had returned to his "usual self," suggesting a primary diagnosis of schizophrenoform disorder, in which psychotic symptoms last between one to six months. . . .

In April, the State's psychiatrist, Dr. Albert Drukteinis, filed a report concurring in Dr. Linder's opinion that defendant was psychotic at the time of the offense, but concluding that it was caused solely by defendant's voluntary use of illegal drugs. Although Dr. Drukteinis observed signs of a personality disorder with narcissistic features, he found no evidence that defendant suffered from a major thought disorder such as schizophrenia. At a subsequent hearing on the State's motion to amend defendant's conditions of release, defendant's treating psychiatrist, Dr. Margaret Bolton, also diagnosed defendant as having a personality disorder, and agreed that defendant did not suffer from any major mental illness such as schizophrenia, as reported by Dr. Linder, or borderline personality, as suggested in an earlier report by [another psychiatrist].

In July 2002, the State filed a motion in limine seeking to prevent defendant from presenting an insanity defense at trial, arguing that Vermont law does not recognize temporary insanity caused by the voluntary use of drugs. . . . Defendant, in response, submitted a supplemental letter from Dr. Linder, reaffirming his earlier opinion that defendant was in the midst of a severe psychotic episode at the time of the offense, resulting from either a substance-induced psychosis or an underlying mental illness, such as schizophrenoform disorder, caused by the ingestion of illegal drugs in combination with an underlying psychological vulnerability that predisposed him to such a reaction.

[The trial court] ruled that an individual . . . whose consumption of illegal drugs activates a latent mental disease or defect resulting in a psychotic reaction is entitled to a complete defense to the crime charged, unless the defendant knew or had reason to know that the drugs would elicit such a reaction. . . . [The State filed an interlocutory appeal.]

. . . While the mental state resulting from extreme intoxication may in some cases be "tantamount to insanity," its origin as a self-induced impairment fundamentally distinguishes it for most courts from a naturally occurring mental disease or defect that leads to insanity. Indeed, it is universally recognized that a condition of insanity brought about by an individual's voluntary use of alcohol or drugs will not relieve the actor of criminal responsibility for his or her acts.

The only generally recognized exception to this rule is the doctrine known as "fixed" or "settled" insanity. Nearly every court and commentator that has addressed this doctrine has defined it as a permanent or chronic mental disorder caused by the habitual and long-term abuse of drugs or alcohol. Scholars have traced the origins of the settled insanity defense in this country to the mid-nineteenth century when courts first considered the culpability of chronic alcoholics for crimes committed in the throes of acute alcohol-induced psychoses, typically marked by hallucinations and paranoid delusions.[6]

From its inception to the present, the settled insanity doctrine has been consistently characterized as a state of mind resulting from "long-continued," "habitual," "prolonged," or "chronic" alcohol or drug abuse leading to a more or less permanent or "fixed" state of insanity. . . . The underlying rationale for the settled insanity doctrine is generally explained as an acknowledgment of "the futility of punishment, since the defective mental state is permanent," or, more commonly, as a compassionate concession that at some point a person's earlier voluntary decisions become so temporally and "morally remote" that the cause of the offense can reasonably be ascribed to the resulting insanity rather than the use of intoxicants. . . .

Although, with one exception, every state court to consider the issue has recognized the doctrine of settled insanity, many states—

[6] Historians have noted the extraordinary amount of alcohol, particularly distilled liquors then known as "spirits," that Americans consumed during the first half of the nineteenth century. It is this historical context that helps to explain the origins of the settled insanity doctrine, and the true nature of the condition of the individuals to which it applied. See, e.g., Beasley v. State, 50 Ala. 149, 151 (1874) (holding that it was error to fail to instruct on settled insanity where evidence showed that "for several years before the killing, the accused was 'a great drunkard;' that he was 'generally drunk;' his habits were 'to drink from a half to one gallon of spirits every night, and large quantities before breakfast, and before dinner, and before supper each day;' " that several weeks before the killing "he had an attack of delirium tremens;" and that shortly before the murder he suffered delusions of "seeing witches and devils.").

including Vermont—have simply not addressed it. . . . Defendant tenders this as an appropriate case in which to recognize the doctrine, noting its general acceptance in other states, longevity under the common law, and recognition by the drafters of the Model Penal Code.[9]

We are not persuaded, however, that this appeal presents a suitable factual setting for resolution of the issue. The many cases and articles that consistently require a showing that defendant's mental illness resulted from "long-term," "habitual," or "chronic" drug or alcohol abuse do not, of course, establish any specific time frames relative to the offense, nor is it possible to do so. Yet, by any measure, the circumstances here do not begin to approach the prolonged abuse leading to a fixed insanity that the common law recognized as sufficiently attenuated to excuse the crime. Whatever its merits, the doctrine of settled insanity was developed to address mental illness resulting from long-term substance abuse over many years, gradually leading to organic brain damage, and its justification is based on the humane recognition "that at some point a person's earlier voluntary decisions become morally remote."

By his own admission, defendant's LSD use here began in July 2000, lasted about two months, and ended two to three weeks before the offense in late September 2000. He took the drugs precisely to experience the perceptual distortions that may result from such hallucinogens, and fully expected that the drugs would alter his state of mind.[10] Although he continued to have bizarre thoughts weeks and months after the offense, he was found to have returned to mental competence to speak with the police and stand trial for his offenses within weeks, if not days, after the murder.[11]

In these circumstances, the claim that defendant was operating under a "fixed or settled" insanity at the time of the offense is contrary to the very meaning of the doctrine and its altruistic origins. To retain any moral or legal salience, the doctrine must—if it is ever justified—be limited to those cases where the initial choice to abuse alcohol or drugs has become so attenuated over time that it serves little or no purpose to

---

[9] The commentary to MPC § 2.08, which deals with intoxication rather than insanity, and which has not been adopted in Vermont, provides:

> Under the Model Code as under existing law, it is immaterial that mental disease excluding responsibility was caused by excessive drinking and in that sense is attributable to the defendant. This sort of disease, generally delirium tremens, is said to be "fixed" or "settled." The same treatment is proposed for those periods of temporary disorientation (in alcoholic psychosis) that can occur after a long drinking bout. The Model Code permits such cases to be dealt with under Section 4.01, and nothing in the formulation here undertakes to influence the resolution of the issue whether serious temporary disorientation from reality following intoxication constitutes "mental disease" within the meaning of that section.

Model Penal Code § 2.08, cmt. 2 at 362–63.

[10] From his interviews with defendant and others, Dr. Linder observed that defendant was an "experimenter scientist type" who used LSD out of "an intellectual curiosity" in order to experience changes in his sensory perceptions. Dr. Linder acknowledged that defendant was aware of, and expected, that the drug would alter his state of mind; he was allegedly unaware of the "degree" to which it would affect his perceptions.

[11] A mental health evaluation of defendant the day after the crime conducted by a psychiatrist at the Vermont State Hospital reported "no abnormalities of thought processes, his thoughts were logical and coherent." Defendant was responsive to questioning, his recent and long-term memory were intact, and although he appeared "hypomanic" (agitated) it was "without psychotic features."

hold the defendant accountable for that choice once a permanent mental illness has taken hold through years of chronic substance abuse. To apply the doctrine here, to a crime committed while defendant was either directly under the influence or in the immediate aftermath of a discrete two-month period of using hallucinogenic drugs, would defeat the doctrine's meaning and underlying purposes. While there may indeed be cases that raise a genuine factual issue as to whether a defendant's prior, long-term drug or alcohol abuse has resulted in a fixed insanity, this is not such a case.[12]

Our conclusion applies with equal force to the alternative settled-insanity theory advanced by the trial court in the proposed instruction at issue here. As noted, Dr. Linder offered two possible diagnoses of defendant's psychosis at the time of the offense. The first posited that it was a straight substance-induced psychosis, based on his testimony that LSD may continue to affect the user weeks after its last ingestion. The second was that the LSD triggered a latent mental disease or defect, causing the psychotic episode.[13] The latter diagnosis differs somewhat from the classic etiology of settled insanity because the theory is not that the illegal drugs caused the illness and resulting psychosis, but rather that they exacerbated or activated a preexisting latent illness.

Accepting this theory as a plausible basis for the insanity defense, the trial court crafted an instruction that attempted to articulate its essential elements. Borrowing from a Massachusetts decision, Commonwealth v. Herd, 604 N.E.2d 1294, 1298 (Mass. 1992), the proposed

[12] We recognize that the settled-insanity cases are not entirely uniform in their approach to the required duration of the defendant's mental illness before or after the offense. The dissent relies, in particular, on four cases with some similarities to the facts here. In an often-cited decision, People v. Kelly, 10 Cal. 3d 565, 516 P.2d 875, 877 (1973), the California Supreme Court applied the doctrine to a defendant who had used LSD and mescaline "in the months leading up to the offense," and who remained psychotic for several months after the drugs had worn off. In Porreca v. State, 49 Md. App. 522, 433 A.2d 1204, 1208 (Md. Ct. Spec. App. 1981), the court held that a defendant in a PCP-induced psychosis that lasted three to six months after the offense could invoke the doctrine. In State v. Maik, 60 N.J. 203, 287 A.2d 715, 721–22 (N.J. 1972), the court held that a defendant who had killed an acquaintance in a psychotic state two months after ingesting LSD was entitled to an insanity defense. And in People v. Conrad, 148 Mich. App. 433, 385 N.W.2d 277, 280–81 (Mich. Ct. App. 1986), the court held that a defendant who had used PCP four or five times during the two weeks preceding the murder, and whose psychotic symptoms lasted for several months thereafter, was entitled to invoke the defense. We are not persuaded that these decisions compel a different result here. First, we note that in *Kelly* there was evidence that the defendant had used drugs for three years before the offense, while in *Porreca* the evidence showed that the defendant had abused drugs for two years, including PCP "with some regularity," and in *Maik* there was no evidence that the defendant's "schizophrenic break" was due to his LSD use, as opposed to depression resulting from a failed romantic relationship. Second, while we question whether these decisions are consistent with the uniformly held requirement of a "permanent" or chronic mental illness, we base our holding on the absence of any evidence that defendant here had developed a fixed insanity through long-term substance abuse. Finally, to the extent these decisions hold otherwise, we simply do not agree that the settled insanity doctrine has any application to a defendant who intentionally ingests a mind-altering substance for a period of about two months, and commits an offense shortly thereafter during a psychotic episode that would not have occurred but for the drugs.

[13] Dr. Linder stated that defendant's reaction "was that seen rarely and more commonly manifested, when it does occur, in individuals vulnerable and genetically predisposed where the toxic effects of LSD interact with premorbid vulnerability to produce a sustained psychotic reaction." Dr. Lukas similarly explained that studies had shown that persons with a "genetic predisposition to schizophrenia," or "premorbid" (undiagnosed) schizophrenic disorders "may experience pathological behavior that is temporally related to drug use," and that defendant's "mental health history clearly puts him in this category."

instruction provides that an insanity defense may be predicated upon a mental condition "caused by the voluntary consumption of illegal drugs if the drugs activate a latent mental disease or defect," provided that the defendant did not know or have reason to know the drug would activate the illness; that the resulting disease is recognized medically and existed at the time of the offense "independent of any temporary intoxication or high that the drugs caused"; and that the mental disease "lasted for a substantial time after the drugs had worn off." The instruction went on to reject settled insanity in its traditional form, stating that "[a] mental disease or defect cannot be caused solely by the consumption of an illegal drug." . . . Defendant has not shown, nor have we discovered, any significant movement by jurisdictions outside of Massachusetts to apply the *Herd* formula.

The proposed instruction essentially posits that when the voluntary use of illegal drugs activates a "latent" mental illness resulting in psychosis, we should ignore the fact that illegal drugs were the precipitating cause. This conclusion runs counter to the fundamental principle that defendant is not excused from criminal liability for acts which result from a mental state that is self-induced through the voluntary ingestion of illegal drugs or alcohol. If defendant here suffered, as Dr. Linder asserts, from a latent mental illness, it does not alter the fact that, as Dr. Linder also explained, defendant would not have been in a psychotic state at the time of the offense had he not chosen to use illegal consciousness-altering drugs.[14] Thus, the very evidence on which defendant relies defeats his claim, for it demonstrates that his recent, voluntary use of illegal drugs was an essential causal element of the mental illness and psychotic episode that followed. On these facts, defendant was not entitled to assert an insanity defense. . . .

Our conclusion is not altered by the instruction's additional requirement that defendant neither "knew nor had reason to know that the drug would activate the illness." As we have seen, it is a fundamental tenet of our criminal code that a defendant must be held accountable for the consequences of his or her actions resulting from the voluntary ingestion of illegal drugs or alcohol, and this rule remains unaffected by the possibility that the substance will activate an unknown condition leading to an unexpected reaction. Indeed, many courts have held that a defendant can not reasonably assume the use of illegal drugs will have any predictable effect. See, e.g., People v. Velez, 175 Cal.App.3d 785, 221 (Ct. App. 1985) (rejecting claim that defendant was not responsible for his actions after smoking marijuana cigarette unaware that it was laced with PCP since he could not "assume" that the marijuana would "produce any predictable intoxicating effect").[15]

---

[14] In his final report to the court, Dr. Linder stated that absent defendant's latent predisposition, his drug use probably would not have resulted in a psychotic reaction, and, equally, that but for the drug use, the latent condition probably would not have produced a psychotic reaction at the time of the offense. As he explained: "Without the predisposing elements of his susceptibility, the drug use alone would have probably not led to the resulting psychotic condition. Without the drug use, in an individual susceptible to decompensation as was Mr. Sexton, the deterioration probably would not have occurred within the same time frame and it may have been avoided altogether due to other interceding circumstances." At his deposition, Dr. Linder again agreed that, "but for the drugs" that defendant had consumed, he probably would not have become psychotic.

[15] Contrary to the assertion of our dissenting colleague, it is of no moment that the defendants in these decisions remained under the influence of drugs or alcohol at the time of the

. . . We recognize that mental disease and the abuse of illegal drugs often coexist, and emphasize that nothing in our holding bars an insanity defense where the prior use of drugs is not an essential causal element of defendant's mental state. Indeed, nothing that we have said would preclude this or any other defendant from attempting to prove at trial that the alleged insanity at the time of the offense was caused by a mental disease or defect that rendered them incapable of appreciating the criminality of their acts or of conforming their conduct to the requirements of law. Upon such a showing, however, the State may offer evidence to prove that the voluntary ingestion of intoxicants was an essential causal element of the insanity so as to refute the claim that the insanity absolves the defendant of criminal responsibility. . . .

The fundamental principle underlying the insanity defense is that one should not be punished for criminal acts for which one is not responsible. Consistent with this principle, it is universally recognized that a defendant who intentionally consumes drugs or alcohol resulting in a psychotic state will not be relieved of responsibility for his or her criminal acts. The question presented by this case is whether we are willing to relieve a defendant of criminal responsibility whose psychosis allegedly emerged from a mental illness triggered by the defendant's voluntary use of illegal hallucinogenic drugs for a period of two months preceding the crime. As explained above, we conclude that the law may reduce an individual's culpability in such circumstances,[a] but will not excuse it. Like any other individual asserting an insanity defense, however, defendant remains free to prove that he was not responsible for his conduct as the result of an independently preexisting mental disease or defect that rendered him unable to appreciate the criminality of his acts or to conform his conduct to the requirements of law. . . .

■ DOOLEY, J., dissenting. . . . In my view, the [court's] holding is inconsistent with our insanity defense statute, the Model Penal Code from which our statute is derived, and the established common law. . . .

I.

[E]veryone in this case, including the defendant, agrees that the mental state of intoxication alone cannot be a complete defense to a criminal charge. But faced with expert opinion that defendant's conduct resulted from a preexisting mental illness activated by long-term drug use, the [trial judge] decided that the causative presence of both the preexisting mental illness and the drug-induced psychotic condition, independent of any intoxication, could be found by the jury to be insanity under our statute.

[T]he majority portrays a defendant who did drugs for a very short period of time, went crazy, killed someone, and then returned to a normal state shortly after the killing. [It] ignores the ample evidence that

---

offense while defendant here may not have been under the immediate influence of LSD. Even if it was the "latent" illness from which defendant's psychosis emerged, that illness was allegedly activated by defendant's two-month use of drugs, and he therefore remains liable for its consequences, anticipated or not (at least in the absence of evidence of a fixed insanity resulting from long-term substance abuse).

[a] In an omitted portion of the opinion, the court held that evidence regarding Sexton's psychotic condition was admissible to negate the mens rea for second-degree murder ("wanton disregard" of the risk of death or great bodily harm).—[Footnote by eds.]

is inconsistent with its characterization of the facts. Compare the majority's description of the evidence to the description of defendant's mental condition contained in Dr. Linder's report in defendant's offer of proof:

> Mr. Sexton was experiencing significant dysfunction in his life characterized in part by the loss of a girlfriend relationship, being confronted at gunpoint, nuclear family dysfunction, curfew-mandated isolation, unemployment, legal difficulties and substance use. It was under the cumulative strain of these circumstances that he decompensated into a florid psychotic condition. His substance use contributed to this destabilization. He had been using cannabis, LSD, some cocaine, some psilocybin mushrooms, some Ketamine, some ecstasy and some nitrous oxide.

Under the majority's analysis of the offer of proof, the only relevant word in the above paragraph is LSD. . . .

[T]here are two recognized instances where a defendant who has taken drugs can nevertheless be insane at the time of the criminal act. The first is when the defendant suffers from "fixed" or "settled" insanity as a result of drug usage. The second is when the defendant has a preexisting mental illness and the drug usage activates that mental illness under circumstances where the defendant is unaware that the activation would occur. Uniquely, the trial court required that both instances be present in the same case, a requirement imposed by no other court in the United States.

. . . Even a cursory reading of the cases cited by the majority shows that they involved (i) statutes explicitly foreclosing an insanity defense when drug use is a causal factor and/or (ii) offenses committed while the defendants were under the immediate influence of intoxicating drugs or alcohol-precisely what the trial court's instruction excluded from consideration in this case. I particularly take issue with the majority's summary of the law: "As we have seen, it is well settled that, absent a fixed insanity developed over a prolonged period of abuse, the voluntary use of drugs or alcohol that triggers a psychotic reaction will not absolve a defendant of criminal responsibility." This is not an accurate statement of the common law in situations where the defendant suffered from an underlying mental illness that was a proximate cause of his criminal conduct and he was not under the direct influence of intoxicating drugs at the time of the offense. Nor is it an accurate description of the fixed or settled insanity doctrine as it has evolved in the common law. And even if it were an accurate statement of the law, defendant's offer of proof is sufficient to get to the jury under that standard.

. . . I cannot subscribe to the majority's view that every mentally ill defendant who takes drugs is morally blameworthy for any criminal conduct that occurs. I agree with the Supreme Judicial Court of Massachusetts that the moral fault for using illegal drugs is not equivalent to the moral fault for committing the charged offense, particularly when that offense is murder. See Commonwealth v. Herd, 413 Mass. 834, 604 N.E.2d 1294, 1299 (Mass. 1992) ("We are unwilling, in order to justify a homicide conviction, to permit the moral fault inherent in the unlawful consumption of drugs to substitute for the moral fault that is absent in one who lacks criminal responsibility."). By denying defendant an opportunity to present an insanity defense because of his prior drug use, the majority undermines one of the most basic precepts of our criminal law.

II.

. . . Defendant was eighteen years old when he committed the offense. His father had a history of recurrent depression, alcohol and substance abuse, suicide attempts, and a personality disorder requiring years of mental health treatment. Defendant's mother also suffered from depression. Other extended family members had had "nervous breakdowns" or had attempted suicide. Early on, defendant was diagnosed with emotional and behavioral disabilities that affected his school work. The diagnoses included adjustment disorder with mixed emotional features, mixed receptive-expressive language disorder, appositional defiant disorder, and acute stress disorder.

By the seventh grade, defendant was exhibiting serious behavioral problems and was smoking marijuana. On separate occasions in 1995, he threatened each of his parents with a knife. Crisis services were called, and defendant was briefly hospitalized, after which he continued for some period of time in outpatient psychotherapy. In 1998, he threatened to kill his father after he was grounded for using the family car. Based on that incident, he was charged with domestic assault and placed on probation.

In the spring of 1999, after another confrontation with his father that resulted in his slitting his own wrist, defendant stopped attending school regularly, left home, and began working full time. His drug use escalated after he lost his job in January 2000. In addition to regular marijuana use, he experimented with other psychoactive drugs such as ecstasy, hallucinogenic mushrooms, and cocaine. In July 2000, he began using LSD. Although he claims to have taken up to 300 "hits" in the ensuing two or three months, at least one of the examining psychiatrists opined that such numbers were unlikely because that amount would have prevented defendant from being able to function at any level. Defendant was arrested twice in August 2000, the month before the killing. The first incident occurred when he engaged police in a physical confrontation after they tried to remove him from a private residence. The second incident occurred a week later when he tried to intervene with police officers who were confronting his friends because of their use of his skateboards. He was charged with impeding an officer, disorderly conduct, and resisting arrest.

By all accounts, defendant last took LSD two to three weeks before the killing. He continued to smoke marijuana on a daily basis until three or four days before, and possibly again on the day of, the killing, but apparently took few, if any, other drugs during that period. Nevertheless, he began to experience more pronounced feelings of paranoia in the days leading up to the killing. Witnesses described him as constantly discussing conspiracy theories and feeling that everyone was against him. He believed that his friends were trying to pull something out of him and that there was "a society within a society" that did not include him. He felt like everyone was "in his face" and wanted to kill him because they knew what he was thinking, particularly how miserable they all were. He considered them all to be "robots" who could not control themselves.

He ate very little, had difficulty sleeping, and stopped going outside. He believed that he saw blood coming from his cat and that the cat was in pain and asking him to end its misery. On the evening of the killing, he strangled and stomped the cat to death after he thought he heard it say it was suffering. He imagined that, to be reborn, he had to collect souls and become a new deity. Not wanting to look at the mangled cat, he decided to start collecting souls immediately. He headed upstairs to gather the souls of (i.e., kill) his neighbors, but they were not home, so he went outside and saw the unfortunate victim riding her bike down the street. Although he had never met or seen the woman before, he attacked her without provocation and beat her to death.

The toxicology report done the day after the killing showed residual marijuana metabolites in defendant's blood but no other legal or illegal drugs in his system, except those attributed to medications he had been given at the hospital following his arrest. A court-appointed psychiatrist, Dr. Linder, concluded that defendant had been latently psychotic for years and that recent circumstances-including drug use-had set in motion a complete psychotic breakdown.

While acknowledging that drug use probably played a significant role in activating defendant's mental illness, Dr. Linder did not consider defendant's substance abuse to be the primary factor in his psychosis because of the long period of disordered thinking before defendant began his relatively brief period of using psychoactive drugs. Dr. Linder also opined that defendant could not have known or predicted the magnitude of his psychotic reaction to the drugs he took. Dr. Linder concluded that, by the time of the alleged offense, defendant had reached such a delusional and psychotic state of mind that he could not reflect rationally enough to refrain from killing either his beloved cat or a total stranger.

Following notification of defendant's intent to rely upon an insanity defense, the State obtained permission for Dr. Albert Drukteinis to perform an independent psychiatric evaluation of defendant. In April 2002, Dr. Drukteinis filed a report in which he stated that defendant was suffering from psychotic thought at the time of the killing and thus was not able to appreciate the criminality of his conduct. Dr. Drukteinis concluded, however, that defendant had no prior history of a major thought disorder such as schizophrenia and that, in his opinion, defendant's psychotic state arose in the context of heavy drug abuse. According to Dr. Drukteinis, defendant had acted recklessly by accepting "the loss of contact with reality that the drugs routinely brought which was not altogether different than the psychotic state which they precipitated." Hence, Dr. Drukteinis opined that defendant's voluntary drug use directly resulted in his psychotic state and the ensuing killing. . . .

In an ensuing deposition and follow-up letter, Dr. Linder concluded that defendant had been suffering from either schizophreniform disorder—a condition resembling schizophrenia, but with symptoms lasting only between one and six months—or a substance-induced psychotic disorder at the time of the alleged offense. Dr. Linder stated that defendant's genetic vulnerability and his long history of mental and emotional dysfunction predisposed him to develop a severe psychotic reaction to some of the psychoactive drugs he took in the months preceding the murder. According to Dr. Linder, however, defendant's sustained psychotic state-lasting several weeks after he stopped using the drugs-indicated that the psychosis he experienced was not purely drug-induced. Rather, Dr. Linder surmised that defendant's predisposition towards mental illness, activated by some combination of social, occupational, interpersonal, and substance-use stressors, caused defendant to be insane at the time of the offense.

Dr. Linder also emphasized that the psychotic state defendant experienced was well beyond the ken of altered states of consciousness anticipated or desired by drug users. Dr. Linder recognized that, in using the drugs, defendant anticipated that they might produce odd and unusual mental experiences but concluded that defendant could not have known the potential for the magnitude of the reaction that occurred.

Thus, Dr. Linder opined that defendant's psychosis on the day of the killing was not a "psychedelic experience" from LSD, but rather was a response "seen rarely . . . in individuals vulnerable and genetically predisposed where the toxic effects of LSD interact with a premorbid vulnerability to produce a sustained psychotic reaction."

Accordingly, the court proposed an instruction allowing the jury to accept an insanity defense if (i) defendant's drug consumption activated a medically recognized mental disease that caused him to be insane at the time of the alleged offense; (ii) defendant did not know and had no reason to know that his drug consumption would activate the mental disease; (iii) the mental disease existed independently of any temporary intoxication or high caused by drugs; and (iv) the mental disease lasted for a substantial period of time after the intoxicating effects of the drugs had worn off. The proposed charge also would inform the jury that the defense could not apply if the mental disease was caused solely by the consumption of drugs. Thus, the trial court precluded defendant from raising a defense claiming temporary insanity that resulted from either the direct intoxicating effects of drugs or solely the long-term use of drugs.

In seeking the instruction on insanity, defendant never claimed, and the expert witness never stated, that defendant's actions on the day of the offense were caused by intoxication—that is, an impaired mental state caused by the immediate effects of drugs or alcohol. Instead, defendant relied upon a variation of fixed or settled insanity, a branch of the insanity defense whereby a prolonged, if not permanent, mental disease or defect is caused by long-term alcohol or drug abuse. The trial court rejected the notion that settled insanity caused exclusively by drug use should be recognized as a defense in Vermont but found that this case involved an additional factor often not present in settled insanity cases—evidence that defendant had an underlying mental illness before he started abusing drugs and that his conduct was caused by both the underlying mental illness and his abuse of drugs.

Although the backbone of the district court's language is the Massachusetts defense, the court added additional elements. It recognized that the Massachusetts defense had been applied in cases in which the defendant was allegedly intoxicated at the time of the offense, thereby allowing the jury to determine whether the intoxication was such a controlling factor that it replaced the mental illness as the cause of the conduct. The court rejected this application of the defense, however, requiring instead that the underlying mental illness be activated by long-term drug use in the absence of any intoxication. In that sense, the instruction included aspects of the traditional fixed or settled insanity defense.

[A]part from a few jurisdictions in which the issue is addressed by a specific statute[,] no other court has required all of these elements in a case involving both drug or alcohol consumption and a mental disease or defect. As shown above, however, there were ample facts for a jury to conclude that (i) defendant had engaged in long-term drug use that activated an underlying, medically accepted mental illness; (ii) the mental illness was independent of the intoxicating effects of the drugs and lasted for a substantial period of time after the murder-indeed, defendant's delusional thinking endured at least until the spring of 2001, several months after the killing; and (iii) defendant did not know, nor could have known, that the drug use would trigger an underlying mental illness that would make him insane—in other words, he was incapable of conforming his actions to the requirements of the law.

III.

The statutory test for insanity in Vermont, which is derived from and nearly identical to the Model Penal Code's provision on the insanity defense, is as follows: "A person is not responsible for criminal conduct if at the time of such conduct as a result of mental disease or defect he lacks adequate capacity either to appreciate the criminality of his conduct or to conform his conduct to the requirements of law." 13 V.S.A. § 4801(a)(1). Defendant has the burden to prove insanity "by a preponderance of the evidence." 13 V.S.A. § 4801(b). Because it is undisputed at this juncture of the case that defendant was unable to appreciate the criminality of his conduct or to conform his conduct to the requirements of the law at the time of the killing, the relevant question for purposes of this appeal is whether defendant's inability to do so was "a result of mental disease or defect."

As demonstrated above, there is ample evidence for a jury to conclude that, at the time of the alleged offense, defendant's inability to appreciate the criminality of his conduct or to conform his conduct to the requirements of the law was a result of a latent mental illness triggered by past drug use. Indeed, the majority acknowledges Dr. Linder's opinion that but for the underlying mental illness, defendant's drug use would not have resulted in the psychotic state that led to the killing. Dr. Lukas added that "Mr. Sexton's psychiatric condition is chronic and is not dependent on the use of LSD or other illicit drugs." In other words, there is expert opinion supporting defendant's claim that his preexisting mental illness, independent of the effects of his drug use, was a cause in fact of the victim's death and a substantial factor—that is, a proximate cause-of the death. Even assuming that defendant's psychotic state may not have occurred absent his drug use, there can be more than one proximate cause of defendant's insanity. Thus, under the plain meaning of the statute, defendant made a sufficient showing to enable his insanity defense to go to the jury.

The majority apparently disagrees, holding that defendant may not present an insanity defense under § 4801 even if he is insane as a result of a mental disease or defect, as long as the mental disease or defect would not have occurred absent his voluntary use of illegal drugs. In support of this test, the majority relies upon decisions from jurisdictions with statutes—unlike § 4801—that explicitly preclude an insanity defense when prior drug use is a proximate cause of the defendant's mental condition. See, e.g., Conn. Gen. Stat. § 53a–13(b) (2001) ("It shall not be a defense under this section if such mental disease or defect was proximately caused by the voluntary ingestion, inhalation or injection of intoxicating liquor or any drug or substance. . . . "). In those jurisdictions, if drug use is one of several proximate causes of the alleged criminal conduct, no insanity defense is available.

. . . At best, from the state's perspective, the evidence in this case indicates that defendant's insanity at the time of the alleged offense arose from a combination of his latent mental illness and his prior drug use; neither one of these causes, independently, would have resulted in defendant's insanity, but they both played a substantial and necessary role in creating his psychotic state. Moreover, there was undisputed expert testimony that defendant had no way of anticipating that his drug use would trigger the psychotic state he was in at the time of the killing.

Given this evidence, a jury could consider defendant's mental illness and his drug use to be separate, concurrent causes of his insanity and could conclude that his insanity—his inability to appreciate the criminality of his conduct or to conform his conduct to the requirements of the law—was a result of a mental disease or defect. The Massachusetts defense, used in part by the trial judge, is simply an application of these standard principles of causation to the insanity defense so as to allow the defense to be raised when the evidence would support a jury determination that the mental illness caused—that is, was a cause in fact and a proximate cause of—the conduct for which the defendant is charged.

In contrast, under the majority's standard, a defendant cannot obtain an insanity defense if his insanity was caused to any significant degree by drug abuse. [T]his effectively imposes an insurmountable burden on defendants. . . .

## NOTES ON THE INSANITY DEFENSE AND INTOXICATION

### 1. INTRODUCTION

The *Sexton* court rests its decision squarely on the principle that voluntary intoxication is not a defense to criminal liability. Voluntary intoxication is not an excuse even if the defendant's mental functioning was so impaired by the acute effects of alcohol or other drugs as to establish what otherwise would be a defense of "unconsciousness" or insanity. In cases of incapacitating voluntary intoxication, the law finds the governing moral criterion in the culpable origin of the incapacity rather than in its severity. As Lord Matthew Hale said, a person who commits a crime while drunk "shall have no privilege by this voluntary contracted madness, but shall have the same judgment as if he were in his right senses."[a] However, Hale identified two situations in which the madness induced by intoxication

[a] 1 Matthew Hale, The History of the Pleas of the Crown 32 (Philadelphia 1847) (1st ed. 1736).

would not be contracted voluntarily and therefore would have exculpatory significance:

> [First,] if a person by the unskillfulness of his physician, or by the contrivance of his enemies, eat or drink such a thing as causeth such a temporary or permanent phrenzy, . . . this puts him into the same condition, in reference to crimes, as any other phrenzy, and equally excuseth him. [Second,] although the *simplex* phrenzy occasioned immediately by drunkenness excuses not in criminals, yet if by one or more such practices, an *habitual* or fixed phrenzy be caused, though this madness was contracted by the vice and will of the party, yet this habitual and fixed phrenzy thereby caused puts the man into the same condition in relation to crimes, as if the same were contracted involuntarily at first.

Each of these two propositions now represents settled law in the United States.

### 2. NON-CULPABLE INTOXICATION

The first of the principles mentioned by Hale, typically labeled "involuntary intoxication," covers a variety of cases in which the person cannot fairly be blamed for becoming intoxicated. Cases of intoxication under duress or by contrivance (*A* puts LSD in *B*'s coffee) simply do not appear in the books. Most of the reported cases involve psychoactive side effects of medically-prescribed substances, typically arising in connection with automobile offenses.

The leading case is Minneapolis v. Altimus, 306 Minn. 462, 238 N.W. 2d 851 (1976). The defendant was charged with careless driving and a "hit and run" offense. The evidence showed that he made an illegal left turn from a right-hand lane, crashed into another vehicle, and then continued driving. He was arrested by a policeman who had observed the accident. In his defense, he testified that three days before the incident he started taking Valium (a psychoactive, anti-anxiety drug with muscle-relaxing effects) for back pain pursuant to a physician's prescription. He said that he began experiencing mental confusion and disorientation while driving and remembered nothing about either the accident or the arrest. He also introduced expert testimony regarding the effects of Valium. The court instructed the jury on voluntary intoxication but refused to instruct on "involuntary intoxication." The Minnesota Supreme Court reversed, holding that defendant's evidence that "at the time he committed the acts in question he was intoxicated and unaware of what he was doing due to an unusual and unexpected reaction to drugs prescribed by a physician" was sufficient "to raise the defense of temporary insanity due to involuntary intoxication."

How should the jury be instructed on remand? The court's language suggests that the test has two elements: first, the intoxication must be "involuntary," which means the effect must have been both atypical and "unexpected"; and the unexpected impairment must amount to "insanity," which in Minnesota is defined according to the *M'Naghten* test. Are these the correct criteria? Compare § 2.08 of the Model Penal Code. Does the Model Penal Code formulation differ from the court's test in *Altimus*? How? Is the Model Code approach sound?

In State v. Gardner, 230 Wis.2d 32, 601 N.W.2d 670 (1999), the court held that the involuntary intoxication defense can be available to a person taking medically prescribed drugs as instructed even if the defendant knows of possible intoxicating effects:

> The State acknowledges that the effects of prescription medication may constitute involuntary intoxication, but urges us to add the requirement that the defendant must not know of the intoxicating effect. We acknowledge that ample case law supports this position. The rationale is that if the defendant knows of the intoxicating effect prior to taking the medication, then the intoxication is rendered voluntary. See City of Minneapolis v. Altimus, 306 Minn. 462, 238 N.W.2d 851, 857 (1976) (so holding and citing supporting cases). We see no reason to so limit the defense. Even if forewarned of the intoxicating effect of a prescription drug, a person should have recourse to the defense if the drug renders him or her unable to distinguish between right and wrong. When faced with a medical condition requiring drug treatment, the patient hardly has a choice but to follow the doctor's orders. Intoxication resulting from such compliance with a physician's advice should not be deemed voluntary just because the patient is aware of potential adverse side effects.

Is this a better rule?

### 3. ALCOHOL-RELATED INSANITY

The second principle to which Hale referred was the exculpatory effect of the "fixed phrenzy" produced by chronic intoxication. The clinical predicate for this generally accepted doctrine is that chronic use of alcohol can result in organic brain pathology. Although chronic alcohol use can contribute to the development of "dementia,"[b] the most relevant disorder for present purposes is "alcohol withdrawal delirium" (also called delirium tremens, or "DT's"), which is precipitated by a cessation or reduction of alcohol consumption after many years of heavy use. This condition usually involves delusions, vivid hallucinations, and agitated behavior. A related condition is alcoholic hallucinosis, involving vivid and usually unpleasant auditory hallucinations without the clouding of consciousness characteristic of delirium. Usually this disorder lasts only a few hours or days but can involve significant danger if the individual responds to hallucinatory threats. This condition can occur after a long period of "spree" drinking.

A famous case involving delirium tremens is Beasley v. State, 50 Ala. 149 (1874). Beasley was charged with murder. The evidence showed that the defendant had shot himself in the head, partially paralyzing his left side, 19 years before the offense, and had been chronically drunk for several years before the killing. He frequently experienced hallucinations and had an attack of delirium tremens three weeks before the killing. He testified that he was seeing devils and witches before and during the day of the shooting and that he "imagined that men were after him to kill him." Prosecution evidence showed that the killing was brutal and unprovoked. The trial court refused to instruct on insanity saying, instead, that "drunkenness, in itself, was no palliation or excuse." Beasley was convicted of second-degree murder. On appeal the conviction was reversed because

[b] Dementia is the general term for an organic brain syndrome characterized by intellectual deficits and impaired memory and often by impaired judgment and impulse control. Its most common manifestation is in cases of Alzheimer's Disease.

the intoxication charge failed to distinguish between the "immediate effects of the defendant's drunkenness" and the effects of "mental unsoundness brought on by excessive drinking which remains after the intoxication has subsided." The appellate court held that the jury should have been instructed on insanity.

It is often said that delirium tremens and alcoholic hallucinosis exculpate to the same degree as any other psychotic disorder, notwithstanding the fact that these conditions were "caused" by the defendant's own excessive drinking. In these situations, the law looks not to the original source of the impairment but to its effect. In sum, the defendant's pattern of voluntary decisions loses its moral significance when behavior "ripens" into a pathological condition no longer subject to voluntary control.

What is the basis for this distinction? Why does the idiom of moral discourse shift from voluntariness to involuntariness when one moves from the disabling (and often unanticipated) effects of an acute episode of intoxication to the disabling (and often unanticipated) effects of a pattern of intoxication? What is the crucial moral variable? The chronicity of the condition? The psychotic character of the impairment? The remote connection between a psychotic condition and individual instances of intoxication? Consider the suggestion of Monrad Paulsen in Intoxication as a Defense to Crime, 1961 U.Ill.L.F. 1, 22–23:

> . . . In a sense it is true that an actor, who by drinking destroys his powers of perception or self-control, bears responsibility for his ultimate state. Does it follow that mental disorder produced by long-term alcoholic behavior should be given a different effect in the law from insanity not produced by "voluntary" behavior? The law is clear. Lack of responsibility can be shown by "settled" insanity without regard to the chain of causation. To give the genesis of mental disorder a legal effect is to put upon the processes of litigation an impossible task. If the full exculpatory effect of mental disease were denied to those illnesses which are related to unwise choices in life, many cases other than those of the alcoholics would be involved. We need only recall that general paresis [a type of dementia] was a not-uncommon consequence of syphilis.

Is this persuasive? Is it really an "impossible" task to determine whether the defendant's disorder is attributable to once voluntary choices? Or does the law rest on a moral judgment that a person cannot fairly be said to have voluntarily assumed the risk of becoming "mentally ill"?

Hale emphasized the "fixed" nature of the "phrenzy" and the courts have typically said that an alcohol-related condition must be "settled" to have exculpatory significance. However, recent commentary has taken note of the clinical reality that both delirium and hallucinosis linked to cessation of drinking usually involve temporary impairment incidental to chronic and heavy use. Although the person's heavy drinking has probably caused organic brain damage, the "phrenzy" is in fact not "fixed." This has led one court to note that "the distinction, notwithstanding the language of the cases, is not so much between temporary and permanent insanity as it is one between the direct results of drinking, which are voluntarily sought after, and its remote and undesired consequences." Parker v. State, 7 Md. App. 167, 179, 254 A.2d 381, 388 (1969).

## 4. INSANITY RELATED TO USE OF OTHER DRUGS

The distinction between the acute effects of intoxication on perception and judgment and psychotic symptoms that can be associated with a brain disease caused by chronic alcohol use is fairly straightforward, both clinically and legally. However, the doctrinal picture became considerably blurred by the patterns of psychoactive drug use that emerged in the 1960's. Many of these drugs can affect cognitive functioning in profound ways that bear no resemblance to the effects of alcohol. As one court noted in 1968, "we anticipate . . . that the demands of due process may require adjustment and refinement in traditional and 'stock' instructions on the subject of criminal responsibility in view of the frightening effects of the hallucinatory drugs."[c] As the *Sexton* court observes, there seems to be little clinical similarity between the organic brain disease associated with chronic drinking and the psychopathology associated with hallucinogenic and stimulant drugs. Three distinct clinical situations are explored below.

### (i) *Psychoactive Effects of Intoxication*

Hallucinogenic drugs such as LSD have sometimes been called "psychotomimetic" drugs because the acute effects of ordinary doses "mimic" psychotic symptoms. The perceptual changes include subjective intensification of perceptions, depersonalization, illusion, and visual hallucinations. The direct effects of the intoxication usually last about six hours. Users of high doses of amphetamines and other stimulant drugs may experience delusions or hallucinations; and users of phencyclidine (PCP) and related substances may experience hallucinations and paranoid ideation.

The question is whether the hallucinogenic effects of these drugs warrant any qualification of the rule that voluntary intoxication is no defense regardless of the nature and severity of the impairment. The courts have uniformly rejected this claim. Consider, for example, State v. Hall, 214 N.W.2d 205 (Iowa 1974). Hall was charged with the fatal shooting of his driving companion during the course of a trip from Oregon to Chicago. He testified that before the shooting he had taken a pill (presumably LSD) which he had been told was a "little sunshine" and would make him feel "groovy." He said he drove all the way to Iowa without rest, took the pill at Des Moines and began experiencing hallucinations. The victim, who was sleeping, appeared to make growling sounds and turn into a rabid dog like one he saw his father kill when he was a child. In panic, he seized the victim's gun and shot him three times. The trial court refused an insanity instruction, and the jury convicted defendant of first-degree murder despite an instruction that his intoxication could be considered in connection with the issue of intent. The appellate court affirmed, holding that the acute, psychotomimetic effects of LSD do not justify a departure from the traditional rule that "a temporary mental condition caused by voluntary intoxication . . . does not constitute a complete defense." Three judges dissented, arguing, inter alia:

> . . . The fallacy in the majority's position is that it puts the issue on a *time* basis rather than an *effect* basis. It says the use of drugs is no defense unless mental illness resulting from long-established use is shown because that's what we have said of alcoholic intoxication. But we have said that about alcohol because

[c] Pierce v. Turner, 402 F.2d 109, 112 (10th Cir. 1968).

> ordinarily the use of alcohol produces no mental illness except by long-continued excessive use. On the other hand, that same result can be obtained overnight by the use of modern hallucinatory drugs like LSD.

Is there merit to the view expressed in the *Hall* dissent?

### *(ii) Precipitation of a "Functional" Psychosis*

As the testimony in *Sexton* indicates, use of hallucinogenic or stimulant drugs can precipitate a psychosis in a predisposed individual, even though the person has never previously had an acute psychotic episode.[d] How should a case such as *Sexton* be decided under the principles thus far reviewed? Should *Hall* or *Beasley* control? Should the applicable rule be determined by the pathological nature of the impairment or by the role of voluntary drug use in causing it?

The view taken by the majority in *Sexton* appears to represent the minority view. The prevailing judicial view is illustrated by State v. Maik, 60 N.J. 203, 287 A.2d 715 (1972), where the Supreme Court of New Jersey held that the insanity defense is available in such a case. Chief Justice Weintraub wrote for a unanimous court:

> [The defendant claimed] that the drugs [LSD], acting upon [an] underlying illness, triggered or precipitated a psychotic state which continued after the direct or immediate influence of the drug had dissipated, and that it was the psychosis, rather than the drug, which rendered defendant unable to know right from wrong at the time of the killing. In other words, defendant urges that when a psychosis emerges from a fixed illness, we should not inquire into the identity of the precipitating event or action. Indeed, it may be said to be unlikely that the inquiry would be useful, for when, as here, the acute psychosis could equally be triggered by some other stress, known or unknown, which the defendant could not handle, a medical opinion as to what did in fact precipitate the psychosis is not apt to rise above a speculation among mere possibilities.
>
> We think it compatible with the philosophical basis of [the insanity defense] to accept the fact of a schizophrenic episode without inquiry into its etiology.

What is the basis for the holding in *Maik*? Was an exculpatory defense allowed because the defendant was mentally ill *before* taking the drugs?[e] Or because he was mentally ill *after* taking the drugs? Under what circumstances, if any, would the *Sexton* court allow a defense to a defendant whose "latent" psychosis was triggered by voluntary use of drugs? Does it rule out such a defense altogether because of the "causal" role of the drug use in precipitating the psychotic symptoms? Neither court alludes to the

---

[d] See, e.g., Michael M. Vardy and Stanley R. Kay, LSD Psychosis or LSD-Induced Schizophrenia? A Multimethod Inquiry, 40 Arch. Gen. Psychiatry 877 (1983); Beverly J. Fauman and Michael A. Fauman, Phencyclidine Abuse and Crime: A Psychiatric Perspective, 10 Bull.Amer. Acad. of Psychiatry and Law 171 (1982).

[e] One court has said: "[I]f the pre-existing condition of mind of the accused is not such as would render him legally insane in and of itself, then the recent use of intoxicants causing stimulation or aggravation of the pre-existing condition to the point of insanity cannot be relied upon as a defense. . . . " Evilsizer v. State, 487 S.W.2d 113, 116 (Tex.Cr.App.1972).

fact that the defendant's possession and use of LSD and the other drugs ingested by the respective defendants were criminal acts. Should that make any difference?

### *(iii) Toxic Psychosis*

Assume that both *Hall* and *Maik* are correctly decided. In other words, assume (i) that a defendant is not entitled to an insanity instruction if the claimed mental impairment is directly attributable to the intoxicating effects of the drug—i.e., those effects which result from the direct action of the drug on the central nervous system during the period when it is pharmacologically active, but (ii) that a predisposed defendant whose drug use triggers an underlying psychotic illness may invoke the insanity defense. The courts sometimes characterize the distinction as one between an exogenous cause of the impairment (drugs or alcohol) vs. an endogenous cause (mental illness). Which principle should control in the case of a person without an underlying disorder who uses an hallucinogenic drug and experiences a so-called "toxic psychosis"—i.e., a transient dysfunction of the brain which is directly attributable to the toxic effects of the drug but which outlasts the period of intoxication?

A toxic psychosis may vary in effect and length depending on the drug, the dose, the person's psychological status or "set," and the setting of use. For example, a single dose of PCP (phencyclidine) can cause a condition characterized by paranoid delusions and violent behavior lasting from several days to several weeks.[f] While a single dose of amphetamines would be unlikely to induce a toxic psychosis, a person who has used moderate or high doses of amphetamines for a long period may develop a disorder, characterized by delusions of persecution, indistinguishable from schizophrenia.

Should a toxic psychosis, which is both temporary and unrelated to an underlying disorder be regarded as a "mental disease or defect" for purposes of the insanity defense? Or should the case be governed by the principle that voluntary intoxication is not a defense, even if it produces a psychotic state? Is psychosis within the range of risk voluntarily assumed by a user of hallucinogenic drugs? These questions have recently been addressed in detail by the Supreme Court of Canada in Bouchard-Lebrun v. R., [2011] 3 S.C. R 575, and by the English Court of Appeal in Coley v. R., [2013] EWCA (Crim.) 223 (Eng.).

## 5. *PEOPLE V. KELLY* AND SUBSEQUENT DEVELOPMENTS IN CALIFORNIA

In People v. Kelly, 10 Cal.3d, 111 Cal.Rptr. 171, 516 P.2d 875 (1973), the California Supreme Court reversed the murder conviction of 18-year-old Valerie Dawn Kelly who had stabbed her mother with an array of kitchen knives. The experts were in substantial agreement that "her

---

[f] During the 1960's, PCP was studied experimentally in "normal" volunteers. The major finding of these studies was "that PCP had no equal in its ability to produce brief psychoses nearly indistinguishable from schizophrenia." Generally, these episodes began immediately after ingestion of the drug but lasted for several hours. They were often characterized by violently paranoid behavior. Recent clinical experience with PCP users experiencing toxic psychoses indicates that they can last considerably longer and that the nature and severity of the symptoms varies widely among individuals. See generally Luisada, The Phencyclidine Psychosis: Phenomenology and Treatment, in Robert C. Petersen and Richard C. Stillman (eds.), Phencyclidine (PCP) Abuse: An Appraisal 241 (1978).

voluntary and repeated ingestion of drugs over a two-month period had triggered a legitimate psychosis" so that on the day of the attack, she was unable to distinguish right from wrong. The trial judge concluded that her insanity was not a defense because "it was not of settled and permanent nature" and had been "produced by the voluntary ingestion of hallucinatory drugs." The California Supreme Court followed *Maik,* holding that "such a temporary psychosis which was not limited merely to periods of intoxication . . . and which rendered defendant insane . . . constitutes a settled insanity that is a complete defense . . . " In 1994, the California legislature enacted Penal Code § 25.5, which precludes an insanity defense "solely on the basis of . . . an addiction to, or abuse of, intoxicating substances." As interpreted in People v. Robinson, 72 Cal.App.4th 421 (Cal. App. 1999), this provision "erects an absolute bar prohibiting use of one's voluntary ingestion of intoxicants as the sole basis for an insanity defense, regardless whether the substances caused organic damage or a settled mental defect or disorder which persists after the immediate effects of the intoxicants have worn off."

Was this a proper interpretation of the statute? Would it alter the result in *Kelly*? Was drug abuse the *sole* basis for her insanity defense? Consider, in this connection, the definition of mental disease proposed by Richard Bonnie—and adopted in a number of states—which includes "only those severely abnormal mental conditions that grossly and demonstrably impair a person's perception or understanding of reality and *that are not attributable primarily to the voluntary ingestion of alcohol or other psychoactive substances*." The Moral Basis of the Insanity Defense, 69 A.B.A.J. 194, 197 (1983). What would be the result in *Kelly* under this formulation? In *Sexton*?

## 6. PATHOLOGICAL INTOXICATION: THE PROBLEM OF UNANTICIPATED EFFECTS

Section 2.08(4) of the Model Penal Code provides that intoxication resulting in substantial cognitive or volitional incapacity is a defense if it is not self-induced or if it "is pathological." Paragraph 5(c) defines "pathological intoxication" as "intoxication grossly excessive in degree, given the amount of the intoxicant, to which the actor does not know he is susceptible."

Standing alone, this particular clinical condition is not especially important; it is extremely rare, if it exists at all,[g] and has arisen in litigation only a handful of times.[h] However, it may be useful to ask whether the

[g] The 1980 edition of the psychiatric diagnostic manual, DSM–III, included a diagnosis for pathological intoxication (labeled "alcohol idiosyncratic intoxication"). The essential feature of the diagnosis was said to be "marked behavioral change—usually to aggressiveness—that is due to the recent ingestion of alcohol insufficient to induce intoxication in most people." However, the diagnosis was omitted in the DSM–IV "because of lack of supporting evidence that it is distinct from [the diagnosis of] alcohol intoxication."

[h] For a case involving a successful claim of pathological intoxication, see Leggett v. State, 21 Tex.App. 382, 17 S.W. 159 (1886). For a recent case in which the claim was rejected, see Kane v. United States, 399 F.2d 730 (9th Cir. 1968). Kane was convicted of manslaughter in the killing of his wife. His condition was diagnosed as pathological intoxication by three of four expert psychiatrists and his medical history was strongly supportive of the diagnosis. Kane had suffered three head injuries, including one several months before the shooting. However, in dictum, the court observed that Kane's testimony showed that he had become aware, after the second injury, of the fact that a modest amount of alcohol would cause him to black out and experience amnesia, and that these effects intensified after the third injury.

quoted provision in § 2.08 stands for a more general proposition. Note that pathological intoxication represents the single instance in which the drafters of the Model Code endorsed a claim of excuse based on the direct effects of intoxication by a person who knowingly and voluntarily ingests an intoxicating substance in order to experience its intoxicating properties. In this sense, the provision qualifies the definition of self-induced intoxication. Consider a general statement of this principle: "An extreme mental impairment which could not reasonably have been anticipated will not be regarded as self-induced even though the individual was aware of the tendency of the substance to cause intoxication." Is this better?

Jerome Hall made a similar proposal in General Principles of Criminal Law 554–56 (2d ed. 1966), arguing that the "inexperienced inebriate" should not be held criminally liable for a harm committed under "gross intoxication"—a condition characterized by "severe blunting of the capacity to understand the moral quality of the act in issue combined with a drastic lapse of inhibition." He explained:

> [S]ince drinking alcoholic liquor is not usually followed by gross intoxication and such intoxication does not usually lead to the commission of serious injuries, it follows that persons who commit them while grossly intoxicated should not be punished unless, at the time of sobriety and the voluntary drinking, they had such prior experience as to anticipate their intoxication and that they would become dangerous in that condition.

The commentators generally have been unenthusiastic about Hall's proposal. They have emphasized the practical difficulties involved, and have argued that awareness of the dangers of gross intoxication does not depend on personal experience. Monrad Paulsen's reaction was typical: "Our culture does not fail to give warning about drunkenness. The risks involved are so widely advertised that few can claim surprise and be believed." Does the "culture" give adequate warning to naive users of the potpourri of psychoactive drugs now so widely used? The dissenting judges in the *Hall* case did not think so:

> . . . There is nothing to indicate [that Hall] knew [the drug] could induce hallucinations or lead to the frightening, debilitating effects of mind and body to which the doctors testified. The majority nevertheless holds [that] the defendant's resulting drug intoxication was voluntary. I disagree. . . .
>
> [The term] voluntary as here used should relate to acknowledgeable acceptance of the danger and risk involved. . . .

Is this a better view? What is the Model Penal Code solution to such a case?

## NOTES ON MEDICAL CONDITIONS THAT IMPAIR CONSCIOUSNESS

### 1. FORMS OF IMPAIRED CONSCIOUSNESS

As studied in Chapter II, criminal liability must be based on conduct that includes a voluntary act. Classic illustrations of involuntary movements include those that occur during a stroke, an epileptic seizure, or some other neurological disturbance. In other recognized instances of involuntariness, however, some link between mind and body remains, but that link is sufficiently attenuated to preclude criminal responsibility. These situations characteristically involve disturbances of consciousness in persons who retain the capacity to engage in goal-directed conduct based on prior learned responses. Two important examples are concussion and somnambulism.[a] Because conscious awareness of one's acts is absent during such episodes, such behavior may be said to be "automatic" and the individual so afflicted an "automaton." Hence the law sometimes has dealt with such conditions under the rubric of "automatism" even though use of this term is medically appropriate only in cases of epilepsy. The following notes describe some medical conditions characterized by impaired consciousness and explore the implications of these conditions for criminal liability.[b]

## 2. CONCUSSION

Temporary brain damage due to physical trauma sometimes produces a "black-out" or "confusional state," during which a person may engage in previously learned behavior without full awareness thereof. An example is the football player who continues to go through the motions of the game even though he is not consciously aware of his actions and does not remember them afterwards. Moreover, concussion can compromise the functioning of those brain centers that mediate and inhibit behavioral manifestation of emotion. A person who injures another while in such a state may do what he or she (unconsciously) wanted to do but would not have done had there been conscious control over the behavior. Some courts have found such conduct to be involuntary.[c]

## 3. EPILEPSY

Epilepsy is a chronic neurological disorder characterized by recurring seizures. During a seizure there is brief but strong electrical activity in the brain, affecting mental and physical functioning, typically resulting in a state of grossly disturbed consciousness. After a seizure, during the phase known as "postictal," an epileptic person might experience confusion and disorientation before returning to a state of normal functioning. In rare instances, harmful conduct can occur during this phase before consciousness has been fully recovered. A Virginia prosecution illustrates the excruciating questions that such cases can create for the criminal justice system.

A baby was found dead in a microwave oven. The medical evidence established that the baby was in the oven for at least 10 minutes and had died from thermal injuries caused by overheating of the blood. The infant's mother had a long, well-documented history of epilepsy, and she claimed that she had no recollection of the events immediately preceding the baby's death. She stated that she got up in the middle of the night to feed the baby, that she could remember sitting on the couch burping him, and that she

---

[a] Although intoxication by alcohol or other drugs that depress the central nervous system can result in profound impairment of consciousness, voluntary intoxication, no matter how severe, does not erase criminal liability, as illustrated by DPP v. Majewski in Chapter III. However, a defense of "involuntary intoxication" may be raised in connection with an unforeseeable impairment of consciousness attributable to use of prescription drugs, as described in the preceding Notes on Intoxication and Insanity.

[b] For an elaborate analysis of the voluntary act doctrine, and a proposed reformulation of the Model Penal Code provision, see Deborah W. Denno, Crime and Consciousness: Science and Involuntary Acts, 87 Minn. L. Rev 269 (2002).

[c] See Regina v. Wakefield, 75 W.N. 66 (New South Wales 1957); Coates v. Regina, 96 C.L.R. 353 (1957); Regina v. Minor, 112 Can. Crim. Cases 29 (1959).

must then have suffered a grand-mal seizure after which she mistakenly placed the baby in the oven.

In the immediate aftermath of the death, epilepsy experts divided over the question of whether the mother could have committed the killing unconsciously. Epileptic seizures sometimes are followed by trance-like states, which can last for as long as 30 minutes. Yet, some experts dismissed the mother's claim as implausible, arguing that the most the sufferer can do during the trance is perform "simple repetitive actions." Other experts disagreed, saying that a person in such a trance is "able to carry out complex tasks such as undressing, using a curling iron, even driving a car." Thus, they speculated that the mother may have dropped the baby during her seizure and then reacted to his cries "as an automaton," placing "him in the oven by accident as if he were a bottle.".

Initially, the prosecutor believed that the woman was lying about the seizure in order to cover up her murder of her baby, and he charged her with first-degree murder. A court-appointed neurologist evaluated the mother, and his video-taped findings tended to corroborate her story. In a test designed to simulate the activities that occurred on the night the baby died, the neurologist deprived the mother of her medication and kept her awake for three days. During the test, the woman had a seizure, after which she appeared to be in a "wide-eyed daze," indeed, to be so bewildered that she was unable to recognize her mother. More important, while she was in the trance, the woman was "able to operate a tape recorder without much trouble—but also without much comprehension of what she [was] doing." After viewing the videotape, the prosecutor concluded that there was doubt about the mother's state of mind at the time of the killing. As he put it in comments made to the press, "I was convinced that she maliciously killed the child—until I saw that tape. . . . It created doubt for me, and I had to wonder how the jury would respond. I am not convinced it was an accident, but I will accept the concept it could have been an accident." As the case was on the verge of going to trial, the prosecutor reduced the charge to involuntary manslaughter, to which the mother entered a "no contest plea."[d]

## 4. SOMNAMBULISM (SLEEP DISORDERS)

There is a well-recognized continuum of sleep disorders, ranging from ordinary nightmares to sleepwalking to a more severe form of disturbance known as "night terrors."[e] During mild sleepwalking episodes, the "sleeping" person may move about, although generally in a poorly coordinated, automatic manner. "Night terrors" are characterized by extreme fear and panic, intense vocalization, and frenzied motor activity. Aberrant behavior, including violence, can occur. Moreover, any interference with a person experiencing a somnambulistic episode may precipitate a violent reaction. The courts have generally regarded acts committed during such episodes as involuntary. In one famous English case, an 1859 grand jury refused

[d] For accounts of this case, see Craig Timberg, Mother Charged in Baby's Oven Death, The Washington Post, Sept. 28, 1999, at B1; Josh White, Baby's Death Stirs Debate on Illness vs. Intent in Va., The Washington Post, Jan. 28, 2001, at C1. Josh White, Va. Mother Gets 5 Years in Microwave Death, The Washington Post, Dec. 14, 2000, at B2.

[e] See generally Karl Doghramji, Solange Margery Bertoglia & Clarence Watson, *Forensic Aspects of the Parasomnias*, *in* PARASOMNIAS 463, 469 (Sanjeev V. Kothare & Anna Ivanenko eds., 2013).

to indict a woman who, after dreaming that her house was on fire, arose in a panic, screamed "Save my children!," and threw her baby out the window.[f]

A more recent case involved Kenneth Parks, a 23-year-old Toronto man, who was suffering from insomnia caused by joblessness and debt. After falling asleep on the couch, late one evening, Parks drove to the house of his parents-in-law, entered with his key, stabbed to death his mother-in-law (with whom he had a loving relationship) and assaulted his father-in-law. He then drove to the police station and said "I think I have killed some people," but was unable to relate any details. In his subsequent murder trial, he raised an unconsciousness defense, ("non-insane automatism"). An expert in sleep disorders testified that Parks was experiencing a somnambulistic episode at the time of the offense and that his apparently goal-directed conduct had not been consciously motivated. In reaching this conclusion, the expert relied on his well-documented history of childhood sleep disorders, the escalation of intense psychological stress during the period leading up to the episode, the absence of any anger or hostility toward the family victims, the occurrence an extended period of complex, goal-directed behavior followed by an observed period of mental confusion without any attempt to cover up the crime, and his profound amnesia for the event. Parks was acquitted of both the murder and the assault. On appeal, the decision was upheld by the Canadian Supreme Court. R. v. Parks, [1990] 56 C.C.C. (3d) 449, aff'd [1992] 75 C.C.C. (3d) 287 (1992). See Rosalind Cartwright, Sleepwalking Violence: A Sleep Disorder, a Legal Dilemma, and a Psychological Challenge, 161 Am. J. Psychiat. 7 (2004).

### 5. HYPOGLYCEMIA

There are other situations involving impaired consciousness for which the sufficiency of the "link between mind and body" appears to be an open question. One such instance concerns the behavioral effects of hypoglycemia, or abnormally low blood sugar. Because blood sugar is the exclusive source of energy for brain metabolism, hypoglycemia can lead to impaired functioning of the central nervous system. This condition usually arises when a diabetic takes too much insulin or fails to get sufficient food or sleep. It can also occur, however, in a non-diabetic but biologically susceptible individual whose blood sugar is reduced by starvation or muscular overexertion. In many such cases, the condition is precipitated by the ingestion of alcohol. Hypoglycemic symptoms include tremors, poor coordination, confusion, and irritation. Although the condition may be associated with aggressive behavior, current understanding does not permit confident generalization about the effect of hypoglycemia on control over one's conduct.[g] The question, simply put, is whether this condition differs significantly from any of a number of other metabolic conditions that may lower

---

[f] This case is described in Nigel Walker, Crime and Insanity in England 168–69 (1968). Other well-known somnambulism cases include Fain v. Commonwealth, 78 Ky. 183 (1879), and H.M. Advocate v. Fraser, 4 Couper 70 (Scotland 1878). For an especially intriguing case, see Norval Morris, Somnambulistic Homicide: Ghosts, Spiders and North Koreans, 5 Res. Judicatae 29 (1959).

[g] See generally Anthony Whitlock, Some Medicolegal Consequences of Hypoglycaemia in Robert Bluglass and Paul Bowden (eds.), Principles and Practice of Forensic Psychiatry 287–90 (1990). For a recent case in which a claim of hypoglycemia was rejected by a Texas jury in a prosecution for assaulting a police officer, see Mendenhall v. State, 77 S.W.3d 815 (Tex. Crim. App., 2002).

a person's threshold for aggressive behavior without rendering such conduct involuntary.

## 6. IMPAIRED CONSCIOUSNESS DUE TO PRESCRIBED MEDICATION

An increasing number of cases in recent decades have involved impairments of consciousness due to prescribed medications. Although these cases are typically analyzed as "involuntary act" claims, they are analytically similar to some of the "involuntary intoxication" claims covered in the previous set of notes because the focal issue is typically whether the defendant was aware of, or ought to have been aware of, the risk that the medications would impair consciousness. Many of these cases involve zolpidem, a widely prescribed sleep medication available in the United States since 1992 that has been associated not only with falling asleep at the wheel but also with impairments of consciousness involving complex behaviors such as sleep driving and sleep walking. See generally, Christopher Daley, Dale E. McNiel & Renee L. Binder, *"I Did What"? Zolpidem and the Courts*, 39 J. of Amer. Acad. Psychiat. & Law 535 (2011). For example, in Fortune v. State, 110 So.3d 831 (Miss. Ct. App 2013), defendant accused of fondling an eleven-year-old girl contended that he experienced somnambulism (sleepwalking) after taking zolpidem, but the court held that an instruction was not required because he had taken the drug in conjunction with a muscle relaxant contrary to express instructions of the pharmacist. See also the highly publicized case in which Kerry Kennedy was acquitted of "driving under the influence" after one hour of jury deliberation based on her uncontested testimony that she had mistakenly taken zolpidem thinking it was her thyroid medication.[h]

Many hypoglycemia cases are best analyzed from this perspective because the diabetic defendants are usually under treatment and the central legal issue is often whether the defendant failed to monitor blood glucose levels or manage them properly with insulin. For an excellent discussion of this problem, see John Rumbold & Martin Wasik, *Diabetic Drivers, Hypoglycemic Unawareness, and Automatism*, 11 Crim. L. Rev. 863, 866 (2011), commenting on R. v. Clarke [2009] EWCA Crim. 921, in which a 49-year-old man with a faultless 30-year history of monitoring his blood glucose levels and managing his condition, suffered a hypoglycemic episode while driving, killing a 4-year old pedestrian. The central issue in the case, according to Rumbold and Wasik, was "whether the defendant at some stage had been aware that he was suffering a hypoglycemic attack and had nevertheless continued to drive or whether his medical condition, including his hypoglycemic unawareness, impaired his cognitive ability to the extent that he was not aware."

## 7. DISPOSITIONAL ISSUES

On April 10, 2012, New York City police responded to a 911 call and found Karyn Kay in a pool of blood on her Manhattan kitchen floor—her eye socket, skull, and ribs fractured. Kay told emergency operators that her

[h] Joseph Berger & Marc Santora, *As Kennedy Trial Opens, Questions on Awareness of a Drug's Effects*, N.Y. Times, Feb. 24 2014, available at http://www.nytimes.com/2014/02/25/nyregion/kerry-kennedy-trial-opens-with-questions-about-her-awareness-of-sleeping-aids-effect.html; Joseph Berger, *Fast Acquittal for Kennedy, Whose Name Put Prosecutors in Bind*, N.Y. Times, Feb. 28 2014, *available at* http://www.nytimes.com/2014/03/01/nyregion/kerry-kennedy-is-found-not-guilty-of-driving-while-impaired.html.

nineteen-year-old son, Henry Wachtel, was having an epileptic seizure and was "coming after" her. At the end of the 911 tape, after several minutes of screaming, Henry Wachtel could be heard pleading with his mother, asking her "Mommy, Mommy, please don't die." Her original reason for the call was to seek assistance with her son's epileptic seizure. When police arrived they found Henry Wachtel at the scene "wild eyed" and "covered in blood"; his only response to their question of what had happened was "[i]t was a mistake." Wachtel, a freshman at Fordham, was charged with second degree murder. According to the expert reports in the case, summarized by the prosecution at the time of the court's judgment two years later, the killing took place immediately after Wachtel had experienced a seizure while he was in "postictal state" (neither fully conscious nor unconscious, that follows a seizure and can involve confusion and anxiety. Wachtel had no recollection of the period during which he killed his mother. The evidence also showed that Wachtel had taken the medication prescribed for his epilepsy. Based on this evidence, is this a clear case of automatism? What should the disposition be in such a case? Should a defendant acquitted on the basis of unconsciousness be subject to an automatic commitment order like a defendant acquitted by reason of insanity?

American courts have generally held that defendants who successfully raise an unconsciousness defense are not "insane" and should go free like any other acquitted defendant. For recent cases, see, e.g., Smith v. State, 284 Ga. 33, 663 S.E.2d 155 (2008); State v. Bush, 164 N.C.App. 254, 595 S.E.2d 715 (2004); Mendenhall v. State, 77 S.W.3d 815 (Tex. Crim. App., 2002). However, courts in the United Kingdom and Canada have taken a different approach. In Bratty v. Attorney General for Northern Ireland (1963), the House of Lords distinguished between epilepsy (which it characterized as an "insane automatism") and other medical conditions that may produce unconsciousness, such as a concussion. This was designed to bring epilepsy within the reach of commitment statutes for insanity acquittees. Is this a sensible approach to the problem? Are people with epilepsy 'insane'? What about people with sleeping disorders? In a case in the UK, Brian Thomas was acquitted of murder and released after he strangled his wife during a nightmare in which he dreamed he was protecting his wife from intruders in the van where they were sleeping. See The Times of London, November 21, 2009. For discussion of these dispositional issues, see R.D. Mackay, Mental Condition Defenses in the Criminal Law 1–73 (1995).

As this review suggests, the typical disposition in a case involving epileptic automatism in the United States is acquittal and release. However, according to the agreement reached in Henry Wachtel's case, he was found "not responsible by reason of mental disease or defect" (the name for the NGRI plea in New York) and was advised by the trial court that he would be "confined in a secure facility for what could be the rest of your life." He was then released from custody and transferred to a private inpatient treatment center, to be followed by an indeterminate commitment to the New York Office of Mental Health under the NGRI dispositional statute. In support of the plea agreement and judgment, the prosecutor emphasized that Wachtel had a substantial history of illegal drug use, including heroin, cocaine, PCP and LSD, that he had taken medication for ADHD since he was 12, that he had been prescribed increasing doses of epilepsy medications to control his seizures which might have had psychiatric side effects, and that he had a deteriorating relationship with his mother including fantasies of violence, during the period leading up to the offense.[i] Did the parties reach a sensible disposition in this case? Was it a lawful one?

## SUBSECTION D: MENTAL ABNORMALITY AND MENS REA

### INTRODUCTORY NOTES ON THE MEANING OF DIMINISHED RESPONSIBILITY

#### 1. INTRODUCTION

The terms "diminished capacity" and "diminished responsibility"[a] appear frequently in judicial opinions and scholarly commentary. The terms have no generally recognized meanings, however, and have been used interchangeably to refer to two distinct concepts.

#### 2. RULE OF LOGICAL RELEVANCE

In this country, courts often use the terms "diminished capacity" and "diminished responsibility" to refer to the following rule of evidence: "Evidence of mental abnormality is admissible whenever it is logically relevant to disprove the existence of a mental state required by the definition of an offense or by its grading." As is developed in more detail below, many courts do not always follow this rule of evidence. They either exclude evidence of mental abnormality altogether or restrict its admissibility short of its full logical import, based on doubts as to its reliability and fear that its use will undermine the social-control functions of the criminal law.

The labels "diminished capacity" and "diminished responsibility" apparently have been used to refer to this evidentiary proposition because the legal effect of admitting such evidence normally is to permit a serious offense to be reduced in grade to a less serious offense, thereby "diminishing" the offender's legal responsibility for criminal conduct. For example, the premeditation and deliberation required for first-degree murder may be rebutted in a particular case by evidence of mental abnormality, but the defendant may still be guilty of second-degree murder or manslaughter. Use of the terms "diminished capacity" or "diminished responsibility" to describe this result is misleading, however, because the terms carry the implication that "diminished capacity" or "diminished responsibility" can be proved by showing a "partial" incapacity in contrast to the "total" incapacity of insanity. As the materials on the insanity defense have demonstrated, however, mens rea requirements in the definition of criminal offenses may not be directly related to the criteria of non-responsibility used by the insanity defense. In particular, defendants found legally insane typically have the state of mind required for conviction of the most serious offense charged. On the other hand, in some instances, a mentally abnormal person

---

[i] See http://www.nytimes.com/2014/10/07/nyregion/under-plea-man-is-found-not-responsible-in-mothers-2012-killing.html?_r=0

[a] For discussion of the different meanings of diminished responsibility, see Stephen Morse, Undiminished Confusion in Diminished Capacity, 75 J.Crim.L. and Criminology 1 (1984); Susan F. Mandiberg, Protecting Society and Defendants Too: The Constitutional Dilemma of Mental Abnormality and Intoxication Defenses, 53 Ford.L.Rev. 221 (1984); Stephen Morse, Diminished Capacity: A Moral and Legal Conundrum, 2 Int'l J. of Law & Psychiatry 271 (1979); Peter Arenella, The Diminished Capacity and Diminished Responsibility Defenses: Two Children of a Doomed Marriage, 77 Colum.L.Rev. 827 (1977).

shown to lack the required mens rea may not satisfy the requirements of the insanity defense.

In any event, the question raised by American cases decided under the "diminished capacity" rubric, simply put, is whether and under what circumstances evidence of mental abnormality should be admissible on mens rea issues. This is the question to which the cases and notes in this subsection are addressed.

### 3. PARTIAL RESPONSIBILITY

The term "diminished responsibility" is sometimes—and more appropriately—used to refer to the idea that the law should recognize that some offenders are not fully responsible for their crimes even though they are not entitled to exculpation and even though they had the mens rea required for conviction. Those who are only "partly responsible" in this sense would be entitled to a formal mitigation of their crime to a lesser offense. When used in this way, "diminished responsibility" refers to a substantive limitation on criminal liability rather than an evidentiary rule. Thus, a person found to be legally sane and to have had the requisite intent might nonetheless be regarded as being only partly responsible for the crime because of the disabling effects of mental abnormality. If an intermediate or partial degree of cognitive or volitional impairment is to have independent grading significance, this will call for a "test" of diminished responsibility to supplement the test of insanity.

No American jurisdiction has explicitly adopted this approach to the grading of any criminal offense, including homicide.[b] However, it is reflected in the criteria used in several states for the verdict of "guilty but mentally ill,"[c] in the current generation of death penalty statutes,[d] and in modern sentencing statutes and guidelines.[e] It is discussed in these materials in those contexts.

## Ruffin v. State

Court of Criminal Appeals of Texas, 2008.
270 S.W.3d 586.

■ COCHRAN, J., delivered the opinion of the unanimous Court.

Appellant was charged with first-degree aggravated assault by shooting at ten police officers during an armed "standoff" on his rural property in Coryell County.[a] He contended that he was suffering from

---

[b] In England, a finding of diminished responsibility reduces murder to manslaughter. The English doctrine and related features of the law of homicide in this country are explored in Chapter X.

[c] See, for example, the provisions of the GBMI statutes in Alaska and Delaware quoted in the notes on this subject in Section 3.

[d] The criteria of diminished responsibility as used in modern capital sentencing statutes are discussed in Chapter XI.

[e] For example, § 5K2.13 of the United States Sentencing Guidelines authorizes a downward departure from the guideline sentence if the defendant "committed [a non-violent] offense while suffering from a significantly reduced mental capacity" and "there was a direct causal connection" between the reduced capacity and the offense. See, e.g., United States v. Fairless, 975 F.2d 664 (9th Cir. 1992), and the related notes on the volitional inquiry in Subsection B.

[a] Texas Penal Code Ann. provides in relevant part:

§ 22.02. Aggravated Assault

severe delusions and believed that he was shooting at Muslims, not police officers. He intended to shoot, but not at a public servant. The trial judge excluded testimony by appellant's psychologist about the existence and severity of his mental disease and delusions, ruling that such expert testimony is admissible only when the defendant is accused of homicide or pleads insanity. Appellant was convicted and sentenced to ten years' imprisonment on each of nine charges. The court of appeals affirmed the convictions and held that the trial judge did not abuse his discretion in excluding the expert testimony. We granted appellant's petition for discretionary review. We . . . hold that both lay and expert testimony of a mental disease or defect that directly rebuts the particular mens rea necessary for the charged offense is relevant and admissible unless excluded under a specific evidentiary rule.

I.

Late in the evening of April 14, 2005, one of appellant's neighbors called the Coryell Sheriff's Department to report gunshots from appellant's property. Deputy Carol Brown immediately headed for appellant's property. She had known appellant and his family for more than ten years and had once worked at his skating rink as a security guard. A month earlier, appellant's wife, Lavon, had told Carol that appellant's mental health was deteriorating. Deputy Brown had informed the sheriff's office of appellant's condition, so that evening two officers were dispatched to investigate the gunshots.

Deputy Paniagua arrived shortly after Deputy Brown, and they drove their patrol cars up the dirt driveway, through the woods, toward appellant's home. They parked and started to approach the house, with Deputy Brown calling out "Steve," so he would know that his friend Carol was there. She did not say that they were police officers. Two dogs ran up to them, one was bloody and looked like it had been shot. They heard gunshots from inside[5] and, shortly thereafter, they heard appellant yelling from the woods, "Get the hell out of here!" A few seconds later, they heard more shooting, so they ran back to Carol's patrol car, took cover behind the car door, and radioed for assistance. The

---

(a) A person commits an offense if the person commits assault as defined [elsewhere] and the person:

(1) causes serious bodily injury to another, including the person's spouse; or

(2) uses or exhibits a deadly weapon during the commission of the assault.

(b) An offense under this section is a felony of the second degree, except that the offense is a felony of the first degree if . . . .

(2) . . . the offense is committed . . .

(B) against a person the actor knows is a public servant while the public servant is lawfully discharging an official duty, or in retaliation or on account of an exercise of official power or performance of an official duty as a public servant; . . .

(c) The actor is presumed to have known the person assaulted was a public servant or a security officer if the person was wearing a distinctive uniform or badge indicating the person's employment as a public servant or status as a security officer.—[Footnote by eds.]

5 When the police finally entered appellant's home, they discovered that he had shot his guitar, a chair, and the walls of his home. They found that a third dog had died from gunshot wounds. They also found marijuana and marijuana pipes, four rifles, five handguns, and a considerable amount of ammunition.

wounded dog leapt into the patrol car and wouldn't get out. He kept stepping on the brake pedal, which turned on the brake lights and illuminated the officers hiding behind the patrol car door.

Deputy Brown continued to call out to appellant that "Carol" was here to check on his safety. Appellant yelled back, "Carol, is that you?" When she said "Yes," appellant shouted, "Carol, get the hell out of here before you get hurt." Deputy Paniagua got his AR-15 from his trunk, and the two officers waited for backup. Appellant kept yelling. He repeatedly shouted, "I'm declaring martial law. Carol, get out of here."

More officers arrived, and more shooting came from the wooded areas around appellant's house. At one point, appellant yelled to Carol that he was "jacking off." Deputy Brown thought this was unusual because appellant did not talk that way. He sounded bizarre and irrational. Another time he said that he would not be "coming out" unless there was a "bullet in his head." Throughout the night, appellant sporadically shot at the officers, but injured no one.[6] The officers, exhibiting restraint, never shot back. A DPS helicopter with heat-sensing equipment was dispatched, but appellant apparently shot at it, and the helicopter retreated. At dawn, SWAT officers and a police negotiation team arrived from Waco.

David Turner, appellant's best friend and closest neighbor, drove to the scene and offered to help, but the deputies yelled at him to leave. Mr. Turner told the deputies, "This is not Steve, you know, he doesn't do things like this."[7]

Around 11:00 a.m., the officers set up a special phone number for appellant's house. A hostage negotiator used a bullhorn to ask appellant to pick up his phone, saying that "Scott" wanted to talk to him. Appellant did so. He thought he was talking to a doctor, and, when "Scott" told him to come outside, he followed those instructions. Appellant appeared "startled" when he saw the police and patrol cars outside. He was taken into custody.

Several lay witnesses testified for the defense concerning appellant's mental status. His wife, Lavon, had worked as a lieutenant in the prison system for ten years. She said that appellant's moods worsened in the year before the standoff. He became obsessed with the color orange and thought that everything should be orange. He burned all of the pictures in his house that his mother had painted because they contained colors other than orange. He talked to the television set and thought that it talked back. He would pull his cigarette lighter out and say, "Okay, Johnny, I know you're listening to me," and stick it back in his shirt pocket. He took all of the appliances out of the house because

---

[6] Appellant shot out Deputy Brown's right front tire and, at some point, a bullet hit the side of her patrol car

[7] Mr. Turner told the jury that appellant was, at that time, having mental problems. He explained that appellant called him a few days before the standoff and asked him what his favorite color was. When Mr. Turner said, "Blue," appellant sharply replied, "No, it's orange." He went down to talk to appellant because he was in one of his "spells," but when Mr. Turner walked in the door, appellant held a dagger-like object to his chest and asked him again what his favorite color was. When he again said blue, appellant poked him with the dagger, so Mr. Turner grabbed it. Appellant pulled the dagger back and it cut Mr. Turner's fingers. Mr. Turner left, thinking that appellant had "lost his rocker" and "was in his own world." Appellant sounded like he was living in the past, said he had a castle in Scotland, and was heir to the throne.

they were bugged, and he wore a T-shirt with aluminum foil on it to protect himself from receiving signals from the tower. Lavon finally moved out of their home in March. When she talked to appellant the day before the standoff and he admitted that he needed to see a doctor, she agreed to come back home and help.

Appellant's mother, Reva Ruffin, testified that appellant had been taking Ritalin for the past year after his nephew was diagnosed with ADD and appellant thought that he, too, might be helped by that drug. Ms. Ruffin said that appellant loved Ritalin and thought it was a miracle drug that allowed him to read "like never before." A week before the standoff, she took him to see a psychiatrist, but appellant "fired" the doctor after talking to him for five minutes.

Appellant's nephew, Scotty, testified that, about two months before the standoff, appellant came to visit him in Austin and said that he was going to give Scotty a thousand orange helicopters when he received his kingdom. Scotty was scared because appellant was acting so bizarrely.

Appellant testified that he first realized that something was very wrong when, about a month before the standoff, he was in Gatesville and "the whole town was like a hippy town. It all had psychedelic colors throughout the whole—every building was a different color and just multicolored buildings." He started seeing everything in psychedelic colors. People on TV were communicating with him and ridiculing him. He explained that he had two different voices in his brain, like two towers broadcasting. "One was girls, female, the other one was boys, male. The girls were Christian, the boys were Muslim." They liked each other, but they hated appellant. On the day before the standoff, he stopped at the Sheriff's Department and asked for a badge because he was supreme commander of the whole world. Appellant testified that, on the night of April 14th, he heard a noise from his garage, located about 90 yards from his house, so he went down to investigate. He heard the voices of the boys and girls and "they were laughing at me and I thought it was real people that was stealing my stuff." He heard Carol when she first drove up, but didn't recognize her voice. He thought it was a trespasser, but when she hollered out that it was Carol, he told her that he didn't want to talk to her; "[G]o away, you're trespassing." He didn't see her uniform and didn't know she was acting in her official capacity as a police officer. "To me, she was just Lavon's friend." He said that he shot down at the ground so that she would go away. Then he "fell back to another position" down the dirt road "and I thought the Muslims was hunting me, so I was out there hiding in the bushes." He was shooting Muslims; there were hundreds of Muslims. He moved around a lot in the woods because it was dangerous to stay in one place. "I also do remember at one time I heard people in my house, around the back of my house, and it was Muslims. I fired several rounds on each side of the door. They were waiting to kill me with a knife." Eventually he went to sleep in the house. A doctor called him. He went out the back door, saw police cars outside, and thought he was hallucinating.

Appellant's attorney also made a proffer of the testimony of a psychologist, Dr. William Lee Carter, who said that, in his professional opinion, appellant had fallen into a deep depression in the months before the standoff and had become psychotic. He began to suffer from delusions, paranoid thinking, and irrationality. Dr. Carter had twice seen appellant in the county jail after the standoff, and then saw him three more times in his office. Dr. Carter explained that a person who is delusional typically believes that his delusions are true. And a person who is experiencing paranoia has

> beliefs that people are out to get him, a lot of suspiciousness, considerable mistrust. If that's the case, and I believe that it was with [appellant], then when people say or do things to him, he interprets what they say and do according to his irrational or paranoid thinking, so his response to them is going to be based on his own irrationality as opposed to the other person's more rational state of being.

Dr. Carter also thought that, on April 14th, appellant was suffering from psychotic symptoms such as hearing or seeing things that did not exist. However, he did not think that appellant suffered from schizophrenia because that disease is ongoing whereas appellant had, while he was segregated in jail, pulled himself together and returned to more normal function. Dr. Carter did not think that appellant was legally insane on April 14th, but that he was both delusional and paranoid and "was not fully aware of the effects his behavior was having on other people." He had a "diminished capacity" to make rational judgments.

After this proffer, the trial judge excluded Dr. Carter's testimony because

> [t]he insanity defense is what is indicated and dictated as our way of determining the capacity of the defendant to make a specific mens rea. The procedure for doing that is through the insanity defense.
>
> I think in essence what Doctor Carter's testimony is, is geared toward [appellant's] ability or capacity to make that determination on the night in question. As such, I think it is in effect an insanity defense. I am going to disallow his testimony for those purposes. I do find that under [the rules of evidence] it would be more confusing to the jury because they would tend to interpret it as an insanity defense which has not been raised. And without notice, the State, of course, does not have any experts available to testify on that subject.

Dr. Carter did testify during the sentencing stage.

On appeal, appellant claimed that the trial court abused its discretion in excluding Dr. Carter's testimony that, because of mental illness and delusions, appellant did not know that he was shooting at law-enforcement officers. He argued that Dr. Carter's testimony would support his theory that he was guilty only of the lesser-included offense of second-degree aggravated assault.[8] The court of appeals stated that appellant offered Dr. Carter's testimony not to establish an insanity defense, but to negate the mens rea element of knowing that the persons he was shooting at were police officers.

---

8 The trial judge, based on appellant's testimony and that of the lay witnesses, instructed the jury on the lesser-included offense. He also instructed the jury that "[t]he defendant is presumed to have known the person assaulted was a public servant if he was wearing a distinctive uniform or badge indicating his or her employment as a public servant."

[T]he court of appeals concluded that evidence of a mental illness or defect that negates the mens rea of an offense is admissible only in a murder trial.

II.

Texas law, like that of all American jurisdictions, presumes that a criminal defendant is sane and that he intends the natural consequences of his acts. Texas law, like that of many American jurisdictions, excuses a defendant from criminal responsibility if he proves, by a preponderance of the evidence, the affirmative defense of insanity.[14] This defense excuses the person from criminal responsibility even though the State has proven every element of the offense, including the mens rea, beyond a reasonable doubt.[15] The test for determining insanity is whether, at the time of the conduct charged, the defendant—as a result of a severe mental disease or defect—did not know that his conduct was "wrong." Under Texas law, "wrong" in this context means "illegal."[17] Thus, the question for deciding insanity is this: Does the defendant factually know that society considers this conduct against the law, even though the defendant, due to his mental disease or defect, may think that the conduct is morally justified?

Insanity is the only "diminished responsibility" or "diminished capacity" defense to criminal responsibility in Texas. These "diminished" mental-state defenses, if allowed, would permit exoneration or mitigation of an offense because of a person's supposed psychiatric compulsion

---

[14] Texas Penal Code § 8.01(a) ("It is an affirmative defense to prosecution that, at the time of the conduct charged, the actor, as a result of severe mental disease or defect, did not know that his conduct was wrong.").

[15] Commentators have frequently noted that "persons crazy enough to be legally insane are not necessarily lacking mens rea. Even defendants who are most demonstrably legally insane rarely lack the mens rea for the highest charged offense." Stephen J. Morse, Undiminished Confusion in Diminished Capacity, 75 J. Crim. L. & Criminology 1, 18 (1984). Or, as another commentator has explained,

> There is no necessary connection between a judgment about the defendant's criminal responsibility and his mental capacity to entertain the state of mind required by the crime. As long as the mens rea element is defined in terms of the conscious mind, cognitive and affective functions, it is perfectly plausible that the defendant entertained the specific mental state but was still insane. In fact, most mentally abnormal offenders are fully capable of thinking about their criminal act before they do it, turning it over in their minds, planning the act, and then performing it in accordance with their preconceived plan. Evidence of how [a defendant's] mental abnormality impaired his behavior controls or made it difficult for him to appreciate the act's gravity does not negate the existence of the required mental states; it merely explains them.

Peter Arenella, The Diminished Capacity and Diminished Responsibility Defenses: Two Children of a Doomed Marriage, 77 Colum. L. Rev. 827, 834 (1977).

[17] In Bigby v. State, 892 S.W.2d 864, 878 (Tex. Crim. App. 1994), we explained,

> Several expert witnesses testified appellant knew his conduct was illegal, however, these experts contended that appellant did not know the act was "morally" wrong. In other words, appellant believed that regardless of society's views about this illegal act and his understanding it was illegal, under his "moral" code it was permissible. This focus upon appellant's morality is misplaced. The question of insanity should focus on whether a defendant understood the nature and quality of his action and whether it was an act he ought to do. By accepting and acknowledging his action was "illegal" by societal standards, he understood that others believed his conduct was "wrong."

or an inability to engage in normal reflection or moral judgment.[18] Such defenses refer to a person's lesser or impaired mental ability (compared to the average person) to reason through the consequences of his actions because of a mental disorder.[20] The Texas Legislature has not enacted any affirmative defenses, other than insanity, based on mental disease, defect, or abnormality. Thus, they do not exist in Texas.

But both physical and mental diseases or defects may affect a person's perception of the world just as much as they may affect his rational understanding of his conduct or his capacity to make moral judgments. For example, suppose that a blind person is sitting on his front porch and hears what he thinks is a trespasser coming up his walk. He shoots at the person to scare him away, knowing that it is illegal to shoot at people, even trespassers. The "trespasser" turns out to be a uniformed police officer who is coming to serve a subpoena. The blind man may be prosecuted for aggravated assault with a deadly weapon, but he cannot be convicted of aggravated assault of a police officer if, because of his blindness, he did not see the uniform and did not know that the person was a police officer. Evidence of the defendant's blindness would, of course, be relevant and admissible to rebut the State's assertion that the defendant intended to shoot at a police officer. Such evidence might be elicited from the defendant, a lay witness—mother, brother, friend, or neighbor—or from an expert, an optometrist, physician, etc. Courts routinely admit evidence of a physical abnormality offered to prove a lack of mens rea.

In Texas, the same rule applies to evidence of a mental disease or defect offered to rebut or disprove the defendant's culpable mens rea. If, instead of blindness, the defendant suffers from mental delusions such that he sees a "trespasser" or a "Muslim" when everyone else around him sees a police officer, he cannot be convicted of intentionally shooting at a police officer, although he may be convicted of intentionally shooting at a trespasser or Muslim. Guilt of the greater offense requires that the State prove, beyond a reasonable doubt, that the defendant intended to shoot a police officer,[25] not a trespasser or Muslim. That is the required mens rea and that is the State's constitutional burden of proof.[26]

The defendant's right to present a defense generally includes the due-process right to the admission of competent, reliable, exculpatory

---

[18] See, e.g., United States v. Pohlot, 827 F.2d 889, 890 (3d Cir. 1987) (explaining those concepts and noting that Congress precluded the assertion of a "diminished responsibility" or "diminished capacity" defense in its 1984 Insanity Defense Reform Act).

[20] The court in *Pohlot* quoted the House Judiciary Committee's discussion of the distinction between the "diminished capacity" defense and the use of evidence of a mental disorder to negate mens rea.

The use of mental disorder to negate mental state elements of crimes should not be confused with the "diminished capacity" defense as developed by the California courts during the 1960's and 1970's. Under that doctrine, a defendant could escape responsibility for a crime by demonstrating not that he or she lacked a required specific intent, but rather that his or her capability of entertaining that intent was not, because of mental disorder, commensurate with that of nondisordered persons.

[25] See Texas Penal Code § 22.02(b)(2)(B) (aggravated assault is a second-degree felony, except that it is a felony of the first degree if it is committed "against a person the actor knows is a public servant while the public servant is lawfully discharging an official duty").

[26] In re Winship, 397 U.S. 358 (1970). . . . [*Winship* and the body of law it germinated are discussed in Chapter XII.]—[Addition to Footnote by eds.]

evidence to rebut any of those elements. Indeed, the Supreme Court has repeatedly struck down "arbitrary rules that prevent whole categories of defense witnesses from testifying."[27] Quite recently, however, the Supreme Court upheld Arizona's wholesale exclusion of expert psychiatric testimony concerning mental illness offered to rebut proof of the defendant's mens rea.[28]

This Court, however, had already held that such expert evidence might be relevant, reliable, and admissible to rebut proof of the defendant's mens rea.[29] We, like the dissenting justices in *Clark*,[30] have confidence that our Texas judges and juries are sufficiently sophisticated to evaluate expert mental-disease testimony in the context of rebutting mens rea just as they are in evaluating an insanity or mental-retardation claim. Of course, such evidence may, in a particular case, be

---

[27] See Rock v. Arkansas, 483 U.S. 44 (1987) (striking down a state rule that prevented the defendant from testifying because she had previously been hypnotized and questioned about the issues); Crane v. Kentucky, 476 U.S. 683 (1986) (reversing conviction because of state judicial rule excluding evidence of the circumstances surrounding the defendant's confession); Chambers v. Mississippi, 410 U.S. 284 (1973) (ordering new trial because of, *inter alia*, state evidentiary rule excluding adverse witness's out-of-court confession); Washington v. Texas, 388 U.S. 14 (1967) (striking down Texas statute prohibiting testimony of defendant's alleged accomplice).

[28] Clark v. Arizona, 548 U.S. 735 (2006). In *Clark*, the Supreme Court addressed whether Arizona's judicially crafted state rule excluding evidence of a defendant's mental disorder short of insanity to negate the mens rea element of a crime violated federal due process. Clark was charged with the intentional murder of a police officer. His defensive theories were that he was legally insane at the time of the killing and that he was operating under the paranoid delusion that "aliens" were "trying to kill him, and bullets were the only way to stop them." The trial court allowed the defendant to offer a wealth of lay "observational" testimony concerning his mental illness and delusions and admitted extensive psychiatric evidence bearing on the affirmative defense of insanity. After hearing all of the evidence, the trial court rejected the insanity defense and found the defendant guilty of the intentional murder. The state appellate court found that the trial court could, under Arizona law, exclude Clark's evidence of mental illness to rebut the requisite criminal intent, and the Supreme Court affirmed that holding.

The Supreme Court indicated that lay and expert "observational" testimony was both relevant and admissible "to show what in fact was on Clark's mind when he fired the gun." Nonetheless, the Court stated that Arizona courts could, consistent with the due-process clause, exclude "mental-disease" evidence offered for purposes of rebutting mens rea because of (i) the controversial character of some categories of mental disease; (ii) the potential of mental-disease evidence to mislead; and (iii) the danger of according greater certainty to "capacity" evidence than experts claim for it. Thus, states that decline to admit such expert mental-disease evidence to rebut mens rea do not violate the due-process clause. Conversely, no state is required to exclude such evidence.

[29] Jackson v. State, 160 S.W.3d 568 (Tex. Crim. App. 2005). [*Jackson* stated that "[a]s with the other elements of the offense, relevant evidence may be presented which the jury may consider to negate the mens rea element" and that, if otherwise admissible, "this evidence may sometimes include evidence of a defendant's history of mental illness."]—[Addition to Footnote by eds.]

[30] See Clark, 548 U.S. at 792–96 (Kennedy, J., joined by Stevens and Ginsburg, JJ., dissenting). Justice Breyer noted that a per se ban upon expert mental-disease testimony to rebut mens rea unduly restricts, if not prevents, the jury from making the factual determination of whether the defendant was "unaware that he was shooting a police officer." He noted that states already have the discretion to bar "unreliable or speculative testimony and to adopt rules to ensure the reliability of expert testimony." He stated that the risk of jury confusion did not justify the rule because [the rules of evidence provide] a mechanism to exclude specific expert testimony that is unfairly complex. "The difficulty of resolving a factual issue, though, does not present a sufficient reason to take evidence away from the jury even when it is crucial for the defense. 'We have always trusted juries to sort through complex facts in various areas of the law.' " And the fact that such evidence might be unduly complex and confusing in some cases does not justify an across-the-board ban.

excluded under other evidentiary rules . . . if the probative value of the proffered evidence is substantially outweighed by the danger of unfair prejudice, if the expert is insufficiently qualified, or the testimony is insufficiently relevant or reliable under our state's guidelines for expert testimony.[31] Such evidence may also be excluded if it does not truly negate the required mens rea.[32]

III.

In this case, the court of appeals applied a blanket ban against the admission of expert testimony offered to rebut appellant's mens rea at the time that he shot at the police officers. It stated that such evidence was inadmissible "because [appellant] was not being prosecuted for homicide and was not pursuing an insanity defense[.]" . . . We repeat and reaffirm our holding in Jackson v. State, 160 S.W. 3d 568, 574 (2005), that "relevant evidence may be presented which the jury may consider to negate the mens rea element. And this evidence may sometimes include evidence of a defendant's history of mental illness." . . .

The testimony proffered by Dr. Carter in this case is clearly relevant to the issue of whether appellant intended to shoot at police officers during the standoff or whether, because of a mental disease and the delusions that he suffered as a result of that disease, he believed that he was shooting at Muslims or some other figment of his mind. Although the trial judge permitted numerous lay witnesses, including appellant himself, to testify to "observational evidence" concerning appellant's mental breakdown and delusions, that evidence was never put into a mental-disease context or its psychological significance explained. But expert evidence that would explain appellant's mental disease and when and how paranoid delusions may distort a person's auditory and visual perceptions is admissible as it relates to whether appellant intended to shoot at police officers, unless that evidence is otherwise barred by evidentiary rules. . . .

We therefore reverse the judgment of the court of appeals and remand the case to that court for further proceedings consistent with this opinion.[b]

---

[31] . . . For example, in Hart v. State, 173 S.W.3d 131 (Tex. App. 2005), the court of appeals held that the trial court did not err in excluding defendant's expert testimony that, in her opinion, the defendant was acting under the influence of an alternate identity at the time of the offense and therefore could not have voluntarily or knowingly committed the offense, because he made no claim that he committed the offense while unconscious or in a semiconscious condition.

[32] See, e.g., United States v. Brown, 326 F.3d 1143, 1148 (10th Cir. 2003) (trial court properly excluded expert psychiatric testimony that, because of post-traumatic-stress syndrome and chemical dependency, defendant was unable to make "correct choices"; testimony did not rebut mens rea in prosecution for conspiracy to possess methamphetamine); United States v. Cameron, 907 F.2d 1051, 1067–68 (11th Cir. 1990) (stating, "Evidence offered as 'psychiatric evidence to negate specific intent' is admissible . . . when such evidence focuses on the defendant's specific state of mind at the time of the charged offense," but holding that defendant failed to demonstrate how her expert's generalized psychiatric testimony would negate intent in drug-trafficking prosecution); United States v. White, 766 F.2d 22, 24–25 (1st Cir. 1985) (upholding exclusion of expert psychiatric testimony "to the effect that, because of the influence exerted upon her by her mother, she was unable to resist her mother's request for assistance, and was thus compelled to aid her in her drug dealing" as merely evidence of a "diminished capacity" to control his conduct).

[b] The court added that the trial court had also rested its decision to exclude Dr. Carter's testimony on a finding that it would confuse jurors, who might interpret it as relating to an

## NOTES ON MENTAL ABNORMALITY AND MENS REA

### 1. THE RULE OF RELEVANCE

*Ruffin* takes the position that evidence of mental abnormality should be taken into account whenever it is logically relevant to the existence of the mental state required for conviction, irrespective of whether the defendant enters an insanity plea.[a] Section 4.02(1) of the Model Penal Code adopts the same approach: "Evidence that the defendant suffered from a mental disease or defect is admissible whenever it is relevant to prove that the defendant did or did not have a state of mind which is an element of the offense."

Proponents of this position typically argue that it is illogical and unfair to define mens rea in subjective terms but then to preclude defendants from introducing otherwise competent evidence to support the claim that they in fact did not have the required state of mind. This view has been summarized by Richard Bonnie and Christopher Slobogin, The Role of Mental Health Professionals in the Criminal Process: The Case For Informed Speculation, 66 Va.L.Rev. 427, 477 (1980):

> In a criminal case involving subjective mens rea requirements, the prosecution usually has no direct evidence concerning the defendant's state of mind; it must rely on "common sense" inferences drawn from the defendant's conduct. This has the practical effect of shifting the burden to the defendant to demonstrate that he did not perceive, believe, expect, or intend what an ordinary person would have perceived, believed, expected, or intended under the same circumstances. Restriction of clinical testimony on mens rea thus compromises the defendant's opportunity to present a defense on an issue concerning which he, in reality, bears the burden of proof. The factfinder is likely to view with considerable skepticism the defendant's claim that he did not function as would a normal person under the circumstances. The defendant must establish the plausibility of his claim of abnormality. By precluding the defendant from offering relevant expert testimony, the law unduly enhances the prosecution's advantage on this issue. For this reason, we believe the only limitations on admissibility of mens rea testimony by mental-health professionals should be relevance and the normal requirements for expert opinion.

What reasons might justify exclusion of the type of evidence admitted in *Ruffin* even if it is relevant? Recall that all jurisdictions restrict the admissibility of intoxication evidence considerably short of its logical import, although most jurisdictions do admit such evidence to negate purpose, knowledge, or "specific intent." Would it make sense to treat evidence of intoxication and evidence of mental abnormality on the same terms, admitting the evidence to negate "specific intent" but not otherwise? Some jurisdictions that admit evidence of intoxication to negate specific intent nonetheless exclude evidence of mental abnormality in cases where evidence of

---

insanity defense which had never been raised. It remanded the case to the court of appeals to allow that court an opportunity to review that part of its earlier ruling.—[Footnote by eds.]

[a] The note on mens rea and mental abnormality in Chapter III should be reviewed at this point for a summary of the historical background on this issue.

intoxication would be admitted. Are there good arguments in favor of this approach?

The modern trend is clearly in the direction of the rule of relevance stated in *Ruffin* and in the Model Penal Code. About one-fourth of the states have adopted a rule similar to § 4.02(1) and now admit evidence of mental abnormality in any case involving a subjective mens rea inquiry. Another third of the states admit such evidence whenever the offense requires "specific intent." In about one-fourth of the states, however, evidence of mental abnormality is excluded altogether unless it is offered in support of an insanity plea.

## 2. THE CASE FOR EXCLUSION: *CLARK V. ARIZONA*

The *Ruffin* Court refers to Clark v. Arizona, 548 U.S. 735 (2006). Clark was convicted of first-degree murder for knowingly killing a law enforcement officer in the line of duty. He did not contest the shooting but sought to show that, as a result of his delusional beliefs about aliens symptomatic of paranoid schizophrenia, he did not know that his victim was a police officer. The trial court ruled that he could introduce the evidence to show that he was legally insane, but could not rely on the same evidence to negate mens rea. After his conviction was affirmed by the Arizona courts, the United States Supreme Court, in a 5–4 decision, sustained Clark's conviction against a due process challenge. In the opinion for the Court, Justice Souter explained the state's reasons for excluding the evidence. He began by emphasizing the "presumption of sanity:"

> State law says that evidence of mental disease and incapacity may be introduced and considered, and if sufficiently forceful to satisfy the defendant's burden of proof under the insanity rule, it will displace the presumption of sanity and excuse from criminal responsibility. . . . Clark presses no objection to Arizona's decision to require persuasion to a clear and convincing degree before the presumption of sanity and normal responsibility is overcome. . . . But if a State is to have [the] authority [to impose such a demanding burden of persuasion in insanity cases], . . . it must be able to deny a defendant the opportunity to displace the presumption of sanity more easily when addressing a different issue in the course of the criminal trial. [J]ust such an opportunity would be available if expert testimony of mental disease and incapacity could be considered for whatever a factfinder might think it was worth on the issue of mens rea. [O]nce reasonable doubt was found, acquittal would be required, and the standards established for the defense of insanity would go by the boards. . . .

Justice Souter acknowledged the force of the argument that the excluded evidence might actually raise a reasonable doubt regarding the defendant's guilt of the offense charged, whether or not it proved affirmatively that he was not guilty by reason of insanity, and that one might therefore hold that "it thus violates due process when the State impedes him from using mental-disease and capacity evidence directly to rebut the prosecution's evidence that he did form mens rea." His response was to ask: "Are there . . . characteristics of mental-disease and capacity evidence giving rise to risks that may reasonably be hedged by channeling the consideration of such evidence to the insanity issue on which, in States like Arizona, a defendant has the burden of persuasion? We think there are." He continued:

> To begin with, the diagnosis may mask vigorous debate within the profession about the very contours of the mental disease itself. . . . Though we certainly do not "condem[n] mental-disease evidence wholesale," the consequence of this professional ferment is a general caution in treating psychological classifications as predicates for excusing otherwise criminal conduct.
>
> Next, there is the potential of mental-disease evidence to mislead jurors (when they are the factfinders) through the power of this kind of evidence to suggest that a defendant suffering from a recognized mental disease lacks cognitive, moral, volitional, or other capacity, when that may not be a sound conclusion at all. Even when a category of mental disease is broadly accepted and the assignment of a defendant's behavior to that category is uncontroversial, the classification may suggest something very significant about a defendant's capacity, when in fact the classification tells us little or nothing about the ability of the defendant to form mens rea or to exercise the cognitive, moral, or volitional capacities that define legal sanity. The limits of the utility of a professional disease diagnosis are evident in the dispute between the two testifying experts in this case; they agree that Clark was schizophrenic, but they come to opposite conclusions on whether the mental disease in his particular case left him bereft of cognitive or moral capacity. Evidence of mental disease, then, can easily mislead; it is very easy to slide from evidence that an individual with a professionally recognized mental disease is very different, into doubting that he has the capacity to form mens rea, whereas that doubt may not be justified. And of course, in the cases mentioned before, in which the categorization is doubtful or the category of mental disease is itself subject to controversy, the risks are even greater that opinions about mental disease may confuse a jury into thinking the opinions show more than they do. Because allowing mental-disease evidence on mens rea can thus easily mislead, it is not unreasonable to address that tendency by confining consideration of this kind of evidence to insanity, on which a defendant may be assigned the burden of persuasion.
>
> There are, finally, particular risks inherent in the opinions of the experts who supplement the mental-disease classifications with opinions on incapacity: on whether the mental disease rendered a particular defendant incapable of the cognition necessary for moral judgment or mens rea or otherwise incapable of understanding the wrongfulness of the conduct charged. Unlike observational evidence bearing on mens rea, capacity evidence consists of judgment, and judgment fraught with multiple perils: a defendant's state of mind at the crucial moment can be elusive no matter how conscientious the enquiry, and the law's categories that set the terms of the capacity judgment are not the categories of psychology that govern the expert's professional thinking. Although such capacity judgments may be given in the utmost good faith, their potentially tenuous character is indicated by the candor of the defense expert in this very case. Contrary to the

> State's expert, he testified that Clark lacked the capacity to appreciate the circumstances realistically and to understand the wrongfulness of what he was doing, but he said that "no one knows exactly what was on [his] mind" at the time of the shooting. And even when an expert is confident that his understanding of the mind is reliable, judgment addressing the basic categories of capacity requires a leap from the concepts of psychology, which are devised for thinking about treatment, to the concepts of legal sanity, which are devised for thinking about criminal responsibility. . . . In sum, these empirical and conceptual problems add up to a real risk that an expert's judgment in giving capacity evidence will come with an apparent authority that psychologists and psychiatrists do not claim to have. We think that this risk, like the difficulty in assessing the significance of mental-disease evidence, supports the State's decision to channel such expert testimony to consideration on the insanity defense, on which the party seeking the benefit of this evidence has the burden of persuasion.

Is this right? Do the risks of confusion and mistake attributable to mental health testimony on mens rea justify excluding the evidence on mens rea altogether? How do the pitfalls associated with this evidence compare with those presented by evidence of intoxication? Can these concerns be ameliorated by curtailing the testimony rather than excluding it? On the other hand, if these concerns about mental health testimony are so substantial, should the insanity defense itself be abolished?

### 3. *PEOPLE V. WETMORE*

An additional concern raised by unrestrained admission of relevant evidence of mental disorder on mens rea issues is that potentially dangerous offenders may be able to win outright acquittal of the criminal charges without being subject to the restrictive dispositional consequences that normally accompany an insanity verdict. The tension between subjective criteria of culpability and the social interest in control of dangerous persons is illustrated by the decision of the California Supreme Court in People v. Wetmore, 22 Cal.3d 318, 149 Cal.Rptr. 265, 583 P.2d 1308 (1978). Wetmore was charged with burglary. The evidence was summarized by the Supreme Court:

> [Joseph Cacciatore, the victim of the burglary] testified that he left his apartment on March 7, 1975. When he returned three days later, he discovered defendant in his apartment. Defendant was wearing Cacciatore's clothes and cooking his food. The lock on the front door had been broken; the apartment lay in a shambles. Cacciatore called the police, who arrested defendant for burglary. Later Cacciatore discovered that a ring, a watch, a credit card, and items of clothing were missing.[1]
>
> The psychiatric reports submitted to the court explain defendant's long history of psychotic illness, including at least 10 occasions of hospital confinement for treatment. According to the reports, defendant, shortly after his last release from [a V.A. hospital], found himself with no place to go. He began to believe that he "owned" property and was "directed" to Cacciatore's apartment.

[1] At the preliminary hearing defendant appeared wearing one of Cacciatore's shirts. . . .

> When he found the door unlocked he was sure he owned the apartment. He entered, rearranged the apartment, destroyed some advertising he felt was inappropriate, and put on Cacciatore's clothes. When the police arrived, defendant was shocked and embarrassed, and only then understood that he did not own the apartment. . . .

Wetmore argued that the psychiatric evidence showed that as a result of mental illness he lacked the specific intent required for conviction of burglary. The trial court acknowledged that the evidence might negate specific intent but concluded that, under the controlling precedents, "if a defendant's mental capacity which would preclude the forming of a specific intent is that of insanity," evidence of such a mental condition "is not admissible to establish . . . lack of specific intent due to diminished capacity." The court was also concerned that there was no lesser offense under California law for which Wetmore could be convicted if he were acquitted of burglary. It accordingly found Wetmore guilty of burglary as charged. Pursuant to California's bifurcated trial procedure, the court then considered the question of insanity and found Wetmore not guilty by reason of insanity. At a subsequent hearing, the trial court found that Wetmore "had not recovered his sanity" and ordered him committed.

The Supreme Court of California unanimously reversed the judgment:

> The state bears the burden of proving every element of the offense charged; defendant cannot logically or constitutionally be denied the right to present probative evidence rebutting an element of the crime merely because such evidence also suggests insanity. Defendant's evidence established that he entered an apartment under a delusion that he owned that apartment and thus did not enter with the intent of committing a theft or felony. That evidence demonstrated that defendant lacked the specific intent required for a conviction of burglary; the trial court's refusal to consider the evidence at the guilt phase of the trial therefore constituted prejudicial error.
>
> We reject the suggestion that we sustain the trial court by holding that a defense of diminished capacity cannot be raised whenever, owing to the lack of a lesser included offense, it might result in the defendant's acquittal. A defendant who, because of diminished capacity, does not entertain the specific intent required for a particular crime is entitled to be acquitted of that crime. If he cannot be convicted of a lesser offense and cannot safely be released, the state's remedy is to institute civil commitment proceedings, not to convict him of a specific-intent crime which he did not commit.

The court elaborated on its rejection of the argument that civil commitment provided inadequate social protection:

> A defendant whose criminal activity arises from mental disease or defect usually requires confinement and special treatment. [The penal code provides for] such confinement and treatment for persons found not guilty by reason of insanity. A defendant acquitted because, as a result of diminished capacity, he lacked the specific intent required for the crime cannot be confined pursuant

to [those] sections, yet often he cannot be released without endangering the public safety.

The same danger may arise, however, when a diminished-capacity defense does not result in the defendant's acquittal, but in his conviction for a lesser-included offense. A defendant convicted of a lesser-included misdemeanor, for example, will be confined for a relatively short period in a facility which probably lacks a suitable treatment program, and may later, having served his term, be released to become a public danger. The solution to this problem thus does not lie in barring the defense of diminished capacity when the charged crime lacks a lesser included offense, but in providing for the confinement and treatment of defendants with diminished capacity arising from mental disease or defect.

[California law] provides for the civil commitment of any person who, "as a result of mental disorder, [is] a danger to others, or to himself, or gravely disabled." . . . [I]f evidence adduced in support of a successful diminished capacity defense indicates to the trial judge that the defendant is dangerous, the court is not compelled to foist the defendant upon the public; it may, instead, initiate procedures for civil commitment.

The attorney general points out that a person who commits a crime against property, such as defendant Wetmore, might not be [civilly] commitable . . . unless he were "gravely disabled." A more serious omission lies in the act's failure to provide for long-term commitment of persons dangerous to others; unless found "gravely disabled," a person "who, as a result of mental disorder, presents an imminent threat of substantial physical harm to others" cannot be confined beyond the initial 90-day post-certification treatment period unless "he has threatened, attempted, or actually inflicted physical harm to another during his period of post-certification treatment." If the [civil-commitment statute] does not adequately protect the public against crimes committed by persons with diminished mental capacity, the answer lies either in amendment to that act or in the enactment of legislation that would provide for commitment of persons acquitted by virtue of a successful diminished capacity defense in the same manner as persons acquitted by reason of insanity are presently committed. It does not lie in judicial creation of an illogical—and possibly unconstitutional—rule denying the defense of diminished capacity to persons charged with crimes lacking a lesser included offense.

Has the court properly resolved the tension between subjective criteria of culpability and the social interest in control over mentally disordered persons who have committed anti-social acts? Has the court simply shifted the tension to the civil commitment process? The *Wetmore* court rejected the "illogical" suggestion that evidence of mental abnormality should be inadmissible "whenever, owing to the lack of a lesser-included offense, it might result in the defendant's acquittal." In common law terms, the rejected approach would preclude the use of such evidence to negate "general intent" and would also preclude its use in cases such as *Wetmore* that involve specific-intent crimes with no lesser-included general-intent offense. How should such an approach be implemented in a jurisdiction with a culpability structure based on the Model Penal Code? Would this approach be entirely illogical? Does it represent a useful compromise?

## NOTE ON MENS REA EVIDENCE UNDER FEDERAL LAW

Section 17 (a) of The Federal Insanity Defense Reform Act, discussed in the Introductory Notes to Section 2, provides, inter alia:

> It is an affirmative defense to a prosecution under any Federal Statute that, at the time of the commission of the acts constituting the offense, the defendant, as a result of a severe mental disease or defect, was unable to appreciate the nature and quality or the wrongfulness of his acts. *Mental disease or defect does not otherwise constitute a defense.* [Emphasis added.]

Does the italicized language preclude defendants from introducing evidence of mental abnormality to negate mens rea? This issue has evoked a bewildering array of pronouncements from the federal courts. United States v. Pohlot, 827 F.2d 889 (3rd Cir. 1987), sets forth the prevailing view.

After he was caught attempting to hire a hit man to kill his wife, Pohlot was found guilty of five counts of using interstate commerce facilities in the commission of a crime of violence and one count of conspiring to do the same. The pertinent evidence was summarized by the Circuit Court:

> Until the summer of 1985, Stephen Pohlot was a successful pharmacist and private investor, living with his wife, Elizabeth, and three of their children in Katonah, New York. According to Pohlot, however, beyond this façade lay a strange set of relationships, dominated by his wife. Pohlot testified, for example, that his wife had broken his thumb by crashing a coffee pot down on it; deeply gouged his face with her nails; threatened him with a hunting knife; shot him in the stomach; and often locked him out of their house and bedroom. Pohlot also blamed his wife for the psychiatric illnesses of two of his four children, who were seriously anorexic. Illustrating her behavior, Pohlot said that she had insisted on keeping an enormous number of pets in or about the house: sixty rabbits, six goats, tanks full of fish, tanks full of snakes, a pony, six indoor cats and nine outdoor cats, numerous ducks and dogs, and a variety of birds.
>
> In the summer of 1985, Elizabeth obtained a court order removing Pohlot from their home. In July 1985, she filed for divorce, freezing Pohlot's assets. These events, according to the government, triggered the murder plot. . . .

A defense expert witness testified that as a result of childhood experiences and his wife's abuse, Pohlot had a "compulsive personality, passive dependent personality and passive aggressive personality." Pohlot himself testified that his psychological inability to respond to his wife's abuse led to the murder plot as "a weak attempt to fight back." The expert witness further testified that Pohlot "felt as if he would hire somebody to kill [his wife] and after that happened, they would go home and live together and be happier." The court then summarized the contending positions on the admissibility of this evidence:

> The Government claims that . . . the [Insanity Defense Reform] Act bars a defendant from using evidence of mental

> abnormality to negate mens rea. . . . We disagree. Both the wording of the statute and the legislative history leave no doubt that Congress intended, as the Senate Report stated, to bar only alternative "affirmative defenses" that "excuse" misconduct, not evidence that disproves an element of the crime itself.
>
> Pohlot essentially contends that mental disease or defect is admissible whenever it is relevant to prove that the defendant did or did not have a state of mind that is an element of the offense. Model Penal Code, § 4.02(1) (1962). Although this principle has sometimes been phrased as a version of the diminished capacity defense, it does not provide any grounds for acquittal not provided in the definition of the offense. Properly understood, it is therefore not a defense at all but merely a rule of evidence. As several United States Courts of Appeals have therefore stressed, [t]he use of expert testimony for this purpose is entirely distinct from the use of such testimony to relieve a defendant of criminal responsibility based on the insanity defense or one of its variants, such as diminished capacity.

The court ultimately affirmed Pohlot's conviction because the proffered testimony was not relevant to mens rea and instead was offered in support of "an unacceptable defense of diminished responsibility." Did the court correctly interpret and apply § 17(a)?[a]

## NOTE ON BIFURCATION OF INSANITY AND MENS REA

Cases involving insanity pleas are sometimes tried in two phases. Under this bifurcated procedure, the issues of "guilt or innocence" and "insanity" are tried separately. Although bifurcation is permitted in many states, the procedure is required by statute only in California and a handful of others.[a]

In a jurisdiction that excludes evidence of mental abnormality from the guilt stage, the bifurcated trial can have decided advantages. By deferring psychiatric testimony to the second stage, it avoids confusing the jury and reduces the risk of compromise verdicts. Also, in many cases it helps protect the defendant's privilege against self-incrimination. If the insanity issue were tried simultaneously with the "guilt" issue, many defendants would be forced to make a strategic choice between contesting the issue of guilt or admitting the elements of the offense and attempting to prove insanity. This is because the defendant's own statements are often an integral part of a defense based on his mental condition at the time of the offense. Thus, the bifurcated trial permits the defendant to remain silent during the guilt phase, thereby assuring that the prosecution bears the burden of proving the elements of the offense without the defendant's assistance. If the prosecution is successful, the defendant is then permitted to put on an insanity defense and may choose to testify at that time.

Obviously the advantages of a bifurcated trial are diminished if the defendant is permitted to introduce evidence of mental abnormality to negate

---

[a] See also United States v. White, 766 F.2d 22 (1st Cir. 1985); United States v. Frisbee, 623 F.Supp. 1217 (N.D. Cal. 1985).

[a] In many states, the trial judge has the discretion to bifurcate the trial but is not required to do so. In some states, bifurcation is required upon the defendant's request. Some states forbid the procedure altogether.

mens rea at the guilt stage while the "insanity" issue is deferred. Since this procedure bifurcates the expert testimony, the trial can become highly cumbersome and redundant. For this reason, a judge sitting in a jurisdiction which does not require bifurcation might decide to hold a unified proceeding. However, what is the correct response if bifurcation is required by statute? On the one hand, the California Supreme Court has taken the position that the defendant cannot fairly be precluded from introducing relevant evidence of mental abnormality at the guilt stage even though the insanity issue will be tried separately. This led the court to recommend that the legislature abandon the bifurcated procedure in favor of a unified trial. People v. Wetmore, 22 Cal.3d 318, 331, 149 Cal.Rptr. 265, 274, 583 P.2d 1308, 1317 (1978). On the other hand, the Wisconsin Supreme Court has concluded that the advantages of the bifurcated trial procedure provide another reason, in addition to those rehearsed by Justice Souter in *Clark*, for excluding evidence of mental abnormality on mens rea issues. See Steele v. State, 97 Wis.2d 72, 294 N.W.2d 2 (1980).

## SUBSECTION E: ABOLITION OF THE INSANITY DEFENSE

### NOTES ON ABOLITION OF THE INSANITY DEFENSE

#### 1. APPROACHES TO ABOLITION

Proposals to abolish the insanity defense have been made since the latter part of the 19th century. These proposals have taken two forms.

#### *(i) The Sentencing Approach*

Some abolitionists recommend that all evidence regarding the defendant's mental abnormality be excluded from the "guilt stage" of the criminal proceeding and that such evidence be taken into account only at the sentencing stage. This approach, which was widely discussed during the early years of the 20th century[a] was actually enacted by the state of Washington in 1909:

> It shall be no defense to a person charged with the commission of a crime that at the time of its commission he was unable, by reason of his insanity, idiocy or imbecility, to comprehend the nature and quality of the act committed, or to understand that it was wrong; or that he was afflicted with a morbid propensity to commit prohibited acts; nor shall any testimony or other proof thereof be admitted in evidence.

The statute also provided that the trial judge could order a convicted defendant to be committed to a state hospital or confined in the psychiatric unit of the penitentiary if it was determined that the defendant was insane. This scheme was declared unconstitutional by the Supreme Court of Washington in State v. Strasburg, 60 Wash. 106, 110 P. 1020 (1910). The court concluded that the statute precluded the defendant from offering evidence to negate the constitutionally required predicate for criminal liability:

---

[a] See, e.g., Curtis D. Wilbur, Should the Insanity Defense to a Criminal Charge be Abolished?, 8 A.B.A.J. 631 (1922); John R. Rood, Statutory Abolition of the Defense of Insanity in Criminal Cases, 9 Mich.L.Rev. 126 (1910). More recent endorsements include H.L.A. Hart, Punishment and Responsibility 186–205 (1968).

> [T]he sanity of the accused, at the time of committing the act charged against him, has always been regarded as much a substantive fact, going to make up his guilt, as the fact of his physical commission of the act. It seems to us the law could as well exclude proof of any other substantive fact going to show his guilt or innocence. If he was insane at the time to the extent that he could not comprehend the nature and quality of the act—in other words, if he had no will to control the physical act of his physical body—how can it in truth be said that the act was his act? To take from the accused the opportunity to offer evidence tending to prove this fact is in our opinion as much a violation of his constitutional right of trial by jury as to take from him the right to offer evidence before the jury tending to show that he did not physically commit the act or physically set in motion a train of events resulting in the act.

### *(ii) The Mens Rea Approach*

Concerns such as those expressed by the *Strasburg* court have inspired a less sweeping abolitionist proposal. Under this approach, evidence of mental abnormality would be excluded unless relevant to the mens rea of the offense charged; criteria of criminal responsibility extrinsic to the definition of the offense would be abandoned.

The mens rea variant of the abolitionist proposals has been especially popular in recent years. It has significant support in the academic literature[b] and has been adopted in Montana, Idaho, Utah and Kansas.[c] Section 46–14–201 of Mont.Rev.Codes Ann. provides, in relevant part:

> (1) Evidence of mental disease or defect is not admissible in a trial on the merits unless the defendant . . . files a written notice of his purpose to rely on a mental disease or defect to prove that he did not have a particular state of mind which is an essential element of the offense charged. . . .
>
> (2) When the defendant is found not guilty of the charged offense or offenses or any lesser included offense for the reason that due to a mental disease or defect, he could not have a particular state of mind that is an essential element of the offense charged, the verdict and judgment shall so state.

Assessing the merits of the mens rea approach to mental abnormality is aided by consideration of three questions: (i) Would the outcomes of criminal cases under the mens rea scheme differ significantly from those that would occur under the existing responsibility tests? (ii) How would the dispositional consequences of the mens rea approach differ from those that now obtain? (iii) To the extent that some defendants now acquitted under the insanity tests would be convicted under the mens rea approach, are

---

[b] See, e.g., Joseph Goldstein and Jay Katz, "Abolish the Insanity Defense"—Why Not?, 72 Yale L.J. 853 (1963); Norval Morris, Psychiatry and the Dangerous Criminal, 41 So.Cal.L.Rev. 514 (1968). Morris reiterated and elaborated on his views in Madness and the Criminal Law (1982). See also, Christopher Slobogin, A End to Insanity: Recasting the Role of Mental Disability in Criminal Cases, 86 Va. L Rev 1199 (2000).

[c] The insanity defense was also abolished in Nevada in favor of the mens rea approach, but the Nevada Supreme Court ruled that the legislature could not constitutionally convict a defendant who, due to mental disease, was unable the appreciate the legal wrongfulness of his acts. Finger v. State, 117 Nev. 548, 27 P.3d 66 (2001).

these results morally acceptable? Each of these issues is addressed in the following notes.

## 2. EFFECT ON CASE OUTCOME

In theory, it seems clear that some claims that now fit within the various insanity tests would not be exculpatory under the mens rea approach. First, claims of volitional impairment would have no exculpatory significance outside the narrow confines of the voluntary-act doctrine. Second, claims of cognitive impairment would have exculpatory significance only (i) if the defendant were charged with an offense requiring a subjectively defined level of culpability, and (ii) if the impairment so distorted the defendant's perceptual capacities that the physical nature and consequences of the alleged criminal acts were not perceived or foreseen. Wetmore might be acquitted, but Ruffin was convicted of a lesser included offense and Joy Baker would probably be guilty of manslaughter.

As a practical matter, however, it is possible that case outcomes would remain much the same as they are now. If the expert testimony is admitted on mens rea issues, judges and juries may behave as many observers believe they do now—they may ignore the technical aspects of the legal formulae and decide, very simply, whether the defendant was crazy. If judges and juries do in fact respond to psychiatric evidence in this blunt way, one might be led to expect, as Alan Dershowitz has asserted, Abolishing the Insanity Defense, 9 Crim.L.Bull. 434, 438–39 (1973), that "nothing much will change."

Empirical studies in the abolitionist states tend to support this prediction. A study in Utah showed that there were as many "mental disease/mens rea" acquittals (seven) during the two years following abolition as there had been "insanity" acquittals during the nine years preceding abolition. Moreover, the author concluded that the defendant's impaired mental functioning actually negated mens rea in only one of the seven mens rea acquittals.[d] A study of dispositions in seven Montana counties revealed a similar result, albeit by a different legal route. Unlike in Utah, Montana's abolitionist reform virtually eliminated acquittals based on mental disease: during the 3 ½ years before the change, insanity acquittals averaged about 14 per year; during the 6 ½ years following the change, there were only five acquittals altogether (and three of these occurred during the first year, when judges may have applied the pre-reform law). However, people who would have been acquitted on ground of insanity under the old law were *not* convicted under the new law:

> After the reform . . . they were being found [incompetent to stand trial], their charges were dismissed or deferred, and they ended up being hospitalized in the same settings where NGRI cases had been sent. Faced with the loss of one avenue, the legal and mental health systems simply found another way to accomplish the same end. If a person's mental status was seen as sufficient to warrant reduced criminal responsibility, they were found [incompetent to stand trial] and committed to the same hospital

---

[d] Peter Heinbecker, Two Years' Experience under Utah's Mens Rea Insanity Law, 14 Bulletin of the American Academy of Psychiatry and Law 185 (1986).

and the same wards where they would have been confined if they had been found NGRI.[e]

## 3. DISPOSITIONAL CONSIDERATIONS

Concerns about the need for control of dangerous persons figure prominently in the controversies over commitment of persons acquitted by reason of insanity and the relationship between mental abnormality and mens rea. What are the dispositional implications of proposals to abolish the insanity defense in favor of a mens rea approach? Two separate issues should be considered: First, how would the abolitionists deal with mentally disordered defendants who would have been acquitted by reason of insanity but would now be convicted? Second, how would they deal with persons who are acquitted because they lack the mens rea for any form of criminal liability?

### *(i) Sentencing the Mentally Disordered Offender*

Many proponents of abolition have argued that insanity tests mistakenly focus attention on backward-looking "moral guesses" about the person's blameworthiness at the time of the offense when the real issue is what ought to be done now to prevent further harm. Other abolitionists argue that considerations of responsibility are relevant but should be taken into account in mitigation of punishment rather than exculpation. Both views lead to the conclusion that evidence of mental abnormality should be taken fully into account at sentencing. Consider, in this connection, the relevant provisions of the Montana statute abolishing the insanity defense:

> Section 46–14–311. Consideration of mental disease or defect in sentencing.
>
> Whenever a defendant is convicted on a verdict or a plea of guilty and he claims that at the time of the commission of the offense . . . he was suffering from a mental disease or defect which rendered him unable to appreciate the criminality of his conduct or to conform his conduct to the requirements of law, the sentencing court shall consider any relevant evidence presented at the trial and shall require such additional evidence as it considers necessary for the determination of the issue including examination of the defendant and a report thereof. . . .
>
> Section 46–14–312. Sentence to be imposed.
>
> (1) If the court finds that the defendant at the time of the commission of the offense of which he was convicted did not suffer from a mental disease or defect as described in Section 46–14–311, it shall sentence him [pursuant to otherwise applicable sentencing provisions].
>
> (2) If the court finds that the defendant at the time of the commission of the offense suffered from a mental disease or defect as described in Section 46–14–311, any mandatory minimum sentence prescribed by law for the offense need not apply and the court shall sentence him to be committed to the custody of the director of the department of institutions to be placed in an appropriate institution for custody, care, and treatment for a definite

[e] Henry Steadman et. al., Before and After Hinckley: Evaluating Insanity Defense Reform 136 (1993).

period of time not to exceed the maximum term of imprisonment that could be imposed under Subsection (1)....

(3) A defendant whose sentence has been imposed under Subsection (2) may petition the sentencing court for review of the sentence if the [responsible mental-health professional] certifies that the defendant has been cured of the mental disease or defect. The sentencing court may make any [otherwise authorized order] except that the length of confinement or supervision must be equal to that of the original sentence. The [responsible mental-health professional] shall review the defendant's status each year.

Section 46–14–313. Discharge of defendant from supervision.

At the expiration of the period of commitment or period of treatment specified by the court under Section 46–14–312(2), the defendant must be discharged from custody and further supervision, subject only to the law regarding the civil commitment of persons suffering from serious mental illness.

How do the dispositional consequences of this scheme differ from those that would obtain if the insanity defense had not been "abolished"?[f]

### *(ii) Disposition of Persons Lacking Mens Rea Due to Mental Disease*

One of the arguments against admitting evidence of mental abnormality whenever it is relevant to mens rea is that this could result in release of dangerous persons. The fear is that the procedures for civil commitment of the mentally ill afford inadequate social protection. Not surprisingly, proponents of the mens rea alternative to the insanity defense usually provide for a separate commitment procedure for persons who lack mens rea due to mental disease. Thus, the same questions concerning the proper criteria for commitment of such persons that arise in a jurisdiction that admits evidence on mens rea in addition to the insanity defense would also have to be resolved under the mens rea alternative to the defense.

Consider for example, the applicable Montana provisions.[g] After a person "is acquitted on the ground that due to a mental disease or defect he could not have a particular state of mind that is an essential element of the offense charged," the court is required to commit him to the mental-health department "for custody, care and treatment." The person is entitled to a hearing within 50 days to "determine his present mental condition and whether he may be discharged or released without danger to others." The burden of proof is placed on the defendant to prove "that he may be safely released." The person is committed indefinitely until a court finds that he "may be discharged or released on condition without danger to himself or others." Would this commitment scheme be acceptable if the subjects were persons acquitted by reason of insanity? Does it provide a more or less acceptable basis for committing persons, such as Wetmore, found to lack the

---

[f] Idaho and Utah have similar provisions. These schemes are unusual because they were adopted in lieu of an insanity defense. It should be recalled, however, that at least 12 states have *combined* a similar sentencing scheme with the insanity defense: in those states, a verdict of not guilty by reason of insanity leads to commitment while a "guilty but mentally ill" verdict leads to special sentencing procedures similar to those in Montana. See, e.g., Mich. Comp.Laws Ann. § 768.36.

[g] Mont.Rev.Stat.Ann. §§ 46–14–301, et seq. Unlike Montana, Idaho and Utah did not enact special dispositional procedures for mens rea acquittees. In Idaho and Utah, these individuals are subject to the generally applicable civil commitment statutes.

mens rea required for criminal liability? What about for defendants like Ruffin, who are acquitted of a serious offense but convicted of a lesser included one?

## 4. BLAMEWORTHINESS CONSIDERATIONS

The proposals to abolish the insanity defense implicate fundamental moral concerns. The central question may be put as follows: To the extent that the mens rea approach in fact would reduce the exculpatory significance of mental abnormality, would it require criminal conviction of "a class of persons who, on any common-sense notion of justice, are beyond blaming and ought not to be punished"?[h]

The proponents of the mens rea approach respond that it would not. They argue that the only meaningful line between the blameless and the blameworthy is that represented by mens rea. Although they concede that responsibility may otherwise be diminished by mental disability, they argue that such factors should be taken into account in sentencing, together with other social and psychological information relevant to the offender's responsibility for his behavior. This argument was developed by Norval Morris in Psychiatry and the Dangerous Criminal, 41 So.Cal.L.Rev. 514, 520–21 (1968):

> [T]he moral issue remains central—whether we should include as criminally responsible . . . those whose freedom to choose between criminal and lawful behavior was curtailed by mental illness. It too often is overlooked that one group's exculpation from criminal responsibility confirms the inculpation of other groups. . . . Adverse social and subcultural background is statistically *more* criminogenic than is psychosis; like insanity, it also severely circumscribes the freedom of choice which a non-deterministic criminal law . . . attributes to accused persons. [It will be argued] that insanity destroys, undermines, diminishes man's capacity to reject what is wrong and to adhere to what is right. So does the ghetto—more so. But surely, [it will be replied,] I would not have us punish the sick. Indeed I would, if [society insists] on punishing the grossly deprived. To the extent that criminal sanctions serve punitive purposes, I fail to see the difference between these two defenses. To the extent that they serve rehabilitative, treatment, and curative purposes I fail to see the need for the difference.

Sanford Kadish responded to Professor Morris in The Decline of Innocence, 26 Camb. L.J. 273, 284 (1968), as follows:

> [Morris argues] that we convict and punish persons daily whose ability to conform is impaired by a variety of circumstances—by youthful neglect, by parental inadequacy, by the social and psychical deprivations of growing up in a grossly underprivileged minority subculture, or by countless other contingencies of life. This is perfectly true, but I fail to see that it supports eliminating the insanity defence. First, the argument logically is an argument for extension of the defence of lack of responsibility, not for its abolition. It is never a reason for adding to injustice that we are already guilty of some. Second, confining the defence to patent

[h] Sanford Kadish, The Decline of Innocence, 26 Camb.L.J. 273, 283 (1968).

> and extreme cases of irresponsibility is not a whimsical irrationality. There may well be an injustice in it, but it rests upon the practical concern to avoid vitiating the deterrent impact of the criminal law upon those who are more or less susceptible to its influences. . . . We may accept as a necessary evil—necessary, that is, given our commitment to a punishment system—the criminal conviction of persons whose ability to conform is somewhat impaired and still protest that it is unacceptable for a society to fail to make a distinction for those who are utterly and obviously beyond the reach of the law.

It is noteworthy that Morris and Kadish join issue most clearly on whether a qualitative line can be drawn through claims of volitional impairment. Does agreement with Morris on this issue necessarily entail abolition of the cognitive prong of the insanity defense as well?

The exchange between Morris and Kadish also highlights another dimension of the controversy. Morris argues that persons who are supposedly held blameless on grounds of insanity in fact are punished under the present system of commitment where they are doubly stigmatized because they are regarded as "both insane and criminal, mad and bad. . . ." He also argues that the insanity defense does not provide an efficient arrangement for "mobiliz[ing] clinical resources for the rational treatment of the psychologically disturbed criminal actor." Kadish insists, in response, that "a just and humane legal system" has an obligation to make a distinction between those who are eligible for criminal punishment and those who are not. He acknowledges that NGRI acquittees are stigmatized due to "the misinterpretation placed upon the person's conduct by people in the community," but he argues that "convicting a morally innocent person of a crime" is a "paradigmatic affront to the sense of justice."

Kadish and Morris disagree on where the line must be drawn to separate the blameless from the blameworthy. They also disagree on whether an NGRI acquittal is "punishment." Who is right? Should the insanity defense be abolished?[i]

## 5. CONSTITUTIONALITY OF ABOLITION

The United States Supreme Court has not decided whether abolition of the insanity defense is constitutional. In Clark v. Arizona, 548 U.S. 735 (2006), the Court upheld an Arizona law allowing the insanity defense only if the defendant proved by clear and convincing evidence that "at the time of the commission of the criminal act [he] was afflicted with a mental disease or defect of such severity that [he] did not know the criminal act was wrong." The Court rejected Clark's argument that the Arizona test was constitutionally inadequate due to its failure to include the "nature and quality of the act" language from the *M'Naghten* test, noting that "if a defendant did not know what he was doing when he acted, he could not have

---

[i] Morris reaffirmed his position in Madness and the Criminal Law (1982). His view was endorsed by the American Medical Association in 251 J.Am.Med.Ass'n 2967 (1984). The abolitionist position has been defended by Professor Christopher Slobogin. See, e.g., Minding Justice 23–61 (Harvard U. Press, 2006); An End to Insanity, 86 Virginia Law Review 1199 (2000). The abolitionist position is criticized in Stephen Morse, Excusing the Crazy: The Insanity Defense Reconsidered, 58 So.Cal.L.Rev. 777 (1985); Donald H.J. Hermann, Book Review: Madness and the Criminal Law, 51 G.W.L.Rev. 329 (1983); Peter Arenella, Reflections on Current Proposals to Abolish or Reform the Insanity Defense, 8 Am.J.Leg.Med. 271 (1982).

known that he was performing the wrongful act charged as a crime." In short, the Court ruled that a test allowing an insanity defense only if the defendant lacked capacity to know or appreciate the wrongfulness of his conduct is constitutionally sufficient, but it has not ruled on whether it is constitutionally required.[j]

# SECTION 3: DISPOSITION OF MENTALLY DISORDERED OFFENDERS

## INTRODUCTORY NOTES ON THE DISPOSITION OF MENTALLY DISORDERED OFFENDERS

### 1. BACKGROUND

Individuals with serious mental illness are grossly overrepresented in the criminal justice system and among offenders under correctional supervision. Compared to the general population, the lifetime prevalence rate of persons with serious mental illness in the correctional population is twice as high for both men and women, and experts have estimated that over 1.3 million people with serious mental illness were on probation or parole or in jails or prisons, representing about 1 in 5 offenders under correctional supervision in the United States.[a] These individuals have been convicted and sentenced under the generally applicable criminal statutes, rather than those prescribing special procedures for mentally disordered offenders. When they receive special judicial attention, it is mainly in the context of claims that the conditions of confinement do not satisfy constitutional standards and that states have not provided constitutionally adequate mental health care.

This section addresses formal legal classifications pertaining to mentally disordered offenders. The most visible category is people acquitted by reason of insanity. However, the insanity defense is raised in fewer than one per cent of all felony cases, and is successful in only a small fraction of these. Moreover, persons acquitted by reason of insanity (NGRI's) represent a very small proportion—less than 10 per cent—of those criminal defendants who eventually are placed in institutions for mentally disordered offenders. The great majority of persons sent to such institutions either have been committed after being found incompetent to stand trial or have been placed there after conviction to serve their sentences. The latter group is by far the largest.[b] Another category of offenders that has been subject to a distinct scheme of confinement and control is sex offenders, An earlier generation of sex psychopath laws was largely repealed in the 1970s, but has been succeeded by a new generation of statutes enacted in the late 20th century.

---

[j] The Supreme Court ducked an opportunity to decide this issue in Delling v. Ohio, 568 U.S. ___, 133 S.Ct. 504 (2012)(denying certiorari in a case in which petitioner challenged the constitutionality of Idaho's statute under the due process clause). Three justices dissented from the denial of certiorari "in view of [amicus] submissions" from the American Psychiatric Association and more than 100 Criminal Law and Mental Health Professors.

[a] Jennifer Skeem and Jillian Peterson, Identifying, Treating, and Reducing Risk for Offenders with Mental Illness, in Joan Petersila and Kevin Reitz (eds), The Oxford Handbook of Sentencing and Corrections (2011)

[b] See generally John Monahan and Henry Steadman (eds.), Mentally Disordered Offenders: Perspectives from Law and Social Sciences (1981).

## 2. COMMITMENT OF PERSONS INCOMPETENT TO STAND TRIAL

Every Anglo-American jurisdiction forbids trial of a person who, as a result of mental disease or mental retardation, is incapable of understanding the proceedings or of assisting in the defense. Because this longstanding practice is regarded as "fundamental to an adversary system of justice," the United States Supreme Court has held that a judge is constitutionally required to request a competency determination whenever there is a bona fide doubt about the defendant's competency to proceed. See Drope v. Missouri, 420 U.S. 162 (1975).

If a person is found incompetent to stand trial, the criminal proceedings are suspended while he or she is committed for treatment. In the past, the incompetency commitment mooted the issue of criminal responsibility in most cases because these defendants were held indefinitely and the criminal proceedings were rarely revived. However, in Jackson v. Indiana, 406 U.S. 715 (1972), the Supreme Court held that a defendant committed solely on account of incapacity to stand trial "cannot be held more than a reasonable period of time necessary to determine whether there is a substantial probability that he will attain that capacity in the foreseeable future." If there is no substantial probability that the defendant will be restored to competency within the foreseeable future, or if the treatment provided does not succeed in advancing the defendant toward that goal, the state must either institute civil commitment proceedings or release the defendant. Most states now require such a definitive determination within 18 months. The average length of hospitalization for incompetency commitments is about six months.

The incompetency commitment still functions, in practice, as a substitute for insanity adjudication in many cases involving misdemeanors or less serious felonies. Empirical studies have shown that most persons found incompetent to stand trial are not prosecuted for the criminal offenses that triggered their commitments. The charges against these defendants are routinely dropped when they are released. Only if the charges are especially serious are they likely to be prosecuted; in many of these cases, the insanity defense is then raised.

## 3. SPECIAL SENTENCING PROVISIONS

In the vast majority of cases, the criminal law defers consideration of the offender's mental condition until sentencing. At that time, judges in most states are empowered to take into account the defendant's dangerousness and amenability to treatment, as well as any claim of diminished responsibility, in choosing the type or severity of sentence.[c] In some states, the court's customary sentencing options are augmented by special "mentally disordered offender" provisions that permit the defendant to be confined in special institutions and that may extend the otherwise authorized period of confinement.[d] In a recent development, at least 12 states now

---

[c] The significance of mental disorder in sentencing is discussed in Norval Morris, Madness and the Criminal Law (1982), and Stephen Morse, Justice, Mercy, and Craziness, 36 Stan.L.Rev. 1485 (1984).

[d] These statutes are discussed in Thomas L. Hafemeister and John Petrila, Treating the Mentally Disordered Offender: Society's Uncertain, Conflicted and Changing Views, 21 Fla. St.U. L. Rev. 729 (1994); and George Dix, Special Dispositional Alternatives for Abnormal Offender: Developments in the Law (1981).

permit or require defendants found "guilty but mentally ill" to be placed in secure psychiatric hospitals, in lieu of ordinary correctional facilities, for some portion of the term of imprisonment.[e] Finally, it should also be noted that, even without a special verdict, most states permit mentally disordered prisoners to be transferred from prisons to psychiatric hospitals while they are serving their sentences.

## 4. COMMITMENT OF PERSONS ACQUITTED BY REASON OF INSANITY

Historically, persons acquitted by reason of insanity have been subject to special procedures requiring commitment to institutions for the "criminally insane" until such time as they "recovered their sanity." Little systematic attention was given to the procedures or criteria governing these decisions, or to the conditions in the institutions for the criminally insane, until the early 1970s, when the traditional restrictive approach was challenged on both constitutional and therapeutic grounds. It was argued that the substantial disparity between "ordinary" civil commitment procedures and the NGRI[f] procedures was constitutionally unjustified. Moreover, the mental health community argued that advances in pharmacological treatment had reduced the therapeutic need for long-term hospitalization in most cases. In response to numerous judicial rulings on the subject, every state has revised its NGRI dispositional statute. Although the initial trend was to make the NGRI statutes less restrictive, and to bring them into congruence with ordinary "civil" commitment statutes, increased public concern about premature release of dangerous insanity acquittees led to a second generation of reforms in many states.

This flurry of legislative and judicial activity has left the current generation of NGRI dispositional statutes in considerable disarray.[g] Speaking generally, the statutes fall into three categories. In some states, insanity acquittees are subject to the same criteria and procedures governing civil commitment of the mentally ill. Typically, this means that the acquittee may not be committed unless the state proves, by clear and convincing evidence, that he or she is mentally ill and dangerous. The period of commitment usually does not exceed 180 days. In a second group of states, the procedures, though similar to those governing civil commitment, vary in a few significant respects. For example, while a civilly committed patient may be hospitalized for emergency evaluation for only a short period—up to one week, perhaps—NGRI's may be committed for evaluation for up to 90 days. In addition, whereas a civilly committed patient is entitled to be discharged without judicial approval whenever the medical staff determines that hospitalization is no longer necessary, statutes governing insanity acquittees typically require a judicial order authorizing discharge. Finally, in a third group of states, the procedures differ substantially from those governing civil commitment. Typically, the statutes provide for automatic, indefinite commitment of the insanity acquittee and place the burden on the acquittee to prove that he or she is no longer committable. Even in these states, however, the acquittee is usually entitled to periodic administrative and judicial review of his or her status and the burden of

---

[e] The "guilty but mentally ill" verdict is considered at the end of this Subsection.

[f] The "guilty but mentally ill" verdict is considered at the end of this Subsection.

[g] The statutes are surveyed and discussed in Jan Brakel, After the Verdict: Dispositional Decisions Regarding Criminal Defendants Acquitted by Reason of Insanity, 37 DePaul L. Rev. 181 (1988).

proof may shift to the state if the hospital authorities recommend discharge.

A common feature of most contemporary NGRI commitment statutes is a conditional release program under which released acquittees are aggressively monitored to assure that the conditions of release are satisfied and to prevent reoffending. Recent studies indicate that most NGRI acquittees function well in the community, with low revocation and rearrest rates, especially when receiving mandated treatment. The disposition of insanity acquittees is addressed in Subsection A.

### 5. DANGEROUS SEX OFFENDER STATUTES

Some states provide for indeterminate civil commitment of persons charged with or convicted of specified sex offenses who are found, in a separate proceeding, to be "sexual psychopaths" or "mentally disordered sex offenders." Courts typically have held that these statutes are non-penal in character, the legislative purpose being to treat the person's condition rather than to punish the person for the underlying offense. See, e.g. Allen v. Illinois, 478 U.S. 364 (1986). These commitments differ somewhat from insanity commitments because they are not predicated on a finding of nonresponsibility. Under some sex offender commitment laws, the prosecutor has the authority to invoke the commitment process after arrest as an alternative to criminal prosecution. In other states, the defendant is convicted of the underlying offense and then committed as an alternative to an ordinary criminal sentence. In still other states, commitment is authorized after the offender has already served his sentence. These statutes are addressed in Subsection B.

## SUBSECTION A: DISPOSITION OF INSANITY ACQUITTEES

### INTRODUCTORY NOTE ON *JONES V. UNITED STATES*

### 1. THE FACTS

Although NGRI dispositional statutes were first exposed to intensive constitutional scrutiny in the early 1970s, the Supreme Court did not address the subject until it decided Jones v. United States, 463 U.S. 354 (1983). Michael Jones was charged with attempting to steal a jacket from a department store on September 19, 1975. He pleaded insanity and the government did not contest the plea. After the court found him not guilty by reason of insanity, Jones was automatically committed to St. Elizabeth's hospital. Under the District of Columbia NGRI commitment statute, Jones was entitled 50 or more days thereafter to request a "release hearing" at which he bore the burden of proving that he was no longer mentally ill or dangerous. At Jones' first release hearing on May 25, 1976, the court found that he was not entitled to release. A second release hearing was held on February 22, 1977. Jones' counsel requested at this hearing that he be released or civilly committed, on the ground that his cumulative hospital confinement had exceeded the one-year maximum period of incarceration for the offense charged. The court denied the request and continued Jones' commitment under the NGRI statute. The District of Columbia Court of Appeals affirmed, en banc, with three judges dissenting.

In a five-four decision, the Supreme Court affirmed. The Court addressed two questions: whether the District's automatic commitment procedure after an insanity acquittal violated the due process clause; and, if Jones' initial commitment was constitutional, whether he was entitled to be released or civilly committed upon expiration of the one-year maximum term prescribed for the offense of attempted petit larceny.

## 2. AUTOMATIC COMMITMENT OF INSANITY ACQUITTEES

In the District of Columbia, as in most states, the defendant bears the burden of proving an insanity defense by a preponderance of the evidence. The question before the Court was whether the findings underlying Jones' insanity verdict established a constitutionally adequate basis for his commitment. Justice Powell, writing for the Court, said it did:

> [An insanity verdict] establishes two facts: (i) The defendant committed an act that constitutes a criminal offense, and (ii) he committed the act because of mental illness. Congress has determined that these findings constitute an adequate basis for hospitalizing the acquittee as a dangerous and mentally ill person.... We cannot say that it was unreasonable and therefore unconstitutional for Congress to make this determination.
>
> The fact that a person has been found, beyond a reasonable doubt, to have committed a criminal act certainly indicates dangerousness.... Indeed, the concrete evidence generally may be at least as persuasive as any predictions about dangerousness that might be made in a civil commitment proceeding....
>
> Nor can we say that it was unreasonable for Congress to determine that the insanity acquittal supports an inference of continuing mental illness. It comports with common sense to conclude that someone whose mental illness was sufficient to lead him to commit a criminal act is likely to remain ill and in need of treatment.... Because a hearing is provided within 50 days of the commitment, there is assurance that every acquittee has a prompt opportunity to obtain release if he has recovered....
>
> We hold that when a criminal defendant establishes by a preponderance of the evidence that he is not guilty of a crime by reason of insanity, the Constitution permits the government, on the basis of the insanity judgment, to confine him to a mental institution until such time as he has regained his sanity or is no longer a danger to himself or society. This holding accords with the widely and reasonably held view that insanity acquittees constitute a special class that should be treated differently from other candidates for commitment....

Justice Brennan's dissenting opinion concluded that the insanity verdict did not provide "a constitutionally adequate basis for involuntary, indefinite commitment" and that the government should be required to prove the commitment criteria, in a post-verdict hearing, by clear and convincing evidence as it is required to do in other cases of involuntary psychiatric hospitalization under Addington v. Texas, 441 U.S. 418 (1979).

Even if a state may presume that an insanity acquittee continues to be mentally ill and dangerous, shifting the burden to the acquittee to prove eligibility for release, how long may this presumption remain in force?

Indefinitely? Should the state be required at some point to prove that the acquittee continues to be mentally ill and dangerous? How does this question relate to the criteria for commitment and release? How does it relate to the second issue raised in *Jones*?

### 3. COMMITMENT AND PROPORTIONALITY

The Supreme Court also addressed Jones' contention "that an acquittee's hypothetical maximum sentence provides the conditional limit for his commitment." He argued that a comparison of the NGRI and civil-commitment procedures demonstrated that an NGRI commitment is inescapably based on "punitive" considerations and that, accordingly, the justification for the special procedures lapses after expiration of the maximum sentence authorized for the offense that triggered the commitment. This contention had been accepted by three judges on the District of Columbia Court of Appeals. They reasoned:

> [NGRI] acquittees are not confined to mental institutions for medical reasons alone. They are confined there in part because society is unwilling to allow those who have committed crimes to escape without paying for their crimes. The intent of the statute is partially punitive, and thus the [stricter procedures governing commitment and release of NGRI's] reflect this added burden on the defendant. Because of this punitive purpose, the maximum statutory period of confinement becomes relevant, for at that point society no longer has a valid interest in continued confinement on the basis of a shortcut procedure. . . . Society's right to punish Michael Jones for his first offense, a misdemeanor—[attempting to steal] a coat—has long since expired. . . . Michael Jones should be released unless civilly committed.

The Supreme Court rejected this analysis. Writing for the majority, Justice Powell explained:

> A particular sentence of incarceration is chosen to reflect society's view of the proper response to commission of a particular criminal offense, based on a variety of considerations such as retribution, deterrence, and rehabilitation. The state may punish a person convicted of a crime even if satisfied that he is unlikely to commit further crimes.
>
> Different considerations underlie commitment of an insanity acquittee. As he was not convicted, he may not be punished. His confinement rests on his continuing illness and dangerousness. Thus, under the District of Columbia statute, no matter how serious the act committed by the acquittee, he may be released within 50 days of his acquittal if he has recovered. In contrast, one who committed a less serious act may be confined for a longer period if he remains ill and dangerous. There simply is no necessary correlation between severity of the offense and length of time necessary for recovery. The length of the acquittee's hypothetical criminal sentence therefore is irrelevant to the purposes of his commitment.

In dissent, Justice Brennan argued that since Jones' commitability had not been proved by clear and convincing evidence, he could not be held beyond the maximum sentence for attempted petit larceny. Justice

Brennan did appear to concede, however, that indefinite hospitalization would be permissible if the commitment were predicated upon constitutionally adequate proof.

Did Justice Powell accurately characterize the underlying purpose of NGRI commitment? Is it so clear that an NGRI commitment does not have a "partially punitive" purpose, as claimed by the dissenting judges on the Court of Appeals? Does it have a punitive effect? Assuming that the justifying purpose is therapeutic restraint rather than punishment for an offense, does it follow that the seriousness of the triggering offense should be irrelevant in determining the length of an NGRI commitment? In determining the criteria and procedures governing release? The Supreme Court addressed some of the these questions in Foucha v. Louisiana, 504 U.S. 71 (1992), the next main case.

## Foucha v. Louisiana

Supreme Court of the United States, 1992.
504 U.S. 71.

■ JUSTICE WHITE delivered the opinion of the Court, except as to Part III.

When a defendant in a criminal case pending in Louisiana is found not guilty by reason of insanity, he is committed to a psychiatric hospital unless he proves that he is not dangerous. This is so whether or not he is then insane. After commitment, if the acquittee or the superintendent begins release proceedings, a review panel at the hospital makes a written report on the patient's mental condition and whether he can be released without danger to himself or others. If release is recommended, the court must hold a hearing to determine dangerousness; the acquittee has the burden of proving that he is not dangerous. If found to be dangerous, the acquittee may be returned to the mental institution whether or not he is then mentally ill. Petitioner contends that this scheme denies him due process and equal protection because it allows a person acquitted by reason of insanity to be committed to a mental institution until he is able to demonstrate that he is not dangerous to himself and others, even though he does not suffer from any mental illness.

### I

Petitioner Terry Foucha was charged by Louisiana authorities with aggravated burglary and illegal discharge of a firearm. Two medical doctors were appointed to conduct a pretrial examination of Foucha. The doctors initially reported, and the trial court initially found, that Foucha lacked mental capacity to proceed, but four months later the trial court found Foucha competent to stand trial. The doctors reported that Foucha was unable to distinguish right from wrong and was insane at the time of the offense.[1] On October 12, 1984, the trial court ruled that Foucha was not guilty by reason of insanity, finding that he "is unable to appreciate the usual, natural and probable consequences of his

---

[1] Louisiana law provides: "If the circumstances indicate that because of a mental disease or mental defect the offender was incapable of distinguishing between right and wrong with reference to the conduct in question, the offender shall be exempt from criminal responsibility." La.Rev.Stat.Ann. § 14:14 (West 1986). . . .

acts; that he is unable to distinguish right from wrong; that he is a menace to himself and others; and that he was insane at the time of the commission of the above crimes and that he is presently insane." He was committed to the East Feliciana Forensic Facility until such time as doctors recommend that he be released, and until further order of the court. In 1988, the superintendent of Feliciana recommended that Foucha be discharged or released. A three-member panel was convened at the institution to determine Foucha's current condition and whether he could be released or placed on probation without being a danger to others or himself. On March 21, 1988, the panel reported that there had been no evidence of mental illness since admission and recommended that Foucha be conditionally discharged.[2] The trial judge appointed a two-member sanity commission made up of the same two doctors who had conducted the pretrial examination. Their written report stated that Foucha "is presently in remission from mental illness [but] [w]e cannot certify that he would not constitute a menace to himself or others if released." One of the doctors testified at a hearing that upon commitment Foucha probably suffered from a drug-induced psychosis but that he had recovered from that temporary condition; that he evidenced no signs of psychosis or neurosis and was in "good shape" mentally; that he has, however, an antisocial personality, a condition that is not a mental disease and that is untreatable. The doctor also testified that Foucha had been involved in several altercations at Feliciana and that he, the doctor, would not "feel comfortable in certifying that [Foucha] would not be a danger to himself or to other people."

After it was stipulated that the other doctor, if he were present, would give essentially the same testimony, the court ruled that Foucha was dangerous to himself and others and ordered him returned to the mental institution. The court of appeals refused supervisory writs, and the state supreme court affirmed, holding that Foucha had not carried the burden placed upon him by statute to prove that he was not dangerous, that our decision in Jones v. United States, 463 U.S. 354 (1983), did not require Foucha's release, and that neither the due process clause nor the equal protection clause was violated by the statutory provision permitting confinement of an insanity acquittee based on dangerousness alone.

Because the case presents an important issue and was decided by the court below in a manner arguably at odds with prior decisions of this Court, we granted certiorari.

II

Addington v. Texas, 441 U.S. 418 (1979), held that to commit an individual to a mental institution in a civil proceeding, the state is required by the due process clause to prove by clear and convincing evidence the two statutory preconditions to commitment: that the person sought to be committed is mentally ill and that he requires hospitalization for his own welfare and protection of others. Proof beyond

---

[2] The panel unanimously recommended that petitioner be conditionally discharged with recommendations that he (1) be placed on probation; (2) remain free from intoxicating and mind-altering substances; (3) attend a substance abuse clinic on a regular basis; (4) submit to regular and random urine drug screening; and (5) be actively employed or seeking employment. Although the panel recited that it was charged with determining dangerousness, its report did not expressly make a finding in that regard.

reasonable doubt was not required, but proof by preponderance of the evidence fell short of satisfying due process.[3]

When a person charged with having committed a crime is found not guilty by reason of insanity, however, a state may commit that person without satisfying the *Addington* burden with respect to mental illness and dangerousness. Such a verdict, we observed in *Jones*, "establishes two facts: (i) the defendant committed an act that constitutes a criminal offense, and (ii) he committed the act because of mental illness," id. 463 U.S. at 363, an illness that the defendant adequately proved in this context by a preponderance of the evidence. From these two facts, it could be properly inferred that at the time of the verdict, the defendant was still mentally ill and dangerous and hence could be committed.

We held, however, that "(t)he committed acquittee is entitled to release when he has recovered his sanity or is no longer dangerous," id. at 368; i.e. the acquittee may be held as long as he is both mentally ill and dangerous, but no longer. We relied on O'Connor v. Donaldson, 422 U.S. 563 (1975), which held as a matter of due process that it was unconstitutional for a state to continue to confine a harmless, mentally ill person. Even if the initial commitment was permissible, "it could not constitutionally continue after that basis no longer existed." Id. at 575. In the summary of our holdings in our opinion we stated that "the Constitution permits the government, on the basis of the insanity judgment, to confine him to a mental institution until such time as he has regained his sanity or is no longer a danger to himself or society." Jones, 463 U.S. at 368, 370. The court below was in error in characterizing the above language from *Jones* as merely an interpretation of the pertinent statutory law in the District of Columbia and as having no constitutional significance. In this case, Louisiana does not contend that Foucha was mentally ill at the time of the trial court's hearing. Thus, the basis for holding Foucha in a psychiatric facility as an insanity acquittee has disappeared, and the state is no longer entitled to hold him on that basis. . . .

A state, pursuant to its police power, may of course imprison convicted criminals for the purposes of deterrence and retribution. . . . Here, the state has no such punitive interest. As Foucha was not convicted, he may not be punished. Jones, supra, 463 U.S. at 369. Here, Louisiana has by reason of his acquittal exempted Foucha from criminal responsibility as La.Rev.Stat.Ann. § 14:14 (West 1986) requires. See n.1, supra.

---

[3] Justice Thomas in dissent complains that Foucha should not be released based on psychiatric opinion that he is not mentally ill because such opinion is not sufficiently precise—because psychiatry is not an exact science and psychiatrists widely disagree on what constitutes a mental illness. That may be true, but such opinion is reliable enough to permit the courts to base civil commitments on clear and convincing medical evidence that a person is mentally ill and dangerous and to base release decisions on qualified testimony that the committee is no longer mentally ill or dangerous. It is also reliable enough for the state not to punish a person who by a preponderance of the evidence is found to have been insane at the time he committed a criminal act, to say nothing of not trying a person who is at the time found incompetent to understand the proceedings. And more to the point, medical predictions of dangerousness seem to be reliable enough for the dissent to permit the state to continue to hold Foucha in a mental institution, even where the psychiatrist would say no more than that he would hesitate to certify that Foucha would not be dangerous to himself or others.

The state may also confine a mentally ill person if it shows "by clear and convincing evidence that the individual is mentally ill and dangerous," Jones, 463 U.S. at 362. Here, the state has not carried that burden; indeed, the state does not claim that Foucha is now mentally ill.

We have also held that in certain narrow circumstances persons who pose a danger to others or to the community may be subject to limited confinement and it is on these cases, particularly United States v. Salerno, 481 U.S. 739 (1987), that the state relies in this case.

*Salerno*, unlike this case, involved pretrial detention. We observed in *Salerno* that the "government's interest in preventing crime by arrestees is both legitimate and compelling," id. 481 U.S. at 749, and that the statute involved there was a constitutional implementation of that interest. The statute carefully limited the circumstances under which detention could be sought to those involving the most serious of crimes (crimes of violence, offenses punishable by life imprisonment or death, serious drug offenses, or certain repeat offenders), and was narrowly focused on a particularly acute problem in which the government interests are overwhelming. In addition to first demonstrating probable cause, the government was required, in a "full-blown adversary hearing," to convince a neutral decisionmaker by clear and convincing evidence that no conditions of release can reasonably assure the safety of the community or any person, i.e., that the "arrestee presents an identified and articulable threat to an individual or the community." Furthermore, the duration of confinement under the act was strictly limited. The arrestee was entitled to a prompt detention hearing and the maximum length of pretrial detention was limited by the "stringent time limitations of the Speedy Trial Act." If the arrestee were convicted, he would be confined as a criminal proved guilty; if he were acquitted, he would go free. Moreover, the act required that detainees be housed, to the extent practicable, in a facility separate from persons awaiting or serving sentences or awaiting appeal.

*Salerno* does not save Louisiana's detention of insanity acquittees who are no longer mentally ill. Unlike the sharply focused scheme at issue in *Salerno,* the Louisiana scheme of confinement is not carefully limited. Under the state statute, Foucha is not now entitled to an adversary hearing at which the state must prove by clear and convincing evidence that he is demonstrably dangerous to the community. Indeed, the state need prove nothing to justify continued detention, for the statute places the burden on the detainee to prove that he is not dangerous. At the hearing which ended with Foucha's recommittal, no doctor or any other person testified positively that in his opinion Foucha would be a danger to the community, let alone gave the basis for such an opinion. There was only a description of Foucha's behavior at Feliciana and his antisocial personality, along with a refusal to certify that he would not be dangerous. When directly asked whether Foucha would be dangerous, Dr. Ritter said only "I don't think I would feel comfortable in certifying that he would not be a danger to himself or to other people." This, under the Louisiana statute, was enough to defeat Foucha's interest in physical liberty. It is not enough to defeat Foucha's liberty interest under the constitution in being freed from indefinite confinement in a mental facility.

Furthermore, if Foucha committed criminal acts while at Feliciana, such as assault, the state does not explain why its interest would not be vindicated by the ordinary criminal processes involving charge and conviction, the use of enhanced sentences for recidivists, and other permissible ways of dealing with patterns of criminal conduct. These are the normal means of dealing with persistent criminal conduct. Had they been employed against Foucha when he assaulted other inmates, there is little doubt that if then sane he could have been convicted and incarcerated in the usual way.

It was emphasized in *Salerno* that the detention we found constitutionally permissible was strictly limited in duration. 481 U.S. at 747. Here, in contrast, the state asserts that because Foucha once committed a criminal act and now has an antisocial personality that sometimes leads to aggressive conduct, a disorder for which there is no effective treatment, he may be held indefinitely. This rationale would permit the state to hold indefinitely any other insanity acquittee not mentally ill who could be shown to have a personality disorder that may lead to criminal conduct. The same would be true of any convicted criminal, even though he has completed his prison term. It would also be only a step away from substituting confinements for dangerousness for our present system which, with only narrow exceptions and aside from permissible confinements for mental illness, incarcerates only those who are proved beyond reasonable doubt to have violated a criminal law.

"In our society liberty is the norm, and detention prior to trial or without trial is the carefully limited exception." United States v. Salerno, supra, 481 U.S. at 755. The narrowly focused pretrial detention of arrestees permitted by the Bail Reform Act was found to be one of those carefully limited exceptions permitted by the due process clause. We decline to take a similar view of a law like Louisiana's, which permits the indefinite detention of insanity acquittees who are not mentally ill but who do not prove they would not be dangerous to others.[6]

III

It should be apparent from what has been said earlier in this opinion that the Louisiana statute also discriminates against Foucha in violation of the equal protection clause of the fourteenth amendment. *Jones* established that insanity acquittees may be treated differently in some respects from those persons subject to civil commitment, but Foucha, who is not now thought to be insane, can no longer be so

---

[6] Justice Thomas' dissent firmly embraces the view that the state may indefinitely hold an insanity acquittee who is found by a court to have been cured of his mental illness and who is unable to prove that he would not be dangerous. This would be so even though, as in this case, the court's finding of dangerousness is based solely on the detainee's antisocial personality that apparently has caused him to engage in altercations from time to time. The dissent, however, does not challenge the holding of our cases that a convicted criminal may not be held as a mentally ill person without following the requirements for civil commitment, which would not permit further detention based on dangerousness alone. Yet it is surely strange to release sane but very likely dangerous persons who have committed a crime knowing precisely what they were doing but continue to hold indefinitely an insanity detainee who committed a criminal act at a time when, as found by a court, he did not know right from wrong. The dissent's rationale for continuing to hold the insanity acquittee would surely justify treating the convicted felon in the same way, and if put to it, it appears that the dissent would permit it. But as indicated in the text, this is not consistent with our present system of justice. . . .

classified. The state nonetheless insists on holding him indefinitely because he at one time committed a criminal act and does not now prove he is not dangerous. Louisiana law, however, does not provide for similar confinement for other classes of persons who have committed criminal acts and who cannot later prove they would not be dangerous. Criminals who have completed their prison terms, or are about to do so, are an obvious and large category of such persons. Many of them will likely suffer from the same sort of personality disorder that Foucha exhibits. However, state law does not allow for their continuing confinement based merely on dangerousness. Instead, the state controls the behavior of these similarly situated citizens by relying on other means, such as punishment, deterrence, and supervised release. Freedom from physical restraint being a fundamental right, the state must have a particularly convincing reason, which it has not put forward, for such discrimination against insanity acquittees who are no longer mentally ill.

Furthermore, in civil commitment proceedings the state must establish the grounds of insanity and dangerousness permitting confinement by clear and convincing evidence. Addington, 441 U.S. at 425–433. Similarly, the state must establish insanity and dangerousness by clear and convincing evidence in order to confine an insane convict beyond his criminal sentence, when the basis for his original confinement no longer exists. However, the state now claims that it may continue to confine Foucha, who is not now considered to be mentally ill, solely because he is deemed dangerous, but without assuming the burden of proving even this ground for confinement by clear and convincing evidence. The court below gave no convincing reason why the procedural safeguards against unwarranted confinement which are guaranteed to insane persons and those who have been convicted may be denied to a sane acquittee, and the state has done no better in this Court.

For the foregoing reasons the judgment of the Louisiana Supreme Court is reversed.

So ordered.

■ JUSTICE O'CONNOR, concurring in part and concurring in the judgment.

Louisiana asserts that it may indefinitely confine Terry Foucha in a mental facility because, although not mentally ill, he might be dangerous to himself or to others if released. For the reasons given in Part II of the Court's opinion, this contention should be rejected. I write separately, however, to emphasize that the Court's opinion addresses only the specific statutory scheme before us, which broadly permits indefinite confinement of sane insanity acquittees in psychiatric facilities. This case does not require us to pass judgment on more narrowly drawn laws that provide for detention of insanity acquittees, or on statutes that provide for punishment of persons who commit crimes while mentally ill.

I do not understand the Court to hold that Louisiana may never confine dangerous insanity acquittees after they regain mental health. Under Louisiana law, defendants who carry the burden of proving insanity by a preponderance of the evidence will "escape punishment," but this affirmative defense becomes relevant only after the prosecution establishes beyond a reasonable doubt that the defendant committed criminal acts with the required level of criminal intent. Although insanity acquittees may not be incarcerated as criminals or penalized for asserting the insanity defense, see Jones v. United States, 463 U.S. 354 (1983), this finding of criminal conduct sets them apart from ordinary citizens.

We noted in *Jones* that a judicial determination of criminal conduct provides "concrete evidence" of dangerousness. Id. at 364. By contrast, " '[t]he only certain thing that can be said about the present state of knowledge and therapy regarding mental disease is that science has not reached finality of judgment. . . .' " Id. at 365, n.13. Given this uncertainty, "courts should pay particular deference to reasonable legislative judgments" about the relationship between dangerous behavior and mental illness. Louisiana evidently has determined that the inference of dangerousness drawn from a verdict of not guilty by reason of insanity continues even after a clinical finding of sanity, and that judgment merits judicial deference.

It might therefore be permissible for Louisiana to confine an insanity acquittee who has regained sanity if, unlike the situation in this case, the nature and duration of detention were tailored to reflect pressing public safety concerns related to the acquittee's continuing dangerousness. Although the dissenters apparently disagree, I think it clear that acquittees could not be confined as mental patients absent some medical justification for doing so; in such a case the necessary connection between the nature and purposes of confinement would be absent. Nor would it be permissible to treat all acquittees alike, without regard for their particular crimes. For example, the strong interest in liberty of a person acquitted by reason of insanity but later found sane might well outweigh the governmental interest in detention where the only evidence of dangerousness is that the acquittee committed a non-violent or relatively minor crime. Cf. Salerno, supra, 481 U.S. at 750 (interest in pretrial detention is "overwhelming" where only individuals arrested for "a specific category of extremely serious offenses" are detained and "Congress specifically found that these individuals are far more likely to be responsible for dangerous acts in the community after arrest"). Equal protection principles may set additional limits on the confinement of sane but dangerous acquittees. Although I think it unnecessary to reach equal protection issues on the facts before us, the permissibility of holding an acquittee who is not mentally ill longer than a person convicted of the same crimes could be imprisoned is open to serious question.

The second point to be made about the Court's holding is that it places no new restriction on the states' freedom to determine whether and to what extent mental illness should excuse criminal behavior. The Court does not indicate that states must make the insanity defense available. See Idaho Code § 18–207(a) (1987) (mental condition not a defense to criminal charges); Mont.Code Ann. § 46–14–102 (1991) (evidence of mental illness admissible to prove absence of state of mind that is an element of the offense). It likewise casts no doubt on laws providing for prison terms after verdicts of "guilty but mentally ill." See, e.g., Del.Code Ann., Tit. 11, § 408(b) (1987); Ill.Rev.Stat., ch. 38, P 1005–2–6 (1989); Ind.Code § 35–36–2–5 (Supp.1991). If a state concludes that mental illness is best considered in the context of criminal sentencing, the holding of this case erects no bar to implementing that judgment.

Finally, it should be noted that the great majority of states have adopted policies consistent with the Court's holding. . . .

Today's holding follows directly from our precedents and leaves the states appropriate latitude to care for insanity acquittees in a way consistent with public welfare. Accordingly, I concur in Parts I and II of the Court's opinion and in the judgment of the Court.

■ JUSTICE KENNEDY, with whom CHIEF JUSTICE REHNQUIST joins, dissenting. . . .

This is a criminal case. It began one day when petitioner, brandishing a .357 revolver, entered the home of a married couple, intending to steal. He chased them out of their home and fired on police officers who confronted him as he fled. Petitioner was apprehended and charged with aggravated burglary and the illegal use of a weapon. . . . There is no question that petitioner committed the criminal acts charged. Petitioner's response was to deny criminal responsibility based on his mental illness when he committed the acts. He contended his mental illness prevented him from distinguishing between right and wrong with regard to the conduct in question.

Mental illness may bear upon criminal responsibility, as a general rule, in either of two ways: First, it may preclude the formation of *mens rea*, if the disturbance is so profound that it prevents the defendant from forming the requisite intent as defined by state law; second, it may support an affirmative plea of legal insanity. Depending on the content of state law, the first possibility may implicate the state's initial burden, under In re Winship, 397 U.S. 358 (1970), to prove every element of the offense beyond a reasonable doubt, while the second possibility does not. Patterson v. New York, 432 U.S. 197 (1977); Leland v. Oregon, 343 U.S. 790 (1952).

The power of the states to determine the existence of criminal insanity following the establishment of the underlying offense is well established. In *Leland v. Oregon*, we upheld a state law that required the defendant to prove insanity beyond a reasonable doubt, observing that this burden had no effect on the state's initial burden to prove every element of the underlying criminal offense. . . .

Louisiana law follows the pattern in *Leland* with clarity and precision. [T]he petitioner entered a dual plea of not guilty and not guilty by reason of insanity. The dual plea, which the majority does not discuss or even mention, ensures that the *Winship* burden remains on the state prove all the elements of the crime. . . .

Compliance with the standard of proof beyond a reasonable doubt is the defining, central feature in criminal adjudication, unique to the criminal law. . . . We have often subjected to heightened due process scrutiny, with regard to both purpose and duration, deprivations of physical liberty imposed before a judgment is rendered under this standard. . . . The same heightened due process scrutiny does not obtain, though, once the state has met its burden of proof and obtained an adjudication. It is well settled that upon compliance with *In re Winship*, the state may incarcerate on any reasonable basis.

. . . A verdict of not guilty by reason of insanity is neither equivalent nor comparable to a verdict of not guilty standing alone. We would not allow a state to evade its burden of proof by replacing its criminal law with a civil system in which there is no presumption of innocence and the defendant has the burden of proof. Nor should we entertain the proposition that this case differs from a conviction of guilty because petitioner has been adjudged "not guilty by reason of insanity," rather than "guilty but insane." Petitioner has suggested no grounds on which to distinguish the liberty interests involved or procedural protections afforded as a consequence of the state's ultimate choice of nomenclature. The due process implications ought not to vary under these circumstances. This is a criminal case in which the state has complied with the rigorous demands of *In re Winship*. . . .

. . . Petitioner in *Jones* contended that *Addington* and *O'Connor* applied to criminal proceedings as well as civil, requiring the government to prove insanity and dangerousness by clear and convincing evidence before commitment. We rejected that contention. In *Jones* we distinguished criminal from civil commitment, holding that the due process clause permits automatic incarceration after a criminal adjudication and without further process. The majority today in effect overrules that holding. . . .

The majority's opinion is troubling at a further level, because it fails to recognize or account for profound differences between clinical insanity and state-law definitions of criminal insanity. It is by now well established that insanity as defined by the criminal law has no direct analog in medicine or science. . . . As provided by Louisiana law, and consistent with both federal criminal law and the law of a majority of the states, petitioner was found not guilty by reason of insanity under the traditional *M'Naghten* test. . . .

Because the *M'Naghten* test for insanity turns on a finding of criminal irresponsibility at the time of the offense, it is quite wrong to place reliance on the fact, as the majority does, that Louisiana does not contend that petitioner is now insane. This circumstance should come as no surprise, since petitioner was competent at the time of his plea, and indeed could not have entered a plea otherwise, see Drope v. Missouri, 420 U.S. 162 (1975). Present sanity would have relevance if petitioner had been committed as a consequence of civil proceedings, in which dangerous conduct in the past was used to predict similar conduct in the future. It has no relevance here, however. Petitioner has not been confined based on predictions about future behavior but rather for past criminal conduct. Unlike civil commitment proceedings, which attempt to divine the future from the past, in a criminal trial whose outcome turns on *M'Naghten*, findings of past insanity and past criminal conduct possess intrinsic and ultimate significance. . . .

The establishment of a criminal act and of insanity under the *M'Naghten* regime provides a legitimate basis for confinement. Although Louisiana has chosen not to punish insanity acquittees, the state has not surrendered its interest in incapacitative incarceration. . . . "[I]solation of the dangerous has always been considered an important function of the criminal law," Powell v. Texas, 392 U.S. at 539 (Black, J., concurring), and insanity acquittees are a special class of offenders proved dangerous beyond their own ability to comprehend.

The wisdom of incarceration under these circumstances is demonstrated by its high level of acceptance. . . .

It remains to be seen whether the majority, by questioning the legitimacy of incapacitative incarceration, puts in doubt the confinement of persons other than insanity acquittees. Parole release provisions often place the burden of proof on the prisoner to prove his lack of dangerousness. . . . It is difficult for me to reconcile the rationale of incapacitative incarceration, which underlies these regimes, with the opinion of the majority, which discounts its legitimacy. . . .

I submit that today's decision is unwarranted and unwise. I share the Court's concerns about the risks inherent in requiring a committed person to prove what can often be imprecise, but as Justice Thomas observes in his dissent, this is not a case in which the period of confinement exceeds the gravity of the offense or in which there are reasons to believe the release proceedings are pointless or a sham. Petitioner has been incarcerated for less than one-third the statutory maximum for the offenses proved by the state. See La.Rev.Stat. Ann. §§ 14:60 (aggravated burglary) and 14:94 (illegal use of a weapon) (West 1986). In light of these facts, the majority's repeated reference to "indefinite detention," with apparent reference to the potential duration of confinement, and not its lack of a fixed end point, has no bearing on this case. It is also significant to observe that this is not a case in which the incarcerated subject has demonstrated his nondangerousness. Within the two months before his release hearing, petitioner had been sent to a maximum security section of the Feliciana Forensic Facility because of altercations with another patient. Further, there is evidence in the record which suggests that petitioner's initial claim of insanity may have been feigned. The medical panel that reviewed petitioner's request for release stated that "there is no evidence of mental illness," and indeed that there was "never any evidence of mental illness or disease since admission." In sum, it would be difficult to conceive of a less compelling situation for the imposition of sweeping new constitutional commands such as the majority imposes today.

Because the majority conflates the standards for civil and criminal commitment, treating this criminal case as though it were civil, it upsets a careful balance relied upon by the states, not only in determining the conditions for continuing confinement, but also in defining the defenses permitted for mental incapacity at the time of the crime in question. In my view, having adopted a traditional and well-accepted test for determining criminal insanity, and having complied with the rigorous demands of *In re Winship*, the state possesses the constitutional authority to incarcerate petitioner for the protection of society. I submit my respectful dissent.

■ JUSTICE THOMAS, with whom CHIEF JUSTICE REHNQUIST and JUSTICE SCALIA join, dissenting. . . .

The Court today attempts to circumvent Jones v. United States, 463 U.S. 354 (1983) by declaring that a state's interest in treating insanity acquittees differently from civil committees evaporates the instant an acquittee "becomes sane." I do not agree. As an initial matter, I believe that it is unwise, given our present understanding of the human mind, to suggest that a determination that a person has "regained sanity" is precise. . . . In this very case, the panel that evaluated Foucha in

1988 concluded that there was "never any evidence of mental illness or disease since admission," the trial court, of course, concluded that Foucha was "presently insane," at the time it accepted his plea and sent him to Feliciana.

The distinction between civil committees and insanity acquittees, after all, turns not on considerations of present sanity, but instead on the fact that the latter have "already unhappily manifested the reality of anti-social conduct. . . . " While a state may renounce a punitive interest by offering an insanity defense, it does not follow that, once the acquittee's sanity is "restored," the state is required to ignore his criminal act, and to renounce all interest in protecting society from him.

Furthermore, the federal constitution does not require a state to "ignore the danger of 'calculated abuse of the insanity defense.' " A state that decides to offer its criminal defendants an insanity defense, which the defendant himself is given the choice of invoking, is surely allowed to attach to that defense certain consequences that prevent abuse. A state may reasonably decide that the integrity of an insanity-acquittal scheme requires the continued commitment of insanity acquittees who remain dangerous. Surely, the citizenry would not long tolerate the insanity defense if a serial killer who convinces a jury that he is not guilty by reason of insanity is returned to the streets immediately after trial by convincing a different factfinder that he is not in fact insane. . . .

In its arguments before this Court, Louisiana chose to place primary reliance on our decision in United States v. Salerno, 481 U.S. 739 (1987) in which we upheld provisions of the Bail Reform Act of 1984 that allowed limited pretrial detention of criminal suspects. That case, as the Court notes, is readily distinguishable. Insanity acquittees, in sharp and obvious contrast to pretrial detainees, have had their day in court. Although they have not been convicted of crimes, neither have they been exonerated, as they would have been upon a determination of "not guilty" simpliciter. Insanity acquittees thus stand in a fundamentally different position from persons who have not been adjudicated to have committed criminal acts. That is what distinguishes this case (and what distinguished *Jones*) from *Salerno* and Jackson v. Indiana, 406 U.S. 715 (1972). In *Jackson*, as in *Salerno*, the state had not proven beyond a reasonable doubt that the accused had committed criminal acts or otherwise was dangerous. The Court disregards this critical distinction, and apparently deems applicable the same scrutiny to pretrial detainees as to persons determined in a judicial proceeding to have committed a criminal act.[16] . . .

---

[16] The Court asserts that the principles set forth in this dissent necessarily apply not only to insanity acquittees, but also to convicted prisoners. "The dissent's rationale for continuing to hold the insanity acquittee would surely justify treating the convicted felon in the same way, and, if put to it, it appears that the dissent would permit it." That is obviously not so. If Foucha had been convicted of the crimes with which he was charged and sentenced to the statutory maximum of 32 years in prison, the state would not be entitled to extend his sentence at the end of that period. To do so would obviously violate the prohibition on ex post facto laws set forth in Art. I, § 10, cl. 1. But Foucha was not sentenced to incarceration for any definite period of time; to the contrary, he pleaded not guilty by reason of insanity and was ordered institutionalized until he was able to meet the conditions statutorily prescribed for his release. To acknowledge, as I do, that it is constitutionally permissible for a state to provide for the continued confinement of an insanity acquittee who remains dangerous is obviously quite different than to assert that the state is allowed to confine anyone who is dangerous for as long as it wishes.

I respectfully dissent.

## NOTES ON THE DISPOSITION OF PERSONS ACQUITTED BY REASON OF INSANITY

### 1. QUESTIONS AND COMMENTS ON *FOUCHA*

*Foucha* presents many interesting issues.[a] At the most general level, the Justices are delineating the constitutional predicates for non-criminal confinement. Detention of deportable aliens and quarantine of individuals with infectious diseases are well-established cases. In *Salerno*, the Court upheld preventive definition of dangerous defendants before trial. The Court's decisions in *Addington*, *Jackson* and *Jones* pertain to the three usual variations of civil commitment of persons with mental illness—ordinary involuntary psychiatric hospitalization, commitment of persons found incompetent to stand trial and commitment of insanity acquittees. In *Foucha*, Justice White suggests that the Louisiana statute, which dispenses with mental illness as a predicate for civil commitment of insanity acquittees, is "only a step away from substituting confinements for dangerousness for our present system" of criminal punishment. Is he right?

*Foucha* also raises basic questions about the nature and meaning of the insanity defense. Justice White, quoting *Jones*, says that "as Foucha was not convicted, he may not be punished." By contrast, Justice Kennedy argues that the insanity verdict is equivalent to a criminal conviction, and that the state may "incarcerate [insanity acquittees] on any reasonable basis." Which view reflects a better understanding of the insanity defense?

Justices Kennedy and Thomas both suggest that Louisiana's statute may have been designed in part to deter abuses of the insanity defense, and Justice Kennedy even hints that Foucha's own insanity claim may have been fabricated. Such an assessment of the facts strengthens the intuition that Foucha himself should not be released, but does it provide an acceptable rationale for Louisiana's statutory scheme?

On another account of the facts, Foucha's insanity claim was predicated on a genuine drug-induced psychotic state which receded during the months following the offense. Although one might have doubts about the moral basis for such insanity claim, it was apparently accepted under Louisiana law. Should the dispositional scheme for insanity acquittees be designed to prolong the hospitalization of acquittees whose mental disorders were drug-induced?

Consider finally the implications of *Foucha* for acquittees whose admittedly severe mental illnesses go into remission during hospitalization. This means that they no longer are experiencing the symptoms of the disorder, and they no longer are acutely mentally ill; from a purely clinical standpoint, they no longer need to be in the hospital. Does *Foucha* apply to these cases?

---

[a] For an analysis of *Foucha*, see James W. Ellis, Limits on the State's Power to Confine Dangerous Persons: Constitutional Implications of *Foucha v. Louisiana*, 15 U. of Puget Sound L. Rev. 635 (1992).

## 2. DANGEROUSNESS

As the constitutional issue was presented in *Foucha*, the Court assumes that Foucha's continued commitment was predicated on a finding of dangerousness. Note, however, that under the Louisiana statute, Foucha was not entitled to release, even on conditions, unless he could prove that he was no longer dangerous. Recall that the Feliciana psychiatrist said he would not "feel comfortable" certifying that Foucha would not be dangerous. Would you? How can an insanity acquittee prove that he will *not* be dangerous?

*Jones* held that the state is justified in presuming dangerousness based on proof of the criminal act. Does the criminal act retain its predictive value indefinitely? Should the state be required to reassume the burden of proof on the dangerousness issue at some point?

Predictive judgments of this sort are confounded by the lack of evidence about the acquittee's response to conditions outside the hospital. How should one balance the acquittee's interest in regaining freedom against the public's interest in avoiding premature release? One possibility is to provide trials of freedom with strict community supervision and expeditious rehospitalization in response to non-compliance. In recent years, a number of states have established administrative review boards to implement programs of conditional release. For an in-depth study of the operation of Oregon's "psychiatric security review board," see Joseph Bloom and Mary Williams, Management and Treatment of Insanity Acquittees: A Model for the 1990's (1994).

## 3. *STATE V. RANDALL*

Justice O'Connor's separate opinion in *Foucha* suggests that the Louisiana approach might have survived constitutional scrutiny if "the nature and duration of detention" had been more narrowly tailored to reflect "pressing public safety concerns." What does she have in mind? Consider in this connection the Wisconsin Supreme Court's decision in State v. Randall, 192 Wis.2d 800, 532 N.W.2d 94 (1995).

Alan Randall pleaded not guilty by reason of insanity to a variety of charges rising out of a 1976 incident in which he shot and killed two police officers and used their squad car to commit a burglary. He was found guilty, in the first stage of a bifurcated trial, of two counts of first-degree murder, one count of burglary, and one count of operating a motor vehicle without consent. In the second phase of the trial, the state entered into a stipulation agreeing that Randall was suffering from paranoid schizophrenia and that he was not guilty by reason of insanity of these offenses. Randall was then committed to a state psychiatric hospital. In January, 1990, Randall petitioned for release under Wisconsin's insanity commitment statute which authorizes discharge or conditional release "if the court is satisfied that [the acquittee] may be safely discharged or released without danger to himself or others."

At the hearing before a six-person jury, psychiatrists and mental health experts described Randall's treatment since his 1977 commitment and testified that he was no longer mentally ill. Other witnesses described his extensive experience with off-grounds privileges between 1981 until 1989 when the hospital terminated its off-grounds privilege policy. In 1986, for example, Randall "participated in numerous activities throughout

Wisconsin on at least 200 different occasions." As a result of these activities, which included attendance at college and steady employment at a local business, he "functioned under normal conditions," outside the hospital for more than 1,300 hours during that year. Despite this evidence, the jury found that Randall could not be "safely discharged," and the court denied his petition for release.

In 1992, after the Supreme Court's decision in *Foucha*, Randall filed a petition seeking immediate release on the ground that Wisconsin's "dangerousness only" release criterion was unconstitutional. The Wisconsin Supreme Court held that Wisconsin's dispositional scheme was distinguishable from the Louisiana scheme struck down in *Foucha*:

> The inference of continuing dangerousness provides the basis for the acquittee's initial commitment to a mental health facility following the insanity acquittal. Under Wisconsin's statutory scheme, the acquittee, once committed, is subject to treatment programs specifically designed to treat both mental and behavioral disorders. Treatment designed to reduce those behavioral disorders which render the individual dangerous may continue even after clinical signs of mental illness are no longer apparent. Such treatment is necessary to realize the ultimate goal of safely returning the acquittee into the community. Because this state's mental health facilities provide such comprehensive treatment we cannot conclude that it is punitive to continue an acquittee's confinement based on dangerousness alone. Rather, we conclude that there is a reasonable relationship between the commitment and the purposes for which the individual is committed and, therefore, that insanity acquittees are treated in a manner consistent with the purposes of their commitment. . . .
>
> Furthermore, unlike the Louisiana statutory scheme held unconstitutional in *Foucha*, we find that the Wisconsin scheme provides sufficient procedural safeguards to insure an acquittee's right to due process. Under the Louisiana statutory scheme, an insanity acquittee could be held in a mental institution for an indefinite and unlimited duration until the acquittee could prove, by a preponderance of the evidence, that he or she was no longer dangerous. Under the Wisconsin procedure, the state, rather than the acquittee, bears the burden to prove by clear and convincing evidence that the commitment should continue because the individual is presently a danger to himself, herself or others. Moreover, commitment is not imposed for an indefinite period of time. [The] commitment may not exceed the maximum term of imprisonment which could have been imposed for the offenses charged.[b] Once the maximum period of the sentence which could have been imposed has elapsed, the court must order the discharge of the insanity acquittee subject to the state's right to commence civil commitment proceedings. . . .

In a separate concurring opinion, Justice Abrahamson expressed doubts about whether the Wisconsin statute, as interpreted in *Randall*, is compatible with *Foucha*:

---

[b] Wisconsin law now limits the acquittee's confinement to two-thirds of the maximum sentence which could have been imposed.—[Footnote by eds.]

> [The statute] is silent about the relationship of mental illness, behavioral disability, medical justification, or treatment to the continued confinement of an acquittee based on dangerousness. The majority opinion appears to graft these requirements onto [the statute] because it concludes that such an interpretation . . . is needed to render it constitutional. The majority is appropriately heeding a teaching of *Foucha*: "Due process requires that the nature of commitment bear some reasonable relation to the purpose for which the individual is committed."
>
> I cannot join the majority opinion, however, because I conclude that the majority's interpretation violates another teaching of *Foucha*. . . . *Foucha* rejected the notion that the state could confine an acquittee in a mental institution on the basis of a condition which is not a mental illness, would not have justified the insanity commitment and was not the basis of that commitment at trial. Thus a "behavioral disorder" (an important concept in the majority opinion but undefined) that renders the acquittee dangerous may be analogous to the antisocial personality condition in *Foucha*, which did not rise to the level of a mental illness or defect on which an insanity commitment could be based.
>
> I recognize that *Foucha* is a troublesome decision and the subject of conflicting interpretations by courts and commentators. The majority struggles to avoid the conclusion mandated by *Foucha*, that mental illness as well as dangerousness are necessary grounds to continue confinement. If I read the majority opinion correctly, the state can continue to confine an acquittee who is not mentally ill but is behaviorally disordered and dangerous if the state can treat the acquittee, but the state must release an acquittee who is not mentally ill but is dangerous if no treatment is available at the institution.

Is the Wisconsin statute, as interpreted in Randall's case compatible with *Foucha*? Would it satisfy Justice O'Connor's concerns?

## NOTE ON THE VERDICT OF GUILTY BUT MENTALLY ILL

At least 12 states have established a separate verdict of "guilty but mentally ill" (GBMI) as an optional verdict in cases in which the defendant pleads insanity.[a] The GBMI concept, as adopted in these states, should be distinguished from two other concepts to which this or similar terminology may refer. First, the GBMI verdict is available in conjunction with, rather than in lieu of, the verdict of "not guilty by reason of insanity"; this procedure should therefore be distinguished from proposals to abolish the insanity defense and to establish, in its stead, a special dispositional procedure for guilty but mentally ill defendants. Second, the consequence of a GBMI verdict is conviction and a criminal sentence; the procedure should therefore be distinguished from proposals to rename the insanity verdict ("guilty but insane" rather than "not guilty by reason of insanity") without altering

---

[a] For general commentary on the GBMI verdict, see Christopher Slobogin, The Guilty But Mentally Ill Verdict: An Idea Whose Time Should Not Have Come, 53 G.W.L.Rev. 494 (1985); Bradley D. McGraw, Diana Farthing-Capowich, and Ingo Keilitz, The Guilty But Mentally Ill Verdict & Current State of Knowledge, 30 Vill.L.Rev. 117 (1984); Ralph Slovenko, Commentaries on Psychiatry and Law: Guilty But Mentally Ill, 10 J.Amer.Acad.Psychiatry and L. 541 (1982).

its dispositional consequences—i.e., subjecting the defendant only to therapeutic restraint under a civil commitment statute.

Procedures under GBMI legislation vary significantly from state to state. However, the statutes typically provide that upon entry of the verdict, the trial judge must impose a criminal sentence. The defendant is then evaluated by correctional or mental health authorities for the purpose of determining his or her suitability for psychiatric treatment. If the evaluators conclude that psychiatric treatment is needed, the person is hospitalized and, upon discharge, is returned to prison to serve the remainder of the sentence. In effect, whether the prisoner will actually be placed in a mental health facility is typically a discretionary determination.

The GBMI verdict is predicated upon different findings in different states. Under most of the statutes, the dispositive finding is that the defendant was "mentally ill" (though not legally insane) at the time of the offense; the definition of "mental illness" is typically drawn from the state's civil commitment statute. In Michigan, for example, mental illness is defined as "a substantial disorder of thought or mood which significantly impairs judgment, behavior, capacity to recognize reality, or ability to cope with the ordinary demands of life."

In a few states, the required finding is linked to criteria of criminal responsibility. In Delaware, for example, the exclusive criterion of insanity is "lack of substantial capacity to appreciate wrongfulness," whereas the GBMI verdict can be based on volitional impairment (that the defendant suffered from a "psychiatric disorder" which "left [him] with insufficient will-power to choose whether he would do the act or refrain from doing it. . . ."). In Alaska, the exclusive criterion of exculpation is that the defendant was "unable . . . to appreciate the nature and quality of his conduct," whereas the criteria for the GBMI verdict are derived from the Model Penal Code insanity test.

The debate about GBMI legislation focuses in part on its dispositional consequences. Its proponents claim that it is designed to establish a procedure other than the NGRI verdict to facilitate psychiatric treatment of mentally disordered offenders who would otherwise be untreated. Critics respond that the procedure is misleading because it does not, in fact, assure treatment; further, they argue, a separate verdict is unnecessary to accomplish dispositional objectives because all states either operate psychiatric hospitals within the correctional system or have well-established procedures for transferring prisoners to secure mental health facilities. Finally, the critics say, a jury verdict based on evidence of past mental condition is an awkward device for triggering placement decisions based on the defendant's mental condition at the time of sentence.

As these observations suggest, the impact of the GBMI procedure on the sentencing and correctional process is ancillary to its effect on the adjudication of criminal responsibility. What is the intended effect of the optional verdict? Is it designed to subvert the insanity defense by offering juries a compromise verdict in cases in which an insanity acquittal would otherwise be proper? Or is it designed to establish a criterion of diminished responsibility to take into account psychological impairments that do not meet the criteria for insanity? Regardless of the legislative purpose, what is the likely effect of the GBMI procedure on the frequency of NGRI pleas and acquittals?[b]

## SUBSECTION B: CIVIL COMMITMENT OF DANGEROUS SEX OFFENDERS

### INTRODUCTORY NOTE ON CIVIL COMMITMENT OF DANGEROUS SEX OFFENDERS

As noted at the beginning of this Section, some states provide for indeterminate civil commitment of persons charged with or convicted of specified sex offenses who are found, in a separate proceeding, to be "sexual psychopaths" or "mentally disordered sex offenders." Courts typically have held that these statutes are non-penal in character, the legislative purpose being to treat the person's condition rather than to punish the person for the underlying offense. See, e.g. Allen v. Illinois, 478 U.S. 364 (1986). These commitments differ somewhat from insanity commitments because they are not predicated on a finding of non-responsibility.

The first of these so-called sex psychopath laws was enacted in 1937 and by the mid-1960s about half of the states had enacted such legislation. However, in the wake of libertarian reforms of other types of civil commitment legislation and a deepening skepticism about the prospects for successful treatment of sex offenders, most states repealed their sex psychopath legislation in the 1970s and 80s.[a]

A new generation of sex offender legislation appeared in the 1990s. The first and most well-known example of this new trend was Washington's Sexually Violent Predator Law enacted in 1990.[b] Under the Washington statute, persons found to be "sexually violent predators" are subject to indeterminate commitment after they have completed serving the criminal sentence for their underlying offenses. The legislature explained the need for this approach in the preamble to the statute:

> In contrast to persons appropriate for [ordinary] civil commitment, sexually violent predators generally have antisocial personality features which are unamenable to existing mental illness treatment modalities and those features render them likely to engage in sexually violent behavior. . . . The legislature further finds that the prognosis for curing sexually violent offenders is poor [and] the treatment needs of this population are very long-term. . . .

Under the statute, a "sexually violent predator" is defined as someone "who has been convicted of or charged with a crime of sexual violence and who suffers from a mental abnormality or personality disorder which

---

[b] For empirical studies of the GBMI procedure, see Henry J. Steadman et al., Before and After Hinckley: Evaluating Insanity Defense Reform (1993); National Center for State Courts, The Guilty But Mentally Ill Verdict: An Empirical Study (1985); Gare A. Smith and James A. Hall, Evaluating Michigan's Guilty But Mentally Ill Verdict: An Empirical Study, 16 Mich.J. L.Reform 77 (1982).

[a] See generally, Samuel Brakel and James Cavanaugh, Jr., Of Psychopaths and Pendulums: Legal and Psychiatric Treatment of Sex Offenders in The United States, 30 N.M.L Rev. 69 (2000); American Bar Association, Criminal Justice Mental Health Standards, Std 7–8.1 (recommending repeal of sex psychopath statutes) and commentary, pages 417–25 (1986).

[b] The Washington Legislature had repealed its older sex psychopath law in 1984.

makes the person likely to engage in predatory acts of sexual violence." Crimes of sexual violence include crimes not usually considered sex offenses if they are determined beyond a reasonable doubt to have been "sexually motivated." The term "personality disorder" is not defined by the statute, but the term "mental abnormality" is defined as "a congenital or acquired condition affecting the emotional or volitional capacity which predisposes the person to the commission of criminal sexual acts." "Predatory" acts are those directed at strangers or individuals groomed by the offender for the purpose of victimization.

When a person's sentence for a sexually violent offense has expired or is about to expire, the state is authorized to file a petition alleging the person to be a sexually violent predator. If the state proves, beyond a reasonable doubt, that the detainee is a sexually violent predator, the detainee is committed to a facility "for control, care, and treatment" until "safe to be at large." All treatment centers in Washington are located within correctional institutions.

Over the decade after Washington enacted its Sexually Violent Predator (SVP) law, about one-third of the states enacted similar statutes. In fact, many of the legislatures copied Washington's SVP statute almost word-for-word. One of these states was Kansas. Constitutional challenges to the SVP laws have been addressed by the Supreme Court in the context of the Kansas statute in the following cases.

## Kansas v. Hendricks

Supreme Court of the United States, 1997.
521 U.S. 346.

■ JUSTICE THOMAS delivered the opinion of the Court.

In 1994, Kansas enacted the Sexually Violent Predator Act, which establishes procedures for the civil commitment of persons who, due to a "mental abnormality" or a "personality disorder," are likely to engage in "predatory acts of sexual violence." Kan. Stat. Ann. § 59–29a01 *et seq.* (1994). The state invoked the Act for the first time to commit Leroy Hendricks, an inmate who had a long history of sexually molesting children, and who was scheduled for release from prison shortly after the Act became law. Hendricks challenged his commitment on, inter alia, "substantive" due process, double jeopardy, and ex post facto grounds. The Kansas Supreme Court invalidated the Act, holding that its precommitment condition of a "mental abnormality" did not satisfy what the court perceived to be the "substantive" due process requirement that involuntary civil commitment must be predicated on a finding of "mental illness." . . . We granted certiorari . . . and now reverse the judgment below.

I

A

The Kansas legislature enacted the Sexually Violent Predator Act (Act) in 1994 to grapple with the problem of managing repeat sexual offenders. Although Kansas already had a statute addressing the involuntary commitment of those defined as "mentally ill," the legislature determined that existing civil commitment procedures were inadequate to confront the risks presented by "sexually violent predators." In the Act's preamble, the legislature explained:

> [A] small but extremely dangerous group of sexually violent predators exist who do not have a mental disease or defect that renders them appropriate for involuntary treatment pursuant to the [general involuntary civil commitment statute]. . . . In contrast to persons appropriate for civil commitment under the [general involuntary civil commitment statute], sexually violent predators generally have anti-social personality features which are unamenable to existing mental illness treatment modalities and those features render them likely to engage in sexually violent behavior. The legislature further finds that sexually violent predators' likelihood of engaging in repeat acts of predatory sexual violence is high. The existing involuntary commitment procedure . . . is inadequate to address the risk these sexually violent predators pose to society. The legislature further finds that the prognosis for rehabilitating sexually violent predators in a prison setting is poor, the treatment needs of this population are very long term and the treatment modalities for this population are very different than the traditional treatment modalities for people appropriate for commitment under the [general involuntary civil commitment statute].

. . . The Act defined a "sexually violent predator" as "any person who has been convicted of or charged with a sexually violent offense and who suffers from a mental abnormality or personality disorder which makes the person likely to engage in the predatory acts of sexual violence." A "mental abnormality" was defined, in turn, as a "congenital or acquired condition affecting the emotional or volitional capacity which predisposes the person to commit sexually violent offenses in a degree constituting such person a menace to the health and safety of others."

As originally structured, the Act's civil commitment procedures pertained to: (i) a presently confined person who, like Hendricks, "has been convicted of a sexually violent offense" and is scheduled for release; (ii) a person who has been "charged with a sexually violent offense" but has been found incompetent to stand trial; (iii) a person who has been found "not guilty by reason of insanity of a sexually violent offense"; and (iv) a person found "not guilty" of a sexually violent offense because of a mental disease or defect. . . .

B

In 1984, Hendricks was convicted of taking "indecent liberties" with two 13-year-old boys. After serving nearly 10 years of his sentence, he was slated for release to a halfway house. Shortly before his scheduled release, however, the state filed a petition in state court seeking Hendricks' civil confinement as a sexually violent predator. . . . During [the] trial, Hendricks' own testimony revealed a chilling history of repeated child sexual molestation and abuse, beginning in 1955 when he exposed his genitals to two young girls. At that time, he pleaded guilty to indecent exposure. Then, in 1957, he was convicted of lewdness involving a young girl and received a brief jail sentence. In 1960, he molested two young boys while he worked for a carnival. After serving two years in prison for that offense, he was paroled, only to be rearrested for molesting a 7-year-old girl. Attempts were made to treat him for his sexual deviance, and in 1965 he was considered "safe to be at large," and was discharged from a state psychiatric hospital.

Shortly thereafter, however, Hendricks sexually assaulted another young boy and girl—he performed oral sex on the 8-year-old girl and fondled the 11-year-old boy. He was again imprisoned in 1967, but refused to participate in a sex offender treatment program, and thus remained incarcerated until his parole in 1972. Diagnosed as a pedophile, Hendricks entered into, but then abandoned, a treatment program. He testified that despite having received professional help for his pedophilia, he continued to harbor sexual desires for children. Indeed, soon after his 1972 parole, Hendricks began to abuse his own stepdaughter and stepson. He forced the children to engage in sexual activity with him over a period of approximately four years. Then, as noted above, Hendricks was convicted of "taking indecent liberties" with two adolescent boys after he attempted to fondle them. As a result of that conviction, he was once again imprisoned, and was serving that sentence when he reached his conditional release date in September 1994.

Hendricks admitted that he had repeatedly abused children whenever he was not confined. He explained that when he "get[s] stressed out," he "can't control the urge" to molest children. Although Hendricks recognized that his behavior harms children, and he hoped he would not sexually molest children again, he stated that the only sure way he could keep from sexually abusing children in the future was "to die." Hendricks readily agreed with the state physician's diagnosis that he suffers from pedophilia and that he is not cured of the condition; indeed, he told the physician that "treatment is bull ____."

The jury unanimously found beyond a reasonable doubt that Hendricks was a sexually violent predator. The trial court subsequently determined, as a matter of state law, that pedophilia qualifies as a "mental abnormality" as defined by the Act, and thus ordered Hendricks committed to the secretary's custody.

Hendricks appealed, claiming, among other things, that application of the Act to him violated the Federal Constitution's Due Process, Double Jeopardy, and Ex Post Facto clauses. The Kansas Supreme Court accepted Hendricks' due process claim. The court declared that in order to commit a person involuntarily in a civil proceeding, a state is required by "substantive" due process to prove by clear and convincing evidence that the person is both mentally ill and a danger to himself or to others. The court then determined that the Act's definition of "mental abnormality" did not satisfy what it perceived to be this Court's "mental illness" requirement in the civil commitment context. As a result, the court held that "the Act violates Hendricks' substantive due process rights." . . .

II

A

Kansas argues that the Act's definition of "mental abnormality" satisfies "substantive" due process requirements. We agree. Although freedom from physical restraint "has always been at the core of the liberty protected by the due process clause from arbitrary governmental action," Foucha v. Louisiana, 504 U.S. 71 (1992), that liberty interest is not absolute. The Court has recognized that an individual's constitutionally protected interest in avoiding physical restraint may be overridden even in the civil context. . . . Accordingly, states have in certain narrow circumstances provided for the forcible civil detainment of people who are unable to control their behavior and who thereby pose a danger to the public health and safety. We have consistently upheld such involuntary commitment statutes provided the confinement takes place pursuant to proper procedures and evidentiary standards. It thus cannot be said that the involuntary civil confinement of a limited subclass of dangerous persons is contrary to our understanding of ordered liberty.

The challenged Act unambiguously requires a finding of dangerousness either to one's self or to others as a prerequisite to involuntary confinement. Commitment proceedings can be initiated only when a person "has been convicted of or charged with a sexually violent offense," and "suffers from a mental abnormality or personality disorder which makes the person likely to engage in the predatory acts of sexual violence." The statute thus requires proof of more than a mere predisposition to violence; rather, it requires evidence of past sexually violent behavior and a present mental condition that creates a likelihood of such conduct in the future if the person is not incapacitated. As we have recognized, "[p]revious instances of violent behavior are an important indicator of future violent tendencies," Heller v. Doe, 509 U.S. 312, 323 (1993).

A finding of dangerousness, standing alone, is ordinarily not a sufficient ground upon which to justify indefinite involuntary commitment. We have sustained civil commitment statutes when they have coupled proof of dangerousness with the proof of some additional factor, such as a "mental illness" or "mental abnormality." See e.g., *Heller v. Doe*, at 314–15 (Kentucky statute permitting commitment of mentally retarded or mentally ill and dangerous individuals); Allen v. Illinois, 478 U.S. 364, 366 (1986) (Illinois statute permitting commitment of "mentally ill" and dangerous individual). . . . These added statutory requirements serve to limit involuntary civil confinement to those who suffer from a volitional impairment rendering them dangerous beyond their control. The Kansas Act is plainly of a kind with these other civil commitment statutes: It requires a finding of future dangerousness, and then links that finding to the existence of a "mental abnormality" or "personality disorder" that makes it difficult, if not impossible, for the person to control his dangerous behavior. The precommitment requirement of a "mental abnormality" or "personality disorder" is consistent with the requirements of these other statutes that we have upheld in that it narrows the class of persons eligible for confinement to those who are unable to control their dangerousness.

Hendricks nonetheless argues that our earlier cases dictate a finding of "mental illness" as a prerequisite for civil commitment, citing *Foucha*. . . . He then asserts that a "mental abnormality" is *not* equivalent to a "mental illness" because it is a term coined by the Kansas legislature, rather than by the psychiatric community. Contrary to Hendricks' assertion, the term "mental illness" is devoid of any talismanic significance. Not only do "psychiatrists disagree widely and frequently on what constitutes mental illness," but the Court itself has used a variety of expressions to describe the mental condition of those properly subject to civil confinement. Indeed, we have never required state legislatures to adopt any particular nomenclature in drafting civil commitment statutes. Rather, we have traditionally left to legislators the task of defining terms of a medical nature that have legal signifycance. As a consequence, the states have, over the years, developed numerous specialized terms to define mental health concepts. Often, those definitions do not fit precisely with the definitions employed by the medical community. The legal definitions of "insanity" and "competency," for example, vary substantially from their psychiatric counterparts. See, *e.g.,* Jules Gerard, The Usefulness of the Medical Model to the Legal System, 39 Rutgers L.Rev. 377, 391–394 (1987) (discussing differing purposes of legal system and the medical profession in recognizing mental illness). Legal definitions, however, which must "take into account such issues as individual responsibility . . . and competency," need not mirror those advanced by the medical profession. American Psychiatric Association, Diagnostic and Statistical Manual of Mental Disorders xxiii, xxvii (4th ed.1994).

To the extent that the civil commitment statutes we have considered set forth criteria relating to an individual's inability to control his dangerousness, the Kansas Act sets forth comparable criteria and Hendricks' condition doubtless satisfies those criteria. The mental health professionals who evaluated Hendricks diagnosed him as suffering from pedophilia, a condition the psychiatric profession itself classifies as a serious mental disorder. Hendricks even conceded that, when he becomes "stressed out," he cannot "control the urge" to molest children. This admitted lack of volitional control, coupled with a prediction of future dangerousness, adequately distinguishes Hendricks from other dangerous persons who are perhaps more properly dealt with exclusively through criminal proceedings. Hendricks' diagnosis as a pedophile, which qualifies as a "mental abnormality" under the Act, thus plainly suffices for due process purposes.

B

[The Court then addressed Hendricks' argument that the Act violates the constitution's Double Jeopardy prohibition and its ban on Ex Post Facto lawmaking:]

The thrust of Hendricks' argument is that the Act establishes criminal proceedings; hence confinement under it necessarily constitutes punishment. He contends that where, as here, newly enacted "punishment" is predicated upon past conduct for which he has already been convicted and forced to serve a prison sentence, the constitution's Double Jeopardy and Ex Post Facto clauses are violated. We are unpersuaded by Hendricks' argument that Kansas has established criminal proceedings.

The categorization of a particular proceeding as civil or criminal "is first of all a question of statutory construction." *Allen,* supra, 478 U.S. at 368. We must initially ascertain whether the legislature meant the statute to establish "civil" proceedings. If so, we ordinarily defer to the legislature's stated intent. Here, Kansas' objective to create a civil proceeding is evidenced by its placement of the Act within the Kansas probate code, instead of the criminal code, Kan. Stat. Ann., Article 29

(1994) ("Care and Treatment for Mentally Ill Persons"), as well as its description of the Act as creating a "*civil commitment procedure*" (emphasis added). Nothing on the face of the statute suggests that the legislature sought to create anything other than a civil commitment scheme designed to protect the public from harm.

Although we recognize that a "civil label is not always dispositive," *Allen,* supra, at 369, we will reject the legislature's manifest intent only where a party challenging the statute provides "the clearest proof" that "the statutory scheme [is] so punitive either in purpose or effect as to negate [the State's] intention" to deem it "civil," United States v. Ward, 448 U.S. 242, 248–49 (1980). In those limited circumstances, we will consider the statute to have established criminal proceedings for constitutional purposes. Hendricks, however, has failed to satisfy this heavy burden.

As a threshold matter, commitment under the Act does not implicate either of the two primary objectives of criminal punishment: retribution or deterrence. The Act's purpose is not retributive because it does not affix culpability for prior criminal conduct. Instead, such conduct is used solely for evidentiary purposes, either to demonstrate that a "mental abnormality" exists or to support a finding of future dangerousness. We have previously concluded that an Illinois statute was nonpunitive even though it was triggered by the commission of a sexual assault, explaining that evidence of the prior criminal conduct was "received not to punish past misdeeds, but primarily to show the accused's mental condition and to predict future behavior." *Allen,* supra, at 371. In addition, the Kansas Act does not make a criminal conviction a prerequisite for commitment—persons absolved of criminal responsibility may nonetheless be subject to confinement under the Act. An absence of the necessary criminal responsibility suggests that the state is not seeking retribution for a past misdeed. Thus, the fact that the Act may be "tied to criminal activity" is "insufficient to render the statut[e] punitive." United States v. Ursery, 518 U.S. 267 (1996).

Moreover, unlike a criminal statute, no finding of scienter is required to commit an individual who is found to be a sexually violent predator; instead, the commitment determination is made based on a "mental abnormality" or "personality disorder" rather than on one's criminal intent. The existence of a scienter requirement is customarily an important element in distinguishing criminal from civil statutes. See Kennedy v. Mendoza-Martinez, 372 U.S. 144, 168 (1963). The absence of such a requirement here is evidence that confinement under the statute is not intended to be retributive.

Nor can it be said that the legislature intended the Act to function as a deterrent. Those persons committed under the Act are, by definetion, suffering from a "mental abnormality" or a "personality disorder" that prevents them from exercising adequate control over their behavior. Such persons are therefore unlikely to be deterred by the threat of confinement. And the conditions surrounding that confinement do not suggest a punitive purpose on the state's part. The State has represented that an individual confined under the Act is not subject to the more restrictive conditions placed on state prisoners, but instead experiences essentially the same conditions as any involuntarily committed patient in the state mental institution. Because none of the parties argues that people institutionalized under the Kansas general civil commitment statute are subject to punitive conditions, even though they may be involuntarily confined, it is difficult to conclude that persons confined under this Act are being "punished."

Although the civil commitment scheme at issue here does involve an affirmative restraint, "the mere fact that a person is detained does not inexorably lead to the conclusion that the government has imposed punishment." United States v. Salerno, 481 U.S. 739, 746 (1987). The state may take measures to restrict the freedom of the dangerously mentally ill. This is a legitimate nonpunitive governmental objective and has been historically so regarded. The Court has, in fact, cited the confinement of "mentally unstable individuals who present a danger to the public" as one classic example of nonpunitive detention. Id. at 748–49. If detention for the purpose of protecting the community from harm *necessarily* constituted punishment, then all involuntary civil commitments would have to be considered punishment. But we have never so held.

Hendricks focuses on his confinement's potentially indefinite duration as evidence of the state's punitive intent. That focus, however, is misplaced. Far from any punitive objective, the confinement's duration is instead linked to the stated purposes of the commitment, namely, to hold the person until his mental abnormality no longer causes him to be a threat to others. Cf. *Jones v. United States*, 463 U.S. at 368 (noting with approval that "because it is impossible to predict how long it will take for any given individual to recover [from insanity] or indeed whether he will ever recover—Congress has chosen . . . to leave the length of commitment indeterminate, subject to periodic review of the patients' suitability for release"). If, at any time, the confined person is adjudged "safe to be at large," he is statutorily entitled to immediate release.

Furthermore, commitment under the Act is only *potentially* indefinite. The maximum amount of time an individual can be incapacitated pursuant to a single judicial proceeding is one year. If Kansas seeks to continue the detention beyond that year, a court must once again determine beyond a reasonable doubt that the detainee satisfies the same standards as required for the initial confinement. This requirement again demonstrates that Kansas does not intend an individual committed pursuant to the Act to remain confined any longer than he suffers from a mental abnormality rendering him unable to control his dangerousness.

Hendricks next contends that the state's use of procedural safeguards traditionally found in criminal trials makes the proceedings here criminal rather than civil. In *Allen,* we confronted a similar argument. There, the petitioner "place[d] great reliance on the fact that proceedings under the Act are accompanied by procedural safeguards usually found in criminal trials" to argue that the proceedings were civil in name only. We rejected that argument, however, explaining that the state's decision "to provide some of the safeguards applicable in criminal trials cannot itself turn these proceedings into criminal prosecutions." The numerous procedural and evidentiary protections afforded here demonstrate that the Kansas legislature has taken great care to confine only a narrow class of particularly dangerous individuals, and then only after meeting the strictest procedural standards. That Kansas chose to afford such procedural protections does not transform a civil commitment proceeding into a criminal prosecution.

Finally, Hendricks argues that the Act is necessarily punitive because it fails to offer any legitimate "treatment." Without such treatment, Hendricks asserts, confinement under the Act amounts to little more than disguised punishment. Hendricks' argument assumes that treatment for his condition is available, but that the state has failed (or refused) to provide it. The Kansas Supreme Court, however, apparently rejected this assumption, explaining:

> It is clear that the overriding concern of the legislature is to continue the segregation of sexually violent offenders from the public. Treatment with the goal of reintegrating them into society is incidental, at best. The record reflects that treatment for sexually violent predators is all but nonexistent. The legislature concedes that sexually violent predators are not amenable to treatment under [the existing Kansas involuntary commitment statute]. If there is nothing to treat under [that statute], then there is no mental illness. In that light, the provisions of the Act for treatment appear somewhat disingenuous.

It is possible to read this passage as a determination that Hendricks' condition was *untreatable* under the existing Kansas civil commitment statute, and thus the Act's sole purpose was incapacitation. Absent a treatable mental illness, the Kansas court concluded, Hendricks could not be detained against his will.

Accepting the Kansas court's apparent determination that treatment is not possible for this category of individuals does not obligate us to adopt its legal conclusions. We have already observed that, under the appropriate circumstances and when accompanied by proper procedures, incapacitation may be a legitimate end of the civil law. See *Allen*, supra, at 373; *Salerno*, 481 U.S. at 748–49. Accordingly, the Kansas court's determination that the Act's "overriding concern" was the continued "segregation of sexually violent offenders" is consistent with our conclusion that the Act establishes civil proceedings, especially when that concern is coupled with the state's ancillary goal of providing treatment to those offenders, if such is possible. While we have upheld state civil commitment statutes that aim both to incapacitate and to treat, see *Allen*, supra, we have never held that the constitution prevents a state from civilly detaining those for whom no treatment is available, but who nevertheless pose a danger to others. A state could hardly be seen as furthering a "punitive" purpose by involuntarily confining persons afflicted with an untreatable, highly contagious disease. Accord, Compagnie Francaise de Navigation a Vapeur v. Louisiana Bd. of Health, 186 U.S. 380 (1902) (permitting involuntary quarantine of persons suffering from communicable diseases). Similarly, it would be of little value to require treatment as a precondition for civil confinement of the dangerously insane when no acceptable treatment existed. To conclude otherwise would obligate a state to release certain confined individuals who were both mentally ill and dangerous simply because they could not be successfully treated for their afflictions.

Alternatively, the Kansas Supreme Court's opinion can be read to conclude that Hendricks' condition is treatable, but that treatment was not the state's "overriding concern," and that no treatment was being provided (at least at the time Hendricks was committed). Even if we accept this determination that the provision of treatment was not the Kansas Legislature's "overriding" or "primary" purpose in passing the Act, this does not rule out the possibility that an ancillary purpose of the Act was to provide treatment, and it does not require us to conclude that the Act is punitive. Indeed, critical language in the Act itself demonstrates that the Secretary, under whose custody sexually violent predators are committed, has an obligation to provide treatment to individuals like Hendricks. ("If the court or jury determines that the person is a sexually violent predator, the person shall be committed to the custody of the secretary of social and rehabilitation services for *control, care and treatment* until such time as the person's mental abnormality or personality disorder has so changed that the person is safe to be at large" (emphasis added)). Other of the Act's sections echo this obligation to provide treatment for committed persons.

Although the treatment program initially offered Hendricks may have seemed somewhat meager, it must be remembered that he was the first person committed under the Act. That the state did not have all of its treatment procedures in place is thus not surprising. What is significant, however, is that Hendricks was placed under the supervision of the Kansas Department of Health and Social and Rehabilitative Services, housed in a unit segregated from the general prison population and operated not by employees of the Department of Corrections, but by other trained individuals. And, before this Court, Kansas declared "[a]bsolutely" that persons committed under the Act are now receiving in the neighborhood of "31½ hours of treatment per week."

Where the state has "disavowed any punitive intent;" limited confinement to a small segment of particularly dangerous individuals; provided strict procedural safeguards; directed that confined persons be segregated from the general prison population and afforded the same status as others who have been civilly committed; recommended treatment if such is possible; and permitted immediate release upon a showing that the individual is no longer dangerous or mentally impaired, we cannot say that it acted with punitive intent. We therefore hold that the Act does not establish criminal proceedings and that involuntary confinement pursuant to the Act is not punitive. Our conclusion that the Act is nonpunitive thus removes an essential prerequisite for both Hendricks' double jeopardy and ex post facto claims.

1

The Double Jeopardy clause provides: "[N]or shall any person be subject for the same offence to be twice put in jeopardy of life or limb." . . . Hendricks argues that, as applied to him, the Act violates double jeopardy principles because his confinement under the Act, imposed after a conviction and a term of incarceration, amounted to both a second prosecution and a second punishment for the same offense. We disagree.

Because we have determined that the Kansas Act is civil in nature, initiation of its commitment proceedings does not constitute a second prosecution. Cf. Jones v. United States, 463 U.S. 354 (1983) (permitting involuntary civil commitment after verdict of not guilty by reason of insanity). Moreover, as commitment under the Act is not tantamount to "punishment," Hendricks' involuntary detention does not violate the Double Jeopardy clause, even though that confinement may follow a prison term. Indeed, in Baxstrom v. Herold, 383 U.S. 107 (1966), we expressly recognized that civil commitment could follow the expiration of a prison term without offending double jeopardy principles. We reasoned that "there is no conceivable basis for distinguishing the commitment of a person who is nearing the end of a penal term from all other civil commitments." If an individual otherwise meets the requirements for involuntary civil commitment, the state is under no obligation to release that individual simply because the detention would follow a period of incarceration. . . .

2

Hendricks' ex post facto claim is similarly flawed. The Ex Post Facto clause, which " 'forbids the application of any new punitive measure to a crime already consummated,' " has been interpreted to pertain exclusively to penal statutes. California Dept. of Corrections v. Morales, 514 U.S. 499, 505 (1995). As we have previously determined, the Act does not impose punishment; thus, its application does not raise ex post facto concerns. Moreover, the Act clearly does not have retroactive effect. Rather, the Act permits involuntary confinement based upon a determination that the person *currently* both suffers from a "mental abnormality" or "personality disorder" and is likely to pose a future danger to the public. To the extent that past behavior is taken into account, it is used, as noted above, solely for evidentiary purposes. Because the Act does not criminalize conduct legal before its enactment, nor deprive Hendricks of any defense that was available to him at the time of his crimes, the Act does not violate the ex post facto clause.

III

We hold that the Kansas Sexually Violent Predator Act comports with due process requirements and neither runs afoul of double jeopardy principles nor constitutes an exercise in impermissible ex post facto lawmaking. Accordingly, the judgment of the Kansas Supreme Court is reversed.

It is so ordered.

■ JUSTICE KENNEDY, concurring.

I join the opinion of the Court in full and add these additional comments.

Though other issues were argued to us, as the action has matured it turns on whether the Kansas statute is an ex post facto law. A law enacted after commission of the offense and which punishes the offense by extending the term of confinement is a textbook example of an ex post facto law. If the object or purpose of the Kansas law had been to provide treatment but the treatment provisions were adopted as a sham or mere pretext, there would have been an indication of the forbidden purpose to punish. The Court's opinion gives a full and complete explanation why an ex post facto challenge based on this contention cannot succeed in the action before us. All this, however, concerns Hendricks alone. My brief, further comment is to caution against dangers inherent when a civil confinement law is used in conjunction with the criminal process, whether or not the law is given retroactive application.

It seems the dissent, too, would validate the Kansas statute as to persons who committed the crime after its enactment, and it might even validate the statute as to Hendricks, assuming a reasonable level of treatment. As all members of the Court seem to agree, then, the power of the state to confine persons who, by reason of a mental disease or mental abnormality, constitute a real, continuing, and serious danger to society is well established. Confinement of such individuals is permitted even if it is pursuant to a statute enacted after the crime has been committed and the offender has begun serving, or has all but completed serving, a penal sentence, provided there is no object or purpose to punish. See Baxstrom v. Herold, 383 U.S. 107, 111–12 (1966). The Kansas law, with its attendant protections, including yearly review and review at any time at the instance of the person confined, is within this pattern and tradition of civil confinement. In this action, the mental abnormality—pedophilia—is at least described in the DSM–IV. American Psychiatric Association, Diagnostic and Statistical Manual of Mental Disorders 524–525, 527–28 (4th ed. 1994).

Notwithstanding its civil attributes, the practical effect of the Kansas law may be to impose confinement for life. At this stage of medical knowledge, although future treatments cannot be predicted, psychiatrists or other professionals engaged in treating pedophilia may be reluctant to find measurable success in treatment even after a long period and may be unable to predict that no serious danger will come from release of the detainee.

A common response to this may be, "A life term is exactly what the sentence should have been anyway".... The point, however, is not how long Hendricks and others like him should serve a criminal sentence. With his criminal record, after all, a life term may well have been the only sentence appropriate to protect society and vindicate the wrong. The concern instead is whether it is the criminal system or the civil system which should make the decision in the first place. If the civil system is used simply to impose punishment after the state makes an improvident plea bargain on the criminal side, then it is not performing its proper function. These concerns persist whether the civil confinement statute is put on the books before or after the offense. We should bear in mind that while incapacitation is a goal common to both the criminal and civil systems of confinement, retribution and general deterrence are reserved for the criminal system alone.

On the record before us, the Kansas civil statute conforms to our precedents. If, however, civil confinement were to become a mechanism for retribution or general deterrence, or if it were shown that mental abnormality is too imprecise a category to offer a solid basis for concluding that civil detention is justified, our precedents would not suffice to validate it.

■ JUSTICE BREYER, with whom JUSTICE STEVENS and JUSTICE SOUTER join, and with whom JUSTICE GINSBURG joins as to Parts II and III, dissenting.

I agree with the majority that the Kansas Sexually Violent Predator Act's "definition of 'mental abnormality' " satisfies the "substantive" requirements of the Due Process clause. Kansas, however, concedes that Hendricks' condition is treatable; yet the Act did not provide Hendricks (or others like him) with any treatment until after his release date from prison and only inadequate treatment thereafter. These, and certain other, special features of the Act convince me that it was not simply an effort to commit Hendricks civilly, but rather an effort to inflict further punishment upon him. The Ex Post Facto clause therefore prohibits the Act's application to Hendricks, who committed his crimes prior to its enactment.

I

I begin with the area of agreement. This Court has held that the civil commitment of a "mentally ill" and "dangerous" person does not automatically violate the due process clause provided that the commitment takes place pursuant to proper procedures and evidentiary standards. See *Foucha v. Louisiana*. The Kansas Supreme Court, however, held that the due process clause forbids application of the Act to Hendricks for "substantive" reasons, i.e., irrespective of the procedures or evidentiary standards used. The court reasoned that Kansas had not satisfied the "mentally ill" requirement of the Due Process clause because Hendricks was not "mentally ill." Moreover, Kansas had not satisfied what the court believed was an additional "substantive due process" requirement, namely, the provision of treatment. I shall consider each of these matters briefly.

A

In my view, the due process clause permits Kansas to classify Hendricks as a mentally ill and dangerous person for civil commitment purposes. *Allen v. Illinois*. I agree with the majority that the constitution gives states a degree of leeway in making this kind of determination. But, because I do not subscribe to all of its reasoning, I shall set forth three sets of circumstances that, taken together, convince me that Kansas has acted within the limits that the due process clause substantively sets.

First, the psychiatric profession itself classifies the kind of problem from which Hendricks suffers as a serious mental disorder. E.g., American Psychiatric Assn., Diagnostic and Statistical Manual of Mental Disorders 524–525, 527–28 (4th ed. 1994) (describing range of paraphilias and discussing how stress aggravates pedophilic behavior). . . . I concede that professionals also debate whether or not this disorder should be called a mental "illness." But the very presence and vigor of this debate is important. The constitution permits a state to follow one reasonable professional view, while rejecting another. The psychiatric debate, therefore, helps to inform the law by setting the bounds of what is reasonable, but it cannot here decide just how states must write their laws within those bounds.

Second, Hendricks' abnormality does not consist simply of a long course of antisocial behavior, but rather it includes a specific serious, and highly unusual inability to control his actions. (For example, Hendricks testified that, when he gets "stressed out," he cannot "control the urge" to molest children.) The law traditionally has considered this kind of abnormality akin to insanity for purposes of confinement. See, e.g., Minnesota ex rel. Pearson v. Probate Court of Ramsey Cty., 309

U.S. 270, 274 (1940) (upholding against a due process challenge the civil confinement of a dangerous person where the danger flowed from an " 'utter lack of power to control . . . sexual impulses' "). . . . Indeed, the notion of an "irresistible impulse" often has helped to shape criminal law's insanity defense and to inform the related recommendations of legal experts as they seek to translate the insights of mental health professionals into workable legal rules. See also American Law Institute, Model Penal Code § 4.01 (insanity defense, in part, rests on inability "to conform . . . conduct to the requirements of law"); Abraham Goldstein, The Insanity Defense 67–79 (1967) (describing "irresistible impulse" test).

Third, Hendricks' mental abnormality also makes him dangerous. Hendricks "has been convicted of . . . a sexually violent offense," and a jury found that he "suffers from a mental abnormality . . . which makes" him "likely to engage" in similar "acts of sexual violence" in the future. The evidence at trial favored the state. Dr. Befort, for example, explained why Hendricks was likely to commit further acts of sexual violence if released. And Hendricks' own testimony about what happens when he gets "stressed out" confirmed Dr. Befort's diagnosis.

Because (i) many mental health professionals consider pedophilia a serious mental disorder; and (ii) Hendricks suffers from a classic case of irresistible impulse, namely, he is so afflicted with pedophilia that he cannot "control the urge" to molest children; and (iii) his pedophilia presents a serious danger to those children, I believe that Kansas can classify Hendricks as "mentally ill" and "dangerous" as this Court used those terms in *Foucha*. . . .

B

The Kansas Supreme Court also held that the Due Process clause requires a state to provide treatment to those whom it civilly confines (as "mentally ill" and "dangerous"). It found that Kansas did not provide Hendricks with significant treatment. And it concluded that Hendricks' confinement violated the Due Process clause for this reason as well.

This case does not require us to consider whether the due process clause *always* requires treatment—whether, for example, it would forbid civil confinement of an *untreatable* mentally ill, dangerous person. To the contrary, Kansas argues that pedophilia is an "abnormality" or "illness" that can be treated. Two groups of mental health professionals agree [citing amicus briefs]. Indeed, no one argues the contrary. Hence the legal question before us is whether the clause forbids Hendricks' confinement unless Kansas provides him with treatment *that it concedes is available.*

Nor does anyone argue that Kansas somehow could have violated the Due Process clause's *treatment* concerns had it provided Hendricks with the treatment that is potentially available (and I do not see how any such argument could succeed). Rather, the basic substantive due process treatment question is whether that clause requires Kansas to provide treatment that it concedes is potentially available to a person whom it concedes is treatable. This same question is at the heart of my discussion of whether Hendricks' confinement violates the Constitution's Ex Post Facto clause. For that reason, I shall not consider the substantive due process treatment question separately, but instead shall simply turn to the Ex Post Facto clause discussion. As Justice Kennedy points out some of the matters there discussed may later prove relevant to substantive due process analysis.

II

Kansas' 1994 Act violates the federal constitution's prohibition of "any . . . ex post facto Law" if it "inflicts" upon Hendricks "a greater punishment" than did the law "annexed to" his "crime[s]" when he "committed" those crimes in 1984. Calder v. Bull, 3 Dall. 386, 390 (1798) (opinion of Chase, J.); U.S. Const., Art. I, § 10. The majority agrees that the clause " 'forbids the application of any *new punitive measure* to a crime already consummated.' " California Dept. of Corrections v. Morales, 514 U.S. 499, 505 (1995). But it finds the Act is not "punitive." With respect to that basic question, I disagree with the majority.

Certain resemblances between the Act's "civil commitment" and traditional criminal punishments are obvious. Like criminal imprisonment, the Act's civil commitment amounts to "secure" confinement and "incarceration against one's will," In re Gault, 387 U.S. 1 (1967). In addition, a basic objective of the Act is incapacitation, which, as Blackstone said in describing an objective of criminal law, is to "depriv[e] the party injuring of the power to do future mischief." 4 W. Blackstone, Commentaries *11–*12 (incapacitation is one important purpose of criminal punishment). . . . Moreover, the Act, like criminal punishment, imposes its confinement (or sanction) only upon an individual who has previously committed a criminal offense. And the Act imposes that confinement through the use of persons (county prosecutors), procedural guarantees (trial by jury, assistance of counsel, psychiatric evaluations), and standards ("beyond a reasonable doubt") traditionally associated with the criminal law.

These obvious resemblances by themselves, however, are not legally sufficient to transform what the Act calls "civil commitment" into a criminal punishment. Civil commitment of dangerous, mentally ill individuals by its very nature involves confinement and incapacitation. Yet "civil commitment," from a constitutional perspective, nonetheless remains civil. *Allen v. Illinois*. Nor does the fact that criminal behavior triggers the Act make the critical difference. The Act's insistence upon a prior crime, by screening out those whose past behavior does not concretely demonstrate the existence of a mental problem or potential future danger, may serve an important noncriminal evidentiary purpose. Neither is the presence of criminal law-type procedures determinative. Those procedures can serve an important purpose that in this context one might consider noncriminal, namely, helping to prevent judgmental mistakes that would wrongly deprive a person of important liberty.

If these obvious similarities cannot by themselves prove that Kansas' "civil commitment" statute is criminal, neither can the word "civil" written into the statute by itself prove the contrary. . . .

In this circumstance, with important features of the Act pointing in opposite directions, I would place particular importance upon those features that would likely distinguish between a basically punitive and a basically nonpunitive purpose. And I note that the Court, in an earlier civil commitment case, *Allen v. Illinois* looked primarily to the law's concern for treatment as an important distinguishing feature. I do not believe that *Allen* means that a particular law's lack of concern for treatment, by itself, is enough to make an incapacitative law punitive. But, for reasons I will point out, when a state believes that treatment does exist, and then couples that admission with a legislatively required delay of such treatment until a person is at the end of his jail term (so that further incapacitation is therefore necessary), such a legislative scheme begins to look punitive. . . .

The *Allen* Court's focus upon treatment, as a kind of touchstone helping to distinguish civil from punitive purposes, is not surprising, for one would expect a nonpunitive statutory scheme to confine, not simply in order to protect, but also in order to cure. That is to say, one would expect a nonpunitively motivated legislature that confines *because of* a dangerous mental abnormality to seek to help the individual himself overcome that abnormality (at least insofar as professional treatment for the abnormality exists and is potentially helpful, as Kansas, supported by some groups of mental health professionals, argues is the case here). Conversely, a statutory scheme that provides confinement that does not reasonably fit a practically available, medically oriented treatment objective, more likely reflects a primarily punitive legislative purpose.

Several important treatment-related factors—factors of a kind that led the five-member *Allen* majority to conclude that the Illinois legislature's purpose was primarily civil, not punitive—in this action suggest precisely the opposite. First, the state supreme court here, unlike the state court in *Allen,* has held that treatment is not a significant objective of the Act. The Kansas court wrote that the Act's purpose is "segregation of sexually violent offenders," with "treatment" a matter that was "incidental at best." . . .

Second, the Kansas statute, insofar as it applies to previously convicted offenders such as Hendricks, commits, confines, and treats those offenders *after* they have served virtually their entire criminal sentence. That time-related circumstance seems deliberate. The Act explicitly defers diagnosis, evaluation, and commitment proceedings until a few weeks prior to the "anticipated release" of a previously convicted offender from prison. But why, one might ask, does the Act not commit and require treatment of sex offenders sooner, say, soon after they begin to serve their sentences? . . . [T]he timing provisions of the statute confirm the Kansas Supreme Court's view that treatment was not a particularly important legislative objective. . . .

Third, the statute, at least as of the time Kansas applied it to Hendricks, did not require the committing authority to consider the possibility of using less restrictive alternatives, such as postrelease supervision, halfway houses, or other methods. . . . This Court has said that a failure to consider, or to use, "alternative and less harsh methods" to achieve a nonpunitive objective can help to show that legislature's "purpose . . . was to punish." Bell v. Wolfish, 441 U.S. 520, 539, n.20 (1979). . . .

Fourth, the laws of other states confirm, through comparison, that Kansas' "civil commitment" objectives do not require the statutory features that indicate a punitive purpose. I have found 17 States with laws that seek to protect the public from mentally abnormal, sexually dangerous individuals through civil commitment or other mandatory treatment programs. Ten of those statutes, unlike the Kansas statute, begin treatment of an offender soon after he has been apprehended and charged with a serious sex offense. Only seven, like Kansas, delay "civil" commitment (and treatment) until the offender has served his criminal sentence (and this figure includes the Acts of Minnesota and New Jersey, both of which generally do not delay treatment). Of these seven, however, six (unlike Kansas) require consideration of less restrictive alternatives. . . .

The majority suggests in the alternative that recent evidence shows that Kansas is now providing treatment. That evidence comes from two sources: First, a statement by the Kansas Attorney General at oral argument that those committed under the Act are now receiving treatment; and second, in a footnote, a Kansas trial judge's statement, in a state habeas proceeding nearly one year after Hendricks was committed, that Kansas is providing treatment. I do not see how either of these statements can be used to justify the validity of the Act's application to Hendricks at the time he filed suit. . . .

. . . Kansas points to United States v. Salerno, 481 U.S. 739 (1987), a case in which this Court held preventive detention of a dangerous accused person pending trial constitutionally permissible. *Salerno,* however, involved the brief detention of that person, after a finding of "probable cause" that he had committed a crime that would justify further imprisonment, and only pending a speedy judicial determination of guilt or innocence. This Court, in *Foucha,* emphasized the fact that the confinement at issue in *Salerno* was "strictly limited in duration." It described that "pretrial detention of arrestees" as "one of those carefully limited exceptions permitted by the due process clause." And it held that *Salerno* did not authorize the indefinite detention, on grounds of dangerousness, of "insanity acquittees who are not mentally ill but who do not prove they would not be dangerous to others." 504 U.S. at 83. Whatever *Salerno* 's "due process" implications may be, it does not focus upon, nor control, the question at issue here, the question of "punishment" for purposes of the ex post facto clause. . . .

III

To find that the confinement the Act imposes upon Hendricks is "punishment" is to find a violation of the ex post facto clause. Kansas does not deny that the 1994 Act changed the legal consequences that attached to Hendricks' earlier crimes, and in a way that significantly "disadvantage[d] the offender."

To find a violation of that clause here, however, is not to hold that the clause prevents Kansas, or other states, from enacting dangerous sexual offender statutes. A statute that operates prospectively, for example, does not offend the ex post facto clause. Neither does it offend the ex post facto clause for a state to sentence offenders to the fully authorized sentence, to seek consecutive, rather than concurrent, sentences, or to invoke recidivism statutes to lengthen imprisonment. Moreover, a statute that operates retroactively, like Kansas' statute, nonetheless does not offend the clause *if the confinement that it imposes is not punishment*—if, that is to say, the legislature does not simply add a later criminal punishment to an earlier one.

The statutory provisions before us do amount to punishment primarily because, as I have said, the legislature did not tailor the statute to fit the nonpunitive civil aim of treatment, which it concedes exists in Hendricks' case. The clause in these circumstances does not stand as an obstacle to achieving important protections for the public's safety; rather it provides an assurance that, where so significant a restriction of an individual's basic freedoms is at issue, a state cannot cut corners. Rather, the legislature must hew to the constitution's liberty-protecting line. See The Federalist No. 78, p. 466 (C. Rossiter ed. 1961) (A. Hamilton).

I therefore would affirm the judgment below.

## Kansas v. Crane

Supreme Court of the United States, 2002.
534 U.S. 407.

■ JUSTICE BREYER delivered the opinion of the Court.

This case concerns the constitutional requirements substantively limiting the civil commitment of a dangerous sexual offender—a matter that this Court considered in Kansas v. Hendricks, 521 U.S. 346 (1997). The State of Kansas argues that the Kansas Supreme Court has interpreted our decision in *Hendricks* in an overly restrictive manner. We agree and vacate the Kansas court's judgment. . . .

II

. . . The state here seeks the civil commitment of Michael Crane, a previously convicted sexual offender who, according to at least one of the state's psychiatric witnesses, suffers from both exhibitionism and antisocial personality disorder. . . . After a jury trial, the Kansas district court ordered Crane's civil commitment. But the Kansas Supreme Court reversed. In that court's view, the Federal Constitution as interpreted in *Hendricks* insists upon "a finding that the defendant cannot control his dangerous behavior"—even if (as provided by Kansas law) problems of "emotional capacity" and not "volitional capacity" prove the "source of bad behavior" warranting commitment. And the trial court had made no such finding.

Kansas now argues that the Kansas Supreme Court wrongly read *Hendricks* as requiring the state *always* to prove that a dangerous individual is *completely* unable to control his behavior. That reading, says Kansas, is far too rigid.

III

We agree with Kansas insofar as it argues that *Hendricks* set forth no requirement of *total* or *complete* lack of control. *Hendricks* referred to the Kansas Act as requiring a "mental abnormality" or "personality disorder" that makes it "*difficult,* if not impossible, for the [dangerous] person to control his dangerous behavior." The word "difficult" indicates that the lack of control to which this Court referred was not absolute. Indeed, as different amici on opposite sides of this case agree, an absolutist approach is unworkable. Cf. Brief for American Psychiatric Association et al. as Amici Curiae; cf.also American Psychiatric Association, Statement on the Insanity Defense (1982) (" 'The line between an irresistible impulse and an impulse not resisted is probably no sharper than that between twilight and dusk' "). Moreover, most severely ill people—even those commonly termed "psychopaths"—retain some ability to control their behavior. See Stephen Morse, Culpability and Control, 142 U. Pa. L.Rev. 1587, 1634–35 (1994); cf. Bruce Winick, Sex Offender Law in the 1990s: A Therapeutic Jurisprudence Analysis, 4 Psychol. Pub. Pol'y & L. 505, 520–25 (1998). Insistence upon absolute lack of control would risk barring the civil commitment of highly dangerous persons suffering severe mental abnormalities.

We do not agree with the state, however, insofar as it seeks to claim that the constitution permits commitment of the type of dangerous sexual offender considered in *Hendricks* without *any* lack-of-control determination. *Hendricks* underscored the constitutional importance of distinguishing a dangerous sexual offender subject to civil commitment "from other dangerous persons who are perhaps more properly dealt with exclusively through criminal proceedings." That distinction is necessary lest "civil commitment" become a "mechanism for retribution or general deterrence"—functions properly those of criminal law, not civil commitment. The presence of what the "psychiatric profession itself classifie[d] . . . as a serious mental disorder" helped to make that distinction in *Hendricks*. And a critical distinguishing feature of that "serious . . . disorder" there consisted of a special and serious lack of ability to control behavior.

In recognizing that fact, we did not give to the phrase "lack of control" a particularly narrow or technical meaning. And we recognize that in cases where lack of control is at issue, "inability to control behavior" will not be demonstrable with mathematical precision. It is enough to say that there must be proof of serious difficulty in controlling behavior. And this, when viewed in light of such features of the case as the nature of the psychiatric diagnosis, and the severity of the mental abnormality itself, must be sufficient to distinguish the dangerous sexual offender whose serious mental illness, abnormality, or disorder subjects him to civil commitment from the dangerous but typical recidivist convicted in an ordinary criminal case. See Foucha v. Louisiana, 504 U.S.71 (1992) (rejecting an approach to civil commitment that would permit the indefinite confinement "of any convicted criminal" after completion of a prison term).

We recognize that *Hendricks* as so read provides a less precise constitutional standard than would those more definite rules for which the parties have argued. But the constitution's safeguards of human liberty in the area of mental illness and the law are not always best enforced through precise bright-line rules. For one thing, the States retain considerable leeway in defining the mental abnormalities and personality disorders that make an individual eligible for commitment. For another, the science of psychiatry, which informs but does not control ultimate legal determinations, is an ever-advancing science, whose distinctions do not seek precisely to mirror those of the law. See also, e.g., DSM–IV xxx ("concept of mental disorder . . . lacks a consistent operational definition"); id. at xxxii-xxxiii (noting the "imperfect fit between the questions of ultimate concern to the law and the information contained in [the DSM's] clinical diagnosis"). Consequently, we have sought to provide constitutional guidance in this area by proceeding deliberately and contextually, elaborating generally stated constitutional standards and objectives as specific circumstances require. *Hendricks* embodied that approach.

IV

The State also questions how often a volitional problem lies at the heart of a dangerous sexual offender's serious mental abnormality or disorder. It points out that the Kansas Supreme Court characterized its state statute as permitting commitment of dangerous sexual offenders who suffered from a mental abnormality properly characterized by an "emotional" impairment and suffered no "volitional" impairment. It adds that, in the Kansas court's view, *Hendricks* absolutely forbids the commitment of any such person. And the State argues that it was wrong to read *Hendricks* in this way.

We agree that *Hendricks* limited its discussion to volitional disabilities. And that fact is not surprising. The case involved an individual suffering from pedophilia—a mental abnormality that critically involves what a lay person might describe as a lack of control. DSM–IV 571–572 (listing as a diagnostic criterion for pedophilia that an individual have acted on, or been affected by, "sexual urges" toward children). Hendricks himself stated that he could not " 'control the urge' " to molest children. In addition, our cases suggest that civil commitment of dangerous sexual offenders will normally involve individuals who find it particularly difficult to control their behavior—in the general sense described above. And it is often appropriate to say of such individuals, in ordinary English, that they are "unable to control their dangerousness."

Regardless, *Hendricks* must be read in context. The Court did not draw a clear distinction between the purely "emotional" sexually related mental abnormality and the "volitional." Here, as in other areas of psychiatry, there may be "considerable overlap between a . . . defective understanding or appreciation and . . . [an] ability to control . . . behavior." American Psychiatric Association Statement on the Insanity Defense, 140 Am. J. Psychiatry 681, 685 (1983) (discussing "psychotic" individuals). Nor, when considering civil commitment, have we ordinarily distinguished for constitutional purposes among volitional, emotional, and cognitive impairments. See, e.g., Jones v. United States, 463 U.S. 354 (1983). The Court in *Hendricks* had no occasion to consider whether confinement based solely on "emotional" abnormality would be constitutional, and we likewise have no occasion to do so in the present case.

* * *

For these reasons, the judgment of the Kansas Supreme Court is vacated, and the case is remanded for further proceedings not inconsistent with this opinion.

It is so ordered.

■ JUSTICE SCALIA, with whom JUSTICE THOMAS joins, dissenting. . . .

I

Respondent was convicted of lewd and lascivious behavior and pleaded guilty to aggravated sexual battery for two incidents that took place on the same day in 1993. In the first, respondent exposed himself to a tanning salon attendant. In the second, 30 minutes later, respondent entered a video store, waited until he was the only customer present, and then exposed himself to the clerk. Not stopping there, he grabbed the clerk by the neck, demanded she perform oral sex on him, and threatened to rape her, before running out of the store. Following respondent's plea to aggravated sexual battery, the State filed a petition in state district court to have respondent evaluated and adjudicated a sexual predator under the SVPA. That Act permits the civil detention of a person convicted of any of several enumerated sexual offenses, if it is proven beyond a reasonable doubt that he suffers from a "mental abnormality"—a disorder affecting his "emotional or volitional capacity which predisposes the person to commit sexually violent offenses"—or a "personality disorder," either of "which makes the person likely to engage in repeat acts of sexual violence."

Several psychologists examined respondent and determined he suffers from exhibitionism and antisocial personality disorder. Though exhibitionism alone would not support classification as a sexual predator, a psychologist concluded that the two in combination did place respondent's condition within the range of disorders covered by the SVPA, "cit[ing] the increasing frequency of incidents involving [respondent], increasing intensity of the incidents, [respondent's] increasing disregard for the rights of others, and his increasing daring and aggressiveness." Another psychologist testified that respondent's behavior was marked by "impulsivity or failure to plan ahead," indicating his unlawfulness "was a combination of willful and uncontrollable behavior." The state's experts agreed, however, that "'[r]espondent's mental disorder does not impair his volitional control to the degree he cannot control his dangerous behavior.'"

Respondent moved for summary judgment, arguing that for his detention to comport with substantive due process the State was required to prove not merely what the statute requires—that by reason of his mental disorder he is "likely to engage in repeat acts of sexual violence"—but also that he is unable to control his violent behavior. The trial court denied this motion, and instructed the jury pursuant to the terms of the statute. The jury found, beyond a reasonable doubt, that respondent was a sexual predator as defined by the SVPA. The Kansas Supreme Court reversed, holding the SVPA unconstitutional as applied to someone, like respondent, who has only an emotional or personality disorder within the meaning of the Act, rather than a volitional impairment. For such a person, it held, the state must show not merely a likelihood that the defendant would engage in repeat acts of sexual violence, but also an inability to control violent behavior. It based this holding solely on our decision in *Hendricks*.

II

. . . The first words of [*Hendricks*] dealing with the merits of the case were as follows: "Kansas argues that the Act's definition of 'mental abnormality' satisfies 'substantive' due process requirements. We agree." And the *reason* it found substantive due process satisfied was clearly stated:

> The Kansas Act is plainly of a kind with these other civil commitment statutes [that we have approved]: It requires a finding of future dangerousness [viz., that the person committed is "likely to engage in repeat acts of sexual violence"], and then links that finding to the existence of a "mental abnormality" or

"personality disorder" *that makes it difficult, if not impossible, for the person to control his dangerous behavior*. (Emphasis added.)

It is the italicized language in the foregoing excerpt that today's majority relies upon as establishing the requirement of a separate *finding* of inability to control behavior.

That is simply not a permissible reading of the passage, for several reasons. First, because the authority cited for the statement . . . is the section of the SVPA that defines "mental abnormality," *which contains no requirement of inability to control*. What the opinion was obviously saying was that the SVPA's required finding of a *causal connection* between the likelihood of repeat acts of sexual violence and the existence of a "mental abnormality" or "personality disorder" *necessarily* establishes "difficulty if not impossibility" in controlling behavior . . . .

The Court relies upon the fact that "*Hendricks* underscored the constitutional importance of distinguishing a dangerous sexual offender subject to civil commitment 'from other dangerous persons who are perhaps more properly dealt with exclusively through criminal proceedings.'" But the SVPA as written—without benefit of a supplemental control finding—already achieves that objective. It conditions civil commitment not upon a mere finding that the sex offender is likely to reoffend, but only upon the additional finding (beyond a reasonable doubt) that the *cause* of the likelihood of recidivism is a "mental abnormality or personality disorder." Ordinary recidivists *choose* to reoffend and are therefore amenable to deterrence through the criminal law; those subject to civil commitment under the SVPA, because their mental illness is an affliction and not a choice, are unlikely to be deterred. We specifically pointed this out in *Hendricks*. "Those persons committed under the Act," we said, "are, by definition, suffering from a 'mental abnormality' or a 'personality disorder' that prevents them from exercising adequate control over their behavior. Such persons are therefore unlikely to be deterred by the threat of confinement."

III

. . . I cannot resist observing that the distinctive status of volitional impairment which the Court mangles *Hendricks* to preserve would not even be worth preserving by more legitimate means. There is good reason why, as the Court accurately says, "when considering civil commitment . . . we [have not] ordinarily distinguished for constitutional purposes among volitional, emotional, and cognitive impairments." We have not done so because it makes no sense. It is obvious that a person may be able to exercise volition and yet be unfit to turn loose upon society. The man who has a will of steel, but who delusionally believes that every woman he meets is inviting crude sexual advances, is surely a dangerous sexual predator.

IV

I not only disagree with the Court's gutting of our holding in *Hendricks;* I also doubt the desirability, and indeed even the coherence, of the new constitutional test which (on the basis of no analysis except a misreading of *Hendricks*) it substitutes. Under our holding in *Hendricks,* a jury in an SVPA commitment case would be required to find, beyond a reasonable doubt, that the person previously convicted of one of the enumerated sexual offenses is suffering from a mental abnormality or personality disorder, and that this condition renders him likely to commit future acts of sexual violence. Both of these findings are coherent, and (with the assistance of expert testimony) well within the capacity of a normal jury. Today's opinion says that the constitution requires the addition of a third finding: that the subject suffers from an inability to control behavior—not utter inability, and not even inability in a particular constant degree, but rather inability in a degree that will vary "in light of such features of the case as the nature of the psychiatric diagnosis, and the severity of the mental abnormality itself."

This formulation of the new requirement certainly displays an elegant subtlety of mind. Unfortunately, it gives trial courts, in future cases under the many commitment statutes similar to Kansas's SVPA, *not a clue* as to how they are supposed to charge the jury! Indeed, it does not even provide a clue to the trial court, on remand, *in this very case.* What is the judge to ask the jury to find? It is fine and good to talk about the desirability of our "proceeding deliberately and contextually, elaborating generally stated constitutional standards and objectives as specific circumstances require," but one would think that this plan would at least produce the "elaboration" of what the jury charge should be in the "specific circumstances" of the present case. "[P]roceeding deliberately" is not synonymous with not proceeding at all.

I suspect that the reason the Court avoids any elaboration is that elaboration which passes the laugh test is impossible. How *is* one to frame for a jury the degree of "inability to control" which, in the particular case, "the nature of the psychiatric diagnosis, and the severity of the mental abnormality" require? Will it be a percentage ("Ladies and gentlemen of the jury, you may commit Mr. Crane under the SVPA only if you find, beyond a reasonable doubt, that he is 42% unable to control his penchant for sexual violence")? Or a frequency ratio ("Ladies and gentlemen of the jury, you may commit Mr. Crane under the SVPA only if you find, beyond a reasonable doubt, that he is unable to control his penchant for sexual violence 3 times out of 10")? Or merely an adverb ("Ladies and gentlemen of the jury, you may commit Mr. Crane under the SVPA only if you find, beyond a reasonable doubt, that he is appreciably—or moderately, or substantially, or almost totally—unable to control his penchant for sexual violence")? None of these seems to me satisfactory.

But if it is indeed possible to "elaborate" upon the Court's novel test, surely the Court has an obligation to do so in the "specific circumstances" of the present case, so that the trial court will know what is expected of it on remand. It is irresponsible to leave the law in such a state of utter indeterminacy. . . .

## NOTES ON *HENDRICKS* AND *CRANE*

### 1. LEGISLATIVE PURPOSE OR JUSTIFICATION

Judging from the Court's opinion in *Hendricks*, the constitutionality of the SVP law depends heavily on how its underlying purpose or justification is characterized. How should it be characterized?

*(i) Punishment*

The threshold issue in resolving Hendricks' ex post facto and double jeopardy claims is whether his detention under the SVP law amounts to punishment for constitutional purposes. Obviously the label deployed in the statute cannot be determinative. What factors were determinative in the majority judgment? In that of the dissent? The dissenters concluded that the SVP imposed additional punishment on offenders who had committed their predicate sex offenses before the law was enacted and had already served the terms for which they had been sentenced. Does it follow that post-sentence commitment would violate the double jeopardy provision even if it were applied prospectively?

*(ii) Treatment*

In *Allen*, the Court found that treatment was one of the legislative goals. The majority equivocates on this issue in *Hendricks*, while the dissent regards the absence of a therapeutic objective as evidence that the goal is punitive. Exactly what is the constitutional significance of treatment? On the one hand, could the legislative purpose be both punitive and therapeutic? On the other, could it be neither? Regardless of declared purpose, does it matter whether treatment is provided? Whether it is efficacious?

*(iii) Incapacitation*

If incapacitation were the *sole* purpose of SVP commitment, does that mean it is not punitive for constitutional purposes? Assuming that a commitment law with an exclusively incapacitative objective would pass muster under the double jeopardy and ex post facto provisions, would it be permissible under the due process clause? Does *Foucha* have any bearing on the answer?

## 2. THE SIGNIFICANCE OF MENTAL DISORDER

How does the SVP requirement of a "mental abnormality or personality disorder" relate to the questions about legislative purpose raised in the previous note? To what extent does this requirement support Kansas' argument that the legislative purpose is not punitive? That it is partly therapeutic?

Assuming again that the statutory purpose of SVP laws is primarily or exclusively incapacitative, is some sort of mental disorder constitutionally required under *Foucha*? If so, what type of mental disorder is necessary? Some critics of the SVP laws object to the statutory definition of "mental abnormality" on the ground that it is essentially a legal definition, not a clinical or scientific one. Is that right? Recall the debate over the criteria for the insanity defense. Clearly these are legal criteria, not medical ones. What bearing, if any, does that have on the propriety of the definition of "mental abnormality" in the SVP statutes?

## 3. THE RELATION BETWEEN MENTAL DISORDER AND DANGEROUS CONDUCT

In the SVP commitment proceedings against Hendricks and Crane, the juries were apparently instructed in the bare language of the statute. In *Hendricks*, the Court upheld the statute on its face and as applied.

However, in *Crane*, the Court held that the law had been unconstitutionally applied. Why? How do the cases differ? How should the jury be instructed on remand in *Crane*?

## 4. VOLITIONAL AND EMOTIONAL IMPAIRMENT

Is a finding of volitional impairment the only constitutionally permissible basis for commitment under an SVP statute? If so, does this imply that NGRI commitments must be predicated on a similar finding? If not, what alternative predicate could support civil commitment? Would such a finding be supportable in *Crane*?[a]

[a] For analysis of *Hendricks* and *Crane* and further reading on SVP laws, see Stephen Morse, Uncontrollable Urges and Irrational People, 88 Va. L. Rev 1025 (2002); Eric S. Janus, *Hendricks* and the Moral Terrain of Police Power Civil Commitment, 4 Psychol. Pub Pol'y & L. 505 (1998); Bruce J. Winick and John Q. LaFond (eds), Protecting Society from Sexually Dangerous Offenders (2003).

# CHAPTER IX

# SEXUAL OFFENSES

## SECTION 1: INTRODUCTION

### INTRODUCTORY NOTES

#### 1. PRELIMINARY COMMENTS

Within contemporary culture, the tasks of defining and enforcing the law of rape and other sexual offenses are complicated and contentious. Much of the controversy is exacerbated, if not directly produced, by gender politics. During the past several decades, feminist commentators have made the elimination of violence against women a central focus of their campaign for social justice. As part of this agenda, many feminists and their allies have worked to persuade lawmakers to expand the definition of rape. Other feminists have approached this project cautiously since they believe that legal intervention in sexual matters largely has served to constrain the sexual activity of women, not that of men. Like other strategists for political change, the advocates have injected these issues into mainstream discourse, where they have provoked an energetic and, at times, angry debate. The popular debate often divides along gender lines, and sophisticated feminist arguments sometimes degenerate into simple claims that represent women and men as opponents: women are raped and thus share the complainant's interests; men rape and thus share the accused's interests.

While it is difficult to foresee all of the long-term implications of these claims for rape doctrine and for gender relations, they have moved legislatures in almost every state to codify new definitions of rape and sexual assault. Likewise, the American Law Institute recently released proposed new sexual assault offenses. As the drafters explain, it is necessary to replace the provisions set out in the 1962 Model Penal Code because "dramatic social and cultural change quickly overtook its formulations, rendering them outmoded and in some instances even offensive to new sensibilities." ALI, Model Penal Code: Sexual Assault and Related Offenses, Tentative Draft No. 1, at p. 11 (April 30, 2014).

Of course, for the participants in individual rape prosecutions, long-term developments are eclipsed by the judgment in their own case. As Catharine MacKinnon has remarked, the debate over competing sexual norms abruptly loses its abstract quality when the conduct of a real defendant is at stake: "someone either is or is not going to jail." Catharine A. MacKinnon, Toward Feminist Jurisprudence, 34 Stan. L. Rev. 703, 728 (1982). The integrity of the criminal process demands that punishment be imposed or withheld in individual cases; with each conviction or acquittal, the criminal process resolves the contest over the underlying social norms, at least for purposes of the actors in that case. Moreover, since so many people regularly have and/or want to have sex, legislators and courts must weigh the policies favoring stable criminal norms (e.g., providing notice that certain conduct is a crime) against arguments that support redefining the crime of rape in accordance with evolving norms about sexuality and gender equality.

According to contemporary wisdom, rape accusations involve two different kinds of sexual encounters, each of which presents distinct challenges to law enforcement. Susan Estrich was one of the first commentators to identify these different categories of rape and their legal significance. See Susan Estrich, Real Rape (1987). Like any other generalization, this one does not wholly withstand close scrutiny, but a brief description of these categories provides a useful way of distinguishing the issues that will be emphasized in this chapter from those that will be given passing treatment.

In the first type of case, the alleged rapist and the complainant are strangers to each other. In these cases, there often is no reasonable doubt that a crime occurred, particularly where the survivor was physically injured. Professor Estrich calls this "real rape." Here, the difficult task for law enforcement personnel is identifying the perpetrator. Often, the survivor is the only witness to the crime and the events leading up to it. Because the attacker is a stranger and his conduct so traumatic, the survivor may have trouble describing him. Depending on the physical evidence connecting the perpetrator to the survivor and to the crime scene, police officers may be unable to locate and apprehend him. If they do make an arrest and the case is strong enough to proceed to trial, the most hotly contested issue likely will be the identity of the rapist. The suspect may offer a variety of arguments (e.g., alibi, mistaken eyewitness identification, mishandling of physical evidence) designed to persuade jurors that, though a crime occurred, some other person committed it. These cases raise problems that are of great importance in the enforcement of rape laws, but the problems usually implicate investigatory procedures and evidence rules. In other words, these cases tend not to raise the most difficult substantive questions. Once jurors are convinced that the accused is the person who had sex with the survivor, they often are ready to agree that the elements of the offense are satisfied.

By contrast, the second category of cases presents difficult questions about the substantive definition of rape. Here, the parties to the sex act are acquaintances, and, in the most vexing cases, they are dating or are married to or sexually involved with each other. These cases raise few of the investigatory problems mentioned above. The complainant can identify the suspect by name, as well as provide an accurate physical description, and the police usually are able promptly to arrest him. In these cases, the suspect often concedes that he is the person who had sex with the complainant on the occasion she claims she was raped. However, he sharply disputes her characterization of their encounter as a rape; instead, he takes the position that the encounter was an ordinary act of sexual intercourse. Most of the materials in this chapter will focus on the substantive issues that legislators, courts, and jurors must resolve in order to adjudicate between these competing accounts.

## 2. PROPOSED REVISION OF MODEL PENAL CODE SEXUAL ASSAULT PROVISIONS

At various points below, this Chapter discusses the details of some of the substantive offenses that were submitted to the American Law Institute for consideration at its April 30, 2014, meeting as proposed revisions of

Article 213 of the Model Penal Code. All of the suggested new offenses are collected in one place here to facilitate their study as an integrated whole:[a]

**Section 213.0. Definitions**

In this Article, unless a different definition is plainly required:

(1) The definitions given in Section 210.0 apply;

(2) "Commercial sex act" means any act of sexual intercourse or sexual contact in exchange for which any money, property, or services are given to or received by any person.

(3) "Consent" means a person's positive agreement, communicated by either words or actions, to engage in sexual intercourse or sexual contact.

(4) "Nonconsent" means a person's refusal to consent to sexual intercourse or sexual contact, communicated by either words or actions; a verbally expressed refusal establishes nonconsent in the absence of subsequent words or actions indicating positive agreement.

(5) "Recklessly" shall carry only the meaning designated in Model Penal Code § 2.02(2)(c); the provisions of Model Penal Code § 2.08(2) shall not apply to this Article.

(6) "Sexual contact" means . . . . [*reserved*].

(7) "Sexual intercourse" means:

(a) any act involving penetration, however slight, of the anus or vagina by any object or body part, unless done for bona fide medical, hygienic, or law-enforcement purposes; or

(b) direct contact between the mouth or tongue of one person and the anus, penis, or vagina of another person.

**Section 213.1. Rape and Related Offenses**

(1) An actor is guilty of rape, a felony of the second degree, if he or she knowingly or recklessly:

(a) uses physical force, physical restraint, or an implied or express threat of physical force, bodily injury, or physical restraint to cause another person to engage in an act of sexual intercourse with anyone; or

(b) causes another person to engage in an act of sexual intercourse by threatening to inflict bodily injury on someone other than such person or by threatening to commit any other crime of violence; or

(c) has, or enables another person to have, sexual intercourse with a person who, at the time of such act of sexual intercourse:

[a] It is important to understand that these provisions do not at this point represent the position of the American Law Institute and are not, as yet, approved revisions of the Model Penal Code. They were submitted for discussion as a tentative draft, and may well undergo significant revisions before they are approved as replacements for the current Article 213. They do, nonetheless, represent the considered preliminary views of experts who were appointed to undertake the task of revision.

(i) is less than 12 years old; or

(ii) is sleeping, unconscious, or physically unable to express nonconsent to engage in such act of sexual intercourse; or

(iii) lacks the capacity to express nonconsent to engage in such act of sexual intercourse, because of mental disorder or disability, whether temporary or permanent; or

(iv) lacks substantial capacity to appraise or control his or her conduct because of drugs, alcohol, or other intoxicating or consciousness-altering substances that the actor administered or caused to be administered, without the knowledge of such other person, for the purpose of impairing such other person's capacity to express nonconsent to such act of sexual intercourse.

(2) An actor is guilty of aggravated rape, a felony of the first degree, if he or she violates subsection (1) of this Section and:

(a) uses a deadly weapon to cause the other person to engage in such act of sexual intercourse; or

(b) acts with the active participation or assistance of one or more other persons who are present at the time of the act of sexual intercourse; or

(c) knowingly or recklessly causes serious bodily injury to the other person or to anyone else for the purpose of causing such other person to engage in the act of sexual intercourse; or

(d) the act of sexual intercourse in violation of subsection (2) of this Section is a commercial sex act.

**Section 213.2. Sexual Intercourse by Coercion or Imposition**

(1) An actor is guilty of sexual intercourse by coercion, a felony of the third degree, if he or she:

(a) knowingly or recklessly has, or enables another person to have, sexual intercourse with a person who at the time of the act of sexual intercourse:

(i) has by words or conduct expressly indicated nonconsent to such act of sexual intercourse; or

(ii) is undressed or is in the process of undressing for the purpose of receiving nonsexual professional services from the actor, and has not given consent to sexual activity; or

(b) obtains the other person's consent by threatening to:

(i) accuse anyone of a criminal offense or of a failure to comply with immigration regulations; or

(ii) expose any information tending to impair the credit or business repute of any person; or

(iii) take or withhold action in an official capacity, whether public or private, or cause another person to take or withhold action in an official capacity, whether public or private; or

(iv) inflict any substantial economic or financial harm that would not benefit the actor; or

(c) knows or recklessly disregards the risk that the other person:

(i) is less than 18 years old and the actor is a parent, foster parent, guardian, teacher, educational or religious counselor, school administrator, extracurricular instructor, or coach of such person; or

(ii) is on probation or parole and that the actor holds any position of authority or supervision with respect to such person's probation or parole; or

(iii) is detained in a hospital, prison, or other custodial institution, and that the actor holds any position of authority at such facility.

(2) An actor is guilty of aggravated sexual intercourse by coercion, a felony of the second degree, if he or she violates subsection (1)(b) or (1)(c) of this Section and in doing so causes a person to engage in a commercial sex act involving sexual intercourse.

(3) An actor is guilty of sexual intercourse by imposition, a felony of the third degree, if he or she knowingly or recklessly has, or enables another person to have, sexual intercourse with a person who, at the time of the act of sexual intercourse:

(a) lacks the capacity to express nonconsent to such act of sexual intercourse, because of intoxication, whether voluntary or involuntary, and regardless of the identity of the person who administered such intoxicants; or

(b) is less than 16 years old and the actor is more than four years older than such person; or

(c) is mentally disabled, developmentally disabled, or mentally incapacitated, whether temporarily or permanently, to the extent that such person is incapable of understanding the physiological nature of sexual intercourse, its potential for causing pregnancy, or its potential for transmitting disease; or

(d) is mentally or developmentally disabled to the extent that such person's social or intellectual capacities are no greater than that of a person who is less than 12 years old.

(4) An actor is guilty of aggravated sexual intercourse by imposition, a felony of the second degree, if he or she violates subsection (3) of this Section and in doing so causes a person to engage in a commercial sex act involving sexual intercourse.

**Section 213.3. Sexual Intercourse by Exploitation**

An actor is guilty of sexual intercourse by exploitation, a felony of the fourth degree, if he or she has sexual intercourse with another person and:

(1) is engaged in providing professional treatment, assessment, or counseling for a mental or emotional illness, symptom, or condition of such person over a period concurrent with or substantially contemporaneous with the time when the act of sexual intercourse occurs, regardless of the location where such act of sexual intercourse occurs and regardless of whether the actor is formally licensed to provide such treatment; or

(2) represents that the act of sexual intercourse is for purposes of medical treatment or that such person is in danger of physical injury or illness which the act of sexual intercourse may serve to mitigate or prevent; or

(3) knowingly leads such person to believe falsely that he or she is someone with whom such person has been sexually intimate.

**Section 213.4. Sexual Intercourse Without Consent**

An actor is guilty of sexual intercourse without consent, a misdemeanor, if the actor knowingly or recklessly has, or enables another person to have, sexual intercourse with a person who at the time of the act of sexual intercourse has not given consent to that act.

**Section 213.5. Criminal Sexual Contact [*Reserved*]**

**Section 213.6. Sexual Offenses Involving Spouses And Other Intimate Partners [*Reserved*]**

## SECTION 2: RAPE

## SUBSECTION A: THE TRADITIONAL APPROACH TO RAPE

### INTRODUCTORY NOTE

The common law defined rape as "the carnal knowledge of a woman forcibly and against her will." 4 William Blackstone, Commentaries *210. This concise prohibition remains influential today. The durability of this particular definition is itself noteworthy: cultural attitudes towards sexuality changed, possibly radically, over the course of the twentieth century, and rape has been the topic of law reform projects for the past several decades. Yet, as the following materials reflect, the common law definition continues to play an important role in shaping contemporary rape doctrine.

Many aspects of rape are not in dispute. By now, almost every state has departed from the common law approach by defining rape in gender-neutral terms. That is, statutory formulations now provide that the crime occurs whenever a "person" (rather than "man") forces another "person" (rather than "woman") to have sex. However, in the vast majority of cases, rape remains a crime that men perpetrate against women, though men do rape other men with some frequency. The psychological literature contains several accounts of women forcibly raping adult men, but the case reporters mention no prosecutions of women for this crime. Usually, both rapist and survivor are young. Children and adolescents are the most frequent targets of sexual assault, and most rapists are under the age of 30. Many rape survivors are well-acquainted with, if not related by blood or marriage to, their attackers. In most cases, survivor and perpetrator are members of the same race. Poor women are much more likely to be raped than those who are affluent. Finally, rape is one of the most, if not the most, under-reported violent crimes. The reporting rate is particularly low in cases where the perpetrator is an acquaintance or intimate partner of the survivor.

The actus reus of rape is some form of sexual physical touching. At common law, the requisite touching was "carnal knowledge." While modern courts treat this phrase as a synonym for "sexual intercourse," Perkins and Boyce explain that the phrase also conveyed the requirement that the sexual connection be "unlawful." Rollin M. Perkins and Ronald N. Boyce, Criminal Law 202–03 (3d ed. 1982). Until very recently, sexual intercourse was unlawful when the participants were not married to each other. While the requirement that the intercourse be "unlawful" had a number of implications for rape doctrine, one significant practical implication was that a man could not be convicted for raping his wife since sex within marriage was not unlawful. At early common law, there was a conflict in authority over whether the completed crime required *both* penetration of the vagina by the penis *and* emission of semen, or whether penetration alone was enough. A consensus soon emerged that the slightest penetration sufficed.

Contemporary statutes define the actus reus of rape in various ways. A significant minority of statutes continue to define the sexual act as vaginal intercourse. One statute retains the phrase "carnal knowledge." In recent years, many states have expanded this definition to include penetration of mouth or anus, as well as vagina. Another legislative innovation treats different types of sexual touching as distinct offenses with different penalties. These statutory variations reflect a disagreement over what kinds of physical touching should be classified as sexual and over how they should be ranked for grading. For the most part, however, once a given state's legislators have resolved these disagreements to their satisfaction, the definitions do not raise significant difficulties in application.

The common law required that the intercourse be done "forcibly" and "against [the woman's] will." Under the common law and early rape statutes, each of these elements was satisfied by proof that the woman had "physically resisted" the man's sexual advances. Verbal resistance did not suffice, since courts took the view that the woman who offered verbal, but not physical, opposition in fact had consented. "[T]hough she object verbally, if she make no outcry and no resistance, she by her conduct consents, and the act is not rape in the man." Mills v. United States, 164 U.S. 644 (1897). Although every jurisdiction agreed that resistance was required, the decisions disagreed over the degree of resistance the woman must offer. Many courts demanded "earnest" or "utmost" resistance, which required the woman to do all that she was physically capable of doing to repel the man and to "resist until exhausted or overpowered." People v. Dohring, 59 N.Y. 374 (1874). By contrast, some courts rejected the "utmost" resistance requirement and held that the resistance must only be sufficient to establish that the woman's lack of consent was "honest and real." See Commonwealth v. McDonald, 110 Mass. 405 (1872).

Some early codifications explicitly included resistance as an element of the crime. For example, a 19th-century California provision defined rape as "sexual intercourse accomplished with a female, not the wife of the perpetrator . . . where she resists, but her resistance was overcome by force or violence." See People v. Fleming, 94 Cal. 308, 29 P. 647 (1892). Even where statutes made no reference to resistance, courts defined the two most contested elements in terms of the victim's resistance. By her physical resistance, the woman established that she did not consent to the encounter, and for sexual intercourse to occur despite the woman's resistance, the man must have used force.

Early opinions do not identify clearly the cultural values underlying the resistance requirement. One intriguing and, to modern lawyers, annoying feature of these opinions is most judges' refusal to narrate facts they deemed unsavory, let alone describe their understanding of human sexuality. A comment by the Supreme Court of Pennsylvania is representative: "This case discloses an amount of social and moral degradation that is not pleasant to contemplate. Its discussion will be confined within the narrowest possible bounds." Commonwealth v. Allen, 135 Pa. 483, 19 A. 957 (1890). From the few remarks that judges ventured, they apparently believed that the resistance requirement was the product of "common sense applied to the nature of a virtuous woman." Hollis v. State, 27 Fla. 387, 9 So. 67 (1891). See also People v. Dohring, 59 N.Y. 374, 384 (1874):

> Can the mind conceive of a woman, in the possession of her faculties and powers, revoltingly unwilling that this deed should be done upon her, who would not resist so hard and so long as she was able? And if a woman, aware that it will be done unless she does resist, does not resist to the extent of her ability on the occasion, must it not be that she is not entirely reluctant?

These and similar comments also reveal why the courts believed that women would be "revoltingly unwilling" to submit. Utmost resistance was expected because "a woman jealous of her chastity, shuddering at the bare thought of dishonor, and flying from pollution" would not adopt a "passive policy" or engage in "half-way" measures. State v. Burgdorf, 53 Mo. 65 (1873).

Anne Coughlin argues that one of the primary functions of the traditional elements of rape was to provide an excuse for women who would otherwise be guilty of fornication or adultery. Today, most courts and commentators assert that the parties' "consent" is the line that divides lawful from unlawful sexual intercourse. Where the sex is consensual, no crime is committed; where it is non-consensual, one of the parties (invariably, the male) is guilty of sexual assault. However, Coughlin points out that the understanding that consensual sexual intercourse is lawful "is in conflict with the fundamental moral and legal premises of the culture from which the rape prohibition emerged and even with a basic ingredient of the traditional rape crime." Anne M. Coughlin, Sex and Guilt, 84 Va. L. Rev. 1, 20 (1998). According to the traditional morés that shaped the rape crime, the line between lawful and unlawful sex was not the parties' consent, but their marriage. In that world, all marital sex was lawful; all nonmarital sex was unlawful; and, depending on their marital status and that of their sexual partners, males and females who engaged in nonmarital sex would be punished for fornication or adultery. Coughlin argues that the prohibitions on fornication and adultery could be expected to and did exert a powerful influence on the substantive definition of rape:

> How would judges who believed that consensual nonmarital intercourse was a crime define rape? . . . By unearthing our ancestors' belief that *all* nonmarital intercourse should be criminalized, we may begin to understand, even as we reject, the inclination of courts to approach rape complaints with deep suspicion. Since, under our ancestors' system, the underlying sexual activity in which a rape complainant engaged (albeit, by her own testimony, unwillingly) was criminal misconduct, her complaint logically could be construed as a plea to be relieved of responsibility for committing that crime. A court would be receptive to such a plea only if the woman could establish that, although she had participated in a sexual transgression, she did so under circumstances that afforded her a defense to criminal liability. Significantly, careful examination of rape doctrine reveals that the elements of the rape offense (almost) are a mirror image of the defenses we would expect from women accused of fornication or adultery. Such traditional defensive strategies would include the claim that the woman had committed no actus reus, that she lacked the mens rea for fornication or adultery, or that she had submitted to the intercourse under duress. For example, just as courts allowed perpetrators of nonsexual crimes to interpose a duress defense, so we must assume that they would be willing to excuse those women suspected of fornication or adultery who could prove that their accomplices had forced them to offend under threat of death or grievous bodily harm. According to this account, the features of rape law to which the critics most strenuously object—namely, the peculiar definitions of the nonconsent and force elements of the crime—are better understood as criteria that excuse the woman for committing an illegal sexual infraction, than as ingredients of the man's offense. Curiously, when we acknowledge, rather than ignore or minimize the long-standing and explicit connection our culture has made between sexual intercourse and criminal guilt, we produce a description of rape law that incorporates a justification for thorough doctrinal reform. That is, if we now are prepared to agree that fornication and adultery should no longer be criminalized—whether because those offenses violate contemporary constitutional guarantees or contemporary moral and political judgments (to the extent that such judgments differ from constitutional guarantees)—then there appears to be no justification for adhering to a definition of rape that treats the rapist's victim as a lawbreaker who must plead for an excuse from criminal responsibility.

Nonetheless, the force and nonconsent elements remain difficult for modern lawmakers to define and apply. Accordingly, the materials in this section largely will focus on the meaning of these elements. For purposes of clarity, many of the notes treat these elements, just as judicial opinions and statutes frequently do, as if they are distinct. Yet, as the following case reflects, the nature of that distinction and, indeed, the question of whether it should be abandoned altogether, are among the most difficult unresolved issues in rape law today.

# State v. Jones

Supreme Court of Idaho, 2013.
154 Idaho 412, 299 P.3d 219.

■ J. JONES, JUSTICE.

Russell G. Jones appealed his conviction by an Elmore County jury on two counts of rape. The case was initially heard by the Idaho Court of Appeals, which affirmed on one count and reversed on the second. Jones sought review, which we granted in order to consider the force and resistance necessary with respect to a charge of forcible rape.

## I.

## Factual and Procedural History

In the spring of 2008, Jones, Craig Carpenter, and the victim, A.S., were longtime friends. Carpenter and A.S. were engaged and had children together but, unbeknownst to Carpenter, Jones and A.S. had been sexually involved for approximately four years. On May 22, 2008, after spending the night together in Jackpot, Nevada, A.S. and Jones drove back to Idaho and decided they would end their affair. But despite this, they returned to A.S.'s apartment and engaged in consensual sex that morning.

Afterwards, A.S. went to the bathroom and then returned to the bedroom, where Jones was looking at pornographic material on the computer. Jones sat next to A.S. on the bed and started touching her, and she responded by telling him that "I thought we had decided that the time before [ ] was the last time and it wasn't going to happen anymore." A.S. stated that at that point:

> I was laying on my stomach on the bed, and [Jones] got behind me. And I wasn't sure what he was doing, and I got up on my elbows to see what he was doing, and he was undoing his pants. . . . I told him, no, that I wasn't going to do this, and I looked back down, and that's when he leaned forward, and I was pushed down, like this, to where I couldn't get up, and he started having sex with me.

A.S. clarified that when she stated she was pushed down "like this" she meant that Jones "leaned forward to where his body was pushing on [hers]" and that her "hands were underneath [her] and she couldn't turn around." Jones then moved A.S.'s underwear to the side and had intercourse with her, while she "kept yelling at him and pleading for him to stop and please quit," which he ignored. Jones apologized to A.S. afterwards, asked her if she was okay, and admitted that he "lost control." He stated that if A.S. "wanted to press charges that [she] could because he was out of line." After Jones eventually left, A.S. contacted the Boise State University Women's Center. She told a counselor that she had been raped and was advised to call the police, which she did not do. Thereafter, A.S. continued to be in contact with Jones and subsequently went to Jackpot with him again.

On May 27, Jones went to A.S.'s apartment to watch movies. He spent the night and remained there in the morning after Carpenter left for work and A.S.'s children went to school. At the time, A.S. was taking an antihistamine for a bee sting and a prescription anti-anxiety medication, both of which caused her to feel drowsy. As a result of her drowsiness she laid down on the living room couch and started to "drift off." Jones went into the living room, sat next to her, and started stroking her hair. A.S. testified that after he "grabbed a handful of hair and pulled" hard enough to hurt her, she was nonresponsive in hopes that "if [she] just laid there and didn't move he would leave [her] alone." She further stated that:

> After he was done pulling my hair, he left me alone for a little bit. And then he grabbed my chest and squeezed my breast really hard. . . . He apparently didn't get the reaction he wanted, and he moved down to my vaginal area. . . . He started touching me outside, and then he started putting his fingers inside me really hard.

Jones then proceeded to pull down A.S.'s pants and underwear, and "pushed [her] legs apart and started having sex with [her]." In response, A.S. "just froze," and testified that she was "paralyzed" with fear.

Afterwards, Jones and A.S. went to the bedroom and shared a cigarette. Jones helped A.S. into bed and once again started to have sexual intercourse with her. She testified that:

> [A]bout a little ways into it he stopped, and then he said, "Baby, I do have a problem." He said, "What am I doing?" . . . He got off me and pulled his clothes back on and put mine back on. And then he sat me back up and asked me if he could have sex with me. And I just kept saying over and over again, no, my kids are going to be home soon.

Eventually, Jones left the apartment.

A.S. drove to Carpenter's brother's house and told the brother's girlfriend that she had been raped. They took A.S. to the hospital where she told the staff that she had been sexually assaulted, but that she did not want to press charges. But law enforcement was contacted, and A.S. provided a statement to police while at the hospital.

On May 29, A.S. met with a detective, who arranged for A.S. to make a recorded call to Jones. A.S. confronted Jones regarding the incidents, and Jones is heard on tape apologizing for both incidents, conceding that he "continued" with sexual intercourse despite her protests in the first incident and her not responding during the second and admitting that after the first incident he sent her text messages[2] "promising [her] it wouldn't happen again." . . . Toward the end of the tape, A.S. asks Jones to describe what he did to her—he states that: "I think that I

---

[2] The text messages sent by Jones to A.S. were written down by Detective Bob Chaney and admitted into evidence:

May 22 1116: I'm so sorry yet Another Fuck up I'm good at it I'm in ur Hands tell me what to do

May 22 1130: I lost control, seem to be doing that a lot lately

May 22 1132: Its my fault neither can I

May 22 1134: That scared me what should I do

May 22 1137[:] Please don't hate me, I hate myself

May 22 1148[:] I Take Full Responsibility if u want 2 press charges I understand I took From someone I Love

May 23 256[:] Im sorry I have not been better 2u I hate what ive become

pushed things too far and I guess it's rape. I did it. You obviously didn't want any part of it."

Based on the May 22 incident in the bedroom (Count I) and the May 28 incident on the couch (Count II), Jones was charged with two counts of forcible rape . . . . At trial, A.S. testified regarding the events of both days. She admitted she had never informed police that she and Jones were sexually involved during the four years prior to the incidents. She also admitted her statements to the police were incomplete—specifically, she did not reveal that she and Jones had had consensual sex earlier in the day on May 22. Moreover, although she had shared text messages from Jones that she thought were incriminating, she did not show officers text messages sent by her to Jones that indicated that she loved him (and that would have revealed their relationship). A.S. also admitted that even at the time of trial, she was still concealing her relationship with Jones from Carpenter.

During cross-examination, defense counsel focused on a letter that A.S. wrote, had notarized, and gave to the prosecution before trial. In it, she recanted her allegations of rape, asserted that Jones was wrongfully charged, and characterized the incidents as a misunderstanding between her and Jones. But A.S. subsequently sent another letter to the prosecutor that retracted her retraction—she maintained that counseling had induced a change of heart and that she indeed wished to go forward with the charges.

The State then presented the testimony of the nurse who examined A.S. after the second incident. The nurse stated that A.S. was "visibly frightened" during their interaction: crying, avoiding eye contact, and speaking very softly. During the examination, A.S. "had her knees to her chest, kind of holding herself" and afterwards she laid down and "just kind of curled up." The nurse further testified that she found no physical evidence of trauma consistent with rape—there was no bruising, scrapes, or scratches on A.S.'s body. . . .

The State then called its final witness, detective Bob Chaney, who met with A.S. following the incidents and who arranged the taped call to Jones. That tape was played . . . for the jury. Detective Chaney then testified that he read and copied several text messages from Jones to A.S, which were admitted into evidence, but that he did not inspect any messages sent from A.S. to Jones—including those in which she told Jones that she loved him. He was unaware that Jones and A.S. had been in a long-term consensual sexual relationship, and that the two had engaged in consensual intercourse on May 22, prior to the first incident. Chaney testified that the lab report he received following A.S.'s examination yielded no traces of semen.

Jones moved for a directed verdict at the close of evidence, alleging that the State failed to prove: 1) that A.S. resisted sexual intercourse and 2) that her resistance was overcome by force. The district court denied the motion, and the jury convicted Jones of both counts of forcible rape. He was sentenced to concurrent 25-year sentences, with five years determinate for each. Jones appealed.

On appeal, the Court of Appeals determined that verbal resistance was sufficient to substantiate a charge of forcible rape and further concluded that the force overcoming that resistance would need to be greater than the force inherent in sexual intercourse. The Court applied these standards and affirmed the Count I conviction, but reversed on Count II. . . . Jones petitioned for, and we granted, review.

II.

Issues on Appeal

I. Whether there is sufficient evidence to support a conviction for forcible rape as alleged in Count I.

II. Whether there is sufficient evidence to support a conviction for forcible rape as alleged in Count II. . . .

III.

Discussion

A. Standard of Review.

. . . In assessing the sufficiency of evidence, we "will uphold a judgment of conviction entered upon a jury verdict so long as there is substantial evidence upon which a rational trier of fact could conclude that the prosecution proved all essential elements of the crime beyond a reasonable doubt." . . . On appeal, this Court must view the evidence in the light most favorable to the prosecution. Further, we "will not substitute our own judgment for that of the jury on matters such as the credibility of witnesses, the weight to be given to certain evidence, and the reasonable inferences to be drawn from the evidence." . . .

B. There was sufficient evidence to convict Jones on Count I.

The first question before this Court is whether there is sufficient evidence that Jones forcibly raped A.S. on May 22. Resolving this brings up two broader issues: whether verbal resistance qualifies as resistance under Idaho's forcible rape statute and the amount of force required to overcome this resistance.

Jones argues that scant Idaho case law illuminates the meaning of "force" and "resistance" and that "unless and until the [L]egislature affirmatively modifies the common law" of forcible rape, this Court must adhere to the common law understanding that "some quantum of physical resistance is required." He claims that A.S.'s purely verbal resistance to Jones on May 22 would be insufficient to support a charge of forcible rape. Jones additionally contends that the "extrinsic force standard" should apply, i.e., that a charge of forcible rape requires more force than is inherent in the sexual act. He asserts there was no evidence that he used any force that exceeded what "was required to achieve penetration." As he puts it:

> [A.S.] was already lying outstretched in a prone position on her stomach on the bed immediately prior to the intercourse at issue. . . . Given her physical position, it was necessary for Mr. Jones to position himself on top of [A.S.] in order to accomplish penetration. Additionally, [A.S.] testified that her arms were already underneath her prior to the intercourse—Mr. Jones did not physically hold her arms down or place her arms where they were pinned underneath [A.S.'s] body. . . . Finally, the act of pulling aside [A.S.'s] underwear was also incidental to the act of penetration.

Jones thus posits that the State failed to provide evidence of resistance or force that would support a conviction for the forcible rape charge in Count I.

With regard to resistance, the State responds that this Court has not followed the common law standard of "resistance to the utmost" for "at least 105 years," citing State v. Neil, 13 Idaho 539, 90 P. 860 (1907), and State v. Andreason, 44 Idaho 396, 257 P. 370 (1927). It argues that in Idaho the resistance factor exists "simply to show two elements of the crime—the assailant's intent to use force in order to have carnal knowledge and the woman's nonconsent." Because A.S. said no and "was effectively prevented from further resistance by being pushed onto the bed with her arms pinned," the State contends that there was sufficient evidence of resistance. Further, with regard to force, the State argues against the extrinsic force standard. Its contention is that "the only 'quantum' of force required by the statute is that necessary to 'effect' the penetration over the victim's resistance." The State argues that that much force was present here. We will first address the resistance issue.

1. Resistance.

The Court freely reviews issues of statutory interpretation. "When [this] Court must engage in statutory construction, it has the duty to ascertain the legislative intent and give effect to that intent." In order to ascertain the intent of the Legislature, "not only must the literal words of the statute be examined, but also the context of those words, the public policy behind the statute and its legislative history."

The Idaho Code defines forcible rape as follows:

> Rape is defined as the penetration, however slight, of the oral, anal or vaginal opening with the perpetrator's penis accomplished with a female under any one (1) of the following circumstances: . . .
>
> (3) Where she resists but her resistance is overcome by force or violence.

The term "resistance" is not defined in the statute and there is no legislative history to provide guidance. Thus, we begin our review by considering the common law. "At common law, [a] state had to prove beyond a reasonable doubt that the woman resisted her assailant to the utmost of her physical capacity to prove that an act of sexual intercourse was rape." Michelle J. Anderson, Reviving Resistance in Rape Law, U. Ill. L.Rev.. 953, 962 (1998). Thus, under the utmost-physical-resistance standard, "verbal resistance was simply inadequate to prove anything."

The utmost-resistance requirement, beyond producing some severely inequitable results at trial,[5] proved to be nearly impossible to

[5] This is exemplified by the outcome in Brown v. State, 127 Wis. 193, 106 N.W. 536 (1906). There, the victim testified that:

> I tried as hard as I could to get away. I was trying all the time to get away just as hard as I could. I was trying to get up; I pulled at the grass; I screamed as hard as I could, and he told me to shut up, and I didn't, and then he held his hand on my mouth until I was almost strangled.

Despite this, the Court held that the victim had not sufficiently resisted, because she only yelled "let me go" once, her screams were inarticulate, and she failed to resist with "hands and limbs and pelvic muscles."

establish. Anderson, supra, at 964 (noting that under it, even "if a woman struggled to the utmost of her physical capacity until doing so appeared futile to her, and only then acquiesced to the rapist's advances, she . . . was not raped"). Thus, the utmost-resistance standard has since been abandoned to varying degrees. Approximately thirty-two states, the Model Penal Code, the District of Columbia Code, and the Uniform Code of Military Justice have done away with the resistance requirement completely, allowing prosecutors to establish a rape without any resistance present. Six more states' criminal codes expressly state that physical resistance is not required for a rape conviction.

As the State notes, Idaho began its departure from the common law rule about 105 years ago. In *Neil*, this Court examined a charge of assault with intent to commit rape, and particularly, the defendant's argument that in order to prove every element of rape, "the state must show . . . that the female 'showed the utmost reluctance and used the utmost resistance.'" We rejected that approach in this oft-quoted passage:

> A large number of authorities are cited by counsel for appellant, to the effect that the state must show in such cases that the female "showed the utmost reluctance and used the utmost resistance." To our minds the trouble with a number of these authorities is that they reverse the order of the inquiry. They go about inquiring into the kind, character, and nature of the fight put up by the woman, rather than the nature of the assault and evident and manifest purpose and intent of the assailant. For the purpose of reaching the conclusions announced in some of these cases, it is necessary to assume that, in the first place, a man has a right to approach a woman, lay hold on her person, take indecent liberties with her, and that, unless she "kicks, bites, scratches, and screams" to the "utmost of her power and ability," she will be deemed to have consented, and indeed to have invited the familiarity. Such is neither justice, law, nor sound reason.

This early departure from the utmost resistance requirement gained much favorable comment.

This Court reaffirmed *Neil*, and clarified the meaning of the resistance requirement, in *State v. Andreason*. There, the appellant was walking with a woman who he forcibly pulled toward him. She tried to get away, and they fell on the ground, at which point he "placed his hand over the girl's mouth when she attempted to scream, and while holding her on the ground, raised her dress." But she managed to get up, pushed the appellant away, and ran to safety. After escaping, "one of her arms was bleeding, her dress was torn, and she was bereft of one shoe"—she testified "that she was completely exhausted from the scuffle, and that perhaps she could not have gotten away if appellant had not wanted to let her go."

The appellant in *Andreason* argued that "the law [requires] an intent to accomplish the act [of rape] in spite of any resistance that the victim may put forth." Or, in other words, he argued that because the woman escaped his assault, or because he relented and "wanted to let her go," that he had not assaulted her with intent to commit rape. The Court characterized his argument as "a misconception, or at least an overemphasis, as to the necessity for resistance on the part of the woman attacked." We then clarified, "The importance of resistance by the woman is simply to show two elements of the crime—the assailant's intent to use force in order to have carnal knowledge, and the woman's nonconsent." We held that if the "appellant finally desisted in his efforts to accomplish the object which the jury found he had intended, and that [because he ended] the encounter . . . he did not consummate his purpose, this would not justify the conclusion of an absence of a lecherous desire before he withdrew from the struggle." The Court held there was sufficient evidence to uphold a verdict of assault with intent to commit rape. . . .

Given the plain language of Idaho's forcible rape statute and Idaho's well-established case law regarding resistance, we hold the statute does not require that rape victims resist to their utmost physical ability and that verbal resistance is sufficient resistance to substantiate a charge of forcible rape. For one thing, there is no language in [the statute] requiring "physical" resistance. The statute only requires "resistance." It does not differentiate between physical or verbal resistance. Furthermore, *Neil* and *Andreason* have expressly rejected the common law utmost physical resistance standard. As a result, the English common law regarding forcible rape has not applied in Idaho for over a century. Therefore, in this State verbal resistance is sufficient for a charge of forcible rape. Whether the evidence establishes the element of resistance is a fact-sensitive determination based on the totality of the circumstances, including the victim's words and conduct.

Beyond this, allowing verbal resistance to support a charge of forcible rape is sound policy. Requiring physical resistance by a rape victim naturally "increases the likelihood of the attacker's use of violence." State v. McKnight, 54 Wash.App. 521, 774 P.2d 532, 534 (1989) (where the court found "no rational basis for requiring resistance to be manifest in all cases by physical means, and in fact, [was] persuaded that public policy considerations militate against such a requirement"); see also People v. Barnes, 42 Cal.3d 284, 228 Cal.Rptr. 228, 721 P.2d 110, 119 (1986) (citing studies reporting that "the likelihood of receiving injuries requiring medical treatment nearly doubled when victims resisted assailants" and that "resistance is inadvisable since it may provoke greater injury").

The State highlights the inequity of requiring physical resistance in situations in which the victim is restrained and unable to physically resist, as was the case here. It argued that because "Jones applied sufficient force to effectively prevent physical resistance" by A.S., it would be a "miscarriage of justice" to then hold that forcible rape did not occur due to merely verbal resistance. We agree. As this Court observed in *Neil*, an inquiry "into the kind, character, and nature of the fight put up by the woman, rather than the nature of the assault and evident and manifest purpose and intent of the assailant," is in effect, backwards.

Based on the evidence before it, the jury certainly had sufficient basis to find that on May 22, A.S. resisted Jones' advances. She testified that she "kept yelling at him and pleading for him to stop and please quit, and he just kept ignoring her." When asked if she tried to "strike out," she responded that "[she] couldn't," because "[her] hands were pinned down, and Jones' weight was on [her] on the bed." In sum, A.S.'s verbal resistance, in the form of repeated pleas for Jones to stop, was sufficient evidence of resistance . . . .

2. Physical force or violence overcoming resistance.

The next issue before us is the meaning of "force or violence" overcoming resistance, for the purposes of [the forcible rape statute]. There are two primary approaches for addressing this issue: the extrinsic force standard, which defines "force" as anything beyond that which is inherent or incidental to the sexual act itself and the intrinsic force standard, which deems the force inherent in intercourse as sufficient to substantiate a charge of forcible rape.

The extrinsic force standard is the traditional view and "is still the most commonly adopted." The standard, as stated by the Washington Court of Appeals in *McKnight*, is that:

> The *force* to which reference is made in forcible compulsion "is not the force inherent in the act of penetration but the force used or threatened to overcome or prevent resistance by the female." . . . Where the degree of force exerted by the perpetrator is the distinguishing feature between second and third degree rape, to establish second degree rape the evidence must be sufficient to show that the force exerted was directed at overcoming the victim's resistance and was more than that which is normally required to achieve penetration.

The primary justification for the extrinsic force standard seems to be textual. That is, if a forcible rape statute by definition requires penetration, then for an additional requirement of force to be meaningful, it necessarily must mean some force beyond that inherent in penetration. . . .

The intrinsic force standard, on the other hand, represents the more modern trend. It provides that any amount of force—even that which is inherent in intercourse—can substantiate a charge of rape. The seminal case adopting this standard is In re M.T.S., 129 N.J. 422, 609 A.2d 1266 (1992). In *M.T.S.*, the Supreme Court of New Jersey considered "whether the element of 'physical force' is met simply by an act of non-consensual penetration involving no more force than necessary to accomplish" the act. There, the victim had been sleeping, and woke up to realize her clothes were removed, and that the assailant was on top of her, in the act of penetration. After examining the state's "reformed statute," which defined rape without reference to a victim's resistance or submission, the court there found that:

> The understanding of sexual assault as a criminal battery, albeit one with especially serious consequences, follows necessarily from the Legislature's decision to eliminate non-consent and resistance from the substantive definition of the offense. Under the new law, the victim no longer is required to resist and therefore need not have said or done anything in order for the sexual penetration to be unlawful. The alleged victim is not put on trial, and his or her responsive or defensive behavior is rendered immaterial. We are thus satisfied that an interpretation of the statutory crime of sexual assault to require physical force in addition to that entailed in an act of involuntary or unwanted sexual penetration would be fundamentally

> inconsistent with the legislative purpose to eliminate any consideration of whether the victim resisted or expressed nonconsent.

Other jurisdictions, with similar statutes, have adopted the intrinsic force standard. See State v. Sedia, 614 So.2d 533, 535 (Fla.App.1993); State v. Chandler, 939 So.2d 574, 580 (La.App.2006).

Based on the plain language of [our forcible rape statute], we hold that the extrinsic force standard applies in Idaho. [Our statute] defines forcible rape as "penetration, however slight," "[w]here [a woman] resists but her resistance is overcome by force or violence." Were we to construe "force" as encompassing the act of penetration itself, it would effectively render the force element moot. Force would *always* be present and never have to be proven, so long as there was sexual intercourse. Generally speaking, "it is incumbent upon a court to give a statute an interpretation which will not render it a nullity." Thus, in order to give full effect to the complete text of the statute, we adopt the extrinsic force standard. Beyond this, the intrinsic force standard is typically instituted in jurisdictions where the legislature has stepped in to amend its rape statute. But in Idaho, the Legislature has not undertaken any such reform. We must work within the confines of the statute as written. Thus, we conclude that some force beyond that which is inherent in the sexual act is required for a charge of forcible rape.

Even with the extrinsic force standard, a jury had sufficient evidence before it to conclude beyond a reasonable doubt that Jones used force that overcame A.S.'s resistance. This is because Jones used more force than is inherent in the sexual act during the incident on May 22. As A.S. testified, Jones "leaned forward" and she "was pushed down . . . to where [she] couldn't get up"; he "leaned forward to where his body was pushing on [hers]," pinning her hands underneath her so she could not turn around; and he removed her underwear to the side. Jones argues that all these actions were merely incidental to the act of intercourse. But Jones' use of his body weight to trap A.S.'s hands under her, and effectively forestall any struggle, seems in particular less "incidental" to sex and far more like force employed to overcome her resistance. Thus, a jury could well have found beyond a reasonable doubt that Jones used force to overcome A.S.'s resistance during the incident on May 22. Because both the resistance and force elements were present for this incident, we hold that there is sufficient evidence to sustain a conviction for forcible rape, and accordingly affirm Count I.

### C. Because A.S. neither physically nor verbally resisted sexual intercourse on May 28, there was insufficient evidence to convict Jones on Count II.

Jones contends that there was insufficient evidence to support a conviction for forcible rape on Count II, particularly that A.S. never even verbally communicated to him that she did not want to engage in sexual activity or that he used force or violence to overcome any resistance. The State counters that "A.S.'s resistance was in feigning sleep—passive resistance," and that this was enough to show A.S.'s lack of consent to intercourse during the May 28 incident. Jones replies that "the State's position that non-resistance is proof of resistance," is untenable, not in accord with the plain language of [the forcible rape statute], and would effectively render the explicit resistance requirement a nullity.

We hold that there is insufficient evidence to support a charge of forcible rape based on Count II. By her own admission, A.S. "didn't respond" physically, or even verbally, to Jones' advances on May 28—she "just froze." Idaho's forcible rape statute expressly requires resistance. Satisfying this element with inactivity strains the definition of resistance, essentially nullifying the resistance requirement. Though studies have shown that "freezing up" is indeed a legitimate, understandable reaction of victims of sexual assault,[6] this Court has no authority to jettison the resistance requirement—modifying this State's statutes is the Legislature's province alone. As the statute is plainly written, some quantum of resistance is required, and A.S. did not resist Jones' advances on May 28. There was insufficient evidence on the element of resistance to support the conviction of forcible rape on Count II so we need not consider the issue of force. The conviction on Count II is accordingly reversed. . . .

IV.

Conclusion

We affirm Jones' conviction on Count I, and reverse his conviction on Count II.

## NOTES ON THE CONDUCT AND CIRCUMSTANCE ELEMENTS OF RAPE

### 1. REFORM OF THE RESISTANCE REQUIREMENT

As *Jones* reveals, the physical resistance requirement has been a favorite target of the rape reform movement. Advocates for reform have advanced several different objections to the requirement.

First, the physical resistance requirement may expose survivors to increased risk of physical injury. Empirical studies report that some rapists become "more violent in response to victim resistance." People v. Barnes, 42 Cal.3d 284, 721 P.2d 110, 228 Cal.Rptr. 228 (1986). While other studies indicate that resistance deters rapists in some circumstances, it may be difficult to determine whether resistance will thwart, rather than incite, a particular rapist. If the best that can be said is that resistance may prevent the rape or "prove an invitation to death or serious harm," the law should not prescribe resistance as the only appropriate response to a sexual assailant. ALI, Model Penal Code and Commentaries § 213.1, pp. 304–05 (1980).

---

[6] See *Barnes*, 228 Cal.Rptr. 228, 721 P.2d at 118–19 ("For example, some studies have demonstrated that while some women respond to sexual assault with active resistance, others 'freeze.' . . . One researcher found that many women demonstrate 'psychological infantilism'—a frozen fright response—in the face of sexual assault. . . . The 'frozen fright' response resembles cooperative behavior. . . . Indeed, . . . the 'victim may smile, even initiate acts, and may appear relaxed and calm.' . . . Subjectively, however, she may be in a state of terror. [Also] the victim may make submissive signs to her assailant and engage in propitiating behavior in an effort to inhibit further aggression. . . . These findings belie the traditional notion that a woman who does not resist has consented. They suggest that lack of physical resistance may reflect a 'profound primal terror' rather than consent.").

Second, resistance may be an imprecise proxy for nonconsent. Although the common-law judges believed that women naturally resist unwanted sexual attention, the reformers offer recent studies that contradict this assumption. Rather than fighting their attackers, "many women demonstrate . . . a frozen fright response." *People v. Barnes*, supra. In some cases, "the 'frozen fright' response resembles cooperative behavior," but the response is not evidence of consent because it is produced by a "profound primal terror," not by willingness to have sexual intercourse. In short, "while the presence of resistance may well be probative on the issue of force or nonconsent, its absence may not."

Third, as *Jones* explains, a law that focuses on the woman's resistance is, in effect, "backwards." By imposing a "duty" to resist, the law puts the crime victim, rather than the perpetrator, on trial. Jurors are instructed to scrutinize the survivor's behavior, and, if they find her opposition to be insufficiently "earnest," they are advised to acquit the defendant, notwithstanding evidence of his culpability. Reformers have pointed out that survivors of other crimes, such as robbery, kidnaping, and assault, are not required to resist physically even though nonconsent is also an element of those crimes. Reformers attribute this unique feature of rape trials to misogyny. By refusing to credit women's verbal objections to intercourse, the law denies women rights of sexual self-determination and confers on men broad sexual access to women. It is not enough for women to "just say no." If they do no more, men are free to have sex with them. Accordingly, one of the most vehement messages of feminist reformers is that the resistance standard should be eliminated and jurors admonished that "no means no." Susan Estrich, Real Rape 102 (1987).

In response to the reformers' arguments, most jurisdictions have revised the resistance requirement. The "earnest" or "utmost" resistance standard has been all but abolished. Only Alabama continues to define the force element as "physical force that overcomes earnest resistance. . . ." Ala. Crim. Code Ann. § 13A–6–60(8) (Michie 2010). A number of statutory provisions purport to reject the resistance requirement altogether. However, many states continue to recognize the significance of physical resistance by acknowledging that its absence may show that the sexual intercourse was consensual. Still, as the drafters of the Model Penal Code's proposed new sexual assault provisions explain, the law is converging on a position under which a verbal "no" may suffice to prove that the sexual contact was not consensual. In the words of the drafters, an actor "who seeks sexual intimacy with another should heed that person's expressed preferences to engage in, refuse, or desist from specific acts. Permitting persistence in the face of verbal or behavioral indicia of unwillingness unjustly privileges the desires of the aggressor over those of his or her partner." ALI, Model Penal Code: Sexual Assault and Related Offenses, Tentative Draft No. 1, at 43 (April 30, 2014).

## 2. DEFINING FORCE

As *Jones* also reveals, there is a conflict in authority over the question of how "force" should be defined for purposes of contemporary rape law. According to *Jones*, the cases contain two different definitions. First, the majority of courts recognize "the extrinsic force standard," which requires some force beyond that which is incidental to the sex act itself. Second, a distinct minority applies an "intrinsic force standard," which treats the "force inherent in intercourse as sufficient to substantiate a charge of forcible rape." In *Jones* itself, the court announced that it was compelled to adopt the "extrinsic force" approach in order to avoid conflating the ostensibly distinct "force" and "penetration" elements contained in the "forcible rape" statute, and thereby rendering the "force" element a nullity.

A decision by the Supreme Court of Pennsylvania illustrates the distinction between these two approaches and the role that they play in some jurisdictions in separating the greater crime of "rape" from lesser ones. In Commonwealth v. Berkowitz, 537 Pa. 143, 641 A.2d 1161 (1994), the defendant was convicted of rape, a first-degree felony, and indecent assault, a second-degree misdemeanor. The rape statute defined the crime as "sexual intercourse with another person . . . by forcible compulsion." The indecent assault statute defined the offense as "indecent contact with another . . . without the consent of the other person." The court reversed the rape conviction on the ground that the record contained insufficient evidence of "forcible compulsion." The fact that the complainant had "stated 'no' throughout the encounter" was "relevant to the issue of consent," but did not establish that the intercourse was "forcible." The court acknowledged that the defendant "penetrated [the complainant's] vagina with his penis," but, in the court's view, "the weight of his body on top of her was the only force applied." Under the court's holding, such "force" does not satisfy the "forcible compulsion" element of rape. On the other hand, the court decided that the evidence was sufficient to support the conviction for indecent assault, which required proof of nonconsent but not proof of forcible compulsion. Since "[t]he victim testified that she repeatedly said 'no' throughout the encounter, . . . the jury reasonably could have inferred that the victim did not consent to the indecent contact." If the complainant in *Berkowitz* had pushed against the defendant's shoulders as he lay on top of her and penetrated her, would he be guilty of rape? If so, why is that fact determinative of the outcome?

In its proposed new sexual assault provisions, the ALI endorses the "extrinsic force" standard for purposes of liability for "rape" and the "intrinsic force" standard for purposes of liability for "sexual intercourse by coercion." Thus, under § 213.1(1)(a), "rape" occurs where an actor "uses physical force, physical restraint, or an implied or express threat of physical force, bodily injury, or physical restraint to cause another person to engage in an act of sexual intercourse with anyone." "Rape" is graded as a "felony of the second degree." By contrast, under § 213.2(1)(a)(i), "sexual intercourse by coercion" occurs where an actor "has, or enables another person to have, sexual intercourse with a person who at the time of the act of sexual intercourse . . . has by words or conduct expressly indicated nonconsent to such act." "Sexual intercourse by coercion" is graded as a "felony of the third degree," and the offense is designed to enforce "a legal obligation to respect expressions of nonconsent, on pain of criminal sanctions, . . . even in the absence of other coercive circumstances," such as physical force. See ALI, Model Penal Code: Sexual Assault and Related Offenses, Tentative Draft No. 1, at pp. 24, 40, 46 (April 30, 2014).

### 3. DEFINING CONSENT

The court in *Jones* refers to the "intrinsic force standard" as the modern trend, and it cites State ex rel. M.T.S., 129 N.J. 422, 609 A.2d 1266 (1992), as the "seminal case adopting this standard." While it is true that

*M.T.S.* is a watershed decision in rape jurisprudence, the *Jones* opinion does not offer an accurate description of the facts or the complete holding in *M.T.S.*

In *M.T.S.,* the Supreme Court of New Jersey upheld a delinquency adjudication based on the commission of sexual assault. The complainant was a 15-year-old girl, who was a "good friend[ ]" of the 17-year-old male defendant. At the time of the alleged assault, the girl and the defendant were engaged in a "heavy petting" session, as they had done several times before. The trial judge found that they "had been kissing and petting, had undressed and had gotten into the girl's bed. . . ." The defendant penetrated the girl's vagina with his penis. The girl slapped the defendant on the face and pushed him off her. The defendant immediately got dressed and left the girl's room.

The defendant was charged with "second-degree sexual assault" under a statute that defined the crime "as an act of sexual penetration with another person [by the use of] physical force or coercion." The trial judge concluded that the crime had occurred. Although "the victim had consented to a session of kissing and heavy petting with [the defendant,] she had not consented to the actual sexual act." On appeal, the intermediate appellate court reversed. In that court's opinion, the only evidence of force was the act of sexual penetration, which by itself was insufficient to satisfy the "physical force" element. The state appealed, and the Supreme Court of New Jersey reversed and reinstated the delinquency judgment. As that court explained, since 1978 the New Jersey penal code "has referred to the crime that was once known as 'rape' as 'sexual assault.' " In part through this change in nomenclature, the New Jersey legislature manifested its intention to redefine rape "consistent with the law of assault and battery." Significantly, under the law of assault and battery, "any unauthorized touching of another" is a crime. The court then explained how this definition applies in the context of "sexual assault":

> [A]ny act of sexual penetration engaged in by the defendant without the affirmative and freely-given permission of the victim to the specific act of penetration constitutes the offense of sexual assault. Therefore, physical force in excess of that inherent in the act of sexual penetration is not required for such penetration to be unlawful. The definition of "physical force" is satisfied . . . if the defendant applies any amount of force against another person in the absence of what a reasonable person would believe to be affirmative and freely-given permission to the act of sexual penetration.
>
> Under the reformed statute, permission to engage in sexual penetration must be affirmative and it must be given freely, but that permission may be inferred either from acts or statements reasonably viewed in light of the surrounding circumstances. Persons need not, of course, expressly announce their consent to engage in intercourse for there to be affirmative permission. Permission to engage in an act of sexual penetration can be and indeed often is indicated through physical actions rather than words. Permission is demonstrated when the evidence, in whatever form, is sufficient to demonstrate that a reasonable person would have believed that the alleged victim had affirmatively and freely given authorization to the act.

Applying this standard to the facts of the case, the court found no reason to disturb the trial court's finding that "the victim had not expressed consent to the act of intercourse, either through her words or actions."

As the foregoing description makes clear, *M.T.S.* does not merely adopt the "intrinsic force approach" described in *Jones*. Rather, the decision also provides an alternative approach to defining the "consent" element of rape. Under *M.T.S.*, sex is consensual not when the actor's partner does not "say no," or offers no other verbal or physical resistance to sexual penetration. Rather, sex is consensual only when the partner provides "affirmative and freely-given permission" to the act. For this reason, *M.T.S.* is widely understood to have adopted a "yes means yes" approach to defining consent, in sharp contrast to the "no means no" approach to defining nonconsent that is reflected in *Jones*.

Under *M.T.S.*, what kinds of "physical actions" express affirmative permission to engage in sexual intercourse? The New Jersey Supreme Court deferred to, but did not analyze, the trial court's finding that the complainant did not give permission, notwithstanding her consensual participation in "heavy petting." Rather, the court chose to emphasize that the New Jersey statute "places no burden on the alleged victim to have expressed non-consent or to have denied permission, and no inquiry is made into what he or she thought or desired or why he or she did not resist or protest." According to Donald Dripps, the court erred by placing on men the burden of seeking permission. Dripps believes that the better approach is to put the burden on women to express refusal. He rests his case on empirical as well as normative grounds:

> In practice couples do not discuss in advance each specific sex act that one or another might initiate, and there is no strong reason why the law should encourage them to do so. Suppose, for example, [that a woman performs fellatio on a man] without asking permission. Suppose, further, that he has religious or other scruples about oral sex. He protests . . . , and she stops [immediately]. Still, under [*M.T.S.*], she is guilty of sexual assault. If uncertainty and spontaneity can enhance the pleasures of love-making, people of either sex might prefer not being asked—so long as they can be sure that behavior they don't like will be stopped on demand. The interest in freedom from wrong guesses by one's bedmates is not so great as to call the criminal law into play.

Donald A. Dripps, Beyond Rape: An Essay on the Difference Between the Presence of Force and the Absence of Consent, 92 Colum. L. Rev. 1780, 1793 n.41 (1992).

Douglas Husak and George Thomas acknowledge that an approach to rape like that endorsed by *M.T.S.* would eliminate the "potential for error" in sexual encounters and the pain that such errors inflict. However, since social norms about sexual intercourse do not currently demand explicit affirmations of consent, they argue that punishing a defendant merely for departing from the *M.T.S.* model

> can be justified only on Holmes's view that "[p]ublic policy sacrifices the individual to the general good," and that it is more important to encourage the social convention to change or to vindicate a particular view of women's autonomy than to do justice in an individual case. But if the law should deal justly with each

> individual defendant, it is objectionable to punish someone to promote an ideology or to effect a change in societal views.

Douglas N. Husak & George C. Thomas III, Date Rape, Social Convention, and Reasonable Mistakes, 11 Law & Phil. 95, 108–09, 112 (1992). Does the law ever punish or, for that matter, refuse to punish someone without promoting an ideology?

The drafters of the proposed new Model Penal Code sexual assault provisions may be poised to recommend that the law should punish an actor who has sex with another without obtaining permission. The formulation is provided in § 213.4, Sexual Intercourse Without Consent:

> An actor is guilty of sexual intercourse, without consent, a misdemeanor, if the actor knowingly or recklessly has, or enables another person to have, sexual intercourse with a person who at the time of the act of sexual intercourse has not given consent to that act.

ALI, Model Penal Code: Sexual Assault and Related Offenses, Tentative Draft No. 1, at pp. 4, 67–70 (April 30, 2014).

According to its drafters, this provision "rests on the increasing recognition that sexual assault is an offense against the . . . individual's right to control the boundaries of his or her sexual experience, rather than a mere exercise of physical dominance." The provision also codifies an aspiration for "more open and honest expressions of sexual needs," which "remains disputed" and which may be "frequently honored in the breach." Nonetheless, in the drafters' view, a balancing of costs and benefits supports the decision to codify an affirmative consent norm: "[G]iven that the harm of unwanted sexual imposition greatly exceeds any harm entailed in having to make arguably awkward efforts to clarify the situation or (temporarily) missing an opportunity for a mutually desired encounter, the appropriate default position clearly is to err in the direction of protecting individuals against unwanted sexual imposition." At the same time, the drafters emphatically reject the grading decision reflected in *M.T.S.*, under which the absence of affirmative permission warranted imposition of felony sanctions. Instead, they insist that "[h]owever unjustifiable, intercourse without affirmative consent is distinctly less reprehensible than intercourse imposed over an express statement of unwillingness or intercourse achieved by force." Accordingly, they propose that this new offense be classified as a misdemeanor.

### 4. COMPETENCE TO CONSENT AND INTOXICATION

Sexual intercourse with a person who is incompetent to consent to the act has long been punished as a form of rape. This crime requires no increment of force beyond that required to achieve penetration. That is, as *Jones* would put it, courts everywhere follow the "intrinsic force" approach in these cases. Incompetent actors include persons who are unconscious or asleep, as well as persons who lack the mental capacity to consent to sexual relations. One difficult issue is the standard to be used to evaluate mental competence to consent to sexual intercourse. Under the law in many jurisdictions, a person is competent to consent if she possesses sufficient mental capacity to understand the "nature and consequences" of sexual intercourse. However, courts have disagreed over the scope of the "nature and consequences" test. For example, some courts require only that the person understand the physiological nature and consequences of intercourse, while others also require some understanding of its moral status and social consequences. See State v. Olivio, 123 N.J. 550, 589 A.2d 597 (1991).

When the complainant was intoxicated at the time of the intercourse, the prosecution may proceed on the theory that she was incompetent to consent. Cultural norms regarding alcohol consumption and sexuality make such cases very difficult to resolve. According to the drafters of the Model Code's proposed new sexual assault provisions, "a great deal of unwanted sexual activity . . . occurs between intoxicated parties." At the same time, "a great deal of desired sexual activity occurs between intoxicated parties," since many people use alcohol "as a welcome means of lowering sexual inhibitions." ALI, Model Penal Code: Sexual Assault and Related Offenses, Tentative Draft No. 1, at 58 (April 30, 2014). For these reasons, lawmakers have struggled to identify the standard to separate the intoxicated intercourse which is criminal from that which is not.

The most common and least controversial prosecutions have involved complainants who had imbibed to the point of unconsciousness and thus were physically incapable of consenting to the sexual intercourse in which the defendant engaged. Every jurisdiction agrees that intercourse with an unconscious person should be a crime. Likewise, there is widespread agreement that a crime occurs when an actor forces or dupes a sexual partner into imbibing an intoxicant that renders the partner physically helpless.

The more difficult cases are those in which the complainant drank voluntarily and never lost consciousness. In such cases, the prosecution will proceed on the theory that she was so drunk that she temporarily lacked mental capacity to consent. The accused will argue that the complainant may have been feeling the effects of the alcohol, but that she remained capable of consenting and that she did, in fact, consent. The accused also will invoke pervasive views about alcohol's sexually disinhibiting effects: because the woman was drinking, she was more likely to and, in fact, did desire to engage in sexual intercourse. See William H. George et al., Perceptions of Postdrinking Female Sexuality: Effects of Gender, Beverage Choice, and Drink Payment, 18 J. Applied Soc. Psychol. 1295 (1988).

As it turns out, most state statutes and case law do not provide clear guidelines concerning the criteria to be used to determine when a person is too drunk to consent to sex. Instead, they include general formulations under which the jury is authorized to convict if it finds that, because of the consumption of drugs or alcohol, the complainant was "so impaired as to be incapable of consenting to sexual intercourse." See Commonwealth v. Blache, 450 Mass. 583, 880 N.E.2d 736 (2008). Moreover, the media tends to depict these cases as all but impossible to adjudicate by asserting that they always pose the so-called "he said, she said"—or, in less heterosexist terms, "word against word"—conundrum. As the following excerpt from *Commonwealth v. Blache* suggests, however, there will be cases in which there is evidence that corroborates the complainant's testimony that she was so grossly intoxicated as to lack the capacity to consent. Even so, such prosecutions are likely to be controversial.

In *Commonwealth v. Blache*, the Supreme Judicial Court of Massachusetts found that there was sufficient evidence of the complainant's intoxication to warrant an incapacity instruction that embodied the standard quoted above. The court offered this summary of the evidence:

On August 17, 2000, the complainant, who was twenty-six years old, went out with a female friend to a bar in Haverhill. The complainant was five feet, two inches tall and weighed 110 pounds. Before leaving home at around 7 p.m., the complainant smoked marijuana and took an antianxiety medication called Klonopin. She had not eaten any food all day. The complainant had "[a] couple" of alcoholic drinks at the first bar she visited, and drank "[a] lot" at a second bar, where she spent the latter part of the evening. Between 11:30 p.m. and midnight, the complainant and her friend were joined by David MacRae, whom the complainant had been dating for about one week, and his friend Allan Castro. By that time, the complainant was "very drunk," and she had only intermittent memories of the remainder of the evening. When the group left the bar shortly before it closed, the complainant was "causing a scene," was argumentative, had difficulty walking, and fell twice. The complainant's friend took her keys to drive her home. Ultimately, however, Castro drove the complainant's friend home in the complainant's truck, and then he, MacRae, and the complainant drove to MacRae's house in Methuen.

At MacRae's house, the complainant continued to behave belligerently. She attempted to leave MacRae's house but drove her truck into his fence and then backed up into the house itself, at which point MacRae took her keys. Castro telephoned the police, and MacRae told them he needed assistance with an unwanted and very intoxicated female guest. Before the police arrived, the complainant returned to the house and "passed out" for some time.

The Methuen police dispatched the defendant, Officer David Blache, to respond to the call; he arrived at MacRae's house just before 2 a.m. When the defendant arrived, the complainant woke up; she was "still drunk," and Castro saw her fall "straight back and hit her head . . . [o]n the wall." The defendant spent about forty-five minutes at the house gathering information for an accident report and arranging for the complainant's truck to be towed. During this time, according to MacRae, Castro, the defendant, and the tow truck driver, the complainant exhibited sexually aggressive behavior toward the defendant. She touched him, tried to kiss him and "grab[ ] his crotch," asked him if he wanted to have sex with her, licked the windows of his police cruiser, and pulled down her pants to show the defendant her genitals. Witnesses also testified that at this time she was still drunk; she slurred her speech; and she pulled down her pants and began to urinate in the street in front of MacRae's house when he refused to allow her back inside to use his bathroom. While the defendant was speaking with MacRae, he allowed the complainant to sit in the front seat of his cruiser because she was cold; after she twice turned on the cruiser's lights and siren, he transferred her to the back seat.

After arranging to have the complainant's truck towed, the defendant obtained permission from police headquarters to transport her home to Haverhill because she did not have enough money to pay for a taxi. The complainant testified that she did not remember leaving MacRae's house in the cruiser, and that the next thing she remembered was the car pulling up next to a dumpster. Once the car stopped, the defendant opened the driver's side rear door, pulled down the complainant's pants, and vaginally raped her in the back seat of the cruiser. She testified that she told him she "didn't want to do that," and tried to kick the defendant and the partition between the front and rear seats, but she was unable to open the opposite door because there was no interior handle. She further testified that the defendant then drove her home, and when he dropped her off he warned her that the police have a "code of silence" and they would not believe her.

The defendant also testified at trial. He admitted having intercourse with the complainant, but he claimed that it was consensual and occurred at her house. According to the defendant, he dropped the complainant at home and cleared the call with headquarters, then he knocked on her door and asked to use her bathroom. He testified that when he emerged from the bathroom, the complainant was completely naked; they embraced, she performed oral sex on him, and they had consensual intercourse on her couch.

Although the complainant did not remember making any telephone calls after she returned home, the prosecutor played recordings of two 911 calls she placed to the Haverhill police. Additionally, Castro testified that he answered two calls from the complainant at MacRae's house about one-half hour after the complainant had left with the defendant. In the first call, she said in a "bragging" or "sarcastic" tone, "Tell Dave [MacRae] thanks for the best fuck of my life," and hung up. In the second call, a few minutes later, she said, "Tell Dave I'm going to go for the whole rape thing," and hung up.

Haverhill police responded to the complainant's 911 calls at about 3:30 a.m. and convinced her to go to the hospital for a sexual assault examination. Two female officers who assisted the complainant that morning testified as fresh complaint witnesses; they described the complainant as quite upset and still intoxicated. The vaginal swab taken from the complainant as part of the examination contained sperm cells, but the oral swab did not. The deoxyribonucleic acid (DNA) of the sperm cells collected matched a blood sample submitted by the defendant. Sperm was also detected in a stain on the zipper area of the defendant's uniform pants but not in the back seat of the cruiser. The complainant's blood was drawn at 7:30 a.m.; testing revealed a blood alcohol level at that time of 0.14 per cent, as well as evidence of marijuana. Using retrograde extrapolation, a toxicology expert testified that the complainant's blood alcohol level at 2:30 to 3 a.m. would have been between 0.176 and 0.24 per cent, a level that typically causes disorientation, loss of judgment, impaired perception, lethargy, imbalance, slurred speech, loss of memory, impaired comprehension, and confusion.

In his opinion concurring and dissenting in *Blache*, Justice Spina faulted the majority for, among other things, rejecting the common-law formulation for incapacity to consent, which could be satisfied only by a showing that the complainant was "wholly insensible," "utterly stupefied," or "unconscious." In his view, the majority's new standard "needlessly complicates certain rape cases, and has great potential to produce unfair results for defendants and unwanted intrusions into the private affairs of complainants." Finally, he warned that, "[in] the future we can expect the Commonwealth to try rape cases, as here, like drunk driving cases." Are these criticisms fair?

The drafters of the Model Penal Code's proposed new sexual assault provisions are poised to recommend criteria for deciding when a person is too drunk to consent to sex. Section 213.2(3)(a) of the tentative draft would make it a felony of the third degree to have sex with another who "lacks the capacity to express nonconsent to such act of sexual intercourse, because of intoxication, whether voluntary or involuntary, and regardless of the identity of the person who administered such intoxicants." ALI, Model Penal Code: Sexual Assault and Related Offenses, Tentative Draft No. 1, at 3, 40–41 (April 30, 2014). Is there a meaningful difference between the *Blache* approach—which asks whether the complainant was so impaired as to be incapable of consenting—and the proposed MPC approach—which asks whether the complainant, because of intoxication, lacks the capacity to express nonconsent? Which is better?

In date rape cases where both participants have been drinking and thus experiencing alcohol's sexually disinhibiting effects, how should the law distinguish the perpetrator from the victim? Probably, such cases occur frequently, since empirical studies suggest that "one third to two thirds of rapists, and many rape victims, are intoxicated." Charlene L. Muehlenhard and Melaney A. Linton, Date Rape and Sexual Aggression in Dating Situations: Incidence and Risk Factors, 34 J. Counseling Psychol. 186, 187 (1987). Moreover, depending on the standard used to evaluate capacity to consent to sex, it is possible for both participants to be so intoxicated as to lack such capacity. In such a case, may one of them be held responsible for raping the other, and if so, what grounds should be used to identify the responsible actor? This problem will be revisited below, in the materials on the mens rea of rape.

### 5. WITHDRAWAL OF CONSENT

Is rape committed if a woman who initially consented to intercourse then withdraws her consent, but the male continues to have sex with her? This contentious issue was considered by the California Supreme Court in In re John Z., 29 Cal.4th 756, 60 P.3d 183, 128 Cal.Rptr.2d 783 (2003). The court took the case to resolve questions created by People v. Vela, 172 Cal. App.3d 237, 218 Cal.Rptr. 161 (1985), in which the California Court of Appeal had held that "the presence or absence of consent at the moment of initial penetration appears to be the crucial point in the crime of rape." According to *Vela*, "the essence of the crime of rape is the outrage to the person and feelings of the female resulting from the nonconsensual violation of her womanhood." Although a woman who withdraws her consent may feel outraged if the man ignores her wishes, "the sense of outrage . . . could hardly be of the same magnitude" as that in cases where the woman initially refused consent. Hence, *Vela* reasoned, "the essential guilt of rape . . . is lacking in the withdrawn consent scenario."

The Supreme Court of California was not persuaded:

> With due respect to *Vela* and the two sister state cases on which it relied, we find their reasoning unsound. First, contrary to

*Vela's* assumption, we have no way of accurately measuring the level of outrage the victim suffers from being subjected to continued sexual intercourse following withdrawal of her consent. We must assume that the sense of outrage is substantial. [More important, the California rape statute does not provide, nor any California case hold] that the victim's outrage is an element of the crime of rape. . . .

*Vela* appears to assume that, to constitute rape, the victim's objections must be raised, or a defendant's use of force must be applied, before intercourse commences, but that argument is clearly flawed. One can readily imagine situations in which the defendant is able to obtain penetration before the victim can express an objection or attempt to resist. Surely, if the defendant thereafter ignores the victim's objections and forcibly continues the act, he has committed "an act of sexual intercourse accomplished . . . against a person's will by means of force. . . ."

Defendant, candidly acknowledging *Vela's* flawed reasoning, contends that, in cases involving an initial consent to intercourse, the male should be permitted a "reasonable amount of time" in which to withdraw, once the female raises an objection to further intercourse. As defendant argues, "By essence of the act of sexual intercourse, a male's primal urge to reproduce is aroused. It is therefore unreasonable for a female and the law to expect a male to cease having sexual intercourse immediately upon her withdrawal of consent. It is only natural, fair and just that a male be given a reasonable amount of time in which to quell his primal urge. . . ."

We disagree with defendant's argument. Aside from the apparent lack of supporting authority for defendant's "primal urge" theory, the principal problem with his argument is that it is contrary to the language of [the rape statute. Nothing in the statutory language] or the case law suggests that the defendant is entitled to persist in intercourse once his victim withdraws her consent.

In any event, even were we to accept defendant's "reasonable time" argument, in the present case he clearly was given ample time to withdraw but refused to do so despite Laura's resistance and objections. Although defendant testified he withdrew as soon as Laura objected, for purposes of appeal we need not accept this testimony as true in light of Laura's contrary testimony. As noted above, Laura testified that she struggled to get away when she was on top of defendant, but that he grabbed her waist and pushed her down onto him. At this point, Laura told defendant that if he really cared about her, he would respect her wishes and stop. Thereafter, she told defendant three times that she needed to go home and that she did not accept his protestations he just needed a "minute." Defendant continued the sex act for at least four or five minutes after Laura first told him she had to go home. According to Laura, after the third time she asked to leave, defendant continued to insist that he needed more time and "just stayed inside of me and kept like basically forcing it on me," for about a "minute, minute and [a] half." Contrary to the dissent's concerns the force defendant exerted in resisting Laura's attempts to stop the act was clearly ample to satisfy [the requirement that the defendant use "force" above and beyond that necessary for the sex act itself].

Although the dissent . . . would prefer more guidance for future cases, this is an appeal from a juvenile court adjudication rather than a jury trial, and the briefing does not address what pinpoint instructions, if any, might be appropriate in these withdrawn consent cases. Accordingly, we do not explore or recommend instructional language governing such matters as the defendant's knowledge of the victim's withdrawal of consent, the possibly equivocal nature of that withdrawal, or the point in time at which defendant must cease intercourse once consent is withdrawn.

### 6. GRADING

The preceding notes have referred to various factors that contemporary statutes invoke for purposes of grading rape and sexual assault offenses. As it turns out, the grading of rape into multiple offenses of different punishment levels is a modern phenomenon. As the drafters of the Model Penal Code explained, the common law placed "different forms of rape . . . in a single category for grading purposes. The effect of [such definition] was to authorize grave sanctions for a range of conduct that included offenses plainly less serious than the most aggravated forms of rape." ALI, Model Penal Code and Commentaries § 213.1, at p. 278 (1980). At the time that the Model Code was being drafted in the 1950's, there "already was . . . an emerging consensus that departure from the single-category approach to the punishment of rape was appropriate and that legislative attention should be addressed to the creation of meaningful grading distinctions among the different forms of the offenses." Over the years that consensus has taken hold almost everywhere, but there remains a conflict over what these grading distinctions should be.

The sexual assault statute at issue in *M.T.S.* represents one approach to grading.[a] As the court in *M.T.S.* explained, the New Jersey legislature replaced the common law "rape" crime with an offense known as "sexual assault." The statute divides sexual assault into two categories, namely, "aggravated sexual assault" and "sexual assault." "Aggravated sexual assault" occurs when an actor sexually penetrates the body of another person under specified aggravating circumstances. Such circumstances include the sexual penetration of a person who is under age 13, commission of the sexual penetration during the perpetration of another serious felony, the threatened use of a weapon, the presence of several attackers, and the use of physical force or coercion accompanied by the infliction of "severe personal injury" on the survivor. "Aggravated sexual assault" is punishable by 10 to 20 years in prison.

By contrast, an actor commits the crime of "sexual assault" when he or she sexually penetrates another under circumstances that are blameworthy, but less serious than those involved in aggravated sexual assault. For example, as was found to be the case in *M.T.S.*, an actor is guilty of "sexual

[a] The relevant New Jersey statutes are reproduced in Appendix B, together with rape statutes from Michigan and Virginia.

assault" when he sexually penetrates another person by the use of "physical force or coercion," but he does not severely injure the other person. "Sexual assault" is punishable by five to 10 years in prison.

The New Jersey Penal Code also includes the offense of "criminal sexual contact." The actus reus of this offense is sexual touching not amounting to sexual penetration. This offense also is divided into two categories for grading purposes, namely, "aggravated criminal sexual contact" and "criminal sexual contact," and these categories are distinguished by the presence or absence of aggravating factors similar to those enumerated in the sexual assault provisions. "Aggravated criminal sexual contact" is punishable by three to five years in prison, while "criminal sexual contact" is punishable by up to 18 months in prison.

*M.T.S.* involved a juvenile delinquency proceeding, and the reported opinions do not reflect what penalty the judge imposed on M.T.S. for the sexual assault. Is the penalty (five to 10 years in prison) authorized by the statute an appropriate one?

### 7. A FEMINIST CRITIQUE OF THE REQUIREMENT OF FORCE

In *Berkowitz*, "forcible compulsion" was the line that divided the felony of rape from the misdemeanor of indecent assault. The trial judge sentenced Berkowitz to concurrent terms of one to four years on the rape count and six to 12 months on the indecent assault count. With the rape conviction reversed on appeal, Berkowitz served six months in county jail. Under the traditional definition of rape, force is the line that divides the crime of rape from noncriminal sexual intercourse. These grading schemes appear to rest, in part, on a judgment that "forcible" intercourse inflicts injuries more serious than those imposed by intercourse that is only "nonconsensual."

According to Donald Dripps, this judgment is sound because "people generally, male and female, would rather be subjected to unwanted sex than be shot, slashed, or beaten with a tire iron. . . . [A]s a general matter unwanted sex is not as bad as violence. I think it follows that those who press sexual advances in the face of refusal act less wickedly [and should be punished less severely] than those who shoot, slash, or batter." Donald A. Dripps, Beyond Rape: An Essay on the Difference Between the Presence of Force and the Absence of Consent, 92 Colum. L. Rev. 1780, 1801 (1992).

Many feminist commentators reject this conclusion. For example, Robin West argues that the distinction between "forcible" and "nonconsensual" intercourse is illusory. West explains that the distinction ignores "the violence, and hence the injury, of the penetration itself. From the victim's perspective, unwanted sexual penetration involves unwanted force, and unwanted force is violent—it is physically painful, sometimes resulting in internal tearing and often leaving scars." Robin L. West, Legitimating the Illegitimate: A Comment on Beyond Rape, 93 Colum. L. Rev. 1442, 1448 (1993). The distinction also ignores the psychological injuries imposed by nonconsensual intercourse. As West remarks, "[r]ape accompanied by additional acts of violence is no doubt a worse experience than what we misleadingly think of as 'nonviolent' rape. [But both] involve violent assaults upon the body. Both are experienced, and typically described, as . . . spiritual murder."

Catharine MacKinnon criticizes feminists and other commentators who argue that rape should be understood as a violent (rather than sexual) act against women. According to MacKinnon, those who assert that rape is a crime of violence, not sex, are attempting to characterize sexuality as "a preexisting natural sphere to which domination is alien." MacKinnon argues that such characterization is mistaken because in our culture there is no "uncoerced context for sexual expression." Rather, "sexuality [is] a social sphere of male power to which forced sex is paradigmatic." In a culture in which normal men are expected to be dominant and sexually aggressive, normal "sex, in the legal perspective, can entail a lot of force." Moreover, since "coercion has become integral to [normal] male sexuality," rape cases find high levels of force to be unobjectionable because judges interpret sexual encounters from the perspective of "normal male sexual behavior, rather than [from] the victim's, or women's, point of violation." MacKinnon insists that, if feminists intend to dismantle "male supremacy," they must persuade lawmakers that "the elements 'with force and without consent' [are] redundant. Force is present because consent is absent." She continues:

> The deeper problem is that women are socialized to passive receptivity; may have or perceive no alternative to acquiescence; may prefer it to the escalated risk of injury and the humiliation of a lost fight; submit to survive. . . . Sexual intercourse may be deeply unwanted, the woman would never have initiated it, yet no force may be present. . . . Force may be used, yet the woman may prefer the sex—to avoid more force or because she, too, eroticizes dominance. Women and men know this. Considering rape as violence not sex evades, at the moment it most seems to confront, the issue of who controls woman's sexuality and the dominance/submission dynamic that has defined it.

Catharine A. MacKinnon, Toward a Feminist Theory of the State 172–74 (1989).

## NOTES ON THE CRIMINALIZATION OF SEX OBTAINED BY COERCION OR FRAUD

Should the law punish people who obtain sex by threats of harm other than physical injury or who obtain sex by deception? The following notes identify several different kinds of nonviolent practices that have formed the basis for criminal prosecutions.

### 1. PSYCHOLOGICAL COERCION

In Commonwealth v. Mlinarich, 518 Pa. 247, 542 A.2d 1335 (1988), the defendant was convicted of rape and attempted rape for his sexual contacts with a 14-year-old girl. Mlinarich was the girl's guardian. Prior to going to live in his home, the girl had been committed to a juvenile detention facility for stealing her brother's ring. Mlinarich and his wife requested custody of the girl, and a court released her into their care. Soon thereafter, Mlinarich began to fondle her. She told him that "he shouldn't do that," but he ignored her "protestations, desisting only if she began to cry." During several of these encounters, Mlinarich attempted and, on one occasion, achieved intercourse with the girl. Each time, she "insisted that she 'did not want to do anything,'" and, during the first unsuccessful attempt, she "experienced pain and 'scream[ed], holler[ed]' and cried." However, Mlinarich persisted, and she submitted to the activity after he "threatened to send her back to the detention home" if she refused him.

On appeal, the intermediate appellate court reversed the rape and attempted rape convictions on the ground that these crimes require "forcible compulsion," which is not satisfied by "threats to do non-violent acts." Commonwealth v. Mlinarich, 345 Pa.Super. 269, 498 A.2d 395 (1985).[a] The Supreme Court of Pennsylvania affirmed by an equally divided court. 518 Pa. 247, 542 A.2d 1335. All of the Justices agreed that the term "forcible compulsion" is not limited to physical violence, but also includes "psychological duress." They divided over the question of whether Mlinarich's threat rose to that level. According to the three Justices who voted to affirm, a threat inflicts psychological duress only where it attacks the woman's will rather than her intellect. They explained:

> The critical distinction is where the compulsion overwhelms the will of the victim in contrast to a situation where the victim can make a deliberate choice to avoid the encounter even though the alternative may be an undesirable one. Indeed, the victim in this instance apparently found the prospect of being returned to the detention home a repugnant one. Notwithstanding, she was left with a choice and therefore the submission was the result of a deliberate choice and was not an involuntary act. . . .
>
> . . . The purpose of [the forcible compulsion element is] to distinguish between assault upon the will and the forcing of the victim to make a choice regardless how repugnant. Certainly difficult choices have a coercive effect but the result is the product of the reason, albeit unpleasant and reluctantly made. . . .

For the three Justices who voted to reverse and reinstate the convictions, the threat of incarceration constituted forcible compulsion. As Justice McDermott put it, "all threats, however compelling in the mind of the actor, leave a choice in the victim. . . . The question is not whether she could make a choice to yield or be confined, but whether the law should allow such a choice at all. The purpose of law is to narrow the choices that may be offered to compel others in order to gain an end of one's own." Thus, the magnitude of the threat, the dread it inspired in the girl, and whether it overcame her reasonable resolve were questions the jury should weigh in light of all the circumstances in the case.

*Mlinarich* was a divisive opinion for the Justices who decided it, and it proved to be controversial for commentators and members of the popular press. In 1995, the Pennsylvania legislature responded to criticisms of *Mlinarich* and cases that followed it by enacting this definition of "forcible compulsion" for purposes of the rape statute: "Compulsion by use of physical, intellectual, moral, emotional, or psychological force, either express or implied." 18 Pa. Cons. Stat. Ann. § 3101 (2000). If a case similar to *Mlinarich* were to be tried under this definition, what would the result be? Assuming that *Mlinarich* was a "problem," as many commentators argued,

---

[a] In addition to the rape and attempted rape counts, Mlinarich was convicted of involuntary deviate sexual intercourse and corrupting the morals of a child. The trial court had imposed "an aggregate term of three to eight years imprisonment in the county jail." With the rape and attempted rape convictions reversed on appeal, Mlinarich's sentence was reduced to a term of two to five years in prison. The state could not try Mlinarich for statutory rape because the girl was over the age of consent. In Pennsylvania, the age of consent for purposes of statutory rape is 14, and Mlinarich began sexually molesting her on her 14th birthday.

is this revision an appropriate "fix"? Does the revision go far enough? Too far?

## 2. EXTORTION

In some jurisdictions, the sexual offenses chapter of the penal code punishes the extortion of sexual relations. A dearth of reported cases of sex by extortion suggests that this theory is rarely invoked by prosecutors. In jurisdictions whose penal codes do not specifically prohibit sex by extortion, the question is whether such activity may be prosecuted under a general extortion statute, as in the following case.

### *(i) Is Sex a Thing of Value?*

In United States v. Hicks, 24 M.J. 3 (1987), the complainant, a woman named Julie, was visiting her boyfriend at his military base. Sergeant Hicks was the leader of the section to which Julie's boyfriend was assigned. When Hicks learned that Julie was staying in the barracks in violation of a regulation, he advised her boyfriend to bring her to Hicks's room where she would not be detected by the staff duty officer. Soon after the boyfriend followed this advice, Hicks returned to his room. He informed "Julie that he was preparing a charge sheet," under which her boyfriend would "lose his pay and privileges" and "probably get thrown in the brig." Hicks then told Julie that "if she 'wanted to get . . . [her boyfriend] out of that trouble,'" she should have sex with him. After a further exchange during which Hicks made additional threatening comments, Julie submitted to sexual intercourse with him. Based on this episode, Hicks was convicted of rape[b] and extortion of sexual favors, and sentenced to confinement for 30 years.

Hicks appealed, and the United States Court of Military Appeals affirmed. To convict Hicks for extortion, the prosecution had to prove two elements: "(1) communication of a threat; (2) 'with the intention thereby to obtain anything of value or any acquittance, advantage, or immunity.'" Hicks attacked only the second element, arguing that it did not encompass "sexual favors or the fulfillment of subjective desires." The court disagreed, holding that "[i]t is sufficient if there is some 'value' or 'advantage' to the accused in the thing sought. 'Value' and 'advantage' are broad concepts and are not limited to pecuniary or material gain." Accordingly, "[t]he extortion offense was complete upon communication of the threat to report [the boyfriend] with the requisite intent."

---

[b] Hicks was convicted of rape under a statute that required proof that the sexual intercourse was accomplished "by force and without [the victim's] consent." The court held that there was sufficient evidence to support the rape conviction, relying in part on Julie's testimony that, after threatening to report her boyfriend, Hicks took her hand and stated, "It doesn't matter if you cooperate or not, I'm going to give it to you anyway." According to the court, this testimony established that Hicks intended "to use whatever force was necessary to accomplish intercourse." The court also concluded that Julie "was placed in fear of bodily harm; she remembered being advised by various articles and television programs [primarily, talk shows] that it was better not to resist unless you are sure you can hurt your assailant to such an extent as to make good your escape." The court also decided that convicting Hicks for both rape and extortion did not violate the double jeopardy clause, which provides that no person "shall be subject for the same offence to be twice put in jeopardy of life or limb." In this case, rape and extortion were not the "same offense" for double jeopardy purposes because "[t]here are elements in each offense which are not contained within the other, and neither offense is a lesser-included offense of the other. The extortion offense was complete upon communication of the threat to report [the boyfriend] with the requisite intent; the rape was accomplished by means of placing the victim in fear of bodily harm."

Not all courts have been receptive to the claim that "sexual favors" satisfy the second element of extortion. In State v. Stockton, 97 Wash.2d 528, 647 P.2d 21 (1982), the Supreme Court of Washington reversed an extortion conviction based on letters threatening to kill a woman and her husband if she did not agree to have sex with the defendant. Extortion was defined as "knowingly to obtain or attempt to obtain by threats property or services." After examining the definition of services provided in the statute, as well as the language of predecessor statutes, the court held that the only "services" contemplated were "those for which compensation is usually received . . . and not the sexual favors which defendant was asking to be freely given to him." The court implied that the defendant could have been tried under a "coercion" statute, which punished threats uttered to "induce[ ] a person to engage in conduct which [she] has a legal right to abstain from." Noting that coercion is only a misdemeanor, the court conceded that it was anomalous to punish as a felony threats to obtain commercial services, while a threat to obtain sexual favors was punished less severely. However, the legislature had created, and was the appropriate body to resolve, that anomaly.

### *(ii) Nature of the Threat*

If sexual contacts satisfy the second element of extortion, the nature of the threat determines whether a crime occurred. Not surprisingly, threats of serious violence suffice for an extortion conviction, but so do other threats. Threats to injure the victim financially, to harm the victim's reputation, and to confine the victim all have been held sufficient in cases involving the extortion of pecuniary assets. While the threat element of extortion thus encompasses a wider variety of coercive pressures than does the traditional definition of rape, extortion does not prohibit inducements to behavior that fall short of a threat to cause an injury. In State v. Hilton, 1991 WL 168608 (Tenn. Crim. App. 1991), a man who had sexual intercourse with his 17-year-old stepdaughter was convicted of incest and rape. To support the rape conviction, the prosecutor argued that the defendant had extorted the sexual contacts because he demanded that the girl have sex with him "for permission to go places, do things, or get things." While sex by extortion is a form of rape under the Tennessee penal code,[c] the appellate court found that there was insufficient evidence of a threat to injure the girl. Rather than being coerced by a threat, she agreed to engage in sexual intercourse "because she wanted the defendant to buy her something. [S]ex was the price she paid for receiving things which her sisters did not have." How clear is the line between a threat to injure someone if they refuse to submit and a promise to compensate them if they acquiesce?

In order to identify this line, the drafters of the Model Code's proposed new sexual assault provisions recommend that the law adopt "as the criteria for impermissible coercion the tests that have long been the measure of illegality in connection with monetary demands. The need to distinguish coercion from legitimate bargaining is just as fundamental in the area of monetary exchange as it is in connection with sexual interaction,

---

[c] The Tennessee statute construed in *Hilton* provides that rape is "unlawful sexual penetration of another [where] force or coercion is used to accomplish the act." Tenn. Code Ann. § 39–2–604(a)(1) (1982). Under the statute, the term "coercion" is defined, among other things, as "extortion." § 39–2–602(1). A subsequent revision of the Tennessee sex offenses retains these provisions. See Tenn. Code Ann. §§ 39–13–501(1), 39–13–503(a)(1) (1991).

and factual judgments are of course inescapable." As the drafters explain, the "elements of extortion have a long-standing pedigree and are given content in an extensive body of case law." ALI, Model Penal Code: Sexual Assault and Related Offenses, Tentative Draft No. 1, at pp. 52–53 (April 30, 2014). Thus, the Code's proposed new definition of "sexual intercourse by coercion," which is graded as a "felony of the third degree," would cover four specific categories of threats, namely, threats to "accuse anyone of a criminal offense or of a failure to comply with immigration regulations," to "expose any information tending to impair the credit or business repute of any person," to "take or withhold action in an official capacity," or to "inflict any substantial economic or financial harm that would not benefit the actor." Id. at pp. 2–3, 40.

### *(iii) Should Sexual Harassment Be a Form of Rape?*

A threat by a supervisor to fire or fail to promote an employee unless the employee has sex with the supervisor is known as "quid pro quo" sexual harassment. Title VII of the Civil Rights Act of 1964, 42 U.S.C. § 2000e, and state tort law provide civil remedies to victims of such harassment. By uttering a quid pro quo threat, would the supervisor also commit the crime of extortion under *Hicks*? If the employee acquiesced and had sex with the supervisor, would the supervisor be guilty of rape under *Hilton* or "sexual intercourse by coercion" under the Model Penal Code's proposed new approach?

The military justice system has taken some decisive steps to criminalize quid pro quo sexual harassment. Military courts first began to move tentatively in that direction when they recognized that the element of "force" for purposes of rape law includes not only the application of actual, physical force, but also "constructive force." Thus, like courts in other jurisdictions, military tribunals have held that the force element may be satisfied "by proof of a coercive atmosphere that includes, for example, threats to injure others or statements that resistance would be futile." United States v. Simpson, 58 M.J. 368, 377 (Ct. App. Armed Forces 2003). Moreover, when deciding whether the alleged perpetrator used constructive force, it is proper for the members of the court-martial to consider the disparity between his rank and that of the complaining witness. In *Simpson*, the Court of Appeals for the Armed Forces cautioned that constructive force requires more than proof of rank disparity. Still, the fact that the accused was the complainant's superior officer could go a long way towards satisfying the force element. As *Simpson* observed, for example, there is a "special relationship between non-commissioned officers and trainees" such that the non-commissioned officer

> cannot create by his own actions an environment of isolation and fear and then seek excusal from the crime of rape by claiming the absence of force especially where, as here, passive acquiescence is prompted by the unique situation of dominance and control presented by appellant's superior rank and position.

More recently, Congress revised Article 120 of the Uniform Code of Military Justice, which punishes rape and other sex crimes. The new statute appears to impose liability directly for some forms of quid pro quo harassment itself. The revised version of Article 120 separates rape into different forms for grading purposes. Under the new provision, the crime of "rape" occurs when a member of the armed forces commits a sexual act upon another person by, among other things, "threatening or placing that other person in fear that any person will be subjected to death, grievous bodily harm, or kidnapping." See 10 U.S.C. § 920(a)(3).[d] The related crime of "sexual assault" occurs when the actor commits a sexual act upon another by causing or threatening harms not as grave as those required for a rape conviction. For purposes of the "sexual assault" crime, such lesser harms include "threatening or placing that other person in fear." The term "threatening or placing that other person in fear" is defined as "a communication or action that is of sufficient consequence to cause a reasonable fear that non-compliance will result in the victim or another person being subjected to the wrongful action contemplated by the communication or action." Presumably, the term "wrongful action" covers a threat by a superior officer to harm the subordinate's career prospects. Is there a policy justification for limiting this definition of sexual assault to the military context, or should it also be applied in the domain of civilian employment?

## 3. SEX BY FRAUD

A number of state statutes punish as rape sexual intercourse or penetration accomplished "by fraud." The scope of this prohibition is determined by the meaning of the term "fraud." Traditionally, the courts have construed the term narrowly by holding that sexual intercourse procured by fraud is a rape in cases of "fraud in the factum" but not in cases of "fraud in the inducement." As the United States Court of Military Appeals has explained, "fraud in the factum" is a "deception [that] causes a misunderstanding as to the fact itself." United States v. Booker, 25 M.J. 114 (1987). The most common perpetrator of rape by fraud in the factum is the doctor who sexually penetrates the body of a patient who is unaware that the act is occurring because she believes she is submitting to a routine medical examination or procedure. E.g., McNair v. State, 108 Nev. 53, 825 P.2d 571 (1992); People v. Ogunmola, 193 Cal.App.3d 274, 238 Cal.Rptr. 300 (1987). By contrast, "fraud in the inducement" is a "deception [that] relate[s] not to the thing done but merely to some collateral matter." *United States v. Booker* elaborates the distinction:

> Clearly, fraud in the inducement includes such general knavery as: "No, I'm not married"; "Of course I'll respect you in the morning"; "We'll get married as soon as. . . . "; "I'll pay you [ ] dollars"; and so on. Whatever else such tactics amount to, they are not rape.
>
> The question is—what is fraud in the factum in the context of consensual intercourse? The better view is that the "factum" involves both the nature of the act and the identity of the participant. Thus in the "doctor" cases, consent would not be present unless the patient realized that the "procedure" being employed was not medical, but sexual. Further while it is arguable that there may be people who are willing to hop into bed with absolutely anyone, we take it that even the most uninhibited people ordinarily make some assessment of a potential sex partner and exercise some modicum of discretion before consenting to sexual

[d] The complete text of Article 120 is reproduced in Appendix B.

> intercourse. Thus, consent to the act is based on the identity of the prospective partner.[2]

Under *Booker*, what kinds of misrepresentations about the "identity" of one's sexual partner constitute fraud in the factum?[e]

The traditional distinction between fraud in the factum and fraud in the inducement may be eroding. At least one court has stated that "fraud" in this context is not limited to fraud in the factum. In State v. Tizard, 897 S.W.2d 732 (Tenn. Crim. App. 1994), the complainant was a 17-year-old male high school student who approached the defendant, a physician, and requested steroids to enhance his athletic performance. During the boy's third appointment, Dr. Tizard physically examined him as on past visits. Towards the end of the examination, the doctor "rubbed the shaft of the [victim's] penis with his hand for a couple of minutes until it was erect." The victim testified that "he was embarrassed and thought that what the defendant did . . . was not right, but he returned for . . . two [more] visits because he wanted steroids." During two subsequent examinations, Dr. Tizard again rubbed the boy's penis until it was erect. On their last appointment, Dr. Tizard continued this activity "for five to ten minutes" until the boy ejaculated. Dr. Tizard was convicted of two counts of sexual battery by fraud. On appeal, the defense argued that the crime required fraud in the factum and that the prosecution had failed to prove such fraud because the boy was not under any misunderstanding as to the act itself. To the contrary, "the victim was completely aware of what was happening and indicated a belief that the defendant's conduct was improper, but returned to obtain steroids while allowing the defendant to commit the act upon which the convictions are based." The Tennessee Court of Criminal Appeals rejected this argument, holding that "the definition of fraud . . . is not limited to any particular type of fraud. [F]raud comprises 'anything calculated to deceive, including all acts, omissions, and concealments involving a breach of legal or equitable duty, trust, or confidence justly reposed, resulting in damage to another, or by which an undue and unconscientious [sic] advantage is taken of another.' "

Why is *Tizard* an example of sexual battery by fraud? Assuming that the case does involve fraud, did Dr. Tizard commit fraud in the factum or fraud in the inducement? Boro v. Superior Court, 163 Cal.App.3d 1224, 210 Cal.Rptr. 122 (1985), is often cited as an example of sex by fraud in the inducement, which the court there held was not punishable as rape. The defendant in *Boro* telephoned a woman, represented that he was a doctor, and told her that "she had contracted a dangerous, highly infectious and perhaps fatal disease." He further advised her that, happily, there were two available cures: the first was a painful form of surgery, which cost $9,000.00, and the second was sexual intercourse with "an anonymous donor" who had been injected with a special serum, which cost only $4,500.00.

---

[2] . . . To be more basic, for there to be actual consent, a woman must be agreeable to the penetration of her body by a particular 'membrum virile': it is quite irrelevant whether she knows the "real" identity of the owner thereof.

[e] The proposed new Model Penal Code provisions on sexual assault would punish some instances of sex by fraud in the factum. Section 213.3 provides that an actor commits "sexual intercourse by exploitation" if he or she has sex with another person and "represents that the act is for purposes of medical treatment . . ." or "knowingly leads such person to believe falsely that he or she is someone with whom such person has been sexually intimate." ALI, Model Penal Code: Sexual Assault and Related Offenses, Tentative Draft No. 1, at pp. 3–4, 66 (April 30, 2014).

The woman chose the second alternative, met the defendant at a hotel, and had intercourse with him. The court in *Boro* issued a writ of prohibition, restraining prosecution of the defendant on charges of rape.[f] Although the woman had "succumbed to [the defendant's] fraudulent blandishments" because she was afraid that otherwise she might die, she "precisely understood the 'nature of the act'" to which she was submitting and thus was merely the victim of noncriminal sex by fraud in the inducement.

Under the definition of fraud quoted by the *Tizard* court, would the examples of sex by fraud in the inducement that *Booker* viewed as "general knavery" be rape? Should those incidents be punishable as rape?

Richard Posner believes that it is appropriate for the law to be reluctant to punish the actor who obtains sex, rather than money, by fraud in the inducement. In his view, when a woman "is not averse to having sex with a particular man," the only wrong is "in the lies . . . rather than in an invasion of her bodily integrity," and our law ordinarily does not punish lies made "in social settings." However, this thinking does not hold in cases where the man pretends to be the woman's husband or "claims to be administering medical treatment to the woman rather than to be inserting his penis in her." In these latter cases, Posner suggests, the act is "disgusting as well as humiliating, rather than merely humiliating." He goes on:

> Ordinarily, to be sure, the law does not place the burden of preventing fraud on the victim; it is cheaper for the potential injurer not to commit fraud than for the victim to take measures of self-protection against it. Nevertheless, a person who has acted the fool is likely to feel slightly less offended at having been fleeced. The problems of proof of seduction by false pretenses—in particular the problem of distinguishing by the methods of litigation between a false statement of one's feelings and a change in those feelings—are exquisitely difficult and argue for making a difference in degree a difference in legal kind, substituting victim self-protection for legal remedies. . . .

Richard A. Posner, Sex and Reason 392–93 (1992).

According to Anne Coughlin, courts recognized the crime of rape "by fraud in the factum" but not by "fraud in the inducement" because, in the former cases, the woman lacked the mens rea necessary to convict her for fornication or adultery, and, hence, it was appropriate to convict only the man for the illegal sex act:

> [T]he rule that sex by fraud constitutes rape only in the context of "fraud in the factum" singles out for prosecution as rape the few cases in which a woman engaged in fornication or adultery only through an exculpatory mistake of fact. The argument proceeds as follows: Though the woman in fact had participated in an act of nonmarital intercourse, she was innocent because she neither knew nor should have known that her conduct was of the forbidden character. This argument would be successful in only two types of cases. First, the argument would be accepted in cases were the woman showed that she reasonably believed that her conduct was nonsexual, such as participating in a routine medical procedure, but the man had used the procedure as a subterfuge to

---

[f] Based on this episode, the defendant also was charged with attempted grand theft and burglary. He did not challenge those counts of the information.

> perpetrate sexual intercourse. Second, a mistake of fact argument might prevail where the woman believed that the sex act constituted marital (i.e., lawful) intercourse because she believed that she was having sex with her husband, when in fact the paramour was someone else. That the woman was induced to engage in sexual intercourse based on some other mistaken belief that she held, even if such belief was created by active deception on the man's part, would be irrelevant to her mental state and, ultimately, to her guilt. In such cases, standard mistake of fact analysis instructs that the woman knew or should have known that she was engaging in nonmarital intercourse, and therefore she, as well as her partner, deserved to be punished for that crime.

Anne M. Coughlin, Sex and Guilt, 84 Va. L. Rev. 1, 32–33 (1998).

## SUBSECTION B: NONCONSENT AND MENS REA

### State v. Smith

Supreme Court of Connecticut, 1989.
210 Conn. 132, 554 A.2d 713.

■ SHEA, JUDGE. After a jury trial the defendant was convicted of sexual assault in the first degree. [On appeal he claims that evidence of the victim's nonconsent was insufficient.] We find no error.

. . . On March 18, 1987, the victim, *T*, a 26-year old woman, and her girlfriend, *A*, a visitor from Idaho, went to a bar in West Haven. *T* was introduced by a friend to the defendant, who bought her a drink. The defendant invited her and *A*, together with a male acquaintance *A* had met at the bar, to dinner at a restaurant across the street. After dinner, the defendant having paid for *T's* share, the four left the restaurant. The defendant proposed that they all go to his apartment in West Haven. Because *A's* acquaintance had a motorcycle, the defendant gave them directions to the apartment so that they could ride there, while he and *T* walked.

After a 20 minute walk, the defendant and *T* arrived at the apartment at about 10 p.m. *A* and her acquaintance were not there and never arrived at the apartment. When *T* and the defendant had entered the apartment they sat on the couch in the living room to watch television. After a while the defendant put his arm around *T* and told her he wanted a kiss. She gave him a kiss. She testified that "He wouldn't back off. He wouldn't let go of me. So I said, look, I am not kidding. I really don't want to do anything. I don't know you and whatnot." The defendant still held onto *T*. She testified that he was "still right in my face wanting to kiss me. You know, saying so, saying that you don't think I paid for dinner for nothing, do you."

*T* testified that she was scared: "At first I didn't know what to do. I did spit in his face and he didn't even take it seriously. Then I tried kicking him off, which was to no avail. He was way too big for me." *T* described the defendant as "at least six foot two" and "at least two hundred pounds." She testified: "He told me he could make it hard on me or I could make it easy on myself, which I finally decided was probably my best bet." *T* understood that the defendant was determined to "have sex" with her and that either he would hurt her or she "was going to go along with it." At the point where *T* ceased resistance, she was "down on the couch" and the defendant was "on top of" her.

*T* testified that she had informed the defendant that she had to pick up her daughter, had insulted him, and had told him that he was "a big man to have to force a woman." She testified, however, that after she decided to "give in," she tried to convince the defendant that she was not going to fight and "was going to go along with him and enjoy it."

The defendant removed *T's* clothing as she remained on the couch and led her into the bedroom. When she declined his request for oral sex, he did not insist upon it, but proceeded to engage in vaginal intercourse with her. After completion of the act, the defendant said that he knew the victim felt that she had been raped, but that she could not prove it and had really enjoyed herself.

After they both had dressed, the defendant requested *T's* telephone number, but she gave him a number she concocted as a pretense. He also offered her some sherbet, which she accepted and ate while she waited for a cab that the defendant had called. *T*, however, placed her pink cigarette lighter underneath the couch, so that she would be able to prove she had been in the apartment. When the cab arrived, she left the apartment. She told the cab driver to take her to the police station because she had been raped. At the station she gave her account of the event to the police. The defendant was arrested. The police found *T's* lighter under the couch in his living room, where *T* had informed them it was located.

I

Although the defendant claims insufficiency of the evidence as the basis for his claim that he was entitled to an acquittal, he actually seeks to have this court impose a requirement of mens rea, or guilty intent, as an essential element of the crime of sexual assault in the first degree. In fact, he concedes in his reply brief that, if conviction for sexual assault in the first degree requires only a general intent, he cannot prevail on his claim that the evidence was insufficient to support his conviction. This court has held that our [sexual assault] statute requires proof of only a general intent to perform the physical acts that constitute that crime. "No specific intent is made an element of the crime of first degree sexual assault. . . . It is well settled that first degree sexual assault is a general intent crime."

The defendant, nevertheless, urges that we adopt a construction . . . making the mental state of the defendant the touchstone for the resolution of the issue of consent when presented in a prosecution for first degree sexual assault. He refers to this mental state as a mens rea, a guilty mind, and describes it as an awareness on the part of a man that he is forcing sex upon a woman against her will and that he intends to do so. In the context of the evidence in this case, the defendant claims, though he did not testify at trial, that he honestly believed that at the time the sexual act occurred that *T* had consented to it. He bases this claim upon her testimony that, after their preliminary encounter on the couch, and his remark that he could "make it hard" for her or she could "make it easy" on herself, she ceased resisting his advances and decided to "go along with it." *T* also testified that, once she decided to "give in," she acted as if she were "going to go along with him and enjoy it."

The position advocated by the defendant that the requisite mens rea should be an element of the crime of sexual assault in the first degree is supported by a widely publicized decision of the British House of Lords in 1975, Director of Public Prosecutions v. Morgan, 1976 App. Cas. 182, 205, 2 W.L.R. 913, 2 All E.R. 347 (H.L. 1975).[a] majority of the court held that a defendant cannot properly be convicted of rape if he in fact believed that the woman had consented, even though the basis for his belief may not have been reasonable. Lord Hailsham expressed the view that, for the crime of rape at common law, "the prohibited act is and always has been intercourse without the consent of the victim and the mental element is and always has been the intention to commit that act, or the equivalent intention to have intercourse willy-nilly, not caring whether the victim consents or no." A similar position has been adopted in Alaska, where it is held that the state has the burden of proving at least "that the defendant acted 'recklessly' regarding his putative victim's lack of consent." The Supreme Court of California has concluded that a wrongful intent is an element of a rape offense, but, contrary to *Morgan*, has held that this element would be negated if a defendant entertained a "reasonable and bona fide belief" that the complainant had consented. . . .

Most courts have rejected the proposition that a specific intention to have intercourse without the consent of the victim is an element of the crime of rape or sexual assault. . . . One of the complications that might arise, if such a mental element were required, involves the problem of intoxication, which is generally held to be relevant to negate a crime of specific intent but not a crime of general intent. The difficulty of convicting a thoroughly intoxicated person of rape, if awareness of lack of consent were an element of the crime, would diminish the protection that our statutes presently afford to potential victims from lustful drunkards. Another related problem would be the admissibility of evidence of other similar behavior of a defendant charged with rape to prove his intent to disregard any lack of consent. Such evidence is now usually excluded as more prejudicial than probative, because only a general intent is necessary to constitute the offense. . . .

---

[a] In *Morgan*, a woman was in bed sleeping when her husband and his three drinking companions entered the room. "[S]he was aroused from her sleep, . . . held by each of her limbs, . . . while [her husband's companions] in turn had intercourse with her in front of the others." The woman testified that she "made her opposition to what was being done very plain indeed." Nonetheless, the three men claimed that they believed she was consenting. According to their testimony, the woman's husband had suggested that they have intercourse with her, and he also had "told them that they must not be surprised if his wife struggled a bit, since she was 'kinky' and this was the only way in which she could get 'turned on.' " The House of Lords agreed with the defendants that the trial judge erred by failing to charge the jury that an honest belief that the woman was consenting negated the mental state for rape. However, the Lords refused to overturn the convictions on the ground that, despite the erroneous instruction, "no miscarriage of justice has or conceivably could have occurred." Subsequently, Parliament codified a new definition of rape, which rejects the mens rea level set by *Morgan*. Under the new provision, a mistake as to the victim's consent is exculpatory only if it is "reasonable." The statute also provides that, in deciding whether such a mistake is reasonable, the factfinder must take account of "all the circumstances, including any steps" taken by the defendant to ascertain whether the victim consented. See Sexual Offenses Act, 2003, c. 42, § 1.—[Footnote by eds.]

While the word "consent" is commonly regarded as referring to the state of mind of the complainant in a sexual assault case, it cannot be viewed as a wholly subjective concept. Although the actual state of mind of the actor in a criminal case may in many instances be the issue upon which culpability depends, a defendant is not chargeable with knowledge of the internal workings of the minds of others except to the extent that he should reasonably have gained such knowledge from his observations of their conduct. The law of contract has come to recognize that a true "meeting of the minds" is no longer essential to the formation of a contract and that rights and obligations may arise from acts of the parties, usually their words, upon which a reasonable person would rely. Similarly, whether a complainant has consented to intercourse depends upon her manifestations of such consent as reasonably construed. If the conduct of the complainant under all the circumstances should reasonably be viewed as indicating consent to the act of intercourse, a defendant should not be found guilty because of some undisclosed mental reservation on the part of the complainant. Reasonable conduct ought not to be deemed criminal. . . .

Thus we adhere to the view expressed in our earlier decisions that no specific intent, but only a general intent to perform the physical acts constituting the crime, is necessary for the crime of first degree sexual assault. We reject the position of the British courts, as well as that adopted in Alaska, that the state must prove either an actual awareness on the part of the defendant that the complainant had not consented or a reckless disregard of her nonconsenting status. We agree, however, with the California courts that a defendant is entitled to a jury instruction that a defendant may not be convicted of this crime if the words or conduct of the complainant under all the circumstances would justify a reasonable belief that she had consented.

[I]t is clear that the jury could properly have found beyond a reasonable doubt that *T's* words and actions could not reasonably be viewed to indicate her consent to intercourse with the defendant. According to her uncontradicted testimony, she expressly declined his advances, explaining that she did not know him and wanted to pick up her child. She spat in his face and "tried kicking him off." She "gave in" only after the defendant declared that "he could make it hard" for her if she continued to resist. This statement she could reasonably have regarded as a threat of physical injury. Only by entertaining the fantasy that "no" meant "yes," and that a display of distaste meant affection, could the defendant have believed that *T's* behavior toward him indicated consent. Such a distorted view of her conduct would not have been reasonable. The evidence was more than sufficient to support the verdict. . . .

There is no error.

In this opinion the other Justices concurred.

## NOTES ON NONCONSENT AND MENS REA

### 1. AVAILABILITY OF THE MISTAKE OF FACT DEFENSE

Notably, *Smith* fails to mention that a few courts have held that even an honest and reasonable mistake as to nonconsent is not exculpatory. See, e.g., Commonwealth v. Ascolillo, 405 Mass. 456, 541 N.E.2d 570 (1989). Under these decisions, nonconsent apparently is treated as a strict liability element. In one such case, the court claimed that this treatment is "in harmony with the analogous rule" in "statutory rape" cases. Commonwealth v. Simcock, 31 Mass.App.Ct. 184, 575 N.E.2d 1137 (1991). Statutory rape provisions criminalize sex with children and adolescents who are below the age at which persons are deemed competent to consent to sexual activity. A majority of jurisdictions treat the age of the victim as a strict liability element. Is the statutory rape analogy cited by *Simcock* persuasive? In Commonwealth v. Lopez, 433 Mass. 722, 745 N.W.2d 961 (2001), the Supreme Judicial Court of Massachusetts offered another rationale for refusing to recognize a "mistake of fact 'defense'" in rape cases. Under the Massachusetts rape statute, the prosecution can obtain a conviction only if it proves that the defendant compelled the complainant to submit "by use of physical force; nonphysical, constructive force; or threat of force." In the court's view, "[p]roof of the element of force, therefore, should negate any possible mistake as to consent." Is this analysis more convincing than the statutory rape analogy?

In jurisdictions in which a mistaken belief as to consent is exculpatory, trial courts must determine when sufficient evidence has been offered to warrant a jury instruction concerning mistake. The Supreme Court of California decided that trial judges are not required to give such an instruction whenever a defendant claims that the encounter was consensual. Rather, the instruction is required only where the record contains "substantial evidence of equivocal conduct that would have led a defendant to reasonably and in good faith believe consent existed where it did not." People v. Williams, 4 Cal.4th 354, 841 P.2d 961, 14 Cal.Rptr.2d 441 (1992). In *Williams*, there was no such evidence. Rather, the victim and the defendant provided dramatically different versions of the victim's behavior, neither of which was equivocal. The victim claimed that she submitted to sexual intercourse only after the defendant punched and threatened to harm her, while the defendant asserted that the victim initiated and participated aggressively in the intercourse. According to the court, the jurors had to identify the credible account, and, once they did, they could find only the presence or absence of "actual consent. . . . These wholly divergent accounts create no middle ground from which Williams could argue he reasonably misinterpreted Deborah's conduct."

## 2. RESOLVING THE FACTS

In rape prosecutions, as in every other trial, the adversaries often offer conflicting stories about the underlying events. Date rape trials frequently present poignant conflicts of this kind. See Kate E. Bloch, A Rape Law Pedagogy, 7 Yale J.L. & Feminism 307 (1995). In the most difficult cases, the parties' factual accounts are substantially similar: they agree that the intercourse occurred, and they even agree as to what each participant said and did before, during, and after the sexual encounter. The dispute arises because each actor offers a different interpretation of the same events, and its resolution depends on whose perspective—the survivor's or the defendant's—the court adopts. For example, it is not uncommon for the question of what conduct constitutes "force" to receive different answers, depending on the perspective invoked. Likewise, one of the most frequently recurring and divisive issues in date rape cases is the interpretation to be given the word "no." In *Smith*, the court dismisses as a "fantasy" the notion that a woman who says "no" to a sexual invitation may mean "yes." Fantasy or not, rape defendants continue to testify to precisely this understanding. The defendant in *Berkowitz* testified that the woman said "no, no, no," when he "started massaging her breasts with [his] mouth," but he understood those words to be "passionate no's" and a "positive response" to his sexual advances. Commonwealth v. Berkowitz, Record at 134–35, 141 (Ct. Common Pleas, Monroe County, No. 241–1988); see also, e.g., United States v. Johnson, 25 M.J. 691 (1987).

Some empirical reports suggest that these kinds of misunderstandings are not uncommon. One researcher who studied college students claims that often it is difficult for people "to decide whether certain words or actions are signs of platonic friendliness or of sexual attraction" because there is an "overlap in the cues used to convey friendliness and seduction," particularly in the early stages of a relationship. Antonia Abbey, Misperception as an Antecedent of Acquaintance Rape: A Consequence of Ambiguity in Communication Between Men and Women, in Acquaintance Rape: The Hidden Crime 96 (Andrea Parrot & Laurie Bechhofer eds. 1991). The study also found that men tend to mistake friendly overtures for sexual ones more often than women do. The potential for misunderstanding is exacerbated by the reluctance of men and women to express their sexual intentions directly. "When people become used to 'yes' being conveyed through subtle hints, it is not surprising that they frequently mistake a 'no' for a 'yes' and feel that it is appropriate to persist after being rebuffed." Worse complications will arise if some women sometimes say "no" to a sexual overture when they mean "yes," as several studies have found. For example, in a study of 610 female undergraduates at Texas A & M University, 39.3% of the respondents "reported saying no to sexual intercourse" even though they "*had every intention to and were willing to engage in sexual intercourse*." Charlene L. Muehlenhard & Lisa C. Hollabaugh, Do Women Sometimes Say No When They Mean Yes? The Prevalence and Correlates of Women's Token Resistance to Sex, 54 J. Person. & Soc. Psychol. 872, 874 (1988). If women engage in such indirection—and if men understand that women do so—then men may tend to interpret "no" as a token form of resistance, which they feel safe to ignore, even when the word is uttered by a woman who means it.

Other empirical data suggest that men and women perceive differently the kind of "heavy petting" that occurred in *M.T.S.* A study of self-disclosed date rapists suggests that men tend to view heavy petting as foreplay that culminates in intercourse. By contrast, women may see petting as a sexual end in itself, rather than as a prelude to vaginal penetration. The study showed that all of the rapes were preceded by consensual sexual activity and, indeed, that the overwhelming majority followed consensual, genital play. According to the author of the study, the men "experienced a rather exaggerated selective perception of the female's receptivity." Most of the men explained that they committed rape in these cases because they found it "difficult to take [the women's] rejections seriously considering the advanced intimacy already achieved." The author went on to discuss the women's perspective. Some observers might be inclined to fault the women in these cases on the ground that they had "instituted high levels of exposure to risk:"

> On the other hand, many of these women did make efforts to evoke agreements and promises regarding the limits of sexual

> involvement. In 68 percent of the cases of consensual genital play the female was reported to have stipulated or made an effort to stipulate that this was to be her maximum level of sexual activity. . . . These delimiting pronouncements were not taken seriously since they were viewed to be the usual show of reticence that respectable females demonstrate in order to ward off the impression of being "easy." The perpetuation of this classic stereotype inevitably leads to a frustration of female sexual self-determination.

Eugene J. Kanin, Date Rape: Unofficial Criminals and Victims, 9 Victimology 95, 99–104 (1984).

### 3. THE RELATIONSHIP BETWEEN MENS REA AND ACTUS REUS

Some commentators have expressed the view that the mens rea for rape and related offenses must be recalibrated to take account of new definitions of "force" that have been proposed by reformers and endorsed by legislators. For example, the members of the Criminal Instructions Subcommittee of the Pennsylvania Supreme Court Committee suggest that, in some date rape cases (those not involving high levels of physical violence), the mens rea should not be gross negligence, but recklessness or, even, knowledge:

> In the opinion of the Subcommittee there may be cases, especially now that [the legislature] has extended the definition of force to psychological, moral and intellectual force, where a defendant might non-recklessly or even reasonably, but wrongly, believe that his words and conduct do not constitute force or the threat of force and that a non-resisting female is consenting. An example might be "date rape" resulting from mutual misunderstanding. The boy does not intend or suspect the intimidating potential of his vigorous wooing. The girl, misjudging the boy's character, believes he will become violent if thwarted; she feigns willingness, even some pleasure. In our opinion the defendant in such a case ought not to be convicted of rape.

Pennsylvania Suggested Standard Criminal Jury Instructions, Subcommittee Note, at 15.3121A. Why should the girl, and not the boy, have to bear the risk of their "mutual misunderstanding"? Is there some other doctrinal revision that might resolve this situation?

### 4. MENS REA AND INTOXICATION

One of the most vexing and contentious questions in contemporary rape jurisprudence is whether or not an accused person's voluntary intoxication may mitigate culpability for the crime. Under the majority approach to voluntary intoxication generally, the answer to this question would seem to be "no," at least in those jurisdictions where rape is a "general intent" crime or, in Model Penal Code nomenclature, a crime for which liability is based on recklessness or negligence. The vast majority of states appear to reason that intoxication cannot, as a logical matter, negate negligence because the "reasonable" actor is always sober. Likewise, for policy reasons related to the connection between intoxication and violent misconduct, most jurisdictions rule out intoxication claims for crimes that require proof of recklessness.

In the past few years, however, some courts and commentators have become uneasy applying this approach to sexual assault cases, especially when the prosecution proceeds on the premise that the crime occurred because the complaining witness was so intoxicated as to lack capacity to consent to the intercourse. In many such cases, both parties to the intercourse are intoxicated, at least to some extent. If so, the accused is likely to argue that it is unfair to hold him responsible for conduct that he committed while intoxicated, while letting the complainant off the hook for hers. Indeed, the accused may be inclined to argue that, like the complaining witness, he too lacked the capacity to consent to sex, with the upshot being that she "raped" him or each "raped" the other. As is the case on so many other fronts, this aspect of the law of rape is in transition.

The Supreme Judicial Court of Massachusetts recently considered this problem. In Commonwealth v. Mountry, 463 Mass. 80, 972 N.E.2d 438 (2012), the defendant was convicted for rape on the ground that he had sexual intercourse with a 16-year-old girl who was so intoxicated as to lack capacity to consent. The evidence showed that, over the course of an evening, the defendant plied the girl with alcohol; that he consumed alcohol too; that he made sexual advances to her, which she twice refused; and that he waited until she passed out in bed, at which point he had sex with her. On appeal, the defendant argued, among other things, that it was error for the trial judge to refuse to instruct the jury that it could consider the defendant's state of intoxication when deciding whether he reasonably should have known of the victim's incapacity to consent. The Supreme Judicial Court decided that, in a proper case, the trial judge should include such an instruction in the jury charge:

> In Commonwealth v. Blache, 450 Mass. 583, 880 N.E.2d 736 (2008), we held that where the Commonwealth relies on evidence that a rape victim was incapable of consent in its effort to establish the element of lack of consent and thereby reduce the degree of required force to only such force as is necessary to effect penetration, "the Commonwealth should also prove the defendant's knowledge of the complainant's incapacitated state." . . . *Blache* did not present an opportunity to address the question of a defendant's incapacity to know whether a victim was incapable of consent. This case presents that occasion.
>
> It is true, as the Commonwealth argues, that intoxication has no mitigating effect on general intent crimes such as rape. However, when proof of knowledge is an element of the crime charged, as here, a defendant's mental impairment by intoxication or otherwise "bears on [his] ability to possess the requisite knowledge of the circumstances in which he acted." . . . [General intent] is a mix of both subjective and objective components on which a defendant's mental capacity has relevance. Thus, even as to general intent crimes, a defendant's intoxication is relevant if the crime contains an element of knowledge. . . .
>
> The instruction in *Blache* has two alternative elements of knowledge. The first, actual knowledge, is a subjective element for which a defendant's state of intoxication has relevance. The second alternative, that the *defendant* reasonably should have known of the victim's incapacity, contains a mix of subjective and objective components . . . . The subjective component focuses on

the defendant's capacity to possess the requisite knowledge, for which his state of intoxication has relevance. The objective component focuses on what the average prudent person possessing the defendant's knowledge would have understood regarding the victim's incapacity. We conclude that, in a rape prosecution in which the Commonwealth must prove that a defendant knew or reasonably should have known that a victim's condition rendered him or her incapable of consenting, and where there is credible evidence of a defendant's mental impairment, a defendant is entitled to the jury's consideration of his mental condition as it relates to his ability to possess the requisite knowledge.

Turning to the instructions in this case, the judge gave a correct instruction on the question whether the defendant actually, or subjectively, knew that the victim was incapable of consent. He told the jury they could consider credible evidence that the defendant was impaired by reason of voluntary intoxication. However, the instruction on the alternative element, that the jury could consider what "the average, reasonable person, *not intoxicated*, and observing the situation as it existed, would have known" concerning the victim's capacity to consent, was error. It effectively foreclosed consideration of evidence of the defendant's intoxication as to the alternative element of knowledge. Contrary to the judge's instruction, this element of knowledge is not purely objective. The Commonwealth had to prove what "*the defendant* reasonably should have known," not what the average reasonable unintoxicated person would have known. A defendant's impaired state of mind is relevant to the jury's consideration of this element. . . . [T]he judge should have instructed the jury that the Commonwealth must prove that in the circumstances known to the defendant, a reasonable person would have known that the victim was incapable of consent, and that when deciding whether the Commonwealth has met its burden of proof, they could consider any credible evidence that the defendant was affected by the voluntary consumption of alcohol.

We hasten to emphasize that our decision today . . . is confined to cases in which the Commonwealth relies on proof that a victim was incapable of consent.

We turn to the question of prejudice. A conviction may be affirmed in the face of an error that has been preserved for review only if we are convinced that the error did not influence to jury, or had but very slight effect. We are satisfied there was no prejudice. The defendant was not entitled to an instruction on voluntary intoxication because there was no evidence of debilitating intoxication that would have hindered him from possessing actual knowledge that the victim was incapable of consent or from possessing knowledge that reasonably would have led him to such an understanding.

The evidence of his impaired state was weak. The defendant may have consumed a substantial amount of vodka, but it is not clear whether he actually did so and how much. After drinking, he was able to drive to a package store, purchase more vodka, and drive back to his apartment with no evidence of difficulty. He also

> was able to understand that the victim was not interested in his advances when she pushed his hand away awhile they drove to purchase more alcohol. Further, he was able to understand that the victim wanted neither conversation nor more alcohol after they returned . . . . The defendant's son observed him because they slept together in the son's room while the victim was staying in the defendant's room. There was no indication from the son that the defendant was experiencing difficulty from intoxication or that he was even drunk. The son testified only that he could smell alcohol on the defendant. The only evidence of the defendant's condition is his own statement to police that he had been drunk and had difficulty remembering what had happened, which alone does not signify an inability to appreciate the victim's incapacity. Moreover, he told police the victim had been too drunk to remember, which suggests he actually had appreciated her incapacity to consent. This does not qualify as "debilitating intoxication." He was not entitled to a voluntary intoxication instruction.

The drafters of the Model Code's proposed new sexual assault provisions would go even further than *Mountry* by suspending the Code's ordinary approach to voluntary intoxication for *all* sexual assault offenses. Section 2.08(2) of the 1962 Model Code endorses the common-law approach to voluntary intoxication by providing that, "[w]hen recklessness establishes an element of the offense, if the actor, due to self-induced intoxication, is unaware of a risk of which he would have been aware had he been sober, such unawareness is immaterial." In the proposed new provisions on sexual assault, however, the definitions section stipulates that the word "recklessly" "shall carry only the meaning designated in Model Penal Code § 2.02(2)(c); the provisions of Model Penal Code § 2.08(2) shall not apply." See ALI, Model Penal Code: Sexual Assault and Related Offenses, Tentative Draft No. 1, § 212.0(5), at p.1, 21 (April 30, 2014). When explaining this recommendation, the drafters mention that the basic premise of § 2.08, "which in effect equates awareness of the risks entailed in heavy drinking with awareness of a substantial and unjustifiable risk of causing a particular kind of harm . . . , has been a target of forceful criticism." When it comes to sexual offenses, this equation is particularly unfair, in the drafters' view because it is often the case that both parties to the intercourse are intoxicated. Since that is so, the drafters reason:

> In such situations, intoxication clouds not only the complainant's capacity and judgment in expressing consent or nonconsent, but also the accused's capacity to accurately understand the complainant's condition. When a complainant is physically able to express nonconsent but, as a result of intoxication, lacks sufficient mental coherence to do so, and when, at the same time, the aggressor, as a result of intoxication, fails to appreciate the degree to which the complainant's mental state is compromised, the subsequent activity is not fairly labeled criminal on the basis of those circumstances alone.

Id. at 76. Is this rationale convincing? Do the drafters undercut their own analysis by referring to the accused in this scenario as "the aggressor"?

In 2012, Congress amended Article 120 of the Uniform Code of Military Justice, which punishes a variety of forms of sexual misconduct.[a] This new codification appears to reject the notion that an accused's voluntary intoxication should possess exculpatory power in a prosecution for a sexual offense. Under Article 120, the most serious offense is "rape," and it occurs when, among other circumstances, an actor causes another person to engage in a sexual act by "first rendering that other person unconscious" or by "administering to that other person by force or threat of force, or without the knowledge or consent of that person, a drug, intoxicant, or other similar substance and thereby substantially impairing the ability of that other person to appraise or control conduct." See 10 U.S.C. § 920(a). As for the question of whether criminal liability should be imposed on a member of the armed forces who has sex with another person who is voluntarily intoxicated, Congress determined that punishment is appropriate in some such cases, albeit for the crime of "sexual assault" and not for the crime of "rape." Under Article 120(b)(3)(A), sexual assault occurs when the actor "commits a sexual act upon another person when the other person is incapable of consenting . . . due to impairment by any drug, intoxicant, or other similar substance, and that condition is known or reasonably should be known" by the actor. From all that appears in the legislative history and the few cases construing the new codification, it seems fair to assume that Congress used the phrase "reasonably should be known" to endorse the notion that an accused may be found guilty of sexual assault if a reasonable, sober actor would have known that the other person was so drunk as to be incapable of consenting to sex.

## 5. FEMINIST PERSPECTIVES ON THE MISTAKE DEFENSE

Although feminists are determined to vindicate women's perspectives on sexuality and sexual violence, feminist legal scholars do not necessarily agree on how the criminal law should incorporate those perspectives. Susan Estrich endorses the majority approach to the mens rea requirement, under which reasonable mistakes as to consent are exculpatory. According to Estrich, strict liability will disadvantage rape victims, even though it appears to simplify the prosecution's case. By eschewing any inquiry into the defendant's culpability, strict liability invites jurors to scrutinize the victim's actions and attitude. A negligence standard is preferable because it assures that the trial remains focused on "the man's blameworthiness instead of the woman's." Susan Estrich, Real Rape 94–100 (1987).

Catharine MacKinnon argues that, in societies in which the sexes are unequal, the mistake-of-fact defense inevitably validates male perspectives and experiences. As she asserts, rape is an injury from the "woman's point of view," but it is a crime "from the male point of view, explicitly including that of the accused." Since that is the case, the mistake-of-fact defense serves to define "reality" from the male point of view:

> Now reconsider to what extent the man's perceptions should determine whether a rape occurred. From whose standpoint, and in whose interest, is a law that allows one person's conditioned unconsciousness to contraindicate another's experienced violation? This aspect of the rape law reflects the sex inequality of the society not only in conceiving a cognizable injury from the viewpoint of

[a] The complete text of Article 120 is reproduced in Appendix B.

the reasonable rapist, but in affirmatively rewarding men with acquittals for not comprehending women's point of view on sexual encounters.

[T]he deeper problem is the rape law's assumption that a single, objective state of affairs existed, one which merely needs to be determined by evidence, when many (maybe even most) rapes involve honest men and violated women. When the reality is split—a woman is raped, but not by a rapist?—the law tends to conclude that a rape did not happen. [Thus, the reasonable mistake standard] is one-sided: male-sided.

Catharine A. MacKinnon, Feminism, Marxism, Method, and the State: Toward Feminist Jurisprudence, 8 Signs 635, 654 (1983).

## NOTE ON MARITAL RAPE

For the better part of the 20th century, most states recognized some form of "marital exemption" for rape. Under the marital exemption, a married man who raped his wife was not subject to criminal liability. In the closing decades of the century, the marital exemption was widely (but by no means completely) abrogated as a result of legislative and judicial action.

The defendant in People v. Liberta, 64 N.Y.2d 152, 485 N.Y.S.2d 207 (1984), was convicted of forcibly raping his wife. At the time of the rape, the defendant and his wife were separated, and he was under court order to stay away from her. Although the New York rape statute codified the marital exemption, the statute treated the defendant as an unmarried man since he was living apart from his wife pursuant to a court order. The defendant argued that the rape statute violated the equal protection clause because it burdened "some, but not all males (all but those within the 'marital exemption')." The New York Court of Appeals agreed that the marital exemption constituted a violation of equal protection. *Liberta* is widely cited for its concise summary of the policies offered to support the marital exemption and its reasons for finding those polices irrational:

> The assumption . . . that a man could not be guilty of raping his wife is traceable to a statement made by the 17th century English jurist Lord Hale, who wrote: "[The] husband cannot be guilty of a rape committed by himself upon his lawful wife, for by their mutual matrimonial consent and contract the wife hath given up herself in this kind unto her husband, which she cannot retract." Although Hale cited no authority for his statement it was relied on by state legislatures which enacted rape statutes with a marital exemption and by courts which established a common law exemption for husbands. . . .
>
> Presently, over 40 states still retain some form of marital exemption for rape. While the marital exemption is subject to an equal protection challenge, because it classifies unmarried men differently than married men, the equal protection clause does not prohibit a state from making classifications, provided the statute does not arbitrarily burden a particular group of individuals. Where a statute draws a distinction based upon marital status, the classification must be reasonable and must be based upon "some ground of difference that rationally explains the different treatment." . . .

We find that there is no rational basis for distinguishing between marital rape and nonmarital rape. The various rationales which have been asserted in defense of the exemption are either based upon archaic notions about the consent and property rights incident to marriage or are simply unable to withstand even the slightest scrutiny. . . .

Lord Hale's notion of an irrevocable implied consent by a married woman to sexual intercourse has been cited most frequently in support of the marital exemption. Any argument based on a supposed consent, however, is untenable. Rape is not simply a sexual act to which one party does not consent. Rather, it is a degrading, violent act which violates the bodily integrity of the victim and frequently causes severe, long-lasting physical and psychic harm. To ever imply consent to such an act is irrational and absurd. . . . Certainly, then, a marriage license should not be viewed as a license for a husband to forcibly rape his wife with impunity. A married woman has the same right to control her own body as does an unmarried woman. If a husband feels "aggrieved" by his wife's refusal to engage in sexual intercourse, he should seek relief in the courts governing domestic relations, not in "violent or forceful self-help."

The other traditional justifications for the marital exemption were the common law doctrines that a woman was the property of her husband and that the legal existence of the woman was "incorporated and consolidated into that of the husband." Both these doctrines, of course, have long been rejected in this state. . . .

Because the traditional justifications for the marital exemption no longer have any validity, other arguments have been advanced in its defense. The first of these recent rationales . . . is that the marital exemption protects against governmental intrusion into marital privacy and promotes reconciliation of the spouses, and thus that elimination of the exemption would be disruptive to marriages. While protecting marital privacy and encouraging reconciliation are legitimate state interests, there is no rational relation between allowing a husband to forcibly rape his wife and these interests. The marital exemption simply does not further marital privacy because this right of privacy protects consensual acts, not violent sexual assaults. Just as a husband cannot invoke a right of marital privacy to escape liability for beating his wife, he cannot justifiably rape his wife under the guise of a right to privacy.

Similarly, it is not tenable to argue that elimination of the marital exemption would disrupt marriages because it would discourage reconciliation. Clearly, it is the violent act of rape and not the subsequent attempt of the wife to seek protection through the criminal justice system which "disrupts" a marriage. Moreover, if the marriage has already reached the point where intercourse is accomplished by violent assault it is doubtful that there is anything left to reconcile. This, of course, is particularly true if the wife is willing to bring criminal charges against her husband which could result in a lengthy jail sentence.

Another rationale sometimes advanced in support of the marital exemption is that marital rape would be a difficult crime to prove. A related argument is that allowing such prosecutions could lead to fabricated complaints by "vindictive" wives. The difficulty of proof argument is based on the problem of showing lack of consent. Proving lack of consent, however, is often the most difficult part of any rape prosecution, particularly where the rapist and the victim had a prior relationship. Similarly, the possibility that married women will fabricate complaints would seem to be no greater than the possibility of unmarried women doing so. The criminal justice system, with all of its built-in safeguards, is presumed to be capable of handling any false complaints. Indeed, if the possibility of fabricated complaints were a basis for not criminalizing behavior which would otherwise be sanctioned, virtually all crimes other than homicides would go unpunished.

The final argument in defense of the marital exemption is that marital rape is not as serious an offense as other rape and is thus adequately dealt with by the possibility of prosecution under criminal statutes, such as assault statutes, which provide for less severe punishment. The fact that rape statutes exist, however, is a recognition that the harm caused by a forcible rape is different, and more severe, than the harm caused by an ordinary assault. "Short of homicide, [rape] is the ultimate violation of self." . . .

Moreover, there is no evidence to support the argument that marital rape has less severe consequences than other rape. On the contrary, numerous studies have shown that marital rape is frequently quite violent and generally has *more* severe, traumatic effects on the victim than other rape.

Among the recent decisions in this country addressing the marital exemption, only one court has concluded that there is a rational basis for it. See People v. Brown, 632 P.2d 1025 (Colo. 1981). We agree with the other courts which have analyzed the exemption, which have been unable to find any present justification for it. Justice Holmes wrote: "It is revolting to have no better reason for a rule of law than that so it was laid down in the time of Henry IV. It is still more revolting if the grounds upon which it was laid down have vanished long since, and the rule simply persists from blind imitation of the past." This statement is an apt characterization of the marital exemption; it lacks a rational basis, and therefore violates the equal protection clauses of both the federal and state constitutions.

After declaring the marital exemption unconstitutional, the court considered what the remedy should be. The court rejected the defendant's invitation to invalidate the rape statute in its entirety because the effect of invalidation "would have a disastrous effect on the public interest and safety." Rather, the court concluded that the marital exemption "must be read out of the statutes prohibiting forcible rape," and, therefore, it affirmed the defendant's conviction.

Do any of the policy arguments supporting the marital exemption retain vitality today? This question is important because the marital exemption, albeit in an attenuated form, continues its influence. The law of marital rape is difficult to summarize concisely because the law is in transition, and a variety of approaches exist.[a] As *Liberta* illustrates, a number of states have eliminated the marital rape exemption completely. In these states, the fact that the participants in the sexual encounter are married is of no relevance in a rape prosecution. However, many rape statutes draw some distinctions between marital and nonmarital rape. Some states have replaced the marital exemption with a distinct crime of marital rape, which usually is graded less severely than a rape that occurs between persons who are not married to each other. In other states, marital rape is a crime, but only when the rapist uses a degree of force greater than that required to establish nonmarital rape. Under yet another approach, the marital exemption is not a defense to a first-degree rape charge, but the exemption continues to bar prosecution of husbands who perpetrate lesser sexual assaults against their wives.

## SECTION 3: STATUTORY RAPE

### INTRODUCTORY NOTE

The phrase "statutory rape" originally was used to distinguish sexual intercourse with a minor, an offense created by statute, from rape, the common law crime requiring force and nonconsent. Under one of the earliest statutes of this kind, which was enacted in 1576, the crime was committed if the "woman child was under the age of 10 years; in which case the consent or non-consent is immaterial, as by reason of her tender years she is incapable of judgment and discretion." 4 William Blackstone, Commentaries *212. Over the course of the 19th and 20th centuries, state legislatures gradually raised the age of consent. Modern penal codes are in conflict over the age at which people are mature enough to have sex. The age ranges from 12 to 18, with most states fixing the age of consent at 13 or 14. Today, the most difficult questions posed by these laws involve sexual activity by adolescents.

### Garnett v. State

Court of Appeals of Maryland, 1993.
332 Md. 571, 632 A.2d 797.

■ MURPHY, JUDGE. Maryland's "statutory rape" law prohibiting sexual intercourse with an underage person is codified in Maryland Code Art. 27, § 463, which reads in [part]:

> Second degree rape.
>
> (a) What constitutes.—A person is guilty of rape in the second degree if the person engages in vaginal intercourse with another person: . . .
>
> (3) Who is under 14 years of age and the person performing the act is at least four years older than the victim.
>
> (b) Penalty.—Any person violating the provisions of this section is guilty of a felony and upon conviction is subject to imprisonment for a period of not more than 20 years.

---

[a] For a summary of the law of marital rape, see Jaye Sitton, Old Wine in New Bottles: The "Marital" Rape Allowance, 72 N.C. L. Rev. 261 (1993).

Subsection (a)(3) represents the current version of a statutory provision dating back to the first comprehensive codification of the criminal law by the Legislature in 1809.[6] Now we consider whether under the present statute, the state must prove that a defendant knew the complaining witness was younger than 14 and, in a related question, whether it was error at trial to exclude evidence that he had been told, and believed, that she was 16 years old.

I

Raymond Lennard Garnett is a young retarded man. At the time of the incident in question he was 20 years old. He has an I.Q. of 52. His [school] guidance counselor . . . described him as a mildly retarded person who read on the third-grade level, did arithmetic on the fifth-grade level, and interacted with others socially at school at the level of someone 11 or 12 years of age. . . . Raymond attended special education classes and for at least one period of time was educated at home when he was afraid to return to school due to his classmates' taunting. Because he could not understand the duties of the jobs given him, he failed to complete vocational assignments; he sometimes lost his way to work. As Raymond was unable to pass any of the state's functional tests required for graduation, he received only a certificate of attendance rather than a high-school diploma.

In November or December 1990, a friend introduced Raymond to Erica Frazier, then aged 13; the two subsequently talked occasionally by telephone. On February 28, 1991, Raymond, apparently wishing to call for a ride home, approached the girl's house at about nine o'clock in the evening. Erica opened her bedroom window, through which Raymond entered; he testified that "she just told me to get a ladder and climb up her window." The two talked, and later engaged in sexual intercourse. Raymond left at about 4:30 a.m. the following morning. On November 19, 1991, Erica gave birth to a baby, of which Raymond is the biological father.

Raymond was tried before the Circuit Court for Montgomery County on one count of second degree rape under § 463(a)(3). . . . At trial, the defense twice proffered evidence to the effect that Erica herself and her friends had previously told Raymond that she was 16 years old, and that he had acted with that belief. The trial court excluded such evidence as immaterial, explaining [that statutory rape is a strict liability offense]. The court found Raymond guilty. It sentenced him to a term of five years in prison, suspended the sentence and imposed five years of probation, and ordered that he pay restitution to Erica and the Frazier family. . . .

II

. . . Section 463(a)(3) does not expressly set forth a requirement that the accused have acted with a criminal state of mind, or mens rea. The state insists that the statute, by design, defines a strict liability

6 "If any person shall carnally know and abuse any woman-child under the age of 10 years, every such carnal knowledge shall be deemed felony, and the offender, being convicted thereof, shall, at the discretion of the court, suffer death by hanging . . . or undergo a confinement in the penitentiary for a period not less than one year nor more than 21 years." . . . The minimum age of the child was raised from 10 years to 14 years in Chapter 410 of the Acts of 1890.

offense, and that its essential elements were met in the instant case when Raymond, age 20, engaged in vaginal intercourse with Erica, a girl under 14 and more than 4 years his junior. Raymond replies that the criminal law exists to assess and punish morally culpable behavior. He says such culpability was absent here. He asks us either to engraft onto subsection (a)(3) an implicit mens rea requirement, or to recognize an affirmative defense of reasonable mistake as to the complainant's age. Raymond argues that it is unjust, under the circumstances of this case which led him to think his conduct lawful, to brand him a felon and rapist.

III

Raymond asserts that the events of this case were inconsistent with the criminal sexual exploitation of a minor by an adult. As earlier observed, Raymond entered Erica's bedroom at the girl's invitation; she directed him to use a ladder to reach her window. They engaged voluntarily in sexual intercourse. They remained together in the room for more than seven hours before Raymond departed at dawn. With an I.Q. of 52, Raymond functioned at approximately the same level as the 13-year-old Erica; he was mentally an adolescent in an adult's body. Arguably, had Raymond's chronological age, 20, matched his socio-intellectual age, about 12, he and Erica would have fallen well within the four-year age difference obviating a violation of the statute, and Raymond would not have been charged with any crime at all.

The precise legal issue here rests on [the trial court's refusal to entertain] a defense of reasonable mistake of Erica's age, by which defense Raymond would have asserted that he acted innocently without a criminal design. At common law, a crime occurred only upon the concurrence of an individual's act and his guilty state of mind. . . . The requirement that an accused have acted with a culpable mental state is an axiom of criminal jurisprudence. . . .

To be sure, legislative bodies since the mid-19th century have created strict liability criminal offenses requiring no mens rea. Almost all such statutes responded to the demands of public health and welfare arising from the complexities of society after the Industrial Revolution. Typically misdemeanors involving only fines or other light penalties, these strict liability laws regulated food, milk, liquor, medicines and drugs, securities, motor vehicles and traffic, the labeling of goods for sale, and the like. Statutory rape, carrying the stigma of felony as well as a potential sentence of 20 years in prison, contrasts markedly with the other strict liability regulatory offenses and their light penalties.

Modern scholars generally reject the concept of strict criminal liability. Professors LaFave and Scott summarize the consensus that punishing conduct without reference to the actor's state of mind fails to reach the desired end and is unjust:

> It is inefficacious because conduct unaccompanied by an awareness of the factors making it criminal does not mark the actor as one who needs to be subjected to punishment in order to deter him or others from behaving similarly in the future, nor does it single him out as a socially dangerous individual who needs to be incapacitated or reformed. It is unjust because the actor is subjected to the stigma of a criminal conviction

> without being morally blameworthy. Consequently, on either a preventive or retributive theory of criminal punishment, the criminal sanction is inappropriate in the absence of mens rea. . . .

The commentators similarly disapprove of statutory rape as a strict liability crime. [T]hey observe that statutory rape prosecutions often proceed even when the defendant's judgment as to the age of the complainant is warranted by her appearance, her sexual sophistication, her verbal misrepresentations, and the defendant's careful attempts to ascertain her true age. Voluntary intercourse with a sexually mature teenager lacks the features of psychic abnormality, exploitation, or physical danger that accompanies such conduct with children.

Two sub-parts of the rationale underlying strict criminal liability require further analysis at this point. Statutory rape laws are often justified on the "lesser legal wrong" theory or the "moral wrong" theory; by such reasoning, the defendant acting without mens rea nonetheless deserves punishment for having committed a lesser crime, fornication, or for having violated moral teachings that prohibit sex outside of marriage. Maryland has no law against fornication. It is not a crime in this state. Moreover, the criminalization of an act, performed without a guilty mind, deemed immoral by some members of the community rests uneasily on subjective and shifting norms. "[D]etermining precisely what the 'community ethic' actually is [is] not an easy task in a heterogeneous society in which our public pronouncements about morality often are not synonymous with our private conduct." The drafters of the Model Penal Code remarked:

> [T]he actor who reasonably believes that his partner is above that age [of consent] lacks culpability with respect to the factor deemed critical to liability. Punishing him anyway simply because his intended conduct would have been immoral under the facts as he supposed them to be postulates a relation between criminality and immorality that is inaccurate on both descriptive and normative grounds. The penal law does not try to enforce all aspects of community morality, and any thoroughgoing attempt to do so would extend the prospect of criminal sanctions far into the sphere of individual liberty and create a regime too demanding for all save the best among us.

We acknowledge here that it is uncertain to what extent Raymond's intellectual and social retardation may have impaired his ability to comprehend imperatives of sexual morality in any case.

IV

The legislatures of 17 states have enacted laws permitting a mistake of age defense in some form in cases of sexual offenses with underage persons. . . . In some states, the defense is available in instances where the complainant's age rises above a statutorily prescribed level, but is not available when the complainant falls below the defining age. In other states, the availability of the defense depends on the severity of the sex offense charged to the accused.

In addition, the highest appellate courts of four states have determined that statutory rape laws by implication required an element of mens rea as to the complainant's age. In the landmark case of People v.

Hernandez, 61 Cal.2d 529, 39 Cal.Rptr. 361, 393 P.2d 673 (1964), the California Supreme Court . . . questioned the assumption that age alone confers a sophistication sufficient to create legitimate consent to sexual relations: "the sexually experienced 15-year-old may be far more acutely aware of the implications of sexual intercourse than her sheltered cousin who is beyond the age of consent." The court then rejected the traditional view that those who engage in sex with young persons do so at their peril, assuming the risk that their partners are underage:

> [If the perpetrator] participates in a mutual act of sexual intercourse, believing his partner to be beyond the age of consent, with reasonable grounds for such belief, where is his criminal intent? In such circumstances he has not consciously taken any risk. Instead he has subjectively eliminated the risk by satisfying himself on reasonable evidence that the crime cannot be committed. If it occurs that he has been misled, we cannot realistically conclude for such reason alone the intent with which he undertook the act suddenly becomes more heinous. . . .

V

We think it sufficiently clear, however, that Maryland's second-degree rape statute defines a strict liability offense that does not require the state to prove mens rea; it makes no allowance for a mistake-of-age defense. The plain language of § 463, viewed in its entirety, and the legislative history of its creation lead to this conclusion.

It is well settled that in interpreting a statute to ascertain and effectuate its goal, our first recourse is to the words of the statute, giving them their ordinary and natural import. While penal statutes are to be strictly construed in favor of the defendant, the construction must ultimately depend upon discerning the intention of the legislature when it drafted and enacted the law in question. . . .

Section 463(a)(3) prohibiting sexual intercourse with underage persons makes no reference to the actor's knowledge, belief, or other state of mind. As we see it, this silence as to mens rea results from legislative design. First, subsection (a)(3) stands in stark contrast to the provision immediately before it, [which prohibits] vaginal intercourse with incapacitated or helpless persons. In subsection (a)(2), the legislature expressly provided as an element of the offense that "the person performing the act knows or should reasonably know the other person is mentally defective, mentally incapacitated, or physically helpless." In drafting this subsection, the legislature showed itself perfectly capable of recognizing and allowing for a defense that obviates criminal intent; if the defendant objectively did not understand that the sex partner was impaired, there is no crime. That it chose not to include similar language in subsection (a)(3) indicates that the legislature aimed to make statutory rape with underage persons a more severe prohibition based on strict criminal liability.

Second, an examination of the drafting history of § 463 during the 1976 revision of Maryland's sexual offense laws reveals that the statute was viewed as one of strict liability from its inception and throughout the amendment process. . . .

This interpretation is consistent with the traditional view of statutory rape as a strict liability crime designed to protect young persons from the dangers of sexual exploitation by adults, loss of chastity, physical injury, and, in the case of girls, pregnancy. The majority of states retain statutes which impose strict liability for sexual acts with underage complainants. We observe again, as earlier, that even among those states providing for a mistake-of-age defense in some instances, the defense often is not available where the sex partner is 14 years old or less; the complaining witness in the instant case was only 13. The majority of appellate courts . . . have held statutory rape to be a strict liability crime.

VI

Maryland's second degree rape statute is by nature a creature of legislation. Any new provision introducing an element of mens rea, or permitting a defense of reasonable mistake of age, with respect to the offense of sexual intercourse with a person less than 14, should properly result from an act of the legislature itself, rather than judicial fiat. Until then, defendants in extraordinary cases, like Raymond, will rely upon the tempering discretion of the trial court at sentencing.

■ ELDRIDGE, JUDGE, dissenting: Both the majority opinion and Judge Bell's dissenting opinion view the question in this case to be whether, on the one hand, § 463(a)(3), is entirely a strict liability statute without any mens rea requirement or, on the other hand, contains the requirement that the defendant knew that the person with whom he or she was having sexual relations was under 14 years of age. . . .

In my view, the [mens rea] issue is not limited to a choice between one of these extremes. . . . I agree with the majority that an ordinary defendant's mistake about the age of his or her sexual partner is not a defense to [statutory rape. Moreover, I am not persuaded by the argument made by Judge Bell that the federal and state constitutions require that a defendant's honest mistake as to the victim's age be a defense.] This does not mean, however, that the statute contains no mens rea requirement at all. . . .

. . . In enacting [§ 463(a)(3)], the General Assembly assumed that a defendant is able to appreciate the risk involved by intentionally and knowingly engaging in sexual activities with a young person. There is no indication that the General Assembly intended that criminal liability attach to one who, because of his or her mental impairment, was unable to appreciate that risk.

It is unreasonable to assume that the legislature intended for one to be convicted under § 463(a)(3), . . . regardless of his or her mental state. Suppose, for example, that Raymond Garnett had not had an I.Q. of 52, but rather, had . . . an I.Q. of 25–30, was physiologically capable of [fathering] a child, but was unable to comprehend the act of sexual intercourse, or even to understand the difference between the sexes. If someone so disabled, having reached Raymond's chronological age, then had "consensual" sexual intercourse with a person younger than 14 years of age, I do not believe that he or she would have violated § 463(a)(3). Under the view that [the statute defines] pure strict liability offenses without any regard for the defendant's mental state, presumably a 20-year-old, who passes out because of drinking too many alcoholic beverages, would be guilty of a sexual offense if a 13-year-old engages in various sexual activities with the 20-year-old while the latter is unconscious. I cannot imagine that the General Assembly intended any such result. . . .

[The dissenting opinion of Judge Bell is omitted.]

## NOTES ON STATUTORY RAPE

### 1. QUESTIONS AND COMMENTS ON *GARNETT*

As the court in *Garnett* explains, a majority of jurisdictions treat statutory rape as a strict liability offense. Courts and commentators approach this instance of strict liability as one that requires careful justification because conviction exposes the accused to significant criminal penalties. *Garnett* describes and criticizes two theories that have been offered to support strict liability in this context, namely, the "lesser legal wrong" and "moral wrong" theories. The court rejects the "lesser legal wrong" theory on the ground that "Maryland has no law against fornication." In states that continue to criminalize fornication (assuming that such laws do not violate any constitutional guarantees), does the "lesser legal wrong" theory support the classification of statutory rape as a strict liability offense?

The court in *Garnett* also criticizes the "moral wrong" theory on the ground that such theory requires judges to identify and enforce community norms, which are "subjective and shifting." In the court's view, what is the problem with imposing punishment on one who may be unaware that he is violating the criminal law, but whose conduct violates a moral norm? Peter Brett argues that the "moral wrong" theory is "clearly in accord with principle. It reflects the view that we learn our duties, not by studying the statute book, but by living in a community. [Therefore, a] defense of mistake rests ultimately on the defendant's being able to say that he has observed the community ethic. . . . " Peter Brett, An Inquiry into Criminal Guilt 149 (1963). Can a defendant who has sex with an adolescent "say that he has observed the community ethic"? If not, why is it unfair to punish him?

Richard Posner argues that strict liability may promote efficiency in the context of statutory rape:

> The girl may look 16 (let us assume 16 is the age of consent), but if she is younger, a reasonable mistake will not excuse the male. . . . [In these cases,] we do not care about deterring activity bordering on the activity that the basic criminal prohibition is aimed at. Because we do not count the avoidance of that activity as a social cost, it pays to reduce the costs of prosecution by eliminating the issue of intent (more precisely, an issue of intent). The male can avoid liability for statutory rape by keeping away from young girls . . . . In effect we introduce a degree of strict liability into criminal law as into tort law when a change in activity level is an efficient method of avoiding a social cost.

Richard A. Posner, An Economic Theory of the Criminal Law, 85 Colum. L. Rev. 1193, 1222 (1985). Is Posner's argument a version of the "moral wrong" theory criticized by the court in *Garnett*?

## 2. STATUTORY RAPE UNDER THE MODEL CODE

The proposed new sexual assault provisions of the Model Penal Code "depart[ ] from the widely prevalent view in American law imposing strict liability with respect to mistake of age in sexual offenses." ALI, Model Penal Code: Sexual Assault and Related Offenses, Tentative Draft No. 1, at pp. 76–77 (April 30, 2014). Indeed, the new provisions depart from the position previously taken by the Model Code, which imposed strict liability for offenses against children under the age of 10 and which authorized liability based on negligence for offenses against children older than 10. See MPC § 213.6(1). The Code's proposed new sections include two different provisions that proscribe sexual intercourse with minors, and both of them require proof that the actor was, at a minimum, reckless with respect to the fact that the child was under the age of consent. Section 213.1(1)(c)(i) states that an "actor is guilty of rape, a felony of the second degree, if he or she knowingly or recklessly . . . has . . . sexual intercourse with a person who . . . is less than 12 years old." Under § 213.2(3)(b), an "actor is guilty of sexual intercourse by imposition, a felony of the third degree, if he or she knowingly or recklessly has . . . sexual intercourse with a person who . . . is less than 16 years old and the actor is more than four years older than such person." To support their decision to reject strict liability and negligence in this context, the drafters offer the following claims. First, consistent with the Model Code's general emphasis on the essential role played by subjective culpability, the drafters insist that "there should be no room for punishment for a sexual offense," which exposes the accused to imprisonment and severe collateral consequences, "in the absence of proof of some degree of fault." Second, if adopted, the new provisions will move the age of consent from 10 to 12 years. In the drafters' view, this development will pose a far greater risk of substantive injustice to the accused because children younger than 12 "may more understandably be perceived as above the age of legal consent" than those who are younger than 10. Moreover, the drafters assert, even if actors manage to escape liability under § 213.1(1)(c)(i) on the ground that they were unaware of the risk that a complainant was younger than 12, they are likely to be punished under § 213.2(3)(b).

## 3. HARM

What policies are served by laws forbidding adults to have sex with children and adolescents? Are those policies implicated in cases where an adolescent previously has engaged in sexual activity? In the past, many courts held that consensual sex with a minor was a crime only if the minor was "of previously chaste character." Today, only one or two states retain the "unchaste victim exception" to statutory rape. See McBrayer v. State, 467 So.2d 647 (Miss. 1985). What policies support the unchaste victim exception? Does a sexual experience confer on children the wisdom or maturity necessary to give meaningful consent to future sexual activity? Or does the exception suggest that the sole purpose of the statutory rape law is to protect minors from loss of chastity?

In most jurisdictions today, lawmakers assert that sex between a minor and an adult subjects the minor, whether chaste or unchaste, to a range of injuries. Moreover, minors are said to incur these injuries even when they claim that they desired the sexual contact and do not perceive that they have been harmed. For example, in Jones v. State, 640 So.2d 1084 (Fla. 1994), two men, one 19 and the other 20 years old, were convicted for having sexual intercourse with girls under the age of 16. "The parties stipulated at trial that the girls with whom the defendants had sexual intercourse were 14 years of age and consented to having intercourse. Neither girl desired to prosecute and the charges were instituted by" the girls' relatives. On appeal, defense counsel "argue[d] that the statute is unconstitutional as applied because the girls in this case have not been harmed; they wanted to have the personal relationships they entered into with these men; and, they do not want the 'protections' advanced by the state." The Supreme Court of Florida rebuffed these claims:

> We are of the opinion that sexual activity with a child opens the door to sexual exploitation, physical harm, and sometimes psychological damage, regardless of the child's maturity or lack of chastity. [N]either the level of intimacy nor the degree of harm are relevant when an adult and a child under the age of 16 engage in sexual intercourse. The statutory protection . . . assures that, to the extent the law can prevent such activity, minors will not be sexually harmed. "Sexual exploitation of children is a particularly pernicious evil that sometimes may be concealed behind the zone of privacy that normally shields the home. The state unquestionably has a very compelling interest in preventing such conduct."
>
> . . . The legislature enacted [the statutory rape provision] based on a "morally neutral judgment" that sexual intercourse with a child under the age of 16, with or without consent, is potentially harmful to the child. Although the right to be let alone protects adults from government intrusion into matters relating to marriage, contraception, and abortion, the state "may exercise control over the sexual conduct of children beyond the scope of its authority to control adults."

The Supreme Court of Florida has held that this reasoning does not apply where a minor is prosecuted for having sex with another minor. In B.B. v. State, 659 So.2d 256 (Fla. 1995), a 16-year-old boy was charged with "unlawful carnal intercourse," a felony, for having consensual sex with a 16-year-old girl, who was "of previous chaste character." The court decided that, as applied to this activity, the statute violated the defendant's state constitutional right to privacy:

> While we do recognize that Florida does have an obligation and a compelling interest in protecting children from sexual activity before their minds and bodies have sufficiently matured to make it appropriate, safe, and healthy for them and that this interest pertains to one minor engaging in carnal intercourse with another, the crux of the state's interest in an adult-minor situation is the prevention of exploitation of the minor by the adult. Whereas in this minor-minor situation, the crux of the state's interest is in protecting the minor from the sexual activity itself for reasons of health and quality of life. Having distinguished between the state's interest in the adult-minor situation and in the minor-minor situation, we conclude that the state has failed to demonstrate . . . that the adjudication of B.B. as a delinquent . . . is the least intrusive means of furthering what we have determined to be the state's compelling interest. . . .
>
> At present, we will not debate morality in respect to the statute or debate whether this century-old statute fits within

> the contemporary "facts of life." We do say that if our decision was what should be taught and reasoned to minors, the unequivocal text of our message would be abstinence. We are all too aware of the real-life crisis of children having children. . . . We recognize the plague of AIDS and the evidence that this epidemic and the rampant spread of serious communicative disease are the sad product of sexual promiscuity. However, our decision is not about what should be taught but about what can be adjudicated to be delinquency as a second-degree felony.

Many states' penal codes no longer criminalize consensual sex between adolescents. These provisions are similar to the statute at issue in *Garnett*, under which the crime occurs only when the minor has sex with an actor who is a specified number of years older than the minor. What policy choices support these provisions?

### 4. HARM AND GENDER DIFFERENCES

Are boys and girls similarly situated with respect to loss of chastity and other injuries these laws were designed to prevent? In Michael M. v. Superior Court of Sonoma County, 450 U.S. 464 (1981), the Supreme Court concluded that there were important reasons why a state legislature might answer this question in the negative. There, the Court decided that California's statutory rape law, which imposed criminal liability only on men, did not violate the equal protection clause of the 14th amendment.[a] The following excerpt is from the plurality opinion authored by Justice Rehnquist:

> We need not be medical doctors to discern that young men and young women are not similarly situated with respect to the problems and risks of sexual intercourse. Only women may become pregnant, and they suffer disproportionately the profound physical, emotional, and psychological consequences of sexual activity. The statute at issue here protects women from sexual intercourse at an age when those consequences are particularly severe. . . .
>
> Because virtually all of the significant harmful and inescapably identifiable consequences of teenage pregnancy fall on the young female, a legislature acts well within its authority when it elects to punish only the participant who, by nature, suffers few of the consequences of his conduct. It is hardly unreasonable for a legislature acting to protect minor females to exclude them from punishment. Moreover, the risk of pregnancy itself constitutes a substantial deterrence to young females. No similar natural sanctions deter males. A criminal sanction imposed solely on males thus serves to roughly "equalize" the deterrents on the sexes. . . .

*Michael M.* tends to provide the focal point for feminist criticism of statutory rape laws. Today, the vast majority of these laws are neutral with

[a] The provision at issue in *Michael M.* defined "unlawful sexual intercourse as 'an act of sexual intercourse accomplished with a female not the wife of the perpetrator, where the female is under the age of 18 years.' " At the time of the incident that gave rise to his prosecution under this statute, the defendant in *Michael M.* was 17½ years old, and the young woman with whom he had intercourse was 16½.

respect to the gender of potential offender and victim.[b] Statutes in a few states continue to define the crime as one that is perpetrated by a male against a female. See, e.g., Ga. Code Ann. § 16–6–3 (1992); Idaho Code § 18–6101(1) (Supp. 1994). However, as they are applied in actual prosecutions, these laws generally assign responsibility for the sexual encounter based on gender: males are perpetrators, and females are victims. According to some feminists, statutory rape laws thus operate to reinforce invidious stereotypes, under which "men are always responsible for initiating sexual intercourse and females must always be protected against their aggression." Nadine Taub & Elizabeth M. Schneider, Women's Subordination and the Role of Law 170, in The Politics of Law (David Kairys ed., 1990). Arguments by other feminists suggest that it is difficult to decide how the criminal law should participate in breaking down these stereotypes. As Frances Olsen remarks, the "double standard of sexual morality" assumes that "[f]or males, sex is an accomplishment; they gain something through intercourse. For women, sex entails giving something up." Frances Olsen, Statutory Rape: A Feminist Critique of Rights Analysis, 63 Tex. L. Rev. 387, 405 (1984). The problem for feminists who reject these assumptions as archaic stereotypes is that the stereotypes may influence the ways in which people actually experience sex. That is, young women may experience their first sexual encounter as a stigmatizing loss, while young men experience it as an honorable acquisition. If so, should those who make and enforce statutory rape laws ignore these different experiences and perspectives? Should the law treat adolescent boys, as well as girls, as if they require protection from sexual activity? Should it punish adolescent girls, as well as boys, for having sex?

### 5. EXTENDING STATUTORY RAPE LAWS

In 1996, the Governor of New York signed into law a bill criminalizing all sexual intercourse, whether coerced or consensual, between prison employees and prison inmates. See N.Y. Penal Law § 130.05(3)(3) (Consol. 2003). The theory underlying this statute is that "the imbalance of power between inmates and officers" is so great that it "negates the possibility of true consent." Monte Williams, Bill Seeks to Protect Inmates From Guards Who Seek Sex, N.Y. Times, Apr. 23, 1996, at A1. Under the statute, therefore, the inmate is defined as a "person deemed incapable of consent" to sex, so that liability for any intercourse between guard and inmate is thrown entirely on the guard. According to the law's proponents, it is difficult to prosecute guards under forcible rape statutes because guards rarely resort to the kind of physical force that such statutes require. Yet, the proponents claimed, sexual intercourse in this context inevitably is coercive. "Female inmates have no capacity to say, 'No' " to sexual advances from corrections officers because the officers have the power to penalize inmates in a variety of formal and informal ways. Opponents of the bill argued that women prisoners sometimes initiate sexual encounters because they "just want the sex," and they contended that the population of female inmates includes many litigious persons who are likely to file false accusations. Notice that

---

[b] In 1993, the California legislature revised that state's statutory rape provision so that it punishes "[a]ny person" who has sexual intercourse with a "person under the age of 18 years." Cal. Penal Code § 261.5 (West Supp. 1995). This change in the law reportedly was prompted by two cases in which prosecutors were unable to bring statutory rape charges against adult women who had sex with underage boys. See Mark Gladstone and Daniel M. Weintraub, "New Law Broadens the Provisions of Statutory Rape," L.A. Times, Oct. 2, 1993.

both sides of this debate seem to have assumed that the guard-perpetrators in these cases inevitably would be male and the inmate-victims would be female. Is that a fair assumption? Do male inmates not need protection from female guards?

Is it fair to assume that all sexual intercourse between guards and inmates is so inherently coercive that it should be criminalized and the guards (alone) held liable for it? If so, this type of statutory rape law might be extended to other relationships in which the participants do not possess equivalent power. Lawmakers could identify such relationships and simply outlaw all sexual intercourse between the parties thereto. Possible candidates include relationships between teachers and students, employers and employees, and superior officers and their military subordinates. Are there other relationships that "negate the possibility of true consent"? What kind of "power" over the life of another person has that effect? Does this approach provide a desirable way to resolve some of the enforcement problems encountered under forcible rape statutes? Are such laws likely to have any adverse consequences?

# CHAPTER X

# HOMICIDE

## SECTION 1: INTRODUCTION

### INTRODUCTORY NOTES ON THE HISTORY OF CRIMINAL HOMICIDE

#### 1. THE EARLY LAW

From a modern perspective, the most important aspect of early English law was the development of the separate offenses of murder and manslaughter.[a] Prior to 1496, murder was the only homicide offense, and the penalty was death. For those who could come within its terms, however, benefit of clergy was available to avoid the death penalty. By the late 15th century, the categories of offenders who could claim this mitigation had expanded to include virtually all literate persons.

A series of statutes enacted between 1496 and 1547 led to the development of manslaughter as a distinct and lesser homicide offense. The effect of these statutes was to exclude certain of the more serious forms of murder from the benefit of clergy. Those convicted of the excluded offenses became subject to the death penalty, unless they could obtain a royal pardon. As the law matured, the dividing line between murder and manslaughter came to be the concept of "malice prepense" or "malice aforethought." In time, murder came to include all homicides committed with "malice aforethought," and manslaughter all criminal homicides committed without "malice aforethought." As the law evolved, to paraphrase Sir James Fitzjames Stephen, the judges allocated criminal homicides between murder and manslaughter—and gave meaning to the determinative term "malice aforethought"—according to which offenders deserved to be hanged.[b] This initial effort at grading criminal homicide offenses thus used the definition of murder as the device for isolating those homicides for which the death penalty was imposed.[c]

---

[a] The history of criminal homicide is recounted in ALI, Model Penal Code and Commentaries, §§ 210.0 to .6, pp. 1–171 (1980). Additional sources are cited in the Model Code commentary. Among the more useful are Royal Comm'n on Capital Punishment, Report, CMND. No. 8932 (1953); 3 Sir James Fitzjames Stephen, A History of the Criminal Law of England 1–107 (1883); Herbert Wechsler and Jerome Michael, A Rationale of the Law of Homicide, 37 Colum.L.Rev. 701, 1261 (1937).

[b] See Royal Comm'n on Capital Punishment, CMND. No. 8932, at 28 (1953). What Stephen actually said (in 1866), was that "the loose term 'malice' was used, and then when a particular state of mind came to their notice the judges called it 'malice' or not according to their view of the propriety of hanging particular people. That is, in two words, the history of the definition of murder."

[c] The traditional definition of murder, as paraphrased from Coke's rendition in the 17th century, was: "When a man of sound memory and of the age of discretion unlawfully kills any reasonable creature in being and under the King's peace, with malice aforethought, either express or implied by the law, the death taking place within a year and a day." See 3 Coke, Institutes * 47; Royal Comm'n on Capital Punishment, CMND. No. 8932, at 28 (1953).

## 2. THE DISTINCTION BETWEEN MURDER AND MANSLAUGHTER

The remaining common law history of murder and manslaughter principally concerns the content assigned to the two categories as they expanded in scope. Murder came to encompass four different kinds of killings:

(i) those where the actor intended to kill or knew that death would result;

(ii) those where the actor intended to inflict grievous bodily harm or knew that such harm would result;

(iii) those where the actor manifested reckless indifference to death—a state of mind variously described as a "depraved mind," an "abandoned and malignant heart," or "wickedness of disposition, hardness of heart, cruelty, recklessness of consequences, and a mind regardless of social duty";

and (iv) those where the death occurred while the actor was engaged in the commission of a felony.

Malice aforethought became a term of art, if not, as Glanville Williams has said, a term of deception,[d] that encompassed all of these various circumstances and states of mind. The term was thus a token, an arbitrary symbol, used to collect under a single label a wide variety of cases having no more in common than that they were at one time or another deemed appropriate situations for imposition of the death penalty.

Manslaughter was defined as homicide that was committed without malice aforethought. Common law manslaughter came to include three distinct types of killings:

(i) those where the actor intended to kill but committed the offense in a sudden heat of passion engendered by adequate provocation;

(ii) those where the actor engaged in reckless or negligent behavior that was insufficiently culpable to constitute murder but more culpable than ordinary civil negligence; and

(iii) those where the death occurred while the actor was engaged in the commission of an unlawful act not amounting to a felony.

The term "voluntary manslaughter" was used to refer to the first category. The term "involuntary manslaughter" was used to designate the second and third categories. The distinction between voluntary and involuntary manslaughter had no significance at early common law, although modern statutes frequently use these terms to describe different grading categories.[e]

## 3. MODERN DEVELOPMENTS

The common law structure has survived in England, although grading provisions designed to restrict use of the death penalty were adopted in 1957 and the death penalty was abandoned altogether in 1965. In the middle of the last century, England also abolished the felony murder rule.

---

[d] Glanville Williams, Textbook of Criminal Law 208 (1978).

[e] See, e.g., the Virginia statutes reproduced in Appendix B.

In the United States, there have been two broad developments in the law of homicide, each of which has generated a rich and complex jurisprudence. The first development, which began in the 18th century and continues to this day, is the emergence of distinct grades of homicide offenses, each of which carries its own penalty and stigmatic value. As the following materials demonstrate, the common law structure was enormously influential in the development of modern homicide statutes. That structure remains intact in a few jurisdictions, and, during the codification process, most state legislatures explicitly built upon it. The states continue to treat murder and manslaughter as distinct offense categories, and as they began to subdivide those categories into a number of separate offenses they borrowed heavily from common law thinking about homicide and fault. Thus, the common law of homicide retains a powerful hold over our legal and popular understandings of which killings are most culpable and why.

For example, despite years of scholarly criticism of the "malice aforethought" construct, many states continue to use the distinct conditions encompassed by the term "malice" as the basis for identifying different degrees of murder. Likewise, many modern statutes rely on the distinction between voluntary and involuntary manslaughter to describe different grading categories.

The second noteworthy development arose from the movement by the United States Supreme Court to constrain the imposition of capital punishment. Commencing in the late 1960s, the Supreme Court entertained a host of procedural and substantive challenges to prevailing capital crime definitions and capital punishment schemes. This litigation produced a series of complicated opinions in which a deeply divided Court struggled to decide when, if ever, imposition of the death penalty was compatible with contemporary constitutional value judgments. Ultimately, the Court upheld the constitutional status of capital punishment in general, but along the way it created a new and complicated body of constitutional death-penalty law. In their turn, the new Supreme Court decisions produced a number of innovations in state capital punishment schemes, which generated new constitutional questions, and so on. Suffice it to say that death-penalty law expanded dramatically in the past several decades, and it now occupies a discrete and unique niche in the criminal homicide landscape.

### 4. PLAN OF THE CHAPTER

This Chapter is divided into four sections. Sections 1 and 2 deal with basic divisions between murder and manslaughter in modern law. Section 1 deals with all categories of murder except felony murder, which is postponed because it is advisable to deal with causation first. Section 2 considers manslaughter. Section 3 covers causation, which sets the stage for the treatment of felony murder in Section 4. Chapter XI considers the capital punishment issue as it applies to murder and other offenses.

## SECTION 2: MURDER

### State v. Brown

Supreme Court of Tennessee, 1992.
836 S.W.2d 530.

■ MARTHA CRAIG DAUGHTREY, JUDGE. This capital case arose from the death of four-year-old Eddie Eugene Brown and the subsequent conviction of his father for first-degree murder, as well as for child neglect. After careful review, we have reached the conclusion that the evidence introduced at trial is not sufficient to support a conviction for first-degree murder. We therefore hold that the defendant's conviction must be reduced to second-degree murder.

1. Factual Background

The victim in this case, Eddie Eugene Brown, was born in early February 1982, the son of defendant Mack Edward Brown and his co-defendant, Evajean Bell Brown, who were not living together at the time of Eddie's birth and were later divorced. Evajean was not able to nurse Eddie immediately after his birth because she was hospitalized with hypotoxemia.

According to his pediatrician, this hospitalization and inability to nurse may have contributed to Eddie's being, as the doctor described him, a "failure to thrive baby." When the physician first saw Eddie on March 17, 1982, at a little more than five weeks old, the infant was in good health but smaller than the median for his age. Mack and Evajean were still separated at that time, and relations between them eventually worsened to the point that Evajean asked the pediatrician to change Eddie's name on his records to Justin Michael Brown. Because Eddie had not begun to talk by age two-and-a-half, he was referred to the University of Tennessee Speech and Hearing Clinic. The clinic's report indicates that by age three years and four months, he was not yet toilet-trained and could speak single words, but not whole sentences. Evajean brought Eddie to see his pediatrician on November 5, 1984, because, as the doctor testified, she said he had fallen down fifteen carpeted stairs the night before. Although the physician found no injuries consistent with such a fall, he did note that Eddie's penis was red, swollen, and tender to the touch. His medical records do not give a reason for this condition. Eddie's last visit to his pediatrician's office was on October 16, 1985, with his mother and father, who by that time had reconciled.

According to a Department of Human Services social worker who had investigated the Brown home, Eddie was a hyperactive child with a severe speech problem. She reported that he also had severe emotional and behavioral problems. As an example of his behavior, she reported that during her visit, he ran down the hall directly into a wall. . . .

Mack had been living with his wife and his son for less than a year when Eddie died. The Brown's next-door neighbor testified that, at around 3:40 a m. on April 10, 1986, she heard yelling and screaming in their apartment. She distinctly heard a man's voice say, "Shut up. Get your ass over here. Sit down. Shut up. I know what I'm doing." She also heard a woman's voice say, "Stop, don't do that. Leave me alone. Stop, don't do that." She testified that the fight went on for 30 minutes and that she heard a sound which she described as a "thump, like something heavy hit the wall." The only other evidence introduced concerning the events of that morning was the tape of Evajean's call for an ambulance. At 8:59 a.m. she telephoned for help for her son, stating that he "fell down some steps and he's not breathing."

The paramedics who answered the call tried to revive Eddie but were unsuccessful. His heartbeat was reestablished at the hospital, but as it turned out, he was already clinically brain-dead. One of the treating nurses later testified that at that point, Eddie was being kept alive only for purposes of potential organ donation.

Various examinations indicated that the child had suffered two, and possibly three, skull fractures. The CT scan revealed a hairline fracture in the front right temporal portion of his skull, as well as a blood clot and swelling in that area of the head. The scan also revealed the possibility of a second fracture in the middle of the frontal bone. Finally, blood coming from Eddie's ear indicated that he had a fracture at the base of his skull which had caused an injury to the middle ear.

The CT scan showed a cerebral edema or swelling of the brain, which was more pronounced on the right side of the brain than the left, and which had shifted the midline of Eddie's brain toward the left. The pathologist who performed the autopsy noted the presence of vomit in Eddie's lungs and explained that swelling in the brain can cause vomiting. He theorized that repeated blows to Eddie's head caused cerebral hemorrhages and swelling. According to the expert, this pressure in the skull resulted in Eddie's aspiration of his own vomit and his ultimate death.

A neurological surgeon testified that Eddie's brain injuries were, at least in part, consistent with contrecoup[4] injuries, which occur when the head is violently shaken back and forth. The surgeon explained that there is a limited amount of fluid between the brain and the skull. That fluid generally serves as a shock absorber, but when the skull and brain are moving at a sufficient velocity and the skull suddenly stops, the fluid is not an adequate buffer between the delicate brain tissue and the hard skull surface. As he described this phenomenon at trial, "when the skull stops the brain slaps up against it," resulting in severe bruising and swelling of the brain.

In addition to his cranial and cerebral injuries, Eddie had several internal injuries. When Eddie's internal organs were removed for donation, the county medical examiner observed hemorrhaging in the duodenum section of his intestine. He testified that such localized hemorrhaging was consistent with a blow by a fist to the upper portion of the abdomen. Additionally, blood was found in the child's stool and urine, and his liver enzymes were elevated. There was testimony to the effect that these conditions may have resulted from cardiac arrest, but that they are also consistent with blows to the abdomen, liver, and kidneys.

Finally, Eddie had bruises of varying ages on his face, scalp, ears, neck, chest, hips, legs, arms, buttocks, and scrotum. He had a large abrasion on his shoulder, scratches on his neck and face, and a round, partially healed wound on his big toe which, according to one of his treating nurses, was consistent with a cigarette burn. He had

---

[4] The neurological surgeon testified that "contrecoup" is French for "back and forth."

lacerations on both his ears at the scalp. He had linear bruises consistent with being struck with a straight object. The autopsy revealed an old lesion at the base of his brain which was evidence of a head injury at least two weeks before his death. X-rays revealed a broken arm which had not been treated and which had occurred three to five weeks before his death. The injury to his arm was confirmed by a witness who had noticed his arm hanging limply and then later noticed it in a homemade sling.

The defendant's statement to the police verified the fact that Eddie's broken arm was never properly treated, but Mack Brown also told them that he had tried to help Eddie by making a splint for his arm himself. He explained that he did not take Eddie for medical treatment because he was terrified that no one would believe that he and his wife had not inflicted this injury on the child. He could not explain the old bruises on Eddie's body. He stated that although sometimes they disciplined Eddie by spanking him, they did attempt to discipline him in, as he described it, "alternative ways" such as sending him to his room to let him know that they were upset and wanted him to mind.

Brown's statement indicates that around two or three o'clock on the morning of April 10, 1986, he and his wife both spanked Eddie because Eddie had urinated and defecated on the floor. The defendant admitted to another spanking, after he had sent Eddie to bed, and after he and his wife had a fight over money. As the defendant described it, it was during this spanking that his "mood began to kind of snap and let go." He said that he remembered going to Eddie's bedroom and remembered ordering Evajean out of the room. Although he denied remembering anything other than spanking Eddie's bottom with the open part of his hand, he stated that he was afraid he had beaten Eddie during the time that everything "went blank." The only thing he clearly recalled before that point was Eddie "staring at [him] mean" and saying, "I hate you! I hate you!" He stated that his next memory was of going downstairs and hearing Eddie behind him, falling onto the landing and into the door.

When the police questioned the defendant, his right hand was badly swollen. He explained that several days prior to April 10, he had injured his hand while working on his car and had sought medical treatment at Fort Sanders Hospital. They put a splint on his hand and gave him pain medication. He denied having struck Eddie with his right hand, saying that "it hurts so bad there ain't no way." The hospital's records indicate that on April 3, the defendant's hand was x-rayed and splinted. The records do not indicate that there was any break in the skin on the hand.

With the consent of the defendant, the police searched the apartment and recovered numerous items stained with blood consistent with Eddie's blood type, including an adult pajama top, a brown paper bag from the living room floor, and several towels and wash cloths. Police also found a bandage under the kitchen sink which was stained with blood consistent with Eddie's blood type. The blood on this bandage material was on the outside near the adhesive tape, not on the inner surface, which would have been next to the skin of the person wearing the bandage. The pants the defendant was wearing at the time of his arrest also had blood stains on them that were consistent with Eddie's blood type. A number of other items collected from the apartment tested positive for human blood, but the type of blood could not be determined because there was too little blood or they had been washed. These items included the couch cover, a pillow case and sheets taken from Eddie's bed, paint chips from the wall in Eddie's room, a child's undershirt and socks, and a three-by-five inch section of the living room rug. . . .

2. Sufficiency of the Evidence

We are asked . . . to decide whether the evidence was sufficient to support the verdict of first-degree murder. The defendant argues principally that premeditation was not shown. . . .

Our consideration of the sufficiency of the evidence is governed by the "well-settled rule that all conflicts in testimony, upon a conviction in the trial court, are resolved in favor of the State, and that upon appeal the State is entitled to the strongest legitimate view of the trial evidence and all reasonable or legitimate inferences which may be drawn therefrom." Nevertheless, the record must demonstrate that the state carried its burden at trial of establishing that the homicide in question was, indeed, first-degree murder. In this case, we conclude, the prosecution failed to discharge its burden. . . .

The statute in effect at the time of the homicide in this case defined first-degree murder as follows:

> Every murder perpetrated by means of poison, lying in wait, or by other kind of willful, deliberate, malicious, and premeditated killing, or committed in the perpetration of, or attempt to perpetrate, any murder in the first degree, arson, rape, robbery, burglary, larceny, kidnaping, aircraft piracy, or the unlawful throwing, placing or discharging of a destructive device or bomb, is murder in the first degree.

Based upon our review of the record, we conclude that the evidence in this case is insufficient to establish deliberation and premeditation. Hence, the defendant's conviction for first-degree murder cannot stand. However, we do find the evidence sufficient to sustain a conviction of second-degree murder. . . .

At common law, there were no degrees of murder, but the tendency to establish a subdivision by statute took root relatively early in the development of American law. The pattern was set by a 1794 Pennsylvania statute that identified the more heinous kinds of murder as murder in the first degree, with all other murders deemed to be murder in the second degree. Some states have subdivided the offense into three or even four degrees of murder, but since the enactment of the first such statute in 1829, Tennessee has maintained the distinction at two. It is one which this Court has found to be "not only founded in mercy and humanity, but . . . well fortified by reason."

From the beginning, the statutory definition of first-degree murder required the state to prove that "the killing [was] done willfully, that is, of purpose, with intent that the act by which the life of a party is taken should have that effect; deliberately, that is, with cool purpose; maliciously, that is, with malice aforethought; and with premeditation, that is, a design must be formed to kill, before the act, by which the death is produced, is performed." Because conviction of second-degree murder also requires proof of intent and malice, the two distinctive elements of first-degree murder are deliberation and premeditation.

Even as early as 1872, however, prosecutors and judges had apparently fallen into the error of commingling these two elements by using the terms interchangeably. In Poole v. State, 61 Tenn. 28 (1872), for example, Justice Turney expounded upon the statutory distinction between deliberation and premeditation and the need to maintain them as separate elements of the first-degree murder:

> Proof must be adduced to satisfy the mind that the death of the party slain was the ultimate result which the conquering will, deliberation and premeditation of the party accused sought, making a marked distinction and independence between the terms "deliberation" and "premeditation" and excluding the idea of the substitution of the one for the other, or of the tautology in their use.

Intent to kill had long been the hallmark of common law murder, and in distinguishing manslaughter from murder on the basis of intent, the courts recognized, in the words of an early Tennessee Supreme Court decision, that the law knows of no specific time within which an intent to kill must be formed so as to make it murder [rather than manslaughter]. If the will accompanies the act, a moment antecedent to the act itself which causes death, it seems to be as completely sufficient to make the offence murder, as if it were a day or any other time. Anderson v. State, 2 Tenn. (2 Overt.) 6, 9 (1804). Of course, the *Anderson* opinion predates the statutory subdivision of murder into first and second degrees. But the temporal concept initially associated in that case with intent, i.e., that no definite period of time is required for the formation of intent, was eventually carried over and applied to the analysis of premeditation. Hence, by the time the opinion in Lewis v. State, 40 Tenn. (3 Head) 127, 147–48, was announced in 1859, the Court had begun the process of commingling the concepts of intent, premeditation, and deliberation, as the following excerpt demonstrates:

> The distinctive characteristic of murder in the first degree, is premeditation. This element is superadded, by the statute, to the common law definition of murder. Premeditation involves a previously formed design, or actual intention to kill. But such design, or intention, may be conceived, and deliberately formed, in an instant. It is not necessary that it should have been conceived, or have pre-existed in the mind, any definite period of time anterior to its execution. It is sufficient that it preceded the assault, however short the interval. The length of time is not of the essence of this constituent of the offense. The purpose to kill is no less premeditated, in the legal sense of the term, if it were deliberately formed but a moment preceding the act by which the death is produced, than if it had been formed an hour before.

It is this language ("premeditation may be formed in an instant") for which *Lewis* is frequently cited. What is often overlooked is the following language, also taken from *Lewis*:

> The mental state of the assailant at the moment, rather than the length of time the act may have been premeditated, is

> the material point to be considered. The mental process, in the formation of the purpose to kill, may have been instantaneous, and the question of vital importance is—was the mind, at that moment, so far free from the influence of excitement, or passion, as to be capable of reflecting and acting with a sufficient degree of coolness and deliberation of purpose; and was the death of the person assaulted, the object to be accomplished—the end determined upon.

Hence, perhaps the two most oft-repeated propositions with regard to the law of first-degree murder, that the essential ingredient of first-degree murder is premeditation and that premeditation may be formed in an instant, are only partially accurate, because they are rarely quoted in context. In order to establish first-degree murder, the premeditated killing must also have been done deliberately, that is, with coolness and reflection. As noted in Rader v. State, 73 Tenn. 610, 619–20 (1880):

> When the murder is not committed in the perpetration of, or attempt to perpetrate any of the felonies named in the [statute], then, in order to constitute murder in the first degree, it must be perpetrated by poison or lying in wait, or some other kind of willful, deliberate, malicious, and premeditated killing; that is to say, the deliberation and premeditation must be akin to the deliberation and premeditation manifested where the murder is by poison or lying in wait—the cool purpose must be formed and the deliberate intention conceived in the mind, in the absence of passion, to take the life of the person slain. Murder by poison or lying in wait, are given as instances of this sort of deliberate and premeditated killing, and in such cases no other evidence of the deliberation and premeditation is required; but where the murder is by other means, proof of deliberation and premeditation is required. It is true it has been held several times that the purpose need not be deliberated upon any particular length of time—it is enough if it precede the act, but in all such cases the purpose must be coolly formed, and not in passion, or, if formed in passion, it must be executed after the passion has had time to subside. . . . If the purpose to kill is formed in passion . . . , and executed without time for the passion to cool, it is not murder in the first degree, but murder in the second degree.

The obvious point to be drawn from this discussion is that even if intent (or "purpose to kill") and premeditation ("design") may be formed in an instant, deliberation requires some period of reflection, during which the mind is "free from the influence of excitement, or passion."

Despite admonitions in the opinions of the Tennessee Supreme Court during the nineteenth century and early part of the twentieth century regarding the necessity of maintaining a clear line of demarcation between first-and second-degree murder, that line has been substantially blurred in later cases. The culprit appears to be the shortcutting of analysis, commonly along three or four different tracks.

One of those has been the same error decried by Justice Turney in 1872, i.e., the use of the terms "premeditation" and "deliberation" interchangeably, or sometimes collectively, to refer to the same concept. Thus, in Sikes v. State, 524 S.W.2d 483, 485 (Tenn. 1975), the Court said: "Deliberation and premeditation involve a prior intention or design on the part of the defendant to kill, however short the interval between the plan and its execution." While this statement focuses on premeditation, nowhere in the brief discussion that follows is there any reference to the coolness of purpose or reflection that is required under the older cases to establish deliberation as a separate and distinct element of first-degree murder. . . .

Another weakness in our more recent opinions is the tendency to overemphasize the speed with which premeditation may be formed. The cases convert the proposition that no specific amount of time between the formation of the design to kill and its execution is required to prove first-degree murder, into one that requires virtually no time lapse at all, overlooking the fact that while intent (and perhaps even premeditation) may indeed arise instantaneously, the very nature of deliberation requires time to reflect, a lack of impulse, and, as the older cases had held at least since 1837, a "cool purpose." . . .

One further development in Tennessee law has tended to blur the distinction between the essential elements of first-and second-degree murder, and that is the matter of evidence of "repeated blows" being used as circumstantial evidence of premeditation. Obviously, there may be legitimate first-degree murder cases in which there is no direct evidence of the perpetrator's state of mind. Since that state of mind is crucial to the establishment of the elements of the offense, the cases have long recognized that the necessary elements of first-degree murder may be shown by circumstantial evidence. Relevant circumstances recognized by other courts around the country have included the fact "that a deadly weapon was used upon an unarmed victim; that the homicidal act was part of a conspiracy to kill persons of a particular class; that the killing was particularly cruel; that weapons with which to commit the homicide were procured; that the defendant made declarations of his intent to kill the victim; or that preparations were made before the homicide for concealment of the crime, as by the digging of a grave." This list, although obviously not intended to be exclusive, is notable for the omission of "repeated blows" as circumstantial evidence of premeditation or deliberation.

In Tennessee, the use of repeated blows to establish the premeditation necessary to first-degree murder apparently traces to Bass v. State, 191 Tenn. 259, 231 S.W.2d 707 (1950). There the Court, after noting that "both premeditation and deliberation may be inferred from the circumstances of a homicide," went on to list a series of facts from which the Court concluded that the victim's death constituted first-degree murder. The first (but not the only) such circumstance mentioned was that "the deceased was not only struck and killed by a blow from an iron poker but apparently from the number and nature of his wounds, was beaten to death by a whole series of blows." While the *Bass* court did not interpret the fact of repeated blows to be sufficient, in and of itself, to constitute premeditation and deliberation, subsequent cases have done so. In Houston v. State, 593 S.W.2d 267, 273 (Tenn. 1980), for example, the only circumstance relied upon by the majority to establish premeditation and deliberation was the fact that the victim had sustained "repeated shots or blows."

Logically, of course, the fact that repeated blows (or shots) were inflicted on the victim is not sufficient, by itself, to establish first-degree murder. Repeated blows can be delivered in the heat of passion, with no design or reflection. Only if such blows are inflicted as the result of premeditation and deliberation can they be said to prove first-degree murder. . . .

This discussion leads us inevitably to the conclusion that Mack Brown's conviction for first-degree murder in this case cannot be sustained. . . .

Here, there simply is no evidence in the record that in causing his son's death, Mack Brown acted with the premeditation and deliberation required to establish first-degree murder. There is proof, circumstantial in nature, that the defendant acted maliciously toward the child, in the heat of passion or anger,[10] and without adequate provocation—all of which would make him guilty of second-degree murder. The only possible legal basis upon which the state might argue that a first-degree conviction can be upheld in this case is the proof in the record that the victim had sustained "repeated blows." It was on this basis, and virtually no other, that we upheld a similar first-degree murder conviction for the death of a victim of prolonged child abuse in State v. LaChance, 524 S.W.2d 933 (Tenn. 1975). In view of our foregoing discussion concerning the shortcomings of such an analysis, we find it necessary to depart from much of the rationale underlying that decision.

In abandoning *LaChance*, we are following the lead of a sister state. In Midgett v. State, 292 Ark. 278, 729 S.W.2d 410 (Ark. 1987), the Arkansas Supreme Court was asked to affirm the first-degree murder conviction of a father who had killed his eight-year-old son by repeated blows of his fist. As was the case here, there was a shocking history of physical abuse to the child, established both by eyewitness testimony and by proof of old bruises and healed fractures.

The Arkansas court faced a precedent much like *LaChance* in Burnett v. State, 287 Ark. 158, 697 S.W.2d 95 (1985). There the court had described the injuries sustained by the child victim and held, without more, that the "required mental state for first-degree murder can be inferred from the evidence of abuse, which is substantial." In confessing error in *Burnett*, the *Midgett* court noted:

> The appellant argues, and we must agree, that in a case of child abuse of long duration the jury could well infer that the perpetrator comes not to expect death of the child from his action, but rather that the child will live so that the abuse may be administered again and again. Had the appellant planned his son's death, he could have accomplished it in a previous beating. . . .
>
> The evidence in this case supports only the conclusion that the appellant intended not to kill his son but to further abuse him or that his intent, if it was to kill the child, was developed in a drunken, heated, rage while disciplining the child. Neither of those supports a finding of premeditation or deliberation.

---

[10] "Passion" has been defined as "any of the emotions of the mind [reflecting] anger, rage, sudden resentment, or terror, rendering the mind incapable of cool reflection."

The Arkansas court, in strengthening the requirements for proof of premeditation and deliberation in a first-degree murder case involving a victim of child abuse, found it necessary to overrule prior case law to the extent that it was inconsistent with the opinion in *Midgett*. We do the same here. Like the *Midgett* court, we do not condone the homicide in this case, or the sustained abuse of the defenseless victim, Eddie Brown. We simply hold that in order to sustain the defendant's conviction, the proof must conform to the statute. Because the state has failed to establish sufficient evidence of first-degree murder, we reduce the defendant's conviction to second-degree murder and remand the case for resentencing.

## NOTES ON FIRST-DEGREE MURDER

### 1. THE "PREMEDITATION AND DELIBERATION" FORMULA

As *Brown* explains, Pennsylvania was the first state to recognize degrees of murder. The innovation was introduced by a Pennsylvania statute adopted in 1794, which created a distinction between "first-degree" and "second-degree" murder. The statute provided:

> [A]ll murder, which shall be perpetrated by means of poison, or by lying in wait, or by any other kind of wilful, deliberate and premeditated killing, or which shall be committed in the perpetration or attempt to perpetrate any arson, rape, robbery, or burglary, shall be deemed murder in the first degree; and all other kinds of murder shall be deemed murder in the second degree.

The purpose of this legislation was to confine the capital sanction, which remained the mandatory penalty,[a] to first-degree murder. The statute was influential. The majority of American jurisdictions adopted similar provisions early in the 19th century. By 1959, the statutes in 34 jurisdictions were closely derived from the original Pennsylvania formula.

By far the most litigated issue under this statute was the meaning of the phrase "by any other kind of wilful, deliberate and premeditated killing." It clearly referred to an intentional killing, but the question was whether it was meant to include all intentional killings or to be limited to an intent to kill formed in a particular manner.[b]

#### *(i) The Pennsylvania Construction*

In his article, History of the Pennsylvania Statute Creating Degrees of Murder, 97 U.Pa.L.Rev. 759, 771–73 (1949), Edwin R. Keedy concluded that the Pennsylvania legislature originally intended the words "deliberate" and "premeditated" to be read literally. Nevertheless, the Pennsylvania courts did not construe the language in this manner: "Soon

---

[a] All states retained the mandatory death penalty for the most serious form of murder until 1838, when Tennessee adopted the first discretionary death penalty statute. Twenty-three American jurisdictions followed suit by the turn of the century, and by 1962 all American jurisdictions had adopted this modification of the common law system.

[b] Note that the statute begins with the words "all murder," then describes those forms of "murder" that fall into the first-degree category, and concludes by classifying "all other kinds of murder" as of the second degree. The statute thus built upon the common law definition of murder. Any form of common law murder not included in the first-degree category fell into the residual second-degree category.

after the statute was enacted the judges began to nullify its requirements by refusing to give effect to the meaning of the words 'deliberate' and 'premeditated,' and by announcing the proposition that killing with an intent to kill constitutes first-degree murder." As early as 1794, the year the degree statute was enacted, a Pennsylvania trial judge adopted this construction. Later pronouncements of the Pennsylvania courts were to the same effect. In Keenan v. Commonwealth, 44 Pa. 55, 56 (1862), the Pennsylvania Supreme Court summarized prior decisions with the comment that "our reported jurisprudence is very uniform in holding that the true criterion of the first degree is the intent to take life."

Modern Pennsylvania decisions reaffirmed this interpretation. In Commonwealth v. Carroll, 412 Pa. 525, 526, 194 A.2d 911, 915 (1963), the court said:

> The specific intent to kill which is necessary to constitute . . . murder in the first degree may be found from a defendant's words or conduct or from the attendant circumstances together with all reasonable inferences therefrom, and may be inferred from the intentional use of a deadly weapon on a vital part of the body of another human being. . . . Whether the intention to kill and the killing, that is, the premeditation and the fatal act, were within a brief space of time or a long space of time is immaterial if the killing was in fact intentional, wilful, deliberate and premeditated.

This approach was by no means limited to Pennsylvania. Herbert Wechsler and Jerome Michael, in their classic article, A Rationale of the Law of Homicide I, 37 Colum.L.Rev. 701, 707–09 (1937), summarized the evolution of the American law of murder. "Malice aforethought," they said, was translated into "a term of art signifying neither 'malice' nor 'aforethought' in the popular sense." The same was true in some jurisdictions of the terms "deliberation" and "premeditation," which often were interpreted "to exclude the two elements which the words normally signify: a determination to kill reached (i) calmly and (ii) some appreciable time prior to the homicide." Prior to the 1967 revision based on the philosophy of the Model Penal Code, for example, New York law required a "deliberate and premeditated design to kill" for first degree murder and a "design" to kill "but without deliberation and premeditation" for second degree.[c] The elimination of calm reflection an appreciable time before the homicide from the first degree offense

> leaves, as Judge Cardozo pointed out, nothing precise as the critical state of mind but intention to kill. . . . The trial judge must solemnly distinguish in his charge between the two degrees in terms which frequently render them quite indistinguishable, a procedure which obviously confers on the jury a discretion to follow one aspect of the charge or the other, if not a valid excuse for neglecting the charge entirely. The statutory scheme was apparently intended to limit administrative discretion in the selection of capital cases. As so frequently occurs, the discretion which the

[c] The New York homicide statutes in effect when Michael and Wechsler wrote are reproduced in Appendix B.—[Footnote by eds.]

> legislature threw out the door was let in through the window by the courts.[d]

The reference to Judge Cardozo in the preceding excerpt was to a lecture given to the Academy of Medicine in 1928, subsequently published in Law and Literature 97–101 (1931). Judge Cardozo referred to New York decisions holding that "deliberate and premeditate" did not require planning "as where one lies in wait for one's enemy or places poison in his food or drink." All that was required "is that the act must not be the result of immediate or spontaneous impulse." It was sufficient if the defendant made "a choice . . . as the result of thought, however short." He concluded that the law was too vague to be continued in its then present form: .

> If intent is deliberate and premeditated whenever there is choice, then in truth it is always deliberate and premeditated, since choice is involved in the hypothesis of the intent. What we have is merely a privilege offered to the jury to find the lesser degree, when the suddenness of the intent, the vehemence of the passion, seems to call irresistibly for the exercise of mercy. I have no objection to giving them this dispensing power, but it should be given to them directly and not in a mystifying cloud of words. The present distinction is so obscure that no jury hearing it for the first time can fairly be expected to assimilate and understand it. . . . Upon the basis of this fine distinction with its obscure and mystifying psychology, scores of men have gone to their death. . . .

### *(ii) People v. Anderson*

As *Brown* illustrates, other courts have given the formula a more literal meaning. Consider, for example, People v. Anderson, 70 Cal.2d 15, 73 Cal.Rptr. 550, 447 P.2d 942 (1968). Anderson was convicted of the first-degree murder of a 10-year old girl and sentenced to death. He had been living with the girl's mother for about eight months prior to the homicide. On the morning of the murder, the mother went to work, leaving Anderson at home alone with the girl. Anderson had not worked for two days and had been drinking heavily. The girl's nude body was discovered in her bedroom by her brother that evening after the mother returned from work. More than 60 knife wounds, some severe and some superficial, were found on her body, including the partial amputation of her tongue and a post-mortem cut extending from the rectum through the vagina. There was no evidence of sexual molestation prior to the death. Blood was found in every room of the house.

The court held that there was insufficient evidence of premeditation and deliberation and that the killing therefore should be reduced to murder in the second degree. It began by noting that it was "well established that the brutality of a killing cannot in itself support a finding that the killer acted with premeditation and deliberation." The court continued:

> [W]e find no indication that the legislature intended to give the words "deliberate" and "premeditated" other than their ordinary dictionary meanings. Moreover, we have repeatedly pointed

[d] The early New York cases as well as those of four states that patterned their law on the New York model are analyzed in James K. Knudson, Murder by the Clock, 24 Wash. U.L.Q. 305 (1939). The results confirm the general conclusions advanced by Wechsler and Michael.—[Footnote by eds.]

> out that the legislative classification of murder into two degrees would be meaningless if "deliberation" and "premeditation" were construed as requiring no more reflection than may be involved in the mere formation of a specific intent to kill.
>
> Thus we have held that in order for a killing with malice aforethought to be first-rather than second-degree murder, " '[t]he intent to kill must be . . . formed upon a *pre-existing* reflection' [and must have] been the subject of actual deliberation or *forethought*." We have therefore [required that the killer act] "as a result of careful thought and weighing of considerations; as a *deliberate* judgment or plan; carried on coolly and steadily, [especially] according to a *preconceived design*."

The court then held that evidence of premeditation and deliberation generally fell into three patterns: evidence of "planning" activity, evidence of "motive," and evidence as to the "manner" of the killing that showed a preconceived design to kill. Most first-degree verdicts that it had sustained, the court said, contained evidence of all three types, though some had consisted of the second in conjunction with one of the other two. But Anderson's case, the court concluded, "lacks evidence of any of the three types." There was no evidence of planning or motive. And "the only inference" which the evidence as to the manner of the killing supports "is that the killing resulted from a 'random,' violent, indiscriminate attack rather than from deliberately placed wounds inflicted according to a preconceived design."[e]

## 2. QUESTIONS AND COMMENTS ON *BROWN*

In *Brown*, the court endeavored to reverse years of judicial erosion of the distinction between killings that merely are intentional, on the one hand, and those that are premeditated and deliberate, on the other. The distinction is of practical significance: the latter killings are eligible for the most severe punishments known to our law, while the former killings are punished less harshly. The court aimed to give each word—"intentional," "premeditated," "deliberate," as well as "maliciously"—a distinct meaning. At one early point in its opinion, the court quoted this effort to define these crucial words:

> [The state must] prove that "the killing [was] done willfully, that is, of purpose, with intent that the act by which the life of a party is taken should have that effect; deliberately, that is, with cool purpose; maliciously, that is with malice aforethought; and with premeditation, that is, a design must be formed to kill, before the act, by which the death is produced, is performed."

---

[e] Compare Washington v. Bingham, 40 Wash.App. 553, 699 P.2d 262 (1985), where the court said:

> [R]eview of [prior Washington] cases reveals that in each one where the evidence has been found sufficient, there has been some evidence beyond time from which a jury could infer the fact of deliberation. This evidence has included, inter alia, motive, acquisition of a weapon, and planning directly related to the killing.
>
> Unless evidence of both time for and fact of deliberation are required, premeditation could be inferred in any case where the means of effecting death requires more than a moment in time. For all practical purposes, it would merge with intent; proof of intent would become proof of premeditation. However, the two elements are separate. Premeditation cannot be inferred from intent.

Thereafter, the court tried to clarify and illustrate each of these distinctions. Was it successful?

This rhetorical exercise takes on added urgency when one contemplates the need to draft instructions in terms that allow jurors to understand their function and to grasp and apply the crucial terms. Presumably, some version of the preceding language provides the basis for jury instructions in homicide cases in Tennessee. If so, are jurors likely to understand the nuances in meaning that the court has in mind and, most crucially, those that determine the fate of defendants such as Mack Brown? How would one rewrite these instructions to make them more accessible to jurors?

Quite apart from the question of how to define the state of mind signified by "premeditation and deliberation" is the question of how the state proves that a particular killer acted with that state of mind. *Brown* refers to some of the circumstantial evidence that courts have cited as creating an inference of premeditation and deliberation. Such evidence has:

> included the fact "that a deadly weapon was used upon on an unarmed victim; that the homicidal act was part of a conspiracy to kill persons of a particular class; that the killing was particularly cruel; that weapons with which to commit the homicide were procured; that the defendant made declarations of his intent to kill the victim; or that preparations were made before the homicide for concealment of the crime, as by the digging of a grave."

According to the court, the prosecutors who tried Mack Brown produced no such evidence, but relied exclusively on the fact that Brown killed Eddie with "repeated blows." The court then rejects the notion that proof that "repeated blows (or shots) were inflicted on the victim" alone can be sufficient to satisfy the requirements for first-degree murder. If the prosecutors in *Brown* could have predicted that the Tennessee Supreme Court would use this case as the occasion for reinvigorating the distinctions between "intent" and "premeditation-deliberation," is there some other strategy they might have pursued in an effort to prove that Mack Brown did premeditate and deliberate? For example, does further scrutiny of the fact pattern provided by the case yield any of the "circumstantial evidence" of premeditation and deliberation that the court approves? Consider too the various items on that list. Does each of them—alone or in some combination—permit an inference of premeditation and deliberation?

The court reduced Brown's conviction from first-degree murder to second-degree murder. Why is he guilty of second-degree murder? At one point, the court asserted that a conviction for second-degree murder requires proof of "intent and malice." If so and if by "intent" the court means "purpose," does the case contain any evidence that Brown intended to kill Eddie? At the time that Brown was prosecuted, Tennessee authorized second-degree murder liability in some categories of non-intentional homicides, such as those where the actor intended (only) to inflict grievous bodily harm and those that demonstrated extreme indifference to the value of human life. Although it does not say so, the court might have had one or both of those possibilities in mind when reducing Brown's conviction to second-degree murder.

### 3. MODERN UTILITY OF THE FORMULA

A number of states retain the premeditation-deliberation doctrine to describe the highest category of criminal homicide. Some newer statutes, however, have followed the Model Penal Code in abandoning that formula. In states where the phrase had been interpreted to include every intentional killing, deleting the language in favor of a phrase such as "intent to kill" merely clarifies the inquiry the jury is expected to undertake. In states where the formula had been taken more literally, some legislatures have been convinced that it does not accurately separate the more heinous forms of murder from the less heinous, regardless of whether the most serious class of offenses is punishable by death. They have concluded, in essence, that the formula does not reflect an intelligible policy for the grading of criminal homicides. Long ago, Sir James Fitzjames Stephen asked the question vividly:

> As much cruelty, as much indifference to the life of others, a disposition at least as dangerous to society, probably even more dangerous, is shown by sudden as by premeditated murders. The following cases appear to me to set this in a clear light. A man passing along the road, sees a boy sitting on a bridge over a deep river and, out of mere wanton barbarity, pushes him into it and so drowns him. A man makes advances to a girl who repels him. He deliberately but instantly cuts her throat. A man civilly asked to pay a just debt pretends to get the money, loads a rifle and blows out his creditor's brains. In none of these cases is there premeditation unless the word is used in a sense as unnatural as "aforethought" in "malice aforethought," but each represents even more diabolical cruelty and ferocity than that which is involved in murders premeditated in the natural sense of the word.

3 A History of the Criminal Law of England 94 (1883).

Quite apart from concerns about capital punishment, does the premeditation-deliberation formula serve a modern function? Should Anderson be included in the highest category of murder? Brown?

Samuel Pillsbury argues that, as a proxy for the worst forms of homicide, the formula is under-and over-inclusive. As he puts it, "[p]remeditation assumes that the worst wrongs involve the most extended, dispassionate consideration of wrongdoing, and while this is often so, it is not always."[f] Pillsbury agrees with Stephen that the spontaneous killer may be as, and sometimes more, culpable than the actor who broods over his crime. He also argues that some premeditated and deliberate killings (say, those committed for profit) are far more culpable than others (say, those committed to relieve the pain of a person who is seriously ill). In other words, "what premeditation misses is the moral importance of the motive for homicide." Hence, Pillsbury proposes that the most serious degree of murder should be defined as a "purposeful" killing that is committed for one of several statutorily specified motives, including "to assert cruel power over another." Would a jury be justified in finding that Mack Brown had killed for that motive?

---

[f] Samuel H. Pillsbury, Judging Evil: Rethinking the Law of Murder and Manslaughter 99 (1998).

The Tennessee legislature ultimately came to agree that homicides similar to that perpetrated by Mack Brown should be defined as first-degree murder. Their solution was to add "aggravated child abuse" and "aggravated child neglect" to the list of predicate felonies whose commission qualify offenders for felony murder liability where the consequence of the abuse or neglect is a death. Is that solution preferable to the more general, open-ended approach endorsed by Pillsbury?

## People v. Roe

Court of Appeals of New York, 1989.
74 N.Y.2d 20, 544 N.Y.S.2d 297, 542 N.E.2d 610.

■ HANCOCK, JUDGE. In defendant's appeal from his conviction for depraved indifference murder[1] for the shooting death of a 13-year-old boy, the sole question we address is the legal sufficiency of the evidence. Defendant, a 15½-year-old high school student, deliberately loaded a mix of "live" and "dummy" shells at random into the magazine of a 12-gauge shotgun. He pumped a shell into the firing chamber not knowing whether it was a "dummy" or a "live" round. He raised the gun to his shoulder and pointed it directly at the victim, Darrin Seifert, who was standing approximately 10 feet away. As he did so, he exclaimed "Let's play Polish roulette" and asked "Who is first?" When he pulled the trigger, the gun discharged sending a "live" round into Darrin's chest. Darrin died as a result of the massive injuries.

Defendant was convicted after a bench trial and the Appellate Division unanimously affirmed, holding that the evidence was legally sufficient to establish defendant's guilt. . . . On our review of the record, we conclude, as did the Appellate Division, that the proof is legally sufficient. Accordingly, there should be an affirmance. . . .

Before analyzing the evidence and its legal sufficiency, a brief examination of the crime of depraved indifference murder and its elements is instructive. Depraved indifference murder, like reckless manslaughter, is a nonintentional homicide. It differs from manslaughter, however, in that it must be shown that the actor's reckless conduct is imminently dangerous and presents a grave risk of death; in manslaughter, the conduct need only present the lesser "substantial risk" of death. See People v. Register, 60 N.Y.2d 270, 276, 469 N.Y.S.2d 599, 457 N.E.2d 704 (1983); see also People v. Gomez, 65 N.Y.2d 9, 11, 489 N.Y.S.2d 156, 478 N.E.2d 759 (1985). Whether the lesser risk sufficient for manslaughter is elevated into the very substantial risk present in murder depends upon the wantonness of defendant's acts—i.e., whether they were committed "[under] circumstances evincing a depraved indifference to human life." This is not a mens rea element which focuses "upon the subjective intent of the defendant, as it is with intentional murder"; rather it involves "an objective assessment of the degree of risk presented by defendant's reckless conduct."

---

[1] Penal Law § 125.25 [provides:]

A person is guilty of murder in the second degree when . . .

2. Under circumstances evincing a depraved indifference to human life, he recklessly engages in conduct which creates a grave risk of death to another person, and thereby causes the death of another person.

The only culpable mental state required for [depraved indifference] murder . . . is recklessness—the same mental state required for [second-degree] manslaughter. In a trial for [depraved indifference] murder, proof of defendant's subjective mental state is, of course, relevant to the element of recklessness, the basic element required for both manslaughter in the second degree and depraved indifference murder. Evidence of the actor's subjective mental state, however, is not pertinent to a determination of the additional element required for depraved indifference murder: whether the objective circumstances bearing on the nature of a defendant's reckless conduct are such that the conduct creates a very substantial risk of death.

Generally, the assessment of the objective circumstances evincing the actor's "depraved indifference to human life"—i.e., those which elevate the risk to the gravity required for a murder conviction—is a qualitative judgment to be made by the trier of the facts. If there is evidence which supports the jury's determination, it is this court's obligation to uphold the verdict. Examples of conduct which have been held sufficient to justify a jury's finding of depraved indifference include: driving an automobile on a city sidewalk at excessive speeds and striking a pedestrian without applying the brakes, see *Gomez*;[4] firing several bullets into a house, see People v. Jernatowski, 238 N.Y. 188, 144 N.E. 497 (1924); continually beating an infant over a five-day period, see People v. Poplis, 30 N.Y.2d 85, 330 N.Y.S.2d 365, 281 N.E.2d 167 (1972); and playing "Russian roulette" with one "live" shell in a six-cylinder gun, see Commonwealth v. Malone, 354 Pa. 180, 47 A.2d 445 (1946).

With this background, we turn to the issue before us, now more fully stated: whether, viewing the evidence in the light most favorable to the People, any rational trier of the facts could have concluded that the objective circumstances surrounding defendant's reckless conduct so elevated the gravity of the risk created as to evince the depraved indifference to human life necessary to sustain the murder conviction. A brief summary of the evidence is necessary.

On the afternoon of August 14, 1984, the day of the shooting, defendant was at his home in the Village of Buchanan, Westchester County. There is uncontraverted proof that defendant, who had completed his first year in high school, had an intense interest in and detailed knowledge of weapons, including firearms of various kinds. He was familiar with his father's 12-gauge shotgun and, indeed, had cleaned it approximately 50 times. The cleaning process involved oiling the firing pin and pulling the trigger, using a "dummy" shell to avoid "dry firing" the weapon.[6]

At approximately 3:00 p.m., Darrin and his friend, Dennis Bleakley, also a 13-year-old, stopped by to await the arrival of Darrin's older brother who was expected shortly. Defendant entertained the two boys by showing them his sawed-off shotgun, gravity knife, and Chuka

---

[4] In attempting to "emphasize the particular escalating depravity facts" in *Gomez,* the dissent overlooks the fact that in *Gomez* we upheld two counts of depraved indifference murder—one for the first victim struck and one for the second. Thus, we obviously did not find it necessary that one person be struck first for the conduct to constitute depraved indifference.

[6] According to defendant, "dry firing" is releasing the firing pin when there is no cartridge in the chamber and nothing for the pin to strike against. To avoid the damage to the pin which "dry firing" can cause, "dummy" cartridges are used.

sticks which he kept in a bag under his bed; he demonstrated how he assembled and disassembled the sawed-off shotgun.

Defendant then escorted Darrin and Dennis to his parents' room where he took out his father's 12-gauge shotgun. He asked Darrin to go back to his bedroom to get the five shotgun shells which were on the shelf. Defendant knew that three of these shells were "live" and two were "dummies." He randomly loaded four of the five shells into the magazine and pumped the shotgun, thereby placing one shell in the firing chamber. Because he loaded the magazine without any regard to the order in which the shells were inserted, he did not know if he had chambered a "live" or "dummy" round.

It was at this point, according to Dennis's testimony, that defendant raised the shotgun, pointed it directly at Darrin, and said "Let's play Polish roulette. Who is first?" He pulled the trigger discharging a "live" round which struck the 82-pound Darrin at close range. The shot created a gaping wound in Darrin's upper right chest, destroyed most of his shoulder, produced extensive damage to his lung, and eventually caused his death.

Defendant disputed this version of the incident. He testified that he had one foot on his parents' bed and was resting the butt of the gun on his inner thigh with the barrel pointing up and away from the victim. While he was demonstrating how the gun worked, he claimed, his foot slipped and the shotgun became airborne momentarily. Defendant testified that when he attempted to catch the gun, the butt kicked up under his armpit and he accidentally hit the trigger and discharged the gun.

The evidence of the objective circumstances surrounding defendant's point-blank discharge of the shotgun is, in our view, sufficient to support a finding of the very serious risk of death required for depraved indifference murder. Because the escalating factor—depraved indifference to human life—is based on an objective assessment of the circumstances surrounding the act of shooting and not the mens rea of the actor, the evidence stressed by the dissent concerning defendant's mens rea—his emotional condition in the aftermath of the killing—is beside the point.[7] Also without relevance are the dissent's references to defendant's claimed ignorance concerning the order in which cartridges, once loaded in the magazine, would enter the firing chamber. Such lack of knowledge can make no difference when, as is concededly the case here, the shooter knowingly loaded the mix of "live" and "dummy" cartridges with no regard to the order of their insertion into the magazine.

The comparable case here is not that of a person, uneducated in use of weapons, who, while playing with a gun that he does not know is loaded, accidentally discharges it; rather, the apt analogy is a macabre game of chance where the victim's fate—life or death—may be decreed by the flip of a coin or a roll of a die. It is no different where the odds

---

[7] 2 LaFave & Scott, Substantive Criminal Law § 7.4 (b), at 204–205, cited by the dissent is not to the contrary. Evidence of defendant's conduct and emotional state after the shooting might be relevant to show his subjective awareness of the risk—an element essential to establish the underlying mens rea of recklessness. Here, however, there is no dispute that defendant acted recklessly. The only question is whether the crime conduct creates the very substantial risk of death necessary for depraved indifference. *Gomez* and *Register* make it clear that this element is to be objectively assessed and that defendant's subjective mens rea is not relevant on this point.

are even that the shell pumped into the firing chamber of a 12-gauge shotgun is a "live" round, the gun is aimed at the victim standing close by, and the trigger is pulled. See 2 Wayne R. LaFave & Austin W. Scott, Jr., Substantive Criminal Law § 7.4, at 202 (1986) ("Russian roulette" with one "live" shell in a six-chamber gun is a classic example of depraved indifference murder).

The sheer enormity of the act—putting another's life at such grave peril in this fashion—is not diminished because the sponsor of the game is a youth of 15. As in *Register*, where bullets which might kill or seriously injure someone, or hit no one at all, were fired at random into a crowded bar, the imminent risk of death was present here. That in one case the gamble is that a bullet might not hit anyone and in the other that the gun might not fire is of no moment. In each case, the fact finder could properly conclude that the conduct was so wanton as to amount to depraved indifference to human life.

It is conceivable that another trier of fact hearing this evidence could have been persuaded to arrive at a different verdict. From the dissenter's extensive discussion of the proof and the inferences he would draw therefrom, it is evident that he would have done so. Our proper function on appeal, however, is vastly different from that of the prosecutor in determining which crimes to charge, that of the Judge or jury in hearing the evidence and making factual conclusions, or that of the Appellate Division in reviewing the facts and exercising, where it chooses, its interest of justice jurisdiction. We do not find facts or exercise such discretion. Our sole authority is to review legal questions such as the one considered here: whether the evidence was legally insufficient. As to this question, we have little difficulty in concluding that the unanimous Appellate Division correctly held that the evidence was sufficient to support the verdict. . . .

■ BELLACOSA, JUDGE, dissenting. I vote to reverse this conviction of a 15-year-old person for the highest degree of criminal homicidal responsibility—depraved indifference murder. The evidence adduced, the statutory scheme under which defendant was charged, and the legislative intent behind it do not support the disproportionate level of maximum blameworthiness imposed here. Moreover, this result finalizes the obliteration of the classical demarcation between murder and manslaughter in this State. . . .

From common law times to modern penal code days, the tragic incident at the heart of this case has qualified as the paradigmatic manslaughter with recklessness as the culpable mental state or mens rea. . . .

One of the three definitions of murder in this State is recklessly engaging in conduct which creates a grave risk of death and causing the death of another under circumstances evincing a depraved indifference to human life. That is the one at issue in this case. Manslaughter, second degree, is defined as recklessly causing the death of another person. This court has held that both of those crimes (the first an "A–I" felony carrying a mandatory sentence of at least 15 years to life, and the lesser being a "C" felony qualifying for 4½ to 15 years) require the same culpable mental state, i.e., acting recklessly when aware of and consciously disregarding a substantial and unjustifiable risk. But that culpable mental state, taken alone, supports and defines only manslaughter unless elevated to murder by reckless conduct, which additionally creates a grave risk under circumstances evincing a depraved indifference to human life. The catapulting ingredients are gravity and depravity. Other synonyms used to try to understand the essence of the escalating difference include malignant, malicious, callous, cruel, wanton, unremorseful, reprehensible and the like. The semantics alone prove that the analysis necessarily includes some subjective, gradational assessment.

While the tangible content of "depraved indifference to human life" is thus elusive, the wantonness of the conduct augmenting the reckless culpable mental state must also manifest a level of callousness and extreme cruelty as to be "equal in blameworthiness to intentional murder." I allude to some of the same case illustrations in this regard as the majority does, except I emphasize the particular escalating depravity facts that the majority avoids: firing a gun three times in a packed barroom, having boasted in advance an intention to kill someone, see People v. Register, 60 N.Y.2d 270, 469 N.Y.S.2d 599, 457 N.E.2d 704 (1983); driving a car at high speed on a crowded urban street and failing to apply the brakes after striking one person, see People v. Gomez, 65 N.Y.2d 9, 489 N.Y.S.2d 156, 478 N.E.2d 759 (1985); continuously beating a young child over a five-day period, see People v. Poplis, 30 N.Y.2d 85, 330 N.Y.S.2d 365, 281 N.E.2d 167 (1972).

The depraved indifference category of murder reflects the Legislature's policy refinement that there is a type of reckless homicide that is so horrendous as to qualify, in a legal fiction way, for blameworthiness in the same degree as the taking of another's life intentionally, purposefully, and knowingly. It is treated equally with the common law antecedent of premeditated murder with malice aforethought. Early cases reveal that the concept of "depraved mind" murder as an escalating factor emerged from this common law notion and was applied in cases where, despite evidence that a defendant had no desire to kill, the conduct nonetheless demonstrated a substitutive aggravating "malice in the sense of a wicked disposition." Modern statutes have borrowed and recast the concept "of a wicked disposition" to speak in terms of "extreme indifference to the value of human life." The predecessor of New York's present statute used an "act imminently dangerous to others" and was interpreted to apply, consistent with its exceptionability, only in cases where defendant's conduct created a danger to a multitude of persons rather than to just one individual. The language of the statute was expanded in 1967 to apply to persons who engage in "conduct which creates a grave risk of death to another person" and has been construed to apply to an attack directed at a single person.

The latest significant case, involving far more egregious conduct than is present in the instant case and held to constitute depraved indifference murder, evoked a warning, albeit in dissent, of the "evisceration" of the "distinction" between manslaughter and murder, see *Register*, at 284 (Jasen, J., dissenting). In my view, today's application completes the homogenization. . . .

I disagree that defendant's conduct qualifies for this lofty homicidal standard. He acted recklessly, of that there can be no doubt. . . . But the accusation and the conviction at the highest homicidal level, predicated on callous depravity and complete indifference to human life, are not supportable against this 15-year-old on a sufficiency review and are starkly contradicted by the whole of the evidence adduced.

This "crime is classified as murder and the murder penalty should be imposed 'only when the degree of risk approaches certainty; that is, at the point where reckless homicide becomes knowing homicide.'" Here, defendant's actions cannot be said to have created an almost certain risk of death. The mathematical probabilities, the objective state of mind evidence at and around the critical moment, the ambiguity in the evidence as to the operational order in the firing of the weapon, and all the circumstances surrounding this tragic incident all render the risk uncertain and counterindicate depravity, callousness, and indifference of the level fictionally equalling premeditated, intentional murder. That central and essential element of the crime charged was not proved beyond a reasonable doubt and that has been for a very long time a classically reviewable issue in this court. . . .

The testimony of the only other eyewitness, Dennis Bleakley, established that defendant was shaken and distraught immediately upon realizing that he had shot their companion. Defendant also immediately ran to his victim and instructed Dennis to call an ambulance; the neighbor testified that when she arrived on the scene, seconds after hearing the shot, defendant was kneeling over his friend's body and crying. Similarly, the police officer who arrived on the scene testified that defendant was extremely distraught and overcome with grief. This is not evidence beyond a reasonable doubt of that hardness of heart or that malignancy of attitude qualifying as "depraved indifference." Frankly, the evidence proves the opposite.

Nor should evidence of the "objective circumstances surrounding the act of the shooting"—the essential elevating element of the crime—be discarded as "beside the point" and artificially cut off as of the moment of the flash of the weapon. This is a substantial and new evidentiary restriction and one that has been rejected by a leading authority. See 2 LaFave & Scott, supra, § 7.4, at 204–05. Indeed, the very section of that text relied upon by the majority is antithetical to the majority's approach and supports the view advanced in this dissent in this regard: "[on] balance, it would seem that, to convict of murder, with its drastic personal consequences, subjective realization should be required," and evidence of a defendant's conduct in stopping and aiding a victim, whom he had struck and fatally injured, was admissible "to 'negative the idea of wickedness of disposition and hardness of heart' required for depraved-heart murder." Under the majority's cramped approach, one must wonder whether res gestae conduct will be foreclosed in a prosecution attempt to prove a real depravity set of circumstances in some other depraved murder case. More to the point here and for the defense side of cases yet to come, the majority appears also to be significantly preventing the evidentiary development of ameliorating or contradicting factors with respect to depravity. Both sides and the truth-seeking process itself lose with this antiseptic evidentiary embargo. . . .

By . . . catapulting the defendant's admittedly reckless criminal act to one "evincing depraved indifference to human life," the court functionally and finally discards and disregards the legislatively drawn distinction between manslaughter and murder. Prosecutors will find the temptation legally and strategically irresistible, and overcharging traditional reckless manslaughter conduct as the more serious murderous conduct will become standard operating procedure in view of the authorized template given for that course of action. Some very disproportionate miscarriages of justice—this case is one of them—will certainly ensue from this prosecutorial leverage in elevating reckless manslaughter to murder. It is difficult to imagine, after this case, any intentional murder situation not being presented to the Grand Jury with a District Attorney's request for a depraved indifference murder count as well. Thus, the exception designed as a special fictional and functional equivalent to intentional murder becomes an automatic alternative and additional top count accusation, carrying significant prejudicial baggage in its terminology alone. That devastating advantage, among others, given to the prosecution provides an unjust double opportunity for a top count murder conviction and an almost certain fallback for conviction on the lesser included crime of manslaughter. . . .

[T]o uphold this defendant's conviction on the uppermost and most heinous level of criminal homicidal responsibility cheapens the gravity with which we treat far more serious murders, e.g., cold-blooded contract killings and the like. In the eyes of the law all the slayers are now made alike, when the perpetrators themselves know and our best instincts and intelligence tell us, too, that they are very different. Justice is disfigured by the punishment of offenders so homogeneously and, yet, so disproportionately.

## NOTES ON SECOND-DEGREE MURDER

### 1. COMMON LAW BACKGROUND

Leaving aside the felony murder doctrine, which is covered later in this chapter, the common law recognized two kinds of unintentional homicide as murder. The first was based on intent to inflict grievous bodily injury. The second, which effectively subsumes the first, was based on a theory of recklessness or negligence that reached a high degree of callousness or indifference to life.

### *(i) Commonwealth v. Malone*

The second theory is illustrated by the well-known case of Commonwealth v. Malone, 354 Pa. 180, 47 A.2d 445 (1946). Malone, then 17 years old, engaged in a game of Russian Roulette with a 13-year-old friend. He loaded one chamber of a pistol that held five bullets and, with his friend's consent, held the gun to his friend's side and pulled the trigger three times. The gun fired on the third try and Malone's friend died from the wound two days later. Malone was convicted of second-degree murder.

The conviction was affirmed on appeal. The court reasoned that "the 'grand criterion' which 'distinguished murder from other killing' was malice on the part of the killer and this malice was not necessarily 'malevolent to the deceased particularly' but 'any evil design in general; the dictate of a wicked, depraved and malignant heart.'" The court continued:

> When an individual commits an act of gross recklessness for which he must reasonably anticipate that death to another is likely to result, he exhibits that "wickedness of disposition, hardness of heart, cruelty, recklessness of consequences, and a mind

regardless of social duty" which proved that there was at that time in him "the state or frame of mind termed malice." This court has declared that if a driver "wantonly, recklessly, and in disregard of consequences" hurls "his car against another, or into a crowd" and death results from that act "he ought . . . to face the same consequences that would be meted out to him if he had accomplished death by wantonly and wickedly firing a gun." . . .

The killing . . . resulted from an act intentionally done . . . , in reckless and wanton disregard of the consequences. . . . The killing was, therefore, murder, for malice in the sense of a wicked disposition is evidenced by the intentional doing of an uncalled-for-act in callous disregard of its likely harmful effects on others. The fact that there was no motive for this homicide does not exculpate the accused. In a trial for murder proof of motive is always relevant but never necessary.

### *(ii) Questions and Comments*

As *Malone* reveals, American common law found the existence of malice in unintentional homicides—and distinguished between murder and manslaughter—on the basis of epithetical descriptions of the defendant's behavior. Did Malone have a "wicked, depraved and malignant heart"? Did Roe? How is a jury to be expected to answer such a question?

## 2. THE DEGREE OF CULPABILITY SUFFICIENT FOR MURDER

The New York statute at issue in *Roe* is derived from § 210.2(1)(b) of the Model Penal Code, which provides that it is murder if a homicide "is committed recklessly under circumstances manifesting extreme indifference to the value of human life." The Model Penal Code provision, in turn, is derived from the "depraved heart" formulation that constituted malice, and hence justified a murder conviction, at common law. What is the justification for grading this form of murder at the same level as intentional homicide? Are the Model Code and New York formulations an improvement over the questions asked in common law jurisdictions? Are the differences in language between the New York provision and the Model Penal Code significant? Which is better?

Note also that the Model Penal Code, in abandoning the Pennsylvania degree formulation, treats "extreme indifference" homicide in the highest category of murder. Is this justified? The New York grading structure is set forth in Appendix B. Did New York place people like Roe in the right grading category?

In *Roe*, the majority divides the inquiry to be made by factfinders into two parts. First, the jury must determine whether the defendant acted with a mens rea of recklessness. Second, the jury must determine whether the "objective circumstances bearing on the nature of a defendant's reckless conduct are such that the conduct creates a very substantial risk of death." If each of these determinations is made in the affirmative, the jury may convict the defendant of depraved indifference murder. Does the dissenting judge disagree with this statement of doctrine or merely with the sufficiency of the evidence to support the necessary findings?

More generally, precisely what is the element that distinguishes depraved indifference murder from involuntary manslaughter? Does "depraved indifference" refer to a unique mens rea element—to some special kind of recklessness focusing more on the defendant's subjective state of mind? Or does it create an additional objective standard, one that elevates the nature and degree of the risks taken by the actor? How, if at all, will the answer to these questions influence the course of litigation in these cases?

### 3. *NORTHINGTON V. STATE*

The revised Alabama statute provides that a person commits murder if:

> Under circumstances manifesting extreme indifference to human life, he recklessly engages in conduct which creates a grave risk of death to a person other than himself, and thereby causes the death of another person.

Northington v. State, 413 So.2d 1169 (Ala.Cr.App.1981), involved a mother convicted of murder for allowing her five-month old daughter to starve to death. The court reversed the conviction because it interpreted the statute to require "universal malice" and no such malice was shown in this case:

> Under whatever name, the doctrine of universal malice, depraved heart murder, or reckless homicide manifesting extreme indifference to human life is intended to embrace those cases where a person has no deliberate intent to kill or injure any *particular* individual. "The element of 'extreme indifference to human life,' by definition, does not address itself to the life of the victim, but to human life generally." People By and Through Russel v. District Court, 185 Colo. 78, [83,] 521 P.2d 1254, 1256 (1974). . . .
>
> The state presented no evidence that the defendant engaged in conduct "under circumstances manifesting extreme indifference to human life" for, while the defendant's conduct did indeed evidence an extreme indifference to the life of her child, there was nothing to show that the conduct displayed an extreme indifference to human life generally. Although the defendant's conduct created a grave risk of death to another and thereby caused the death of that person, the acts of the defendant were aimed at the particular victim and no other. Not only did the defendant's conduct create a grave risk of death to only her daughter and no other, but the defendant's actions (or inactions) were directed specifically against the young infant. This evidence does not support a conviction of murder. . . . The function of this section is to embrace those homicides caused by such acts as driving an automobile in a grossly wanton manner, shooting a firearm into a crowd or a moving train, and throwing a timber from a roof onto a crowded street.[a]

The court concluded by saying that it was "extremely reluctant to reverse the conviction" because of "the revolting and heartsickening details of

---

[a] The court quoted extensively from State v. Berge, 25 Wash.App. 433, 607 P.2d 1247 (1980), in support of this interpretation of the Alabama statute. *Berge,* in turn, identifies Darry v. People, 10 N.Y. 120 (1854), as the origin of the notion that "depraved mind" murder refers, as the court in *Darry* put it, to "general malice" and not "any affection of the mind having for its object a particular individual."—[Footnote by eds.]

this case."[b] "Yet, because our system is one of law and not of men, we have no other choice." Can this be right?

## SECTION 3: MANSLAUGHTER

### Freddo v. State

Supreme Court of Tennessee, 1913.
127 Tenn. 376, 155 S.W. 170.

■ WILLIAMS, J. The plaintiff in error, Raymond Freddo, was indicted . . . for the crime of murder in the first degree . . . and was found by the jury guilty of murder in the second degree; his punishment being fixed at 10 years imprisonment. [I]t is . . . urged . . . that the facts adduced did not warrant a verdict of guilty of a crime of degree greater than voluntary manslaughter, if guilt of any crime be shown.

[I]n the roundhouse department of the shops of the Nashville & Chattanooga Railway Company from 50 to 60 men were employed, among them being . . . Freddo and the deceased, Higginbotham. Freddo was at the time about 19 years of age; he had been from the age of four years an orphan; he had been reared thereafter in an orphanage, and yet later in the family of a Nashville lady, with result that he had been morally well trained. The proof shows him to have been a quiet, peaceable, high-minded young man of a somewhat retiring disposition. Due, perhaps, to the loss of his mother in his infancy, and to his gratitude to his foster mother, he respected womanhood beyond the average young man, and had a decided antipathy to language of obscene trend or that reflected on womanhood.

Deceased, Higginbotham, was about six years older than Freddo, [was taller than Freddo and outweighed him by about 30 pounds,] and was one of a coterie of the roundhouse employees, . . . given to the use . . . of the expression "son of a bitch"—meant to be taken as an expression of good fellowship or of slight deprecation. Deceased, prior to the date of the difficulty, had applied this epithet to . . . Freddo without meaning offense, but was requested by the latter to discontinue it, as it was not appreciated, but resented. It was not discontinued, but repeated, and Freddo so chafed under it that he again warned deceased not to repeat it; and the fact of Freddo's sensitiveness being noted by the mechanic, J.J. Lynch, under whom Freddo served as helper, Lynch sought out deceased in Freddo's behalf and warned him to desist. On Lynch's telling deceased of the offense given to plaintiff in error, and that "he will hurt you some day," deceased replied, "The son of a bitch, he won't do nothing of the kind." [D]eceased is shown to have been habitually foul-mouthed, overbearing, and "nagging and tormenting" in language, and at times in conduct.

On the afternoon of the tragedy, Higginbotham and Freddo were engaged . . . in the packing of a locomotive cylinder. . . . Deceased, so engaged, was in a squatting posture, holding a pinch bar. It appears that some one, thought by deceased to have been Freddo, had spilled oil on deceased's tool box, and as he proceeded with his work the latter, in hearing of the crew, remarked: "Freddo, what in the hell did you want

[b] The court's opinion did not elaborate on the facts beyond this cryptic statement.

to spill that oil on that box for. If some one spilled oil on your box, you would be raising hell, wouldn't you, you son of a bitch?" Freddo asked Higginbotham if he meant to call the former a son of a bitch, and was replied to in an angry and harsh tone: "Yes, you are a son of a bitch." The plaintiff in error, standing to the left of and about eight feet away from deceased, seeing deceased preparing to rise or rising from his squatting posture, seized a steel bar, one yard long and one inch thick, lying immediately at hand, and advancing struck deceased a blow on the side of his head, above the left ear, and extending slightly to the front and yet more to the rear of the head, but not shown to have been delivered from the rear. Deceased in rising had not gained an erect posture, but is described as stooping at the time the blow was delivered.

Plaintiff in error testified that deceased, in rising, was apparently coming at him; that deceased made a gesture, and had his hand behind him all the time; that he (Freddo) believed that Higginbotham was going to strike; and that he struck because of anger at the epithet and to defend himself, but would not have struck but for deceased's movement. It appears, however, that deceased had not gained a position where he could strike the accused, and it does not appear that he had anything in his hand with which to attack; and the evidence preponderates against the prisoner on the point of deceased's having his hand behind him.

[W]e deem the facts sufficient to show that plaintiff in error killed deceased under the impulse of sudden heat of passion; but, no matter how strong his passionate resentment was, it did not suffice to reduce the grade of the crime from murder to voluntary manslaughter, unless that passion were due to a provocation such as the law deemed reasonable and adequate—that is, a provocation of such a character as would, in the mind of an average reasonable man, stir resentment likely to cause violence, obscuring the reason, and leading to action from passion rather than judgment.

While the testimony indicates that plaintiff in error was peculiarly sensitive in respect of the use by another, as applied to him, of the opprobrious epithet used by deceased, yet we believe the rule to be firmly fixed on authority to the effect that the law proceeds in testing the adequacy of the provocation upon the basis of a mind ordinarily constituted—of the fair average mind and disposition. . . .

The rule in this state is, as it was at common law, that the law regards no mere epithet or language, however violent or offensive, as sufficient provocation for taking life. . . .

It is contended, however, that while the use of such an epithet may not of itself be sufficient cause for provocation, yet that, looked to in connection with the conduct of the deceased at the time of its utterance, in rising from a squatting to a stooping posture, just reached as the blow was delivered, the epithet and the act in combination make a cause of adequate provocation.

The common-law rule appears to be that an assault, too slight in itself to be a sufficient provocation, may become such when accompanied by offensive language. [But the jury was correctly charged on the] proper definitions of and distinctions between murder in the second degree and manslaughter. . . . The stroke having been delivered by plaintiff in error at a moment when deceased may have been found by the jury not to have been in a position to assault him, and since the determination of the fact whether the provocation relied upon in such a case is adequate or reasonable is, under a proper charge, for the jury, we hold that the errors assigned and here treated of are not well taken. . . .

Affirmed.

In view of the very good character of the young plaintiff in error, as disclosed in the record, and of the peculiar motive and the circumstances under which he acted, we feel constrained to and do recommend to the governor of the state that his sentence be commuted to such punishment as the executive may, in the light of this record and opinion, in his discretion think proper. To allow time for such application, execution of sentence is ordered stayed for 10 days from this date.

## NOTES ON THE MITIGATION OF MURDER TO MANSLAUGHTER

### 1. THE PROVOCATION FORMULA

At common law, the distinction between murder and manslaughter originally emerged as a device for isolating a class of offenders who would be subjected to capital punishment. Those convicted of murder received the mandatory death penalty; those convicted of manslaughter received a lesser sentence. It was in this context that the law of provocation developed. When American jurisdictions narrowed the category of murder to which capital punishment applied, the law continued to recognize the distinction between murder and manslaughter as a grading device. The provocation doctrine has proved to be remarkably durable. Today, every state employs some variation of the provocation formula to distinguish between two distinct grades of non-capital criminal homicide.

The origins of the doctrine and its early meaning were summarized in A.J. Ashworth, The Doctrine of Provocation, 35 Camb.L.J. 292, 293 (1976). Provocation emerged as a recognized mitigation in the 17th Century. It was presumed by the law that a killer acted from malice, which could be express or implied. Malice was implied in all cases where express malice was not proved. Provocation then entered the picture as a rebuttal to implied malice, "the theory being that such evidence showed that the cause of the killing lay not in some secret hatred or design in the breast of the slayer but rather in provocation given by the deceased which inflamed the slayer's passions." The various forms of provocation that would suffice for this purpose

> were conveniently summarised by Lord Holt, C.J., in his judgment in Mawgridge, [1707] Kel. 119, where the categories of provocation are set forth. It was generally agreed that any striking of the accused would be sufficient provocation, and Lord Holt discussed four further types of provocation which had been legally sufficient to rebut the implication of malice: (i) angry words followed by an assault, (ii) the sight of a friend or relative being beaten, (iii) the sight of a citizen being unlawfully deprived of his liberty, and (iv) the sight of a man in adultery with the accused's wife. The categories of provocation insufficient to reduce murder to manslaughter were (i) words alone, (ii) affronting gestures, (iii) trespass to property, (iv) misconduct by a child or servant, and (v) breach of contract.

The rule applied in *Freddo* that "the law regards no mere epithet . . . as sufficient provocation" is thus consistent with early descriptions of provocation. The same rule would be applied with equal rigor in many jurisdictions today. In such jurisdictions, courts refuse to give voluntary manslaughter instructions in cases where the alleged provoking event consisted of "words alone." Similarly, many jurisdictions continue to restrict the events that may constitute sufficient provocation to the categories identified by Ashworth. Where the defendant's evidence of provocation falls outside those categories, the evidence will be excluded. See 1 Paul H. Robinson, Criminal Law Defenses 484–86 (1984).

Beginning in the middle of the 19th century, however, a competing approach to provocation began to develop. For example, Maher v. People, 10 Mich. 212, 220–22 (1862), offered the following description of the provocation doctrine:

> The principle involved . . . would seem to suggest as the true general rule, that reason should, at the time of the act, be disturbed or obscured by passion to an extent which *might render* ordinary men, of fair average disposition, *liable* to act rashly or without due deliberation or reflection, and from passion, rather than judgment. . . .
>
> The judge, it is true, must, to some extent, assume to decide upon the sufficiency of the alleged provocation, when the question arises upon the admission of testimony, and when it is so clear as to admit of no reasonable doubt upon any theory, that the alleged provocation could not have had any tendency to produce such state of mind, in ordinary men, he may properly exclude the evidence; but, if the alleged provocation be such as to admit of any reasonable doubt, whether it might not have had such tendency, it is much safer, . . . and more in accordance with principle, to let the evidence go to the jury under the proper instructions. [T]he question of the reasonableness or adequacy of the provocation must depend upon the facts of each particular case. . . . The law can not with justice assume, by the light of past decisions, to catalogue all the various facts and combinations of facts which shall be held to constitute reasonable or adequate provocation. . . .

By rejecting the notion that the law should identify the precise categories of events that constitute adequate provocation, the *Maher* formulation represents a considerable departure from the traditional view of provocation. *Maher* implies that *any* event—not only those allowed by the traditional doctrine—may be sufficient provocation, as long as the event would inspire a "heat of passion" in the reasonable person. Rather than simply replacing the traditional doctrine with the *Maher* formulation, however, most jurisdictions appear to have merged the two approaches and thereby created a three-stage analysis: (i) the defendant must in fact have acted in a heat of passion based on sudden provocation; (ii) the provoking event must have been "legally adequate," i.e., the courts continue to exclude certain events, such as "mere epithets," from the mitigation even though the event may in fact have provoked "heat of passion" in the defendant; and (iii) the provocation must also have been of a sufficient degree to have excited the passions of a reasonable person. How many of these steps are applied in *Freddo?* Is the *Maher* approach preferable? The pre-19th century rule that ignores the third step?

## 2. RATIONALE FOR THE PROVOCATION FORMULA

These questions can be answered only by thinking about why the rule of provocation developed and, particularly, what (if anything) its modern function should be. It is helpful to subdivide this inquiry into three stages corresponding to the three analytical steps mentioned above.

### *(i) Defendant in Fact Provoked*

Why should it matter that the defendant killed in the "heat of passion" produced by a provoking event? The traditional answer to this question is that a killing which "is the result of temporary excitement" is substantially less blameworthy than a killing which is the result of "wickedness of heart or innate recklessness of disposition." State v. Gounagias, 88 Wash. 304, 311, 153 P. 9, 12 (1915). Glanville Williams offered a utilitarian refinement of this point when he remarked in Provocation and the Reasonable Man, [1954] Crim.L.Rev. 740, 742, that:

> Surely the true view of provocation is that it is a concession to "the frailty of human nature" in those exceptional cases where the legal prohibition fails of effect. It is a compromise, neither conceding the propriety of the act nor exacting the full penalty for it.

Are these explanations satisfactory? Is the person who kills in a "heat of passion" less dangerous than the "cold-blooded" killer? Is "heat of passion" more justified as a mitigation that excludes persons from the death penalty (its original function) than as a mitigation authorizing different terms of imprisonment (its modern function)?

### *(ii) Legally Adequate Provocation*

The notion that provocation should be limited to "legally adequate" categories has been rejected by the Model Penal Code and by many American statutes that have followed its lead. The drafters of the Model Code defend this result on the ground that blameworthiness "cannot be resolved successfully by categorization of conduct" and that the correct approach, as *Maher* suggested, is "to abandon preconceived notions of what constitutes adequate provocation and to submit that question to the jury's deliberation." ALI, Model Penal Code and Commentaries, § 210.3, p. 61 (1980). Which formulation is preferable? Does the concept of legally adequate provocation reduce the opportunity for ad hoc determinations by juries and thus contribute to the fairness of the criminal process? Should the requirement be retained for this or any other reason?

### *(iii) The Objective Standard*

Why should an objective standard be used to measure the mitigating significance of the provocation to which the defendant reacted? If a reasonable person would have been provoked to the point of losing self-control, is it fair to punish the defendant at all?[a] If the defendant was in fact provoked

---

[a] Compare Glanville Williams, Provocation and the Reasonable Man, [1954] Crim. L. Rev. 740, 742:

> Plausible as this formulation may appear, it creates a serious problem. In the law of contract and tort, and elsewhere in the criminal law, the test of the reasonable man indicates an ethical standard .... [Not so here.] The reason why provoked hom-

and acted in the "heat of passion," should not the grade of the offense at least be reduced below that of unprovoked intent-to-kill murders, however confident we are that ordinary people would have remained calm in the face of the provocation? On the other hand, does deterrence theory suggest that provocation should not be recognized as a mitigation, no matter how understandable the accused's passionate reaction? Consider the observations of Jerome Michael and Herbert Wechsler in A Rationale of the Law of Homicide II, 37 Colum.L.Rev. 1261, 1281–82 (1937), in connection with these questions. If it is to recognize provocation at all, the law must draw a difficult line:

> While it is true, it is also beside the point, that most men do not kill on even the gravest provocation; the point is that the more strongly they would be moved to kill by circumstances of the sort which provoked the actor to the homicidal act, and the more difficulty they would experience in resisting the impulse to which he yielded, the less does his succumbing serve to differentiate his character from theirs. But the slighter the provocation, the more basis there is for ascribing the actor's act to an extraordinary susceptibility to intense passion, to an unusual deficiency in those other desires which counteract in most men the desires which impel them to homicidal acts, or to an extraordinary weakness of reason and consequent inability to bring such desires into play.

Compare the observations in A.J. Ashworth, The Doctrine of Provocation, 35 Camb.L.J. 292, 307–09 (1976). He argues that the provocation mitigation rests on the ethics of justification as well as the ethics of excuse. He calls this "partial justification" in order to express "the moral notion that the punishment of wrongdoers is justifiable." But, he said:

> This is not to argue that it is ever morally right to kill a person who does wrong. Rather, the claim implicit in partial justification is that an individual is *to some extent* morally justified in making a punitive return against someone who intentionally causes him serious offence, and that this serves to differentiate someone who is provoked to lose his self-control and kill from the unprovoked killer. . . . The victim plays an important role in provocation cases, either as instigator of the conflict or by doing something which the accused regards as a wrong against him. . . . The complicity of the victim cannot and should not be ignored, for the blameworthiness of his conduct has a strong bearing on the court's judgment of the seriousness of the provocation and the reasonableness of the accused's failure to control himself. . . .

But, he continues, the idea of partial justification "should not be overemphasized." If allowed to dominate thinking about provocation, it could "lead the courts to indulge those who take the law into their own hands and deliberately wreak vengeance upon those who insult or wrong them." The subjective element of loss of self-control is an

---

icide is punished is to deter people from committing the offence; and it is a curious confession of failure on the part of the law to suppose that, notwithstanding the possibility of heavy punishment, an ordinary person will commit it. If the assertion were correct, it would raise serious doubts whether the offense should continue to be punished. [H]ow can it be admitted that the paragon of virtue, the reasonable man, gives way to provocation?

essential component. But an objective qualifier is equally essential, lest all provoked losses of temper be judged suitable for the mitigation.[b]

## 3. COOLING TIME

The traditional provocation doctrine includes a requirement that the killing occur before a sufficient interval has passed "to permit the passions to cool and to allow thought and reflection and reason to reassert itself."[c] Many courts have followed a three-step analysis of the cooling-time question similar to that employed for the main body of the provocation rule: (i) the defendant's passion must not in fact have abated; (ii) the passage of a period of time sufficient for reason to be restored will preclude the defense as a matter of law; and (iii) it is in any event a question for the jury whether a reasonable person would have cooled off in the interval between the provocation and the act of killing.

State v. Gounagias, 88 Wash. 304, 153 P. 9 (1915), is a vivid illustration of the operation of the cooling-time requirement. On the evening of April 19, 1914, the defendant got drunk—so drunk that he fell on the floor almost unconscious. The deceased made many insulting remarks about the defendant and his wife, and then sodomized the defendant while he lay there helpless. The next day, the defendant confronted the deceased about the sodomy; when they parted, the defendant asked the deceased not to tell anyone what had happened. However, the deceased spread the story widely, and numerous acquaintances taunted the defendant about the incident. On April 30, a revolver that the defendant had ordered on April 18 arrived, and he placed it in the mattress of his bed. The continual taunting caused the defendant severe emotional distress and frequent headaches. As a result, he stayed home from work on May 6. That evening, he went to a coffeehouse, where he again was taunted by about 10 of his acquaintances. He became so excited and enraged that, as he sought to testify, "he lost all control of his reason," and resolved to kill the deceased. He went home, picked up his gun and loaded it, went to the house where the deceased lived, entered the house, found the deceased asleep, and, without waking him, emptied the revolver into the deceased's head. He then returned to his house, removed the discharged cartridges, put the gun back in his mattress, and went to bed. He was arrested shortly thereafter.

The trial court excluded evidence of provocation, and the defendant was convicted of murder. On appeal, the Washington Supreme Court affirmed the conviction. The court first reviewed the law on provocation and the cooling-time requirement, and then reasoned:

---

[b] The ethical basis of the provocation mitigation is explored in Joshua Dressler, Rethinking Heat of Passion: A Defense in Search of a Rationale, 73 J.Crim.Law & Criminology 421 (1982). Dressler concludes that the mitigation should be derived from the ethics of excuse, not the ethics of justification. In particular, he argues that the provoked defendant is less blameworthy because his capacity for choice has been limited by the provoking situation. He also argues that under some circumstances—those "which would render the ordinarily reasonable and law-abiding person in the same situation liable to become so emotionally upset that he would be wholly incapable of controlling his conduct"—provocation should be a complete defense. For discussion of the exculpatory effect of situational excuse under present law, see the notes on duress and situational compulsion in Chapter VII.—[Footnote by eds.]

[c] State v. Lee, 36 Del. 11, 19, 171 A. 195, 198 (1933). Compare the language of the pre-*Furman* Georgia statute reproduced in Appendix B.

> The offered evidence makes it clear that the appellant knew and appreciated for days before the killing the full meaning of the words, signs, and vulgar gestures of his [acquaintances] which, as the offer shows, he had encountered from day to day for about three weeks following the original outrage, wherever he went. The final demonstration in the coffeehouse was nothing new. It was exactly what the appellant, from his experience for the prior three weeks, must have anticipated. To say that it alone tended to create the sudden passion and heat of blood essential to mitigation is to ignore the admitted fact that the same thing had created no such condition on its repeated occurrence during the prior three weeks. To say that these repeated demonstrations, coupled with the original outrage, *culminated* in a sudden passion and heat of blood when he encountered the same character of demonstration in the coffeehouse on the night of the killing, is to say that sudden passion and heat of blood in the mitigative sense may be a cumulative result of repeated reminders of a single act of provocation occurring weeks before, and this, whether that provocation be regarded as the original outrage or the spreading of the story among appellant's associates, both of which he knew and fully realized for three weeks before the fatal night. This theory of the cumulative effect of reminders of former wrongs, not of new acts of provocation by the deceased, is contrary to the idea of sudden anger as understood in the doctrine of mitigation. In the nature of the thing *sudden* anger cannot be cumulative. A provocation which does not cause instant resentment, but which is only resented after being thought upon and brooded over, is not a provocation sufficient in law to reduce intentional killing from murder to manslaughter. . . .
>
> The evidence offered had no tendency to prove sudden anger and resentment. On the contrary, it did tend to prove brooding thought, resulting in the design to kill. It was therefore properly excluded.

By contrast, the Supreme Court of California has suggested that the kind of evidence proffered in *Gounagias* may be mitigating, in spite (or, perhaps, because) of the passage of time involved. In People v. Berry, 18 Cal.3d 509, 134 Cal.Rptr. 415, 556 P.2d 777 (1976), the defendant killed his wife, whose name was Rachel, after a 10-day period during which she kept taunting him with the fact that she was sexually attracted to another man. Rachel disclosed that she recently had sexual relations with the other man, claimed she might be pregnant by him, showed the defendant pictures of herself with the other man, and demanded a divorce. On one occasion while the defendant and Rachel were driving, she "demanded immediate sexual intercourse with defendant in the car, which was achieved; however upon reaching their apartment, she again stated that she loved [the other man] and that she would not have intercourse with the defendant in the future." Three days before the killing occurred, the defendant and Rachel engaged in heavy petting at a movie theater. Later, in bed at home, Rachel announced that she had intended to have sex with the defendant, but explained that she had changed her mind because she was saving herself for the other man. The defendant began preparing to leave the apartment, and Rachel started screaming and yelling at him. At this point, the defendant "choked her into unconsciousness," but did not kill her. Rather, he took her to a hospital. A day later, the defendant went to the apartment to talk to Rachel. She was out, and he waited for her there for about 20 hours. When Rachel returned home, she said to the defendant, "I suppose you have come here to kill me." The defendant made an ambivalent response, and Rachel again started screaming. "Defendant grabbed her by the shoulder and tried to stop her screaming. She continued. They struggled and finally defendant strangled her with a telephone cord."

At the defendant's homicide trial, the court refused his request for an instruction on voluntary manslaughter, and the jury convicted him of murder. On appeal, the Supreme Court of California reversed the conviction, agreeing with the defendant's contention "that there is sufficient evidence in the record to show that he committed the homicide while in a state of uncontrollable rage caused by provocation." The court explained:

> [T]here is no specific type of provocation required by [the voluntary manslaughter statute] and . . . verbal provocation may be sufficient. [For example, as we held in a prior case,] evidence of admissions of infidelity by the defendant's paramour, taunts directed to him and other conduct, "supports a finding that the defendant killed in wild desperation induced by long continued provocatory conduct." We find this reasoning persuasive in the case now before us. Defendant's testimony chronicles a two-week period of provocatory conduct by his wife Rachel that could arouse a passion of jealousy, pain and sexual rage in an ordinary man of average disposition such as to cause him to act rashly from this passion. . . .
>
> The Attorney General contends that the killing could not have been done in the heat of passion because there was a cooling period, defendant having waited in the apartment for 20 hours. However, the long course of provocatory conduct, which had resulted in intermittent outbreaks of rage under specific provocation in the past, reached its final culmination in the apartment when Rachel began screaming. Both defendant and [his expert witness] testified that defendant killed in a state of uncontrollable rage, of passion, and there is ample evidence in the record to support the conclusion that this passion was the result of the long course of provocatory conduct by Rachel. . . .

## 4. THE OBJECTIVE STANDARD

Both the sufficiency of the provocation and the passage of adequate time to cool down are measured by an objective standard. How "objective" should the inquiry be? To put the question another way, what facts—about the situation leading up to the killing and about the accused—are pertinent to an "objective" inquiry? Especially vexing is the question of whether characteristics personal to the accused should be taken into account. If so, which characteristics? Should the inquiry exclude individual traits that may have made the defendant more or less excitable than the average person? The court in *Maher* reasoned that "the average of men . . . of fair average mind and disposition should be taken as the standard—*unless* . . . the person whose guilt is in question be shown to have some peculiar weakness of mind or infirmity of temper, not arising from wickedness of heart or cruelty of disposition."

At the other extreme is the holding in Bedder v. Director of Public Prosecutions, [1954] 2 All E.R. 801. The defendant was an 18-year-old youth who was sexually impotent and emotionally distressed by his condition. On the night of the offense, he approached a prostitute, who led him to a quiet court off the street. There he attempted in vain to have intercourse with her. She responded by jeering at him and trying to get away. He tried to hold her, and she slapped him in the face and punched him in the stomach. He grabbed her shoulders and pushed her back, whereupon she kicked him in the groin. He then pulled a knife and stabbed her twice. Defendant testified that: "She kicked me in the privates. Whether it was her knee or foot, I do not know. After that I do not know what happened till she fell." She died from the knife wounds, and the defendant was prosecuted for murder. The trial judge instructed on the nature of the objective standard as follows:

> The reasonable person, the ordinary person, is the person you must consider when you are considering the effect which any acts, any conduct, any words, might have to justify the steps which were taken in response thereto, so that an unusually excitable or pugnacious individual, or drunken one or a man who is sexually impotent is not entitled to rely on provocation which would not have led an ordinary person to have acted in the way which was in fact carried out.

Defendant argued on appeal that this instruction was wrong, but his conviction was affirmed. Lord Simonds reasoned in part that:

> It would be plainly illogical not to recognize an unusually excitable or pugnacious temperament in the accused as a matter to be taken into account [as a prior case had established] but yet to recognize for that purpose some unusual physical characteristic, be it impotence or another. Moreover, the proposed distinction appears to me to ignore the fundamental fact that the temper of a man which leads him to react in such and such a way to provocation, is, or may be, itself conditioned by some physical defect. It is too subtle a refinement for my mind or, I think, for that of a jury to grasp that the temper may be ignored but the physical defect taken into account.

Is Lord Simonds correct when he asserts that it is both illogical and too difficult to take account of the accused's physical, but not temperamental, characteristics? Using the facts of *Bedder* as an example, why should the jurors not be instructed to judge the severity of the provocation from the perspective of a sexually impotent man who possesses a reasonable temper?

More recently, in People v. Ogen, 168 Cal.App.3d 611, 215 Cal.Rptr. 16 (1985), the Court of Appeals of California explained why the adequacy of provocation should not be judged by reference to the accused's special sensitivities:

> [T]here are substantial policy reasons to restrict the application of the heat of passion defense to cases where the circumstances are sufficiently provocative to trigger violent reactions in a reasonable person. As members of society, each of us is constantly in contact with family members, friends, acquaintances and strangers under countless circumstances. No social

> interaction is so placid as to be utterly devoid of interpersonal stress and friction including, we speculate, monastic existence short of becoming a hermit. [The defendant's] suggested rule would limit homicides to manslaughter upon any fancied slight so long as the perpetrator was sufficiently sensitive. Ethnic, racial, or religious slurs, and sexual innuendoes trigger violent reactions and occasionally killings. However, society has a strong interest in deterring violent and homicidal conduct by not allowing individuals to justify their acts by their own standard of conduct. "[Thus], no man of extremely violent passion could so justify or excuse himself if the exciting cause be not adequate, nor could an excessively cowardly man justify himself unless the circumstances were such as to arouse the fears of the ordinarily courageous man."

By contrast, Richard Singer argues that the "solution . . . is to adopt a totally subjective approach" to provocation. Richard Singer, The Resurgence of Mens Rea: I—Provocation, Emotional Disturbance, and the Model Penal Code, 27 B.C. L. Rev. 243, 315 (1986). Since the provocation standard should be defined by reference to the purposes served by criminal punishment, Singer believes that lawmakers must focus on "the question . . . whether a person who has killed in the heat of passion is, for a utilitarian, less deterrable, less dangerous or less in need of rehabilitation than a murderer, or for a retributivist, less morally blameworthy than a murderer and therefore less deserving of the punishment imposed upon a murderer." For Singer, the "singular purpose of the criminal law" is "to measure moral blameworthiness and punish it proportionately." Accordingly, in provocation cases,

> [t]he law should ask only whether (1) the defendant lost control due to some emotional event or series of events; (2) in losing that control, was the defendant as morally blameworthy as a person who deliberately or recklessly kills. In assessing this liability, the jury should consider only the defendant and his emotional characteristics; no suggestions of "reasonable" people or "adequate" provocation should be allowed. This view . . . has the virtue of focusing on the critical inquiry: was the defendant blameworthy for having lost his temper, given everything known about the defendant? If so, then his "blameworthy conduct" is in failing to control his temper, *not* in killing once his temper had "replaced his reason."

## 5. BOYS' RULES?[d]

Over the past few years, a number of lawyers and commentators have criticized the provocation doctrine on the ground that it incorporates a model of human behavior that may be true of men, but is not true of women. These critics claim that the doctrine was designed and continues to be receptive to the violent rages of the ordinary "man," not those of the ordinary "person." The "sight of adultery" cases are offered to support this claim. The overwhelming majority of defendants in such cases are men who have killed their wives or their wives' lovers. By contrast, when women kill their spouses, they typically do so for reasons other than jealousy

[d] "Most of the time a criminal law that reflects male views and male standards imposes its judgment on men who have injured other men. It is 'boys' rules' applied to a boy's fight." Susan Estrich, Real Rape 60 (1987).

over sexual infidelity, but the provocation doctrine does not recognize such reasons as factors that should mitigate their punishment. Thus, for the critics, the assertion that the provocation doctrine is a "concession to the frailty of human nature" is false as a descriptive matter. The doctrine is a concession to the frailty of "male nature," and, as such, it rests not on an "objective" perspective, but on a "male" perspective.

This criticism has been extended by critical race scholars and practitioners, who claim that the provocation formula (like other legal doctrines) endorses the perceptions and experiences of whites, not of blacks or members of other racial minorities. These commentators attack the reasoning employed by the court in *Ogen*, under which "ethnic, racial, or religious slurs" are not "sufficiently provocative to trigger violent reactions in a reasonable person." According to these critics, such reasoning is insensitive to the experiences that tend to provoke rage in minority citizens, including especially the experience of racial discrimination.

These descriptive criticisms have generated different normative criticisms of the provocation doctrine. First, the assertion that the doctrine embodies a male perspective may imply that the doctrine should be abolished altogether. If men, but not women, fly into a homicidal passion when they discover that their spouse has been sexually unfaithful, why should the law recognize such passion as a *mitigating* factor? Why should a man who experiences an overpowering rage in these circumstances not be viewed as more, rather than less, culpable, since a woman would not be similarly provoked? In When "Heterosexual" Men Kill "Homosexual" Men: Reflections on Provocation Law, Sexual Advances, and the "Reasonable Man" Standard, 85 J. Crim. L. & Criminology 726, 735–37, 750–51 (1995), Joshua Dressler agrees that the provocation defense "is a male-oriented doctrine," but he argues that the law should retain it. There would be, he admits, important deterrent gains if the law did not recognize provocation as a mitigation. But:

> Deterrence . . . is not the exclusive goal of the criminal law. Another purpose of the law is to differentiate between more and less serious offenses, and "to safeguard offenders against excessive, disproportionate or arbitrary punishment." These goals of the criminal law require consideration of matters of personal culpability. . . . A system of laws that refuses to recognize any excusing conditions might deter violence and, therefore, might be justifiable in a purely utilitarian system. But excuses, including provocation, are recognized for a non-utilitarian (even counter-utilitarian) reason: they stem from the commitment to afford justice to individual wrongdoers—ensuring that they are not blamed and punished in excess of their personal desert.

Some propose revising the provocation doctrine so that it accords mitigating significance to events that provoke violence in persons who are members of disempowered groups. In Is the Reasonable Man Obsolete? A Critical Perspective on Self-Defense and Provocation, 14 Loyola of L.A.L.Rev. 435 (1981), Delores Donovan and Stephanie Wildman argue that the law of provocation should take account of such factors as race, sex, socio-economic background, traumatic personal experiences, and other factors relevant to the "social reality" of the defendant's behavior. For example, a woman who kills an abusive spouse under circumstances not amounting to self defense should be permitted to offer proof of the abuse in support of a provocation instruction. Donovan and Wildman offer the following jury instruction for cases where provocation is asserted:

> In determining whether the killing was done with malice aforethought, you must consider whether, in light of all the evidence in the case, the accused was honestly and understandably aroused to the heat of passion. In determining whether [he or she] was understandably aroused to the heat of passion, you must ask yourselves whether [he or she] could have been fairly expected to avoid the act of homicide.

According to Donovan and Wildman, this instruction does not abandon the requirement that an "objective" judgment be made. Rather, the instruction conveys that requirement to the jury in terms that are more likely to produce just results. How does this instruction differ from the "totally subjective approach" proposed by Richard Singer?

## 6. THE RELEVANCE OF MISTAKE

In Criminal Law 578 (1972), Wayne R. LaFave and Austin W. Scott, Jr., assert that:

> It would seem that the provocation is adequate to reduce the homicide to voluntary manslaughter if the killer reasonably believes that the injury to him exists, though actually he has not been injured. In other words, a man's passion directed against another person is reasonable if (i) he reasonably believes that he has been injured by the other, and (ii) a reasonable man who actually has suffered such an injury would be put in a passion directed against the other.

The leading American case for this proposition is State v. Yanz, 74 Conn. 177, 50 A. 37 (1901), where an instruction that "[i]f, in fact, no adultery was going on, and the husband is mistaken as to the fact, though the circumstances were such as to justify a belief . . . of adultery, the offense would not be reduced to manslaughter" was held to be reversible error. The court said that:

> The excitement is the effect of a belief, from ocular evidence, of the actual commission of adultery. It is the belief, so reasonably formed, that excites the uncontrollable passion. Such a belief, though a mistaken one, is calculated to induce the same emotions as would be felt were the wrongful act in fact committed.

One judge dissented, reasoning in part that when anger

> is provoked by the wrongful act of the person slain, who thus brings upon himself the fatal blow, given in the first outbreak of rage, caused by himself, the offense is manslaughter; not only because the voluntary act is, in a way, compelled by an ungovernable rage, but also because the victim is the aggressor; and his wrong, although it cannot justify, may modify, the nature of the homicide thus induced. The court therefore correctly told the jury that to make the offense manslaughter, the injury claimed as a provocation must in fact have been done. Our law of homicide recognizes no provocation as legally competent to so modify the cruelty of intentional, unlawful killing as to reduce the offense to

manslaughter, except the provocation involved in an actual and adequate injury and insult.

In Provocation and the Reasonable Man, [1954] Crim.L.Rev. 740, 752–53, Glanville Williams disagrees with LaFave and Scott and with both the majority and the dissent in *Yanz,* at least as to what the law ought to be:

> It is . . . submitted that . . . the mistake need not be reasonable. . . . This is not a denial of the objective test of provocation, for the objective test operates only on the facts as they were believed by the accused to exist. The question asked by the objective test is whether, assuming the facts to be as the accused believed them to be, those facts would come within the legal categories of provocation, or would be provocation for an ordinary man. What the objective test discountenances is unusual deficiency of self-control, not the making of an error of observation or inference in point of fact.

How should mistakes be treated in the context of provocation? Should mistakes induced by intoxication be treated differently? Williams argued that, where the charge was an offense that required intent or recklessness, the facts should be taken as the intoxicated defendant supposed them to be.

## 7. THE RELEVANCE OF MENTAL ABNORMALITY

To what extent is evidence of mental abnormality logically relevant to the criteria governing the reduction of murder to manslaughter? There are two principal contexts in which this question has arisen.

### (i) *Provocation*

Is evidence of mental abnormality relevant to the ordinary provocation inquiry? Clearly, such evidence can be probative as to one component of the mitigation—that the defendant in fact acted in the heat of passion generated by the provoking event. For this reason, several courts have admitted such evidence to show that the defendant actually was provoked. But unless the "reasonable person" is to be imbued with the peculiar mental characteristics of the defendant—a step which the courts uniformly have refused to take—the defendant's mental abnormality would not be relevant to whether it was "reasonable" to have been provoked under similar circumstances. Thus, the fact that the standard of adequate provocation requires the application of an objective measure of liability eliminates such evidence from consideration on this branch of the inquiry.

Since evidence of mental abnormality would be relevant on the subjective dimension of the inquiry but not the objective one, should the evidence be admitted or excluded? Could the admission of testimony about the defendant's abnormality mislead and confuse a jury that is told to consider it for one purpose but ignore it for another? Could admission of such evidence push the inquiry too far in a subjective direction? On the other hand, is it fair to foreclose the defendant from a reliable source of evidence on one important aspect of the inquiry?

### (ii) *"Imperfect" Justification*

It is a defense to an intentional killing if it can be shown that the defendant believed it a necessary response to unlawful deadly force and that the response was reasonable under the circumstances. Moreover, many courts reduce the offense from murder to manslaughter if only the subjective component of this inquiry is met. The term "imperfect justification" is often used to describe the rule that permits such mitigation.

In jurisdictions that follow this rule, it seems plain that evidence of mental abnormality can be logically relevant to the subjective consideration that will suffice for mitigation of the offense to manslaughter. Such evidence was held admissible in People v. Wells, 33 Cal.2d 330, 202 P.2d 53 (1949), where the defendant was prosecuted under a statute that read: "Every person undergoing a life sentence in a state prison . . . who, with malice aforethought, commits an assault upon the person of another . . . by any means of force likely to produce great bodily injury, is punishable with death." The defendant sought to introduce evidence that he suffered from a condition that produced an abnormal fear for his own safety causing him to overreact to conduct which he perceived as threatening. He did not claim that he met the objective criterion for exoneration on the ground of self-defense. The court held that "malice aforethought" in the quoted statute had the same meaning as it would in a prosecution for murder, and that because such evidence would be admissible to negate the malice aforethought required for murder (reducing the offense to manslaughter), it was also logically relevant and admissible to negate an essential element of the offense charged.

Suppose Wells had also claimed self-defense and had sought to show that the objective component of that defense had been satisfied. Would the expert testimony be admissible for that purpose? If not, does this cast doubt on whether it should be admitted in a case where both the complete defense and the mitigation are claimed and the evidence is offered for the sole purpose of establishing the mitigation? Can the jury be expected to keep the two issues separate? Is the provocation situation sufficiently different to suggest that the expert testimony might be excluded entirely in provocation cases but admitted for a limited purpose in a case where the defendant claims both complete and imperfect justification?

## NOTES ON "EXTREME EMOTIONAL DISTURBANCE" AS A MITIGATION OF MURDER TO MANSLAUGHTER

### 1. THE MODEL PENAL CODE FORMULATION

Section 210.3(b) of the Model Penal Code proposes the following codification of the circumstances that should mitigate murder to manslaughter:

> Criminal homicide constitutes manslaughter when . . . a homicide which would otherwise be murder is committed under the influence of extreme mental or emotional disturbance for which there is reasonable explanation or excuse. The reasonableness of such explanation or excuse shall be determined from the viewpoint of a person in the actor's situation under the circumstances as he believes them to be.

As the drafters of the Code explain, this provision is designed to modify the common law provocation doctrine. Indeed, their objective in describing the mitigating condition as "extreme mental or emotional disturbance" was to endorse a "substantially enlarged version of the rule of provocation." Thus, the commentary to § 210.3(b) explains:

. . . This formulation effects substantial changes in the traditional notion of provocation. For one thing, the Code does not require that the actor's emotional distress arise from some injury, affront, or other provocative act perpetrated upon him by the deceased. Under the Code, mitigation may be appropriate where the actor believes that the deceased is responsible for some injustice to another or even where he strikes out in a blinding rage and kills an innocent bystander. In some such cases, the cause and intensity of the actor's emotion may be less indicative of moral depravity than would be a homicidal response to a blow to one's person. By eliminating any reference to provocation in the ordinary sense of improper conduct by the deceased, the Model Code avoids arbitrary exclusion of some circumstances that may justify reducing murder to manslaughter.

Section 210.3 also sweeps away the rigid rules that limited provocation to certain defined circumstances. Instead, it casts the issue in phrases that have no common law antecedents and hence no accumulated doctrinal content. Where there is evidence of extreme mental or emotional disturbance, it is for the trier of fact to decide, in light of all the circumstances of the case, whether there exists a reasonable explanation or excuse for the actor's mental condition. The issue cannot be resolved successfully by categorization of conduct. It must be confronted directly on the facts of each case. By restating the ultimate inquiry, [the section] avoids the strictures of early precedents and puts the issue in the terms in which it should be considered. This development reflects the trend of many modern decisions to abandon preconceived notions of what constitutes adequate provocation and to submit that question to the jury's deliberation.

Most importantly, the Model Code qualifies the rigorous objectivity with which the common law determined adequacy of provocation. Of course, [the section] does require that the actor's emotional distress be based on "reasonable explanation or excuse." This language preserves the essentially objective character of the inquiry and erects a barrier against debilitating individualization of the legal standard. But the statute further provides that the "reasonableness of such explanation or excuse shall be determined from the viewpoint of a person in the actor's situation under the circumstances as he believes them to be." The last clause clarifies the role of mistake. The trier of fact must evaluate the actor's conduct under the circumstances that the actor believed to exist. Thus, for example, a man who reasonably but mistakenly identifies his wife's rapist and kills the wrong person may be eligible for mitigation if his extreme emotional disturbance were otherwise subject to reasonable explanation or excuse.

The critical element in the Model Code formulation is the clause requiring that reasonableness be assessed "from the viewpoint of a person in the actor's situation." The word "situation" is designedly ambiguous. On the one hand, it is clear that personal handicaps and some external circumstances must be taken into account. Thus, blindness, shock from traumatic injury, and extreme grief are all easily read into the term "situation."

> This result is sound, for it would be morally obtuse to appraise a crime for mitigation of punishment without reference to these factors. On the other hand, it is equally plain that idiosyncratic moral values are not part of the actor's situation. An assassin who kills a political leader because he believes it is right to do so cannot ask that he be judged by the standard of a reasonable extremist. Any other result would undermine the normative message of the criminal law. In between these two extremes, however, there are matters neither as clearly distinct from individual blameworthiness as blindness or handicap nor as integral a part of moral depravity as a belief in the rightness of killing. Perhaps the classic illustration is the unusual sensitivity to the epithet "bastard" of a person born illegitimate. An exceptionally punctilious sense of personal honor or an abnormally fearful temperament may also serve the differentiate an individual actor from the hypothetical reasonable man, yet none of these factors is wholly irrelevant to the ultimate issue of culpability. The proper role of such factors cannot be resolved satisfactorily by abstract definition of what may constitute adequate provocation ..... In the end, the question is whether the actor's loss of self-control can be understood in terms that arouse sympathy in the ordinary citizen. Section 210.3 faces this issue squarely and leaves the ultimate judgment to the ordinary citizen in the function of a juror assigned to resolve the specific case.

The Model Penal Code has led to a reformulation of the law of provocation in at least a dozen states, New York among them. It is clear that it significantly broadens the common law standard in a number of respects.

Exactly how does it do so? Review the sequence of notes following *Freddo v. State*, supra. How does the Model Code formula differ from common law provocation on the issues treated in those notes? How would the Model Code be applied to the facts in *Freddo* and the cases discussed in the notes following *Freddo*? Does it do a better job, or is it too permissive and not sufficiently protective of human life? The Oregon statute, reproduced in Appendix B, infra, is worded differently from the Model Code. Is it an improvement?[a]

## 2. *PEOPLE V. CASASSA*

Victor Casassa was charged with murder in the stabbing death of Victoria Lo Consolo. He waived a jury and was tried by the court. The defense conceded that Casassa had killed Ms. Lo Consolo, but claimed that he had done so "under the influence of extreme mental or emotional disturbance," and that his offense should be mitigated to manslaughter as provided by § 125.25(1)(a) of the New York Penal Law, which is identical to the Model Penal Code formulation.[b]

The evidence showed that Casassa and the victim met in August 1976 as a result of their residence in the same apartment complex. Shortly thereafter, he asked her to accompany him to a social function and she agreed. The two apparently dated casually on other occasions until

---

[a] The Oregon statute is extensively considered in State v. Ott, 297 Or. 375, 686 P.2d 1001 (1984).

[b] The applicable New York statutes are reproduced in Appendix B.

November, 1976 when Ms. Lo Consolo informed him that she was not "falling in love" with him. Devastated by this rejection, Casassa became obsessed with Ms. Lo Consolo. Aware that she was seeing other men, he broke into the apartment below Ms. Lo Consolo's on several occasions to eavesdrop. Thereafter, on one occasion, he broke into her apartment while she was out. He took nothing, but, instead, observed the apartment, disrobed and lay for a time in Miss Lo Consolo's bed. During this break-in, defendant was armed with a knife which, he later told police, he carried "because he knew that he was either going to hurt Victoria or Victoria was going to cause him to commit suicide." Cassasa's final visit to his victim's apartment occurred on February 28, 1977. He brought several bottles of wine and liquor with him to offer as a gift. Upon Ms. Lo Consolo's rejection of this offering, defendant produced a steak knife which he had brought with him, stabbed her several times in the throat, dragged her body to the bathroom and submerged it in a bathtub full of water to "make sure she was dead."

The defense presented only one witness, a psychiatrist, who testified, in essence, that the defendant had become obsessed with Miss Lo Consolo and that the course which their relationship had taken, combined with several personality attributes peculiar to defendant, caused him to be under the influence of extreme emotional disturbance at the time of the killing. In rebuttal, the state's psychiatrist testified that although Casassa was emotionally disturbed, he was not under the influence of "extreme emotional disturbance" within the meaning of § 125.25(1)(a) of the Penal Law because his disturbed state was not the product of external factors but rather was "a stress he created from within himself, dealing mostly with a fantasy, a refusal to accept the reality of the situation."

The trial court in resolving this issue noted that the affirmative defense of extreme emotional disturbance may be based upon a series of events, rather than a single precipitating cause. In order to be entitled to the defense, the court held, a defendant must show that his reaction to such events was reasonable. In determining whether defendant's emotional reaction was reasonable, the court considered the appropriate test to be whether in the totality of the circumstances the finder of fact could understand how a person might have his reason overcome. Concluding that the test was not to be applied solely from the viewpoint of defendant, the court found that defendant's emotional reaction at the time of the commission of the crime was so peculiar to him that it could not be considered reasonable so as to reduce the conviction to manslaughter in the first degree. Accordingly, the trial court found defendant guilty of murder in the second degree. The Court of Appeals affirmed:

> By suggesting a standard of evaluation which contains both subjective and objective elements, we believe that the drafters of the code adequately achieved their dual goals of broadening the "heat of passion" doctrine to apply to a wider range of circumstances while retaining some element of objectivity in the process. The result of their draftsmanship is a statute which offers the defendant a fair opportunity to seek mitigation without requiring that the trier of fact find mitigation in each case where an emotional disturbance is shown—or as the drafters put it, to offer "room for argument as to the reasonableness of the explanations or excuses offered."

We note also that this interpretation comports with what has long been recognized as the underlying purpose of any mitigation statute. In the words of Mr. Justice Cardozo, referring to an earlier statute: "What we have is merely a privilege offered to the jury to find the lesser degree when the suddenness of the intent, the vehemence of the passion, seems to call irresistibly for the exercise of mercy. I have no objection to giving them this dispensing power, but it should be given to them directly and not in a mystifying cloud of words." Benjamin Cardozo, Law and Literature 100–01.[c] In the end, we believe that what the legislature intended in enacting the statute was to allow the finder of fact the discretionary power to mitigate the penalty when presented with a situation which, under the circumstances, appears to them to have caused an understandable weakness in one of their fellows. Perhaps the chief virtue of the statute is that it allows such discretion without engaging in a detailed explanation of individual circumstances in which the statute would apply, thus avoiding the "mystifying cloud of words" which Mr. Justice Cardozo abhorred.[d]

We conclude that the trial court, in this case, properly applied the statute. The court apparently accepted, as a factual matter, that defendant killed Miss Lo Consolo while under the influence of "extreme emotional disturbance," a threshold question which must be answered in the affirmative before any test of reasonableness is required. The court, however, also recognized that in exercising its function as trier of fact, it must make a further inquiry into the reasonableness of that disturbance. In this regard, the court considered each of the mitigating factors put forward by defendant, including his claimed mental disability, but found that the excuse offered by defendant was so peculiar to him that it was unworthy of mitigation. The court obviously made a sincere effort to understand defendant's "situation" and "the circumstances as defendant believed them to be," but concluded that the murder in this case was the result of defendant's malevolence rather than an understandable human response deserving of mercy. We cannot say, as a matter of law, that the court erred in so concluding. Indeed, to do so would subvert the purpose of the statute.

In our opinion, this statute would not require that the jury or the court as trier of fact find mitigation on any particular set of facts, but, rather, allows the finder of fact the opportunity to do so, such opportunity being conditional only upon a finding of extreme emotional disturbance in the first instance. In essence, the statute requires mitigation to be afforded an emotionally disturbed defendant only when the trier of fact, after considering a broad range of mitigating circumstances, believes that such leniency is justified. Since the trier of fact found that defendant failed to establish that he was acting "under the influence of extreme

---

[c] The passage from which this quotation is taken is reproduced in context in Note 1(i) in the Notes on First-Degree Murder in Section 1 of this Chapter.—[Footnote by eds.]

[d] But see Robert M. Byrn, Homicide Under the Proposed New York Penal Law, 33 Fordham L.Rev. 173, 179 (1964) ("All that has happened is that 'one mystifying cloud of words' has been substituted for another.")—[Footnote by eds.]

emotional disturbance for which there was a reasonable explanation or excuse," defendant's conviction of murder in the second degree should not be reduced to the crime of manslaughter in the first degree.

Did the Court of Appeals properly apply the Model Penal Code mitigation to Casassa? What if the case had been tried before a jury and the trial judge had refused to give the jury a manslaughter instruction under § 125.25(1)(a) on the ground that the evidence was legally insufficient to show that there was "a reasonable explanation or excuse" for Casassa's emotional disturbance? How would the Court of Appeals have ruled in that case? What did the drafters of the Model Penal Code intend?

Victoria Nourse has sharply criticized the reforms prompted by the MPC formulation, especially in connection with claims for mitigation such as those presented in *Casassa*. In Passion's Progress: Modern Law Reform and the Provocation Defense, 106 Yale L.J. 1331 (1997), Nourse argues that the reforms "have led us to change our understandings of intimate homicide in ways that we might never have expected." The drafters of the Model Code intended to introduce "modern and enlightened" ways of thinking about the provocation doctrine, but the appellate cases from reform states suggest that the "extreme emotional disturbance" formulation instead has had a pernicious effect. By allowing claims like Casassa's, the formulation "perpetuates . . . ideas about men, women, and their relationships that society long ago abandoned." Although the law of domestic relations now acknowledges that women have the right to divorce or separate from their male partners, the reforms of the provocation doctrine have "yielded precisely the opposite result, binding women to the emotional claims of husbands or boyfriends" those women had lawfully and properly rejected. Thus, Nourse wonders whether the Model Code's approach to provocation is an improvement at all. As she puts it, "[i]n this upside-down world of gender relations [promoted by the MPC formulation], it should not be surprising to learn that the common law approach toward the provocation defense, deemed an antique by most legal scholars, provides greater protection for women than do purportedly liberal versions of the defense."

In this connection, note that New York authorizes a maximum prison sentence of 25 years for a person whose offense is mitigated from murder to manslaughter by an "extreme emotional disturbance." The maximum in Oregon is 20 years. By contrast, the maximum in Virginia, which follows the traditional common law provocation formula, is 10 years. See Appendix B. Is the appropriate choice of formula related to the severity with which the mitigated offense can be punished? Is changing the label from murder to manslaughter under more relaxed standards more tolerable if the offense is still subject to severe punishments approaching those for murder?

### 3. DIMINISHED RESPONSIBILITY IN ENGLAND

In the Homicide Act, 1957, 5 & 6 Eliz. 2, c. 11, § 2, England amended the common law homicide structure as follows:

> Persons suffering from diminished responsibility.
>
> (1) Where a person kills or is a party to the killing of another, he shall not be convicted of murder if he was suffering from such abnormality of mind (whether arising from a condition of arrested or retarded development of mind or any inherent causes or

> induced by disease or injury) as substantially impaired his mental responsibility for his acts and omissions in doing or being a party to the killing.
>
> (2) On a charge of murder, it shall be for the defence to prove that the person charged is by virtue of this section not liable to be convicted of murder.
>
> (3) A person who but for this section would be liable, whether as principal or as accessory, to be convicted of murder shall be liable instead to be convicted of manslaughter.
>
> (4) The fact that one party to a killing is by virtue of this section not liable to be convicted of murder shall not affect the question whether the killing amounted to murder in the case of any other party to it.

The term "abnormality of mind" has since been defined in Regina v. Byrne, [1960] 2 Q.B. 396, 403, in the following terms:

> "Abnormality of mind," which has to be contrasted with the time-honoured expression in the *M'Naghten* rules, "defect of reason," means a state of mind so different from that of ordinary human beings that the reasonable man would term it abnormal. It appears to us to be wide enough to cover the mind's activities in all its aspects, not only the perception of physical acts and matters and the ability to form a rational judgment whether an act is right or wrong, but also the ability to exercise will-power to control physical acts in accordance with that rational judgment.

The English statute was adopted as part of a package of legislation designed to limit the range of offenses for which the death penalty could be imposed. The death penalty itself was abolished in England in 1965, but the 1957 diminished-responsibility provisions were retained. Note that the effect of the 1957 legislation was to broaden the substantive criteria under which evidence of "abnormality of mind" could be considered as a mitigating factor to reduce murder to manslaughter. Functionally, therefore, it operates much as does the provocation mitigation. Like provocation, it provides the jury with a substantive basis for reducing the grade of the offense, and in so doing broadens the base of evidence that can be introduced for this purpose. Note that it makes evidence of mental abnormality relevant in ways not encompassed by the *M'Naghten* formulation of the insanity defense and also not encompassed by the provocation mitigation. Is this a desirable development?

### 4. DIMINISHED RESPONSIBILITY UNDER THE "EXTREME EMOTIONAL DISTURBANCE" FORMULATION

In what ways does the "extreme emotional disturbance" formulation broaden the base of psychiatric testimony that can be considered for the purpose of reducing an offense from murder to manslaughter? If a defendant is not insane within the applicable definition used by a given jurisdiction for that defense, is it nonetheless desirable that evidence of mental abnormality be considered as a grading factor to distinguish murder from manslaughter? Did the court so use such evidence in *Casassa?* Should it have? Do those states that use the Model Penal Code approach now have a diminished responsibility basis for reducing murder to manslaughter analogous to the English concept discussed above? How is the Model Code formula different from the English concept? Which is the better approach?

5. BURDEN OF PERSUASION

New York places the burden of persuasion on the defendant to prove "extreme emotional disturbance" by a preponderance of the evidence. As a matter of legislative policy,[e] on whom should the burden be placed on this issue? What factors should be taken into account in resolving this question?

## United States v. Robertson

United States Court of Military Appeals, 1993.
37 M.J. 432.

■ WISS, JUDGE. After a contested trial, a general court-martial of officer and enlisted members convicted appellant of involuntary manslaughter. . . . The members sentenced appellant to a bad-conduct discharge, confinement for 1 year, and reduction to the lowest enlisted grade. . . .

On appeal, the Court of Military Review concluded that "there is insufficient evidence to support a finding of culpable negligence, and thus the manslaughter conviction cannot stand." In the court's view, however, the evidence was both legally and factually sufficient "to support a finding of negligent homicide." Accordingly, the court affirmed only a finding of negligent homicide and, on reassessment of the sentence "on the basis of the errors noted and the entire record," a sentence extending only to reduction to the grade of E–5.

On appellant's petition, this Court agreed to review: "Whether the Army court erred in finding the evidence to be sufficient as a matter of law to support a finding of guilty to negligent homicide. . . ." On further consideration of the decision below, we agree with one prong of appellant's multi-faceted attack within this issue: We hold that the evidence of appellant's negligence—even the simple negligence that is in issue in negligent homicide—is insufficient as a matter of law to support the finding affirmed below.

I

The opinion of the Court of Military Review told the truly sad story of the anorexic/bulimic mission that appellant's son Brad set for himself and the tragic, fatal consequences. Added to this human tragedy for appellant was his own court-martial for alleged negligence in letting his son pursue his suicidal course. . . .

II.A

[Brad lived with his mother after his parents divorced] in 1981, and appellant had not seen his son since then until he visited Brad at his home in Kansas during Christmas of 1987. Their relationship renewed, Brad visited his father in New Jersey during spring break in 1988.

At the time he arrived in New Jersey in early April, Brad was well along on his journey toward self-destruction. . . . Brad began this

[e] Constitutional questions posed by placing the burden of persuasion on this issue on the defendant are postponed to Chapter XII. For now it should be assumed, as the United States Supreme Court held in Patterson v. New York, 432 U.S. 197 (1977), that the Constitution permits this issue to be resolved as a matter of legislative policy.

pattern of abuse when he discovered during a virus that he had contracted in the fall of 1986 that, if he vomited and did not eat, he would lose weight—a noteworthy discovery to Brad, who had been "quite chunky" at "one point in his life." Before he came into appellant's care in April 1988, Brad already had been hospitalized once for a week in connection with his difficulty in eating and his weight loss, [and he made numerous visits to a medical doctor and a psychiatrist, neither of whom diagnosed anorexia in part because Brad's mother did not tell them about Brad's weight loss and hospitalization.]

[Moreover,] "appellant received essentially no information from Brad's mother at the time of the boy's arrival to alert him to Brad's previous weight loss and erratic eating habits." Appellant's wife testified [that Brad's mother told her only that Brad's stomach was "iffy" because he had a "stomach virus."]

Appellant and his wife noticed, on Brad's arrival, that Brad looked thin. Over the next couple of weeks, Brad seemed mostly to pick at his food rather than to eat much of it. On April 17, Brad complained of dizziness, so appellant took him to the hospital emergency room, where Brad was examined and referred to the pediatric clinic.

On April 20, appellant and Brad saw Dr. (Lieutenant Colonel) Grace Nadhiry at the clinic. . . . Dr. Nadhiry weighed Brad during her examination, finding that he then weighed 122 pounds; she plotted this weight on a weight chart for boys of Brad's age and found that he was at the 50th percentile. She did notice that his weight on that occasion was less than the 125 pounds that had been recorded as his weight in the emergency room 3 days earlier. When asked, however, whether that weight loss had caused her "any concern," she answered, "Not from the appearance that Brad had. Brad clinically looked perfectly in good health."

Dr. Nadhiry talked to both Brad and appellant about anorexia and the problems associated with it. She talked to Brad in a way intended to elicit his confidence and friendship and asked to have his records from Kansas brought to her. Because the word "psychiatrist really scares most children from Brad's stage and with his type of attitude, which was unfriendly," Dr. Nadhiry "talked to him about a psychologist and counseling." Brad responded that "he didn't need that." . . .

Over the next 3 weeks, appellant noticed that Brad still was not eating much, which he believed to be atypical for a 15-year-old. That factor, plus Dr. Nadhiry's advice that she should see him again in 3 to 4 weeks, led appellant to decide that [he should take Brad for a follow-up meeting with Dr. Nadhiry. However, Brad resisted the suggestion; indeed, appellant stated that he thought Brad was going to punch him when he heard about the plan to visit Dr. Nadhiry.]

[A]ppellant decided that physically forcing Brad to return [to the clinic] would be counterproductive. . . . Brad had told him in conversations about the "stress and turmoil" in the family situation in Kansas, and appellant believed that it was important for Brad to feel comfortable and accepted by appellant. Accordingly, appellant decided on a more "low-keyed" approach of trying to persuade Brad to be more receptive to medical attention (like he had been earlier to eye and dental exams). [Appellant testified that he believed this strategy was working. Brad was scheduled to return to Kansas for a family party, and, about 10 days before his trip, he phoned his mother and asked her to make an appointment with his doctor.]

Throughout the approximately 3 months that Brad spent with appellant and his wife, Brad had followed a pattern of conscious deceit concerning his eating and his weight. For instance, Brad always wore very loose clothes . . . ; and, since he was almost 15 years old, neither appellant nor his wife ever saw him undressed. Moreover, Brad was an excellent cook, and typically appellant and his wife would arrive home from work about 7:00 p.m. and find that Brad had dinner waiting for them. When they would ask why he was not eating too, he would answer that he had eaten while cooking. . . .

Appellant put Brad on an airplane back to Kansas on July 27, and Brad had an appointment with the doctor the next day. His mother picked him up at the airport, took him home at Brad's insistence even though he looked "[h]ideous," unsuccessfully tried to get him to eat something, and finally let him go to bed. Brad's mother called a doctor that night and was told she could bring him in when the office opened the next morning. She found Brad dead in his bed at 7:00 a.m. The conclusion of the subsequent autopsy was death caused by "cardiac failure due to starvation."

Although a number of witnesses, both expert and lay, testified on both sides on the merits, the only expert witness who addressed actions and reactions of parents of an anorexic or bulimic child was Dr. Neal Satin, a psychiatrist with expertise in eating disorders. . . . In response to questions asking how parents of anorexic/bulimic children respond and concerning, specifically, appellant's responses [to Brad, Dr. Satin testified:]

> I think that invariably with families, they're no villains, they're only victims. Parents do the best that they can. They often do things that I wouldn't do as an expert, but they try to do what they can to get the individuals either to seek treatment, to eat, to change their behavior, and they are almost invariably unsuccessful. . . . And so I don't think that in these instances, parents can do anything right or wrong because there isn't a clear answer of what is right or wrong. I think that the best that parents can do is attempt to get the children to accept treatment and to hope that the people that are training are sufficiently competent and have enough expertise in the field that they can raise the likelihood of success a slight higher percentage. . . .

II.B

[I]n the face of a challenge to the legal sufficiency of the evidence, this Court's charge is to answer "whether, considering the evidence in the light most favorable to the prosecution, a reasonable factfinder could have found all the essential elements beyond a reasonable doubt."

One of the elements of negligent homicide, of course, is simple negligence. See para. 85b(4), Part IV, Manual, supra. Paragraph 85c(2) defines simple negligence for purposes of this crime as follows:

> Simple negligence is the absence of due care, that is, an act or omission of a person who is under a duty to use due care which

> exhibits a lack of that degree of care of the safety of others which a reasonably careful person would have exercised under the same or similar circumstances.

At the risk of over-simplification, appellant's approach to getting his son the continued medical treatment that appellant ultimately recognized was needed was to persuade his nearly 15-year-old, strong-minded son, who had demonstrated a willingness to physically fight appellant's effort to get him to a doctor. Some parents . . . might have pursued more authoritative action, just like some parents are more authoritative than others with their children on virtually all aspects of their upbringing.

[U]rging that negligence cannot be judged by hindsight or by the ultimate result, in essence appellant asks: If the boy's death were unknown (in order to preclude any subconscious impact), does the evidence establish beyond reasonable doubt that his approach was a negligent one? Stated in terms of paragraph 85c(2), did appellant's approach to parenting exhibit a lack of that degree of care for his son which a reasonably prudent parent would have exercised under the same or similar circumstances?

Measured against this standard, we conclude that the evidence is such that a reasonable factfinder could not find beyond a reasonable doubt that appellant's approach to caring for his son was negligent. The uncontroverted evidence demonstrates the following: Appellant had no knowledge of Brad's past medical difficulties relating to eating disorders or weight loss, except for being told Brad had an "iffy" stomach; Brad consciously and creatively concealed both the severity of his weight loss and his non-eating; even when appellant did become aware of these related symptoms, he did not fully appreciate their magnitude because of Brad's determined effort to hide them; and when Brad did exhibit a medical difficulty—dizziness—appellant promptly obtained medical attention for him.

Thereafter, he followed Dr. Nadhiry's advice and closely watched his son, tried to get him to eat, and asked his wife and friends of the family to assist him to persuade his son to eat; when it appeared 3 to 4 weeks later that it was not working, he set out to call Dr. Nadhiry, prompting a physical confrontation with his son who adamantly refused to return to her. Rather than fight his 15-year-old son who was physically and emotionally determined to resist, appellant set out to watch him closely and to persistently try to persuade his son that he needed medical help; indeed, appellant ultimately did exactly that, and his son called his mother to ask her to make an appointment with a doctor back home whom he had seen before.

In light of Dr. Satin's testimony, we are at a loss how reasonable factfinders could find appellant's course of caring for his son to be criminally at odds with what "a reasonably careful" parent would have done under the same or similar circumstances. Absence of negligence does not require that judgment [to be] right, only that it reflect what a reasonably careful person would do. Brad died—and that truly is tragic. But that regrettable result does not necessarily mean that appellant was not reasonably careful. Indeed, Dr. Satin's testimony makes it clear that it does not necessarily mean even that appellant's actions were "wrong."

III

The decision of the United States Army Court of Military Review is reversed. The findings and sentence are set aside. The charge is dismissed.

■ GIERKE, JUDGE, concurring. I agree with the principal opinion. I write separately only to articulate an additional rationale that led me to the conclusion that the evidence in this case is legally insufficient to support appellant's conviction.

Appellant's negligence was based on the allegation that he failed "to provide proper medical and/or psychiatric care" for his son . . . , such "failure" being the "proximate cause of" his son's death. The Government's theory was that appellant did not do the "right" thing which, in essence, would have required appellant to physically force his recalcitrant son to go to the hospital at some time prior to his son's death. During her final argument, trial counsel told the members:

> And ask yourselves, if this was your son, if he had gone from healthy to this, 40 pounds less in 3 months, what would you do? Would you let your son say, "I don't want to go to the doctor?" I think what you'd do is tie him up and put him in the car and take him to the hospital and have him admitted. But even if you wouldn't even go that far, you'd go to a doctor. You'd get some care for him.[1]

On appeal, the Government still contends that forced hospitalization would have saved appellant's son's life (or, at least, prolonged it temporarily), and implies that anything short of enlisting the assistance of health care professionals should be considered negligence under the circumstances.

[T]he question is whether there was any evidence to prove that a reasonable person in appellant's position would have recognized that at some time prior to his son's scheduled appointment, the need for immediate medical intervention made forced hospitalization the only rational option. The evidence is uncontradicted that appellant attempted to persuade his son to seek medical help and was ultimately successful in convincing his son to have his mother schedule an appointment with a doctor in Kansas. More significantly, however, I believe that the evidence fails to establish that a reasonable person in appellant's position would have known, prior to appellant's son's death, that immediate medical intervention was necessary. Accordingly, I concur that the evidence is legally insufficient to support appellant's conviction.

A parent's legal duty to provide medical assistance for his or her children is based upon the "inherent dependency of a child upon his parent to obtain medical aid, i.e., the incapacity of a child to evaluate

---

[1] As a general rule, it is improper for counsel to identify the "reasonable person" with members of the very jury which is to apply the reasonable person standard. Although there was no objection, trial counsel's suggestion that the members ask themselves what they would do with their own son advocated an incorrect legal standard. Cf. United States v. Shamberger, 1 MJ 377, 379 (CMA 1976) (asking members to place themselves in position of victim's relative invites them to improperly judge issue from a personal rather than objective perspective). Appellant's decision to persuade rather than force his son to receive medical treatment may have been based in part on the unique circumstances facing him as the new guardian of a headstrong teenager whom he previously had not even seen for 7 years.

his condition and summon aid by himself, supports imposition of such a duty upon the parent." Commonwealth v. Konz, 498 Pa. 639 (1982). Thus, when a parent knows or should know that his or her child needs immediate medical intervention, failure to act within a reasonable time to seek such aid may be a breach of that duty. Cf. Bergmann v. State, 486 N.E.2d 653 (Ind.App. 4 Dist.1985) (affirming reckless homicide conviction of parents who "treated" 9-month-old daughter who died of bacterial meningitis with prayers and fasting instead of seeking medical care).

On the other hand, consideration must be given to alternative courses of conduct available to a parent. "Parents are vested with a reasonable discretion in regard to when medical attention is needed for their children." It follows then that, absent evidence that a reasonable person would recognize the need for immediate medical intervention, the decision to persuade rather than use force or trickery to get a reluctant adolescent to receive medical care is also within a parent's discretion.

A conviction of negligent homicide requires proof that death resulted from the simple negligence of the accused. Proof of simple negligence requires a showing that the accused failed to use "that degree of care [for] the safety of others which a reasonably careful person would have exercised under the same or similar circumstances." Such a person "is not necessarily a supercautious individual devoid of human frailties." As the late Chief Justice Holmes once noted, a choice "may be mistaken and yet prudent." . . .

Appellant cannot be held criminally responsible for knowledge of medical risks which are neither readily apparent nor known to him. Cf. Fabritz v. Traurig, 583 F.2d 697, 698 (4th Cir.1978) (child-abuse conviction vacated where record lacked evidence indicating that mother had knowledge of fatal nature of 3-year-old daughter's condition when she deferred seeking professional medical care for her). The mere fact that Dr. Nadhiry discussed the "problems" associated with a disease that she did not diagnose appellant's son as having is hardly sufficient evidence to place appellant on notice of the future seriousness of his son's need for medical care.

No evidence established that, at any time during his stay with appellant, appellant's son's illness rendered him helpless and unable to summon aid by himself. Appellant's son suffered from an unusual, long-term psychiatric eating disorder in which receptiveness to treatment was important for its cure. He resisted treatment while continuing to stay active. He attended school and performed routine activities that included mowing a friend's lawn just 2 days before he left appellant.

While likely to become noticeable over a significant period of time, the steady weight loss of appellant's son would be almost imperceptible on a daily basis, especially where the uncontradicted evidence indicates that his son attempted to hide his weight loss and deceive appellant about his eating habits. To say that appellant was negligent for failing to force his son to get medical care sooner than his scheduled appointment based on his son's physical condition at the time of his death begs the question of how much sooner: after his son initially refused to get a follow-up examination?; after his son lost 20 more pounds?; 30 pounds?; 35½ pounds? The negligence of an individual's conduct (or lack of it) must be determined "in the light of the possibilities apparent to him at the time, and not by looking backward 'with the wisdom born of the event.'" Once appellant was aware his son had an appointment to see a doctor upon his son's return to Kansas, he had no apparent reason to force his son to seek medical treatment in New Jersey ahead of his scheduled appointment.[3] To be sure, there was nothing magic about the fact that his son died of cardiac failure at the weight of 80 pounds. Uncontradicted evidence in the record indicated that, while anorexics may die suddenly after extreme weight loss, they may also live at much lower body weights than Brad's without complication. . . .

■ COX, JUDGE, with whom JUDGE CRAWFORD joins, dissenting. Viewing the evidence in the light most favorable to the prosecution, which is the appropriate mode for reviewing the legal sufficiency of evidence, there can be no serious question that the evidence of appellant's negligence is sufficient to sustain his conviction. The obvious reason for our viewing evidence in the light most favorable to the prosecution is that the defense evidence, for one reason or another, did not sway the factfinder. . . . The question then is whether the prosecution presented enough evidence such that "any rational trier of fact could have found the essential elements of the crime beyond a reasonable doubt." The logical place to look, therefore, is the prosecution's evidence. . . .

The record does not reveal how much appellant knew, prior to Brad's moving to New Jersey, about his physical and mental condition. [Brad's mother testified that, at the time Brad moved to New Jersey, he weighed between 135 and 140 pounds.] However, there is evidence that appellant was specifically made aware of the general nature of the situation shortly after Brad's arrival. This came about because, on April 17, 1988—2 ½ to 3 ½ weeks after his arrival, Brad paid a visit to an emergency room at Fort Dix, due to dizziness and difficulty breathing. By that time, his weight had dropped to 125 pounds.

Three days later, on April 20, he was seen on a follow-up basis by Dr. Grace Nadhiry, a pediatrician at Fort Dix. By this time, Brad's weight had dropped to 122 pounds. . . . Dr. Nadhiry [testified that she discussed anorexia with Brad and appellant. She made appellant "aware of the problems that could come up," and she asked him to make a follow-up appointment for Brad.]

The April 20 visit with Dr. Nadhiry was Brad's last contact with a doctor until his death—just over 3 months later—when Brad's weight had dropped to about 80 pounds! Despite the multitude of medical, psychological, psychiatric, and social resources available without cost to service-members and their dependents by merely picking up a telephone, there is no evidence that appellant ever took any meaningful action during that interval to enlist the assistance of any health care or social professional or agency. Indeed there is no indication that appellant ever so much as notified any person in a position of public trust or authority, or any agency, that he was having a problem with his son! This wholesale failure to seek professional assistance—particularly if

[3] Even the mother of appellant's son admitted that, although she was shocked by her son's condition when she had picked him up at the airport in Kansas and moved up his appointment by several hours, she did not immediately force her son to go to the hospital before taking him to her house because she "didn't honestly believe that he was going to die."

normal parental suasion was not working—is the precise theory of negligence upon which appellant was prosecuted and convicted.

Brad flew back to Kansas on July 27, 1988, and was found dead in bed by his mother on the morning of July 28, 1988. An autopsy was conducted July 29, and the pathologist, Dr. (Colonel) Mani Bala, determined the cause of death to be "emaciation and cachexia due to starvation, cardiac failure due to starvation." . . . Dr. Bala described Brad's appearance as

> just like wasted away to the point you can see the bones on the body. It's like—almost like having skin shot on a skeleton. That's what cachexia means, wasted down to the bones. . . . [T]he muscles were all wasted down to the bones. The pictures will tell you all the details,[3] but he was really burned down or cachectic to the point it's almost like a mummy dug out of [the] grave and—

Asked, "If an individual weighed 122 pounds and dropped to 80 within about three and a half months, would that weight loss be noticeable?," Dr. Bala responded, "You bet, absolutely."

Such was the strapping lad appellant feared would "punch . . . [his] running lights out" if appellant sought medical attention. Dr. Bala was confident that, had Brad received medical attention as little as 24 hours before his death, he would have survived.

Dr. Bala's description of Brad's appearance was corroborated by other witnesses. Brad's mother [testified that, when she first saw him at the airport, he was hideous.] "He looked like a walking skeleton." . . . The safety pins he used to hold up his pants caused "sores on his side" that had to be covered by band-aids. . . .

A teacher at Sylvan Learning Center in New Jersey, where Brad received approximately 24 hours of coaching between May and July, 1988, also noted his deterioration. By late July, the teacher described him as being

> very, very thin. I mean his skin was white. You could almost—it's almost like you could see through it. And he had cuts—little cuts down his arm and he was very weak. He had trouble making it through the last hour that I taught with him and he complained that he was perspiring and thirsty.

He had to stop the session because "he said he was getting dizzy spells and he was perspiring and he just couldn't concentrate."

Appellant gave the Learning Center director the impression that Brad had recently been released from the hospital and that everything that could be done for Brad was being done. The director "probed a little bit to find out what the illness had been, [but] there was resistance to sharing it with me and so . . . [she] respected their privacy." The general supposition at the Center was that Brad had either "AIDS or cancer." . . .

---

[3] Defense counsel objected to admission of the pictures on the ground that "a couple of the photographs . . . looked like they are straight from Dachau." Indeed, these post-mortem photographs, a number of which were received in evidence, are virtually sufficient in and of themselves to overcome a legal sufficiency challenge. They portray a young man who is a virtual skeleton—nothing but skin and bones.

[L]ooking only to the prosecution's evidence, I am satisfied it was more than sufficient to sustain the findings of guilty. As I view the prosecution's evidence, the legal adequacy of the evidence of neglect and proximate cause, inter alia, are beyond dispute.

## NOTES ON INVOLUNTARY MANSLAUGHTER

### 1. THE DEGREE OF CULPABILITY SUFFICIENT FOR INVOLUNTARY MANSLAUGHTER

The common law defined involuntary manslaughter as a killing caused by reckless or negligent conduct that was insufficiently blameworthy to constitute murder but more culpable than ordinary civil negligence. Thus, for purposes of isolating involuntary manslaughter as a distinct degree of homicide, the doctrinal task has been to identify a species of killings that (1) are *less* reckless than those manifesting the "depraved indifference to human life" required for a second-degree murder conviction and (2) are *more* negligent than those required for tort, as opposed to criminal, liability. As the *Roe* case and the note materials on second-degree murder explain, the common law courts tended to fall back on epithets and hyperbole when forced to articulate the difference between depraved-indifference murder and involuntary manslaughter. Thus, according to *Roe*, "[w]hether the lesser risk [of death] sufficient for manslaughter is elevated into the very substantial risk present in murder depends on the wantonness of defendant's acts—i.e., whether they were committed '[under] circumstances evincing a depraved indifference to human life.' "

When it came time to describe the difference between the ordinary negligence sufficient for tort liability and that degree of negligence that will support a conviction for involuntary manslaughter, the common law courts tended to be no more precise. Most agree that it takes "more" negligence than will suffice for an ordinary tort, but there is surprisingly little attention in common law cases to how that additional ingredient can be formulated in a way that effectively communicates to juries the judgment to be made. Is it likely that a jury would understand the standard the court means to be applying?

#### *(i) Commonwealth v. Sostilio*

In Commonwealth v. Sostilio, 325 Mass. 143, 89 N.E.2d 510 (1949), the court said:

> The question in this case is whether there is evidence of wanton or reckless conduct on the part of the defendant. Wanton or reckless conduct has been defined as "intentional conduct, by way either of commission or omission where there is a duty to act, which conduct involves a high degree of likelihood that substantial harm will result to another." Wanton or reckless conduct is the legal equivalent of intentional conduct. If by wanton or reckless conduct bodily injury is caused to another, the person guilty of such conduct is guilty of assault and battery. And since manslaughter is simply a battery that causes death, if death results he is guilty of manslaughter.

The court applied this standard to uphold the manslaughter conviction of a driver of midget race-cars who killed another competitor by causing a crash while trying to pass by fitting his four-foot car into a two-foot space.

### *(ii) Commonwealth v. Agnew*

Contrast Commonwealth v. Agnew, 263 Pa.Super. 424, 398 A.2d 209 (1979). The defendant was a farmer who was driving his tractor home after disking a field. It was close to midnight and the road, a two-lane highway bounded by guard rails, was unlighted. The road was 33 feet wide from guard rail to guard rail, and the disk the farmer was towing behind his tractor was 17 feet, four inches wide. No lights were placed on the disk. An oncoming car traveling at about 55 miles per hour saw the tractor but not the disk, never slowed down, and hit the disk. The driver and his passenger were killed. The policeman who came to the scene testified that he was unable to see the disk, even with the aid of headlights, until he came to within 30 or 40 feet of the tractor.

The court reversed a conviction of involuntary manslaughter. It reasoned as follows:

> The state of mind or mens rea which characterizes involuntary manslaughter is recklessness or gross negligence: a great departure from the standard of ordinary care evidencing a disregard for human life or an indifference to the possible consequences of the actor's conduct. . . .
>
> We feel that the facts in the instant case . . . fail to show Agnew's indifference to the possible consequences of his actions. While the evidence shows that Agnew committed two summary offenses under the Motor Vehicle Code[a] which were substantial factors in bringing about the accident, this in itself is not sufficient to sustain a charge of involuntary manslaughter. However, the commonwealth argues that since Agnew drove his tractor at night knowing that the unlighted extremities of the towed disk would encroach upon the oncoming lane, the requisite mens rea was present. However, what must be shown is *disregard* for human life, and an *indifference* to consequences. Here the record shows that Agnew was quite aware of the risk he created and took positive steps to reduce the risk. He placed flashing yellow lights on the top of the tractor cab, placed warning signs on the tractor disk, and proceeded at a slow rate of speed. Obviously, as the opinion of the lower court concludes, "[t]he precautions were tragically inadequate." Still, the fact that Agnew took these precautions negates the requisite *disregard* of human life. Additionally, when Agnew perceived the oncoming car, he took every possible step to avoid a collision, pulling his tractor over to the right so far as the guard rails would allow . . . , and slowing his tractor down to a stop. This is not indifference to potential consequences, but a conscientious attempt to reduce the risk of an accident. Unhappily, the [driver of the] oncoming car never saw the towed disk in his lane and drove into it at full speed. While a jury could find

[a] He violated prohibitions limiting the maximum width of farm equipment on a highway and requiring that one-half of the roadway be yielded to an oncoming vehicle.—[Footnote by eds.]

Agnew guilty of ordinary negligence and impose civil liability on him, we assume, his actions disprove the "disregard of human life and indifference to consequences" mens rea necessary to support the criminal charge of involuntary manslaughter.

## 2. THE DEGREE OF CULPABILITY SUFFICIENT FOR MANSLAUGHTER AND NEGLIGENT HOMICIDE UNDER THE MODEL CODE

The Model Penal Code divides the former common law offense of involuntary manslaughter into two offenses. Section 210.3 punishes a homicide as manslaughter if "recklessly" committed and § 210.4 punishes a homicide as negligent homicide if "negligently" committed. Many American jurisdictions have followed this approach, both before and after the Model Penal Code was drafted. It is thus not uncommon, as *Robertson* illustrates, for the law of a particular jurisdiction to reflect three grades or levels of criminal homicide based on blameworthy inadvertence: an extreme recklessness that will justify a conviction of some form of murder, a type of recklessness or negligence that will justify a conviction of manslaughter, and a degree of negligence that will warrant a conviction of negligent homicide. What is unique about the Model Penal Code, therefore, is the care with which it attempts to define the concepts of "recklessness" and "negligence" that will suffice.

Is the Model Penal Code approach an improvement over the common law? Are the grading distinctions intelligible? Desirable?

## 3. QUESTIONS AND COMMENTS ON *ROBERTSON*

Unlike *Roe*, which explores the distinction between depraved-indifference murder and involuntary manslaughter, *Robertson* addresses the distinction between involuntary manslaughter and negligent homicide, and, indeed, the ultimate distinction between criminal liability and (potential) tort liability. Robertson was prosecuted for involuntary manslaughter in connection with Brad's death, which required the government to prove that his behavior "amounted to culpable negligence." The Military Judge's Benchbook offers the following definition of "culpable negligence" to be used when instructing the jury on the elements of involuntary manslaughter:

> Culpable negligence is a degree of carelessness greater than simple negligence. Simple negligence is the absence of due care. The law requires everyone at all times to demonstrate the care for the safety of others that a reasonably careful person would demonstrate under the same or similar circumstances; this is what "due care" means. Culpable negligence is a negligent act or failure to act accompanied by a gross, reckless, wanton or deliberate disregard for the foreseeable results to others.

Presumably, the judge who presided over Robertson's trial gave a version of this instruction to the members of the court-martial, and they found Robertson guilty. On appeal, the Court of Military Review reduced the conviction from involuntary manslaughter to negligent homicide. In the opinion reproduced above, the Court of Military Appeals reversed again, finding that the evidence was insufficient to support even the finding of "simple negligence" required for conviction of negligent homicide Which body of decisionmakers—the members of the court-martial, the judges on the Court of Military Review, the majority on the Court of Military Appeals—got it right? Was either of the courts of appeal justified in rejecting as insufficient the evidence of Robertson's guilt—either of involuntary manslaughter, as the members of the court-martial found, or of negligent homicide, as the Court of Military Review found? In most jurisdictions, there is a distinction between criminal negligence and tort negligence. Normally, the standard that justifies civil recovery of damages is not an adequate basis for the imposition of a criminal sanction. Did the Court of Military Appeals keep this straight?

In connection with *Robertson*, it is useful to revisit the doctrinal analysis applied in cases where criminal liability is sought to be imposed on the basis of an "omission" rather than an "affirmative act." Presumably, each of the judges on the Court of Military Appeals agreed that Robertson owed a duty of care to Brad, which extended to providing him with medical attention in an emergency. However, it is possible that the judges did not agree on the precise scope of that duty and that this disagreement in part explains their disagreement over the ultimate question of criminal liability. In his concurring opinion, Judge Gierke implies that Robertson had a duty to obtain medical assistance for Brad only when Brad's "illness rendered him helpless and unable to summon aid by himself." Is that a correct statement of the duties that parents owe to their children? To infants? To teenagers? Does the duty of care analysis differ in cases involving failure to assist a person who is suffering from a mental, as opposed to physical, illness or condition?

Might the outcome of the case have been different if Robertson had been Brad's mother rather than his father? If Brad had been a girl instead of a boy? Should these differences matter?

## SECTION 4: CAUSATION

### State v. Pelham

Supreme Court of New Jersey, 2003.
824 A.2d 1082.

■ LAVECCHIA, JUSTICE. This criminal appeal focuses on a disputed jury instruction involving the subject of causation. Defendant was convicted of second-degree death by auto. At trial, the court instructed the jury that a car-accident victim's voluntary removal from a respirator was legally insufficient as an independent intervening cause and thus incapable of breaking the chain of causality between defendant's acts and the victim's death. . . . The Appellate Division reversed and remanded for a new trial because, in its view, "the charge to the jury on intervening cause deprived defendant of his constitutional right to have the jury in a criminal trial . . . decide all elements of the charged offense." We reverse.

It is beyond dispute that individuals have the right to self-determination in respect of medical care generally and, specifically, in respect of rejecting or removing life support devices or techniques. We conclude that the jury may be instructed, as a matter of law, that a victim's determination to be removed from life support is a foreseeable event that does not remove or lessen criminal responsibility for death.

I.

The facts of the horrific car accident in which defendant, Sonney Pelham, was involved are summarized from the trial record. On the evening of December 29, 1995, William Patrick, a sixty-six-year-old lawyer, was driving his Chrysler LeBaron in the right lane of northbound Route 1 in South Brunswick. At approximately 11:42 p.m., a 1993 Toyota Camry driven by defendant struck the LeBaron from behind. The LeBaron sailed over the curb and slid along the guardrail, crashing into a utility pole before it ultimately came to rest 152 feet from the site of impact. The Camry traveled over a curb and came to rest in a grassy area on the side of the highway.

Two nearby police officers heard the collision and rushed to the scene. The officers found Patrick, still wearing his seatbelt, unconscious and slumped forward in the driver's seat. The rear of the LeBaron was crumpled through to the rear tire and the backseat, and the convertible top was crushed. Patrick was making "gurgling" and "wheezing" sounds, and appeared to have difficulty breathing. His passenger, Jocelyn Bobin, was semi-conscious. Emergency crews extricated the two using the "jaws of life" and transported them to [a hospital]. Bobin was treated and later released.

At the accident scene, Officer Heistand smelled an odor of alcohol on defendant's breath, and noted that he was swaying from side to side and front to back. He had no injuries, but was "belligerent." Heistand believed defendant was intoxicated. . . . Defendant failed [three field sobriety tests. Experts later estimated that his blood alcohol content was] between .19 and .22 at the time of the accident.

Patrick's condition was critical on his arrival at [the hospital]. He had suffered a constellation of injuries, including a spinal column fracture that left him paralyzed from the chest down and a "flailed chest," a condition in which the ribs are broken in multiple places causing uneven chest wall movement during each breath. . . . The catastrophic injuries Patrick experienced made it virtually impossible for him to breathe on his own. . . . He was placed on a ventilator. Within five days of the accident, [Patrick's lungs began] to fail. His heart beat was rapid and irregular, and his blood pressure was dropping because of the turmoil within his body. Low blood pressure triggered the start of kidney failure.

Patrick's paralysis rendered him at an increased risk for pulmonary thromboemboli, or blood clots. Accordingly, doctors implanted a vena cava filter through the major vein in the groin area and into the major blood vessel to the heart. The filters were intended to trap clots that form in the lower extremities. A ventilator tube inserted through Patrick's throat was converted to a surgical airway through his neck and into his windpipe. Because Patrick was unable to feed himself, he was fed initially by a tube inserted through his nose to the stomach, and later by a tube directly into the stomach. In addition, because paralysis left him unable to control his bladder or bowels, a Foley catheter was inserted. . . .

On March 13, 1996, Patrick was transferred to [a hospital that] specialized in the care of patients with spinal cord injuries. When he arrived, Patrick was unable to breathe on his own, and was suffering from multi-organ system failure. Medication was required to stabilize his heart rhythm. He was extremely weak, with blood-protein levels that placed him at high risk of death. He was unable to clear secretions in his airways, and thus his oxygen levels would drop requiring medical personnel repeatedly to clear the secretions. Complications from the ventilator caused pneumonia to recur due to his inability to cough or to protect himself from bacteria. Bowel and urinary tract infections continued.

. . . Patrick also was monitored by psychiatric staff. He presented as depressed, confused, uncooperative, and not engaged psychologically. At times he was "hallucinating," even "psychotic." The staff determined that he was "significantly" brain injured. Nonetheless, Patrick was aware of his physical and cognitive disabilities. During lucid moments, he expressed his unhappiness with his situation, and, on occasion, tried to remove his ventilator.

Patrick improved somewhat during the month of April, but then his condition rapidly regressed. By early May, severe infections returned, as well as pneumonia. It was undisputed at trial that Patrick had expressed to his family a preference not to be kept alive on life support. Because of his brain damage, his lack of improvement, and his severe infections Patrick's family decided to act in accordance with his wishes and remove the ventilator. [W]ithin two hours of the ventilator's removal on May 30, 1996, he was pronounced dead. The Deputy Middlesex County Medical Examiner determined that the cause of death was sepsis and bronchopneumonia resulting from multiple injuries from the motor vehicle accident.

Defendant was charged with first-degree aggravated manslaughter. . . .

. . . At trial, [defendant offered no expert testimony] to refute the causal connection between Patrick's death and his accident injuries.

[T]he trial court included in its jury charge on causation an instruction concerning intervening cause and a victim's determination to remove life support. On those points, the trial court instructed the jury as follows:

> To establish causation the State must prove two elements beyond a reasonable doubt. First, that but for defendant's conduct William Patrick wouldn't have died. Second, William Patrick's death must have been within the risk of which the defendant was aware. If not it must involve the same kind of injury or harm as the probable result of the defendant's conduct and must also not be too remote, too accidental in its occurrence or too dependant [sic] upon another's volitional act to have a just bearing on the defendant's liability or on the gravity of the offense. In other words, the State must prove beyond a reasonable doubt that William Patrick's death was not so unexpected or unusual that it would be unjust to find the defendant guilty of aggravated manslaughter.
>
> Now, it is alleged that the victim William Patrick died approximately five months after the collision which occurred on December 29, 1995. With regard to the issue of remoteness there is no requirement that the State prove that the victim

died immediately or within a certain period of time after the collision. Nevertheless, you may consider the time that elapsed between the collision and Mr. Patrick's death along with all of the other evidence in the case in determining whether the State has proven beyond a reasonable doubt that the defendant caused William Patrick's death as I've defined that term.

The State alleges that William Patrick died as a result of medical complications from the injuries which he sustained in the collision. Subject to the definition of causation which I have already given you the State may satisfy its burden of proving causation by proving beyond a reasonable doubt that William Patrick died from medical complications that resulted from injuries which he sustained in the collision provided that these injuries and medical complications were the precipitating and contributing causes of his death.

With regard to the issue of accident, if you find that Mr. Patrick's death resulted from preexisting medical conditions independent of the injuries and accompanying medical complications which he received as a result of the collision . . . then you must find [the defendant] not guilty. If you find that Mr. Patrick died as a result of prior medical conditions being exacerbated or made worse by the collision you are instructed that criminal liability is not lessened because the victim is not in excellent health.

In other words, if you find beyond a reasonable doubt that the defendant's conduct accelerated or worsened any preexisting medical conditions or illness which Mr. Patrick had thereby resulting in his death and meets the other conditions of causation then you should find the defendant caused Mr. Patrick's death.

Let me now instruct you on what an intervening cause is and what it's not. An intervening cause is a cause which breaks the original chain of causation. In that regard you have heard testimony that on May 30, 1996 William Patrick was taken off the ventilator pursuant to his wishes and that he died several hours later. I instruct you that the removal of life supports, in this case a ventilator, is not a sufficient intervening cause to relieve the defendant of criminal liability. In other words, the removal of life supports from Mr. Patrick who is not brain dead was not a sufficient intervening cause to relieve Mr. Pelham from criminal liability.[2]

If you find that the defendant's actions set in motion the victim's need for life support the causal link between the defendant's actions and the victim's death is not broken by the

[2] We do not approve of language in the last two sentences of this paragraph. Nonetheless, reviewing the charge as a whole, we believe that the jury did not misunderstand its obligation to determine the factual question concerning causation in this case, namely, whether Patrick's death resulted from the natural progression of his accident injuries and their complications. To emphasize that the jury must make the causation determination, the court should have added language such as: "Should you make the finding that Mr. Patrick died from medical complications that resulted from injuries he sustained in the collision. . . ." . . .

> removal or refusal of life support as long as you find that the death was the natural result of the defendant's actions.

The jury acquitted defendant of aggravated manslaughter, but convicted him of the lesser-included offense of second-degree vehicular homicide. He was sentenced to a custodial term of seven years with a mandatory parole ineligibility period of three years. . . .

II.

New Jersey has been in the forefront of recognizing an individual's right to refuse medical treatment. It is now well settled that competent persons have the right to refuse life-sustaining treatment. Even incompetent persons have the right to refuse life-sustaining treatment through a surrogate decision maker.

The parameters of the right to refuse medical treatment were first addressed in the seminal case In re Quinlan, 70 N.J. 10, 355 A.2d 647, cert. denied sub nom. Garger v. New Jersey, 429 U.S. 922 (1976). We concluded that the right to decide whether to forego life-sustaining treatment was "a valuable incident [to the] right of privacy" afforded by both the New Jersey and United States Constitutions. Any interest the State might have in preservation of life "weakens and the individual's right to privacy grows as the degree of bodily invasion increases and the prognosis dims."

As we explained, because Karen Ann Quinlan's prognosis was "extremely poor," any State-asserted interest in preserving life was outweighed by her right to self-determination. The "bodily invasion" involved in her care was extensive, including constant nursing care, antibiotics, a catheter, a respirator, and a feeding tube. We held that the only practical way to protect Ms. Quinlan's right to refuse treatment when she was incompetent was to permit her guardian to determine whether Ms. Quinlan would have refused life-sustaining treatment. Cognizant of the liability risk attendant when physicians carry out such wishes, we also made clear that a doctor's termination of treatment, and consequent acceleration of death, is not homicide. Since the 1976 decision in *Quinlan*, numerous other courts, including the United States Supreme Court, have recognized the so-called "right to die." See Cruzan v. Director, Missouri Dept. of Health, 497 U.S. 261 (1990) (recognizing that competent person has Fourteenth Amendment liberty interest in refusing unwanted medical treatment).

[In cases following *Quinlan*, we] observed that the right of self-determination is tempered by the State's countervailing interests, including: (1) preservation of life; (2) prevention of suicide; (3) protection of innocent third parties; and (4) safeguarding the integrity of the medical profession. However, those state interests usually will not preclude a competent person from refusing treatment for himself or herself. As we explained,

> refusing medical intervention merely allows the disease to take its natural course; if death were eventually to occur, it would be the result, primarily, of the underlying disease, and not the result of a self-inflicted injury. . . .

[T]he public policy of this State, as developed by case law and through legislative enactment,[a] clearly recognizes that an individual has the right to refuse devices or techniques for sustaining life, including the withholding of food and the removal of life support. We turn then to examine the effect to be given to a victim's exercise of that right in the context of a homicide trial.

III. A.

Defendant was charged with aggravated manslaughter, which, according to the New Jersey Code of Criminal Justice (Code), occurs when one "recklessly causes death under circumstances manifesting extreme indifference to human life." The trial court charged the jury on aggravated manslaughter and the lesser-included offense of second-degree vehicular homicide, defined as "criminal homicide . . . caused by driving a vehicle or vessel recklessly." Causation is an essential element of those homicide charges.

The Code defines "causation" as follows:

> a. Conduct is the cause of a result when:
>
> (1) It is an antecedent but for which the result in question would not have occurred; and
>
> (2) The relationship between the conduct and result satisfies any additional causal requirements imposed by the code or by the law defining the offense. . . .
>
> c. When the offense requires that the defendant recklessly or criminally negligently cause a particular result, the actual result must be within the risk of which the actor is aware or, in the case of criminal negligence, of which he should be aware, or, if not, the actual result must involve the same kind of injury or harm as the probable result and must not be too remote, accidental in its occurrence, or dependent on another's volitional act to have a just bearing on the actor's liability or on the gravity of his offense.

The causation requirement of our Code contains two parts, a "but-for" test under which the defendant's conduct is "deemed a cause of the event if the event would not have occurred without that conduct" and, when applicable, a culpability assessment. Under the culpability assessment,

> when the actual result is of the same character, but occurred in a different manner from that designed or contemplated [or risked], it is for the jury to determine whether intervening causes or unforeseen conditions lead to the conclusion that it is unjust to find that the defendant's conduct is the cause of the actual result. Although the jury may find that the defendant's conduct was a "but-for" cause of the victim's death . . . it may nevertheless conclude . . . that the death differed in kind from that designed or contemplated [or risked] or that the death

[a] In 1991, the New Jersey legislature passed a statute that identified procedures for making "living wills," by which people provide "advance directives" concerning their future medical care. The legislative findings included a statement declaring that patients have the right "to accept, to reject, or to choose among alternative courses" of health-care treatment.—[Footnote by eds.]

was too remote, accidental in its occurrence, or dependent on another's volitional act to justify a murder conviction.

Our Code, like the Model Penal Code (MPC), does not identify what may be an intervening cause. Instead, the Code "deals only with the ultimate criterion by which the significance of such possibilities ought to be judged." Removal of life support, as it relates to causation, should be judged only by the criteria of the Code, assuming that the law recognizes the possibility that removal can be an intervening cause. The dissent . . . suggests that the [Code's] reference to "another's volitional act" supports having the jury determine whether a crime victim's removal from life support constitutes an independent intervening cause. While "another's volitional act" undoubtedly would require a jury to consider whether, for example, a doctor's malpractice in treating a crime victim constituted an intervening cause that had broken the chain of causation after a criminal defendant's act, we do not believe, as the dissent suggests, that the Legislature intended the reference to "another's volitional act" to include a crime victim's decision to be removed from life support.

"Intervening cause" is defined as "an event that comes between the initial event in a sequence and the end result, thereby altering the natural course of events that might have connected a wrongful act to an injury." Generally, to avoid breaking the chain of causation for criminal liability, a variation between the result intended or risked and the actual result of defendant's conduct must not be so out of the ordinary that it is unfair to hold defendant responsible for that result. A defendant may be relieved of criminal liability for a victim's death if an "independent" intervening cause has occurred, meaning "an act of an independent person or entity that destroys the causal connection between the defendant's act and the victim's injury and, thereby becomes the cause of the victim's injury." The question we address, then, is whether the removal of the victim's life support may constitute, as a matter of law, an "independent intervening cause," the significance of which a jury may evaluate as part of a culpability analysis.

B.

The longstanding, clear policy of this State recognizes the constitutional, common law, and now statutorily based right of an individual to accept, reject, or discontinue medical treatment in the form of life supporting devices or techniques. An ill or injured person has that personal right and is free to exercise it, at his or her discretion, directly or through a family member or guardian acting in accordance with the person's wishes. In other words, a person's choice to have himself or herself removed from life support cannot be viewed as unexpected or extraordinary.

Decisions from other jurisdictions have reasoned similarly and have held that removal of life support is not an independent intervening cause in varied, but related, settings. Courts have confronted whether a victim's removal from life support renders a homicide verdict against the weight of the evidence and have rejected the contention that there was insufficient evidence to support a conviction when the victim expired following his or her removal from life support. . . .

Thus, in People v. Bowles, 461 Mich. 555, 607 N.W.2d 715 (2000), the defendant contended on appeal that the State's evidence on causation was insufficient because "the victim's death was caused by the intervening cause of removal from life support systems that were required to sustain the life of the victim." In its affirmance of the defendant's conviction, the Supreme Court of Michigan observed that "the implementation of a decision to terminate life-support treatment is not the cause of the patient's subsequent death. Instead, the discontinuance of life-support measures merely allows the patient's injury or illness to take its natural and inevitable course." The court concluded that the case involved "no separate intervening cause. Rather, we find in these facts only the unsuccessful efforts of the medical community to overcome the harm inflicted by the defendant, and the acceptance by the victim's family of the reality of the fatal injuries."

Similarly, courts have denied requests by defendants for a jury instruction charging that a victim's removal from life support constitutes an independent intervening cause sufficient to relieve the defendant of criminal liability. . . .

The California Court of Appeals reasoned . . . in People v. Funes, 23 Cal. App. 4th 1506, 28 Cal. Rptr. 2d 758 (1994), that the defendant was not entitled to an instruction on intervening causes because "as a matter of law, the decision to withhold antibiotics was not an independent intervening cause. Consequently, the court was not required to instruct on [that] issue." The court noted that a duty exists to instruct on an issue that is supported by the evidence, and conversely, that no such duty arises in respect of an issue unsupported by the evidence. Because an independent intervening cause absolving the defendant from criminal liability must be "unforeseeable" or an "extraordinary and abnormal occurrence," the Court concluded that on the facts of the case before it "the decision to withhold antibiotics was, as a matter of law, not an independent intervening cause. Instead, it was a normal and reasonably foreseeable result of defendant's original [criminal] act." There was no other reasonable inference from the evidence; the removal of life support was determined not to be independent from the defendant's criminal act. . . .

We agree with the widely-recognized principle that removal of life support, as a matter of law, may not constitute an independent intervening cause for purposes of lessening a criminal defendant's liability. Removal of life support in conformity with a victim's expressed wishes is not a legally cognizable cause of death in New Jersey. As aptly put by the District of Columbia Court of Appeals, "the defendant's desire to mitigate his liability may never legally override, in whole, or in part, the decisions of the physicians and the family regarding the treatment of the victim." . . .

Causation is a factual determination for the jury to consider, but the jury may consider only that which the law permits it to consider. The purpose of the charge to the jury is to inform the jury on the law and what the law requires. . . .

Our courts have recognized other circumstances in which a jury is not permitted to consider certain facts. For example, a defendant's criminal liability is not lessened by the existence in the victim of a medical condition that, unbeknownst to the defendant, made the victim particularly vulnerable to attack. The trial court here recognized as much when it correctly instructed the jury to that effect. Similarly, we now hold that a defendant's criminal liability may not be lessened by a victim's subsequent decision to discontinue life support. Therefore, although the trial court must be careful not to suggest that it is directing a verdict on causation, here, the court's instruction viewed in its entirety informed the jury that it could not consider the victim's removal from life support as an intervening cause of his death so long as the death was the natural result of defendant's actions. That is, if defendant's actions set in motion the victim's need for life support, without which death would naturally result, then the causal link is not broken by an unforeseen, extraordinary act when the victim exercises his or her right to be removed from life support and thereupon expires unless there was an intervening volitional act of another, such as gross malpractice by a physician. The trial court's statement was correct as a matter of law and its effect was not the equivalent of directing a verdict when the charge is read as a whole.

. . . In this case, the court did not direct a verdict on causation; rather the jury was instructed on what it could not consider as part of its determination of the causation question. Further, the jury properly was told that it could consider remoteness in respect of the length of time that passed between the date of the accident and the date on which Patrick expired after having been removed from life support (as well as the cause and progression of his medical complications). Thus, the jury could not consider removal as the cause of death when determining causation but it could consider whether the causal link was broken by remoteness in time of death.

IV.

In conclusion, we hold that there was no error in instructing the jury that a victim's decision to invoke his right to terminate life support may not, as a matter of law, be considered an independent intervening cause capable of breaking the chain of causation triggered by defendant's wrongful actions. The judgment of the Appellate Division is reversed and the matter remanded to the trial court for reinstatement of the judgment of conviction.

■ ALBIN, JUSTICE, with whom JUSTICE LONG joins, dissenting. "Hard facts make bad law" is an old saw and an apt description of the resolution of this appeal. In this vehicular homicide case, William Patrick, a sixty-six-year-old lawyer, suffered multiple devastating injuries when his car, which was stopped at a light, was rear-ended by this drunk-driving defendant. The majority opinion describes at length the victim's gruesome injuries, painful hospitalizations, and medical treatment. After the passage of five months during which his condition continued to deteriorate, Patrick, in accordance with his wishes, was taken off a ventilator, and died several hours later. . . .

Proof of causation is an element of every criminal offense and, until today, was no different from other elements that must be submitted to the jury. The New Jersey Code of Criminal Justice (Code) reserves to the jury the ultimate authority to determine whether intervening circumstances break the chain of causation of criminal culpability. In this case, the Code required the jury to determine whether the manner of Patrick's death, which followed from the voluntary removal of life support, was "too remote, accidental in its occurrence, or dependent on another's volitional act to have a just bearing on the actor's liability or on the gravity of his offense." The general and broad language of that provision was intended to apply to the infinite number of variables that arise in the unique circumstances of each new case, including that of this defendant. Causation was a matter that the jury should have been trusted to decide correctly.

Instead, the majority ignores the statutory language that governs this case and imports into the law of causation its own moral and philosophical preferences as it departs from the bedrock principle that a judge cannot direct a verdict against a defendant on an element of an offense, even where evidence of guilt appears overwhelming. The majority has carved from the Code's broad language on causation an inflexible rule that, in all cases, a victim's termination of medical care to support life may never be considered an independent intervening circumstance capable of breaking the chain of causation. The majority has come to that conclusion because it finds that the victim's removal of life-sustaining treatment is always foreseeable.

I object not so much to the wisdom of that new rule of law, as to its failure to find any support in the text of the Code. The Code's drafters left to the jury the commonsense judgment of distinguishing those cases in which intervening circumstances "would have a just bearing on the actor's liability or on the gravity of his offense." Our jurisprudence has traditionally deferred to the jury the delicate and difficult task of deciding the facts on which a defendant's guilt or innocence depends.

The majority's new rule is not only at odds with the Code and the fundamental right of an accused to have the jury decide each element of an offense, but will also have unanticipated consequences as it is reflexively applied to future cases. The jury will no longer be permitted to consider whether the chain of causation is broken in homicide cases where the victim refuses to take antibiotics or other benign medication necessary to sustain life without interfering with the enjoyment of life; where the victim declines a blood transfusion for religious or other reasons; or where the victim decides that he no longer wishes to continue using a medical device, such as a respirator or dialysis machine. The removal of a ventilator or the refusal to take medication or to allow a blood transfusion, all of which may be necessary to sustain life, may or may not, depending on the circumstances, "have a just bearing on the actor's liability or on the gravity of his offense," but the ultimate decision always has been one for the jury.

The application of a general rule, such as the Code's on intervening circumstances, necessarily will lead to varied outcomes, depending on the facts of a particular case. The understanding that two separate juries might decide the same case differently is an acknowledgment of the lack of perfection in our system of justice. That jurors, through their collective experience and humanity, are the conscience of the community is not a weakness, but a strength and the reason why, I suspect, we have not lost faith in the jury as the best means of delivering justice. . . .

[The] patient's right to refuse or terminate life-sustaining medical treatment is . . . not in conflict with a defendant's right to have a jury decide whether he should be held criminally liable for causing the death of a victim who elects to terminate his life. The defendant and prosecutor have no standing to interfere with the patient's decision-making process regarding the course of his medical treatment. It is highly improbable that a crime victim would remain on life support solely for the purpose of assuring that a defendant who victimized him would not be charged with homicide. It is equally improbable that a victim would decline medical intervention for the purpose of assuring a homicide prosecution. . . .

Our causation provision, although not identical to its MPC source, is firmly rooted in MPC § 2.03, and has been construed by this Court accordingly. The premise underlying each code's causation provision is that variations between the actual result of a defendant's conduct and that contemplated, designed, or probable under the circumstances are to be treated as "problems of culpability rather than metaphysical problems of causation." Both codes avoid the vague concept of "proximate cause," and focus on whether a remote result of which a defendant's conduct was a "but-for" cause "bears on the defendant's culpability for the offense."

New Jersey is only one of two states that have adopted MPC § 2.03 and explicitly added the intervening volitional conduct of others as a factor to be considered in determining causation. The inclusion of that factor in cases of human intervention is based on "deeply engrained common sense ideas about causality and responsibility," where the issue "properly turns on the voluntariness of the intervening actor's conduct—to the extent that his intervention is independent and voluntary, the defendant's liability should be diminished." Moreover, only New Jersey has incorporated the term "just" bearing into its causation provision. Despite the American Law Institute's debate on the wisdom of putting "undefined questions of justice to the jury" by including the optional term "just" in its final MPC provision, our Code's drafters, by adopting that term, surely believed its proponents' rationale that its inclusion "had the merit of putting it clearly to the jury that the issue it must decide is whether . . . it would be just to accord" significance to the actual result's remoteness, accidental quality, or dependence on another's volitional act in determining liability.

[The New Jersey causation provisions] "deal explicitly with variations between the actual result and that designed, contemplated or risked." "The actual result is 'to be contrasted with the designed or contemplated [ ]or . . . probable[ ] result in terms of its specific character and manner of occurrence.' " "Thus, when the actual result occurs in the same manner and is of the same character as the designed or contemplated [or probable] result, the causation requirement is satisfied." On the other hand, if the actual result does not occur in the same manner as the designed, contemplated, or probable result, " 'the culpability requirement is not established unless the actual result involved the same kind of injury or harm as that [probable,] designed or contemplated but the precise injury inflicted was different or occurred in a different way.' " Our Code

> makes no attempt to catalogue the possibilities, e.g., to deal with the intervening or concurrent causes, natural or human; unexpected physical conditions; distinctions between the infliction of mortal or non-mortal wounds. It deals only with the ultimate criterion by which the significance of such possibilities

ought to be judged, i.e., that the question to be faced is whether the actual result is too accidental in its occurrence or too dependent on another's volitional act to have a just bearing on the actor's liability or on the gravity of his offense.

Holding

. . . In sum, the drafters of our Code clearly contemplated, as previously recognized by this Court, that "when the actual result is of the same character, but occurred in a different manner . . . , it is for the jury to determine whether intervening causes or unforeseen conditions lead to the conclusion that it is unjust to find that the defendant's conduct is the cause of the actual result." This is just such a case.

[D]efendant does not dispute that his conduct was a "but-for" cause of the victim's death. Instead, he claims that the State must prove the additional requirement . . . that he recklessly caused the actual result, i.e., the victim's death, five months after the accident and two hours after the victim and his family elected to disconnect his ventilator. In order for this defendant to be guilty of vehicular homicide, the State must prove that the specific character and manner of the victim's death was either: (1) within the risk of which defendant was aware; or, (2) if not, then not "too remote, accidental in its occurrence, or dependent on another's volitional act to have a just bearing" on defendant's liability or the gravity of his offense.

The majority holds, in essence, that the risk that a victim will elect to reject or terminate some life-sustaining measure as a result of his injuries is, as a matter of law, within the risk of which defendants are aware. I part with the majority on this point. Whether defendant was aware of the risk was a question for the jury. I do not doubt that under the circumstances of this case, a jury could have found that the manner of Patrick's death was not "too remote, accidental in its occurrence, or dependent on another's volitional act to have a just bearing" on defendant's liability. However, by directing a verdict to the effect that the victim's decision to terminate his life was not a sufficient intervening circumstance to relieve defendant of criminal liability, the trial court deprived defendant of the right to have a jury decide the issue of causation. That ruling directly contravened the Legislature's intent that intervening circumstances be put "squarely to the jury's sense of justice." This Court's affirmance of that ruling eviscerates not only the right to trial by jury, but also the Legislature's intent that our causation provision be "flexible for application to the infinite variety of cases likely to arise."

While asserting the hard-and-fast rule that a victim's decision "to terminate life support, may not, as a matter of law, be considered an independent intervening cause," the majority maintains that a remoteness assessment is viable pursuant to the Code. In approving the trial court's charge, the majority finds that "the jury could not consider removal as the cause of death when determining causation but it could consider whether the causal link was broken by remoteness in time of death." Therefore, the majority must be suggesting that after a period of time, to be fixed by the jury, a victim's decision to terminate life support will not transform an aggravated assault into a homicide. The various factors set forth in the Code that were to have a "just bearing on the actor's liability or on the gravity of his offense" were not meant to be compartmentalized and detached from one another, but considered as a whole in reaching a just verdict. The drafters of the Code expected a jury to consider the interplay between remoteness and the volitional act of another as breaking the chain of causation. In making no allowance for the varied circumstances in which life support may be terminated by a victim, the majority does not permit the jury to consider the level of medical assistance required to sustain life, for example, whether the medical regimen is so burdensome as to deny even a minimal quality of life, or is relatively benign in comparison. The nature and scope of the medical care and the quality of life of the victim are factors that should be considered along with remoteness in determining whether intervening circumstances—including the voluntary termination of life support—should have a just bearing on the outcome of the case. . . .

## NOTES ON CAUSATION

### 1. THE RELEVANCE OF CAUSATION

Issues of causation arise in the criminal law whenever the definition of the offense specifies a result as an actus reus element. The causation inquiry, as *Pelham* illustrates, concerns a relationship or linkage between the defendant's conduct and the result such that the defendant can properly be punished for the result. Offenses against the person are the predominant contexts where issues of causation arise, and homicide is the offense where most causation problems are litigated.

Both issues of grading and liability can turn on causation. This point can be illustrated by assuming on the *Pelham* facts that the court had found that the decision to remove Patrick from life support was an "independent intervening cause" of Patrick's death and that Pelham therefore could not be convicted of homicide in connection with that death. Are there other crimes for which Pelham could be convicted? If so, are the penalties for those other crimes comparable to those imposed for second-degree vehicular homicide? Should they be?

A number of states have adopted reckless-endangering statutes derived from § 211.2 of the Model Penal Code. These offenses require proof that the actor created a grave risk of death, not that he or she caused the risked result. Presumably, Pelham could be prosecuted under such a statute, but the available penalty most likely would be less severe, and probably far less severe, than that imposed for vehicular homicide. Hence, a significant grading differential turns on the causation inquiry.

The differential is greater still when the defendant is merely negligent. If a death is "caused" by the right quantum of negligence, a conviction of negligent homicide may follow. There may be, in the context of operation of a vehicle, for example, various laws that were broken by a defendant's negligent behavior. But it is rare for there to be a generic "negligent endangering" statute. The Model Penal Code does not contain such a provision, nor does the law of all but a very few states. So the difference in many cases of negligent behavior may be between a fairly serious crime and no crime at all.

Causation may have more significance still. Compare the issues explored in Chapter V. To paraphrase a problem presented there, assume an actor who, in the terms of the New Jersey vehicular homicide statute, created a risk that another human being would die by driving a vehicle recklessly. If no death is "caused" by such behavior can there be a conviction for *attempted* vehicular homicide? Are the issues presented by debate of that question similar to those presented by the hypothetical variation of *Pelham* presented above? Why should results matter so much?

Elaborate treatment of these issues can be found in Stephen J. Schulhofer, Harm and Punishment: A Critique of Emphasis on the Results of Conduct in the Criminal Law, 122 U. Pa. L. Rev. 1497 (1974). Schulhofer concludes that "many problems associated with mens rea and the law of attempts have never been resolved satisfactorily, due to the absence of acceptable or coherent reasons for attributing significance to the harm caused; the entire field of causation in criminal law is utterly bankrupt for the same reason. Identification of the precise policies served by emphasis on results should provide a basis for more meaningful efforts to tackle these problems." What might these "precise policies" be?

## 2. THE COMMON LAW APPROACH TO CAUSATION

Most descriptions of the common law approach to causation divide the problem into two questions. The first is one of factual causation, frequently measured by the so-called "but for" test. This inquiry states a necessary but not sufficient condition of liability, i.e., that the result would not have occurred "but for" the defendant's antecedent conduct. A simple illustration of when this test would not be satisfied would be a case where *A* inflicts a minor flesh wound on *B*, and *C*—acting independently—shoots *B* through the heart and kills *B* instantly. *A*'s conduct in this instance would plainly not be a "but for" cause of *B*'s death, even though *A* may have intended to kill *B*.

It is clear, however, that the law cannot stop by asking the "but for" question. Consider the following case. *D* attempts to kill his wife and fails, and as a result she leaves home, goes to live on a farm with her family, falls off a horse while riding in the woods, lands on a rattlesnake, and dies from the bite of the snake. In this case, *D*'s conduct is related to his wife's death in a "but for" sense; were it not for his attempt to kill her, she would not have left home, would not have been riding in the woods, would not have fallen off her horse, etc. But, although *D* is guilty of attempted murder for his initial conduct, it is clear that he could not be convicted of murder following her death.

The concept used by the common law to describe this conclusion is called "proximate" or "legal" cause. If the defendant's conduct is a "but for" cause of death, the second question that must be asked is whether it was also the "proximate cause" of the death. It is this inquiry that is ordinarily crucial. When deciding whether the actor's conduct was the "sufficiently direct" and, hence, the "proximate" cause of death, courts often ask whether some other cause "intervened" in the chain of events begun by the defendant's conduct such that the defendant should not be held responsible for the ultimate result. The common law vocabulary for analyzing this question often used the terms "dependent intervening cause" to describe a more immediate causal factor that would not exculpate (e.g., the victim actually died from an infection that resulted from wounds inflicted by the defendant) and "independent intervening cause" to describe a causal factor that would exculpate (e.g., the wife's decision to go horseback riding in the hypothetical used above).

The difficulty with these terms is that they are merely labels that can be attached to conclusions already reached. They do not describe the process or the criteria by which one could reason to those conclusions. They do not explain why a particular actor should be guilty, nor do they establish criteria that can be applied to the next case.

### 3. THE MODEL CODE APPROACH

It is said in H.L.A. Hart and Tony Honoré, Causation in the Law 353 (1959), that "[t]he most lucid, comprehensive, and successful attempt to simplify problems of 'proximate cause' in the criminal law is that contained in the . . . Model Penal Code prepared by the American Law Institute." The Model Code made a deliberate attempt "to cut loose from the 'encrusted precedents' of 'proximate cause.' " In doing so, it substituted a new vocabulary and discarded the old common law terms for reasoning about the proximate-cause question. The New Jersey statute involved in *Pelham* was derived from the Model Code.

The key to the Model Code analysis of causation is recognition that the problem of proximate cause is not a problem of describing physical relationships, but one of assessing their legal significance. Moreover, the criteria against which their significance should be assessed are closely related to the criteria used for measuring responsibility in the criminal law. The question, in other words, is not quantitative, but qualitative; it turns on a judgment of blameworthiness and responsibility and should be thought of in those terms, not in terms of physical causation.

Section 2.03 of the Model Code provides:

(1) Conduct is the cause of a result when:

(a) it is an antecedent but for which the result in question would not have occurred; and

(b) the relationship between the conduct and result satisfies any additional causal requirements imposed by the Code or by the law defining the offense.

(2) When purposely or knowingly causing a particular result is an element of an offense, the element is not established if the actual result is not within the purpose or the contemplation of the actor unless:

(a) the actual result differs from that designed or contemplated, as the case may be, only in the respect that a different person or different property is injured or affected or that the injury or harm designed or contemplated would have been more serious or more extensive than that caused; or

(b) the actual result involves the same kind of injury or harm as that designed or contemplated and is not too remote or accidental in its occurrence to have a [just] bearing on the actor's liability or on the gravity of his offense.

(3) When recklessly or negligently causing a particular result is an element of the offense, the element is not established if the actual result is not within the risk of which the actor is aware or, in the case of negligence, of which he should be aware unless:

(a) the actual result differs from the probable result only in the respect that a different person or different property is injured or affected or that the probable injury or harm would have been more serious or more extensive than that caused; or

(b) the actual result involves the same kind of injury or harm as the probable result and is not too remote or accidental in its occurrence to have a [just] bearing on the actor's liability or on the gravity of his offense.

(4) When causing a particular result is a material element of an offense for which absolute liability is imposed by law, the element is not established unless the actual result is a probable consequence of the actor's conduct.

## 4. PROBLEMS WITH THE MODEL CODE

The Model Code provisions on causation have not been received uncritically. Many recently revised codes have not included a comparable provision, at least partly on the ground that the Model Code provision is too complex. There have also been a number of substantive criticisms, among them the following:

### *(i) Concurrent Causes*

In 1 Working Papers of the Nat'l Comm'n on Reform of Federal Criminal Laws 144–45 (1970), the Model Code reliance on "but-for" causation in § 2.03(1)(a) is criticized because it "ignores the cases in which ['but-for' causation] is not essential for liability." The example given is a case of concurrent causation:

> Even though all of the senators may have intended to kill Caesar and all of them stabbed him, under the Model Penal Code's formulation none would be criminally liable for his death since (so I shall assume) he would have died even though any one of them had held back his knife. Even a senator who stabbed Caesar through the heart would not be liable, since so Anthony tells us (act 3, scene 2) "sweet Caesar's blood" was streaming from all the wounds.

Is this a likely situation? Is it adequately dealt with by the Model Code?[a] What result under the Model Code if *A* inflicts a mortal wound on *B* with intent to kill, but *C* kills *B* before *A*'s wound can have its natural effect? Should *A* be guilty of murder?

---

[a] The membership of the American Law Institute debated this issue, "but decided that the language [of the Code] should not be complicated further in an attempt to make more explicit the treatment of extraordinary cases in which persons act concurrently but independently to produce the forbidden consequence." ALI, Model Penal Code and Commentaries, § 2.03, pp. 259–60 (1985). The commentary adds that "[a]ll who have considered the issue agree that each of the assailants should be liable, and it was the intent of the Institute to make them liable." It explains that there is no difficulty when multiple persons act in concert, since each is liable for the acts of the others and in sum "but for" cause is established. "The only difficult case is one that arises most infrequently, when the conduct of two actors is completely independent, and each actor's conduct would have been sufficient by itself to produce death. . . ." This situation should perhaps be characterized, the commentary concludes, as " 'death from two mortal blows.' So described, the victim's demise has as but-for causes each assailant's blow."

### *(ii) Transferred Intent*

Consider the following situation. *A* shoots at *B* with intent to kill. Because it was aimed badly, the shot misses, ricochets off a rock, and kills *C*. The common law would have resolved this case by using the fictional concept of "transferred intent"—by magically "transferring" *A*'s intent from *B* to *C* and holding *A* liable for murder. Under the Model Code, *A* would be liable for murder because *A* acted purposely with respect to the death of another and because the causation requirements of § 2.03(2)(a) would be satisfied; the actual result would have differed from the intended result "only in the respect that a different person . . . is injured."

It is argued in Note, Causation in the Model Penal Code, 78 Colum.L. Rev. 1249, 1267–72 (1978), that the common law transferred-intent doctrine is a species of strict liability and that the Model Code resolution in effect continues that result and is thus inconsistent with its normal approach to strict liability:

> A difference in victims is not simply a trivial variation in the manner in which harm occurs; the identity of the victim is apt to be of great significance both to the offender and to those affected by the killing. No one would suppose that an offender who fails to kill his intended victim has achieved his basic objective if he inadvertently kills someone else. Admittedly, the harm that ultimately results may be as great as that which would have occurred if the offender had accomplished his precise objective. But if the magnitude of resulting harm were the sole prerequisite for the imposition of liability, there would be no need for any proximity requirement.

The suggested solution is to treat the actor in the transferred-intent situation under the provisions of § 210.2(1)(b) of the Model Code, by adding a presumption of the required recklessness in cases where the death occurs during the attempted murder of another. Is this a better resolution? Does the Model Code embrace a form of strict liability in § 2.03(2)(a)? Is the transferred-intent situation properly treated as a causation problem?

## 5. QUESTIONS AND COMMENTS ON *PELHAM*

Some of the most difficult causation problems arise when the defendant sets in motion a series of events that is interrupted by the voluntary action of another person. The Model Code would resolve such a case by asking in § 2.03(3)(b) whether the actual result was "not too remote or accidental in its occurrence to have a [just] bearing on the actor's liability or the gravity of his offense." The words "remote or" were added to an earlier draft, partially in response to the criticism of Hart and Honoré that the words "too accidental" put the crucial inquiry in this kind of case "in quite unfamiliar terms." New Jersey responded to this problem by modifying the applicable standard. As *Pelham* explains, New Jersey adopts the basic Model Code structure but modifies § 2.03(3)(b) as follows: "the actual result must involve the same kind of injury or harm as the probable result and must not be too remote, accidental in its occurrence, or dependent on another's volitional act to have a just bearing on the actor's liability or on the gravity of his offense." N.J.Stat.Ann. § 2C:2–3(c). Is the New Jersey statute an improvement on the Model Code? How should liability in this situation be measured?

## SECTION 5: FELONY MURDER

### INTRODUCTORY NOTES ON FELONY MURDER

#### 1. THE RULE AND ITS TRADITIONAL LIMITATIONS

The original statement of the felony murder rule was that a person who commits any felony and all accomplices in that felony are guilty of murder if a death occurs during the commission or attempted commission of the felony. Liability is strict, in the sense that no inquiry need be made into the felons' culpability as to the death; their culpability for the underlying felony is sufficient. As the Supreme Court of Kansas put the point, "the killer's malignant purpose is established by proof of the collateral felony." State v. Goodseal, 220 Kan. 487, 553 P.2d 279 (1976). Thus, if two persons undertake to commit a robbery, they are both guilty of murder if a victim of the robbery is killed during the commission of the offense, whether or not either robber would have been guilty of murder by the application of the normal mens rea requirements for murder.

The history of felony murder is marked by judicial efforts to limit its scope. The premise of these efforts is that the rule should not be activated by "any" felony, because not all felonies present a likelihood of danger to human life. To pick just a few examples, the list of modern felonies includes offenses related to election returns and voting, securities and insurance violations, conflict of interest, fraud, and a wide variety of other activity in which the prospect of violence or other life-endangering activity is at best remote. Assuming that the rationale for the rule is based on the tendency of certain felonies to threaten life, it follows that some limitation on the kinds of felonies that support application of the felony murder rule is needed.

The courts have used essentially three devices for limiting the situations to which the rule applies: (i) a requirement that the felony be inherently dangerous, either in general or on the particular facts; (ii) a causation limitation, usually expressed as a requirement that the death be a "natural and probable result" of the felonious conduct; and (iii) a requirement that the felony be "independent" of the homicide, often stated to exclude lesser-included homicide and assault offenses from those felonies to which the rule applies. The first limitation is sometimes expressed as a requirement that the felony must be malum in se rather than malum prohibitum, though this is an obvious overgeneralization since not all malum in se offenses are dangerous to life. The third device is often identified as a "merger" rule; an assault with intent to kill, for example, may be said to "merge" into a resulting homicide and thus not to be an "independent" felony that can result in a felony murder conviction.

In many states, a form of the first limitation is imposed by statute. For example, murder statutes in those states that have followed the original Pennsylvania degree structure generally include a list of "inherently dangerous" felonies that will support a first-degree murder conviction. Most such statutes define second-degree murder as "all other kinds of murder" recognized by the common law. Thus, in these jurisdictions, second-degree murder includes a residual category of felony murder based on felonies not found on the first-degree list. Thus the need to address appropriate limitations on the unadorned felony murder rule exists in states where the highest grade of murder encompasses homicides that occur during the commission of "any" felony,[a] as well as in those states in which a lower grade of murder includes a residual category composed of other homicides that would constitute "murder" at common law.[b]

## 2. RATIONALE FOR THE RULE

The felony murder rule has two principal consequences. First, it criminalizes behavior that absent the rule would not be an independent homicide offense at all. The defendant will be guilty of murder without proof that any traditional culpability standard, independent of that required for the felony that triggered the rule, was satisfied. Thus, an entirely accidental killing—one for which neither an intent to kill nor recklessness or negligence as to the death can be shown—may result in a conviction for murder if it occurs during the commission of a qualifying felony. Second, the felony murder rule upgrades homicidal behavior that otherwise might be classified as a lesser offense. A negligent killing, for example, might be punished as involuntary manslaughter under normal circumstances, but is upgraded to murder if committed during the course of a qualifying felony. Similarly, provocation that ordinarily might reduce an offense to manslaughter may not have that effect if the charge is felony murder.

Why has the law provided for these results? Given the general reluctance of the common law system to rely on strict liability, why is strict liability used for one of the most serious criminal offenses? The usual answer is the one endorsed by the Supreme Court of Kansas in *Goodseal*: "The only rational function of the felony murder rule is to furnish an added deterrent to the perpetration of felonies which, by their nature or by the attendant circumstances, create a foreseeable risk of death." A well-known defense, though not necessarily an endorsement, of the rule was offered by Oliver Wendell Holmes in The Common Law 59 (1881):

> [I]f experience shows, or is deemed by the lawmaker to show, that somehow or other deaths which the evidence makes accidental happen disproportionately often in connection with other felonies, or with resistance to officers, or if on any other ground of policy it is deemed desirable to make special efforts for the prevention of such deaths, the lawmaker may consistently treat acts which, under the known circumstances, are felonious, or constitute resistance to officers, as having a sufficiently dangerous tendency to be put under a special ban. The law may, therefore, throw on the actor the peril, not only of the consequences foreseen by him, but also of consequences which, although not predicted by common experience, the legislator apprehends.

It is often noted in response to this contention that there is little empirical evidence that homicides "which the evidence makes accidental happen disproportionately often in connection with other felonies." In ALI, Model Penal Code and Commentaries, § 210.2, p. 38 (1980), statistics are reproduced which show that of 16,273 robberies in New Jersey in 1975, only 66 homicides (or homicides in .41 per cent of the cases) were committed.

---

[a] See, e.g., the Kansas statute quoted in State v. Goodseal, 220 Kan. 487, 553 P.2d 279 (1976): "Murder in the first degree is the killing of a human being committed maliciously, willfully, deliberately and with premeditation or committed in the perpetration or attempt to perpetrate any felony."

[b] See, e.g., the original Pennsylvania degree statute quoted in the Notes on First-Degree Murder following *State v. Brown*, above.

Similar figures are cited for other felonies and other jurisdictions. Do these statistics show that the felony murder rule is unnecessary, or that it works? Is Holmes right in considering only those homicides "which the evidence makes accidental"? Are these the only homicides as to which a special rule may be needed?

In an article entitled In Defense of the Felony Murder Doctrine, 8 Harv.J.Law & Pub.Policy 359 (1985), David Crump and Susan Waite Crump offer six rationales for retaining felony murder. First, they argue that the rule "reflects a societal judgment that an intentionally committed robbery that causes . . . death . . . is qualitatively more serious than an identical robbery that does not." As they remark, the law often classifies offenses on the basis of results. Murder and attempted murder, for example, may be committed with the same mens rea, yet attempted murder is usually graded less severely. The only factor that can account for this grading differential is that the murderer has caused a death. If it is not irrational to grade murder more seriously than attempted murder, they conclude, it is similarly not irrational to classify robbery-that-causes-a-death more seriously than robbery. Second, they argue that the "reinforcement of societal norms" associated with the function of condemnation supports placing the label "murder" on a death that occurs during certain felonies that are by their nature violent. They think this particularly appropriate when, as they argue is the case with felony murder, common social judgment coincides with the classification. Third, they argue that the "felony murder rule is just the sort of simple, commonsense, readily enforceable, and widely known principle that is likely to result in deterrence."

Their remaining arguments list advantages of the rule that they do not advance as independent justifications, but that ought to be considered, in their view, in any rational debate. Their fourth argument is that "the aim of consistent and predictable adjudication" is better served by the felony murder rule than by the convoluted rules that are often used to describe the mens rea of murder. Fifth, the "rule has beneficial allocative consequences because it clearly defines the offense, simplifies the task of judge and jury with respect to questions of law and fact, and thereby promotes efficient administration of justice." Finally, they argue that the rule reduces the incentive to commit perjury by removing defenses that can most readily be proved by the defendant's own testimony.

### 3. JUDICIAL REJECTION OF THE RULE: *PEOPLE V. AARON*

The felony murder rule was rejected by the Michigan Supreme Court in People v. Aaron, 409 Mich. 672, 299 N.W.2d 304 (1980). The court first addressed the history of the doctrine, noting that "the rule is of questionable origin" and "the reasons for the rule no longer exist, making it an anachronistic remnant, 'a historic survivor for which there is no logical or practical basis for existence in modern law.'" As to its origins, the court referred to scholarship[c] suggesting that the 16th century cases commonly thought to have established the rule were misinterpreted by Lord Coke and some of the other early writers. As to its initial rationale, the court said:

---

[c] E.g., J.M. Kaye, The Early History of Murder and Manslaughter, Part II, 83 Quarterly Rev. 569 (1967); Recent Developments, Felony-Murder-Rule—Felon's Responsibility for Death of Accomplice, 65 Colum.L.Rev. 1496 (1965); Note, Felony Murder as a First Degree Offense: An Anachronism Retained, 66 Yale L.J. 427 (1957).

The failure of the felony murder rule to consider the defendant's moral culpability is explained by examining the state of the law at the time of the rule's inception. The concept of culpability was not an element of homicide at early common law. The early history of malice aforethought was vague. The concept meant little more than intentional wrongdoing with no other emphasis on intention except to exclude homicides that were committed by misadventure or in some otherwise pardonable manner. Thus, under this early definition of malice aforethought, an intent to commit the felony would itself constitute malice. Furthermore, as all felonies were punished alike, it made little difference whether the felon was hanged for the felony or for the death.

Thus, the felony murder rule did not broaden the concept of murder at the time of its origin because proof of the intention to commit a felony met the test of culpability based on the vague definition of malice aforethought governing at that time. Today, however, malice is a term of art. It does not include the nebulous definition of intentional wrongdoing. Thus, although the felony murder rule did not broaden the definition of murder at early common law, it does so today. We find this enlargement of the scope of murder unacceptable, because it is based on a concept of culpability which is "totally incongruous with the general principles of our jurisprudence" today.

The Michigan statute at issue in *Aaron* was based on the original Pennsylvania degree structure:

> Murder which is perpetrated by means of poison, lying in wait, or other wilful, deliberate, and premeditated killing, or which is committed in the perpetration or attempt to perpetrate [certain listed felonies], is murder in the first degree. . . .

The court held that the purpose of the statute was only "to graduate punishment"; it "only serves to raise an already established *murder* to the first-degree level, not to transform a death, without more, into a murder." Thus, the "use of the term 'murder' in the . . . statute requires that a murder first be established before the statute is applied to elevate the degree."

The question, then, was what constituted a "murder" that could be elevated to "murder in the first degree" when committed in the course of one of the listed felonies. The prosecutor argued that the undefined term "murder" referred to the common law, and that the common law included a felony murder rule that could trigger the statute. The court recognized the logic of this argument, but held that it was an unsound rule that was "no longer acceptable":

> Accordingly we hold today that malice is the intention to kill, the intention to do great bodily harm, or the wanton and wilful disregard of the likelihood that the natural tendency of the defendant's behavior is to cause death or great bodily harm. We further hold that malice is an essential element of any murder, as that term is judicially defined, whether the murder occurs in the course of a felony or otherwise. The facts and circumstances involved in the perpetration of a felony may evidence an intent to kill, an intent to cause great bodily harm, or a wanton and wilful disregard of the likelihood that the natural tendency of

> the defendant's behavior is to cause death or great bodily harm; however, the conclusion must be left to the jury to infer from all the evidence.

Finally, the court addressed the practical effect of its abolition of the felony murder rule. It said:

> From a practical standpoint, the abolition of the category of malice arising from the intent to commit the underlying felony should have little effect on the result of the majority of cases. In many cases where the felony murder rule has been applied, the use of the doctrine was unnecessary because the other types of malice could have been inferred from the evidence.
>
> Abrogation of this rule does not make irrelevant the fact that a death occurred in the course of a felony. A jury can properly *infer* malice from evidence that a defendant set in motion a force likely to cause death or great bodily harm. Thus, whenever a killing occurs in the perpetration or attempted perpetration of an inherently dangerous felony, in order to establish malice the jury may consider the "nature of the underlying felony and the circumstances surrounding its commission." If the jury concludes that malice existed, they can find murder and, if they determine that the murder occurred in the perpetration or attempted perpetration of one of the enumerated felonies, by statute the murder would become first-degree murder.
>
> The difference is that the jury may not find malice from the intent to commit the underlying felony alone. The defendant will be permitted to assert any of the applicable defenses relating to mens rea which he would be allowed to assert if charged with premeditated murder. The latter result is reasonable in light of the fact that felony murder is certainly no more heinous than premeditated murder. The prosecution will still be able to prove first-degree murder without proof of premeditation when a homicide is committed with malice, as we have defined it, and the perpetration or attempted perpetration of an enumerated felony is established. Hence, our first-degree statute continues to elevate to first-degree murder a *murder* which is committed in the perpetration or attempted perpetration of one of the enumerated felonies.

Two justices wrote separately to explain the rationale on which they agreed with the result reached by the court's opinion. There were no dissents.

## 4. THE MODEL PENAL CODE AND MODERN STATUTES

The Model Penal Code takes the position that the felony murder rule is indefensible in principle because it bases the most severe sanctions known to the criminal law on strict liability. The Model Code suggests instead that ordinary principles of criminal homicide, causation, and complicity should be used for the prosecution of homicides that occur during the commission of a felony. It does, however, make one concession to the historical momentum of the rule. This is contained in § 210.2(1)(b), which reads as follows:

> [C]riminal homicide constitutes murder when . . . it is committed recklessly under circumstances manifesting extreme indifference to the value of human life. Such recklessness and

> indifference are presumed if the actor is engaged or is an accomplice in the commission of, or an attempt to commit, or flight after committing or attempting to commit robbery, rape or deviate sexual intercourse by force or threat of force, arson, burglary, kidnapping or felonious escape.

The effect of a presumption under the Model Code is dealt with in § 1.12(5). It really amounts to no more than an authorized inference. Is this an effective compromise? Is compromise appropriate?

Among the states in which recent penal-code revisions have been undertaken, only Hawaii and Kentucky have abolished the felony murder rule completely, and only New Hampshire has adopted the Model Penal Code solution. A couple of states have restricted the rule by engrafting an additional mens rea showing onto the traditional felony murder elements. For example, Delaware requires that the actor "recklessly cause the death of another person" in order to be guilty of first-degree murder under the felony murder doctrine, and reduces the offense to second-degree murder if the actor is negligent.

Among the other states, the most important revision is New York's, which is reproduced in Appendix B. The Model Code commentary reports that the New York approach has been copied in at least seven enacted codes. Is the New York approach a more principled compromise of the felony murder debate? What accounts for its greater popularity? What explains the persistence of the felony murder rule?

## People v. Hansen

Supreme Court of California, 1994.
9 Cal.4th 300, 36 Cal.Rptr.2d 609, 885 P.2d 1022.

■ GEORGE, JUSTICE. In this case we must determine whether the offense of discharging a firearm at an inhabited dwelling house is a felony "inherently dangerous to human life" for purposes of the second-degree felony murder doctrine, and, if so, whether that doctrine nonetheless is inapplicable in the present case under the so-called "merger" doctrine applied in People v. Ireland, 70 Cal.2d 522, 75 Cal.Rptr. 188, 450 P.2d 580 (1969), and its progeny. For the reasons explained hereafter, we conclude that this offense, for such purposes, is a felony inherently dangerous to human life and does not "merge" with a resulting homicide so as to preclude application of the felony murder doctrine. Because the Court of Appeal reached a similar conclusion, we affirm the judgment of that court upholding defendant's conviction of second-degree murder.

### I

On September 19, 1991, defendant Michael Hansen, together with Rudolfo Andrade and Alexander Maycott, planned to purchase $40 worth of methamphetamine. With that purpose, defendant, accompanied by his girlfriend Kimberly Geldon and Maycott, drove in defendant's Camaro to an apartment duplex located in the City of San Diego. Upon arriving at the duplex, defendant pounded on the door of the upstairs apartment where Christina Almenar resided with her two children. When he received no response, defendant proceeded to return to his automobile and was approached by Michael Echaves.

Echaves resided in the downstairs apartment with Martha Almenar (Christina's sister) and Martha's two children, Diane Rosalez, 13 years of age, and Louie Miranda, 5 years of age. At the time, Diane and Louie were outside with Echaves helping him with yard work. In response to a question from Echaves, defendant said he was looking for Christina. When Echaves stated he had not seen her, defendant asked whether Echaves would be able to obtain some crystal methamphetamine (speed). After making a telephone call, Echaves informed defendant that he would be able to do so. Defendant said he would attempt to purchase the drug elsewhere but, if unsuccessful, would return.

Defendant and his companions departed but returned approximately 20 minutes later. Defendant, accompanied by Echaves, Maycott, and Geldon, then drove a short distance to another apartment complex. Defendant parked his vehicle, gave Echaves two $20 bills, and told Echaves he would wait while Echaves obtained the methamphetamine. Echaves said he would be back shortly.

When Echaves failed to return, defendant and his companions proceeded to Echaves's apartment. Defendant knocked on the door and the windows. Diane and Louie were inside the apartment alone but did not respond. Their mother, Martha, had left the apartment to meet Echaves, who had telephoned her after eluding defendant. After meeting Echaves at a hardware store, Martha telephoned her children from a public telephone booth. Diane answered and told her mother that the "guys in the Camaro" had returned, pounded on the door, and then had left.

Meanwhile, defendant, Maycott, and Geldon returned to the location where Andrade was waiting for them, acquiring en route a handgun from an acquaintance. The three men then decided to return to Echaves's apartment with the objective either of recovering their money or physically assaulting Echaves. At approximately 7:30 p.m., defendant approached the apartment building in his automobile with the lights turned off, and then from the vehicle fired the handgun repeatedly at the dwelling. At the time, Diane was inside the apartment, in the living room with her brother. The kitchen and living room lights were on. Diane was struck fatally in the head by one of the bullets fired by defendant . . .

The trial court instructed the jury on several theories of murder, including second-degree felony murder as an unlawful killing that occurs during the commission or attempted commission of a felony inherently dangerous to human life, and further instructed that the felony of shooting at an inhabited dwelling is inherently dangerous to human life. The jury returned a verdict finding defendant guilty of second-degree murder. . . .

On appeal, defendant asserted, among other contentions, that the trial court erred in instructing the jury on second-degree felony murder based upon the underlying felony of discharging a firearm at an inhabited dwelling, because the latter offense merged with the resulting homicide within the meaning of *People v. Ireland.* [T]he Court of Appeal affirmed the conviction of second-degree murder. . . .

II

Murder is the unlawful killing of a human being, or a fetus, with malice aforethought. (§ 187, subd. (a).) Second degree murder is the unlawful killing of a human being with malice, but without the additional elements (i.e., willfulness, premeditation, and deliberation) that would support a conviction of first degree murder. (§§ 187, subd. (a); 189.)

Malice may be express or implied. (§ 188.) It is express "when there is manifested a deliberate intention unlawfully to take away the life of a fellow creature." (§ 188.) It is implied "when no considerable provocation appears, or when the circumstances attending the killing show an abandoned and malignant heart." (§ 188.) We have held that implied malice has both a physical and a mental component, the physical component being the performance of " 'an act, the natural consequences of which are dangerous to life,' " and the mental component being the requirement that the defendant " 'knows that his conduct endangers the life of another and . . . acts with a conscious disregard for life.' " (People v. Patterson, 49 Cal.3d 615, 626, 262 Cal.Rptr. 195, 778 P.2d 549 (1989); People v. Watson, 30 Cal.3d 290, 300, 179 Cal.Rptr. 43, 637 P.2d 279 (1981).)

The felony murder rule imputes the requisite malice for a murder conviction to those who commit a homicide during the perpetration of a felony inherently dangerous to human life. "Under well-settled principles of criminal liability a person who kills—whether or not he is engaged in an independent felony at the time—is guilty of murder if he acts with malice aforethought. The felony murder doctrine, whose ostensible purpose is to deter those engaged in felonies from killing negligently or accidentally, operates to posit the existence of that crucial mental state—and thereby to render irrelevant evidence of actual malice or the lack thereof—when the killer is engaged in a felony whose inherent danger to human life renders logical an imputation of malice on the part of all who commit it." (People v. Satchell, 6 Cal.3d 28, 43, 98 Cal.Rptr. 33, 489 P.2d 1361 (1971).)

The felony murder rule applies to both first-and second-degree murder. Application of the first-degree felony murder rule is invoked by the perpetration of one of the felonies enumerated in [the first-degree murder statute]. In People v. Ford, 60 Cal.2d 772, 795, 36 Cal. Rptr. 620, 388 P.2d 892 (1964), the court restricted the felonies that could support a conviction of second-degree murder, based upon a felony murder theory, to those felonies that are "inherently dangerous to human life." We have explained that the justification for the imputation of implied malice under these circumstances is that, "when society has declared certain inherently dangerous conduct to be felonious, a defendant should not be allowed to excuse himself by saying he was unaware of the danger to life. . . . " (*Patterson*, supra, 49 Cal.3d at 626.) We also have reasoned that, " '[i]f the felony is not inherently dangerous, it is highly improbable that the potential felon will be deterred; he will not anticipate that any injury or death might arise solely from the fact that he will commit the felony.' " (People v. Burroughs, 35 Cal.3d 824, 829, 201 Cal.Rptr. 319, 678 P.2d 894 (1984).) Thus, under the latter circumstances the commission of the felony could not serve logically as the basis for imputation of malice.

In determining whether a felony is inherently dangerous, the court looks to the elements of the felony in the abstract, "not the 'particular' facts of the case," i.e., not to the defendant's specific conduct. (People v. Williams, 63 Cal.2d 452, 47 Cal.Rptr. 7, 406 P.2d 647 (1965).)

Past decisions of this court have explained further the concept of an inherently dangerous felony. In *People v. Burroughs*, supra, we held that an inherently dangerous felony is one which, "by its very nature, . . . cannot be committed without creating a substantial risk that someone will be killed. . . . " And, most recently, in *People v. Patterson*, supra, we specified that, "for purposes of the second degree felony murder doctrine, an 'inherently dangerous felony' is an offense carrying 'a high probability' that death will result."

Felonies that have been found inherently dangerous to human life, in the abstract—thus supporting application of the second-degree felony murder rule—include furnishing a poisonous substance (methyl alcohol), reckless or malicious possession of a destructive device, and kidnapping for ransom.

The initial question presented in the case before us is whether the underlying felony involved—willful discharge of a firearm at an inhabited dwelling—is an inherently dangerous felony for purposes of the second-degree felony murder rule. The offense in question is defined in section 246, which provides in pertinent part:

> Any person who shall maliciously and willfully discharge a firearm at an inhabited dwelling house . . . is guilty of a felony. . . . As used in this section, "inhabited" means currently being used for dwelling purposes, whether occupied or not.

As we shall explain, we conclude that this felony, considered in the abstract, involves a high probability that death will result and therefore is an inherently dangerous felony under the governing principles set forth above, for purposes of the second degree felony murder doctrine.

Although our court has not had occasion previously to render a direct holding on the question whether [this] offense . . . is an inherently dangerous felony for purposes of the second-degree felony murder doctrine, the reasoning and language of one of our prior decisions provide a rather clear indication of this court's view on this issue. In *People v. Satchell*, the court held the felony of possession of a concealable firearm by a felon, considered in the abstract, was not inherently dangerous to human life and therefore would not support an instruction on second-degree felony murder. The court concluded that "mere passive possession" of a firearm, even by a felon, could not properly supply the element of malice in a murder prosecution. The court went on to say, however, that if passive possession ripened into a felonious act in which danger to human life was inherent, the purposes of the felony murder rule would be served by its application, because "it is the deterrence of such acts by felons which the rule is designed to accomplish." The court noted that a "ready example" of such a felony was the act [of] discharging a firearm at an inhabited dwelling.

Although the pertinent language in *Satchell* clearly was dictum, the reasoning underlying this language remains sound. . . . The discharge of a firearm at an inhabited dwelling house . . . is a felony whose commission inherently involves a danger to human life. An inhabited dwelling house is one in which persons reside and where occupants "are generally in or *around* the premises." (People v. White, 4 Cal.App.4th 1299, 1303, 6 Cal.Rptr.2d 259 (1992).) In firing a gun at such a structure, there always will exist a significant likelihood that an occupant may be present. Although it is true that a defendant may be guilty of this felony even if, at the time of the shooting, the residents of the inhabited dwelling happen to be absent, the offense nonetheless is one that, viewed in the abstract . . . , poses a great risk or "high probability" of death. . . .

Furthermore, application of the second-degree felony murder rule to a homicide resulting from [such felony] directly would serve the fundamental rationale of the felony murder rule—the deterrence of negligent or accidental killings in the course of the commission of dangerous felonies. The tragic death of innocent and often random victims, both young and old, as the result of the discharge of firearms, has become an alarmingly common occurrence in our society—a phenomenon of enormous concern to the public. By providing notice to persons inclined to willfully discharge a firearm at an inhabited dwelling—even to those individuals who would do so merely to frighten or intimidate the occupants, or to "leave their calling card"—that such persons will be guilty of murder should their conduct result in the all-too-likely fatal injury of another, the felony murder rule may serve to deter this type of reprehensible conduct, which has created a climate of fear for significant numbers of Californians even in the privacy of their own homes.

Accordingly, we hold that the offense of discharging a firearm at an inhabited dwelling is an "inherently dangerous felony" for purposes of the second-degree felony murder rule.

III

Defendant contends that, even if the . . . felony of discharging a firearm is inherently dangerous to human life, the commission of that felony in the present case "merged" with the resulting homicide, within the meaning of *People v. Ireland,* thereby precluding application of the second-degree felony murder rule.

[D]efendant's contention rests upon an unduly expansive view of the scope of the "merger" doctrine. . . . Prior to our decision in *Ireland*, the "merger" doctrine had been developed in other jurisdictions as a shorthand explanation for the conclusion that the felony murder rule should not be applied in circumstances where the only underlying (or "predicate") felony committed by the defendant was assault. The name of the doctrine derived from the characterization of the assault as an offense that "merged" with the resulting homicide. In explaining the basis for the merger doctrine, courts and legal commentators reasoned that, because a homicide generally results from the commission of an assault, every felonious assault ending in death automatically would be elevated to murder in the event a felonious assault could serve as the predicate felony for purposes of the felony murder doctrine. Consequently, application of the felony murder rule to felonious assaults would usurp most of the law of homicide, relieve the prosecution in the great majority of homicide cases of the burden of having to prove malice in order to obtain a murder conviction, and thereby frustrate the Legislature's intent to punish certain felonious assaults resulting in death (those committed with malice aforethought, and therefore punishable as murder) more harshly than other felonious assaults that happened to result in death (those committed without malice aforethought, and therefore punishable as manslaughter). [T]he merger rule applied to assaults is supported by the policy of preserving some meaningful domain in which the Legislature's careful gradation of homicide offenses can be implemented.

In *People v. Ireland,* we adopted the merger rule in a case involving the underlying felony of assault with a deadly weapon, where the defendant had shot and killed his wife. The jury was instructed that it could return a second-degree felony murder verdict based upon the underlying felony of assault with a deadly weapon, and the defendant was convicted of second-degree murder.

On appeal, this court reversed, reasoning that "[t]o allow such use of the felony murder rule would effectively preclude the jury from considering the issue of malice aforethought in all cases wherein homicide has been committed as a result of a felonious assault—a category which includes the great majority of all homicides. This kind of bootstrapping finds support neither in logic nor in law." The court therefore concluded that the offense of assault with a deadly weapon, which was "an integral part of" and "included in fact" within the homicide, could not support a second-degree felony murder instruction.

Subsequent decisions have applied the *Ireland* rule to other felonies involving assault . . . , [such as felony child abuse of the assaultive category, burglary with intent to commit the felony of assault with a deadly weapon, and assault with a deadly weapon].

Our court, however, has not extended the *Ireland* doctrine beyond the context of assault, even under circumstances in which the underlying felony plausibly could be characterized as "an integral part of" and "included in fact within" the resulting homicide. The decision in People v. Mattison, 4 Cal.3d 177, 93 Cal.Rptr. 185, 481 P.2d 193 (1971), provides an apt example. In that case, the defendant and the victim both were inmates of a correctional institution. The defendant worked as a technician in the medical laboratory. He previously had offered to sell alcohol to inmates, leading the victim, an alcoholic, to seek alcohol from him. The defendant supplied the victim with methyl alcohol, resulting in the victim's death by methyl alcohol poisoning.

At trial, the court instructed on felony murder based upon the felony of mixing poison with a beverage, an offense proscribed by the then-current version of section 347 ("Every person who wilfully mingles any poison with any food, drink or medicine, with intent that the same shall be taken by any human being to his injury, is guilty of a felony.") The defendant was convicted of second-degree murder. On appeal, contending that the trial court had erred in instructing the jury on felony murder, the defendant maintained that, on the facts of his case, the underlying felony was "an integral part of" and "included in fact within" the resulting murder, precluding application of the felony murder rule.

In *Mattison,* [we rejected the defendant's contention because] we found that the predicate felony presented an "entirely different situation from the one that confronted us in *Ireland,*" where the underlying felony was assault with a deadly weapon. We concluded that the merger rule was inapplicable because, in furnishing the methyl alcohol to the victim, the defendant exhibited a collateral and independent felonious design that was separate from the resulting homicide. [W]e held that where the underlying felony is committed with a design collateral to, or independent of, an intent to cause injury that would result in death, "[g]iving a felony murder instruction in such a situation serves rather than subverts the purpose of the rule."

The Court of Appeal's decision in People v. Taylor, 11 Cal.App.3d 57, 89 Cal.Rptr. 697 (1970), upon which *Mattison* explicitly relied, provides additional guidance. . . . In *Taylor*, the victim died as a result of an overdose of heroin, which had been furnished to her by the defendant. The defendant was convicted of second degree murder, and the question presented was whether application of the felony murder rule constituted error under *Ireland*. The Court of Appeal in *Taylor* first acknowledged the confusion that arose from the circumstance that, although *Ireland* involved an assault with a deadly weapon (a felony to which the merger rule traditionally has been applied), the broad language of *Ireland* could be interpreted as extending that rule to all felonies that constitute "an integral part of the homicide," potentially encompassing all felonies closely related to a homicide (and therefore possibly every felony inherently dangerous to human life). . . .

[In *Taylor*, the court decided] that *Ireland's* "integral part of the homicide" language did not constitute the crucial test [for] merger. [It] held that a felony does not merge with a homicide where the act causing death was committed with a collateral and independent felonious design separate from the intent to inflict the injury that caused death. The court explained its reasoning as follows: when the Legislature has prescribed that an assault resulting in death constitutes second degree murder if the felon acts with malice, it would subvert the legislative intent for a court to apply the felony murder rule automatically to elevate all felonious assaults resulting in death to second degree murder even where the felon does not act with malice. In other words, if the felony murder rule were applied to felonious assaults, all such assaults ending in death would constitute murder, effectively eliminating the requirement of malice—a result clearly contrary to legislative intent. The court in *Taylor* further explained, however, that when the underlying or predicate felony is not assault, but rather is a felony such as the furnishing of heroin . . . , application of the felony murder rule would not subvert the legislative intent, because "this is simply not a situation where the Legislature has demanded a showing of actual malice, as distinguished from malice implied in law by way of the felony murder rule."

We agree . . . that *Ireland's* "integral part of the homicide" language [is not the test for] merger. Such a test would be inconsistent with the underlying rule that only felonies "inherently dangerous to human life" are sufficiently indicative of a defendant's culpable mens rea to warrant application of the felony murder rule. The more dangerous the felony, the more likely it is that a death may result directly from the commission of the felony, but resort to the "integral part of the homicide" language would preclude application of the felony murder rule for those felonies that are most likely to result in death and that are, consequently, the felonies as to which the felony murder doctrine is most likely to act as a deterrent (because the perpetrator could foresee the great likelihood that death may result, negligently or accidentally).

[However, we reject *Taylor's* conclusion that merger never applies in cases where the predicate felony was] "committed with a collateral and independent felonious design." Under such a test, a felon who acts with a purpose other than specifically to inflict injury upon someone—for example, with the intent to sell narcotics for financial gain, or to discharge a firearm at a building solely to intimidate the occupants—is subject to greater criminal liability for an act resulting in death than a person who actually intends to injure the person of the victim. Rather than rely upon a somewhat artificial test that may lead to an anomalous result, we focus upon the principles and rationale underlying the foregoing language in *Taylor*, namely, that with respect to certain inherently dangerous felonies, their use as the predicate felony supporting application of the felony murder rule will not elevate all felonious assaults to murder or otherwise subvert the legislative intent.

In the present case, as in *Mattison* and *Taylor*, application of the second-degree felony murder rule would not [subvert] legislative intent. Most homicides do not result from [the felony involved here], and thus, unlike the situation in *People v. Ireland,* application of the felony murder doctrine in the present context will not have the effect of "preclud[ing] the jury from considering the issue of malice aforethought . . . [in] the great majority of all homicides." Similarly, application of the felony murder doctrine in the case before us would not frustrate the Legislature's deliberate calibration of punishment for assaultive conduct resulting in death, based upon the presence or absence of malice aforethought. [Moreover,] application of the felony murder rule [here] clearly is consistent with the traditionally recognized purpose of the . . . doctrine—namely the deterrence of negligent or accidental killings that occur in the course of the commission of dangerous felonies.

The Texas Court of Criminal Appeals recently applied similar reasoning in upholding a murder conviction that occurred after a jury was instructed on felony murder based upon underlying felonious conduct involving the discharge of a firearm into an occupied dwelling. See Aguirre v. State, 732 S.W.2d 320 (Tex.Crim.App. 1982). The court viewed the defendant's conduct of "attempting to blow open a door with a shotgun" as an offense that did not "merge" with the resulting homicide. . . .

holding

For the foregoing reasons, we conclude that the offense of discharging a firearm at an inhabited dwelling house does not "merge" with a resulting homicide within the meaning of the *Ireland* doctrine, and therefore that this offense will support a conviction of second-degree felony murder. . . .

■ WERDEGAR, JUSTICE, concurring. . . . I write separately to express my understanding of the "merger" doctrine, as articulated in People v. Ireland, 70 Cal.2d 522, 75 Cal.Rptr. 188, 450 P.2d 580 (1969), and succeeding decisions, and as applied here.

I join the majority in rejecting the premise [that] *Ireland's* "integral part of the homicide" language is decisive of the merger issue in this case. In my view, however, People v. Mattison, 4 Cal.3d 177, 93 Cal.Rptr. 185, 481 P.2d 193 (1971), adopting the reasoning of the Court of Appeal in People v. Taylor, 11 Cal.App.3d 57, 89 Cal.Rptr. 697 (1970), sets forth the operative test. Those cases require us to determine whether the underlying felony was committed with a "collateral and independent felonious design." Unlike the majority, I see no reason not to follow those decisions. I do not share the majority's concern that application of the *Mattison* and *Taylor* rule leads to the anomalous result of punishing one who does not intend to injure more harshly than one who does. One who commits a felony inherently dangerous to human life with the intent to inflict injury is, in all probability, guilty of second degree murder under the implied malice theory. It follows there likely will be no disparity in the respective criminal liability of the two offenders; thus, the anomaly the majority fears is more apparent than real.

The evidence in this case supports the conclusion defendant entertained a collateral and independent felonious design under *Mattison* and *Taylor*, namely to intimidate Echaves by firing shots into his house. Accordingly, I join in the disposition this court's judgment will effect.

■ MOSK, JUSTICE, dissenting. . . . I dissent from the judgment to the extent that it affirms the judgment of the Court of Appeal affirming defendant's conviction of murder in the second degree. . . . This conviction was affected by reversible error when the superior court instructed the jury on second-degree felony murder based on discharge of a firearm at an inhabited dwelling house.

I

. . . At issue is the second-degree felony murder rule. This doctrine arises not from any statute enacted by the Legislature but rather from the common law made by the courts. "[T]he second degree felony murder rule remains, as it has been since 1872, a judge-made doctrine without any express"—or implied—"basis in the Penal Code. . . ." Contrary to the majority's assertion, the rule does not "impute" the element of malice aforethought. Rather, it omits that element altogether. . . .

The purpose of the . . . felony murder rule is simply "to deter [persons] engaged in felonies from killing negligently or accidentally. . . ." Contrary to the majority's implication at points, the objective is not to deter such persons from committing the underlying felonies themselves.

Pursuant to the so-called "merger" doctrine, the second-degree felony murder rule is not applicable when, on the evidence adduced at trial, the underlying felony was an "integral part" of, and "included in fact" within, the resulting homicide.

A felony may be so characterized when "there was a single course of conduct with a single purpose," viz., to commit "the very assault which resulted in death. . . ." It has been held that assault is simply a willful act "likely to result in . . . physical force" against another.

A felony, however, cannot be so characterized when "there [was] an independent felonious purpose," such as to steal. . . .

At bottom, then, the "merger" doctrine is predicated on, and limited by, the following rationale. When a felony is undertaken with the purpose to engage in an assault, in the sense of a willful act "likely to result in . . . physical force" against another, the second-degree felony murder rule cannot be invoked because its objective—to deter the perpetrator from killing negligently or accidentally—is not likely to be attained. It "can hardly be much of a deterrent to a defendant who has decided" to so act. By contrast, when a felony is undertaken with a different purpose, the rule is allowed to operate because its objective can be reached.

Critique

II

At trial, the superior court instructed the jury on the crime of murder, [including second-degree felony murder]. . . . After six days of deliberations—almost as much time as was devoted to evidence, arguments, and instructions—the jury returned a verdict finding defendant guilty of murder in the second degree.[4]

III

. . . The applicability of the second-degree felony murder rule, under the governing law, depends on an affirmative answer to this threshold question: is discharge of a firearm at an inhabited dwelling house, considered in the abstract, a felony inherently dangerous to human life? The answer, however, is negative. . . . Logic dictates that discharge of a firearm at an inhabited dwelling house cannot carry " 'a high probability' that death will result" when [the statute] expressly does not require the presence of any occupant. Experience provides confirmation: to judge from reported appellate decisions, the prohibited conduct has resulted in death only in rare instances. . . . Surely, if the dwelling is not occupied at the time of the shooting, the "probability" of death is not "high"—it is zero.

[Thus, the majority errs when it reasons] that "there will always exist a significant likelihood that an occupant may be killed". . . . At any given time, all occupants may be absent from the dwelling. School, work, shopping, leisure pursuits, and other activities may demand attendance outside, often for the greater part of the day. Even if an occupant is present, he may be in a part of the dwelling away from the shooting. The resident is necessarily smaller than the residence. Usually, thousands of times so. For example, an average adult man may stand in 1 square foot of floor space and take up 6 cubic feet of a room; by contrast, even a modest house may cover as many as 1,500 square feet and, with 8-foot ceilings, fill as much as 12,000 cubic feet. But even if an occupant happens to be near the shooting, the dwelling itself provides significant protection. . . .

Moreover, even if "the offense . . . pose[d] a great risk . . . of death," it would not matter. The prohibited conduct might be deemed "inherently dangerous to human life" under the former, less demanding definition, which was satisfied by nothing more than a "substantial risk that someone will be killed. . . . " But it would not qualify under the present, more stringent definition, which requires " 'a high probability' that death will result." The implication that a "great risk . . . of death" is a " 'high probability' of death" is dead wrong.

The majority then assert: "[A]pplication of the second-degree felony murder rule to a homicide resulting from [discharging a firearm at a habitation] directly would serve the fundamental rationale of the felony

[4] It was apparently the second-degree felony murder rule and not the facts of the case that caused the jury to have trouble reaching its verdict. Ironically, it was also the rule and not the facts that ultimately produced the determination of guilt. One juror subsequently stated: "It makes me sick and ashamed to have been part of a system that would convict someone like [defendant] of murder. Not everyone deserves a second chance but [he] does. The law is what dictated the verdict, not the jury." Another juror added: "If it wasn't for the scenario which said that the murder was a result of an intentional act of shooting into a dwelling which is a felony, then my vote would be for manslaughter. I do think that what [defendant] did was very serious but I would not rank him as a cold blooded killer."

murder rule—the deterrence of negligent or accidental killings in the course of the commission of dangerous felonies." Are we then to conclude that the rule would lead a person who is minded to discharge a firearm at an inhabited dwelling house—"maliciously and willfully," as [the Penal Code] requires—to blaze away with due caution and circumspection? To ask the question is to provide its answer. As stated above, the rule "can hardly be much of a deterrent to a defendant who has decided" to undertake an assault, in the sense of a willful act "likely to result in . . . physical force" against another. That [the felony involved here] does not bear the label of "assault" is not dispositive. It embraces its substance. Because it does, it appears in the Penal Code in the chapter entitled "Assault and Battery."

Next, to the question under the "merger" doctrine, "On the evidence adduced at trial, was defendant's discharge of a firearm at the inhabited dwelling house in question an 'integral part' of, and 'included in fact' within, the resulting homicide?," the majority answer, "No." Again, they are wrong.

In part, the majority would avoid the "merger" doctrine by limiting it to "circumstances where the only underlying . . . felony committed by the defendant was assault." Even if this limitation is sound—and apparently it is not—it would not yield the result desired. That is because the only underlying felony committed by defendant here was in fact assault, in the sense of a willful act "likely to result in . . . physical force" against another.

Additionally, the majority would avoid the "merger" doctrine by applying it purportedly in accordance with People v. Mattison, 4 Cal.3d 177, 93 Cal.Rptr. 185, 481 P.2d 193 (1971) and People v. Taylor, 11 Cal.App.3d 57, 89 Cal.Rptr. 697 (1970). They recognize that *Mattison* and *Taylor* each held the doctrine unavailable because the evidence adduced at trial therein revealed an "independent felonious purpose." But they seem not to recognize that, as explained, the evidence adduced at trial in this case reveals no such "independent felonious purpose," but only an intent to commit an assault, in the sense indicated above. . . .

Further, the majority attempt to avoid the "merger" doctrine by invoking Aguirre v. State, 732 S.W.2d 320 (Tex.Crim.App. 1982). *Aguirre* is distinguishable. In that case, the felony underlying the resulting homicide was "criminal mischief," a "property offense," which comprised an "attemp[t] to blow open a door with a shotgun;" it was undertaken with the "independent felonious purpose"—in our phrase—to effect an unlawful entrance into a residence. In this case, by contrast, the felony underlying the resulting homicide was discharge of a firearm at an inhabited dwelling house, a crime against the person; it was undertaken simply to effect the ultimately fatal assault, in the sense indicated above.

Unable to avoid the "merger" doctrine, the majority come close to rendering it void. They reason that the doctrine is not available in this case because "[m]ost homicides do not result" from discharge of a firearm at an inhabited dwelling house. It follows that the doctrine would not be available in any case because most homicides do not result from any one felony. Such an outcome is untenable.

■ KENNARD, JUSTICE, concurring and dissenting. . . . The majority concludes, and I agree, that the offense of discharging a firearm at an inhabited dwelling is indeed an inherently dangerous felony for purposes of the second-degree felony murder rule because it is "an offense carrying 'a high probability' that death will result." This court has never held that for a felony to pose a high probability of death, death must result from the commission of the felony in a majority, or even in a great percentage, of instances. Nor is it necessary in this case to define the outer limits of that term. The drive-by shootings that now plague our cities frequently result in the death of someone inside a residence. Even with no one present in the targeted house, the act of shooting at an inhabited house or apartment creates a substantial or serious risk of death to occupants of neighboring houses or to passersby. . . .

I disagree with the majority, however, when it concludes that the felony of discharging a weapon at an inhabited dwelling is one that does not "merge" with the resulting homicide within the meaning of our decision in People v. Ireland, 70 Cal.2d 522, 75 Cal.Rptr. 188, 450 P.2d 580 (1969). Under *Ireland*, which has been the law of this state for more than 25 years, a conviction for second degree felony murder cannot rest on a felony assault "that is an integral part of the homicide" and that, based on the prosecution's evidence, is "included in fact" within the resulting homicide. Later decisions have added that a defendant's commission of a felony will support a felony murder conviction only if the defendant entertained some "independent felonious purpose" beyond mere assault. Here, the prosecution's evidence did not show that defendant had any independent felonious purpose for discharging the firearm at the Echaves residence. That conduct satisfies this court's definition of an assault. As Justice Mosk observes, it was "a willful act 'likely to result in . . . physical force' against another." As such, in this case the underlying felony of discharging a firearm at an inhabited dwelling house "merges" with the resulting homicide and cannot support the second-degree murder conviction.

Although from the facts of this case a jury could find that the defendant harbored malice and accordingly could base a second-degree murder conviction on an implied malice theory (rather than a felony murder theory), I agree with Justice Mosk that defendant's second-degree felony murder conviction must be reversed because the record does not reveal whether the jury ever made the findings necessary to support a second-degree murder conviction premised on implied malice. I would remand this case to give the prosecution the opportunity to retry the murder charge on a theory of implied malice.

## NOTES ON FELONY MURDER

### 1. QUESTIONS AND COMMENTS ON *HANSEN*

Each of the traditional limitations on the felony murder rule summarized in the introductory notes to this section has the effect of modifying the rule by importing some measure of culpability for the offender's conduct in relation to the victim's death—though not that normally associated with murder. The scope of the felony murder rule in a given jurisdiction thus can be seen as an adjustment of the tension between the deterrent objectives of the rule and limitations based on individual blameworthiness. The arguments made by Judge Mosk in his dissent in *Hansen* are among those frequently offered to illustrate the anomalous results that can arise from such compromises. Do they indicate the fundamental unsoundness of the rule? Or are they inevitable byproducts of the need to draw lines in the implementation of a desirable legislative policy?

Consider also the following aspects of the *Hansen* opinion.

### *(i) Determination of Inherent Dangerousness*

In *Hansen,* the court applies one of the traditional, judge-made prerequisites for second-degree felony murder liability, namely, the requirement that the felony be "inherently dangerous to human life." The court also identifies the methodology to be used in making this essential evaluation: "In determining whether a felony is inherently dangerous, the court looks to the elements of the felony in the abstract." *Hansen* thus demands that felonies be classified according to their general tendencies, not by the facts and circumstances of the particular offense. Other courts have rejected the abstract approach, holding instead that the facts and circumstances surrounding the particular misconduct should be considered in deciding which felonies qualify for operation of the felony murder rule. Which of these views states the preferable position? Do the purposes of the felony murder rule suggest an answer?

abstract v facts

From another perspective, consider the purposes that are served by the felony murder rule. Do any of the opinions in *Hansen* clearly articulate a rationale for this strict-liability doctrine? Judge Mosk chides the majority for misstating the objectives of the rule. Does Judge Mosk's opinion offer a convincing explanation for felony murder? An explanation that supports the outcome he prefers?

If the offense is to be classified in the abstract, as *Hansen* concludes, the question to be determined would appear to be one of law for the court. But if the circumstances of the offense are to be considered, should the question be determined by the court or the jury?

### *(ii) Merger*

In the *Ireland* case, discussed in *Hansen*, the defendant shot and killed his wife "by firing into her at close range two .38 caliber bullets" from his pistol. The defendant was convicted of second-degree murder based on a jury charge that included instructions authorizing the jury to rely on the felony murder rule. The theory underlying this instruction was that the defendant had assaulted his wife with a deadly weapon and, in the course of committing that felony, he had caused her death. The court reversed the conviction:

> We have concluded that the utilization of the felony murder rule in circumstances such as those before us extends the operation of that rule "beyond any rational function that it is designed to serve." To allow such use of the felony murder rule would effectively preclude the jury from considering the issue of malice aforethought in all cases wherein homicide has been committed as a result of a felonious assault—a category which includes the great majority of all homicides. This kind of bootstrapping finds support neither in logic nor in law.

The court's reasoning in *Ireland* seems irrefutable in one respect: if there were no merger rule of any kind, every person guilty of any felonious grade of homicide would automatically be guilty of felony murder—in effect, for example, one who committed manslaughter would automatically be guilty of murder if the crime of manslaughter could supply the basis for a charge of felony murder. The absence of some merger doctrine thus would erase altogether the distinctions traditionally drawn in grading serious homicides. No court has refused to apply a version of the merger doctrine in this context.

The disputed issue is whether application of the felony murder rule can be predicated on a felonious assault. In most jurisdictions, intent to injure or recklessness concerning the risk of injury is sufficient to establish the mens rea for some form of felonious assault. What is the proper approach in this situation? Should the felony murder rule be applied in such a case or should the assault be said to merge with the homicide?

Consider State v. Wanrow, 91 Wash.2d 301, 588 P.2d 1320 (1978), in this connection. The Washington second-degree murder statute covered the killing of a human being, not justifiable or excusable, "committed with a design to effect the death of the person killed or of another, but without premeditation" (subsection (1)) or perpetrated during the commission of "a felony other than those enumerated" on the first-degree list (subsection (2)). The prosecution theory was that the defendant committed a felonious assault when she "wilfully assault[ed]" the victim with a gun, and that this offense established the predicate felony for second-degree felony murder even if she did not intend to kill the victim. The defense argued that this construction of the statute would effectively eliminate the requirement of intent to kill as an element of second-degree murder, and that application of the merger doctrine was necessary to ameliorate the otherwise harsh application of the felony murder rule.[a] The court rejected these arguments.[b] Was this the proper result?[c]

## 2. DISTRIBUTION OF CONTROLLED SUBSTANCES

Should the felony murder rule be applicable to deaths caused by the distribution of controlled substances? At least one state has addressed the question by statute. Section 782.04(1)(a)(3) of the Florida penal code provides that:

> The unlawful killing of a human being . . . which resulted from the unlawful distribution of opium or any synthetic or

---

[a] Ms. Wanrow also attacked the felony murder rule on constitutional grounds. In rejecting her argument, the court noted that the Supreme Court of the United States had in effect upheld the constitutionality of the rule by its summary order in Thompson v. Washington, 434 U.S. 898 (1977).

[b] The court said that subsection (1) of the statute was not rendered meaningless by its decision "because there are many conceivable circumstances in which an intent to kill is both present and clearly manifested. In these circumstances the state may properly charge under subsection (1). In practice it may be that most second-degree murders are proved through subsection (2), but as long as clear cases of unpremeditated acts with a manifest intent to kill are conceivable, subsection (1) is not meaningless."

[c] The court cited decisions in four other states that had not adopted a merger rule in this context, but added that at least seven states had adopted such a rule.

The merger doctrine is applied in some jurisdictions only where the victim of the assault is also the victim of the homicide. In those jurisdictions, therefore, a felony murder conviction becomes possible where the defendant assaults one person and accidentally kills another.

> natural salt, compound, derivative, or preparation of opium by a person 18 years of age or older, when such drug is proven to be the proximate cause of the death of the user, is murder in the first degree and constitutes a capital felony. . . . [d]

Does this statute establish a wise public policy? What does it mean by "proximate cause"?

In the absence of legislative guidance, this contentious question has been left to the courts, and it has tended to divide them. In *Hansen*, the court cites with approval the decision by the California Court of Appeal in *Taylor*, which held that the "furnishing of heroin" is an appropriate predicate felony for purposes of felony murder liability. Which of the following cases states the better view?

### *(i) Heacock v. Commonwealth*

The Virginia statutes contain a traditional category of first-degree felony murder based on the Pennsylvania model, and also provide that the "killing of one accidentally, contrary to the intention of the parties, while in the prosecution of some felonious act other than those specified [in the first-degree statute], is murder of the second degree." In Heacock v. Commonwealth, 228 Va. 397, 323 S.E.2d 90 (1984), the court affirmed the felony murder conviction of a person who supplied cocaine to the participants at a "drug party." The defendant, with another, "prepared the narcotic mixture in a spoon" prior to a fatal injection and was present at the time of the injection.

The court rejected the "inherently dangerous felony" limitation, concluding that the statute applied to "all felonious acts" except those particularly named in the first-degree statute. The court then said that even if it were prepared to accept that limitation, "which we are not," the evidence was that the defendant "knew, or should have known" that the dosage he helped prepare was inherently dangerous. It based this conclusion on the fact that another person had suffered a violent reaction to the same substance prior to the lethal injection, on medical testimony that "any amount" of cocaine could cause such a reaction in "anyone," and on the fact that the legislature had classified cocaine distribution as a very serious felony (40 years for the first offense; life imprisonment for a second). "Accordingly, we hold as a matter of law, that the unlawful distribution of cocaine is conduct potentially dangerous to human life."

The court then held that any proximate cause limitation that might apply to this class of homicide was satisfied here: "The underlying felony was distribution of cocaine, a drug the defendant should have known was inherently dangerous to human life; [the victim] ingested that drug and, as we have said, it is immaterial who made the injection; [the victim] died of 'acute intravenous cocainism'; thus cause and effect were proximately interrelated." The court concluded:

> [W]e hold that where, as here, death results from ingestion of a controlled substance, classified in law as dangerous to human life, the homicide constitutes murder of the second degree . . . if

---

[d] The capital punishment aspect of this statute may well be unconstitutional under Enmund v. Florida, 458 U.S. 782 (1982). *Enmund* does not speak, however, to when a non-capital sentence can be imposed for felony murder.

that substance had been distributed to the decedent in violation of the felony statutes of this commonwealth.

### *(ii) Sheriff, Clark County v. Morris*

By contrast, in Sheriff, Clark County v. Morris, 99 Nev. 109, 659 P.2d 852 (1983), the court carefully limited the circumstances that would support conviction of a drug-seller for second-degree felony murder:

> First, it must be established by the evidence that the unauthorized sale and ingestion of [a controlled substance] in the quantities involved are inherently dangerous in the abstract, i.e., without reference to the specific victim. Second, there must be an immediate and causal relationship between the felonious conduct of the defendant and the death of the [victim]. By the term "immediate" we mean without the intervention of some other source or agency. Third, the causal relationship must extend beyond the unlawful sale of the drugs to an involvement by commission or omission in the ingestion of a lethal dosage by the decedent. This element of the rule would be satisfied by the unlawful selling or providing of the drugs and helping the recipient of the drugs to ingest a lethal dose or by unlawfully selling or dispensing the drugs and being present during the consumption of a lethal dose. Thus, absent more, the rule would not apply to a situation involving a sale only or a sale with a nonlethal dosage ingested in the defendant's presence. Although it may be cogently argued that an unlawful sale of drugs is inherently dangerous per se, and therefore an appropriate basis for a charge of murder when death occurs, we leave such a determination to the legislature.

### *(iii) State v. Randolph*

In State v. Randolph, 676 S.W.2d 943 (Tenn. 1984), the court declined to embrace a felony murder theory, but suggested that ordinary principles of culpability could be used in some contexts to convict a drug-seller of second-degree murder or involuntary manslaughter for the death of a drug-purchaser. On the question of causation, the court said "we are of the opinion that the act of the customer in injecting himself is not necessarily so unexpected, unforeseeable or remote as to insulate the seller from criminal responsibility as a matter of law."

## 3. ATTEMPTED FELONY MURDER

In Amlotte v. Florida, 456 So.2d 448 (Fla.1984), the court held that "attempted felony murder is a crime in Florida" and that the "essential elements of the crime are the perpetration or attempt to perpetrate an enumerated felony, together with an intentional overt act, or the aiding and abetting of such an act, which could, but does not, cause the death of another." It added: "Because the attempt occurs during the commission of a felony, the law, as under the felony murder doctrine, presumes the existence of the specific intent required to prove attempt." The court made these statements in the context of an attempted robbery where two of the felons returned gunfire when a victim of the robbery tried to shoot them. Is this a sound extension of the felony murder rule?

## State v. Sophophone

Supreme Court of Kansas, 2001.
270 Kan. 703, 19 P.3d 70.

■ LARSON, JUDGE. This is Sanexay Sophophone's direct appeal of his felony murder conviction for the death of his co-felon during flight from an aggravated burglary in which both men participated.

The facts are not in dispute. Sophophone and three other individuals conspired to and broke into a house in Emporia. The resident reported the break-in to the police.

Police officers responded to the call, saw four individuals leaving the back of the house, shined a light on the suspects, identified themselves as police officers, and ordered them to stop. The individuals, one being Sophophone, started to run away. One officer ran down Sophophone, hand-cuffed him, and placed him in a police car.

Other officers arrived to assist in apprehending the other individuals as they were running from the house. An officer chased one of the suspects later identified as Somphone Sysoumphone. Sysoumphone crossed railroad tracks, jumped a fence, and then stopped. The officer approached with his weapon drawn and ordered Sysoumphone to the ground and not to move. Sysoumphone was lying face down but raised up and fired at the officer, who returned fire and killed him. . . .

Sophophone was charged with . . . aggravated burglary and felony murder. . . .

Sophophone moved to dismiss the felony murder charges, contending the complaint was defective because it alleged that he and not the police officer had killed Sysoumphone and further because he was in custody and sitting in the police car when the deceased was killed and therefore not attempting to commit or even fleeing from an inherently dangerous felony. His motion to dismiss was denied by the trial court.

Sophophone was convicted by a jury of all counts. His motion for judgment of acquittal was denied. He was sentenced on all counts. He appeals only his conviction of felony murder. . . .

We consider only the question of law, upon which our review is unlimited, of whether Sophophone can be convicted of felony murder for the killing of a co-felon not caused by his acts but by the lawful acts of a police officer acting in self-defense in the course and scope of his duties in apprehending the co-felon fleeing from an aggravated burglary.

The applicable provisions of K.S.A. 21–3401 read as follows:

> Murder in the first degree is the killing of a human being committed: . . .
>
> (b) in the commission of, attempt to commit, or flight from an inherently dangerous felony as defined in K.S.A. 21–3436. . . .

Aggravated burglary is one of the inherently dangerous felonies as enumerated by K.S.A. 21–3436(10).

Sophophone does not dispute that aggravated burglary is an inherently dangerous felony which given the right circumstances would support a felony murder charge. His principal argument centers on his being in custody at the time his co-felon was killed by the lawful act of the officer which he contends was a "break in circumstances" sufficient to insulate him from further criminal responsibility.

This "intervening cause" or "break in circumstances" argument has no merit under the facts of this case. We have held in numerous cases that "time, distance, and the causal relationship between the underlying felony and a killing are factors to be considered in determining whether the killing occurs in the commission of the underlying felony and the defendant is therefore subject to the felony murder rule." Based on the uncontroverted evidence in this case, the killing took place during flight from the aggravated burglary, and it is only because the act which resulted in the killing was a lawful one by a third party that a question of law exists as to whether Sophophone can be convicted of felony murder. . . . [a]

Our cases are legion in interpreting the felony murder statute, but we have not previously decided a case where the killing was not by the direct acts of the felon but rather where a co-felon was killed during his flight from the scene of the felony by the lawful acts of a third party (in our case, a law enforcement officer).

A similar scenario took place in State v. Murrell, 224 Kan. 689, 585 P.2d 1017 (1978), where Murrell was charged with felony murder for the death of his co-felon who had been shot by the robbery victim who had returned gunfire from Murrell. However, Murrell was acquitted of felony murder and his appeal involved only issues relating to his other convictions.

Although there were clearly different facts, we held in State v. Hoang, 243 Kan. 40, 755 P.2d 7 (1988), that felony murder may include the accidental death of a co-felon during the commission of arson. The decedents had conspired with Hoang to burn down a building housing a Wichita restaurant/club but died when they were trapped inside the building while starting the fire. Hoang was an active participant in the felony and present at the scene, although he remained outside the building while his three accomplices entered the building with containers of gasoline to start the fire.

We held, in a split decision, that the decedents were killed during the perpetration of a felony inherently dangerous to human life and there was nothing in the statute to exclude the killing of co-felons from its application. It must be pointed out that the facts in *Hoang* involved the wrongful acts of a co-felon which were directly responsible for the deaths of his co-felons.

The dissent in *Hoang* noted that in previous cases the felony murder rule had been applied only to the deaths of innocents and not to the deaths of co-felons. The result was deemed by the dissent to be contrary to legislative intent and the strict construction of criminal statutes that is required.

With this brief background of our prior Kansas cases, we look to the prevailing views concerning the applicability of the felony murder doctrine where the killing has been caused by the acts of a third

---

[a] The court identified two purposes of felony murder in omitted portions of its opinion. One was "to deter those engaged in felonies from killing negligently or accidentally." The other was "to relieve the state of the burden of proving premeditation and malice when the victim's death is caused by the killer while he is committing another felony."—[Footnote by eds.]

party. . . . In Joshua Dressler, Understanding Criminal Law (1987), the question is posed of whether the felony murder rule should apply when the fatal act is performed by a non-felon. Dressler [identifies two approaches]:

> . . . The "Agency" Approach
>
> The majority rule is that the felony murder doctrine does not apply if the person who directly causes the death is a non-felon. . . .
>
> The reasoning of this approach stems from accomplice liability theory. Generally speaking, the acts of the primary party (the person who directly commits the offense) are imputed to an accomplice on the basis of the agency doctrine. It is as if the accomplice says to the primary party: "Your acts are my acts." It follows that [a co-felon] cannot be convicted of the homicides because the primary party was not the person with whom she was an accomplice. It is not possible to impute the acts of the antagonistic party—[the non-felon or] the police officer—to [a co-felon] on the basis of agency.
>
> . . . The "Proximate Causation" Approach
>
> An alternative theory, followed by a few courts . . . , holds that a felon may be held responsible under the felony murder rule for a killing committed by a non-felon if the felon set in motion the acts which resulted in the victim's death.
>
> Pursuant to this rule, the issue becomes one of proximate causation: if an act by one felon is the proximate cause of the homicidal conduct by [the non-felon] or the police officer, murder liability is permitted.

In 2 Wayne R. LaFave & Austin W. Scott, Jr., Substantive Criminal Law (1986), the author opines: "Although it is now generally accepted that there is no felony murder liability when one of the felons is shot and killed by the victim, a police officer, or a bystander, it is not easy to explain why this is so."

The author discusses foreseeability, [concludes] that it is not correct to say that a felon is never liable when the death is lawful because it is "justifiable," and goes on to state:

> A more plausible explanation, it is submitted, is the feeling that it is not justice (though it may be poetic justice) to hold the felon liable for murder on account of the death, which the felon did not intend, of a co-felon willingly participating in the risky venture. It is true that it is no defense to intentional homicide crimes that the victim voluntarily placed himself in danger of death at the hands of the defendant, or even that he consented to his own death: a mercy killing constitutes murder; and aiding suicide is murder unless special legislation reduces it to manslaughter. But with unintended killings it would seem proper to take the victim's willing participation into account. . . .

As we noted in *Hoang*, it is not very helpful to review case law from other states because of differences in statutory language; however, the high courts which have considered this precise question are divided between the agency approach and the proximate cause approach.

The leading case adopting the agency approach is Commonwealth v. Redline, 391 Pa. 486 (1958), where the underlying principle of the agency theory is described as follows:

> In adjudging a felony murder, it is to be remembered at all times that the thing which is imputed to a felon for a killing incidental to his felony is malice and not the act of killing. The mere coincidence of homicide and felony is not enough to satisfy the felony murder doctrine.

The following statement from *Redline* is more persuasive for Sophophone:

> In the present instance, the victim of the homicide was one of the robbers who, while resisting apprehension in his effort to escape, was shot and killed by a policeman in the performance of his duty. Thus, the homicide was justifiable and, obviously, could not be availed of, on any rational legal theory, to support a charge of murder. How can anyone, no matter how much of an outlaw he may be, have a criminal charge lodged against him for the consequences of the lawful conduct of another person? The mere question carries with it its own answer. . . .

The minority of the states whose courts have adopted the proximate cause theory believe their legislatures intended that any person . . . who commits an inherently dangerous felony should be held responsible for any death which is a direct and foreseeable consequence of the actions of those committing the felony. These courts apply the civil law concept of proximate cause to felony murder situations. . . .

It should be mentioned that some courts have been willing to impose felony murder liability even where the shooting was by a person other than one of the felons in the so-called "shield" situations where it has been reasoned "that a felon's act of using a victim as a shield in compelling a victim to occupy a place or position of danger constitutes a direct lethal act against the victim."

[We did not] adopt the proximate cause approach . . . in State v. Shaw, 260 Kan. 396, 921 P.2d 779 (1996), where we held that a defendant who bound and gagged an 86-year-old robbery victim with duct tape was liable for the victim's death when he died of a heart attack while so bound and gagged. Although we may speak of causation in such a case, our ruling in *Shaw* is better described [as follows:] "The victim must be taken as the defendant finds him. Death resulting from a heart attack will support a felony murder conviction if there is a causal connection between the heart attack and the felonious conduct of the defendant." This is not the embracing of a proximate cause approach under the facts we face.

[The State also urges that] in State v. Lamae, 268 Kan. 544, 998 P.2d 106 (2000), we recognized that the killing could be perpetrated ["by the defendant *or another*"]. The case involved the death of a participant in a methamphetamine fire. Our opinion did state: "It is true that there must be a direct causal connection between the commission of the felony and the homicide to invoke the felony murder rule. However, the general rules of proximate cause used in civil actions do not apply." This language, if taken in isolation, is much more favorable to Sophophone's position. However, we believe that neither this statement nor the "or another" language in *Lamae* should be given undue consideration when we resolve the different question we face here.

There is language in K.S.A. 21–3205(2) that predicates criminal responsibility to an aider or abettor for "any other crime committed in pursuance of the intended crime if reasonably foreseeable by such person as a probable consequence of committing or attempting to commit the crime intended." This wording does not assist us for the killing of the co-felon in our case where it was the lawful act by a law enforcement officer who was in no manner subject to these aider and abettor provisions.

The overriding fact which exists in our case is that neither Sophophone nor any of his accomplices "killed" anyone. The law enforcement officer acted lawfully in committing the act which resulted in the death of the co-felon. This does not fall within the language of K.S.A. 21–3205 since the officer committed no crime.

[To] impute the act of killing to Sophophone when the act was the lawful and courageous one of a law enforcement officer acting in the line of his duties is contrary to the strict construction we are required to give criminal statutes. There is considerable doubt about the meaning of K.S.A. 21–3401(b) as applied to the facts of this case, and we believe that making one criminally responsible for the lawful acts of a law enforcement officer is not the intent of the felony murder statute as it is currently written. . . .

It does little good to suggest one construction over another would prevent the commission of dangerous felonies or that it would deter those who engage in dangerous felonies from killing purposely, negligently, or accidentally. Actually, innocent parties and victims of crimes appear to be those who are sought to be protected rather than co-felons.

We hold that under the facts of this case where the killing resulted from the lawful acts of a law enforcement officer in attempting to apprehend a co-felon, Sophophone is not criminally responsible for the resulting death of Somphone Sysoumphone, and his felony murder conviction must be reversed.

This decision is in no manner inconsistent with our rulings in *Hoang* or *Lamae*, which are based on the direct acts of a co-felon and are simply factually different from our case. . . .

Reversed.

■ ABBOT, JUDGE, with whom CHIEF JUDGE MCFARLAND and JUDGE DAVIS join, dissenting. The issue facing the court in this case is whether Sophophone may be legally convicted under the felony murder statute when he did not pull the trigger and where the victim was one of the co-felons. The majority holds that Sophophone cannot be convicted of felony murder. I dissent. . . .

When an issue requires statutory analysis and the statute is unambiguous, we are limited by the wording chosen by the legislature. We are not free to alter the statutory language, regardless of the result. In the present case, the felony murder statute does not require us to adopt the "agency" theory favored by the majority. Indeed, there is nothing in the statute which establishes an agency approach. The statute does not address the issue at all. The requirements, according to the statute, are: (1) there must be a killing, and (2) the killing must be committed in the commission, attempt to commit, or flight from an inherently dangerous felony. The statute simply does not contain the limitations discussed by the majority. . . .

Moreover, there are sound reasons to adopt the proximate cause approach described in the majority opinion. In State v. Hoang, 243 Kan. 40, 755 P.2d 7 (1988), this court took such an approach, although never referring to it by name. In *Hoang*, Chief Justice McFarland, writing for the court, discussed at length the requirements of the felony murder rule in Kansas and stated:

> In felony murder cases, the elements of malice, deliberation, and premeditation which are required for murder in the first degree are deemed to be supplied by felonious conduct alone if a homicide results. To support a conviction for felony murder, all that is required is to prove that a felony was being committed, which felony was inherently dangerous to human life, and that the homicide which followed was a direct result of the commission of that felony. In a felony murder case, evidence of who the triggerman is is irrelevant and all participants are principals.
>
> The purpose of the felony murder doctrine is to deter all those engaged in felonies from killing negligently or accidentally. . . .
>
> It is argued in the case before us that felony murder applies only to the deaths of "innocents" rather than co-felons. There is nothing in our statute on which to base such a distinction. . . .
>
> Dung and Thuong, the decedents herein, were human beings who were killed in the perpetration of a felony. . . . Defendant was an active participant in the felony and present on the scene during all pertinent times. There is nothing in the statute excluding the killing of the co-felons herein from its application. For this court to exclude the co-felons would constitute judicial amendment of a statute on philosophic rather than legal grounds. This would be highly improper. The legislature has defined felony murder. If this definition is to be amended to exclude the killing of co-felons therefrom under circumstances such as are before us, it is up to the legislature to make [the] amendment. . . .

The majority in this case points out that the majority of states have adopted the agency approach when faced with the death of a co-felon. They acknowledge, however, that because statutes vary significantly from state to state, reference to a "majority" rule and a "minority" rule is meaningless. Indeed, an in-depth analysis of the current case law in this area leads me to the following conclusions: (1) While a majority of states would agree with the majority opinion in this case, the margin is slim; (2) many of the states that have adopted the so-called "agency" approach have done so because the statutory language in their state requires them to do so; and (3) several of the states that have adopted the "proximate cause" approach have done so because their statutes are silent on the issue, like Kansas. . . .

In my opinion, our statute is unambiguous and simply does not require the defendant to be the direct cause of the victim's death, nor does it limit application of the felony murder rule to the death of "innocents."

In People v. Lowery, 178 Ill. 2d 462, 687 N.E.2d 973 (1997), the Illinois Supreme Court discussed the public policy reasons justifying application of a proximate cause approach, stating:

> It is equally consistent with reason and sound public policy to hold that when a felon's attempt to commit a forcible felony sets in motion a chain of events which were or should have been within his contemplation when the motion was initiated, he should be held responsible for any death which by direct and almost inevitable sequence results from the initial criminal act. Thus, there is no reason why the principle underlying the doctrine of proximate cause should not apply to criminal cases. Moreover, we believe that the intent behind the felony murder doctrine would be thwarted if we did not hold felons responsible for the foreseeable consequences of their actions.

In Sheckles v. State, 684 N.E.2d 201 (Ind. Ct. App. 1997), the Indiana Court of Appeals opined:

> [A] person who commits or attempts to commit one of the offenses designated in the felony murder statute is criminally responsible for a homicide which results from the act of one who was not a participant in the original criminal activity. Where the accused reasonably should have . . . foreseen that the commission of or attempt to commit the contemplated felony would likely create a situation which would expose another to the danger of death at the hands of a nonparticipant in the felony, and where death in fact occurs as was foreseeable, the creation of such a dangerous situation is a . . . medium in effecting or bringing about the death of the victim.

Likewise, the Supreme Court of New Jersey discussed the historical justification for application of the proximate cause rule in felony murder cases in State v. Martin, 119 N.J. 2, 573 A.2d 1359 (1990), stating:

> More recently, felony murder has been viewed not as a crime of transferred intent, but as one of absolute or strict liability. Whether the offense is viewed as a crime of transferred intent or as one of absolute liability, the continuing justification for the felony murder rule is that in some circumstances one who commits a felony should be liable for a resulting, albeit unintended, death. Conversely, other deaths are so remotely related to the underlying felony that the actor should not be held culpable for them. Our task is to ascertain the circumstances in which the Legislature has decided that one who commits a felony should also be culpable for a resulting death.
>
> The historical justification for the rule is that it serves as a general deterrent against the commission of violent crimes. The rationale is that if potential felons realize that they will be culpable as murderers for a death that occurs during the

commission of a felony, they will be less likely to commit the felony. From this perspective, the imposition of strict liability without regard to the intent to kill serves to deter the commission of serious crimes.

Here, Sophophone set in motion acts [that] could have very easily resulted in the death of a law enforcement officer, and in my opinion this is exactly the type of case the legislature had in mind when it adopted the felony murder rule. . . .

## FURTHER NOTES ON FELONY MURDER

### 1. HOMICIDE COMMITTED BY A NON-PARTICIPANT

Situations where the homicide is actually committed by the police or a victim have proved particularly troublesome in American litigation over the proper scope of the felony murder rule. As the opinions in *Sophophone* vividly illustrate, courts have divided sharply over this question, adopting two different approaches to the problem. The first, sometimes called the "proximate-cause" theory, is illustrated by State v. Canola, 135 N.J.Super. 224, 343 A.2d 110 (1975). Four men were engaged in an armed robbery. One of them shot a victim of the offense, who in turn drew a weapon and shot his assailant. Both men died. The defendant was convicted of felony murder for *both* deaths, and his convictions were affirmed. The court said that "[t]he proximate-cause theory simply stated is that when a felon sets in motion a chain of events which were or should have been within his contemplation when the motion was initiated, the felon, and those acting in concert with him, should be held responsible for any death which by direct and almost inevitable consequences results from the initial criminal act."

Canola's conviction for the murder of his accomplice was reversed by the New Jersey Supreme Court, 73 N.J. 206, 374 A.2d 20 (1977). The court rejected the "proximate cause" theory and adopted instead the so-called "agency theory," applied in Commonwealth v. Redline, 391 Pa. 486, 137 A.2d 472 (1958). In *Redline,* the defendant and a co-felon were engaged in the commission of an armed robbery. They engaged in a gun battle with the police, during which the co-felon was killed by police bullets. The Pennsylvania Supreme Court held that "in order to convict for felony murder, the killing must have been done by the defendant or by an accomplice or confederate or by one acting in furtherance of the felonious undertaking." As described in *Canola,* "the [*Redline*] court held that in order to convict for felony murder the killing must have been done by defendant or someone acting in concert with him in furtherance of the felonious undertaking; that the death must be a consequence of the felony and not merely coincidental; and that a justifiable homicide could not be availed of to support a charge of murder."

What would be the result on the *Canola* facts under *Sophophone*? Does Kansas squarely endorse the "agency" theory of felony murder over the "proximate cause" theory? Which theory is to be preferred?

### 2. *PEOPLE V. WASHINGTON*

In order to answer the last question, one must have in mind the general rationales for felony murder. What justifications for the rule are cited by the majority in *Sophophone*? Which justifications does the dissent endorse? Do the judges explain why those justifications support one approach over the other? Consider as well the arguments of Chief Justice Traynor in People v. Washington, 62 Cal.2d 777, 44 Cal.Rptr. 442, 402 P.2d 130 (1965). The defendant was convicted of felony murder for participating in a robbery in which his accomplice was killed by a victim of the robbery. In reversing the conviction, the court reasoned:

> The purpose of the felony murder rule is to deter felons from killing negligently or accidentally by holding them strictly responsible for killings they commit. This purpose is not served by punishing them for killings committed by their victims.
>
> It is contended, however, that another purpose of the felony murder rule is to prevent the commission of robberies. Neither the common law rationale of the rule nor the penal code supports this contention. In every robbery there is a possibility that the victim will resist and kill. The robber has little control over such a killing once the robbery is undertaken. . . . To impose an additional penalty for the killing would discriminate between robbers, not on the basis of any difference in their own conduct, but solely on the basis of the response by others that the robber's conduct happened to induce. An additional penalty for a homicide committed by the victim would deter robbery haphazardly at best. To "prevent stealing, [the law] would do better to hang one thief in every thousand by lot." Oliver Wendell Holmes, The Common Law 58 (1881). . . .
>
> A defendant need not do the killing himself, however, to be guilty of murder. He may be vicariously responsible under the rules defining principals and criminal conspiracies. All persons aiding and abetting the commission of a robbery are guilty of first-degree murder when one of them kills while acting in furtherance of the common design. Moreover, when the defendant intends to kill or intentionally commits acts that are likely to kill with a conscious disregard for life, he is guilty of murder even though he uses another person to accomplish his objective.
>
> Defendants who initiate gun battles may also be found guilty of murder if their victims resist and kill. Under such circumstances, "the defendant for a base, anti-social motive and with wanton disregard for human life, does an act that involves a high degree of probability that it will result in death" and it is unnecessary to imply malice by invoking the felony murder doctrine. To invoke the felony murder doctrine to imply malice in such a case is unnecessary and overlooks the principles of criminal liability that should govern the responsibility of one person for a killing committed by another.
>
> To invoke the felony murder doctrine when the killing is not committed by the defendant or by his accomplice could lead to absurd results. Thus, two men rob a grocery store and flee in opposite directions. The owner of the store follows one of the robbers and kills him. Neither robber may have fired a shot. Neither robber may have been armed with a deadly weapon. If the felony murder doctrine applied, however, the surviving robber could be convicted of first-degree murder, even though he was captured by a policeman and placed under arrest at the time his accomplice was killed.

> The felony murder rule has been criticized on the grounds that in almost all cases in which it is applied it is unnecessary and that it erodes the relation between criminal liability and moral culpability. Although it is the law in this state, it should not be extended beyond any rational function that it is designed to serve. Accordingly, for a defendant to be guilty of murder under the felony murder rule the act of killing must be committed by the defendant or by his accomplice acting in furtherance of their common design.

Is Chief Justice Traynor's opinion internally consistent? Why is the deterrent purpose of the felony murder rule accomplished by punishing felons for accidental killings committed by them, but not for intentional or accidental killings committed by their victims? Does the proximate-cause approach extend the rule "beyond any rational function that it is designed to serve"?

### 3. RELATION TO PRINCIPLES OF CAUSATION

Causation problems can arise in two distinct ways in connection with felony murder situations:

#### *(i) Application of Felony Murder Rule*

The first concerns the principles of causation that should control the operation of the felony murder rule itself. The debate between the "proximate-cause" theory and the "agency" theory for analyzing cases where the homicide is committed by a victim or the police is illustrative. Are those courts which adopt the "agency" theory in effect applying narrower notions of proximate cause to the felony murder rule than would otherwise be applicable in a prosecution for criminal homicide? If the answer is "yes," then it would seem that a special doctrine of causation is being applied to limit the scope of the felony murder rule. On the other hand, if the answer is "no," then it would seem that courts adopting the "proximate cause" approach are creating a special doctrine of causation in order to extend the felony murder rule beyond the limits that ordinary principles of criminal liability would suggest. Which is the more accurate answer to the question? Should special causation principles be applied to limit or to extend the scope of the felony murder rule?

#### *(ii) Independent Prosecution for Murder*

The second way in which causation principles become relevant concerns the possibility of a murder prosecution without resort to the felony murder rule. Consider the following hypothetical. If *A* initiates a gun battle with intent to kill or in reckless disregard of human life, and if the victim returns fire and accidentally kills a bystander, would normal principles of causation permit *A*'s conviction of murder? Is the action of the victim an "independent intervening cause" of the bystander's death? If the answer to this question is "no," then—as *Washington* indicates—ordinary principles of causation and accessorial liability could handle many cases which have tested the limits of the felony murder rule.

Note also the relationship between these two ways in which causation can be relevant. If an independent prosecution for murder is possible in those cases where the defendant is culpable as to death (albeit not necessarily the one that actually occurred), does this then make the use of narrower causation principles in connection with the operation of the felony murder rule more justifiable? Should the felony murder doctrine be discarded entirely in favor of such independent prosecutions for murder? What kinds of murder convictions would be excluded by such an approach? Is the loss significant to the deterrent purposes of the law?

## 4. RELATION TO PRINCIPLES OF ACCESSORIAL LIABILITY

The felony murder rule also intersects with problems of accessorial liability. It is again helpful in thinking about this relationship to focus separately on the operation of the felony murder rule itself and the possibility of an independent prosecution for murder.

### *(i) Application of Felony Murder Rule*

The felony murder rule operates as an independent basis for accomplice liability. This aspect of the felony murder rule does not depend on the debate between the "agency" and "proximate cause" theories of felony murder. Under any formulation of the rule, once its scope is determined all participants in the felony are guilty of murder if any one of them commits an included homicide.

Does this aspect of the felony murder rule represent an extension of the ordinary principles of accessorial liability that would otherwise determine responsibility for the acts of a confederate? Do the policies underlying the felony murder rule suggest the need for a separate set of more inclusive principles of accomplice liability? Or is the felony murder rule on this point simply redundant, i.e., does it lead to the result that ordinary principles of accomplice liability would otherwise accomplish in any event?[a]

### *(ii) Independent Prosecution for Murder*

In situations to which the felony murder rule does not apply, as in *Sophophone*, the way is nonetheless open for the prosecutor to rely on ordinary principles of accomplice liability in an effort to secure a murder conviction. Given the possibility of an ordinary murder prosecution and conviction of accomplices under ordinary principles, is there any need for a special felony murder rule for accomplices?

## 5. *PEOPLE V. ANTICK*

People v. Antick, 15 Cal.3d 79, 123 Cal.Rptr. 475, 539 P.2d 43 (1975), provides a testing situation for application of these principles. Antick was charged, inter alia, with burglary and murder. The burglary was said to have been committed by two people—Antick and Bose. Bose was confronted after the burglary when police spotted him sitting in a stopped car. A person later thought to be Antick was walking away from the car as the police approached. Bose initiated a gun battle, and was killed by a policeman in

---

[a] The relationship of the felony murder rule to principles of accessorial liability is further complicated by the possibility of a conspiracy charge. As developed in the materials on conspiracy in Chapter VI, the liability of a conspirator for crimes committed by other conspirators is frequently measured by the law of conspiracy without reference to the law of accomplice liability. Thus, in felony murder situations there are three possible bases of accomplice liability: (i) liability under ordinary complicity rules; (ii) liability as a co-conspirator; and (iii) liability under the felony murder rule.

the exchange of fire. Antick was not apprehended at the scene, but was later identified as the second person involved in the burglary and presumably the person who was walking away from the car when the police approached. The prosecution of Antick for felony murder was based on the theory, as charged in the information, that "during the perpetration of the [September 28] burglary [defendant's] co-partner in the burglary, Donald Joseph Bose, initiated a gun battle which was the direct and unlawful cause of the death of the said Donald Joseph Bose."

Antick was convicted of both burglary and murder, but the murder conviction was set aside on appeal. The court began its discussion as follows:

> [D]efendant's conviction of first-degree murder may have been based upon either of two theories: (i) his participation in the commission of a burglary which resulted in the death of his accomplice, or (ii) his vicarious liability for the crimes of his accomplice. Defendant contends that on the present record he cannot be convicted of murder under either theory.
>
> Our consideration of defendant's contention requires us at the start to briefly review the basic principles underlying the crime of murder, the felony murder doctrine and the theory of accomplice liability. A defendant is not guilty of murder unless he is legally chargeable, either by virtue of his own conduct or that of an accomplice, with the two component elements of the crime: its actus reus, a homicide, and its mens rea, malice.[8] "Homicide is the killing of a human being by another human being." Malice is the state of mind of one who has "an intent to kill or an intent with conscious disregard for life to commit acts likely to kill."[9] In addition, "[t]he felony murder doctrine ascribes malice . . . to the felon who kills in the perpetration of an inherently dangerous felony."[10]
>
> The imputation of malice by application of the felony murder doctrine has been limited by this court to those cases in which the actual killing is committed by the defendant or his accomplice.
>
>> When a killing is not committed by a robber or by his accomplice but by his victim, malice aforethought is not attributable to the robber, for the killing is not committed by him in the perpetration or attempt to perpetrate robbery. It is not enough that the killing was a risk reasonably to be foreseen and that the robbery might therefore be regarded as a proximate cause of the killing. Section 189 requires that the felon or his accomplice commit the killing, for if he does not, the killing is not committed to perpetrate the felony. Indeed, in the present case the killing was committed to thwart

[8] Cal.Penal Code § 187 provides in pertinent part: "(a) Murder is the unlawful killing of a human being . . . with malice aforethought."

[9] Cal.Penal Code § 188 defines "malice" for purposes of murder: "Such malice may be express or implied. It is express when there is manifested a deliberate intention unlawfully to take away the life of a fellow creature. It is implied, when no considerable provocation appears, or when the circumstances attending the killing show an abandoned and malignant heart."

[10] Under Cal.Penal Code § 189, "[a]ll murder . . . which is committed in the perpetration of, or attempt to perpetrate, arson, rape, robbery, burglary, mayhem, or any act punishable under Section 288 [lewd or lascivious acts against children], is murder of the first degree. . . ."

> a felony. To include such killings within Section 189 would expand the meaning of the words "murder . . . which is committed in the perpetration [of] robbery . . . " beyond common understanding.

People v. Washington, 62 Cal.2d 777, 781, 44 Cal.Rptr. 442, 445, 402 P.2d 130, 133 (1965).

The court then summarized the applicable principles:

> The operation of these principles can best be illustrated by the following example. Three persons agree to commit a robbery, and during its commission *one* of them initiates a gun battle in which the victim or a police officer in reasonable response to such act kills *another* of the robbers. Since the immediate cause of death is the act of the victim or the officer, the felony murder rule is not applicable to convert the killing into a murder. Nevertheless, the robber initiating the gun battle and the third accomplice are guilty of murder. The former commits a homicide, since his conduct is the proximate cause of the death of another human being; the intervening act of the victim or police officer is not an independent superseding cause, eliminating responsibility for the killing. Furthermore, in initiating the shootout the robber acts with malice, having intentionally and with conscious disregard for life engaged in conduct likely to kill. That this malice is directed at someone other than his crime partner who as a proximate result of the robber's acts is eventually killed "does not prevent the killing from constituting the offense of murder [since] the law transfers the felonious intent from the original object of his attempt to the person killed and the homicide so committed is murder." Since in the posited situation the robber initiating the gun battle is acting in furtherance of the common design of all three participants, the third robber as well may be held vicariously liable for the murder.

The conclusion was:

> Applying these principles to the case at bench, we first observe that on the uncontradicted evidence defendant himself did not participate in the immediate events which preceded his accomplice's death. Under the People's version of the facts, which we accept as accurate for purposes of this discussion, Bose initiated a gun battle with the police in order to escape apprehension for a burglary which he and defendant had recently committed. The police officer responded by killing Bose. As the immediate cause of death was the act of the officer, it is clear that the felony murder rule does not operate to convert the killing into a murder for which defendant may be liable by virtue of his participation in the underlying burglary.[11] *People v. Washington,* supra.
>
> Nor may defendant be held legally accountable for Bose's death based upon his vicarious liability for the crimes of his accomplice. In order to predicate defendant's guilt upon this theory,

[11] The People concede in their brief on appeal that the felony murder instruction was erroneous and that the only possible legal basis for defendant's murder conviction is his vicarious liability for the consequences of Bose's act in initiating the shootout with the police officers.

it is necessary to prove that Bose committed a murder, in other words, that he caused the death of another human being [and] that he acted with malice.

It is well settled that Bose's conduct in initiating a shootout with police officers may establish the requisite malice. As we have noted on a number of occasions, a person who initiates a gun battle in the course of committing a felony intentionally and with a conscious disregard for life commits an act that is likely to cause death. However, Bose's malicious conduct did not result in the unlawful killing of *another* human being, but rather in Bose's own death. The only homicide which occurred was the justifiable killing of Bose by the police officer. Defendant's criminal liability certainly cannot be predicated upon the actions of the officer. As Bose could not be found guilty of murder in connection with his own death, it is impossible to base defendant's liability for this offense upon his vicarious responsibility for the crime of his accomplice.

In summary defendant's conviction of the murder of his accomplice Bose cannot be upheld either on the doctrine of felony murder or on a theory of vicarious liability. We are therefore compelled to conclude that on the instant record defendant as a matter of law cannot be found guilty of murder and that the verdict of the jury to that effect is against the law and the evidence.

### 6. QUESTIONS AND COMMENTS ON *ANTICK*

Focus on the three-person example given by the *Antick* court. One accomplice (*A1*) is killed by the police after another (*P1*) initiates a gun battle. *P1* is guilty of murder, not because of the felony murder rule but based the application of ordinary actus reus, mens rea, and causation principles. The other accomplice (*A2*) is also guilty of murder, in this case again not because of the felony murder rule but because of the application of ordinary principles of liability as an accessory.

In Antick's case, however, he cannot be convicted of murder under any theory. Felony murder principles do not apply because California adopts the "agency" theory. Accomplice liability principles do not apply either, because Bose did not commit murder. But in terms of personal culpability, personal responsibility, or any other principles relevant to the appropriate imposition of criminal sanctions, how is Antick different from *A2*? Why should he go free of a murder conviction when *A2* is convicted?

Consider the potential application of two Model Penal Code provisions to Antick's situation. Section 2.06(4) provides:

> When causing a particular result is an element of an offense, an accomplice in the conduct causing such result is an accomplice in the commission of that offense, if he acts with the kind of culpability, if any, with respect to that result that is sufficient for the commission of the offense.

And § 5.01(3) states:

> A person who engages in conduct designed to aid another to commit a crime which would establish his complicity under Section 2.06 if the crime were committed by such other person, is

> guilty of an attempt to commit the crime, although the crime is not committed or attempted by such other person.

Does this mean that Antick could be convicted of attempted murder under the Model Code? Is this the right outcome?

### 7. DURATION OF THE FELONY

Sophophone moved to dismiss the felony murder charges on the ground that the killing did not occur during the commission or attempted commission of a felony. Indeed, Sophophone argued that the killing did not even take place during a period of flight from the felony because, at the time the officer shot his co-felon, Sophophone "was in custody and sitting in the police car." Since the killing occurred during this "break in the circumstances," he argued, homicide liability could not rest on the felony murder doctrine.

This argument raises the general problem of determining the operative time span during which the felony murder rule can be applied—when, in other words, the felony to which the rule attaches begins and when it ends. The normal statement of the rule is that the felony murder doctrine applies from the time when an attempt to commit the felony has occurred, through its actual commission, and through the period of immediate flight therefrom. One of the ways in which the felony murder rule can be contracted or expanded is by tinkering with the time during which the felony can be said to be in process. Are there ways in which this issue can be intelligently addressed? Does the purpose of the felony murder rule suggest how lines of this sort should be drawn? Consider the comments in Herbert Wechsler & Jerome Michael, A Rationale of the Law of Homicide I, 37 Colum.L.Rev. 701, 716–17 (1937):

> The rule has . . . been restricted by the contraction of the period during which the felony can be said to be "in the course of" commission. Thus, if a person in flight kills a policeman attempting to interfere with his escape, it is not felony murder if he was not carrying away spoils. Conceding the ever present legislative necessity for reconciling extremes by drawing arbitrary lines the justice of which must be viewed from afar, the limits of intelligent casuistry have clearly been reached when the question whether judgment of death shall be imposed on a man who went no further than to participate in the planning of a robbery depends upon whether his accomplice shot the victim in his store or on the sidewalk outside.

The court summarily rejected Sophophone's argument as having "no merit under the facts of this case." In the court's view, the "uncontroverted evidence" established that "the killing took place during flight from the aggravated burglary." Is this the right answer?

### 8. MODERN STATUTES

Most current penal codes do not speak specifically to the situations described in *Antick* and the preceding notes, and the courts are accordingly left to the development of common law principles to decide such cases. There are, however, exceptions. The criminal code revisions adopted in New York in 1965 were widely copied on the question of felony murder. Section 125.25(3) provided that it would be felony murder when:

> Acting either alone or with one or more other persons, he commits or attempts to commit robbery, burglary, kidnapping, arson, rape in the first degree, sodomy in the first degree, sexual abuse in the first degree, aggravated sexual abuse, escape in the first degree, or escape in the second degree, and, in the course of and in furtherance of such crime or of immediate flight therefrom, he, or another participant, if there be any, causes the death of a person other than one of the participants, except that in any prosecution under this subdivision, in which the defendant was not the only participant in the underlying crime, it is an affirmative defense that the defendant:
>
> (a) Did not commit the homicidal act or in any way solicit, request, command, importune, cause or aid the commission thereof; and
>
> (b) Was not armed with a deadly weapon, or any instrument, article or substance readily capable of causing death or serious physical injury and of a sort not ordinarily carried in public places by law-abiding persons; and
>
> (c) Had no reasonable ground to believe that any other participant was armed with such a weapon, instrument, article or substance; and
>
> (d) Had no reasonable ground to believe that any other participant intended to engage in conduct likely to result in death or serious physical injury.

Contrast § 782.04(3) of the Florida penal code, which provides:

> When a person is killed in the perpetration of, or in the attempt to perpetrate, any [one of a series of enumerated felonies] by a person other than the person engaged in the perpetration of or attempt to perpetrate such felony, the person perpetrating or attempting to perpetrate such felony is guilty of murder in the second degree, . . . punishable by imprisonment for a term of years not exceeding life. . . .

## NOTE ON MISDEMEANOR MANSLAUGHTER

Manslaughter was typically defined at common law as causing the death of another by an unlawful act or by a lawful act committed in an unlawful manner. The second part of this definition is a reference to liability for recklessness or negligence, which has been dealt with above. The first part is a reference to the so-called misdemeanor manslaughter rule. This rule provides that when a death occurs during the commission of or attempt to commit a misdemeanor, all participants in the offensive conduct are guilty of manslaughter. As it has been applied in some jurisdictions, the rule encompasses all "unlawful" behavior, i.e., it includes conduct that was not criminal but that only involved the breach of civil standards of liability. In most jurisdictions, however, the rule has been limited to misdemeanors, hence the derivation of the name by which the doctrine is normally called. As in the case of felony murder, liability is strict as to death in those jurisdictions that follow the rule, and all participants are liable regardless of their culpability as to the death. Analytically, the problems of implementing the misdemeanor manslaughter rule are directly analogous to problems encountered with felony murder.

The history of the misdemeanor manslaughter rule also parallels the felony murder rule. In the main, it consists of a series of judicially derived limitations on its reach, such as by applying it only when the misdemeanor is dangerous to life or limb. As with felony murder, a limitation of this type could be applied based on the general characteristics of the misdemeanor or it could take into account the manner in which the misdemeanor was actually committed. For a comments on the rule and some of its qualifications, see Herbert Wechsler and Jerome Michael, A Rationale of the Law of Homicide I, 37 Colum.L. Rev. 701, 722–23 (1937)..

The Model Penal Code does not include a counterpart to the misdemeanor manslaughter rule. It is reported in ALI, Model Penal Code and Commentaries, § 210.3, p. 77 (1980), that 22 enacted codes and proposals agreed with the Model Code and abolished the rule in its entirety. Eleven codes and one proposal, on the other hand, retained some form of the rule. There are a number of jurisdictions that have not revised their penal codes in response to the Model Penal Code and that still retain some version of the common law rule. Should the rule be retained?

# CHAPTER XI

# CAPITAL PUNISHMENT

## SECTION 1: THE SUPREME COURT AND CAPITAL PUNISHMENT

### INTRODUCTORY NOTES ON THE SUPREME COURT AND CAPITAL PUNISHMENT

#### 1. BACKGROUND

Capital punishment was an established feature of American law at the time the Constitution and the Bill of Rights were adopted, as well as when the Fourteenth Amendment was ratified following the Civil War. In most states, the common law crime of murder had been divided into degrees. First-degree murder, which generally required that the killing be "willful, deliberate, and premeditated," remained eligible for the penalty of death. Second-degree murder did not. Although a movement to abolish the death penalty altogether surfaced during the 1830s, only a few states (Michigan, Rhode Island, and Wisconsin) eliminated the capital sanction before the Civil War. Thereafter, occasional surges of abolitionist sentiment led to a gradual reduction of offenses punishable by death.

Abolitionist sentiment emerged on a broad scale after World War II. Seven state legislatures eliminated capital punishment between 1957 and 1965, bringing to 10 the number of abolitionist states. Meanwhile, the penalty was carried out with declining frequency: the average annual number of executions dropped from 167 during the 1930s to less than 50 during the late 1950s and early 1960s.

In the early 1960s, death penalty opponents began to focus on the courts. Although the constitutionality of capital punishment had long been regarded as settled, there was reason to believe that the Supreme Court might be receptive to the abolitionist cause. The Court had recently shown its willingness—in the school desegregation and reapportionment cases—to use constitutional litigation as a mechanism for changing traditional social and political practices. Moreover, the claim that the death penalty had been administered in a racially discriminatory fashion[a] implicated one of the central concerns of the Warren Court.

As opponents of capital punishment prepared to take their challenge to the Supreme Court in the 1960s, 40 states authorized (but did not require) the death penalty for the highest form of murder. Kidnapping was a capital offense in two-thirds of the states, and treason and rape were punishable by death in about half. In trials for capital offenses, juries in most states typically returned a sentence recommendation (often binding) together with the verdict of guilt. No additional criteria or standards were spelled out in the instructions to explain how the jury's discretion should be exercised.

---

[a] Of the 3,859 persons executed between 1930 and 1968, 2,066 were black. Of the 455 executed for rape during this period, 405 were black. Of the 2,306 persons executed in the South during these years, 72 percent were black.

Moreover, because the jury decisions on guilt and sentence were made at the same time, no evidence beyond that admissible on the question of guilt was directed specifically to the propriety of a capital sentence. Since evidence concerning the defendant's character, personal background, and prior criminal record is normally inadmissible to determine guilt, the jury was required in many cases to make its sentencing decision without such information.

Litigation was brought challenging the constitutionality of capital sentencing procedures. In 1968, the Supreme Court invalidated procedures that permitted the prosecution to exclude "for cause" any jurors who had "conscientious scruples" against the death penalty. The Court held, in Witherspoon v. Illinois, 391 U.S. 510 (1968), that the exclusion of jurors for cause should be limited to those who were unequivocally opposed to the death penalty in all cases; exclusion of jurors with more ambiguous attitudes, the Court ruled, tended to produce a "hanging jury." The *Witherspoon* decision had the effect of invalidating most death sentences pending at the time. A de facto moratorium on executions then took hold.[b]

## 2. *MCGAUTHA V. CALIFORNIA*

In McGautha v. California, 402 U.S. 183 (1971), the Court considered two claims that called into question the constitutionality of every capital sentencing statute then in use. First, the challengers contended that the practice of leaving the sentencing decision to unguided jury discretion was fundamentally unfair because it invited arbitrary and ad-hoc determinations. Second, they argued that the practice of submitting both guilt and punishment to the jury in a single proceeding excluded relevant sentencing information from the jury and thereby deprived the defendant of a fair sentencing hearing.[c] In a six-three decision, the Court held that discretionary jury sentencing, even in a single proceeding, did not violate due process.

## 3. *FURMAN V. GEORGIA*

One month after *McGautha* was decided, the Court granted certiorari in four cases to decide whether "the imposition and carrying out of the death penalty [in these cases] constitutes cruel and unusual punishment in violation of the Eighth and Fourteenth Amendments."[d] The cases involved two death sentences for rape and one each for felony murder and murder by a person previously convicted of murder. A year later, a five-four majority set aside the death sentences in all four cases. The result was announced in a short per curiam opinion without supporting explanation. Furman v. Georgia, 408 U.S. 238 (1972). Each member of the Court wrote separately in opinions occupying more than 230 pages in the United States Reports.

The opinions fall into three categories. Justices Brennan and Marshall concluded that the death penalty was unconstitutional across the board.

---

[b] This information could be considered by the judge, however, in states where the jury recommendation was not binding.

[c] Although California was one of the few states with a bifurcated sentencing process, *McGautha* had been consolidated for decision with an Ohio case in which the death penalty had been imposed in a unitary proceeding.

[d] As students of constitutional law will know, the Eighth Amendment in terms applies only to the federal government. The Court had previously held, however, that the Cruel-and-Unusual-Punishment Clause of the Eighth Amendment applied to the states through the Fourteenth Amendment.

Justices Douglas, Stewart, and White concurred on narrower grounds. They were concerned with the risk that unguided jury discretion would degenerate into unacceptably inconsistent judgments. Chief Justice Burger and Justices Blackmun, Powell, and Rehnquist dissented. The views of each group of Justices are summarized below.

### *(i) Brennan and Marshall*

Justice Brennan found the death penalty to be incompatible with evolving conceptions of human dignity for four reasons. First, he argued that the death penalty is so extreme in its severity and so degrading in its character as to be equivalent to the "barbaric punishments condemned by history," such as the rack, the thumbscrew, and the iron boot. Second, he thought that capital punishment, as administered, was incompatible with the principle that the state "must not arbitrarily inflict a severe punishment." Third, he concluded that the infrequency with which executions actually occurred demonstrated that capital punishment had become morally unacceptable to contemporary society. Finally, Justice Brennan canvassed the various purposes of punishment and concluded that, as administered, the death penalty "serves no penal purpose more effectively than a less severe punishment." He discounted deterrence as "speculative," and concluded that retribution could not justify a penalty so inconsistently and infrequently imposed.

Justice Marshall was aligned with Brennan. He said that the average American citizen, if fully informed on the issue, would find the death penalty "shocking to his conscience and sense of justice." He also argued that the death penalty was unconstitutionally excessive because it made no measurable contribution to legitimate legislative objectives. He concluded that "retribution for its own sake is improper" and that the available statistical evidence demonstrated that the death penalty had no significant deterrent effect.

### *(ii) Douglas, Stewart, and White*

Justices Douglas, Stewart, and White concluded that the sentencing procedures then in use were constitutionally defective. Justice Douglas noted that discretionary capital sentencing statutes are, in operation, "pregnant with discrimination" against poor, black defendants. Justice Stewart observed that the death penalty is "wantonly and freakishly imposed" and that "death sentences are cruel and unusual in the same way that being struck by lightning is cruel and unusual." Justice White added that "there is no meaningful basis for distinguishing the few cases in which [the death penalty] is imposed from the many cases in which it is not."

### *(iii) The Dissenters*

The dissenters noted that capital punishment was widely used when the Constitution and the Bill of Rights were adopted, that it had been in continuous use since then, and that the declining frequency of imposition indicated that the penalty was being reserved for the most extreme cases and not that it was no longer socially acceptable. As for the argument that the death penalty does not serve valid penological objectives, the dissenters concluded that the Court should defer to rational legislative judgments regarding its retributive and deterrent value.

## 4. THE AFTERMATH OF *FURMAN*

Even to the practiced eye, the meaning of *Furman* was obscure, but it at least made clear that the states were not allowed to commit death sentences to unguided jury discretion. Since all states followed that procedure, the effect of the decision was to invalidate every death penalty statute then in force.

Thirty-five states responded to *Furman* by reformulating their capital sentencing provisions to restrict sentencing discretion. Two approaches seemed plausible, and the states were evenly divided on which would succeed. Eighteen states attempted to eliminate sentencing discretion altogether by making death the mandatory punishment for conviction of a capital crime. The remaining 17 states attempted to structure and control the exercise of sentencing discretion, usually in provisions patterned after the Model Penal Code, which provided for bifurcated proceedings and required consideration of specified aggravating and mitigating factors.[e]

## 5. THE 1976 DECISIONS

The Court considered a representative group of these statutes in five cases decided in 1976.[f] The Court was again closely divided. Justices Brennan and Marshall adhered to their view that the death penalty was unconstitutional in all cases. Burger, White, Blackmun, and Rehnquist voted to sustain all five statutes, holding that the defect identified in *Furman* could be remedied either by making the death penalty mandatory or by requiring consideration of specified aggravating and mitigating circumstances. The three remaining Justices—Stewart, Powell and Stevens[g]—voted to invalidate the mandatory death penalties but to uphold the statutes that specified criteria to structure the exercise of discretion. Together, the various opinions in these five cases occupy 210 pages in the United States Reports.

One might have thought that a mandatory death penalty would be the perfect cure for too much discretion. The situation was complicated, however, by the way some states responded to *Furman*. Most states prescribed mandatory death penalties for narrow categories of criminal homicide, such as murder of a police officer or murder by someone already serving a life sentence. North Carolina, however, (and also New Mexico) made death the mandatory penalty for *all* first-degree murder. Any homicide found "wilful, deliberate, and premeditated," which previously would have been death-*eligible*, now became death-*mandatory*. Faced with a vast expansion of capital punishment for which the Supreme Court itself was in some sense responsible, the Justices balked. The decisive bloc of Stewart, Powell, and Stevens held that the ostensibly mandatory nature of the North Carolina death penalty simply "papered over" the problem of unchecked discretion. The reason was that juries retained the power not to convict of the

---

[e] In 2009 the American Law Institute "withdrew" the Model Penal Code's capital punishment provision "in light of the currently intractable institutional and structural obstacles to ensuring a minimally adequate system for administering capital punishment.

[f] Gregg v. Georgia, 428 U.S. 153 (1976); Proffitt v. Florida, 428 U.S. 242 (1976); Jurek v. Texas, 428 U.S. 262 (1976); Woodson v. North Carolina, 428 U.S. 280 (1976); Roberts v. Louisiana, 428 U.S. 325 (1976). The statutes involved in these five decisions are reproduced in Appendix B.

[g] Stevens had succeeded Douglas.

mandatory offense, and history showed they would often do so: "North Carolina's mandatory death-penalty statute provides no standards to guide the jury in its inevitable exercise of the power to determine which first-degree murderers shall live and which shall die. And there is no way under the North Carolina law for the judiciary to check arbitrary and capricious exercise of that power through a review of death sentences."

Moreover, said the trio, the mandatory statute was deficient in "its failure to allow the particularized consideration of relevant aspects of the character and record of each convicted defendant before the imposition upon him of a sentence of death":

> A process that accords no significance to relevant facets of the character and record of the individual offender or the circumstances of the particular offense excludes from consideration in fixing the ultimate punishment of death the possibility of compassionate or mitigating factors stemming from the diverse frailties of humankind. It treats all persons convicted of a designated offense not as uniquely individual human beings, but as members of a faceless, undifferentiated mass to be subjected to the blind infliction of the penalty of death.[h]

Although Stewart, Powell, and Stevens (joined by Brennan and Marshall) refused to allow mandatory death penalties, they (joined in this instance by Burger, White, Blackmun, and Rehnquist) approved statutes based on the Model Penal Code, of which the Georgia statute was illustrative:

> The basic concern of *Furman* centered on those defendants who were being condemned to death capriciously and arbitrarily. Under the procedures before the Court in that case, sentencing authorities were not directed to give attention to the nature or circumstances of the crime committed or to the character or record of the defendant. Left unguided, juries imposed the death sentence in a way that could only be called freakish. The new Georgia sentencing procedures, by contrast, focus the jury's attention on the particularized nature of the crime and the particularized characteristics of the individual defendant. While the jury is permitted to consider any aggravating or mitigating circumstances, it must find and identify at least one statutory aggravating factor before it may impose a penalty of death. In this way the jury's discretion is channeled. No longer can a jury wantonly and freakishly impose the death sentence; it is always circumscribed by the legislative guidelines. In addition, the review function of the Supreme Court of Georgia affords additional assurance that the concerns that prompted our decision in *Furman* are not present to any significant degree in the Georgia procedure applied here.

The plurality rejected two major arguments against the Georgia system. The first was that the prosecutor in charging and plea bargaining, the jury in convicting the defendant of a non-capital form of criminal homicide,

---

[h] The Court has subsequently made it clear that mandatory death penalty provisions are categorically unconstitutional. In Roberts v. Louisiana, 431 U.S. 633 (1977), it struck down a mandatory death penalty for murder of an on-duty policeman, and in Sumner v. Shuman, 483 U.S. 66 (1987), it invalidated Nevada statute that made a death sentence mandatory for a prison inmate who had been convicted of murder while serving a life sentence without possibility of parole.—[Footnote by eds.]

and the governor in exercising the pardon power all exercise discretion inconsistent with the concerns of *Furman.* The plurality responded that:

> Nothing in any of our cases suggests that the decision to afford an individual defendant mercy violates the Constitution. *Furman* held only that, in order to minimize the risk that the death penalty would be imposed on a capriciously selected group of offenders, the decision to impose it had to be guided by standards so that the sentencing authority would focus on the particularized circumstances of the crime and the defendant.

The second argument was that the standards adopted by the Georgia statute were so broad and vague as to provide no meaningful guidance. The plurality held that in context, particularly given the reviewing function exercised by the Georgia Supreme Court, the provisions were not unacceptably vague. The plurality was unwilling to construe *Furman* as requiring that all possibility of arbitrary action be eliminated. A reasonable effort to guide and control the discretion of the jury was all that could be expected. A more rigid approach would have the effect of outlawing capital punishment altogether.

## 6. *LOCKETT, EDDINGS,* AND *PENRY*

Subsequent cases elaborated on "constitutionally indispensable" requirement of an individualized determination of the death penalty.

Sandra Lockett was waiting in a car when an accomplice committed a homicide during the course of a pawn shop robbery.[i] She was convicted of murder under the ordinary rules of complicity. She claimed mitigation on the grounds that she was a secondary participant in the offense, that she had not previously committed any major crimes, and that her youth (she was 21) should be taken into account. Under the Ohio statute, the judge was required to impose the death penalty unless the defendant proved statutorily specified mitigating circumstances. Since none of the three claims advanced by Lockett was listed,[j] the trial judge had "no alternative" but to impose a death sentence.

In Lockett v. Ohio, 438 U.S. 586 (1978), the Supreme Court struck down her death sentence with only one dissent:

> The Eighth and Fourteenth Amendments require that the sentencer, in all but the rarest kind of capital case, not be precluded from considering, *as a mitigating factor,* any aspect of a defendant's character or record and any of the circumstances of the offense that the defendant proffers as a basis for a sentence less than death.

Justice Rehnquist's dissent argued that the effect of the plurality decision was to resurrect the discretionary sentencing practices—and the risk of arbitrariness—that *Furman* was designed to eliminate.

---

[i] The person who actually fired the fatal shot pleaded guilty to a non-capital murder charge and was the chief prosecution witness. Lockett twice refused to plead guilty to a reduced charge which would have been punishable by a mandatory life sentence.

[j] Ohio authorized mitigation where the victim had induced or facilitated the offense, where the defendant was "under duress, coercion or strong provocation," or where the offense was "primarily the product of psychosis or mental deficiency."

*Lockett* was followed in Eddings v. Oklahoma, 455 U.S. 104 (1982), where a five-to-four majority relied on *Lockett* to strike down a death sentence imposed on a 16-year-old defendant for killing a police officer.[k] The Court ruled that the sentencing judge had failed to consider evidence of Eddings' "turbulent family history, of beatings by a harsh father and of severe emotional disturbance." Justice Powell explained for the Court that "the sentencer [and the appellate court] may determine the weight to be given relevant mitigating evidence. But they may not give it no weight by excluding such evidence from their consideration" as a matter of law. Chief Justice Burger dissented, joined by Justices White, Blackmun and Rehnquist.

In Penry v. Lynaugh, 492 U.S. 302 (1989), a five-to-four majority relied on *Lockett* and *Eddings* to invalidate Texas' jury instructions, as applied to Penry, because they failed to allow the jury "to consider and give effect to mitigating evidence" he had introduced regarding his mental retardation and abused background. The standard Texas instruction directed the jury to impose a death sentence upon affirmative answers to three special issues: whether the killing was deliberate, whether it was unreasonable in response to any provocation, and whether the defendant would constitute a future danger to society. The problem with this instruction, Justice O'Connor observed, was that

> if a juror concluded that Penry acted deliberately and was likely to be dangerous in the future, but also concluded that because of his mental retardation he was not sufficiently culpable to deserve the death penalty, that juror would be unable to give effect to that mitigating evidence under the instruction given in this case. . . . In the absence of instructions informing the jury that it could consider and give effect to the mitigating evidence of Penry's mental retardation and abused background by declining to impose the death penalty, we conclude that the jury was not provided with a vehicle for expressing its 'reasoned moral response' to that evidence in rendering its sentencing decision.

Justice Scalia dissented, joined by Chief Justice Rehnquist and Justices White and Kennedy. In holding that the jury had to be free to deem Penry's mental retardation and sad childhood relevant for whatever purpose it wished," Justice Scalia concluded, "the Court has come full circle, not only permitting but requiring what *Furman* once condemned."

## 7. *ZANT V. STEPHENS*

There is undeniable tension between two themes that underlie the death penalty cases—that capital sentencing decisions must be structured so as to promote consistency and reduce the risk of arbitrariness and that the states may not either eliminate discretion or structure it in a way that compromises the defendant's right to an individualized determination of sentence. In Zant v. Stephens, 462 U.S. 862 (1983), the Court addressed this tension. The case involved the Georgia statute upheld in 1976. The

[k] The Court granted certiorari to consider the constitutionality of a death sentence for minors, but did not reach that question in *Eddings*. It subsequently addressed the permissibility of the death penalty for minors in Thompson v. Oklahoma, 487 U.S. 815 (1988), Stanford v. Kentucky, 492 U.S. 361 (1989), and Roper v. Simmons, 543 U.S. 551 (2005). *Roper* held that the Eighth Amendment barred execution of offenders who were under 18 when they committed the crime. These cases are summarized below.

statute permitted the jury to consider evidence in aggravation beyond the statutory list of aggravating factors and also permitted the jury to exercise unconstrained discretion in determining whether the death penalty should be imposed after a statutory aggravating circumstance was found.

In his opinion for the Court, Justice Stevens summarized the governing constitutional imperatives in the administration of capital sentencing statutes:

> The [*Gregg* Court's] approval of Georgia's capital sentencing procedure rested primarily on two features of the scheme: that the jury was required to find at least one valid statutory aggravating circumstance and to identify it in writing, and that the state supreme court reviewed the record of every death penalty proceeding to determine whether the sentence was arbitrary or disproportionate. These elements, the opinion concluded, adequately protected against the wanton and freakish imposition of the death penalty. This conclusion rested . . . on the fundamental requirement that . . . an aggravating circumstance must genuinely narrow the class of persons eligible for the death penalty and must reasonably justify the imposition of a more severe sentence on the defendant compared to others found guilty of murder. . . .
>
> Our cases indicate, then, that the statutory aggravating circumstances play a constitutionally necessary function at the stage of legislative definition; they circumscribe the class of persons eligible for the death penalty. But the Constitution does not require the jury to ignore other possible aggravating factors in the process of selecting, from among that class, those defendants who will actually be sentenced to death. What is important at the selection stage is an *individualized* determination on the basis of the character of the individual and the circumstances of the crime.
>
> The Georgia scheme provides for categorical narrowing at the definition stage, and for individualized determination and appellate review at the selection stage. We therefore remain convinced, as we were in 1976, that the structure of the statute is constitutional. . . .

Does this help?

## 8. ADDITIONAL CASES ON CAPITAL PUNISHMENT

The remaining material in this chapter explores several key themes of the Supreme Court's death penalty decisions in further depth. Section 2 continues to trace the Court's struggle to assure that the states have put in place procedures that assure that there is a "meaningful difference" between the cases in which the death penalty is imposed and those in which it is not. Section 3 presents a series of decisions in which the Court has ruled that the death penalty is a "grossly disproportionate" punishment for certain offenses (e,g., rape) and for certain offenders (e.g., who were younger that 18 at the time of the capital offense or had an intellectual disability). Finally, Section 4 covers an important decision in which the Court rejected claims that the death penalty was being applied in a racially discriminatory fashion.

In studying the Supreme Court's continuing constitutional encounter with capital punishment, it is well to keep in mind the empirical context and the ongoing political debate about the death penalty. Among the 38 states that have authorized capital punishment during the modern period (i.e., after the 1976 decisions), 34 states have executed at least one person. There are currently more than 3,000 inmates on death row, about half of whom are in California, Florida, and Texas. Recent executions tend to be concentrated in a few states, most notably Texas, Florida and Oklahoma. Although the number of death sentences steadily increased each year for two decades, the annual nationwide number of death sentences then began a steady decline, dropping from more than 300 per year in 1996 to less than 80 in 2012. Similarly, the annual number of executions peaked at 98 in 1999 and dropped to 39 in 2013. Meanwhile political support for abolition has grown in recent years, and six states abolished capital punishment between 2007 and 2013. Aside from arguments about the morality of capital punishment and the fairness of the process, key empirical aspects of the debate include the risk of convicting and executing innocent people, the cost of maintaining death rows and funding death penalty litigation, and the deterrent effects of authorizing and administering capital punishment.

## SECTION 2: ARBITRARINESS

### Godfrey v. Georgia

Supreme Court of the United States, 1980.
446 U.S. 420.

■ MR. JUSTICE STEWART announced the judgment of the Court and delivered an opinion, in which MR. JUSTICE BLACKMUN, MR. JUSTICE POWELL, and MR. JUSTICE STEVENS joined.

Under Georgia law, a person convicted of murder may be sentenced to death if it is found beyond a reasonable doubt that the offense "was outrageously or wantonly vile, horrible or inhuman in that it involved torture, depravity of mind, or an aggravated battery to the victim." In Gregg v. Georgia, 428 U.S. 153 (1976), the Court held that this statutory aggravating circumstance (Subsection (b)(7)) is not unconstitutional on its face.[a] . . . Nearly four years have passed since the *Gregg* decision, and during that time many death sentences based in whole or in part on Subsection (b)(7) have been affirmed by the Supreme Court of Georgia. The issue now before us is whether, in affirming the imposition of the sentences of death in the present case, the Georgia Supreme Court has adopted such a broad and vague construction of the Subsection (b)(7) aggravating circumstance as to violate the Eighth and Fourteenth Amendments to the United States Constitution.[2]

---

[a] The Georgia statute before the Court in *Gregg* and again in *Godfrey* is reprinted in Appendix B.—[Footnote by eds.]

[2] The other statutory aggravating circumstances upon which a death sentence may be based after conviction of murder in Georgia are considerably more specific or objectively measurable than Subsection (b)(7). . . .

In [a prior decision], the Supreme Court of Georgia held unconstitutional the portion of the first statutory aggravating circumstance encompassing persons who have a "substantial history of serious assaultive criminal convictions" because it did not set "sufficiently 'clear and objective standards.' "

I

On a day in early September in 1977, the petitioner and his wife of 28 years had a heated argument in their home. During the course of this altercation, the petitioner, who had consumed several cans of beer, threatened his wife with a knife and damaged some of her clothing. At this point, the petitioner's wife declared that she was going to leave him, and departed to stay with relatives. That afternoon she went to a justice of the peace and secured a warrant charging the petitioner with aggravated assault. A few days later, while still living away from home, she filed suit for divorce. Summons was served on the petitioner, and a court hearing was set on a date some two weeks later. Before the date of the hearing, the petitioner on several occasions asked his wife to return to their home. Each time his efforts were rebuffed. At some point during this period, his wife moved in with her mother. The petitioner believed that his mother-in-law was actively instigating his wife's determination not to consider a possible reconciliation.

In the early evening of September 20, according to the petitioner, his wife telephoned him at home. Once again they argued. She asserted that reconciliation was impossible and allegedly demanded all the proceeds from the planned sale of their house. The conversation was terminated after she said that she would call back later. This she did in an hour or so. The ensuing conversation was, according to the petitioner's account, even more heated than the first. His wife reiterated her stand that reconciliation was out of the question, said that she still wanted all the proceeds from the sale of their house, and mentioned that her mother was supporting her position. Stating that she saw no further use in talking or arguing, she hung up.

At this juncture, the petitioner got out his shotgun and walked with it down the hill from his home to the trailer where his mother-in-law lived. Peering through a window, he observed his wife, his mother-in-law, and his 11-year-old daughter playing a card game. He pointed the shotgun at his wife through the window and pulled the trigger. The charge from the gun struck his wife in the forehead and killed her instantly. He proceeded into the trailer, striking and injuring his fleeing daughter with the barrel of the gun. He then fired the gun at his mother-in-law, striking her in the head and killing her instantly.

The petitioner then called the local sheriff's office, identified himself, said where he was, explained that he had just killed his wife and mother-in-law, and asked that the sheriff come and pick him up. Upon arriving at the trailer, the law-enforcement officers found the petitioner seated on a chair in open view near the driveway. He told one of the officers that "they're dead, I killed them" and directed the officer to the place where he had put the murder weapon. Later the petitioner told a police officer: "I've done a hideous crime, . . . but I have been thinking about it for eight years . . . I'd do it again."

The petitioner was subsequently indicted on two counts of murder and one of aggravated assault. He pleaded not guilty and relied primarily on a defense of temporary insanity at his trial. The jury returned verdicts of guilty on all three counts.

The sentencing phase of the trial was held before the same jury. No further evidence was tendered, but counsel for each side made arguments to the jury. Three times during the course of his argument, the prosecutor stated that the case involved no allegation of "torture" or of an "aggravated battery." When counsel had completed their arguments, the trial judge instructed the jury orally and in writing on the standards that must guide them in imposing sentence. Both orally and in writing, the judge quoted to the jury the statutory language of the Subsection (b)(7) aggravating circumstance in its entirety.

The jury imposed sentences of death on both of the murder convictions. As to each, the jury specified that the aggravating circumstance they had found beyond a reasonable doubt was "that the offense of murder was outrageously or wantonly vile, horrible and inhuman."

In accord with Georgia law in capital cases, the trial judge prepared a report in the form of answers to a questionnaire for use on appellate review. One question on the form asked whether or not the victim had been "physically harmed or tortured." The trial judge's response was "No, as to both victims, excluding the actual murdering of the two victims."[4]

The Georgia Supreme Court affirmed the judgments of the trial court in all respects . . . . The court found no evidence that the sentence had been "imposed under the influence of passion, prejudice, or any other arbitrary factor," held that the sentence was neither excessive nor disproportionate to the penalty imposed in similar cases, and stated that the evidence supported the jury's finding of the Subsection (b)(7) statutory aggravating circumstance. Two justices dissented.

II

In Furman v. Georgia, 408 U.S. 238 (1972), the Court held that the penalty of death may not be imposed under sentencing procedures that create a substantial risk that the punishment will be inflicted in an arbitrary and capricious manner. *Gregg* reaffirmed this holding . . . . :

A capital-sentencing scheme must, in short, provide a "meaningful basis for distinguishing the few cases in which [the penalty] is imposed from the many cases in which it is not."

This means that if a state wishes to authorize capital punishment it has a constitutional responsibility to tailor and apply its law in a manner that avoids the arbitrary and capricious infliction of the death penalty. Part of a state's responsibility in this regard is to define the crimes for which death may be the sentence in a way that obviates "standardless [sentencing] discretion." It must channel the sentencer's discretion by "clear and objective standards" that provide "specific and detailed guidance," and that "make rationally reviewable the process for imposing a sentence of death." . . .

In the case before us, the Georgia Supreme Court has affirmed a sentence of death based upon no more than a finding that the offense was "outrageously or wantonly vile, horrible and inhuman." There is nothing in these few words, standing alone, that implies any inherent restraint on the arbitrary and capricious infliction of the death sentence. A person of ordinary sensibility could fairly characterize almost

[4] Another question on the form asked the trial judge to list the mitigating circumstances that were in evidence. The judge noted that the petitioner had no significant history of prior criminal activity.

every murder as "outrageously or wantonly vile, horrible and inhuman." Such a view may, in fact, have been one to which the members of the jury in this case subscribed. If so, their preconceptions were not dispelled by the trial judge's sentencing instructions. These gave the jury no guidance concerning the meaning of any of Subsection (b)(7)'s terms. In fact, the jury's interpretation of Subsection (b)(7) can only be the subject of sheer speculation.

The standardless and unchanneled imposition of death sentences in the uncontrolled discretion of a basically uninstructed jury in this case was in no way cured by the affirmance of those sentences by the Georgia Supreme Court. Under state law that court may not affirm a judgment of death until it has independently assessed the evidence of record and determined that such evidence supports the trial judge's or jury's finding of an aggravating circumstance.

In past cases the state supreme court has apparently understood this obligation as carrying with it the responsibility to keep Subsection (b)(7) within constitutional bounds. Recognizing that "there is a possibility of abuse of [the Subsection (b)(7)] statutory aggravating circumstance," the court has emphasized that it will not permit the language of that subsection simply to become a "catchall" for cases which do not fit within any other statutory aggravating circumstance. Thus, in exercising its function of death-sentence review, the court has said that it will restrict its "approval of the death penalty under this statutory aggravating circumstance to those cases that lie at the core."

When *Gregg* was decided by this Court in 1976, the Georgia Supreme Court had affirmed two death sentences based wholly on Subsection (b)(7). The homicide in [the first case] was "a horrifying torture-murder." There, the victim had been beaten, burned, raped, and otherwise severely abused before her death by strangulation. The homicide in [the second case] was of a similar ilk. In that case, the convicted murderer had choked two seven-year-old boys to death after having forced each of them to submit to anal sodomy.

[Subsequent decisions] suggest that the Georgia Supreme Court had by 1977 reached three separate but consistent conclusions respecting the Subsection (b)(7) aggravating circumstance. The first was that the evidence that the offense was "outrageously or wantonly vile, horrible or inhuman" had to demonstrate "torture, depravity of mind, or an aggravated battery to the victim." The second was that the phrase, "depravity of mind," comprehended only the kind of mental state that led the murderer to torture or to commit an aggravated battery before killing his victim. The third . . . was that the word, "torture," must be construed in pari materia with "aggravated battery" so as to require evidence of serious physical abuse of the victim before death. Indeed, the circumstances proved in a number of the Subsection (b)(7) death-sentence cases affirmed by the Georgia Supreme Court have met all three of these criteria.

The Georgia courts did not, however, so limit Subsection (b)(7) in the present case. No claim was made, and nothing in the record before us suggests, that the petitioner committed an aggravated battery upon his wife or mother-in-law or, in fact, caused either of them to suffer any physical injury preceding their deaths. Moreover, in the trial court, the prosecutor repeatedly told the jury—and the trial judge wrote in his sentencing report—that the murders did not involve "torture." Nothing said on appeal by the Georgia Supreme Court indicates that it took a different view of the evidence. The circumstances of this case, therefore, do not satisfy the criteria laid out by the Georgia Supreme Court itself in [the prior] cases. In holding that the evidence supported the jury's Subsection (b)(7) finding, the state Supreme Court simply asserted that the verdict was "factually substantiated."

Thus, the validity of the petitioner's death sentences turns on whether, in light of the facts and circumstances of the murders that Godfrey was convicted of committing, the Georgia Supreme Court can be said to have applied a constitutional construction of the phrase "outrageously or wantonly vile, horrible or inhuman in that [they] involved . . . depravity of mind. . . ."[15] We conclude that the answer must be no. The petitioner's crimes cannot be said to have reflected a consciousness materially more "depraved" than that of any person guilty of murder. His victims were killed instantaneously.[16] They were members of his family who were causing him extreme emotional trauma. Shortly after the killings, he acknowledged his responsibility and the heinous nature of his crimes. These factors certainly did not remove the criminality from the petitioner's acts. But . . . it "is of vital importance to the defendant and to the community that any decision to impose the death sentence be, and appear to be, based on reason rather than caprice or emotion."

That cannot be said here. There is no principled way to distinguish this case, in which the death penalty was imposed, from the many cases in which it was not. Accordingly, the judgment of the Georgia Supreme Court insofar as it leaves standing the petitioner's death sentences is reversed, and the case is remanded to that court for further proceedings.

It is so ordered.

■ MR. JUSTICE MARSHALL, with whom MR. JUSTICE BRENNAN joins, concurring in the judgment. . . .

In Gregg v. Georgia, 428 U.S. 153 (1976), the Court rejected the position, expressed by my Brother Brennan and myself, that the death penalty is in all circumstances cruel and unusual punishment forbidden by the Eighth and Fourteenth Amendments. . . . For reasons I expressed in Furman v. Georgia, 408 U.S. 238 (1972), and *Gregg*, I believe that the death penalty may not constitutionally be imposed even if it were possible to do so in an evenhanded manner. But events since *Gregg* make that possibility seem increasingly remote. Nearly every week of every year, this Court is presented with at least one petition for certiorari raising troubling issues of non-compliance with the strictures of *Gregg* and its progeny. On numerous occasions since *Gregg*, the Court has reversed decisions of state supreme courts upholding the imposition

---

15 The sentence of death in this case rested exclusively on Subsection (b)(7). Accordingly, we intimate no view as to whether or not the petitioner might constitutionally have received the same sentences on some other basis. Georgia does not, as do some states, make multiple murders an aggravating circumstance, as such.

16 In light of this fact, it is constitutionally irrelevant that the petitioner used a shotgun instead of a rifle as the murder weapon, resulting in a gruesome spectacle in his mother-in-law's trailer. An interpretation of Subsection (b)(7) so as to include all murders resulting in gruesome scenes would be totally irrational.

of capital punishment, [citing 14 cases over a three-year period], frequently on the ground that the sentencing proceeding allowed undue discretion, causing dangers of arbitrariness in violation of *Gregg* and its companion cases. These developments, coupled with other pervasive evidence,[6] strongly suggest that appellate courts are incapable of guaranteeing the kind of objectivity and evenhandedness that the Court contemplated and hoped for in *Gregg*. The disgraceful distorting effects of racial discrimination and poverty continue to be painfully visible in the imposition of death sentences.[7] And while hundreds have been placed on death row in the years since *Gregg*,[8] only three persons have been executed.[9] Two of them made no effort to challenge their sentence and were thus permitted to commit what I have elsewhere described as "state-administered suicide." The task of eliminating arbitrariness in the infliction of capital punishment is proving to be one which our criminal justice system—and perhaps any criminal justice system—is unable to perform.... The issue presented in this case usefully illustrates the point. The Georgia Supreme Court has given no real content to Subsection (b)(7) in by far the majority of the cases in which it has had an opportunity to do so. In the four years since *Gregg,* the Georgia court has *never* reversed a jury's finding of a Subsection (b)(7) aggravating circumstance. With considerable frequency the Georgia court has, as here, upheld the imposition of the death penalty on the basis of a simple conclusory statement that the evidence supported the jury's finding under Subsection (b)(7). Instances of a narrowing construction are difficult to find, and those narrowing constructions that can be found have not been adhered to with any regularity. In no case has the Georgia court required a narrowing construction to be given to the jury—an indispensable method for avoiding the "standardless and unchanneled imposition of death sentences." Genuinely independent review has been exceedingly rare....

The Georgia court's inability to administer its capital-punishment statute in an evenhanded fashion is not necessarily attributable to any bad faith on its part; it is, I believe, symptomatic of a deeper problem that is proving to be genuinely intractable. Just five years before *Gregg,* Mr. Justice Harlan stated for the Court that the tasks of identifying "before the fact those characteristics of criminal homicides and their perpetrators which call for the death penalty, and [of] express[ing]

[6] See generally George Dix, Appellate Review of the Decision To Impose Death, 68 Geo.L.J. 97 (1979). Dix's meticulous study of the process of appellate review in Georgia, Florida, and Texas since 1976 demonstrates that "objective standards" for the imposition of the death penalty have not been achieved and probably are impossible to achieve, and concludes that *Gregg* and its companion cases "mandate pursuit of an impossible goal."

[7] On April 20, 1980, for example, over 40 percent of the persons on death row were Negroes.

[8] See NAACP Legal Defense and Educational Fund, Death Row, U.S.A. (April 20, 1980) (642 people on death row); U.S. Department of Justice, Capital Punishment 1978, p. 1 (1979) (445 people on death row as of December 31, 1978).

[9] In *Furman,* my Brothers Stewart and White concurred in the judgment largely on the ground that the death penalty had been so infrequently imposed that it made no contribution to the goals of punishment. Mr. Justice Stewart stated that "the petitioners are among a capriciously selected random handful upon whom the sentence of death has in fact been imposed." Mr. Justice White relied on his conclusion that "the penalty is so infrequently imposed that the threat of execution is too attenuated to be of substantial service to criminal justice." These conclusions have proved to be equally valid under the sentencing schemes upheld in *Gregg.*

these characteristics in language which can be fairly understood and applied by the sentencing authority, appear to be . . . beyond present human ability." McGautha v. California, 402 U.S. 183, 204 (1971). From this premise, the Court in *McGautha* drew the conclusion that the effort to eliminate arbitrariness in the imposition of the death penalty need not be attempted at all. In *Furman,* the Court concluded that the arbitrary infliction of the death penalty was constitutionally intolerable. And in *Gregg,* the Court rejected the premise of *McGautha* and approved a statutory scheme under which, as the Court then perceived it, the death penalty would be imposed in an evenhanded manner.

There can be no doubt that the conclusion drawn in *McGautha* was properly repudiated in *Furman,* where the Court made clear that the arbitrary imposition of the death penalty is forbidden by the Eighth and Fourteenth Amendments. But I believe that the Court in *McGautha* was substantially correct in concluding that the task of selecting in some objective way those persons who should be condemned to die is one that remains beyond the capacities of the criminal justice system. For this reason, I remain hopeful that even if the Court is unwilling to accept the view that the death penalty is so barbaric that it is in all circumstances cruel and unusual punishment forbidden by the Eighth and Fourteenth Amendments, it may eventually conclude that the effort to eliminate arbitrariness in the infliction of that ultimate sanction is so plainly doomed to failure that it—and the death penalty—must be abandoned altogether.

■ MR. CHIEF JUSTICE BURGER, dissenting.

After murdering his wife and mother-in-law, petitioner informed the police that he had committed a "hideous" crime. The dictionary defines hideous as "morally offensive," "shocking," or "horrible." Thus, the very curious feature of this case is that petitioner himself characterized his crime in terms equivalent to those employed in the Georgia statute. For my part, I prefer petitioner's characterization of his conduct to the plurality's effort to excuse and rationalize that conduct as just another killing. The jurors in this case, who heard all relevant mitigating evidence obviously shared that preference; they concluded that this "hideous" crime was "outrageously or wantonly vile, horrible and inhuman" within the meaning of Subsection (b)(7).

More troubling than the plurality's characterization of petitioner's crime is the new responsibility that it assumes with today's decision—the task of determining on a case-by-case basis whether a defendant's conduct is egregious enough to warrant a death sentence. . . . I am convinced that the course the plurality embarks on today is sadly mistaken. . . .

■ MR. JUSTICE WHITE, with whom MR. JUSTICE REHNQUIST joins, dissenting. . . .

The question [is] whether the facts of this case bear sufficient relation to Subsection (b)(7) to conclude that the Georgia Supreme Court responsibly and constitutionally discharged its review function. I believe that they do.

[P]etitioner, in a cold blooded executioner's style, murdered his wife and his mother-in-law and, in passing, struck his young daughter on the head with the barrel of his gun. The weapon, a shotgun, is hardly known for the surgical precision with which it perforates its target. The murder scene, in consequence, can only be described in the most unpleasant terms. Petitioner's wife lay prone on the floor. Mrs. Godfrey's head had a hole described as "[a]pproximately the size of a silver dollar" on the side where the shot entered, and much less decipherable and more extensive damage on the side where the shot exited. Pellets that had passed through Mrs. Godfrey's head were found embedded in the kitchen cabinet.

It will be remembered that after petitioner inflicted this much damage, he took out time not only to strike his daughter on the head, but also to reload his single-shot shotgun and to enter the house. Only then did he get around to shooting his mother-in-law, Mrs. Wilkerson, whose last several moments as a sentient being must have been as terrifying as the human mind can imagine. The police eventually found her face down on the floor with a substantial portion of her head missing and her brain, no longer cabined by her skull, protruding for some distance onto the floor. Blood not only covered the floor and table, but dripped from the ceiling as well.

The Georgia Supreme Court held that these facts supported the jury's finding of the existence of statutory aggravating circumstance Subsection (b)(7). A majority of this Court disagrees. But this disagreement, founded as it is on the notion that the lower court's construction of the provision was overly broad, in fact reveals a conception of this Court's role in backstopping the Georgia Supreme Court that is itself overly broad. Our role is to correct genuine errors of constitutional significance resulting from the application of Georgia's capital sentencing procedures; our role is not to peer majestically over the lower court's shoulder so that we might second-guess its interpretation of facts that quite reasonably—perhaps even quite plainly—fit within the statutory language.[2]

Who is to say that the murders of Mrs. Godfrey and Mrs. Wilkerson were not "vile," or "inhuman," or "horrible"? In performing his murderous chore, petitioner employed a weapon known for its disfiguring effects on targets, human or other, and he succeeded in creating a scene so macabre and revolting that, if anything, "vile," "horrible," and "inhuman" are descriptively inadequate.

And who among us can honestly say that Mrs. Wilkerson did not feel "torture" in her last sentient moments. Her daughter, an instant ago a living being sitting across the table from Mrs. Wilkerson, lay prone on the floor, a bloodied and mutilated corpse. The seconds ticked

---

[2] The plurality opinion states that "[A]n interpretation of Subsection (b)(7) so as to include all murders resulting in gruesome scenes would be totally irrational" and that the fact that both "victims were killed instantaneously" makes the gruesomeness of the scene irrelevant. This view ignores the indisputable truth that Mrs. Wilkerson did not die "instantaneously"; she had many moments to contemplate her impending death, assuming that the stark terror she must have felt permitted any contemplation. More importantly, it also ignores the obvious correlation between gruesomeness and "depravity of mind," between gruesomeness and "aggravated battery," between gruesomeness and "horrible," between gruesomeness and "vile," and between gruesomeness and "inhuman." Mere gruesomeness, to be sure, would not itself serve to establish the existence of Subsection (b)(7). But it certainly fares sufficiently well as an indicator of this particular aggravating circumstance to signal to a reviewing court the distinct possibility that the terms of the provision, upon further investigation, might well be met in the circumstances of the case.

by; enough time for her son-in-law to reload his gun, to enter the home, and to take a gratuitous swipe at his daughter. What terror must have run through her veins as she first witnessed her daughter's hideous demise and then came to terms with the imminence of her own. Was this not torture? And if this was not torture, can it honestly be said that petitioner did not exhibit a "depravity of mind" in carrying out this cruel drama to its mischievous and murderous conclusion? I should have thought, moreover, that the Georgia court could reasonably have deemed the scene awaiting the investigating policemen as involving "an aggravated battery to the victim[s]."

The point is not that, in my view, petitioner's crimes were definitively vile, horrible, or inhuman, or that, as I assay the evidence, they beyond *any* doubt involved torture, depravity of mind, or an aggravated battery to the victims. Rather, the lesson is a much more elementary one, an instruction that, I should have thought, this Court would have taken to heart long ago. Our mandate does not extend to interfering with factfinders in state criminal proceedings or with state courts that are responsibly and consistently interpreting state law, unless that interference is predicated on a violation of the Constitution. No convincing showing of such a violation is made here, for, as Mr. Justice Stewart has written in another place, the issue here is not what *our* verdict would have been, but whether "any rational factfinder" could have found the existence of aggravating circumstance Subsection (b)(7). Faithful adherence to this standard of review compels our affirmance of the judgment below. . . .

Under the present statutory regime, adopted in response to *Furman,* the Georgia Supreme Court has responsibly and consistently performed its review function pursuant to the Georgia capital-sentencing procedures. The state reports, that at the time its brief was written, the Georgia Supreme Court had reviewed some 99 cases in which the death penalty has been imposed. Of these, 66 had been affirmed, five had been reversed for errors in the guilt phase; and 22 had been reversed for errors in the sentencing phase. This reversal rate of over 27 percent is not substantially lower than the historic reversal rate of state supreme courts. See Courting Reversal: The Supervisory Role of State Supreme Courts, 87 Yale L.J. 1191, 1198, 1209 (1978), where it is indicated that 16 state supreme courts over a 100-year period, in deciding 5,133 cases, had a reversal rate of 38.5 percent; for criminal cases, the reversal rate was 35.6 percent. To the extent that the reversal rate is lower than the historic level, it doubtless can be attributed to the great and admirable extent to which discretion and uncertainty have been removed from Georgia's capital-sentencing procedures since our decision in *Furman* and to the fact that review is mandatory.

The Georgia Supreme Court has vacated a death sentence where it believed that the statutory sentencing procedures, as passed by the legislature, were defective; it has held that jurors must be instructed that they can impose a life sentence even though they find the existence of a statutory aggravating circumstance; it has reversed the imposition of the death penalty where the prosecutor made an improper comment during his argument to the jury in the sentencing phase; it has reversed a trial court's decision limiting the type of mitigating evidence that could be presented; it has set aside a death sentence when jurors failed to specify which aggravating circumstances they found to exist; it has reversed a death sentence imposed on a partial finding of an aggravating circumstance; it has disapproved a death penalty because of errors in admitting evidence; it has reversed a capital sentence where a codefendant received only a life sentence; and it has held a statutory aggravating circumstance to be unconstitutional.

The Georgia Supreme Court has also been responsible and consistent in its construction of Subsection (b)(7). The provision has been the exclusive or nonexclusive basis for imposition of the death penalty in over 30 cases. In one excursus on the provision's language, the court in effect held that the section is to be read as a whole, construing "depravity of mind," "torture," and "aggravated battery" to flesh out the meaning of "vile," "horrible," and "inhuman." I see no constitutional error resulting from this understanding of the provision. . . . And the court has noted that it would apply the provision only in "core" cases and would not permit Subsection (b)(7) to become a "catchall."

Nor do the facts of this case stand out as an aberration. A jury found Subsection (b)(7) satisfied, for example, when a child was senselessly and ruthlessly executed by a murderer who, like petitioner, accomplished this end with a shotgun. The Georgia Supreme Court affirmed. The court has also affirmed a jury's finding of Subsection (b)(7) where, as here, there was substantial disfigurement of the victim, and where, as arguably with Mrs. Wilkerson, there was torture of the victim.

The majority's attempt to drive a wedge between this case and others in which Subsection (b)(7) has been applied is thus unconvincing, as is any suggestion that the Georgia Supreme Court has somehow failed overall in performance of its review function.

In the circumstances of this case, the majority today endorses the argument that I thought we had rejected in *Gregg*: namely, "that no matter how effective the death penalty may be as a punishment, government, created and run as it must be by humans, is inevitably incompetent to administer it." The Georgia Supreme Court, faced with a seemingly endless train of macabre scenes, has endeavored in a responsible, rational, and consistent fashion to effectuate its statutory mandate as illuminated by our judgment in *Gregg*. Today, a majority of this Court, its arguments shredded by its own illogic, informs the Georgia Supreme Court that, to some extent, its efforts have been outside the Constitution. I reject this as an unwarranted invasion into the realm of state law, for, as in *Gregg*, "I decline to interfere with the manner in which Georgia has chosen to enforce [its] laws" until a genuine error of constitutional magnitude surfaces.

I would affirm the judgment of the Supreme Court of Georgia.

## NOTE ON *GODFREY*

Although the Supreme Court held that Godfrey's death sentence was unconstitutional, the rationale for the decision is elusive. Did the Court hold that subsection (b)(7) is void for vagueness? If not, what did it hold?

The plurality and dissenting opinions appear to view the outcome in *Godfrey* through different lenses. Justice White asserts that the case does not "stand out as an aberration" when compared with other cases in which death sentences had been imposed under subsection (b)(7). In contrast, Justice Stewart observes that "there is no meaningful way to distinguish [Godfrey's] case in which the death penalty was imposed from the many cases in which it was not." Which is the right question to ask? How did Justice Stewart know about the cases in which the death penalty had not been imposed?

After Godfrey's case was remanded to the Georgia courts, the prosecution again sought the death penalty. This time another statutory circumstance was advanced to establish the predicate for a death sentence—that the murder "was committed while the offender was engaged in the commission of another capital felony." The jury found that this circumstance had been proved and recommended death sentences for each murder. On appeal, the Georgia Supreme Court affirmed. Godfrey v. State, 248 Ga. 616, 284 S.E.2d 422 (1981). The court rejected Godfrey's contention that the particular aggravating circumstance had been improperly applied:

> [Godfrey] argues that since both murders were separate in time, although only moments apart, and each was instantaneous, one could not have occurred while in the commission of another. However, this argument has been raised before and decided in a manner contrary to Godfrey's position [citing a 1981 case]. Furthermore, under the plain meaning of the statute, multiple murders are included as "another capital felony."

## NOTE ON THE STRUCTURE OF MODERN CAPITAL SENTENCING

The Supreme Court has established certain conditions that must be met by capital sentencing procedures. Although the Court's decisions have not yet marked a clear line regarding the level of culpability that is constitutionally required to support a death sentence, it appears that intent to kill (or to use lethal force) or extreme indifference to the value of human life must be shown.[a] In addition, the line of decisions culminating in *Zant v. Stephens* stands for the proposition that the state is required to establish additional substantive criteria so as to "genuinely narrow the class of persons eligible for the death penalty." The state may provide such criteria in the definition of the elements of capital homicide, as has been done in Texas and Virginia, or in the definition of aggravating circumstances that must be proved at the sentencing stage, as has been done in Georgia and Florida.

The Supreme Court has also specified constitutional criteria of exclusion. It has held that the Eighth Amendment precludes execution of defendants who are mentally retarded[b] or under 18 years of age at the time of the homicide.[c]

Once the legislature has defined the class of intentional homicides for which the death penalty is permissible, what additional criteria should be considered? The Supreme Court has made it clear that the death sentence cannot be mandatory and that the sentencer is constitutionally required to "consider" any evidence proffered by the defendant in mitigation. Within this framework, should the sentencer's discretion be subject to normative

[a] See Enmund v. Florida, 458 U.S. 782 (1982), and Tison v. Arizona, 481 U.S. 137 (1987), discussed below.

[b] See Atkins v. Virginia, 536 U.S. 304 (2002), discussed below.

[c] See Roper v. Simmons, 543 U.S. 551 (2005), discussed below.

constraint or guidance? In this connection, compare the Model Penal Code and the Georgia and Florida statutes reproduced in Appendix B. Under the Georgia statute, the sentencer's discretion "to recommend" a death sentence for a death-eligible offender is unconstrained by normative criteria. In contrast, the Model Penal Code provides that the sentencing court is permitted to consider a death sentence only if it (or the jury) finds that "there are no mitigating circumstances sufficiently substantial to call for leniency." Even in the absence of such a finding, it appears that the court has residual discretion to impose a life sentence. The Florida statute appears to tip the scale in the other direction, requiring a death sentence to be imposed if "there are insufficient mitigating circumstances to outweigh the aggravating circumstances." Are these variations significant? Which is preferable?

Finally, there is the widespread practice of comparative review. Appellate review in capital cases serves the same functions as elsewhere—assuring, for example, that the trial court has properly interpreted and applied the governing law and that the evidence is legally sufficient to establish the necessary substantive predicates for the conviction and death sentence. In addition, appellate courts in most states also have a unique responsibility in capital cases to conduct "comparative review" of each death sentence to determine whether the imposition of the capital sanction is consistent with the sentences imposed in similar cases. Although the Supreme Court has held that comparative review is not constitutionally required, Pulley v. Harris, 465 U.S. 37 (1984), most state statutes include provisions, modeled on the Georgia statute, which direct the appellate court to determine "whether the sentence of death is excessive or disproportionate to the penalty imposed in similar cases, considering both the crime and the defendant." Comparative review is designed to promote consistency in the administration of the death penalty in each state and thereby to respond to the concerns underlying the Supreme Court's decision in *Furman.* Can it work for this purpose? On what data should the comparisons be based? Are any two offenses likely to be identical in *all* relevant respects? What kinds of variations are tolerable?

## SECTION 3: PROPORTIONALITY

### Coker v. Georgia

Supreme Court of the United States, 1977.
433 U.S. 584.

■ MR. JUSTICE WHITE announced the judgment of the Court and filed an opinion in which MR. JUSTICE STEWART, MR. JUSTICE BLACKMUN, and MR. JUSTICE STEVENS, joined.

. . . Petitioner Coker was convicted of rape and sentenced to death. Both the conviction and the sentence were affirmed by the Georgia Supreme Court. Coker was granted a writ of certiorari limited to the single claim, rejected by the Georgia court, that the punishment of death for rape violates the Eighth Amendment, which proscribes "cruel and unusual punishments" and which must be observed by the states as well as the federal government. Robinson v. California, 370 U.S. 660 (1962).

I

While serving various sentences for murder, rape, kidnapping, and aggravated assault, petitioner escaped from the Ware Correctional Institution near Waycross, Ga., on September 2, 1974. At approximately 11 o'clock that night, petitioner entered the house of Allen and Elnita Carver through an unlocked kitchen door. Threatening the couple with a "board," he tied up Mr. Carver in the bathroom, obtained a knife from the kitchen, and took Mr. Carver's money and the keys to the family car. Brandishing the knife and saying "you know what's going to happen to you if you try anything, don't you," Coker then raped Mrs. Carver. Soon thereafter, petitioner drove away in the Carver car, taking Mrs. Carver with him. Mr. Carver, freeing himself, notified the police; and not long thereafter petitioner was apprehended. Mrs. Carver was unharmed.

Petitioner was [tried on charges of] escape, armed robbery, motor vehicle theft, kidnapping, and rape. . . . The jury returned a verdict of guilty, rejecting his general plea of insanity. A sentencing hearing was then conducted in accordance with the procedures dealt with at length in Gregg v. Georgia, 428 U.S. 153 (1976). . . . The jury's verdict on the rape count was death by electrocution. . . .

II

[The Court's prior capital punishment decisions] make unnecessary the recanvassing of certain critical aspects of the controversy about the constitutionality of capital punishment. It is now settled that the death penalty is not invariably cruel and unusual punishment within the meaning of the Eighth Amendment; it is not inherently barbaric or an unacceptable mode of punishment for crime; neither is it always disproportionate to the crime for which it is imposed. . . .

In sustaining the imposition of the death penalty, however, the Court [has] firmly embraced the holdings and dicta from prior cases, to the effect that the Eighth Amendment bars not only those punishments that are "barbaric" but also those that are "excessive" in relation to the crime committed. Under *Gregg v. Georgia,* supra, a punishment is "excessive" and unconstitutional if it (i) makes no measurable contribution to acceptable goals of punishment and hence is nothing more than the purposeless and needless imposition of pain and suffering; or (ii) is grossly out of proportion to the severity of the crime. A punishment might fail the test on either ground. Furthermore, these Eighth Amendment judgments should not be, or appear to be, merely the subjective views of individual Justices; judgment should be informed by objective factors to the maximum possible extent. To this end, attention must be given to the public attitudes concerning a particular sentence—history and precedent, legislative attitudes, and the response of juries reflected in their sentencing decisions are to be consulted. In *Gregg,* after giving due regard to such sources, the Court's judgment was that the death penalty for deliberate murder was neither the purposeless imposition of severe punishment nor a punishment grossly disproportionate to the crime. But the Court reserved the question of the constitutionality of the death penalty when imposed for other crimes.

III

That question, with respect to rape of an adult woman, is now before us. We have concluded that a sentence of death is grossly disproportionate and excessive punishment for the crime of rape and is therefore forbidden by the Eighth Amendment as cruel and unusual punishment.

A

As advised by recent cases, we seek guidance in history and from the objective evidence of the country's present judgment concerning the acceptability of death as a penalty for rape of an adult woman. At no time in the last 50 years have a majority of the states authorized death as a punishment for rape. In 1925, 18 states, the District of Columbia, and the federal government authorized capital punishment for the rape of an adult female. By 1971 just prior to the decision in Furman v. Georgia, 408 U.S. 238 (1972), that number had declined, but not substantially, to 16 states plus the federal government. *Furman* then invalidated most of the capital-punishment statutes in this country, including the rape statutes, because, among other reasons, of the manner in which the death penalty was imposed and utilized under those laws.

With their death-penalty statutes for the most part invalidated, the states were faced with the choice of enacting modified capital-punishment laws in an attempt to satisfy the requirements of *Furman* or of being satisfied with life imprisonment as the ultimate punishment for *any* offense. Thirty-five states immediately reinstituted the death penalty for at least limited kinds of crime. This public judgment as to the acceptability of capital punishment, evidenced by the immediate, post-*Furman* legislative reaction in a large majority of the states, heavily influenced the Court to sustain the death penalty for murder in *Gregg v. Georgia,* supra. . . .

In reviving death-penalty laws to satisfy *Furman's* mandate, none of the states that had not previously authorized death for rape chose to include rape among capital felonies. Of the 16 states in which rape had been a capital offense, only three provided the death penalty for rape of an adult woman in their revised statutes—Georgia, North Carolina, and Louisiana. In the latter two states, the death penalty was mandatory for those found guilty, and those laws were invalidated by Woodson v. North Carolina, 428 U.S. 280 (1976), and Roberts v. Louisiana, 428 U.S. 325 (1976). When Louisiana and North Carolina, responding to those decisions, again revised their capital punishment laws, they reenacted the death penalty for murder but not for rape; none of the seven other legislatures that to our knowledge have amended or replaced their death penalty statutes since July 2, 1976, . . . included rape among the crimes for which death was an authorized punishment.

Georgia argues that 11 of the 16 states that authorized death for rape in 1972 attempted to comply with *Furman* by enacting arguably mandatory death-penalty legislation and that it is very likely that, aside from Louisiana and North Carolina, these states simply chose to eliminate rape as a capital offense rather than to *require* death for *each* and *every* instance of rape. The argument is not without force; but four of the 16 states did not take the mandatory course and also did *not* continue rape of an adult woman as a capital offense. Further, as we have indicated, the legislatures of six of the 11 arguably mandatory states have revised their death-penalty laws since *Woodson* and *Roberts* without enacting a new death penalty for rape. And this is to say nothing of 19 other states that enacted nonmandatory, post-*Furman* statutes and chose not to sentence rapists to death. . . .

Georgia is the sole jurisdiction in the United States at the present time that authorizes a sentence of death when the rape victim is an adult woman and only two other jurisdictions provide capital punishment when the victim is a child.

The current judgment with respect to the death penalty for rape is not wholly unanimous among state legislatures, but it obviously weighs very heavily on the side of rejecting capital punishment as a suitable penalty for raping an adult woman.[10]

B

It was also observed in *Gregg* that "[t]he jury . . . is a significant and reliable objective index of contemporary values because it is so directly involved," and that it is thus important to look to the sentencing decisions that juries have made in the course of assessing whether capital punishment is an appropriate penalty for the crime being tried. . . . According to the factual submissions in this Court, out of all rape convictions in Georgia since 1973—and that total number has not been tendered—63 cases had been reviewed by the Georgia Supreme Court as of the time of oral argument; and of these, six involved a death sentence, one of which was set aside, leaving five convicted rapists now under sentence of death in the state of Georgia. Georgia juries have thus sentenced rapists to death six times since 1973. This obviously is not a negligible number; and the state argues that as a practical matter juries simply reserve the extreme sanction for extreme cases of rape and that recent experience surely does not prove that jurors consider the death penalty to be a disproportionate punishment for every conceivable instance of rape, no matter how aggravated. Nevertheless, it is true that in the vast majority of cases, at least nine out of 10, juries have not imposed the death sentence.

IV

These recent events evidencing the attitude of state legislatures and sentencing juries do not wholly determine this controversy, for the Constitution contemplates that in the end our own judgment will be brought to bear on the question of the acceptability of the death penalty under the Eighth Amendment. Nevertheless, the legislative rejection of capital punishment for rape strongly confirms our own judgment, which is that death is indeed a disproportionate penalty for the crime of raping an adult woman.

We do not discount the seriousness of rape as a crime. It is highly reprehensible, both in a moral sense and in its almost total contempt for the personal integrity and autonomy of the female victim and for the latter's privilege of choosing those with whom intimate relationships

---

[10] In Trop v. Dulles, 356 U.S. 86, 102 (1958), the plurality took pains to note the climate of international opinion concerning the acceptability of a particular punishment. It is thus not irrelevant here that out of 60 major nations in the world surveyed in 1965, only three retained the death penalty for rape where death did not ensue. United Nations, Department of Economic and Social Affairs, Capital Punishment 40, 86 (1968).

are to be established. Short of homicide, it is the "ultimate violation of self." It is also a violent crime because it normally involves force, or the threat of force or intimidation, to overcome the will and the capacity of the victim to resist. Rape is very often accompanied by physical injury to the female and can also inflict mental and psychological damage. Because it undermines the community's sense of security, there is public injury as well.

Rape is without doubt deserving of serious punishment; but in terms of moral depravity and of the injury to the person and to the public, it does not compare with murder, which does involve the unjustified taking of human life. Although it may be accompanied by another crime, rape by definition does not include the death of or even the serious injury to another person. The murderer kills; the rapist, if no more than that, does not. Life is over for the victim of the murderer; for the rape victim, life may not be nearly so happy as it was, but it is not over and normally is not beyond repair. We have the abiding conviction that the death penalty, which "is unique in its severity and irrevocability," is an excessive penalty for the rapist who, as such, does not take human life.

This does not end the matter; for under Georgia law, death may not be imposed for any capital offense, including rape, unless the jury or judge finds one of the statutory aggravating circumstances and then elects to impose that sentence. For the rapist to be executed in Georgia, it must therefore be found not only that he committed rape but also that one or more of the following aggravating circumstances were present: (i) that the rape was committed by a person with a prior record of conviction for a capital felony; (ii) that the rape was committed while the offender was engaged in the commission of another capital felony, or aggravated battery; or (iii) the rape "was outrageously or wantonly vile, horrible or inhuman in that it involved torture, depravity of mind, or aggravated battery to the victim."[a] Here, the first two of these aggravating circumstances were alleged and found by the jury.

Neither of these circumstances, nor both of them together, change our conclusion that the death sentence imposed on Coker is a disproportionate punishment for rape. Coker had prior convictions for capital felonies—rape, murder, and kidnapping—but these prior convictions do not change the fact that the instant crime being punished is a rape not involving the taking of life.

It is also true that the present rape occurred while Coker was committing armed robbery, a felony for which the Georgia statutes authorize the death penalty. But Coker was tried for the robbery offense as well as for rape and received a separate life sentence for this crime; the jury did not deem the robbery itself deserving of the death penalty, even though accompanied by the aggravating circumstance, which was stipulated, that Coker had been convicted of a prior capital crime.[16]

---

[a] The applicable Georgia statutes are reprinted in Appendix B.—[Footnote by eds.]

[16] Where the accompanying capital crime is murder, it is most likely that the defendant would be tried for murder, rather than rape; and it is perhaps academic to deal with the death sentence for rape in such a circumstance. It is likewise unnecessary to consider the rape-felony murder—a rape accompanied by the death of the victim which was unlawfully but nonmaliciously caused by the defendant.

We note finally that in Georgia a person commits murder when he unlawfully and with malice aforethought, either express or implied, causes the death of another human being. He also commits that crime when in the commission of a felony he causes the death of another human being, irrespective of malice. But even where the killing is deliberate, it is not punishable by death absent proof of aggravating circumstances. It is difficult to accept the notion, and we do not, that the rapist, with or without aggravating circumstances, should be punished more heavily than the deliberate killer as long as the rapist does not himself take the life of his victim. The judgment of the Georgia Supreme Court upholding the death sentence is reversed, and the case is remanded to that court for further proceedings not inconsistent with this opinion.

So ordered.

■ MR. JUSTICE BRENNAN, concurring in the judgment.

Adhering to my view that the death penalty is in all circumstances cruel and unusual punishment prohibited by the eighth and Fourteenth Amendments, I concur in the judgment of the Court setting aside the death sentence imposed under the Georgia rape statute.

■ MR. JUSTICE MARSHALL, concurring in the judgment.

. . . I continue to adhere to [my previously expressed view that the death penalty is a cruel and unusual punishment prohibited by the eighth and Fourteenth Amendments] in concurring in the judgment of the Court in this case.

■ MR. JUSTICE POWELL, concurring in the judgment in part and dissenting in part.

I concur in the judgment of the Court on the facts of this case, and also in the plurality's reasoning supporting the view that ordinarily death is disproportionate punishment for the crime of raping an adult woman. Although rape invariably is a reprehensible crime, there is no indication that petitioner's offense was committed with excessive brutality or that the victim sustained serious or lasting injury. The plurality, however, does not limit its holding to the case before us or to similar cases. Rather, in an opinion that ranges well beyond what is necessary, it holds that capital punishment *always*—regardless of the circumstances—is a disproportionate penalty for the crime of rape.

The Georgia statute specifies [three] aggravating circumstances [for the crime of rape]: (i) the offense was committed by a person with a prior record of conviction for a capital felony; (ii) the offense was committed while the offender was engaged in another capital felony or in aggravated battery; and (iii) the offense was "outrageously or wantonly vile, horrible or inhuman in that it involved torture, depravity of mind, or an aggravated battery to the victim." Only the third circumstance describes in general the offense of aggravated rape, often identified as a separate and more heinous offense than rape. See, e.g., ALI, Model

Where the third aggravating circumstance mentioned in the text is present—that the rape is particularly vile or involves torture or aggravated battery—it would seem that the defendant could very likely be convicted, tried, and appropriately punished for this additional conduct.

Penal Code § 213.1. That third circumstance was not submitted to the jury in this case, as the evidence would not have supported such a finding. It is therefore quite unnecessary for the plurality to write in terms so sweeping as to foreclose each of the 50 state legislatures from creating a narrowly defined substantive crime of aggravated rape punishable by death.[1] . . .

Today, in a case that does not require such an expansive pronouncement, the plurality draws a bright line between murder and all rapes—regardless of the degree of brutality of the rape or the effect upon the victim. I dissent because I am not persuaded that such a bright line is appropriate. "[There] is extreme variation in the degree of culpability of rapists." The deliberate viciousness of the rapist may be greater than that of the murderer. Rape is never an act committed accidentally. Rarely can it be said to be unpremeditated. There also is wide variation in the effect on the victim. The plurality opinion says that "[l]ife is over for the victim of the murderer; for the rape victim, life may not be nearly so happy as it was, but it is not over and normally is not beyond repair." But there is indeed "extreme variation" in the crime of rape. Some victims are so grievously injured physically or psychologically that life *is* beyond repair. . . .

It has not been shown that society finds the penalty disproportionate for all rapes. In a proper case a more discriminating inquiry than the plurality undertakes well might discover that both juries and legislatures have reserved the ultimate penalty for the case of an outrageous rape resulting in serious, lasting harm to the victim. I would not prejudge the issue. To this extent, I respectfully dissent.

■ MR. CHIEF JUSTICE BURGER, with whom MR. JUSTICE REHNQUIST joins, dissenting. . . .

In striking down the death penalty imposed upon the petitioner in this case, the Court has overstepped the bounds of proper constitutional adjudication by substituting its policy judgment for that of the state legislature. I accept that the Eighth Amendment's concept of disproportionality bars the death penalty for minor crimes. But rape is not a minor crime. . . .

(1)

On December 5, 1971, the petitioner, Ehrlich Anthony Coker, raped and then stabbed to death a young woman. Less than eight months later Coker kidnapped and raped a second young woman. After twice raping this 16-year-old victim, he stripped her, severely beat her with a club, and dragged her into a wooded area where he left her for dead. He was apprehended and pleaded guilty to offenses stemming from these incidents. He was sentenced by three separate courts to three life terms, two 20-year terms, and one eight-year term of imprisonment. Each judgment specified that the sentences it imposed were to run consecutively rather than concurrently. Approximately one and one-half

---

[1] It is not this Court's function to formulate the relevant criteria that might distinguish aggravated rape from the more usual case, but perhaps a workable test would embrace the factors identified by Georgia: the cruelty or viciousness of the offender, the circumstances and manner in which the offense was committed, and the consequences suffered by the victim. The legislative task of defining, with appropriate specificity, the elements of the offense of aggravated rape would not be easy, but certainly this Court should not assume that the task is impossible. . . .

years later, on September 2, 1974, petitioner escaped from the state prison where he was serving these sentences. He promptly raped another 16-year-old woman in the presence of her husband, abducted her from her home, and threatened her with death and serious bodily harm. It is this crime for which the sentence now under review was imposed.

The Court today holds that the state of Georgia may not impose the death penalty on Coker. In so doing, it prevents the state from imposing any effective punishment upon Coker for his latest rape. The Court's holding, moreover, bars Georgia from guaranteeing its citizens that they will suffer no further attacks by this habitual rapist. In fact, given the lengthy sentences Coker must serve for the crimes he has already committed, the Court's holding assures that petitioner—as well as others in his position—will henceforth feel no compunction whatsoever about committing further rapes as frequently as he may be able to escape from confinement and indeed even within the walls of the prison itself. To what extent we have left states "elbow-room" to protect innocent persons from depraved human beings like Coker remains in doubt.

(2)

My first disagreement with the Court's holding is its unnecessary breadth. The narrow issue here presented is whether the state of Georgia may constitutionally execute this petitioner for the particular rape which he has committed, in light of all the facts and circumstances shown by this record. The plurality opinion goes to great lengths to consider societal mores and attitudes toward the generic crime of rape and the punishment for it; however, the opinion gives little attention to the special circumstances which bear directly on whether imposition of the death penalty is an appropriate societal response to Coker's criminal acts: (i) On account of his prior offenses, Coker is already serving such lengthy prison sentences that imposition of additional periods of imprisonment would have no incremental punitive effect; (ii) by his life pattern Coker has shown that he presents a particular danger to the safety, welfare, and chastity of women, and on his record the likelihood is therefore great that he will repeat his crime at the first opportunity; (iii) petitioner escaped from prison, only a year and a half after he commenced serving his latest sentences; he has nothing to lose by further escape attempts; and (iv) should he again succeed in escaping from prison, it is reasonably predictable that he will repeat his pattern of attacks on women—and with impunity since the threat of added prison sentences will be no deterrent.

Unlike the plurality, I would narrow the inquiry in this case to the question actually presented: Does the Eighth Amendment's ban against cruel and unusual punishment prohibit the state of Georgia from executing a person who has, within the space of three years, raped three separate women, killing one and attempting to kill another, who is serving prison terms exceeding his probable lifetime and who has not hesitated to escape confinement at the first available opportunity? Whatever one's view may be as to the state's constitutional power to impose the death penalty upon a rapist who stands before a court convicted for the first time, this case reveals a chronic rapist whose continuing danger to the community is abundantly clear.

Mr. Justice Powell would hold the death sentence inappropriate in *this* case because "there is no indication that petitioner's offense was committed with excessive brutality or that the victim sustained serious or lasting injury." Apart from the reality that rape is inherently one of the most egregiously brutal acts one human being can inflict upon another, there is nothing in the Eighth Amendment that so narrowly limits the factors which may be considered by a state legislature in determining whether a particular punishment is grossly excessive. Surely recidivism, especially the repeated commission of heinous crimes, is a factor which may properly be weighed as an aggravating circumstance, permitting the imposition of a punishment more severe than for one isolated offense. . . . As a factual matter, the plurality opinion is correct in stating that Coker's "prior convictions do not change the fact that the instant crime being punished is a rape not involving the taking of life"; however, it cannot be disputed that the existence of these prior convictions makes Coker a substantially more serious menace to society than a first-time offender:[4]

> There is a widely held view that those who present the strongest case for severe measures of incapacitation are not murderers as a group (their offenses often are situational) *but rather those who have repeatedly engaged in violent, combative behavior*. A well-demonstrated propensity for life-endangering behavior is thought to provide a more solid basis for infliction of the most severe measures of incapacitation than does the fortuity of a single homicidal incident. Packer, Making the Punishment Fit the Crime, 77 Harv.L.Rev. 1071, 1080 (1964). (Emphasis added.)

In my view, the Eighth Amendment does not prevent the state from taking an individual's "well-demonstrated propensity for life-endangering behavior" into account in devising punitive measures which will prevent inflicting further harm upon innocent victims. Only one year ago Mr. Justice White succinctly noted: "[D]eath finally forecloses the possibility that a prisoner will commit further crimes, whereas life imprisonment does not." . . .

Since the Court now invalidates the death penalty as a sanction for all rapes of adults at all times under all circumstances, I reluctantly turn to what I see as the broader issues raised by this holding.

(3)

The plurality acknowledges the gross nature of the crime of rape. A rapist not only violates a victim's privacy and personal integrity, but inevitably causes serious psychological as well as physical harm in the process. The long-range effect upon the victim's life and health is likely to be irreparable; it is impossible to measure the harm which results. Volumes have been written by victims, physicians, and psychiatric specialists on the lasting injury suffered by rape victims. Rape is not a mere physical attack—it is destructive of the human personality. The

[4] This special danger is demonstrated by the very record in this case. After tying and gagging the victim's husband, and raping the victim, petitioner sought to make his getaway in their automobile. Leaving the victim's husband tied and gagged in his bathroom, Coker took the victim with him. As he started to leave, he brandished the kitchen knife he was carrying and warned the husband that "if he would get pulled over or the police was following him in any way that he would kill—he would kill my wife. *He said he didn't have nothing to lose—that he was in prison for the rest of his life, anyway. . . .*" Testimony of the victim's husband, App. 121 (emphasis added).

remainder of the victim's life may be gravely affected, and this in turn may have a serious detrimental effect upon her husband and any children she may have. I therefore wholly agree with Mr. Justice White's conclusion as far as it goes—that "[s]hort of homicide, [rape] is the ultimate violation of self." Victims may recover from the physical damage of knife or bullet wounds, or a beating with fists or a club, but recovery from such a gross assault on the human personality is not healed by medicine or surgery. To speak blandly, as the plurality does, of rape victims who are "unharmed," or to classify the human outrage of rape, as does Mr. Justice Powell, in terms of "excessively brutal," versus "moderately brutal," takes too little account of the profound suffering the crime imposes upon the victims and their loved ones.

Despite its strong condemnation of rape, the Court reaches the inexplicable conclusion that "the death penalty . . . is an excessive penalty" for the perpetrator of this heinous offense. This, the Court holds, is true even though in Georgia the death penalty may be imposed only where the rape is coupled with one or more aggravating circumstances. . . .

The analysis of the plurality opinion is divided into two parts: (i) an "objective" determination that most American jurisdictions do not presently make rape a capital offense, and (ii) a subjective judgment that death is an excessive punishment for rape because the crime does not, in and of itself, cause the death of the victim. I take issue with each of these points.

(a)

The plurality opinion bases its analysis, in part, on the fact that "Georgia is the sole jurisdiction in the United States at the present time that authorizes a sentence of death when the rape victim is an adult woman." Surely, however, this statistic cannot be deemed determinative, or even particularly relevant. As the opinion concedes, two other states—Louisiana and North Carolina—have enacted death penalty statutes for adult rape since this Court's 1972 decision in *Furman v. Georgia.* If the Court is to rely on some "public opinion" process, does this not suggest the beginning of a "trend"?

More to the point, however, it is myopic to base sweeping constitutional principles upon the narrow experience of the past five years. Considerable uncertainty was introduced into this area of the law by this Court's *Furman* decision. A large number of states found their death-penalty statutes invalidated; legislatures were left in serious doubt by the expressions vacillating between discretionary and mandatory death penalties, as to whether this Court would sustain *any* statute imposing death as a criminal sanction. Failure of more states to enact statutes imposing death for rape of an adult woman may thus reflect hasty legislative compromise occasioned by time pressures following *Furman,* a desire to wait on the experience of those states which did enact such statutes, or simply an accurate forecast of today's holding.

In any case, when considered in light of the experience since the turn of this century, where more than one-third of American jurisdictions have consistently provided the death penalty for rape, the plurality's focus on the experience of the immediate past must be viewed as truly disingenuous. . . . However, even were one to give the most charitable acceptance to the plurality's statistical analysis, it still does not, to my mind, support its conclusion. The most that can be claimed is that for the past year Georgia has been the only state whose adult rape death penalty statute has not otherwise been invalidated; two other state legislatures had enacted rape death penalty statutes in the last five years, but these were invalidated for reasons unrelated to rape under the Court's decisions. . . . Even if these figures could be read as indicating that no other states view the death penalty as an appropriate punishment for the rape of an adult woman, it would not necessarily follow that Georgia's imposition of such sanction violates the Eighth Amendment. . . .

The question of whether the death penalty is an appropriate punishment for rape is surely an open one. It is arguable that many prospective rapists would be deterred by the possibility that they could suffer death for their offense; it is also arguable that the death penalty would have only minimal deterrent effect. It may well be that rape victims would become more willing to report the crime and aid in the apprehension of the criminals if they knew that community disapproval of rapists was sufficiently strong to inflict the extreme penalty; or perhaps they would be reluctant to cooperate in the prosecution of rapists if they knew that a conviction might result in the imposition of the death penalty. Quite possibly, the occasional, well-publicized execution of egregious rapists may cause citizens to feel greater security in their daily lives; or, on the contrary, it may be that members of a civilized community will suffer the pangs of a heavy conscience because such punishment will be perceived as excessive.[13] We cannot know which among this range of possibilities is correct, but today's holding forecloses the very exploration we have said federalism was intended to foster. It is difficult to believe that Georgia would long remain alone in punishing rape by death if the next decade demonstrated a drastic reduction in its incidence of rape, an increased cooperation by rape victims in the apprehension and prosecution of rapists, and a greater confidence in the rule of law on the part of the populace. . . .

(b)

The subjective judgment that the death penalty is simply disproportionate to the crime of rape is even more disturbing than the "objective" analysis discussed supra. The plurality's conclusion on this point is based upon the bare fact that murder necessarily results in the physical death of the victim, while rape does not. However, no member of the Court explains why this distinction has relevance, much less constitutional significance. It is, after all, not irrational—nor constitutionally impermissible—for a legislature to make the penalty more severe than the criminal act it punishes in the hope it would deter wrongdoing. . . .

It begs the question to state, as does the plurality opinion: "Life is over for the victim of the murderer; for the rape victim, life may not be nearly so happy as it was, but it is not over and normally is not beyond repair." Until now, the issue under the Eighth Amendment has not been the state of any particular victim after the crime, but rather

---

[13] Obviously I have no special competence to make these judgments, but by the same token no other member of the Court is competent to make a contrary judgment. This is why our system has, until now, left these difficult policy choices to the state legislatures, which may be no wiser, but surely are more attuned to the mores of their communities, than are we.

whether the punishment imposed is grossly disproportionate to the evil committed by the perpetrator. As a matter of constitutional principle, that test cannot have the primitive simplicity of "life for life, eye for eye, tooth for tooth." Rather states must be permitted to engage in a more sophisticated weighing of values in dealing with criminal activity which consistently poses serious danger of death or grave bodily harm. If innocent life and limb are to be preserved I see no constitutional barrier in punishing by death all who engage in such activity, regardless of whether the risk comes to fruition in any particular instance.

. . . The clear implication of today's holding appears to be that the death penalty may be properly imposed only as to crimes resulting in death of the victim. This casts serious doubt upon the constitutional validity of statutes imposing the death penalty for a variety of conduct which, though dangerous, may not necessarily result in any immediate death, e.g., treason, airplane hijacking, and kidnapping. In that respect, today's holding does even more harm than is initially apparent. We cannot avoid taking judicial notice that crimes such as airplane hijacking, kidnapping, and mass terrorist activity constitute a serious and increasing danger to the safety of the public. It would be unfortunate indeed if the effect of today's holding were to inhibit states and the federal government from experimenting with various remedies—including possibly imposition of the penalty of death—to prevent and deter such crimes.

Some sound observations, made only a few years ago, deserve repetition:

> Our task here, as must so frequently be emphasized and re-emphasized, is to pass upon the constitutionality of legislation that has been enacted and that is challenged. This is the sole task for judges. We should not allow our personal preferences as to the wisdom of legislative and congressional action, or our distaste for such action, to guide our judicial decision in cases such as these. The temptations to cross that policy line are very great. In fact, as today's decision reveals, they are almost irresistible. Furman v. Georgia, 408 U.S. at 411 (Blackmun, J., dissenting).

Whatever our individual views as to the wisdom of capital punishment, I cannot agree that it is constitutionally impermissible for a state legislature to make the "solemn judgment" to impose such penalty for the crime of rape. Accordingly, I would leave to the states the task of legislating in this area of the law.

## NOTES ON OFFENSES PUNISHABLE BY DEATH

### 1. QUESTIONS AND COMMENTS ON *COKER*

Obviously, *Coker* is an easy case if one takes the view that capital punishment is always unconstitutional. It is a case worth talking about as a problem independent of the legitimacy of capital punishment in general only if one is prepared to assume that the capital sanction is sometimes constitutional.

On this assumption, the case may be evaluated from at least two perspectives. The first concerns the Court's methodology. Justice White argues that the judgment involved "should not be, or appear to be, merely the subjective views of individual Justices; judgment should be informed by objective factors to the maximum possible extent." To what "objective factors" does he look? Does Chief Justice Burger disagree about what factors are relevant, or only about their application to the case at hand? Are the factors to which either opinion looks really "objective," or does the case in the end turn on "merely the subjective views of the individual Justices?"

Secondly, there is the question on the merits: whether rapists in general, or Coker in particular, can appropriately be distinguished from those murderers constitutionally punishable by death. Do you agree with Justice White's treatment of this issue? With the Chief Justice's? Or should Justice Powell's view—that some rapists may be executed but not Coker—prevail?

### 2. *ENMUND V. FLORIDA*

The Court addressed the use of capital punishment for an accomplice to murder in Enmund v. Florida, 458 U.S. 782 (1982). Enmund planned the robbery of an elderly couple, Thomas and Eunice Kersey, who were known to keep large sums of cash in their home. He waited in a car some distance from the victims' house while two accomplices, Sampson and Jeanette Armstrong, approached the house on the pretense of asking for water for an overheated radiator. After Thomas Kersey retrieved a water jug, Sampson Armstrong held a gun to him while Jeanette tried to get his wallet. Hearing her husband's cry for help, Eunice Kersey came around the side of the house with a gun and shot Jeanette Armstrong. Sampson, and perhaps Jeanette, returned Eunice's fire, killing both her and her husband. They then dragged the bodies into the kitchen, took what money they could find, and fled in the waiting car. Enmund and Sampson Armstrong were sentenced to death. Jeanette Armstrong was given three consecutive life sentences for two counts of second-degree murder and one of robbery

Under Florida law, no finding was required as to whether Enmund planned the killings or actually anticipated that lethal force might be used. It was enough that he qualified as a principal in the second degree, which the Florida courts found him to be.

The Supreme Court, by a vote of five to four, set aside Enmund's sentence, holding that the Eighth Amendment does not permit "imposition of the death penalty on one such as Enmund who aids and abets a felony in the course of which a murder is committed by others but who does not himself kill, attempt to kill or intend that a killing take place or that lethal force will be employed

#### *(i) The Indicators of Societal Judgment*

Justice White wrote for the Court. He began by referring to the methodology of *Coker:*

> [I]t was stressed that our judgment "should be informed by objective factors to the maximum possible extent." Accordingly, the Court looked to the historical development of the punishment at issue, legislative judgments, international opinion, and the sentencing decisions juries have made before bringing its own judgment to bear on the matter. We proceed to analyze the punishment at issue in this case in a similar manner.

White then analyzed the felony-murder provisions of the 36 American jurisdictions that authorize the death penalty. Essentially, he divided the states into three categories: (i) nine states in which the death penalty is authorized "solely for participation in a robbery in which another robber takes life"; (ii) nine states in which conviction of a capital offense for felony murder would be permissible only with various combinations of aggravating and mitigating; and (iii) the remainder of the states, in which felony murder would not be a capital offense on these facts or in which some culpability as to the death would have to be proved in order to justify conviction of a capital crime. He added:

> Thus only a small minority of jurisdictions—nine—allow the death penalty to be imposed solely because the defendant somehow participated in a robbery in the course of which a murder was committed. Even if the nine states are included where such a defendant could be executed for an unintended felony murder if sufficient aggravating circumstances are present to outweigh mitigating circumstances—which often include the defendant's minimal participation in the murder—only about a third of American jurisdictions would ever permit a defendant who somehow participated in a robbery where a murder occurred to be sentenced to die.

White concluded that this review of current legislative judgment "weighs on the side of rejecting capital punishment for the crime at issue."

He then turned to the second "objective" factor relied upon in *Coker*. He asserted that "[s]ociety's rejection of the death penalty for accomplice liability in felony murders is also indicated by the sentencing decisions that juries have made. . . . The evidence is overwhelming that American juries have repudiated imposition of the death penalty for crimes such as petitioner's." White cited in support of this conclusion a search by Enmund's lawyer of all reported appellate court decisions since 1954 involving defendants who were executed for homicide. The study revealed only six cases (all in 1955) in which a "nontriggerman felony murderer was executed."

Justice White also cited a study by counsel of the nation's death row population as of October 1, 1981. There were 796 inmates under a capital sentence for homicide. Of the 739 for whom the data were sufficient, only 41 did not actually participate in the fatal assault. Of these 41, only 16 were not actually present at the homicide, and 13 of these 16 either hired or solicited someone else to commit the offense or participated in a scheme designed to kill the victim. Thus only three offenders, including Enmund, did not take life themselves, attempt to take life, or intend to take life.

"[W]e are not aware," White concluded, "of a single person convicted of felony murder over the past quarter century who did not kill or attempt to kill, and did not intend the death of the victim, who has been executed." And "only three persons in that category are presently sentenced to die."

Justice O'Connor's dissent accepted the premise that the factors to be examined were those identified by the *Coker* plurality, but concluded that "the available data do not show that society has rejected conclusively the death penalty for felony murderers." She first noted that historically—beginning with the English law from which the American tradition is derived—the death penalty was an accepted sanction for felony murder. She then examined the study of reported appellate opinions since 1954, the examination of the prisoners currently on death row, and the conclusions drawn from current death penalty legislation:

> Impressive as these statistics are at first glance, they cannot be accepted uncritically. So stated, the data do not reveal the number or fraction of homicides that were charged as felony murders, or the number or fraction of cases in which the state sought the death penalty for an accomplice guilty of felony murder. Consequently, we cannot know the fraction of cases in which juries rejected the death penalty for accomplice felony murder. Moreover, . . . much of these data classify defendants by whether they "personally committed homicidal assault," and do not show the fraction of capital defendants who were shown to have an intent to kill. While the petitioner relies on the fact that he did not pull the trigger, his principal argument is, and must be, that death is an unconstitutional penalty absent an intent to kill, for otherwise, defendants who hire others to kill would escape the death penalty. Thus, the data he presents are not entirely relevant. Even accepting the petitioner's facts as meaningful, they may only reflect that sentencers are especially cautious in imposing the death penalty, and reserve that punishment for those defendants who are sufficiently involved in the homicide, whether or not there was specific intent to kill.

With respect to the third point—the current status of state legislation authorizing the death penalty for felony murder—Justice O'Connor disagreed with Justice White's characterization of the statutes. On her analysis, the laws of 24 states an execution that would violate the principle underlying the majority opinion, whereas Justice White considered that only nine—or at most 18—would permit such an execution. Justice O'Connor concluded as follows:

> Thus, in nearly half the states, and in two-thirds of the states that permit the death penalty for murder, a defendant who neither killed the victim nor specifically intended that the victim die may be sentenced to death for his participation in the robbery-murder. Far from "[w]eighing very heavily on the side of rejecting capital punishment as a suitable penalty for" felony murder, these legislative judgments indicate that our "evolving standards of decency" still embrace capital punishment for this crime. For this reason, I conclude that the petitioner has failed to meet the standards in *Coker* . . . that the "two crucial indicators of evolving standards of decency . . . —jury determinations and legislative enactments—*both point conclusively* to the repudiation of capital punishment for felony murder. In short, the death penalty for felony murder does not fall short of our national standards of decency."

### *(ii) The "Ultimate" Judgment*

After his review of the "objective" indicators of society's judgment on the death penalty for persons in Enmund's situation, Justice White concluded his opinion for the Court as follows:

> We have no doubt that robbery is a serious crime deserving serious punishment. It is not, however, a crime "so grievous an affront to humanity that the only adequate response may be the

penalty of death." "[I]t does not compare with murder, which does involve the unjustified taking of human life. Although it may be accompanied by another crime, [robbery] by definition does not include the death of or even the serious injury to another person. The murderer kills; the [robber], if no more than that, does not. Life is over for the victim of the murderer; for the [robbery] victim, life . . . is not over and normally is not beyond repair." Coker v. Georgia, 433 U.S. 584, 598 (1977). As was said of the crime of rape in *Coker,* we have the abiding conviction that the death penalty, which is "unique in its severity and irrevocability," is an excessive penalty for the robber who, as such, does not take human life.

Here the robbers did commit murder; but they were subjected to the death penalty only because they killed as well as robbed. The question before us is not the disproportionality of death as a penalty for murder, but is rather the validity of capital punishment for Enmund's own conduct. The focus must be on *his* culpability, not on that of those who committed the robbery and shot the victims, for we insist on "individualized consideration as a constitutional requirement in imposing the death sentence," which means that we must focus on "relevant facets of the character and record of the individual offender."[a] Enmund himself did not kill or attempt to kill; and as construed by the Florida Supreme Court, the record before us does not warrant a finding that Enmund had any intention of participating in or facilitating a murder. . . .

In Gregg v. Georgia, 428 U.S. 153, 183 (1976), the prevailing opinion observed that "[t]he death penalty is said to serve two principal social purposes: retribution and deterrence of capital crimes by prospective offenders." Unless the death penalty when applied to those in Enmund's position measurably contributes to one or both of these goals, it "is nothing more than the purposeless and needless imposition of pain and suffering," and hence an unconstitutional punishment. We are quite unconvinced, however, that the threat that the death penalty will be imposed for murder will measurably deter one who does not kill and has no intention or purpose that life will be taken. Instead, it seems likely that "capital punishment can serve as a deterrent only when murder is the result of premeditation and deliberation". . . .

It would be very different if the likelihood of a killing in the course of a robbery were so substantial that one should share the blame for the killing if he somehow participated in the felony. But [the evidence shows] that only about one-half of one per cent of robberies resulted in homicide.[b] The most recent national crime statistics strongly support this conclusion. In addition to the evidence that killings only rarely occur during robberies is the fact,

---

[a] The reference is to the individualization requirements of *Lockett* and *Eddings,* which are discussed in the Section 1 introductory notes on the Supreme Court and capital punishment in this chapter.—[Footnote by eds.]

[b] Model Penal Code § 210.1, Comment at 38 & n.96 (Official Draft and Revised Comments, 1980). The cited discussion occurs in the context of whether there should be a felony-murder rule in the first place, not whether the death penalty should be authorized if there is to be such a rule. As discussed in Chapter X, the Model Penal Code rejects the traditional formulation of the felony-murder rule.—[Footnote by eds.]

> already noted, that however often death occurs in the course of a felony such as robbery, the death penalty is rarely imposed on one only vicariously guilty of the murder, a fact which further attenuates its possible utility as an effective deterrent.
>
> As for retribution as a justification for executing Enmund, we think this very much depends on the degree of Enmund's culpability—what Enmund's intentions, expectations, and actions were. American criminal law has long considered a defendant's intention—and therefore his moral guilt—to be critical to "the degree of [his] criminal culpability" and the Court has found criminal penalties to be unconstitutionally excessive in the absence of intentional wrongdoing.
>
> For purposes of imposing the death penalty, Enmund's criminal culpability must be limited to his participation in the robbery, and his punishment must be tailored to his personal responsibility and moral guilt. Putting Enmund to death to avenge two killings that he did not commit and had no intention of committing or causing does not measurably contribute to the retributive end of ensuring that the criminal gets his just deserts. This is the judgment of most of the legislatures that have recently addressed the matter, and we have no reason to disagree with that judgment for purposes of construing and applying the Eighth Amendment.

Justice O'Connor's dissent also addressed the requirement of *Coker* that "the penalty imposed in a capital case be proportional to the harm caused and the defendant's blameworthiness." On this point, she concluded:

> Although the Court disingenuously seeks to characterize Enmund as only a "robber," it cannot be disputed that he is responsible, along with Sampson and Jeanette Armstrong, for the murders of the Kerseys. There is no dispute that their lives were unjustifiably taken, and that the petitioner, as one who aided and abetted the armed robbery, is legally liable for their deaths. Quite unlike the defendant in *Coker,* the petitioner cannot claim that the penalty imposed is "grossly out of proportion" to the harm for which he admittedly is at least partly responsible.
>
> The Court's holding today is especially disturbing because it makes intent a matter of federal constitutional law, requiring this Court both to review highly subjective definitional problems customarily left to state criminal law and to develop an Eighth Amendment meaning of intent. . . . Although the Court's opinion suggests that intent can be ascertained as if it were some historical fact, in fact it is a legal concept, not easily defined. Thus, while proportionality requires a nexus between the punishment imposed and the defendant's blameworthiness, the Court fails to explain why the Eighth Amendment concept of proportionality requires rejection of standards of blameworthiness based on other levels of intent, such as, for example, the intent to commit an armed robbery coupled with knowledge that armed robberies involve substantial risk of death or serious injury to other persons. Moreover, the intent-to-kill requirement is crudely crafted; it fails to take into account the complex picture of the defendant's knowledge of his accomplice's intent and whether he was armed, the defendant's contribution to the planning and success of the crime, and

the defendant's actual participation during the commission of the crime. Under the circumstances, the determination of the degree of blameworthiness is best left to the sentencer, who can sift through the facts unique to each case. . . .

In sum, the petitioner and the Court have failed to show that contemporary standards, as reflected in both jury determinations and legislative enactments, preclude imposition of the death penalty for accomplice felony murder. Moreover, examination of the qualitative factors underlying the concept of proportionality do not show that the death penalty is disproportionate as applied to Earl Enmund. In contrast to the crime in *Coker,* the petitioner's crime involves the very type of harm that this Court has held justifies the death penalty. Finally, because of the unique and complex mixture of facts involving a defendant's actions, knowledge, motives, and participation during the commission of a felony murder, I believe that the factfinder is best able to assess the defendant's blameworthiness. Accordingly, I conclude that the death penalty is not disproportionate to the crime of felony murder even though the defendant did not actually kill or intend to kill his victims.

At this point, Justice O'Connor appended a footnote:

The petitioner and the Court also contend that capital punishment for felony murder violates the Eighth Amendment because it "makes no measurable contribution to acceptable goals of punishment." In brief, the petitioner and the Court reason that since he did not specifically intend to kill the Kerseys, since the probability of death during an armed robbery is so low, and since the death penalty is so rarely imposed on nontriggermen, capital punishment could not have deterred him or anyone else from participating in the armed robbery. The petitioner and the Court also reject the notion that the goal of retribution might be served because his "moral guilt" is too insignificant.

At their core, these considerations are legislative judgment decisions regarding the efficacy of capital punishment as a tool in achieving retributive justice and deterring violent crime. Surely, neither the petitioner nor the Court has shown that capital punishment is ineffective as a deterrent for his crime; the most the Court can do is speculate as to its effect on other felony murderers and rely on "competent observers" rather than legislative judgments. Moreover, the decision of whether or not a particular punishment serves the admittedly legitimate goal of retribution seems uniquely suited to legislative resolution. Because an armed robber takes a serious risk that someone will die during the course of his crime, and because of the obviousness of that risk, we cannot conclude that the death penalty "makes no measurable contribution to acceptable goals of punishment."

### 3. *TISON V. ARIZONA*

The principle announced by the majority in *Enmund* was modified in Tison v. Arizona, 481 U.S. 137 (1987), another five-to-four decision,[c] in which the Court set aside death sentences imposed on two brothers, Raymond and Ricky Tison. The facts were summarized in Justice O'Connor's opinion for the Court:

> Gary Tison was sentenced to life imprisonment as the result of a prison escape during the course of which he had killed a guard. After he had been in prison a number of years, Gary Tison's wife, their three sons Donald, Ricky, and Raymond, Gary's brother Joseph, and other relatives made plans to help Gary Tison escape again. The Tison family assembled a large arsenal of weapons for this purpose. Plans for escape were discussed with Gary Tison, who insisted that his cellmate, Randy Greenawalt, also a convicted murderer, be included in the prison break. The following facts are largely evidenced by [Raymond and Ricky Tison's] detailed confessions given as part of a plea bargain according to the terms of which the State agreed not to seek the death sentence. The Arizona courts interpreted the plea agreement to require that petitioners testify to the planning stages of the breakout. When they refused to do so, the bargain was rescinded and they were tried, convicted, and sentenced to death.
>
> On July 30, 1978, the three Tison brothers entered the Arizona State Prison at Florence carrying a large ice chest filled with guns. The Tisons armed Greenawalt and their father, and the group, brandishing their weapons, locked the prison guards and visitors present in a storage closet. The five men fled the prison grounds in the Tisons' Ford Galaxy automobile. No shots were fired at the prison.
>
> After leaving the prison, the men abandoned the Ford automobile and proceeded on to an isolated house in a white Lincoln automobile that the brothers had parked at a hospital near the prison. At the house, the Lincoln automobile had a flat tire; the only spare tire was pressed into service. After two nights at the house, the group drove towards Flagstaff. As the group traveled on back roads and secondary highways through the desert, another tire blew out. The group decided to flag down a passing motorist and steal a car. Raymond stood out in front of the Lincoln; the other four armed themselves and laid in wait by the side of the road. One car passed by without stopping, but a second car, a Mazda occupied by John Lyons, his wife Donelda, his two-year-old son Christopher and his 15-year-old niece, Theresa Tyson, pulled over to render aid.
>
> As Raymond showed John Lyons the flat tire on the Lincoln, the other Tisons and Greenawalt emerged. The Lyons family was forced into the back seat of the Lincoln. Raymond and Donald drove the Lincoln down a dirt road off the highway and then down a gas line service road farther into the desert; Gary Tison, Ricky

---

[c] The *Tison* majority comprised Justices O'Connor and Powell and Chief Justice Rehnquist (all of whom dissented in *Enmund*), Justice White (who wrote the majority opinion in *Enmund*), and Justice Scalia (who had succeeded Chief Justice Burger).

Tison and Randy Greenawalt followed in the Lyons' Mazda. The two cars were parked trunk to trunk and the Lyons family was ordered to stand in front of the Lincoln's headlights. The Tisons transferred their belongings from the Lincoln into the Mazda. They discovered guns and money in the Mazda which they kept and they put the rest of the Lyons' possessions in the Lincoln.

Gary Tison then told Raymond to drive the Lincoln still farther into the desert. Raymond did so, and, while the others guarded the Lyons and Theresa Tyson, Gary fired his shotgun into the radiator, presumably to completely disable the vehicle. The Lyons and Theresa Tyson were then escorted to the Lincoln and again ordered to stand in its headlights. Ricky Tison reported that John Lyons begged, in comments "more or less directed at everybody," "Jesus, don't kill me." Gary Tison said he was "thinking about it." John Lyons asked the Tisons and Greenawalt to "[g]ive us some water . . . just leave us out here, and you all go home." Gary Tison then told his sons to go back to the Mazda and get some water. Raymond later explained that his father "was like in conflict with himself . . . [w]hat it was, I think it was the baby being there and all this, and he wasn't sure about what to do."

The petitioners' statements diverge to some extent, but it appears that both of them went back towards the Mazda, along with Donald, while Randy Greenawalt and Gary Tison stayed at the Lincoln guarding the victims. Raymond recalled being at the Mazda filling the water jug "when we started hearing the shots." Ricky said that the brothers gave the water jug to Gary Tison who then, with Randy Greenawalt went behind the Lincoln where they spoke briefly, then raised the shotguns and started firing. In any event, petitioners agree they saw Greenawalt and their father brutally murder their four captives with repeated blasts from their shotguns. Neither made an effort to help the victims, though both later stated they were surprised by the shooting. The Tisons got into the Mazda and drove away, continuing their flight. Physical evidence suggested that Theresa Tyson managed to crawl away from the bloodbath, severely injured. She died in the desert after the Tisons left.

Several days later the Tisons and Greenawalt were apprehended after a shootout at a police roadblock. Donald Tison was killed. Gary Tison escaped into the desert where he subsequently died of exposure. . . .

[Raymond and Ricky Tison were tried] for capital murder of the four victims as well as for the associated crimes of armed robbery, kidnaping, and car theft. The capital murder charges were based on Arizona felony-murder law providing that a killing occurring during the perpetration of robbery or kidnaping is capital murder, and that each participant in the kidnaping or robbery is legally responsible for the acts of his accomplices. Each [was] convicted of the four murders under these accomplice liability and felony-murder statutes.

The trial judge sentenced each of the Tison brothers to death based on findings of three aggravating factors which he found to outweigh the mitigating factors, including the brothers' youth and the absence of any prior felony record. He also specifically found that their "participation . . . in the crimes giving rise to the application of the felony murder rule" had been "very substantial," and that each of them "could reasonably have foreseen that his conduct . . . would cause or create a grave risk of . . . death." On direct appeal, the Arizona Supreme Court affirmed the death sentences, noting that:

> The record establishes that both Ricky and Raymond Tison were present when the homicides took place and that they occurred as part of and in the course of the escape and continuous attempt to prevent recapture. The deaths would not have occurred but for their assistance. That they did not specifically intend that the Lyonses and Theresa Tyson die, that they did not plot in advance that these homicides would take place, or that they did not actually pull the triggers on the guns which inflicted the fatal wounds is of little significance.

In state habeas proceedings brought after the Supreme Court's decision in *Enmund*, the Tisons sought to set aside the death sentences on the ground that *Enmund* required a finding of intent to kill. Finding that the Tisons "could anticipate the use of lethal force" and "played an active part in the events that led to the murders," the Arizona Supreme Court held that this amounted to "intent to kill" within the meaning of *Enmund*, because "intent to kill includes the situation in which the defendant intended, contemplated, or anticipated that lethal force would or might be used or that life would or might be taken in accomplishing the underlying felony."

Justice O'Connor acknowledged that the Arizona Supreme Court's definition of intent "is broader than that described by the *Enmund* Court" and that the Tisons "do not fall within the 'intent to kill' category of felony murderers for which *Enmund* explicitly finds the death penalty permissible. . . . " On the other hand, she observed, "it is equally clear" that they "fall outside the category of felony murderers for whom *Enmund* explicitly held the death penalty disproportional"—cases involving "the minor actor in an armed robbery, not on the scene, who neither intended to kill nor was found to have had any culpable mental state." She continued:

> [The] facts not only indicate that the Tison brothers' participation in the crime was anything but minor, they also would clearly support a finding that they both subjectively appreciated that their acts were likely to result in the taking of innocent life. The issue raised by this case is whether the Eighth Amendment prohibits the death penalty in the intermediate case of the defendant whose participation is major and whose mental state is one of reckless indifference to the value of human life. *Enmund* does not specifically address this point. We now take up the task of determining whether the Eighth Amendment proportionality requirement bars the death penalty under these circumstances.
>
> Like the *Enmund* Court, we find the state legislatures' judgment as to proportionality in these circumstances relevant to this constitutional inquiry. The largest number of States still fall into the two intermediate categories discussed in *Enmund*. Four States authorize the death penalty in felony-murder cases upon a showing of culpable mental state such as recklessness or extreme indifference to human life. Two jurisdictions require that the defendant's participation be substantial and the statutes of at least

six more, including Arizona, take minor participation in the felony expressly into account in mitigation of the murder. These requirements significantly overlap both in this case and in general, for the greater the defendant's participation in the felony murder, the more likely that he acted with reckless indifference to human life. At a minimum, however, it can be said that all these jurisdictions, as well as six States which *Enmund* classified along with Florida as permitting capital punishment for felony-murder *simpliciter*, and the three States which simply require some additional aggravation before imposing the death penalty upon a felony murderer, specifically authorize the death penalty in a felony-murder case where, though the defendant's mental state fell short of intent to kill, the defendant was a major actor in a felony in which he knew death was highly likely to occur. On the other hand, even after *Enmund*, only 11 States authorizing capital punishment forbid imposition of the death penalty even though the defendant's participation in the felony murder is major and the likelihood of killing is so substantial as to raise an inference of extreme recklessness. This substantial and recent legislative authorization of the death penalty for the crime of felony murder regardless of the absence of a finding of an intent to kill powerfully suggests that our society does *not* reject the death penalty as grossly excessive under these circumstances.

Moreover, a number of state courts have interpreted *Enmund* to permit the imposition of the death penalty in such aggravated felony murders. . . .

Against this backdrop, we now consider the proportionality of the death penalty in these mid range felony-murder cases for which the majority of American jurisdictions clearly authorize capital punishment and for which American courts have not been nearly so reluctant to impose death as they are in the case of felony-murder *simpliciter*.

A critical facet of the individualized determination of culpability required in capital cases is the mental state with which the defendant commits the crime. Deeply ingrained in our legal tradition is the idea that the more purposeful is the criminal conduct, the more serious is the offense, and, therefore, the more severely it ought to be punished. . . .

A narrow focus on the question of whether or not a given defendant "intended to kill," however, is a highly unsatisfactory means of definitively distinguishing the most culpable and dangerous of murderers. . . . [S]ome nonintentional murderers may be among the most dangerous and inhumane of all—the person who tortures another not caring whether the victim lives or dies, or the robber who shoots someone in the course of the robbery, utterly indifferent to the fact that the desire to rob may have the unintended consequence of killing the victim as well as taking the victim's property. This reckless indifference to the value of human life may be every bit as shocking to the moral sense as an "intent to kill." Indeed it is for this very reason that the common law and modern criminal codes alike have classified behavior such as occurred in this case along with intentional murders. *Enmund* held that when "intent to kill" results in its logical though not inevitable consequence—the taking of human life—the Eighth Amendment permits the State to exact the death penalty after a careful weighing of the aggravating and mitigating circumstances. Similarly, we hold that the reckless disregard for human life implicit in knowingly engaging in criminal activities known to carry a grave risk of death represents a highly culpable mental state, a mental state that may be taken into account in making a capital sentencing judgment when that conduct causes its natural, though also not inevitable, lethal result.

Only a small minority of those jurisdictions imposing capital punishment for felony murder have rejected the possibility of a capital sentence absent an intent to kill and we do not find this minority position constitutionally required. We will not attempt to precisely delineate the particular types of conduct and states of mind warranting imposition of the death penalty here. Rather, we simply hold that major participation in the felony committed, combined with reckless indifference to human life, is sufficient to satisfy the *Enmund* culpability requirement. . . .

The Court concluded that the Arizona courts had "clearly found" that the Tison brothers were major participants in the felony, but had not specifically found that they satisfied the reckless indifference standard. Accordingly, it set aside the death sentences and remanded the case to the Arizona Supreme Court.[d]

Justice Brennan dissented, in an opinion joined by Justices Marshall, Blackmun and Stevens:

. . . Creation of a new category of culpability is not enough to distinguish this case from *Enmund*. The Court must also establish that death is a proportionate punishment for individuals in this category. In other words, the Court must demonstrate that major participation in a felony with a state of mind of reckless indifference to human life deserves the same punishment as intending to commit a murder or actually committing a murder. The Court does not attempt to conduct a proportionality review of the kind performed in past cases raising a proportionality question.

One reason the Court offers for its conclusion that death is proportionate punishment for persons falling within its new category is that limiting the death penalty to those who intend to kill "is a highly unsatisfactory means of definitively distinguishing the most culpable and dangerous of murderers." To illustrate that intention cannot be dispositive, the Court offers as examples "the person *who tortures* another not caring whether the victim lives or

---

[d] What happened to the Tison brothers? The Arizona Supreme Court remanded to the trial court for resentencing. The trial judge then reimposed the death penalty based on the record evidence without holding a new hearing. On appeal of that decision, the Arizona Supreme Court held that a new fact hearing was required. State v. Tison, 160 Ariz. 501, 774 P.2d 805 (1989). The trial court held the hearing, and again imposed the death penalty. According to newspaper accounts, the next step was a ruling by "the state Supreme Court [that] the prosecution had failed to prove the brothers had shown reckless indifference toward human life, since their father and Greenawalt had done the shootings. They were resentenced to life in prison." See http:www.lubbockonline.com/news/012097/memberof.htm. Greenawalt was executed 18½ years after the prison breakout. See http://www.deathpenaltyinfo.org/randy-greenawalt.—[Footnote by eds.]

dies, or the robber *who shoots* someone in the course of the robbery, utterly indifferent to the fact that the desire to rob may have the unintended consequence of killing the victim as well as taking the victim's property." (Emphasis added.) Influential commentators and some States have approved the use of the death penalty for persons, like those given in the Court's examples, *who kill* others in circumstances manifesting an extreme indifference to the value of human life. Thus an exception to the requirement that only intentional murders be punished with death might be made for persons who actually commit an act of homicide; *Enmund*, by distinguishing from the accomplice case "those who kill," clearly reserved that question. But the constitutionality of the death penalty for those individuals is no more relevant to this case than it was to *Enmund*, because this case, like *Enmund*, involves accomplices *who did not kill*. Thus, although some of the "most culpable and dangerous of murderers" may be those who killed without specifically intending to kill, it is considerably more difficult to apply that rubric convincingly to those who not only did not intend to kill, but who also have not killed.

It is precisely in this context—where the defendant has not killed—that a finding that he or she nevertheless intended to kill seems indispensable to establishing capital culpability. It is important first to note that such a defendant has not committed an *act* for which he or she could be sentenced to death. The applicability of the death penalty therefore turns entirely on the defendant's mental state with regard to an act committed by another. Factors such as the defendant's major participation in the events surrounding the killing or the defendant's presence at the scene are relevant insofar as they illuminate the defendant's mental state with regard to the killings. They cannot serve, however, as independent grounds for imposing the death penalty.

Second, when evaluating such a defendant's mental state, a determination that the defendant acted with intent is qualitatively different from a determination that the defendant acted with reckless indifference to human life. The difference lies in the nature of the choice each has made. The reckless actor has not *chosen* to bring about the killing in the way the intentional actor has. The person who chooses to act recklessly and is indifferent to the possibility of fatal consequences often deserves serious punishment. But because that person has not chosen to kill, his or her moral and criminal culpability is of a different degree than that of one who killed or intended to kill. . . . The Court's decision today to approve the death penalty for accomplices who lack this mental state is inconsistent with *Enmund* and with the only justifications this Court has put forth for imposing the death penalty in any case.

In *Enmund*, the Court explained at length the reasons a finding of intent is a necessary prerequisite to the imposition of the death penalty. In any given case, the Court said, the death penalty must "measurably contribut[e]" to one or both of the two "social purposes"—deterrence and retribution—which this Court has accepted as justifications for the death penalty. . . . The

Court's second reason for abandoning the intent requirement is based on its survey of state statutes authorizing the death penalty for felony murder, and on a handful of state cases. On this basis, the Court concludes that "[o]nly a small minority *of those jurisdictions imposing capital punishment for felony murder have* rejected the possibility of a capital sentence absent an intent to kill and we do not find this minority position constitutionally required." (Emphasis added.) The Court would thus have us believe that "the majority of American jurisdictions clearly authorize capital punishment" in cases such as this. This is not the case. First, the Court excludes from its survey those jurisdictions that have abolished the death penalty and those that have authorized it only in circumstances different from those presented here. When these jurisdictions are included, and are considered with those jurisdictions that require a finding of intent to kill in order to impose the death sentence for felony murder, one discovers that approximately three-fifths of American jurisdictions do not authorize the death penalty for a non-triggerman absent a finding that he intended to kill. Thus, contrary to the Court's implication that its view is consonant with that of "the majority of American jurisdictions," the Court's view is itself distinctly the minority position.

Second, it is critical examine not simply those jurisdictions that authorize the death penalty in a given circumstance, but those that actually *impose* it. Evidence that a penalty is imposed only infrequently suggests not only that jurisdictions are reluctant to apply it but also that, when it is applied, its imposition is arbitrary and therefore unconstitutional. Thus, the Court in *Enmund* examined the relevant statistics on the imposition of the death penalty for accomplices in a felony murder. . . .

The Court today neither reviews nor updates this evidence. Had it done so, it would have discovered that, even including the 65 executions since *Enmund*, "[t]he fact remains that we are not aware of a single person convicted of felony murder over the past quarter century who did not kill or attempt to kill, and did not intend the death of the victim, who has been executed. . . ." Of the 64 persons on death row in Arizona, all of those who have raised and lost an *Enmund* challenge in the Arizona Supreme Court have been found either to have killed or to have specifically intended to kill. Thus, like Enmund, the Tisons' sentence appears to be an aberration within Arizona itself as well as nationally and internationally. The Court's objective evidence that the statutes of roughly 20 States appear to authorize the death penalty for defendants in the Court's new category is therefore an inadequate substitute for a proper proportionality analysis, and is not persuasive evidence that the punishment that was unconstitutional for Enmund is constitutional for the Tisons.

### 4. QUESTIONS ON *ENMUND* AND *TISON*

Can *Tison* be reconciled with *Enmund*? What culpability should a state supreme court regard as constitutionally prerequisite to the imposition of a death sentence on an accomplice to a felony-murder? Justice Brennan argues that reckless indifference to human life should not be constitutionally sufficient for an accomplice even though it might be sufficient for the killer. Is this a defensible position?

It is also helpful to think about *Enmund* and *Tison* from the standpoint of constitutional interpretation. Consider the methodology employed in the various opinions. Do the Justices disagree about what "objective" factors are relevant or only about their application to the cases at hand? And on the merits of the "ultimate" issue, did the Court reach the right results in these two cases?[e]

## 5. RAPE OF A CHILD: *KENNEDY V. LOUISIANA*

The plurality opinion in *Coker* explicitly framed the issue before the Court as whether the death penalty is excessive for the rape "of an adult woman," leaving open whether the death penalty might be permissible for rape of a child. The Court addressed that question three decades later in Kennedy v. Louisiana, 554 U.S. 407 (2008). In a five-to-four decision, the Court invalidated Patrick Kennedy's death sentence for the brutal rape of his nine-year-old stepdaughter, drawing a line between "intentional first-degree murder on the one hand and non-homicide crimes against individual persons, including child rape, on the other." Justice Kennedy's majority opinion was careful to emphasize that the ruling was "limited to crimes against individual persons" and did not address the constitutionality of capital punishment for "treason, espionage, terrorism, and drug kingpin activity, which are offenses against the state."

Reviewing the "objective indicia" of contemporary values, Justice Kennedy noted that only six states permitted the death penalty for child rape and that Louisiana was the only state since 1964 to impose a death sentence for that crime. Such a "national consensus" is entitled to "great weight," said Justice Kennedy, although the conclusion that the death penalty is disproportionate to the seriousness of the child rape rested "in the end" on the Court's "own independent judgment." He explained:

> It must be acknowledged that there are moral grounds to question a rule barring capital punishment for a crime against an individual that did not result in death. These facts illustrate the point. Here the victim's fright, the sense of betrayal, and the nature of her injuries caused more prolonged physical and mental suffering than, say, a sudden killing by an unseen assassin. The attack was not just on her but on her childhood. For this reason, we should be most reluctant to rely upon the language of the plurality in *Coker*, which posited that, for the victim of rape, "life may not be nearly so happy as it was" but it is not beyond repair. Rape has a permanent psychological, emotional, and sometimes physical impact on the child. We cannot dismiss the years of long anguish that must be endured by the victim of child rape.
>
> It does not follow, though, that capital punishment is a proportionate penalty for the crime. The constitutional prohibition against excessive or cruel and unusual punishments mandates that the State's power to punish "be exercised within the limits of civilized standards." Evolving standards of decency that mark the

[e] For a thorough discussion of *Enmund* and *Tison*, see David McCord, State Death Sentencing for Felony Murder Accomplices under the *Enmund* and *Tison* Standards, 32 Ariz. St. L. J. 843 (2000).

> progress of a maturing society counsel us to be most hesitant before interpreting the Eighth Amendment to allow the extension of the death penalty, a hesitation that has special force where no life was taken in the commission of the crime. It is an established principle that decency, in its essence, presumes respect for the individual and thus moderation or restraint in the application of capital punishment. . . . As it relates to crimes against individuals, the death penalty should not be expanded to instances where the victim's life was not taken. . . .
>
> Consistent with evolving standards of decency and the teachings of our precedents we conclude that, in determining whether the death penalty is excessive, there is a distinction between intentional first-degree murder on the one hand and non-homicide crimes against individual persons, even including child rape, on the other. The latter crimes may be devastating in their harm, as here, but "in terms of moral depravity and of the injury to the person and to the public," they cannot be compared to murder in their "severity and irrevocability."

Justice Alito dissented in an opinion joined by Chief Justice Roberts and Justices Scalia and Thomas:

> The Court's [principal] justification for its holding is that murder is unique in its moral depravity and in the severity of the injury that it inflicts on the victim and the public. But the Court makes little attempt to defend these conclusions. . . . With respect to the question of moral depravity, is it really true that every person who is convicted of capital murder and sentenced to death is more morally depraved than every child rapist? Consider the following two cases. In the first, a defendant robs a convenience store and watches as his accomplice shoots the store owner. The defendant acts recklessly, but was not the triggerman and did not intend the killing. See, e.g., Tison v. Arizona, 481 U.S. 137 (1987). In the second case, a previously convicted child rapist kidnaps, repeatedly rapes, and tortures multiple child victims. Is it clear that the first defendant is more morally depraved than the second? . . . I have no doubt that, under the prevailing standards of our society, robbery, the crime that the petitioner in Enmund v. Florida, 458 U.S. 782 (1982), intended to commit, does not evidence the same degree of moral depravity as the brutal rape of a young child. Indeed, I have little doubt that, in the eyes of ordinary Americans, the very worst child rapists—predators who seek out and inflict serious physical and emotional injury on defenseless young children—are the epitome of moral depravity.
>
> With respect to the question of the harm caused by the rape of child in relation to the harm caused by murder, it is certainly true that the loss of human life represents a unique harm, but that does not explain why other grievous harms are insufficient to permit a death sentence. And the Court does not take the position that no harm other than the loss of life is sufficient. The Court takes pains to limit its holding to "crimes against individual persons" and to exclude "offenses against the State," a category that the Court stretches—without explanation—to include "drug kingpin activity." But the Court makes no effort to explain why the

harm caused by such crimes is necessarily greater than the harm caused by the rape of young children. This is puzzling in light of the Court's acknowledgment that "[r]ape has a permanent psychological, emotional, and sometimes physical impact on the child." As the Court aptly recognizes, "[w]e cannot dismiss the years of long anguish that must be endured by the victim of child rape."

The rape of any victim inflicts great injury, and "[s]ome victims are so grievously injured physically or psychologically that life *is* beyond repair." Coker v. Georgia, 433 U.S. 584, 603 (1977) (opinion of Powell, J.). "The immaturity and vulnerability of a child, both physically and psychologically, adds a devastating dimension to rape that is not present when an adult is raped." Meister, Murdering Innocence: The Constitutionality of Capital Child Rape Statutes, 45 Ariz. L. Rev. 197, 208–09 (2003). Long-term studies show that sexual abuse is "grossly intrusive in the lives of children and is harmful to their normal psychological, emotional and sexual development in ways which no just or humane society can tolerate." C. Bagley & K. King, Child Sexual Abuse: The Search for Healing 2 (1990).

It has been estimated that as many as 40% of 7– to 13-year-old sexual assault victims are considered "seriously disturbed." Psychological problems include sudden school failure, unprovoked crying, dissociation, depression, insomnia, sleep disturbances, nightmares, feelings of guilt and inferiority, and self-destructive behavior, including an increased incidence of suicide.

The deep problems that afflict child-rape victims often become society's problems as well. Commentators have noted correlations between childhood sexual abuse and later problems such as substance abuse, dangerous sexual behaviors or dysfunction, inability to relate to others on an interpersonal level, and psychiatric illness. . . .

The harm that is caused to the victims and to society at large by the worst child rapists is grave. It is the judgment of the Louisiana lawmakers and those in an increasing number of other States that these harms justify the death penalty. The Court provides no cogent explanation why this legislative judgment should be overridden. . . .

Justice Kennedy offered several other reasons why allowing use of the death penalty for child rape would have undesirable consequences, including further distress to the child victims themselves, especially if they are required to testify against the abuser. He also took note of the number of executions that would have been allowed if Louisiana's statute had been upheld:

The crime of child rape, considering its reported incidents, occurs more often than first-degree murder. Approximately 5,702 incidents of vaginal, anal, or oral rape of a child under the age of 12 were reported nationwide in 2005; this is almost twice the total incidents of intentional murder for victims of all ages (3,405) reported during the same period. See Inter-University Consortium for Political and Social Research, National Incident-Based Reporting System, 2005, Study No. 4720, http://www.icpsr.umich.edu (as

> visited June 12, 2008, and available in Clerk of Court's case file). Although we have no reliable statistics on convictions for child rape, we can surmise that, each year, there are hundreds, or more, of these convictions just in jurisdictions that permit capital punishment. As a result of existing rules, only 2.2% of convicted first-degree murderers are sentenced to death, see Blume, Eisenberg, & Wells, Explaining Death Row's Population and Racial Composition, 1 J. of Empirical Legal Studies 165, 171 (2004). But under [Louisiana's] approach, the 36 States that permit the death penalty could sentence to death all persons convicted of raping a child less than 12 years of age. This could not be reconciled with our evolving standards of decency and the necessity to constrain the use of the death penalty.
>
> It might be said that narrowing aggravators could be used in this context, as with murder offenses, to ensure the death penalty's restrained application. We find it difficult to identify standards that would guide the decisionmaker so the penalty is reserved for the most severe cases of child rape and yet not imposed in an arbitrary way. Even were we to forbid, say, the execution of first-time child rapists, or require as an aggravating factor a finding that the perpetrator's instant rape offense involved multiple victims, the jury still must balance, in its discretion, those aggravating factors against mitigating circumstances. In this context, which involves a crime that in many cases will overwhelm a decent person's judgment, we have no confidence that the imposition of the death penalty would not be so arbitrary as to be "freakis[h]" [citing Justice Stewart's opinion in Furman v. Georgia, 408 U.S. 238 (1972)]. We cannot sanction this result when the harm to the victim, though grave, cannot be quantified in the same way as death of the victim.

Justice Alito responded:

> The Court's argument regarding the structuring of sentencing discretion is hard to comprehend. The Court finds it "difficult to identify standards that would guide the decisionmaker so the penalty is reserved for the most severe cases of child rape and yet not imposed in an arbitrary way." Even assuming that the age of a child is not alone a sufficient factor for limiting sentencing discretion, the Court need only examine the child-rape laws recently enacted in Texas, Oklahoma, Montana, and South Carolina, all of which use a concrete factor to limit quite drastically the number of cases in which the death penalty may be imposed. In those states, a defendant convicted of the rape of a child may be sentenced to death only if the defendant has a prior conviction for a specified felony sex offense.

Given *Coker*, is it possible to defend a constitutional rule that would allow the death penalty for rape of a 12-year old girl but preclude it for rape of a 16-year old teenager (the age of Coker's victim) or a 66-year old woman? Would allowing the death penalty for child rape lead to a significant "expansion" of capital punishment, as Justice Kennedy feared? Is that reason enough to preclude it, as he implied?

## NOTES ON OFFENDERS WITH MENTAL RETARDATION: *ATKINS V. VIRGINIA*

### 1. INTRODUCTION

*Coker* and the preceding notes address the constitutionally necessary *offense* elements (conduct and mens rea) required for capital punishment. Another line of cases has addressed the capacities of *offenders*—specifically the levels of maturity and intellectual capacity that are constitutionally necessary predicates for execution. In both contexts, it has been argued that death is a grossly disproportionate punishment even though the offender's youthfulness or intellectual deficiency does not bar criminal conviction and punishment.

### 2. *PENRY V. LYNAUGH*

In Penry v. Lynaugh, 492 U.S. 302 (1989), a five-to-four majority of the Supreme Court held that the death penalty is not categorically precluded for mentally retarded defendants. At the time *Penry* was decided, only one state (Georgia) and the federal government explicitly barred execution of a retarded person who had been convicted of a capital crime, and no data were available on sentencing practices. Thus, neither of the "objective indicators" utilized in previous cases demonstrated an evolving societal consensus against execution of the mentally retarded. Justice Scalia, joined by Chief Justice Rehnquist and Justices White and Kennedy, thought that the Court's inquiry was at an end. The plurality refused to undertake any "subjective" analysis of proportionality, which "has no place in our Eighth-Amendment jurisprudence." If "an objective examination of laws and jury determinations fails to demonstrate society's disapproval of it, the punishment is not unconstitutional even if out of accord with the theories of penology favored by the Justices of the Court."

The five remaining Justices endorsed the legitimacy of the proportionality inquiry, and all except Justice O'Connor were prepared to bar execution of mentally retarded defendants. The basis for this conclusion was most fully developed by Justice Brennan, in an opinion joined by Justice Marshall, concluded that "[t]he impairment of a mentally retarded offender's reasoning abilities, control over impulsive behavior and moral development in my view limits his culpability so that, whatever other punishment might be appropriate, the ultimate penalty of death is always and necessarily disproportionate to his blameworthiness and hence is unconstitutional."

Justice O'Connor's vote was determinative: "On the record before the Court today, . . .I cannot conclude that all mentally retarded people of Penry's ability—by virtue of their mental retardation alone, and apart from any individualized consideration of their personal responsibility—inevitably lack the cognitive, volitional, and moral capacity to act with the degree of culpability associated with the death penalty."

### 3. *ATKINS V. VIRGINIA*

Thirteen years after *Penry*, the Court revisited the issue in Atkins v. Virginia, 536 U.S. 304 (2002). By this time, 17 states had joined Georgia in enacting statutes prohibiting the execution of mentally retarded offenders. The Court's opinion, written by Justice Stevens and joined by Justices

O'Connor, Kennedy, Souter, Ginsburg and Breyer, concluded a societal consensus had formed against the use of the death penalty for mentally retarded defendants:

> Much has changed since [*Penry*]. Responding to the national attention received by [a juvenile] execution and our decision in *Penry*, state legislatures across the country began to address the issue. . . .
>
> It is not so much the number of these states that is significant, but the consistency of the direction of change. Given the well-known fact that anticrime legislature is far more popular than legislation providing protections for persons guilty of violent crime, the large number of states prohibiting the execution of mentally retarded persons (and the complete absence of states passing legislation reinstating the power to conduct such executions) provides powerful evidence that today our society views mentally retarded offenders as categorically less culpable than the average criminal. The evidence carries even greater force when it is noted that the legislatures that have addressed the issue have voted overwhelmingly in favor of the prohibition. Moreover, in those states that allow the execution of mentally retarded offenders, the practice is uncommon. Some states, for example New Hampshire and New Jersey, continue to authorize executions, but none have been carried out in decades. Thus there is little need to pursue legislation barring the execution of the mentally retarded in those States. And it appears that even among those states that regularly execute offenders and that have no prohibition with regard to the mentally retarded, only five have executed offenders possessing a known IQ less than 70 since we decided *Penry*. The practice, therefore, has become truly unusual, and it is fair to say that a national consensus has developed against it. . . .
>
> This consensus unquestionably reflects widespread judgment about the relative culpability of mentally retarded offenders, and the relationship between mental retardation and the penological purposes served by the death penalty. Additionally, it suggests that some characteristics of mental retardation undermine the strength of the procedural protections that our capital jurisprudence steadfastly guards.
>
> [C]linical definitions of mental retardation require not only subaverage intellectual functioning, but also significant limitations in adaptive skills such as communications, self-care, and self-direction that became manifest before age 18. Mentally retarded persons frequently know the difference between right and wrong and are competent to stand trial. Because of their impairments, however, by definition they have diminished capacities to understand and process information, to communicate, to abstract from mistakes and learn from experience, to engage in logical reasoning, to control impulses, and to understand the reactions of others. There is no evidence that they are more likely to engage in criminal conduct than others, but there is abundant evidence that they often act on impulse rather than pursuant to a premeditated plan, and that in group settings they are followers rather than leaders. Their deficiencies do not warrant an exemption from

> criminal sanctions, but they do diminish their personal culpability.
>
> In light of these deficiencies, our death penalty jurisprudence provides two reasons consistent with the legislative consensus that the mentally retarded should be categorically excluded from execution. First, there is a serious question as to whether either justification that we have recognized as a basis for the death penalty applies to mentally retarded offenders. *Gregg v. Georgia* identified "retribution and deterrence of capital crimes by prospective offenders" as the social purposes served by the death penalty. Unless the imposition of the death penalty on a mentally retarded person "measurably contributes" to one or both of these goals, it "is nothing more than the purposeless and needless imposition of pain and suffering," and hence an unconstitutional punishment. *Enmund*. . . .
>
> Our independent evaluation of the issue reveals no reason to disagree with the judgments of "the legislatures that have recently addressed the matter" and concluded that death is not a suitable punishment for a mentally retarded criminal. We are not persuaded that the execution of mentally retarded criminals will measurably advance the deterrent or the retributive purpose of the death penalty. Construing and applying the Eighth Amendment in the light of our "evolving standards of decency," we therefore conclude that such punishment is excessive and that the constitution "places a substantive restriction on the state's power to take the life" of a mentally retarded offender.

Chief Justice Rehnquist and Justices Scalia and Thomas dissented. In his dissenting opinion, Justice Scalia objected to the Court's methodology as well as to its result:

> Today's decision is the pinnacle of our Eighth Amendment death-is-different jurisprudence. Not only does it, like all of that jurisprudence, find no support in the text or history of the Eighth Amendment; it does not even have support in current social attitudes regarding the conditions that render an otherwise just death penalty inappropriate. Seldom has an opinion of this Court rested so obviously upon nothing but the personal views of its members. . . .
>
> [Atkins'] mental retardation was a *central issue* at sentencing. The jury concluded, however, that his alleged retardation was not a compelling reason to exempt him from the death penalty in light of the brutality of his crime and his long demonstrated propensity for violence. In upsetting this particularized judgment on the basis of a constitutional absolute, the Court concludes that no one who is even slightly mentally retarded can have sufficient moral responsibility to be subjected to capital punishment for any crime. As a sociological and moral conclusion that is implausible; and it is doubly implausible as an interpretation of the United States constitution.
>
> The Court makes no pretense that execution of the mildly mentally retarded would have been considered "cruel and unusual" in 1791. Only the *severely* or *profoundly* mentally retarded,

commonly known as "idiots," enjoyed any special status under the law at that time. . . . Mentally retarded offenders with less severe impairments—those who were not "idiots"—suffered criminal prosecution and punishment, including capital punishment. . . .

The Court is left to argue, therefore, that execution of the mildly retarded is inconsistent with the "evolving standards of decency that mark the progress of a maturing society." . . . [It] miraculously extracts a "national consensus" forbidding execution of the mentally retarded . . . from the fact that 18 states—less than *half* (47%) of the 38 States that permit capital punishment (for whom the issue exists)—have very recently enacted legislation barring execution of the mentally retarded. Even that 47% figure is a distorted one. If one is to say, as the Court does today, that *all* executions of the mentally retarded are so morally repugnant as to violate our national "standards of decency," surely the "consensus" it points to must be one that has set its righteous face against *all* such executions. Not 18 States, but only seven—18% of death penalty jurisdictions—have legislation of that scope. Eleven of those that the Court counts enacted statutes prohibiting execution of mentally retarded defendants *convicted after, or convicted of crimes committed after, the effective date* of the legislation; those already on death row, or consigned there before the statute's effective date, or even (in those State using the date of the crime as the criterion of retroactivity) tried in the future for murders committed many years ago, could be put to death. That is not a statement of absolute moral repugnance, but one of current preference between two tolerable approaches. Two of these States permit execution of the mentally retarded in other situations as well: Kansas apparently permits execution of all except the *severely* mentally retarded; New York permits execution of the mentally retarded who commit murder in a correctional facility. . . .

Moreover, a major fact that the Court entirely disregards is that the legislation of all 18 states it relies on is still in its infancy. The oldest of the statutes is only 14 years old; five were enacted last year; over half were enacted within the past eight years. Few, if any, of the States have had sufficient experience with these laws to know whether they are sensible in the long term. It is "myopic to base sweeping constitutional principles upon the narrow experience of [a few] years." . . .

The genuinely operative portion of the opinion, then, is the Court's statement of the reasons why it agrees with the contrived consensus it has found, that the "diminished capacities" of the mentally retarded render the death penalty excessive. The Court's analysis rests on two fundamental assumptions: that the Eighth Amendment prohibits excessive punishments, and that sentencing juries or judges are unable to account properly for the "diminished capacities" of the retarded. The first assumption is wrong, as I explained at length in Harmelin v. Michigan, 501 U.S. 957, 966–990 (1991).[a] The Eighth Amendment is addressed to always-

[a] In *Harmelin,* a closely divided Court held that a mandatory life sentence without possibility of parole for possessing 672 grams of cocaine did not violate the Eighth Amendment.—[Footnote by eds.]

and-everywhere "cruel" punishments, such as the rack and the thumbscrew. But where the punishment is in itself permissible, "[t]he Eighth Amendment is not a ratchet, whereby a temporary consensus on leniency for a particular crime fixes a permanent constitutional maximum, disabling the States from giving effect to altered beliefs and responding to changed social conditions." The second assumption—inability of judges or juries to take proper account of mental retardation—is not only unsubstantiated, but contradicts the immemorial belief, here and in England, that they play an *indispensable* role in such matters. . . .

[W]hat scientific analysis can possibly show that a mildly retarded individual who commits an exquisite torture-killing is "no more culpable" than the "average" murderer in a holdup-gone-wrong or a domestic dispute? Or a moderately retarded individual who commits a series of 20 exquisite torture-killings? Surely culpability, and deservedness of the most severe retribution, depends not merely (if at all) upon the mental capacity of the criminal (above the level where he is able to distinguish right from wrong) but also upon the depravity of the crime—which is precisely why this sort of question has traditionally been thought answerable not by a categorical rule of the sort the Court today imposes upon all trials, but rather by the sentencer's weighing of the circumstances (both degree of retardation and depravity of crime) in the particular case. The fact that juries continue to sentence mentally retarded offenders to death for extreme crimes shows that society's moral outrage sometimes demands execution of retarded offenders. By what principle of law, science, or logic can the Court pronounce that this is wrong? There is none. Once the Court admits (as it does) that mental retardation does not render the offender morally *blameless*, there is no basis for saying that the death penalty is *never* appropriate retribution, no matter *how* heinous the crime. As long as a mentally retarded offender knows "the difference between right and wrong," only the sentencer can assess whether his retardation reduces his culpability enough to exempt him from the death penalty for the particular murder in question. . . .

[S]urely the deterrent effect of a penalty is adequately vindicated if it successfully deters many, but not all, of the target class. Virginia's death penalty, for example, does not fail of its deterrent effect simply because *some* criminals are unaware that Virginia *has* the death penalty. In other words, the supposed fact that *some* retarded criminals cannot fully appreciate the death penalty has nothing to do with the deterrence rationale, but is simply an echo of the arguments denying a retribution rationale, discussed and rejected above. . . .

Today's opinion adds one more to the long list of substantive and procedural requirements impeding imposition of the death penalty imposed under this Court's assumed power to invent a death-is-different jurisprudence. . . .

This newest invention promises to be more effective than any of the others in turning the process of capital trial into a game. One need only read the definitions of mental retardation adopted by the American Association on Mental Retardation and the American Psychiatric Association to realize that the symptoms of this condition can readily be feigned. . . .

Perhaps these practical difficulties will not be experienced by the minority of capital-punishment States that have very recently changed mental retardation from a mitigating factor (to be accepted or rejected by the sentencer) to an absolute immunity. Time will tell—and the brief time those States have had the new disposition in place (an average of 6.8 years) is surely not enough. But if the practical difficulties do not appear, and if the other states share the Court's perceived moral consensus that *all* mental retardation renders the death penalty inappropriate for *all* crimes, then that majority will presumably follow suit. But there is no justification for this Court's pushing them into the experiment—and turning the experiment into a permanent practice—on constitutional pretext. Nothing has changed the accuracy of Matthew Hale's endorsement of the common law's traditional method for taking account of guilt-reducing factors, written over three centuries ago:

> [Determination of a person's incapacity] is a matter of great difficulty, partly from the easiness of counterfeiting this disability . . . and partly from the variety of the degrees of this infirmity, whereof some are sufficient, and some are insufficient to excuse persons in capital offenses. . . .
>
> Yet the law of England hath afforded the best method of trial, that is possible, of this and all other matters of fact, namely, by a jury of twelve men all concurring in the same judgment, by the testimony of witnesses . . . , and by the inspection and direction of the judge. 1 Pleas of the Crown, at 32–33.

### 4. QUESTIONS ON *ATKINS*

*Atkins* raises many interesting questions of both theory and implementation. On the methodology of proportionality analysis, who has the better of the argument, Justice Stevens or Justice Scalia? What should be the relative weight of the "objective indicators" of societal consensus and the Court's "subjective" judgment about the suitability of the death penalty in relation to the culpability of the offender? How significant was the legislative activity between 1989 and 2002? In omitted portions of the opinions, the Justices disagreed about the relevance of evidence of international law and practice and public opinion polls. Should international human rights norms have any bearing on the interpretation of the Eighth Amendment?

### 5. DEFINING INTELLECTUAL DISABILITY: *HALL V. FLORIDA*

One of the intriguing aspects of *Atkins* is that the Court declined to define mental retardation (now called intellectual disability[b]), leaving it to the states to do so. Most states have adopted a clinical definition drawn from the diagnostic criteria in the American Psychiatric Association's

[b] The leading professional organizations in the field replaced the term "mental retardation" with "intellectual disability" between the decisions in *Atkins* and *Hall,* The Supreme Court adopted the new terminology in *Hall*.

diagnostic manual (the current version is DSM–V) or the manual of the American Association on Intellectual and Developmental Disabilities.[c] Under the prevailing definition, intellectual disability is characterized by significant deficits in both intellectual and adaptive functioning. Typically the diagnosis must be based on the defendant's performance on standardized measures of intelligence and "adaptive behavior" that is two standard deviations from the mean. But a score on any psychological test is subject to measurement error, so a score of, say 70 does not "mean" 70—it means a prediction that, for example, the person would score between 66 and 74 on this test 66% of the time. Ultimately, the diagnosis requires a clinical judgment that takes account of all of the evidence regarding impairments in both intellectual and adaptive functioning. Thus, it is possible that a person who demonstrably exhibits significant deficits in adaptive behavior might be diagnosed as mentally retarded even if the scoring on an IQ test is somewhat higher than 70. (Similarly, a person who scores below 70 on an IQ test might not be diagnosed as intellectually disabled if adaptive behavior is not significantly impaired.)

Although the Florida statute codified the professional definition of intellectual disability, the Florida Supreme Court ruled that a person whose IQ test score is above 70 does not, as a matter of law, have an intellectual disability and is barred from presenting other evidence to establish the diagnosis. This rule was applied to Freddie Lee Hall, despite 7 scores ranging from 71 to 80 over a 40-year period and lifelong diagnoses of intellectual disability.[d] The Florida Supreme Court upheld his death sentence, but the Supreme Court reversed by a five-to-four vote. Hall v. Florida, ___ U.S. ___, 134 S.Ct. 1986 (2014). In an opinion by Justice Kennedy, the Court noted that Florida's "70 IQ" rule "disregards established medical practice in two interrelated ways. It takes an IQ score as final and conclusive evidence of a defendant's intellectual capacity when experts in the field would consider other evidence. It also relies on a purportedly scientific measurement of the defendant's abilities, his IQ score, while refusing to recognize that the score is, on its own terms, imprecise." The Court continued:

> Intellectual disability is a condition, not a number. . . . [I]n using these scores to assess a defendant's eligibility for the death penalty, a state must afford these test scores the same studied skepticism that those who design and use the tests do, and understand that a IQ test score represents a range rather than a fixed number. A state that ignores the inherent imprecision of these tests risks executing a person who suffers from an intellectual disability. [W]hen a defendant's test score falls within the test's acknowledged and inherent margin of error, the defendant must be able to present additional evidence of intellectual disability, including testimony regarding adaptive deficits. . . . The Florida statute, as interpreted by its courts, misuses IQ score on its own

[c] As Justice Scalia pointed out in *Atkins*, one state (Kansas) exempts offenders with mental retardation only if they are found to meet the Model Penal Code criteria for the insanity defense (lack of substantial capacity to appreciate the wrongfulness of the conduct or conform conduct to the requirements of law). Is this constitutional?

[d] Hall had two scores below 70, but they were excluded for evidentiary reasons For discussion of the challenges of implementing *Atkins*, see Richard J. Bonnie and Katherine Gustafson, The Challenge of Implementing *Atkins v. Virginia*: How Legislatures and Courts Can Promote Accurate Assessments and Adjudications of Mental Retardation in Death Penalty Cases, 41 U. Rich. L Rev. 811 (2007).

terms; and this in turn, bars consideration of evidence that must be considered in determining whether a defendant in a capital case has intellectual disability.

Justice Alito's dissenting opinion accused the Court of discarding its ruling in *Atkins* that the Eighth Amendment "does not mandate the use of a single method for identifying" intellectually disabled defendants and substituting "the positions adopted by private professional associations" for the "evolving standards of a maturing society" as the grounding for Eighth Amendment analysis. Is he right? Who should define "intellectual disability" for constitutional purposes? And who should decide whether a particular defendant is intellectually disabled? Under *Atkins* and *Hall*, is this determination a legal judgment informed by expert opinion? Or is the ultimate issue simply a factual question about the proper clinical diagnosis? Are there any other contexts in the criminal law where the defendant's guilt or punishment is authoritatively determined by a clinical diagnosis?

## Roper v. Simmons

Supreme Court of the United States, 2005.
543 U.S. 551.

■ JUSTICE KENNEDY delivered the opinion of the Court.

This case requires us to address, for the second time in a decade and a half, whether it is permissible under the Eighth and Fourteenth Amendments to the Constitution of the United States to execute a juvenile offender who was older than 15 but younger than 18 when he committed a capital crime. In Stanford v. Kentucky, 492 U. S. 361 (1989), a divided Court rejected the proposition that the Constitution bars capital punishment for juvenile offenders in this age group. We reconsider the question.

I

At the age of 17, when he was still a junior in high school, Christopher Simmons, committed murder. About nine months later, after he had turned 18, he was tried and sentenced to death. There is little doubt that Simmons was the instigator of the crime. Before its commission Simmons said he wanted to murder someone. In chilling, callous terms he talked about his plan, discussing it for the most part with two friends, Charles Benjamin and John Tessmer, then aged 15 and 16 respectively. Simmons proposed to commit burglary and murder by breaking and entering, tying up a victim, and throwing the victim off a bridge. Simmons assured his friends they could "get away with it" because they were minors.

The three met at about 2 a.m. on the night of the murder, but Tessmer left before the other two set out. (The State later charged Tessmer with conspiracy, but dropped the charge in exchange for his testimony against Simmons.) Simmons and Benjamin entered the home of the victim, Shirley Crook, after reaching through an open window and unlocking the back door. Simmons turned on a hallway light. Awakened, Mrs. Crook called out, "Who's there?" In response Simmons entered Mrs. Crook's bedroom, where he recognized her from a previous car accident involving them both. Simmons later admitted this confirmed his resolve to murder her.

Using duct tape to cover her eyes and mouth and bind her hands, the two perpetrators put Mrs. Crook in her minivan and drove to a state park. They reinforced the bindings, covered her head with a towel, and walked her to a railroad trestle spanning the Meramec River. There they tied her hands and feet together with electrical wire, wrapped her whole face in duct tape and threw her from the bridge, drowning her in the waters below.

By the afternoon of September 9, Steven Crook had returned home from an overnight trip, found his bedroom in disarray, and reported his wife missing. On the same afternoon fishermen recovered the victim's body from the river. Simmons, meanwhile, was bragging about the killing, telling friends he had killed a woman "because the bitch seen my face." . . .

The state charged Simmons with burglary, kidnaping, stealing, and murder in the first degree. As Simmons was 17 at the time of the crime, he was outside the criminal jurisdiction of Missouri's juvenile court system. He was tried as an adult. At trial the State introduced Simmons' confession and the videotaped reenactment of the crime, along with testimony that Simmons discussed the crime in advance and bragged about it later. The defense called no witnesses in the guilt phase. The jury having returned a verdict of murder, the trial proceeded to the penalty phase.

The state sought the death penalty. As aggravating factors, the state submitted that the murder was committed for the purpose of receiving money; was committed for the purpose of avoiding, interfering with, or preventing lawful arrest of the defendant; and involved depravity of mind and was outrageously and wantonly vile, horrible, and inhuman. The state called Shirley Crook's husband, daughter, and two sisters, who presented moving evidence of the devastation her death had brought to their lives.

In mitigation Simmons' attorneys first called an officer of the Missouri juvenile justice system, who testified that Simmons had no prior convictions and that no previous charges had been filed against him. Simmons' mother, father, two younger half brothers, a neighbor, and a friend took the stand to tell the jurors of the close relationships they had formed with Simmons and to plead for mercy on his behalf. Simmons' mother, in particular, testified to the responsibility Simmons demonstrated in taking care of his two younger half brothers and of his grandmother and to his capacity to show love for them.

During closing arguments, both the prosecutor and defense counsel addressed Simmons' age, which the trial judge had instructed the jurors they could consider as a mitigating factor. Defense counsel reminded the jurors that juveniles of Simmons' age cannot drink, serve on juries, or even see certain movies, because "the legislatures have wisely decided that individuals of a certain age aren't responsible enough." Defense counsel argued that Simmons' age should make "a huge difference to [the jurors] in deciding just exactly what sort of punishment to make." In rebuttal, the prosecutor gave the following response: "Age, he says. Think about age. Seventeen years old. Isn't that scary? Doesn't that scare you? Mitigating? Quite the contrary I submit. Quite the contrary."

The jury recommended the death penalty after finding the state had proved each of the three aggravating factors submitted to it. Accepting the jury's recommendation, the trial judge imposed the death penalty. . . .

After [initial post-conviction proceedings] in Simmons' case had run their course, this Court held that the Eighth and Fourteenth Amendments prohibit the execution of a mentally retarded person. Atkins v. Virginia, 536 U. S. 304 (2002). Simmons filed a new petition for state postconviction relief, arguing that the reasoning of *Atkins* established that the Constitution prohibits the execution of a juvenile who was under 18 when the crime was committed. The Missouri Supreme Court agreed. [I]t set aside Simmons' death sentence and resentenced him to life imprisonment without eligibility for probation, parole, or release. . . . We granted certiorari and now affirm.

II

. . . In Thompson v. Oklahoma, 487 U. S. 815 (1988), a plurality of the Court determined that our standards of decency do not permit the execution of any offender under the age of 16 at the time of the crime. . . . The next year, in Stanford v. Kentucky, 492 U. S. 361 (1989), the Court, over a dissenting opinion joined by four Justices, referred to contemporary standards of decency in this country and concluded the Eighth and Fourteenth Amendments did not proscribe the execution of juvenile offenders over 15 but under 18. . . . Just as the *Atkins* Court reconsidered the issue decided in *Penry*, we now reconsider the issue decided in *Stanford*. The beginning point is a review of objective indicia of consensus, as expressed in particular by the enactments of legislatures that have addressed the question. This data gives us essential instruction. We then must determine, in the exercise of our own independent judgment, whether the death penalty is a disproportionate punishment for juveniles.

III

A

The evidence of national consensus against the death penalty for juveniles is similar, and in some respects parallel, to the evidence *Atkins* held sufficient to demonstrate a national consensus against the death penalty for the mentally retarded. When *Atkins* was decided, 30 States prohibited the death penalty for the mentally retarded. This number comprised 12 that had abandoned the death penalty altogether, and 18 that maintained it but excluded the mentally retarded from its reach. By a similar calculation in this case, 30 States prohibit the juvenile death penalty, comprising 12 that have rejected the death penalty altogether and 18 that maintain it but, by express provision or judicial interpretation, exclude juveniles from its reach. *Atkins* emphasized that even in the 20 States without formal prohibition, the practice of executing the mentally retarded was infrequent. Since *Penry*, only five States had executed offenders known to have an IQ under 70. In the present case, too, even in the 20 States without a formal prohibition on executing juveniles, the practice is infrequent. Since *Stanford*, six States have executed prisoners for crimes committed as juveniles. In the past 10 years, only three have done so: Oklahoma, Texas, and Virginia. In December 2003 the Governor of Kentucky decided to spare the life of Kevin Stanford, and commuted his sentence to one of life imprisonment without parole, with the declaration that "[w]e ought not be executing people who, legally, were children." By this act the Governor ensured Kentucky would not add itself to the list of States that have executed juveniles within the last 10 years even by the execution of the very defendant whose death sentence the Court had upheld in *Stanford v. Kentucky*.

There is, to be sure, at least one difference between the evidence of consensus in *Atkins* and in this case. Impressive in *Atkins* was the rate of abolition of the death penalty for the mentally retarded. Sixteen States that permitted the execution of the mentally retarded at the time of *Penry* had prohibited the practice by the time we heard *Atkins*. By contrast, the rate of change in reducing the incidence of the juvenile death penalty, or in taking specific steps to abolish it, has been slower. Five States that allowed the juvenile death penalty at the time of *Stanford* have abandoned it in the intervening 15 years—four through legislative enactments and one through judicial decision.

Though less dramatic than the change from *Penry* to *Atkins*, we still consider the change from *Stanford* to this case to be significant. . . . The number of States that have abandoned capital punishment for juvenile offenders since *Stanford* is smaller than the number of States that abandoned capital punishment for the mentally retarded after *Penry;* yet we think the same consistency of direction of change has been demonstrated. Since *Stanford*, no State that previously prohibited capital punishment for juveniles has reinstated it. This fact, coupled with the trend toward abolition of the juvenile death penalty, carries special force in light of the general popularity of anticrime legislation, and in light of the particular trend in recent years toward cracking down on juvenile crime in other respects. Any difference between this case and *Atkins* with respect to the pace of abolition is thus counterbalanced by the consistent direction of the change.

The slower pace of abolition of the juvenile death penalty over the past 15 years, moreover, may have a simple explanation. When we heard *Penry*, only two death penalty States had already prohibited the execution of the mentally retarded. When we heard *Stanford*, by contrast, 12 death penalty States had already prohibited the execution of any juvenile under 18, and 15 had prohibited the execution of any juvenile under 17. If anything, this shows that the impropriety of executing juveniles between 16 and 18 years of age gained wide recognition earlier than the impropriety of executing the mentally retarded. . . .

Petitioner cannot show national consensus in favor of capital punishment for juveniles but still resists the conclusion that any consensus exists against it. Petitioner supports this position with, in particular, the observation that when the Senate ratified the International Covenant on Civil and Political Rights (ICCPR), Dec. 19, 1966, 999 U. N. T. S. 171 (entered into force Mar. 23, 1976), it did so subject to the President's proposed reservation regarding Article 6(5) of that treaty, which prohibits capital punishment for juveniles. This reservation at best provides only faint support for petitioner's argument. First, the reservation was passed in 1992; since then, five States have abandoned capital punishment for juveniles. Second, Congress considered the issue when enacting the Federal Death Penalty Act in 1994, and determined that the death penalty should not extend to juveniles. See 18 U. S. C. § 3591. The reservation to Article 6(5) of the ICCPR provides minimal evidence that there is not now a national consensus against juvenile executions.

As in *Atkins*, the objective indicia of consensus in this case—the rejection of the juvenile death penalty in the majority of States; the infrequency of its use even where it remains on the books; and the consistency in the trend toward abolition of the practice—provide sufficient evidence that today our society views juveniles, in the words *Atkins* used respecting the mentally retarded, as "categorically less culpable than the average criminal."

B

A majority of States have rejected the imposition of the death penalty on juvenile offenders under 18, and we now hold this is required by the Eighth Amendment.

Because the death penalty is the most severe punishment, the Eighth Amendment applies to it with special force. Capital punishment must be limited to those offenders who commit " 'a narrow category of the most serious crimes' and whose extreme culpability makes them 'the most deserving of execution.' " *Atkins*. . . .

Three general differences between juveniles under 18 and adults demonstrate that juvenile offenders cannot with reliability be classified among the worst offenders. First, as any parent knows and as the scientific and sociological studies respondent and his amici cite tend to confirm, "[a] lack of maturity and an underdeveloped sense of responsibility are found in youth more often than in adults and are more understandable among the young. These qualities often result in impetuous and ill-considered actions and decisions." It has been noted that "adolescents are overrepresented statistically in virtually every category of reckless behavior." Arnett, Reckless Behavior in Adolescence: A Developmental Perspective, 12 Developmental Review 339 (1992). In recognition of the comparative immaturity and irresponsibility of juveniles, almost every State prohibits those under 18 years of age from voting, serving on juries, or marrying without parental consent.

The second area of difference is that juveniles are more vulnerable or susceptible to negative influences and outside pressures, including peer pressure. This is explained in part by the prevailing circumstance that juveniles have less control, or less experience with control, over their own environment. See Steinberg & Scott, Less Guilty by Reason of Adolescence: Developmental Immaturity, Diminished Responsibility, and the Juvenile Death Penalty, 58 Am. Psychologist 1009, 1014 (2003) (hereinafter Steinberg & Scott) ("[A]s legal minors, [juveniles] lack the freedom that adults have to extricate themselves from a criminogenic setting").

The third broad difference is that the character of a juvenile is not as well formed as that of an adult. The personality traits of juveniles are more transitory, less fixed. See generally E. Erikson, Identity: Youth and Crisis (1968).

These differences render suspect any conclusion that a juvenile falls among the worst offenders. The susceptibility of juveniles to immature and irresponsible behavior means "their irresponsible conduct is not as morally reprehensible as that of an adult." Their own vulnerability and comparative lack of control over their immediate surroundings mean juveniles have a greater claim than adults to be forgiven for failing to escape negative influences in their whole environment. The reality that juveniles still struggle to define their identity means it is less supportable to conclude that even a heinous crime committed by a juvenile is evidence of irretrievably depraved character. From a moral standpoint it would be misguided to equate the failings of a minor with those of an adult, for a greater possibility exists that a minor's character deficiencies will be reformed. Indeed, "[t]he relevance of youth as a mitigating factor derives from the fact that the signature qualities of youth are transient; as individuals mature, the impetuousness and recklessness that may dominate in younger years can subside."

In *Thompson*, a plurality of the Court recognized the import of these characteristics with respect to juveniles under 16, and relied on them to hold that the Eighth Amendment prohibited the imposition of the death penalty on juveniles below that age. We conclude the same reasoning applies to all juvenile offenders under 18.

Once the diminished culpability of juveniles is recognized, it is evident that the penological justifications for the death penalty apply to them with lesser force than to adults. We have held there are two distinct social purposes served by the death penalty: "retribution and deterrence of capital crimes by prospective offenders." As for retribution, we remarked in *Atkins* that "[i]f the culpability of the average murderer is insufficient to justify the most extreme sanction available to the state, the lesser culpability of the mentally retarded offender surely does not merit that form of retribution." The same conclusions follow from the lesser culpability of the juvenile offender. Whether viewed as an attempt to express the community's moral outrage or as an attempt to right the balance for the wrong to the victim, the case for retribution is not as strong with a minor as with an adult. Retribution is not proportional if the law's most severe penalty is imposed on one whose culpability or blameworthiness is diminished, to a substantial degree, by reason of youth and immaturity.

As for deterrence, it is unclear whether the death penalty has a significant or even measurable deterrent effect on juveniles, as counsel for the petitioner acknowledged at oral argument. In general we leave to legislatures the assessment of the efficacy of various criminal penalty schemes. Here, however, the absence of evidence of deterrent effect is of special concern because the same characteristics that render juveniles less culpable than adults suggest as well that juveniles will be less susceptible to deterrence. In particular, as the plurality observed in *Thompson*, "[t]he likelihood that the teenage offender has made the kind of cost-benefit analysis that attaches any weight to the possibility of execution is so remote as to be virtually nonexistent." To the extent the juvenile death penalty might have residual deterrent effect, it is worth noting that the punishment of life imprisonment without the possibility of parole is itself a severe sanction, in particular for a young person.

In concluding that neither retribution nor deterrence provides adequate justification for imposing the death penalty on juvenile offenders, we cannot deny or overlook the brutal crimes too many juvenile offenders have committed. Certainly it can be argued, although we by no means concede the point, that a rare case might arise in which a juvenile offender has sufficient psychological maturity, and at the same time demonstrates sufficient depravity, to merit a sentence of death. Indeed, this possibility is the linchpin of one contention pressed by petitioner and his amici. They assert that even assuming the truth of the observations we have made about juveniles' diminished culpability in general, jurors nonetheless should be allowed to consider mitigating arguments related to youth on a case-by-case basis, and in some cases to impose the death penalty if justified. A central feature of death penalty sentencing is a particular assessment of the circumstances of the crime and the characteristics of the offender. The system is designed to consider both aggravating and mitigating circumstances, including youth, in every case. Given this Court's own insistence on individualized consideration, petitioner maintains that it is both arbitrary and unnecessary to adopt a categorical rule barring imposition of the death penalty on any offender under 18 years of age.

We disagree. The differences between juvenile and adult offenders are too marked and well understood to risk allowing a youthful person to receive the death penalty despite insufficient culpability. An unacceptable likelihood exists that the brutality or cold-blooded nature of any particular crime would overpower mitigating arguments based on youth as a matter of course, even where the juvenile offender's objective immaturity, vulnerability, and lack of true depravity should require a sentence less severe than death. In some cases a defendant's youth may even be counted against him. In this very case, as we noted above, the prosecutor argued Simmons' youth was aggravating rather than mitigating. While this sort of overreaching could be corrected by a particular rule to ensure that the mitigating force of youth is not overlooked, that would not address our larger concerns.

It is difficult even for expert psychologists to differentiate between the juvenile offender whose crime reflects unfortunate yet transient immaturity, and the rare juvenile offender whose crime reflects irreparable corruption. See Steinberg & Scott 1014–1016. As we understand it, this difficulty underlies the rule forbidding psychiatrists from diagnosing any patient under 18 as having antisocial personality disorder, a disorder also referred to as psychopathy or sociopathy, and which is characterized by callousness, cynicism, and contempt for the feelings, rights, and suffering of others. American Psychiatric Association, Diagnostic and Statistical Manual of Mental Disorders 701–06 (4th ed. text rev. 2000). If trained psychiatrists with the advantage of clinical testing and observation refrain, despite diagnostic expertise, from assessing any juvenile under 18 as having antisocial personality disorder, we conclude that States should refrain from asking jurors to issue a far graver condemnation—that a juvenile offender merits the death penalty. When a juvenile offender commits a heinous crime, the State can exact forfeiture of some of the most basic liberties, but the State cannot extinguish his life and his potential to attain a mature understanding of his own humanity.

Drawing the line at 18 years of age is subject, of course, to the objections always raised against categorical rules. The qualities that distinguish juveniles from adults do not disappear when an individual turns 18. By the same token, some under 18 have already attained a level of maturity some adults will never reach. For the reasons we have discussed, however, a line must be drawn. The plurality opinion in *Thompson* drew the line at 16. In the intervening years the *Thompson* plurality's conclusion that offenders under 16 may not be executed has not been challenged. The logic of *Thompson* extends to those who are under 18. The age of 18 is the point where society draws the line for many purposes between childhood and adulthood. It is, we conclude, the age at which the line for death eligibility ought to rest.

These considerations mean *Stanford v. Kentucky* should be deemed no longer controlling on this issue. . . .

IV

Our determination that the death penalty is disproportionate punishment for offenders under 18 finds confirmation in the stark reality that the United States is the only country in the world that continues to give official sanction to the juvenile death penalty. This reality does not become controlling, for the task of interpreting the Eighth Amendment remains our responsibility. Yet at least from the time of the Court's decision in *Trop*, the Court has referred to the laws of other countries and to international authorities as instructive for its interpretation of the Eighth Amendment's prohibition of "cruel and unusual punishments." (plurality opinion) ("The civilized nations of the world are in virtual unanimity that statelessness is not to be imposed as punishment for crime"). . . .

As respondent and a number of amici emphasize, Article 37 of the United Nations Convention on the Rights of the Child, which every country in the world has ratified save for the United States and Somalia, contains an express prohibition on capital punishment for crimes committed by juveniles under 18. United Nations Convention on the Rights of the Child, Art. 37, Nov. 20, 1989, 1577 U.N.T.S. 3, 28 I.L.M. 1448, 1468–1470 (entered into force Sept. 2, 1990) . . . Parallel prohibitions are contained in other significant international covenants. See ICCPR, Art. 6(5), 999 U.N.T.S., at 175 (prohibiting capital punishment for anyone under 18 at the time of offense) (signed and ratified by the United States subject to a reservation regarding Article 6(5), as noted, *supra*); American Convention on Human Rights: Pact of San Jose, Costa Rica, Art. 4(5), Nov. 22, 1969, 1144 U.N.T.S. 146 (entered into force July 19, 1978) (same); African Charter on the Rights and Welfare of the Child, Art. 5(3), OAU Doc. CAB/LEG/24.9/49 (1990) (entered into force Nov. 29, 1999) (same).

Respondent and his amici have submitted, and petitioner does not contest, that only seven countries other than the United States have executed juvenile offenders since 1990: Iran, Pakistan, Saudi Arabia, Yemen, Nigeria, the Democratic Republic of Congo, and China. Since then each of these countries has either abolished capital punishment for juveniles or made public disavowal of the practice. In sum, it is fair to say that the United States now stands alone in a world that has turned its face against the juvenile death penalty. . . .

The Eighth and Fourteenth Amendments forbid imposition of the death penalty on offenders who were under the age of 18 when their crimes were committed. The judgment of the Missouri Supreme Court setting aside the sentence of death imposed upon Christopher Simmons is affirmed.

It is so ordered.

■ JUSTICE STEVENS, with whom JUSTICE GINSBURG joins, concurring.

Perhaps even more important than our specific holding today is our reaffirmation of the basic principle that informs the Court's interpretation of the Eighth Amendment. If the meaning of that Amendment had been frozen when it was originally drafted, it would impose no impediment to the execution of seven-year-old children today. The evolving standards of decency that have driven our construction of this critically important part of the Bill of Rights foreclose any such reading of the Amendment. In the best tradition of the common law, the pace of that evolution is a matter for continuing debate; but that our understanding of the Constitution does change from time to time has been settled since John Marshall breathed life into its text. If great lawyers of his day—Alexander Hamilton, for example—were sitting with us today, I would expect them to join Justice Kennedy's opinion for the Court. In all events, I do so without hesitation.

■ JUSTICE O'CONNOR, dissenting.

The Court's decision today establishes a categorical rule forbidding the execution of any offender for any crime committed before his 18th birthday, no matter how deliberate, wanton, or cruel the offense. Neither the objective evidence of contemporary societal values, nor the Court's moral proportionality analysis, nor the two in tandem suffice to justify this ruling.

Although the Court finds support for its decision in the fact that a majority of the States now disallow capital punishment of 17-year-old offenders, it refrains from asserting that its holding is compelled by a genuine national consensus. Indeed, the evidence before us fails to demonstrate conclusively that any such consensus has emerged in the brief period since we upheld the constitutionality of this practice in Stanford v. Kentucky, 492 U. S. 361 (1989).

Instead, the rule decreed by the Court rests, ultimately, on its independent moral judgment that death is a disproportionately severe punishment for any 17-year-old offender. I do not subscribe to this judgment. Adolescents *as a class* are undoubtedly less mature, and therefore less culpable for their misconduct, than adults. But the Court has adduced no evidence impeaching the seemingly reasonable conclusion reached by many state legislatures: that at least *some* 17-year-old murderers are sufficiently mature to deserve the death penalty in an appropriate case. Nor has it been shown that capital sentencing juries are incapable of accurately assessing a youthful defendant's maturity or of giving due weight to the mitigating characteristics associated with youth.

On this record—and especially in light of the fact that so little has changed since our recent decision in *Stanford*—I would not substitute our judgment about the moral propriety of capital punishment for 17-year-old murderers for the judgments of the Nation's legislatures. Rather, I would demand a clearer showing that our society truly has set its face against this practice before reading the Eighth Amendment categorically to forbid it.

I

Let me begin by making clear that I agree with much of the Court's description of the general principles that guide our Eighth Amendment jurisprudence. The Amendment bars not only punishments that are inherently "barbaric," but also those that are "excessive in relation to the crime committed".... It is by now beyond serious dispute that the Eighth Amendment's prohibition of "cruel and unusual punishments" is not a static command. Its mandate would be little more than a dead letter today if it barred only those sanctions—like the execution of children under the age of seven—that civilized society had already repudiated in 1791....

II

Although the general principles that guide our Eighth Amendment jurisprudence afford some common ground, I part ways with the Court in applying them to the case before us.... Here, as in *Atkins*, the objective evidence of a national consensus is weaker than in most prior cases in which the Court has struck down a particular punishment under the Eighth Amendment [citing *Coker* and *Enmund*]. In my view, the objective evidence of national consensus, standing alone, was insufficient to dictate the Court's holding in *Atkins*. Rather, the compelling moral proportionality argument against capital punishment of mentally retarded offenders played a *decisive* role in persuading the Court that the practice was inconsistent with the Eighth Amendment....

It is beyond cavil that juveniles as a class are generally less mature, less responsible, and less fully formed than adults, and that these differences bear on juveniles' comparative moral culpability.... But even accepting this premise, the Court's proportionality argument fails to support its categorical rule.

First, the Court adduces no evidence whatsoever in support of its sweeping conclusion, that it is only in "rare" cases, if ever, that 17-year-old murderers are sufficiently mature and act with sufficient depravity to warrant the death penalty. The fact that juveniles are generally *less* culpable for their misconduct than adults does not necessarily mean that a 17-year-old murderer cannot be *sufficiently* culpable to merit the death penalty. At most, the Court's argument suggests that the average 17-year-old murderer is not as culpable as the average adult murderer. But an especially depraved juvenile offender may nevertheless be just as culpable as many adult offenders considered bad enough to deserve the death penalty. Similarly, the fact that the availability of the death penalty may be *less* likely to deter a juvenile from committing a capital crime does not imply that this threat cannot *effectively* deter some 17-year-olds from such an act. Surely there is an age below which no offender, no matter what his crime, can be deemed to have the cognitive or emotional maturity necessary to warrant the death penalty. But at least at the margins between adolescence and adulthood—and especially for 17-year-olds such as respondent—the relevant differences between "adults" and "juveniles" appear to be a matter of degree, rather than of kind. It follows that a legislature may reasonably conclude that at least *some* 17-year-olds can act with sufficient moral culpability, and can be sufficiently deterred by the threat of execution, that capital punishment may be warranted in an appropriate case.

Indeed, this appears to be just such a case. Christopher Simmons' murder of Shirley Crook was premeditated, wanton, and cruel in the extreme. Well before he committed this crime, Simmons declared that he wanted to kill someone. On several occasions, he discussed with two friends (ages 15 and 16) his plan to burglarize a house and to murder the victim by tying the victim up and pushing him from a bridge. Simmons said they could "get away with it" "because they were minors." In accord with this plan, Simmons and his 15-year-old accomplice broke into Mrs. Crook's home in the middle of the night, forced her from her bed, bound her, and drove her to a state park. There, they walked her to a railroad trestle spanning a river, "hog-tied" her with electrical cable, bound her face completely with duct tape, and pushed her, still alive, from the trestle. She drowned in the water below. One can scarcely imagine the terror that this woman must have suffered throughout the ordeal leading to her death. Whatever can be said about the comparative moral culpability of 17-year-olds as a general matter, Simmons' actions unquestionably reflect "a consciousness materially more depraved than that of . . . the average murderer." See *Atkins*. And Simmons' prediction that he could murder with impunity because he had not yet turned 18—though inaccurate—suggests that he *did* take into account the perceived risk of punishment in deciding whether to commit the crime. Based on this evidence, the sentencing jury certainly had reasonable grounds for concluding that, despite Simmons' youth, he "ha[d] sufficient psychological maturity when he committed this horrific murder, and at the same time demonstrate[d] sufficient depravity, to merit a sentence of death."

The Court's proportionality argument suffers from a second and closely related defect: It fails to establish that the differences in maturity between 17-year-olds and young "adults" are both universal enough and significant enough to justify a bright-line prophylactic rule against capital punishment of the former. The Court's analysis is premised on differences *in the aggregate* between juveniles and adults, which frequently do not hold true when comparing individuals. Although it may be that many 17-year-old murderers lack sufficient maturity to deserve the death penalty, some juvenile murderers may be quite mature. Chronological age is not an unfailing measure of psychological development, and common experience suggests that many 17-year-olds are more mature than the average young "adult." In short, the class of offenders exempted from capital punishment by today's decision is too broad and too diverse to warrant a categorical prohibition. Indeed, the age-based line drawn by the Court is indefensibly arbitrary—it quite likely will protect a number of offenders who are mature enough to deserve the death penalty and may well leave vulnerable many who are not.

For purposes of proportionality analysis, 17-year-olds as a class are qualitatively and materially different from the mentally retarded. "Mentally retarded" offenders, as we understood that category in *Atkins*, are *defined* by precisely the characteristics which render death an excessive punishment. A mentally retarded person is, "by definition," one whose cognitive and behavioral capacities have been proven to fall below a certain minimum. Accordingly, for purposes of our decision in *Atkins*, the mentally retarded are not merely *less* blameworthy for their misconduct or *less* likely to be deterred by the death penalty than others. Rather, a mentally retarded offender is one whose demonstrated impairments make it so highly unlikely that he is culpable enough to deserve the death penalty or that he could have been deterred by the threat of death, that execution is not a defensible punishment. There is no such inherent or accurate fit between an offender's chronological age and the personal limitations which the Court believes make capital punishment excessive for 17-year-old murderers. Moreover, it defies common sense to suggest that 17-year-olds as a class are somehow equivalent to mentally retarded persons with regard to culpability or susceptibility to deterrence. Seventeen-year-olds may, on average, be less mature than adults, but that lesser maturity simply cannot be equated with the major, lifelong impairments suffered by the mentally retarded.

The proportionality issues raised by the Court clearly implicate Eighth Amendment concerns. But these concerns may properly be addressed not by means of an arbitrary, categorical age-based rule, but rather through individualized sentencing in which juries are required to give appropriate mitigating weight to the defendant's immaturity, his susceptibility to outside pressures, his cognizance of the consequences of his actions, and so forth. In that way the constitutional response can be tailored to the specific problem it is meant to remedy. . . .

Although the prosecutor's apparent attempt to use respondent's youth as an aggravating circumstance in this case is troubling, that conduct was never challenged with specificity in the lower courts and is not directly at issue here. As the Court itself suggests, such "overreaching" would best be addressed, if at all, through a more narrowly tailored remedy. The Court argues that sentencing juries cannot accurately evaluate a youthful offender's maturity or give appropriate weight to the mitigating characteristics related to youth. But, again, the Court presents no real evidence—and the record appears to contain none—supporting this claim. Perhaps more importantly, the Court fails to explain why this duty should be so different from, or so much more difficult than, that of assessing and giving proper effect to any other qualitative capital sentencing factor. I would not be so quick to conclude that the constitutional safeguards, the sentencing juries, and the trial judges upon which we place so much reliance in all capital cases are inadequate in this narrow context.

I turn, finally, to the Court's discussion of foreign and international law. Without question, there has been a global trend in recent years towards abolishing capital punishment for under-18 offenders. Very few, if any, countries other than the United States now permit this practice in law or in fact. While acknowledging that the actions and views of other countries do not dictate the outcome of our Eighth Amendment inquiry, the Court asserts that "the overwhelming weight of international opinion against the juvenile death penalty . . . does provide respected and significant confirmation for [its] own conclusions." Because I do not believe that a genuine *national* consensus against the juvenile death penalty has yet developed, and because I do not believe the Court's moral proportionality argument justifies a categorical, age-based constitutional rule, I can assign no such *confirmatory* role to the international consensus described by the Court. In short, the evidence of an international consensus does not alter my determination that the Eighth Amendment does not, at this time, forbid capital punishment of 17-year-old murderers in all cases.

Nevertheless, I disagree with Justice Scalia's contention that foreign and international law have no place in our Eighth Amendment jurisprudence. Over the course of nearly half a century, the Court has consistently referred to foreign and international law as relevant to its assessment of evolving standards of decency. . . . [T]his Nation's evolving understanding of human dignity certainly is neither wholly isolated from, nor inherently at odds with, the values prevailing in other countries. On the contrary, we should not be surprised to find congruence between domestic and international values, especially where the international community has reached clear agreement—expressed in international law or in the domestic laws of individual countries—that a particular form of punishment is inconsistent with fundamental human rights. At least, the existence of an international consensus of this nature can serve to confirm the reasonableness of a consonant and genuine American consensus. The instant case presents no such domestic consensus, however, and the recent emergence of an otherwise global consensus does not alter that basic fact.

Reasonable minds can differ as to the minimum age at which commission of a serious crime should expose the defendant to the death penalty, if at all. Many jurisdictions have abolished capital punishment altogether, while many others have determined that even the most heinous crime, if committed before the age of 18, should not be punishable by death. Indeed, were my office that of a legislator, rather than a judge, then I, too, would be inclined to support legislation setting a minimum age of 18 in this context. But a significant number of States, including Missouri, have decided to make the death penalty potentially available for 17-year-old capital murderers such as respondent. Without a clearer showing that a genuine national consensus forbids the execution of such offenders, this Court should not substitute its own "inevitably subjective judgment" on how best to resolve this difficult moral question for the judgments of the Nation's democratically elected legislatures. I respectfully dissent.

■ JUSTICE SCALIA, with whom THE CHIEF JUSTICE [Rehnquist] and JUSTICE THOMAS join, dissenting. . . .

Because I do not believe that the meaning of our Eighth Amendment, any more than the meaning of other provisions of our Constitution, should be determined by the subjective views of five Members of this Court and like-minded foreigners, I dissent. . . .

I

Words have no meaning if the views of less than 50% of death penalty States can constitute a national consensus. Our previous cases have required overwhelming opposition to a challenged practice, generally over a long period of time. In *Coker*, a plurality concluded the Eighth Amendment prohibited capital punishment for rape of an adult woman where only one jurisdiction authorized such punishment. The plurality also observed that "[a]t no time in the last 50 years ha[d] a majority of States authorized death as a punishment for rape." In Ford v. Wainwright, 477 U. S. 399, 408 (1986), we held execution of the insane unconstitutional, tracing the roots of this prohibition to the common law and noting that "no State in the union permits the execution of the insane." In *Enmund*, we invalidated capital punishment imposed for participation in a robbery in which an accomplice committed murder, because 78% of all death penalty States prohibited this punishment. Even there we expressed some hesitation, because the legislative judgment was neither "wholly unanimous among state legislatures . . . nor as compelling as the legislative judgments considered in *Coker*." By contrast, agreement among 42% of death penalty States in *Stanford*, which the Court appears to believe was correctly decided at the time, was insufficient to show a national consensus.

In an attempt to keep afloat its implausible assertion of national consensus, the Court throws overboard a proposition well established in our Eighth Amendment jurisprudence. "It should be observed," the Court says, "that the *Stanford* Court should have considered those States that had abandoned the death penalty altogether as part of the consensus against the juvenile death penalty . . . ; a State's decision to bar the death penalty altogether of necessity demonstrates a judgment that the death penalty is inappropriate for all offenders, including juveniles." The insinuation that the Court's new method of counting contradicts only "the *Stanford* Court" is misleading. *None* of our cases dealing with an alleged constitutional limitation upon the death penalty has counted, as States supporting a consensus in favor of that limitation, States that have eliminated the death penalty entirely. . . .

Recognizing that its national-consensus argument was weak compared with our earlier cases, the *Atkins* Court found additional support in the fact that 16 States had prohibited execution of mentally retarded individuals since *Penry v. Lynaugh*. Indeed, the *Atkins* Court distinguished *Stanford* on that very ground, explaining that "[a]lthough we decided *Stanford* on the same day as *Penry*, apparently *only two* state legislatures have raised the threshold age for imposition of the death penalty." Now, the Court says a legislative change in four States is "significant" enough to trigger a constitutional prohibition. It is amazing to think that this subtle shift in numbers can take the issue entirely off the table for legislative debate. . . .

II

Of course, the real force driving today's decision is not the actions of four state legislatures, but the Court's "own judgment" that murderers younger than 18 can never be as morally culpable as older counterparts. . . .

Today's opinion provides a perfect example of why judges are ill equipped to make the type of legislative judgments the Court insists on making here. To support its opinion that States should be prohibited from imposing the death penalty on anyone who committed murder before age 18, the Court looks to scientific and sociological studies, picking and choosing those that support its position. It never explains why those particular studies are methodologically sound; none was ever entered into evidence or tested in an adversarial proceeding.

We need not look far to find studies contradicting the Court's conclusions. As petitioner points out, the American Psychological Association (APA), which claims in this case that scientific evidence shows persons under 18 lack the ability to take moral responsibility for their decisions, has previously taken precisely the opposite position before this very Court. In its brief in *Hodgson v. Minnesota,* 497 U.S. 417 (1990), the APA found a "rich body of research" showing that juveniles are mature enough to decide whether to obtain an abortion without parental involvement. The APA brief, citing psychology treatises and studies too numerous to list here, asserted: "[B]y middle adolescence (age 14–15) young people develop abilities similar to adults in reasoning about moral dilemmas, understanding social rules and laws, [and] reasoning about interpersonal relationships and interpersonal problems." Given the nuances of scientific methodology and conflicting views, courts—which can only consider the limited evidence on the record before them—are ill equipped to determine which view of science is the right one. Legislatures "are better qualified to weigh and 'evaluate the results of statistical studies in terms of their own local conditions and with a flexibility of approach that is not available to the courts.' " McCleskey v. Kemp, 481 U.S. 279, 319 (1987).

Even putting aside questions of methodology, the studies cited by the Court offer scant support for a categorical prohibition of the death penalty for murderers under 18. At most, these studies conclude that, *on average*, or *in most cases*, persons under 18 are unable to take moral responsibility for their actions. Not one of the cited studies opines that all individuals under 18 are unable to appreciate the nature of their crimes.

Moreover, the cited studies describe only adolescents who engage in risky or antisocial behavior, as many young people do. Murder, however, is more than just risky or antisocial behavior. It is entirely consistent to believe that young people often act impetuously and lack judgment, but, at the same time, to believe that those who commit premeditated murder are—at least sometimes—just as culpable as adults. Christopher Simmons, who was only seven months shy of his 18th birthday when he murdered Shirley Crook, described to his friends *beforehand*—"[i]n chilling, callous terms," as the Court puts it—the murder he planned to commit. He then broke into the home of an innocent woman, bound her with duct tape and electrical wire, and threw her off a bridge alive and conscious. In their amici brief, the States of Alabama, Delaware, Oklahoma, Texas, Utah, and Virginia offer additional examples of murders committed by individuals under 18 that involve truly monstrous acts. . . . Though these cases are assuredly the exception rather than the rule, the studies the Court cites in no way justify a constitutional imperative that prevents legislatures and juries from treating exceptional cases in an exceptional way—by determining that some murders are not just the acts of happy-go-lucky teenagers, but heinous crimes deserving of death.

That "almost every State prohibits those under 18 years of age from voting, serving on juries, or marrying without parental consent," is patently irrelevant—and is yet another resurrection of an argument that this Court gave a decent burial in *Stanford*. . . . As we explained in *Stanford*, it is "absurd to think that one must be mature enough to drive carefully, to drink responsibly, or to vote intelligently, in order to be mature enough to understand that murdering another human being is profoundly wrong, and to conform one's conduct to that most minimal of all civilized standards." Serving on a jury or entering into marriage also involve decisions far more sophisticated than the simple decision not to take another's life.

Moreover, the age statutes the Court lists "set the appropriate ages for the operation of a system that makes its determinations in gross, and that does not conduct individualized maturity tests." The criminal justice system, by contrast, provides for individualized consideration of each defendant. In capital cases, this Court requires the sentencer to make an individualized determination, which includes weighing aggravating factors and mitigating factors, such as youth. In other contexts where individualized consideration is provided, we have recognized that at least some minors will be mature enough to make difficult decisions that involve moral considerations. For instance, we have struck down abortion statutes that do not allow minors deemed mature by courts to bypass parental notification provisions. See, e.g., Bellotti v. Baird, 443 U.S. 622, 643–44 (1979) (opinion of Powell, J.); Planned Parenthood of Central Mo. v. Danforth, 428 U.S. 52, 74–75 (1976). It is hard to see why this context should be any different. Whether to obtain an abortion is surely a much more complex decision for a young person than whether to kill an innocent person in cold blood.

The Court concludes, however, that juries cannot be trusted with the delicate task of weighing a defendant's youth along with the other mitigating and aggravating factors of his crime. This startling conclusion undermines the very foundations of our capital sentencing system, which entrusts juries with "mak[ing] the difficult and uniquely human judgments that defy codification and that 'buil[d] discretion, equity, and flexibility into a legal system.'" *McCleskey*, supra, at 311 (quoting H. Kalven & H. Zeisel, The American Jury 498 (1966)). The Court says that juries will be unable to appreciate the significance of a defendant's youth when faced with details of a brutal crime. This assertion is based on no evidence; to the contrary, the Court itself acknowledges that the execution of under-18 offenders is "infrequent" even in the States "without a formal prohibition on executing juveniles," suggesting that juries take seriously their responsibility to weigh youth as a mitigating factor.

Nor does the Court suggest a stopping point for its reasoning. If juries cannot make appropriate determinations in cases involving murderers under 18, in what other kinds of cases will the Court find jurors deficient? We have already held that no jury may consider whether a mentally deficient defendant can receive the death penalty, irrespective of his crime. Why not take other mitigating factors, such as considerations of childhood abuse or poverty, away from juries as well? Surely jurors "overpower[ed]" by "the brutality or cold-blooded nature" of a crime, could not adequately weigh these mitigating factors either.

The Court's contention that the goals of retribution and deterrence are not served by executing murderers under 18 is also transparently false. The argument that "[r]etribution is not proportional if the law's most severe penalty is imposed on one whose culpability or blameworthiness is diminished," is simply an extension of the earlier, false generalization that youth *always* defeats culpability. The Court claims that "juveniles will be less susceptible to deterrence" because "[t]he likelihood that the teenage offender has made the kind of cost-benefit analysis that attaches any weight to the possibility of execution is so remote as to be virtually nonexistent." The Court unsurprisingly finds no support for this astounding proposition, save its own case law. The facts of this very case show the proposition to be false. Before committing the crime, Simmons encouraged his friends to join him by assuring them that they could "get away with it" because they were minors. This fact may have influenced the jury's decision to impose capital punishment despite Simmons' age. Because the Court refuses to entertain the possibility that its own unsubstantiated generalization about juveniles could be wrong, it ignores this evidence entirely.

III

Though the views of our own citizens are essentially irrelevant to the Court's decision today, the views of other countries and the so-called international community take center stage.

[T]he basic premise of the Court's argument—that American law should conform to the laws of the rest of the world—ought to be rejected out of hand. In fact the Court itself does not believe it. In many significant respects the laws of most other countries differ from our law—including not only such explicit provisions of our Constitution as the right to jury trial and grand jury indictment, but even many interpretations of the Constitution prescribed by this Court itself. The Court-pronounced exclusionary rule, for example, is distinctively American. . . .

The Court has been oblivious to the views of other countries when deciding how to interpret our Constitution's requirement that "Congress shall make no law respecting an establishment of religion . . . " Most other countries—including those committed to religious neutrality—do not insist on the degree of separation between church and state that this Court requires. . . . And let us not forget the Court's abortion jurisprudence, which makes us one of only six countries that allow abortion on demand until the point of viability. . . .

The Court should either profess its willingness to reconsider all these matters in light of the views of foreigners, or else it should cease putting forth foreigners' views as part of the *reasoned basis* of its decisions. . . .

## NOTES ON OFFENDERS PUNISHABLE BY DEATH

### 1. QUESTIONS ON *SIMMONS*

The majority and dissenting opinions in *Simmons* closely track the fault lines in *Atkins*, ranging from disputes about the methodology of Eighth Amendment proportionality review to the propriety of basing a categorical constitutional rule on indisputably continuous concepts such as age or degree of intellectual disability. Among the six Justices in the majority in *Atkins*, only Justice O'Connor dissented in *Simmons*. She rests her *Simmons* dissent on what she regards as the "flawed" argument that no 17-year-old is sufficiently culpable to deserve the death penalty, and that a categorical constitutional rule drawing the line at 18 is therefore unjustified. If Justice O'Connor is right about this, why isn't a line drawn at a particular IQ score equally flawed? Does a constitutional bar against executing 17-year-olds necessarily rest on the belief that no 17-year-old murderer deserves the death penalty? What other justifications might be offered for drawing categorical lines in these contexts?

Scientific evidence shows that adolescents and young adults continue to develop capacities for emotional self-regulation, long-term thinking, and mature judgment into their 20s. See Elizabeth S. Scott and Laurence Steinberg, Less Guilty by Reason of Adolescence, 47 American Psychologist 723 (2003). This evidence has played an important role in legislative debates about the minimum drinking age. Nevertheless, no societal consensus currently exists forbidding execution of offenders who were 18 or 19 at the time of their offenses.

### 2. MENTAL ILLNESS AND THE EIGHTH AMENDMENT

Not surprisingly, the Supreme Court's receptiveness to proportionality claims based on limited capacity in *Atkins* and *Simmons* has spawned efforts to extend the principle to mental illness. See, e.g., Bruce J. Winick, The Supreme Court's Evolving Death Penalty Jurisprudence: Severe Mental Illness as the Next Frontier, 50 B.C. L. Rev. 785 (2009). Is the reasoning deployed by the Court in *Atkins* and *Simmons* applicable to other mental conditions that can impair responsibility, such as schizophrenia? Would a categorical rule based on medical diagnosis be appropriate in this context?

Note that the Supreme Court has held that the Eighth Amendment forbids execution of an inmate who, at the time of the scheduled execution, is unable to understand the nature of the punishment and the reason for it, even though the death sentence itself is constitutionally valid. See Panetti v. Quarterman, 551 U.S. 930 (2007). Inmates whose "competence for execution" is questionable typically have been diagnosed with a severe mental disorder earlier in their lives and have unsuccessfully sought mitigation on the basis of diminished responsibility at their capital trials, leading some observers to argue that the criminal justice system is giving inadequate attention to the disabling effects of severe mental illness in capital adjudications. See American Bar Association Task Force on Mental Disability and the Death Penalty, 30 Mental and Physical Disability Law Reporter 668 (2006). The ABA Task Force, joined by the American Psychiatric Association and the American Psychological Association, have recommended that diminished responsibility based on mental disability, which is now treated as a mitigating circumstance under most state statutes, should bar a death sentence altogether.

## SECTION 4: RACE AND THE DEATH PENALTY

### McCleskey v. Kemp

Supreme Court of the United States, 1987.
481 U.S. 279.

■ JUSTICE POWELL delivered the opinion of the Court.

This case presents the question whether a complex statistical study that indicates a risk that racial considerations enter into capital sentencing determinations proves that petitioner McCleskey's capital sentence is unconstitutional under the Eighth or 14th Amendment. . . .

McCleskey, a black man, was convicted of two counts of armed robbery and one count of murder in the Superior Court of Fulton County, Georgia, on October 12, 1978. McCleskey's convictions arose out of the robbery of a furniture store and the killing of a white police officer during the course of the robbery. The evidence at trial indicated that McCleskey and three accomplices planned and carried out the robbery. All four were armed. McCleskey entered the front of the store while the other three entered the rear. McCleskey secured the front of the store by rounding up the customers and forcing them to lie face down on the floor. The other three rounded up the employees in the rear and tied them up with tape. The manager was forced at gunpoint to turn over the store receipts, his watch, and six dollars. During the course of the robbery, a police officer, answering a silent alarm, entered the store through the front door. As he was walking down the center aisle of the store, two shots were fired. Both struck the officer. One hit him in the face and killed him.

Several weeks later, McCleskey was arrested in connection with an unrelated offense. He confessed that he had participated in the furniture store robbery, but denied that he had shot the police officer. At trial, the state introduced evidence that at least one of the bullets that struck the officer was fired from a .38 caliber Rossi revolver. This description matched the description of the gun that McCleskey had carried during the robbery. The state also introduced the testimony of two witnesses who had heard McCleskey admit to the shooting.

The jury convicted McCleskey of murder.[1] At the penalty hearing,[2] the jury heard arguments as to the appropriate sentence. Under Georgia law, the jury could not consider imposing the death penalty unless it found beyond a reasonable doubt that the murder was accompanied by one of the statutory aggravating circumstances. The jury in this case found two aggravating circumstances to exist beyond a reasonable doubt: the murder was committed during the course of an armed robbery; and the murder was committed upon a peace officer engaged in the performance of his duties. In making its decision whether to impose the death sentence, the jury considered the mitigating and aggravating circumstances of McCleskey's conduct. McCleskey offered no mitigating evidence. The jury recommended that he be sentenced to death on the murder charge and to consecutive life sentences on the armed robbery charges. The court followed the jury's recommendation and sentenced McCleskey to death.

[McCleskey's death sentence was affirmed on direct appeal and in state habeas corpus proceedings, and he next filed a habeas corpus

---

[1] The Georgia Code contains only one degree of murder. A person commits murder "when he unlawfully and with malice aforethought, either express or implied, causes the death of another human being." Ga. Code Ann. § 16–5–1(a) (1984). A person convicted of murder "shall be punished by death or by imprisonment for life." § 16–5–1(d).

[2] Georgia Code Ann. § 17–10–2(c) (1982) provides that when a jury convicts a defendant of murder, "the court shall resume the trial and conduct a presentence hearing before the jury." This subsection suggests that a defendant convicted of murder always is subjected to a penalty hearing at which the jury considers imposing a death sentence. But as a matter of practice, penalty hearings seem to be held only if the prosecutor affirmatively seeks the death penalty. If he does not, the defendant receives a sentence of life imprisonment. See David C. Baldus, Charles R. Pulaski, Jr., and George Woodworth, Comparative Review of Death Sentences: An Empirical Study of the Georgia Experience, 74 J. Crim. L. & C. 661, 674, n. 56 (1983).

petition in the federal district court.] His petition raised 18 claims, one of which was that the Georgia capital sentencing process is administered in a racially discriminatory manner in violation of the Eighth and 14th Amendments to the United States constitution. In support of his claim, McCleskey proffered a statistical study performed by Professors David C. Baldus, Charles Pulaski, and George Woodworth (the Baldus study) that purports to show a disparity in the imposition of the death sentence in Georgia based on the race of the murder victim and, to a lesser extent, the race of the defendant. The Baldus study is actually two sophisticated statistical studies that examine over 2,000 murder cases that occurred in Georgia during the 1970s. The raw numbers collected by Professor Baldus indicate that defendants charged with killing white persons received the death penalty in 11 percent of the cases, but defendants charged with killing blacks received the death penalty in only one percent of the cases. The raw numbers also indicate a reverse racial disparity according to the race of the defendant: four percent of the black defendants received the death penalty, as opposed to seven percent of the white defendants.

Baldus also divided the cases according to the combination of the race of the defendant and the race of the victim. He found that the death penalty was assessed in 22 percent of the cases involving black defendants and white victims; eight percent of the cases involving white defendants and white victims; one percent of the cases involving black defendants and black victims; and three percent of the cases involving white defendants and black victims. Similarly, Baldus found that prosecutors sought the death penalty in 70 percent of the cases involving black defendants and white victims; 32 percent of the cases involving white defendants and white victims; 15 percent of the cases involving black defendants and black victims; and 19 percent of the cases involving white defendants and black victims.

Baldus subjected his data to an extensive analysis, taking account of 230 variables that could have explained the disparities on nonracial grounds. One of his models concludes that, even after taking account of 39 nonracial variables, defendants charged with killing white victims were 4.3 times as likely to receive a death sentence as defendants charged with killing blacks. According to this model, black defendants were 1.1 times as likely to receive a death sentence as other defendants. Thus, the Baldus study indicates that black defendants, such as McCleskey, who kill white victims have the greatest likelihood of receiving the death penalty.[5]

The district court held an extensive evidentiary hearing on McCleskey's petition. . . . It concluded that McCleskey's "statistics do not demonstrate a prima facie case in support of the contention that the

[5] Baldus' 230-variable model divided cases into eight different ranges, according to the estimated aggravation level of the offense. Baldus argued in his testimony to the district court that the effects of racial bias were most striking in the midrange cases. "When the cases become tremendously aggravated so that everybody would agree that if we're going to have a death sentence, these are the cases that should get it, the race effects go away. It's only in the mid-range of cases where the decision-makers have a real choice as to what to do. If there's room for the exercise of discretion, then the [racial] factors begin to play a role." Under this model, Baldus found that 14.4 percent of the black-victim midrange cases received the death penalty, and 34.4 percent of the white-victim cases received the death penalty. According to Baldus, the facts of McCleskey's case placed it within the midrange.

death penalty was imposed upon him because of his race, because of the race of the victim, or because of any Eighth Amendment concern." As to McCleskey's Fourteenth Amendment claim, the court found that the methodology of the Baldus study was flawed in several respects. Because of these defects, the court held that the Baldus study "fail[ed] to contribute anything of value" to McCleskey's claim. Accordingly, the court denied the petition insofar as it was based upon the Baldus study.

The Court of Appeals for the Eleventh Circuit, sitting en banc, carefully reviewed the district court's decision on McCleskey's claim. It assumed the validity of the study itself and addressed the merits of McCleskey's Eighth and Fourteenth Amendment claims. That is, the court assumed that the study "showed that systematic and substantial disparities existed in the penalties imposed upon homicide defendants in Georgia based on race of the homicide victim, that the disparities existed at a less substantial rate in death sentencing based on race of defendants, and that the factors of race of the victim and defendant were at work in Fulton County." Even assuming the study's validity, the court of appeals found the statistics "insufficient to demonstrate discriminatory intent or unconstitutional discrimination in the Fourteenth Amendment context, [and] insufficient to show irrationality, arbitrariness and capriciousness under any kind of Eighth Amendment analysis." . . .

The Court of Appeals affirmed the denial by the district court of McCleskey's petition for a writ of habeas corpus insofar as the petition was based upon the Baldus study, with three judges dissenting as to McCleskey's claims based on the Baldus study. We granted certiorari and now affirm.

[The Court rejected McClesky's equal protection challenge to Georgia's capital sentencing statute on the ground that the evidence failed to show either that any of the decision-makers in his case acted with a discriminatory purpose or that the Georgia Legislature had enacted or perpetuated its capital sentencing statute to further a racially discriminatory purpose. The court then turned to his Eighth Amendment claim.]

In light of our precedents under the Eighth Amendment, McCleskey cannot argue successfully that his sentence is "disproportionate to the crime in the traditional sense." See Pulley v. Harris, 465 U.S. 37, 43 (1984). He does not deny that he committed a murder in the course of a planned robbery, a crime for which this Court has determined that the death penalty constitutionally may be imposed. Gregg v. Georgia, 428 U.S. 153, 187 (1976). His disproportionality claim "is of a different sort." *Pulley v. Harris*, supra. McCleskey argues that the sentence in his case is disproportionate to the sentences in other murder cases.

On the one hand, he cannot base a constitutional claim on an argument that his case differs from other cases in which defendants did receive the death penalty. On automatic appeal, the Georgia Supreme Court found that McCleskey's death sentence was not disproportionate to other death sentences imposed in the state. The court supported this conclusion with an appendix containing citations to 13 cases involving generally similar murders. See Ga. Code Ann. § 17–10–35(e) (1982). Moreover, where the statutory procedures adequately channel the sentencer's discretion, such proportionality review is not constitutionally required. *Pulley v. Harris*, supra.

On the other hand, absent a showing that the Georgia capital punishment system operates in an arbitrary and capricious manner, McCleskey cannot prove a constitutional violation by demonstrating that other defendants who may be similarly situated did not receive the death penalty. In *Gregg*, the Court confronted the argument that "the opportunities for discretionary action that are inherent in the processing of any murder case under Georgia law," specifically the opportunities for discretionary leniency, rendered the capital sentences imposed arbitrary and capricious. We rejected this contention:

> The existence of these discretionary stages is not determinative of the issues before us. At each of these stages an actor in the criminal justice system makes a decision which may remove a defendant from consideration as a candidate for the death penalty. *Furman*, in contrast, dealt with the decision to impose the death sentence on a specific individual who had been convicted of a capital offense. Nothing in any of our cases suggests that the decision to afford an individual defendant mercy violates the constitution. *Furman* held only that, in order to minimize the risk that the death penalty would be imposed on a capriciously selected group of offenders, the decision to impose it had to be guided by standards so that the sentencing authority would focus on the particularized circumstances of the crime and the defendant.[28]

Because McCleskey's sentence was imposed under Georgia sentencing procedures that focus discretion "on the particularized nature of the crime and the particularized characteristics of the individual defendant," we lawfully may presume that McCleskey's death sentence was not "wantonly and freakishly" imposed, and thus that the sentence is not disproportionate within any recognized meaning under the Eighth Amendment.

Although our decision in *Gregg* as to the facial validity of the Georgia capital punishment statute appears to foreclose McCleskey's disproportionality argument, he further contends that the Georgia capital punishment system is arbitrary and capricious in application, and therefore his sentence is excessive, because racial considerations may influence capital sentencing decisions in Georgia. We now address this claim.

To evaluate McCleskey's challenge, we must examine exactly what the Baldus study may show. Even Professor Baldus does not contend that his statistics *prove* that race enters into any capital sentencing

---

[28] The constitution is not offended by inconsistency in results based on the objective circumstances of the crime. Numerous legitimate factors may influence the outcome of a trial and a defendant's ultimate sentence, even though they may be irrelevant to his actual guilt. If sufficient evidence to link a suspect to a crime cannot be found, he will not be charged. The capability of the responsible law enforcement agency can vary widely. Also, the strength of the available evidence remains a variable throughout the criminal justice process and may influence a prosecutor's decision to offer a plea bargain or to go to trial. Witness availability, credibility, and memory also influence the results of prosecutions. Finally, sentencing in state courts is generally discretionary, so a defendant's ultimate sentence necessarily will vary according to the judgment of the sentencing authority. The foregoing factors necessarily exist in varying degrees throughout our criminal justice system.

decisions or that race was a factor in McCleskey's particular case. Statistics at most may show only a likelihood that a particular factor entered into some decisions. There is, of course, some risk of racial prejudice influencing a jury's decision in a criminal case. There are similar risks that other kinds of prejudice will influence other criminal trials. The question "is at what point that risk becomes constitutionally unacceptable." McCleskey asks us to accept the likelihood allegedly shown by the Baldus study as the constitutional measure of an unacceptable risk of racial prejudice influencing capital sentencing decisions. This we decline to do.

Because of the risk that the factor of race may enter the criminal justice process, we have engaged in "unceasing efforts" to eradicate racial prejudice from our criminal justice system. Batson v. Kentucky, 476 U.S. 79, 85 (1986).[30] Our efforts have been guided by our recognition that "the inestimable privilege of trial by jury . . . is a vital principle, underlying the whole administration of criminal justice." Thus, it is the jury that is a criminal defendant's fundamental "protection of life and liberty against race or color prejudice." Strauder v. West Virginia, 100 U.S. 303, 309 (1880). Specifically, a capital sentencing jury representative of a criminal defendant's community assures a " 'diffused impartiality,' " in the jury's task of "express[ing] the conscience of the community on the ultimate question of life or death," Witherspoon v. Illinois, 391 U.S. 510, 519 (1968).

Individual jurors bring to their deliberations "qualities of human nature and varieties of human experience, the range of which is unknown and perhaps unknowable." Peters v. Kiff, 407 U.S. 493, 503 (1972) (opinion of Marshall, J.). The capital sentencing decision requires the individual jurors to focus their collective judgment on the unique characteristics of a particular criminal defendant. It is not surprising that such collective judgments often are difficult to explain. But the inherent lack of predictability of jury decisions does not justify their condemnation. On the contrary, it is the jury's function to make the difficult and uniquely human judgments that defy codification and that "buil[d] discretion, equity, and flexibility into a legal system." Harry Kalven and Hans Zeisel, The American Jury 498 (1966).

McCleskey's argument that the constitution condemns the discretion allowed decisionmakers in the Georgia capital sentencing system is antithetical to the fundamental role of discretion in our criminal justice system. Discretion in the criminal justice system offers substantial benefits to the criminal defendant. Not only can a jury decline to impose the death sentence, it can decline to convict, or choose to convict of a lesser offense. Whereas decisions against a defendant's interest may be

---

[30] This Court has repeatedly stated that prosecutorial discretion cannot be exercised on the basis of race. Nor can a prosecutor exercise peremptory challenges on the basis of race. Batson v. Kentucky, 476 U.S. 79 (1986). More generally, this Court has condemned state efforts to exclude blacks from grand and petit juries. Vasquez v. Hillery, 474 U.S. 254 (1986). . . .

Other protections apply to the trial and jury deliberation process. Widespread bias in the community can make a change of venue constitutionally required. The constitution prohibits racially biased prosecutorial arguments. If the circumstances of a particular case indicate a significant likelihood that racial bias may influence a jury, the constitution requires questioning as to such bias. Finally, in a capital sentencing hearing, a defendant convicted of an interracial murder is entitled to such questioning without regard to the circumstances of the particular case. Turner v. Murray, 476 U.S. 28 (1986).

reversed by the trial judge or on appeal, these discretionary exercises of leniency are final and unreviewable. Similarly, the capacity of prosecutorial discretion to provide individualized justice is "firmly entrenched in American law." As we have noted, a prosecutor can decline to charge, offer a plea bargain, or decline to seek a death sentence in any particular case. Of course, "the power to be lenient [also] is the power to discriminate," but a capital-punishment system that did not allow for discretionary acts of leniency "would be totally alien to our notions of criminal justice." *Gregg v. Georgia*.

At most, the Baldus study indicates a discrepancy that appears to correlate with race. Apparent disparities in sentencing are an inevitable part of our criminal justice system.[35] The discrepancy indicated by the Baldus study is "a far cry from the major systemic defects identified in *Furman*," *Pulley v. Harris*, supra.[36] As this Court has recognized, any mode for determining guilt or punishment "has its weaknesses and the potential for misuse." Specifically, "there can be 'no perfect procedure for deciding in which cases governmental authority should be used to impose death.'" Despite these imperfections, our consistent rule has been that constitutional guarantees are met when "the mode [for determining guilt or punishment] itself has been surrounded with safeguards to make it as fair as possible." Where the discretion that is fundamental to our criminal process is involved, we decline to assume that what is unexplained is invidious. In light of the safeguards designed to minimize racial bias in the process, the fundamental value of jury trial in our criminal justice system, and the benefits that discretion provides to criminal defendants, we hold that the Baldus study does not demonstrate a constitutionally significant risk of racial bias affecting the Georgia capital-sentencing process.

Two additional concerns inform our decision in this case. First, McCleskey's claim, taken to its logical conclusion, throws into serious question the principles that underlie our entire criminal justice system. The Eighth Amendment is not limited in application to capital punishment, but applies to all penalties. Solem v. Helm, 463 U.S. 277 (1983). Thus, if we accepted McCleskey's claim that racial bias has impermissibly tainted the capital sentencing decision, we could soon be faced with similar claims as to other types of penalty.[38] Moreover, the claim that

---

[35] Congress has acknowledged that existence of such discrepancies in criminal sentences, and in 1984 created the United States Sentencing Commission to develop sentencing guidelines. The objective of the guidelines 'is to avoid *unwarranted* sentencing disparities among defendants with similar records who have been found guilty of similar criminal conduct, while maintaining sufficient flexibility to permit individualized sentencing when warranted by mitigating or aggravating factors not taken into account in the guidelines.' 52 Fed. Reg. 3920 (1987) (emphasis added). No one contends that all sentencing disparities can be eliminated. The guidelines, like the safeguards in the *Gregg*-type statute, further an essential need of the Anglo-American criminal justice system—to balance the desirability of a high degree of uniformity against the necessity for the exercise of discretion.

[36] The Baldus study in fact confirms that the Georgia system results in a reasonable level of proportionality among the class of murderers eligible for the death penalty. As Professor Baldus confirmed, the system sorts out cases where the sentence of death is highly likely and highly unlikely, leaving a mid-range of cases where the imposition of the death penalty in any particular case is less predictable.

[38] Studies already exist that allegedly demonstrate a racial disparity in the length of prison sentences. See, e.g., Cassia Spohn, John Gruhl, and Susan Welch, The Effect of Race on Sentencing: A Reexamination of an Unsettled Question, 16 Law & Soc. Rev. 71 (1981–1982);

his sentence rests on the irrelevant factor of race easily could be extended to apply to claims based on unexplained discrepancies that correlate to membership in other minority groups, and even to gender. Similarly, since McCleskey's claim relates to the race of his victim, other claims could apply with equally logical force to statistical disparities that correlate with the race or sex of other actors in the criminal justice system, such as defense attorneys, or judges. Also, there is no logical reason that such a claim need be limited to racial or sexual bias. If arbitrary and capricious punishment is the touchstone under the Eighth Amendment, such a claim could at least in theory be based upon any arbitrary variable, such as the defendant's facial characteristics, or the physical attractiveness of the defendant or the victim, that some statistical study indicates may be influential in jury decisionmaking. As these examples illustrate, there is no limiting principle to the type of challenge brought by McCleskey. The constitution does not require that a state eliminate any demonstrable disparity that correlates with a potentially irrelevant factor in order to operate a criminal justice system that includes capital punishment. As we have stated specifically in the context of capital punishment, the Constitution does not "plac[e] totally unrealistic conditions on its use." *Gregg v. Georgia*.

Second, McCleskey's arguments are best presented to the legislative bodies. It is not the responsibility—or indeed even the right—of this Court to determine the appropriate punishment for particular crimes. It is the legislatures, the elected representatives of the people, that are "constituted to respond to the will and consequently the moral values of the people." Legislatures also are better qualified to weigh and "evaluate the results of statistical studies in terms of their own local conditions and with a flexibility of approach that is not available to the courts." Capital punishment is now the law in more than two thirds of our states. It is the ultimate duty of courts to determine on a case-by-case basis whether these laws are applied consistently with the constitution. Despite McCleskey's wide ranging arguments that basically challenge the validity of capital punishment in our multi-racial society, the only question before us is whether in his case, the law of Georgia was properly applied. We agree with the district court and the Court of Appeals for the Eleventh Circuit that this was carefully and correctly done in this case. . . .

■ JUSTICE BRENNAN, with whom JUSTICE MARSHALL joins, and with whom JUSTICE BLACKMUN and JUSTICE STEVENS join in all but Part I, dissenting.

I

Adhering to my view that the death penalty is in all circumstances cruel and unusual punishment forbidden by the Eighth and 14th Amendments, I would vacate the decision below insofar as it left undisturbed the death sentence imposed in this case. Gregg v. Georgia, 428 U.S. 153, 227 (1976) (Brennan, J., dissenting). The Court observes that "the *Gregg*-type statute imposes unprecedented safeguards in the special context of capital punishment," which "ensure a degree of care in

---

James D. Unnever, Charles E. Frazier, and John C. Henretta, Race Differences in Criminal Sentencing, 21 Sociological Q. 197 (1980).

the imposition of the death penalty that can be described only as unique." Notwithstanding these efforts, murder defendants in Georgia with white victims are more than four times as likely to receive the death sentence as are defendants with black victims. Nothing could convey more powerfully the intractable reality of the death penalty: "that the effort to eliminate arbitrariness in the infliction of that ultimate sanction is so plainly doomed to failure that it—and the death penalty—must be abandoned altogether." Godfrey v. Georgia, 446 U.S. 420, 442 (1980) (Marshall, J., concurring in judgment).

Even if I did not hold this position, however, I would reverse the Court of Appeals, for petitioner McCleskey has clearly demonstrated that his death sentence was imposed in violation of the Eighth and 14th Amendments. . . .

II

At some point in this case, Warren McCleskey doubtless asked his lawyer whether a jury was likely to sentence him to die. A candid reply to this question would have been disturbing. First, counsel would have to tell McCleskey that few of the details of the crime or of McCleskey's past criminal conduct were more important than the fact that his victim was white. Furthermore, counsel would feel bound to tell McCleskey that defendants charged with killing white victims in Georgia are 4.3 times as likely to be sentenced to death as defendants charged with killing blacks. In addition, frankness would compel the disclosure that it was more likely than not that the race of McCleskey's victim would determine whether he received a death sentence: six of every 11 defendants convicted of killing a white person would not have received the death penalty if their victims had been black, while, among defendants with aggravating and mitigating factors comparable to McCleskey's, 20 of every 34 would not have been sentenced to die if their victims had been black. Finally, the assessment would not be complete without the information that cases involving black defendants and white victims are more likely to result in a death sentence than cases featuring any other racial combination of defendant and victim. The story could be told in a variety of ways, but McCleskey could not fail to grasp its essential narrative line: there was a significant chance that race would play a prominent role in determining if he lived or died.

The Court today holds that Warren McCleskey's sentence was constitutionally imposed. It finds no fault in a system in which lawyers must tell their clients that race casts a large shadow on the capital sentencing process. The Court arrives at this conclusion by stating that the Baldus study cannot "prove that race enters into any capital sentencing decisions or that race was a factor in McCleskey's particular case." Since, according to Professor Baldus, we cannot say "to a moral certainty" that race influenced a decision, we can identify only "a likelihood that a particular factor entered into some decisions," and "a discrepancy that appears to correlate with race." This "likelihood" and "discrepancy," holds the Court, is insufficient to establish a constitutional violation. The Court reaches this conclusion by placing four factors on the scales opposite McCleskey's evidence: the desire to encourage sentencing discretion, the existence of "statutory safeguards" in the Georgia scheme, the fear of encouraging widespread challenges to other sentencing decisions, and the limits of the judicial role. The Court's evaluation of the significance of petitioner's evidence is fundamentally at odds with our consistent concern for rationality in capital sentencing, and the considerations that the majority invokes to discount that evidence cannot justify ignoring its force.

III

A

. . . The Court assumes the statistical validity of the Baldus study, and acknowledges that McCleskey has demonstrated a risk that racial prejudice plays a role in capital sentencing in Georgia. Nonetheless, it finds the probability of prejudice insufficient to create constitutional concern. Close analysis of the Baldus study, however, in light of both statistical principles and human experience, reveals that the risk that race influenced McCleskey's sentence is intolerable by any imaginable standard.

B

The Baldus study indicates that, after taking into account some 230 nonracial factors that might legitimately influence a sentencer, the jury more likely than not would have spared McCleskey's life had his victim been black. The study distinguishes between those cases in which (1) the jury exercises virtually no discretion because the strength or weakness of aggravating factors usually suggests that only one outcome is appropriate;[2] and (2) cases reflecting an "intermediate" level of aggravation, in which the jury has considerable discretion in choosing a sentence.[3] McCleskey's case falls into the intermediate range. In such cases, death is imposed in 34 percent of white-victim crimes and 14 percent of black-victim crimes, a difference of 139 percent in the rate of imposition of the death penalty. In other words, just under 59 percent—almost six in 10—defendants comparable to McCleskey would not have received the death penalty if their victims had been black.[4]

Furthermore, even examination of the sentencing system as a whole, factoring in those cases in which the jury exercises little discretion, indicates the influence of race on capital sentencing. For the Georgia system as a whole, race accounts for a six percentage point difference in the rate at which capital punishment is imposed. Since

---

2 The first two and the last of the study's eight case categories represent those cases in which the jury typically sees little leeway in deciding on a sentence. Cases in the first two categories are those that feature aggravating factors so minimal that juries imposed no death sentences in the 88 cases with these factors during the period of the study. Cases in the Eighth category feature aggravating factors so extreme that the jury imposed the death penalty in 88 percent of the 58 cases with these factors in the same period. Ibid.

3 In the five categories characterized as intermediate, the rate at which the death penalty was imposed ranged from eight percent to 41 percent. The overall rate for the 326 cases in these categories was 20 percent.

4 The considerable racial disparity in sentencing rates among these cases is consistent with the "liberation hypothesis" of H. Kalven and H. Zeisel in their landmark work, The American Jury (1966). These authors found that, in close cases in which jurors were most often in disagreement, "the closeness of the evidence makes it possible for the jury to respond to sentiment by liberating it from the discipline of the evidence." While "the jury does not often consciously and explicitly yield to sentiment in the teeth of the law . . . it yields to sentiment in the apparent process of resolving doubts as to evidence. The jury, therefore, is able to conduct its revolt from the law within the etiquette of resolving issues of fact." Thus, it is those cases in which sentencing evidence seems to dictate neither life imprisonment nor the death penalty that impermissible factors such as race play the most prominent role.

death is imposed in 11 percent of all white-victim cases, the rate in comparably aggravated black-victim cases is five percent. The rate of capital sentencing in a white-victim case is thus 120 percent greater than the rate in a black-victim case. Put another way, over half—55 percent—of defendants in white-victim crimes in Georgia would not have been sentenced to die if their victims had been black. Of the more than 200 variables potentially relevant to a sentencing decision, race of the victim is a powerful explanation for variation in death sentence rates—as powerful as nonracial aggravating factors such as a prior murder conviction or acting as the principal planner of the homicide.[5]

These adjusted figures are only the most conservative indication of the risk that race will influence the death sentences of defendants in Georgia. Data unadjusted for the mitigating or aggravating effect of other factors show an even more pronounced disparity by race. The capital sentencing rate for all white-victim cases was almost 11 times greater than the rate for black-victim cases. Furthermore, blacks who kill whites are sentenced to death at nearly 22 times the rate of blacks who kill blacks, and more than seven times the rate of whites who kill blacks. In addition, prosecutors seek the death penalty for 70 percent of black defendants with white victims, but for only 15 percent of black defendants with black victims, and only 19 percent of white defendants with black victims. Since our decision upholding the Georgia capital sentencing system in *Gregg*, the state has executed seven persons. All of the seven were convicted of killing whites, and six of the seven executed were black.[6] Such execution figures are especially striking in light of the fact that, during the period encompassed by the Baldus study, only 9.2 percent of Georgia homicides involved black defendants and white victims, while 60.7 percent involved black victims. . . .

The statistical evidence in this case thus relentlessly documents the risk that McCleskey's sentence was influenced by racial considerations. This evidence shows that there is a better than even chance in Georgia that race will influence the decision to impose the death penalty: a majority of defendants in white-victim crimes would not have been sentenced to die if their victims had been black. In determining whether this risk is acceptable, our judgment must be shaped by the awareness that "the risk of racial prejudice infecting a capital sentencing proceeding is especially serious in light of the complete finality of the death sentence," Turner v. Murray, 476 U.S. 28, 35 (1986), and that "it is of vital importance to the defendant and to the community that any decision to impose the death sentence be, and appear to be, based on reason rather than caprice or emotion." Gardner v. Florida, 430 U.S. 349, 358 (1977). In determining the guilt of a defendant, a state must prove its case beyond a reasonable doubt. That is, we refuse to convict if the chance of error is simply less likely than not. Surely, we should not be willing to take a person's life if the chance that his death sentence was irrationally imposed is more likely than not. In light of the gravity of the interest at stake, petitioner's statistics on their face are a powerful

---

[5] The fact that a victim was white accounts for a nine percentage point difference in the rate at which the death penalty is imposed, which is the same difference attributable to a prior murder conviction or the fact that the defendant was the "prime mover" in planning a murder.

[6] NAACP Legal Defense and Educational Fund, Death Row, U. S. A. 4 (Aug. 1, 1986).

demonstration of the type of risk that our Eighth Amendment jurisprudence has consistently condemned.

C

Evaluation of McCleskey's evidence cannot rest solely on the numbers themselves. We must also ask whether the conclusion suggested by those numbers is consonant with our understanding of history and human experience. Georgia's legacy of a race-conscious criminal justice system, as well as this Court's own recognition of the persistent danger that racial attitudes may affect criminal proceedings, indicates that McCleskey's claim is not a fanciful product of mere statistical artifice.

For many years, Georgia operated openly and formally precisely the type of dual system the evidence shows is still effectively in place. The criminal law expressly differentiated between crimes committed by and against blacks and whites, distinctions whose lineage traced back to the time of slavery. During the colonial period, black slaves who killed whites in Georgia, regardless of whether in self-defense or in defense of another, were automatically executed. A. Leon Higginbotham, Jr., In the Matter of Color: Race in the American Legal Process 256 (1978).

By the time of the Civil War, a dual system of crime and punishment was well established in Georgia. See Ga. Penal Code (1861). The state criminal code contained separate sections for "Slaves and Free Persons of Color," and for all other persons. The code provided, for instance, for an automatic death sentence for murder committed by blacks, but declared that anyone else convicted of murder might receive life imprisonment if the conviction were founded solely on circumstantial testimony or simply if the jury so recommended. The code established that the rape of a free white female by a black "shall be" punishable by death. However, rape by anyone else of a free white female was punishable by a prison term not less than two nor more than 20 years. The rape of blacks was punishable "by fine and imprisonment, at the discretion of the court." A black convicted of assaulting a free white person with intent to murder could be put to death at the discretion of the court, but the same offense committed against a black, slave or free, was classified as a "minor" offense whose punishment lay in the discretion of the court, as long as such punishment did not "extend to life, limb, or health." Assault with intent to murder by a white person was punishable by a prison term of from two to 10 years. While sufficient provocation could reduce a charge of murder to manslaughter, the code provided that "obedience and submission being the duty of a slave, much greater provocation is necessary to reduce a homicide of a white person by him to voluntary manslaughter, than is prescribed for white persons."

In more recent times, some 40 years ago, Gunnar Myrdal's epochal study of American race relations produced findings mirroring McCleskey's evidence:

> As long as only Negroes are concerned and no whites are disturbed, great leniency will be shown in most cases. . . . The sentences for even major crimes are ordinarily reduced when the victim is another Negro. . . .

> For offenses which involve any actual or potential danger to whites, however, Negroes are punished more severely than whites. . . .
>
> On the other hand, it is quite common for a white criminal to be set free if his crime was against a Negro. Gunnar Myrdal, An American Dilemma 551–553 (1944).

This Court has invalidated portions of the Georgia capital sentencing system three times over the past 15 years. The specter of race discrimination was acknowledged by the Court in striking down the Georgia death penalty statute in *Furman*. . . .

Five years later, the Court struck down the imposition of the death penalty in Georgia for the crime of rape. Coker v. Georgia, 433 U.S. 584 (1977). Although the Court did not explicitly mention race, the decision had to have been informed by the specific observations on rape by both the Chief Justice and Justice Powell in *Furman*. Furthermore, evidence submitted to the Court indicated that black men who committed rape, particularly of white women, were considerably more likely to be sentenced to death than white rapists. For instance, by 1977 Georgia had executed 62 men for rape since the federal government began compiling statistics in 1930. Of these men, 58 were black and 4 were white. . . .

[This] historical review of Georgia criminal law is not intended as a bill of indictment calling the state to account for past transgressions. Citation of past practices does not justify the automatic condemnation of current ones. But it would be unrealistic to ignore the influence of history in assessing the plausible implications of McCleskey's evidence. . . .

The ongoing influence of history is acknowledged, as the majority observes, by our " 'unceasing efforts' to eradicate racial prejudice from our criminal justice system." These efforts, however, signify not the elimination of the problem but its persistence. Our cases reflect a realization of the myriad of opportunities for racial considerations to influence criminal proceedings: in the exercise of peremptory challenges, Batson v. Kentucky, 476 U.S. 79 (1986); in the selection of the grand jury, Vasquez v. Hillery, 474 U.S. 254 (1986); in the selection of the petit jury, Whitus v. Georgia, 385 U.S. 545 (1967); in the exercise of prosecutorial discretion, Wayte v. United States, 470 U.S. 598 (1985); in the conduct of argument, Donnelly v. DeChristoforo, 416 U.S. 637 (1974); and in the conscious or unconscious bias of jurors, Turner v. Murray, 476 U.S. 28 (1986); Ristaino v. Ross, 424 U.S. 589 (1976).

The discretion afforded prosecutors and jurors in the Georgia capital sentencing system creates such opportunities. No guidelines govern prosecutorial decisions to seek the death penalty, and Georgia provides juries with no list of aggravating and mitigating factors, nor any standard for balancing them against one another. Once a jury identifies one aggravating factor, it has complete discretion in choosing life or death, and need not articulate its basis for selecting life imprisonment. The Georgia sentencing system therefore provides considerable opportunity for racial considerations, however subtle and unconscious, to influence charging and sentencing decisions.

History and its continuing legacy thus buttress the probative force of McCleskey's statistics. Formal dual criminal laws may no longer be in effect, and intentional discrimination may no longer be prominent. Nonetheless, as we acknowledged in *Turner*, "subtle, less consciously held racial attitudes" continue to be of concern and the Georgia system gives such attitudes considerable room to operate. The conclusions drawn from McCleskey's statistical evidence are therefore consistent with the lessons of social experience.

The majority thus misreads our Eighth Amendment jurisprudence in concluding that McCleskey has not demonstrated a degree of risk sufficient to raise constitutional concern. The determination of the significance of his evidence is at its core an exercise in human moral judgment, not a mechanical statistical analysis. . . . It is true that every nuance of decision cannot be statistically captured, nor can any individual judgment be plumbed with absolute certainty. Yet the fact that we must always act without the illumination of complete knowledge cannot induce paralysis when we confront what is literally an issue of life and death. Sentencing data, history, and experience all counsel that Georgia has provided insufficient assurance of the heightened rationality we have required in order to take a human life.

IV

The Court cites four reasons for shrinking from the implications of McCleskey's evidence: the desirability of discretion for actors in the criminal justice system, the existence of statutory safeguards against abuse of that discretion, the potential consequences for broader challenges to criminal sentencing, and an understanding of the contours of the judicial role. While these concerns underscore the need for sober deliberation, they do not justify rejecting evidence as convincing as McCleskey has presented. . . .

Our desire for individualized moral judgments may lead us to accept some inconsistencies in sentencing outcomes. Since such decisions are not reducible to mathematical formulae, we are willing to assume that a certain degree of variation reflects the fact that no two defendants are completely alike. There is thus a presumption that actors in the criminal justice system exercise their discretion in responsible fashion, and we do not automatically infer that sentencing patterns that do not comport with ideal rationality are suspect.

As we made clear in Batson v. Kentucky, 476 U.S. 79 (1986), however, that presumption is rebuttable. *Batson* dealt with another arena in which considerable discretion traditionally has been afforded, the exercise of peremptory challenges. Those challenges are normally exercised without any indication whatsoever of the grounds for doing so. The rationale for this deference has been a belief that the unique characteristics of particular prospective jurors may raise concern on the part of the prosecution or defense, despite the fact that counsel may not be able to articulate that concern in a manner sufficient to support exclusion for cause. As with sentencing, therefore, peremptory challenges are justified as an occasion for particularized determinations related to specific individuals, and, as with sentencing, we presume that such challenges normally are not made on the basis of a factor such as race. As we said in *Batson*, however, such features do not justify imposing a "crippling burden of proof," in order to rebut that presumption. The Court in this case apparently seeks to do just that. On the basis of the need for individualized decisions, it rejects evidence, drawn from the most sophisticated capital sentencing analysis ever performed, that reveals that race more likely than not infects capital sentencing decisions. The Court's position converts a rebuttable presumption into a virtually conclusive one. . . .

It has now been over 13 years since Georgia adopted the provisions upheld in *Gregg*. Professor Baldus and his colleagues have compiled data on almost 2,500 homicides committed during the period 1973–79. They have taken into account the influence of 230 nonracial variables, using a multitude of data from the state itself, and have produced striking evidence that the odds of being sentenced to death are significantly greater than average if a defendant is black or his or her victim is white. The challenge to the Georgia system is not speculative or theoretical; it is empirical. As a result, the Court cannot rely on the statutory safeguards in discounting McCleskey's evidence, for it is the very effectiveness of those safeguards that such evidence calls into question. . . .

The Court next states that its unwillingness to regard petitioner's evidence as sufficient is based in part on the fear that recognition of McCleskey's claim would open the door to widespread challenges to all aspects of criminal sentencing. Taken on its face, such a statement seems to suggest a fear of too much justice. Yet surely the majority would acknowledge that if striking evidence indicated that other minority groups, or women, or even persons with blond hair, were disproportionately sentenced to death, such a state of affairs would be repugnant to deeply rooted conceptions of fairness. The prospect that there may be more widespread abuse than McCleskey documents may be dismaying, but it does not justify complete abdication of our judicial role. . . .

In fairness, the Court's fear that McCleskey's claim is an invitation to descend a slippery slope also rests on the realization that any humanly imposed system of penalties will exhibit some imperfection. Yet to reject McCleskey's powerful evidence on this basis is to ignore both the qualitatively different character of the death penalty and the particular repugnance of racial discrimination, considerations which may properly be taken into account in determining whether various punishments are "cruel and unusual." Furthermore, it fails to take account of the unprecedented refinement and strength of the Baldus study. . . .

Finally, the Court justifies its rejection of McCleskey's claim by cautioning against usurpation of the legislatures' role in devising and monitoring criminal punishment. The Court is, of course, correct to emphasize the gravity of constitutional intervention and the importance that it be sparingly employed. The fact that "capital punishment is now the law in more than two thirds of our states," however, does not diminish the fact that capital punishment is the most awesome act that a state can perform. The judiciary's role in this society counts for little if the use of governmental power to extinguish life does not elicit close scrutiny. . . .

Those whom we would banish from society or from the human community itself often speak in too faint a voice to be heard above society's demand for punishment. It is the particular role of courts to hear these voices, for the constitution declares that the majoritarian chorus may not alone dictate the conditions of social life. The Court thus fulfills, rather than disrupts, the scheme of separation of powers by closely scrutinizing the imposition of the death penalty, for no decision of a society is more deserving of "sober second thought." Harlan F. Stone, The Common Law in the United States, 50 Harv. L. Rev. 4, 25 (1936).

V

At the time our Constitution was framed 200 years ago this year, blacks "had for more than a century before been regarded as beings of an inferior order, and altogether unfit to associate with the white race, either in social or political relations; and so far inferior, that they had no rights which the white man was bound to respect." Dred Scott v. Sandford, 60 U.S. (19 How.) 393, 407 (1857). Only 130 years ago, this Court relied on these observations to deny American citizenship to blacks. A mere three generations ago, this Court sanctioned racial segregation, stating that "if one race be inferior to the other socially, the Constitution of the United States cannot put them upon the same plane." Plessy v. Ferguson, 163 U.S. 537, 552 (1896).

In more recent times, we have sought to free ourselves from the burden of this history. Yet it has been scarcely a generation since this Court's first decision striking down racial segregation, and barely two decades since the legislative prohibition of racial discrimination in major domains of national life. These have been honorable steps, but we cannot pretend that in three decades we have completely escaped the grip of a historical legacy spanning centuries. Warren McCleskey's evidence confronts us with the subtle and persistent influence of the past. His message is a disturbing one to a society that has formally repudiated racism, and a frustrating one to a Nation accustomed to regarding its destiny as the product of its own will. Nonetheless, we ignore him at our peril, for we remain imprisoned by the past as long as we deny its influence in the present.

It is tempting to pretend that minorities on death row share a fate in no way connected to our own, that our treatment of them sounds no echoes beyond the chambers in which they die. Such an illusion is ultimately corrosive, for the reverberations of injustice are not so easily confined. "The destinies of the two races in this country are indissolubly linked together," id. at 560 (Harlan, J., dissenting), and the way in which we choose those who will die reveals the depth of moral commitment among the living.

The Court's decision today will not change what attorneys in Georgia tell other Warren McCleskeys about their chances of execution. Nothing will soften the harsh message they must convey, nor alter the prospect that race undoubtedly will continue to be a topic of discussion. McCleskey's evidence will not have obtained judicial acceptance, but that will not affect what is said on death row. However many criticisms of today's decision may be rendered, these painful conversations will serve as the most eloquent dissents of all.[a]

■ JUSTICE STEVENS, with whom JUSTICE BLACKMUN joins, dissenting. . . .

In this case it is claimed—and the claim is supported by elaborate studies which the Court properly assumes to be valid—that the jury's sentencing process was likely distorted by racial prejudice. The studies

[a] Justice Blackmun's dissenting opinion has been omitted.—[Footnote by eds.]

demonstrate a strong probability that McCleskey's sentencing jury, which expressed "the community's outrage—its sense that an individual has lost his moral entitlement to live," Spaziano v. Florida, 468 U.S. 447, 469 (1984) (Stevens, J., dissenting)—was influenced by the fact that McCleskey is black and his victim was white, and that this same outrage would not have been generated if he had killed a member of his own race. This sort of disparity is constitutionally intolerable. It flagrantly violates the Court's prior "insistence that capital punishment be imposed fairly, and with reasonable consistency, or not at all." Eddings v. Oklahoma, 455 U.S. 104, 112 (1982).

The Court's decision appears to be based on a fear that the acceptance of McCleskey's claim would sound the death knell for capital punishment in Georgia. If society were indeed forced to choose between a racially discriminatory death penalty (one that provides heightened protection against murder "for whites only") and no death penalty at all, the choice mandated by the constitution would be plain. But the Court's fear is unfounded. One of the lessons of the Baldus study is that there exist certain categories of extremely serious crimes for which prosecutors consistently seek, and juries consistently impose, the death penalty without regard to the race of the victim or the race of the offender. If Georgia were to narrow the class of death-eligible defendants to those categories, the danger of arbitrary and discriminatory imposition of the death penalty would be significantly decreased, if not eradicated. As Justice Brennan has demonstrated in his dissenting opinion, such a restructuring of the sentencing scheme is surely not too high a price to pay.

Like Justice Brennan, I would therefore reverse the judgment of the Court of Appeals. I believe, however, that further proceedings are necessary in order to determine whether McCleskey's death sentence should be set aside. First, the Court of Appeals must decide whether the Baldus study is valid. I am persuaded that it is, but orderly procedure requires that the Court of Appeals address this issue before we actually decide the question. Second, it is necessary for the District Court to determine whether the particular facts of McCleskey's crime and his background place this case within the range of cases that present an unacceptable risk that race played a decisive role in McCleskey's sentencing.

Accordingly, I respectfully dissent

## NOTES ON RACE AND THE DEATH PENALTY

### 1. INTRODUCTION

The risk of arbitrariness in capital sentencing condemned in *Furman* has two dimensions: (i) random or capricious decisions that are not grounded in any discernible normative criteria that could justify differential outcomes; and (ii) "discriminatory" decisions that are based on impermissible factors. The preceding materials have focused mainly on the first dimension of *Furman*. *McCleskey* addresses the second.

Empirical studies conducted before *Furman* suggested two respects in which the death penalty may have been discriminatory: first, black defendants were more likely to receive the death penalty than white defendants in the South, although this finding was not consistently demonstrated elsewhere; and second, the death penalty was less likely to be imposed for homicides with black victims than for those with white victims.[a] In 1976, a majority of the Supreme Court expressed confidence that the new generation of reformed capital sentencing statutes had substantially reduced the risk of discrimination in the administration of the death penalty. During the following decade, social scientists sought to test the Court's supposition in studies of sentencing patterns under the post-*Furman* statutes. Although the Baldus study is generally acknowledged to be the most sophisticated of these investigations, other rigorous studies were conducted during the 1970s in Florida,[b] South Carolina,[c] and North Carolina.[d] This body of research yields a surprisingly consistent pattern: most investigators found no systematic evidence of discrimination based on race of the defendant, as had been expected, but almost all of the studies found a pronounced race-of-victim effect similar to the one found by Baldus and his colleagues.

## 2. THE GROSS AND MAURO STUDY

The pervasiveness of the race-of-victim effect in the post-*Furman* time frame is evident in a multi-state study conducted by Samuel Gross and Robert Mauro. They examined death sentencing patterns from 1976 through 1980 in eight states, using data obtained primarily from reports on homicide cases filed by local police agencies with the FBI. The FBI reports included data on: (i) the sex, age, and race of the victim(s); (ii) the sex, age, and race of the suspect(s); (iii) the date and place of the homicide; (iv) the weapon used; (v) the commission of any accompanying felony; and (vi) the relationship between the victim(s) and the suspected killer(s). The findings from this study are described and discussed in Samuel Gross and Robert Mauro, Patterns of Death: An Analysis of Racial Disparities in Capital Sentencing and Homicide Victimization, 37 Stan.L.Rev. 27 (1984).

In reporting their findings, the authors focused on the three states (Georgia, Florida, and Illinois) that had the highest number of death sentences. In each of those states, a large proportion of homicide victims were African-American, but those who killed whites (whether themselves white or not) were several times more likely be sentenced to death than those who killed blacks.

Gross and Mauro also looked at the relation between outcome and the nonracial variables included in the FBI data. They found that three of

---

[a] These studies are summarized in Gary Kleck, Racial Discrimination in Criminal Sentencing: A Critical Evaluation of the Evidence with Additional Evidence on the Death Penalty, 46 Am.Soc.Rev. 783 (1981).

[b] William Bowers and Glenn Pierce, Arbitrariness and Discrimination Under Post-Furman Capital Statutes, 26 Crime and Delinq. 563 (1980); Michael Radalet, Racial Characteristics and the Imposition of the Death Penalty, 46 Amer. Sociolog. Rev. 918 (1981); Hans Zeisel, Race Bias in the Administration of the Death Penalty: The Florida Experience, 95 Harv. L. Rev. 456 (1981); Linda Foley and Richard Powell, The Discretion of Prosecutors, Judges and Juries in Capital Cases, 7 Crim. Just. Rev. 16 (1982); Steven Arkin, Discrimination and Arbitrariness in Capital Punishment: An Analysis of Post-Furman Murder Cases in Dade County, Florida, 1973–1976, 33 Stan. L. Rev. 75 (1980); William Bowers, The Pervasiveness of Arbitrariness and Discrimination Under Post-Furman Capital Statutes, 74 J. Crim. L. and Criminol. 1067 (1983).

[c] Raymond Paternoster, Prosecutorial Discretion in Requesting the Death Penalty: A Case of Victim-Based Racial Discrimination, 18 L. & Soc'y Rev. 437 (1984).

[d] Barry Nakell and Kenneth Hardy, The Arbitrariness of the Death Penalty (1987).

these factors had a strong aggregate effect on the likelihood of death sentences in each state: the commission of a homicide in the course of another felony, the killing of a stranger, and the killing of multiple victims. They then sought to determine whether the race-of-victim disparities could be explained by any of these nonracial effects, and concluded, after taking these variables into account, that the race of the victim continued to have a large effect on the likelihood of a capital sentence.

Gross and Mauro also tried to anticipate the methodological objections that could be raised to their analysis. In particular, they focus on the possibility that information not included in the FBI files (concerning the strength of evidence or the suspects' prior record, for example) could account for the observed racial disparities. Although they concede that the inclusion of information on other variables would probably affect the magnitude of the effects yielded by the regression analysis, they insist that there is little likelihood that the omitted variables would substantially explain the racial disparities. "In sum," they conclude, "we are aware of no plausible alternative hypothesis that might explain the observed racial patterns in capital sentencing in legitimate, nondiscriminatory terms."

### 3. QUESTIONS AND COMMENTS ON *MCCLESKEY*

Justice Powell concluded that the Baldus study failed to demonstrate "a constitutionally significant risk of racial bias" in the administration of Georgia's dealth penalty. Why not? Would the result have been different if the Baldus study had revealed an equally pronounced race-of-defendant effect? Would it have mattered if the race-of-victim effect had been larger or more pervasive (e.g. if it had appeared in the most aggravated cases as well as in the mid-range cases)? In their comments on the *McCleskey* decision, Baldus and his colleagues suggest that the Court's refusal "to accept statistical proof of discrimination to support an Eighth Amendment claim" reflects "an unwillingness to destabilize the capital sentencing process.[e] Assume that McCleskey had prevailed. What would have been the impact of such a ruling on other death sentences in Georgia? On death sentences in other states?

### 4. POST-*MCCLESKEY* RESEARCH

In the wake of *McCleskey*, Congress asked the Government Accounting Office (GAO) to determine the extent to which race was a factor in the administration of the death penalty. The GAO's 1990 report summarized post-*Furman* research regarding race-of-victim discrimination as follows:

> In 82% of the studies, race-of-victim was found to influence the likelihood of being charged with capital murder or receiving a death sentence. . . . This finding was remarkably consistent across data sets, states, data collection methods, and analytic techniques.

With regard to race-of-defendant discrimination, the GAO concluded that the evidence was more equivocal. Although more than half of the studies found that race-of-defendant influenced the likelihood of being charged

---

[e] David C. Baldus, George Woodworth & Charles R. Pulaski, Jr., Equal Justice and the Death Penalty and A Legal and Empirical Analysis 380 (1990).

with a capital crime or receiving the death penalty, the nature of the relationship varied across studies.

Between 1990, when the GOA report was prepared, and 2003, 18 additional studies were published. David Baldus & George Woodworth, Race Discrimination in the Administration of the Death Penalty: An Overview of the Empirical Evidence with Special Emphasis on the Post-1990 Research, 39 Crim. L Bull. 194 (2003), summarized the findings of these studies as follows:

> Overall, their results indicate that the patterns documented in the GAO study persist. Specifically, on the issue of race-of-victim discrimination, there is a consistent pattern of white-victim disparities across the systems for which we have data. However, they are not apparent in all jurisdictions [or] at all stages of the charging and sentencing processes in which they do occur. On the issue of race-of-defendant discrimination in the system, with few exceptions the pre-1990 pattern of minimal minority-defendant disparities persists, although in some states, black defendants in white victim cases are at higher risk of being charged capitally and sentenced to death than are all other cases with different defendant/victim racial combinations.

Since the Baldus and Woodworth review in 2003, additional studies have been conducted in Connecticut,[f] Delaware,[g] Maryland,[h] North Carolina,[i] Texas,[j] and Washington,[k] providing additional evidence in support of victim-related disparities and defendant-related disparities. In a study on the administration of the death penalty in the United States Armed Forces between 1984 and 2005, David Baldus and several colleagues documented white-victim and minority defendant/white victim disparities in charging and sentencing outcomes similar to the findings repeatedly found over three decades of research in state courts, but also identified independent minority defendant disparities of a magnitude rarely seen in state court systems. David Baldus, Catherine Grosso, George Woodworth and Richard Newell, Racial Discrimination in the Administration of the Death Penalty: The Experience of the United States Armed Forces, 101 J.Crim.L. & Criminol. 1227 (2012).

---

[f] John J. Donahue III, An Empirical Examination of the Connecticut Death Penalty System since 1973: Are there Unlawful Racial, Gender, and Geographic Disparities? 11 J.E.L.S. 637 (2014)

[g] Sheri Lynn Johnson, John H. Blume, Theodore Eisenberg, Valerie P. Hans & Martin T. Wells, The Delaware Death Penalty: An Empirical Study, 97 Iowa L. Rev. 1925 (2011–12).

[h] Raymond Paternoster, Robert Brame, Sarah Bacon & Andrew Ditchfield, Justice by Geography and Race: The Administration of the Death Penalty in Maryland, 1978–1999, 4 Margins: Md. L. J. on Race, Religion, Gender & Class 1 (2004).

[i] Isaac Unah, Empirical Analysis of Race and the Process of Capital Punishment in North Carolina, 2011 Mich. St. L Rev. 609.

[j] Scott Phillips, Continued Racial Disparities in the Capital of Capital Punishment: The Rosenthal Era, 50 Hous. L Rev. 131 (2012).

[k] Katherine Beckett & Heather Evans, The Role of Race in Washington State Capital Sentencing, 1981–2012 (2014) available at http://www.deathpenaltyinfo.org/documents/WashRaceStudy2014.pdf.

# CHAPTER XII

# PROOF BEYOND A REASONABLE DOUBT

## SECTION 1: MITIGATIONS AND DEFENSES

### NOTES ON PROOF OF MITIGATIONS AND DEFENSES

1. *IN RE WINSHIP*

Proof beyond a reasonable doubt has long been a fundamental premise of American criminal justice. It was not until 1970, however, that the Supreme Court explicitly held that the Constitution required this standard of proof in criminal cases.

The issue arose in a New York juvenile delinquency proceeding in which conviction was permitted based on proof by a preponderance of the evidence. In re Winship, 397 U.S. 358 (1970), held that the Constitution required the same standard of proof for both adult criminal prosecutions and juvenile delinquency proceedings. The Court's conclusion was unmistakably plain: "Lest there remain any doubt about the constitutional stature of the reasonable-doubt standard, we explicitly hold that the Due Process Clause protects the accused against conviction except upon proof beyond a reasonable doubt of every fact necessary to constitute the crime with which he is charged."

By the time of *Winship,* every American jurisdiction required that criminal conviction of an adult be based on proof beyond a reasonable doubt. Aside from extending that standard to juvenile delinquency proceedings, *Winship* seemed at first to have little impact. The issue lurking in *Winship,* however, was the scope of the reasonable-doubt requirement. What, exactly, was included in the phrase "every fact necessary to constitute the crime . . . charged?" Should it cover only those facts formally made elements of the crime by the definition of the offense? Should it also include matters technically extrinsic to the definition of the offense, such as a fact relevant only to a defense? Should it apply to matters taken into account at the sentencing stage that were "necessary" predicates of a long prison sentence? Should it perhaps be limited to those facts constitutionally necessary to constitute the crime charged? If so, how does one determine which facts are "constitutionally necessary"?

These and other possible interpretations surfaced in the years following *Winship.* Before too long, a constitutional pronouncement that originally had seemed largely symbolic had become the subject of intense debate that still presents major issues for Supreme Court consideration. The essential problem is how to mesh a judicial requirement of proof beyond a reasonable doubt with legislative control over the substance of the penal law. The Supreme Court's efforts to address this issue are covered in the materials that follow.

## 2. *MULLANEY V. WILBUR*

The Supreme Court's confrontation with the implications of *Winship* began five years later in Mullaney v. Wilbur, 421 U.S. 684 (1975). Maine law included the standard common law provision that a defendant charged with murder could be convicted only of manslaughter if the homicidal act occurred "in the heat of passion on sudden provocation." In most states, if the defendant offered some evidence to support a claim of provocation, the prosecution was required disprove the claim beyond a reasonable doubt. In Maine, the defendant was required to establish provocation by a preponderance of the evidence.

There was a good bit of debate in the lower courts and the briefs about exactly how Maine law should be described. But the Supreme Court stated the issue as follows:

> The Maine law of homicide, as it bears on this case, can be stated succinctly: Absent justification or excuse, all intentional or criminally reckless killings are felonious homicides. Felonious homicide is punished as murder . . . unless the defendant proves by a fair preponderance of the evidence that it was committed in the heat of passion on sudden provocation, in which case it is punished as manslaughter. . . . The issue is whether the Maine rule requiring the defendant to prove that he acted in the heat of passion on sudden provocation accords with due process.[a]

Justice Powell's opinion for a unanimous Court concluded that the Constitution was violated. He first examined the "historical context." While the early common law cases placed the burden on the defendant to prove provocation, Justice Powell concluded that:

> This historical review establishes two important points. First, the fact at issue here—the presence or absence of the heat of passion on sudden provocation—has been, almost from the inception of the common law of homicide, the single most important factor in determining the degree of culpability attaching to an unlawful homicide. And, second, the clear trend has been toward requiring the prosecution to bear the ultimate burden of proving this fact.

He continued:

> [T]he criminal law of Maine, like that of other jurisdictions, is concerned not only with guilt or innocence in the abstract but also with the degree of criminal culpability. Maine has chosen to distinguish those who kill in the heat of passion from those who kill in the absence of this factor. Because the former are less

---

[a] In an earlier portion of its opinion, the Court described the Maine rule somewhat differently:

> [The trial] court charged that "malice aforethought is an essential and indispensable element of the crime of murder," without which the homicide would be manslaughter. The jury was further instructed, however, that if the prosecution established that the homicide was both intentional and unlawful, malice aforethought was to be conclusively implied unless the defendant proved by a fair preponderance of the evidence that he acted in the heat of passion on sudden provocation. The court emphasized that "malice aforethought and heat of passion on sudden provocation are two inconsistent things"; thus, by proving the latter the defendant would negate the former and reduce the homicide from murder to manslaughter.

This difference was to prove important in the Court's later decision in *Patterson v. New York*, summarized below.—[Footnote by eds.]

"blameworth[y]," they are subject to substantially less severe penalties. By drawing this distinction, while refusing to require the prosecution to establish beyond a reasonable doubt the fact upon which it turns, Maine denigrates the interests found critical in *Winship*.

The safeguards of due process are not rendered unavailing simply because a determination may already have been reached that would stigmatize the defendant and that might lead to a significant impairment of personal liberty. The fact remains that the consequences resulting from a verdict of murder, as compared with a verdict of manslaughter, differ significantly. Indeed, when viewed in terms of the potential difference in restrictions of personal liberty attendant to each conviction, the distinction established by Maine between murder and manslaughter may be of greater importance than the difference between guilt or innocence for many lesser crimes.

Moreover, if *Winship* were limited to those facts that constitute a crime as defined by state law, a state could undermine many of the interests that decision sought to protect without effecting any substantive change in its law. It would only be necessary to redefine the elements that constitute different crimes, characterizing them as factors that bear solely on the extent of punishment. An extreme example of this approach can be fashioned from the law challenged in this case. Maine divides the single generic offenses of felonious homicide into three distinct punishment categories—murder, voluntary manslaughter, and involuntary manslaughter. Only the first two of these categories require that the homicidal act either be intentional or the result of criminally reckless conduct. But under Maine law these facts of intent are not general elements of the crime of felonious homicide. Instead, they bear only on the appropriate punishment category. Thus, if petitioners' argument were accepted, Maine could impose a life sentence for any felonious homicide—even those that traditionally might be considered involuntary manslaughter—unless the *defendant* was able to prove that his act was neither intentional nor criminally reckless.[24]

*Winship* is concerned with substance rather than this kind of formalism. The rationale of that case requires an analysis that looks to the "operation and effect of the law as applied and enforced by the state," and to the interests of both the state and the defendant as affected by the allocation of the burden of proof.

In *Winship* the Court emphasized the societal interests in the reliability of jury verdicts:

> The requirement of proof beyond a reasonable doubt has [a] vital role in our criminal procedure for cogent reasons. The accused during a criminal prosecution has at stake interests of immense importance, both because of the

[24] Many states impose different statutory sentences on different degrees of assault. If *Winship* were limited to a state's definition of the elements of a crime, these states could define all assaults as a single offense and then require the defendant to disprove the elements of aggravation—e.g., intent to kill or intent to rob. . . .

possibility that he may lose his liberty upon conviction and because of the certainty that he would be stigmatized by the conviction. . . .

Moreover, use of the reasonable-doubt standard is indispensable to command the respect and confidence of the community in applications of the criminal law. It is critical that the moral force of the criminal law not be diluted by a standard of proof that leaves people in doubt whether innocent men are being condemned.

The interests are implicated to a greater degree in this case than they were in *Winship* itself. Petitioner there faced an 18-month sentence, with a maximum possible extension of an additional four and one-half years, whereas respondent here faces a differential in sentencing ranging from a nominal fine to a mandatory life sentence. Both the stigma to the defendant and the community's confidence in the administration of the criminal law are also of greater consequence in this case, since the adjudication of delinquency involved in *Winship* was "benevolent" in intention, seeking to provide "a generously conceived program of compassionate treatment."

Not only are the interests underlying *Winship* implicated to a greater degree in this case, but in one respect the protection afforded those interests is less here. In *Winship* the ultimate burden of persuasion remained with the prosecution, although the standard had been reduced to proof by a fair preponderance of the evidence. In this case, by contrast, the state has affirmatively shifted the burden of proof to the defendant. The result, in a case such as this one where the defendant is required to prove the critical fact in dispute, is to increase further the likelihood of an erroneous murder conviction. . . .

Nor is the requirement of proving a negative unique in our system of criminal jurisprudence. Maine itself requires the prosecution to prove the absence of self-defense beyond a reasonable doubt. Satisfying this burden imposes an obligation that, in all practical effect, is identical to the burden involved in negating the heat of passion on sudden provocation. Thus, we discern no unique hardship on the prosecution that would justify requiring the defendant to carry the burden of proving a fact so critical to criminal culpability. . . .

Maine law requires a defendant to establish by a preponderance of the evidence that he acted in the heat of passion on sudden provocation in order to reduce murder to manslaughter. Under this burden of proof a defendant can be given a life sentence when the evidence indicates that it is *as likely as not* that he deserves a significantly lesser sentence. This is an intolerable result in a society where, to paraphrase Mr. Justice Harlan, it is far worse to sentence one guilty only of manslaughter as a murderer than to sentence a murderer for the lesser crime of manslaughter. *In re Winship*, 397 U.S. at 372 (concurring opinion). We therefore hold that the Due Process Clause requires the prosecution to prove beyond a reasonable doubt the absence of the heat of passion on sudden provocation when the issue is properly presented in a homicide case.

### 3. BURDEN OF PROOF ON INSANITY DEFENSE: *LELAND* AND *RIVERA*

The Court held in Leland v. Oregon, 343 U.S. 790 (1952), that the Constitution did not require the prosecution to disprove an alleged insanity defense beyond a reasonable doubt. It was acceptable to place the burden of establishing the insanity defense on the defendant.[b]

Joined by Chief Justice Burger, Justice Rehnquist wrote a concurring opinion in *Mullaney*, the main objective of which was to argue that *Leland* survived *Mullaney*:

> The Court noted in *Leland* that the issue of insanity as a defense to a criminal charge was considered by the jury only after it had found that all elements of the offense, including the mens rea, if any, required by state law, had been proved beyond a reasonable doubt. Although as the state court's instructions in *Leland* recognized evidence relevant to insanity as defined by state law may also be relevant to whether the required means rea was present, the existence or nonexistence of legal insanity bears no necessary relationship to the existence or nonexistence of the required mental elements of the crime. For this reason, Oregon's placement of the burden of proof of insanity on *Leland*, unlike Maine's redefinition of homicide in the instant case, did not effect an unconstitutional shift in the State's traditional burden of proof beyond a reasonable doubt of all necessary elements of the offense. Both the Court's opinion and the concurring opinion of Mr. Justice Harlan in *In re Winship* stress the importance of proof beyond a reasonable doubt in a criminal case as "bottomed on a fundamental value determination of our society that it is far worse to convict an innocent man than to let a guilty man go free." Having once met that rigorous burden of proof that, for example, in a case such as this, the defendant not only killed a fellow human being, but did it with malice aforethought, the State could quite consistently with such a constitutional principle conclude that a defendant who sought to establish the defense of insanity, and thereby escape any punishment whatever for a heinous crime, should bear the laboring oar on such an issue.

The *Leland* issue came back to the Court a year after *Mullaney*. In Rivera v. Delaware, 429 U.S. 877 (1976), the Court dismissed an appeal for want of a substantial federal question.[c] Justice Stevens stated that he

---

[b] Indeed, in Oregon at the time, the *defendant* was required to establish insanity beyond a reasonable doubt. Today, no state retains such an onerous requirement, although the federal government and a number of states require defense proof that is "clear and convincing." Other states put the burden on the defendant by a preponderance of the evidence. Less than half require the prosecution to disprove the defense beyond a reasonable doubt.

[c] As a formal matter, this means, in Supreme Court practice, that the federal issue presented to the Court was frivolous, that it was so insubstantial and so obviously correctly decided by the lower court that the Supreme Court lacked jurisdiction to hear the case. Moreover, the Court's disposition stands as precedent for the correctness of the disposition below of the federal question presented to it for review.

would have noted probable jurisdiction.[d] Joined by Justice Marshall, Justice Brennan dissented. He started by describing the issue:

> [T]he constitutionality of a Delaware statute that requires a criminal defendant raising an insanity defense to prove mental illness or defect by a preponderance of the evidence was sustained [by the Delaware Supreme Court. That Court] held that *Leland* required its conclusion, because *Leland* has not been overruled by *Mullaney* . . . either expressly or implicitly. Because I believe this case presents the substantial federal question whether *Leland* can be reconciled with our recent holdings in *Winship* and *Mullaney*, I would note probable jurisdiction and set the case for oral argument.

Justice Brennan then summarized Justice Rehnquist's defense of *Leland* in *Mullaney*, concluding:

> I do not think that the logic of this view is self-evident. Like the state rule invalidated in *Mullaney*, . . . the plea of insanity, whether or not the State chooses to characterize it as an affirmative defense, relates to the accused's state of mind, an essential element of the crime, and bears upon the appropriate form of punishment. Nor is it sufficient after *Mullaney* to say, as the Court did in *Leland*, that a State may characterize the insanity defense as it chooses. We said in *Mullaney* that the requirement of *Winship* that the State prove all elements of the crime was one of substance, not limited to "a State's definition of the elements of the crime. . . ."

## 4. QUESTIONS AND COMMENTS

Consider two questions before reading the next Note: What is the principle for which *Mullaney* stands? Why is it consistent with that principle to place the burden of proof of insanity on the defendant? Neither of these questions is easy. The first one, at least, is made much more complex by the decision, only two years after *Mullaney*, in *Patterson v. New York*.

## 5. *PATTERSON V. NEW YORK*

Under the New York law at issue in Patterson v. New York, 432 U.S. 197 (1977), a person could be convicted of second degree murder on proof of causing the death of another person with intent to do so. It was an "affirmative defense," on which the defendant had the burden of proof by a preponderance of the evidence, if the defendant "acted under the influence of extreme emotional disturbance for which there was a reasonable

---

[d] That is, he voted to hear the case on the merits.

explanation or excuse.[e] The question was whether this structure was acceptable after *Mullaney*. The Court held that it was.[f]

For the Court, Justice White said:

> In convicting Patterson under its murder statute, New York did no more than *Leland* and *Rivera* permitted it to do without violating the Due Process Clause. Under those cases, once the facts constituting a crime are established beyond a reasonable doubt, based on all the evidence including the evidence of the defendant's mental state, the State may refuse to sustain the affirmative defense of insanity unless demonstrated by a preponderance of the evidence.
>
> The New York law on extreme emotional disturbance follows this pattern. This affirmative defense, which the Court of Appeals described as permitting the defendant to show that his actions were caused by a mental infirmity not arising to the level of insanity, and that he is less culpable for having committed them, does not serve to negative any facts of the crime which the State is to prove in order to convict of murder. It constitutes a separate issue on which the defendant is required to carry the burden of persuasion; and unless we are to overturn *Leland* and *Rivera*, New York has not violated the Due Process Clause, and Patterson's conviction must be sustained.
>
> We are unwilling to reconsider *Leland* and *Rivera*. But even if we were to hold that a State must prove sanity to convict once that fact is put in issue, it would not necessarily follow that a State must prove beyond a reasonable doubt every fact, the existence or nonexistence of which it is willing to recognize as an exculpatory or mitigating circumstance affecting the degree of culpability or the severity of the punishment. Here, in revising its criminal code, New York provided the affirmative defense of extreme emotional disturbance, a substantially expanded version of the older heat-of-passion concept; but it was willing to do so only if the facts making out the defense were established by the defendant with sufficient certainty. The State was itself unwilling to undertake to establish the absence of those facts beyond a reasonable doubt, perhaps fearing that proof would be too difficult and that too many persons deserving treatment as murderers would escape that punishment if the evidence need merely raise a reasonable doubt about the defendant's emotional state. It has been

---

[e] Successful assertion of this "affirmative defense" would result in conviction of manslaughter in the first degree. The relevant statute provided: "A person is guilty of manslaughter in the first degree when . . . [w]ith intent to cause the death of another person, he causes the death of such person or of a third person under circumstances which do not constitute murder because he acts under the influence of extreme emotional disturbance, as defined in [the second degree murder statute]. The fact that homicide was committed under the influence of extreme emotional disturbance constitutes a mitigating circumstance reducing murder to manslaughter in the first degree and need not be proved in any prosecution initiated under this subdivision."

[f] A majority of five Justices reached this conclusion, in an opinion by Justice White. Justice Rehnquist did not participate. Justice Powell, joined by Justices Brennan and Marshall, dissented. Four of the Justices in the *Patterson* majority had voted in *Mullaney* to hold the Maine law unconstitutional. They were Chief Justice Burger and Justices White, Stewart, and Blackmun. Justice Stevens also voted with the majority in *Patterson*. He had replaced Justice Douglas in the interval between the decisions in *Mullaney* and *Patterson*.

said that the new criminal code of New York contains some 25 affirmative defenses which exculpate or mitigate but which must be established by the defendant to be operative.[10] The Due Process Clause, as we see it, does not put New York to the choice of abandoning those defenses or undertaking to disprove their existence in order to convict of a crime which otherwise is within its constitutional powers to sanction by substantial punishment.

The requirement of proof beyond a reasonable doubt in a criminal case is bottomed on a fundamental value determination of our society that it is far worse to convict an innocent man than to let a guilty man go free. *Winship*, 397 U.S. at 372 (Harlan, J., concurring). The social cost of placing the burden on the prosecution to prove guilt beyond a reasonable doubt is thus an increased risk that the guilty will go free. While it is clear that our society has willingly chosen to bear a substantial burden in order to protect the innocent, it is equally clear that the risk it must bear is not without limits; and Mr. Justice Harlan's aphorism provides little guidance for determining what those limits are. Due process does not require that every conceivable step be taken, at whatever cost, to eliminate the possibility of convicting an innocent person. Punishment of those found guilty by a jury, for example, is not forbidden merely because there is a remote possibility in some instances that an innocent person might go to jail.

It is said that the common-law rule permits a State to punish one as a murderer when it is as likely as not that he acted in the heat of passion or under severe emotional distress and when, if he did, he is guilty only of manslaughter. But this has always been the case in those jurisdictions adhering to the traditional rule. It is also very likely true that fewer convictions of murder would occur if New York were required to negative the affirmative defense at issue here. But in each instance of a murder conviction under the present law New York will have proved beyond a reasonable doubt that the defendant has intentionally killed another person, an act which it is not disputed the State may constitutionally criminalize and punish. If the State nevertheless chooses to recognize a factor that mitigates the degree of criminality or punishment, we think the State may assure itself that the fact has been established with reasonably certainty. To recognize at all a mitigating circumstance does not require the State to prove its nonexistence in each case in which the fact is put in issue, if in its judgment this would be too cumbersome, too expensive, and too inaccurate.

---

[10] The State of New York is not alone in this result:

Since the Model Penal Code was completed in 1962, some 22 states have codified and reformed their criminal laws. At least 12 of these jurisdictions have used the concept of an "affirmative defense" and have defined that phrase to require that the defendant prove the existence of an "affirmative defense" by a preponderance of the evidence. Additionally, at least six proposed state codes and each of the four successive versions of a revised federal code use the same procedural device. Finally, many jurisdictions that do not generally employ this concept of "affirmative defense" nevertheless shift the burden of proof to the defendant on particular issues.

Peter W. Low & John C. Jeffries, Jr., DICTA: Constitutionalizing the Criminal Law?, 29 Va. Law Weekly, No. 18, p. 1 (1977) (footnotes omitted). . . .

We thus decline to adopt as a constitutional imperative, operative countrywide, that a State must disprove beyond a reasonable doubt every fact constituting any and all affirmative defenses related to the culpability of an accused. Traditionally, due process has required that only the most basic procedural safeguards be observed; more subtle balancing of society's interests against those of the accused have been left to the legislative branch. We therefore will not disturb the balance struck in previous cases holding that the Due Process Clause requires the prosecution to prove beyond a reasonable doubt all of the elements included in the definition of the offense of which the defendant is charged. Proof of the nonexistence of all affirmative defenses has never been constitutionally required; and we perceive no reason to fashion such a rule in this case and apply it to the statutory defense at issue here.

This view may seem to permit state legislatures to reallocate burdens of proof by labeling as affirmative defenses at least some elements of the crimes now defined in their statutes. But there are obviously constitutional limits beyond which the States may not go in this regard. . . . Long before *Winship*, the universal rule in this country was that the prosecution must prove guilt beyond a reasonable doubt. At the same time, the long-accepted rule was that it was constitutionally permissible to provide that various affirmative defenses were to be proved by the defendant. This did not lead to such abuses or to such widespread redefinition of crime and reduction of the prosecution's burden that a new constitutional rule was required.[12] This was not the problem to which *Winship* was addressed. Nor does the fact that a majority of the States have now assumed the burden of disproving affirmative defenses for whatever reasons mean that those States that strike a different balance are in violation of the Constitution.

What, then, is *Mullaney* to mean? The Court responded:

*Mullaney*'s holding, it is argued, is that the State may not permit the blameworthiness of an act or the severity of punishment authorized for its commission to depend on the presence or absence of an identified fact without assuming the burden of proving the presence or absence of that fact, as the case may be, beyond a reasonable doubt.[15] In our view, the *Mullaney* holding

[12] Whenever due process guarantees are dependent upon the law as defined by the legislative branches, some consideration must be given to the possibility that legislative discretion may be abused to the detriment of the individual. The applicability of the reasonable-doubt standard, however, has always been dependent on how a State defines the offense that is charged in any given case; yet there has been no great rush by the States to shift the burden of disproving traditional elements of the criminal offenses to the accused.

[15] There is some language in *Mullaney* that has been understood as perhaps construing the Due Process Clause to require the prosecution to prove beyond a reasonable doubt any fact affecting the degree of criminal culpability. It is said that such a rule would deprive legislatures of any discretion whatsoever in allocating the burden of proof, the practical effect of which might be to undermine legislative reform of our criminal justice system. See . . . P. Low & J. Jeffries, supra, n.10. Carried to its logical extreme, such a reading of *Mullaney* might also, for example, discourage Congress from enacting pending legislation to change the felony-murder rule by permitting the accused to prove by a preponderance of the evidence the affirmative defense that the homicide committed was neither a necessary nor a reasonably

should not be so broadly read. The concurrence of two Justices in *Mullaney* was necessarily contrary to such a reading; and a majority of the Court refused to so understand and apply *Mullaney* when *Rivera* was dismissed for want of a substantial federal question.

*Mullaney* surely held that a State must prove every ingredient of an offense beyond a reasonable doubt, and that it may not shift the burden of proof to the defendant by presuming that ingredient upon proof of the other elements of the offense. This is true even though the State's practice, as in Maine, had been traditionally to the contrary. Such shifting of the burden of persuasion with respect to a fact which the State deems so important that it must be either proved or presumed is impermissible under the Due Process Clause.

It was unnecessary to go further in *Mullaney*. The Maine Supreme Judicial Court made it clear that malice aforethought, which was mentioned in the statutory definition of the crime, was not equivalent to premeditation and that the presumption of malice traditionally arising in intentional homicide cases carried no factual meaning insofar as premeditation was concerned. Even so, a killing became murder in Maine when it resulted from a deliberate, cruel act committed by one person against another, suddenly without any, or without a considerable provocation. Premeditation was not within the definition of murder; but malice, in the sense of the absence of provocation, was part of the definition of that crime. Yet malice, i. e., lack of provocation, was presumed and could be rebutted by the defendant only by proving by a preponderance of the evidence that he acted with heat of passion upon sudden provocation. In *Mullaney* we held that however traditional this mode of proceeding might have been, it is contrary to the Due Process Clause as construed in *Winship*.

### 6. *MARTIN V. OHIO*

Ohio was one of two states that placed the burden of persuasion on a defendant who wished to assert a claim of self defense in a murder prosecution. The question in Martin v. Ohio, 480 U.S. 228 (1987), was whether that rule was consistent with *Mullaney-Patterson*.

Justice White's opinion for the Court held that, as applied, the Ohio rule did not violate due process:

As in *Patterson*, the jury was here instructed that to convict it must find, in light of all the evidence, that each of the elements of the crime of aggravated murder has been proved by the state beyond reasonable doubt and that the burden of proof with respect to these elements did not shift. To find guilt, the jury had to be convinced that none of the evidence, whether offered by the state or by Martin in connection with her plea of self-defense, raised a reasonable doubt that Martin had killed her husband,

---

foreseeable consequence of the underlying felony. The Court did not intend *Mullaney* to have such far-reaching effect.

> that she had the specific purpose and intent to cause his death, or that she had done so with prior calculation and design. . . .
>
> We agree with the State . . . that this conviction did not violate the Due Process Clause. The state did not exceed its authority in defining the crime of murder as purposely causing the death of another with prior calculation or design. It did not seek to shift to Martin the burden of proving any of those elements, and the jury's verdict reflects that none of her self-defense evidence raised a reasonable doubt about the state's proof that she purposefully killed with prior calculation and design. She nevertheless had the opportunity under state law and the instructions given to justify the killing and show herself to be blameless by proving that she acted in self-defense. . . . It would be quite different if the jury had been instructed that self-defense evidence could not be considered in determining whether there was a reasonable doubt about the state's case, i.e., that self-defense evidence must be put aside for all purposes unless it satisfied the preponderance standard. Such instruction would relieve the state of its burden and plainly run afoul of *Winship*'s mandate.

7. QUESTIONS AND COMMENTS

Can the decisions in *Mullaney* and *Patterson* be reconciled? Or did the Court, after only two years and no determinative shift in personnel, simply change its mind? There is a case to be made for the proposition that *Patterson* rewrote *Mullaney* into obscurity and that, as now construed, *Mullaney* is of little modern significance. The spirit of *Mullaney*, however, is far from dead. The materials in Section 2 of this Chapter make clear that the tension between the cases has modern purchase. It is therefore of current importance to think about the principles that ought to determine those "elements" of crime on which the prosecution should bear the burden of proof beyond a reasonable doubt. Consider the following efforts to do so.

*(i) The Procedural Interpretation of Winship and Mullaney*

Under what might be called the "procedural" interpretation of *Winship* and *Mullaney*, the constitutional commitment to proof beyond a reasonable doubt should extend to every fact determinative of criminal liability. The prosecution would be required to prove beyond a reasonable doubt not only every element of the offense charged but also the absence of justification, excuse, or other grounds of defense or mitigation. This is termed the procedural interpretation of *Winship* because it treats the reasonable-doubt standard as a procedural requirement to be enforced without regard to legislative control over the substance of the penal law. In other words, the value of requiring proof beyond a reasonable doubt is thought to be entirely independent of the substantive issue of what must be proved.

An articulate statement of this approach can be found in Barbara Underwood, The Thumb on the Scales of Justice: Burdens of Persuasion in Criminal Cases, 86 Yale L.J. 1299 (1977). She postulates two distinct purposes for requiring proof beyond a reasonable doubt: "First, the rule is meant to affect the outcome of individual cases, reducing the likelihood of an erroneous conviction. Second, the rule is meant to symbolize for society the great significance of a criminal conviction." In Underwood's view, the fact that a defense is gratuitous—i.e., that it may be granted or withheld at the legislature's option—provides no basis for treating it as an exception to the reasonable-doubt requirement. Shifting the burden of persuasion to the defendant, she argues, "limits the defense to those for whom the evidence is most abundant." It does not necessarily identify those who are in fact the least culpable or most deserving of the defense. She concludes:

> [A] constitutional valuation of the relative costs of errors cannot be avoided by legislative fiat. So long as the factual determination has the function and consequences that characterize other issues in a criminal case, such as enhanced stigma and an increased period of potential incarceration, the reasons for the constitutional rule remain. The costs of erroneous convictions and erroneous acquittals are not different by virtue of the gratuitous character of the defense. . . .

### (ii) *Preservation of the Gratuitous Defense*

A contrary view is stated in John C. Jeffries, Jr. and Paul B. Stephan III, Defenses, Presumptions, and Burden of Proof in the Criminal Law, 88 Yale L.J. 1325 (1979).[g] In their opinion, the rationales for the reasonable-doubt requirement demand that *something* be proved beyond a reasonable doubt, but "do not establish that *every* fact relevant to the imposition or grade of penal liability be subject to that standard." They focus squarely on the gratuitous defense. In their view, the constitutional insistence on proof beyond a reasonable doubt "no longer makes sense" when applied to a gratuitous defense. "Such a rule would purport to preserve individual liberty and the societal sense of commitment to it by forcing the government *either* to disprove the defense beyond a reasonable doubt *or* to eliminate the defense altogether." The government could cure the purported unconstitutionality *either* by proving more *or* by proving less, as it saw fit. "The latter solution results in an extension of penal liability despite the presence of mitigating or exculpatory facts. It is difficult to see this result as constitutionally compelled and harder still to believe that it flows from a general policy, whether actual or symbolic, in favor of individual liberty." It is likely, they thought, that denying to the legislature the option of shifting the burden of persuasion to the defendant would "thwart legislative reform of the penal law," "stifle efforts to undo injustice in the traditional law of crimes," and risk "a harsh and regressive expansion in the definition of guilt":

> In order to test this proposition, we surveyed the practices of the 33 American states that have recently enacted comprehensive revisions of their penal laws. . . . Eight of these states provide no statutory guidance on this point, and six more expressly require that the prosecution bear the burden of proof beyond a reasonable doubt for every fact needed to obtain conviction. However, 19 states have enacted revised codes that include burden-shifting defenses. Virtually all of these uses of the burden-shifting defense mark instances of benevolent innovation in the penal law. Thirteen states recognize an affirmative defense of renunciation for the crime of attempt. Nine permit reasonable mistake as to age as

[g] See also Ronald J. Allen, The Restoration of *In re Winship*: A Comment on Burdens of Persuasion in Criminal Cases After *Patterson* v. *New York*, 76 Mich.L.Rev. 30 (1977), and Ronald J. Allen, *Mullaney* v. *Wilbur*, The Supreme Court and the Substantive Criminal Law—An Examination of the Limits of Legitimate Intervention, 55 Tex.L.Rev. 269 (1977).

> an affirmative defense to statutory rape. Eight create an affirmative defense to liability for felony murder, and six exonerate the accused [who] can show reasonable reliance on an official misstatement of law. In each of these cases, the affirmative defense is used to introduce a new ground of exculpation, often in circumstances where an obligation to disprove its existence beyond a reasonable doubt would be especially onerous. None of the named defenses existed at common law, and none is a traditional feature of American statutes. A plausible conclusion is that shifting the burden of proof is often politically necessary to secure legislative reform. It seems quite possible, therefore, that disallowance of this procedural device would work to inhibit reform and induce retrogression in the penal law.

### *(iii) An Alternative Reformulation of Mullaney: The Patterson and Martin Dissents*

Justice Powell accused the *Patterson* majority of running "a constitutional boundary line through the barely visible space that separates Maine's law from New York's," doing so "on the basis of distinctions in language that are formalistic rather than substantive," and adopting a rationale that "bears little resemblance to the basic rationale of [the *Mullaney*] decision." He continued:

> But this is not the cause of greatest concern. The test the Court today establishes allows a legislature to shift, virtually at will, the burden of persuasion with respect to any factor in a criminal case, so long as it is careful not to mention the non-existence of that factor in the statutory language that defines the crime. . . .
>
> Perhaps the Court's interpretation of *Winship* is consistent with the letter of the holding in that case. But little of the spirit survives. . . . With all respect, this type of constitutional adjudication is indefensibly formalistic. A limited but significant check on possible abuses in the criminal law now becomes an exercise in arid formalities. What *Winship* and *Mullaney* had sought to teach about the limits a free society places on its procedures to safeguard the liberty of its citizens becomes a rather simplistic lesson in statutory draftsmanship. Nothing in the Court's opinion prevents a legislature from applying this new learning to many of the classical elements of the crimes it punishes.[8] It would be preferable, if the Court has found reason to reject the rationale of *Winship* and *Mullaney*, simply and straightforwardly to overrule those precedents.
>
> The Court understandably manifests some uneasiness that its formalistic approach will give legislatures too much latitude in shifting the burden of persuasion. And so it issues a warning that "there are obviously constitutional limits beyond which the states

---

[8] For example, a state statute could pass muster under the only solid standard that appears in the Court's opinion if it defined murder as mere physical contact between the defendant and the victim leading to the victim's death, but then set up an affirmative defense leaving it to the defendant to prove that he acted without culpable mens rea. The state, in other words, could be relieved altogether of responsibility for proving *anything* regarding the defendant's state of mind, provided only that the face of the statute meets the Court's drafting formulas. . . .

> may not go in this regard." The Court thereby concedes that legislative abuses may occur and that they must be curbed by the judicial branch. But if the state is careful to conform to the drafting formulas articulated today, the constitutional limits are anything but "obvious." This decision simply leaves us without a conceptual framework for distinguishing abuses from legitimate legislative adjustments of the burden of persuasion in criminal cases.

So what is the appropriate conceptual framework? Justice Powell's answer was:

> [There are two] principles that should govern this case. The Due Process Clause requires that the prosecutor bear the burden of persuasion beyond a reasonable doubt only if the factor at issue makes a substantial difference in punishment and stigma. The requirement of course applies a fortiori if the factor makes the difference between guilt and innocence. But a substantial difference in punishment alone is not enough. It also must be shown that in the Anglo-American legal tradition the factor in question historically has held that level of importance. If either branch of the test is not met, then the legislature retains its traditional authority over matters of proof. But to permit a shift in the burden of persuasion when both branches of this test are satisfied would invite the undermining of the presumption of innocence, "that bedrock 'axiomatic and elementary' principle whose 'enforcement lies at the foundation of the administration of our criminal law.' "

He elaborated:

> The Court beats its retreat from *Winship* apparently because of a concern that otherwise the federal judiciary will intrude too far into the substantive choices concerning the content of a state's criminal law. The concern is legitimate, but misplaced. *Winship* and *Mullaney* are no more than what they purport to be: decisions addressing the procedural requirements that states must meet to comply with due process. They are not outposts for policing the substantive boundaries of the criminal law.
>
> The *Winship/Mullaney* test identifies those factors of such importance, historically, in determining punishment and stigma that the Constitution forbids shifting to the defendant the burden of persuasion when such a factor is at issue. *Winship* and *Mullaney* specify only the procedure that is required when a state elects to use such a factor as part of its substantive criminal law. They do not say that the state must elect to use it. For example, where a state has chosen to retain the traditional distinction between murder and manslaughter, as have New York and Maine, the burden of persuasion must remain on the prosecution with respect to the distinguishing factor, in view of its decisive historical importance. But nothing in *Mullaney* or *Winship* precludes a state from abolishing the distinction between murder and manslaughter and treating all unjustifiable homicide as murder.[13]

[13] Perhaps under other principles of due-process jurisprudence, certain factors are so fundamental that a state could not, as a substantive matter, refrain from recognizing them so long as it chooses to punish given conduct as a crime. . . . But substantive limits were not at issue in *Winship* or *Mullaney*, and they are not at issue here. . . .

> In this significant respect, neither *Winship* nor *Mullaney* eliminates the substantive flexibility that should remain in legislative hands.
>
> Moreover, it is unlikely that more than a few factors—although important ones—for which a shift in the burden of persuasion seriously would be considered will come within the *Mullaney* holding. With some exceptions, then, the state has the authority "to recognize a factor that mitigates the degree of criminality or punishment" without having "to prove its nonexistence in each case in which the fact is put in issue." New ameliorative affirmative defenses, about which the Court expresses concern, generally remain undisturbed by the holdings in *Winship* and *Mullaney*—and need not be disturbed by a sound holding reversing Patterson's conviction.

This theme was repeated in Justice Powell's dissent in *Martin*,[h] where he said that there are "at least two benefits" to the approach he outlined in *Patterson*:

> First, it ensures that the critical facts necessary to sustain a conviction will be proved by the state. Because the Court would be willing to look beyond the text of a state statute, legislatures would have no incentive to redefine essential elements of an offense to make them part of an affirmative defense, thereby shifting the burden of proof in a manner inconsistent with *Winship* and *Mullaney*. Second, it would leave the states free in all other respects to recognize new factors that may mitigate the degree of criminality or punishment, without requiring that they also bear the burden of disproving these defenses.

Justice Powell refocused his position in *Mullaney*, introducing a different calculus to measure the constitutional limits on burden-shifting defenses. What is the appropriate role of the "Anglo-American legal tradition" in decisions of this sort? Should the constitutionality of modern legislation depend on its consistency with the early common law? If so, what is to be made in *Mullaney* of the fact that initially the common law placed the burden of persuasion on the defendant in provocation cases? And how should crimes be treated that have no common law counterparts? Should the legislature be completely free to allocate the burden of persuasion in offenses governing securities, antitrust, organized crime, corporate ethics, taxes, gun control, drugs, food stamps, medicare, and the many, many other situations without common law antecedents to which the modern criminal law extends?

Also to be considered is the relationship between procedural and substantive limitations. If history is to be decisive in limiting shifts in the burden of persuasion, should it also be decisive in limiting legislative power over the substance of the law? If the historic importance of provocation in the law of homicide precludes the legislature from shifting the burden of persuasion, why does it not also prevent the legislature from taking the much greater step of eliminating the provocation mitigation altogether?

---

[h] He was joined in this dissent by Justices Brennan, Marshall, and Blackmun.

### *(iv) Burden of Proof and Substantive Justice*

It seems clear that the underlying concern in much of the debate over burden of proof is not procedural regularity but substantive justice. This concern surfaces in the "horror stories" used to describe what a legislature might do if burden shifting were allowed. Recall, for example, the *Patterson* footnote where Justice Powell speculates that a state might define murder "as mere physical contact between the defendant and the victim leading to the victim's death, but then set up an affirmative defense leaving it to the defendant to prove that he acted without culpable mens rea." By this device, says Justice Powell, the prosecution "could be relieved altogether of responsibility for proving *anything* regarding the defendant's state of mind. . . . " Barbara Underwood advances a similar concern. What if, she asks, the legislature were to replace the entire range of homicide and assault offenses with the single crime of "personal attack"? Unless burden shifting were disallowed, she continues, the legislature could authorize major penalties "on proof of a trivial assault, with the burden on the defendant to establish the mitigating defenses of the victim's survival, his freedom from injury, or the defendant's lack of intent to harm or injure." These hypotheticals have much in common. Both envision serious punishment on proof beyond a reasonable doubt of no more than trivial wrongdoing. The result would be the use of burden shifting defenses to impose criminal penalties far out of proportion to any proven misconduct by the accused.

Do the dangers posed by these hypotheticals have any necessary connection to shifts in the burden of proof? Justice Powell recognized the potential need for an independent limitation in footnote 13 of his *Patterson* dissent. Consider also the response of Jeffries and Stephan:

> The trouble [with this argument] lies in the unspoken assumption that excessive punishment is somehow a product of shifting the burden of proof. In fact, use of a burden-shifting defense . . . does not necessarily result in excessive punishment, nor does excessive punishment necessarily involve reallocation of the burden of proof. . . . The hypothetical legislature that would assign the fact of the victim's survival to an affirmative defense to a "personal attack" charge just as easily could eliminate the victim's death as a grading factor for assaultive behavior. The state could simply authorize serious sanctions for any physical assault, whether fatal or trivial, and leave distinctions among cases to the sentencing stage. This scheme involves no reallocation of the burden of proof, but it is just as objectionable as Underwood's original hypothetical. Both schemes would authorize major felony sanctions on proof of nothing more than a trivial assault; both involve the infliction of punishment grossly disproportionate to any proven blameworthiness of the defendant.

### *(v) Facts Constitutionally Required to Be Proved*

Jeffries and Stephan conclude that the constitutional insistence on proof beyond a reasonable doubt should extend only to those facts that are essential to provide "a constitutionally adequate basis for imposing the punishment authorized." The state could shift to the defendant the burden of persuasion for any additional or gratuitous factor which it chose to take into account. The focus would be not on what the government invited the defendant to prove by way of mitigation or excuse, but rather on what the prosecution had to prove beyond a reasonable doubt in order to establish liability in the first instance.

For Jeffries and Stephan, therefore, the question in both *Mullaney* and *Patterson* would be whether the facts required to be proved beyond a reasonable doubt established a constitutionally adequate basis for imposing the authorized maximum of life imprisonment. If so, "nothing would bar the state from going beyond the constitutional minimum to allow mitigation when the defendant can prove his claim to it." If not, the state would be required to establish a constitutionally adequate basis for life imprisonment by disproving heat of passion or extreme emotional disturbance beyond a reasonable doubt.

### *(vi) Proportionality Review*

The difficulty with the argument that the focus should be on facts constitutionally required to be proved is how to determine which elements are required to be established by "constitutionally adequate" proof. Justice Powell suggests in his *Patterson* footnote 13 the possibility of a due process limitation. Litigation on this issue, however, has usually proceeded under the Cruel and Unusual Punishment Clause, and has resulted in all cases that have reached the Supreme Court save one in the denial of relief.[i]

In Harmelin v. Michigan, 501 U.S. 957 (1991), Justice Scalia, joined by Chief Justice Rehnquist, concluded, simply, that "the Eighth Amendment contains no proportionality guarantee." In Ewing v. California, 538 U.S. 11 (2003), Justice Thomas associated himself with this position. Four Justices—Stevens, Souter, Ginsburg, and Breyer—said in *Ewing* that proportionality review is both capable of judicial application and required by the Cruel and Unusual Punishment Clause of the Eighth Amendment. They would have granted relief in that case. Justices O'Connor and Kennedy (joined in this instance by Chief Justice Rehnquist) examined the proportionality issue on the merits in *Ewing*, but did so through a lens that foreclosed relief in all but the most extreme cases. In their view, the Eighth Amendment "does not require strict proportionality between crime and sentence" but "forbids only extreme sentences that are 'grossly disproportionate' to the crime." They make it clear that "gross disproportionality" is a high threshold indeed, and that no further inquiry is needed if that threshold is not met.[j] No case involving legislative manipulation of the sort imagined by the *Mullaney* supporters has ever reached the Court.

---

[i] The one case in which relief was granted was Solem v. Helm, 463 U.S. 277 (1983), a five-to-four decision in which Justices Powell, Brennan, Marshall, Stevens, and Blackmun formed the majority. Helm was sentenced to life without parole for a seventh non-violent felony, the last of which was uttering a "no account" check for $100. Cases in which relief was denied include Rummel v. Estelle, 445 U.S. 263 (1980) (life with the possibility of parole for a third felony conviction; the first was in 1964 for fraudulent use of a credit card to obtain $80 worth of goods or services, the second a 1969 conviction for passing a forged check in the amount of $28.36, and the third a 1973 conviction for obtaining $120.75 by false pretenses); Hutto v. Davis, 454 U.S. 370 (1982) (consecutive 20-year terms for possession with intent to distribute nine ounces of marijuana and distribution of marijuana); Harmelin v. Michigan, 501 U.S. 957 (1991) (mandatory life in prison without the possibility of parole for a first-offense conviction of possession of 672 grams of cocaine); Ewing v. California, 538 U.S. 11 (2003) (25 years to life for four "serious" prior felony convictions and a triggering conviction, while on parole, for stealing three golf clubs each valued at $399).

[j] Justice Kennedy's opinion in *Harmelin* states what appears to be the controlling view to be derived from the cases cited in the previous footnote. He repeated prior injunctions that

### (vii) Concluding Comments

As noted above, debate over the meaning of *Mullaney*, particularly given *Patterson*, would seem to be dated and of modest current interest. There is little controversy today over shifting the burden of proof on defenses or whether the "gratuitous" defense must be disproved by the prosecution beyond a reasonable doubt. *Patterson* has settled these questions. But, as revealed below, precisely the same issues, leading to a substantially identical debate, have arisen in more recent decisions having to do with the procedures applicable to sentencing. In this context, the Supreme Court appears to have taken its guidance from *Mullaney*, not *Patterson*.

## SECTION 2: SENTENCING

### INTRODUCTORY NOTES ON SENTENCING ALTERNATIVES

#### 1. INTRODUCTORY COMMENTS

Prior to *Apprendi*, the next main case, there were three basic approaches to the exercise of sentencing authority in non-capital cases. One is that the legislature provided a "mandatory" penalty that was required to be imposed on all who were convicted of a given offense. Sometimes the legislature would require that a particular term of years be imposed. More often it would prescribe a minimum below which the sentence could not go, as in "not less than 10 but no more than 25." One criticism of mandatory sentences is that not all offenders will fit the stereotypical defendant on which such legislation is likely to be based. Given the incentives in the legislative arena, the penalty will be fixed with the most egregious offenders in mind. These offenders, in turn, are likely to be some fraction of all who will be convicted of the offense, with the result that sentences for many, if not most, who violate such a law will be unjustly long. Another criticism is that mandatory penalties amount in practice to an unwarranted enhancement of largely unreviewable prosecutorial power. Prosecutors can, in effect, choose the sentence by selecting the charge, and can gain considerable leverage in plea bargaining and in inducing cooperation by one defendant against another by using the mandatory penalty as a threat. Over the years, most legislatures have nonetheless favored mandatory sentences—particularly mandatory minimums—for at least some offenses. They still do.

A second approach was to allow the jury to select the sentence, either based on the evidence introduced at the guilt stage or after a bifurcated proceeding at which evidence relevant to the sentence is offered for consideration. Common criticisms of this approach are either that the sentence will be based on too limited a view of the factors that ought to be taken into

---

proportionality review should be informed by "objective factors to the maximum possible extent." Objectivity, the Court had previously observed, can be gained by a comparative analysis, looking at how other crimes in the same jurisdiction are treated and the sentences imposed for the same crime in other jurisdictions. But a "better reading of our cases," Justice Kennedy said in *Harmelin*, "leads to the conclusion that intrajurisdictional and interjurisdictional analyses are appropriate only in the rare case in which a threshold comparison of the crime committed and the sentence imposed leads to an inference of gross disproportionality. . . . The proper role for comparative analysis of sentences . . . is to validate an initial judgment that a sentence is grossly disproportionate to a crime."

account (prior record, for example, ordinarily is not admissible at the guilt stage of a criminal case) or that the sentencing proceeding will be too expensive to be used routinely (bifurcation). Another criticism often leveled at jury sentencing is that the results are likely to be disparate and random. Members of a jury are likely to impose a sentence only once. Juries will bring no experience or expertise to the decision, and there is no opportunity to develop institutional norms and traditions. Nonetheless, a small minority of American jurisdictions still rely on jury sentencing in cases where guilt is contested before a jury.

But by far the most common sentencing option in use in this country—throughout the 20th Century and at present—has been the third, under which the trial judge selects the sentence after a post-conviction process designed to inform the decision.[a] In time, variations emerged on the extent to which the sentencing discretion exercised by the judge under such a system came to be regulated by criteria or other limiting standards. Three approaches to this question are outlined below, as a preface to consideration of cases on this topic.

## 2. *WILLIAMS V. NEW YORK*

The approach to judicial sentencing in this country for much of the early part of the 20th Century was for many years quite simple. Penal codes provided a range of penalties—say, from 0 to 20 years, from 5 to 25 years, from no imprisonment to life—and authorized judges to choose a sentence within that range based on whatever facts and whatever criteria the judge thought relevant. Under the standard procedure, the judge would have access to a presentence report prepared by an officer of the court, which contained factual evidence about the defendant's background deemed relevant to sentence. The judge would then hold a hearing at which contested facts could be resolved—by the judge, not a jury, and by a standard of proof far less than "proof beyond a reasonable doubt." The judge was typically not required to state factual conclusions, nor to state reasons for choosing one sentence over another. And typically there was no appellate review of the sentence, save in instances where the judge chose to state a reason on the record that was clearly discriminatory or otherwise plainly unacceptable. Justice Black's opinion for the Court in Williams v. New York, 337 U.S. 241 (1949), is typical of the tolerance for this approach:

> . . . The question [before us] relates to the rules of evidence applicable to the manner in which a judge may obtain information to guide him in the imposition of sentence upon an already convicted defendant. Within limits fixed by statutes, New York judges are given a broad discretion to decide the type and extent of punishment for convicted defendants. Here, for example, the judge's discretion was to sentence to life imprisonment or death. To aid a judge in exercising this discretion intelligently the New York procedural policy encourages him to consider information about the convicted person's past life, health, habits, conduct, and mental and moral propensities. The sentencing judge may consider such information even though obtained outside the courtroom

[a] Typically, this procedure would also be followed in cases where the legislature prescribed a range between a maximum and a mandatory minimum. That is, in a "not less than 10 but no more than 25" option, the judge would decide whether to impose more than the minimum and, if so, how much more up to the allowable maximum.

from persons whom a defendant has not been permitted to confront or cross-examine. It is the consideration of information obtained by a sentencing judge in this manner that is the basis for appellant's broad constitutional challenge. . . .

Tribunals passing on the guilt of a defendant always have been hedged in by strict evidentiary procedural limitations. But both before and since the American colonies became a nation, courts in this country and in England practiced a policy under which a sentencing judge could exercise a wide discretion in the sources and types of evidence used to assist him in determining the kind and extent of punishment to be imposed within limits fixed by law. . . .

In addition to the historical basis for different evidentiary rules governing trial and sentencing procedures there are sound practical reasons for the distinction. In a trial before verdict the issue is whether a defendant is guilty of having engaged in certain criminal conduct of which he has been specifically accused. Rules of evidence have been fashioned for criminal trials which narrowly confine the trial contest to evidence that is strictly relevant to the particular offense charged. These rules rest in part on a necessity to prevent a time consuming and confusing trial of collateral issues. They were also designed to prevent tribunals concerned solely with the issue of guilt of a particular offense from being influenced to convict for that offense by evidence that the defendant had habitually engaged in other misconduct. A sentencing judge, however, is not confined to the narrow issue of guilt. His task within fixed statutory or constitutional limits is to determine the type and extent of punishment after the issue of guilt has been determined. Highly relevant—if not essential—to his selection of an appropriate sentence is the possession of the fullest information possible concerning the defendant's life and characteristics. And modern concepts individualizing punishment have made it all the more necessary that a sentencing judge not be denied an opportunity to obtain pertinent information by a requirement of rigid adherence to restrictive rules of evidence properly applicable to the trial. . . .

New York criminal statutes set wide limits for maximum and minimum sentences. Under New York statutes a state judge cannot escape his grave responsibility of fixing sentence. In determining whether a defendant shall receive a one-year minimum or a twenty-year maximum sentence, we do not think the federal Constitution restricts the view of the sentencing judge to the information received in open court. The Due Process Clause should not be treated as a device for freezing the evidential procedure of sentencing in the mold of trial procedure. So to treat the Due Process Clause would hinder if not preclude all courts—state and federal—from making progressive efforts to improve the administration of criminal justice.

### 3. THE MODEL PENAL CODE

There was widespread criticism of this approach by the middle of the 20th Century. Disparity among sentences was the primary reason.

Similarly situated defendants were given widely different sentences, it was alleged and often demonstrated by statistics and anecdotal evidence, based on arbitrary differences in the predilections of different judges. Some judges were seen as giving harsh sentences, some lenient sentences, some inconsistent sentences from case to case. Different judges pursued different sentencing philosophies. Law, in short, was not brought to bear on the sentencing process. No criteria were required to be followed, no reasons were expected or given, and no accountability to principle or to a higher court was enforced. Trial judges did what they wanted. Their word was law.

The Model Penal Code, drafted in the late 1950s and published in final form in 1962, offered a partial solution to this criticism called the "extended term." As implemented in Sections 6.07, 6.09, 7.03, and 7.04, the idea was that most sentence levels should be set with the "ordinary" offender in mind, but that persons who satisfied stated criteria could be sentenced to a higher "extended term." Judges were still permitted to hold sentencing hearings along the informal lines described in Justice Black's *Williams* opinion. The idea was to control disparity by limiting the range within which it could occur, and to permit sentences in the longer ranges only if stated criteria were satisfied and defended. Former legislation that authorized the judge to sentence a convicted offender from 0 to 10 years, for example, would be recast so that the judge would be limited to 0 to 5 unless findings were made that specified criteria justified an "extended term" in the 5- to 10-year range.

## 4. SENTENCING GUIDELINES

A more sophisticated version of the Model Penal Code idea was developed shortly thereafter, under which an agency was created to draft specific and detailed criteria for the imposition of sentences that trial judges were required, with varying degrees of rigidity, to follow. To continue the simple example used above, instead of one waystation at five years in the old 0–10 sentencing range, one might say that the typical prison sentence for a person convicted of this offense was 2–4 years. The judge could add increments on top of the four years if this or that criterion was satisfied, or could subtract increments from the two years based on other factors stated in the formal criteria. Typically, the judge was required to explain on the record how the facts fit the criteria, and both the defendant and the state could initiate appellate review to make sure the criteria were followed.

Various versions of this approach were adopted, and prevail today in many states.[b] The most rigorous and wooden of these reforms was found in the Federal Sentencing Guidelines. Congress established the United States Sentencing Commission in the Sentencing Reform Act of 1984.[c] In due course, the Commission produced detailed guidelines for federal sentences.[d]

---

[b] A good source for exploring some of the variations can be found in ALI, Model Penal Code: Sentencing, Tentative Draft No. 1 (April 9, 2007). See also ALI, Model Penal Code: Sentencing, Discussion Draft (April 17, 2006); ALI, Model Penal Code: Sentencing, Report (April 11, 2003).

[c] The constitutionality of the basic structure of the Sentencing Commission was upheld in Mistretta v. United States, 488 U.S. 361 (1989).

[d] The Guidelines themselves and other useful materials are available on the Commission's website at http://www.ussc.gov. In their printed form, the Guidelines extend to hundreds of pages—596 in 2014—and grow every year as new wrinkles are added. They resemble in scope and complexity, and arguably in attention to minute details, the Internal Revenue Code and the NCAA regulations governing intercollegiate athletics.

Basically, each listed offense included a "heartland sentence," that is, a sentence that served as a starting point for a person convicted of that crime who was to be incarcerated.[e] The "heartland sentence" was determined by ascertaining the "base offense level" for the offense at issue. The "base offense level" was a number, say, 20 for the crime of robbery. Points were then added to or subtracted from this number based on the applicability of stated criteria. For example, add four if there was serious bodily injury, add another seven if a firearm was discharged, subtract four if the defendant was a minimal participant, subtract two if the defendant clearly accepts responsibility, etc.[f] At the end of this process, a number was generated that established the "offense level." One then computed the defendant's "criminal history points" based on the number of prior convictions, their relationship over time, etc. A matrix that had 43 "offense levels" on the vertical axis and six "criminal history" categories on the horizontal axis could then be applied. The matrix yielded a fixed and limited range—say, between 70 and 87 months—within which the defendant was to be sentenced, subject to a complex set of "departure" rules that themselves were based on additional criteria or on factors that had not been taken into account in the Guidelines.[g] Stated reasons were required for each sentence, and appellate review was available for both the prosecution and defense to argue that the Guidelines were not properly followed.

## 5. PRE-*APPRENDI* CASE LAW

The reforms described above were designed to regulate the substance of sentencing, i.e., the length of the sentence the convicted offender would receive. None governed the procedures by which the facts underlying the application of sentencing criteria were to be determined. They all assumed business as usual on this front, i.e., that the judge would conduct fact hearings and resolve the facts as seemed appropriate based on the presentence report and such evidence as the parties wished to introduce at the sentencing hearing. In *Apprendi v. New Jersey*, the next main case, the Supreme Court launched a procedural revolution in this arena. Three cases deserve consideration as a prelude to *Apprendi*.

### *(i) McMillan v. Pennsylvania*

The statute at issue in McMillan v. Pennsylvania, 477 U.S. 79 (1986), provided that a five-year mandatory minimum sentence was to be imposed on any offender who "visibly possessed a firearm" during the commission of

---

[e] Fines, probation, etc., were available in stated instances.

[f] The educational materials available at http://www.ussc.gov/training/educat.htm include an example of how the guidelines can be applied.

[g] R. Barry Ruback & Jonathan Wroblewski, The Federal Sentencing Guidelines, 7 Psychol. Pub. Pol'y & Law 739 (2001), point out that if all possible combinations are calculated, "there are 18,579,456 possible ways in which the guidelines characterize robberies." They guess that more than 99% of the distinctions for robbery have never been used, and add:

> Note that these calculations are just for robbery, one of 148 different classes of crimes in the guidelines. Although there are only 258 cells in the matrix of the U.S. Sentencing Guidelines, the guidelines themselves make millions of distinctions.

And the ultimate irony, they point out in a footnote, is that the matrix approach to sentencing guidelines, developed in Minnesota in 1980, has been criticized for "oversimplifying the complexity of sentencing."

certain listed offenses.[h] The available maximum sentence exceeded five years for each of the listed offenses. McMillan argued that *Winship* and *Mullaney* required that proof of the "visible possession" was required to be made by the prosecutor beyond a reasonable doubt. In a five-to-four decision, written by Chief Justice Rehnquist, the Court held that "the present case is controlled by *Patterson* . . . rather than by *Mullaney*." A "sentencing factor" is not an "element" of the offense.[i]

Two aspects of *McMillan* are worthy of comment. The first is that Chief Justice Rehnquist observed that McMillan's claim "would have at least more superficial appeal if a finding of visible possession exposed [him] to greater or additional punishment." The second is that Justice Stevens argued in dissent that "[o]nce a state defines a criminal offense, the Due Process Clause requires it to prove any component of the prohibited transaction that gives rise to both a special stigma and a special punishment beyond a reasonable doubt." The Chief Justice, in other words, recognized the possibility that an increase in the *maximum* available sentence based on factual findings might be subject to the proof-beyond-a-reasonable-doubt requirement. Justice Stevens, in contrast, offered a different interpretation of the *Mullaney-Patterson* line: proof beyond a reasonable doubt is required for all "conduct that [the state] targets for severe criminal penalties" that affect the sentence in any respect.[j]

### *(ii) Almendarez-Torres v. United States*

In Almendarez-Torres v. United States, 523 U.S. 224 (1998), the defendant argued that an enhanced sentence as a recidivist was not permissible unless the indictment alleged the prior offenses upon which it was based. The Court, again in a five-to-four decision, rejected the claim, holding that recidivism was "as typical a sentencing factor as one might imagine." Justice Breyer continued for the Court:

> . . . *Mullaney*'s language, if read literally, suggests that the Constitution requires that most, if not all, sentencing factors be treated as elements. But *Patterson* suggests the exact opposite, namely, that the Constitution requires scarcely any sentencing factors to be treated in that way. The cases, taken together, cannot significantly help petitioner, for the statute here involves a

---

[h] The Pennsylvania statute explicitly provided that visible possession of a firearm "shall not be an element of the crime" and that the trial court should resolve factual disputes "by a preponderance of the evidence" at the sentencing proceeding.

[i] In a phrase that has often been quoted since, the Chief Justice said at one point that the "statute gives no impression of having been tailored to permit the visible possession finding to be a tail which wags the dog of the substantive offense." By this he meant that the statute did not appear to be an attempt by the legislature to evade substantive or procedural constitutional limitations.

[j] Justice Stevens explained that *Patterson* was consistent with his view because it dealt with exculpatory or mitigating circumstances. The state is free, in his view, to allocate the burden on such factors to the prosecutor by a lesser standard or to the defendant. But everything having to do with a special stigma or punishment associated with the behavior that the state seeks to punish—the "prohibited transaction" in his vocabulary—must be established by the prosecutor beyond a reasonable doubt. Thus, to illustrate, the state may require the defendant to prove facts associated with provocation, duress, or an insanity defense—facts associated with these claims will reduce or eliminate the criminal sanction. But the state must require the prosecutor to prove beyond a reasonable doubt facts such as drug quantity, the status of the perpetrator or the victim, or gun possession that it identifies as aggravating the offense or increasing the penalty.

> sentencing factor—the prior commission of an aggravated felony—that is neither "presumed" to be present, nor need be "proved" to be present, in order to prove the commission of the relevant crime. Indeed, as we have said, it involves one of the most frequently found factors that affects sentencing—recidivism.

In dissent, Justice Scalia, joined by Justices Stevens, Souter, and Ginsburg, said that he would have construed the statute to contain the recidivist component as an element, in large part to avoid the constitutional question resolved by the majority. Significantly, for reasons that will appear below, Justice Thomas provided the critical fifth vote for the *Almendarez-Torres* result.

### *(iii) Jones v. United States*

Jones v. United States, 526 U.S. 227 (1999), was the immediate precursor to *Apprendi*. *Jones* involved the federal carjacking statute, which set forth the elements of the offense and then added three sentencing alternatives: a 15-year maximum, which was increased to 25 years if "serious bodily injury results," and to any number of years or life "if death results." In the end, the majority opinion by Justice Souter construed the sentence aggravations as elements of the offense, and held that the prosecutor had to prove "serious bodily injury" beyond a reasonable doubt in order to justify a 25-year sentence. This "better reading" of the statute was appropriate "particularly in light of the rule that any interpretive uncertainty should be resolved to avoid serious questions about the statute's constitutionality."

Justice Kennedy's dissent, joined by Chief Justice Rehnquist and by Justices O'Connor and Breyer, challenged the Court to state the constitutional principle that it was avoiding. Justice Souter responded:

> The seriousness of the due process issue is evident from *Mullaney*'s insistence that a State cannot manipulate its way out of *Winship*, and from *Patterson*'s recognition of a limit on state authority to reallocate traditional burdens of proof; the substantiality of the jury claim is evident from the practical implications of assuming Sixth Amendment indifference to treating a fact that sets the sentencing range as a sentencing factor, not an element.

To this he appended a footnote:

> The dissent repeatedly chides us for failing to state precisely enough the principle animating our view that the carjacking statute, as construed by the government, may violate the Constitution. The preceding paragraph in the text expresses that principle plainly enough, and we restate it here: under the Due Process Clause of the Fifth Amendment and the notice and jury trial guarantees of the Sixth Amendment, any fact (other than prior conviction) that increases the maximum penalty for a crime must be charged in an indictment, submitted to a jury, and proven beyond a reasonable doubt. Because our prior cases suggest rather than establish this principle, our concern about the Government's reading of the statute rises only to the level of doubt, not certainty.
>
> Contrary to the dissent's suggestion, the constitutional proposition that drives our concern in no way "call[s] into question the principle that the definition of the elements of a criminal offense

is entrusted to the legislature." The constitutional guarantees that give rise to our concern in no way restrict the ability of legislatures to identify the conduct they wish to characterize as criminal or to define the facts whose proof is essential to the establishment of criminal liability. The constitutional safeguards that figure in our analysis concern not the identity of the elements defining criminal liability but only the required procedures for finding the facts that determine the maximum permissible punishment; these are the safeguards going to the formality of notice, the identity of the factfinder, and the burden of proof.

## Apprendi v. New Jersey

Supreme Court of the United States, 2000.
530 U.S. 466.

■ JUSTICE STEVENS delivered the opinion of the Court.

A New Jersey statute classifies the possession of a firearm for an unlawful purpose as a "second-degree" offense. Such an offense is punishable by imprisonment for "between five years and 10 years." A separate statute, described by that State's Supreme Court as a "hate crime" law, provides for an "extended term" of imprisonment if the trial judge finds, by a preponderance of the evidence, that "the defendant in committing the crime acted with a purpose to intimidate an individual or group of individuals because of race, color, gender, handicap, religion, sexual orientation or ethnicity." The extended term authorized by the hate crime law for second-degree offenses is imprisonment for "between 10 and 20 years."

The question presented is whether the Due Process Clause of the Fourteenth Amendment requires that a factual determination authorizing an increase in the maximum prison sentence for an offense from 10 to 20 years be made by a jury on the basis of proof beyond a reasonable doubt.

I

At 2:04 a.m. on December 22, 1994, petitioner Charles C. Apprendi, Jr., fired several .22-caliber bullets into the home of an African-American family that had recently moved into a previously all-white neighborhood in Vineland, New Jersey. Apprendi was promptly arrested and, at 3:05 a.m., admitted that he was the shooter. After further questioning, at 6:04 a.m., he made a statement—which he later retracted—that even though he did not know the occupants of the house personally, "because they are black in color he does not want them in the neighborhood."

A New Jersey grand jury returned a [multi]-count indictment. . . . The charges alleged shootings on four different dates, as well as the unlawful possession of various weapons. None of the counts referred to the hate crime statute, and none alleged that Apprendi acted with a racially biased purpose.

The parties entered into a plea agreement, pursuant to which Apprendi pleaded guilty [to several offenses, including] second-degree possession of a firearm for an unlawful purpose. . . . Under state law, a second-degree offense carries a penalty range of 5 to 10 years. . . . As part of the plea agreement, however, the State reserved the right to request the court to impose a higher "enhanced" sentence on [the] count . . . based on the December 22 shooting . . . on the ground that that offense was committed with a biased purpose. Apprendi, correspondingly, reserved the right to challenge the hate crime sentence enhancement on the ground that it violates the United States Constitution.

At the plea hearing, the trial judge heard sufficient evidence to establish Apprendi's guilt . . . ; the judge then confirmed that Apprendi understood the maximum sentences that could be imposed. . . . After the trial judge accepted the . . . guilty plea[ ], the prosecutor filed a formal motion for an extended term. The trial judge thereafter held an evidentiary hearing on the issue of Apprendi's "purpose" for the shooting on December 22. Apprendi adduced evidence from a psychologist and from seven character witnesses who testified that he did not have a reputation for racial bias. He also took the stand himself, explaining that the incident was an unintended consequence of overindulgence in alcohol, denying that he was in any way biased against African-Americans, and denying that his statement to the police had been accurately described. The judge, however, found the police officer's testimony credible, and concluded that the evidence supported a finding "that the crime was motivated by racial bias." Having found "by a preponderance of the evidence" that Apprendi's actions were taken "with a purpose to intimidate" as provided by the statute, the trial judge held that the hate crime enhancement applied. Rejecting Apprendi's constitutional challenge to the statute, the judge sentenced him to a 12-year term of imprisonment [for the December 22 shooting].

Apprendi appealed, arguing, inter alia, that the Due Process Clause of the United States Constitution requires that the finding of bias upon which his hate crime sentence was based must be proved to a jury beyond a reasonable doubt. [The lower courts rejected the claim.] We granted certiorari and now reverse. . . .

II

. . . The question whether *Apprendi* had a constitutional right to have a jury find such bias on the basis of proof beyond a reasonable doubt is starkly presented. Our answer to that question was foreshadowed by our opinion in Jones v. United States, 526 U.S. 227 (1999), construing a federal statute. We there noted that under the Due Process Clause of the Fifth Amendment and the notice and jury trial guarantees of the Sixth Amendment, any fact (other than prior conviction) that increases the maximum penalty for a crime must be charged in an indictment, submitted to a jury, and proven beyond a reasonable doubt. The Fourteenth Amendment commands the same answer in this case involving a state statute.

III

In his 1881 lecture on the criminal law, Oliver Wendell Holmes, Jr., observed: "The law threatens certain pains if you do certain things, intending thereby to give you a new motive for not doing them. If you persist in doing them, it has to inflict the pains in order that its threats may continue to be believed." New Jersey threatened Apprendi with certain pains if he unlawfully possessed a weapon and with additional pains if he selected his victims with a purpose to intimidate them because of their race. As a matter of simple justice, it seems obvious that the procedural safeguards designed to protect Apprendi from unwarranted pains should apply equally to the two acts that New Jersey has singled out for punishment. Merely using the label "sentence enhancement" to describe the latter surely does not provide a principled basis for treating them differently.

At stake in this case are constitutional protections of surpassing importance: the proscription of any deprivation of liberty without "due process of law," and the guarantee that "in all criminal prosecutions, the accused shall enjoy the right to a speedy and public trial, by an impartial jury." Taken together, these rights indisputably entitle a criminal defendant to "a jury determination that [he] is guilty of every element of the crime with which he is charged, beyond a reasonable doubt." [T]he historical foundation for our recognition of these principles extends down centuries into the common law. . . .

Any possible distinction between an element of a felony offense and a sentencing factor was unknown to the practice of criminal indictment, trial by jury, and judgment by court as it existed during the years surrounding our Nation's founding. As a general rule, criminal proceedings were submitted to a jury after being initiated by an indictment containing "all the facts and circumstances which constitute the offence, . . . stated with such certainty and precision, that the defendant . . . may be enabled to determine the species of offence they constitute, in order that he may prepare his defence accordingly . . . and *that there may be no doubt as to the judgment which should be given,* if the defendant be convicted." J. Archbold, Pleading and Evidence in Criminal Cases 44 (15th ed. 1862) (emphasis added). The defendant's ability to predict with certainty the judgment from the face of the felony indictment flowed from the invariable linkage of punishment with crime. . . .

We should be clear that nothing in this history suggests that it is impermissible for judges to exercise discretion—taking into consideration various factors relating both to offense and offender—in imposing a judgment *within the range* prescribed by statute. We have often noted that judges in this country have long exercised discretion of this nature in imposing sentence *within statutory limits* in the individual case. See, e.g., Williams v. New York, 337 U.S. 241, 246 (1949). . . . As in *Williams,* our periodic recognition of judges' broad discretion in sentencing—since the 19th-century shift in this country from statutes providing fixed-term sentences to those providing judges discretion within a permissible range—has been regularly accompanied by the qualification that that discretion was bound by the range of sentencing options prescribed by the legislature. . . .[11]

Since *Winship*, we have made clear beyond peradventure that *Winship's* due process and associated jury protections extend, to some degree, "to determinations that [go] not to a defendant's guilt or innocence, but simply to the length of his sentence." *Almendarez-Torres*, 523 U.S. at 251 (Scalia, J., dissenting). This was a primary lesson of Mullaney v. Wilbur, 421 U.S. 684 (1975), in which we invalidated a Maine statute that presumed that a defendant who acted with an intent

[11] . . . Nothing in *Williams* implies that a judge may impose a more severe sentence than the maximum authorized by the facts found by the jury. . . .

to kill possessed the "malice aforethought" necessary to constitute the State's murder offense (and therefore, was subject to that crime's associated punishment of life imprisonment). The statute placed the burden on the defendant of proving, in rebutting the statutory presumption, that he acted with a lesser degree of culpability, such as in the heat of passion, to win a reduction in the offense from murder to manslaughter (and thus a reduction of the maximum punishment of 20 years).

The state had posited in *Mullaney* that requiring a defendant to prove heat-of-passion intent to overcome a presumption of murderous intent did not implicate *Winship* protections because, upon conviction of either offense, the defendant would lose his liberty and face societal stigma just the same. Rejecting this argument, we acknowledged that criminal law "is concerned not only with guilt or innocence in the abstract, but also with the degree of criminal culpability" assessed. Because the "*consequences*" of a guilty verdict for murder and for manslaughter differed substantially, we dismissed the possibility that a State could circumvent the protections of *Winship* merely by "redefining the elements that constitute different crimes, characterizing them as factors that bear solely on the extent of punishment."[12]

IV

It was in McMillan v. Pennsylvania, 477 U.S. 79 (1986), that this Court, for the first time, coined the term "sentencing factor" to refer to a fact that was not found by a jury but that could affect the sentence imposed by the judge. . . . We did not, however, there budge from the position that (1) constitutional limits exist to states' authority to define away facts necessary to constitute a criminal offense, and (2) that a state scheme that keeps from the jury facts that "expose [defendants] to greater or additional punishment," may raise serious constitutional concern. As we explained:

> [The Pennsylvania statute] neither alters the maximum penalty for the crime committed nor creates a separate offense calling for a separate penalty; it operates solely to limit the sentencing court's discretion in selecting a penalty within the range already available to it without the special finding of visible possession of a firearm. . . . Petitioners' claim that visible possession under the Pennsylvania statute is "really" an element of the offenses for which they are being punished—that Pennsylvania has in effect defined a new set of upgraded felonies—would have at least more superficial appeal if a finding

[12] Contrary to the principal dissent's suggestion, Patterson v. New York, 432 U.S. 197 (1977), posed no direct challenge to this aspect of *Mullaney*. In upholding a New York law allowing defendants to raise and prove extreme emotional distress as an affirmative defense to murder, *Patterson* made clear that the state law still required the State to prove every element of that State's offense of murder and its accompanying punishment. "No further facts are either presumed or inferred in order to constitute the crime." New York, unlike Maine, had not made malice aforethought, or any described mens rea, part of its statutory definition of second-degree murder; one could tell from the face of the statute that if one intended to cause the death of another person and did cause that death, one could be subject to sentence for a second-degree offense. Responding to the argument that our view could be seen "to permit state legislatures to reallocate burdens of proof by labeling as affirmative defenses at least some elements of the crimes now defined in their statutes," the Court made clear in the very next breath that there were "obviously constitutional limits beyond which the States may not go in this regard."

of visible possession exposed them to greater or additional punishment, . . . but it does not.[13]

[Justice Stevens examined Almendarez-Torres v. United States, 523 U.S. 224 (1998), and Jones v. United States, 526 U.S. 227 (1999), and continued:]

Even though it is arguable that *Almendarez-Torres* was incorrectly decided, . . . Apprendi does not contest the decision's validity and we need not revisit it for purposes of our decision today to treat the case as a narrow exception to the general rule we recalled at the outset. Given its unique facts, it surely does not warrant rejection of the otherwise uniform course of decision during the entire history of our jurisprudence.

In sum, our reexamination of our cases in this area, and of the history upon which they rely, confirms the opinion that we expressed in *Jones*. Other than the fact of a prior conviction, any fact that increases the penalty for a crime beyond the prescribed statutory maximum must be submitted to a jury, and proved beyond a reasonable doubt. With that exception, we endorse the statement of the rule set forth in the concurring opinions in that case: [I]t is unconstitutional for a legislature to remove from the jury the assessment of facts that increase the prescribed range of penalties to which a criminal defendant is exposed. It is equally clear that such facts must be established by proof beyond a reasonable doubt.[16]

---

[13] The principal dissent accuses us of today "overruling *McMillan*." We do not overrule *McMillan*. We limit its holding to cases that do not involve the imposition of a sentence more severe than the statutory maximum for the offense established by the jury's verdict—a limitation identified in the *McMillan* opinion itself. Conscious of the likelihood that legislative decisions may have been made in reliance on *McMillan*, we reserve for another day the question whether stare decisis considerations preclude reconsideration of its narrower holding.

[16] The principal dissent would reject the Court's rule as a "meaningless formalism," because it can conceive of hypothetical statutes that would comply with the rule and achieve the same result as the New Jersey statute. While a state could, hypothetically, undertake to revise its entire criminal code in the manner the dissent suggests—extending all statutory maximum sentences to, for example, 50 years and giving judges guided discretion as to a few specially selected factors within that range—this possibility seems remote. Among other reasons, structural democratic constraints exist to discourage legislatures from enacting penal statutes that expose *every* defendant convicted of, for example, weapons possession, to a maximum sentence exceeding that which is, in the legislature's judgment, generally proportional to the crime. This is as it should be. Our rule ensures that a state is obliged "to make its choices concerning the substantive content of its criminal laws with full awareness of the consequence, unable to mask substantive policy choices" of exposing all who are convicted to the maximum sentence it provides. *Patterson v. New York* (Powell, J., dissenting). So exposed, "the political check on potentially harsh legislative action is then more likely to operate."

In all events, if such an extensive revision of the state's entire criminal code were enacted for the purpose the dissent suggests, or if New Jersey simply reversed the burden of the hate crime finding (effectively assuming a crime was performed with a purpose to intimidate and then requiring a defendant to prove that it was not), we would be required to question whether the revision was constitutional under this Court's prior decisions.

Finally, the principal dissent ignores the distinction the Court has often recognized, see, e.g., Martin v. Ohio, 480 U.S. 228 (1987), between facts in aggravation of punishment and facts in mitigation. If facts found by a jury support a guilty verdict of murder, the judge is authorized by that jury verdict to sentence the defendant to the maximum sentence provided by the murder statute. If the defendant can escape the statutory maximum by showing, for example, that he is a war veteran, then a judge that finds the fact of veteran status is neither exposing the defendant to a deprivation of liberty greater than that authorized by the verdict according to statute, nor is the Judge imposing upon the defendant a greater stigma than that

V

[New Jersey's argument that] the required finding of biased purpose is not an "element" of a distinct hate crime offense, but rather the traditional "sentencing factor" of motive . . . is nothing more than a disagreement with the rule we apply today. Beyond this, we do not see how the argument can succeed on its own terms. . . . The defendant's intent in committing a crime is perhaps as close as one might hope to come to a core criminal offense "element." . . . Despite what appears to us the clear "elemental" nature of the factor here, the relevant inquiry is one not of form, but of effect—does the required finding expose the defendant to a greater punishment than that authorized by the jury's guilty verdict?[19] . . .

New Jersey's reliance on *Almendarez-Torres* is . . . unavailing. The reasons supporting an exception from the general rule for the statute construed in that case do not apply to the New Jersey statute. Whereas recidivism does not relate to the commission of the offense itself, 523 U.S. at 230, New Jersey's biased purpose inquiry goes precisely to what happened in the commission of the offense. Moreover, there is a vast difference between accepting the validity of a prior judgment of conviction entered in a proceeding in which the defendant had the right to a jury trial and the right to require the prosecutor to prove guilt beyond a reasonable doubt, and allowing the judge to find the required fact under a lesser standard of proof. . . .

The New Jersey procedure challenged in this case is an unacceptable departure from the jury tradition that is an indispensable part of our criminal justice system. Accordingly, the judgment of the Supreme Court of New Jersey is reversed, and the case is remanded for further proceedings not inconsistent with this opinion.

It is so ordered.

■ JUSTICE SCALIA, concurring.

[Justice Scalia wrote a short concurrence responding to the Breyer dissent, in the course of which he said:]

. . . What ultimately demolishes the case for the dissenters is that they are unable to say what the right to trial by jury *does* guarantee if, as they assert, it does not guarantee—what it has been assumed to guarantee throughout our history—the right to have a jury determine those facts that determine the maximum sentence the law allows. They provide no coherent alternative.

Justice Breyer proceeds on the erroneous and all-too-common assumption that the Constitution means what we think it ought to mean.

---

accompanying the jury verdict alone. Core concerns animating the jury and burden-of-proof requirements are thus absent from such a scheme.

[19] This is not to suggest that the term "sentencing factor" is devoid of meaning. The term appropriately describes a circumstance, which may be either aggravating or mitigating in character, that supports a specific sentence *within the range* authorized by the jury's finding that the defendant is guilty of a particular offense. On the other hand, when the term "sentence enhancement" is used to describe an increase beyond the maximum authorized statutory sentence, it is the functional equivalent of an element of a greater offense than the one covered by the jury's guilty verdict. Indeed, it fits squarely within the usual definition of an "element" of the offense.

It does not; it means what it says. And the guarantee that "[i]n all criminal prosecutions, the accused shall enjoy the right to . . . trial, by an impartial jury," has no intelligible content unless it means that all the facts which must exist in order to subject the defendant to a legally prescribed punishment *must* be found by the jury.

■ JUSTICE THOMAS, with whom JUSTICE SCALIA joins as to Parts I and II, concurring.

I join the opinion of the Court in full. I write separately to explain my view that the Constitution requires a broader rule than the Court adopts.

I

[A long line of] authority establishes that a "crime" includes every fact that is by law a basis for imposing or increasing punishment (in contrast with a fact that mitigates punishment). Thus, if the legislature defines some core crime and then provides for increasing the punishment of that crime upon a finding of some aggravating fact—of whatever sort, including the fact of a prior conviction—the core crime and the aggravating fact together constitute an aggravated crime, just as much as grand larceny is an aggravated form of petit larceny. The aggravating fact is an element of the aggravated crime. Similarly, if the legislature, rather than creating grades of crimes, has provided for setting the punishment of a crime based on some fact—such as a fine that is proportional to the value of stolen goods—that fact is also an element. . . . One need only look to the kind, degree, or range of punishment to which the prosecution is by law entitled for a given set of facts. Each fact necessary for that entitlement is an element.

II

Cases from the founding to roughly the end of the Civil War establish the rule that I have described, applying it to all sorts of facts, including recidivism. As legislatures varied common-law crimes and created new crimes, American courts, particularly from the 1840's on, readily applied to these new laws the common-law understanding that a fact that is by law the basis for imposing or increasing punishment is an element.[2]

[Justice Thomas then undertook a substantial review of mid-to-late 19th century cases and treatises. He concluded:]

[The] traditional understanding—that a "crime" includes every fact that is by law a basis for imposing or increasing punishment—continued well into the 20th century, at least until the middle of the century. In fact, it is fair to say that *McMillan* began a revolution in the law regarding the definition of "crime." Today's decision, far from being a sharp break with the past, marks nothing more than a return to the

---

2 It is strange that Justice O'Connor faults me for beginning my analysis with cases primarily from the 1840's, rather from the time of the founding. As . . . she concedes, the very idea of a sentencing enhancement was foreign to the common law of the time of the founding. Justice O'Connor therefore, and understandably, does not contend that any history from the founding supports her position. As far as I have been able to tell, the argument that a fact that was by law the basis for imposing or increasing punishment might not be an element did not seriously arise (at least not in reported cases) until the 1840's. As I explain below, from that time on—for at least a century—essentially all authority rejected that argument, and much of it did so in reliance upon the common law. I find this evidence more than sufficient.

status quo ante—the status quo that reflected the original meaning of the Fifth and Sixth Amendments.

III

The consequence of the above discussion for our decisions in Almendarez-Torres, 523 U.S. 229 (1998), and McMillan, 477 U.S. 81 (1986), should be plain enough, but a few points merit special mention.

First, it is irrelevant to the question of which facts are elements that legislatures have allowed sentencing judges discretion in determining punishment (often within extremely broad ranges). Bishop, immediately after setting out the traditional rule on elements, explained why:

> The reader should distinguish between the foregoing doctrine, and the doctrine . . . that, within the limits of any discretion as to the punishment which the law may have allowed, the judge, when he pronounces sentence, may suffer his discretion to be influenced by matter shown in aggravation or mitigation, not covered by the allegations of the indictment. . . . The aggravating circumstances spoken of cannot swell the penalty above what the law has provided for the acts charged against the prisoner, and they are interposed merely to check the judicial discretion in the exercise of the permitted mercy [in finding mitigating circumstances]. This is an entirely different thing from punishing one for what is not alleged against him.

1 J. Bishop, Law of Criminal Procedure § 85, at 54 (2d ed. 1872). . . . In other words, establishing what punishment is available by law and setting a specific punishment within the bounds that the law has prescribed are two different things.[9] Thus, it is one thing to consider what the Constitution requires the prosecution to do in order to entitle itself to a particular kind, degree, or range of punishment of the accused, and quite another to consider what constitutional constraints apply either to the imposition of punishment within the limits of that entitlement or to a legislature's ability to set broad ranges of punishment. In answering the former constitutional question, I need not, and do not, address the latter.

Second, one of the chief errors of *Almendarez-Torres*—an error to which I succumbed—was to attempt to discern whether a particular fact is traditionally (or typically) a basis for a sentencing court to increase an offender's sentence. For the reasons I have given, it should be clear that this approach just defines away the real issue. What matters is the way by which a fact enters into the sentence. If a fact is by law the basis for imposing or increasing punishment—for establishing or increasing the prosecution's entitlement—it is an element. (To put the point differently, I am aware of no historical basis for treating as a non-element a fact that by law sets or increases punishment.) When one considers the question from this perspective, it is evident why the fact of a prior conviction is an element under a recidivism statute. . . . One reason frequently offered for treating recidivism differently, a reason on which we relied in *Almendarez-Torres*, is a concern for prejudicing the jury by informing it of the prior conviction. But this concern, of which earlier courts were well aware, does not make the

[9] This is not to deny that there may be laws on the borderline of this distinction. . . .

traditional understanding of what an element is any less applicable to the fact of a prior conviction.[10]

Third, I think it clear that the common law rule would cover the *McMillan* situation of a mandatory minimum sentence (in that case, for visible possession of a firearm during the commission of certain crimes). No doubt a defendant could, under such a scheme, find himself sentenced to the same term to which he could have been sentenced absent the mandatory minimum. The range for his underlying crime could be 0 to 10 years, with the mandatory minimum of 5 years, and he could be sentenced to 7. (Of course, a similar scenario is possible with an increased maximum.) But it is equally true that his expected punishment has increased as a result of the narrowed range and that the prosecution is empowered, by invoking the mandatory minimum, to require the judge to impose a higher punishment than he might wish. The mandatory minimum "entitles the government" to more than it would otherwise be entitled (5 to 10 years, rather than 0 to 10 and the risk of a sentence below 5). . . .

For the foregoing reasons, as well as those given in the Court's opinion, I agree that the New Jersey procedure at issue is unconstitutional.

■ JUSTICE O'CONNOR, with whom . . . CHIEF JUSTICE [REHNQUIST], JUSTICE KENNEDY, and JUSTICE BREYER join, dissenting.

. . . Today, in what will surely be remembered as a watershed change in constitutional law, the Court imposes as a constitutional rule the principle it first identified in Jones v. United States, 526 U.S. 227 (1999).

## I

Our Court has long recognized that not every fact that bears on a defendant's punishment need be charged in an indictment, submitted to a jury, and proved by the government beyond a reasonable doubt. Rather, we have held that the "legislature's definition of the elements of the offense is usually dispositive." McMillan v. Pennsylvania, 477 U.S. 79, 85 (1986); see also Almendarez-Torres v. United States, 523 U.S. 224, 228 (1998); Patterson v. New York, 432 U.S. 197, 210, 211, n.12 (1977). Although we have recognized that "there are obviously constitutional limits beyond which the States may not go in this regard," and that "in certain limited circumstances *Winship*'s reasonable-doubt requirement applies to facts not formally identified as elements of the offense charged," we have proceeded with caution before deciding that a certain fact must be treated as an offense element despite the legislature's choice not to characterize it as such. We have therefore declined to establish any bright-line rule for making such judgments and have instead approached each case individually, sifting through the considerations most relevant to determining whether the legislature has acted properly within its broad power to define crimes and their punishments

[10] In addition, it has been common practice to address this concern by permitting the defendant to stipulate to the prior conviction, in which case the charge of the prior conviction is not read to the jury, or, if the defendant decides not to stipulate, to bifurcate the trial, with the jury only considering the prior conviction after it has reached a guilty verdict on the core crime. . . .

or instead has sought to evade the constitutional requirements associated with the characterization of a fact as an offense element.

In one bold stroke the Court today casts aside our traditional cautious approach and instead embraces a universal and seemingly bright-line rule limiting the power of Congress and state legislatures to define criminal offenses and the sentences that follow from convictions thereunder. The Court states: "Other than the fact of a prior conviction, any fact that increases the penalty for a crime beyond the prescribed statutory maximum must be submitted to a jury, and proved beyond a reasonable doubt." In its opinion, the Court marshals virtually no authority to support its extraordinary rule. Indeed, it is remarkable that the Court cannot identify a *single instance*, in the over 200 years since the ratification of the Bill of Rights, that our Court has applied, as a constitutional requirement, the rule it announces today.

According to the Court, its constitutional rule emerges from our history and case law. None of the history contained in the Court's opinion requires the rule it ultimately adopts. . . . No Member of this Court questions the proposition that a State must charge in the indictment and prove at trial beyond a reasonable doubt the actual elements of the offense. This case, however, concerns the distinct question of when a fact that bears on a defendant's punishment, but which the legislature has not classified as an element of the charged offense, must nevertheless be treated as an offense element. The excerpts drawn from [a 19th Century] treatise do not speak to this question at all. The history on which the Court's opinion relies provides no support for its increase in the maximum penalty rule.

In his concurring opinion, Justice Thomas cites additional historical evidence that, in his view, dictates an even broader rule than that set forth in the Court's opinion. The history cited by Justice Thomas does not require, as a matter of federal constitutional law, the application of the rule he advocates. To understand why, it is important to focus on the basis for Justice Thomas' argument. First, he claims that the Fifth and Sixth Amendments codified pre-existing common law. Second, he contends that the relevant common law treated any fact that served to increase a defendant's punishment as an element of an offense. Even if Justice Thomas' first assertion were correct—a proposition this Court has not before embraced—he fails to gather the evidence necessary to support his second assertion. Indeed, for an opinion that purports to be founded upon the original understanding of the Fifth and Sixth Amendments, Justice Thomas' concurrence is notable for its failure to discuss any historical practice, or to cite any decisions, predating (or contemporary with) the ratification of the Bill of Rights. Rather, Justice Thomas divines the common-law understanding of the Fifth and Sixth Amendment rights by consulting decisions rendered by American courts well after the ratification of the Bill of Rights, ranging primarily from the 1840's to the 1890's. Whatever those decisions might reveal about the way American state courts resolved questions regarding the distinction between a crime and its punishment under general rules of criminal pleading or their own state constitutions, the decisions fail to demonstrate any settled understanding with respect to the definition of a crime under the relevant, pre-existing common law. Thus, there is a crucial disconnect between the historical evidence Justice Thomas cites and the proposition he seeks to establish with that evidence. [Moreover], Justice Thomas' collection of state-court opinions is . . . of marginal assistance in determining the original understanding of the Fifth and Sixth Amendments. While the decisions Justice Thomas cites provide some authority for the rule he advocates, they certainly do not control our resolution of the *federal constitutional* question presented in the instant case and cannot, standing alone, justify overruling three decades' worth of decisions by this Court.

In contrast to Justice Thomas, the Court asserts that its rule is supported by "our cases in this area." That the Court begins its review of our precedent with a quotation from a dissenting opinion speaks volumes about the support that actually can be drawn from our cases for the "increase in the maximum penalty" rule announced today. See ante, quoting *Almendarez-Torres,* 523 U.S. at 251 (Scalia, J., dissenting). The Court then cites our decision in *Mullaney v. Wilbur* to demonstrate the "lesson" that due process and jury protections extend beyond those factual determinations that affect a defendant's guilt or innocence. The Court explains *Mullaney* as having held that the due process proof-beyond-a-reasonable-doubt requirement applies to those factual determinations that, under a State's criminal law, make a difference in the degree of punishment the defendant receives. The Court chooses to ignore, however, the decision we issued two years later, *Patterson v. New York,* which clearly rejected the Court's broad reading of *Mullaney.*

In *Patterson,* the jury found the defendant guilty of second-degree murder. Under New York law, the fact that a person intentionally killed another while under the influence of extreme emotional disturbance distinguished the reduced offense of first-degree manslaughter from the more serious offense of second-degree murder. Thus, the presence or absence of this one fact was the defining factor separating a greater from a lesser punishment. . . .

Although we characterized the factual determination under New York law as one going to the mitigation of culpability, as opposed to the aggravation of the punishment, it is difficult to understand why the rule adopted by the Court in today's case (or the broader rule advocated by Justice Thomas) would not require the overruling of *Patterson.* Unless the Court is willing to defer to a legislature's formal definition of the elements of an offense, it is clear that the fact that Patterson did not act under the influence of extreme emotional disturbance, in substance, increase[d] the penalty for [his] crime beyond the prescribed statutory maximum for first-degree manslaughter. Nonetheless, we held that New York's requirement that the defendant, rather than the State, bear the burden of proof on this factual determination comported with the Fourteenth Amendment's Due Process Clause.

*Patterson* is important because it plainly refutes the Court's expansive reading of *Mullaney.* Indeed, the defendant in *Patterson* characterized *Mullaney* exactly as the Court has today and we *rejected* that interpretation:

> *Mullaney*'s holding, it is argued, is that the State may not permit the blameworthiness of an act *or the severity of punishment authorized for its commission* to depend on the presence or absence of an identified fact without assuming the burden of proving the presence or absence of that fact, as the case

may be, beyond a reasonable doubt. In our view, the *Mullaney* holding should not be so broadly read.

We explained *Mullaney* instead as holding only "that a state must prove every ingredient of an offense beyond a reasonable doubt, and that it may not shift the burden of proof to the defendant by presuming that ingredient upon proof of the other elements of the offense." Because nothing had been presumed against Patterson under New York law, we found no due process violation. Ever since our decision in *Patterson*, we have consistently explained the holding in *Mullaney* in these limited terms and have rejected the broad interpretation the Court gives *Mullaney* today. . . .

[Justice O'Connor then argued that the Court could not derive its principle from *McMillan* and that, apart] from *Mullaney* and *McMillan*, the Court does not claim to find support for its rule in any other pre-*Jones* decision. . . . Thus, . . . the Court's statement that its increase in the maximum penalty rule emerges from the history and case law that it cites is simply incorrect. . . .

II

. . . [T]here appear to be several plausible interpretations of the constitutional principle on which the Court's decision rests.

For example, under one reading, the Court appears to hold that the Constitution requires that a fact be submitted to a jury and proved beyond a reasonable doubt only if that fact, as a formal matter, extends the range of punishment *beyond the prescribed statutory maximum*. A state could, however, remove from the jury (and subject to a standard of proof below "beyond a reasonable doubt") the assessment of those facts that define narrower ranges of punishment, *within the overall statutory range*, to which the defendant may be sentenced. Thus, apparently New Jersey could cure its sentencing scheme, and achieve virtually the same results, by drafting its weapons possession statute in the following manner: First, New Jersey could prescribe, in the weapons possession statute itself, a range of 5 to 20 years' imprisonment for one who commits that criminal offense. Second, New Jersey could provide that only those defendants convicted under the statute who are found by a judge, by a preponderance of the evidence, to have acted with a purpose to intimidate an individual on the basis of race may receive a sentence greater than 10 years' imprisonment. . . .

Under another reading of the Court's decision, it may mean only that the Constitution requires that a fact be submitted to a jury and proved beyond a reasonable doubt if it, as a formal matter, *increases* the range of punishment *beyond that which could legally be imposed absent that fact*. A state could, however, remove from the jury (and subject to a standard of proof below "beyond a reasonable doubt") the assessment of those facts that, as a formal matter, *decrease* the range of punishment *below that which could legally be imposed absent that fact*. Thus, consistent with our decision in *Patterson*, New Jersey could cure its sentencing scheme, and achieve virtually the same results, by drafting its weapons possession statute in the following manner: First, New Jersey could prescribe, in the weapons possession statute itself, a range of 5 to 20 years' imprisonment for one who commits that criminal offense. Second, New Jersey could provide that a defendant convicted under the statute whom a judge finds, by a preponderance of the evidence, *not* to have acted with a purpose to intimidate an individual on the basis of race may receive a sentence no greater than 10 years' imprisonment.

The rule that Justice Thomas advocates in his concurring opinion embraces this precise distinction between a fact that increases punishment and a fact that decreases punishment. . . . [W]hether a fact is responsible for an increase or a decrease in punishment rests in the eye of the beholder. Again, it is difficult to understand, and neither the Court nor Justice Thomas explains, why the Constitution would require a state legislature to follow such a meaningless and formalistic difference in drafting its criminal statutes.

If either of the above readings is all that the Court's decision means, "the Court's principle amounts to nothing more than chastising [the New Jersey legislature] for failing to use the approved phrasing in expressing its intent as to how [unlawful weapons possession] should be punished." *Jones*, 526 U.S. at 267 (Kennedy, J., dissenting). If New Jersey can, consistent with the Constitution, make precisely the same differences in punishment turn on precisely the same facts, and can remove the assessment of those facts from the jury and subject them to a standard of proof below "beyond a reasonable doubt," it is impossible to say that the Fifth, Sixth, and Fourteenth Amendments require the Court's rule. For the same reason, the "structural democratic constraints" that might discourage a legislature from enacting either of the above hypothetical statutes would be no more significant than those that would discourage the enactment of New Jersey's present sentence-enhancement statute. In all three cases, the legislature is able to calibrate punishment perfectly, and subject to a maximum penalty only those defendants whose cases satisfy the sentence-enhancement criterion. As Justice Kennedy explained in *Jones,* "[n]o constitutional values are served by so formalistic an approach, while its constitutional costs in statutes struck down . . . are real."

Given the pure formalism of the above readings of the Court's opinion, one suspects that the constitutional principle underlying its decision is more far reaching. The actual principle underlying the Court's decision may be that any fact (other than prior conviction) that has the effect, *in real terms*, of increasing the maximum punishment beyond an otherwise applicable range must be submitted to a jury and proved beyond a reasonable doubt. ("The relevant inquiry is one not of form, but of effect—does the required finding expose the defendant to a greater punishment than that authorized by the jury's guilty verdict?"). The principle thus would apply not only to schemes like New Jersey's, under which a factual determination exposes a defendant to a sentence beyond the prescribed statutory maximum, but also to all determinate-sentencing schemes in which the length of a defendant's sentence within the statutory range turns on specific factual determinations (e.g., the federal sentencing guidelines). . . . I would reject any such principle. . . .

As the Court acknowledges, we have never doubted that the Constitution permits Congress and the state legislatures to define criminal offenses, to prescribe broad ranges of punishment for those offenses, and to give judges discretion to decide where within those ranges a particular defendant's punishment should be set. That view accords with historical practice under the Constitution. "From the beginning of the Republic, federal judges were entrusted with wide sentencing discretion. The great majority of federal criminal statutes have stated only a maximum term of years and a maximum monetary fine, permitting the sentencing judge to impose any term of imprisonment and any fine up to the statutory maximum." Kate Stith & Jose Cabranes, Fear of Judging: Sentencing Guidelines in the Federal Courts 9 (1998) (footnote omitted). Under discretionary-sentencing schemes, a judge bases the defendant's sentence on any number of facts neither presented at trial nor found by a jury beyond a reasonable doubt. . . .[a]

Under our precedent, then, a state may leave the determination of a defendant's sentence to a judge's discretionary decision within a prescribed range of penalties. When a judge, pursuant to that sentencing scheme, decides to increase a defendant's sentence on the basis of certain contested facts, those facts need not be proved to a jury beyond a reasonable doubt. The judge's findings, whether by proof beyond a reasonable doubt or less, suffice for purposes of the Constitution. Under the Court's decision today, however, it appears that once a legislature constrains judges' sentencing discretion by prescribing certain sentences that may only be imposed (or must be imposed) in connection with the same determinations of the same contested facts, the Constitution requires that the facts instead be proved to a jury beyond a reasonable doubt. I see no reason to treat the two schemes differently. See, e.g., *McMillan* ("We have some difficulty fathoming why the due process calculus would change simply because the legislature has seen fit to provide sentencing courts with additional guidance"). In this respect, I agree with the Solicitor General that "[a] sentence that is constitutionally permissible when selected by a court on the basis of whatever factors it deems appropriate does not become impermissible simply because the court is permitted to select that sentence only after making a finding prescribed by the legislature." Although the Court acknowledges the legitimacy of discretionary sentencing by judges, it never provides a sound reason for treating judicial factfinding under determinate-sentencing schemes differently under the Constitution. . . .

Consideration of the purposes underlying the Sixth Amendment's jury trial guarantee further demonstrates why our acceptance of judge-made findings in the context of discretionary sentencing suggests the approval of the same judge-made findings in the context of determinate sentencing as well. One important purpose of the Sixth Amendment's jury trial guarantee is to protect the criminal defendant against potentially arbitrary judges. It effectuates this promise by preserving, as a constitutional matter, certain fundamental decisions for a jury of one's peers, as opposed to a judge. . . . Clearly, the concerns animating the Sixth Amendment's jury trial guarantee, if they were to extend to the sentencing context at all, would apply with greater strength to a discretionary-sentencing scheme than to determinate sentencing. In the former scheme, the potential for mischief by an arbitrary judge is much greater, given that the judge's decision of where to set the defendant's sentence within the prescribed statutory range is left almost entirely to discretion. In contrast, under a determinate-sentencing system, the discretion the judge wields within the statutory range is tightly constrained. Accordingly, our approval of discretionary-sentencing

[a] Justice O'Connor cited *Williams v. New York* for this proposition.—[Footnote by eds.]

schemes, in which a defendant is not entitled to have a jury make factual findings relevant to sentencing despite the effect those findings have on the severity of the defendant's sentence, demonstrates that the defendant should have no right to demand that a jury make the equivalent factual determinations under a determinate-sentencing scheme.

The Court appears to hold today, however, that a defendant is entitled to have a jury decide, by proof beyond a reasonable doubt, every fact relevant to the determination of sentence under a determinate-sentencing scheme. If this is an accurate description of the constitutional principle underlying the Court's opinion, its decision will have the effect of invalidating significant sentencing reform accomplished at the federal and state levels over the past three decades. . . .

Prior to the most recent wave of sentencing reform, the federal government and the states employed indeterminate-sentencing schemes in which judges and executive branch officials (e.g., parole board officials) had substantial discretion to determine the actual length of a defendant's sentence. . . . Studies of indeterminate-sentencing schemes found that similarly situated defendants often received widely disparate sentences. Although indeterminate sentencing was intended to soften the harsh and uniform sentences formerly imposed under mandatory-sentencing systems, some studies revealed that indeterminate sentencing actually had the opposite effect. . . .

In response, Congress and the state legislatures shifted to determinate-sentencing schemes that aimed to limit judges' sentencing discretion and, thereby, afford similarly situated offenders equivalent treatment. The most well known of these reforms was the federal Sentencing Reform Act of 1984. In the Act, Congress created the United States Sentencing Commission, which in turn promulgated the Sentencing Guidelines that now govern sentencing by federal judges. Whether one believes the determinate-sentencing reforms have proved successful or not—and the subject is one of extensive debate among commentators—the apparent effect of the Court's opinion today is to halt the current debate on sentencing reform in its tracks and to invalidate with the stroke of a pen three decades' worth of nationwide reform, all in the name of a principle with a questionable constitutional pedigree. Indeed, it is ironic that the Court, in the name of constitutional rights meant to protect criminal defendants from the potentially arbitrary exercise of power by prosecutors and judges, appears to rest its decision on a principle that would render unconstitutional efforts by Congress and the state legislatures to place constraints on that very power in the sentencing context. . . .

Finally, perhaps the most significant impact of the Court's decision will be a practical one—its unsettling effect on sentencing conducted under current federal and state determinate-sentencing schemes. As I have explained, the Court does not say whether these schemes are constitutional, but its reasoning strongly suggests that they are not. Thus, with respect to past sentences handed down by judges under determinate-sentencing schemes, the Court's decision threatens to unleash a flood of petitions by convicted defendants seeking to invalidate their sentences in whole or in part on the authority of the Court's decision today. Statistics compiled by the United States Sentencing Commission reveal that almost a half-million cases have been sentenced under the

Sentencing Guidelines since 1989. Federal cases constitute only the tip of the iceberg. In 1998, for example, federal criminal prosecutions represented only about 0.4% of the total number of criminal prosecutions in federal and state courts. ([In]1998, 57,691 criminal cases were filed in federal court compared to 14,623,330 in state courts). Because many states, like New Jersey, have determinate-sentencing schemes, the number of individual sentences drawn into question by the Court's decision could be colossal.

The decision will likely have an even more damaging effect on sentencing conducted in the immediate future under current determinate-sentencing schemes. Because the Court fails to clarify the precise contours of the constitutional principle underlying its decision, federal and state judges are left in a state of limbo. Should they continue to assume the constitutionality of the determinate-sentencing schemes under which they have operated for so long, and proceed to sentence convicted defendants in accord with those governing statutes and guidelines? The Court provides no answer, yet its reasoning suggests that each new sentence will rest on shaky ground. The most unfortunate aspect of today's decision is that our precedents did not foreordain this disruption in the world of sentencing. Rather, our cases traditionally took a cautious approach to questions like the one presented in this case. The Court throws that caution to the wind and, in the process, threatens to cast sentencing in the United States into what will likely prove to be a lengthy period of considerable confusion.

III

Because I do not believe that the Court's "increase in the maximum penalty" rule is required by the Constitution, I would evaluate New Jersey's sentence-enhancement statute by analyzing the factors we have examined in past cases. First, the New Jersey statute does not shift the burden of proof on an essential ingredient of the offense by presuming that ingredient upon proof of other elements of the offense. Second, the magnitude of the New Jersey sentence enhancement, as applied in petitioner's case, is constitutionally permissible. Under New Jersey law, the weapons possession offense to which petitioner pleaded guilty carries a sentence range of 5 to 10 years' imprisonment. The fact that petitioner, in committing that offense, acted with a purpose to intimidate because of race exposed him to a higher sentence range of 10 to 20 years' imprisonment. The 10-year increase in the maximum penalty to which petitioner was exposed falls well within the range we have found permissible. Third, the New Jersey statute gives no impression of having been enacted to evade the constitutional requirements that attach when a State makes a fact an element of the charged offense. For example, New Jersey did not take what had previously been an element of the weapons possession offense and transform it into a sentencing factor.

In sum, New Jersey "simply took one factor that has always been considered by sentencing courts to bear on punishment"—a defendant's motive for committing the criminal offense—"and dictated the precise weight to be given that factor" when the motive is to intimidate a person because of race. . . .

The New Jersey statute resembles the Pennsylvania statute we upheld in *McMillan* in every respect but one. That difference—that the

New Jersey statute increases the maximum punishment to which petitioner was exposed—does not persuade me that New Jersey "sought to evade the constitutional requirements associated with the characterization of a fact as an offense element." There is no question that New Jersey could prescribe a range of 5 to 20 years' imprisonment as punishment for its weapons possession offense. Thus, as explained above, the specific means by which the State chooses to control judges' discretion within that permissible range is of no moment. Cf. *Patterson* ("The Due Process Clause, as we see it, does not put New York to the choice of abandoning [the affirmative defense] or undertaking to disprove [its] existence in order to convict of a crime which otherwise is within its constitutional powers to sanction by substantial punishment"). . . .

■ JUSTICE BREYER, with whom . . . CHIEF JUSTICE [REHNQUIST] joins, dissenting.

The majority holds that the Constitution contains the following requirement: "any fact [other than recidivism] that increases the penalty for a crime beyond the prescribed statutory maximum must be submitted to a jury, and proved beyond a reasonable doubt." This rule would seem to promote a procedural ideal—that of juries, not judges, determining the existence of those facts upon which increased punishment turns. But the real world of criminal justice cannot hope to meet any such ideal. It can function only with the help of procedural compromises, particularly in respect to sentencing. And those compromises, which are themselves necessary for the fair functioning of the criminal justice system, preclude implementation of the procedural model that today's decision reflects. At the very least, the impractical nature of the requirement that the majority now recognizes supports the proposition that the Constitution was not intended to embody it.

I

In modern times the law has left it to the sentencing judge to find those facts which (within broad sentencing limits set by the legislature) determine the sentence of a convicted offender. The judge's factfinding role is not inevitable. One could imagine, for example, a pure "charge offense" sentencing system in which the degree of punishment depended only upon the crime charged (e.g., eight mandatory years for robbery, six for arson, three for assault). But such a system would ignore many harms and risks of harm that the offender caused or created, and it would ignore many relevant offender characteristics. See United States Sentencing Commission, Sentencing Guidelines and Policy Statements, Part A, at 1.5 (1987) (hereinafter Sentencing Guidelines or Guidelines) (pointing out that a "charge offense" system by definition would ignore any fact "that did not constitute [a] statutory element of the offense of which the defendant was convicted"). Hence, that imaginary "charge offense" system would not be a fair system, for it would lack proportionality, i.e., it would treat different offenders similarly despite major differences in the manner in which each committed the same crime.

There are many such manner-related differences in respect to criminal behavior. Empirical data collected by the Sentencing Commission makes clear that, before the Guidelines, judges who exercised discretion within broad legislatively determined sentencing limits (say, a range of 0 to 20 years) would impose very different sentences upon offenders engaged in the same basic criminal conduct, depending, for example, upon the amount of drugs distributed (in respect to drug crimes), the amount of money taken (in respect to robbery, theft, or fraud), the presence or use of a weapon, injury to a victim, the vulnerability of a victim, the offender's role in the offense, recidivism, and many other offense-related or offender-related factors. The majority does not deny that judges have exercised, and, constitutionally speaking, *may* exercise sentencing discretion in this way.

Nonetheless, it is important for present purposes to understand why *judges*, rather than *juries*, traditionally have determined the presence or absence of such sentence-affecting facts in any given case. And it is important to realize that the reason is not a theoretical one, but a practical one. It does not reflect an ideal of procedural "fairness," but rather an administrative need for procedural *compromise*. There are, to put it simply, far too many potentially relevant sentencing factors to permit submission of all (or even many) of them to a jury. As the Sentencing Guidelines state the matter,

> [a] bank robber with (or without) a gun, which the robber kept hidden (or brandished), might have frightened (or merely warned), injured seriously (or less seriously), tied up (or simply pushed) a guard, a teller or a customer, at night (or at noon), for a bad (or arguably less bad) motive, in an effort to obtain money for other crimes (or for other purposes), in the company of a few (or many) other robbers, for the first (or fourth) time that day, while sober (or under the influence of drugs or alcohol), and so forth.

The Guidelines note that "a sentencing system tailored to fit every conceivable wrinkle of each case can become unworkable and seriously compromise the certainty of punishment and its deterrent effect." To ask a jury to consider all, or many, such matters would do the same.

At the same time, to require jury consideration of all such factors—say, during trial where the issue is guilt or innocence—could easily place the defendant in the awkward (and conceivably unfair) position of having to deny he committed the crime yet offer proof about how he committed it, e.g., "I did not sell drugs, but I sold no more than 500 grams." And while special postverdict sentencing juries could cure this problem, they have seemed (but for capital cases) not worth their administrative costs. Hence, before the Guidelines, federal sentencing judges typically would obtain relevant factual sentencing information from probation officers' presentence reports, while permitting a convicted offender to challenge the information's accuracy at a hearing before the judge without benefit of trial-type evidentiary rules. See Williams v. New York, 337 U.S. 241, 249–51 (1949) (describing the modern "practice of individualizing punishments" under which judges often consider otherwise inadmissible information gleaned from probation reports).

It is also important to understand how a judge traditionally determined which factors should be taken into account for sentencing purposes. In principle, the number of potentially relevant behavioral characteristics is endless. A judge might ask, for example, whether an unlawfully possessed knife was "a switchblade, drawn or concealed, opened or closed, large or small, used in connection with a car theft (where victim confrontation is rare), a burglary (where confrontation is unintended) or a robbery (where confrontation is intentional)." Again, the method reflects practical, rather than theoretical, considerations. Prior to the Sentencing Guidelines, federal law left the individual sentencing judge free to determine which factors were relevant. That freedom meant that each judge, in an effort to tailor punishment to the individual offense and offender, was guided primarily by experience, relevance, and a sense of proportional fairness. . . .

Finally, it is important to understand how a legislature decides which factual circumstances among all those potentially related to generally harmful behavior it should transform into elements of a statutorily defined crime (where they would become relevant to the guilt or innocence of an accused), and which factual circumstances it should leave to the sentencing process (where, as sentencing factors, they would help to determine the sentence imposed upon one who has been found guilty). Again, theory does not provide an answer. Legislatures, in defining crimes in terms of elements, have looked for guidance to common law tradition, to history, and to current social need. And, traditionally, the Court has left legislatures considerable freedom to make the element determination.

. . . A sentencing system in which judges have discretion to find sentencing-related factors is a workable system and one that has long been thought consistent with the Constitution; why, then, would the Constitution treat sentencing *statutes* any differently?

II

As Justice Thomas suggests, until fairly recent times many legislatures rarely focused upon sentencing factors. Rather, it appears they simply identified typical forms of antisocial conduct, defined basic "crimes," and attached a broad sentencing range to each definition—leaving judges free to decide how to sentence within those ranges in light of such factors as they found relevant. But the Constitution does not freeze 19th-century sentencing practices into permanent law. And dissatisfaction with the traditional sentencing system (reflecting its tendency to treat similar cases differently) has led modern legislatures to write new laws that refer specifically to sentencing factors. . . .

Legislatures have tended to address the problem of too much judicial sentencing discretion in two ways. First, legislatures sometimes have created sentencing commissions armed with delegated authority to make more uniform judicial exercise of that discretion. Congress, for example, has created a federal Sentencing Commission, giving it the power to create guidelines that (within the sentencing range set by individual statutes) reflect the host of factors that might be used to determine the actual sentence imposed for each individual crime. Federal judges must apply those guidelines in typical cases (those that lie in the "heartland" of the crime as the statute defines it) while retaining freedom to depart in atypical cases.

Second, legislatures sometimes have directly limited the use (by judges or by a commission) of particular factors in sentencing, either by specifying statutorily how a particular factor will affect the sentence imposed or by specifying how a commission should use a particular factor when writing a guideline. Such a statute might state explicitly, for example, that a particular factor, say, use of a weapon, recidivism, injury to a victim, or bad motive, "shall" increase, or "may" increase, a particular sentence in a particular way. See, e.g., McMillan v. Pennsylvania, 477 U.S. 79 (1986) (Pennsylvania statute expressly treated "visible possession of a firearm" as a sentencing consideration that subjected a defendant to a mandatory 5-year term of imprisonment).

The issue the Court decides today involves this second kind of legislation. The Court holds that a legislature cannot enact such legislation (where an increase in the maximum is involved) unless the factor at issue has been charged, tried to a jury, and found to exist beyond a reasonable doubt. My question in respect to this holding is, simply, "*why* would the Constitution contain such a requirement"?

III

. . . [T]he majority raises no objection to traditional pre-Guidelines sentencing procedures under which judges, not juries, made the factual findings that would lead to an increase in an individual offender's sentence. How does a legislative determination differ in any significant way? For example, if a judge may on his or her own decide that victim injury or bad motive should increase a bank robber's sentence from 5 years to 10, why does it matter that a legislature instead enacts a statute that increases a bank robber's sentence from 5 years to 10 based on this same judicial finding?

. . . [T]he majority also makes no constitutional objection to a legislative delegation to a commission of the authority to create guidelines that determine how a judge is to exercise sentencing discretion. But if the Constitution permits guidelines, why does it not permit Congress similarly to guide the exercise of a judge's sentencing discretion? That is, if the Constitution permits a delegatee (the commission) to exercise sentencing-related rulemaking power, how can it deny the delegator (the legislature) what is, in effect, the same rulemaking power?

The majority appears to offer two responses. First, it argues for a limiting principle that would prevent a legislature with broad authority from transforming (jury-determined) facts that constitute elements of a crime into (judge-determined) sentencing factors, thereby removing procedural protections that the Constitution would otherwise require ("constitutional limits" prevent states from "defining away facts necessary to constitute a criminal offense"). The majority's cure, however, is not aimed at the disease.

The same "transformational" problem exists under traditional sentencing law, where legislation, silent as to sentencing factors, grants the judge virtually unchecked discretion to sentence within a broad range. Under such a system, judges or prosecutors can similarly "transform" crimes, punishing an offender convicted of one crime as if he had committed another. A prosecutor, for example, might charge an offender with five counts of embezzlement (each subject to a 10-year maximum penalty), while asking the judge to impose maximum and consecutive sentences because the embezzler murdered his employer. And, as part of the traditional sentencing discretion that the majority concedes judges retain, the judge, not a jury, would determine the last-mentioned relevant fact, i.e., that the murder actually occurred.

This egregious example shows the problem's complexity. The source of the problem lies not in a legislature's power to enact sentencing factors, but in the traditional legislative power to select elements defining a crime, the traditional legislative power to set broad sentencing ranges, and the traditional judicial power to choose a sentence within that range on the basis of relevant offender conduct. Conversely, the solution to the problem lies, not in prohibiting legislatures from enacting sentencing factors, but in sentencing rules that determine punishments on the basis of properly defined relevant conduct, with sensitivity to the need for procedural protections where sentencing factors are determined by a judge (for example, use of a "reasonable doubt" standard), and invocation of the Due Process Clause where the history of the crime at issue, together with the nature of the facts to be proved, reveals unusual and serious procedural unfairness. Cf. *McMillan* (upholding statute in part because it "gives no impression of having been tailored to permit the [sentencing factor] to be a tail which wags the dog of the substantive offense").

Second, the majority, in support of its constitutional rule, emphasizes the concept of a statutory "maximum." The Court points out that a sentencing judge (or a commission) traditionally has determined, and now still determines, sentences *within* a legislated range capped by a maximum (a range that the legislature itself sets). I concede the truth of the majority's statement, but I do not understand its relevance.

From a defendant's perspective, the legislature's decision to cap the possible range of punishment at a statutorily prescribed "maximum" would affect the actual sentence imposed no differently than a sentencing commission's (or a sentencing judge's) similar determination. Indeed, as a practical matter, a legislated mandatory "minimum" is far more important to an actual defendant. A judge and a commission, after all, are legally free to select any sentence below a statute's maximum, but they are not free to subvert a statutory minimum. And, as Justice Thomas indicates, all the considerations of fairness that might support submission to a jury of a factual matter that increases a statutory maximum, apply a fortiori to any matter that would increase a statutory minimum. To repeat, I do not understand why, when a legislature *authorizes* a judge to impose a higher penalty for bank robbery (based, say, on the court's finding that a victim was injured or the defendant's motive was bad), a new crime is born; but where a legislature *requires* a judge to impose a higher penalty than he otherwise would (within a preexisting statutory range) based on similar criteria, it is not.

IV

. . . [I] am willing . . . to assume that the majority's rule would provide a degree of increased procedural protection in respect to those particular sentencing factors currently embodied in statutes. I nonetheless believe that any such increased protection provides little practical help and comes at too high a price. For one thing, by leaving mandatory minimum sentences untouched, the majority's rule simply encourages any legislature interested in asserting control over the sentencing process to do so by creating those minimums. That result would mean significantly less procedural fairness, not more.

For another thing, this Court's case law led legislatures to believe that they were permitted to increase a statutory maximum sentence on the basis of a sentencing factor [and] legislatures may well have relied upon that belief. See, e.g., 21 U.S.C. § 841(b) (1994 ed. and Supp. III) (providing penalties for, among other things, possessing a "controlled substance" with intent to distribute it, which sentences vary dramatically depending upon the amount of the drug possessed, without requiring jury determination of the amount); N. J. Stat. Ann. §§ 2C:43–6, 2C:43–7, 2C:44–1a-f, 2C:44–3 (West 1995 and Supp. 1999–2000) (setting sentencing ranges for crimes, while providing for lesser or greater punishments depending upon judicial findings regarding certain "aggravating" or "mitigating" factors); Cal. Penal Code Ann. § 1170 (West Supp. 2000) (similar); see also Cal. Court Rule 420(b) (1996) (providing that "circumstances in aggravation and mitigation" are to be established by the sentencing judge based on "the case record, the probation officer's report, [and] other reports and statements properly received").

As Justice O'Connor points out, the majority's rule creates serious uncertainty about the constitutionality of such statutes and about the constitutionality of the confinement of those punished under them. . . .

Finally, the Court's new rule will likely impede legislative attempts to provide authoritative guidance as to how courts should respond to the presence of traditional sentencing factors. The factor at issue here—motive—is such a factor. Whether a robber takes money to finance other crimes or to feed a starving family can matter, and long has mattered, when the length of a sentence is at issue. The state of New Jersey has determined that one motive—racial hatred—is particularly bad and ought to make a difference in respect to punishment for a crime. That determination is reasonable. The procedures mandated are consistent with traditional sentencing practice. Though additional procedural protections might well be desirable, for the reasons Justice O'Connor discusses and those I have discussed, I do not believe the Constitution requires them where ordinary sentencing factors are at issue. Consequently, in my view, New Jersey's statute is constitutional.

I respectfully dissent.

## NOTES ON THE AFTERMATH OF *APPRENDI*

### 1. CAPITAL SENTENCING

Under all contemporary capital sentencing statutes, a defendant convicted of a capital offense cannot be sentenced to death unless the prosecution proves one or more "aggravating circumstances" at the sentencing phase of the case. Most capital sentencing statutes require the substantive factual predicates for a death sentence to be proved in a bifurcated proceeding to a jury beyond a reasonable doubt. However, some states repose capital sentencing authority in judges and until recently did not require the requisite findings to be made beyond a reasonable doubt.

When the issue first came before the Supreme Court in Walton v. Arizona, 497 U.S. 639 (1990), the Court held that the specific findings required for imposition of a death sentence are not constitutionally equivalent to elements of the offense, and that the Constitution did not require them to be determined by a jury. *Walton* also implied that the findings need not be made beyond a reasonable doubt. The precedential implications of *Walton* were much debated in the *Apprendi* opinions. The dissenters thought the two decisions irreconcilable and cited *Walton* in support of their position.

The view of the dissenters that the cases were inconsistent proved to be right. The Court overruled *Walton* in Ring v. Arizona, 536 U.S. 584 (2002), holding that these findings must be made by a jury.[a] Although the Court had no reason to say so explicitly in *Ring*, the implication is inescapable that they must be proved beyond a reasonable doubt.[b]

## 2. SENTENCING GUIDELINES: *BLAKELY* AND *BOOKER*

The most important question left open after *Apprendi* was its impact on sentencing guideline systems. The answers came in Blakely v. Washington, 542 U.S. 961 (2004), and United States v. Booker, 543 U.S. 220 (2005).

### (i) *Blakely*

Blakely pleaded guilty to second-degree kidnaping involving domestic violence and use of a firearm. Under Washington law, this was a Class B felony, which carried a maximum of 10 years in prison. The Washington guidelines provided that the "standard range" for this offense was 49 to 53 months. A sentence above this range could be imposed if the judge found "substantial and compelling reasons justifying an exceptional sentence." An illustrative, but not exhaustive, list of aggravating factors was provided in the statute. The judge could impose an exceptional sentence based on one or more of these factors, or any others that were not already taken into account in setting the standard range. Findings of fact and conclusions of law thought to establish the exceptional sentence were required, and the decision to impose such a sentence was subject to appeal under a "clearly erroneous" standard of review.

The judge sentenced Blakely to 90 months, based on the ground that he had acted with "deliberate cruelty." "Deliberate cruelty" was one of the statutory grounds permitting an exceptional sentence in domestic violence cases. The Washington courts upheld the sentence, but the Supreme Court reversed. Justice Scalia wrote for the same majority that decided *Apprendi*:

> In this case, petitioner was sentenced to more than three years above the 53-month statutory maximum of the standard range because he had acted with deliberate cruelty. The facts supporting that finding were neither admitted by petitioner nor found by a jury. The State nevertheless contends that there was no *Apprendi* violation because the relevant statutory maximum is not 53 months, but the 10-year maximum for class B felonies. . . . It observes that no exceptional sentence may exceed that limit.

---

[a] The case was decided on the same day as *Harris*. The vote was 7–2. Joined by Chief Justice Rehnquist, Justice O'Connor dissented. Justice Kennedy indicated that he was ready to accept *Apprendi* as the law, but not to extend it. He agreed that *Walton* could not stand given *Apprendi*. Justice Breyer went further than the majority. He argued that the Constitution required that the capital punishment decision itself must be made by the jury.

[b] The Court held in Schriro v. Summerlin, 542 U.S. 348 (2004), that *Ring* was not to be retroactively applied to cases that were final when *Ring* was decided. The vote in that case was along more predictable lines. Justice Scalia wrote for the Court, and was joined by Chief Justice Rehnquist and Justices O'Connor, Kennedy, and Thomas. Justice Breyer dissented, joined by Justices Stevens, Souter, and Ginsburg. Although the issue was not before the Court, the implication is clear that neither *Apprendi* nor its other progeny will be applied to invalidate sentences imposed in cases that were final when the relevant new principle was established. In contrast, the law is clear that decisions of this type are fully applicable to cases pending at trial or on appeal at the time the new decision is reached.

> Our precedents make clear, however, that the statutory maximum for *Apprendi* purposes is the maximum sentence a judge may impose solely on the basis of the facts reflected in the jury verdict or admitted by the defendant. In other words, the relevant statutory maximum is not the maximum sentence a judge may impose after finding additional facts, but the maximum he may impose without any additional findings. When a judge inflicts punishment that the jury's verdict alone does not allow, the jury has not found all the facts which the law makes essential to the punishment, and the judge exceeds his proper authority.
>
> The judge in this case could not have imposed the exceptional 90-month sentence solely on the basis of the facts admitted in the guilty plea. Those facts alone were insufficient. . . . Had the judge imposed the 90-month sentence solely on the basis of the plea, he would have been reversed. The maximum sentence is no more 10 years here than it was 20 years in *Apprendi* (because that is what the judge could have imposed upon finding a hate crime) or death in *Ring* (because that is what the judge could have imposed upon finding an aggravator).

Justice Scalia also defended *Apprendi* in principle:

> Our commitment to *Apprendi* in this context reflects not just respect for longstanding precedent, but the need to give intelligible content to the right of jury trial. That right is no mere procedural formality, but a fundamental reservation of power in our constitutional structure. Just as suffrage ensures the people's ultimate control in the legislative and executive branches, jury trial is meant to ensure their control in the judiciary. *Apprendi* carries out this design by ensuring that the judge's authority to sentence derives wholly from the jury's verdict. Without that restriction, the jury would not exercise the control that the Framers intended.
>
> Those who would reject *Apprendi* are resigned to one of two alternatives. The first is that the jury need only find whatever facts the legislature chooses to label elements of the crime, and that those it labels sentencing factors—no matter how much they may increase the punishment—may be found by the judge. This would mean, for example, that a judge could sentence a man for committing murder even if the jury convicted him only of illegally possessing the firearm used to commit it—or of making an illegal lane change while fleeing the death scene. Not even *Apprendi*'s critics would advocate this absurd result. The jury could not function as circuitbreaker in the State's machinery of justice if it were relegated to making a determination that the defendant at some point did something wrong, a mere preliminary to a judicial inquisition into the facts of the crime the State *actually* seeks to punish.[10]
>
> The second alternative is that legislatures may establish legally essential sentencing factors *within limits*—limits crossed

[10] Justice O'Connor believes that a built-in political check will prevent lawmakers from manipulating offense elements in this fashion. But the many immediate practical advantages of judicial factfinding suggest that political forces would, if anything, pull in the opposite direction. In any case, the Framers' decision to entrench the jury-trial right in the Constitution shows that they did not trust government to make political decisions in this area.

> when, perhaps, the sentencing factor is a tail which wags the dog of the substantive offense. McMillan v. Pennsylvania, 477 U.S. 79, 88 (1986). What this means in operation is that the law must not go *too far*—it must not exceed the judicial estimation of the proper role of the judge.
>
> The subjectivity of this standard is obvious. Petitioner argued below that second-degree kidnaping with deliberate cruelty was essentially the same as first-degree kidnaping, the very charge he had avoided by pleading to a lesser offense. The court conceded this might be so but held it irrelevant. Petitioner's 90-month sentence exceeded the 53-month standard maximum by almost 70%; the Washington Supreme Court in other cases has upheld exceptional sentences 15 times the standard maximum. Did the court go too far in any of these cases? There is no answer that legal analysis can provide. With *too far* as the yardstick, it is always possible to disagree with such judgments and never to refute them.
>
> Whether the Sixth Amendment incorporates this manipulable standard rather than *Apprendi*'s bright-line rule depends on the plausibility of the claim that the Framers would have left definition of the scope of jury power up to judges' intuitive sense of how far is *too far*. We think that claim not plausible at all, because the very reason the Framers put a jury-trial guarantee in the Constitution is that they were unwilling to trust government to mark out the role of the jury.

Speaking also for Chief Justice Rehnquist and Justices Breyer and Kennedy, Justice O'Connor dissented:[c]

> One need look no further than the history leading up to and following the enactment of Washington's guidelines scheme to appreciate the damage that today's decision will cause. Prior to 1981, Washington, like most other States and the Federal Government, employed an indeterminate sentencing scheme. Washington's criminal code separated all felonies into three broad categories: class A, carrying a sentence of 20 years to life; class B, carrying a sentence of 0 to 10 years; and class C, carrying a sentence of 0 to 5 years. Sentencing judges, in conjunction with parole boards, had virtually unfettered discretion to sentence defendants to prison terms falling anywhere within the statutory range, including probation—i.e., no jail sentence at all.
>
> This system of unguided discretion inevitably resulted in severe disparities in sentences received and served by defendants committing the same offense and having similar criminal histories. Indeed, rather than reflect legally relevant criteria, these disparities too often were correlated with constitutionally suspect variables such as race.
>
> To counteract these trends, the state legislature passed the Sentencing Reform Act of 1981. The Act had the laudable purposes of "mak[ing] the criminal justice system accountable to the public," and "[e]nsur[ing] that the punishment for a criminal offense is proportionate to the seriousness of the offense . . . [and]

[c] Justices Kennedy and Breyer also submitted separate dissents.

commensurate with the punishment imposed on others committing similar offenses." Wash. Rev.Code Ann. § 9.94A.010 (2000). The Act neither increased any of the statutory sentencing ranges for the three types of felonies (though it did eliminate the statutory mandatory minimum for class A felonies), nor reclassified any substantive offenses. It merely placed meaningful constraints on discretion to sentence offenders within the statutory ranges, and eliminated parole. There is thus no evidence that the legislature was attempting to manipulate the statutory elements of criminal offenses or to circumvent the procedural protections of the Bill of Rights. Rather, lawmakers were trying to bring some much-needed uniformity, transparency, and accountability to an otherwise labyrinthine sentencing and corrections system that lack[ed] any principle except unguided discretion.

Far from disregarding principles of due process and the jury trial right, as the majority today suggests, Washington's reform has served them. Before passage of the Act, a defendant charged with second degree kidnaping, like petitioner, had no idea whether he would receive a 10-year sentence or probation. The ultimate sentencing determination could turn as much on the idiosyncrasies of a particular judge as on the specifics of the defendant's crime or background. A defendant did not know what facts, if any, about his offense or his history would be considered relevant by the sentencing judge or by the parole board. After passage of the Act, a defendant charged with second degree kidnaping knows what his presumptive sentence will be; he has a good idea of the types of factors that a sentencing judge can and will consider when deciding whether to sentence him outside that range; he is guaranteed meaningful appellate review to protect against an arbitrary sentence. Criminal defendants still face the same statutory maximum sentences, but they now at least know, much more than before, the real consequences of their actions.

Washington's move to a system of guided discretion has served equal protection principles as well. Over the past 20 years, there has been a substantial reduction in racial disparity in sentencing across the State. The reduction is directly traceable to the constraining effects of the guidelines-namely, their "presumptive range[s]" and limits on the imposition of "exceptional sentences" outside of those ranges. . . .

Justice O'Connor also addressed the principle of the matter:

Washington's Sentencing Reform Act did not alter the statutory maximum sentence to which petitioner was exposed. Petitioner was informed in the charging document, his plea agreement, and during his plea hearing that he faced a potential statutory maximum of 10 years in prison. As discussed above, the guidelines served due process by providing notice to petitioner of the consequences of his acts; they vindicated his jury trial right by informing him of the stakes of risking trial; they served equal protection by ensuring petitioner that invidious characteristics such as race would not impact his sentence.

Given these observations, it is difficult for me to discern what principle besides doctrinaire formalism actually motivates today's decision. The majority chides the *Apprendi* dissenters for preferring a nuanced interpretation of the Due Process Clause and Sixth Amendment jury trial guarantee that would generally defer to legislative labels while acknowledging the existence of constitutional constraints—what the majority calls the law must not go too far approach. If indeed the choice is between adopting a balanced case-by-case approach that takes into consideration the values underlying the Bill of Rights, as well as the history of a particular sentencing reform law, and adopting a rigid rule that destroys everything in its path, I will choose the former.

But even were one to accept formalism as a principle worth vindicating for its own sake, it would not explain *Apprendi*'s, or today's, result. A rule of deferring to legislative labels has no less formal pedigree. It would be more consistent with our decisions leading up to *Apprendi*. It also would be easier to administer than the majority's rule, inasmuch as courts would not be forced to look behind statutes and regulations to determine whether a particular fact does or does not increase the penalty to which a defendant was exposed.

The majority is correct that rigid adherence to such an approach *could conceivably* produce absurd results; but, as today's decision demonstrates, rigid adherence to the majority's approach *does and will continue* to produce results that disserve the very principles the majority purports to vindicate. The pre-*Apprendi* rule of deference to the legislature retains a built-in political check to prevent lawmakers from shifting the prosecution for crimes to the penalty phase proceedings of lesser included and easier-to-prove offenses—e.g., the majority's hypothesized prosecution of murder in the guise of a traffic offense sentencing proceeding. There is no similar check, however, on application of the majority's "any fact that increases the upper bound of judicial discretion" by courts.

The majority claims the mantle of history and original intent. But as I have explained elsewhere, a handful of state decisions in the mid-19th century and a criminal procedure treatise have little if any persuasive value as evidence of what the Framers of the Federal Constitution intended in the late 18th century. Because broad judicial sentencing discretion was foreign to the Framers, they were never faced with the constitutional choice between submitting every fact that increases a sentence to the jury or vesting the sentencing judge with broad discretionary authority to account for differences in offenses and offenders.

### *(ii) Questions and Comments on Blakely*

Consider the two alternatives to *Apprendi* posed by Justice Scalia. One was to allow legislative labels to control, an approach that would "mean, for example, that a judge could sentence a man for committing murder even if the jury convicted him only of illegally possessing the firearm used to commit it—or of making an illegal lane change while fleeing the death scene." The other was that legislative decisions would control "within limits," limits that would be transgressed when the legislature went "too far." Neither of these results is acceptable, Scalia argues, and *Apprendi* avoids both.

But does it? Suppose a legislature authorized a sentence of anywhere from zero to life for one of Justice Scalia's hypothesized offenses, and then left it to the judge to determine the actual sentence based on unstated reasons of the judge's choosing. If a defendant is sentenced to life after conviction by a jury of one of these offenses because the judge believes the defendant to have committed a murder, does *Apprendi* come into play?[d] If not, how could the Court address the situation? Is it inevitable, in other words, that a runaway legislature that is clever about it could force the Supreme Court to decide whether it went "too far"? Why, in any event, should the possibility that a legislature might do something that no American legislature has ever done or is likely to do have any persuasive force in the *Apprendi* debate?

*Blakely* cast doubt on the constitutionality under *Apprendi* of numerous guideline systems around the country.[e] One widely debated question concerned the impact of *Blakely* on the Federal Sentencing Guidelines. Justice Scalia's *Blakely* opinion said in a footnote that the "Federal Sentencing Guidelines are not before us, and we express no opinion on them." But the implication that *Blakely* put the federal guidelines at risk was clear, and lower federal judges faced an immediate quandary about how to handle cases pending before them.

The reaction was swift. *Blakely* was decided on June 24, 2004. On July 9, just over two weeks later, United States v. Booker, 375 F.3d 508 (7th Cir. 2004), was decided. In an opinion by Judge Richard A. Posner, the Court held that *Blakely* was indistinguishable and that *Apprendi* applied to the federal guidelines. Judge Frank H. Easterbrook dissented, concluding his opinion with the observation that "[t]oday's decision will discombobulate the whole criminal-law docket. I trust that our superiors will have something to say about this. Soon."

They did. A petition for certiorari was filed on July 21, less than two weeks after the Court of Appeals decision. The petition was granted on August 2, 12 days later. The case was argued on October 4, and decided on January 12. This is lightning speed for the United States Supreme Court.

### *(iii) United States v. Booker: The Merits*

The decision in United States v. Booker, 543 U.S. 220 (2005), was complicated by the fact that there were two opinions for the Court, composed of different majorities, that dealt on the one hand with whether *Apprendi* applied to the federal sentencing guidelines and, on the other, with the appropriate remedy once a majority held that it did.

Booker was charged with possession with intent to distribute at least 50 grams of crack. The jury found him guilty, based on evidence that 92.5 grams were found in his duffle bag. The relevant statute required a minimum of 10 years in prison for this offense and a maximum of life. The Guidelines provided for a "heartland" sentence of 210 to 262 months based on Booker's criminal history and the quantity of drugs found by the jury. At a post-trial sentencing proceeding, the judge found that Booker had

[d] Recall the *Mullaney-Patterson* discussion in Note 7(iv) on Burden of Proof and Substantive Justice in Section 1.

[e] The Court subsequently held that the California system, the details of which are not important for now, could not continue to operate as before. See Cunningham v. California, 549 U.S. 270 (2007).

possessed an additional 566 grams of crack and that he had obstructed justice. These findings required the judge to impose a sentence of between 360 months and life. Booker was sentenced to 30 years. Without these findings, his maximum would have been 21 years and 10 months.[f]

Joined by Justices Scalia, Souter, Thomas, and Ginsburg, Justice Stevens wrote the opinion for the Court on the question whether *Apprendi* applied to the Federal Sentencing Guidelines. He had no trouble concluding that it did:

> [T]here is no distinction of constitutional significance between the Federal Sentencing Guidelines and the Washington procedures at issue in that case. . . . This conclusion rests on the premise, common to both systems, that the relevant sentencing rules are mandatory and impose binding requirements on all sentencing judges.
>
> If the Guidelines as currently written could be read as merely advisory provisions that recommended, rather than required, the selection of particular sentences in response to differing sets of facts, their use would not implicate the Sixth Amendment. We have never doubted the authority of a judge to exercise broad discretion in imposing a sentence within a statutory range. See *Apprendi*, 530 U.S. at 481; Williams v. New York, 337 U.S. 241, 246 (1949). Indeed, everyone agrees that the constitutional issues presented by these cases would have been avoided entirely if Congress had omitted . . . the provisions that make the Guidelines binding on district judges. . . . For when a trial judge exercises his discretion to select a specific sentence within a defined range, the defendant has no right to a jury determination of the facts that the judge deems relevant.
>
> The Guidelines as written, however, are not advisory; they are mandatory and binding on all judges. . . . [O]ur conclusion [is] that our holding in *Blakely* applies to the Sentencing Guidelines. We recognize, as we did in *Jones*, *Apprendi*, and *Blakely*, that in some cases jury factfinding may impair the most expedient and efficient sentencing of defendants. But the interest in fairness and reliability protected by the right to a jury trial—a common-law right that defendants enjoyed for centuries and that is now enshrined in the Sixth Amendment—has always outweighed the interest in concluding trials swiftly. . . .
>
> Accordingly, we reaffirm our holding in *Apprendi*: Any fact (other than a prior conviction) which is necessary to support a sentence exceeding the maximum authorized by the facts established by a plea of guilty or a jury verdict must be admitted by the defendant or proved to a jury beyond a reasonable doubt.

---

[f] *United States v. Fanfan* was a companion case presenting similar issues. It was decided in the same opinions. In *Fanfan*, the trial court held that *Apprendi* applied to the Guidelines and therefore imposed a sentence based on the jury verdict rather than a finding of additional drug possession at the sentencing hearing. The government filed a notice of appeal in the Circuit Court, and immediately filed a petition for certiorari before judgment. That petition was granted, and the case was consolidated for argument and decision with *Booker*.

Predictably, Justice Breyer dissented from this holding. Also predictably, he was joined in dissent by Chief Justice Rehnquist and Justices O'Connor and Kennedy.

### *(iv) United States v. Booker: The Remedy*

The truly surprising feature of *Booker* was its holding on the appropriate remedy. On this question, Justice Breyer wrote the opinion for the Court. He was joined by his usual allies in this arena, Chief Justice Rehnquist and Justices O'Connor and Kennedy. The surprise was that Justice Ginsburg joined with these four to form a remedial majority.[g] Two aspects of the Court's holding are worthy of note.

First, the Court excised from the acts of Congress establishing the Guidelines all provisions that made them mandatory. This made the Guidelines advisory, and they accordingly then fell within the unanimous view of the Court, as quoted above, that "[i]f the Guidelines as currently written could be read as merely advisory provisions that recommended, rather than required, the selection of particular sentences in response to differing sets of facts, their use would not implicate the Sixth Amendment. We have never doubted the authority of a judge to exercise broad discretion in imposing a sentence within a statutory range."

Second, the Court modified the Congressional provisions on appellate review. Congress had tightened the appellate review standard in order to make the Guidelines more mandatory. The Court instead adopted an earlier standard of review: "We infer appropriate review standards from related statutory language, the structure of the statute, and the 'sound administration of justice'. . . . [T]hose factors, in addition to the past two decades of appellate practice in cases involving departures, imply a practical standard of review already familiar to appellate courts: review for 'unreasonable[ness].' "[h]

## 3. THE FEDERAL GUIDELINES AFTER *BOOKER*

So how are the Federal Sentencing Guidelines to be implemented after *Booker*? The Court gave its answer in Gall v. United States, 552 U.S. 38 (2007):

> [A] district court should begin all sentencing proceedings by correctly calculating the applicable Guidelines range. As a matter of administration and to secure nationwide consistency, the Guidelines should be the starting point and the initial benchmark. The Guidelines are not the only consideration, however. Accordingly, after giving both parties an opportunity to argue for whatever sentence they deem appropriate, the district judge should then consider all of the [18 U.S.C.] § 3553(a) factors to determine whether they support the sentence requested by a party.[6] In so

---

[g] Justices Stevens, Scalia, Souter, and Thomas dissented on the remedial issue in three separate opinions.

[h] How the Court got to these conclusions and whether they are within the proper scope of its powers raise questions far beyond the subject matter of this book. In the view of the dissenters, the Court substantially exceeded its powers. They thought the Court had no authority to "amend" the statutes in the manner it did.

[6] Section 3553(a) lists seven factors that a sentencing court must consider. The first factor is a broad command to consider the "nature and circumstances of the offense and the history and characteristics of the defendant." The second factor requires the consideration of the

doing, he may not presume that the Guidelines range is reasonable. He must make an individualized assessment based on the facts presented. If he decides that an outside-Guidelines sentence is warranted, he must consider the extent of the deviation and ensure that the justification is sufficiently compelling to support the degree of the variance. We find it uncontroversial that a major departure should be supported by a more significant justification than a minor one. After settling on the appropriate sentence, he must adequately explain the chosen sentence to allow for meaningful appellate review and to promote the perception of fair sentencing.

Regardless of whether the sentence imposed is inside or outside the Guidelines range, the appellate court must review the sentence under an abuse-of-discretion standard. It must first ensure that the district court committed no significant procedural error, such as failing to calculate (or improperly calculating) the Guidelines range, treating the Guidelines as mandatory, failing to consider the § 3553(a) factors, selecting a sentence based on clearly erroneous facts, or failing to adequately explain the chosen sentence—including an explanation for any deviation from the Guidelines range. Assuming that the district court's sentencing decision is procedurally sound, the appellate court should then consider the substantive reasonableness of the sentence imposed under an abuse-of-discretion standard. When conducting this review, the court will, of course, take into account the totality of the circumstances, including the extent of any variance from the Guidelines range. If the sentence is within the Guidelines range, the appellate court may, but is not required to, apply a presumption of reasonableness.[i] But if the sentence is outside the Guidelines range, the court may not apply a presumption of unreasonableness.[j] It may consider the extent of the deviation, but must give due deference to the district court's decision that the § 3553(a) factors, on a whole, justify the extent of the variance. The fact that the appellate court might reasonably have concluded that a different

general purposes of sentencing, including: the "need for the sentence imposed—(A) to reflect the seriousness of the offense, to promote respect for the law, and to provide just punishment for the offense; (B) to afford adequate deterrence to criminal conduct; (C) to protect the public from further crimes of the defendant; and (D) to provide the defendant with needed educational or vocational training, medical care, or other correctional treatment in the most effective manner." The third factor pertains to "the kinds of sentences available"; the fourth to the Sentencing Guidelines; the fifth to any relevant policy statement issued by the Sentencing Commission; the sixth to "the need to avoid unwarranted sentence disparities"; and the seventh to "the need to provide restitution to any victim." Preceding this list is a general directive to "impose a sentence sufficient, but not greater than necessary, to comply with the purposes" of sentencing described in the second factor. The fact that § 3553(a) explicitly directs sentencing courts to consider the Guidelines supports the premise that district courts must begin their analysis with the Guidelines and remain cognizant of them throughout the sentencing process.

[i] This was the Court's holding in Rita v. United States, 551 U.S. 338 (2007).—[Footnote by eds.]

[j] Nor is it necessarily impermissible for the district court to disagree with a sentencing policy reflected in the Guidelines. Kimbrough v. United States, 552 U.S. 864 (2007), involved a Guidelines provision that, as summarized by the Court, said that "a drug trafficker dealing in crack cocaine is subject to the same sentence as one dealing in 100 times more powder cocaine." The sentencing judge disagreed and imposed a sentence based on a different principle. The sentence was upheld.—[Footnote by eds.]

sentence was appropriate is insufficient to justify reversal of the district court.

### 4. *OREGON V. ICE*

Most states follow the common law tradition of allowing the sentencing judge to determine, unfettered by limiting criteria, whether sentences for conviction of multiple offenses must be served consecutively or concurrently. Some states provide that sentences on multiple counts will run consecutively, unless the sentencing judge orders them to run concurrently for cause shown. Oregon followed yet a third path. It provided that sentences will run concurrently, unless the sentencing judge made certain factual findings that would warrant a consecutive sentence. The question in Oregon v. Ice, 555 U.S. 160 (2009), was how *Apprendi* and *Blakely* applied to this system. In an opinion by Justice Ginsburg, the Court concluded: "We hold, in light of historical practice and the authority of States over administration of their criminal justice systems, that the Sixth Amendment does not exclude Oregon's choice."

On two separate occasions the defendant sexually assaulted an 11-year-old girl. He was convicted of three crimes for each episode: burglary for entering with intent to commit a felony and two separate sexual assault offenses for his behavior once in the presence of his victim. At sentencing, the judge made findings that permitted, but did not require, the imposition of consecutive sentences. Specifically, the judge found that the burglaries were "separate incidents." This authorized consecutive sentences for the two burglaries. Secondly, the judge found that Ice's behavior exhibited a "willingness to commit more than one . . . offense" during each episode and that his conduct "caused or created a risk of causing greater, qualitatively different loss, injury, or harm to the victim." These findings permitted a consecutive sentence for each of the two sexual assault offenses that could then be consecutive to each associated burglary crime. The judge added these on too. If the judge had ordered concurrent sentences for all of the offenses, the penalty would have been 90 months in prison. As it was, and adding everything together, the judge imposed a sentence of 340 months.

The Court's prior decisions, Justice Ginsburg noted, "involved sentencing for a discrete crime, not—as here—for multiple offenses different in character or committed at different times." She continued:

> Our application of *Apprendi*'s rule must honor the "longstanding common-law practice" in which the rule is rooted. The rule's animating principle is the preservation of the jury's historic role as a bulwark between the State and the accused at the trial for an alleged offense. Guided by that principle, our opinions make clear that the Sixth Amendment does not countenance legislative encroachment on the jury's traditional domain. We accordingly considered whether the finding of a particular fact was understood as within "the domain of the jury . . . by those who framed the Bill of Rights." Harris v. United States, 536 U.S. 545, 557 (2002) (plurality opinion). In undertaking this inquiry, we remain cognizant that administration of a discrete criminal justice system is among the basic sovereign prerogatives States retain.
>
> These twin considerations—historical practice and respect for state sovereignty—counsel against extending *Apprendi*'s rule to

> the imposition of sentences for discrete crimes. The decision to impose sentences consecutively is not within the jury function that "extends down centuries into the common law." *Apprendi,* 530 U.S. at 477. Instead, specification of the regime for administering multiple sentences has long been considered the prerogative of state legislatures.

As to the history, she elaborated:

> The historical record demonstrates that the jury played no role in the decision to impose sentences consecutively or concurrently. Rather, the choice rested exclusively with the judge. . . . In light of this history, legislative reforms regarding the imposition of multiple sentences do not implicate the core concerns that prompted our decision in *Apprendi*. There is no encroachment here by the judge upon facts historically found by the jury, nor any threat to the jury's domain as a bulwark at trial between the State and the accused. Instead, the defendant—who historically may have faced consecutive sentences by default—has been granted by some modern legislatures statutory protections meant to temper the harshness of the historical practice.

On the question of respect for state sovereignty, she argued:

> States' interest in the development of their penal systems, and their historic dominion in this area, also counsel against the extension of *Apprendi* that Ice requests. Beyond question, the authority of States over the administration of their criminal justice systems lies at the core of their sovereign status. We have long recognized the role of the States as laboratories for devising solutions to difficult legal problems. This Court should not diminish that role absent impelling reason to do so.
>
> It bears emphasis that state legislative innovations like Oregon's seek to rein in the discretion judges possessed at common law to impose consecutive sentences at will. Limiting judicial discretion to impose consecutive sentences serves the "salutary objectives" of promoting sentences proportionate to "the gravity of the offense," *Blakely,* 542 U.S. at 308, and of reducing disparities in sentence length. All agree that a scheme making consecutive sentences the rule, and concurrent sentences the exception, encounters no Sixth Amendment shoal. To hem in States by holding that they may not equally choose to make concurrent sentences the rule, and consecutive sentences the exception, would make scant sense. Neither *Apprendi* nor our Sixth Amendment traditions compel straitjacketing the States in that manner.
>
> Further, it is unclear how many other state initiatives would fall under Ice's proposed expansion of *Apprendi*. As 17 States have observed in an amici brief supporting Oregon, States currently permit judges to make a variety of sentencing determinations other than the length of incarceration. Trial judges often find facts about the nature of the offense or the character of the defendant in determining, for example, the length of supervised release following service of a prison sentence; required attendance at drug rehabilitation programs or terms of community service; and the imposition of statutorily prescribed fines and orders of restitution.

> Intruding *Apprendi*'s rule into these decisions on sentencing choices or accoutrements surely would cut the rule loose from its moorings.
>
> Moreover, the expansion that Ice seeks would be difficult for States to administer. The predicate facts for consecutive sentences could substantially prejudice the defense at the guilt phase of a trial. As a result, bifurcated or trifurcated trials might often prove necessary. We will not so burden the Nation's trial courts absent any genuine affront to *Apprendi*'s instruction. . . .
>
> Members of this Court have warned against "wooden, unyielding insistence on expanding the *Apprendi* doctrine far beyond its necessary boundaries." Cunningham v. California, 549 U.S. 270, 295 (Kennedy, J., dissenting). The jury-trial right is best honored through a "principled rationale" that applies the rule of the *Apprendi* cases "within the central sphere of their concern." 549 U.S. at 295. Our disposition today—upholding an Oregon statute that assigns to judges a decision that has not traditionally belonged to the jury—is faithful to that aim.

Joined by Chief Justice Roberts and by Justices Souter and Thomas, Justice Scalia dissented. The essence of Scalia's dissent is captured in the following:

> The rule of Apprendi v. New Jersey, 530 U.S. 466 (2000), is clear: Any fact—other than that of a prior conviction—that increases the maximum punishment to which a defendant may be sentenced must be admitted by the defendant or proved beyond a reasonable doubt to a jury. Oregon's sentencing scheme allows judges rather than juries to find the facts necessary to commit defendants to longer prison sentences, and thus directly contradicts what we held eight years ago and have reaffirmed several times since. The Court's justification of Oregon's scheme is a virtual copy of the dissents in those cases.

Consider the holding in *Oregon v. Ice* from two perspectives. First, can it be reconciled with *Apprendi* and *Blakely*? Second, does it signal a retreat from the full implications of those decisions? This possibility, combined perhaps with substantial changes in personnel since *Apprendi* was decided,[k] could be read as suggesting that the glory days of *Apprendi* are over.

It is clear, however, that this is not the case. The Court held by a 6–3 majority[l] in Southern Union Co. v. United States, 567 U.S. ___, 132 S.Ct. 2344 (2012), that *Apprendi* was fully applicable to facts authorizing an increase in fines: "[W]e see no principled basis . . . for treating criminal fines differently" from imprisonment or the death sentence. And the Court has since extended *Apprendi* to mandatory minimum sentences as related below.

---

[k] The *Apprendi* majority was Stevens (since replaced by Kagan), Souter (since replaced by Sotomayor), Scalia, Ginsburg, and Thomas. The dissenters were O'Connor (since replaced by Alito), Rehnquist (since replaced by Roberts), Breyer, and Kennedy.

[l] Justice Sotomayor wrote for the Court. Justice Breyer dissented, joined by Kennedy and Alito.

## INTRODUCTORY NOTE ON *MCMILLAN* AND *HARRIS*

Another important post-*Apprendi* question was whether the Court's holding in McMillan v. Pennsylvania, 477 U.S. 79 (1986), was still viable. *McMillan*, recall from the Introductory Notes to this Section, held that facts specified by the legislature that required a mandatory minimum sentence were not required to be submitted to the jury. The question first returned to the Court in Harris v. United States, 536 U.S. 545 (2002).

Harris sold marijuana to an undercover agent on two occasions. Both times he was carrying a handgun in an unconcealed holster. He pleaded guilty to drug distribution and, after a bench trial, was also convicted of carrying a firearm "during and in relation to any crime of violence or drug trafficking." At sentencing, applying a preponderance standard, the District Court found that Harris had "brandished" his handgun during one of the drug sales. That finding triggered a seven-year mandatory minimum sentence (as compared to the five-year mandatory minimum otherwise applicable). Harris was sentenced to the seven-year minimum. The maximum available sentence was life.

*McMillan* survived, even though five Justices thought the decision inconsistent with *Apprendi*. Justice Kennedy wrote for a plurality, joined by Chief Justice Rehnquist and Justices O'Connor and Scalia. His conclusion was:

> *McMillan* and *Apprendi* are consistent because there is a fundamental distinction between the factual findings that were at issue in those two cases. *Apprendi* said that any fact extending the defendant's sentence beyond the maximum authorized by the jury's verdict would have been considered an element of an aggravated crime—and thus the domain of the jury—by those who framed the Bill of Rights. The same cannot be said of a fact increasing the mandatory minimum (but not extending the sentence beyond the statutory maximum), for the jury's verdict has authorized the judge to impose the minimum with or without the finding. As *McMillan* recognized, a statute may reserve this type of factual finding for the judge without violating the Constitution.

Justice Breyer disagreed with the rationale, but agreed with the conclusion:

> I cannot easily distinguish *Apprendi* from this case in terms of logic. For that reason, I cannot agree with the plurality's opinion insofar as it finds such a distinction. At the same time, I continue to believe that the Sixth Amendment permits judges to apply sentencing factors—whether those factors lead to a sentence beyond the statutory maximum (as in *Apprendi*) or the application of a mandatory minimum (as here). And because I believe that extending *Apprendi* to mandatory minimums would have adverse practical, as well as legal, consequences, I cannot yet accept its rule. I therefore join the Court's judgment, and I join its opinion to the extent that it holds that *Apprendi* does not apply to mandatory minimums.

Joined by Justices Stevens, Souter, and Ginsburg, Justice Thomas dissented:

> I would reaffirm *Apprendi* [and] overrule *McMillan*. . . . As a matter of common sense, an increased mandatory minimum heightens the loss of liberty and represents the increased stigma society attaches to the offense. Consequently, facts that trigger an increased mandatory minimum sentence warrant constitutional safeguards. . . . Whether one raises the floor or raises the ceiling it is impossible to dispute that the defendant is exposed to greater punishment than is otherwise prescribed.

The Court revisited this issue in the main case below.

## Alleyne v. United States

Supreme Court of the United States, 2013.
570 U.S. ___, 133 S. Ct. 2151.

■ JUSTICE THOMAS announced the judgment of the Court and delivered the opinion of the Court with respect to Parts I, III–B, III–C, and IV, and an opinion with respect to Parts II and III–A, in which JUSTICE GINSBURG, JUSTICE SOTOMAYOR, and JUSTICE KAGAN join.

In Harris v. United States, 536 U.S. 545 (2002), this Court held that judicial factfinding that increases the mandatory minimum sentence for a crime is permissible under the Sixth Amendment. We granted certiorari to consider whether that decision should be overruled.

*Harris* drew a distinction between facts that increase the statutory maximum and facts that increase only the mandatory minimum. We conclude that this distinction is inconsistent with our decision in Apprendi v. New Jersey, 530 U.S. 466 (2000), and with the original meaning of the Sixth Amendment. Any fact that, by law, increases the penalty for a crime is an "element" that must be submitted to the jury and found beyond a reasonable doubt. Mandatory minimum sentences increase the penalty for a crime. It follows, then, that any fact that increases the mandatory minimum is an "element" that must be submitted to the jury. Accordingly, *Harris* is overruled.

### I

Petitioner Allen Ryan Alleyne and an accomplice devised a plan to rob a store manager as he drove the store's daily deposits to a local bank. By feigning car trouble, they tricked the manager to stop. Alleyne's accomplice approached the manager with a gun and demanded the store's deposits, which the manager surrendered. Alleyne was later charged with multiple federal offenses, including robbery affecting interstate commerce, 18 U.S.C. § 1951(a), and using or carrying a firearm in relation to a crime of violence, § 924(c)(1)(A). Section 924(c)(1)(A) provides, in relevant part, that anyone who "uses or carries a firearm" in relation to a "crime of violence" shall:

> (i) be sentenced to a term of imprisonment of not less than 5 years;
>
> (ii) if the firearm is brandished, be sentenced to a term of imprisonment of not less than 7 years; and

(iii) if the firearm is discharged, be sentenced to a term of imprisonment of not less than 10 years.

The jury convicted Alleyne. The jury indicated on the verdict form that Alleyne had "[u]sed or carried a firearm during and in relation to a crime of violence," but did not indicate a finding that the firearm was "[b]randished."

The presentence report recommended a 7-year sentence on the § 924(c) count, which reflected the mandatory minimum sentence for cases in which a firearm has been "brandished." Alleyne objected to this recommendation. He argued that it was clear from the verdict form that the jury did not find brandishing beyond a reasonable doubt and that he was subject only to the 5-year minimum for "us[ing] or carr[ying] a firearm." Alleyne contended that raising his mandatory minimum sentence based on a sentencing judge's finding that he brandished a firearm would violate his Sixth Amendment right to a jury trial.

The District Court overruled Alleyne's objection. It explained that, under *Harris,* brandishing was a sentencing factor that the court could find by a preponderance of evidence without running afoul of the Constitution. It found that the evidence supported a finding of brandishing, and sentenced Alleyne to seven years' imprisonment on the § 924(c) count. The Court of Appeals affirmed, likewise noting that Alleyne's objection was foreclosed by *Harris.*

II

[In Part II of his opinion, Justice Thomas summarized the *McMillan* and *Harris* decisions.]

III

Alleyne contends that *Harris* was wrongly decided and that it cannot be reconciled with our reasoning in *Apprendi*. We agree.

A

The touchstone for determining whether a fact must be found by a jury beyond a reasonable doubt is whether the fact constitutes an "element" or "ingredient" of the charged offense. In *Apprendi,* we held that a fact is by definition an element of the offense and must be submitted to the jury if it increases the punishment above what is otherwise legally prescribed. While *Harris* declined to extend this principle to facts increasing mandatory minimum sentences, *Apprendi*'s definition of "elements" necessarily includes not only facts that increase the ceiling, but also those that increase the floor. Both kinds of facts alter the prescribed range of sentences to which a defendant is exposed and do so in a manner that aggravates the punishment. Facts that increase the mandatory minimum sentence are therefore elements and must be submitted to the jury and found beyond a reasonable doubt. . . .

B

Consistent with common-law and early American practice, *Apprendi* concluded that any "facts that increase the prescribed range of penalties to which a criminal defendant is exposed" are elements of the crime.[1] We held that the Sixth Amendment provides defendants with the right to have a jury find those facts beyond a reasonable doubt. While *Harris* limited *Apprendi* to facts increasing the statutory maximum, the principle applied in *Apprendi* applies with equal force to facts increasing the mandatory minimum.

It is indisputable that a fact triggering a mandatory minimum alters the prescribed range of sentences to which a criminal defendant is exposed. But for a finding of brandishing, the penalty is five years to life in prison; with a finding of brandishing, the penalty becomes seven years to life. Just as the maximum of life marks the outer boundary of the range, so seven years marks its floor. And because the legally prescribed range *is* the penalty affixed to the crime, it follows that a fact increasing either end of the range produces a new penalty and constitutes an ingredient of the offense.

It is impossible to dissociate the floor of a sentencing range from the penalty affixed to the crime. Indeed, criminal statutes have long specified both the floor and ceiling of sentence ranges, which is evidence that both define the legally prescribed penalty. This historical practice allowed those who violated the law to know, ex ante, the contours of the penalty that the legislature affixed to the crime—and comports with the obvious truth that the floor of a mandatory range is as relevant to wrongdoers as the ceiling. A fact that increases a sentencing floor, thus, forms an essential ingredient of the offense.

Moreover, it is impossible to dispute that facts increasing the legally prescribed floor *aggravate* the punishment. Elevating the low-end of a sentencing range heightens the loss of liberty associated with the crime: the defendant's "expected punishment has increased as a result of the narrowed range" and "the prosecution is empowered, by invoking the mandatory minimum, to require the judge to impose a higher punishment than he might wish." *Apprendi,* 530 U.S. at 522 (Thomas, J., concurring). Why else would Congress link an increased mandatory minimum to a particular aggravating fact other than to heighten the consequences for that behavior? This reality demonstrates that the core crime and the fact triggering the mandatory minimum sentence together constitute a new, aggravated crime, each element of which must be submitted to the jury.[2]

Defining facts that increase a mandatory statutory minimum to be part of the substantive offense enables the defendant to predict the legally applicable penalty from the face of the indictment. It also preserves the historic role of the jury as an intermediary between the State and criminal defendants.

---

[1] In *Almendarez-Torres v. United States,* 523 U.S. 224 (1998), we recognized a narrow exception to this general rule for the fact of a prior conviction. Because the parties do not contest that decision's vitality, we do not revisit it for purposes of our decision today.

[2] Juries must find any facts that increase either the statutory maximum or minimum because the Sixth Amendment applies where a finding of fact both alters the legally prescribed range *and* does so in a way that aggravates the penalty. Importantly, this is distinct from factfinding used to guide judicial discretion in selecting a punishment "within limits fixed by law." *Williams v. New York,* 337 U.S. 241, 246 (1949). While such findings of fact may lead judges to select sentences that are more severe than the ones they would have selected without those facts, the Sixth Amendment does not govern that element of sentencing.

In adopting a contrary conclusion, *Harris* relied on the fact that the 7-year minimum sentence could have been imposed with or without a judicial finding of brandishing, because the jury's finding already authorized a sentence of five years to life. The dissent repeats this argument today. While undoubtedly true, this fact is beside the point.

As noted, the essential Sixth Amendment inquiry is whether a fact is an element of the crime. When a finding of fact alters the legally prescribed punishment so as to aggravate it, the fact necessarily forms a constituent part of a new offense and must be submitted to the jury. It is no answer to say that the defendant could have received the same sentence with or without that fact. It is obvious, for example, that a defendant could not be convicted and sentenced for assault, if the jury only finds the facts for larceny, even if the punishments prescribed for each crime are identical. One reason is that each crime has different elements and a defendant can be convicted only if the jury has found each element of the crime of conviction.

Similarly, because the fact of brandishing aggravates the legally prescribed range of allowable sentences, it constitutes an element of a separate, aggravated offense that must be found by the jury, regardless of what sentence the defendant *might* have received if a different range had been applicable. . . . The essential point is that the aggravating fact produced a higher range, which, in turn, conclusively indicates that the fact is an element of a distinct and aggravated crime. It must, therefore, be submitted to the jury and found beyond a reasonable doubt.

Because there is no basis in principle or logic to distinguish facts that raise the maximum from those that increase the minimum, *Harris* was inconsistent with *Apprendi*. It is, accordingly, overruled.

C

In holding that facts that increase mandatory minimum sentences must be submitted to the jury, we take care to note what our holding does not entail. Our ruling today does not mean that any fact that influences judicial discretion must be found by a jury. We have long recognized that broad sentencing discretion, informed by judicial factfinding, does not violate the Sixth Amendment.[6] . . . Our decision today is wholly consistent with the broad discretion of judges to select a sentence within the range authorized by law.

IV

Here, the sentencing range supported by the jury's verdict was five years' imprisonment to life. The District Court imposed the 7-year mandatory minimum sentence based on its finding by a preponderance of evidence that the firearm was "brandished." Because the finding of brandishing increased the penalty to which the defendant was subjected, it was an element, which had to be found by the jury beyond a reasonable doubt. The judge, rather than the jury, found brandishing, thus violating petitioner's Sixth Amendment rights.

---

[6] See . . . Williams v. New York, 337 U.S. 241, 246 (1949) ("[B]oth before and since the American colonies became a nation, courts in this country and in England practiced a policy under which a sentencing judge could exercise a wide discretion in the sources and types of evidence used to assist him in determining the kind and extent of punishment to be imposed within limits fixed by law").

Accordingly, we vacate the Fourth Circuit's judgment with respect to Alleyne's sentence on the § 924(c)(1)(A) conviction and remand the case for resentencing consistent with the jury's verdict.

It is so ordered.

■ JUSTICE SOTOMAYOR, with whom JUSTICE GINSBURG and JUSTICE KAGAN join, concurring.

I join the opinion of the Court, which persuasively explains why Harris v. United States, 536 U.S. 545 (2002), and McMillan v. Pennsylvania, 477 U.S. 79 (1986), were wrongly decided. Under the reasoning of our decision in Apprendi v. New Jersey, 530 U.S. 466 (2000), and the original meaning of the Sixth Amendment, facts that increase the statutory minimum sentence (no less than facts that increase the statutory maximum sentence) are elements of the offense that must be found by a jury and proved beyond a reasonable doubt.

[The remainder of Justice Sotomayor's opinion, in which she explained why overruling *Harris* was consistent with the doctrine of stare decisis, is omitted.]

■ JUSTICE BREYER, concurring in part and concurring in the judgment.

Eleven years ago, in Harris v. United States, 536 U.S. 545 (2002), I wrote that "I cannot easily distinguish Apprendi v. New Jersey, 530 U.S. 466 (2000), from this case in terms of logic." I nonetheless accepted *Harris*' holding because I could "[n]ot yet accept [*Apprendi* 's] rule." I continue to disagree with *Apprendi*. But *Apprendi* has now defined the relevant legal regime for an additional decade. And, in my view, the law should no longer tolerate the anomaly that the *Apprendi/Harris* distinction creates.

The Court's basic error in *Apprendi,* I believe, was its failure to recognize the law's traditional distinction between elements of a crime (facts constituting the crime, typically for the jury to determine) and sentencing facts (facts affecting the sentence, often concerning, e.g., the manner in which the offender committed the crime, and typically for the judge to determine). The early historical references that this Court's opinions have set forth in favor of *Apprendi* refer to *offense elements,* not to *sentencing facts*. . . . [T]he best answer to Justice Scalia's implicit question in *Apprendi*—what, exactly, does the "right to trial by jury" guarantee?—is that it guarantees a jury's determination of facts that constitute the elements of a crime.

. . . [It] seems to me highly anomalous to read *Apprendi* as insisting that juries find sentencing facts that *permit* a judge to impose a higher sentence while not insisting that juries find sentencing facts that *require* a judge to impose a higher sentence.

To overrule *Harris* and to apply *Apprendi*'s basic jury-determination rule to mandatory minimum sentences would erase that anomaly. Where a *maximum* sentence is at issue, *Apprendi* means that a judge who *wishes* to impose a higher sentence cannot do so unless a jury finds the requisite statutory factual predicate. Where a *mandatory minimum* sentence is at issue, application of *Apprendi* would mean that the government cannot force a judge who *does not wish* to impose a higher sentence to do so unless a jury finds the requisite statutory factual predicate. In both instances the matter concerns higher sentences;

in both instances factfinding must trigger the increase; in both instances jury-based factfinding would act as a check: in the first instance, against a sentencing judge wrongly imposing the higher sentence that the judge believes is appropriate, and in the second instance, against a sentencing judge wrongly being required to impose the higher sentence that the judge believes is inappropriate.

While *Harris* has been the law for 11 years, *Apprendi* has been the law for even longer; and I think the time has come to end this anomaly in *Apprendi*'s application. Consequently, I vote to overrule *Harris*. I join Parts I, III–B, III–C, and IV of the Court's opinion and concur in its judgment.

■ CHIEF JUSTICE ROBERTS, with whom JUSTICE SCALIA and JUSTICE KENNEDY join, dissenting.

Suppose a jury convicts a defendant of a crime carrying a sentence of five to ten years. And suppose the judge says he would sentence the defendant to five years, but because he finds that the defendant used a gun during the crime, he is going to add two years and sentence him to seven. No one thinks that this violates the defendant's right to a jury trial in any way.

Now suppose the legislature says that two years should be added to the five year minimum, if the judge finds that the defendant used a gun during the crime. Such a provision affects the role of the judge—limiting his discretion—but has no effect on the role of the jury. And because it does not affect the jury's role, it does not violate the jury trial guarantee of the Sixth Amendment.

The Framers envisioned the Sixth Amendment as a protection for defendants from the power of the Government. The Court transforms it into a protection for judges from the power of the legislature. For that reason, I respectfully dissent.

I

In a steady stream of cases decided over the last 15 years, this Court has sought to identify the historical understanding of the Sixth Amendment jury trial right and determine how that understanding applies to modern sentencing practice. Our key sources in this task have been 19th-century treatises and common law cases identifying which facts qualified as "elements" of a crime, and therefore had to be alleged in the indictment and proved to a jury beyond a reasonable doubt. With remarkable uniformity, those authorities provided that an element was "whatever is in law essential to the punishment sought to be inflicted." 1 J. Bishop, Criminal Procedure 50 (2d ed. 1872).

Judging that this common law rule best reflects what the Framers understood the Sixth Amendment jury right to protect, we have struck down sentencing schemes that were inconsistent with the rule. In *Apprendi,* for example, the defendant pleaded guilty to a crime that carried a maximum sentence of ten years. After his plea, however, the trial judge determined that the defendant had committed the crime with a biased purpose. Under a New Jersey law, that finding allowed the judge to impose up to ten additional years in prison. Exercising that authority, the judge sentenced the defendant to 12 years.

Because the sentence was two years longer than would have been possible without the finding of bias, that finding was "essential to the punishment" imposed. Thus, in line with the common law rule, we held the New Jersey procedure unconstitutional.

Subsequent cases have worked out how this principle applies in other contexts, such as capital sentencing regimes, state and federal sentencing guidelines, or criminal fines. Through all of them, we have adhered to the rule, rooted in the common law understanding described above, that we laid down in *Apprendi*: "Other than the fact of a prior conviction, any fact that increases the penalty for a crime beyond the prescribed statutory maximum must be submitted to a jury, and proved beyond a reasonable doubt."

We have embraced this 19th-century common law rule based not only on a judgment that it reflects the understanding in place when the Sixth Amendment was ratified, but also on the "need to give intelligible content to the right of jury trial." As Justice Scalia wrote in *Apprendi,* it is unclear "what the right to trial by jury *does* guarantee if . . . it does not guarantee . . . the right to have a jury determine those facts that determine the maximum sentence the law allows." 530 U.S. at 498–99 (concurring opinion).

After all, if a judge's factfinding could authorize a sentence beyond that allowed by the jury's verdict alone, the jury trial would be "a mere preliminary to a judicial inquisition into the facts of the crime the State *actually* seeks to punish." *Blakely,* 542 U.S. at 306–07. The Framers clearly envisioned a more robust role for the jury. They appreciated the danger inherent in allowing "justices . . . named by the crown" to "imprison, dispatch, or exile any man that was obnoxious to the government, by an instant declaration, that such is their will and pleasure." 4 W. Blackstone, Commentaries on the Laws of England 343 (1769). To guard against this "violence and partiality of judges appointed by the crown," the common law "wisely placed th[e] strong . . . barrier, of . . . trial by jury, between the liberties of the people, and the prerogative of the crown." Id. The Sixth Amendment therefore provided for trial by jury as a "double security, against the prejudices of judges, who may partake of the wishes and opinions of the government, and against the passions of the multitude, who may demand their victim with a clamorous precipitancy." J. Story, Commentaries on the Constitution of the United States § 924, p. 657 (Abr. 1833); see also The Federalist No. 83, p. 499 (C. Rossiter ed. 1961) (A. Hamilton) (discussing criminal jury trial as a protection against "judicial despotism"). Our holdings that a judge may not sentence a defendant to more than the jury has authorized properly preserve the jury right as a guard against judicial overreaching.

II

There is no such risk of judicial overreaching here. Under 18 U.S.C. § 924(c)(1)(A)(i), the jury's verdict fully authorized the judge to impose a sentence of anywhere from five years to life in prison. No additional finding of fact was "essential" to any punishment within the range. After rendering the verdict, the jury's role was completed, it was discharged, and the judge began the process of determining where within that range to set Alleyne's sentence.

Everyone agrees that in making that determination, the judge was free to consider any relevant facts about the offense and offender, including facts not found by the jury beyond a reasonable doubt.

"[B]oth before and since the American colonies became a nation, courts . . . practiced a policy under which a sentencing judge could exercise a wide discretion in the sources and types of evidence used to assist him in determining the kind and extent of punishment to be imposed within limits fixed by law." Williams v. New York, 337 U.S. 241 (1949).

As *Apprendi* itself recognized, "nothing in this history suggests that it is impermissible for judges to exercise discretion—taking into consideration various factors relating both to offense and offender—in imposing a judgment within the range prescribed by statute." And the majority does not dispute the point. Thus, under the majority's rule, in the absence of a statutory mandatory minimum, there would have been no constitutional problem had the judge, exercising the discretion given him by the jury's verdict, decided that seven years in prison was the appropriate penalty for the crime *because of* his finding that the firearm had been brandished during the offense.

In my view, that is enough to resolve this case. The jury's verdict authorized the judge to impose the precise sentence he imposed for the precise factual reason he imposed it. As we have recognized twice before, the Sixth Amendment demands nothing more. See Harris v. United States, 536 U.S. 545, 568–69 (2002); McMillan v. Pennsylvania, 477 U.S. 79, 93 (1986).

III

This approach is entirely consistent with *Apprendi*. As I have explained, *Apprendi*'s constraint on the normal legislative control of criminal procedure draws its legitimacy from two primary principles: (1) common law understandings of the "elements" of a crime, and (2) the need to preserve the jury as a "strong barrier" between defendants and the State. Neither of those principles supports the rule the majority adopts today.

First, there is no body of historical evidence supporting today's new rule. The majority does not identify a single case holding that a fact affecting only the sentencing floor qualified as an element or had to be found by a jury, nor does it point to any treatise language to that effect. To be sure, the relatively recent vintage of mandatory minimum sentencing enhancements means that few, if any, 19th-century courts would have encountered such a fact pattern. So I do not mean to suggest that the absence of historical condemnation of the practice conclusively establishes its constitutionality today. But given that *Apprendi*'s rule rests heavily on affirmative historical evidence about the practices to which we have previously applied it, the lack of such evidence on statutory minimums is a good reason not to extend it here.

Nor does the majority's extension of *Apprendi* do anything to preserve the role of the jury as a safeguard between the defendant and the State. That is because even if a jury does not find that the firearm was brandished, a judge can do so and impose a harsher sentence because of his finding, so long as that sentence remains under the statutory maximum. The question here is about the power of judges, not juries. Under the rule in place until today, a legislature could tell judges that certain facts carried certain weight, and require the judge to devise a sentence based on that weight—so long as the sentence remained within the range authorized by the jury. Now, in the name of the jury right that formed a barrier between the defendant and the State, the majority has erected a barrier between judges and legislatures, establishing that discretionary sentencing is the domain of judges. Legislatures must keep their respectful distance.

I find this new rule impossible to square with the historical understanding of the jury right as a defense *from* judges, not a defense *of* judges. Just as the Sixth Amendment "limits judicial power only to the extent that the claimed judicial power infringes on the province of the jury," *Blakely,* 542 U.S. at 308, so too it limits *legislative* power only to the extent *that* power infringes on the province of the jury. Because the claimed infringement here is on the province of the judge, not the jury, the jury right has no work to do.

IV

The majority offers several arguments to the contrary. I do not find them persuasive.

First, the majority asserts that "because the legally prescribed range *is* the penalty affixed to the crime, it follows that a fact increasing either end of the range produces a new penalty and constitutes an ingredient of the offense." The syllogism trips out of the gate, for its first premise—that the constitutionally relevant "penalty" includes the bottom end of the statutory range—simply assumes the answer to the question presented. . . .

Second, the majority observes that "criminal statutes have long specified both the floor and ceiling of sentence ranges, which is evidence that both define the legally prescribed penalty." Again, though, this simply assumes the core premise: That the constitutionally relevant "penalty" involves both the statutory minimum and the maximum. Unless one accepts that premise on faith, the fact that statutes have long specified both floor and ceiling is evidence of nothing more than that statutes have long specified both the floor and the ceiling. Nor does it help to say that "the floor of a mandatory range is as relevant to wrongdoers as the ceiling." The meaning of the Sixth Amendment does not turn on what wrongdoers care about most. . . . That a minimum sentence is "relevant" to punishment, and that a statute defines it, does not mean it must be treated the same as the maximum sentence the law allows.

Third, the majority offers that "it is impossible to dispute that facts increasing the legally prescribed floor *aggravate* the punishment." This argument proves too much, for it would apply with equal force to any fact which leads the judge, in the exercise of his own discretion, to choose a penalty higher than he otherwise would have chosen. The majority nowhere explains what it is about the jury right that bars a determination by Congress that brandishing (or any other fact) makes an offense worth two extra years, but not an identical determination by a judge. Simply calling one "aggravation" and the other "discretion" does not do the trick.

Fourth, the majority argues that "[i]t is no answer to say that the defendant could have received the same sentence with or without" a particular factual finding, pointing out "that a defendant could not be convicted and sentenced for assault, if the jury only finds the facts for larceny, even if the punishments prescribed for each crime are identical." In that hypothetical case, the legislature has chosen to define two crimes with two different sets of elements. Courts must, of course, respect that legislative judgment. But that tells us nothing about when courts can override the legislature's decision *not* to create separate crimes, and instead to treat a particular fact as a trigger for a minimum sentence within the already-authorized range.

* * *

... [B]ecause I believe the majority's new rule—safeguarding the power of judges, not juries—finds no support in the history or purpose of the Sixth Amendment, I respectfully dissent.

■ JUSTICE ALITO, dissenting....

If the Court is of a mind to reconsider existing precedent, a prime candidate should be Apprendi v. New Jersey, 530 U.S. 466 (2000). Although *Apprendi* purported to rely on the original understanding of the jury trial right, there are strong reasons to question the Court's analysis on that point....

[In support of this assertion, Justice Alito referred to post-*Apprendi* literature which concluded, inter alia, that there was no 18th Century evidence linking the Court's 19th Century evidence back to the Framing, that *Apprendi* was "undoubtedly founded on an erroneous historical understanding of the Framers' views in 1790 when they wrote the 6th Amendment's jury-trial guarantee," that "*Apprendi*'s historical claim that sentencing enhancements were treated as 'elements' of offenses whenever they increased a defendant's maximum punishment is demonstrably mistaken," and that "the platitudes from ... nineteenth-century treatises, which the pro-*Apprendi* Justices repeatedly invoke ... are patently false and did not accurately describe the law in actual court decisions of that era."

[At the end of his dissent, he added a footnote:

> In my view, *Harris'* force is not vitiated by the Court's *Apprendi* line of cases, for two reasons. First, that line of cases is predicated on a purported Sixth Amendment requirement that juries find facts that increase maximum penalties, not mandatory minimums. Accordingly, as the Chief Justice's dissent persuasively explains, *Apprendi* and its progeny have no impact on the distinct question resolved by *Harris,* which does not bear on the jury right. Second, the *Apprendi* line is now too intellectually incoherent to undermine any "contrary" precedents. If the rationale of *Apprendi*—which, as broadly construed by the Court in this case, is that "[a]ny fact that, by law, increases the penalty for a crime is an 'element' that must be submitted to the jury and found beyond a reasonable doubt,"—were taken seriously, discretionary sentencing ... should also be held to violate the Sixth Amendment. But a majority of the Court has not been willing to go where its reasoning leads....

[Justice Alito had previously elaborated on this second point in his dissent in Gall v. United States, 552 U.S. 38, 64–66 (2007):

> It would be a coherent principle to hold that any fact that increases a defendant's sentence beyond the minimum required by the jury's verdict of guilt must be found by a jury. Such a holding, however, would clash with accepted sentencing practice at the time of the adoption of the Sixth Amendment. By that time, many States had enacted criminal statutes that gave trial judges the discretion to select a sentence from within a prescribed range, and the First Congress enacted federal criminal statutes that were cast in this mold.
>
> Under a sentencing system of this type, trial judges inevitably make findings of fact (albeit informally) that increase sentences beyond the minimum required by the jury's verdict. For example, under a statute providing that the punishment for burglary is, say, imprisonment for up to *x* years, the sentencing court might increase the sentence that it would have otherwise imposed by some amount based on evidence introduced at trial that the defendant was armed or that, before committing the crime, the defendant had told a confederate that he would kill the occupants if they awakened during the burglary. The only difference between this sort of factfinding and the type that occurs under a guidelines system is that factfinding under a guidelines system is explicit and the effect of each critical finding is quantified. But in both instances, facts that cause a defendant to spend more time in prison are found by judges, not juries, and therefore no distinction can be drawn as a matter of Sixth Amendment principle.

[Justice Alito concluded his *Alleyne* footnote with the following observation:

[O]ther than the fact that there are currently five Justices willing to vote to overrule *Harris,* and not five Justices willing to overrule *Apprendi,* there is no compelling reason why the Court overrules the former rather than the latter.]

APPENDIX A

# THE MODEL PENAL CODE

## INTRODUCTORY NOTE ON THE MODEL PENAL CODE

The American Law Institute was founded in 1923. It is a private organization of lawyers, judges, and law teachers. Together with the American Bar Association, the Institute sponsors an extensive program of continuing legal education. It has published Restatements of American law in numerous areas, including property, torts, contracts, agency, conflict of laws, trusts, and employment law. It has prepared model statutes on subjects as diverse as federal income taxation, federal securities, evidence, criminal procedure, federal jurisdiction, and land development. And it was a major contributor to the drafting of the Uniform Commercial Code. Of more relevance to students of the criminal law, the Institute published the Model Penal Code in 1962.

Examination of the substantive criminal law in the United States was on the Institute's initial agenda in 1923. An early proposal to restate the law was rejected, however, largely on the ground that a more prescriptive document, looking toward major reform, should be attempted. The first proposal for a "model code" of criminal law was considered in 1931. For various reasons, the project was sidetracked until 1950, when an Advisory Committee was established to take another look at the problem. By 1952, funds had been secured from the Rockefeller Foundation, and the drafting of a model penal code began in earnest.

Herbert Wechsler of the Columbia University Law School was appointed the Chief Reporter for the project. Louis B. Schwartz of the University of Pennsylvania Law School became the Reporter for Part II of the Code, which was to contain the provisions defining specific crimes. The elaborate process of producing the Model Code extended over a period of 10 years. Drafts were reviewed by a specially appointed Advisory Committee, by the Council of the Institute, and by the entire Institute membership at annual meetings. During the period from 1953 to 1962, Tentative Drafts of the Model Code, numbered one through 13, were published and reviewed at the annual meetings. A Proposed Final Draft was reviewed by the membership in 1961, and the text of the Proposed Official Draft was approved in 1962.

Extensive explanatory commentary was included in the various Tentative Drafts. This commentary provides a rich source of research and reflection on the content of the criminal law. Shortly after the completion of the text of the Model Code in 1962, an effort was undertaken to prepare a final commentary on each provision. Although that project was also delayed for various reasons, three volumes, consisting of commentary on Part II (specific crimes), were published in the fall of 1980. Three additional volumes on Part I (the general provisions) were published in 1985, together with a fourth volume containing the final text of the Code. This commentary explains the rationale underlying each section of the Model Code and examines the extent to which the Code provisions have been influential in reform efforts.

It is impossible to estimate the number of people who have had a hand in the Model Penal Code since the inception of the project in 1950. What can be said, however, is that the list of those who participated at one time or another is a virtual Who's Who of practitioners, judges, and academics interested in the subject of criminal law both in the United States and abroad. Additionally, the Tentative Drafts of the Code sparked a considerable body of commentary from academics, judges, and practitioners, all of which was taken into account as the drafting process progressed. Suffice it to say that the Model Penal Code is the product of an impressive intellectual effort. Moreover, it has been, as Sanford Kadish put it in 1978, "stunningly successful in accomplishing the comprehensive rethinking of the criminal law that Wechsler and his colleagues sought."[a]

Wechsler stated the objective of the Institute in promulgating a Model Penal Code as follows:

> It should be noted . . . that it was not the purpose of the Institute to achieve uniformity in penal law throughout the nation, since it was deemed inevitable that substantial differences of social situation or of point of view among the states should be reflected in substantial variation in their penal laws. The hope was rather that the model would stimulate and facilitate the systematic re-examination of the subject needed to assure that the prevailing law does truly represent the mature sentiment of our respective jurisdictions, sentiment formed after a fresh appraisal of the problems and their possible solutions. Of course, the Institute was not without ambition that in such an enterprise the model might seem worthy of adoption or, at least, of adaptation.[b]

One need only examine the volume of criminal code reform that occurred in this country shortly after the Model Code project was undertaken in order to appreciate the extent to which this ambition has been achieved. Prior to 1952, the date the drafting of the Model Code was begun, only one state—Louisiana in 1942—had significantly revised its criminal code in the 20th century. As a result, criminal codes in the United States were a clumsy collection of common-law principles and ad hoc modifications. Dramatic inconsistencies, particularly in penalty structure but also in the definition of offenses, could easily be found in virtually any penal code. Legislatures had responded piecemeal over the years to particular problems as they arose or were perceived, and little effort was devoted to examining the criminal code as a whole or to integrating newly adopted provisions into an overall scheme or plan. The result was statutory hodge-podge.

Although four states prepared new codes while the Model Code was being drafted, the first new enactment that was animated entirely by the spirit of the Model Code was adopted in New York in 1965 and became effective in 1967.[c] The New York penal code itself became a kind of model. Subsequent enactments in other states were influenced substantially both

---

[a] Sanford Kadish, Codifiers of the Criminal Law: Wechsler's Predecessors, 78 Colum. L. Rev. 1098, 1140 (1978).

[b] Herbert Wechsler, Codification of Criminal Law in the United States: The Model Penal Code, 68 Colum. L. Rev. 1425, 1427 (1968). See also Herbert Wechsler, The Challenge of a Model Penal Code, 65 Harv. L. Rev. 1097 (1952), which was prepared at the outset of the Model Code project.—[Footnote by eds.]

[c] Wechsler himself was actively involved—and influential—in the process leading to the New York revision.

by the fact that criminal code reform had been successful in New York and by the particular adaptations of the Model Code enacted in that state.

Code revision proceeded at a moderate pace over the next several years. During the decade of the 1970's, however, substantial reform was achieved in many American jurisdictions. By May of 1982, new legislation in 37 American jurisdictions had been substantially influenced by the Model Penal Code. In at least 11 more, new criminal codes had been completed as of 1982 but had failed of enactment. The remaining states were at one stage or another in study of the question.[d] Some of the states in which new legislation based on the Model Penal Code was enacted adopted only minor revisions, essentially retaining the common-law orientation of their previous codes. But in many, a thorough re-examination of fundamental issues was conducted by a locally-appointed drafting body and the codes were substantially revised along lines suggested by the Model Penal Code and/or the new legislation in New York.[e]

The days of comprehensive legislative reform based on the Model Penal Code have long since passed. But the extent to which the judiciary has been influenced—and continues to be influenced—by the Model Code must also be taken into account. Many of the cases reproduced in this book illustrate that influence. More subtly, many of the analytical techniques of the Model Code have become an integral part of judicial reasoning about the criminal law. The vocabulary of the Model Code—particularly its culpability structure—has also been influential in this manner. The Model Code is to a considerable degree working its way into the common law of the country even in jurisdictions that have not explicitly adopted its provisions by legislation.

The Model Penal Code is worth careful study because to a large extent it represents existing law in many American jurisdictions. Perhaps more importantly, however, the provisions of the Model Code define the terms of debate even today on numerous issues of penal law of general significance. The Model Code thus rewards study on its own terms in a basic course on criminal law.[f] Development of the criminal law in the United States has

---

[d] This information was extracted from the Annual Report of the American Law Institute, May 1982. For a slightly different count of enacted laws and a list of the affected states, see Dannye Holley, The Influence of the Model Penal Code's Culpability Provisions on State Legislatures: A Study of Lost Opportunities, Including Abolishing the Mistake of Fact Doctrine, 27 Sw. U. L. Rev. 229 & n.2 (1997) (criminal laws in "approximately thirty six" states have, as Wechsler noted, "been influenced in varying degrees")

[e] For one example, see Dannye Holley, The Influence of the Model Penal Code's Culpability Provisions on State Legislatures: A Study of Lost Opportunities, Including Abolishing the Mistake of Fact Doctrine, 27 Sw. U. L. Rev. 229, 236–49 (1997), where it is reported that 22 states have revised their basic culpability structure based on the Model Code.

[f] There are, to be sure, respects in which the Model Code has become obsolete. For example, some aspects of the Code's treatment of the crime of rape now appear archaic when measured against modern developments that have dramatically changed the general approach to that offense. At the same time, other aspects of the Code's rape provisions continue to appear radical today, even though they were initially formulated in May of 1955. These developments are covered in Chapter IX of this book.

There is also one major respect in which the American Law Institute has reconsidered a position taken in the Model Code and two others in which it is currently doing so. As explained in the footnotes to § 210.2 and § 210.6, the Institute has changed its position on the availability of capital punishment. As explained in the footnotes to Article 6 and Article 7, it is currently reconsidering its approach to sentencing. And as explained in the footnote to Article 213, the Institute is also in the midst of a major reconsideration of its provisions on sexual offenses.

been dominated by the Model Penal Code for many years. Its influence has been and remains pervasive.

# AMERICAN LAW INSTITUTE MODEL PENAL CODE[a] (OFFICIAL DRAFT, 1962)



Table of Contents

## PART I. GENERAL PROVISIONS

### ARTICLE 1. PRELIMINARY



### ARTICLE 2. GENERAL PRINCIPLES OF LIABILITY



[a] The Model Penal Code consists of four parts. Parts I and II are reproduced in full on the following pages. Part III (dealing with treatment and correction) and Part IV (dealing with organization of correctional facilities) have been omitted.

### ARTICLE 224. FORGERY AND FRAUDULENT PRACTICES



## OFFENSES AGAINST THE FAMILY

### ARTICLE 230. OFFENSES AGAINST THE FAMILY



## OFFENSES AGAINST PUBLIC ADMINISTRATION

### ARTICLE 240. BRIBERY AND CORRUPT INFLUENCE

---

## PART I. GENERAL PROVISIONS

---

## ARTICLE 1. PRELIMINARY

### Section 1.01. Title and Effective Date

(1) This Act is called the Penal and Correctional Code and may be cited as P.C.C. It shall become effective on. . . .

(2) Except as provided in Subsections (3) and (4) of this Section, the Code does not apply to offenses committed prior to its effective date and prosecutions for such offenses shall be governed by the prior law, which is continued in effect for that purpose, as if this Code were not in force. For the purposes of this Section, an offense was committed prior to the

effective date of the Code if any of the elements of the offense occurred prior thereto.

(3) In any case pending on or after the effective date of the Code, involving an offense committed prior to such date:

(a) procedural provisions of the Code shall govern, insofar as they are justly applicable and their application does not introduce confusion or delay;

(b) provisions of the Code according a defense or mitigation shall apply, with the consent of the defendant;

(c) the Court, with the consent of the defendant, may impose sentence under the provisions of the Code applicable to the offense and the offender.

(4) Provisions of the Code governing the treatment and the release or discharge of prisoners, probationers and parolees shall apply to persons under sentence for offenses committed prior to the effective date of the Code, except that the minimum or maximum period of their detention or supervision shall in no case be increased.

**Section 1.02. Purposes; Principles of Construction**

(1) The general purposes of the provisions governing the definition of offenses are:

(a) to forbid and prevent conduct that unjustifiably and inexcusably inflicts or threatens substantial harm to individual or public interests;

(b) to subject to public control persons whose conduct indicates that they are disposed to commit crimes;

(c) to safeguard conduct that is without fault from condemnation as criminal;

(d) to give fair warning of the nature of the conduct declared to constitute an offense;

(e) to differentiate on reasonable grounds between serious and minor offenses.

(2) The general purposes of the provisions governing the sentencing and treatment of offenders are:

(a) to prevent the commission of offenses;

(b) to promote the correction and rehabilitation of offenders;

(c) to safeguard offenders against excessive, disproportionate or arbitrary punishment;

(d) to give fair warning of the nature of the sentences that may be imposed on conviction of an offense;

(e) to differentiate among offenders with a view to a just individualization in their treatment;

(f) to define, coordinate and harmonize the powers, duties and functions of the courts and of administrative officers and agencies responsible for dealing with offenders;

(g) to advance the use of generally accepted scientific methods and knowledge in the sentencing and treatment of offenders;

(h) to integrate responsibility for the administration of the correctional system in a State Department of Correction [or other single department or agency].

(3) The provisions of the Code shall be construed according to the fair import of their terms but when the language is susceptible of differing constructions it shall be interpreted to further the general purposes stated in this Section and the special purposes of the particular provision involved. The discretionary powers conferred by the Code shall be exercised in accordance with the criteria stated in the Code and, insofar as such criteria are not decisive, to further the general purposes stated in this Section.

**Section 1.03. Territorial Applicability**

(1) Except as otherwise provided in this Section, a person may be convicted under the law of this State of an offense committed by his own conduct or the conduct of another for which he is legally accountable if:

(a) either the conduct which is an element of the offense or the result which is such an element occurs within this State; or

(b) conduct occurring outside the State is sufficient under the law of this State to constitute an attempt to commit an offense within the State; or

(c) conduct occurring outside the State is sufficient under the law of this State to constitute a conspiracy to commit an offense within the State and an overt act in furtherance of such conspiracy occurs within the State; or

(d) conduct occurring within the State establishes complicity in the commission of, or an attempt, solicitation or conspiracy to commit, an offense in another jurisdiction which also is an offense under the law of this State; or

(e) the offense consists of the omission to perform a legal duty imposed by the law of this State with respect to domicile, residence or a relationship to a person, thing or transaction in the State; or

(f) the offense is based on a statute of this State which expressly prohibits conduct outside the State, when the conduct bears a reasonable relation to a legitimate interest of this State and the actor knows or should know that his conduct is likely to affect that interest.

(2) Subsection (1)(a) does not apply when either causing a specified result or a purpose to cause or danger of causing such a result is an element of an offense and the result occurs or is designed or likely to occur only in another jurisdiction where the conduct charged would not constitute an offense, unless a legislative purpose plainly appears to declare the conduct criminal regardless of the place of the result.

(3) Subsection (1)(a) does not apply when causing a particular result is an element of an offense and the result is caused by conduct occurring outside the State which would not constitute an offense if the result had occurred there, unless the actor purposely or knowingly caused the result within the State.

(4) When the offense is homicide, either the death of the victim or the bodily impact causing death constitutes a "result," within the mean-

ing of Subsection (1)(a) and if the body of a homicide victim is found within the State, it is presumed that such result occurred within the State.

(5) This State includes the land and water and the air space above such land and water with respect to which the State has legislative jurisdiction.

### Section 1.04. Classes of Crimes; Violations

(1) An offense defined by this Code or by any other statute of this State, for which a sentence of [death or of] imprisonment is authorized, constitutes a crime. Crimes are classified as felonies, misdemeanors or petty misdemeanors.

(2) A crime is a felony if it is so designated in this Code or if persons convicted thereof may be sentenced [to death or] to imprisonment for a term which, apart from an extended term, is in excess of one year.

(3) A crime is a misdemeanor if it is so designated in this Code or in a statute other than this Code enacted subsequent thereto.

(4) A crime is a petty misdemeanor if it is so designated in this Code or in a statute other than this Code enacted subsequent thereto or if it is defined by a statute other than this Code which now provides that persons convicted thereof may be sentenced to imprisonment for a term of which the maximum is less than one year.

(5) An offense defined by this Code or by any other statute of this State constitutes a violation if it is so designated in this Code or in the law defining the offense or if no other sentence than a fine, or fine and forfeiture or other civil penalty is authorized upon conviction or if it is defined by a statute other than this Code which now provides that the offense shall not constitute a crime. A violation does not constitute a crime and conviction of a violation shall not give rise to any disability or legal disadvantage based on conviction of a criminal offense.

(6) Any offense declared by law to constitute a crime, without specification of the grade thereof or of the sentence authorized upon conviction, is a misdemeanor.

(7) An offense defined by any statute of this State other than this Code shall be classified as provided in this Section and the sentence that may be imposed upon conviction thereof shall hereafter be governed by this Code.

### Section 1.05. All Offenses Defined by Statute; Application of General Provisions of the Code

(1) No conduct constitutes an offense unless it is a crime or violation under this Code or another statute of this State.

(2) The provisions of Part I of the Code are applicable to offenses defined by other statutes, unless the Code otherwise provides.

(3) This Section does not affect the power of a court to punish for contempt or to employ any sanction authorized by law for the enforcement of an order or a civil judgment or decree.

**Section 1.06. Time Limitations**

(1) A prosecution for murder may be commenced at any time.

(2) Except as otherwise provided in this Section, prosecutions for other offenses are subject to the following periods of limitation:

(a) a prosecution for a felony of the first degree must be commenced within six years after it is committed;

(b) a prosecution for any other felony must be commenced within three years after it is committed;

(c) a prosecution for a misdemeanor must be commenced within two years after it is committed;

(d) a prosecution for a petty misdemeanor or a violation must be commenced within six months after it is committed.

(3) If the period prescribed in Subsection (2) has expired, a prosecution may nevertheless be commenced for:

(a) any offense a material element of which is either fraud or a breach of fiduciary obligation within one year after discovery of the offense by an aggrieved party or by a person who has legal duty to represent an aggrieved party and who is himself not a party to the offense, but in no case shall this provision extend the period of limitation otherwise applicable by more than three years; and

(b) any offense based upon misconduct in office by a public officer or employee at any time when the defendant is in public office or employment or within two years thereafter, but in no case shall this provision extend the period of limitation otherwise applicable by more than three years.

(4) An offense is committed either when every element occurs, or, if a legislative purpose to prohibit a continuing course of conduct plainly appears, at the time when the course of conduct or the defendant's complicity therein is terminated. Time starts to run on the day after the offense is committed.

(5) A prosecution is commenced either when an indictment is found [or an information filed] or when a warrant or other process is issued, provided that such warrant or process is executed without unreasonable delay.

(6) The period of limitation does not run:

(a) during any time when the accused is continuously absent from the State or has no reasonably ascertainable place of abode or work within the State, but in no case shall this provision extend the period of limitation otherwise applicable by more than three years; or

(b) during any time when a prosecution against the accused for the same conduct is pending in this State.

**Section 1.07. Method of Prosecution When Conduct Constitutes More Than One Offense**

(1) Prosecution for Multiple Offenses; Limitation on Convictions. When the same conduct of a defendant may establish the commission of more than one offense, the defendant may be prosecuted for each such offense. He may not, however, be convicted of more than one offense if:

(a) one offense is included in the other, as defined in Subsection (4) of this Section; or

(b) one offense consists only of a conspiracy or other form of preparation to commit the other; or

(c) inconsistent findings of fact are required to establish the commission of the offenses; or

(d) the offenses differ only in that one is defined to prohibit a designated kind of conduct generally and the other to prohibit a specific instance of such conduct; or

(e) the offense is defined as a continuing course of conduct and the defendant's course of conduct was uninterrupted, unless the law provides that specific periods of such conduct constitute separate offenses.

(2) Limitation on Separate Trials for Multiple Offenses. Except as provided in Subsection (3) of this Section, a defendant shall not be subject to separate trials for multiple offenses based on the same conduct or arising from the same criminal episode, if such offenses are known to the appropriate prosecuting officer at the time of the commencement of the first trial and are within the jurisdiction of a single court.

(3) Authority of Court to Order Separate Trials. When a defendant is charged with two or more offenses based on the same conduct or arising from the same criminal episode, the Court, on application of the prosecuting attorney or of the defendant, may order any such charge to be tried separately, if it is satisfied that justice so requires.

(4) Conviction of Included Offense Permitted. A defendant may be convicted of an offense included in an offense charged in the indictment [or the information]. An offense is so included when:

(a) it is established by proof of the same or less than all the facts required to establish the commission of the offense charged; or

(b) it consists of an attempt or solicitation to commit the offense charged or to commit an offense otherwise included therein; or

(c) it differs from the offense charged only in the respect that a less serious injury or risk of injury to the same person, property or public interest or a lesser kind of culpability suffices to establish its commission.

(5) Submission of Included Offense to Jury. The Court shall not be obligated to charge the jury with respect to an included offense unless there is a rational basis for a verdict acquitting the defendant of the offense charged and convicting him of the included offense.

### Section 1.08. When Prosecution Barred by Former Prosecution for the Same Offense

When a prosecution is for a violation of the same provision of the statutes and is based upon the same facts as a former prosecution, it is barred by such former prosecution under the following circumstances:

(1) The former prosecution resulted in an acquittal. There is an acquittal if the prosecution resulted in a finding of not guilty by the trier of fact or in a determination that there was insufficient evidence to

warrant a conviction. A finding of guilty of a lesser included offense is an acquittal of the greater inclusive offense, although the conviction is subsequently set aside.

(2) The former prosecution was terminated, after the information had been filed or the indictment found, by a final order or judgment for the defendant, which has not been set aside, reversed, or vacated and which necessarily required a determination inconsistent with a fact or a legal proposition that must be established for conviction of the offense.

(3) The former prosecution resulted in a conviction. There is a conviction if the prosecution resulted in a judgment of conviction which has not been reversed or vacated, a verdict of guilty which has not been set aside and which is capable of supporting a judgment, or a plea of guilty accepted by the Court. In the latter two cases failure to enter judgment must be for a reason other than a motion of the defendant.

(4) The former prosecution was improperly terminated. Except as provided in this Subsection, there is an improper termination of a prosecution if the termination is for reasons not amounting to an acquittal, and it takes place after the first witness is sworn but before verdict. Termination under any of the following circumstances is not improper:

(a) The defendant consents to the termination or waives, by motion to dismiss or otherwise, his right to object to the termination.

(b) The trial court finds that the termination is necessary because:

(1) it is physically impossible to proceed with the trial in conformity with law; or

(2) there is a legal defect in the proceedings which would make any judgment entered upon a verdict reversible as a matter of law; or

(3) prejudicial conduct, in or outside the courtroom, makes it impossible to proceed with the trial without injustice to either the defendant or the State; or

(4) the jury is unable to agree upon a verdict; or

(5) false statements of a juror on voir dire prevent a fair trial.

### Section 1.09. When Prosecution Barred by Former Prosecution for Different Offense

Although a prosecution is for a violation of a different provision of the statutes than a former prosecution or is based on different facts, it is barred by such former prosecution under the following circumstances:

(1) The former prosecution resulted in an acquittal or in a conviction as defined in Section 1.08 and the subsequent prosecution is for:

(a) any offense of which the defendant could have been convicted on the first prosecution; or

(b) any offense for which the defendant should have been tried on the first prosecution under Section 1.07, unless the Court ordered a separate trial of the charge of such offense; or

(c) the same conduct, unless (i) the offense of which the defendant was formerly convicted or acquitted and the offense for which he is subsequently prosecuted each requires proof of a fact not required by the other and the law defining each of such offenses is intended to prevent a substantially different harm or evil, or (ii) the second offense was not consummated when the former trial began.

(2) The former prosecution was terminated, after the information was filed or the indictment found, by an acquittal or by a final order or judgment for the defendant which has not been set aside, reversed or vacated and which acquittal, final order or judgment necessarily required a determination inconsistent with a fact which must be established for conviction of the second offense.

(3) The former prosecution was improperly terminated, as improper termination is defined in Section 1.08, and the subsequent prosecution is for an offense of which the defendant could have been convicted had the former prosecution not been improperly terminated.

### Section 1.10. Former Prosecution in Another Jurisdiction: When a Bar

When conduct constitutes an offense within the concurrent jurisdiction of this State and of the United States or another State, a prosecution in any such other jurisdiction is a bar to a subsequent prosecution in this State under the following circumstances:

(1) The first prosecution resulted in an acquittal or in a conviction as defined in Section 1.08 and the subsequent prosecution is based on the same conduct, unless (a) the offense of which the defendant was formerly convicted or acquitted and the offense for which he is subsequently prosecuted each requires proof of a fact not required by the other and the law defining each of such offenses is intended to prevent a substantially different harm or evil or (b) the second offense was not consummated when the former trial began; or

(2) The former prosecution was terminated, after the information was filed or the indictment found, by an acquittal or by a final order or judgment for the defendant which has not been set aside, reversed or vacated and which acquittal, final order or judgment necessarily required a determination inconsistent with a fact which must be established for conviction of the offense of which the defendant is subsequently prosecuted.

### Section 1.11. Former Prosecution Before Court Lacking Jurisdiction or When Fraudulently Procured by the Defendant

A prosecution is not a bar within the meaning of Sections 1.08, 1.09 and 1.10 under any of the following circumstances:

(1) The former prosecution was before a court which lacked jurisdiction over the defendant or the offense; or

(2) The former prosecution was procured by the defendant without the knowledge of the appropriate prosecuting officer and with the purpose of avoiding the sentence which might otherwise be imposed; or

(3) The former prosecution resulted in a judgment of conviction which was held invalid in a subsequent proceeding on a writ of habeas corpus, coram nobis or similar process.

**Section 1.12. Proof Beyond a Reasonable Doubt; Affirmative Defenses; Burden of Proving Fact When Not an Element of an Offense; Presumptions**

(1) No person may be convicted of an offense unless each element of such offense is proved beyond a reasonable doubt. In the absence of such proof, the innocence of the defendant is assumed.

(2) Subsection (1) of this Section does not:

(a) require the disproof of an affirmative defense unless and until there is evidence supporting such defense; or

(b) apply to any defense which the Code or another statute plainly requires the defendant to prove by a preponderance of evidence.

(3) A ground of defense is affirmative, within the meaning of Subsection (2)(a) of this Section, when:

(a) it arises under a section of the Code which so provides; or

(b) it relates to an offense defined by a statute other than the Code and such statute so provides; or

(c) it involves a matter of excuse or justification peculiarly within the knowledge of the defendant on which he can fairly be required to adduce supporting evidence.

(4) When the application of the Code depends upon the finding of a fact which is not an element of an offense, unless the Code otherwise provides:

(a) the burden of proving the fact is on the prosecution or defendant, depending on whose interest or contention will be furthered if the finding should be made; and

(b) the fact must be proved to the satisfaction of the Court or jury, as the case may be.

(5) When the Code establishes a presumption with respect to any fact which is an element of an offense, it has the following consequences:

(a) when there is evidence of the facts which give rise to the presumption, the issue of the existence of the presumed fact must be submitted to the jury, unless the Court is satisfied that the evidence as a whole clearly negatives the presumed fact; and

(b) when the issue of the existence of the presumed fact is submitted to the jury, the Court shall charge that while the presumed fact must, on all the evidence, be proved beyond a reasonable doubt, the law declares that the jury may regard the facts giving rise to the presumption as sufficient evidence of the presumed fact.

(6) A presumption not established by the Code or inconsistent with it has the consequences otherwise accorded it by law.

### Section 1.13. General Definitions

In this Code, unless a different meaning plainly is required:

(1) "statute" includes the Constitution and a local law or ordinance of a political subdivision of the State;

(2) "act" or "action" means a bodily movement whether voluntary or involuntary;

(3) "voluntary" has the meaning specified in Section 2.01;

(4) "omission" means a failure to act;

(5) "conduct" means an action or omission and its accompanying state of mind, or, where relevant, a series of acts and omissions;

(6) "actor" includes, where relevant, a person guilty of an omission;

(7) "acted" includes, where relevant, "omitted to act";

(8) "person," "he" and "actor" include any natural person and, where relevant, a corporation or an unincorporated association;

(9) "element of an offense" means (i) such conduct or (ii) such attendant circumstances or (iii) such a result of conduct as

(a) is included in the description of the forbidden conduct in the definition of the offense; or

(b) establishes the required kind of culpability; or

(c) negatives an excuse or justification for such conduct; or

(d) negatives a defense under the statute of limitations; or

(e) establishes jurisdiction or venue;

(10) "material element of an offense" means an element that does not relate exclusively to the statute of limitations, jurisdiction, venue or to any other matter similarly unconnected with (i) the harm or evil, incident to conduct, sought to be prevented by the law defining the offense, or (ii) the existence of a justification or excuse for such conduct;

(11) "purposely" has the meaning specified in Section 2.02 and equivalent terms such as "with purpose," "designed" or "with design" have the same meaning;

(12) "intentionally" or "with intent" means purposely;

(13) "knowingly" has the meaning specified in Section 2.02 and equivalent terms such as "knowing" or "with knowledge" have the same meaning;

(14) "recklessly" has the meaning specified in Section 2.02 and equivalent terms such as "recklessness" or "with recklessness" have the same meaning;

(15) "negligently" has the meaning specified in Section 2.02 and equivalent terms such as "negligence" or "with negligence" have the same meaning;

(16) "reasonably believes" or "reasonable belief" designates a belief which the actor is not reckless or negligent in holding.

## ARTICLE 2. GENERAL PRINCIPLES OF LIABILITY

### Section 2.01. Requirement of Voluntary Act; Omission as Basis of Liability; Possession as an Act

(1) A person is not guilty of an offense unless his liability is based on conduct which includes a voluntary act or the omission to perform an act of which he is physically capable.

(2) The following are not voluntary acts within the meaning of this Section:

(a) a reflex or convulsion;

(b) a bodily movement during unconsciousness or sleep;

(c) conduct during hypnosis or resulting from hypnotic suggestion;

(d) a bodily movement that otherwise is not a product of the effort or determination of the actor, either conscious or habitual.

(3) Liability for the commission of an offense may not be based on an omission unaccompanied by action unless:

(a) the omission is expressly made sufficient by the law defining the offense; or

(b) a duty to perform the omitted act is otherwise imposed by law.

(4) Possession is an act, within the meaning of this Section, if the possessor knowingly procured or received the thing possessed or was aware of his control thereof for a sufficient period to have been able to terminate his possession.

### Section 2.02. General Requirements of Culpability

(1) Minimum Requirements of Culpability. Except as provided in Section 2.05, a person is not guilty of an offense unless he acted purposely, knowingly, recklessly or negligently, as the law may require, with respect to each material element of the offense.

(2) Kinds of Culpability Defined.

(a) Purposely.

A person acts purposely with respect to a material element of an offense when:

(i) if the element involves the nature of his conduct or a result thereof, it is his conscious object to engage in conduct of that nature or to cause such a result; and

(ii) if the element involves the attendant circumstances, he is aware of the existence of such circumstances or he believes or hopes that they exist.

(b) Knowingly.

A person acts knowingly with respect to a material element of an offense when:

(i) if the element involves the nature of his conduct or the attendant circumstances, he is aware that his conduct is of that nature or that such circumstances exist; and

(ii) if the element involves a result of his conduct, he is aware that it is practically certain that his conduct will cause such a result.

(c) Recklessly.

A person acts recklessly with respect to a material element of an offense when he consciously disregards a substantial and unjustifiable risk that the material element exists or will result from his conduct. The risk must be of such a nature and degree that, considering the nature and purpose of the actor's conduct and the circumstances known to him, its disregard involves a gross deviation from the standard of conduct that a law-abiding person would observe in the actor's situation.

(d) Negligently.

A person acts negligently with respect to a material element of an offense when he should be aware of a substantial and unjustifiable risk that the material element exists or will result from his conduct. The risk must be of such a nature and degree that the actor's failure to perceive it, considering the nature and purpose of his conduct and the circumstances known to him, involves a gross deviation from the standard of care that a reasonable person would observe in the actor's situation.

(3) Culpability Required Unless Otherwise Provided. When the culpability sufficient to establish a material element of an offense is not prescribed by law, such element is established if a person acts purposely, knowingly or recklessly with respect thereto.

(4) Prescribed Culpability Requirement Applies to All Material Elements. When the law defining an offense prescribes the kind of culpability that is sufficient for the commission of an offense, without distinguishing among the material elements thereof, such provision shall apply to all the material elements of the offense, unless a contrary purpose plainly appears.

(5) Substitutes for Negligence, Recklessness and Knowledge. When the law provides that negligence suffices to establish an element of an offense, such element also is established if a person acts purposely, knowingly or recklessly. When recklessness suffices to establish an element, such element also is established if a person acts purposely or knowingly. When acting knowingly suffices to establish an element, such element also is established if a person acts purposely.

(6) Requirement of Purpose Satisfied if Purpose Is Conditional. When a particular purpose is an element of an offense, the element is established although such purpose is conditional, unless the condition negatives the harm or evil sought to be prevented by the law defining the offense.

(7) Requirement of Knowledge Satisfied by Knowledge of High Probability. When knowledge of the existence of a particular fact is an element of an offense, such knowledge is established if a person is aware of a high probability of its existence, unless he actually believes that it does not exist.

(8) Requirement of Wilfulness Satisfied by Acting Knowingly. A requirement that an offense be committed wilfully is satisfied if a person acts knowingly with respect to the material elements of the offense, unless a purpose to impose further requirements appears.

(9) Culpability as to Illegality of Conduct. Neither knowledge nor recklessness or negligence as to whether conduct constitutes an offense or as to the existence, meaning or application of the law determining the elements of an offense is an element of such offense, unless the definition of the offense or the Code so provides.

(10) Culpability as Determinant of Grade of Offense. When the grade or degree of an offense depends on whether the offense is committed purposely, knowingly, recklessly or negligently, its grade or degree shall be the lowest for which the determinative kind of culpability is established with respect to any material element of the offense.

**Section 2.03. Causal Relationship Between Conduct and Result; Divergence Between Result Designed or Contemplated and Actual Result or Between Probable and Actual Result**

(1) Conduct is the cause of a result when:

(a) it is an antecedent but for which the result in question would not have occurred; and

(b) the relationship between the conduct and result satisfies any additional causal requirements imposed by the Code or by the law defining the offense.

(2) When purposely or knowingly causing a particular result is an element of an offense, the element is not established if the actual result is not within the purpose or the contemplation of the actor unless:

(a) the actual result differs from that designed or contemplated, as the case may be, only in the respect that a different person or different property is injured or affected or that the injury or harm designed or contemplated would have been more serious or more extensive than that caused; or

(b) the actual result involves the same kind of injury or harm as that designed or contemplated and is not too remote or accidental in its occurrence to have a [just] bearing on the actor's liability or on the gravity of his offense.

(3) When recklessly or negligently causing a particular result is an element of an offense, the element is not established if the actual result is not within the risk of which the actor is aware or, in the case of negligence, of which he should be aware unless:

(a) the actual result differs from the probable result only in the respect that a different person or different property is injured or affected or that the probable injury or harm would have been more serious or more extensive than that caused; or

(b) the actual result involves the same kind of injury or harm as the probable result and is not too remote or accidental in its occurrence to have a [just] bearing on the actor's liability or on the gravity of his offense.

(4) When causing a particular result is a material element of an offense for which absolute liability is imposed by law, the element is not established unless the actual result is a probable consequence of the actor's conduct.

## Section 2.04. Ignorance or Mistake

(1) Ignorance or mistake as to a matter of fact or law is a defense if:

(a) the ignorance or mistake negatives the purpose, knowledge, belief, recklessness or negligence required to establish a material element of the offense; or

(b) the law provides that the state of mind established by such ignorance or mistake constitutes a defense.

(2) Although ignorance or mistake would otherwise afford a defense to the offense charged, the defense is not available if the defendant would be guilty of another offense had the situation been as he supposed. In such case, however, the ignorance or mistake of the defendant shall reduce the grade and degree of the offense of which he may be convicted to those of the offense of which he would be guilty had the situation been as he supposed.

(3) A belief that conduct does not legally constitute an offense is a defense to a prosecution for that offense based upon such conduct when:

(a) the statute or other enactment defining the offense is not known to the actor and has not been published or otherwise reasonably made available prior to the conduct alleged; or

(b) he acts in reasonable reliance upon an official statement of the law, afterward determined to be invalid or erroneous, contained in (i) a statute or other enactment; (ii) a judicial decision, opinion or judgment; (iii) an administrative order or grant of permission; or (iv) an official interpretation of the public officer or body charged by law with responsibility for the interpretation, administration or enforcement of the law defining the offense.

(4) The defendant must prove a defense arising under Subsection (3) of this Section by a preponderance of evidence.

## Section 2.05. When Culpability Requirements Are Inapplicable to Violations and to Offenses Defined by Other Statutes; Effect of Absolute Liability in Reducing Grade of Offense to Violation

(1) The requirements of culpability prescribed by Sections 2.01 and 2.02 do not apply to:

(a) offenses which constitute violations, unless the requirement involved is included in the definition of the offense or the Court determines that its application is consistent with effective enforcement of the law defining the offense; or

(b) offenses defined by statutes other than the Code, insofar as a legislative purpose to impose absolute liability for such offenses or with respect to any material element thereof plainly appears.

(2) Notwithstanding any other provision of existing law and unless a subsequent statute otherwise provides:

(a) when absolute liability is imposed with respect to any material element of an offense defined by a statute other than the Code and a conviction is based upon such liability, the offense constitutes a violation; and

(b) although absolute liability is imposed by law with respect to one or more of the material elements of an offense defined by a statute other than the Code, the culpable commission of the offense may be charged and proved, in which event negligence with respect to such elements constitutes sufficient culpability and the classification of the offense and the sentence that may be imposed therefor upon conviction are determined by Section 1.04 and Article 6 of the Code.

**Section 2.06. Liability for Conduct of Another; Complicity**

(1) A person is guilty of an offense if it is committed by his own conduct or by the conduct of another person for which he is legally accountable, or both.

(2) A person is legally accountable for the conduct of another person when:

(a) acting with the kind of culpability that is sufficient for the commission of the offense, he causes an innocent or irresponsible person to engage in such conduct; or

(b) he is made accountable for the conduct of such other person by the Code or by the law defining the offense; or

(c) he is an accomplice of such other person in the commission of the offense.

(3) A person is an accomplice of another person in the commission of an offense if:

(a) with the purpose of promoting or facilitating the commission of the offense, he

(i) solicits such other person to commit it; or

(ii) aids or agrees or attempts to aid such other person in planning or committing it; or

(iii) having a legal duty to prevent the commission of the offense, fails to make proper effort so to do; or

(b) his conduct is expressly declared by law to establish his complicity.

(4) When causing a particular result is an element of an offense, an accomplice in the conduct causing such result is an accomplice in the commission of that offense, if he acts with the kind of culpability, if any, with respect to that result that is sufficient for the commission of the offense.

(5) A person who is legally incapable of committing a particular offense himself may be guilty thereof if it is committed by the conduct of another person for which he is legally accountable, unless such liability is inconsistent with the purpose of the provision establishing his incapacity.

(6) Unless otherwise provided by the Code or by the law defining the offense, a person is not an accomplice in an offense committed by another person if:

(a) he is a victim of that offense; or

(b) the offense is so defined that his conduct is inevitably incident to its commission; or

(c) he terminates his complicity prior to the commission of the offense and

(i) wholly deprives it of effectiveness in the commission of the offense; or

(ii) gives timely warning to the law enforcement authorities or otherwise makes proper effort to prevent the commission of the offense.

(7) An accomplice may be convicted on proof of the commission of the offense and of his complicity therein, though the person claimed to have committed the offense has not been prosecuted or convicted or has been convicted of a different offense or degree of offense or has an immunity to prosecution or conviction or has been acquitted.

**Section 2.07. Liability of Corporations, Unincorporated Associations and Persons Acting, or Under a Duty to Act, in Their Behalf**

(1) A corporation may be convicted of the commission of an offense if:

(a) the offense is a violation or the offense is defined by a statute other than the Code in which a legislative purpose to impose liability on corporations plainly appears and the conduct is performed by an agent of the corporation acting in behalf of the corporation within the scope of his office or employment, except that if the law defining the offense designates the agents for whose conduct the corporation is accountable or the circumstances under which it is accountable, such provisions shall apply; or

(b) the offense consists of an omission to discharge a specific duty of affirmative performance imposed on corporations by law; or

(c) the commission of the offense was authorized, requested, commanded, performed or recklessly tolerated by the board of directors or by a high managerial agent acting in behalf of the corporation within the scope of his office or employment.

(2) When absolute liability is imposed for the commission of an offense, a legislative purpose to impose liability on a corporation shall be assumed, unless the contrary plainly appears.

(3) An unincorporated association may be convicted of the commission of an offense if:

(a) the offense is defined by a statute other than the Code which expressly provides for the liability of such an association and the conduct is performed by an agent of the association acting in behalf of the association within the scope of his office or employment, except that if the law defining the offense designates the agents for whose conduct the association is accountable or the circumstances under which it is accountable, such provisions shall apply; or

(b) the offense consists of an omission to discharge a specific duty of affirmative performance imposed on associations by law.

(4) As used in this Section:

(a) "corporation" does not include an entity organized as or by a governmental agency for the execution of a governmental program;

(b) "agent" means any director, officer, servant, employee or other person authorized to act in behalf of the corporation or association and, in the case of an unincorporated association, a member of such association;

(c) "high managerial agent" means an officer of a corporation or an unincorporated association, or, in the case of a partnership, a partner, or any other agent of a corporation or association having duties of such responsibility that his conduct may fairly be assumed to represent the policy of the corporation or association.

(5) In any prosecution of a corporation or an unincorporated association for the commission of an offense included within the terms of Subsection (1)(a) or Subsection (3)(a) of this Section, other than an offense for which absolute liability has been imposed, it shall be a defense if the defendant proves by a preponderance of evidence that the high managerial agent having supervisory responsibility over the subject matter of the offense employed due diligence to prevent its commission. This paragraph shall not apply if it is plainly inconsistent with the legislative purpose in defining the particular offense.

(6) (a) A person is legally accountable for any conduct he performs or causes to be performed in the name of the corporation or an unincorporated association or in its behalf to the same extent as if it were performed in his own name or behalf.

(b) Whenever a duty to act is imposed by law upon a corporation or an unincorporated association, any agent of the corporation or association having primary responsibility for the discharge of the duty is legally accountable for a reckless omission to perform the required act to the same extent as if the duty were imposed by law directly upon himself.

(c) When a person is convicted of an offense by reason of his legal accountability for the conduct of a corporation or an unincorporated association, he is subject to the sentence authorized by law when a natural person is convicted of an offense of the grade and the degree involved.

**Section 2.08. Intoxication**

(1) Except as provided in Subsection (4) of this Section, intoxication of the actor is not a defense unless it negatives an element of the offense.

(2) When recklessness establishes an element of the offense, if the actor, due to self-induced intoxication, is unaware of a risk of which he would have been aware had he been sober, such unawareness is immaterial.

(3) Intoxication does not, in itself, constitute mental disease within the meaning of Section 4.01.

(4) Intoxication which (a) is not self-induced or (b) is pathological is an affirmative defense if by reason of such intoxication the actor at the time of his conduct lacks substantial capacity either to appreciate its

criminality [wrongfulness] or to conform his conduct to the requirements of law.

(5) Definitions. In this Section unless a different meaning plainly is required:

(a) "intoxication" means a disturbance of mental or physical capacities resulting from the introduction of substances into the body;

(b) "self-induced intoxication" means intoxication caused by substances which the actor knowingly introduces into his body, the tendency of which to cause intoxication he knows or ought to know, unless he introduces them pursuant to medical advice or under such circumstances as would afford a defense to a charge of crime;

(c) "pathological intoxication" means intoxication grossly excessive in degree, given the amount of the intoxicant, to which the actor does not know he is susceptible.

## Section 2.09. Duress

(1) It is an affirmative defense that the actor engaged in the conduct charged to constitute an offense because he was coerced to do so by the use of, or a threat to use, unlawful force against his person or the person of another, which a person of reasonable firmness in his situation would have been unable to resist.

(2) The defense provided by this Section is unavailable if the actor recklessly placed himself in a situation in which it was probable that he would be subjected to duress. The defense is also unavailable if he was negligent in placing himself in such a situation, whenever negligence suffices to establish culpability for the offense charged.

(3) It is not a defense that a woman acted on the command of her husband, unless she acted under such coercion as would establish a defense under this Section. [The presumption that a woman, acting in the presence of her husband, is coerced is abolished.]

(4) When the conduct of the actor would otherwise be justifiable under Section 3.02, this Section does not preclude such defense.

## Section 2.10. Military Orders

It is an affirmative defense that the actor, in engaging in the conduct charged to constitute an offense, does no more than execute an order of his superior in the armed services which he does not know to be unlawful.

## Section 2.11. Consent

(1) In General. The consent of the victim to conduct charged to constitute an offense or to the result thereof is a defense if such consent negatives an element of the offense or precludes the infliction of the harm or evil sought to be prevented by the law defining the offense.

(2) Consent to Bodily Harm. When conduct is charged to constitute an offense because it causes or threatens bodily harm, consent to such conduct or to the infliction of such harm is a defense if:

(a) the bodily harm consented to or threatened by the conduct consented to is not serious; or

(b) the conduct and the harm are reasonably foreseeable hazards of joint participation in a lawful athletic contest or competitive sport; or

(c) the consent establishes a justification for the conduct under Article 3 of the Code.

(3) Ineffective Consent. Unless otherwise provided by the Code or by the law defining the offense, assent does not constitute consent if:

(a) it is given by a person who is legally incompetent to authorize the conduct charged to constitute the offense; or

(b) it is given by a person who by reason of youth, mental disease or defect or intoxication is manifestly unable or known by the actor to be unable to make a reasonable judgment as to the nature or harmfulness of the conduct charged to constitute the offense; or

(c) it is given by a person whose improvident consent is sought to be prevented by the law defining the offense; or

(d) it is induced by force, duress or deception of a kind sought to be prevented by the law defining the offense.

**Section 2.12. De Minimis Infractions**

The Court shall dismiss a prosecution if, having regard to the nature of the conduct charged to constitute an offense and the nature of the attendant circumstances, it finds that the defendant's conduct:

(1) was within a customary license or tolerance, neither expressly negatived by the person whose interest was infringed nor inconsistent with the purpose of the law defining the offense; or

(2) did not actually cause or threaten the harm or evil sought to be prevented by the law defining the offense or did so only to an extent too trivial to warrant the condemnation of conviction; or

(3) presents such other extenuations that it cannot reasonably be regarded as envisaged by the legislature in forbidding the offense.

The Court shall not dismiss a prosecution under Subsection (3) of this Section without filing a written statement of its reasons.

**Section 2.13. Entrapment**

(1) A public law enforcement official or a person acting in cooperation with such an official perpetrates an entrapment if for the purpose of obtaining evidence of the commission of an offense, he induces or encourages another person to engage in conduct constituting such offense by either:

(a) making knowingly false representations designed to induce the belief that such conduct is not prohibited; or

(b) employing methods of persuasion or inducement which create a substantial risk that such an offense will be committed by persons other than those who are ready to commit it.

(2) Except as provided in Subsection (3) of this Section, a person prosecuted for an offense shall be acquitted if he proves by a preponderance of evidence that his conduct occurred in response to an entrapment. The issue of entrapment shall be tried by the Court in the absence of the jury.

(3) The defense afforded by this Section is unavailable when causing or threatening bodily injury is an element of the offense charged and the prosecution is based on conduct causing or threatening such injury to a person other than the person perpetrating the entrapment.

## ARTICLE 3. GENERAL PRINCIPLES OF JUSTIFICATION

### Section 3.01. Justification an Affirmative Defense; Civil Remedies Unaffected

(1) In any prosecution based on conduct which is justifiable under this Article, justification is an affirmative defense.

(2) The fact that conduct is justifiable under this Article does not abolish or impair any remedy for such conduct which is available in any civil action.

### Section 3.02. Justification Generally: Choice of Evils

(1) Conduct which the actor believes to be necessary to avoid a harm or evil to himself or to another is justifiable, provided that:

(a) the harm or evil sought to be avoided by such conduct is greater than that sought to be prevented by the law defining the offense charged; and

(b) neither the Code nor other law defining the offense provides exceptions or defenses dealing with the specific situation involved; and

(c) a legislative purpose to exclude the justification claimed does not otherwise plainly appear.

(2) When the actor was reckless or negligent in bringing about the situation requiring a choice of harms or evils or in appraising the necessity for his conduct, the justification afforded by this Section is unavailable in a prosecution for any offense for which recklessness or negligence, as the case may be, suffices to establish culpability.

### Section 3.03. Execution of Public Duty

(1) Except as provided in Subsection (2) of this Section, conduct is justifiable when it is required or authorized by:

(a) the law defining the duties or functions of a public officer or the assistance to be rendered to such officer in the performance of his duties; or

(b) the law governing the execution of legal process; or

(c) the judgment or order of a competent court or tribunal; or

(d) the law governing the armed services or the lawful conduct of war; or

(e) any other provision of law imposing a public duty.

(2) The other sections of this Article apply to:

(a) the use of force upon or toward the person of another for any of the purposes dealt with in such sections; and

(b) the use of deadly force for any purpose, unless the use of such force is otherwise expressly authorized by law or occurs in the lawful conduct of war.

(3) The justification afforded by Subsection (1) of this Section applies:

(a) when the actor believes his conduct to be required or authorized by the judgment or direction of a competent court or tribunal or in the lawful execution of legal process, notwithstanding lack of jurisdiction of the court or defect in the legal process; and

(b) when the actor believes his conduct to be required or authorized to assist a public officer in the performance of his duties, notwithstanding that the officer exceeded his legal authority.

**Section 3.04. Use of Force in Self-Protection**

(1) Use of Force Justifiable for Protection of the Person. Subject to the provisions of this Section and of Section 3.09, the use of force upon or toward another person is justifiable when the actor believes that such force is immediately necessary for the purpose of protecting himself against the use of unlawful force by such other person on the present occasion.

(2) Limitations on Justifying Necessity for Use of Force.

(a) The use of force is not justifiable under this Section:

(i) to resist an arrest which the actor knows is being made by a peace officer, although the arrest is unlawful; or

(ii) to resist force used by the occupier or possessor of property or by another person on his behalf, where the actor knows that the person using the force is doing so under a claim of right to protect the property, except that this limitation shall not apply if:

(1) the actor is a public officer acting in the performance of his duties or a person lawfully assisting him therein or a person making or assisting in a lawful arrest; or

(2) the actor has been unlawfully dispossessed of the property and is making a re-entry or recaption justified by Section 3.06; or

(3) the actor believes that such force is necessary to protect himself against death or serious bodily harm.

(b) The use of deadly force is not justifiable under this Section unless the actor believes that such force is necessary to protect himself against death, serious bodily harm, kidnapping or sexual intercourse compelled by force or threat; nor is it justifiable if:

(i) the actor, with the purpose of causing death or serious bodily harm, provoked the use of force against himself in the same encounter; or

(ii) the actor knows that he can avoid the necessity of using such force with complete safety by retreating or by surrendering possession of a thing to a person asserting a claim of right thereto or by complying with a demand that he abstain from any action which he has no duty to take, except that:

(1) the actor is not obliged to retreat from his dwelling or place of work, unless he was the initial aggressor or is assailed in his place of work by another person whose place of work the actor knows it to be; and

(2) a public officer justified in using force in the performance of his duties or a person justified in using force in his assistance or a person justified in using force in making an arrest or preventing an escape is not obliged to desist from efforts to perform such duty, effect such arrest or prevent such escape because of resistance or threatened resistance by or on behalf of the person against whom such action is directed.

(c) Except as required by paragraphs (a) and (b) of this Subsection, a person employing protective force may estimate the necessity thereof under the circumstances as he believes them to be when the force is used, without retreating, surrendering possession, doing any other act which he has no legal duty to do or abstaining from any lawful action.

(3) Use of Confinement as Protective Force. The justification afforded by this Section extends to the use of confinement as protective force only if the actor takes all reasonable measures to terminate the confinement as soon as he knows that he safely can, unless the person confined has been arrested on a charge of crime.

**Section 3.05. Use of Force for the Protection of Other Persons**

(1) Subject to the provisions of this Section and of Section 3.09, the use of force upon or toward the person of another is justifiable to protect a third person when:

(a) the actor would be justified under Section 3.04 in using such force to protect himself against the injury he believes to be threatened to the person whom he seeks to protect; and

(b) under the circumstances as the actor believes them to be, the person whom he seeks to protect would be justified in using such protective force; and

(c) the actor believes that his intervention is necessary for the protection of such other person.

(2) Notwithstanding Subsection (1) of this Section:

(a) when the actor would be obliged under Section 3.04 to retreat, to surrender the possession of a thing or to comply with a demand before using force in self-protection, he is not obliged to do so before using force for the protection of another person, unless he knows that he can thereby secure the complete safety of such other person; and

(b) when the person whom the actor seeks to protect would be obliged under Section 3.04 to retreat, to surrender the possession of a thing or to comply with a demand if he knew that he could obtain complete safety by so doing, the actor is obliged to try to cause him to do so before using force in his protection if the actor knows that he can obtain complete safety in that way; and

(c) neither the actor nor the person whom he seeks to protect is obliged to retreat when in the other's dwelling or place of work to any greater extent than in his own.

**Section 3.06. Use of Force for the Protection of Property**

(1) Use of Force Justifiable for Protection of Property. Subject to the provisions of this Section and of Section 3.09, the use of force upon or toward the person of another is justifiable when the actor believes that such force is immediately necessary:

(a) to prevent or terminate an unlawful entry or other trespass upon land or a trespass against or the unlawful carrying away of tangible, movable property, provided that such land or movable property is, or is believed by the actor to be, in his possession or in the possession of another person for whose protection he acts; or

(b) to effect an entry or re-entry upon land or to retake tangible movable property, provided that the actor believes that he or the person by whose authority he acts or a person from whom he or such other person derives title was unlawfully dispossessed of such land or movable property and is entitled to possession, and provided, further, that:

(i) the force is used immediately or on fresh pursuit after such dispossession; or

(ii) the actor believes that the person against whom he uses force has no claim of right to the possession of the property and, in the case of land, the circumstances, as the actor believes them to be, are of such urgency that it would be an exceptional hardship to postpone the entry or re-entry until a court order is obtained.

(2) Meaning of Possession. For the purposes of Subsection (1) of this Section:

(a) a person who has parted with the custody of property to another who refuses to restore it to him is no longer in possession, unless the property is movable and was and still is located on land in his possession;

(b) a person who has been dispossessed of land does not regain possession thereof merely by setting foot thereon;

(c) a person who has a license to use or occupy real property is deemed to be in possession thereof except against the licensor acting under claim of right.

(3) Limitations on Justifiable Use of Force.

(a) Request to Desist. The use of force is justifiable under this Section only if the actor first requests the person against whom such force is used to desist from his interference with the property, unless the actor believes that:

(i) such request would be useless; or

(ii) it would be dangerous to himself or another person to make the request; or

(iii) substantial harm will be done to the physical condition of the property which is sought to be protected before the request can effectively be made.

(b) Exclusion of Trespasser. The use of force to prevent or terminate a trespass is not justifiable under this Section if the actor knows that the exclusion of the trespasser will expose him to substantial danger or serious bodily harm.

(c) Resistance of Lawful Re-entry or Recaption. The use of force to prevent an entry or re-entry upon land or the recaption of movable property is not justifiable under this Section, although the actor believes that such re-entry or recaption is unlawful, if:

(i) the re-entry or recaption is made by or on behalf of a person who was actually dispossessed of the property; and

(ii) it is otherwise justifiable under paragraph (1)(b) of this Section.

(d) Use of Deadly Force. The use of deadly force is not justifiable under this Section unless the actor believes that:

(i) the person against whom the force is used is attempting to dispossess him of his dwelling otherwise than under a claim of right to its possession; or

(ii) the person against whom the force is used is attempting to commit or consummate arson, burglary, robbery or other felonious theft or property destruction and either:

(1) has employed or threatened deadly force against or in the presence of the actor; or

(2) the use of force other than deadly force to prevent the commission or the consummation of the crime would expose the actor or another in his presence to substantial danger of serious bodily harm.

(4) Use of Confinement as Protective Force. The justification afforded by this Section extends to the use of confinement as protective force only if the actor takes all reasonable measures to terminate the confinement as soon as he knows that he can do so with safety to the property, unless the person confined has been arrested on a charge of crime.

(5) Use of Device to Protect Property. The justification afforded by this Section extends to the use of a device for the purpose of protecting property only if:

(a) the device is not designed to cause or known to create a substantial risk of causing death or serious bodily harm; and

(b) the use of the particular device to protect the property from entry or trespass is reasonable under the circumstances, as the actor believes them to be; and

(c) the device is one customarily used for such a purpose or reasonable care is taken to make known to probable intruders the fact that it is used.

(6) Use of Force to Pass Wrongful Obstructor. The use of force to pass a person whom the actor believes to be purposely or knowingly and

unjustifiably obstructing the actor from going to a place to which he may lawfully go is justifiable, provided that:

(a) the actor believes that the person against whom he uses force has no claim of right to obstruct the actor; and

(b) the actor is not being obstructed from entry or movement on land which he knows to be in the possession or custody of the person obstructing him, or in the possession or custody of another person by whose authority the obstructor acts, unless the circumstances, as the actor believes them to be, are of such urgency that it would not be reasonable to postpone the entry or movement on such land until a court order is obtained; and

(c) the force used is not greater than would be justifiable if the person obstructing the actor were using force against him to prevent his passage.

**Section 3.07. Use of Force in Law Enforcement**

(1) Use of Force Justifiable to Effect an Arrest. Subject to the provisions of this Section and of Section 3.09, the use of force upon or toward the person of another is justifiable when the actor is making or assisting in making an arrest and the actor believes that such force is immediately necessary to effect a lawful arrest.

(2) Limitations on the Use of Force.

(a) The use of force is not justifiable under this Section unless:

(i) the actor makes known the purpose of the arrest or believes that it is otherwise known by or cannot reasonably be made known to the person to be arrested; and

(ii) when the arrest is made under a warrant, the warrant is valid or believed by the actor to be valid.

(b) The use of deadly force is not justifiable under this Section unless:

(i) the arrest is for a felony; and

(ii) the person effecting the arrest is authorized to act as a peace officer or is assisting a person whom he believes to be authorized to act as a peace officer; and

(iii) the actor believes that the force employed creates no substantial risk of injury to innocent persons; and

(iv) the actor believes that:

(1) the crime for which the arrest is made involved conduct including the use or threatened use of deadly force; or

(2) there is a substantial risk that the person to be arrested will cause death or serious bodily harm if his apprehension is delayed.

(3) Use of Force to Prevent Escape From Custody. The use of force to prevent the escape of an arrested person from custody is justifiable when the force could justifiably have been employed to effect the arrest under which the person is in custody, except that a guard or other person authorized to act as a peace officer is justified in using any force, including deadly force, which he believes to be immediately necessary to

prevent the escape of a person from a jail, prison, or other institution for the detention of persons charged with or convicted of a crime.

(4) Use of Force by Private Person Assisting an Unlawful Arrest.

(a) A private person who is summoned by a peace officer to assist in effecting an unlawful arrest, is justified in using any force which he would be justified in using if the arrest were lawful, provided that he does not believe the arrest is unlawful.

(b) A private person who assists another private person in effecting an unlawful arrest, or who, not being summoned, assists a peace officer in effecting an unlawful arrest, is justified in using any force which he would be justified in using if the arrest were lawful, provided that (i) he believes the arrest is lawful, and (ii) the arrest would be lawful if the facts were as he believes them to be.

(5) Use of Force to Prevent Suicide or the Commission of a Crime.

(a) The use of force upon or toward the person of another is justifiable when the actor believes that such force is immediately necessary to prevent such other person from committing suicide, inflicting serious bodily harm upon himself, committing or consummating the commission of a crime involving or threatening bodily harm, damage to or loss of property or a breach of the peace, except that:

(i) any limitations imposed by the other provisions of this Article on the justifiable use of force in self-protection, for the protection of others, the protection of property, the effectuation of an arrest or the prevention of an escape from custody shall apply notwithstanding the criminality of the conduct against which such force is used; and

(ii) the use of deadly force is not in any event justifiable under this Subsection unless:

(1) the actor believes that there is a substantial risk that the person whom he seeks to prevent from committing a crime will cause death or serious bodily harm to another unless the commission or the consummation of the crime is prevented and that the use of such force presents no substantial risk of injury to innocent persons; or

(2) the actor believes that the use of such force is necessary to suppress a riot or mutiny after the rioters or mutineers have been ordered to disperse and warned, in any particular manner that the law may require, that such force will be used if they do not obey.

(b) The justification afforded by this Subsection extends to the use of confinement as preventive force only if the actor takes all reasonable measures to terminate the confinement as soon as he knows that he safely can, unless the person confined has been arrested on a charge of crime.

## Section 3.08. Use of Force by Persons With Special Responsibility for Care, Discipline or Safety of Others

The use of force upon or toward the person of another is justifiable if:

(1) the actor is the parent or guardian or other person similarly responsible for the general care and supervision of a minor or a person acting at the request of such parent, guardian or other responsible person and:

(a) the force is used for the purpose of safeguarding or promoting the welfare of the minor, including the prevention or punishment of his misconduct; and

(b) the force used is not designed to cause or known to create a substantial risk of causing death, serious bodily harm, disfigurement, extreme pain or mental distress or gross degradation; or

(2) the actor is a teacher or a person otherwise entrusted with the care or supervision for a special purpose of a minor and:

(a) the actor believes that the force used is necessary to further such special purpose, including the maintenance of reasonable discipline in a school, class or other group, and that the use of such force is consistent with the welfare of the minor; and

(b) the degree of force, if it had been used by the parent or guardian of the minor, would not be unjustifiable under Subsection (1)(b) of this Section; or

(3) the actor is the guardian or other person similarly responsible for the general care and supervision of an incompetent person; and:

(a) the force is used for the purpose of safeguarding or promoting the welfare of the incompetent person, including the prevention of his misconduct, or, when such incompetent person is in a hospital or other institution for his care and custody, for the maintenance of reasonable discipline in such institution; and

(b) the force used is not designed to cause or known to create a substantial risk of causing death, serious bodily harm, disfigurement, extreme or unnecessary pain, mental distress, or humiliation; or

(4) the actor is a doctor or other therapist or a person assisting him at his direction, and:

(a) the force is used for the purpose of administering a recognized form of treatment which the actor believes to be adapted to promoting the physical or mental health of the patient; and

(b) the treatment is administered with the consent of the patient or, if the patient is a minor or an incompetent person, with the consent of his parent or guardian or other person legally competent to consent in his behalf, or the treatment is administered in an emergency when the actor believes that no one competent to consent can be consulted and that a reasonable person, wishing to safeguard the welfare of the patient, would consent; or

(5) the actor is a warden or other authorized official of a correctional institution, and:

(a) he believes that the force used is necessary for the purpose of enforcing the lawful rules or procedures of the institution, unless his belief in the lawfulness of the rule or procedure sought to be enforced is erroneous and his error is due to ignorance or mistake as to the provisions of the Code, any other provision of the criminal law or the law governing the administration of the institution; and

(b) the nature or degree of force used is not forbidden by Article 303 or 304 of the Code; and

(c) if deadly force is used, its use is otherwise justifiable under this Article; or

(6) the actor is a person responsible for the safety of a vessel or an aircraft or a person acting at his direction, and:

(a) he believes that the force used is necessary to prevent interference with the operation of the vessel or aircraft or obstruction of the execution of a lawful order, unless his belief in the lawfulness of the order is erroneous and his error is due to ignorance or mistake as to the law defining his authority; and

(b) if deadly force is used, its use is otherwise justifiable under this Article; or

(7) the actor is a person who is authorized or required by law to maintain order or decorum in a vehicle, train or other carrier or in a place where others are assembled, and:

(a) he believes that the force used is necessary for such purpose; and

(b) the force used is not designed to cause or known to create a substantial risk of causing death, bodily harm, or extreme mental distress.

**Section 3.09. Mistake of Law as to Unlawfulness of Force or Legality of Arrest; Reckless or Negligent Use of Otherwise Justifiable Force; Reckless or Negligent Injury or Risk of Injury to Innocent Persons**

(1) The justification afforded by Sections 3.04 to 3.07, inclusive, is unavailable when:

(a) the actor's belief in the unlawfulness of the force or conduct against which he employs protective force or his belief in the lawfulness of an arrest which he endeavors to effect by force is erroneous; and

(b) his error is due to ignorance or mistake as to the provisions of the Code, any other provision of the criminal law or the law governing the legality of an arrest or search.

(2) When the actor believes that the use of force upon or toward the person of another is necessary for any of the purposes for which such belief would establish a justification under Sections 3.03 to 3.08 but the actor is reckless or negligent in having such belief or in acquiring or failing to acquire any knowledge or belief which is material to the justifiability of his use of force, the justification afforded by those Sections is unavailable in a prosecution for an offense for which recklessness or negligence, as the case may be, suffices to establish culpability.

(3) When the actor is justified under Sections 3.03 to 3.08 in using force upon or toward the person of another but he recklessly or negligently injures or creates a risk of injury to innocent persons, the justifi-

cation afforded by those Sections is unavailable in a prosecution for such recklessness or negligence towards innocent persons.

**Section 3.10. Justification in Property Crimes**

Conduct involving the appropriation, seizure or destruction of, damage to, intrusion on or interference with property is justifiable under circumstances which would establish a defense of privilege in a civil action based thereon, unless:

(1) the Code or the law defining the offense deals with the specific situation involved; or

(2) a legislative purpose to exclude the justification claimed otherwise plainly appears.

**Section 3.11. Definitions**

In this Article, unless a different meaning plainly is required:

(1) "unlawful force" means force, including confinement, which is employed without the consent of the person against whom it is directed and the employment of which constitutes an offense or actionable tort or would constitute such offense or tort except for a defense (such as the absence of intent, negligence, or mental capacity; duress; youth; or diplomatic status) not amounting to a privilege to use the force. Assent constitutes consent, within the meaning of this Section, whether or not it otherwise is legally effective, except assent to the infliction of death or serious bodily harm.

(2) "deadly force" means force which the actor uses with the purpose of causing or which he knows to create a substantial risk of causing death or serious bodily harm. Purposely firing a firearm in the direction of another person or at a vehicle in which another person is believed to be constitutes deadly force. A threat to cause death or serious bodily harm, by the production of a weapon or otherwise, so long as the actor's purpose is limited to creating an apprehension that he will use deadly force if necessary, does not constitute deadly force;

(3) "dwelling" means any building or structure, though movable or temporary, or a portion thereof, which is for the time being the actor's home or place of lodging.

## ARTICLE 4. RESPONSIBILITY

**Section 4.01. Mental Disease or Defect Excluding Responsibility**

(1) A person is not responsible for criminal conduct if at the time of such conduct as a result of mental disease or defect he lacks substantial capacity either to appreciate the criminality [wrongfulness] of his conduct or to conform his conduct to the requirements of law.

(2) As used in this Article, the terms "mental disease or defect" do not include an abnormality manifested only by repeated criminal or otherwise anti-social conduct.

### Section 4.02. Evidence of Mental Disease or Defect Admissible When Relevant to Element of the Offense; [Mental Disease or Defect Impairing Capacity as Ground for Mitigation of Punishment in Capital Cases]

(1) Evidence that the defendant suffered from a mental disease or defect is admissible whenever it is relevant to prove that the defendant did or did not have a state of mind which is an element of the offense.

[(2) Whenever the jury or the Court is authorized to determine or to recommend whether or not the defendant shall be sentenced to death or imprisonment upon conviction, evidence that the capacity of the defendant to appreciate the criminality [wrongfulness] of his conduct or to conform his conduct to the requirements of law was impaired as a result of mental disease or defect is admissible in favor of sentence of imprisonment.]

### Section 4.03. Mental Disease or Defect Excluding Responsibility Is Affirmative Defense; Requirement of Notice; Form of Verdict and Judgment When Finding of Irresponsibility Is Made

(1) Mental disease or defect excluding responsibility is an affirmative defense.

(2) Evidence of mental disease or defect excluding responsibility is not admissible unless the defendant, at the time of entering his plea of not guilty or within ten days thereafter or at such later time as the Court may for good cause permit, files a written notice of his purpose to rely on such defense.

(3) When the defendant is acquitted on the ground of mental disease or defect excluding responsibility, the verdict and the judgment shall so state.

### Section 4.04. Mental Disease or Defect Excluding Fitness to Proceed

No person who as a result of mental disease or defect lacks capacity to understand the proceedings against him or to assist in his own defense shall be tried, convicted or sentenced for the commission of an offense so long as such incapacity endures.

### Section 4.05. Psychiatric Examination of Defendant With Respect to Mental Disease or Defect

(1) Whenever the defendant has filed a notice of intention to rely on the defense of mental disease or defect excluding responsibility, or there is reason to doubt his fitness to proceed, or reason to believe that mental disease or defect of the defendant will otherwise become an issue in the cause, the Court shall appoint at least one qualified psychiatrist or shall request the Superintendent of the _______ Hospital to designate at least one qualified psychiatrist, which designation may be or include himself, to examine and report upon the mental condition of the defendant. The Court may order the defendant to be committed to a hospital or other suitable facility for the purpose of the examination for a period of not exceeding sixty days or such longer period as the Court determines to be necessary for the purpose and may direct that a qualified

psychiatrist retained by the defendant be permitted to witness and participate in the examination.

(2) In such examination any method may be employed which is accepted by the medical profession for the examination of those alleged to be suffering from mental disease or defect.

(3) The report of the examination shall include the following: (a) a description of the nature of the examination; (b) a diagnosis of the mental condition of the defendant; (c) if the defendant suffers from a mental disease or defect, an opinion as to his capacity to understand the proceedings against him and to assist in his own defense; (d) when a notice of intention to rely on the defense of irresponsibility has been filed, an opinion as to the extent, if any, to which the capacity of the defendant to appreciate the criminality [wrongfulness] of his conduct or to conform his conduct to the requirements of law was impaired at the time of the criminal conduct charged; and (e) when directed by the Court, an opinion as to the capacity of the defendant to have a particular state of mind which is an element of the offense charged.

If the examination can not be conducted by reason of the unwillingness of the defendant to participate therein, the report shall so state and shall include, if possible, an opinion as to whether such unwillingness of the defendant was the result of mental disease or defect.

The report of the examination shall be filed [in triplicate] with the clerk of the Court, who shall cause copies to be delivered to the district attorney and to counsel for the defendant.

**Section 4.06. Determination of Fitness to Proceed; Effect of Finding of Unfitness; Proceedings if Fitness Is Regained [; Post-Commitment Hearing]**

(1) When the defendant's fitness to proceed is drawn in question, the issue shall be determined by the Court. If neither the prosecuting attorney nor counsel for the defendant contests the finding of the report filed pursuant to Section 4.05, the Court may make the determination on the basis of such report. If the finding is contested, the Court shall hold a hearing on the issue. If the report is received in evidence upon such hearing, the party who contests the finding thereof shall have the right to summon and to cross-examine the psychiatrists who joined in the report and to offer evidence upon the issue.

(2) If the Court determines that the defendant lacks fitness to proceed, the proceeding against him shall be suspended, except as provided in Subsection (3) [Subsections (3) and (4)] of this Section, and the Court shall commit him to the custody of the Commissioner of Mental Hygiene [Public Health or Correction] to be placed in an appropriate institution of the Department of Mental Hygiene [Public Health or Correction] for so long as such unfitness shall endure. When the Court, on its own motion or upon the application of the Commissioner of Mental Hygiene [Public Health or Correction] or the prosecuting attorney, determines, after a hearing if a hearing is requested, that the defendant has regained fitness to proceed, the proceeding shall be resumed. If, however, the Court is of the view that so much time has elapsed since the commitment of the defendant that it would be unjust to resume the criminal proceeding, the Court may dismiss the charge and may order the defendant to be discharged or, subject to the law governing the civil

commitment of persons suffering from mental disease or defect, order the defendant to be committed to an appropriate institution of the Department of Mental Hygiene [Public Health].

(3) The fact that the defendant is unfit to proceed does not preclude any legal objection to the prosecution which is susceptible of fair determination prior to trial and without the personal participation of the defendant.

[Alternative: (3) At any time within ninety days after commitment as provided in Subsection (2) of this Section, or at any later time with permission of the Court granted for good cause, the defendant or his counsel or the Commissioner of Mental Hygiene [Public Health or Correction] may apply for a special post-commitment hearing. If the application is made by or on behalf of a defendant not represented by counsel, he shall be afforded a reasonable opportunity to obtain counsel, and if he lacks funds to do so, counsel shall be assigned by the Court. The application shall be granted only if the counsel for the defendant satisfies the Court by affidavit or otherwise that as an attorney he has reasonable grounds for a good faith belief that his client has, on the facts and the law, a defense to the charge other than mental disease or defect excluding responsibility.

[(4) If the motion for a special post-commitment hearing is granted, the hearing shall be by the Court without a jury. No evidence shall be offered at the hearing by either party on the issue of mental disease or defect as a defense to, or in mitigation of, the crime charged. After hearing, the Court may in an appropriate case quash the indictment or other charge, or find it to be defective or insufficient, or determine that it is not proved beyond a reasonable doubt by the evidence, or otherwise terminate the proceedings on the evidence or the law. In any such case, unless all defects in the proceedings are promptly cured, the Court shall terminate the commitment ordered under Subsection (2) of this Section and order the defendant to be discharged or, subject to the law governing the civil commitment of persons suffering from mental disease or defect, order the defendant to be committed to an appropriate institution of the Department of Mental Hygiene [Public Health].]

## Section 4.07. Determination of Irresponsibility on Basis of Report; Access to Defendant by Psychiatrist of His Own Choice; Form of Expert Testimony When Issue of Responsibility Is Tried

(1) If the report filed pursuant to Section 4.05 finds that the defendant at the time of the criminal conduct charged suffered from a mental disease or defect which substantially impaired his capacity to appreciate the criminality [wrongfulness] of his conduct or to conform his conduct to the requirements of law, and the Court, after a hearing if a hearing is requested by the prosecuting attorney or the defendant, is satisfied that such impairment was sufficient to exclude responsibility, the Court on motion of the defendant shall enter judgment of acquittal on the ground of mental disease or defect excluding responsibility.

(2) When, notwithstanding the report filed pursuant to Section 4.05, the defendant wishes to be examined by a qualified psychiatrist or other expert of his own choice, such examiner shall be permitted to have

reasonable access to the defendant for the purposes of such examination.

(3) Upon the trial, the psychiatrists who reported pursuant to Section 4.05 may be called as witnesses by the prosecution, the defendant or the Court. If the issue is being tried before a jury, the jury may be informed that the psychiatrists were designated by the Court or by the Superintendent of the _______ Hospital at the request of the Court, as the case may be. If called by the Court, the witness shall be subject to cross-examination by the prosecution and by the defendant. Both the prosecution and the defendant may summon any other qualified psychiatrist or other expert to testify, but no one who has not examined the defendant shall be competent to testify to an expert opinion with respect to the mental condition or responsibility of the defendant, as distinguished from the validity of the procedure followed by, or the general scientific propositions stated by, another witness.

(4) When a psychiatrist or other expert who has examined the defendant testifies concerning his mental condition, he shall be permitted to make a statement as to the nature of his examination, his diagnosis of the mental condition of the defendant at the time of the commission of the offense charged and his opinion as to the extent, if any, to which the capacity of the defendant to appreciate the criminality [wrongfulness] of his conduct or to conform his conduct to the requirements of law or to have a particular state of mind which is an element of the offense charged was impaired as a result of mental disease or defect at that time. He shall be permitted to make any explanation reasonably serving to clarify his diagnosis and opinion and may be cross-examined as to any matter bearing on his competency or credibility or the validity of his diagnosis or opinion.

### Section 4.08. Legal Effect of Acquittal on the Ground of Mental Disease or Defect Excluding Responsibility; Commitment; Release or Discharge

(1) When a defendant is acquitted on the ground of mental disease or defect excluding responsibility, the Court shall order him to be committed to the custody of the Commissioner of Mental Hygiene [Public Health] to be placed in an appropriate institution for custody, care and treatment.

(2) If the Commissioner of Mental Hygiene [Public Health] is of the view that a person committed to his custody, pursuant to paragraph (1) of this Section, may be discharged or released on condition without danger to himself or to others, he shall make application for the discharge or release of such person in a report to the Court by which such person was committed and shall transmit a copy of such application and report to the prosecuting attorney of the county [parish] from which the defendant was committed. The Court shall thereupon appoint at least two qualified psychiatrists to examine such person and to report within sixty days, or such longer period as the Court determines to be necessary for the purpose, their opinion as to his mental condition. To facilitate such examination and the proceedings thereon, the Court may cause such person to be confined in any institution located near the place where the Court sits, which may hereafter be designated by the

Commissioner of Mental Hygiene [Public Health] as suitable for the temporary detention of irresponsible persons.

(3) If the Court is satisfied by the report filed pursuant to paragraph (2) of this Section and such testimony of the reporting psychiatrists as the Court deems necessary that the committed person may be discharged or released on condition without danger to himself or others, the Court shall order his discharge or his release on such conditions as the Court determines to be necessary. If the Court is not so satisfied, it shall promptly order a hearing to determine whether such person may safely be discharged or released. Any such hearing shall be deemed a civil proceeding and the burden shall be upon the committed person to prove that he may safely be discharged or released. According to the determination of the Court upon the hearing, the committed person shall thereupon be discharged or released on such conditions as the Court determines to be necessary, or shall be recommitted to the custody of the Commissioner of Mental Hygiene [Public Health], subject to discharge or release only in accordance with the procedure prescribed above for a first hearing.

(4) If, within [five] years after the conditional release of a committed person, the court shall determine, after hearing evidence, that the conditions of release have not been fulfilled and that for the safety of such person or for the safety of others his conditional release should be revoked, the Court shall forthwith order him to be recommitted to the Commissioner of Mental Hygiene [Public Health], subject to discharge or release only in accordance with the procedure prescribed above for a first hearing.

(5) A committed person may make application for his discharge or release to the Court by which he was committed, and the procedure to be followed upon such application shall be the same as that prescribed above in the case of an application by the Commissioner of Mental Hygiene [Public Health]. However, no such application by a committed person need be considered until he has been confined for a period of not less than [six months] from the date of the order of commitment, and if the determination of the Court be adverse to the application, such person shall not be permitted to file a further application until [one year] has elapsed from the date of any preceding hearing on an application for his release or discharge.

### Section 4.09. Statements for Purposes of Examination or Treatment Inadmissible Except on Issue of Mental Condition

A statement made by a person subjected to psychiatric examination or treatment pursuant to Sections 4.05, 4.06 or 4.08 for the purposes of such examination or treatment shall not be admissible in evidence against him in any criminal proceeding on any issue other than that of his mental condition but it shall be admissible upon that issue, whether or not it would otherwise be deemed a privileged communication [, unless such statement constitutes an admission of guilt of the crime charged].

### Section 4.10. Immaturity Excluding Criminal Conviction; Transfer of Proceedings to Juvenile Court

(1) A person shall not be tried for or convicted of an offense if:

(a) at the time of the conduct charged to constitute the offense he was less than sixteen years of age [, in which case the Juvenile Court shall have exclusive jurisdiction]; or

(b) at the time of the conduct charged to constitute the offense he was sixteen or seventeen years of age, unless:

(i) the Juvenile Court has no jurisdiction over him, or,

(ii) the Juvenile Court has entered an order waiving jurisdiction and consenting to the institution of criminal proceedings against him.

(2) No court shall have jurisdiction to try or convict a person of an offense if criminal proceedings against him are barred by Subsection (1) of this Section. When it appears that a person charged with the commission of an offense may be of such an age that criminal proceedings may be barred under Subsection (1) of this Section, the Court shall hold a hearing thereon, and the burden shall be on the prosecution to establish to the satisfaction of the Court that the criminal proceeding is not barred upon such grounds. If the Court determines that the proceeding is barred, custody of the person charged shall be surrendered to the Juvenile Court, and the case, including all papers and processes relating thereto, shall be transferred.

## ARTICLE 5. INCHOATE CRIMES

### Section 5.01. Criminal Attempt

(1) Definition of Attempt. A person is guilty of an attempt to commit a crime if, acting with the kind of culpability otherwise required for commission of the crime, he:

Impossibility

(a) purposely engages in conduct which would constitute the crime if the attendant circumstances were as he believes them to be; or

Last Proximate Act

(b) when causing a particular result is an element of the crime, does or omits to do anything with the purpose of causing or with the belief that it will cause such result without further conduct on his part; or

Residual
Incomplete conduct

(c) purposely does or omits to do anything which, under the circumstances as he believes them to be, is an act or omission constituting a substantial step in a course of conduct planned to culminate in his commission of the crime.

(2) Conduct Which May Be Held Substantial Step Under Subsection (1)(c). Conduct shall not be held to constitute a substantial step under Subsection (1)(c) of this Section unless it is strongly corroborative of the actor's criminal purpose. Without negativing the sufficiency of other conduct, the following, if strongly corroborative of the actor's criminal purpose, shall not be held insufficient as a matter of law:

(a) lying in wait, searching for or following the contemplated victim of the crime;

(b) enticing or seeking to entice the contemplated victim of the crime to go to the place contemplated for its commission;

(c) reconnoitering the place contemplated for the commission of the crime;

(d) unlawful entry of a structure, vehicle or enclosure in which it is contemplated that the crime will be committed;

(e) possession of materials to be employed in the commission of the crime, which are specially designed for such unlawful use or which can serve no lawful purpose of the actor under the circumstances;

(f) possession, collection or fabrication of materials to be employed in the commission of the crime, at or near the place contemplated for its commission, where such possession, collection or fabrication serves no lawful purpose of the actor under the circumstances;

(g) soliciting an innocent agent to engage in conduct constituting an element of the crime.

(3) Conduct Designed to Aid Another in Commission of a Crime. A person who engages in conduct designed to aid another to commit a crime which would establish his complicity under Section 2.06 if the crime were committed by such other person, is guilty of an attempt to commit the crime, although the crime is not committed or attempted by such other person.

(4) Renunciation of Criminal Purpose. When the actor's conduct would otherwise constitute an attempt under Subsection (1)(b) or (1)(c) of this Section, it is an affirmative defense that he abandoned his effort to commit the crime or otherwise prevented its commission, under circumstances manifesting a complete and voluntary renunciation of his criminal purpose. The establishment of such defense does not, however, affect the liability of an accomplice who did not join in such abandonment or prevention.

Within the meaning of this Article, renunciation of criminal purpose is not voluntary if it is motivated, in whole or in part, by circumstances, not present or apparent at the inception of the actor's course of conduct, which increase the probability of detection or apprehension or which make more difficult the accomplishment of the criminal purpose. Renunciation is not complete if it is motivated by a decision to postpone the criminal conduct until a more advantageous time or to transfer the criminal effort to another but similar objective or victim.

### Section 5.02. Criminal Solicitation

(1) Definition of Solicitation. A person is guilty of solicitation to commit a crime if with the purpose of promoting or facilitating its commission he commands, encourages or requests another person to engage in specific conduct which would constitute such crime or an attempt to commit such crime or which would establish his complicity in its commission or attempted commission.

(2) Uncommunicated Solicitation. It is immaterial under Subsection (1) of this Section that the actor fails to communicate with the person he solicits to commit a crime if his conduct was designed to effect such communication.

(3) Renunciation of Criminal Purpose. It is an affirmative defense that the actor, after soliciting another person to commit a crime, persuaded him not to do so or otherwise prevented the commission of the crime, under circumstances manifesting a complete and voluntary renunciation of his criminal purpose.

**Section 5.03. Criminal Conspiracy**

(1) Definition of Conspiracy. A person is guilty of conspiracy with another person or persons to commit a crime if with the purpose of promoting or facilitating its commission he:

(a) agrees with such other person or persons that they or one or more of them will engage in conduct which constitutes such crime or an attempt or solicitation to commit such crime; or

(b) agrees to aid such other person or persons in the planning or commission of such crime or of an attempt or solicitation to commit such crime.

(2) Scope of Conspiratorial Relationship. If a person guilty of conspiracy, as defined by Subsection (1) of this Section, knows that a person with whom he conspires to commit a crime has conspired with another person or persons to commit the same crime, he is guilty of conspiring with such other person or persons, whether or not he knows their identity, to commit such crime.

(3) Conspiracy With Multiple Criminal Objectives. If a person conspires to commit a number of crimes, he is guilty of only one conspiracy so long as such multiple crimes are the object of the same agreement or continuous conspiratorial relationship.

(4) Joinder and Venue in Conspiracy Prosecutions.

(a) Subject to the provisions of paragraph (b) of this Subsection, two or more persons charged with criminal conspiracy may be prosecuted jointly if:

(i) they are charged with conspiring with one another; or

(ii) the conspiracies alleged, whether they have the same or different parties, are so related that they constitute different aspects of a scheme of organized criminal conduct.

(b) In any joint prosecution under paragraph (a) of this Subsection:

(i) no defendant shall be charged with a conspiracy in any county [parish or district] other than one in which he entered into such conspiracy or in which an overt act pursuant to such conspiracy was done by him or by a person with whom he conspired; and

(ii) neither the liability of any defendant nor the admissibility against him of evidence of acts or declarations of another shall be enlarged by such joinder; and

(iii) the Court shall order a severance or take a special verdict as to any defendant who so requests, if it deems it necessary or appropriate to promote the fair determination of his guilt or innocence, and shall take any other proper measures to protect the fairness of the trial.

(5) Overt Act. No person may be convicted of conspiracy to commit a crime, other than a felony of the first or second degree, unless an overt act in pursuance of such conspiracy is alleged and proved to have been done by him or by a person with whom he conspired.

(6) Renunciation of Criminal Purpose. It is an affirmative defense that the actor, after conspiring to commit a crime, thwarted the success of the conspiracy, under circumstances manifesting a complete and voluntary renunciation of his criminal purpose.

(7) Duration of Conspiracy. For purposes of Section 1.06(4):

(a) conspiracy is a continuing course of conduct which terminates when the crime or crimes which are its object are committed or the agreement that they be committed is abandoned by the defendant and by those with whom he conspired; and

(b) such abandonment is presumed if neither the defendant nor anyone with whom he conspired does any overt act in pursuance of the conspiracy during the applicable period of limitation; and

(c) if an individual abandons the agreement, the conspiracy is terminated as to him only if and when he advises those with whom he conspired of his abandonment or he informs the law enforcement authorities of the existence of the conspiracy and of his participation therein.

## Section 5.04. Incapacity, Irresponsibility or Immunity of Party to Solicitation or Conspiracy

(1) Except as provided in Subsection (2) of this Section, it is immaterial to the liability of a person who solicits or conspires with another to commit a crime that:

(a) he or the person whom he solicits or with whom he conspires does not occupy a particular position or have a particular characteristic which is an element of such crime, if he believes that one of them does; or

(b) the person whom he solicits or with whom he conspires is irresponsible or has an immunity to prosecution or conviction for the commission of the crime.

(2) It is a defense to a charge of solicitation or conspiracy to commit a crime that if the criminal object were achieved, the actor would not be guilty of a crime under the law defining the offense or as an accomplice under Section 2.06(5) or 2.06(6)(a) or (b).

## Section 5.05. Grading of Criminal Attempt, Solicitation and Conspiracy; Mitigation in Cases of Lesser Danger; Multiple Convictions Barred

(1) Grading. Except as otherwise provided in this Section, attempt, solicitation and conspiracy are crimes of the same grade and degree as the most serious offense which is attempted or solicited or is an object of

the conspiracy. An attempt, solicitation or conspiracy to commit a [capital crime or a] felony of the first degree is a felony of the second degree.

(2) Mitigation. If the particular conduct charged to constitute a criminal attempt, solicitation or conspiracy is so inherently unlikely to result or culminate in the commission of a crime that neither such conduct nor the actor presents a public danger warranting the grading of such offense under this Section, the Court shall exercise its power under Section 6.12 to enter judgment and impose sentence for a crime of lower grade or degree or, in extreme cases, may dismiss the prosecution.

(3) Multiple Convictions. A person may not be convicted of more than one offense defined by this Article for conduct designed to commit or to culminate in the commission of the same crime.

**Section 5.06. Possessing Instruments of Crime; Weapons**

(1) Criminal Instruments Generally. A person commits a misdemeanor if he possesses any instrument of crime with purpose to employ it criminally. "Instrument of crime" means:

(a) anything specially made or specially adapted for criminal use; or

(b) anything commonly used for criminal purposes and possessed by the actor under circumstances which do not negative unlawful purpose.

(2) Presumption of Criminal Purpose from Possession of Weapon. If a person possesses a firearm or other weapon on or about his person, in a vehicle occupied by him, or otherwise readily available for use, it is presumed that he had the purpose to employ it criminally, unless:

(a) the weapon is possessed in the actor's home or place of business;

(b) the actor is licensed or otherwise authorized by law to possess such weapon; or

(c) the weapon is of a type commonly used in lawful sport.

"Weapon" means anything readily capable of lethal use and possessed under circumstances not manifestly appropriate for lawful uses which it may have; the term includes a firearm which is not loaded or lacks a clip or other component to render it immediately operable, and components which can readily be assembled into a weapon.

(3) Presumptions as to Possession of Criminal Instruments in Automobiles. Where a weapon or other instrument of crime is found in an automobile, it shall be presumed to be in the possession of the occupant if there is but one. If there is more than one occupant, it shall be presumed to be in the possession of all, except under the following circumstances:

(a) where it is found upon the person of one of the occupants;

(b) where the automobile is not a stolen one and the weapon or instrument is found out of view in a glove compartment, car trunk, or other enclosed customary depository, in which case it shall be presumed to be in the possession of the occupant or occupants who own or have authority to operate the automobile;

(c) in the case of a taxicab, a weapon or instrument found in the passengers' portion of the vehicle shall be presumed to be in the possession of all the passengers, if there are any, and, if not, in the possession of the driver.

### Section 5.07. Prohibited Offensive Weapons

A person commits a misdemeanor if, except as authorized by law, he makes, repairs, sells, or otherwise deals in, uses, or possesses any offensive weapon. "Offensive weapon" means any bomb, machine gun, sawed-off shotgun, firearm specially made or specially adapted for concealment or silent discharge, any blackjack, sandbag, metal knuckles, dagger, or other implement for the infliction of serious bodily injury which serves no common lawful purpose. It is a defense under this Section for the defendant to prove by a preponderance of evidence that he possessed or dealt with the weapon solely as a curio or in a dramatic performance, or that he possessed it briefly in consequence of having found it or taken it from an aggressor, or under circumstances similarly negativing any purpose or likelihood that the weapon would be used unlawfully. The presumptions provided in Section 5.06(3) are applicable to prosecutions under this Section.

## ARTICLE 6. AUTHORIZED DISPOSITION OF OFFENDERS[b]

### Section 6.01. Degrees of Felonies

(1) Felonies defined by this Code are classified, for the purpose of sentence, into three degrees, as follows:

(a) felonies of the first degree;

(b) felonies of the second degree;

(c) felonies of the third degree.

A felony is of the first or second degree when it is so designated by the Code. A crime declared to be a felony, without specification of degree, is of the third degree.

(2) Notwithstanding any other provision of law, a felony defined by any statute of this State other than this Code shall constitute for the purpose of sentence a felony of the third degree.

### Section 6.02. Sentence in Accordance With Code; Authorized Dispositions

(1) No person convicted of an offense shall be sentenced otherwise than in accordance with this Article.

[(2) The Court shall sentence a person who has been convicted of murder to death or imprisonment, in accordance with Section 210.6.]

(3) Except as provided in Subsection (2) of this Section and subject to the applicable provisions of the Code, the Court may suspend the

---

[b] Because "the architecture of the 1962 [Model Penal] Code's sentencing provisions no longer fits current realities," ALI, Model Penal Code: Sentencing, Tentative Draft No. 1 xxix (April 9, 2007), the American Law Institute is in the process of rewriting Articles 6 and 7 from scratch to take account of the modern movement to sentencing guidelines. See also ALI, Model Penal Code: Sentencing, Tentative Draft No. 3 (April 24, 2014).—[Footnote by eds.]

imposition of sentence on a person who has been convicted of a crime, may order him to be committed in lieu of sentence, in accordance with Section 6.13, or may sentence him as follows:

(a) to pay a fine authorized by Section 6.03; or

(b) to be placed on probation [, and, in the case of a person convicted of a felony or misdemeanor to imprisonment for a term fixed by the Court not exceeding thirty days to be served as a condition of probation]; or

(c) to imprisonment for a term authorized by Sections 6.05, 6.06, 6.07, 6.08, 6.09, or 7.06; or

(d) to fine and probation or fine and imprisonment, but not to probation and imprisonment [, except as authorized in paragraph (b) of this Subsection].

(4) The Court may suspend the imposition of sentence on a person who has been convicted of a violation or may sentence him to pay a fine authorized by Section 6.03.

(5) This Article does not deprive the Court of any authority conferred by law to decree a forfeiture of property, suspend or cancel a license, remove a person from office, or impose any other civil penalty. Such a judgment or order may be included in the sentence.

**Section 6.03. Fines**

A person who has been convicted of an offense may be sentenced to pay a fine not exceeding:

(1) $10,000, when the conviction is of a felony of the first or second degree;

(2) $5,000, when the conviction is of a felony of the third degree;

(3) $1,000, when the conviction is of a misdemeanor;

(4) $500, when the conviction is of a petty misdemeanor or a violation;

(5) any higher amount equal to double the pecuniary gain derived from the offense by the offender;

(6) any higher amount specifically authorized by statute.

**Section 6.04. Penalties Against Corporations and Unincorporated Associations; Forfeiture of Corporate Charter or Revocation of Certificate Authorizing Foreign Corporation to Do Business in the State**

(1) The Court may suspend the sentence of a corporation or an unincorporated association which has been convicted of an offense or may sentence it to pay a fine authorized by Section 6.03.

(2) (a) The [prosecuting attorney] is authorized to institute civil proceedings in the appropriate court of general jurisdiction to forfeit the charter of a corporation organized under the laws of this State or to revoke the certificate authorizing a foreign corporation to conduct business in this State. The Court may order the charter forfeited or the certificate revoked upon finding (i) that the board of directors or a high managerial agent acting in behalf of the corporation has, in conducting the corporation's affairs, purposely engaged in a persistent course of

criminal conduct and (ii) that for the prevention of future criminal conduct of the same character, the public interest requires the charter of the corporation to be forfeited and the corporation to be dissolved or the certificate to be revoked.

(b) When a corporation is convicted of a crime or a high managerial agent of a corporation, as defined in Section 2.07, is convicted of a crime committed in the conduct of the affairs of the corporation, the Court, in sentencing the corporation or the agent, may direct the [prosecuting attorney] to institute proceedings authorized by paragraph (a) of this Subsection.

(c) The proceedings authorized by paragraph (a) of this Subsection shall be conducted in accordance with the procedures authorized by law for the involuntary dissolution of a corporation or the revocation of the certificate authorizing a foreign corporation to conduct business in this State. Such proceedings shall be deemed additional to any other proceedings authorized by law for the purpose of forfeiting the charter of a corporation or revoking the certificate of a foreign corporation.

### Section 6.05. Young Adult Offenders

(1) Specialized Correctional Treatment. A young adult offender is a person convicted of a crime who, at the time of sentencing, is sixteen but less than twenty-two years of age. A young adult offender who is sentenced to a term of imprisonment which may exceed thirty days [alternatives: (1) ninety days; (2) one year] shall be committed to the custody of the Division of Young Adult Correction of the Department of Correction, and shall receive, as far as practicable, such special and individualized correctional and rehabilitative treatment as may be appropriate to his needs.

(2) Special Term. A young adult offender convicted of a felony may, in lieu of any other sentence of imprisonment authorized by this Article, be sentenced to a special term of imprisonment without a minimum and with a maximum of four years, regardless of the degree of the felony involved, if the Court is of the opinion that such special term is adequate for his correction and rehabilitation and will not jeopardize the protection of the public.

[(3) Removal of Disabilities; Vacation of Conviction.

(a) In sentencing a young adult offender to the special term provided by this Section or to any sentence other than one of imprisonment, the Court may order that so long as he is not convicted of another felony, the judgment shall not constitute a conviction for the purposes of any disqualification or disability imposed by law upon conviction of a crime.

(b) When any young adult offender is unconditionally discharged from probation or parole before the expiration of the maximum term thereof, the Court may enter an order vacating the judgment of conviction.]

[(4) Commitment for Observation. If, after pre-sentence investigation, the Court desires additional information concerning a young adult offender before imposing sentence, it may order that he be committed, for a period not exceeding ninety days, to the custody of the Division of Young Adult Correction of the Department of Correction for observation and study at an appropriate reception or classification center. Such Division of the Department of Correction and the [Young Adult Division of the] Board of Parole shall advise the Court of their findings and recommendations on or before the expiration of such ninety-day period.]

**Section 6.06. Sentence of Imprisonment for Felony; Ordinary Terms**

A person who has been convicted of a felony may be sentenced to imprisonment, as follows:

(1) in the case of a felony of the first degree, for a term the minimum of which shall be fixed by the Court at not less than one year nor more than ten years, and the maximum of which shall be life imprisonment;

(2) in the case of a felony of the second degree, for a term the minimum of which shall be fixed by the Court at not less than one year nor more than three years, and the maximum of which shall be ten years;

(3) in the case of a felony of the third degree, for a term the minimum of which shall be fixed by the Court at not less than one year nor more than two years, and the maximum of which shall be five years.

**Alternate Section 6.06. Sentence of Imprisonment for Felony; Ordinary Terms**

A person who has been convicted of a felony may be sentenced to imprisonment, as follows:

(1) in the case of a felony of the first degree, for a term the minimum of which shall be fixed by the Court at not less than one year nor more than ten years, and the maximum at not more than twenty years or at life imprisonment;

(2) in the case of a felony of the second degree, for a term the minimum of which shall be fixed by the Court at not less than one year nor more than three years, and the maximum at not more than ten years;

(3) in the case of a felony of the third degree, for a term the minimum of which shall be fixed by the Court at not less than one year nor more than two years, and the maximum at not more than five years.

No sentence shall be imposed under this Section of which the minimum is longer than one-half the maximum, or, when the maximum is life imprisonment, longer than ten years.

**Section 6.07. Sentence of Imprisonment for Felony; Extended Terms**

In the cases designated in Section 7.03, a person who has been convicted of a felony may be sentenced to an extended term of imprisonment, as follows:

(1) in the case of a felony of the first degree, for a term the minimum of which shall be fixed by the Court at not less than five years nor more than ten years, and the maximum of which shall be life imprisonment;

(2) in the case of a felony of the second degree, for a term the minimum of which shall be fixed by the Court at not less than one year nor more than five years, and the maximum of which shall be fixed by the Court at not less than ten nor more than twenty years;

(3) in the case of a felony of the third degree, for a term the minimum of which shall be fixed by the Court at not less than one year nor more than three years, and the maximum of which shall be fixed by the Court at not less than five nor more than ten years.

**Section 6.08. Sentence of Imprisonment for Misdemeanors and Petty Misdemeanors; Ordinary Terms**

A person who has been convicted of a misdemeanor or a petty misdemeanor may be sentenced to imprisonment for a definite term which shall be fixed by the Court and shall not exceed one year in the case of a misdemeanor or thirty days in the case of a petty misdemeanor.

**Section 6.09. Sentence of Imprisonment for Misdemeanors and Petty Misdemeanors; Extended Terms**

(1) In the cases designated in Section 7.04, a person who has been convicted of a misdemeanor or a petty misdemeanor may be sentenced to an extended term of imprisonment, as follows:

(a) in the case of a misdemeanor, for a term the minimum of which shall be fixed by the Court at not more than one year and the maximum of which shall be three years;

(b) in the case of a petty misdemeanor, for a term the minimum of which shall be fixed by the Court at not more than six months and the maximum of which shall be two years.

(2) No such sentence for an extended term shall be imposed unless:

(a) the Director of Correction has certified that there is an institution in the Department of Correction, or in a county, city [or other appropriate political subdivision of the State] which is appropriate for the detention and correctional treatment of such misdemeanants or petty misdemeanants, and that such institution is available to receive such commitments; and

(b) the [Board of Parole] [Parole Administrator] has certified that the Board of Parole is able to visit such institution and to assume responsibility for the release of such prisoners on parole and for their parole supervision.

**Section 6.10. First Release of All Offenders on Parole; Sentence of Imprisonment Includes Separate Parole Term; Length of Parole Term; Length of Recommitment and Reparole After Revocation of Parole; Final Unconditional Release**

(1) First Release of All Offenders on Parole. An offender sentenced to an indefinite term of imprisonment in excess of one year under Section 6.05, 6.06, 6.07, 6.09 or 7.06 shall be released conditionally on parole at or before the expiration of the maximum of such term, in accordance with Article 305.

(2) Sentence of Imprisonment Includes Separate Parole Term; Length of Parole Term. A sentence to an indefinite term of imprisonment in excess of one year under Section 6.05, 6.06, 6.07, 6.09 or 7.06 includes as a separate portion of the sentence a term of parole or of recommitment for violation of the conditions of parole which governs the duration of parole or recommitment after the offender's first conditional release on parole. The minimum of such term is one year and

the maximum is five years, unless the sentence was imposed under Section 6.05(2) or Section 6.09, in which case the maximum is two years.

(3) Length of Recommitment and Reparole After Revocation of Parole. If an offender is recommitted upon revocation of his parole, the term of further imprisonment upon such recommitment and of any subsequent reparole or recommitment under the same sentence shall be fixed by the Board of Parole but shall not exceed in aggregate length the unserved balance of the maximum parole term provided by Subsection (2) of this Section.

(4) Final Unconditional Release. When the maximum of his parole term has expired or he has been sooner discharged from parole under Section 305.12, an offender shall be deemed to have served his sentence and shall be released unconditionally.

### Section 6.11. Place of Imprisonment

(1) When a person is sentenced to imprisonment for an indefinite term with a maximum in excess of one year, the Court shall commit him to the custody of the Department of Correction [or other single department or agency] for the term of his sentence and until released in accordance with law.

(2) When a person is sentenced to imprisonment for a definite term, the Court shall designate the institution or agency to which he is committed for the term of his sentence and until released in accordance with law.

### Section 6.12. Reduction of Conviction by Court to Lesser Degree of Felony or to Misdemeanor

If, when a person has been convicted of a felony, the Court, having regard to the nature and circumstances of the crime and to the history and character of the defendant, is of the view that it would be unduly harsh to sentence the offender in accordance with the Code, the Court may enter judgment of conviction for a lesser degree of felony or for a misdemeanor and impose sentence accordingly.

### Section 6.13. Civil Commitment in Lieu of Prosecution or of Sentence

(1) When a person prosecuted for a [felony of the third degree,] misdemeanor or petty misdemeanor is a chronic alcoholic, narcotic addict [or prostitute] or person suffering from mental abnormality and the Court is authorized by law to order the civil commitment of such person to a hospital or other institution for medical, psychiatric or other rehabilitative treatment, the Court may order such commitment and dismiss the prosecution. The order of commitment may be made after conviction, in which event the Court may set aside the verdict or judgment of conviction and dismiss the prosecution.

(2) The Court shall not make an order under Subsection (1) of this Section unless it is of the view that it will substantially further the rehabilitation of the defendant and will not jeopardize the protection of the public.

## ARTICLE 7. AUTHORITY OF COURT IN SENTENCING[c]

### Section 7.01. Criteria for Withholding Sentence of Imprisonment and for Placing Defendant on Probation

(1) The Court shall deal with a person who has been convicted of a crime without imposing sentence of imprisonment unless, having regard to the nature and circumstances of the crime and the history, character and condition of the defendant, it is of the opinion that his imprisonment is necessary for protection of the public because:

(a) there is undue risk that during the period of a suspended sentence or probation the defendant will commit another crime; or

(b) the defendant is in need of correctional treatment that can be provided most effectively by his commitment to an institution; or

(c) a lesser sentence will depreciate the seriousness of the defendant's crime.

(2) The following grounds, while not controlling the discretion of the Court, shall be accorded weight in favor of withholding sentence of imprisonment:

(a) the defendant's criminal conduct neither caused nor threatened serious harm;

(b) the defendant did not contemplate that his criminal conduct would cause or threaten serious harm;

(c) the defendant acted under a strong provocation;

(d) there were substantial grounds tending to excuse or justify the defendant's criminal conduct, though failing to establish a defense;

(e) the victim of the defendant's criminal conduct induced or facilitated its commission;

(f) the defendant has compensated or will compensate the victim of his criminal conduct for the damage or injury that he sustained;

(g) the defendant has no history of prior delinquency or criminal activity or has led a law-abiding life for a substantial period of time before the commission of the present crime;

(h) the defendant's criminal conduct was the result of circumstances unlikely to recur;

(i) the character and attitudes of the defendant indicate that he is unlikely to commit another crime;

(j) the defendant is particularly likely to respond affirmatively to probationary treatment;

(k) the imprisonment of the defendant would entail excessive hardship to himself or his dependents.

(3) When a person who has been convicted of a crime is not sentenced to imprisonment, the Court shall place him on probation if he is

---

[c] See footnote b to Article 6, supra.—[Footnote by eds.]

in need of the supervision, guidance, assistance or direction that the probation service can provide.

### Section 7.02. Criteria for Imposing Fines

(1) The Court shall not sentence a defendant only to pay a fine, when any other disposition is authorized by law, unless having regard to the nature and circumstances of the crime and to the history and character of the defendant, it is of the opinion that the fine alone suffices for protection of the public.

(2) The Court shall not sentence a defendant to pay a fine in addition to a sentence of imprisonment or probation unless:

(a) the defendant has derived a pecuniary gain from the crime; or

(b) the Court is of opinion that a fine is specially adapted to deterrence of the crime involved or to the correction of the offender.

(3) The Court shall not sentence a defendant to pay a fine unless:

(a) the defendant is or will be able to pay the fine; and

(b) the fine will not prevent the defendant from making restitution or reparation to the victim of the crime.

(4) In determining the amount and method of payment of a fine, the Court shall take into account the financial resources of the defendant and the nature of the burden that its payment will impose.

### Section 7.03. Criteria for Sentence of Extended Term of Imprisonment; Felonies

The Court may sentence a person who has been convicted of a felony to an extended term of imprisonment if it finds one or more of the grounds specified in this Section. The finding of the Court shall be incorporated in the record.

(1) The defendant is a persistent offender whose commitment for an extended term is necessary for protection of the public.

The Court shall not make such a finding unless the defendant is over twenty-one years of age and has previously been convicted of two felonies or of one felony and two misdemeanors, committed at different times when he was over [insert Juvenile Court age] years of age.

(2) The defendant is a professional criminal whose commitment for an extended term is necessary for protection of the public.

The Court shall not make such a finding unless the defendant is over twenty-one years of age and:

(a) the circumstances of the crime show that the defendant has knowingly devoted himself to criminal activity as a major source of livelihood; or

(b) the defendant has substantial income or resources not explained to be derived from a source other than criminal activity.

(3) The defendant is a dangerous, mentally abnormal person whose commitment for an extended term is necessary for protection of the public.

The Court shall not make such a finding unless the defendant has been subjected to a psychiatric examination resulting in the conclusions that his mental condition is gravely abnormal; that his criminal conduct has been characterized by a pattern of repetitive or compulsive behavior or by persistent aggressive behavior with heedless indifference to consequences; and that such condition makes him a serious danger to others.

(4) The defendant is a multiple offender whose criminality was so extensive that a sentence of imprisonment for an extended term is warranted.

The Court shall not make such a finding unless:

(a) the defendant is being sentenced for two or more felonies, or is already under sentence of imprisonment for felony, and the sentences of imprisonment involved will run concurrently under Section 7.06; or

(b) the defendant admits in open court the commission of one or more other felonies and asks that they be taken into account when he is sentenced; and

(c) the longest sentences of imprisonment authorized for each of the defendant's crimes, including admitted crimes taken into account, if made to run consecutively would exceed in length the minimum and maximum of the extended term imposed.

### Section 7.04. Criteria for Sentence of Extended Term of Imprisonment; Misdemeanors and Petty Misdemeanors

The Court may sentence a person who has been convicted of a misdemeanor or petty misdemeanor to an extended term of imprisonment if it finds one or more of the grounds specified in this Section. The finding of the Court shall be incorporated in the record.

(1) The defendant is a persistent offender whose commitment for an extended term is necessary for protection of the public.

The Court shall not make such a finding unless the defendant has previously been convicted of two crimes, committed at different times when he was over [insert Juvenile Court age] years of age.

(2) The defendant is a professional criminal whose commitment for an extended term is necessary for protection of the public.

The Court shall not make such a finding unless:

(a) the circumstances of the crime show that the defendant has knowingly devoted himself to criminal activity as a major source of livelihood; or

(b) the defendant has substantial income or resources not explained to be derived from a source other than criminal activity.

(3) The defendant is a chronic alcoholic, narcotic addict, prostitute or person of abnormal mental condition who requires rehabilitative treatment for a substantial period of time.

The Court shall not make such a finding unless, with respect to the particular category to which the defendant belongs, the Director of Correction has certified that there is a specialized institution or facility which is satisfactory for the rehabilitative treatment of such persons and which otherwise meets the requirements of Section 6.09, Subsection (2).

(4) The defendant is a multiple offender whose criminality was so extensive that a sentence of imprisonment for an extended term is warranted.

The Court shall not make such a finding unless:

(a) the defendant is being sentenced for a number of misdemeanors or petty misdemeanors or is already under sentence of imprisonment for crime of such grades, or admits in open court the commission of one or more such crimes and asks that they be taken into account when he is sentenced; and

(b) maximum fixed sentences of imprisonment for each of the defendant's crimes, including admitted crimes taken into account, if made to run consecutively, would exceed in length the maximum period of the extended term imposed.

**Section 7.05. Former Conviction in Another Jurisdiction; Definition and Proof of Conviction; Sentence Taking into Account Admitted Crimes Bars Subsequent Conviction for Such Crimes**

(1) For purposes of paragraph (1) of Section 7.03 or 7.04, a conviction of the commission of a crime in another jurisdiction shall constitute a previous conviction. Such conviction shall be deemed to have been of a felony if sentence of death or of imprisonment in excess of one year was authorized under the law of such other jurisdiction, of a misdemeanor if sentence of imprisonment in excess of thirty days but not in excess of a year was authorized and of a petty misdemeanor if sentence of imprisonment for not more than thirty days was authorized.

(2) An adjudication by a court of competent jurisdiction that the defendant committed a crime constitutes a conviction for purposes of Sections 7.03 to 7.05 inclusive, although sentence or the execution thereof was suspended, provided that the time to appeal has expired and that the defendant was not pardoned on the ground of innocence.

(3) Prior conviction may be proved by any evidence, including fingerprint records made in connection with arrest, conviction or imprisonment, that reasonably satisfies the Court that the defendant was convicted.

(4) When the defendant has asked that other crimes admitted in open court be taken into account when he is sentenced and the Court has not rejected such request, the sentence shall bar the prosecution or conviction of the defendant in this State for any such admitted crime.

**Section 7.06. Multiple Sentences; Concurrent and Consecutive Terms**

(1) Sentences of Imprisonment for More Than One Crime. When multiple sentences of imprisonment are imposed on a defendant for more than one crime, including a crime for which a previous suspended sentence or sentence of probation has been revoked, such multiple sentences shall run concurrently or consecutively as the Court determines at the time of sentence, except that:

(a) a definite and an indefinite term shall run concurrently and both sentences shall be satisfied by service of the indefinite term; and

(b) the aggregate of consecutive definite terms shall not exceed one year; and

(c) the aggregate of consecutive indefinite terms shall not exceed in minimum or maximum length the longest extended term authorized for the highest grade and degree of crime for which any of the sentences was imposed; and

(d) not more than one sentence for an extended term shall be imposed.

(2) Sentences of Imprisonment Imposed at Different Times. When a defendant who has previously been sentenced to imprisonment is subsequently sentenced to another term for a crime committed prior to the former sentence, other than a crime committed while in custody:

(a) the multiple sentences imposed shall so far as possible conform to Subsection (1) of this Section; and

(b) whether the Court determines that the terms shall run concurrently or consecutively, the defendant shall be credited with time served in imprisonment on the prior sentence in determining the permissible aggregate length of the term or terms remaining to be served; and

(c) when a new sentence is imposed on a prisoner who is on parole, the balance of the parole term on the former sentence shall be deemed to run during the period of the new imprisonment.

(3) Sentence of Imprisonment for Crime Committed While on Parole. When a defendant is sentenced to imprisonment for a crime committed while on parole in this State, such term of imprisonment and any period of reimprisonment that the Board of Parole may require the defendant to serve upon the revocation of his parole shall run concurrently, unless the Court orders them to run consecutively.

(4) Multiple Sentences of Imprisonment in Other Cases. Except as otherwise provided in this Section, multiple terms of imprisonment shall run concurrently or consecutively as the Court determines when the second or subsequent sentence is imposed.

(5) Calculation of Concurrent and Consecutive Terms of Imprisonment.

(a) When indefinite terms run concurrently, the shorter minimum terms merge in and are satisfied by serving the longest minimum term and the shorter maximum terms merge in and are satisfied by discharge of the longest maximum term.

(b) When indefinite terms run consecutively, the minimum terms are added to arrive at an aggregate minimum to be served equal to the sum of all minimum terms and the maximum terms are added to arrive at an aggregate maximum equal to the sum of all maximum terms.

(c) When a definite and an indefinite term run consecutively, the period of the definite term is added to both the minimum and maximum of the indefinite term and both sentences are satisfied by serving the indefinite term.

(6) Suspension of Sentence or Probation and Imprisonment; Multiple Terms of Suspension and Probation. When a defendant is

sentenced for more than one offense or a defendant already under sentence is sentenced for another offense committed prior to the former sentence:

(a) the Court shall not sentence to probation a defendant who is under sentence of imprisonment [with more than thirty days to run] or impose a sentence of probation and a sentence of imprisonment [, except as authorized by Section 6.02(3)(b)]; and

(b) multiple periods of suspension or probation shall run concurrently from the date of the first such disposition; and

(c) when a sentence of imprisonment is imposed for an indefinite term, the service of such sentence shall satisfy a suspended sentence on another count or a prior suspended sentence or sentence to probation; and

(d) when a sentence of imprisonment is imposed for a definite term, the period of a suspended sentence on another count or a prior suspended sentence or sentence to probation shall run during the period of such imprisonment.

(7) Offense Committed While Under Suspension of Sentence or Probation. When a defendant is convicted of an offense committed while under suspension of sentence or on probation and such suspension or probation is not revoked:

(a) if the defendant is sentenced to imprisonment for an indefinite term, the service of such sentence shall satisfy the prior suspended sentence or sentence to probation; and

(b) if the defendant is sentenced to imprisonment for a definite term, the period of the suspension or probation shall not run during the period of such imprisonment; and

(c) if sentence is suspended or the defendant is sentenced to probation, the period of such suspension or probation shall run concurrently with or consecutively to the remainder of the prior periods, as the Court determines at the time of sentence.

**Section 7.07. Procedure on Sentence; Pre-sentence Investigation and Report; Remand for Psychiatric Examination; Transmission of Records to Department of Correction**

(1) The Court shall not impose sentence without first ordering a pre-sentence investigation of the defendant and according due consideration to a written report of such investigation where:

(a) the defendant has been convicted of a felony; or

(b) the defendant is less than twenty-two years of age and has been convicted of a crime; or

(c) the defendant will be [placed on probation or] sentenced to imprisonment for an extended term.

(2) The Court may order a pre-sentence investigation in any other case.

(3) The pre-sentence investigation shall include an analysis of the circumstances attending the commission of the crime, the defendant's history of delinquency or criminality, physical and mental condition, family situation and background, economic status, education,

occupation and personal habits and any other matters that the probation officer deems relevant or the Court directs to be included.

(4) Before imposing sentence, the Court may order the defendant to submit to psychiatric observation and examination for a period of not exceeding sixty days or such longer period as the Court determines to be necessary for the purpose. The defendant may be remanded for this purpose to any available clinic or mental hospital or the Court may appoint a qualified psychiatrist to make the examination. The report of the examination shall be submitted to the Court.

(5) Before imposing sentence, the Court shall advise the defendant or his counsel of the factual contents and the conclusions of any pre-sentence investigation or psychiatric examination and afford fair opportunity, if the defendant so requests, to controvert them. The sources of confidential information need not, however, be disclosed.

(6) The Court shall not impose a sentence of imprisonment for an extended term unless the ground therefor has been established at a hearing after the conviction of the defendant and on written notice to him of the ground proposed. Subject to the limitation of Subsection (5) of this Section, the defendant shall have the right to hear and controvert the evidence against him and to offer evidence upon the issue.

(7) If the defendant is sentenced to imprisonment, a copy of the report of any pre-sentence investigation or psychiatric examination shall be transmitted forthwith to the Department of Correction [or other state department or agency] or, when the defendant is committed to the custody of a specific institution, to such institution.

## Section 7.08. Commitment for Observation; Sentence of Imprisonment for Felony Deemed Tentative for Period of One Year; Re-sentence on Petition of Commissioner of Correction

(1) If, after pre-sentence investigation, the Court desires additional information concerning an offender convicted of a felony or misdemeanor before imposing sentence, it may order that he be committed, for a period not exceeding ninety days, to the custody of the Department of Correction, or, in the case of a young adult offender, to the custody of the Division of Young Adult Correction, for observation and study at an appropriate reception or classification center. The Department and the Board of Parole, or the Young Adult Divisions thereof, shall advise the Court of their findings and recommendations on or before the expiration of such ninety-day period. If the offender is thereafter sentenced to imprisonment, the period of such commitment for observation shall be deducted from the maximum term and from the minimum, if any, of such sentence.

(2) When a person has been sentenced to imprisonment upon conviction of a felony, whether for an ordinary or extended term, the sentence shall be deemed tentative, to the extent provided in this Section, for the period of one year following the date when the offender is received in custody by the Department of Correction [or other state department or agency].

(3) If, as a result of the examination and classification by the Department of Correction [or other state department or agency] of

a person under sentence of imprisonment upon conviction of a felony, the Commissioner of Correction [or other department head] is satisfied that the sentence of the Court may have been based upon a misapprehension as to the history, character or physical or mental condition of the offender, the Commissioner, during the period when the offender's sentence is deemed tentative under Subsection (2) of this Section shall file in the sentencing Court a petition to re-sentence the offender. The petition shall set forth the information as to the offender that is deemed to warrant his re-sentence and may include a recommendation as to the sentence to be imposed.

(4) The Court may dismiss a petition filed under Subsection (3) of this Section without a hearing if it deems the information set forth insufficient to warrant reconsideration of the sentence. If the Court is of the view that the petition warrants such reconsideration, a copy of the petition shall be served on the offender, who shall have the right to be heard on the issue and to be represented by counsel.

(5) When the Court grants a petition filed under Subsection (3) of this Section, it shall re-sentence the offender and may impose any sentence that might have been imposed originally for the felony of which the defendant was convicted. The period of his imprisonment prior to re-sentence and any reduction for good behavior to which he is entitled shall be applied in satisfaction of the final sentence.

(6) For all purposes other than this Section, a sentence of imprisonment has the same finality when it is imposed that it would have if this Section were not in force.

(7) Nothing in this Section shall alter the remedies provided by law for vacating or correcting an illegal sentence.

**Section 7.09. Credit for Time of Detention Prior to Sentence; Credit for Imprisonment Under Earlier Sentence for the Same Crime**

(1) When a defendant who is sentenced to imprisonment has previously been detained in any state or local correctional or other institution following his [conviction of] [arrest for] the crime for which such sentence is imposed, such period of detention following his [conviction] [arrest] shall be deducted from the maximum term, and from the minimum, if any, of such sentence. The officer having custody of the defendant shall furnish a certificate to the Court at the time of sentence, showing the length of such detention of the defendant prior to sentence in any state or local correctional or other institution, and the certificate shall be annexed to the official records of the defendant's commitment.

(2) When a judgment of conviction is vacated and a new sentence is thereafter imposed upon the defendant for the same crime, the period of detention and imprisonment theretofore served shall be deducted from the maximum term, and from the minimum, if any, of the new sentence. The officer having custody of the defendant shall furnish a certificate to the Court at the time of sentence, showing the period of imprisonment served under the original sentence, and the certificate shall be annexed to the official records of the defendant's new commitment.

# PART II. DEFINITION OF SPECIFIC CRIMES

## OFFENSES AGAINST EXISTENCE OR STABILITY OF THE STATE

[Reporter's note: This category of offenses, including treason, sedition, espionage and like crimes, was excluded from the scope of the Model Penal Code. These offenses are peculiarly the concern of the federal government. The Constitution itself defines treason: "Treason against the United States shall consist only in levying War against them, or in adhering to their Enemies, giving them Aid and Comfort. . . . " Article III, Section 3; cf. Pennsylvania v. Nelson, 350 U.S. 497 (1956)(supersession of state sedition legislation by federal law). Also, the definition of offenses against the stability of the state is inevitably affected by special political considerations. These factors militated against the use of the Institute's limited resources to attempt to draft "model" provisions in this area. However we provide at this point in the Plan of the Model Penal Code for an Article 200, where definitions of offenses against the existence or stability of the state may be incorporated.]

## OFFENSES INVOLVING DANGER TO THE PERSON

## ARTICLE 210. CRIMINAL HOMICIDE

### Section 210.0. Definitions

In Articles 210–213, unless a different meaning plainly is required:

(1) "human being" means a person who has been born and is alive;

(2) "bodily injury" means physical pain, illness or any impairment of physical condition;

(3) "serious bodily injury" means bodily injury which creates a substantial risk of death or which causes serious, permanent disfigurement, or protracted loss or impairment of the function of any bodily member or organ;

(4) "deadly weapon" means any firearm, or other weapon, device, instrument, material or substance, whether animate or inanimate, which in the manner it is used or is intended to be used is known to be capable of producing death or serious bodily injury.

### Section 210.1. Criminal Homicide

(1) A person is guilty of criminal homicide if he purposely, knowingly, recklessly or negligently causes the death of another human being.

(2) Criminal homicide is murder, manslaughter or negligent homicide.

### Section 210.2. Murder

(1) Except as provided in Section 210.3(1)(b), criminal homicide constitutes murder when:

(a) it is committed purposely or knowingly; or

(b) it is committed recklessly under circumstances manifesting extreme indifference to the value of human life. Such recklessness and indifference are presumed if the actor is engaged or is an accomplice in the commission of, or an attempt to commit, or flight after committing or attempting to commit robbery, rape or deviate sexual intercourse by force or threat of force, arson, burglary, kidnapping or felonious escape.

(2) Murder is a felony of the first degree [but a person convicted of murder may be sentenced to death, as provided in Section 210.6 [d]].

### Section 210.3. Manslaughter

(1) Criminal homicide constitutes manslaughter when:

(a) it is committed recklessly; or

(b) a homicide which would otherwise be murder is committed under the influence of extreme mental or emotional disturbance for which there is reasonable explanation or excuse. The reasonableness of such explanation or excuse shall be determined from the viewpoint of a person in the actor's situation under the circumstances as he believes them to be.

(2) Manslaughter is a felony of the second degree.

### Section 210.4. Negligent Homicide

(1) Criminal homicide constitutes negligent homicide when it is committed negligently.

(2) Negligent homicide is a felony of the third degree.

### Section 210.5. Causing or Aiding Suicide

(1) Causing Suicide as Criminal Homicide. A person may be convicted of criminal homicide for causing another to commit suicide only if he purposely causes such suicide by force, duress or deception.

(2) Aiding or Soliciting Suicide as an Independent Offense. A person who purposely aids or solicits another to commit suicide is guilty of a felony of the second degree if his conduct causes such suicide or an attempted suicide, and otherwise of a misdemeanor.

---

[d] In the original formulation of the Model Penal Code, the American Law Institute took no position on whether capital punishment should be authorized. The bracketed portion of this provision, as well as § 210.6, were included to address the procedures for imposition of the death penalty for jurisdictions that wished to retain it. As explained in the footnote to § 210.6, the Institute has since changed its position on this point.—[Footnote by eds.]

## [Section 210.6. Sentence of Death for Murder; Further Proceedings to Determine Sentence[e]

(1) Death Sentence Excluded. When a defendant is found guilty of murder, the Court shall impose sentence for a felony of the first degree if it is satisfied that:

(a) none of the aggravating circumstances enumerated in Subsection (3) of this Section was established by the evidence at the trial or will be established if further proceedings are initiated under Subsection (2) of this Section; or

(b) substantial mitigating circumstances, established by the evidence at the trial, call for leniency; or

(c) the defendant, with the consent of the prosecuting attorney and the approval of the Court, pleaded guilty to murder as a felony of the first degree; or

(d) the defendant was under 18 years of age at the time of the commission of the crime; or

(e) the defendant's physical or mental condition calls for leniency; or

(f) although the evidence suffices to sustain the verdict, it does not foreclose all doubt respecting the defendant's guilt.

(2) Determination by Court or by Court and Jury. Unless the Court imposes sentence under Subsection (1) of this Section, it shall conduct a separate proceeding to determine whether the defendant should be sentenced for a felony of the first degree or sentenced to death. The proceeding shall be conducted before the Court alone if the defendant was convicted by a Court sitting without a jury or upon his plea of guilty or if the prosecuting attorney and the defendant waive a jury with respect to sentence. In other cases it shall be conducted before the Court sitting with the jury which determined the defendant's guilt or, if the Court for good cause shown discharges that jury, with a new jury empaneled for the purpose.

In the proceeding, evidence may be presented as to any matter that the Court deems relevant to sentence, including but not limited to the nature and circumstances of the crime, the defendant's character, background, history, mental and physical condition and any of the

---

[e] The American Law Institute has withdrawn this provision of its Model Code. Its official announcement—available at http://www.ali.org/_news/10232009.htm—follows:

On October 23, 2009, the ALI Council voted overwhelmingly, with some abstentions, to accept the resolution of the capital punishment matter as approved by the Institute's membership at the 2009 Annual Meeting in May. The resolution adopted at the Annual Meeting and now accepted by the Council reads as follows:

For reasons stated in Part V of the Council's report to the membership, the Institute withdraws Section 210.6 of the Model Penal Code in light of the current intractable institutional and structural obstacles to ensuring a minimally adequate system for administering capital punishment.

The report to the membership referenced in this resolution is dated April 15, 2009, and is accessible at http://www.ali.org/doc/Capital Punishment_web.pdf.

Having achieved the consensus of the membership at the Annual Meeting and now of the Council, this resolution is the official position of the Institute. Efforts will be made to communicate this position wherever the Model Penal Code is published or otherwise available and to the public generally.—[Footnote by eds.]

aggravating or mitigating circumstances enumerated in Subsections (3) and (4) of this Section. Any such evidence, not legally privileged, which the Court deems to have probative force, may be received, regardless of its admissibility under the exclusionary rules of evidence, provided that the defendant's counsel is accorded a fair opportunity to rebut such evidence. The prosecuting attorney and the defendant or his counsel shall be permitted to present argument for or against sentence of death.

The determination whether sentence of death shall be imposed shall be in the discretion of the Court, except that when the proceeding is conducted before the Court sitting with a jury, the Court shall not impose sentence of death unless it submits to the jury the issue whether the defendant should be sentenced to death or to imprisonment and the jury returns a verdict that the sentence should be death. If the jury is unable to reach a unanimous verdict, the Court shall dismiss the jury and impose sentence for a felony of the first degree.

The Court, in exercising its discretion as to sentence, and the jury, in determining upon its verdict, shall take into account the aggravating and mitigating circumstances enumerated in Subsections (3) and (4) and any other facts that it deems relevant, but it shall not impose or recommend sentence of death unless it finds one of the aggravating circumstances enumerated in Subsection (3) and further finds that there are no mitigating circumstances sufficiently substantial to call for leniency. When the issue is submitted to the jury, the Court shall so instruct and also shall inform the jury of the nature of the sentence of imprisonment that may be imposed, including its implication with respect to possible release upon parole, if the jury verdict is against sentence of death.

**Alternative formulation of Subsection (2):**

(2) Determination by Court. Unless the Court imposes sentence under Subsection (1) of this Section, it shall conduct a separate proceeding to determine whether the defendant should be sentenced for a felony of the first degree or sentenced to death. In the proceeding, the Court, in accordance with Section 7.07, shall consider the report of the pre-sentence investigation and, if a psychiatric examination has been ordered, the report of such examination. In addition, evidence may be presented as to any matter that the Court deems relevant to sentence, including but not limited to the nature and circumstances of the crime, the defendant's character, background, history, mental and physical condition and any of the aggravating or mitigating circumstances enumerated in Subsections (3) and (4) of this Section. Any such evidence, not legally privileged, which the Court deems to have probative force, may be received, regardless of its admissibility under the exclusionary rules of evidence, provided that the defendant's counsel is accorded a fair opportunity to rebut such evidence. The prosecuting attorney and the defendant or his counsel shall be permitted to present argument for or against sentence of death.

The determination whether sentence of death shall be imposed shall be in the discretion of the Court. In exercising such discretion, the Court shall take into account the aggravating and mitigating circumstances enumerated in Subsections (3) and (4) and any other facts that it deems relevant but shall not impose sentence of death unless it finds one of the aggravating circumstances enumerated in Subsection (3) and further finds that there are no mitigating circumstances sufficiently substantial to call for leniency.

(3) Aggravating Circumstances.

(a) The murder was committed by a convict under sentence of imprisonment.

(b) The defendant was previously convicted of another murder or of a felony involving the use or threat of violence to the person.

(c) At the time the murder was committed the defendant also committed another murder.

(d) The defendant knowingly created a great risk of death to many persons.

(e) The murder was committed while the defendant was engaged or was an accomplice in the commission of, or an attempt to commit, or flight after committing or attempting to commit robbery, rape or deviate sexual intercourse by force or threat of force, arson, burglary or kidnapping.

(f) The murder was committed for the purpose of avoiding or preventing a lawful arrest or effecting an escape from lawful custody.

(g) The murder was committed for pecuniary gain.

(h) The murder was especially heinous, atrocious or cruel, manifesting exceptional depravity.

(4) Mitigating Circumstances.

(a) The defendant has no significant history of prior criminal activity.

(b) The murder was committed while the defendant was under the influence of extreme mental or emotional disturbance.

(c) The victim was a participant in the defendant's homicidal conduct or consented to the homicidal act.

(d) The murder was committed under circumstances which the defendant believed to provide a moral justification or extenuation for his conduct.

(e) The defendant was an accomplice in a murder committed by another person and his participation in the homicidal act was relatively minor.

(f) The defendant acted under duress or under the domination of another person.

(g) At the time of the murder, the capacity of the defendant to appreciate the criminality [wrongfulness] of his conduct or to conform his conduct to the requirements of law was impaired as a result of mental disease or defect or intoxication.

(h) The youth of the defendant at the time of the crime.]

## ARTICLE 211. ASSAULT; RECKLESS ENDANGERING; THREATS

### Section 211.0. Definitions

In this Article, the definitions given in Section 210.0 apply unless a different meaning plainly is required.

### Section 211.1. Assault

(1) Simple Assault. A person is guilty of assault if he:

(a) attempts to cause or purposely, knowingly or recklessly causes bodily injury to another; or

(b) negligently causes bodily injury to another with a deadly weapon; or

(c) attempts by physical menace to put another in fear of imminent serious bodily injury.

Simple assault is a misdemeanor unless committed in a fight or scuffle entered into by mutual consent, in which case it is a petty misdemeanor.

(2) Aggravated Assault. A person is guilty of aggravated assault if he:

(a) attempts to cause serious bodily injury to another, or causes such injury purposely, knowingly or recklessly under circumstances manifesting extreme indifference to the value of human life; or

(b) attempts to cause or purposely or knowingly causes bodily injury to another with a deadly weapon.

Aggravated assault under paragraph (a) is a felony of the second degree; aggravated assault under paragraph (b) is a felony of the third degree.

### Section 211.2. Recklessly Endangering Another Person

A person commits a misdemeanor if he recklessly engages in conduct which places or may place another person in danger of death or serious bodily injury. Recklessness and danger shall be presumed where a person knowingly points a firearm at or in the direction of another, whether or not the actor believed the firearm to be loaded.

### Section 211.3. Terroristic Threats

A person is guilty of a felony of the third degree if he threatens to commit any crime of violence with purpose to terrorize another or to cause evacuation of a building, place of assembly, or facility of public transportation, or otherwise to cause serious public inconvenience, or in reckless disregard of the risk of causing such terror or inconvenience.

## ARTICLE 212. KIDNAPPING AND RELATED OFFENSES; COERCION

### Section 212.0. Definitions

In this Article, the definitions given in Section 210.0 apply unless a different meaning plainly is required.

## Section 212.1. Kidnapping

A person is guilty of kidnapping if he unlawfully removes another from his place of residence or business, or a substantial distance from the vicinity where he is found, or if he unlawfully confines another for a substantial period in a place of isolation, with any of the following purposes:

(a) to hold for ransom or reward, or as a shield or hostage; or

(b) to facilitate commission of any felony or flight thereafter; or

(c) to inflict bodily injury on or to terrorize the victim or another; or

(d) to interfere with the performance of any governmental or political function.

Kidnapping is a felony of the first degree unless the actor voluntarily releases the victim alive and in a safe place prior to trial, in which case it is a felony of the second degree. A removal or confinement is unlawful within the meaning of this Section if it is accomplished by force, threat or deception, or, in the case of a person who is under the age of 14 or incompetent, if it is accomplished without the consent of a parent, guardian or other person responsible for general supervision of his welfare.

## Section 212.2. Felonious Restraint

A person commits a felony of the third degree if he knowingly:

(a) restrains another unlawfully in circumstances exposing him to risk of serious bodily injury; or

(b) holds another in a condition of involuntary servitude.

## Section 212.3. False Imprisonment

A person commits a misdemeanor if he knowingly restrains another unlawfully so as to interfere substantially with his liberty.

## Section 212.4. Interference With Custody

(1) Custody of Children. A person commits an offense if he knowingly or recklessly takes or entices any child under the age of 18 from the custody of its parent, guardian or other lawful custodian, when he has no privilege to do so. It is an affirmative defense that:

(a) the actor believed that his action was necessary to preserve the child from danger to its welfare; or

(b) the child, being at the time not less than 14 years old, was taken away at its own instigation without enticement and without purpose to commit a criminal offense with or against the child.

Proof that the child was below the critical age gives rise to a presumption that the actor knew the child's age or acted in reckless disregard thereof. The offense is a misdemeanor unless the actor, not being a parent or person in equivalent relation to the child, acted with knowledge that his conduct would cause serious alarm for the child's safety, or in reckless disregard of a likelihood of causing such alarm, in which case the offense is a felony of the third degree.

(2) Custody of Committed Persons. A person is guilty of a misdemeanor if he knowingly or recklessly takes or entices any committed

person away from lawful custody when he is not privileged to do so. "Committed person" means, in addition to anyone committed under judicial warrant, any orphan, neglected or delinquent child, mentally defective or insane person, or other dependent or incompetent person entrusted to another's custody by or through a recognized social agency or otherwise by authority of law.

**Section 212.5. Criminal Coercion**

(1) Offense Defined. A person is guilty of criminal coercion if, with purpose unlawfully to restrict another's freedom of action to his detriment, he threatens to:

(a) commit any criminal offense; or

(b) accuse anyone of a criminal offense; or

(c) expose any secret tending to subject any person to hatred, contempt or ridicule, or to impair his credit or business repute; or

(d) take or withhold action as an official, or cause an official to take or withhold action.

It is an affirmative defense to prosecution based on paragraphs (b), (c) or (d) that the actor believed the accusation or secret to be true or the proposed official action justified and that his purpose was limited to compelling the other to behave in a way reasonably related to the circumstances which were the subject of the accusation, exposure or proposed official action, as by desisting from further misbehavior, making good a wrong done, refraining from taking any action or responsibility for which the actor believes the other disqualified.

(2) Grading. Criminal coercion is a misdemeanor unless the threat is to commit a felony or the actor's purpose is felonious, in which cases the offense is a felony of the third degree.

## ARTICLE 213. SEXUAL OFFENSES[f]

**Section 213.0. Definitions**

In this Article, unless a different meaning plainly is required:

(1) the definitions given in Section 210.0 apply;

(2) "Sexual intercourse" includes intercourse per os or per anum, with some penetration however slight; emission is not required;

(3) "Deviate sexual intercourse" means sexual intercourse per os or per anum between human beings who are not husband and wife, and any form of sexual intercourse with an animal.

---

[f] The Council of the American Law Institute approved revisiting the provisions in Article 213 in 2012 because "[f]or some time experts have told us that this portion of the MPC needed to be rewritten to fit with contemporary knowledge and values." ALI, Model Penal Code: Sexual Assault and Related Offenses, Discussion Draft ix (April 22, 2013). An initial effort to redraft the substantive offenses contained in Article 213 was presented to the Institute in 2014. See ALI, Model Penal Code: Sexual Assault and Related Offenses, Tentative Draft No. 1 (April 30, 2014). The substantive offenses proposed in the Tentative Draft are discussed where relevant to the topics considered in Chapter IX and are reproduced in full in the Introductory Notes in Section 1 of that Chapter.—[Footnote by eds.]

## Section 213.1. Rape and Related Offenses

(1) Rape. A male who has sexual intercourse with a female not his wife is guilty of rape if:

(a) he compels her to submit by force or by threat of imminent death, serious bodily injury, extreme pain or kidnapping, to be inflicted on anyone; or

(b) he has substantially impaired her power to appraise or control her conduct by administering or employing without her knowledge drugs, intoxicants or other means for the purpose of preventing resistance; or

(c) the female is unconscious; or

(d) the female is less than 10 years old.

Rape is a felony of the second degree unless (i) in the course thereof the actor inflicts serious bodily injury upon anyone, or (ii) the victim was not a voluntary social companion of the actor upon the occasion of the crime and had not previously permitted him sexual liberties, in which cases the offense is a felony of the first degree.

(2) Gross Sexual Imposition. A male who has sexual intercourse with a female not his wife commits a felony of the third degree if:

(a) he compels her to submit by any threat that would prevent resistance by a woman of ordinary resolution; or

(b) he knows that she suffers from a mental disease or defect which renders her incapable of appraising the nature of her conduct; or

(c) he knows that she is unaware that a sexual act is being committed upon her or that she submits because she mistakenly supposes that he is her husband.

## Section 213.2. Deviate Sexual Intercourse by Force or Imposition

(1) By Force or Its Equivalent. A person who engages in deviate sexual intercourse with another person, or who causes another to engage in deviate sexual intercourse, commits a felony of the second degree if:

(a) he compels the other person to participate by force or by threat of imminent death, serious bodily injury, extreme pain or kidnapping, to be inflicted on anyone; or

(b) he has substantially impaired the other person's power to appraise or control his conduct, by administering or employing without the knowledge of the other person drugs, intoxicants or other means for the purpose of preventing resistance; or

(c) the other person is unconscious; or

(d) the other person is less than 10 years old.

(2) By Other Imposition. A person who engages in deviate sexual intercourse with another person, or who causes another to engage in deviate sexual intercourse, commits a felony of the third degree if:

(a) he compels the other person to participate by any threat that would prevent resistance by a person of ordinary resolution; or

(b) he knows that the other person suffers from a mental disease or defect which renders him incapable of appraising the nature of his conduct; or

(c) he knows that the other person submits because he is unaware that a sexual act is being committed upon him.

**Section 213.3. Corruption of Minors and Seduction**

(1) Offense Defined. A male who has sexual intercourse with a female not his wife, or any person who engages in deviate sexual intercourse or causes another to engage in deviate sexual intercourse, is guilty of an offense if:

(a) the other person is less than [16] years old and the actor is at least [four] years older than the other person; or

(b) the other person is less than 21 years old and the actor is his guardian or otherwise responsible for general supervision of his welfare; or

(c) the other person is in custody of law or detained in a hospital or other institution and the actor has supervisory or disciplinary authority over him; or

(d) the other person is a female who is induced to participate by a promise of marriage which the actor does not mean to perform.

(2) Grading. An offense under paragraph (a) of Subsection (1) is a felony of the third degree. Otherwise an offense under this section is a misdemeanor.

**Section 213.4. Sexual Assault**

A person who has sexual contact with another not his spouse, or causes such other to have sexual contact with him, is guilty of sexual assault, a misdemeanor, if:

(1) he knows that the contact is offensive to the other person; or

(2) he knows that the other person suffers from a mental disease or defect which renders him or her incapable of appraising the nature of his or her conduct; or

(3) he knows that the other person is unaware that a sexual act is being committed; or

(4) the other person is less than 10 years old; or

(5) he has substantially impaired the other person's power to appraise or control his or her conduct, by administering or employing without the other's knowledge drugs, intoxicants or other means for the purpose of preventing resistance; or

(6) the other person is less than [16] years old and the actor is at least [four] years older than the other person; or

(7) the other person is less than 21 years old and the actor is his guardian or otherwise responsible for general supervision of his welfare; or

(8) the other person is in custody of law or detained in a hospital or other institution and the actor has supervisory or disciplinary authority over him.

Sexual contact is any touching of the sexual or other intimate parts of the person for the purpose of arousing or gratifying sexual desire.

### Section 213.5. Indecent Exposure

A person commits a misdemeanor if, for the purpose of arousing or gratifying sexual desire of himself or of any person other than his spouse, he exposes his genitals under circumstances in which he knows his conduct is likely to cause affront or alarm.

### Section 213.6. Provisions Generally Applicable to Article 213[g]

(1) Mistake as to Age. Whenever in this Article the criminality of conduct depends on a child's being below the age of 10, it is no defense that the actor did not know the child's age, or reasonably believed the child to be older than 10. When criminality depends on the child's being below a critical age other than 10, it is a defense for the actor to prove by a preponderance of the evidence that he reasonably believed the child to be above the critical age.

(2) Spouse Relationships. Whenever in this Article the definition of an offense excludes conduct with a spouse, the exclusion shall be deemed to extend to persons living as man and wife, regardless of the legal status of their relationship. The exclusion shall be inoperative as respects spouses living apart under a decree of judicial separation. Where the definition of an offense excludes conduct with a spouse or conduct by a woman, this shall not preclude conviction of a spouse or woman as accomplice in a sexual act which he or she causes another person, not within the exclusion, to perform.

(3) Sexually Promiscuous Complainants. It is a defense to prosecution under Section 213.3 and paragraphs (6), (7) and (8) of Section 213.4 for the actor to prove by a preponderance of the evidence that the alleged victim had, prior to the time of the offense charged, engaged promiscuously in sexual relations with others.

(4) Prompt Complaint. No prosecution may be instituted or maintained under this Article unless the alleged offense was brought to the notice of public authority within [3] months of its occurrence or, where the alleged victim was less than [16] years old or otherwise incompetent to make complaint, within [3] months after a parent, guardian or other competent person specially interested in the victim learns of the offense.

(5) Testimony of Complainants. No person shall be convicted of any felony under this Article upon the uncorroborated testimony of the alleged victim. Corroboration may be circumstantial. In any prosecution before a jury for an offense under this Article, the jury shall be

---

[g] This section is eliminated in the proposed revisions of Article 213 in ALI, Model Penal Code: Sexual Assault and Related Offenses, Tentative Draft No. 1 (April 30, 2014). Subsections (3), (4), and (5) are replaced by an elaborate provision on procedural and evidentiary principles applicable to Article 213 that covers topics beyond the scope of these materials. The broad marital exemption recognized at common law is rejected in the new proposals, but the topic of sexual offenses involving spouses and other intimate partners has been reserved for future coverage.

With respect to mistakes as to age covered in § 213.6(1), the proposals adopt a wholly new approach. They reject strict liability and liability based on negligence, and apply the normal mens rea provisions of § 2.02 to such mistakes. The rationale for this recommendation is discussed in the Note on Statutory Rape Under the Model Penal Code in Section 2 of Chapter IX.

instructed to evaluate the testimony of a victim or complaining witness with special care in view of the emotional involvement of the witness and the difficulty of determining the truth with respect to alleged sexual activities carried out in private.

---

## OFFENSES AGAINST PROPERTY

---

## ARTICLE 220. ARSON, CRIMINAL MISCHIEF, AND OTHER PROPERTY DESTRUCTION

### Section 220.1. Arson and Related Offenses

(1) Arson. A person is guilty of arson, a felony of the second degree, if he starts a fire or causes an explosion with the purpose of:

(a) destroying a building or occupied structure of another; or

(b) destroying or damaging any property, whether his own or another's, to collect insurance for such loss. It shall be an affirmative defense to prosecution under this paragraph that the actor's conduct did not recklessly endanger any building or occupied structure of another or place any other person in danger of death or bodily injury.

(2) Reckless Burning or Exploding. A person commits a felony of the third degree if he purposely starts a fire or causes an explosion, whether on his own property or another's, and thereby recklessly:

(a) places another person in danger of death or bodily injury; or

(b) places a building or occupied structure of another in danger of damage or destruction.

(3) Failure to Control or Report Dangerous Fire. A person who knows that a fire is endangering life or a substantial amount of property of another and fails to take reasonable measures to put out or control the fire, when he can do so without substantial risk to himself, or to give a prompt fire alarm, commits a misdemeanor if:

(a) he knows that he is under an official, contractual, or other legal duty to prevent or combat the fire; or

(b) the fire was started, albeit lawfully, by him or with his assent, or on property in his custody or control.

(4) Definitions. "Occupied structure" means any structure, vehicle or place adapted for overnight accommodation of persons, or for carrying on business therein, whether or not a person is actually present. Property is that of another, for the purposes of this section, if anyone other than the actor has a possessory or proprietary interest therein. If a building or structure is divided into separately occupied units, any unit not occupied by the actor is an occupied structure of another.

### Section 220.2. Causing or Risking Catastrophe

(1) Causing Catastrophe. A person who causes a catastrophe by explosion, fire, flood, avalanche, collapse of building, release of poison gas,

radioactive material or other harmful or destructive force or substance, or by any other means of causing potentially widespread injury or damage, commits a felony of the second degree if he does so purposely or knowingly, or a felony of the third degree if he does so recklessly.

(2) Risking Catastrophe. A person is guilty of a misdemeanor if he recklessly creates a risk of catastrophe in the employment of fire, explosives or other dangerous means listed in Subsection (1).

(3) Failure to Prevent Catastrophe. A person who knowingly or recklessly fails to take reasonable measures to prevent or mitigate a catastrophe commits a misdemeanor if:

(a) he knows that he is under an official, contractual or other legal duty to take such measures; or

(b) he did or assented to the act causing or threatening the catastrophe.

### Section 220.3. Criminal Mischief

(1) Offense Defined. A person is guilty of criminal mischief if he:

(a) damages tangible property of another purposely, recklessly, or by negligence in the employment of fire, explosives, or other dangerous means listed in Section 220.2(1); or

(b) purposely or recklessly tampers with tangible property of another so as to endanger person or property; or

(c) purposely or recklessly causes another to suffer pecuniary loss by deception or threat.

(2) Grading. Criminal mischief is a felony of the third degree if the actor purposely causes pecuniary loss in excess of $5,000, or a substantial interruption or impairment of public communication, transportation, supply of water, gas or power, or other public service. It is a misdemeanor if the actor purposely causes pecuniary loss in excess of $100, or a petty misdemeanor if he purposely or recklessly causes pecuniary loss in excess of $25. Otherwise criminal mischief is a violation.

## ARTICLE 221. BURGLARY AND OTHER CRIMINAL INTRUSION

### Section 221.0. Definitions

In this Article, unless a different meaning plainly is required:

(1) "occupied structure" means any structure, vehicle or place adapted for overnight accommodation of persons, or for carrying on business therein, whether or not a person is actually present.

(2) "night" means the period between thirty minutes past sunset and thirty minutes before sunrise.

### Section 221.1. Burglary

(1) Burglary Defined. A person is guilty of burglary if he enters a building or occupied structure, or separately secured or occupied portion thereof, with purpose to commit a crime therein, unless the premises are at the time open to the public or the actor is licensed or privileged to enter. It is an affirmative defense to prosecution for burglary that the building or structure was abandoned.

(2) Grading. Burglary is a felony of the second degree if it is perpetrated in the dwelling of another at night, or if, in the course of committing the offense, the actor:

(a) purposely, knowingly or recklessly inflicts or attempts to inflict bodily injury on anyone; or

(b) is armed with explosives or a deadly weapon.

Otherwise, burglary is a felony of the third degree. An act shall be deemed "in the course of committing" an offense if it occurs in an attempt to commit the offense or in flight after the attempt or commission.

(3) Multiple Convictions. A person may not be convicted both for burglary and for the offense which it was his purpose to commit after the burglarious entry or for an attempt to commit that offense, unless the additional offense constitutes a felony of the first or second degree.

**Section 221.2. Criminal Trespass**

(1) Buildings and Occupied Structures. A person commits an offense if, knowing that he is not licensed or privileged to do so, he enters or surreptitiously remains in any building or occupied structure, or separately secured or occupied portion thereof. An offense under this Subsection is a misdemeanor if it is committed in a dwelling at night. Otherwise it is a petty misdemeanor.

(2) Defiant Trespasser. A person commits an offense if, knowing that he is not licensed or privileged to do so, he enters or remains in any place as to which notice against trespass is given by:

(a) actual communication to the actor; or

(b) posting in a manner prescribed by law or reasonably likely to come to the attention of intruders; or

(c) fencing or other enclosure manifestly designed to exclude intruders.

An offense under this Subsection constitutes a petty misdemeanor if the offender defies an order to leave personally communicated to him by the owner of the premises or other authorized person. Otherwise it is a violation.

(3) Defenses. It is an affirmative defense to prosecution under this Section that:

(a) a building or occupied structure involved in an offense under Subsection (1) was abandoned; or

(b) the premises were at the time open to members of the public and the actor complied with all lawful conditions imposed on access to or remaining in the premises; or

(c) the actor reasonably believed that the owner of the premises, or other person empowered to license access thereto, would have licensed him to enter or remain.

## ARTICLE 222. ROBBERY

### Section 222.1. Robbery

(1) Robbery Defined. A person is guilty of robbery if, in the course of committing a theft, he:

(a) inflicts serious bodily injury upon another; or

(b) threatens another with or purposely puts him in fear of immediate serious bodily injury; or

(c) commits or threatens immediately to commit any felony of the first or second degree.

An act shall be deemed "in the course of committing a theft" if it occurs in an attempt to commit theft or in flight after the attempt or commission.

(2) Grading. Robbery is a felony of the second degree, except that it is a felony of the first degree if in the course of committing the theft the actor attempts to kill anyone, or purposely inflicts or attempts to inflict serious bodily injury.

## ARTICLE 223. THEFT AND RELATED OFFENSES

### Section 223.0. Definitions

In this Article, unless a different meaning plainly is required:

(1) "deprive" means:

(a) to withhold property of another permanently or for so extended a period as to appropriate a major portion of its economic value, or with intent to restore only upon payment of reward or other compensation; or

(b) to dispose of the property so as to make it unlikely that the owner will recover it.

(2) "financial institution" means a bank, insurance company, credit union, building and loan association, investment trust or other organization held out to the public as a place of deposit of funds or medium of savings or collective investment.

(3) "government" means the United States, any State, county, municipality, or other political unit, or any department, agency or subdivision of any of the foregoing, or any corporation or other association carrying out the functions of government.

(4) "movable property" means property the location of which can be changed, including things growing on, affixed to, or found in land, and documents although the rights represented thereby have no physical location. "Immovable property" is all other property.

(5) "obtain" means:

(a) in relation to property, to bring about a transfer or purported transfer of a legal interest in the property, whether to the obtainer or another; or

(b) in relation to labor or service, to secure performance thereof.

(6) "property" means anything of value, including real estate, tangible and intangible personal property, contract rights, choses-in-action and other interests in or claims to wealth, admission or transportation tickets, captured or domestic animals, food and drink, electric or other power.

(7) "property of another" includes property in which any person other than the actor has an interest which the actor is not privileged to infringe, regardless of the fact that the actor also has an interest in the property and regardless of the fact that the other person might be precluded from civil recovery because the property was used in an unlawful transaction or was subject to forfeiture as contraband. Property in possession of the actor shall not be deemed property of another who has only a security interest therein, even if legal title is in the creditor pursuant to a conditional sales contract or other security agreement.

**Section 223.1. Consolidation of Theft Offenses; Grading; Provisions Applicable to Theft Generally**

(1) Consolidation of Theft Offenses. Conduct denominated theft in this Article constitutes a single offense. An accusation of theft may be supported by evidence that it was committed in any manner that would be theft under this Article, notwithstanding the specification of a different manner in the indictment or information, subject only to the power of the Court to ensure fair trial by granting a continuance or other appropriate relief where the conduct of the defense would be prejudiced by lack of fair notice or by surprise.

(2) Grading of Theft Offenses.

(a) Theft constitutes a felony of the third degree if the amount involved exceeds $500, or if the property stolen is a firearm, automobile, airplane, motorcycle, motorboat, or other motor-propelled vehicle, or in the case of theft by receiving stolen property, if the receiver is in the business of buying or selling stolen property.

(b) Theft not within the preceding paragraph constitutes a misdemeanor, except that if the property was not taken from the person or by threat, or in breach of a fiduciary obligation, and the actor proves by a preponderance of the evidence that the amount involved was less than $50, the offense constitutes a petty misdemeanor.

(c) The amount involved in a theft shall be deemed to be the highest value, by any reasonable standard, of the property or services which the actor stole or attempted to steal. Amounts involved in thefts committed pursuant to one scheme or course of conduct, whether from the same person or several persons, may be aggregated in determining the grade of the offense.

(3) Claim of Right. It is an affirmative defense to prosecution for theft that the actor:

(a) was unaware that the property or service was that of another; or

(b) acted under an honest claim of right to the property or service involved or that he had a right to acquire or dispose of it as he did; or

(c) took property exposed for sale, intending to purchase and pay for it promptly, or reasonably believing that the owner, if present, would have consented.

(4) Theft From Spouse. It is no defense that theft was from the actor's spouse, except that misappropriation of household and personal effects, or other property normally accessible to both spouses, is theft only if it occurs after the parties have ceased living together.

**Section 223.2. Theft by Unlawful Taking or Disposition**

(1) Movable Property. A person is guilty of theft if he unlawfully takes, or exercises unlawful control over, movable property of another with purpose to deprive him thereof.

(2) Immovable Property. A person is guilty of theft if he unlawfully transfers immovable property of another or any interest therein with purpose to benefit himself or another not entitled thereto.

**Section 223.3. Theft by Deception**

A person is guilty of theft if he purposely obtains property of another by deception. A person deceives if he purposely:

(1) creates or reinforces a false impression, including false impressions as to law, value, intention or other state of mind; but deception as to a person's intention to perform a promise shall not be inferred from the fact alone that he did not subsequently perform the promise; or

(2) prevents another from acquiring information which would affect his judgment of a transaction; or

(3) fails to correct a false impression which the deceiver previously created or reinforced, or which the deceiver knows to be influencing another to whom he stands in a fiduciary or confidential relationship; or

(4) fails to disclose a known lien, adverse claim or other legal impediment to the enjoyment of property which he transfers or encumbers in consideration for the property obtained, whether such impediment is or is not valid, or is or is not a matter of official record.

The term "deceive" does not, however, include falsity as to matters having no pecuniary significance, or puffing by statements unlikely to deceive ordinary persons in the group addressed.

**Section 223.4. Theft by Extortion**

A person is guilty of theft if he purposely obtains property of another by threatening to:

(1) inflict bodily injury on anyone or commit any other criminal offense; or

(2) accuse anyone of a criminal offense; or

(3) expose any secret tending to subject any person to hatred, contempt or ridicule, or to impair his credit or business repute; or

(4) take or withhold action as an official, or cause an official to take or withhold action; or

(5) bring about or continue a strike, boycott or other collective unofficial action, if the property is not demanded or received for the benefit of the group in whose interest the actor purports to act; or

(6) testify or provide information or withhold testimony or information with respect to another's legal claim or defense; or

(7) inflict any other harm which would not benefit the actor.

It is an affirmative defense to prosecution based on paragraphs (2), (3) or (4) that the property obtained by threat of accusation, exposure, lawsuit or other invocation of official action was honestly claimed as restitution or indemnification for harm done in the circumstances to which such accusation, exposure, lawsuit or other official action relates, or as compensation for property or lawful services.

### Section 223.5. Theft of Property Lost, Mislaid, or Delivered by Mistake

A person who comes into control of property of another that he knows to have been lost, mislaid, or delivered under a mistake as to the nature or amount of the property or the identity of the recipient is guilty of theft if, with purpose to deprive the owner thereof, he fails to take reasonable measures to restore the property to a person entitled to have it.

### Section 223.6. Receiving Stolen Property

(1) Receiving. A person is guilty of theft if he purposely receives, retains, or disposes of movable property of another knowing that it has been stolen, or believing that it has probably been stolen, unless the property is received, retained, or disposed with purpose to restore it to the owner. "Receiving" means acquiring possession, control or title, or lending on the security of the property.

(2) Presumption of Knowledge. The requisite knowledge or belief is presumed in the case of a dealer who:

(a) is found in possession or control of property stolen from two or more persons on separate occasions; or

(b) has received stolen property in another transaction within the year preceding the transaction charged; or

(c) being a dealer in property of the sort received, acquires it for a consideration which he knows is far below its reasonable value.

"Dealer" means a person in the business of buying or selling goods including a pawnbroker.

### Section 223.7. Theft of Services

(1) A person is guilty of theft if he purposely obtains services which he knows are available only for compensation, by deception or threat, or by false token or other means to avoid payment for the service. "Services" includes labor, professional service, transportation, telephone or other public service, accommodation in hotels, restaurants or elsewhere, admission to exhibitions, use of vehicles or other movable property. Where compensation for service is ordinarily paid immediately upon the rendering of such service, as in the case of hotels and restaurants, refusal to pay or absconding without payment or offer to pay gives rise to a presumption that the service was obtained by deception as to intention to pay.

(2) A person commits theft if, having control over the disposition of services of others, to which he is not entitled, he knowingly diverts such services to his own benefit or to the benefit of another not entitled thereto.

### Section 223.8. Theft by Failure to Make Required Disposition of Funds Received

A person who purposely obtains property upon agreement, or subject to a known legal obligation, to make specified payment or other disposition, whether from such property or its proceeds or from his own property to be reserved in equivalent amount, is guilty of theft if he deals with the property obtained as his own and fails to make the required payment or disposition. The foregoing applies notwithstanding that it may be impossible to identify particular property as belonging to the victim at the time of the actor's failure to make the required payment or disposition. An officer or employee of the government or of a financial institution is presumed: (i) to know any legal obligation relevant to his criminal liability under this Section, and (ii) to have dealt with the property as his own if he fails to pay or account upon lawful demand, or if an audit reveals a shortage or falsification of accounts.

### Section 223.9. Unauthorized Use of Automobiles and Other Vehicles

A person commits a misdemeanor if he operates another's automobile, airplane, motorcycle, motorboat, or other motor-propelled vehicle without consent of the owner. It is an affirmative defense to prosecution under this Section that the actor reasonably believed that the owner would have consented to the operation had he known of it.

## ARTICLE 224. FORGERY AND FRAUDULENT PRACTICES

### Section 224.0. Definitions

In this Article, the definitions given in Section 223.0 apply unless a different meaning plainly is required.

### Section 224.1. Forgery

(1) Definition. A person is guilty of forgery if, with purpose to defraud or injure anyone, or with knowledge that he is facilitating a fraud or injury to be perpetrated by anyone, the actor:

(a) alters any writing of another without his authority; or

(b) makes, completes, executes, authenticates, issues or transfers any writing so that it purports to be the act of another who did not authorize that act, or to have been executed at a time or place or in a numbered sequence other than was in fact the case, or to be a copy of an original when no such original existed; or

(c) utters any writing which he knows to be forged in a manner specified in paragraphs (a) or (b).

"Writing" includes printing or any other method of recording information, money, coins, tokens, stamps, seals, credit cards, badges, trade-marks, and other symbols of value, right, privilege, or identification.

(2) Grading. Forgery is a felony of the second degree if the writing is or purports to be part of an issue of money, securities, postage or revenue stamps, or other instruments issued by the government, or part of an issue of stock, bonds or other instruments representing interests in or claims against any property or enterprise. Forgery is a felony of the third degree if the writing is or purports to be a will, deed, contract, release, commercial instrument, or other document evidencing, creating, transferring, altering, terminating, or otherwise affecting legal relations. Otherwise forgery is a misdemeanor.

**Section 224.2. Simulating Objects of Antiquity, Rarity, Etc.**

A person commits a misdemeanor if, with purpose to defraud anyone or with knowledge that he is facilitating a fraud to be perpetrated by anyone, he makes, alters or utters any object so that it appears to have value because of antiquity, rarity, source, or authorship which it does not possess.

**Section 224.3. Fraudulent Destruction, Removal or Concealment of Recordable Instruments**

A person commits a felony of the third degree if, with purpose to deceive or injure anyone, he destroys, removes or conceals any will, deed, mortgage, security instrument or other writing for which the law provides public recording.

**Section 224.4. Tampering With Records**

A person commits a misdemeanor if, knowing that he has no privilege to do so, he falsifies, destroys, removes or conceals any writing or record, with purpose to deceive or injure anyone or to conceal any wrongdoing.

**Section 224.5. Bad Checks**

A person who issues or passes a check or similar sight order for the payment of money, knowing that it will not be honored by the drawee, commits a misdemeanor. For the purposes of this Section as well as in any prosecution for theft committed by means of a bad check, an issuer is presumed to know that the check or order (other than a post-dated check or order) would not be paid, if:

(1) the issuer had no account with the drawee at the time the check or order was issued; or

(2) payment was refused by the drawee for lack of funds, upon presentation within 30 days after issue, and the issuer failed to make good within 10 days after receiving notice of that refusal.

**Section 224.6. Credit Cards**

A person commits an offense if he uses a credit card for the purpose of obtaining property or services with knowledge that:

(1) the card is stolen or forged; or

(2) the card has been revoked or canceled; or

(3) for any other reason his use of the card is unauthorized by the issuer.

It is an affirmative defense to prosecution under paragraph (c) if the actor proves by a preponderance of the evidence that he had the purpose and ability to meet all obligations to the issuer arising out of his use of the card. "Credit card" means a writing or other evidence of an undertaking to pay for property or services delivered or rendered to or upon the order of a designated person or bearer. An offense under this Section is a felony of the third degree if the value of the property or services secured or sought to be secured by means of the credit card exceeds $500; otherwise it is a misdemeanor.

### Section 224.7. Deceptive Business Practices

A person commits a misdemeanor if in the course of business he:

(1) uses or possesses for use a false weight or measure, or any other device for falsely determining or recording any quality or quantity; or

(2) sells, offers or exposes for sale, or delivers less than the represented quantity of any commodity or service; or

(3) takes or attempts to take more than the represented quantity of any commodity or service when as buyer he furnishes the weight or measure; or

(4) sells, offers or exposes for sale adulterated or mislabeled commodities. "Adulterated" means varying from the standard of composition or quality prescribed by or pursuant to any statute providing criminal penalties for such variance, or set by established commercial usage. "Mislabeled" means varying from the standard of truth or disclosure in labeling prescribed by or pursuant to any statute providing criminal penalties for such variance, or set by established commercial usage; or

(5) makes a false or misleading statement in any advertisement addressed to the public or to a substantial segment thereof for the purpose of promoting the purchase or sale of property or services; or

(6) makes a false or misleading written statement for the purpose of obtaining property or credit; or

(7) makes a false or misleading written statement for the purpose of promoting the sale of securities, or omits information required by law to be disclosed in written documents relating to securities.

It is an affirmative defense to prosecution under this Section if the defendant proves by a preponderance of the evidence that his conduct was not knowingly or recklessly deceptive.

### Section 224.8. Commercial Bribery and Breach of Duty to Act Disinterestedly

(1) A person commits a misdemeanor if he solicits, accepts or agrees to accept any benefit as consideration for knowingly violating or agreeing to violate a duty of fidelity to which he is subject as:

(a) partner, agent, or employee of another;

(b) trustee, guardian, or other fiduciary;

(c) lawyer, physician, accountant, appraiser, or other professional adviser or informant;

(d) officer, director, manager or other participant in the direction of the affairs of an incorporated or unincorporated association; or

(e) arbitrator or other purportedly disinterested adjudicator or referee.

(2) A person who holds himself out to the public as being engaged in the business of making disinterested selection, appraisal, or criticism of commodities or services commits a misdemeanor if he solicits, accepts or agrees to accept any benefit to influence his selection, appraisal or criticism.

(3) A person commits a misdemeanor if he confers, or offers or agrees to confer, any benefit the acceptance of which would be criminal under this Section.

### Section 224.9. Rigging Publicly Exhibited Contest

(1) A person commits a misdemeanor if, with purpose to prevent a publicly exhibited contest from being conducted in accordance with the rules and usages purporting to govern it, he:

(a) confers or offers or agrees to confer any benefit upon, or threatens any injury to a participant, official or other person associated with the contest or exhibition; or

(b) tampers with any person, animal or thing.

(2) Soliciting or Accepting Benefit for Rigging. A person commits a misdemeanor if he knowingly solicits, accepts or agrees to accept any benefit the giving of which would be criminal under Subsection (1).

(3) Participation in Rigged Contest. A person commits a misdemeanor if he knowingly engages in, sponsors, produces, judges, or otherwise participates in a publicly exhibited contest knowing that the contest is not being conducted in compliance with the rules and usages purporting to govern it, by reason of conduct which would be criminal under this Section.

### Section 224.10. Defrauding Secured Creditors

A person commits a misdemeanor if he destroys, removes, conceals, encumbers, transfers or otherwise deals with property subject to a security interest with purpose to hinder enforcement of that interest.

### Section 224.11. Fraud in Insolvency

A person commits a misdemeanor if, knowing that proceedings have been or are about to be instituted for the appointment of a receiver or other person entitled to administer property for the benefit of creditors, or that any other composition or liquidation for the benefit of creditors has been or is about to be made, he:

(1) destroys, removes, conceals, encumbers, transfers, or otherwise deals with any property with purpose to defeat or obstruct the claim of any creditor, or otherwise to obstruct the operation of any law relating to administration of property for the benefit of creditors; or

(2) knowingly falsifies any writing or record relating to the property; or

(3) knowingly misrepresents or refuses to disclose to a receiver or other person entitled to administer property for the benefit of creditors, the existence, amount or location of the property, or any other information which the actor could be legally required to furnish in relation to such administration.

### Section 224.12. Receiving Deposits in a Failing Financial Institution

An officer, manager or other person directing or participating in the direction of a financial institution commits a misdemeanor if he receives or permits the receipt of a deposit, premium payment or other investment in the institution knowing that:

(1) due to financial difficulties the institution is about to suspend operations or go into receivership or reorganization; and

(2) the person making the deposit or other payment is unaware of the precarious situation of the institution.

### Section 224.13. Misapplication of Entrusted Property and Property of Government or Financial Institution

A person commits an offense if he applies or disposes of property that has been entrusted to him as a fiduciary, or property of the government or of a financial institution, in a manner which he knows is unlawful and involves substantial risk of loss or detriment to the owner of the property or to a person for whose benefit the property was entrusted. The offense is a misdemeanor if the amount involved exceeds $50; otherwise it is a petty misdemeanor. "Fiduciary" includes trustee, guardian, executor, administrator, receiver and any person carrying on fiduciary functions on behalf of a corporation or other organization which is a fiduciary.

### Section 224.14. Securing Execution of Documents by Deception

A person commits a misdemeanor if by deception he causes another to execute any instrument affecting, purporting to affect, or likely to affect the pecuniary interest of any person.

---

## OFFENSES AGAINST THE FAMILY

---

## ARTICLE 230. OFFENSES AGAINST THE FAMILY

### Section 230.1. Bigamy and Polygamy

(1) Bigamy. A married person is guilty of bigamy, a misdemeanor, if he contracts or purports to contract another marriage, unless at the time of the subsequent marriage:

(a) the actor believes that the prior spouse is dead; or

(b) the actor and the prior spouse have been living apart for five consecutive years throughout which the prior spouse was not known by the actor to be alive; or

(c) a Court has entered a judgment purporting to terminate or annul any prior disqualifying marriage, and the actor does not know that judgment to be invalid; or

(d) the actor reasonably believes that he is legally eligible to remarry.

(2) Polygamy. A person is guilty of polygamy, a felony of the third degree, if he marries or cohabits with more than one spouse at a time in purported exercise of the right of plural marriage. The offense is a continuing one until all cohabitation and claim of marriage with more than one spouse terminates. This section does not apply to parties to a polygamous marriage, lawful in the country of which they are residents or nationals, while they are in transit through or temporarily visiting this State.

(3) Other Party to Bigamous or Polygamous Marriage. A person is guilty of bigamy or polygamy, as the case may be, if he contracts or purports to contract marriage with another knowing that the other is thereby committing bigamy or polygamy.

**Section 230.2. Incest**

A person is guilty of incest, a felony of the third degree, if he knowingly marries or cohabits or has sexual intercourse with an ancestor or descendant, a brother or sister of the whole or half blood [or an uncle, aunt, nephew or niece of the whole blood]. "Cohabit" means to live together under the representation or appearance of being married. The relationships referred to herein include blood relationships without regard to legitimacy, and relationship of parent and child by adoption.

**Section 230.3. Abortion**

(1) Unjustified Abortion. A person who purposely and unjustifiably terminates the pregnancy of another otherwise than by a live birth commits a felony of the third degree or, where the pregnancy has continued beyond the twenty-sixth week, a felony of the second degree.

(2) Justifiable Abortion. A licensed physician is justified in terminating a pregnancy if he believes there is substantial risk that continuance of the pregnancy would gravely impair the physical or mental health of the mother or that the child would be born with grave physical or mental defect, or that the pregnancy resulted from rape, incest, or other felonious intercourse. All illicit intercourse with a girl below the age of 16 shall be deemed felonious for purposes of this Subsection. Justifiable abortions shall be performed only in a licensed hospital except in case of emergency when hospital facilities are unavailable. [Additional exceptions from the requirement of hospitalization may be incorporated here to take account of situations in sparsely settled areas where hospitals are not generally accessible.]

(3) Physicians' Certificates; Presumption From Non-Compliance. No abortion shall be performed unless two physicians, one of whom may be the person performing the abortion, shall have certified in writing the circumstances which they believe to justify the abortion. Such certificate shall be submitted before the abortion to the hospital where it is to be performed and, in the case of abortion following felonious intercourse, to the prosecuting attorney or the police. Failure to comply with any of the requirements of this Subsection gives rise to a presumption that the abortion was unjustified.

(4) Self-Abortion. A woman whose pregnancy has continued beyond the twenty-sixth week commits a felony of the third degree if she purposely terminates her own pregnancy otherwise than by a live birth, or if she uses instruments, drugs or violence upon herself for that purpose.

Except as justified under Subsection (2), a person who induces or knowingly aids a woman to use instruments, drugs or violence upon herself for the purpose of terminating her pregnancy otherwise than by a live birth commits a felony of the third degree whether or not the pregnancy has continued beyond the twenty-sixth week.

(5) Pretended Abortion. A person commits a felony of the third degree if, representing that it is his purpose to perform an abortion, he does an act adapted to cause abortion in a pregnant woman although the woman is in fact not pregnant, or the actor does not believe she is. A person charged with unjustified abortion under Subsection (1) or an attempt to commit that offense may be convicted thereof upon proof of conduct prohibited by this Subsection.

(6) Distribution of Abortifacients. A person who sells, offers to sell, possesses with intent to sell, advertises, or displays for sale anything specially designed to terminate a pregnancy, or held out by the actor as useful for that purpose, commits a misdemeanor, unless:

(a) the sale, offer or display is to a physician or druggist or to an intermediary in a chain of distribution to physicians or druggists; or

(b) the sale is made upon prescription or order of a physician; or

(c) the possession is with intent to sell as authorized in paragraphs (a) and (b); or

(d) the advertising is addressed to persons named in paragraph (a) and confined to trade or professional channels not likely to reach the general public.

(7) Section Inapplicable to Prevention of Pregnancy. Nothing in this Section shall be deemed applicable to the prescription, administration or distribution of drugs or other substances for avoiding pregnancy, whether by preventing implantation of a fertilized ovum or by any other method that operates before, at or immediately after fertilization.

### Section 230.4. Endangering Welfare of Children

A parent, guardian, or other person supervising the welfare of a child under 18 commits a misdemeanor if he knowingly endangers the child's welfare by violating a duty of care, protection or support.

### Section 230.5. Persistent Non-Support

A person commits a misdemeanor if he persistently fails to provide support which he can provide and which he knows he is legally obliged to provide to a spouse, child or other dependent.

# OFFENSES AGAINST PUBLIC ADMINISTRATION

## ARTICLE 240. BRIBERY AND CORRUPT INFLUENCE

### Section 240.0. Definitions

In Articles 240–243, unless a different meaning plainly is required:

(1) "benefit" means gain or advantage, or anything regarded by the beneficiary as gain or advantage, including benefit to any other person or entity in whose welfare he is interested, but not an advantage promised generally to a group or class of voters as a consequence of public measures which a candidate engages to support or oppose;

(2) "government" includes any branch, subdivision or agency of the government of the State or any locality within it;

(3) "harm" means loss, disadvantage or injury, or anything so regarded by the person affected, including loss, disadvantage or injury to any other person or entity in whose welfare he is interested;

(4) "official proceeding" means a proceeding heard or which may be heard before any legislative, judicial, administrative or other governmental agency or official authorized to take evidence under oath, including any referee, hearing examiner, commissioner, notary or other person taking testimony or deposition in connection with any such proceeding;

(5) "party official" means a person who holds an elective or appointive post in a political party in the United States by virtue of which he directs or conducts, or participates in directing or conducting party affairs at any level of responsibility;

(6) "pecuniary benefit" is benefit in the form of money, property, commercial interests or anything else the primary significance of which is economic gain;

(7) "public servant" means any officer or employee of government, including legislators and judges, and any person participating as juror, advisor, consultant or otherwise, in performing a governmental function; but the term does not include witnesses;

(8) "administrative proceeding" means any proceeding, other than a judicial proceeding, the outcome of which is required to be based on a record or documentation prescribed by law, or in which law or regulation is particularized in application to individuals.

### Section 240.1. Bribery in Official and Political Matters

A person is guilty of bribery, a felony of the third degree, if he offers, confers or agrees to confer upon another, or solicits, accepts or agrees to accept from another:

(1) any pecuniary benefit as consideration for the recipient's decision, opinion, recommendation, vote or other exercise of discretion as a public servant, party official or voter; or

(2) any benefit as consideration for the recipient's decision, vote, recommendation or other exercise of official discretion in a judicial or administrative proceeding; or

(3) any benefit as consideration for a violation of a known legal duty as public servant or party official.

It is no defense to prosecution under this section that a person whom the actor sought to influence was not qualified to act in the desired way whether because he had not yet assumed office, or lacked jurisdiction, or for any other reason.

### Section 240.2. Threats and Other Improper Influence in Official and Political Matters

(1) Offenses Defined. A person commits an offense if he:

(a) threatens unlawful harm to any person with purpose to influence his decision, opinion, recommendation, vote or other exercise of discretion as a public servant, party official or voter; or

(b) threatens harm to any public servant with purpose to influence his decision, opinion, recommendation, vote or other exercise of discretion in a judicial or administrative proceeding; or

(c) threatens harm to any public servant or party official with purpose to influence him to violate his known legal duty; or

(d) privately addresses to any public servant who has or will have an official discretion in a judicial or administrative proceeding any representation, entreaty, argument or other communication with purpose to influence the outcome on the basis of considerations other than those authorized by law.

It is no defense to prosecution under this Section that a person whom the actor sought to influence was not qualified to act in the desired way, whether because he had not yet assumed office, or lacked jurisdiction, or for any other reason.

(2) Grading. An offense under this Section is a misdemeanor unless the actor threatened to commit a crime or made a threat with purpose to influence a judicial or administrative proceeding, in which cases the offense is a felony of the third degree.

### Section 240.3. Compensation for Past Official Behavior

A person commits a misdemeanor if he solicits, accepts or agrees to accept any pecuniary benefit as compensation for having, as public servant, given a decision, opinion, recommendation or vote favorable to another, or for having otherwise exercised a discretion in his favor, or for having violated his duty. A person commits a misdemeanor if he offers, confers or agrees to confer compensation acceptance of which is prohibited by this Section.

### Section 240.4. Retaliation for Past Official Action

A person commits a misdemeanor if he harms another by any unlawful act in retaliation for anything lawfully done by the latter in the capacity of public servant.

### Section 240.5. Gifts to Public Servants by Persons Subject to Their Jurisdiction

(1) Regulatory and Law Enforcement Officials. No public servant in any department or agency exercising regulatory functions, or conducting inspections or investigations, or carrying on civil or criminal litigation on behalf of the government, or having custody of prisoners, shall

solicit, accept or agree to accept any pecuniary benefit from a person known to be subject to such regulation, inspection, investigation or custody, or against whom such litigation is known to be pending or contemplated.

(2) Officials Concerned with Government Contracts and Pecuniary Transactions. No public servant having any discretionary function to perform in connection with contracts, purchases, payments, claims or other pecuniary transactions of the government shall solicit, accept or agree to accept any pecuniary benefit from any person known to be interested in or likely to become interested in any such contract, purchase, payment, claim or transaction.

(3) Judicial and Administrative Officials. No public servant having judicial or administrative authority and no public servant employed by or in a court or other tribunal having such authority, or participating in the enforcement of its decisions, shall solicit, accept or agree to accept any pecuniary benefit from a person known to be interested in or likely to become interested in any matter before such public servant or a tribunal with which he is associated.

(4) Legislative Officials. No legislator or public servant employed by the legislature or by any committee or agency thereof shall solicit, accept or agree to accept any pecuniary benefit from any person known to be interested in a bill, transaction or proceeding, pending or contemplated, before the legislature or any committee or agency thereof.

(5) Exceptions. This Section shall not apply to:

(a) fees prescribed by law to be received by a public servant, or any other benefit for which the recipient gives legitimate consideration or to which he is otherwise legally entitled; or

(b) gifts or other benefits conferred on account of kinship or other personal, professional or business relationship independent of the official status of the receiver; or

(c) trivial benefits incidental to personal, professional or business contacts and involving no substantial risk of undermining official impartiality.

(6) Offering Benefits Prohibited. No person shall knowingly confer, or offer or agree to confer, any benefit prohibited by the foregoing Subsections.

(7) Grade of Offense. An offense under this Section is a misdemeanor.

### Section 240.6. Compensating Public Servant for Assisting Private Interests in Relation to Matters Before Him

(1) Receiving Compensation. A public servant commits a misdemeanor if he solicits, accepts or agrees to accept compensation for advice or other assistance in preparing or promoting a bill, contract, claim, or other transaction or proposal as to which he knows that he has or is likely to have an official discretion to exercise.

(2) Paying Compensation. A person commits a misdemeanor if he pays or offers or agrees to pay compensation to a public servant with knowledge that acceptance by the public servant is unlawful.

### Section 240.7. Selling Political Endorsement; Special Influence

(1) Selling Political Endorsement. A person commits a misdemeanor if he solicits, receives, agrees to receive, or agrees that any political party or other person shall receive, any pecuniary benefit as consideration for approval or disapproval of an appointment or advancement in public service, or for approval or disapproval of any person or transaction for any benefit conferred by an official or agency of government. "Approval" includes recommendation, failure to disapprove, or any other manifestation of favor or acquiescence. "Disapproval" includes failure to approve, or any other manifestation of disfavor or nonacquiescence.

(2) Other Trading in Special Influence. A person commits a misdemeanor if he solicits, receives or agrees to receive any pecuniary benefit as consideration for exerting special influence upon a public servant or procuring another to do so. "Special influence" means power to influence through kinship, friendship or other relationship, apart from the merits of the transaction.

(3) Paying for Endorsement or Special Influence. A person commits a misdemeanor if he offers, confers or agrees to confer any pecuniary benefit receipt of which is prohibited by this Section.

## ARTICLE 241. PERJURY AND OTHER FALSIFICATION IN OFFICIAL MATTERS

### Section 241.0. Definitions

In this Article, unless a different meaning plainly is required:

(1) the definitions given in Section 240.0 apply; and

(2) "statement" means any representation, but includes a representation of opinion, belief or other state of mind only if the representation clearly relates to state of mind apart from or in addition to any facts which are the subject of the representation.

### Section 241.1. Perjury

(1) Offense Defined. A person is guilty of perjury, a felony of the third degree, if in any official proceeding he makes a false statement under oath or equivalent affirmation, or swears or affirms the truth of a statement previously made, when the statement is material and he does not believe it to be true.

(2) Materiality. Falsification is material, regardless of the admissibility of the statement under rules of evidence, if it could have affected the course or outcome of the proceeding. It is no defense that the declarant mistakenly believed the falsification to be immaterial. Whether a falsification is material in a given factual situation is a question of law.

(3) Irregularities No Defense. It is not a defense to prosecution under this Section that the oath or affirmation was administered or taken in an irregular manner or that the declarant was not competent to make the statement. A document purporting to be made upon oath or affirmation at any time when the actor presents it as being so verified shall be deemed to have been duly sworn or affirmed.

(4) Retraction. No person shall be guilty of an offense under this Section if he retracted the falsification in the course of the proceeding in which it was made before it became manifest that the falsification was or would be exposed and before the falsification substantially affected the proceeding.

(5) Inconsistent Statements. Where the defendant made inconsistent statements under oath or equivalent affirmation, both having been made within the period of the statute of limitations, the prosecution may proceed by setting forth the inconsistent statements in a single count alleging in the alternative that one or the other was false and not believed by the defendant. In such case it shall not be necessary for the prosecution to prove which statement was false but only that one or the other was false and not believed by the defendant to be true.

(6) Corroboration. No person shall be convicted of an offense under this Section where proof of falsity rests solely upon contradiction by testimony of a single person other than the defendant.

**Section 241.2. False Swearing**

(1) False Swearing in Official Matters. A person who makes a false statement under oath or equivalent affirmation, or swears or affirms the truth of such a statement previously made, when he does not believe the statement to be true, is guilty of a misdemeanor if:

(a) the falsification occurs in an official proceeding; or

(b) the falsification is intended to mislead a public servant in performing his official function.

(2) Other False Swearing. A person who makes a false statement under oath or equivalent affirmation, or swears or affirms the truth of such a statement previously made, when he does not believe the statement to be true, is guilty of a petty misdemeanor, if the statement is one which is required by law to be sworn or affirmed before a notary or other person authorized to administer oaths.

(3) Perjury Provisions Applicable. Subsections (3) to (6) of Section 241.1 apply to the present Section.

**Section 241.3. Unsworn Falsification to Authorities**

(1) In General. A person commits a misdemeanor if, with purpose to mislead a public servant in performing his official function, he:

(a) makes any written false statement which he does not believe to be true; or

(b) purposely creates a false impression in a written application for any pecuniary or other benefit, by omitting information necessary to prevent statements therein from being misleading; or

(c) submits or invites reliance on any writing which he knows to be forged, altered or otherwise lacking in authenticity; or

(d) submits or invites reliance on any sample, specimen, map, boundary-mark, or other object which he knows to be false.

(2) Statements "Under Penalty." A person commits a petty misdemeanor if he makes a written false statement which he does not believe to be true, on or pursuant to a form bearing notice, authorized by law, to the effect that false statements made therein are punishable.

(3) Perjury Provisions Applicable. Subsections (3) to (6) of Section 241.1 apply to the present section.

## Section 241.4. False Alarms to Agencies of Public Safety

A person who knowingly causes a false alarm of fire or other emergency to be transmitted to or within any organization, official or volunteer, for dealing with emergencies involving danger to life or property commits a misdemeanor.

## Section 241.5. False Reports to Law Enforcement Authorities

(1) Falsely Incriminating Another. A person who knowingly gives false information to any law enforcement officer with purpose to implicate another commits a misdemeanor.

(2) Fictitious Reports. A person commits a petty misdemeanor if he:

(a) reports to law enforcement authorities an offense or other incident within their concern knowing that it did not occur; or

(b) pretends to furnish such authorities with information relating to an offense or incident when he knows he has no information relating to such offense or incident.

## Section 241.6. Tampering With Witnesses and Informants; Retaliation Against Them

(1) Tampering. A person commits an offense if, believing that an official proceeding or investigation is pending or about to be instituted, he attempts to induce or otherwise cause a witness or informant to:

(a) testify or inform falsely; or

(b) withhold any testimony, information, document or thing; or

(c) elude legal process summoning him to testify or supply evidence; or

(d) absent himself from any proceeding or investigation to which he has been legally summoned.

The offense is a felony of the third degree if the actor employs force, deception, threat or offer of pecuniary benefit. Otherwise it is a misdemeanor.

(2) Retaliation Against Witness or Informant. A person commits a misdemeanor if he harms another by any unlawful act in retaliation for anything lawfully done in the capacity of witness or informant.

(3) Witness or Informant Taking Bribe. A person commits a felony of the third degree if he solicits, accepts or agrees to accept any benefit in consideration of his doing any of the things specified in clauses (a) to (d) of Subsection (1).

## Section 241.7. Tampering With or Fabricating Physical Evidence

A person commits a misdemeanor if, believing that an official proceeding or investigation is pending or about to be instituted, he:

(1) alters, destroys, conceals or removes any record, document or thing with purpose to impair its verity or availability in such proceeding or investigation; or

(2) makes, presents or uses any record, document or thing knowing it to be false and with purpose to mislead a public servant who is or may be engaged in such proceeding or investigation.

**Section 241.8. Tampering With Public Records or Information**

(1) Offense Defined. A person commits an offense if he:

(a) knowingly makes a false entry in, or false alteration of, any record, document or thing belonging to, or received or kept by, the government for information or record, or required by law to be kept by others for information of the government; or

(b) makes, presents or uses any record, document or thing knowing it to be false, and with purpose that it be taken as a genuine part of information or records referred to in paragraph (a); or

(c) purposely and unlawfully destroys, conceals, removes or otherwise impairs the verity or availability of any such record, document or thing.

(2) Grading. An offense under this Section is a misdemeanor unless the actor's purpose is to defraud or injure anyone, in which case the offense is a felony of the third degree.

**Section 241.9. Impersonating a Public Servant**

A person commits a misdemeanor if he falsely pretends to hold a position in the public service with purpose to induce another to submit to such pretended official authority or otherwise to act in reliance upon that pretense to his prejudice.

## ARTICLE 242. OBSTRUCTING GOVERNMENTAL OPERATIONS; ESCAPES

**Section 242.0. Definitions**

In this Article, unless another meaning plainly is required, the definitions given in Section 240.0 apply.

**Section 242.1. Obstructing Administration of Law or Other Governmental Function**

A person commits a misdemeanor if he purposely obstructs, impairs or perverts the administration of law or other governmental function by force, violence, physical interference or obstacle, breach of official duty, or any other unlawful act, except that this Section does not apply to flight by a person charged with crime, refusal to submit to arrest, failure to perform a legal duty other than an official duty, or any other means of avoiding compliance with law without affirmative interference with governmental functions.

**Section 242.2. Resisting Arrest or Other Law Enforcement**

A person commits a misdemeanor if, for the purpose of preventing a public servant from effecting a lawful arrest or discharging any other duty, the person creates a substantial risk of bodily injury to the public servant or anyone else, or employs means justifying or requiring substantial force to overcome the resistance.

### Section 242.3. Hindering Apprehension or Prosecution

A person commits an offense if, with purpose to hinder the apprehension, prosecution, conviction or punishment of another for crime, he:

(1) harbors or conceals the other; or

(2) provides or aids in providing a weapon, transportation, disguise or other means of avoiding apprehension or effecting escape; or

(3) conceals or destroys evidence of the crime, or tampers with a witness, informant, document or other source of information, regardless of its admissibility in evidence; or

(4) warns the other of impending discovery or apprehension, except that this paragraph does not apply to a warning given in connection with an effort to bring another into compliance with law; or

(5) volunteers false information to a law enforcement officer.

The offense is a felony of the third degree if the conduct which the actor knows has been charged or is liable to be charged against the person aided would constitute a felony of the first or second degree. Otherwise it is a misdemeanor.

### Section 242.4. Aiding Consummation of Crime

A person commits an offense if he purposely aids another to accomplish an unlawful object of a crime, as by safeguarding the proceeds thereof or converting the proceeds into negotiable funds. The offense is a felony of the third degree if the principal offense was a felony of the first or second degree. Otherwise it is a misdemeanor.

### Section 242.5. Compounding

A person commits a misdemeanor if he accepts or agrees to accept any pecuniary benefit in consideration of refraining from reporting to law enforcement authorities the commission or suspected commission of any offense or information relating to an offense. It is an affirmative defense to prosecution under this Section that the pecuniary benefit did not exceed an amount which the actor believed to be due as restitution or indemnification for harm caused by the offense.

### Section 242.6. Escape

(1) Escape. A person commits an offense if he unlawfully removes himself from official detention or fails to return to official detention following temporary leave granted for a specific purpose or limited period. "Official detention" means arrest, detention in any facility for custody of persons under charge or conviction of crime or alleged or found to be delinquent, detention for extradition or deportation, or any other detention for law enforcement purposes; but "official detention" does not include supervision of probation or parole, or constraint incidental to release on bail.

(2) Permitting or Facilitating Escape. A public servant concerned in detention commits an offense if he knowingly or recklessly permits an escape. Any person who knowingly causes or facilitates an escape commits an offense.

(3) Effect of Legal Irregularity in Detention. Irregularity in bringing about or maintaining detention, or lack of jurisdiction of the committing or detaining authority, shall not be a defense to prosecution un-

der this Section if the escape is from a prison or other custodial facility or from detention pursuant to commitment by official proceedings. In the case of other detentions, irregularity or lack of jurisdiction shall be a defense only if:

(a) the escape involved no substantial risk of harm to the person or property of anyone other than the detainee; or

(b) the detaining authority did not act in good faith under color of law.

(4) Grading of Offenses. An offense under this Section is a felony of the third degree where:

(a) the actor was under arrest for or detained on a charge of felony or following conviction of crime; or

(b) the actor employs force, threat, deadly weapon or other dangerous instrumentality to effect the escape; or

(c) a public servant concerned in detention of persons convicted of crime purposely facilitates or permits an escape from a detention facility.

Otherwise an offense under this section is a misdemeanor.

### Section 242.7. Implements for Escape; Other Contraband

(1) Escape Implements. A person commits a misdemeanor if he unlawfully introduces within a detention facility, or unlawfully provides an inmate with, any weapon, tool or other thing which may be useful for escape. An inmate commits a misdemeanor if he unlawfully procures, makes, or otherwise provides himself with, or has in his possession, any such implement of escape. "Unlawfully" means surreptitiously or contrary to law, regulation or order of the detaining authority.

(2) Other Contraband. A person commits a petty misdemeanor if he provides an inmate with anything which the actor knows it is unlawful for the inmate to possess.

### Section 242.8. Bail Jumping; Default in Required Appearance

A person set at liberty by court order, with or without bail, upon condition that he will subsequently appear at a specified time and place, commits a misdemeanor if, without lawful excuse, he fails to appear at that time and place. The offense constitutes a felony of the third degree where the required appearance was to answer to a charge of felony, or for disposition of any such charge, and the actor took flight or went into hiding to avoid apprehension, trial or punishment. This Section does not apply to obligations to appear incident to release under suspended sentence or on probation or parole.

## ARTICLE 243. ABUSE OF OFFICE

### Section 243.0. Definitions

In this Article, unless a different meaning plainly is required, the definitions given in Section 240.0 apply.

### Section 243.1. Official Oppression

A person acting or purporting to act in an official capacity or taking advantage of such actual or purported capacity commits a misdemeanor if, knowing that his conduct is illegal, he:

(1) subjects another to arrest, detention, search, seizure, mistreatment, dispossession, assessment, lien or other infringement of personal or property rights; or

(2) denies or impedes another in the exercise or enjoyment of any right, privilege, power or immunity.

### Section 243.2. Speculating or Wagering on Official Action or Information

A public servant commits a misdemeanor if, in contemplation of official action by himself or by a governmental unit with which he is associated, or in reliance on information to which he has access in his official capacity and which has not been made public, he:

(1) acquires a pecuniary interest in any property, transaction or enterprise which may be affected by such information or official action; or

(2) speculates or wagers on the basis of such information or official action; or

(3) aids another to do any of the foregoing.

---

## OFFENSES AGAINST PUBLIC ORDER AND DECENCY

---

## ARTICLE 250. RIOT, DISORDERLY CONDUCT, AND RELATED OFFENSES

### Section 250.1. Riot; Failure to Disperse

(1) Riot. A person is guilty of riot, a felony of the third degree, if he participates with [two] or more others in a course of disorderly conduct:

(a) with purpose to commit or facilitate the commission of a felony or misdemeanor;

(b) with purpose to prevent or coerce official action; or

(c) when the actor or any other participant to the knowledge of the actor uses or plans to use a firearm or other deadly weapon.

(2) Failure of Disorderly Persons to Disperse Upon Official Order. Where [three] or more persons are participating in a course of disorderly conduct likely to cause substantial harm or serious inconvenience, annoyance or alarm, a peace officer or other public servant engaged in executing or enforcing the law may order the participants and others in the immediate vicinity to disperse. A person who refuses or knowingly fails to obey such an order commits a misdemeanor.

### Section 250.2. Disorderly Conduct

(1) Offense Defined. A person is guilty of disorderly conduct if, with purpose to cause public inconvenience, annoyance or alarm, or recklessly creating a risk thereof, he:

(a) engages in fighting or threatening, or in violent or tumultuous behavior; or

(b) makes unreasonable noise or offensively coarse utterance, gesture or display, or addresses abusive language to any person present; or

(c) creates a hazardous or physically offensive condition by any act which serves no legitimate purpose of the actor.

"Public" means affecting or likely to affect persons in a place to which the public or a substantial group has access; among the places included are highways, transport facilities, schools, prisons, apartment houses, places of business or amusement, or any neighborhood.

(2) Grading. An offense under this Section is a petty misdemeanor if the actor's purpose is to cause substantial harm or serious inconvenience, or if he persists in disorderly conduct after reasonable warning or request to desist. Otherwise disorderly conduct is a violation.

### Section 250.3. False Public Alarms

A person is guilty of a misdemeanor if he initiates or circulates a report or warning of an impending bombing or other crime or catastrophe, knowing that the report or warning is false or baseless and that it is likely to cause evacuation of a building, place of assembly, or facility of public transport, or to cause public inconvenience or alarm.

### Section 250.4. Harassment

A person commits a petty misdemeanor if, with purpose to harass another, he:

(1) makes a telephone call without purpose of legitimate communication; or

(2) insults, taunts or challenges another in a manner likely to provoke violent or disorderly response; or

(3) makes repeated communications anonymously or at extremely inconvenient hours, or in offensively coarse language; or

(4) subjects another to an offensive touching; or

(5) engages in any other course of alarming conduct serving no legitimate purpose of the actor.

### Section 250.5. Public Drunkenness; Drug Incapacitation

A person is guilty of an offense if he appears in any public place manifestly under the influence of alcohol, narcotics or other drug, not therapeutically administered, to the degree that he may endanger himself or other persons or property, or annoy persons in his vicinity. An offense under this Section constitutes a petty misdemeanor if the actor has been convicted hereunder twice before within a period of one year. Otherwise the offense constitutes a violation.

### Section 250.6. Loitering or Prowling

A person commits a violation if he loiters or prowls in a place, at a time, or in a manner not usual for law-abiding individuals under circumstances that warrant alarm for the safety of persons or property in the vicinity. Among the circumstances which may be considered in determining whether such alarm is warranted is the fact that the actor takes flight upon appearance of a peace officer, refuses to identify himself, or manifestly endeavors to conceal himself or any object. Unless flight by the actor or other circumstance makes it impracticable, a peace officer shall prior to any arrest for an offense under this section afford the actor an opportunity to dispel any alarm which would otherwise be warranted, by requesting him to identify himself and explain his presence and conduct. No person shall be convicted of an offense under this Section if the peace officer did not comply with the preceding sentence, or if it appears at trial that the explanation given by the actor was true and, if believed by the peace officer at the time, would have dispelled the alarm.

### Section 250.7. Obstructing Highways and Other Public Passages

(1) A person, who, having no legal privilege to do so, purposely or recklessly obstructs any highway or other public passage, whether alone or with others, commits a violation, or, in case he persists after warning by a law officer, a petty misdemeanor. "Obstructs" means renders impassable without unreasonable inconvenience or hazard. No person shall be deemed guilty of recklessly obstructing in violation of this Subsection solely because of a gathering of persons to hear him speak or otherwise communicate, or solely because of being a member of such a gathering.

(2) A person in a gathering commits a violation if he refuses to obey a reasonable official request or order to move:

(a) to prevent obstruction of a highway or other public passage; or

(b) to maintain public safety by dispersing those gathered in dangerous proximity to a fire or other hazard.

An order to move, addressed to a person whose speech or other lawful behavior attracts an obstructing audience, shall not be deemed reasonable if the obstruction can be readily remedied by police control of the size or location of the gathering.

### Section 250.8. Disrupting Meetings and Processions

A person commits a misdemeanor if, with purpose to prevent or disrupt a lawful meeting, procession or gathering, he does any act tending to obstruct or interfere with it physically, or makes any utterance, gesture or display designed to outrage the sensibilities of the group.

### Section 250.9. Desecration of Venerated Objects

A person commits a misdemeanor if he purposely desecrates any public monument or structure, or place of worship or burial, or if he purposely desecrates the national flag or any other object of veneration by the public or a substantial segment thereof in any public place. "Desecrate" means defacing, damaging, polluting or otherwise physically mistreating in a way that the actor knows will outrage the sensibilities of persons likely to observe or discover his action.

**Section 250.10. Abuse of Corpse**

Except as authorized by law, a person who treats a corpse in a way that he knows would outrage ordinary family sensibilities commits a misdemeanor.

**Section 250.11. Cruelty to Animals**

A person commits a misdemeanor if he purposely or recklessly:

(1) subjects any animal to cruel mistreatment; or

(2) subjects any animal in his custody to cruel neglect; or

(3) kills or injures any animal belonging to another without legal privilege or consent of the owner.

Subsections (1) and (2) shall not be deemed applicable to accepted veterinary practices and activities carried on for scientific research.

**Section 250.12. Violation of Privacy**

(1) Unlawful Eavesdropping or Surveillance. A person commits a misdemeanor if, except as authorized by law, he:

(a) trespasses on property with purpose to subject anyone to eavesdropping or other surveillance in a private place; or

(b) installs in any private place, without the consent of the person or persons entitled to privacy there, any device for observing, photographing, recording, amplifying or broadcasting sounds or events in such place, or uses any such unauthorized installation; or

(c) installs or uses outside a private place any device for hearing, recording, amplifying or broadcasting sounds originating in such place which would not ordinarily be audible or comprehensible outside, without the consent of the person or persons entitled to privacy there.

"Private place" means a place where one may reasonably expect to be safe from casual or hostile intrusion or surveillance, but does not include a place to which the public or a substantial group thereof has access.

(2) Other Breach of Privacy of Messages. A person commits a misdemeanor if, except as authorized by law, he:

(a) intercepts without the consent of the sender or receiver a message by telephone, telegraph, letter or other means of communicating privately; but this paragraph does not extend to (i) overhearing of messages through a regularly installed instrument on a telephone party line or on an extension, or (ii) interception by the telephone company or subscriber incident to enforcement of regulations limiting use of the facilities or incident to other normal operation and use; or

(b) divulges without the consent of the sender or receiver the existence or contents of any such message if the actor knows that the message was illegally intercepted, or if he learned of the message in the course of employment with an agency engaged in transmitting it.

## ARTICLE 251. PUBLIC INDECENCY

### Section 251.1. Open Lewdness

A person commits a petty misdemeanor if he does any lewd act which he knows is likely to be observed by others who would be affronted or alarmed.

### Section 251.2. Prostitution and Related Offenses

(1) Prostitution. A person is guilty of prostitution, a petty misdemeanor, if he or she:

(a) is an inmate of a house of prostitution or otherwise engages in sexual activity as a business; or

(b) loiters in or within view of any public place for the purpose of being hired to engage in sexual activity.

"Sexual activity" includes homosexual and other deviate sexual relations. A "house of prostitution" is any place where prostitution or promotion of prostitution is regularly carried on by one person under the control, management or supervision of another. An "inmate" is a person who engages in prostitution in or through the agency of a house of prostitution. "Public place" means any place to which the public or any substantial group thereof has access.

(2) Promoting Prostitution. A person who knowingly promotes prostitution of another commits a misdemeanor or felony as provided in Subsection (3). The following acts shall, without limitation of the foregoing, constitute promoting prostitution:

(a) owning, controlling, managing, supervising or otherwise keeping, alone or in association with others, a house of prostitution or a prostitution business; or

(b) procuring an inmate for a house of prostitution or a place in a house of prostitution for one who would be an inmate; or

(c) encouraging, inducing, or otherwise purposely causing another to become or remain a prostitute; or

(d) soliciting a person to patronize a prostitute; or

(e) procuring a prostitute for a patron; or

(f) transporting a person into or within this state with purpose to promote that person's engaging in prostitution, or procuring or paying for transportation with that purpose; or

(g) leasing or otherwise permitting a place controlled by the actor, alone or in association with others, to be regularly used for prostitution or the promotion of prostitution, or failure to make reasonable effort to abate such use by ejecting the tenant, notifying law enforcement authorities, or other legally available means; or

(h) soliciting, receiving, or agreeing to receive any benefit for doing or agreeing to do anything forbidden by this Subsection.

(3) Grading of Offenses Under Subsection (2). An offense under Subsection (2) constitutes a felony of the third degree if:

(a) the offense falls within paragraph (a), (b) or (c) of Subsection (2); or

(b) the actor compels another to engage in or promote prostitution; or

(c) the actor promotes prostitution of a child under 16, whether or not he is aware of the child's age; or

(d) the actor promotes prostitution of his wife, child, ward or any person for whose care, protection or support he is responsible.

Otherwise the offense is a misdemeanor.

(4) Presumption from Living off Prostitutes. A person, other than the prostitute or the prostitute's minor child or other legal dependent incapable of self-support, who is supported in whole or substantial part by the proceeds of prostitution is presumed to be knowingly promoting prostitution in violation of Subsection (2).

(5) Patronizing Prostitutes. A person commits a violation if he hires a prostitute to engage in sexual activity with him, or if he enters or remains in a house of prostitution for the purpose of engaging in sexual activity.

(6) Evidence. On the issue whether a place is a house of prostitution the following shall be admissible evidence: its general repute; the repute of the persons who reside in or frequent the place; the frequency, timing and duration of visits by non-residents. Testimony of a person against his spouse shall be admissible to prove offenses under this Section.

## Section 251.3. Loitering to Solicit Deviate Sexual Relations

A person is guilty of a petty misdemeanor if he loiters in or near any public place for the purpose of soliciting or being solicited to engage in deviate sexual relations.

## Section 251.4. Obscenity

(1) Obscene Defined. Material is obscene if, considered as a whole, its predominant appeal is to prurient interest, that is, a shameful or morbid interest, in nudity, sex or excretion, and if in addition it goes substantially beyond customary limits of candor in describing or representing such matters. Predominant appeal shall be judged with reference to ordinary adults unless it appears from the character of the material or the circumstances of its dissemination to be designed for children or other specially susceptible audience. Undeveloped photographs, molds, printing plates, and the like, shall be deemed obscene notwithstanding that processing or other acts may be required to make the obscenity patent or to disseminate it.

(2) Offenses. Subject to the affirmative defense provided in Subsection (3), a person commits a misdemeanor if he knowingly or recklessly:

(a) sells, delivers or provides, or offers or agrees to sell, deliver or provide, any obscene writing, picture, record or other representation or embodiment of the obscene; or

(b) presents or directs an obscene play, dance or performance, or participates in that portion thereof which makes it obscene; or

(c) publishes, exhibits or otherwise makes available any obscene material; or

(d) possesses any obscene material for purposes of sale or other commercial dissemination; or

(e) sells, advertises or otherwise commercially disseminates material, whether or not obscene, by representing or suggesting that it is obscene.

A person who disseminates or possesses obscene material in the course of his business is presumed to do so knowingly or recklessly.

(3) Justifiable and Non-Commercial Private Dissemination. It is an affirmative defense to prosecution under this Section that dissemination was restricted to:

(a) institutions or persons having scientific, educational, governmental or other similar justification for possessing obscene material; or

(b) non-commercial dissemination to personal associates of the actor.

(4) Evidence; Adjudication of Obscenity. In any prosecution under this Section evidence shall be admissible to show:

(a) the character of the audience for which the material was designed or to which it was directed;

(b) what the predominant appeal of the material would be for ordinary adults or any special audience to which it was directed, and what effect, if any, it would probably have on conduct of such people;

(c) artistic, literary, scientific, educational or other merits of the material;

(d) the degree of public acceptance of the material in the United States;

(e) appeal to prurient interest, or absence thereof, in advertising or other promotion of the material; and

(f) the good repute of the author, creator, publisher or other person from whom the material originated.

Expert testimony and testimony of the author, creator, publisher or other person from whom the material originated, relating to factors entering into the determination of the issue of obscenity, shall be admissible. The Court shall dismiss a prosecution for obscenity if it is satisfied that the material is not obscene.

---

## ADDITIONAL ARTICLES

[Reporter's note: At this point, a State enacting a new Penal Code may insert additional Articles dealing with special topics such as narcotics, alcoholic beverages, gambling and offenses against tax and trade laws. The Model Penal Code project did not extend to these, partly because a higher priority on limited time and resources was accorded to branches of the penal law which have not received close legislative scrutiny. Also, in legislation dealing with narcotics, liquor, tax evasion, and the like, penal provisions have been so intermingled with regulatory and procedural provisions that the task of segregating one group from the other presents special difficulty for model legislation.]

# APPENDIX B

# SELECTED PENAL STATUTES

TABLE OF CONTENTS



## (A) FLORIDA STAND YOUR GROUND LAWS

### 1. Florida Statutes (2014)

**776.012. Use or threatened use of force in defense of person**

(1) A person is justified in using or threatening to use force, except deadly force, against another when and to the extent that the person

reasonably believes that such conduct is necessary to defend himself or herself or another against the other's imminent use of unlawful force. A person who uses or threatens to use force in accordance with this subsection does not have a duty to retreat before using or threatening to use such force.

(2) A person is justified in using or threatening to use deadly force if he or she reasonably believes that using or threatening to use such force is necessary to prevent imminent death or great bodily harm to himself or herself or another or to prevent the imminent commission of a forcible felony. A person who uses or threatens to use deadly force in accordance with this subsection does not have a duty to retreat and has the right to stand his or her ground if the person using or threatening to use the deadly force is not engaged in a criminal activity and is in a place where he or she has a right to be.

### 776.013. Home protection; use or threatened use of deadly force; presumption of fear of death or great bodily harm

(1) A person is presumed to have held a reasonable fear of imminent peril of death or great bodily harm to himself or herself or another when using or threatening to use defensive force that is intended or likely to cause death or great bodily harm to another if:

(a) The person against whom the defensive force was used or threatened was in the process of unlawfully and forcefully entering, or had unlawfully and forcibly entered, a dwelling, residence, or occupied vehicle, or if that person had removed or was attempting to remove another against that person's will from the dwelling, residence, or occupied vehicle; and

(b) The person who uses or threatens to use defensive force knew or had reason to believe that an unlawful and forcible entry or unlawful and forcible act was occurring or had occurred.

(2) The presumption set forth in subsection (1) does not apply if:

(a) The person against whom the defensive force is used or threatened has the right to be in or is a lawful resident of the dwelling, residence, or vehicle, such as an owner, lessee, or titleholder, and there is not an injunction for protection from domestic violence or a written pretrial supervision order of no contact against that person; or

(b) The person or persons sought to be removed is a child or grandchild, or is otherwise in the lawful custody or under the lawful guardianship of, the person against whom the defensive force is used or threatened; or

(c) The person who uses or threatens to use defensive force is engaged in a criminal activity or is using the dwelling, residence, or occupied vehicle to further a criminal activity; or

(d) The person against whom the defensive force is used or threatened is a law enforcement officer, as defined in s. 943.10(14), who enters or attempts to enter a dwelling, residence, or vehicle in the performance of his or her official duties and the officer identified himself or herself in accordance with any applicable law or the person using or threatening to use force knew or reasonably should have known that the person entering or attempting to enter was a law enforcement officer.

(3) A person who is attacked in his or her dwelling, residence, or vehicle has no duty to retreat and has the right to stand his or her ground and use or threaten to use force, including deadly force, if he or she uses or threatens to use force in accordance with s. 776.012(1) or (2) or s. 776.031(1) or (2).

(4) A person who unlawfully and by force enters or attempts to enter a person's dwelling, residence, or occupied vehicle is presumed to be doing so with the intent to commit an unlawful act involving force or violence.

(5) As used in this section, the term:

(a) "Dwelling" means a building or conveyance of any kind, including any attached porch, whether the building or conveyance is temporary or permanent, mobile or immobile, which has a roof over it, including a tent, and is designed to be occupied by people lodging therein at night.

(b) "Residence" means a dwelling in which a person resides either temporarily or permanently or is visiting as an invited guest.

(c) "Vehicle" means a conveyance of any kind, whether or not motorized, which is designed to transport people or property.

**776.031. Use or threatened use of force in defense of property**

(1) A person is justified in using or threatening to use force, except deadly force, against another when and to the extent that the person reasonably believes that such conduct is necessary to prevent or terminate the other's trespass on, or other tortious or criminal interference with, either real property other than a dwelling or personal property, lawfully in his or her possession or in the possession of another who is a member of his or her immediate family or household or of a person whose property he or she has a legal duty to protect. A person who uses or threatens to use force in accordance with this subsection does not have a duty to retreat before using or threatening to use such force.

(2) A person is justified in using or threatening to use deadly force only if he or she reasonably believes that such conduct is necessary to prevent the imminent commission of a forcible felony. A person who uses or threatens to use deadly force in accordance with this subsection does not have a duty to retreat and has the right to stand his or her ground if the person using or threatening to use the deadly force is not engaged in a criminal activity and is in a place where he or she has a right to be.

**776.032. Immunity from criminal prosecution and civil action for justifiable use or threatened use of force**

(1) A person who uses or threatens to use force as permitted in s. 776.012, s. 776.013, or s. 776.031 is justified in such conduct and is immune from criminal prosecution and civil action for the use or threatened use of such force by the person, personal representative, or heirs of the person against whom the force was used or threatened, unless the person against whom force was used or threatened is a law enforcement officer, as defined in s. 943.10(14), who was acting in the performance of

his or her official duties and the officer identified himself or herself in accordance with any applicable law or the person using or threatening to use force knew or reasonably should have known that the person was a law enforcement officer. As used in this subsection, the term "criminal prosecution" includes arresting, detaining in custody, and charging or prosecuting the defendant.

(2) A law enforcement agency may use standard procedures for investigating the use or threatened use of force as described in subsection (1), but the agency may not arrest the person for using or threatening to use force unless it determines that there is probable cause that the force that was used or threatened was unlawful.

(3) The court shall award reasonable attorney's fees, court costs, compensation for loss of income, and all expenses incurred by the defendant in defense of any civil action brought by a plaintiff if the court finds that the defendant is immune from prosecution as provided in subsection (1).

### 2. Florida Session Laws 2005, effective October 1, 2005

FLORIDA 2005 SESSION LAW SERVICE, Nineteenth Legislature, First Regular Session

Chapter 2005–27, C.S.C.S.S.B. No. 436

SELF DEFENSE—DEADLY FORCE

An act relating to the protection of persons and property; creating s. 776.013, F.S.; authorizing a person to use force, including deadly force, against an intruder or attacker in a dwelling, residence, or vehicle under specified circumstances; creating a presumption that a reasonable fear of death or great bodily harm exists under certain circumstances; creating a presumption that a person acts with the intent to use force or violence under specified circumstances; providing definitions; amending ss. 776.012 and 776.031, F.S.; providing that a person is justified in using deadly force under certain circumstances; declaring that a person has no duty to retreat and has the right to stand his or her ground and meet force with force if the person is in a place where he or she has a right to be and the force is necessary to prevent death, great bodily harm, or the commission of a forcible felony; creating s. 776.032, F.S.; providing immunity from criminal prosecution or civil action for using deadly force; defining the term "criminal prosecution"; authorizing a law enforcement agency to investigate the use of deadly force but prohibiting the agency from arresting the person unless the agency determines that there is probable cause that the force the person used was unlawful; providing for the award of attorney's fees, court costs, compensation for loss of income, and other expenses to a defendant in a civil suit who was immune from prosecution under this section; providing an effective date.

WHEREAS, the Legislature finds that it is proper for law-abiding people to protect themselves, their families, and others from intruders and attackers without fear of prosecution or civil action for acting in defense of themselves and others, and

WHEREAS, the castle doctrine is a common-law doctrine of ancient origins which declares that a person's home is his or her castle, and

WHEREAS, Section 8 of Article I of the State Constitution guarantees the right of the people to bear arms in defense of themselves, and

WHEREAS, the persons residing in or visiting this state have a right to expect to remain unmolested within their homes or vehicles, and

WHEREAS, no person or victim of crime should be required to surrender his or her personal safety to a criminal, nor should a person or victim be required to needlessly retreat in the face of intrusion or attack, NOW, THEREFORE,

Be It Enacted by the Legislature of the State of Florida:

Section 1. Section 776.013, Florida Statutes, is created to read:

**776.013. Home protection; use of deadly force; presumption of fear of death or great bodily harm**

(1) A person is presumed to have held a reasonable fear of imminent peril of death or great bodily harm to himself or herself or another when using defensive force that is intended or likely to cause death or great bodily harm to another if:

(a) The person against whom the defensive force was used was in the process of unlawfully and forcefully entering, or had unlawfully and forcibly entered, a dwelling, residence, or occupied vehicle, or if that person had removed or was attempting to remove another against that person's will from the dwelling, residence, or occupied vehicle; and

(b) The person who uses defensive force knew or had reason to believe that an unlawful and forcible entry or unlawful and forcible act was occurring or had occurred.

(2) The presumption set forth in subsection (1) does not apply if:

(a) The person against whom the defensive force is used has the right to be in or is a lawful resident of the dwelling, residence, or vehicle, such as an owner, lessee, or titleholder, and there is not an injunction for protection from domestic violence or a written pretrial supervision order of no contact against that person; or

(b) The person or persons sought to be removed is a child or grandchild, or is otherwise in the lawful custody or under the lawful guardianship of, the person against whom the defensive force is used; or

(c) The person who uses defensive force is engaged in an unlawful activity or is using the dwelling, residence, or occupied vehicle to further an unlawful activity; or

(d) The person against whom the defensive force is used is a law enforcement officer, as defined in s. 943.10(14), who enters or attempts to enter a dwelling, residence, or vehicle in the performance of his or her official duties and the officer identified himself or herself in accordance with any applicable law or the person using force knew or reasonably should have known that the person entering or attempting to enter was a law enforcement officer.

(3) A person who is not engaged in an unlawful activity and who is attacked in any other place where he or she has a right to be has no

duty to retreat and has the right to stand his or her ground and meet force with force, including deadly force if he or she reasonably believes it is necessary to do so to prevent death or great bodily harm to himself or herself or another or to prevent the commission of a forcible felony.

(4) A person who unlawfully and by force enters or attempts to enter a person's dwelling, residence, or occupied vehicle is presumed to be doing so with the intent to commit an unlawful act involving force or violence.

(5) As used in this section, the term:

(a) "Dwelling" means a building or conveyance of any kind, including any attached porch, whether the building or conveyance is temporary or permanent, mobile or immobile, which has a roof over it, including a tent, and is designed to be occupied by people lodging therein at night.

(b) "Residence" means a dwelling in which a person resides either temporarily or permanently or is visiting as an invited guest.

(c) "Vehicle" means a conveyance of any kind, whether or not motorized, which is designed to transport people or property.

Section 2. Section 776.012, Florida Statutes, is amended to read:

**776.012. Use of force in defense of person**

A person is justified in using force, except deadly force, against another when and to the extent that the person reasonably believes that such conduct is necessary to defend himself or herself or another against the other's imminent use of unlawful force. However, a person is justified in the use of deadly force and does not have a duty to retreat if:

(a) He or she reasonably believes that such force is necessary to prevent imminent death or great bodily harm to himself or herself or another or to prevent the imminent commission of a forcible felony; or

(b) Under those circumstances permitted pursuant to s. 776.013.

Section 3. Section 776.031, Florida Statutes, is amended to read:

**776.031. Use of force in defense of others**

A person is justified in the use of force, except deadly force, against another when and to the extent that the person reasonably believes that such conduct is necessary to prevent or terminate the ~~such~~ other's trespass on, or other tortious or criminal interference with, either real property other than a dwelling or personal property, lawfully in his or her possession or in the possession of another who is a member of his or her immediate family or household or of a person whose property he or she has a legal duty to protect. However, the person is justified in the use of deadly force only if he or she reasonably believes that such force is necessary to prevent the imminent commission of a forcible felony. A person does not have a duty to retreat if the person is in a place where he or she has a right to be.

Section 4. Section 776.032, Florida Statutes, is created to read:

**776.032. Immunity from criminal prosecution and civil action for justifiable use of force**

(1) A person who uses force as permitted in s. 776.012, s. 776.013, or s. 776.031 is justified in using such force and is immune from criminal prosecution and civil action for the use of such force, unless the person against whom force was used is a law enforcement officer, as defined in s. 943.10(14), who was acting in the performance of his or her official duties and the officer identified himself or herself in accordance with any applicable law or the person using force knew or reasonably should have known that the person was a law enforcement officer. As used in this subsection, the term "criminal prosecution" includes arresting, detaining in custody, and charging or prosecuting the defendant.

(2) A law enforcement agency may use standard procedures for investigating the use of force as described in subsection (1), but the agency may not arrest the person for using force unless it determines that there is probable cause that the force that was used was unlawful.

(3) The court shall award reasonable attorney's fees, court costs, compensation for loss of income, and all expenses incurred by the defendant in defense of any civil action brought by a plaintiff if the court finds that the defendant is immune from prosecution as provided in subsection (1).

---

## (B) CONTEMPORARY RAPE STATUTES

### 1. New Jersey Statutes Annotated:

**§ 2C:14–2. Sexual assault**

a. An actor is guilty of aggravated sexual assault if he commits an act of sexual penetration with another person under any one of the following circumstances:

(1) The victim is less than 13 years old;

(2) The victim is at least 13 but less than 16 years old; and

(a) The actor is related to the victim by blood or affinity to the third degree, or

(b) The actor has supervisory or disciplinary power over the victim by virtue of the actor's legal, professional, or occupational status, or

(c) The actor is a resource family parent, a guardian, or stands in loco parentis within the household;

(3) The act is committed during the commission, or attempted commission, whether alone or with one or more other persons, of robbery, kidnapping, homicide, aggravated assault on another, burglary, arson or criminal escape;

(4) The actor is armed with a weapon or any object fashioned in such a manner as to lead the victim to reasonably believe it to be

a weapon and threatens by word or gesture to use the weapon or object;

(5) The actor is aided or abetted by one or more other persons and the actor uses physical force or coercion;

(6) The actor uses physical force or coercion and severe personal injury is sustained by the victim;

(7) The victim is one whom the actor knew or should have known was physically helpless or incapacitated, intellectually or mentally incapacitated, or had a mental disease or defect which rendered the victim temporarily or permanently incapable of understanding the nature of his conduct, including, but not limited to, being incapable of providing consent

Aggravated sexual assault is a crime of the first degree [20-year maximum].

b. An actor is guilty of sexual assault if he commits an act of sexual contact with a victim who is less than 13 years old and the actor is at least four years older than the victim.

c. An actor is guilty of sexual assault if he commits an act of sexual penetration with another person under any one of the following circumstances:

(1) The actor uses physical force or coercion, but the victim does not sustain severe personal injury;

(2) The victim is on probation or parole, or is detained in a hospital, prison or other institution and the actor has supervisory or disciplinary power over the victim by virtue of the actor's legal, professional or occupational status;

(3) The victim is at least 16 but less than 18 years old and:

(a) The actor is related to the victim by blood or affinity to the third degree; or

(b) The actor has supervisory or disciplinary power of any nature or in any capacity over the victim; or

(c) The actor is a resource family parent, a guardian, or stands in loco parentis within the household;

(4) The victim is at least 13 but less than 16 years old and the actor is at least four years older than the victim.

d. Notwithstanding the provisions of subsection a. of this section, where a defendant is charged with a violation under paragraph (1) of subsection a. of this section, the prosecutor, in consideration of the interests of the victim, may offer a negotiated plea agreement in which the defendant would be sentenced to a specific term of imprisonment of not less than 15 years, during which the defendant shall not be eligible for parole. In such event, the court may accept the negotiated plea agreement and upon such conviction shall impose the term of imprisonment and period of parole ineligibility as provided for in the plea agreement, and may not impose a lesser term of imprisonment or parole or a lesser period of parole ineligibility than that expressly provided in the plea agreement. The Attorney General shall develop guidelines to ensure the uniform exercise of discretion in making determinations regarding a negotiated reduction in the term of imprisonment and period of parole ineligibility set forth in subsection a. of this section.

Sexual assault is a crime of the second degree [10-year maximum].

### § 2C:14–2.1. Right of victim to consult with prosecuting authority

Whenever there is a prosecution for a violation of N.J.S.A.2C: 14–2, the victim of the sexual assault shall be provided an opportunity to consult with the prosecuting authority prior to the conclusion of any plea negotiations.

Nothing contained herein shall be construed to alter or limit the authority or discretion of the prosecutor to enter into any plea agreement which the prosecutor deems appropriate.

### § 2C:14–3. Criminal sexual contact

a. An actor is guilty of aggravated criminal sexual contact if he commits an act of sexual contact with the victim under any of the circumstances set forth in 2C:14–2a. (2) through (7).

Aggravated criminal sexual contact is a crime of the third degree.

b. An actor is guilty of criminal sexual contact if he commits an act of sexual contact with the victim under any of the circumstances set forth in section 2C:14–2c. (1) through (4).

Criminal sexual contact is a crime of the fourth degree [18-month maximum].

## 2. Virginia Code Ann.:

### § 18.2–61 Rape.

A. If any person has sexual intercourse with a complaining witness, whether or not his or her spouse, or causes a complaining witness, whether or not his or her spouse, to engage in sexual intercourse with any other person and such act is accomplished (i) against the complaining witness's will, by force, threat or intimidation of or against the complaining witness or another person; or (ii) through the use of the complaining witness's mental incapacity or physical helplessness; or (iii) with a child under age 13 as the victim, he or she shall be guilty of rape.[a]

B. A violation of this section shall be punishable, in the discretion of the court or jury, by confinement in a state correctional facility for life or for any term not less than five years; and in addition:

---

[a] Prior to 1999, this provision contained the following limitation:

However, no person shall be found guilty under this subsection unless, at the time of the alleged offense,

(i) the spouses were living separate and apart, or

(ii) the defendant caused serious physical injury to the spouse by the use of force or violence.

The phrase "serious physical injury" was changed to "bodily injury" in 1999, and the entire limitation was deleted in 2002.—[Footnote by eds.]

1. For a violation of clause (iii) of subsection A where the offender is more than three years older than the victim, if done in the commission of, or as part of the same course of conduct as, or as part of a common scheme or plan as a violation of (i) subsection A of § 18.2–47 or § 18.2–48, (ii) § 18.2–89, 18.2–90, or 18.2–91, or (iii) § 18.2–51.2, the punishment shall include a mandatory minimum term of confinement of 25 years; or

2. For a violation of clause (iii) of subsection A where it is alleged in the indictment that the offender was 18 years of age or older at the time of the offense, the punishment shall include a mandatory minimum term of confinement for life.

The mandatory minimum terms of confinement prescribed for violations of this section shall be served consecutively with any other sentence. If the term of confinement imposed for any violation of clause (iii) of subsection A, where the offender is more than three years older than the victim, is for a term less than life imprisonment, the judge shall impose, in addition to any active sentence, a suspended sentence of no less than 40 years. This suspended sentence shall be suspended for the remainder of the defendant's life, subject to revocation by the court.

C. Upon a finding of guilt under this section, when a spouse is the complaining witness in any case tried by the court without a jury, the court, without entering a judgment of guilt, upon motion of the defendant who has not previously had a proceeding against him for violation of this section dismissed pursuant to this subsection and with the consent of the complaining witness and the attorney for the Commonwealth, may defer further proceedings and place the defendant on probation pending completion of counseling or therapy, if not already provided, in the manner prescribed [elsewhere]. If the defendant fails to so complete such counseling or therapy, the court may make final disposition of the case and proceed as otherwise provided. If such counseling is completed as prescribed [elsewhere], the court may discharge the defendant and dismiss the proceedings against him if, after consideration of the views of the complaining witness and such other evidence as may be relevant, the court finds such action will promote maintenance of the family unit and be in the best interest of the complaining witness.

### § 18.2–63 Carnal knowledge of child between thirteen and fifteen years of age.

A. If any person carnally knows, without the use of force, a child thirteen years of age or older but under fifteen years of age, such person shall be guilty of a Class 4 felony [10-year maximum].

B. If any person carnally knows, without the use of force, a child thirteen years of age or older but under fifteen years of age who consents to sexual intercourse and the accused is a minor and such consenting child is three years or more the accused's junior, the accused shall be guilty of a Class 6 felony [five-year maximum]. If such consenting child is less than three years the accused's junior, the accused shall be guilty of a Class 4 misdemeanor [maximum: fine not exceeding $250].

In calculating whether such child is three years or more a junior of the accused minor, the actual dates of birth of the child and the accused, respectively, shall be used.

C. For the purposes of this section,

(i) a child under the age of thirteen years shall not be considered a consenting child and

(ii) "carnal knowledge" includes the acts of sexual intercourse, cunnilingus, fellatio, anillingus, anal intercourse, and animate and inanimate object sexual penetration.

### § 18.2–63.1 Death of victim.

When the death of the victim occurs in connection with an offense under this article, it shall be immaterial in the prosecution thereof whether the alleged offense occurred before or after the death of the victim.

### § 18.2–64.1 Carnal knowledge of certain minors.

If any person providing services, paid or unpaid, to juveniles under the purview of the Juvenile and Domestic Relations District Court Law, or to juveniles who have been committed to the custody of the State Department of Juvenile Justice, carnally knows, without the use of force, any minor fifteen years of age or older, when such minor is confined or detained in jail, is detained in any facility mentioned in § 16.1–249, or has been committed to the custody of the Department of Juvenile Justice pursuant to § 16.1–278.8, knowing or having good reason to believe that

(i) such minor is in such confinement or detention status,

(ii) such minor is a ward of the Department of Juvenile Justice, or

(iii) such minor is on probation, furlough, or leave from or has escaped or absconded from such confinement, detention, or custody, he shall be guilty of a Class 6 felony [five-year maximum].

For the purposes of this section, "carnal knowledge" includes the acts of sexual intercourse, cunnilingus, fellatio, anallingus, anal intercourse, and animate and inanimate object sexual penetration.

### § 18.2–67.1 Forcible sodomy.

A. An accused shall be guilty of forcible sodomy if he or she engages in cunnilingus, fellatio, anilingus, or anal intercourse with a complaining witness whether or not his or her spouse, or causes a complaining witness, whether or not his or her spouse, to engage in such acts with any other person, and

1. The complaining witness is less than 13 years of age, or

2. The act is accomplished against the will of the complaining witness, by force, threat or intimidation of or against the complaining witness or another person, or through the use of the complaining witness's mental incapacity or physical helplessness.

B. Forcible sodomy is a felony punishable by confinement in a state correctional facility for life or for any term not less than five years; and in addition:

1. For a violation of subdivision A 1, where the offender is more than three years older than the victim, if done in the commission of, or as part of the same course of conduct as, or as part of a common scheme or plan as a violation of (i) subsection A of § 18.2–47 or § 18.2–48, (ii) § 18.2–89, 18.2–90, or 18.2–91, or (iii) § 18.2–51.2, the punishment shall include a mandatory minimum term of confinement of 25 years; or

2. For a violation of subdivision A 1 where it is alleged in the indictment that the offender was 18 years of age or older at the time of the offense, the punishment shall include a mandatory minimum term of confinement for life.

The mandatory minimum terms of confinement prescribed for violations of this section shall be served consecutively with any other sentence. If the term of confinement imposed for any violation of subdivision A 1, where the offender is more than three years older than the victim, is for a term less than life imprisonment, the judge shall impose, in addition to any active sentence, a suspended sentence of no less than 40 years. This suspended sentence shall be suspended for the remainder of the defendant's life, subject to revocation by the court.

In any case deemed appropriate by the court, all or part of any sentence imposed for a violation under this section against a spouse may be suspended upon the defendant's completion of counseling or therapy, if not already provided, in the manner prescribed under § 19.2–218.1 if, after consideration of the views of the complaining witness and such other evidence as may be relevant, the court finds such action will promote maintenance of the family unit and will be in the best interest of the complaining witness.

C. Upon a finding of guilt under this section, when a spouse is the complaining witness in any case tried by the court without a jury, the court, without entering a judgment of guilt, upon motion of the defendant who has not previously had a proceeding against him for violation of this section dismissed pursuant to this subsection and with the consent of the complaining witness and the attorney for the Commonwealth, may defer further proceedings and place the defendant on probation pending completion of counseling or therapy, if not already provided, in the manner prescribed [elsewhere]. If the defendant fails to so complete such counseling or therapy, the court may make final disposition of the case and proceed as otherwise provided. If such counseling is completed as prescribed [elsewhere], the court may discharge the defendant and dismiss the proceedings against him if, after consideration of the views of the complaining witness and such other evidence as may be relevant, the court finds such action will promote maintenance of the family unit and be in the best interest of the complaining witness.

### § 18.2–67.2 Object sexual penetration; penalty.

A. An accused shall be guilty of inanimate or animate object sexual penetration if he or she penetrates the labia majora or anus of a complaining witness, whether or not his or her spouse, other than for a bona fide medical purpose, or causes such complaining witness to so penetrate his or her own body with an object or causes a complaining witness, whether or not his or her spouse, to engage in such acts with any other person or to penetrate, or to be penetrated by, an animal, and

1. The complaining witness is less than 13 years of age, or

2. The act is accomplished against the will of the complaining witness, by force, threat or intimidation of or against the complaining witness or another person, or through the use of the complaining witness's mental incapacity or physical helplessness.

B. Inanimate or animate object sexual penetration is a felony punishable by confinement in the state correctional facility for life or for any term not less than five years; and in addition:

1. For a violation of subdivision A 1, where the offender is more than three years older than the victim, if done in the commission of, or as part of the same course of conduct as, or as part of a common scheme or plan as a violation of (i) subsection A of § 18.2–47 or § 18.2–48, (ii) § 18.2–89, 18.2–90, or 18.2–91, or (iii) § 18.2–51.2, the punishment shall include a mandatory minimum term of confinement of 25 years; or

2. For a violation of subdivision A 1 where it is alleged in the indictment that the offender was 18 years of age or older at the time of the offense, the punishment shall include a mandatory minimum term of confinement for life.

The mandatory minimum terms of confinement prescribed for violations of this section shall be served consecutively with any other sentence. If the term of confinement imposed for any violation of subdivision A 1, where the offender is more than three years older than the victim, is for a term less than life imprisonment, the judge shall impose, in addition to any active sentence, a suspended sentence of no less than 40 years. This suspended sentence shall be suspended for the remainder of the defendant's life, subject to revocation by the court.

In any case deemed appropriate by the court, all or part of any sentence imposed for a violation under this section against a spouse may be suspended upon the defendant's completion of counseling or therapy, if not already provided, in the manner prescribed under § 19.2–218.1 if, after consideration of the views of the complaining witness and such other evidence as may be relevant, the court finds such action will promote maintenance of the family unit and will be in the best interest of the complaining witness.

C. Upon a finding of guilt under this section, when a spouse is the complaining witness in any case tried by the court without a jury, the court, without entering a judgment of guilt, upon motion of the defendant who has not previously had a proceeding against him for violation of this section dismissed pursuant to this subsection and with the consent of the complaining witness and the attorney for the Commonwealth, may defer further proceedings and place the defendant on probation pending completion of counseling or therapy, if not already provided, in the manner prescribed [elsewhere]. If the defendant fails to so complete such counseling or therapy, the court may make final disposition of the case and proceed as otherwise provided. If such counseling is completed as prescribed [elsewhere], the court may discharge the defendant and dismiss the proceedings against him if, after consideration of the views of the complaining witness and such other evidence as may be relevant, the court finds such action will promote maintenance of the family unit and be in the best interest of the complaining witness.

### § 18.2–67.3 Aggravated sexual battery.

A. An accused shall be guilty of aggravated sexual battery if he or she sexually abuses the complaining witness, and

1. The complaining witness is less than 13 years of age, or

2. The act is accomplished through the use of the complaining witness's mental incapacity or physical helplessness, or

3. The offense is committed by a parent, step-parent, grandparent, or step-grandparent and the complaining witness is at least 13 but less than 18 years of age, or

4. The act is accomplished against the will of the complaining witness by force, threat or intimidation, and

a. The complaining witness is at least 13 but less than 15 years of age, or

b. The accused causes serious bodily or mental injury to the complaining witness, or

c. The accused uses or threatens to use a dangerous weapon.

B. Aggravated sexual battery is a felony punishable by confinement in a state correctional facility for a term of not less than one nor more than 20 years and by a fine of not more than $100,000.

### § 18.2–67.4 Sexual battery.

A. An accused shall be guilty of sexual battery if he or she sexually abuses, as defined in § 18.2–67.10,

(i) the complaining witness against the will of the complaining witness, by force, threat, intimidation or ruse, or

(ii) within a two-year period, more than one complaining witness or one complaining witness on more than one occasion intentionally and without the consent of the complaining witness,

(iii) an inmate who has been committed to jail or convicted and sentenced to confinement in a state or local correctional facility or regional jail, and the accused is an employee or contractual employee of, or a volunteer with, the state or local correctional facility or regional jail; is in a position of authority over the inmate; and knows that the inmate is under the jurisdiction of the state or local correctional facility or regional jail, or

(iv) a probationer, parolee, or a pretrial or posttrial offender under the jurisdiction of the Department of Corrections, a local community-based probation program, a pretrial services program, a local or regional jail for the purposes of imprisonment, a work program or any other parole/probationary or pretrial services program and the accused is an employee or contractual employee of, or a volunteer with, the Department of Corrections, a local community-based probation program, a pretrial services program or a local or regional jail; is in a position of authority over an offender; and knows that the offender is under the jurisdiction of the Department of Corrections, a local community-based probation program, a pretrial services program or a local or regional jail.

B. Sexual battery is a Class 1 misdemeanor [12-month maximum].

**§ 18.2–67.4:1 Infected sexual battery; penalty.**

A. Any person who, knowing he is infected with HIV, syphilis, or hepatitis B, has sexual intercourse, cunnilingus, fellatio, anilingus or anal intercourse with the intent to transmit the infection to another person is guilty of a Class 6 felony [five-year maximum].

B. Any person who, knowing he is infected with HIV, syphilis, or hepatitis B, has sexual intercourse, cunnilingus, fellatio, anilingus or anal intercourse with another person without having previously disclosed the existence of his infection to the other person is guilty of a Class 1 misdemeanor.

C. "HIV" means the human immunodeficiency virus or any other related virus that causes acquired immunodeficiency syndrome (AIDS).

Nothing in this section shall prevent the prosecution of any other crime against persons under Chapter 4 of this title. Any person charged with a violation of this section alleging he is infected with HIV shall be subject to the testing provisions of § 18.2–62.

**§ 18.2–67.5 Attempted rape, forcible sodomy, object sexual penetration, aggravated sexual battery, and sexual battery.**

A. An attempt to commit rape, forcible sodomy, or inanimate or animate object sexual penetration shall be punishable as a Class 4 felony [10-year maximum].

B. An attempt to commit aggravated sexual battery shall be a felony punishable as a Class 6 felony [five-year maximum].

C. An attempt to commit sexual battery is a Class 1 misdemeanor [12-month maximum].

### 3. Michigan Compiled Laws Annotated:

**§ 750.520a. Definitions**

As used in this chapter:

(a) "Actor" means a person accused of criminal sexual conduct.

(b) "Developmental disability" means an impairment of general intellectual functioning or adaptive behavior which meets all of the following criteria:

(*i*) It originated before the person became 18 years of age.

(*ii*) It has continued since its origination or can be expected to continue indefinitely.

(*iii*) It constitutes a substantial burden to the impaired person's ability to perform in society.

(*iv*) It is attributable to 1 or more of the following:

(A) Mental retardation, cerebral palsy, epilepsy, or autism.

(B) Any other condition of a person found to be closely related to mental retardation because it produces a similar impairment or requires treatment and services similar to those required for a person who is mentally retarded.

(c) "Electronic monitoring" means that term as defined in [the corrections code].

(d) "Intellectual disability" means that term as defined in section 100b of the mental health code, 1974 PA 258, MCL 330.1100b

(e) "Intermediate school district" means a corporate body established under [the school code]

(f) "Intimate parts" includes the primary genital area, groin, inner thigh, buttock, or breast of a human being.

(g) "Mental health professional" means that term as defined in [the mental health code].

(h) "Mental illness" means a substantial disorder of thought or mood that significantly impairs judgment, behavior, capacity to recognize reality, or ability to cope with the ordinary demands of life.

(i) "Mentally disabled" means that a person has a mental illness, is mentally retarded, or has a developmental disability.

(j) "Mentally incapable" means that a person suffers from a mental disease or defect that renders that person temporarily or permanently incapable of appraising the nature of his or her conduct.

(k) "Mentally incapacitated" means that a person is rendered temporarily incapable of appraising or controlling his or her conduct due to the influence of a narcotic, anesthetic, or other substance administered to that person without his or her consent, or due to any other act committed upon that person without his or her consent.

(*l*) "Nonpublic school" means a private, denominational, or parochial elementary or secondary school.

(m) "Physically helpless" means that a person is unconscious, asleep, or for any other reason is physically unable to communicate unwillingness to an act.

(n) "Personal injury" means bodily injury, disfigurement, mental anguish, chronic pain, pregnancy, disease, or loss or impairment of a sexual or reproductive organ.

(*o*) "Public school" means a public elementary or secondary educational entity or agency that is established under the [school code].

(p) "School district" means a general powers school district organized under the [school code].

(q) "Sexual contact" includes the intentional touching of the victim's or actor's intimate parts or the intentional touching of the clothing covering the immediate area of the victim's or actor' s intimate parts, if that intentional touching can reasonably be construed as being for the purpose of sexual arousal or gratification, done for a sexual purpose, or in a sexual manner for:

(*i*) Revenge.

(*ii*) To inflict humiliation.

(*iii*) Out of anger.

(r) "Sexual penetration" means sexual intercourse, cunnilingus, fellatio, anal intercourse, or any other intrusion, however slight, of any part of a person's body or of any object into the genital or anal openings of another person's body, but emission of semen is not required.

(s) "Victim" means the person alleging to have been subjected to criminal sexual conduct.

### § 750.520b. Criminal sexual conduct in first degree

(1) A person is guilty of criminal sexual conduct in the first degree if he or she engages in sexual penetration with another person and if any of the following circumstances exists:

(a) That other person is under 13 years of age.

(b) That other person is at least 13 but less than 16 years of age and any of the following:

(*i*) The actor is a member of the same household as the victim.

(*ii*) The actor is related to the victim by blood or affinity to the fourth degree.

(*iii*) The actor is in a position of authority over the victim and used this authority to coerce the victim to submit.

(*iv*) The actor is a teacher, substitute teacher, or administrator of the public school, nonpublic school, school district, or intermediate school district in which that other person is enrolled.

(*v*) The actor is an employee or a contractual service provider of the public school, nonpublic school, school district, or intermediate school district in which that other person is enrolled, or is a volunteer who is not a student in any public school or nonpublic school, or is an employee of this state or of a local unit of government of this state or of the United States assigned to provide any service to that public school, nonpublic school, school district, or intermediate school district, and the actor uses his or her employee, contractual, or volunteer status to gain access to, or to establish a relationship with, that other person.

(*vi*) The actor is an employee, contractual service provider, or volunteer of a child care organization, or a person licensed to operate a foster family home or a foster family group home in which that other person is a resident, and the sexual penetration occurs during the period of that other person's residency. As used in this subparagraph, "child care organization", "foster family home", and "foster family group home" mean those terms as defined in section 1 of 1973 PA 116, MCL 722.111.

(c) Sexual penetration occurs under circumstances involving the commission of any other felony.

(d) The actor is aided or abetted by 1 or more other persons and either of the following circumstances exists:

(*i*) The actor knows or has reason to know that the victim is mentally incapable, mentally incapacitated, or physically helpless.

(*ii*) The actor uses force or coercion to accomplish the sexual penetration. Force or coercion includes, but is not limited to, any of the circumstances listed in subdivision (f).

(e) The actor is armed with a weapon or any article used or fashioned in a manner to lead the victim to reasonably believe it to be a weapon.

(f) The actor causes personal injury to the victim and force or coercion is used to accomplish sexual penetration. Force or coercion includes, but is not limited to, any of the following circumstances:

(*i*) When the actor overcomes the victim through the actual application of physical force or physical violence.

(*ii*) When the actor coerces the victim to submit by threatening to use force or violence on the victim, and the victim believes that the actor has the present ability to execute these threats.

(*iii*) When the actor coerces the victim to submit by threatening to retaliate in the future against the victim, or any other person, and the victim believes that the actor has the ability to execute this threat. As used in this subdivision, "to retaliate" includes threats of physical punishment, kidnapping, or extortion.

(*iv*) When the actor engages in the medical treatment or examination of the victim in a manner or for purposes that are medically recognized as unethical or unacceptable.

(*v*) When the actor, through concealment or by the element of surprise, is able to overcome the victim.

(g) The actor causes personal injury to the victim, and the actor knows or has reason to know that the victim is mentally incapable, mentally incapacitated, or physically helpless.

(h) That other person is mentally incapable, mentally disabled, mentally incapacitated, or physically helpless, and any of the following:

(*i*) The actor is related to the victim by blood or affinity to the fourth degree.

(*ii*) The actor is in a position of authority over the victim and used this authority to coerce the victim to submit.

(2) Criminal sexual conduct in the first degree is a felony punishable as follows:

(a) Except as provided in subdivisions (b) and (c), by imprisonment for life or for any term of years.

(b) For a violation that is committed by an individual 17 years of age or older against an individual less than 13 years of age by imprisonment for life or any term of years, but not less than 25 years.

(c) For a violation that is committed by an individual 18 years of age or older against an individual less than 13 years of age, by imprisonment for life without the possibility of parole if the person was previously convicted of a violation of this section or section 520c, 520d, 520e, or 520g committed against an individual less than 13 years of age or a violation of law of the United States, another state or political subdivision substantially corresponding to a violation of this section or section 520c, 520d, 520e, or 520g committed against an individual less than 13 years of age.

(d) In addition to any other penalty imposed under subdivision (a) or (b), the court shall sentence the defendant to lifetime electronic monitoring under section 520n.

(3) The court may order a term of imprisonment imposed under this section to be served consecutively to any term of imprisonment imposed for any other criminal offense arising from the same transaction.

## § 750.520c. Criminal sexual conduct in second degree

(1) A person is guilty of criminal sexual conduct in the second degree if the person engages in sexual contact with another person and if any of the following circumstances exists:

(a) That other person is under 13 years of age.

(b) That other person is at least 13 but less than 16 years of age and any of the following:

(*i*) The actor is a member of the same household as the victim.

(*ii*) The actor is related by blood or affinity to the fourth degree to the victim.

(*iii*) The actor is in a position of authority over the victim and the actor used this authority to coerce the victim to submit.

(*iv*) The actor is a teacher, substitute teacher, or administrator of the public school, nonpublic school, school district, or intermediate school district in which that other person is enrolled.

(*v*) The actor is an employee or a contractual service provider of the public school, nonpublic school, school district, or intermediate school district in which that other person is enrolled, or is a volunteer who is not a student in any public school or nonpublic school, or is an employee of this state or of a local unit of government of this state or of the United States assigned to provide any service to that public school, nonpublic school, school district, or intermediate school district, and the actor uses his or her employee, contractual, or volunteer status to gain access to, or to establish a relationship with, that other person.

(*vi*) The actor is an employee, contractual service provider, or volunteer of a child care organization, or a person licensed to operate a foster family home or a foster family group home in which that other person is a resident, and the sexual penetration occurs during the period of that other person's residency. As used in this subparagraph, "child care organization", "foster family home", and "foster family group home" mean those terms as defined in section 1 of 1973 PA 116, MCL 722.111.

(c) Sexual contact occurs under circumstances involving the commission of any other felony.

(d) The actor is aided or abetted by 1 or more other persons and either of the following circumstances exists:

(*i*) The actor knows or has reason to know that the victim is mentally incapable, mentally incapacitated, or physically helpless.

(*ii*) The actor uses force or coercion to accomplish the sexual contact. Force or coercion includes, but is not limited to, any of the circumstances listed in section 520b(1)(f).

(e) The actor is armed with a weapon, or any article used or fashioned in a manner to lead a person to reasonably believe it to be a weapon.

(f) The actor causes personal injury to the victim and force or coercion is used to accomplish the sexual contact. Force or coercion includes, but is not limited to, any of the circumstances listed in section 520b(1)(f).

(g) The actor causes personal injury to the victim and the actor knows or has reason to know that the victim is mentally incapable, mentally incapacitated, or physically helpless.

(h) That other person is mentally incapable, mentally disabled, mentally incapacitated, or physically helpless, and any of the following:

(*i*) The actor is related to the victim by blood or affinity to the fourth degree.

(*ii*) The actor is in a position of authority over the victim and used this authority to coerce the victim to submit.

(i) That other person is under the jurisdiction of the department of corrections and the actor is an employee or a contractual employee of, or a volunteer with, the department of corrections who knows that the other person is under the jurisdiction of the department of corrections.

(j) That other person is under the jurisdiction of the department of corrections and the actor is an employee or a contractual employee of, or a volunteer with, a private vendor that operates a youth correctional facility under [the corrections code], who knows that the other person is under the jurisdiction of the department of corrections.

(k) That other person is a prisoner or probationer under the jurisdiction of a county for purposes of imprisonment or a work program or other probationary program and the actor is an employee or a contractual employee of or a volunteer with the county or the department of corrections who knows that the other person is under the county's jurisdiction.

(*l*) The actor knows or has reason to know that a court has detained the victim in a facility while the victim is awaiting a trial or hearing, or committed the victim to a facility as a result of the victim having been found responsible for committing an act that would be a crime if committed by an adult, and the actor is an employee or contractual employee of, or a volunteer with, the facility in which the victim is detained or to which the victim was committed.

(2) Criminal sexual conduct in the second degree is a felony punishable as follows:

(a) By imprisonment for not more than 15 years.

(b) In addition to the penalty specified in subdivision (a), the court shall sentence the defendant to lifetime electronic monitoring . . . if the violation involved sexual contact committed by an individual 17 years of age or older against an individual less than 13 years of age.

## § 750.520d. Criminal sexual conduct in third degree

(1) A person is guilty of criminal sexual conduct in the third degree if the person engages in sexual penetration with another person and if any of the following circumstances exist:

(a) That other person is at least 13 years of age and under 16 years of age.

(b) Force or coercion is used to accomplish the sexual penetration. Force or coercion includes but is not limited to any of the circumstances listed in section 520b(1)(f)(i) to (v).

(c) The actor knows or has reason to know that the victim is mentally incapable, mentally incapacitated, or physically helpless.

(d) That other person is related to the actor by blood or affinity to the third degree and the sexual penetration occurs under circumstances not otherwise prohibited by this chapter. It is an affirmative defense to a prosecution under this subdivision that the other person was in a position of authority over the defendant and used this authority to coerce the defendant to violate this subdivision. The defendant has the burden of proving this defense by a preponderance of the evidence. This subdivision does not apply if both persons are lawfully married to each other at the time of the alleged violation.

(e) That other person is at least 16 years of age but less than 18 years of age and a student at a public school or nonpublic school, and either of the following applies:

(*i*) The actor is a teacher, substitute teacher, or administrator of that public school, nonpublic school, school district, or intermediate school district. This subparagraph does not apply if the other person is emancipated or if both persons are lawfully married to each other at the time of the alleged violation.

(*ii*) The actor is an employee or a contractual service provider of the public school, nonpublic school, school district, or intermediate school district in which that other person is enrolled, or is a volunteer who is not a student in any public school or nonpublic school, or is an employee of this state or of a local unit of government of this state or of the United States assigned to provide any service to that public school, nonpublic school, school district, or intermediate school district, and the actor uses his or her employee, contractual, or volunteer status to gain access to, or to establish a relationship with, that other person.

(f) That other person is at least 16 years old but less than 26 years of age and is receiving special education services, and either of the following applies:

(*i*) The actor is a teacher, substitute teacher, administrator, employee, or contractual service provider of the public school, nonpublic school, school district, or intermediate school district from which that other person receives the special education services. This subparagraph does not apply if both persons are lawfully married to each other at the time of the alleged violation.

(*ii*) The actor is a volunteer who is not a student in any public school or nonpublic school, or is an employee of this state or of a local unit of government of this state or of the United States assigned to provide any service to that public school, nonpublic school, school district, or intermediate school district, and the actor uses his or her employee, contractual, or volunteer status to gain access to, or to establish a relationship with, that other person.

(g) The actor is an employee, contractual service provider, or volunteer of a child care organization, or a person licensed to operate a foster family home or a foster family group home, in which that other person is a resident, that other person is at least 16 years of age, and the sexual penetration occurs during that other person's residency. As used in this subdivision, "child care organization", "foster family home", and "foster family group home" mean those terms as defined in section 1 of 1973 PA 116, MCL 722.111.

(2) Criminal sexual conduct in the third degree is a felony punishable by imprisonment for not more than 15 years.

### § 750.520e. Criminal sexual conduct in fourth degree

(1) A person is guilty of criminal sexual conduct in the fourth degree if he or she engages in sexual contact with another person and if any of the following circumstances exist:

(a) That other person is at least 13 years of age but less than 16 years of age, and the actor is 5 or more years older than that other person.

(b) Force or coercion is used to accomplish the sexual contact. Force or coercion includes, but is not limited to, any of the following circumstances:

(*i*) When the actor overcomes the victim through the actual application of physical force or physical violence.

(*ii*) When the actor coerces the victim to submit by threatening to use force or violence on the victim, and the victim believes that the actor has the present ability to execute that threat.

(*iii*) When the actor coerces the victim to submit by threatening to retaliate in the future against the victim, or any other person, and the victim believes that the actor has the ability to execute that threat. As used in this subparagraph, "to retaliate" includes threats of physical punishment, kidnapping, or extortion.

(*iv*) When the actor engages in the medical treatment or examination of the victim in a manner or for purposes which are medically recognized as unethical or unacceptable.

(*v*) When the actor achieves the sexual contact through concealment or by the element of surprise.

(c) The actor knows or has reason to know that the victim is mentally incapable, mentally incapacitated, or physically helpless.

(d) That other person is related to the actor by blood or affinity to the third degree and the sexual contact occurs under circumstances not otherwise prohibited by this chapter. It is an affirmative defense to a prosecution under this subdivision that the other person was in a position of authority over the defendant and used this authority to coerce the defendant to violate this subdivision. The defendant has the burden of proving this defense by a preponderance of the evidence. This subdivision does not apply if both persons are lawfully married to each other at the time of the alleged violation.

(e) The actor is a mental health professional and the sexual contact occurs during or within 2 years after the period in which the victim is his or her client or patient and not his or her spouse. The consent of the victim is not a defense to a prosecution under this subdivision. A prosecution under this subsection shall not be used as evidence that the victim is mentally incompetent.

(f) That other person is at least 16 years of age but less than 18 years of age and a student at a public school or nonpublic school, and either of the following applies:

(*i*) The actor is a teacher, substitute teacher, or administrator of that public school, nonpublic school, school district, or intermediate school district. This subparagraph does not apply if the other person is emancipated or if both persons are lawfully married to each other at the time of the alleged violation.

(*ii*) The actor is an employee or a contractual service provider of the public school, nonpublic school, school district, or intermediate school district in which that other person is enrolled, or is a volunteer who is not a student in any public school or nonpublic school, or is an employee of this state or of a local unit of government of this state or of the United States assigned to provide any service to that public school, nonpublic school, school district, or intermediate school district, and the actor uses his or her employee, contractual, or volunteer status to gain access to, or to establish a relationship with, that other person.

(g) That other person is at least 16 years old but less than 26 years of age and is receiving special education services, and either of the following applies:

(*i*) The actor is a teacher, substitute teacher, administrator, employee, or contractual service provider of the public school, nonpublic school, school district, or intermediate school district from which that other person receives the special education services. This subparagraph does not apply if both persons are lawfully married to each other at the time of the alleged violation.

(*ii*) The actor is a volunteer who is not a student in any public school or nonpublic school, or is an employee of this state or of a local unit of government of this state or of the United States assigned to provide any service to that public school, nonpublic school, school district, or intermediate school district, and the actor uses his or her employee, contractual, or volunteer status to gain access to, or to establish a relationship with, that other person.

(2) Criminal sexual conduct in the fourth degree is a misdemeanor punishable by imprisonment for not more than 2 years or a fine of not more than $500.00, or both.

### § 750.520f. Sentencing for second or subsequent offenses under §§ 750520b, c, or d

(1) If a person is convicted of a second or subsequent offense under section 520b, 520c, or 520d, the sentence imposed under those sections for the second or subsequent offense shall provide for a mandatory minimum sentence of at least 5 years.

(2) For purposes of this section, an offense is considered a second or subsequent offense if, prior to conviction of the second or subsequent offense, the actor has at any time been convicted under section 520b, 520c, or 520d or under any similar statute of the United States or any state for a criminal sexual offense including rape, carnal knowledge, indecent liberties, gross indecency, or an attempt to commit such an offense.

### § 750.520g. Assault with intent to commit criminal sexual conduct

(1) Assault with intent to commit criminal sexual conduct involving sexual penetration shall be a felony punishable by imprisonment for not more than 10 years.

(2) Assault with intent to commit criminal sexual conduct in the second degree is a felony punishable by imprisonment for not more than 5 years.

## 4. 10 U.S.C. § 920. Art. 120.

### § 920. Art. 120. Rape and sexual assault generally

(a) Rape.—Any person subject to this chapter who commits a sexual act upon another person by—

(1) using unlawful force against that other person;

(2) using force causing or likely to cause death or grievous bodily harm to any person;

(3) threatening or placing that other person in fear that any person will be subjected to death, grievous bodily harm, or kidnapping;

(4) first rendering that other person unconscious; or

(5) administering to that other person by force or threat of force, or without the knowledge or consent of that person, a drug, intoxicant, or other similar substance and thereby substantially impairing the ability of that other person to appraise or control conduct;

is guilty of rape and shall be punished as a court-martial may direct.

(b) Sexual assault.—Any person subject to this chapter who—

(1) commits a sexual act upon another person by—

(A) threatening or placing that other person in fear;

(B) causing bodily harm to that other person;

(C) making a fraudulent representation that the sexual act serves a professional purpose; or

(D) inducing a belief by any artifice, pretense, or concealment that the person is another person;

(2) commits a sexual act upon another person when the person knows or reasonably should know that the other person is asleep, unconscious, or otherwise unaware that the sexual act is occurring; or

(3) commits a sexual act upon another person when the other person is incapable of consenting to the sexual act due to—

(A) impairment by any drug, intoxicant, or other similar substance, and that condition is known or reasonably should be known by the person; or

(B) a mental disease or defect, or physical disability, and that condition is known or reasonably should be known by the person;

is guilty of sexual assault and shall be punished as a court-martial may direct.

(c) Aggravated sexual contact.—Any person subject to this chapter who commits or causes sexual contact upon or by another person, if to do so would violate subsection (a) (rape) had the sexual contact been a sexual act, is guilty of aggravated sexual contact and shall be punished as a court-martial may direct.

(d) Abusive sexual contact. —Any person subject to this chapter who commits or causes sexual contact upon or by another person, if to do so would violate subsection (b) (sexual assault) had the sexual contact been a sexual act, is guilty of abusive sexual contact and shall be punished as a court-martial may direct.

(e) Proof of threat.—In a prosecution under this section, in proving that a person made a threat, it need not be proven that the person actually intended to carry out the threat or had the ability to carry out the threat.

(f) Defenses.—An accused may raise any applicable defenses available under this chapter or the Rules for Court-Martial. Marriage is not a defense for any conduct in issue in any prosecution under this section.

(g) Definitions—In this section:

(1) Sexual act.—The term "sexual act" means—

(A) contact between the penis and the vulva or anus or mouth, and for purposes of this subparagraph contact involving the penis occurs upon penetration, however slight; or

(B) the penetration, however slight, of the vulva or anus or mouth, of another by any part of the body or by any object, with an intent to abuse, humiliate, harass, or degrade any person or to arouse or gratify the sexual desire of any person.

(2) Sexual contact.—The term "sexual contact" means—

(A) touching, or causing another person to touch, either directly or through the clothing, the genitalia, anus, groin, breast, inner thigh, or buttocks of any person, with an intent to abuse, humiliate, or degrade any person; or

(B) any touching, or causing another person to touch, either directly or through the clothing, any body part of any person, if done with an intent to arouse or gratify the sexual desire of any person.

Touching may be accomplished by any part of the body.

(3) Bodily harm.—The term "bodily harm" means any offensive touching of another, however slight, including any nonconsensual sexual act or nonconsensual sexual contact.

(4) Grievous bodily harm.—The term "grievous bodily harm" means serious bodily injury. It includes fractured or dislocated bones, deep cuts, torn members of the body, serious damage to internal organs, and other severe bodily injuries. It does not include minor injuries such as a black eye or a bloody nose.

(5) Force—The term "force" means—

(A) the use of a weapon;

(B) the use of such physical strength or violence as is sufficient to overcome, restrain, or injure a person; or

(C) inflicting physical harm sufficient to coerce or compel submission by the victim.

(6) Unlawful force.—The term "unlawful force" means an act of force done without legal justification or excuse.

(7) Threatening or placing that other person in fear.—The term "threatening or placing that other person in fear" means a

communication or action that is of sufficient consequence to cause a reasonable fear that non-compliance will result in the victim or another person being subjected to the wrongful action contemplated by the communication or action.

(8) Consent.—

(A) The term "consent" means a freely given agreement to the conduct at issue by a competent person. An expression of lack of consent through words or conduct means there is no consent. Lack of verbal or physical resistance or submission resulting from the use of force, threat of force, or placing another person in fear does not constitute consent. A current or previous dating or social or sexual relationship by itself or the manner of dress of the person involved with the accused in the conduct at issue shall not constitute consent.

(B) A sleeping, unconscious, or incompetent person cannot consent. A person cannot consent to force causing or likely to cause death or grievous bodily harm or to being rendered unconscious. A person cannot consent while under threat or in fear or under the circumstances described in subparagraph (C) or (D) of subsection (b)(1).

(C) Lack of consent may be inferred based on the circumstances of the offense. All the surrounding circumstances are to be considered in determining whether a person gave consent, or whether a person did not resist or ceased to resist only because of another person's actions.

---

## (C) VIRGINIA HOMICIDE STATUTES

### 1. 2 Va. Stat. §§ 2, 4, 14 (Shepherd 1796):

II. And whereas, The several offenses which are included under the general denomination of murder, differ so greatly from each other in the degree of their atrociousness, that it is unjust to involve them in the same punishment; Be it . . . enacted, That all murder which shall be perpetrated by means of poison, or by lying in wait, or by any other kind of wilful, deliberate, and premeditated killing, or which shall be committed in the perpetration or attempt to perpetrate any arson, rape, robbery or burglary, shall be deemed murder of the first degree; and all other kinds of murder shall be deemed murder of the second degree. . . .

IV. . . . Every person duly convicted of the crime of murder in the second degree, shall be sentenced to . . . confinement for a period not less than five years, nor more than 18 years. . . .

XIV. Every person convicted of murder of the first degree . . . shall suffer death by hanging by the neck.

### 2. Va. Code, tit. 52 (1887):

**§ 3662. Murder, first and second degree, defined.**—Murder by poison, lying in wait, imprisonment, starving, or any wilful, deliberate, and premeditated killing, or in the commission of, or attempt to commit arson, rape, robbery, or burglary, is murder of the first degree. All other murder is murder of the second degree.

**§ 3663. First degree, how punished.**—Murder of the first degree shall be punished with death.

**§ 3664. Second degree, how punished.**—Murder of the second degree shall be punished by confinement in the penitentiary not less than five nor more than 18 years.

**§ 3665. Voluntary manslaughter, how punished.**—Voluntary manslaughter, shall be punished by confinement in the penitentiary not less than one nor more than five years.

**§ 3666. Involuntary manslaughter, a misdemeanor.**—Involuntary manslaughter, shall be a misdemeanor.

### 3. Va. Acts, ch. 240, § 1 (1914):

1. Be it enacted by the General Assembly of Virginia, That section 3663, be amended and reenacted so as to read as follows:

**Sec. 3663.** Murder of the first degree shall be punished with death, or in the discretion of the jury by confinement in the penitentiary for life.

### 4. Va. Code Ann. (Michie 1996 & Supp. 2009):

**§ 18.2–10. Punishment for conviction of felony; penalty.**—The authorized punishments for conviction of a felony are:

(a) For Class 1 felonies, death, if the person so convicted was 18 years of age or older at the time of the offense and is not determined to be mentally retarded pursuant to § 19.2–264.3:1.1, or imprisonment for life and, subject to subdivision (g), a fine of not more than $100,000. If the person was under 18 years of age at the time of the offense or is determined to be mentally retarded pursuant to § 19.2–264.3:1.1, the punishment shall be imprisonment for life and, subject to subdivision (g), a fine of not more than $100,000.

(b) For Class 2 felonies, imprisonment for life or for any term not less than 20 years and, subject to subdivision (g), a fine of not more than $100,000.

(c) For Class 3 felonies, a term of imprisonment of not less than five years nor more than 20 years and, subject to subdivision (g), a fine of not more than $100,000.

(d) For Class 4 felonies, a term of imprisonment of not less than two years nor more than 10 years and, subject to subdivision (g), a fine of not more than $100,000.

(e) For Class 5 felonies, a term of imprisonment of not less than one year nor more than 10 years, or in the discretion of the jury or the court trying the case without a jury, confinement in jail for not more than 12 months and a fine of not more than $2,500, either or both.

(f) For Class 6 felonies, a term of imprisonment of not less than one year nor more than five years, or in the discretion of the jury or the court trying the case without a jury, confinement in jail for not more than 12 months and a fine of not more than $2,500, either or both.

(g) Except as specifically authorized in subdivision (e) or (f), or in Class 1 felonies for which a sentence of death is imposed, the court shall impose either a sentence of imprisonment together with a fine, or imprisonment only. However, if the defendant is not a natural person, the court shall impose only a fine.

For any felony offense committed (i) on or after January 1, 1995, the court may, and (ii) on or after July 1, 2000, shall, except in cases in which the court orders a suspended term of confinement of at least six months, impose an additional term of not less than six months nor more than three years, which shall be suspended conditioned upon successful completion of a period of post-release supervision pursuant to § 19.2–295.2 and compliance with such other terms as the sentencing court may require. However, such additional term may only be imposed when the sentence includes an active term of incarceration in a correctional facility.

For a felony offense prohibiting proximity to children as described in subsection A of § 18.2–370.2, the sentencing court is authorized to impose the punishment set forth in that section in addition to any other penalty provided by law.

**§ 18.2–30. Murder and manslaughter declared felonies.**—Any person who commits capital murder, murder of the first degree, murder of the second degree, voluntary manslaughter, or involuntary manslaughter, shall be guilty of a felony.

**§ 18.2–31. Capital murder defined; punishment.**—The following offenses shall constitute capital murder, punishable as a Class 1 felony:

1. The willful, deliberate and premeditated killing of any person in the commission of abduction, as defined in § 18.2–48, when such abduction was committed with the intent to extort money, or a pecuniary benefit or with the intent to defile the victim of such abduction;

2. The willful, deliberate, and premeditated killing of any person by another for hire;

3. The willful, deliberate, and premeditated killing of any person by a prisoner confined in a state or local correctional facility as defined in § 53.1–1, or while in the custody of an employee thereof;

4. The willful, deliberate, and premeditated killing of any person in the commission of robbery or attempted robbery;

5. The willful, deliberate, and premeditated killing of any person in the commission of, or subsequent to, rape or attempted rape, forcible sodomy or attempted forcible sodomy or object sexual penetration;

6. The willful, deliberate, and premeditated killing of a law-enforcement officer as defined in § 9.1–101, a fire marshal

appointed pursuant to § 27–30 or a deputy or an assistant fire marshal appointed pursuant to § 27–36, when such fire marshal or deputy or assistant fire marshal has police powers as set forth in §§ 27–34.2 and 27–34.2:1, an auxiliary police officer appointed or provided for pursuant to §§ 15.2–1731 and 15.2–1733, an auxiliary deputy sheriff appointed pursuant to § 15.2–1603, or any law-enforcement officer of another state or the United States having the power to arrest for a felony under the laws of such state or the United States, when such killing is for the purpose of interfering with the performance of his official duties;

7. The willful, deliberate, and premeditated killing of more than one person as a part of the same act or transaction;

8. The willful, deliberate, and premeditated killing of more than one person within a three-year period;

9. The willful, deliberate, and premeditated killing of any person in the commission of or attempted commission of a violation of § 18.2–248, involving a Schedule I or II controlled substance, when such killing is for the purpose of furthering the commission or attempted commission of such violation.

10. The willful, deliberate, and premeditated killing of any person by another pursuant to the direction or order of one who is engaged in a continuing criminal enterprise as defined in subsection I of § 18.2–248;

11. The willful, deliberate, and premeditated killing of a pregnant woman by one who knows that the woman is pregnant and has the intent to cause the involuntary termination of the woman's pregnancy without a live birth;

12. The willful, deliberate, and premeditated killing of a person under the age of fourteen by a person age twenty-one or older; and

13. The willful, deliberate, and premeditated killing of any person by another in the commission of or attempted commission of an act of terrorism as defined in § 18.2–46.4.

14. The willful, deliberate, and premeditated killing of a justice of the Supreme Court, a judge of the Court of Appeals, a judge of a circuit court or district court, a retired judge sitting by designation or under temporary recall, or a substitute judge appointed under § 16.1–69.9:1 when the killing is for the purpose of interfering with his official duties as a judge; and

15. The willful, deliberate, and premeditated killing of any witness in a criminal case after a subpoena has been issued for such witness by the court, the clerk, or an attorney, when the killing is for the purpose of interfering with the person's duties in such case.

If any one or more subsections, sentences, or parts of this section shall be judged unconstitutional or invalid, such adjudication shall not affect, impair, or invalidate the remaining provisions thereof but shall be confined in its operation to the specific provisions so held unconstitutional or invalid.

**§ 18.2–32. First- and second-degree murder defined; punishment.**—Murder, other than capital murder, by poison, lying in wait, imprisonment, starving, or by any willful, deliberate, and premeditated killing, or in the commission of, or attempt to commit, arson, rape, forcible sodomy, inanimate or animate object sexual penetration, robbery, burglary or abduction, except as provided in § 18.2–31, is murder of the first degree, punishable as a Class 2 felony.

All murder other than capital murder and murder in the first degree is murder of the second degree and is punishable by confinement in a state correctional facility for not less than five nor more than forty years.

**§ 18.2–32.1. Murder of a pregnant woman; penalty.**—The willful and deliberate killing of a pregnant woman without premeditation by one who knows that the woman is pregnant and has the intent to cause the involuntary termination of the woman's pregnancy without a live birth shall be punished by a term of imprisonment of not less than ten years nor more than forty years.

**§ 18.2–33. Felony homicide defined; punishment.**—The killing of one accidentally, contrary to the intention of the parties, while in the prosecution of some felonious act other than those specified in §§ 18.2–31 and 18.2–32, is murder of the second degree and is punishable by confinement in a state correctional facility for not less than five years nor more than forty years.

**§ 18.2–35. How voluntary manslaughter punished.**—Voluntary manslaughter is punishable as a Class 5 felony.

**§ 18.2–36. How involuntary manslaughter punished.**—Involuntary manslaughter is punishable as a Class 5 felony.

**§ 19.2–264.2. Conditions for imposition of death sentence.**—In assessing the penalty of any person convicted of an offense for which the death penalty may be imposed, a sentence of death shall not be imposed unless the court or jury shall (1) after consideration of the past criminal record of convictions of the defendant, find that there is a probability that the defendant would commit criminal acts of violence that would constitute a continuing serious threat to society or that his conduct in committing the offense for which he stands charged was outrageously or wantonly vile, horrible or inhuman in that it involved torture, depravity of mind or an aggravated battery to the victim; and (2) recommend that the penalty of death be imposed.

**§ 19.2–264.3. Procedure for trial by jury.**—

A. In any case in which the offense may be punishable by death which is tried before a jury the court shall first submit to the jury the issue of guilt or innocence of the defendant of the offense charged in the indictment, or any other offense supported by the evidence for which a lesser punishment is provided by law and the penalties therefor.

B. If the jury finds the defendant guilty of an offense for which the death penalty may not be imposed, it shall fix the punishment for such offense as provided in § 19.2–295.1.

C. If the jury finds the defendant guilty of an offense which may be punishable by death, then a separate proceeding before the same jury shall be held as soon as is practicable on the issue of the penalty, which shall be fixed as is provided in § 19.2–264.4.

If the sentence of death is subsequently set aside or found invalid, and the defendant or the Commonwealth requests a jury for purposes of resentencing, the court shall impanel a different jury on the issue of penalty.

**§ 19.2–264.4. Sentence proceeding.**—

A. Upon a finding that the defendant is guilty of an offense which may be punishable by death, a proceeding shall be held which shall be limited to a determination as to whether the defendant shall be sentenced to death or life imprisonment. Upon request of the defendant, a jury shall be instructed that for all Class 1 felony offenses committed after January 1, 1995, a defendant shall not be eligible for parole if sentenced to imprisonment for life. In case of trial by jury, where a sentence of death is not recommended, the defendant shall be sentenced to imprisonment for life.

A1. In any proceeding conducted pursuant to this section, the court shall permit the victim, as defined in § 19.2–11.01, upon the motion of the attorney for the Commonwealth, and with the consent of the victim, to testify in the presence of the accused regarding the impact of the offense upon the victim. The court shall limit the victim's testimony to the factors set forth in clauses (i) through (vi) of subsection A of § 19.2–299.1.

B. In cases of trial by jury, evidence may be presented as to any matter which the court deems relevant to sentence, except that reports under the provisions of § 19.2–299, or under any Rule of Court, shall not be admitted into evidence.

Evidence which may be admissible, subject to the rules of evidence governing admissibility, may include the circumstances surrounding the offense, the history and background of the defendant, and any other facts in mitigation of the offense. Facts in mitigation may include, but shall not be limited to, the following:

(i) The defendant has no significant history of prior criminal activity,

(ii) the capital felony was committed while the defendant was under the influence of extreme mental or emotional disturbance,

(iii) the victim was a participant in the defendant's conduct or consented to the act,

(iv) at the time of the commission of the capital felony, the capacity of the defendant to appreciate the criminality of his conduct or to conform his conduct to the requirements of law was significantly impaired,

(v) the age of the defendant at the time of the commission of the capital offense or

(vi) even if § 19.2–264.3:1.1 is inapplicable as a bar to the death penalty, the subaverage intellectual functioning of the defendant.

C. The penalty of death shall not be imposed unless the Commonwealth shall prove beyond a reasonable doubt that there is a probability based upon evidence of the prior history of the defendant or of the circumstances surrounding the commission of the offense of which he is accused that he would commit criminal acts of violence that would constitute a continuing serious threat to society, or that his conduct in committing the offense was outrageously or wantonly vile, horrible or inhuman, in that it involved torture, depravity of mind or aggravated battery to the victim.

D. In the event the jury cannot agree as to the penalty, the court shall dismiss the jury, and impose a sentence of imprisonment for life.

**§ 19.2–264.5. Post sentence reports.**—When the punishment of any person has been fixed at death, the court shall, before imposing sentence, direct a probation officer of the court to thoroughly investigate the history of the defendant and any and all other relevant facts, to the end that the court may be fully advised as to whether the sentence of death is appropriate and just. Reports shall be made, presented and filed as provided in § 19.2–299 except that, notwithstanding any other provision of law, such reports shall in all cases contain a Victim Impact Statement. Such statement shall contain the same information and be prepared in the same manner as Victim Impact Statements prepared pursuant to § 19.2–299.1. After consideration of the report, and upon good cause shown, the court may set aside the sentence of death and impose a sentence of imprisonment for life. Notwithstanding any other provision of law, if the court sets aside the sentence of death and imposes a sentence of imprisonment for life, it shall include in the sentencing order an explanation for the reduction in sentence.

**§ 17.1–313. Review of death sentence.**—

A. A sentence of death, upon the judgment thereon becoming final in the circuit court, shall be reviewed on the record by the Supreme Court.

B. The proceeding in the circuit court shall be transcribed as expeditiously as practicable, and the transcript filed forthwith upon transcription with the clerk of the circuit court, who shall, within ten days after receipt of the transcript, compile the record as provided in Rule 5:14 and transmit it to the Supreme Court.

C. In addition to consideration of any errors in the trial enumerated by appeal, the court shall consider and determine:

1. Whether the sentence of death was imposed under the influence of passion, prejudice or any other arbitrary factor; and

2. Whether the sentence of death is excessive or disproportionate to the penalty imposed in similar cases, considering both the crime and the defendant.

D. In addition to the review and correction of errors in the trial of the case, with respect to review of the sentence of death, the court may:

1. Affirm the sentence of death;

2. Commute the sentence of death to imprisonment for life; or

3. Remand to the trial court for a new sentence proceeding.

E. The Supreme Court may accumulate the records of all capital felony cases tried within such period of time as the court may determine. The court shall consider such records as are available as a guide in determining whether the sentence imposed in the case under review is excessive. Such records as are accumulated shall be made available to the circuit courts.

F. Sentence review shall be in addition to appeals, if taken, and review and appeal may be consolidated. The defendant and the Commonwealth shall have the right to submit briefs within time limits imposed by the court, either by rule or order, and to present oral argument.

G. The Supreme Court shall, in setting its docket, give priority to the review of cases in which the sentence of death has been imposed over other cases pending in the Court. In setting its docket, the Court shall also give priority to the consideration and disposition of petitions for writs of habeas corpus filed by prisoners held under sentence of death.

---

## (D) PRE-*FURMAN* GEORGIA HOMICIDE STATUTES

### 1. Ga. Laws, 1968 Sess., pp. 1276–77, 1335, before the Supreme Court in Furman v. Georgia, 408 U.S. 238 (1972):

**§ 26–1101. Murder.** (a) A person commits murder when he unlawfully and with malice aforethought, either express or implied, causes the death of another human being. Express malice is that deliberate intention unlawfully to take away the life of a fellow creature, which is manifested by external circumstances capable of proof. Malice shall be implied where no considerable provocation appears, and where all the circumstances of the killing show an abandoned and malignant heart.

(b) A person also commits the crime of murder when in the commission of a felony he causes the death of another human being, irrespective of malice.

(c) A person convicted of murder shall be punished by death or by imprisonment for life.

**§ 26–1102. Voluntary Manslaughter.** A person commits voluntary manslaughter when he causes the death of another human being, under circumstances which would otherwise be murder, if he acts solely as the result of a sudden, violent, and irresistible passion resulting from serious provocation sufficient to excite such passion in a reasonable person; however, if there should have been an interval between the provocation and the killing sufficient for the voice of reason and humanity to be heard, of which the jury in all cases shall be the judge, the killing shall be attributed to deliberate revenge and be punished as murder. A person convicted of voluntary manslaughter shall be punished by imprisonment for not less than one nor more than 20 years.

**§ 26–1103. Involuntary Manslaughter.** (a) A person commits involuntary manslaughter in the commission of an unlawful act when he causes the death of another human being without any intention to do so, by the commission of an unlawful act other than a felony. A person convicted under this subsection shall be punished by imprisonment for not less than one year nor more than five years.

(b) A person commits involuntary manslaughter in the commission of a lawful act in an unlawful manner when he causes the death of another human being, without any intention to do so, by the commission of a lawful act in an unlawful manner likely to cause death or great bodily harm. A person convicted under this subsection shall be punished as for a misdemeanor.

**§ 26–3102. Capital Offenses.—Jury Verdict and Sentence.** Where, upon a trial by jury, a person is convicted of an offense which may be punishable by death, a sentence of death shall not be imposed unless the jury verdict includes a recommendation that such sentence be imposed. Where a recommendation of death is made, the court shall sentence the defendant to death. Where a sentence of death is not recommended by the jury, the court shall sentence the defendant to imprisonment as provided by law. Unless the jury trying the case recommends the death sentence in its verdict, the court shall not sentence the defendant to death.

---

## (E) NEW YORK HOMICIDE STATUTES

### 1. Bender's N.Y. Penal Law (1942):

#### § 1044. Murder in first degree defined.

The killing of a human being, unless it is excusable or justifiable, is murder in the first degree, when committed:

1. From a deliberate and premeditated design to effect the death of the person killed, or of another; or,

2. By an act imminently dangerous to others, and evincing a depraved mind, regardless of human life, although without a premeditated design to effect the death of any individual; or without a design to effect death, by a person engaged in the commission of, or in an attempt to commit a felony, either upon or affecting the person killed or otherwise; or

3. When perpetrated in committing the crime of arson in the first degree. . . .

#### § 1045. Punishment for murder in first degree.

Murder in the first degree is punishable by death, unless the jury recommends life imprisonment as provided by section 1045–a.

#### § 1045–a. Life imprisonment for felony murder; jury may recommend.

A jury finding a person guilty of murder in the first degree, as defined by Section 1044(2), may, as a part of its verdict, recommend that the defendant be imprisoned for the term of his natural life. Upon such recommendation, the court may sentence the defendant to imprisonment for the term of his natural life.

**§ 1046. Murder in second degree defined.**

Such killing of a human being is murder in the second degree, when committed with a design to effect the death of the person killed, or of another, but without deliberation and premeditation.

**§ 1048. Punishment for murder in the second degree.**

Murder in the second degree is punishable by imprisonment under an indeterminate sentence, the minimum of which shall be not less than 20 years and the maximum of which shall be for the offender's natural life. . . .

**§ 1049. Manslaughter defined.**

In a case other than one of those specified in Sections 1044 [and] 1046 . . . , homicide, not being justifiable or excusable, is manslaughter.

**§ 1050. Manslaughter in first degree.**

Such homicide is manslaughter in the first degree, when committed without a design to effect death:

1. By a person engaged in committing, or attempting to commit a misdemeanor, affecting the person or property, either of the person killed, or of another; or,

2. In the heat of passion, but in a cruel and unusual manner, or by means of a dangerous weapon. . . .

**§ 1051. Punishment for manslaughter in first degree.**

Manslaughter in the first degree is punishable by imprisonment for a term not exceeding 20 years.

**§ 1052. Manslaughter in second degree defined.**

Such homicide is manslaughter in the second degree, when committed without a design to effect death:

1. By a person committing or attempting to commit a trespass, or other invasion of a private right, either of the person killed, or of another, not amounting to a crime; or,

2. In the heat of passion, but not by a dangerous weapon or by the use of means of either cruel or unusual; or,

3. By any act, procurement or culpable negligence of any person, which, according to the provisions of this article, does not constitute the crime of murder in the first or second degree, nor manslaughter in the first degree. . . .

**§ 1053. Punishment for manslaughter in second degree.**

Manslaughter in the second degree is punishable by imprisonment for a term not exceeding 15 years, or by a fine of not more than $1,000, or by both.

**§ 1053–a. Criminal negligence in operation of a vehicle resulting in death.**

A person who operates or drives any vehicle of any kind in a reckless or culpably negligent manner, whereby a human being is killed, is guilty of criminal negligence in the operation of a vehicle resulting in death.

**§ 1053–b. Punishment for criminal negligence in operation of vehicle resulting in death.**

A person convicted of the crime defined by section 1053–a is punishable by imprisonment for a term of not exceeding five years or by a fine of not more than $1000, or by both.

**2. N.Y. Penal Law (McKinney 1998 & Supp. 2004):**

**§ 125.10. Criminally negligent homicide.**

A person is guilty of criminally negligent homicide when, with criminal negligence, he causes the death of another person.

Criminally negligent homicide is a class E felony [four-year maximum].

**§ 125.15. Manslaughter in the second degree.**

A person is guilty of manslaughter in the second degree when:

1. He recklessly causes the death of another person. . . .

Manslaughter in the second degree is a class C felony [15-year maximum].

**§ 125.20. Manslaughter in the first degree.**

A person is guilty of manslaughter in the first degree when:

1. With intent to cause serious physical injury to another person, he causes the death of such person or of a third person; or

2. With intent to cause the death of another person, he causes the death of such person or of a third person under circumstances which do not constitute murder because he acts under the influence of extreme emotional disturbance, as defined in paragraph (a) of subdivision one of section 125.25. The fact that homicide was committed under the influence of extreme emotional disturbance constitutes a mitigating circumstance reducing murder to manslaughter in the first degree and need not be proved in any prosecution initiated under this subdivision. . . .

Manslaughter in the first degree is a class B felony [25-year maximum].

**§ 125.25. Murder in the second degree.**

A person is guilty of murder in the second degree [punishable by a 20-year minimum and maximum of life imprisonment] when:

1. With intent to cause the death of another person, he causes the death of such person or of a third person; except that in any prosecution under this subdivision, it is an affirmative defense that:

(a) The defendant acted under the influence of extreme emotional disturbance for which there was a reasonable explanation or excuse, the reasonableness of which is to be determined from the viewpoint of a person in the defendant's situation under the circumstances as the defendant believed them to be. Nothing contained in this paragraph shall constitute a defense to a prosecution for, or preclude a conviction of, manslaughter in the first degree or any other crime; or

(b) The defendant's conduct consisted of causing or aiding, without the use of duress or deception, another person to commit suicide. Nothing contained in this paragraph shall constitute a defense to a prosecution for, or preclude a conviction of, manslaughter in the second degree or any other crime; or

2. Under circumstances evincing a depraved indifference to human life, he recklessly engages in conduct which creates a grave risk of death to another person, and thereby causes the death of another person; or

3. Acting either alone or with one or more other persons, he commits or attempts to commit robbery, burglary, kidnapping, arson, rape in the first degree, criminal sexual act in the first degree, sexual abuse in the first degree, aggravated sexual abuse, escape in the first degree, or escape in the second degree, and, in the course of and in furtherance of such crime or of immediate flight therefrom, he, or another participant, if there be any, causes the death of a person other than one of the participants; except that in any prosecution under this subdivision, in which the defendant was not the only participant in the underlying crime, it is an affirmative defense that the defendant:

(a) Did not commit the homicidal act or in any way solicit, request, command, importune, cause or aid the commission thereof; and

(b) Was not armed with a deadly weapon, or any instrument, article or substance readily capable of causing death or serious physical injury and of a sort not ordinarily carried in public places by law-abiding persons; and

(c) Had no reasonable ground to believe that any other participant was armed with such a weapon, instrument, article or substance; and

(d) Had no reasonable ground to believe that any other participant intended to engage in conduct likely to result in death or serious physical injury; or

4. Under circumstances evincing a depraved indifference to human life, and being eighteen years old or more the defendant recklessly engages in conduct which creates a grave risk of serious physical injury or death to another person less than eleven years old and thereby causes the death of such person; or

5. Being eighteen years old or more, while in the course of committing rape in the first, second or third degree, criminal sexual act in the first, second or third degree, sexual abuse in the first degree, aggravated sexual abuse in the first, second, third or fourth degree, or incest in

the first, second or third degree, against a person less than fourteen years old, he or she intentionally causes the death of such person.

Murder in the second degree is a class A–I felony.

### § 125.27. Murder in the first degree.[b]

A person is guilty of murder in the first degree when:

1. With intent to cause the death of another person, he causes the death of such person or of a third person; and

(a) Either:

(i) the intended victim was a police officer . . . who was at the time of the killing engaged in the course of performing his official duties, and the defendant knew or reasonably should have known that the intended victim was a police officer; or

(ii) the intended victim was a peace officer . . . who was at the time of the killing engaged in the course of performing his official duties, and the defendant knew or reasonably should have known that the intended victim was such a uniformed court officer, parole officer, probation officer, or employee of the division for youth; or

(ii–2) the intended victim was a firefighter, emergency medical technician, ambulance driver, paramedic, physician or registered nurse involved in a first response team, or any other individual who, in the course of official duties, performs emergency response activities and was engaged in such activities at the time of killing and the defendant knew or reasonably should have known that the intended victim was such firefighter, emergency medical technician, ambulance driver, paramedic, physician or registered nurse; or

(iii) the intended victim was an employee of a state correctional institution or was an employee of a local correctional facility . . . , who was at the time of the killing engaged in the course of performing his official duties, and the defendant knew or reasonably should have known that the intended victim was an employee of a state correctional institution or a local correctional facility; or

(iv) at the time of the commission of the killing, the defendant was confined in a state correctional institution or was otherwise in custody upon a sentence for the term of his natural life, or upon a sentence commuted to one of natural life, or upon a sentence for an indeterminate term the minimum of which was at least fifteen years and the maximum of which was natural life, or at the time of the commission of the killing, the defendant had escaped from such confinement or custody while serving such a sentence and had not yet been returned to such confinement or custody; or

(v) the intended victim was a witness to a crime committed on a prior occasion and the death was caused for the

---

[b] This section was substantially revised in 1995 when New York revived the death penalty for first-degree murder.—[Footnote by eds.]

purpose of preventing the intended victim's testimony in any criminal action or proceeding whether or not such action or proceeding had been commenced, or the intended victim had previously testified in a criminal action or proceeding and the killing was committed for the purpose of exacting retribution for such prior testimony, or the intended victim was an immediate family member of a witness to a crime committed on a prior occasion and the killing was committed for the purpose of preventing or influencing the testimony of such witness, or the intended victim was an immediate family member of a witness who had previously testified in a criminal action or proceeding and the killing was committed for the purpose of exacting retribution upon such witness for such prior testimony. As used in this subparagraph "immediate family member" means a husband, wife, father, mother, daughter, son, brother, sister, stepparent, grandparent, stepchild or grandchild; or

(vi) the defendant committed the killing or procured commission of the killing pursuant to an agreement with a person other than the intended victim to commit the same for the receipt, or in expectation of the receipt, of anything of pecuniary value from a party to the agreement or from a person other than the intended victim acting at the direction of a party to such agreement; or

(vii) the victim was killed while the defendant was in the course of committing or attempting to commit and in furtherance of robbery, burglary in the first degree or second degree, kidnapping in the first degree, arson in the first degree or second degree, rape in the first degree, criminal sexual act in the first degree, sexual abuse in the first degree, aggravated sexual abuse in the first degree or escape in the first degree, or in the course of and furtherance of immediate flight after committing or attempting to commit any such crime or in the course of and furtherance of immediate flight after attempting to commit the crime of murder in the second degree; provided however, the victim is not a participant in one of the aforementioned crimes and, provided further that, unless the defendant's criminal liability under this subparagraph is based upon the defendant having commanded another person to cause the death of the victim or intended victim . . . , this subparagraph shall not apply where the defendant's criminal liability is based upon the conduct of another . . . ; or

(viii) as part of the same criminal transaction, the defendant, with intent to cause serious physical injury to or the death of an additional person or persons, causes the death of an additional person or persons; provided, however, the victim is not a participant in the criminal transaction; or

(ix) prior to committing the killing, the defendant had been convicted of murder as defined in this section or section 125.25 of this article, or had been convicted in another jurisdiction of an offense which, if committed in this state, would constitute a violation of either of such sections; or

(x) the defendant acted in an especially cruel and wanton manner pursuant to a course of conduct intended to inflict and inflicting torture upon the victim prior to the victim's death. As used in this subparagraph, "torture" means the intentional and depraved infliction of extreme physical pain; "depraved" means the defendant relished the infliction of extreme physical pain upon the victim evidencing debasement or perversion or that the defendant evidenced a sense of pleasure in the infliction of extreme physical pain; or

(xi) the defendant intentionally caused the death of two or more additional persons within the state in separate criminal transactions within a period of twenty-four months when committed in a similar fashion or pursuant to a common scheme or plan; or

(xii) the intended victim was a judge . . . and the defendant killed such victim because such victim was, at the time of the killing, a judge; or

(xiii) the victim was killed in furtherance of an act of terrorism, as defined in paragraph (b) of subdivision one of section 490.05 of this chapter; and

(b) The defendant was more than eighteen years old at the time of the commission of the crime.

2. In any prosecution under subdivision one, it is an affirmative defense that:

(a) The defendant acted under the influence of extreme emotional disturbance for which there was a reasonable explanation or excuse, the reasonableness of which is to be determined from the viewpoint of a person in the defendant's situation under the circumstances as the defendant believed them to be. Nothing contained in this paragraph shall constitute a defense to a prosecution for, or preclude a conviction of, manslaughter in the first degree or any other crime except murder in the second degree; or

(b) The defendant's conduct consisted of causing or aiding, without the use of duress or deception, another person to commit suicide. Nothing contained in this paragraph shall constitute a defense to a prosecution for, or preclude a conviction of, manslaughter in the second degree or any other crime except murder in the second degree.

Murder in the first degree is a class A–I felony.

### 3. N.Y. Crim. Proc. Law (McKinney Supp. 2004)

### § 400.27. Procedure for determining sentence upon conviction for the offense of murder in the first degree.

1. Upon the conviction of a defendant for the offense of murder in the first degree as defined by section 125.27 of the penal law, the court shall promptly conduct a separate sentencing proceeding to determine whether the defendant shall be sentenced to death or to life imprisonment without parole. . . . Nothing in this section shall be deemed to preclude the people at any time from determining that the death penalty

shall not be sought in a particular case, in which case the separate sentencing proceeding shall not be conducted and the court may sentence such defendant to life imprisonment without parole or to a sentence of imprisonment [not less than 20 years] other than a sentence of life imprisonment without parole.

2. The separate sentencing proceeding provided for by this section shall be conducted before the court sitting with the jury that found the defendant guilty. The court may discharge the jury and impanel another jury only in extraordinary circumstances and upon a showing of good cause, which may include, but is not limited to, a finding of prejudice to either party. . . . Before proceeding with the jury that found the defendant guilty, the court shall determine whether any juror has a state of mind that is likely to preclude the juror from rendering an impartial decision based upon the evidence adduced during the proceeding. In making such determination the court shall personally examine each juror individually outside the presence of the other jurors. The scope of the examination shall be within the discretion of the court and may include questions supplied by the parties as the court deems proper. The proceedings provided for in this subdivision shall be conducted on the record; provided, however, that upon motion of either party, and for good cause shown, the court may direct that all or a portion of the record of such proceedings be sealed. In the event the court determines that a juror has such a state of mind, the court shall discharge the juror and replace the juror with the alternate juror whose name was first drawn and called. If no alternate juror is available, the court must discharge the jury and impanel another jury. . . .

3. For the purposes of a proceeding under this section each subparagraph of paragraph (a) of subdivision one of section 125.27 of the penal law shall be deemed to define an aggravating factor. Except as provided in subdivision seven of this section, at a sentencing proceeding pursuant to this section the only aggravating factors that the jury may consider are those proven beyond a reasonable doubt at trial, and no other aggravating factors may be considered. Whether a sentencing proceeding is conducted before the jury that found the defendant guilty or before another jury, the aggravating factor or factors proved at trial shall be deemed established beyond a reasonable doubt at the separate sentencing proceeding and shall not be relitigated. Where the jury is to determine sentences for concurrent counts of murder in the first degree, the aggravating factor included in each count shall be deemed to be an aggravating factor for the purpose of the jury's consideration in determining the sentence to be imposed on each such count. . . .

6. At the sentencing proceeding the people shall not relitigate the existence of aggravating factors proved at the trial or otherwise present evidence, except, subject to the rules governing admission of evidence in the trial of a criminal action, in rebuttal of the defendant's evidence. However, when the sentencing proceeding is conducted before a newly impaneled jury, the people may present evidence to the extent reasonably necessary to inform the jury of the nature and circumstances of the count or counts of murder in the first degree for which the defendant was convicted in sufficient detail to permit the jury to determine the weight to be accorded the aggravating factor or factors established at trial. Whenever the people present such evidence, the court must

instruct the jury in its charge that any facts elicited by the people that are not essential to the verdict of guilty on such count or counts shall not be deemed established beyond a reasonable doubt. Subject to the rules governing the admission of evidence in the trial of a criminal action, the defendant may present any evidence relevant to any mitigating factor set forth in subdivision nine of this section; provided, however, the defendant shall not be precluded from the admission of reliable hearsay evidence. The burden of establishing any of the mitigating factors set forth in subdivision nine of this section shall be on the defendant, and must be proven by a preponderance of the evidence. The people shall not offer evidence or argument relating to any mitigating factor except in rebuttal of evidence offered by the defendant.

7. (a) The people may present evidence at the sentencing proceeding to prove that in the ten-year period prior to the commission of the crime of murder in the first degree for which the defendant was convicted, the defendant has previously been convicted of two or more offenses committed on different occasions; provided, that each such offense shall be either (i) [specified violent felonies or attempted violent felonies] or a felony offense under the penal law a necessary element of which involves either the use or attempted use or threatened use of a deadly weapon or the intentional infliction of or the attempted intentional infliction of serious physical injury or death, or (ii) an offense under the laws of another state or of the United States punishable by a term of imprisonment of more than one year a necessary element of which involves either the use or attempted use or threatened use of a deadly weapon or the intentional infliction of or the attempted intentional infliction of serious physical injury or death. . . . In calculating the ten-year period under this paragraph, any period of time during which the defendant was incarcerated for any reason between the time of commission of any of the prior felony offenses and the time of commission of the crime of murder in the first degree shall be excluded and such ten year period shall be extended by a period or periods equal to the time served under such incarceration. The defendant's conviction of two or more such offenses shall, if proven at the sentencing proceeding, constitute an aggravating factor.

(b) In order to be deemed established, an aggravating factor set forth in this subdivision must be proven by the people beyond a reasonable doubt and the jury must unanimously find such factor to have been so proven. . . .

8. Consistent with the provisions of this section, the people and the defendant shall be given fair opportunity to rebut any evidence received at the separate sentencing proceeding.

9. Mitigating factors shall include the following:

(a) The defendant has no significant history of prior criminal convictions involving the use of violence against another person;

(b) The defendant was mentally retarded at the time of the crime, or the defendant's mental capacity was impaired or his ability to conform his conduct to the requirements of law was impaired but not so impaired in either case as to constitute a defense to prosecution;

(c) The defendant was under duress or under the domination of another person, although not such duress or domination as to constitute a defense to prosecution;

(d) The defendant was criminally liable for the present offense of murder committed by another, but his participation in the offense was relatively minor although not so minor as to constitute a defense to prosecution;

(e) The murder was committed while the defendant was mentally or emotionally disturbed or under the influence of alcohol or any drug, although not to such an extent as to constitute a defense to prosecution; or

(f) Any other circumstance concerning the crime, the defendant's state of mind or condition at the time of the crime, or the defendant's character, background or record that would be relevant to mitigation or punishment for the crime.

10. At the conclusion of all the evidence, the people and the defendant may present argument in summation for or against the sentence sought by the people. The people may deliver the first summation and the defendant may then deliver the last summation. Thereafter, the court shall deliver a charge to the jury on any matters appropriate in the circumstances. In its charge, the court must instruct the jury that with respect to each count of murder in the first degree the jury should consider whether or not a sentence of death should be imposed and whether or not a sentence of life imprisonment without parole should be imposed, and that the jury must be unanimous with respect to either sentence. The court must also instruct the jury that in the event the jury fails to reach unanimous agreement with respect to the sentence, the court will sentence the defendant to a term of imprisonment with a minimum term of between twenty and twenty-five years and a maximum term of life. . . .

11. (a) The jury may not direct imposition of a sentence of death unless it unanimously finds beyond a reasonable doubt that the aggravating factor or factors substantially outweigh the mitigating factor or factors established, if any, and unanimously determines that the penalty of death should be imposed. Any member or members of the jury who find a mitigating factor to have been proven by the defendant by a preponderance of the evidence may consider such factor established regardless of the number of jurors who concur that the factor has been established.

(b) If the jury directs imposition of either a sentence of death or life imprisonment without parole, it shall specify on the record those mitigating and aggravating factors considered and those mitigating factors established by the defendant, if any. . . .

12. (a) Upon the conviction of a defendant for the offense of murder in the first degree as defined in section 125.27 of the penal law, the court shall, upon oral or written motion of the defendant based upon a showing that there is reasonable cause to believe that the defendant is mentally retarded, promptly conduct a hearing without a jury to determine whether the defendant is mentally retarded. Upon the consent of both parties, such a hearing, or a portion thereof, may be conducted by the court contemporaneously with the

separate sentencing proceeding in the presence of the sentencing jury, which in no event shall be the trier of fact with respect to the hearing. At such hearing the defendant has the burden of proof by a preponderance of the evidence that he or she is mentally retarded. The court shall defer rendering any finding pursuant to this subdivision as to whether the defendant is mentally retarded until a sentence is imposed pursuant to this section.

(b) In the event the defendant is sentenced pursuant to this section to life imprisonment without parole or to a term of imprisonment for the class A–I felony of murder in the first degree other than a sentence of life imprisonment without parole, the court shall not render a finding with respect to whether the defendant is mentally retarded.

(c) In the event the defendant is sentenced pursuant to this section to death, the court shall thereupon render a finding with respect to whether the defendant is mentally retarded. If the court finds the defendant is mentally retarded, the court shall set aside the sentence of death and sentence the defendant either to life imprisonment without parole or to a term of imprisonment for the class A–I felony of murder in the first degree other than a sentence of life imprisonment without parole. If the court finds the defendant is not mentally retarded, then such sentence of death shall not be set aside pursuant to this subdivision.

(d) In the event that a defendant is convicted of murder in the first degree pursuant to subparagraph (iii) of paragraph (a) of subdivision one of section 125.27 of the penal law, and the killing occurred while the defendant was confined or under custody in a state correctional facility or local correctional institution, and a sentence of death is imposed, such sentence may not be set aside pursuant to this subdivision upon the ground that the defendant is mentally retarded. Nothing in this paragraph or paragraph (a) of this subdivision shall preclude a defendant from presenting mitigating evidence of mental retardation at the separate sentencing proceeding.

(e) The foregoing provisions of this subdivision notwithstanding, at a reasonable time prior to the commencement of trial the defendant may, upon a written motion alleging reasonable cause to believe the defendant is mentally retarded, apply for an order directing that a mental retardation hearing be conducted prior to trial. If, upon review of the defendant's motion and any response thereto, the court finds reasonable cause to believe the defendant is mentally retarded, it shall promptly conduct a hearing without a jury to determine whether the defendant is mentally retarded. In the event the court finds after the hearing that the defendant is not mentally retarded, the court must, prior to commencement of trial, enter an order so stating, but nothing in this paragraph shall preclude a defendant from presenting mitigating evidence of mental retardation at a separate sentencing proceeding. In the event the court finds after the hearing that the defendant, based upon a preponderance of the evidence, is mentally retarded, the court must, prior to commencement of trial, enter an order so stating. Unless the order is reversed on an appeal by the people or unless the provisions of paragraph (d) of this subdivision apply, a separate sentencing proceeding under this section shall not be conducted if the defendant is thereafter convicted of murder in the first degree. In the event a separate sentencing proceeding is not conducted, the court, upon conviction of a defendant for the crime of murder in the first degree, shall sentence the defendant to life imprisonment without parole or to a sentence of imprisonment for the class A–I felony of murder in the first degree other than a sentence of life imprisonment without parole. Whenever a mental retardation hearing is held and a finding is rendered pursuant to this paragraph, the court may not conduct a hearing pursuant to paragraph (a) of this subdivision. For purposes of this subdivision and paragraph (b) of subdivision nine of this section, "mental retardation" mens significantly subaverage general intellectual functioning existing concurrently with deficits in adaptive behavior which were manifested before the age of eighteen. . . .

**§ 470.30. Determination by court of appeals of appeals . . .**

2. Whenever a sentence of death is imposed, the judgment and sentence shall be reviewed on the record by the court of appeals. Review by the court of appeals . . . may not be waived.

3. With regard to the sentence, the court shall, in addition to exercising the powers and scope of review [otherwise granted], determine:

(a) whether the sentence of death was imposed under the influence of passion, prejudice, or any other arbitrary or legally impermissible factor including whether the imposition of the verdict or sentence was based upon the race of the defendant or a victim of the crime for which the defendant was convicted;

(b) whether the sentence of death is excessive or disproportionate to the penalty imposed in similar cases considering both the crime and the defendant. In conducting such review the court, upon request of the defendant, in addition to any other determination, shall review whether the sentence of death is excessive or disproportionate to the penalty imposed in similar cases by virtue of the race of the defendant or a victim of the crime for which the defendant was convicted; and

(c) whether the decision to impose the sentence of death was against the weight of the evidence.

4. The court shall include in its decision: (a) the aggravating and mitigating factors established in the record on appeal; and (b) those similar cases it took into consideration. . . .

---

# (F) OREGON HOMICIDE AND ASSAULT OFFENSES AND PROVISIONS ON ATTEMPT

## 1. Ore. Rev. Stat. Ann. (West 2003):

### HOMICIDE

### § 163.005. Criminal homicide

(1) A person commits criminal homicide if, without justification or excuse, the person intentionally, knowingly, recklessly or with criminal negligence causes the death of another human being.

(2) "Criminal homicide" is murder, manslaughter, criminally negligent homicide or aggravated vehicular homicide.

(3) "Human being" means a person who has been born and was alive at the time of the criminal act.

### § 163.115. Murder; affirmative defenses; felony murder; sentence

(1) Except as provided in ORS 163.118 and 163.125, criminal homicide constitutes murder:

(a) When it is committed intentionally, except that it is an affirmative defense that, at the time of the homicide, the defendant was under the influence of an extreme emotional disturbance;

(b) When it is committed by a person, acting either alone or with one or more persons, who commits or attempts to commit any of the following crimes and in the course of and in furtherance of the crime the person is committing or attempting to commit, or during the immediate flight therefrom, the person, or another participant if there be any, causes the death of a person other than one of the participants:

(A) Arson in the first degree as defined in ORS 164.325;

(B) Criminal mischief in the first degree by means of an explosive as defined in ORS 164.365;

(C) Burglary in the first degree as defined in ORS 164.225;

(D) Escape in the first degree as defined in ORS 162.165;

(E) Kidnapping in the second degree as defined in ORS 163.225;

(F) Kidnapping in the first degree as defined in ORS 163.235;

(G) Robbery in the first degree as defined in ORS 164.415;

(H) Any felony sexual offense in the first degree defined in this chapter; or

(I) Compelling prostitution as defined in ORS 167.017; or

(J) Assault in the first degree, as defined in ORS 163.185, and the victim is under 14 years of age, or assault in the second degree, as defined in ORS 163.175 (1)(a) or (b), and the victim is under 14 years of age; or

(c) By abuse when a person, recklessly under circumstances manifesting extreme indifference to the value of human life, causes the death of a child under 14 years of age or a dependent person . . . , and:

(A) The person has previously engaged in a pattern or practice of assault or torture of the victim or another child under 14 years of age or a dependent person; or

(B) The person causes the death by neglect or maltreatment. . . .

(3) It is an affirmative defense to a charge of violating subsection (1)(b) of subsection (1) of this section that the defendant:

(a) Was not the only participant in the underlying crime;

(b) Did not commit the homicidal act or in any way solicit, request, command, importune, cause or aid in the commission thereof;

(c) Was not armed with a dangerous or deadly weapon;

(d) Had no reasonable ground to believe that any other participant was armed with a dangerous or deadly weapon; and

(e) Had no reasonable ground to believe that any other participant intended to engage in conduct likely to result in death.

(4) It is an affirmative defense to a charge of violating subsection (1)(c)(B) of this section that the child or dependent person was under care or treatment solely by spiritual means pursuant to the religious beliefs or practices of the child or person or the parent or guardian of the child or person.

(5) (a) Except as [otherwise provided], a person convicted of murder, who was at least 15 years of age at the time of committing the murder, shall be punished by imprisonment for life [with a minimum non-parolable term of 25 years]. . . .

### § 163.118. First degree manslaughter

(1) Criminal homicide constitutes manslaughter in the first degree when:

(a) It is committed recklessly under circumstances manifesting extreme indifference to the value of human life;

(b) It is committed intentionally by a defendant under the influence of extreme emotional disturbance as provided in ORS 163.135, which constitutes a mitigating circumstance reducing the homicide that would otherwise be murder to manslaughter in the first degree and need not be proved in any prosecution; or

(c) A person recklessly causes the death of a child under 14 years of age or a dependent person, as defined in ORS 163.205, and:

(A) The person has previously engaged in a pattern or practice of assault or torture of the victim or another child under 14 years of age or a dependent person; or

(B) The person causes the death by neglect or maltreatment, as defined in ORS 163.115.

"(d) It is committed recklessly or with criminal negligence by a person operating a motor vehicle while under the influence of intoxicants in violation of ORS 813.010 and:

(A) The person has at least three previous convictions for driving while under the influence of intoxicants under ORS 813.010, or its statutory counterpart in any jurisdiction, in the 10 years prior to the date of the current offense; or

(B)

(i) The person has a previous conviction for any of the crimes described in subsection (2) of this section, or their statutory counterparts in any jurisdiction; and

(ii) The victim's serious physical injury in the previous conviction was caused by the person driving a motor vehicle.

(2) The previous convictions to which subsection (1)(d)(B) of this section applies are:

(a) Assault in the first degree under ORS 163.185;

(b) Assault in the second degree under ORS 163.175; or

(c) Assault in the third degree under ORS 163.165.

(3) Manslaughter in the first degree is a Class A felony.

(4) It is an affirmative defense to a charge of violating:

(a) Subsection (1)(c)(B) of this section that the victim was a dependent person who was at least 18 years of age and was under care or treatment solely by spiritual means pursuant to the religious beliefs or practices of the dependent person or the guardian of the dependent person.

(b) Subsection (1)(d)(B) of this section that the defendant was not under the influence of intoxicants at the time of the conduct that resulted in the previous conviction.

### § 163.125. Second Degree Manslaughter

(1) Criminal homicide constitutes manslaughter in the second degree when:

(a) It is committed recklessly;

(b) A person intentionally causes or aids another person to commit suicide; or

(c) A person, with criminal negligence, causes the death of a child under 14 years of age or a dependent person, as defined in ORS 163.205, and:

(A) The person has previously engaged in a pattern or practice of assault or torture of the victim or another child under 14 years of age or a dependent person; or

(B) The person causes the death by neglect or maltreatment, as defined in ORS 163.115.

(2) Manslaughter in the second degree is a Class B felony.

### § 163.135. Extreme emotional disturbance . . .

(1) It is an affirmative defense to murder for purposes of ORS 163.115 (1)(a) that the homicide was committed under the influence of extreme emotional disturbance if the disturbance is not the result of the person's own intentional, knowing, reckless or criminally negligent act and if there is a reasonable explanation for the disturbance. The reasonableness of the explanation for the disturbance must be determined from the standpoint of an ordinary person in the actor's situation under the circumstances that the actor reasonably believed them to be. Extreme emotional disturbance does not constitute a defense to a prosecution for, or preclude a conviction of, manslaughter in the first degree or any other crime. . . .

### § 163.145.

[This section punishes criminally negligent homicide as a Class B felony.]

## ASSAULT AND RELATED OFFENSES

### § 163.160. Assault in the fourth degree.

(1) A person commits the crime of assault in the fourth degree if the person:

(a) Intentionally, knowingly or recklessly causes physical injury to another; or

(b) With criminal negligence causes physical injury to another by means of a deadly weapon.

(2) Assault in the fourth degree is a Class A misdemeanor.

(3) Notwithstanding subsection (2) of this section, assault in the fourth degree is a Class C felony if the person commits the crime of assault in the fourth degree and:

(a) The person has previously been convicted of assaulting the same victim;

(b) The person has previously been convicted at least three times under this section or under equivalent laws of another jurisdiction and all of the assaults involved domestic violence, as defined in ORS 135.230; or

(c) The assault is committed in the immediate presence of, or is witnessed by, the person's or the victim's minor child or stepchild or a minor child residing within the household of the person or victim.

d) The person commits the assault knowing that the victim is pregnant.

(4) For the purposes of subsection (3) of this section, an assault is witnessed if the assault is seen or directly perceived in any other manner by the child.

### § 163.165. Assault in the third degree.

(1) A person commits the crime of assault in the third degree if the person:

(a) Recklessly causes serious physical injury to another by means of a deadly or dangerous weapon;

(b) Recklessly causes serious physical injury to another under circumstances manifesting extreme indifference to the value of human life;

(c) Recklessly causes physical injury to another by means of a deadly or dangerous weapon under circumstances manifesting extreme indifference to the value of human life;

(d) Intentionally, knowingly or recklessly causes, by means other than a motor vehicle, physical injury to the operator of a public transit vehicle while the operator is in control of or operating the vehicle. . . .

(e) While being aided by another person actually present, intentionally or knowingly causes physical injury to another;

(f) While committed to a youth correction facility, intentionally or knowingly causes physical injury to another knowing the other person is a staff member of a youth correction facility while the other person is acting in the course of official duty;

(g) Intentionally, knowingly or recklessly causes physical injury to an emergency medical technician or paramedic, . . . while the technician or paramedic is performing official duties; or

(h) Being at least 18 years of age, intentionally or knowingly causes physical injury to a child 10 years of age or younger.

(i) Intentionally, knowingly or recklessly causes, by means other than a motor vehicle, physical injury to the operator of a taxi while the operator is in control of the taxi.

(2) Assault in the third degree is a Class C felony. . . .

### § 163.175. Assault in the second degree.

(1) A person commits the crime of assault in the second degree if the person:

(a) Intentionally or knowingly causes serious physical injury to another; or

(b) Intentionally or knowingly causes physical injury to another by means of a deadly or dangerous weapon; or

(c) Recklessly causes serious physical injury to another by means of a deadly or dangerous weapon under circumstances manifesting extreme indifference to the value of human life.

(2) Assault in the second degree is a Class B felony.

## § 163.185. Assault in the first degree.

(1) A person commits the crime of assault in the first degree if the person:

(a) Intentionally causes serious physical injury to another by means of a deadly or dangerous weapon;

(b) Intentionally or knowingly causes serious physical injury to a child under six years of age;

(c) Violates ORS 163.175 knowing that the victim is pregnant; or

(d) Intentionally, knowingly or recklessly causes serious physical injury to another while operating a motor vehicle under the influence of intoxicants in violation of ORS 813.010 and:

(A) The person has at least three previous convictions for driving while under the influence of intoxicants under ORS 813.010, or its statutory counterpart in any jurisdiction, in the 10 years prior to the date of the current offense; or

(B)(i) The person has a previous conviction for any of the crimes described in subsection (2) of this section, or their statutory counterparts in any jurisdiction; and

(ii) The victim's death or serious physical injury in the previous conviction was caused by the person driving a motor vehicle.

(2) The previous convictions to which subsection (1)(d)(B) of this section apply are:

(a) Manslaughter in the first degree under ORS 163.118;

(b) Manslaughter in the second degree under ORS 163.125;

(c) Criminally negligent homicide under ORS 163.145;

(d) Assault in the first degree under this section;

(e) Assault in the second degree under ORS 163.175; or

(f) Assault in the third degree under ORS 163.165.

(3) Assault in the first degree is a Class A felony.

(4) It is an affirmative defense to a prosecution under subsection (1)(d)(B) of this section that the defendant was not under the influence of intoxicants at the time of the conduct that resulted in the previous conviction.

## § 163.190. Menacing.

(1) A person commits the crime of menacing if by word or conduct the person intentionally attempts to place another person in fear of imminent serious physical injury.

(2) Menacing is a Class A misdemeanor.

## § 163.195. Recklessly endangering another person.

(1) A person commits the crime of recklessly endangering another person if the person recklessly engages in conduct which creates a substantial risk of serious physical injury to another person.

(2) Recklessly endangering another person is a Class A misdemeanor.

INCHOATE CRIMES

### § 161.405. Attempt

(1) A person is guilty of an attempt to commit a crime when the person intentionally engages in conduct which constitutes a substantial step toward commission of the crime.

(2) An attempt is a:

(a) Class A felony if the offense attempted is murder or treason.

(b) Class B felony if the offense attempted is a Class A felony.

(c) Class C felony if the offense attempted is a Class B felony.

(d) Class A misdemeanor if the offense attempted is a Class C felony or an unclassified felony.

(e) Class B misdemeanor if the offense attempted is a Class A misdemeanor.

(f) Class C misdemeanor if the offense attempted is a Class B misdemeanor.

(g) Violation if the offense attempted is a Class C misdemeanor or an unclassified misdemeanor.

### § 161.425. Impossibility as defense.

In a prosecution for an attempt, it is no defense that it was impossible to commit the crime which was the object of the attempt where the conduct engaged in by the actor would be a crime if the circumstances were as the actor believed them to be.

### § 161.430. Renunciation; defense to attempt

(1) A person is not liable under ORS 161.405 if, under circumstances manifesting a voluntary and complete renunciation of the criminal intent of the person, the person avoids the commission of the crime attempted by abandoning the criminal effort and, if mere abandonment is insufficient to accomplish this avoidance, doing everything necessary to prevent the commission of the attempted crime.

(2) The defense of renunciation is an affirmative defense.

DISPOSITION OF OFFENDERS

### § 161.605. Maximum terms of imprisonment; felonies.

The maximum term of an indeterminate sentence of imprisonment for a felony is as follows:

(1) For a Class A felony, 20 years.

(2) For a Class B felony, 10 years.

(3) For a Class C felony, 5 years.

(4) For an unclassified felony as provided in the statute defining the crime.

### § 161.615. Sentences for misdemeanors.

Sentences for misdemeanors shall be for a definite term. The court shall fix the term of imprisonment within the following maximum limitations:

(1) For a Class A misdemeanor, 1 year.

(2) For a Class B misdemeanor, 6 months.

(3) For a Class C misdemeanor, 30 days.

(4) For an unclassified misdemeanor, as provided in the statute defining the crime.

---

## (G) SELECTED COLORADO STATUTES

### 1. Colo. Rev. Stat. (2003):

PRINCIPLES OF CRIMINAL CULPABILITY

### § 18–1–501. Definitions

The following definitions are applicable to the determination of culpability requirements for offenses defined in this code:

(1) "Act" means a bodily movement, and includes words and possession of property.

(2) "Conduct" means an act or omission and its accompanying state of mind or, where relevant, a series of acts or omissions.

(3) "Criminal negligence". A person acts with criminal negligence when, through a gross deviation from the standard of care that a reasonable person would exercise, he fails to perceive a substantial and unjustifiable risk that a result will occur or that a circumstance exists.

(4) "Culpable mental state" means intentionally, or with intent, or knowingly, or willfully, or recklessly, or with criminal negligence, as these terms are defined in this section.

(5) "Intentionally" or "with intent". All offenses defined in this code in which the mental culpability requirement is expressed as "intentionally" or "with intent" are declared to be specific intent offenses. A person acts "intentionally" or "with intent" when his conscious objective is to cause the specific result proscribed by the statute defining the offense. It is immaterial to the issue of specific intent whether or not the result actually occurred.

(6) "Knowingly" or "willfully". All offenses defined in this code in which the mental culpability requirement is expressed as "knowingly" or "willfully" are declared to be general intent crimes. A person acts "knowingly" or "willfully" with respect to conduct or to a circumstance described by a statute defining an offense when he is aware that his conduct is of such nature or that such circumstance exists. A person acts "knowingly" or "willfully", with respect to a result of his conduct, when he is aware that his conduct is practically certain to cause the result.

(7) "Omission" means a failure to perform an act as to which a duty of performance is imposed by law.

(8) "Recklessly". A person acts recklessly when he consciously disregards a substantial and unjustifiable risk that a result will occur or that a circumstance exists.

(9) "Voluntary act" means an act performed consciously as a result of effort or determination, and includes the possession of property if the actor was aware of his physical possession or control thereof for a sufficient period to have been able to terminate it.

ATTEMPTS

### § 18–2–101. Criminal attempt

(1) A person commits criminal attempt if, acting with the kind of culpability otherwise required for commission of an offense, he engages in conduct constituting a substantial step toward the commission of the offense. A substantial step is any conduct, whether act, omission, or possession, which is strongly corroborative of the firmness of the actor's purpose to complete the commission of the offense. Factual or legal impossibility of committing the offense is not a defense if the offense could have been committed had the attendant circumstances been as the actor believed them to be, nor is it a defense that the crime attempted was actually perpetrated by the accused.

(2) A person who engages in conduct intending to aid another to commit an offense commits criminal attempt if the conduct would establish his complicity under section 18–1–603 were the offense committed by the other person, even if the other is not guilty of committing or attempting the offense.

(3) It is an affirmative defense to a charge under this section that the defendant abandoned his effort to commit the crime or otherwise prevented its commission, under circumstances manifesting the complete and voluntary renunciation of his criminal intent. . . .

(4) Criminal attempt to commit a class 1 felony is a class 2 felony; criminal attempt to commit a class 2 felony is a class 3 felony; criminal attempt to commit a class 3 felony is a class 4 felony; criminal attempt to commit a class 4 felony is a class 5 felony; criminal attempt to commit a class 5 or 6 felony is a class 6 felony. . . .

HOMICIDE

### § 18–3–101. Homicide—Definition of terms.

As used in this part 1, unless the context otherwise requires:

(1) "Homicide" means the killing of a person by another.

(2) "Person," when referring to the victim of a homicide, means a human being who had been born and was alive at the time of the homicidal act.

(2.5) One in a "position of trust" includes, but is not limited to, any person who is a parent or acting in the place of a parent and charged with any of a parent's rights, duties, or responsibilities concerning a child, including a guardian or someone otherwise responsible for the general supervision of a child's welfare, or a person who is charged with any duty or responsibility for the health, education, welfare, or supervision of a child, including foster care, child care, family care, or institutional care, either independently or through another, no matter how brief, at the time of an unlawful act.

(3) The term "after deliberation" means not only intentionally but also that the decision to commit the act has been made after the exercise of reflection and judgment concerning the act. An act committed after deliberation is never one which has been committed in a hasty or impulsive manner.

## § 18–3–102. Murder in the first degree.

(1) A person commits the crime of murder in the first degree if:

(a) After deliberation and with the intent to cause the death of a person other than himself, he causes the death of that person or of another person; or

(b) Acting either alone or with one or more persons, he or she commits or attempts to commit arson, robbery, burglary, kidnapping, sexual assault . . . , or a class 3 felony for sexual assault on a child . . . , or the crime of escape . . . , and, in the course of or in furtherance of the crime that he or she is committing or attempting to commit, or of immediate flight therefrom, the death of a person, other than one of the participants, is caused by anyone; or

(c) By perjury or subornation of perjury he procures the conviction and execution of any innocent person; or

(d) Under circumstances evidencing an attitude of universal malice manifesting extreme indifference to the value of human life generally, he knowingly engages in conduct which creates a grave risk of death to a person, or persons, other than himself, and thereby causes the death of another; or

(e) He or she commits unlawful distribution, dispensation, or sale of a controlled substance to a person under the age of eighteen years on school grounds . . . , and the death of such person is caused by the use of such controlled substance; or

(f) The person knowingly causes the death of a child who has not yet attained twelve years of age and the person committing the offense is one in a position of trust with respect to the victim.

(2) It is an affirmative defense to a charge of violating subsection (1)(b) of this section that the defendant:

(a) Was not the only participant in the underlying crime; and

(b) Did not commit the homicidal act or in any way solicit, request, command, importune, cause, or aid the commission thereof; and

(c) Was not armed with a deadly weapon; and

(d) Had no reasonable ground to believe that any other participant was armed with such a weapon, instrument, article, or substance; and

(e) Did not engage himself in or intend to engage in and had no reasonable ground to believe that any other participant intended to engage in conduct likely to result in death or serious bodily injury; and

(f) Endeavored to disengage himself from the commission of the underlying crime or flight therefrom immediately upon having reasonable grounds to believe that another participant is armed with a deadly weapon, instrument, article, or substance, or intended to engage in conduct likely to result in death or serious bodily injury.

(3) Murder in the first degree is a class 1 felony. . . .

### § 18–3–103. Murder in the second degree

(1) A person commits the crime of murder in the second degree if the person knowingly causes the death of a person.

(2) Diminished responsibility due to self-induced intoxication is not a defense to murder in the second degree.

(3) (a) Except as otherwise provided in paragraph (b) of this subsection (3), murder in the second degree is a class 2 felony.

(b) Notwithstanding the provisions of paragraph (a) of this subsection (3), murder in the second degree is a class 3 felony where the act causing the death was performed upon a sudden heat of passion, caused by a serious and highly provoking act of the intended victim, affecting the defendant sufficiently to excite an irresistible passion in a reasonable person; but, if between the provocation and the killing there is an interval sufficient for the voice of reason and humanity to be heard, the killing is a class 2 felony. . . .

### § 18–3–104. Manslaughter.

(1) A person commits the crime of manslaughter if:

(a) Such person recklessly causes the death of another person[c] . . .

(2) Manslaughter is a class 4 felony.

### § 18–3–105. Criminally negligent homicide.

Any person who causes the death of another person by conduct amounting to criminal negligence commits criminally negligent homicide which is a class 5 felony.

---

[c] Prior to 1996, this section contained a paragraph (c) that read:

> Such person knowingly causes the death of another person under circumstances where the act causing the death was performed upon a sudden heat of passion, caused by a serious and highly provoking act of the intended victim, affecting the person who performs the killing sufficiently to excite an irresistible passion in a reasonable person; but, if between the provocation and the killing there is an interval sufficient for the voice of reason and humanity to be heard, the killing is murder.

The penalty was that of a Class 3 felony. Subsection (b) deals with assisted suicide.—[Footnote by eds.]

## ASSAULTS

### § 18–3–202. Assault in the first degree.

(1) A person commits the crime of assault in the first degree if:

(a) With intent to cause serious bodily injury to another person, he causes serious bodily injury to any person by means of a deadly weapon; or

(b) With intent to disfigure another person seriously and permanently, or to destroy, amputate, or disable permanently a member or organ of his body, he causes such an injury to any person; or

(c) Under circumstances manifesting extreme indifference to the value of human life, he knowingly engages in conduct which creates a grave risk of death to another person, and thereby causes serious bodily injury to any person; or . . .

(2) (a) If assault in the first degree is committed under circumstances where the act causing the injury is performed upon a sudden heat of passion, caused by a serious and highly provoking act of the intended victim, affecting the person causing the injury sufficiently to excite an iresistible passion in a reasonable person, and without an interval between the provocation and the injury sufficient for the voice of reason and humanity to be heard, it is a class 5 felony.

(b) If assault in the first degree is committed without the circumstances provided in paragraph (a) of this subsection (2), it is a class 3 felony. . . .

### § 18–3–203. Assault in the second degree.

(1) A person commits the crime of assault in the second degree if: . . .

(b) With intent to cause bodily injury to another person, he or she causes such injury to any person by means of a deadly weapon; or . . .

(d) He recklessly causes serious bodily injury to another person by means of a deadly weapon; or . . .

(g) With intent to cause bodily injury to another person, he causes serious bodily injury to that person or another.

(2) (a) If assault in the second degree is committed under circumstances where the act causing the injury is performed upon a sudden heat of passion, caused by a serious and highly provoking act of the intended victim, affecting the person causing the injury sufficiently to excite an irresistible passion in a reasonable person, and without an interval between the provocation and the injury sufficient for the voice of reason and humanity to be heard, it is a class 6 felony.

(b) If assault in the second degree is committed without the circumstances provided in paragraph (a) of this subsection (2), it is a class 4 felony. . . .

### § 18–3–204. Assault in the third degree.

(1) A person commits the crime of assault in the third degree if:

(a) The person knowingly or recklessly causes bodily injury to another person or with criminal negligence the person causes bodily injury to another person by means of a deadly weapon; or

(b) The person, with intent to infect, injure, harm, harass, annoy, threaten, or alarm another person whom the actor knows or reasonably should know to be a peace officer, a firefighter, an emergency medical care provider, or an emergency medical service provider, causes the other person to come into contact with blood, seminal fluid, urine, feces, saliva, mucus, vomit, or toxic, caustic, or hazardous material by any means, including throwing, tossing, or expelling the fluid or material.

(2) (a) An adult or juvenile who has had a court find that there is probable cause to believe that he or she has committed an offense pursuant to paragraph (b) of subsection (1) of this section or is convicted of an offense pursuant to paragraph (b) of subsection (1) of this section or any person who is determined to have provided blood, seminal fluid, urine, feces, saliva, mucus, or vomit to a person for whom probable cause has been found or been convicted of such an offense shall be ordered by the court to submit to a medical test for communicable diseases and to supply blood, feces, urine, saliva, or other bodily fluid required for the test. The results of such test shall be reported to the court or the court's designee, who shall then disclose the results to any victim of the offense who requests such disclosure. Review and disclosure of medical test results by the court shall be closed and confidential, and any transaction records relating thereto shall also be closed and confidential. If a person subject to a medical test for communicable diseases pursuant to this subsection (2) voluntarily submits to a medical test for communicable diseases, the fact of the person's voluntary submission shall be admissible in mitigation of sentence if the person is convicted of the charged offense.

(b) In addition to any other penalty provided by law, the court may order any person who is convicted of the offense described in paragraph (b) of subsection (1) of this section to meet all or any portion of the financial obligations of medical tests performed on and treatment prescribed for the victim or victims of the offense.

(3) Assault in the third degree is a class 1 misdemeanor and is an extraordinary risk crime that is subject to the modified sentencing range specified in section 18–1.3–501(3).

(4) "Emergency medical care provider" means a doctor, intern, nurse, nurse's aid, physician's assistant, ambulance attendant or operator, air ambulance pilot, paramedic, or any other member of a hospital or health care facility staff or security force who is involved in providing emergency medical care at a hospital or health care facility, or in an air ambulance or ambulance as defined in section 25–3.5–103(1) and (1.5), C.R.S.

### § 18–3–206. Menacing.

A person commits the crime of menacing if, by any threat or physical action, he or she knowingly places or attempts to place another person in fear of imminent serious bodily injury. Menacing is a class 3 misdemeanor, but, it is a class 5 felony if committed:

(a) By the use of a deadly weapon or any article used or fashioned in a manner to cause a person to reasonably believe that the article is a deadly weapon; or

(b) By the person representing verbally or otherwise that he or she is armed with a deadly weapon.

### § 18–3–208. Reckless endangerment.

A person who recklessly engages in conduct which creates a substantial risk of serious bodily injury to another person commits reckless endangerment, which is a class 3 misdemeanor.

---

## (H) CAPITAL PUNISHMENT STATUTES BEFORE THE SUPREME COURT IN 1976 DECISIONS

### 1. Ga. Laws, 1973 Sess., pp. 164–67, 170, before the Supreme Court in Gregg v. Georgia, 428 U.S. 153 (1976):

**§ 26–3102. Capital offenses; jury verdict and sentence.** Where, upon a trial by jury, a person is convicted of an offense which may be punishable by death, a sentence of death shall not be imposed unless the jury verdict includes a finding of at least one statutory aggravating circumstance and a recommendation that such sentence be imposed. Where a statutory aggravating circumstance is found and a recommendation of death is made, the court shall sentence the defendant to death. Where a sentence of death is not recommended by the jury, the court shall sentence the defendant to imprisonment as provided by law. Unless the jury trying the case makes a finding of at least one statutory aggravating circumstance and recommends the death sentence in its verdict, the court shall not sentence the defendant to death, provided that no such finding of statutory aggravating circumstance shall be necessary in offenses of treason or aircraft hijacking. The provisions of this section shall not affect a sentence when the case is tried without a jury or when the judge accepts a plea of guilty.

**§ 27–2534.1. Mitigating and aggravating circumstances; death penalty.**—(a) The death penalty may be imposed for the offenses of aircraft hijacking or treason, in any case.

(b) In all cases of other offenses for which the death penalty may be authorized, the judge shall consider, or he shall include in his instructions to the jury for it to consider, any mitigating circumstances or aggravating circumstances otherwise authorized by law and any of the following statutory aggravating circumstances which may be supported by the evidence:

(1) The offense of murder, rape, armed robbery, or kidnapping was committed by a person with a prior record of conviction for a

capital felony, or the offense of murder was committed by a person who has a substantial history of serious assaultive criminal convictions.

(2) The offense of murder, rape, armed robbery, or kidnapping was committed while the offender was engaged in the commission of another capital felony, or aggravated battery, or the offense of murder was committed while the offender was engaged in the commission of burglary or arson in the first degree.

(3) The offender by his act of murder, armed robbery, or kidnapping knowingly created a great risk of death to more than one person in a public place by means of a weapon or device which would normally be hazardous to the lives of more than one person.

(4) The offender committed the offense of murder for himself or another, for the purpose of receiving money or any other thing of monetary value.

(5) The murder of a judicial officer, former judicial officer, district attorney or solicitor or former district attorney or solicitor during or because of the exercise of his official duty.

(6) The offender caused or directed another to commit murder or committed murder as an agent or employee of another person.

(7) The offense of murder, rape, armed robbery, or kidnapping was outrageously or wantonly vile, horrible or inhuman in that it involved torture, depravity of mind, or an aggravated battery to the victim.

(8) The offense of murder was committed against any peace officer, corrections employee or fireman while engaged in the performance of his official duties.

(9) The offense of murder was committed by a person in, or who has escaped from, the lawful custody of a peace officer or place of lawful confinement.

(10) The murder was committed for the purpose of avoiding, interfering with, or preventing a lawful arrest or custody in a place of lawful confinement, of himself or another.

(c) The statutory instructions as determined by the trial judge to be warranted by the evidence shall be given in charge and in writing to the jury for its deliberation. The jury, if its verdict be a recommendation of death, shall designate in writing, signed by the foreman of the jury, the aggravating circumstance or circumstances which it found beyond a reasonable doubt. In non-jury cases the judge shall make such designation. Except in cases of treason or aircraft hijacking, unless at least one of the statutory aggravating circumstances enumerated in Code Section 27–2534.1(b) is so found, the death penalty shall not be imposed.

**§ 27–2537. Review of death sentences.**—(a) Whenever the death penalty is imposed, and upon the judgment becoming final in the trial court, the sentence shall be reviewed on the record by the Supreme Court of Georgia. The clerk of the trial court, within ten days after receiving the transcript, shall transmit the entire record and transcript to the Supreme Court of Georgia together with a notice prepared by the clerk and a report prepared by the trial judge. The notice shall set forth the title and docket number of the case, the name of the defendant and the name and address of his attorney, a narrative statement of the judgment, the offense, and the punishment prescribed. The report shall be in the form of a standard questionnaire prepared and supplied by the Supreme Court of Georgia.

(b) The Supreme Court of Georgia shall consider the punishment as well as any errors enumerated by way of appeal.

(c) With regard to the sentence, the court shall determine:

(1) Whether the sentence of death was imposed under the influence of passion, prejudice, or any other arbitrary factor, and

(2) Whether, in cases other than treason or aircraft hijacking, the evidence supports the jury's or judge's finding of a statutory aggravating circumstance as enumerated in Code Section 27–2534.1(b), and

(3) Whether the sentence of death is excessive or disproportionate to the penalty imposed in similar cases, considering both the crime and the defendant.

(d) Both the defendant and the State shall have the right to submit briefs within the time provided by the court, and to present oral argument to the court.

(e) The court shall include in its decision a reference to those similar cases which it took into consideration. In addition to its authority regarding correction of errors, the court, with regard to review of death sentences, shall be authorized to:

(1) Affirm the sentence of death; or

(2) Set the sentence aside and remand the case for resentencing by the trial judge based on the record and argument of counsel. The records of those similar cases referred to by the Supreme Court of Georgia in its decision, and the extracts prepared as hereinafter provided for, shall be provided to the resentencing judge for his consideration.

(f) There shall be an Assistant to the Supreme Court, who shall be an attorney appointed by the Chief Justice of Georgia and who shall serve at the pleasure of the court. The court shall accumulate the records of all capital felony cases in which sentence was imposed after January 1, 1970, or such earlier date as the court may deem appropriate. The Assistant shall provide the court with whatever extracted information it desires with respect thereto, including but not limited to a synopsis or brief of the facts in the record concerning the crime and the defendant.

(g) The court shall be authorized to employ an appropriate staff and such methods to compile such data as are deemed by the Chief Justice to be appropriate and relevant to the statutory questions concerning the validity of the sentence.

(h) The office of the Assistant shall be attached to the office of the Clerk of the Supreme Court of Georgia for administrative purposes.

(i) The sentence review shall be in addition to direct appeal, if taken, and the review and appeal shall be consolidated for consideration. The court shall render its decision on legal errors enumerated, the factual substantiation of the verdict, and the validity of the sentence.

### 2. Fla. Laws, 1975, ch. 75–298, § 6; Fla. Laws, 1972, ch. 72–724, §§ 2, 9, before the Supreme Court in Proffitt v. Florida, 428 U.S. 242 (1976):

**§ 782.04. Murder—**

(1) (a) The unlawful killing of a human being, when perpetrated from a premeditated design to effect the death of the person killed or any human being, or when committed by a person engaged in the perpetration of, or in the attempt to perpetrate, any arson, involuntary sexual battery, robbery, burglary, kidnapping, aircraft piracy, or unlawful throwing, placing, or discharging of a destructive device or bomb, or which resulted from the unlawful distribution of heroin by a person 18 years of age or older when such drug is proven to be the proximate cause of the death of the user, shall be murder in the first degree and shall constitute a capital felony, punishable as provided in § 775.082.

(b) In all cases under this section, the procedure set forth in § 921.141 shall be followed in order to determine sentence of death or life imprisonment.

**§ 775.082. Penalties for felonies and misdemeanors.—**

(1) A person who has been convicted of a capital felony shall be punished by life imprisonment and shall be required to serve no less than 25 calendar years before becoming eligible for parole unless the proceeding held to determine sentence according to the procedure set forth in § 921.141 results in findings by the court that such person shall be punished by death, and in the latter event such person shall be punished by death.

**§ 921.141. Sentence of death or life imprisonment for capital felonies; further proceedings to determine sentence.—**

(1) Upon conviction or adjudication of guilt of a defendant of a capital felony the court shall conduct a separate sentencing proceeding to determine whether the defendant should be sentenced to death or life imprisonment as authorized by Section 775.082. The proceeding shall be conducted by the trial judge before the trial jury as soon as practicable. If the trial jury has been waived or if the defendant pleaded guilty, the sentencing proceeding shall be conducted before a jury empaneled for that purpose unless waived by the defendant. In the proceeding, evidence may be presented as to any matter that the court deems relevant to sentence, and shall include matters relating to any of the aggravating or mitigating circumstances enumerated in Subsections (6) and (7) of this section. Any such evidence which the court deems to have probative value may be received, regardless of its admissibility under the exclusionary rules of evidence, provided that the defendant is accorded a fair opportunity to rebut any hearsay statements; and further provided that this subsection shall not be construed to authorize the introduction of any evidence secured in violation of the Constitution of the United States or of the State of Florida. The state and the defendant or his counsel shall be permitted to present argument for or against sentence of death.

(2) After hearing all the evidence, the jury shall deliberate and render an advisory sentence to the court based upon the following matters:

(a) Whether sufficient aggravating circumstances exist as enumerated in Subsection (6), and

(b) Whether sufficient mitigating circumstances exist as enumerated in Subsection (7), which outweigh aggravating circumstances found to exist, and

(c) Based on these considerations whether the defendant should be sentenced to life or death.

(3) Notwithstanding the recommendation of a majority of the jury, the court after weighing the aggravating and mitigating circumstances shall enter a sentence of life imprisonment or death, but if the court imposes a sentence of death, it shall set forth in writing its findings upon which the sentence of death is based as to the facts:

(a) That sufficient aggravating circumstances exist as enumerated in Subsection (6), and

(b) That there are insufficient mitigating circumstances, as enumerated in Subsection (7), to outweigh the aggravating circumstances.

In each case in which the court imposes the death sentence, the determination of the court shall be supported by specific written findings of fact based upon the circumstances in Subsections (6) and (7) and based upon the records of the trial and the sentencing proceedings.

(4) If the court does not make the findings requiring the death sentence, the court shall impose sentence of life imprisonment in accordance with Section 775.082.

(5) The judgment of conviction and sentence of death shall be subject to automatic review by the Supreme Court of Florida within 60 days after certification by the sentencing court of the entire record unless time is extended an additional period not to exceed 30 days by the Supreme Court for good cause shown. Such review by the Supreme Court shall have priority over all other cases, and shall be heard in accordance with rules promulgated by the Supreme Court.

(6) Aggravating circumstances.—Aggravating circumstances shall be limited to the following:

(a) The capital felony was committed by a person under sentence of imprisonment;

(b) The defendant was previously convicted of another capital felony or of a felony involving the use or threat of violence to the person;

(c) The defendant knowingly created a great risk of death to many persons;

(d) The capital felony was committed while the defendant was engaged or was an accomplice in the commission of, or an attempt to commit, or flight after committing or attempting to commit any robbery, rape, arson, burglary, kidnaping, aircraft piracy, or the unlawful throwing, placing or discharging of a destructive device or bomb;

(e) The capital felony was committed for the purpose of avoiding or preventing a lawful arrest or effecting an escape from custody;

(f) The capital felony was committed for pecuniary gain;

(g) The capital felony was committed to disrupt or hinder the lawful exercise of any governmental function or the enforcement of laws;

(h) The capital felony was especially heinous, atrocious or cruel.

(7) Mitigating circumstances.—Mitigating circumstances shall be the following:

(a) The defendant has no significant history of prior criminal activity;

(b) The capital felony was committed while the defendant was under the influence of extreme mental or emotional disturbance;

(c) The victim was a participant in the defendant's conduct or consented to the act;

(d) The defendant was an accomplice in the capital felony committed by another person and his participation was relatively minor;

(e) The defendant acted under extreme duress or under the substantial domination of another person;

(f) The capacity of the defendant to appreciate the criminality of his conduct or to conform his conduct to the requirements of law was substantially impaired;

(g) The age of the defendant at the time of the crime.

### 3. Tex. Gen. Laws, 63rd Leg., ch. 426, art. 1, § 1, p. 1122, art. 3, § 1, pp. 1125–26, before the Supreme Court in Jurek v. Texas, 428 U.S. 262 (1976):

#### Art. 1257. Punishment for murder.

(a) Except as provided in Subsection (b) of this Article, the punishment for murder shall be confinement in the penitentiary for life or for any term of years not less than two.

(b) The punishment for murder with malice aforethought shall be death or imprisonment for life if:

(1) the person murdered a peace officer or fireman who was acting in the lawful discharge of an official duty and who the defendant knew was a peace officer or fireman;

(2) the person intentionally committed the murder in the course of committing or attempting to commit kidnapping, burglary, robbery, forcible rape, or arson;

(3) the person committed the murder for remuneration or the promise of remuneration or employed another to commit the murder for remuneration or the promise of remuneration;

(4) the person committed the murder while escaping or attempting to escape from a penal institution;

(5) the person, while incarcerated in a penal institution, murdered another who was employed in the operation of the penal institution.

(c) If the jury does not find beyond a reasonable doubt that the murder was committed under one of the circumstances or conditions enumerated in Subsection (b) of this Article, the defendant may be convicted of murder, with or without malice, under Subsection (a) of this Article or of any other lesser included offense. . . .

**Art. 37.071. Procedure in capital case.**

(a) Upon a finding that the defendant is guilty of a capital offense, the court shall conduct a separate sentencing proceeding to determine whether the defendant shall be sentenced to death or life imprisonment. The proceeding shall be conducted in the trial court before the trial jury as soon as practicable. In the proceeding, evidence may be presented as to any matter that the court deems relevant to sentence. This subsection shall not be construed to authorize the introduction of any evidence secured in violation of the Constitution of the United States or of the State of Texas. The state and the defendant or his counsel shall be permitted to present argument for or against sentence of death.

(b) On conclusion of the presentation of the evidence, the court shall submit the following issues to the jury:

(1) whether the conduct of the defendant that caused the death of the deceased was committed deliberately and with the reasonable expectation that the death of the deceased or another would result;

(2) whether there is a probability that the defendant would commit criminal acts of violence that would constitute a continuing threat to society; and

(3) if raised by the evidence, whether the conduct of the defendant in killing the deceased was unreasonable in response to the provocation, if any, by the deceased.

(c) The state must prove each issue submitted beyond a reasonable doubt, and the jury shall return a special verdict of "yes" or "no" on each issue submitted.

(d) The court shall charge the jury that:

(1) it may not answer any issue "yes" unless it agrees unanimously; and

(2) it may not answer any issue "no" unless 10 or more jurors agree.

(e) If the jury returns an affirmative finding on each issue submitted under this article, the court shall sentence the defendant to death. If the jury returns a negative finding on any issue submitted under this article, the court shall sentence the defendant to confinement in the Texas Department of Corrections for life.

(f) The judgment of conviction and sentence of death shall be subject to automatic review by the Court of Criminal Appeals within 60 days after certification by the sentencing court of the entire record unless time is extended an additional period not to exceed 30 days by the Court of Criminal Appeals for good cause shown. Such review by the Court of Criminal Appeals shall have priority over all other cases, and shall be heard in accordance with rules promulgated by the Court of Criminal Appeals.

### 4. N.C. Sess. Laws, 1973, ch. 1201, § 1, p. 323, before the Supreme Court in Woodson v. North Carolina, 428 U.S. 280 (1976):

**§ 14–17. Murder in the first and second degree defined; punishment.**—A murder which shall be perpetrated by means of poison, lying in wait, imprisonment, starving, torture, or by any other kind of willful, deliberate and premeditated killing, or which shall be committed in the perpetration or attempt to perpetrate any arson, rape, robbery, kidnapping, burglary or other felony, shall be deemed to be murder in the first degree and shall be punished with death. All other kinds of murder shall be deemed murder in the second degree, and shall be punished by imprisonment for a term of not less than two years nor more than life imprisonment in the State's prison.

### 5. La. Acts, 1973, No. 109, § 1, p. 218, before the Supreme Court in Roberts v. Louisiana, 428 U.S. 325 (1976):

**§ 30. First-degree murder.**

First-degree murder is the killing of a human being:

(1) When the offender has a specific intent to kill or to inflict great bodily harm and is engaged in the perpetration or attempted perpetration of aggravated kidnapping, aggravated rape or armed robbery; or

(2) When the offender has a specific intent to kill, or to inflict great bodily harm upon, a fireman or a peace officer who was engaged in the performance of his lawful duties; or

(3) Where the offender has a specific intent to kill or to inflict great bodily harm and has previously been convicted of an unrelated murder or is serving a life sentence; or

(4) When the offender has a specific intent to kill or to inflict great bodily harm upon more than one person.

(5) When the offender has specific intent to commit murder and has been offered or has received anything of value for committing the murder.

For the purposes of Paragraph (2) herein, the term peace officer shall be defined and include any constable, sheriff, deputy sheriff, local or state policeman, game warden, federal law enforcement officer, jail or prison guard, parole officer, probation officer, judge, district attorney, assistant district attorney or district attorneys' investigator.

Whoever commits the crime of first-degree murder shall be punished by death.